BARRON'S

GUIDE TO LAW SCHOOLS

15TH EDITION

Introduction by
Gary A. Munneke
Professor of Law
Pace University School of Law

BARRON'S

All inquiries should be addressed to:
Barron's Educational Series, Inc.
250 Wireless Boulevard
Hauppauge, New York 11788
http://www.barronseduc.com

Every effort has been made to ensure the accuracy of the information in this book. Because costs and statistics change from year to year, prospective students should contact the schools to verify this information.

Library of Congress Catalog Card No. 90-40512

International Standard Book No. 0-7641-1783-1

International Standard Serial Number 1062-2489

PRINTED IN THE UNITED STATES OF AMERICA
98765432

Contents

Abbreviations and Degrees

ABBREVIATIONS

AALL—American Association of Law Libraries
AALS—Association of American Law Schools
ABA—American Bar Association
ALAS—Auxiliary Loans to Assist Students
CLEO—Council on Legal Education Opportunity
CPPVE—Council for Private Postsecondary and Vocational Education
CRS—Candidate Referral Service
CSS—College Scholarship Service
CWSP—College Work-Study Program
FAFSA—Free Application for Federal Student Aid
FFS—Family Financial Statement
GAPSFAS—Graduate and Professional School Financial Aid Service
GBBE—Georgia Board of Bar Examiners
GPA—Grade Point Average
GSL—Guaranteed Student Loans
LSAT—Law School Admission Test
LSDAS—Law School Data Assembly Service
MBR—Massachusetts Board of Regents
MSACS—Middle States Association of Colleges and Schools
NASC—Northwest Association of Schools and Colleges
NCACS—North Central Association of Colleges and Schools
NDSL—National Direct Student Loan
NEASC—New England Association of Schools and Colleges
SAAC—Student Aid Application for California
SACS—Southern Association of Colleges and Schools
SBC—State Bar of California
WASC—Western Association of Schools and Colleges
UGPA—Undergraduate Grade Point Average

DEGREES

D.C.L.—Doctor of Civil Law
D.C.L.—Doctor of Comparative Law
J.D.—Doctor of Jurisprudence
J.D./M.B.A.—Juris Doctor/Master of Business Administration
J.M.—Master of Jurisprudence
J.S.D.—Doctor of the Science of Law
J.S.M.—Master of the Science of Law
LL.B.—Bachelor of Laws
LL.M.—Master of Laws
M.A.—Master of Arts
M.Acc.—Master of Accountancy
M.A.L.I.R.—Master of Arts in Labor and Industrial Relations
M.A.P.A.—Master of Arts in Public Administration
M.A.S.—Master of Accounting Science
M.B.A.—Master of Business Administration
M.B.T.—Master of Business Taxation
M.C.J.—Master of Criminal Justice
M.C.L.—Master of Comparative Law
M.C.P.—Master of City Planning
M.C.P.—Master of Community Planning
M.C.R.P.—Master of City and Regional Planning
M.D.—Doctor of Medicine
M.H.A.—Master of Health Administration
M.I.L.R.—Master of Industrial and Labor Relations
M.L.S.—Master of Legal Studies
M.L.S.—Master of Library Science
M.L. & T.—Master of Law and Taxation
M.M.—Master of Management
M.O.B.—Master of Organizational Behavior
M.P.A.—Master of Public Administration
M.P.H.—Master of Public Health
M.P.P.A.—Master of Public Policy Administration
M.P.P.M.—Master of Public and Private Management
M.R.P.—Master of Regional Planning
M.S.—Master of Science
M.S.L.—Master of Studies in Law
M.S.S.A.—Master of Science in Social Administration
M.S.W.—Master of Social Work
M.U.P.—Master of Urban Planning
M.U.R.P.—Master of Urban and Regional Planning
Ph.D.—Doctor of Philosophy
S.J.D.—Doctor of the Science of Law

PART I

Choosing a Law School

CHAPTER 1

Should I Go to Law School?

You picked up this book because you have given some thought to the question of going to law school, or else someone you know is thinking about going to law school. Each year, more than 40,000 students in the United States begin the long and arduous journey associated with attending law school. There was a time when large numbers of attorneys received their legal training by studying law books at home until they were knowledgeable enough to pass an oral examination to become a lawyer. Today, almost all lawyers attend a law school before taking a standardized written bar exam. The educational process takes three or four years, depending on whether the curriculum is full or part time, and whether it is obtained at one of the law schools approved by the American Bar Association, or a handful of other law schools approved in the state where they are located.

Law school is not for everyone. Some individuals cannot cope with the intellectual demands, while others find the psychological stress associated with the study and practice of law to be suffocating. Many bright and ambitious people do not succeed at law because they find other activities more rewarding and challenging. However, many college graduates will find law school to be the most stimulating experience of their lives.

There is a great deal of popular mythology about law school and the legal profession. This book attempts to get past much of the confusing rhetoric facing individuals contemplating a legal education. *Barron's Guide to Law Schools* is full of factual information about law schools and no nonsense devices on the application process, the LSAT, and the decision-making process.

A COMPLEX DECISION

The process of choosing a law school is a complex one, and there are no easy answers along the way. The best choice for one person may be the very worst choice for another. Accordingly, this Guide should be viewed more as a road map to your destination than as the answer to all your questions. A road map may help you find your way, but it cannot replace the experience of getting there yourself.

This book focuses on the choices that each law school applicant must make during the admission process. While you are considering whether and where to attend law school, you will spend considerable energy weighing various options. The fact that you will feel confused (and at times overwhelmed) is normal. Regardless of your background, you cannot escape facing tough decisions that will affect the rest of your life. If you struggle with the choices, it is a sign that you appreciate the importance of the process.

This basic problem (Which school is best for you?) is the same for every applicant. Whether you have many choices or a single acceptance, so much rests on your decision that it is impossible not to feel the pressure. Particularly in a period of national crisis, at a time when the rule of law is under attack, the decision to attend law school is an important one. Similarly, in an era of change in the legal profession, the consequences of career decisions seem magnified.

The publisher and authors of this text have no ax to grind and no personal investment in whether you attend law school or not. Our aim is to provide objective information that will help you make an informed choice about a tough decision. We encourage you to listen to other voices who have opinions on this subject. There certainly is room for divergence of viewpoints on many of the subjects addressed here. One person will tell you that you have to be a lawyer, and the next person will tell you that nobody should be a lawyer. In the end, only you can decide on the best course of action. The best way to assure that your final decision will be the right one for you is to become fully informed on all the issues.

WHY GO TO LAW SCHOOL?

You might choose to go to law school for a number of different reasons. In fact, many lawyers were influenced by a variety of factors: They wanted the prestige, power, and panache that a degree in law provides; they wanted a professional career in which they could make enough money to establish and maintain a comfortable lifestyle; they wanted to change the world in order to make it a little better than it was when they arrived; they wanted to pursue a long family tradition; they wanted to do something different from anyone else in their family; they took an aptitude test during college and the career counselor said that they should become a lawyer; or (my personal reason for attending law school) they went to a prelaw association meeting as a favor to a roommate, got elected president, and couldn't back out. Everyone arrives at the law school door for different reasons. Some of these are valid; some are not. Here are a few of the wrong reasons to go to law school:

Don't go to law school because other people expect you to. Spouses, family, friends, and advisors seem perpetually willing to push their loved one, associate, or advisee in this direction. While these people almost always want what is best for you, their personal motives are inevitably more complex. Look at the source and weigh the advice accordingly.

Don't go to law school because of what you see on television or read in the newspapers about lawyers. Media coverage of high profile cases such as the O.J. Simpson trial or President Clinton's impeachment tend to glamorize or demonize lawyers and the law. Popular television shows such as *The Practice* or *Ally McBeal,* inevitably portray the law practice in a very different light than most lawyers experience in their daily lives. Lawyers are neither as rich, good-looking, and fast-talking, or as weasly, manipulative, and grasping as the stereotypes suggest. Most practicing lawyers will tell you that these images have little in common with their real lives. The fictional world of *Ally McBeal* has about as much in common with the way real lawyers spend their time as WWF wrestling does with war in Afghanistan. We smile bemusedly at the antics of the characters on the popular television series, but in our hearts we know that Ally and her associates could never exist in the flesh. If you want to discover how real-life lawyers work and live, ask them. Visit a law firm, or better yet, get a job in one. Look for lawyers outside the world of work; find out about lawyers in their neighborhoods and communities. Investigate how they live and play when they go home at night. You will probably discover that lawyers are a well-educated and intense (but diverse) lot, who give as much to the community as they do to their jobs.

Don't go to law school because you can't figure out what to do with your life, or because you couldn't find anything else that interested you in four years of college, or you just couldn't find a job. Law school is not the place to go to find yourself. Legal education is no place to buy more time to make a decision because you just can't bear to face the real world.

Whatever other motives may influence your decision to attend law school, make certain that a major consideration is your genuine desire to study law. If you have doubts about whether you want to *study* law (as opposed to *practice* law), do something else for a year or two. Work in a law firm, or join the Peace Corps. If you find you can't get the idea of law school out of your mind, that should be a sign to you. If, on the other hand, you forget about it, forget about it.

These admonitions may fall on deaf ears, but at least you've been warned. Many people find law school to be the most interesting, intellectually stimulating, and challenging experience of their educational lives (despite its many aggravations); others hate it almost more than they can bear. If you find that you fit into the latter group and not the former, don't put yourself through the misery of sitting through three years or more of law school classes.

WHICH LAW SCHOOL?

The decision as to which law school to attend can be even more complicated than the decision whether to attend law school. Beware of law school admissions and recruitment people. They want you—actually they want your seat deposit. Most of them are personable, well-informed, and genuine. They are, however, selling a product: their school. The best defense against the hard sell is comparison shopping. Listen to a number of different pitches before you make a choice. Finally, check out the various claims and promises relying on your own independent investigation rather than stock promotional materials. *Barron's Guide to Law Schools* is particularly suited to help you accomplish this objective (see Part I Chapter 2 and Part III of this Guide for more information).

Beware of family, friends, and prelaw advisors, who push you to attend a particular law school. Utilize impartial advice, particularly guidance from professional counselors and advisors, in making your decision. Their experience and knowledge can be invaluable. But remember! Your prelaw advisor may like a certain school because she graduated from it. Your career counselor may have been particularly impressed by the speech he heard at an open house for a certain law school. Your lawyer friend may or may not be privy to accurate information. Sometimes, opinions masked by objectivity are far from objective. And most important of all, remember that no single school is the right choice for everyone.

Beware of letting your procrastination make decisions for you. There are many critical dates in the law school admission process. Don't be foreclosed from applying to schools, seeking financial aid, or pursuing any alternative because you didn't do it in time. If you want to make the best choice, you should seek to maximize your options, and the best way to maximize your options is to stay on top of the process. Start early. Develop a tickler file to remind you in advance about critical dates. Most calendar programs for personal computers allow you to save important dates. Set aside sufficient time to meet deadlines and accomplish your objectives. Remember that the easiest decision is not always the best one.

Barron's Guide to Law Schools contains chapters on the LSAT (Chapters 10 and 11), the job outlook for graduates, including starting salaries (Chapter 8), financial aid (Chapter 6), and profiles of law schools themselves (Chapters 13 and 14).

The checklist below may help you to clarify your objectives and focus your research efforts as you think about law school. It lists the primary questions you should address as you evaluate law schools. If you can determine what choices are best for you, you not only will increase your chances of being accepted, but also improve the likelihood that law school will be a rewarding experience.

Geographical considerations inevitably come into play. A majority of law school graduates accept positions in the region where they went to law school. Those who do not stay in the same geographic area tend to return to the region where they grew up or where they have family. This is true not only for so-called local and regional law schools, but for national law schools as well. It is easier to find a job if you are physically located in the area where your job search occurs. Thus, if you know where you want to settle after graduation, you may want to consider limiting your applications to law schools in that geographic area.

Although most law school graduates settle in the largest metropolitan areas, both law schools and legal employment are found in a variety of settings. You may want to consider, as an alternative to pursuing a legal education at a school in a big city, attending school or working in a smaller city or town, a suburban area within a larger metropolitan population, or a rural area. You may have business, political, or personal ties to a community that would make it advantageous to target that place for postgraduate employment. You or your family may have ties to a university or law school that would lead you to go to school there.

You may want to give thought to what substantive areas of practice interest you. Although many entering law students do not have a clue about what areas of law they wish to pursue, sometime during the tenure of their legal education, they will have to make those choices. Other law students know before they begin law school that they are interested in a particular type of practice, and may choose a law school because of its curricular concentration in that field. Although the first year curriculum and

CHECKLIST ON CHOOSING A LAW SCHOOL

Where geograpically do you want to go to school?
- ☐ Family considerations
- ☐ Personal considerations
- ☐ Future job prospects
- ☐ Urban, suburban, rural
- ☐ Current job

What areas of practice interest you?
- ☐ School specialization, course offerings
- ☐ Part-time and summer jobs
- ☐ Other life experiences

What kind of school can you afford?
- ☐ State or private
- ☐ Evening (part-time) or Day (full-time)
- ☐ Availability of financial aid, scholarships

What sort of atmosphere do you want?
- ☐ Size of student body and faculty
- ☐ Competitiveness
- ☐ Physical plant
- ☐ Library resources
- ☐ Student services
- ☐ Educational philosphy
- ☐ University community
- ☐ Special programs, concentrations

What schools will accept you?
- ☐ LSAT
- ☐ GPA
- ☐ Special considerations (such as ethnicity)
- ☐ Work, education, or life experiences
- ☐ Other factors that make you unique
- ☐ Recommendations
- ☐ Opportunity for personal interview

many core upper-level electives are common in most law schools, different law schools will have different upper-level course offerings and concentrations. You should look carefully at law school catalogs and talk to school representatives about these differences as part of the decision-making process.

What kind of school can you afford? State law schools are usually less expensive for residents than for nonresidents, or than private schools. Among private schools, tuition may differ considerably depending on the prestige of the institution and other considerations. Schools also differ considerably as to the amount of financial aid and scholarship funds that are available to incoming students. Additionally, schools with part-time or evening programs provide an opportunity for students to attend law school while continuing to work full time.

You should look carefully for information about the school's institutional culture. Although it is hard to discern sometimes, every school has a unique personality. Its geographic location and student body demographic makeup will affect the school's atmosphere. The background of the faculty members will, too. Do most of them have experience practicing law? Or did most come directly into teaching from postgraduate appellate clerkships? What is the size of the student body, the faculty, and average classes? In some ways, a larger law school may seem more vibrant and diverse, while a smaller law school will feel more intimate and supportive. Look at the competitiveness of the institution. Do you want to see how you fare in the most highly charged competitive environment? Do you want to be a big fish in a little pond? Will you be happy just to get accepted? Take a look at the physical plant, the library, and other resources available to the law school. Consider what benefits accrue to the law school from affiliation with its parent university. Think about the history of the university and the law school, and how the institutional roots have molded the law school culture today.

Observe whether current students are satisfied with services, such as financial aid and career services. Consider the availability of cocurricular and extracurricular groups, such as law review, moot court, law school student government, and other student organizations. Ask about the educational philosophy of the institution, whether it is highly theoretical, or practical and skills-oriented. Find out whether the curriculum focuses on the law of a particular jurisdiction, or is concentrated in some other way. All of these factors are important in choosing a law school, and you can learn about many of them through careful research.

Finally, look at which law schools will accept you. If your LSAT and GPA are both very strong, you will have significantly more opportunities than people with less impressive credentials. If either your LSAT or GPA is less stellar, the number of law schools interested in you will inevitably drop. You may need to demonstrate your aptitude through other activities and experiences. If your LSAT and GPA are both low, you may find it challenging to find a single law school that will accept you. A few law schools offer programs that permit applicants to compete for slots during the summer prior to admission.

Some law schools may be located in a geographic area that does not draw as many applications as more populous ones. Some states accredit law schools not approved by the American Bar Association (ABA). Graduates of non-ABA-approved schools usually can only take the bar in the state in which the school is accredited. These schools usually have fewer and less competitive applications, and for some people this may be the only way to go to law school. Before committing to a law school not approved by the ABA you should look carefully at all the factors described in the last paragraph (see also Chapter 14).

As you use this book, it will help if you have identified your priorities. Then, as you look at various possibilities, you can judge how closely each school comes to meeting your needs. Although no option may be perfect, you will at least have some organized basis for comparison.

by Gary A. Munneke, Professor of Law at Pace University School of Law where he teaches Torts, Professional Responsibility and Law Practice Management. Prior to joining the Pace faculty in 1988, he served on the faculty of the Widener University School of Law, and as Assistant Dean at the University of Texas School of Law. Professor Munneke is the author of 16 books and numerous articles about current issues in the legal profession. His other books provide information about choosing law as a career (*Careers in Law* [1997] and *Opportunities in Law Careers* [1993], VGM Career Horizons, Lincolnwood, IL), what to do after you enter law school (*How To Succeed in Law School,* Barron's, NY, 2000), and what to do after you graduate from law school (*The Legal Career Guide: From Law Student to Lawyer* [2002], and *Nonlegal Careers for Lawyers* [2002], American Bar Association, Chicago). In addition, he has lectured extensively on these topics. Professor Munneke is Past Chair of the American Bar Association Law Practice Management Section and previously chaired its Publishing Board. He has served as President and Research Chair of the National Association for Law Placement as well as Chair of the ABA Standing Committee on Professional Utilizational and Career Development. Professor Munneke received his J.D. from the University of Texas Law School in 1973 and is licensed to practice law in Texas and Pennsylvania. He is a Fellow of the American Bar Foundation, and the College of Law Practice Management.

CHAPTER 2

Where Can I Find Information About Law School?

There is both a wealth and paucity of information about law schools. Books and guides of various sorts abound on the shelves of libraries and bookstores. Increasingly, information is available in electronic formats. Information in the form of advice from well-meaning advisors is also easily accessible. If you are thinking about attending law school, the one thing you will find in abundance is advice. What is often in short supply is any way to tell whether the advice you get is good or not. This informational paradox was apparent to the developers of this Guide. The result is a Guide that is easy to use and understand, containing up-to-the-minute information about law schools.

In addition to the *Guide to Law Schools,* Barron's offers other excellent publications, two of which are excerpted in this book. They are *Barron's How to Prepare for the LSAT* by Jerry Bobrow, an in-depth preparation guide for the law school admission test, and *How to Succeed in Law School* by Professor Gary A. Munneke, which describes what law school will be like and what students need to do to maximize their performance and opportunities. A smaller version of the LSAT book, *Pass Key to the LSAT,* is also available. These books should provide you with enough information to tackle the law school challenge. Many readers, however, will want more. For those with the time, energy, and inclination, the following paragraphs discuss many other sources of information.

Prelaw Advisors

Most colleges and universities designate one or more professors as prelaw advisors. Students thinking about law school are routinely funneled to these professors and administrators for guidance. The question of prelaw school education is addressed in more depth in the next chapter: The comments here are aimed more at assessing the pros and cons of utilizing a prelaw advisor at school.

First of all, it is very difficult to make generalizations about the type of individuals who become prelaw advisors or the quality of advice they dispense. Prelaw advisors may come from almost any discipline, although it seems that a high percentage are political science professors. Many, but certainly not all, possess a law degree themselves, in addition to professional credentials in their teaching field. They may be young professors, barely out of school themselves, or wizened veterans who have been advising generations of prospective law students.

Prelaw advisors often come to the table with a distinct set of biases in favor of or against certain law schools, approaches to the application process, and the qualities that are needed to succeed in law school. Keep in mind, however, that the more definite the advisor is in his or her opinions, the more likely it is that there are differing points of view that make as much sense. Some prelaw advisors diligently collect information about law schools, such as law school catalogs or information about former students who have attended certain law schools. Other advisors may have little in the way of written materials, but willingly commit many hours to give to those who want to talk.

Whether or not you should take the advice of your prelaw advisor is a very personal question. Just as it is with doctors, dentists, psychologists, and other professionals, chemistry is important. You need to find someone with whom it is easy to carry on a conversation, someone whose opinion you value, and someone who strikes you as well informed and objective. The same prelaw advisor might hit it off with one student and turn off another. For this reason, it makes sense to get in to talk to your prelaw advisor as early as you can during your college career. If you are not happy with the advice you get, or not comfortable talking to the advisor, you have an opportunity to find another person to fill this role.

You may find that advice from a trusted faculty mentor, such as a club sponsor, academic advisor, or favorite teacher may work just as well for you as the school's official prelaw advisor. While this mentor may not be as well versed on law schools as the regular prelaw advisor, the benefit that you will derive from being able to speak openly and candidly can be invaluable.

Career Services Offices

At some institutions, the office of career services provides information and advice about law schools and legal education. Because career counselors have training and experience in helping people to make career decisions, they may be able to assist you in ways that a faculty member could not. Some career services offices offer testing programs, which attempt to identify things like work values, personality types, and vocational interests. These tests are often validated by comparison to control groups of individuals from particular professions. Thus, you can determine whether your personality type or professional values are similar to the values or personality of other people who have chosen to go into law. Unfortunately, such tests can lay a trap for the unwary. It is one thing to say that you are like other members of a group; it does not necessarily follow that you have to have those traits in order to be successful in a given field. In reality, successful lawyers are as diverse in terms of personality and values as the general population, and while it may be possible to identify characteristics common among typical lawyers, it is not uncommon to find lawyers who do not fit into the mold.

Other Advisors

Nor is it necessary to limit the universe of potential advisors to educational settings. Well-informed family members, work supervisors, friends, and business associates all may have qualities that make them good advisors for you. In fact, nowhere is it written that you can seek advice from only one person. You may want to take a sampling of opinions from various people and reach your own decisions.

Law School Career Days

One of the best ways to get information about law schools is to attend a law school career day. These events come in a variety of forms, from those sponsored by a single university, attended by as few as a single law school, to those sponsored by Law Services in major U.S. cities, sometimes attended by more than one hundred law schools. Law schools typically send representatives to these events, in areas where they hope to draw their students. Individual law schools may schedule a day of interviews through the career service office, or the prelaw advisor. Several colleges may join together to schedule panels or career fairs of law school representatives. The Law Services annual law forums are regional fairs in major cities attended by a large number of American law schools (see page 10 for a listing of the fall 2002 fairs). Law school forums allow you to visit a number of law school representatives in person and in close proximity for easy comparison. The law schools usually bring catalogs, applications, and other literature for you to take, thus providing a quick way to receive materials.

Prelaw Associations

Many colleges and universities have a prelaw association or club committed to supporting prelaw students at those institutions. These student organizations may sponsor programs, collect information, and at universities affiliated with a law school, provide opportunities for direct contact with law school faculty and students.

The Internet

Most law schools provide home pages on the Internet that contain an array of useful segments on various aspects of the law school's life and history. You can find faculty biographies, course descriptions, admission and graduation requirements, schedules, and information about special programs in the law school. Some law schools provide for on-line application. You may be able to contact the admissions officer or faculty members by e-mail with questions. For individuals who are comfortable operating in an electronic environment, much of the work in applying to law school can be completed on-line.

Law School Visits

If you have narrowed the number of law schools to which you plan to apply to two or three, it may make sense for you to visit the schools in person. When you applied to undergraduate schools, you probably visited campuses before you made your final choice. What you learned about the setting, ambiance, and facilities undoubtedly contributed to your final decision. It is no different with the decision to attend law school. Some law schools encourage on-site visits through open houses on specific dates. Most law schools, however, are happy to arrange for a campus visit at any time. It makes sense to try to schedule your visit at a time when classes are in session in order to get a sense of what law school life is like at the school. You may be able to visit classes, talk to students and faculty, and meet with officials about such matters as applications and financial aid.

Interviews

Some law schools incorporate personal interviews into the application process. A few schools utilize interviews as a formal part of the selection process. Some other schools encourage, but do not require, applicants to interview with a representative of the law school as a means of gathering more data about the candidate. An interview is typically a one- or two-on-one process, not unlike a job interview, as distinguished from more informal visits with law school personnel in conjunction with law forums or campus visits. Find out if the schools to which you plan to apply provide for interviews. If they do, decide whether you want to avail yourself of this opportunity. Most applicants welcome the chance to sell themselves directly to the school.

Law-Related Jobs

Part of the information gathering process may include finding out more about what lawyers do. If you grew up in a family of one or more lawyers, you probably learned a great deal about the legal profession and the practice of law through contact with these family members. You probably learned more about lawyers than you realized at the time. The fact that you remain interested in a career in law suggests that something about the lifestyle of a lawyer appeals to you.

If you did not grow up in such a family, or if you did and you want to learn more, one of the best ways to find out whether you want to practice law is to work in a law firm or other legal organization. Even if you visited a law office as part of a career day in high school or college, nothing will give you a first-hand view of legal work better than a job in the law. You might be surprised at how many opportunities there are in the law firms, corporate law departments, government law departments, district attorney and public defender offices, and public service organizations. These organizations include, in addition to the legal staff, a support staff of people who have not attended law school, such as legal assistants, legal secretaries, and file clerks.

The jobs may be full time or part time, depending on the needs of the employer, and the pay may vary widely depending on the qualifications for the job and the marketplace for workers in the area. You may be able to find a job with a law firm or other employer for the summer, or as part of a school-sponsored internship. If you are already working for a company, you may be able to arrange for temporary assignments with the company's legal department, or to take on other law-related tasks.

The greatest number of opportunities in the legal marketplace is probably for permanent support staff positions. For legal assistants (paralegals as they are sometimes called) or legal secretaries, training or experience in the field will be helpful; however, there are no state or national standards for these positions such as there would be for becoming a lawyer in the organization. Some firms try to hire highly intelligent and motivated people, who possess basic skills such as keyboarding, word processing, and other computer skills, and provide the training to these individuals themselves.

It is not uncommon for law students today to have spent two to three years, or more, working in a law firm or other organization, before coming to law school. Many law students continue these prelegal positions while they go to law school, either cutting back on their work hours to part-time status while they are in school, or continuing to work full time, but attending law school part time in the evening. One potential advantage of working in a law-related position before or during law school, is that there may be an increased probability of obtaining employment with that organization as a lawyer after graduation. Even more important, however, employment in a legal setting may help you to decide whether you want to work in law at all. You will see up close that the practice of law is very different from the images of legal work garnered from books, television, and secondhand anecdotal information.

U.S. News and Other Rankings

Each year *U.S. News and World Report* produces a ranking of law schools that is relied on extensively by many law school applicants and their advisors. The rankings, based on both statistical data and surveys of lawyers, judges and legal educators, have a tendency to imbue a

Law School Forums in 2002

If you're considering law school, come to a Law School Forum. Free admission. No preregistration. Once you register on-site, in one place, you can:

- talk with representatives of LSAC—member law schools from across the United States and Canada;
- obtain admission materials, catalogs, and financial aid information;
- view video programs about the law school admission process, legal education and careers, and minority perspectives on legal education, and gay and lesbian issues;
- attend informational sessions on the law school admission process, financing a legal education, and issues of importance to minority applicants; and
- review LSAC publications, videos, software, and LSAT® preparation materials.

Atlanta, GA	Friday-Saturday, October 11-12, 2002 Sheraton Atlanta Hotel
Boston, MA	Saturday, November 2, 2002 Boston Marriott Copley Place
Chicago, IL	Friday-Saturday, September 20-21, 2002 Chicago Marriott Downtown
Dallas (Fort Worth), TX	Saturday, October 19, 2002 Renaissance Worthington
Los Angeles, CA	Friday-Saturday, November 15-16, 2002 Los Angeles Airport Marriott
New York, NY	Saturday-Sunday, September 28-29, 2002
Washington, DC	Saturday, July 6, 2002 Marriott Wardman Park
Bay Area, CA	Monday, November 11, 2002 Hotel Nikko, San Francisco
For further information contact:	**Law School Forums** Law Services Box 40 Newtown, PA 18940-0040 215.968.1001 Internet: *http://www.lsac.org*

Test Dates	Domestic & Canadian Published Test Centers (US/Puerto Rico/US Territories/Canada): Regular Registration by Mail (postmark deadline), Telephone (receipt deadline), and Online (receipt deadline)	Late Registration by Mail (postmark deadline)	Late Registration by Telephone and Online (receipt deadline)	Foreign Published Test Centers: Registration Deadline** by Mail (postmark deadline), Telephone (receipt deadline), and Online (receipt deadline)
Monday, June 10, 2002	May 8, 2002	May 9-15, 2002	May 9-20, 2002	May 3, 2002
Saturday, October 5, 2002 Monday, October 7, 2002†*	September 4, 2002	September 5-11, 2002	September 5-16, 2002	August 30, 2002
Saturday, December 7, 2002 Monday, December 9, 2002†*	November 6, 2002	November 7-13, 2002	November 7-18, 2002	November 1, 2002
Saturday, February 8, 2003* Monday, February 10, 2003†*	January 8, 2003	January 9-15, 2003	January 9-21, 2003	January 3, 2003

Other LSAT Options

Test Dates	Test Center Change†† by Mail (postmark deadline) Telephone (receipt deadline) $28	Test Date Change by Mail (postmark deadline) $28	Nonpublished Test Centers—Domestic & Canadian Test Centers (receipt deadline) $199 plus $103 LSAT fee	Nonpublished Test Centers—Foreign Test Centers (receipt deadline) $266 plus $103 LSAT fee	LSAT Registration Refunds *partial only* (postmark deadline) $39
Monday, June 10, 2002	May 17, 2002 (mail) May 22, 2002 (telephone)	June 15, 2002	May 3, 2002	April 12, 2002	June 7, 2002
Saturday, October 5, 2002 Monday, October 7, 2002†*	September 13, 2002 (mail) September 18, 2002 (telephone)	October 12, 2002	August 30, 2002	August 9, 2002	October 4, 2002
Saturday, December 7, 2002 Monday, December 9, 2002†*	November 15, 2002 (mail) November 20, 2002 (telephone)	December 14, 2002	November 1, 2002	October 11, 2002	December 6, 2002
Saturday, February 8, 2003* Monday, February 10, 2003†*	January 17, 2003 (mail) January 22, 2003 (telephone)	February 15, 2003	January 3, 2003	December 13, 2002	February 7, 2003

LSAT Score Release Dates

Test Dates	LSAT TelScore 215.968.1200 $10 fee	Score Report Mailed (approximated date)
Monday, June 10, 2002	June 29, 2002	July 9, 2002
Saturday, October 5, 2002 Monday, October 7, 2002†*	October 26, 2002	November 5, 2002
Saturday, December 7, 2002 Monday, December 9, 2002†*	January 4, 2003	January 13, 2003
Saturday, February 8, 2003* Monday, February 10, 2003†*	March 1, 2003	March 10, 2003

- **For Telephone Services: 215.968.1001** *(see page 3 for hours)*
- **For Online Services: *www.LSAC.org***
  Registration closes midnight EST on deadline date

† This test is for Saturday Sabbath observers only. For details, please see Saturday Sabbath Observers.

†† Center changes to foreign centers must meet the foreign registration deadline.

* This test is NONDISCLOSED. Persons who take a nondisclosed test receive only their scores. They do not receive their test questions, answer key, or individual responses.

** Late registration is not available for foreign centers.

Note *Walk-in registration on the day of the test is not permitted at any test center for any test administration.*

degree of certainty into the process of evaluating law schools that does not exist in reality. Other similar surveys, reported by different publications, fall into the same trap. They all presume that a single set of measurable criteria will work for all applicants. This is simply not the case.

The American Bar Association has circulated a statement warning students against the uncritical use of law school rankings (see box below). This position is supported by the Law School Admissions Council and most law school deans and admissions officers.

Rating of Law Schools

No rating of law schools beyond the simple statement of their accreditation status is attempted or advocated by the American Bar Association. Qualities that make one kind of school good for one student may not be as important to another. The American Bar Association and its Section of Legal Education and Admissions to the Bar have issued disclaimers of any law school rating system. Prospective law students should consider a variety of factors in making their choice among approved schools.

If you look at a ranking system such as *U.S. News,* do so with a skeptical eye. Remember that reputations in legal education are established over decades. Recognize that different schools are “”best” for different people. And accept the fact that all ABA-approved law schools go through the same rigorous accreditation process.

LITERATURE AND THE MEDIA

Lawyers are portrayed in a variety of lights in literature and the media. Many of the images of lawyers in television and film, as well as in books and the news, are exaggerated, distorted, and stereotypical. It is very difficult to capture the essence of legal work through a literary or cinematic eye. Notwithstanding this limitation, the pervasiveness of media images of lawyers makes it inevitable that we are influenced by these images. Even lawyers themselves are sometimes influenced by their own media hype.

There are a number of excellent books and films on the legal profession, and regular viewing of court proceedings and discussion of legal issues on Court TV, CNN, and C-SPAN can be highly illuminating. Here are a few specific recommendations on books and films:

- *The Bramble Bush* by Carl Llewellyn. Still a classic on the thought process of legal analysis.

- *The Paper Chase* by John Jay Osborne. The book, or the movie with John Houseman as the quintessential law professor who does intellectual battle with his less-than-equal first-year student nemesis, Hart.

- *One L* by Scott Turow. Probably a more realistic picture of law school, based on Turow's school notes about the first year of law school.

- *A Civil Action* by Jonathan Harr. A riveting account of the colossal battle between a brash, aggressive plaintiff lawyer and an icon of the Boston legal establishment in an environmental pollution case in the town of Woburn, Massachusetts—a true story. Read the book; skip the movie.

- *Inherit the Wind.* The book, the play, the movie, all three a fictionalization of the Scopes Monkey Trial, in which a Tennessee science teacher was prosecuted for teaching evolution. The lawyers in the real case were three-time presidential candidate William Jennings Bryan and famed defense counsel Clarence Darrow.

- *A Few Good Men,* with Jack Nicholson and Tom Cruise, tells the story of military justice, after a commander's rigid discipline leads to a soldier's death. We all know that the villain doesn't usually break down on the stand in real life, but Jack makes us believe anyway.

- *Gideon's Trumpet* by Anthony Lewis. If ever you wanted a reason to become a lawyer, this is it: indigent man fights to the Supreme Court for the right to be represented by counsel.

- *To Kill a Mockingbird* by Harper Lee, or the movie with Gregory Peck. A classic in print or film: small town Southern lawyer stands for courage and dignity as he faces the challenges of practicing law, while standing up for truth, justice, and the American way of life.

- Anything by John Grisham. Sure, the plots are far-fetched, and the dialogue hardly Hemingway, but each one of Grisham's tales provides great imagery on different practice settings from plaintiff practice (*The*

Rainmaker), to elite corporate work (*The Firm*), to high profile criminal cases (*A Time to Kill*).

- *Kramer v. Kramer*. Dustin Hoffman and Meryl Streep fight for custody in a courtroom drama that demonstrates how justice isn't always easy to find in the courtroom.

- *Erin Brokavich*. Feisty paralegal played by Julia Roberts helps expose Pacific Gas & Electric pollution coverup. Based on a true story.

The list could go on and on, because lawyers, trials, and the stories of people who encounter the justice system provide such fertile soil for intriguing plotlines. Whether the source is books, movies, or TV (depictions of lawyers on the small screen are legion), it is possible to learn about the work of lawyers by watching how they are depicted in various media. What you learn may not dictate your choices about law school, but it may provide useful clues to help you answer your questions.

It should be apparent to you that in order for you to gather information about law schools, you need to evaluate information from a variety of sources in light of your own aspirations. The decision to attend law school may involve the outlay of one hundred thousand dollars, or more, in direct costs, and require you to forego other income for a period of three or four years. For this reason, the decision to go to law school should not be made lightly. This chapter has provided an overview of the primary sources of information available to help you make this decision. The rest is up to you.

by Gary A. Munneke, Professor of Law, Pace University School of Law (see page 6).

CHAPTER 3

What Course of Prelaw Study Should I Take?

There is no standard prelaw curriculum. Law schools do not require any particular undergraduate degree, course of study, or particular courses in order to gain admission. Statistics on the entering class of every law school will demonstrate that students come from a wide variety of backgrounds. Perhaps the largest number of law students started out as political science majors, but other majors from the arts and social sciences are well represented, including history, English, psychology, and sociology. Law schools generally have a high concentration of business majors, including tax and accounting, general business, economics, criminal justice, and international relations. There are usually smaller but significant numbers from the hard sciences like physics, chemistry, and biology, or engineering. Other majors, such as journalism, environmental science, and art, music, or drama, are likely to be found in a typical first-year class.

Because law schools only require that you complete an undergraduate degree, every degree program is equal, at least in theory. In practice, law schools may find that they have had better success with graduates from certain degree programs at certain universities than others. Individual admissions committee members at different schools may have their own ideas about what kind of prelaw training will prepare students best for law school. Undergraduate advisors may channel prelaw students into certain majors that they perceive to have a nexus with law school. If your research discloses that certain concentrations or degree programs are likely to receive favorable treatment in the admissions process of schools where you plan to apply, you would be wise to pursue such a course of study.

Otherwise, the best advice for your prelegal education is to follow a curriculum that you enjoy and in which you possess an interest independent of law school. There are two important reasons for this: First, chances are that you will do better in a subject area that you enjoy than you will in one that you hate. If you have to struggle each day to get up and go to class, it will undoubtedly be reflected in your grades, and a poor showing will adversely affect your chances to be admitted to law school. Second, if you do not get into law school or decide not to go to law school, you will have pursued a course of study that will help you in some alternative career path.

Much the same advice can be said about specific courses. Take courses that you like, that provide an intellectual challenge for you personally. Study under professors who are interesting and exciting, rather than those who put you to sleep. Take classes that make you want to learn, rather than those that fit into a convenient schedule or guarantee an "A."

There is no washout course for prelaw, like Organic Chemistry for premed majors. There is no one course that every law school applicant must complete. Yet, prelaw students continue to pose the question: What courses will help me most in law school? At the risk of negating the advice of take what you like, the following are this author's personal suggestions:

1. **Logic or reasoning.** Much of law school centers on legal analysis, which is fundamentally deductive logic. Learning about logic and reasoning can help to prepare you for the kind of thinking you will be required to do in law school.

2. **Legal history.** Although you will read historical cases in law school, you may find a paucity of information about the roots of our legal system. A course that traces the development of the law, particularly Anglo-American jurisprudence, will provide you with a useful background throughout your legal career.

3. **Public speaking.** You will be required to speak when called on in class, and you

will need to be able to make oral arguments throughout law school. Courses that polish your speaking ability and the skill of thinking on your feet will make the inevitable speaking requirements of law school more palatable. A course like this might be particularly valuable for someone who is not accustomed to, or afraid of, standing up and speaking publicly.

4. **Research and writing.** Any course that imposes a demanding regimen of critiqued writing based upon academic research will help you in law school. All law students are required to complete research and writing assignments during law school—an activity that does not end with graduation, because much of lawyering involves research and writing. In addition, many law school exams are essay tests, which favor effective writers. The more writing experience you get, the better off you will be in law school.

5. **Basic accounting.** Certain law school courses in the areas of contracts, business and tax, assume a fundamental understanding of financial and accounting terms and principles. Legal practitioners are constantly required to deal with their clients' money, as well as their own. Understanding the basics of accounting and business will prove invaluable.

6. **Speed reading.** You will probably be required to do more reading in law school than you ever have before. You will also be expected to understand the material in greater depth than in the past. Accordingly, the ability to pore over a great amount of reading with a high level of retention is important. Many universities offer such courses on either a credit or noncredit basis; if yours does not, consider taking such a course outside of school.

Here are a few other suggestions for course selection in undergraduate school: Do not be afraid of courses that are intellectually demanding; these classes will train your mind for the rigors of a legal education. Get a well-rounded education; take courses outside your major. Legal problems draw from the experience of humankind, and so lawyers inevitably must be renaissance people in order to understand these legal problems. Master technology; most universities are now wired environments, and students use computers in a variety of ways. Do not think that you can avoid technology by attending law school; conversely, if you embrace technology, you will find that there are many applications for your knowledge in law. Do more than go to classes; get involved in extracurricular activities as well. Evidence of learning is found in more places than transcripts.

If it has been several years since you were in school, you may find yourself experiencing some uneasiness about returning to the world of education. Some of this malaise you should discount out of hand. You will find that your reacclimation to school comes quickly. You will also discover that life experiences gained since college give you valuable perspectives that you will use in the law. The discipline of managing life in the real world will undoubtedly help you to organize your time and maximize your performance in law school. If you have been out of school for a long time, or remain nervous about returning to school for any other reason, then take courses before you apply to law school. These might be undergraduate courses at a local community college or a university, or they might be graduate level courses offered through your employer. Such experiences may help to make the transition go more smoothly.

Although the bulk of this section has dealt with undergraduate education, it is worth noting that a significant number of law school entrants possess advanced degrees, including MBAs, CPAs, master's degrees in a variety of other fields, Ph.D.s, MDs and other medical degrees. You should not be surprised in your first year law school class to find yourself sitting between an anesthesiologist and a history professor. You may have obtained a graduate degree yourself, and wondered if there is room in law school for someone like you. The answer is yes.

People who come to law school with professional degree certification usually fall into one of two groups: those who hope to build upon their prior training with a degree in law, and those who hope to make a complete career change because they are not satisfied with their chosen occupation. Both groups are well represented in law school. Graduate level training can be a useful credential for law school admission and an excellent preparation for the study of law. However, because the admission process typically focuses on undergraduate grades, A's in graduate school will not wipe out C's in college.

Finally, a word about *which* college. Law schools take into consideration the reputations of undergraduate institutions just as other graduate programs do. If you went to a school with an excellent reputation, or a highly regarded degree program, it will help you in the application process. Because law schools are able to compare the performance of admitted students with their undergraduate institutions, they may have evidence to show that students from a particular school or college perform above or below the average of admitted students. This may be because the undergraduate school recommends more or fewer of its better students to a particular law school. It may be that a larger number of applicants coming from a particular university (say a local one) means that admitted students fall within the full range of qualifications in the entering class. Whatever the reasons, your school does make a difference. If you think that law schools may not know enough about your prelegal schools or degree programs to be able to make an accurate assessment of your abilities, send informational material about the school or program with your application.

In the final analysis, your prelegal education can help you in a variety of ways to prepare for the rigors of law school. The absence of specific requirements gives you a great deal of freedom in choosing a path. Select one that builds the skills you will need in law school, that is simultaneously interesting and fulfilling on its own.

by Gary A. Munneke, Professor of Law, Pace University School of Law (see page 6).

CHAPTER 4

How Do I Apply to Law School?

Law school and the legal profession are nebulous concepts for most people. The law school application process that you will complete as an applicant is somewhat analogous to what you will be doing as a law student. You will research the issue, you will analyze the results of your research, and you will reach a conclusion.

An attorney has power and position, and thus great responsibility. You are about to embark upon a process that is just the beginning of a lifetime of continued legal education. The law is an ever changing body of statutes and court opinions. You must become socially aware and involved in your community. Today, we face problems that are different from those faced in the past; the problems of the future will be different from those faced today; none are less important than the others.

The application process must be taken seriously and applicants should investigate all options available to them. Fortunately, there are many sources of information for prospective law students to use. See Chapter 2, particularly the schedule of Law School Forums for 2003.

LSATS AND GPAS

Each applicant to law school is required to take the Law School Admission Test (LSAT). The LSAT is administered four times per year, typically June, October, December, and February. For most law schools the LSAT is one of the most important factors in determining entrance as it is a common denominator for every applicant.

In determining whether a particular application is appropriate, law school representatives will release median numbers. Applicants should know that a median means the middle score. Therefore, there are students enrolled with numbers above and below the median. In addition, should the school release average numbers, it would be the sum of the scores divided by the number of enrolled students. Finally, applicants should recognize that the median for the accepted group of students to a particular school is typically higher than the median for the actual enrolled group for that school. For example, if a law school admitted five students with LSAT scores of 180, 172, 151, 148, 143, their median LSAT would be a 151. By way of contrast, the average LSAT would be a 159. If only the bottom three students enrolled, however, the median would be 148, and the average would be 147.

It would appear to be a rather simple matter to compare law schools based on their medians if that were the only criteria used in admission. However, an applicant's undergraduate career typically plays an equally important role in the decision process. A student's academic record must be analyzed very carefully. Factors such as school(s) attended, classes taken, major, minor, number of hours worked while in school, as well as grade progression are all important factors. Therefore, applicants should acknowledge particular strengths in their academic performance, and point out events such as a change of major that may have had a significant impact on the progression of grades.

FACTORS TO CONSIDER

Choosing a law school is a complex process. You must analyze your own needs and desires. You should consider the atmosphere in which you function well, the location, the reputation, the support services, housing options, financial aid packages, placement opportunities, faculty, student body characteristics, activities, and library facilities. Each will be more or less important to each individual.

Are you happiest in an urban, suburban, or rural area? Is the prestige value of the institution you attend of great importance to you? Do you do best where there is a fair degree of interaction between you and your faculty members? Do you want to attend a large school or a small school? (Keep in mind that a law school with over 1,000 students is considered large.) Do you need a nearby support system of family and friends? Is cost important to you? This list of questions barely scratches the surface. Be honest with yourself in order to assess what law school best suits your needs.

As you begin to review the catalogs, keep in mind the factors that are most important to you. However, remember that you shouldn't base your decision solely on the availability of certain elective courses. Your interest may change once you're in law school.

Review the faculty. Do they come from a wide range of schools? Do they have advanced degrees? Have they clerked for a judge or worked in a law firm? Are there women and members of minority groups on the faculty? Do they teach the substantive required courses? There are no right or wrong answers to these and other questions. But the answers to these and other questions you pose will give you a better picture of the law school.

Next, review the student organizations as they can enrich your legal education experience. The variety and types available will give you a sense of the student body at that given law school.

Review the law school career services office. What type of services do they offer? What type of jobs do the graduates take? Where geographically are they employed? Are you able to speak to alumni who practice in various areas of the law, e.g., environmental, health, criminal, etc.? (An overview of law school career services appears in Chapter 8 of this Guide).

The catalog will also give detailed information on the library: the number of volumes, the advanced technology available, and any specialized collections unique to the school. Most law school libraries have access to the national legal data bases, and law school students are trained to use this valuable research tool.

Items such as faculty-to-student ratio, the ratio of library seats to students, or the number of volumes in the library are factors that are scrutinized by the American Bar Association (ABA). All ABA-approved law schools must meet or exceed national standards as determined by the ABA. (Profiles of ABA-approved law schools appear in Chapters 12 and 13 of this Guide).

At this point the question of attending a non-ABA-approved school may be raised and the answer generally is no. There are some non-ABA-approved law schools that are accredited in their own state. Graduates of state certified schools are usually eligible to take the bar exam in that state. However, problems arise when one of these graduates wants to practice law in another state. The state board of bar examiners in each state sets the requirements for admission to practice in their state as there is no national bar exam. The graduate of a non-ABA-approved law school will find that it is difficult, if not impossible, to get admitted to the bar of any other state. (For more information, see Chapter 14 of this Guide.)

The number of law schools remaining after this cursory review is probably still too large a number for you to consider applying to all. Therefore, look closely at the schools that meet your needs, based on the preliminary information you have gathered. How well do you match up with the profile of these law schools' most recent incoming class? What are the medians of the schools in which you are interested and how do your numerical predictors match up with their numbers?

It may appear that applicants are judged only on the numbers; however, most law schools consider many other aspects of the application as discussed earlier. Applicants must recognize that the LSAT and GPA are the most common factors to each applicant, thus placing everyone at a starting point or on a level playing field. Other factors then become important, such as major, undergraduate institution, advanced degrees, leadership roles in community or within extracurricular activities, letters of recommendation, and the personal essay.

Most applicants submit anywhere from five to seven applications to various law schools. Applying to one law school is probably unwise; likewise, applying to 100 law schools is not necessary and is very expensive.

FILLING OUT THE APPLICATION

Once you have identified the schools you will be applying to, you must complete the applications in a timely manner. Applicants must read the instructions for each school carefully. Complete all questions that are not identified as optional and provide explanations where necessary. Any questions labeled "optional" may be left blank. (See the sample application provided on page 20.)

If you do not have access to a typewriter or word processor, the law school application may be printed clearly. Remember to make copies of each application that is submitted. An increasing number of schools allow you to apply on-line through their web sites. If you are connected to the Internet at your school this option may make sense for you. In addition, applications may be completed by utilizing school specific on-line applications or the LSACD. Produced by Law Services, the LSACD is a Windows(r) compatible, Interactive multimedia CD-ROM. All ABA-approved law schools are included in the LSACD's fully searchable database and easy-to-use application forms.

The Personal Statement

Most law schools in the country do not interview candidates for admission. Therefore, your personal statement is the only place in which you are able to sell yourself to the law school. This may be the only opportunity that the committee has to get to know the person behind the application. It is an opportunity for you to respond to questions you think the admissions committee may have when they review your application and academic record. It is the place to express who you are and what is important to you. You may wish to emphasize any personal or professional experiences and how they have contributed to your growth and/or personal development. Examples of items that applicants might consider including are: a description of work experience and extracurricular activities; explanation of distinct trends or discrepancies among grades; a description of substantial time commitments while attending school; verification that standardized tests have underpredicted academic performance in the past (prior test scores should be provided); cultural, ethnic, educational, or other factors that might cause the LSAT score or GPA to be an inaccurate measure of potential for law study. In addition, you may wish to mention the fact that you are the first member of the family to graduate from college, or you may wish to explain hardships or handicaps that you have overcome in order to achieve your degree.

In sum, the personal statement is a case that you have made for yourself to the admissions committee. Above all, it must be typed carefully and accurately. Correct spelling and grammar are essential.

Letters of Recommendation

Letters of recommendation can be very helpful to the admissions committee. For recent graduates (within two years), at least one faculty appraisal is preferred. Other applicants who would find it difficult to obtain faculty appraisals may request recommendations from individuals who can appraise their ability to perform in law school. Where an institution has a central file for appraisals that are duplicated as needed, or where a committee provides a composite appraisal, typically these alternative procedures are acceptable.

Applicants who have been out of school for a number of years should seek letters of recommendation from individuals who can speak to the applicant's character, leadership abilities, and analytical skills. The quality of the recommendation and content are more important than who writes the letter.

Letters of recommendation are additional pieces of evidence that support your case for admission. Many law schools utilize standard recommendation forms in lieu of or in addition to letters. If the school provides such forms, make sure that your references are complete, then return them.

Most law schools will be utilizing a new service offered by Law Services that will require your letters to be submitted through the LSDAS letter of recommendation service that serves all member schools. The service is included in your LSDAS registration subscription. Your letters will be copied and sent to law schools along with your LSDAS report, or as received. To use this service, follow the directions for submitting letters outlined in the LSAT/LSDAS Registration and Information Book. Be sure to fill out and give each letter writer a letter of recommendation form from the LSAT/LSDAS Registration and Information Book.

DEADLINES, DEADLINES, DEADLINES

All law schools specify deadlines for submission of the application materials to their institution. However, you should begin to explore your options in your junior year of college. This allows you enough time to narrow your choices, gather the appropriate information, and be prepared to submit timely applications in the fall of your senior year. Even if you later decide to work for a period of time after graduation, you keep your choices open by starting early.

First, determine when you are going to take the LSAT exam. Registration materials are available through Law Services. Almost all ABA-approved law schools require the use of the Law School Data Assembly Service (LSDAS), and, therefore, upon registration for the exam, you should register simultaneously for the service. This service analyzes your transcript (you must have one sent to Law Services from each undergraduate institution you have attended) and submits a report of your undergraduate record along with your LSAT score and an unofficial copy of your transcript to the law schools you have indicated.

Application for Admission__2002-03

Pace University School of Law
78 North Broadway
White Plains, NY 10603
Admissions Telephone - (914) 422-4210

Application as:

☒ First year student: Fall term 2002
☐ Reactivation
☐ Transfer student: __________ term __________
☐ Visiting student: __________ term __________
☐ Twenty-four credit student: __________ term __________
(Only for students with foreign law degrees who wish to qualify for bar exam)

Application to enter:

☒ Three-year J.D. (full-time) program*
☐ Four-year J.D. (part-time) program*
☐ Day part-time
☐ Evening part-time

Please type or print in ink:

1. Name *SAMPLE* (Last) *MPLE* (First) *A.* (Middle)

If we will be receiving documents under any other name, please indicate name: *NO*

2. Social Security Number *999-99-9999*

3. Are you at least 18 years of age? ☒ Yes ☐ No Birthdate *02 / 04 / 71* (optional)

4. Present Mailing Address *78 North Broadway White Plains NY 10603 USA* (Number and Street / City / State / Zip Code)

Date when current address no longer applies __________

Home Telephone: *914-422-4210* (Area Code/Number) Business Telephone: *914-422-4282* (Area Code/Number)

If we contact you at your business number, may we identify ourselves as calling from Pace University School of Law? ☒ Yes ☐ No

5. Permanent Address *78 North Broadway* (Number and Street) Home Telephone: *914-422-4210* (Area Code/Number)

White Plains NY 10603 USA (City / State / Zip Code)

6. **Citizenship**
Are you a U.S. Citizen? ☒ Yes ☐ No
Are you a permanent resident of the U.S.? ☐ Yes ☐ No
If you answered NO to either of the above questions, you must complete the Foreign Student Questionnaire attached to the application.

7. Father's Name *Joe Doe* 8. Father's Occupation *Doctor*

9. Mother's Name *Jane Smith* 10. Mother's Occupation *Nurse*

11. If any member of your family has attended Pace University School of Law, please list their name and date of graduation.

____

List the name, address and home and business telephone numbers of a person through whom you can be reached

Name	Address	Telephone #
Jane Smith	*Same as above*	*(914) 422-2222*

*If the program you have checked is closed at the time your application is processed, do you wish to be considered for the alternate division?
☒ Yes ☐ No

12. Please complete the following summary of your academic history in chronological sequence. This form must be completed.

	Name of Institution	College Code Number (See LSAT/LSDAS registration materials.)	Location of school attended	Dates of attendance	Degree or expected degree	Date awarded or expected	Major field of study
Secondary School(s)	*White Plains High School*		*White Plains NY*	*09/88*		*06/99*	
College(s) and/or Universities	*Pace University*	*2644*	*White Plains NY*	*09/92 06/94*	*BA*		*Accounting*
Graduate and/or Law School(s)	*Pace University*	*2644*	*White Plains NY*	*09/94 06/96*	*MBA*		*Accounting*

13. Describe in an addendum, if you wish, any or all extracurricular or community activities which were important to you. Indicate your contribution to each activity. We are primarily concerned with those which demonstrate your leadership, communication, and creative thinking abilities as well as your initiative.

14. List any academic honors, awards, prizes or other recognition you have received ***Who's Who Among American College Graduates, Alumni Academic Scholarship Program***

15. As an undergraduate, were you employed during the academic year? ***Yes***

No. of hours per week: Fr. Year ***0*** Soph. Year ***10*** Jr. Year ***20*** Sr. Year ***20***

Position held: ***Part-time - Office Assistant***

16. Please state your last four positions (paid or volunteer) of full or part-time employment, including summer employment. You may in addition to, or in place of, the following, submit a current resume. There cannot be any missing or unexplained time periods in our reviewing of items 12, 16, and the personal statement.

From	To	Position held	Name and address of employer	Reason for leaving
06/96	*Present*	*Office Coordinator*	*Pepsico*	*N/A*
09/94	*05/96*	*Human Resources Assistant*	*IBM Corporation*	*Position at Pepsico*
09/93	*08/94*	*Office Assistant*	*Career Development Office - Pace Univ.*	*Graduated*

17. Have you ever applied for admission to this law school? ***NO*** If so, in what year and with what result? ______

SAMPLE

Answer all of the following questions:

Answer Yes or No

Have you ever been enrolled (registered) in another law school? 18. *No*
School Name__________ Dates of Attendance ____/____/____ to ____/____/____
______ I am ______ I am not eligible to return to the above school. If not eligible, briefly state the reason(s) why you are ineligible on a supplementary sheet.

Have you ever attended a Summer Conditional Admissions Program sponsored by a law school? 19. *No*
School Name __________ Dates of Attendance ____/____/____ to ____/____/____

Has your college, university, graduate or professional school course been interrupted for one or more terms for any reason? (Interruptions between the end of one degree program and the beginning of another need not be explained.) 20. *No*

Are there any disciplinary charges pending against you? 21. *No*

Have you ever been placed on academic probation during your college, university, graduate, or professional coursework? 22. *No*

Have you ever been placed on academic and or disciplinary probation for actions arising from allegations of academic dishonesty, plagiarism, cheating, during your college, university, graduate or professional coursework? 23. *No*

Have you ever been suspended or required to withdraw from any school or college for scholastic or other reasons? 24. *No*

Have you ever been convicted of a criminal offense other than a minor traffic violation? (NOTE: Repeated moving violations, unpaid parking tickets, or driving while intoxicated or impaired may be viewed by some jurisdictions as serious offenses.) 25. *No*

Are there any criminal charges pending against you? 26. *No*

Note: Admission to law school does not mean that you will meet the character and fitness requirements for admission to the bar of any state. If you are concerned as to whether an event in your life will affect your eligibility for a license to practice law you should discuss the matter with the Board of Bar Examiners in the state(s) where you plan to practice.

If you have ever served on full-time military active duty, was your discharge other than honorable? 27. *No*

If your answer to any of questions 18 - 27 is "yes," please explain fully on a supplemental sheet.

28. Please indicate when you took (or plan to take) the Law School Admissions Test. Date(s) *02/01/02* Score(s) *155*

29. Ethnic Status (Optional): In order to advance the affirmative action plan of the Law School and in accordance with the national goal of equal opportunity, please indicate your ethnic and/or racial background (E.E.O. categories). Please check one:
    - ☐ African-American (non-Hispanic)
    - ☐ American Indian/Alaskan Native (Native American)
    - ☐ Asian/Pacific Islander
    - ☒ Caucasian/White (non-Hispanic)
    - ☐ Chicano/Mexican
    - ☐ Other
    - ☐ Hispanic (black)
    - ☐ Hispanic (white)
    - ☐ Puerto Rican

30. Will you be applying to the Council on Legal Education Opportunity (CLEO) program? *(see description in instructions)*
    ☐ Yes ☒ No

31. Two appraisals must be submitted on your behalf. Please list the names, titles and addresses of those persons from whom you have requested an appraisal: PLEASE PRINT CLEARLY.

a.		b.	
	Jim Burns		*J. White*
	Professor		*Professor*
	Pace University		*Pace University*
	Bedford Rd.		*1 Martin Ave.*

(over)

32. Personal Statement:
On a separate sheet of paper, please complete the required statement as described in the instructions to applicants. The statement must be typed and double-spaced.

33. Please complete. Information regarding the status of my application may be released to the following individual(s). If this section is left blank, information will <u>not</u> be released to anyone except the applicant. Final decisions are <u>not</u> released over the telephone to anyone.

No ____
Name *Relationship*

No ____
Name *Relationship*

34. Did you meet a representative of Pace University School of Law? ☒ Yes ☐ No
If yes, indicate where ____

☒ LSAC Sponsored Law Forum at:
☒ New York ☐ Chicago ☐ Washington, D.C.
☐ Atlanta ☐ Houston
☐ Boston ☐ Los Angeles

35. If you are interested in information concerning a specific area of law, indicate below the area of interest:
☐ Certificate in Environmental Law
☐ Certificate in Health Law
☒ Certificate in International Law
☒ J.D./M.B.A.
☐ J.D./M.P.A.
__ Health Care
__ Government

Please be sure that all of the Instructions to Applicants have been followed. An application will be considered only after it has been completed in full and the Office of Admissions has received all required documents.

I understand that, if I am admitted to the School of Law and register as a student, the School will retain this application and all supporting materials and may make them available to state bar character committees and I consent to such disclosure.

I certify that the information provided by me in this application is true and complete. From time of application through enrollment, I shall promptly advise the Office of Admissions of the School of Law **<u>in writing</u>** of any change in any of the facts indicated in this application. I understand that matriculation and attendance at any other law school (from time of application through enrollment) would render any offer of admission from P[illegible] Univ[illegible]ity Sch[illegible]l of [illegible]

SAMPLE

I understand that notific[illegible] of th[illegible] a[illegible]ica[illegible] w[illegible] av[illegible] [illegible]ial or [illegible]wer, for dismissal from the School of Law. I further agree and authorize Pa[illegible] Univ[illegible] [illegible] pu[illegible]lic [illegible]elations [illegible]poses, any photographs in which I appear.

I understand that my admission to Pace University is a privilege and not a right and I agree that my admission, if granted, my registration and continuance on the rolls and graduation are subject to all policies, rules, regulations and procedures set forth in the current bulletins, catalogs, and other publications and notices of Pace University and as they may be amended, and further, subject to the right of the authorities of Pace University to require my withdrawal for scholastic, disciplinary, or other reasons, under circumstances deemed sufficient by them.

____
Signature of Applicant *Date*

Send the transcript to Law Services once all your junior year courses have been completed. Typically, upward grade trends occur after the first year of college. Some law schools may even require fall grades in your senior year if a significant trend is noted.

The registration date for the LSAT should be made individually by each applicant. Since test preparation is essential, you should allow adequate time to properly prepare for the test. There are many commercial preparation courses, various books such as Barron's *How to Prepare for the LSAT,* as well as preparation materials through Law Services. (See also Chapters 10 and 11 of this Guide.)

You should be prepared the first time you sit for the exam; never enter the exam with the thought of it being a dry run. Since most law schools average repeated scores, multiple test scores can hurt your application.

THE WAITING PERIOD

When all the appropriate materials are filed with the admissions office, you begin a waiting period. The decision-making process takes time.

Once an application is received, the office of admissions opens a file on you, requests the LSDAS report, and, when all materials are received, reviews your application. The process may be held up if, for example, you have left blank questions on the application that were not marked "optional," or do not file a fee with the application, or do not sign the application form.

When you are notified that the file is complete and ready for review by the admissions committee, the process may take anywhere from two weeks to two months. Patience is essential; however, if you have not heard anything from a law school, do not hesitate to contact that school. You may be missing vital information, or your correspondence may have been delayed by the mail.

Every school employs a slightly different approach to making admissions decisions and notifying applicants of their acceptance. Many schools employ automatic acceptance and rejection categories for very high or low LSAT scores and GPAs. Most applicants fall somewhere in the middle, and their applications are reviewed more carefully by the admissions committee. Some schools may send out all acceptance letters at one time, while others notify applicants as decisions are made. Although the notification process may begin prior to January 1 of the academic year preceding admission, most applicants will hear from law schools between February and April. Later decisions may occur for students who are included on a waiting list, from which they are drawn if other accepted students decide not to matriculate at the school. Waiting list decisions may be made as late as August.

A few schools offer conditional summer programs for students with marginal credentials. Typically, the final decision for these applicants is made on the basis of their performance in the summer courses. Although the experience of attending such programs is good preparation for law school itself, ABA standards do not permit schools to give law school credit for preadmission work.

The admissions office at the schools to which you apply will be able to explain the idiosyncrasies of their procedures, and keep you advised on the progress of your application. Don't call them every day, however, because excessive phone calls actually slow down the admissions process. Use common sense in deciding whether to call for assistance and information.

THE FINAL DECISION

Once the admissions committee reaches a final decision, you must begin your decision-making process. Try to visit the law schools to which you have been accepted. (Please note that most schools will require a deposit no earlier than April but as early as two weeks after your offer of admission is made. Therefore, visiting schools should begin as early as the application process does, if possible.)

A visit might include attendance at a first year class, or a meeting with current students and/or a member of the faculty. You will not have to spend much time at a law school to get a feel for its atmosphere and personality.

Cost is always an issue, and you should recognize the need to submit the required financial aid forms in a timely manner. The submission of financial aid forms (Free Application for Federal Student Aid) does not have an impact on the admission decision. The filing of the appropriate forms should be completed at the time of application to the individual schools or as late as March 15. If all the appropriate financial aid materials have been submitted, a law school should be able to provide you with a financial aid package at the time of acceptance, allowing you to make an educated decision. (See Chapter 6 of this Guide for more information on financial aid.)

by Angela D'Agostino, Assistant Dean for students, and Cathy Alexander, Director of Admissions, Pace University School of Law, White Plains, NY.

CHAPTER 5

Your Chances of Law School Admission

A PROFILE OF RECENT FIRST-YEAR LAW STUDENTS

The table in this section provides basic admissions statistics for the law schools that have been approved by the American Bar Association. All these schools offer the J.D. degree. The information has been compiled from the most recent available information received from schools. If you compare your own GPA and your LSAT score and percentile with those of students recently admitted, and if you note the number of students who applied and the number who were accepted, you will be able to get an idea of your chances of admission to any given law school.

Bear in mind that many law schools take into account factors other than strictly academic qualifications. These are discussed in the profiles of the individual schools.

A blank cell on the chart means that information was not available.

LAW SCHOOL	ACADEMIC STATISTICS				ADMISSION STATISTICS		
	Median LSAT Percentile of Enrolled	Median LSAT Score of Enrolled	Lowest LSAT Percentile of Accepted	Median GPA (4.0 scale) of Enrolled	Total Applicants	Applicants Accepted	Applicants Enrolled
Albany Law School 80 New Scotland Avenue Albany, NY 12208 518-445-2326 Fax: 518-445-2369 *admissions@mail.als.edu*	47	150	13	3.24	1468	877	267
American University (Washington College of Law) 4801 Massachusetts Avenue, N.W. Washington, DC 20016-8186 202-274-4101 Fax: 202-274-4107 *wcladmit@wcl.american.edu*	70	157		3.4	6222	2134	395
Appalachian School of Law P.O. Box 2825 Grundy, VA 24614 276-935-4349 Fax: 276-935-8261 *vkeene@asl.edu*	32	146		2.86	546	344	136
Arizona State University (College of Law/Armstrong Hall) Box 877906 Tempe, AZ 85287-7906 480-965-1474 Fax: 480-727-7930 *chitra.damania@asu.edu*	74	157		3.4	2003	489	182
Baylor University (School of Law) P.O. Box 97288 Waco, TX 76798-7288 254-710-1911 Fax: 254-710-2316 *becky-beck@baylor.edu*	75	159	52	3.65	1651	739	179
Boston College (Law School) 885 Centre Street Newton, MA 02459 617-552-4351 Fax: 617-552-2917 *bclawadm@bc.edu*	88	162		3.5	5718	1353	276
Boston University (School of Law) 765 Commonwealth Avenue Boston, MA 02215 617-353-3100 *bulawadm@bu.edu*	90	163	20	3.4	5171	1310	246
Brigham Young University (J. Reuben Clark Law School) 342 JRCB Brigham Young University Provo, UT 84602 801-378-4277 Fax: 801-378-5897 *wilcock@lawgate.byu.edu*	86	161		3.67	677	240	153
Brooklyn Law School 250 Joralemon Street Brooklyn, NY 11201 718-780-7906 Fax: 718-780-0395 *admitq@brooklaw.edu*	74	158	43	3.4	3549	1408	487

LAW SCHOOL	ACADEMIC STATISTICS				ADMISSION STATISTICS		
	Median LSAT Percentile of Enrolled	Median LSAT Score of Enrolled	Lowest LSAT Percentile of Accepted	Median GPA (4.0 scale) of Enrolled	Total Applicants	Applicants Accepted	Applicants Enrolled
California Western School of Law 225 Cedar Street San Diego, CA 92101-3046 619-525-1401 Fax: 619-615-1401 *admissions@cwsl.edu*		150	25	3.09	1745	1131	343
Campbell University **(Norman Adrian Wiggins School of Law)** P.O. Box 158 Buies Creek, NC 27506 910-893-1754 Fax: 910-893-1780 *culaw@webster.campbell.edu*	64	154		3.3	672	225	113
Capital University **(Law School)** 303 East Broad Street Columbus, OH 43215-3200 614-236-6500 Fax: 614-236-6972 *admissions@law.capital.edu*	48	150	36	3.14	1034	599	276
Case Western Reserve University **(School of Law)** 11075 East Boulevard Cleveland, OH 44106 216-368-3600 Fax: 216-368-6144 *lawadmissions@po.cwru.edu* or *lawmoney@po.cwru.edu*	75	157		3.24	1547	861	221
Catholic University of America **(Columbus School of Law)** Cardinal Station Washington, DC 20064 (202) 319-5151 Fax: (202) 319-6285 *admission@law.edu*		155	23	3.1	2165	1033	314
Catholic University of Puerto Rico **(School of Law)** Avenida Las Americas-Station 6 Ponce, PR 00732 809-841-2000	13			2.9			
Chapman University **(School of Law)** One University Drive Orange, CA 92866 714-628-2500 Fax: 714-628-2501 *heyer@chapman.edu*	60	154	24	3.13	962	403	128
City University of New York **at Queens College** **(School of Law)** 65-21 Main Street Flushing, NY 11367-1300 718-340-4210 Fax: 718-340-4435 *admissions@mail.law.cuny.edu*					1351	529	165
Cleveland State University **(Cleveland-Marshall College of Law)** 1801 Euclid Avenue Cleveland, OH 44115 216-687-2304 Fax: 216-687-6881	50	150	5	3	1205	649	292

LAW SCHOOL	ACADEMIC STATISTICS				ADMISSION STATISTICS		
	Median LSAT Percentile of Enrolled	Median LSAT Score of Enrolled	Lowest LSAT Percentile of Accepted	Median GPA (4.0 scale) of Enrolled	Total Applicants	Applicants Accepted	Applicants Enrolled
College of William & Mary (William & Mary Law School) P.O. Box 8795 Williamsburg, VA 23187-8795 757-221-3785 Fax: 757-221-3261 *lawadm@.wm.edu*	90	163	26	3.4	3641	718	205
Columbia University (School of Law) 435 West 116th Street New York, NY 10027 212-854-2670 Fax: 212-854-1109 *admissions@law.columbia.edu*	98	169		3.64	6614	1157	356
Cornell University (Law School) Myron Taylor Hall Ithaca, NY 14853-4901 607-255-5141 Fax: 607-255-7193 *lawadmit@postoffice.law.cornell.edu*	94	165		3.6	3717		189
Creighton University (School of Law) 2500 California Plaza Omaha, NE 68178 402-280-2872 Fax: 402-280-3161 *admit@culaw.creighton.edu*	52	151	21	3.23	681	431	170
De Paul University (College of Law) 25 East Jackson Boulevard Chicago, IL 60604 312-362-6831 Fax: 312-362-5280 *lawinfo@wppost.depaul.edu*	63	154	33	3.27	2606	1093	293
Drake University (Law School) 2507 University Avenue Des Moines, IA 50311 515-271-2782 Fax: 515-271-1990 *lawadmit@drake.edu*	55	152	14	3.28	748	466	144
Duke University (School of Law) Science and Towerview Drive, Box 90393 Durham, NC 27708 919-613-7020 Fax: 919-613-7257 *admissions@law.duke.edu*		166		3.5	3580		229
Duquesne University (School of Law) 900 Locust Street, Hanley Hall Pittsburgh, PA 15282 412-396-6296 *campion@duq.edu*	60	153		3.25			217
Emory University (School of Law) Gambrell Hall Atlanta, GA 30322 404-727-6801 Fax: 404-727-2477 *jbalej@law.emory.edu*	86	161	43	3.52	2983	1037	227

LAW SCHOOL	ACADEMIC STATISTICS				ADMISSION STATISTICS		
	Median LSAT Percentile of Enrolled	Median LSAT Score of Enrolled	Lowest LSAT Percentile of Accepted	Median GPA (4.0 scale) of Enrolled	Total Applicants	Applicants Accepted	Applicants Enrolled
Florida Coastal School of Law 7555 Beach Boulevard Jacksonville, FL 32216 904-680-7710 Fax: 904-680-7776 *admissions@fcsl.edu*	50	150	15	2.9	2156	585	165
Florida State University (College of Law) 425 W. Jefferson St. Tallahassee, FL 32306-1601 850-644-3787 Fax: 850-644-7284 *admissions@law.fsu.edu*	68	155		3.32	2209	765	215
Fordham University (School of Law) 140 West 62nd Street New York, NY 10023 212-626-6810	92	164	48	3.5	5177	1486	510
Franklin Pierce Law Center 2 White Street Concord, NH 03301 603-228-9217 Fax: 603-228-1074 *admissions@fplc.edu*		150		3	916	532	128
George Mason University (School of Law) 3301 North Fairfax Drive Arlington, VA 22201-4426 703-993-8010 Fax: 703-993-8260 *arichar5@gmu.edu*	83	160		3.35	2667	604	246
George Washington University (Law School) 2000 H Street, N.W. Washington, DC 20052 202-739-0648 *jd@main.n/c.gwu.edu*	90	163	37	3.4	8212	1996	460
Georgetown University (Law Center) 600 New Jersey Avenue, N.W. Washington, DC 20001 202-662-9010 Fax: 202-662-9439 *admis@law.georgetown.edu*	96	167	37	3.64	9557	2299	656
Georgia State University (College of Law) P.O. Box 4037 Atlanta, GA 30302-4037 404-651-2048 Fax: (404) 651-2048 *cjjackson@gsu.edu*	74	156	33	3.2	2009	558	237
Golden Gate University (School of Law) 536 Mission Street San Francisco, CA 94105-2968 415-442-6630	36	147		3.1	1546	989	233

	ACADEMIC STATISTICS				ADMISSION STATISTICS		
LAW SCHOOL	Median LSAT Percentile of Enrolled	Median LSAT Score of Enrolled	Lowest LSAT Percentile of Accepted	Median GPA (4.0 scale) of Enrolled	Total Applicants	Applicants Accepted	Applicants Enrolled
Gonzaga University (School of Law) Box 3528 Spokane, WA 99220-3528 509-323-5532 Fax: 509-323-5744 *admissions@lawschool.gonzaga.edu*	52	152	15	3.13	943	568	209
Hamline University (School of Law) 1536 Hewitt Avenue St. Paul, MN 55104-1284 651-523-2461 Fax: 651-523-3064 *lawadm@gw.hamline.edu*	52	151	5	3.2	981	635	219
Harvard University (Harvard Law School) Cambridge, MA 02138 617-495-3179 *jdadmiss@law.harvard.edu*					5916	838	559
Hofstra University (School of Law) 121 Hofstra University Hempstead, NY 11549 516-463-5916 Fax: 516-463-6264 *lawpts@hofstra.edu*	71	156	8	3.3	3066	1073	306
Howard University 2900 Van Ness Street, N.W. Washington, DC 20008 202-806-8008 Fax: 202-806-8162 *admissions@law.howard.edu*	50	151		2.9	1225	372	140
Illinois Institute of Technology (Chicago-Kent College of Law) 565 West Adams Street Chicago, IL 60661 312-906-5020 Fax: 312-906-5274 *admit@kentlaw.edu*	65	156		3.27	2622	1148	316
Indiana University at Bloomington (School of Law) 211 S. Indiana Avenue Bloomington, IN 47405-1001 812-855-4765 Fax: 812-855-0555 *Lawadmis@indiana.edu*	84	160		3.4	1493	692	203
Indiana University-Purdue University at Indianapolis (Indiana University School of Law-Indianapolis) 530 West New York Street Indianapolis, IN 46202-3225 317-274-2459 Fax: 317-274-3955 *khmiller@iupui.edu*	62	155	6	3.3	1259	553	262
Inter-American University of Puerto Rico (School of Law) P.O. Box 70351 San Juan, PR 00936-8351 787-751-1912, ext. 2013		140	2	3.1	1008	295	203

LAW SCHOOL	ACADEMIC STATISTICS				ADMISSION STATISTICS		
	Median LSAT Percentile of Enrolled	Median LSAT Score of Enrolled	Lowest LSAT Percentile of Accepted	Median GPA (4.0 scale) of Enrolled	Total Applicants	Applicants Accepted	Applicants Enrolled
John Marshall Law School 315 South Plymouth Court Chicago, IL 60604 312-987-1406 Fax: 312-427-5136 *admission@jmls.edu*		150		3.4	1543	964	255
Lewis and Clark College (Northwestern School of Law) 10015 Southwest Terwilliger Boulevard Portland, OR 97219 503-768-6613 Fax: 503-768-6850 *lawadmss@lclark.edu*	77	158	11	3.27	1758	880	232
Louisiana State University (Paul M. Hebert Law Center) Baton Rouge, LA 70803 225-578-8646 Fax: 225-578-8647 *mforbe1@lsu.edu*	52	153	7	3.28	998	553	261
Loyola Marymount University (Loyola Law School) 919 S. Albany Street Los Angeles, CA 90015 213-736-1180 *admissions@lls.edu*	78	158	23	3.34	3284	1265	425
Loyola University of Chicago (School of Law) One East Pearson Street Chicago, IL 60611 312-915-7170 Fax: 312-915-7906 *law-admissions@luc.edu*	78	158	36	3.3	2461	938	263
Loyola University of New Orleans (School of Law) 7214 St. Charles Avenue New Orleans, LA 70118 504-861-5575 Fax: 504-861-5772 *ladmit@loyno.edu*	48	150	22	3	1518	839	313
Marquette University (Law School) Office of Admissions, Sensenbrenner Hall, P.O. Box 1881 Milwaukee, WI 53201-1881 414-288-6767 Fax: 414-288-0676 *law.admission@marquette.edu*	64			3.33	1105		202
Mercer University (Walter F. George School of Law) 1021 Georgia Ave. Macon, GA 31207 478-301-2605 Fax: 478-301-2989 *Sutton_me@mercer.edu*		153	25	3.32	954	366	136
Michigan State University (Detroit College of Law) 316 Law College Bldg. East Lansing, MI 48824-1300 517-432-0222 Fax: 517-432-0098 *heatleya@pilot.msu.edu*	50	152	21	3.2	1200	720	250

LAW SCHOOL	ACADEMIC STATISTICS				ADMISSION STATISTICS		
	Median LSAT Percentile of Enrolled	Median LSAT Score of Enrolled	Lowest LSAT Percentile of Accepted	Median GPA (4.0 scale) of Enrolled	Total Applicants	Applicants Accepted	Applicants Enrolled
Mississippi College (School of Law) 151 E. Griffith Street Jackson, MS 39201 601-925-7150 *pevans@mc.edu*	50	149		3	574	342	143
New England School of Law 154 Stuart Street Boston, MA 02116 617-422-7210 Fax: 617-422-7200 *admit@admin.nesi.edu*					2080	1416	342
New York Law School 57 Worth Street New York, NY 10013-2960 212-431-2888 Fax: 212-966-1522 *admissions@nyls.edu*		154		3.1	4194	348	470
New York University (School of Law) 110 West Third Street New York, NY 10012 212-998-6060 Fax: 212-995-4527	98	169		3.6	6887	1436	385
North Carolina Central University (School of Law) 1512 S. Alston Avenue Durham, NC 27707 919-560-6333 Fax: 919-560-6339 *jfaucett@wpo.nccu.edu*	50	148	143	3.1	1080	258	116
Northeastern University (School of Law) 400 Huntington Avenue Boston, MA 02115 617-373-2395 Fax: 617-373-8865 *m.knoll@neu.edu*	74	157	10	3.3	2000	796	194
Northern Illinois University (College of Law) Swen Parson Hall De Kalb, IL 60115-2890 815-753-1420 Fax: 815-753-4501 *lawadm@niu.edu*	60	153		3.1	897	336	109
Northern Kentucky University (Salmon P. Chase College of Law) Louie B. Nunn Hall Highland Heights, KY 41099 859-572-6476 Fax: 859-572-6081 *brayg@nku.edu*	56	152	18	3.1	619	286	127
Northwestern University (School of Law) 357 East Chicago Avenue Chicago, IL 60611 312-503-8465 Fax: 312-503-0178 *nulawadm@law.northwestern.edu*	96	167	45	3.6	4083	796	205

LAW SCHOOL	ACADEMIC STATISTICS				ADMISSION STATISTICS		
	Median LSAT Percentile of Enrolled	Median LSAT Score of Enrolled	Lowest LSAT Percentile of Accepted	Median GPA (4.0 scale) of Enrolled	Total Applicants	Applicants Accepted	Applicants Enrolled
Nova Southeastern University (Shepard Broad Law Center) 3305 College Avenue Fort Lauderdale, FL 33314-7721 954-262-6117 Fax: 954-262-3844 *admission@nsu.law.nova.edu*	37	147	3	2.8	1416	785	334
Ohio Northern University (Claude W. Pettit College of Law) 525 South Main Street Ada, OH 45810 419-772-2211 Fax: 419-772-1487 *l-english@onu.edu*	36	147		3.22	775	460	120
Ohio State University (Michael E. Moritz College of Law) 55 West 12th Avenue, John Deaver Drinko Hall Columbus, OH 43210-1391 614-292-8810 Fax: 614-292-1383 *lawadmit@osu.edu*	78	158		3.6	1902	614	225
Oklahoma City University (School of Law) 2501 North Blackwelder Oklahoma City, OK 73106-1493 405-521-5354 Fax: 405-521-5802 *lawadmit@okcu.edu*	32	145	10	2.9	1447	796	220
Pace University (School of Law) 78 North Broadway White Plains, NY 10603 914-422-4210 Fax: 914-422-4010 *calexander@law.pace.edu*	52	152		3.2	1802	819	230
Pennsylvania State University (Dickinson School of Law) 150 South College Street Carlisle, PA 17013 717-240-5207 Fax: 717-241-3503 *dsladmit@psu.edu*	59	153	19	3.3	1718	824	181
Pepperdine University (School of Law) 24255 Pacific Coast Highway Malibu, CA 90263 310-506-4631 Fax: 310-506-7668 *soladmis@pepperdine.edu*	71	156		3.3	2300	870	212
Quinnipiac University (School of Law) 275 Mt. Carmel Avenue Hamden, CT 06518-1948 203-582-3400 Fax: 203-582-3339 *ladm@quinnipiac.edu*				3	1927	671	190

LAW SCHOOL	ACADEMIC STATISTICS				ADMISSION STATISTICS		
	Median LSAT Percentile of Enrolled	Median LSAT Score of Enrolled	Lowest LSAT Percentile of Accepted	Median GPA (4.0 scale) of Enrolled	Total Applicants	Applicants Accepted	Applicants Enrolled
Regent University (School of Law) 1000 Regent University Drive Virginia Beach, VA 23464-9800 757-226-4584 Fax: 757-226-4139 *lawschool@regent.edu*	45	148	18	3.1	565	368	215
Roger Williams University (Ralph R. Papitto School of Law) Ten Metacom Avenue Bristol, RI 02809-5171 401-254-4555 Fax: 401-254-4516 *admissions@law.rwu.edu*	40	148		3.04	1030	669	240
Rutgers University/Camden (School of Law) Fifth and Penn Streets Camden, NJ 08102 856-225-6102 Fax: 856-225-6537	79	159		3.2	1929	592	244
Rutgers University/Newark (School of Law) Center for Law and Justice, 123 Washington St. Newark, NJ 07102 973-353-5557/5554 Fax: 973-353-3459 *awalton@andromeda.rutgers.edu*	74	157		3.3	2373	699	247
Saint John's University (School of Law) 8000 Utopia Parkway Jamaica, NY 11439 718-990-6474 *rsvp@stjohns.edu*	71	156		3.28	2534	900	300
Saint Louis University (School of Law) 3700 Lindell Boulevard St. Louis, MO 63108 314-977-2800 Fax: 314-977-1464 *admissions@law.slu.edu*	64	154	13	3.34	1351	729	263
Saint Mary's University (School of Law) One Camino Santa Maria San Antonio, TX 78228-8601 210-436-3523 Fax: 210-431-4202 *meryc@law.stmarytx.edu*	46	149	25	3	1066	692	240
Samford University (Cumberland School of Law) 800 Lakeshore Drive Birmingham, AL 35229 205-726-2702 Fax: 205-726-2057 *law.admissions@samford.edu*		152		3.1	886	464	174
Santa Clara University (School of Law) 500 El Camino Real Santa Clara, CA 95053 408-554-4800 Fax: 408-554-7897 *lawadmissions@scu.edu*	68	156		3.27	2597	1272	297

LAW SCHOOL	ACADEMIC STATISTICS				ADMISSION STATISTICS		
	Median LSAT Percentile of Enrolled	Median LSAT Score of Enrolled	Lowest LSAT Percentile of Accepted	Median GPA (4.0 scale) of Enrolled	Total Applicants	Applicants Accepted	Applicants Enrolled
Seattle University (School of Law) 900 Broadway Seattle, WA 98122-4340 206-398-4200 Fax: 206-398-4058 *lawadmis@seattleu.edu*	64	154	11		1379	849	345
Seton Hall University (School of Law) One Newark Center Newark, NJ 07102-5210 973-642-8747 Fax: 973-642-8876 *admitme@shu.edu*	67	155	50	3.2	2384	1035	382
South Texas College of Law 1303 San Jacinto Street Houston, TX 77002-7000 713-646-1810 Fax: 713-646-2906 *admissions@stcl.edu*	43	149	15	2.95	1394	934	436
Southern Illinois University (School of Law) Lesar Law Building, Mail Code 6804 Carbondale, IL 62901-6804 618-453-8767 Fax: 618-453-8769 *lawadmit@siu.edu*	46	151	24	3.17	592	381	128
Southern Methodist University (School of Law) Office of Admissions, P.O. Box 750110 Dallas, TX 75275-0110 214-768-2550 Fax: 214-768-2549 *lawadmit@mail.smu.edu*	75	157		3.3			
Southern University and A & M College (Law Center) Post Office Box 9294 Baton Rouge, LA 70813-9294 225-771-5340 Fax: 225-771-2121 *vwilkerson@sus.edu*		146		2.8	667	234	156
Southwestern University (School of Law) 675 South Westmoreland Avenue Los Angeles, CA 90005-3992 213-738-6717 Fax: 213-383-1688 *admissions@swlaw.edu*					2143	1007	380
St. Thomas University (School of Law) 16400 N.W. 32nd Avenue Miami, FL 33054 305-623-2310 *lamy@stu.edu*	35	147	16	2.8	1466	853	186
Stanford University (Stanford Law School) Crown Quadrangle Stanford, CA 94305-8610 650-723-4985 Fax: 650-723-0838 *law.admissions@forsythe.stanford.edu/*		167		3.83	4211	450	178

LAW SCHOOL	ACADEMIC STATISTICS				ADMISSION STATISTICS		
	Median LSAT Percentile of Enrolled	Median LSAT Score of Enrolled	Lowest LSAT Percentile of Accepted	Median GPA (4.0 scale) of Enrolled	Total Applicants	Applicants Accepted	Applicants Enrolled
State University of New York at Buffalo (Law School) O'Brian Hall Buffalo, NY 14260 716-645-2907 Fax: 716-645-6676 *coxublaw@buffalo.edu*	64	154	17	3.36	1225	484	235
Stetson University (College of Law) 1401 61st Street South St. Petersburg, FL 33707 727-562-7802 Fax: 727-343-0136 *lawadmit@hermes.law.stetson.edu*		151		3.24	1735	845	320
Suffolk University (Law School) 120 Tremont Street Boston, MA 02108-4977 617-573-8144 Fax: 617-523-1367	54	153	32	3.2	2100		525
Syracuse University (College of Law) Office of Admissions and Financial Aid Syracuse, NY 13244-1030 315-443-1962 Fax: 315-443-9568	52	151		3.28	1901		280
Temple University (James E. Beasley School of Law) 1719 N. Broad Street Philadelphia, PA 19122 215-204-8925 Fax: 215-204-1185 *lawadmis@blue.temple.edu*	74	157	32	3.35	3225	1276	345
Texas Southern University (Thurgood Marshall School of Law) 3100 Cleburne Avenue Houston, TX 77004 713-313-7114 Fax: 713-313-1049 *cgardner@tsulaw.edu*		142		2.7	952	417	322
Texas Tech University (School of Law) 1802 Hartford Lubbock, TX 79409 806-742-3990, ext. 273 Fax: 806-742-1629 *donna.williams@ttu.edu*	59	153	25	3.4	1147	548	234
Texas Wesleyan University (School of Law) 1515 Commerce Street Fort Worth, TX 76102 817-212-4040 Fax: 817-212-4002 *law-admissions@law.txwes.edu*		150		3.1	1047	608	249
Thomas Jefferson School of Law 2121 San Diego Avenue San Diego, CA 92110 619-297-9700 Fax: 619-294-4713 *adm@tjsl.edu*		149	9	2.9	1522	1048	226

LAW SCHOOL	ACADEMIC STATISTICS				ADMISSION STATISTICS		
	Median LSAT Percentile of Enrolled	Median LSAT Score of Enrolled	Lowest LSAT Percentile of Accepted	Median GPA (4.0 scale) of Enrolled	Total Applicants	Applicants Accepted	Applicants Enrolled
Thomas M. Cooley Law School 300 South Capitol Avenue Lansing, MI 48901 517-371-5140 Fax: 517-334-5718 *admissions@cooley.edu*		142		2.91	3128	2328	885
Touro College (Jacob D. Fuchsberg Law Center) 300 Nassau Road Huntington, NY 11743 631-421-2244 ext. 312 Fax: 631-421-9708 *admissions@tourolaw.edu*			15		1547	683	224
Tulane University (Law School) Weinmann Hall, 6329 Freret Street New Orleans, LA 70118 504-865-5930 Fax: 504-865-6710 *admissions@law.tulane.edu*	83	159	25	3.4	3140	1221	340
University of Akron (School of Law) Corner of Wolf Ledges and University Avenue Akron, OH 44325-2901 330-972-7331 Fax: 330-258-2343 *lawadmissions@uakron.edu*	59	153		3.19	1419	596	228
University of Alabama (School of Law) Box 870382 Tuscaloosa, AL 35487-0382 205-348-5440 Fax: 205-348-3917 *admissions@law.ua.edu*	86	159		3.3	991	366	186
University of Arizona (James E. Rogers College of Law) Mountain and Speedway P.O. Box 210176 Tucson, AZ 85721-0176 520-621-3477 Fax: 520-621-9140 *admissions@law.arizona.edu*	87	161	36	3.48	1870	430	162
University of Arkansas (School of Law) Robert A. Leflar Law Center, Waterman Hall Fayetteville, AR 72701 501-575-3102		152		3.3	622	338	161
University of Arkansas at Little Rock (UALR William H. Bowen School of Law) 1201 McMath Avenue Little Rock, AR 72202-5142 501-324-9439 Fax: 501-324-9433 *lawadm@ualr.edu*	52	150	23	3.4	430	253	134
University of Baltimore (School of Law) 1420 North Charles Street Baltimore, MD 21201-5779 410-837-4459 Fax: 410-837-4450 *lwadmiss@ubmail.ubalt.edu*	47	150	17	2.9	1770	849	313

LAW SCHOOL	ACADEMIC STATISTICS				ADMISSION STATISTICS		
	Median LSAT Percentile of Enrolled	Median LSAT Score of Enrolled	Lowest LSAT Percentile of Accepted	Median GPA (4.0 scale) of Enrolled	Total Applicants	Applicants Accepted	Applicants Enrolled
University of California (Hastings College of the Law) 200 McAllister Street San Francisco, CA 94102 415-565-4623 Fax: 415-565-4863 *admiss@uchastings.edu*	88	161	23	3.5	4800	1496	420
University of California at Berkeley (Boalt Hall) 5 Boalt Hall Berkeley, CA 94720 510-642-2274 Fax: 510-643-6222	94	165	22	3.73	5632	873	299
University of California at Davis (School of Law) Martin Luther King, Jr. Hall 400 Mrak Hall Drive Davis, CA 95616-5201 530-752-6477 *lawadmissions@ucdavis.edu*	80	159	25	3.55	2779	863	214
University of California at Los Angeles (School of Law) P.O. Box 951445 Los Angeles, CA 90095-1445 310-825-2080 Fax: 310-825-9450 *admissions@law.ucla.edu*	92	164	47	3.63	5091	967	304
University of Chicago (Law School) 1111 East 60th Street Chicago, IL 60637 773-702-9484 Fax: 773-834-0942 *admissions@law.uchicago.edu*	97	169		3.62	3859	749	195
University of Cincinnati (College of Law) P.O. Box 210040 Cincinnati, OH 45221-0040 513-556-6805 *admissions@law.uc.edu*		160	147	3.44	1124	404	97
University of Colorado (School of Law) Campus Box 403 Boulder, CO 80309-0403 303-492-7203	86	161		3.55	2239	601	165
University of Connecticut (School of Law) 55 Elizabeth Street Hartford, CT 06105 860-570-5159 Fax: 860-570-5153 *admit@law.uconn.edu*	80	160		3.34	2063	542	184
University of Dayton (School of Law) 300 College Park Dayton, OH 45469-2760 937-229-3555 Fax: 937-229-4194 *lawinfo@udayton.edu*	51	151	7	3.01	1340	861	172

LAW SCHOOL	ACADEMIC STATISTICS				ADMISSION STATISTICS		
	Median LSAT Percentile of Enrolled	Median LSAT Score of Enrolled	Lowest LSAT Percentile of Accepted	Median GPA (4.0 scale) of Enrolled	Total Applicants	Applicants Accepted	Applicants Enrolled
University of Denver (College of Law) 7039 E. 18th Avenue Denver, CO 80220 303-871-6135 Fax: 303-871-6100 *khigganb@law.du.edu*	61	155	33	3.1	2053	1042	375
University of Detroit Mercy (School of Law) 651 East Jefferson Avenue Detroit, MI 48226 313-596-0264 Fax: 313-596-0280 *udmlawao@udmercy.edu*	37	147	15	3	564	312	96
University of Florida (College of Law) 325 Holland Hall P.O. Box 117622 Gainesville, FL 32611-7622 352-392-2087 Fax: 352-392-2087 *patrick@law.ufl.edu*	75	157		3.5	2328	773	400
University of Georgia (School of Law) Hirsch Hall, 225 Herty Drive Athens, GA 30602-6012 706-542-7060 *ugajd@arches.uga.edu*	88	162	20	3.65	2034	535	236
University of Hawaii at Manoa (William S. Richardson School of Law) 2515 Dole Street Honolulu, HI 96822 808-956-7966 Fax: 808-956-3813 *lawadm@hawaii.educ*	68	156	21	3.4	562	213	81
University of Houston (Law Center) 100 Law Center Houston, TX 77204-6060 713-743-2280 Fax: 713-743-2194 *admission@www.law.uh.edu*	68	157	27	3.4	2389	836	306
University of Idaho (College of Law) P.O. Box 442321 Moscow, ID 83844-2321 208-885-6423 Fax: 208-885-5709 *erickl@uidaho.edu*	57	152	13	3.31	461	280	124
University of Illinois (College of Law) 504 East Pennsylvania Avenue Champaign, IL 61820 217-244-6415 Fax: 217-244-1478 *admissions@law.uiuc.edu*	86	161	33	3.4	1606	609	209
University of Iowa (College of Law) 276 Boyd Law Building, Melrose at Byington Street Iowa City, IA 52242 319-335-9095 or 319-335-9142 Fax: 319-335-9019 *law-admissions@uiowa.edu*	80	159		3.57	1273	535	245

LAW SCHOOL	ACADEMIC STATISTICS				ADMISSION STATISTICS		
	Median LSAT Percentile of Enrolled	Median LSAT Score of Enrolled	Lowest LSAT Percentile of Accepted	Median GPA (4.0 scale) of Enrolled	Total Applicants	Applicants Accepted	Applicants Enrolled
University of Kansas (School of Law) 205 Green Hall Lawrence, KS 66045 785-864-4378 Fax: 785-864-5054 *reitz@law.wpo.ukans.edu*	69	155	20	3.3	861	428	192
University of Kentucky (College of Law) 209 Law Building Lexington, KY 40506-0048 606-257-7938 Fax: n/av *dbakert@uky.edu*	78	158	30	3.5	925	395	131
University of Louisville (Louis D. Brandeis School of Law) University of Louisville Belknap Campus-Wilson W. Wyatt Hall Louisville, KY 40292 502-852-6364 Fax: 502-852-0862 *lawadmissions@louisville.edu*	70	156	16	3.3	796	271	129
University of Maine (School of Law) 246 Deering Avenue Portland, ME 04102 207-780-4341 *mainelaw@usm.maine.edu*		153	16	3.26	529	285	95
University of Maryland (School of Law) 500 West Baltimore Street Baltimore, MD 21201 410-706-3492 Fax: 410-706-4045 *admissions@law.umaryland.edu*	71	156	10	3.4	2718	1016	364
University of Memphis (Cecil C. Humphreys School of Law) 207 Humphreys Law School Memphis, TN 38152-3140 901-678-5403 Fax: 901-678-5210 *lawadmissions@spc75.law.memphis.edu*	60	153	11	3.29	771	320	146
University of Miami (School of Law) P.O. Box 248087, 1311 Miller Drive Coral Gables, FL 33124-8087 305-284-2523 *admissions@law.miami.edu*	63	154	7	3.3	3286	1569	418
University of Michigan (Law School) 625 South State Street Ann Arbor, MI 48109-1215 734-764-0537 Fax: 734-647-3218 *law.jd.admissions@umich.edu*	95	166		3.51	4022	1169	361
University of Minnesota (Law School) 229 19th Avenue S. Minneapolis, MN 55455 612-625-3487 Fax: 612-626-1874	90	163		3.6	1926	662	232

LAW SCHOOL	ACADEMIC STATISTICS				ADMISSION STATISTICS		
	Median LSAT Percentile of Enrolled	Median LSAT Score of Enrolled	Lowest LSAT Percentile of Accepted	Median GPA (4.0 scale) of Enrolled	Total Applicants	Applicants Accepted	Applicants Enrolled
University of Mississippi (L.Q.C. Lamar Hall) Grove Loop University, MS 38677 601-915-6910 Fax: 601-915-1289 *bvinson@olemiss.edu*	59	153	6	3.53	1165	411	163
University of Missouri-Columbia (School of Law) 103 Hulston Hall Columbia, MO 65211 573-882-6042 Fax: 573-882-9625 *CatheyA@missouri.edu*	62	155	28	3.36	733	446	185
University of Missouri-Kansas City (School of Law) 500 East 52nd Street Kansas City, MO 64110-2499 816-235-1644 Fax: 816-235-5276 *brooksdv@umkc.edu*	52	152	20	3.2	717	432	189
University of Montana (School of Law) Missoula, MT 59812 406-243-2698 *lawadmis@selway.umt.edu*	64	154	17	3.2			80
University of Nebraska (College of Law) P.O. Box 830902 Lincoln, NE 68583-0902 402-472-2161 Fax: 402-472-5185 *lawadm@unl.edu*	60	153	11	3.6	551	334	152
University of Nevada, Las Vegas (William S. Boyd School of Law) 4505 Maryland Parkway, Box 451003 Las Vegas, NV 89154-1003 702-895-3671 Fax: 702-895-1095 *request@law.unlv.edu*	64	154	96	3.36	770	241	142
University of New Mexico (School of Law) 1117 Stanford Drive N.E. Albuquerque, NM 87131-1431 505-277-0572 Fax: 505-277-9958	63	154	16	3.24	650	251	110
University of North Carolina at Chapel Hill (School of Law) Campus Box 3380, 101 Van Hecke-Wettach Hall Chapel Hill, NC 27599-3380 919-962-5109 Fax: 919-843-7939 *law_admission@unc.edu*		160	24	3.6	2481	621	237
University of North Dakota (School of Law) Box 9003 Grand Forks, ND 58202 701-777-2104 Fax: 701-777-2217 *linda.kohoutek@thor.law.und.nodak.edu*		150	11	3.3	239	129	64

LAW SCHOOL	ACADEMIC STATISTICS				ADMISSION STATISTICS		
	Median LSAT Percentile of Enrolled	Median LSAT Score of Enrolled	Lowest LSAT Percentile of Accepted	Median GPA (4.0 scale) of Enrolled	Total Applicants	Applicants Accepted	Applicants Enrolled
University of Notre Dame (Notre Dame Law School) P.O. Box R, Notre Dame, IN 46556-0780, 574-631-6626, Fax: 574-631-5474, *lawadmit@nd.edu*	88	162	36	3.51	1902	605	173
University of Oklahoma (College of Law) 300 Timberdell Road, Norman, OK 73019, 405-325-4726, Fax: 405-325-0502, *kmadden@ou.edu*	64	154	64	3.45	746	295	180
University of Oregon (School of Law, William W. Knight Law Center) 1515 Agate Street, Eugene, OR 97403-1221, 541-346-1553, Fax: 541-346-3984, *admissions@law.uoregon.edu*		157	17	3.5	1400	600	171
University of Pennsylvania (Law School) 3400 Chestnut Street, Philadelphia, PA 19104-6204, 215-898-7400, *admissions@oyez.law.upenn.edu*	95	166	45	3.6	3651	838	261
University of Pittsburgh (School of Law) 3900 Forbes Avenue, Pittsburgh, PA 15260, 412-648-1400, Fax: 412-648-2647, *admissions@law.pitt.edu*		156		3.3	1429	732	272
University of Puerto Rico (School of Law) P.O. Box 23349, UPR Station, Rio Piedras, PR 00931-3349, 787-772-1472, Fax: 787-764-4360, *wandi_perez@hotmail.com*	34	145	4	3.5	823	240	214
University of Richmond (The T.C. Williams School of Law) University of Richmond, VA 23173, 804-289-8189, *admissions@uofrlaw.richmond.edu*	74	157		3.2	1545	575	171
University of San Diego (School of Law) 5998 Alcala Park, San Diego, CA 92110, 619-260-4528, Fax: 619-260-2218, *jdinfo@sandiego.edu*	85	161		3.5	3408		346
University of San Francisco (School of Law) 2130 Fulton Street, San Francisco, CA 94117-1080, 415-422-6586, Fax: 415-422-6433	68	155		3.2	2002	928	242

LAW SCHOOL	ACADEMIC STATISTICS				ADMISSION STATISTICS		
	Median LSAT Percentile of Enrolled	Median LSAT Score of Enrolled	Lowest LSAT Percentile of Accepted	Median GPA (4.0 scale) of Enrolled	Total Applicants	Applicants Accepted	Applicants Enrolled
University of South Carolina (School of Law) Main and Greene Streets Columbia, SC 29208 803-777-6605 Fax: 803-777-7751 *usclaw@law.law.sc.edu*	75	156		3.2	1280	459	240
University of South Dakota (School of Law) 414 East Clark Street Vermillion, SD 57069-2390 605-677-5443 Fax: 605-677-5417 *lawreq@usd.edu*	44	149	9	3.3	300	183	81
University of Southern California (Law School) Los Angeles, CA 90089-0074 213-740-2523	92	164		3.55	4669	1140	210
University of Tennessee (College of Law) 1505 W. Cumblerland Avenue Knoxville, TN 37996-1810 865-974-4131 Fax: 865-974-1572 *lawadmit@libra.law.utk.edu*		156	139	3.46	1069	386	156
University of Texas at Austin (School of Law) 727 East Dean Keeton Street Austin, TX 78705 512-232-1200 Fax: 512-471-6988 *admissions@mail.law.utexas.edu*	88	162	16	3.68	4451	1050	484
University of the District of Columbia (David A. Clarke School of Law) 4200 Connecticut Avenue, N.W. Washington, DC 20008 202-274-7341 Fax: 202-274-5583 *vcanty@law.udc.edu*	23	148	13	2.78	427	94	40
University of the Pacific (McGeorge School of Law) 3200 Fifth Avenue Sacramento, CA 95817 916-739-7105 Fax: 916-739-7134 *admissionsmcgeorge@uop.edu*	56	152	22	3.12	1892	1167	386
University of Toledo (College of Law) 2801 West Bancroft Street Toledo, OH 43606-3390 419-530-4131 Fax: 419-530-4345 *law.utoledo.edu*	64	154	26	3.31	983	501	167
University of Tulsa (College of Law) 3120 East Fourth Place Tulsa, OK 74104-2499 918-631-2709 Fax: 918-631-3630 *george-justice@utulsa.edu*	50	149	25	3.1	815	543	223

LAW SCHOOL	ACADEMIC STATISTICS				ADMISSION STATISTICS		
	Median LSAT Percentile of Enrolled	Median LSAT Score of Enrolled	Lowest LSAT Percentile of Accepted	Median GPA (4.0 scale) of Enrolled	Total Applicants	Applicants Accepted	Applicants Enrolled
University of Utah (College of Law) 332 South 1400 East Front Room 101 Salt Lake City, UT 84112 801-581-7479 Fax: 801-581-6897 *aguilarr@law.utah.edu*	77	158	21	3.53	908	344	138
University of Virginia (School of Law) 580 Massie Road Charlottesville, VA 22903-1789 804-924-7351 Fax: 804-982-2128 *lawadmit@virginia.edu*	94	166		3.64	3562	977	350
University of Washington (School of Law) 1100 Northeast Campus Parkway Seattle, WA 98105-6617 206-543-4078 *admissions@law.washington.edu*	88	162	138	3.62	1954	468	177
University of Wisconsin (Law School) 975 Bascom Mall Madison, WI 53706 608-262-5914 Fax: 608-262-5485 *admissions@law.wisc.educ*	83	160	23	3.38	1981	695	236
University of Wyoming (College of Law) P.O. Box 3035 Laramie, WY 82071 307-766-6416 *lawadmis@uwyo.edu*	55	151	9	3.28	435	249	90
Valparaiso University (School of Law) Wesemann Hall Valparaiso, IN 46383-6493 219-465-7829 Fax: 219-465-7808 *marilyn.olson@valpo.edu*	52	150	17	3.21	835	531	173
Vanderbilt University (Law School) 131 21st Avenue South Nashville, TN 37203 615-322-6452 Fax: 615-322-1531	88	162	22	3.68	2341	757	198
Vermont Law School P.O. Box 96, Chelsea Street South Royalton, VT 05068-0096 802-763-8303 Fax: 802-763-7071 *admiss@vermontlaw.edu*	52	151	7	3	781	515	185
Villanova University (School of Law) Garey Hall Villanova, PA 19085 610-519-7010 Fax: 610-519-6291 *admissions@law.vill.edu*	67	157	50	3.4	1789	883	257

LAW SCHOOL	ACADEMIC STATISTICS				ADMISSION STATISTICS		
	Median LSAT Percentile of Enrolled	Median LSAT Score of Enrolled	Lowest LSAT Percentile of Accepted	Median GPA (4.0 scale) of Enrolled	Total Applicants	Applicants Accepted	Applicants Enrolled
Wake Forest University (School of Law) P.O. Box 7206, Reynolda Station Winston-Salem, NC 27109 336-758-5437	86	160	26	3.4	1781	645	169
Washburn University (School of Law) 1700 College Topeka, KS 66621 785-231-1185 Fax: 785-232-8087 *admissions@washburnlaw.edu*		146		3.51	509	363	141
Washington and Lee University (School of Law) Lewis Hall Lexington, VA 24450 540-463-8504 Fax: 540-463-8586 *lawadm@wlu.edu*	94	165	35	3.42	1637	506	122
Washington University in St. Louis (School of Law) Box 1120, One Brookings Drive St. Louis, MO 63130 314-935-4525 Fax: 314-935-6959 *admiss@walaw.wash.edu*	83	162	31	3.5	2440	868	225
Wayne State University (Law School) 471 W. Palmer Detroit, MI 48202 313-577-3937 Fax: 313-577-6000 *linda.sims@wayne.edu*	64	154	20	3.33	1049	531	250
West Virginia University (College of Law) P.O. Box 6130 Morgantown, WV 26506 304-293-5304 Fax: 304-293-6891 *lawaply@wvu.edu*	64	154	13	3.3	585	297	157
Western New England College (School of Law) 1215 Wilbraham Road Springfield, MA 01119 413-782-1406 Fax: 413-796-2067 *lawadmis@wnec.edu*	51	151	15	3	915	538	154
Western State University (College of Law) 1111 North State College Blvd Fullerton, CA 92831 714-738-1000, ext. 2600 Fax: 714-441-1748 *paulb@wsulaw.edu*		145		2.9	974	525	149
Whittier College (School of Law) 3333 Harbor Blvd. Costa Mesa, CA 92626 714-444-4141, ext. 121 Fax: 714-444-0250 *info@law.whittier.edu*	47	150	11	3	1316	776	209

LAW SCHOOL	ACADEMIC STATISTICS				ADMISSION STATISTICS		
	Median LSAT Percentile of Enrolled	Median LSAT Score of Enrolled	Lowest LSAT Percentile of Accepted	Median GPA (4.0 scale) of Enrolled	Total Applicants	Applicants Accepted	Applicants Enrolled
Widener University (School of Law) 4601 Concord Pike, P.O. Box 7474 Wilmington, DE 19803, 302-477-2162 (DE); 717-541-3903 (PA) Fax: 302-477-2224 (DE); 717-541-3999 (PA) *law.admissions@law.widener.edu*	36	148	7	3.03	2849	1324	696
Willamette University (College of Law) 245 Winter Street S.E. Salem, OR 97301 503-370-6282 Fax: 503-370-6375 *law-admission@willamette.edu*	63	154		3.24	742	422	142
William Mitchell College of Law 875 Summit Avenue St. Paul, MN 55105-3076 651-290-6476 Fax: 651-290-6414 *admissions@wmitchell.edu*	59	153	8	3.2	1022	670	319
Yale University (Yale Law School) P.O. Box 208329 New Haven, CT 06520-8329 203-432-4995 *admissions.law@yale.edu*	99	171		3.84	3315	290	187
Yeshiva University (Benjamin N. Cardozo School of Law) 55 Fifth Avenue New York, NY 10003 212-790-0274 Fax: 212-790-0482 *lawinfo@ymail.yu.edu*	81	159		3.4	2993	1085	335

CHAPTER 6

Is Financial Aid Available?

Unless you are independently wealthy, you are probably having some concerns about financing your legal education. The important thing to keep in mind is that funds are available to help you. The bulk of the assistance for law school students takes the form of student loans. There is very little money available for outright grants. Most law school students and their families are willing to take on a heavy debt load as an investment in the future.

There are certain concepts relative to financial aid that all applicants should know. All programs that are federally funded or sponsored have very strict requirements as to eligibility. Law school financial aid offices process the loan applications in accordance with these rules and regulations. They have very little leeway except in the awarding of institutional funds.

Need Based Need-based loans require a demonstration of need based on Federal Methodology.

Merit Based Merit-based aid does not require a showing of need.

Federal Methodology (FM) Federal Methodology is the federally mandated method of determining financial need.

Base Year Base year is the prior calendar year and is used to calculate need under FM.

Independent Student Law school students are deemed to be independent due to their professional student status.

Budget The budget is set by the financial aid office each year. FM allows only *required* student expenses. These expenses are: tuition, fees, books, living expenses including room and board, transportation costs, an allowance for personal expenses, and miscellaneous expenses. Required student expenses will not cover, in most cases, car payments, credit card monthly payments, alimony, or mortgage payments.

Financial Need Financial need is the difference between expected family contribution and the total cost of attendance.

Packaging Policy Packaging policy is set by each law school and delineates the priorities for awarding financial aid.

CAMPUS-BASED PROGRAMS

Certain financial aid programs are referred to as campus-based. First in this category of aid would be scholarships and grants funded entirely by the law school. At most law schools the amount of money available for this form of aid is small. Since the money comes from the institution, the institution sets the requirements for receiving the aid. In most cases these awards will require a showing of need. Occasionally, a law school will have some merit-based aid.

Carl D. Perkins Loans are another form of campus-based aid. Each year the institution receives an allocation from the federal government for this program. It is basically a loan program administered by the institution in that the institution lends the money to the student and the institution is responsible for collecting the loans from the recipients. Perkins loans carry the lowest interest rate and at most schools are reserved for the neediest students. There is a cumulative limit of $30,000 on all Perkins loans, both graduate and undergraduate.

Another type of campus-based aid is the Federal Work Study Program (FWS). Again, the institution receives a yearly allocation from the federal government to fund this program. FWS is a need-based program and may be reserved for the neediest students. The financial aid award will indicate that the law student is eligible to receive a certain amount of money under the FWS program. This money can be earned either by working on campus or off campus. On-campus jobs take the form of working in the library or other law school offices or as research assistants for faculty members. Off-campus jobs can only be with nonprofit or governmental entities. Some examples would be work at a public defender's office, as a law clerk for a judge, or for a state or federal agency. FWS funds do not have to be repaid.

FEDERAL LOAN PROGRAMS

Other federal loan programs are available through banks, credit unions, savings and loan associations, and other private lenders. The Stafford Student Loan (formerly the Guaranteed Student Loan) is a relatively low-interest federal loan available to law school students. Stafford loans are insured by state guarantee agencies and must be approved by that agency. Subsidized Stafford loans require demonstration of financial need. Law school students can borrow a maximum of $18,500 per academic year under this program but may not exceed $138,500 in total Stafford loans for law school.

OTHER LOAN PROGRAMS

Other loan programs are available to law school students but do not receive federal interest subsidies. These loan programs do not require demonstration of financial need and carry the highest interest rates. An applicant may also have to show a good credit rating or creditworthiness.

The Access Group has developed a loan program specifically designed to fit the needs of law school students. Under this program the student can apply for federally subsidized and unsubsidized Stafford loans as well as a private loan from The Access Group. This private loan is the Law Access Loan (LAL). Students with good credit can borrow up to the total cost of attendance.

There are other private loan programs available. Law Loans is one such program. Your financial aid office will have information on these programs.

OUTSIDE FUNDING

Various foundations and business and professional organizations offer assistance in financing your education. Some programs are geared for minority and disadvantaged students such as the Council on Legal Education Opportunity, the Earl Warren Legal Training Program, and the Mexican American Legal Defense Education Fund. The financial aid office can give you complete information on these other programs. As funds for most of these programs are limited, you should apply early.

Another source of outside funding comes from various state and county bar associations that award scholarships. The amounts and requirements will vary, but this possibility should not be overlooked.

Some states also offer grants to needy graduate students. Contact your local state guarantee agency to explore this option. Your financial aid office (both graduate and undergraduate) can supply you with their names and addresses.

Money is available to finance your legal education. But at what cost? The interest rate increases as you move from the Perkins loan (lowest interest) to the Stafford and the private loans. Borrowing decisions should be carefully made as these loans ultimately have to be repaid.

APPLICATION PROCESS

All law schools require that the financial information necessary to determine financial need be submitted to a national processing center. Most schools use the Free Application for Federal Student Aid (FAFSA).

The FAFSA should be filed as early as possible. Processing time for the FAFSA is approximately four to six weeks. Read the forms carefully and answer all required parts. After the FAFSA has been analyzed, a report will be sent to the schools you have designated.

When the law school financial aid office receives your report generated by the FAFSA, it will review your file in accordance with its packaging policy. This means that the expected student contribution will be subtracted from the school budget to arrive at financial need.

Some schools' packaging policies will require that the first level of need be met by the Stafford loan. If there is any remaining need, you may be eligible for Perkins loan funds and Federal Work Study. After the financial aid office determines your level of eligibility for aid, you will receive notification. This may be four to six weeks or longer after the receipt of the FAFSA report.

The loan applications must be completed, signed, and returned to the lender. If a credit report is required, it is done at this time. If the lender/guarantee agency approves your loan, the check will be disbursed. The approval process can take up to six weeks. For most loans the interest starts to accrue when the check is disbursed. In most cases the check will be made co-payable to the student and the law school. When the check arrives, you will be asked to endorse it, and then the school will endorse it and credit it to your account. If the amount credited is more than is owed, the school will process a refund check for you.

DEFERMENT

It is possible to defer repayment on student loans you received as an undergraduate as long as you are a full-time student. You should request deferment forms from your lender. Take these forms to the registrar at your law school. Federal regulations require that you be a matriculated student so these forms will not be signed and sent to your lender until after the semester starts.

It is important to file deferment forms and to know if they have to be filed annually with your lender. If you are not granted a deferment, don't make payments on your undergraduate loans, and are declared in default, you run the risk of being denied loans for your legal education.

REPAYMENT AND CONSOLIDATION

While the money is available to finance your legal education, ultimately it must be repaid. You will have to start making payments six to nine months after graduation. There are several different ways to repay a Federal Direct Loan.

A Standard Repayment Plan has a fixed monthly repayment amount for a fixed period of time, usually 10 years.

An Extended Repayment Plan has a lower fixed monthly payment amount, and loan repayment can be extended beyond the usual 10 years.

A Graduated Repayment Plan usually begins with lower monthly payments, and payment amounts increase at specified times. Payments may be for the usual 10-year period, or they may be extended beyond 10 years.

An Income-contingent Repayment Plan for Direct Stafford loans sets annual repayment amounts based on the borrower's income after leaving school. The loan is repaid over an extended period of time, not to exceed 25 years.

by Angela D'Agostino and Cathy Alexander, adapted from the original article by Christine A. Koterba, Director of Financial Aid, Widener University School of Law.

CHAPTER 7

What Should I Expect in Law School?

[Barron's *How to Succeed in Law School* provides an in-depth look at legal education from the student's point of view, particularly the critical first year. The premise of the book is that being intelligent is not enough; the successful law student needs to know how to play the game. The portion of the book reprinted below provides an overview of the first year; other chapters deal with classroom preparation, studying, test taking, and a variety of other key elements in law school success. Readers who successfully gain admission to law school should read *How to Succeed in Law School* as the next step in their preparation for a career in law. Ed.]

THE LAW SCHOOL CALENDAR

No two people are the same. A key to your success in law school will be your ability to channel the skills you already have into a new educational program, while building new skills that will serve you in the future as a lawyer. It may help you to understand what is happening during the first year of law school by looking at the law school calendar. Although every law school is slightly different from all the others, in many respects they are all much the same. Virtually every law school in the United States models its curriculum, particularly in the first year, after the socratic system promulgated at Harvard Law School in the 1870s. Although legal education has evolved in the past century, the general comment in this chapter will be substantially descriptive of your law school.

Orientation

Law school starts with orientation. Orientation is designed to introduce you to the law school community (and some would say to lull you into a false sense of security about the upcoming ten months). The first step is check-in. Check-in is run by the Admissions Office, and you will be greeted by the smiling countenance of the admissions officer who recruited you or dealt with you during the admissions process. The Admissions Office will want to make sure that you have paid your tuition, that your financial aid is in order, and that your registration is complete. Depending on how check-in is organized, you may or may not have to wait in a long line. If the line is long, it generally portends three to four years of the same thing.

After checking in, and grabbing a cup of hot coffee, you will proceed to an auditorium where you will be subjected to a series of speeches you will not remember. You will hear from the dean, some associate deans, assistant deans, the financial aid officer, placement director, student bar president, law review editor, moot court board chair, head of security, and other administrators and students too numerous to name. They will all tell you how glad they are to see you, how talented you all are, and how their doors will always be open. You will never see most of them again. While most schools have abandoned the tactic, a few of them may still use the old "Look to the right of you; look to the left of you; one of you won't be here next August." The truth is, 90–95 percent of those who enter law school eventually will graduate.

After this convocation, you may be given a tour of the facilities, including the law library, by engaging upperclass students just dying to tell you what law school is "really like." You also may be solicited by various student organizations; they will all be around and still anxious for your membership after the first year.

One of your first lessons in law school will be to separate the wheat from the chaff. Find out where the assignments are posted. Find out how you can sign up for a locker. Learn to recognize The Dean by sight. (There are many deans, but only one Dean.)

At many schools, class assignments for the first day are posted prior to orientation. An assignment sheet for each class will also tell you what books to buy for the course so you can go to the law school bookstore and pick up your books before the crowds arrive. Don't wait until school has started to obtain your books and start reading.

ORIENTATION CHECKLIST

___Admissions
    ___College transcripts (if needed)
    ___Identification
___Financial aid (if applicable)
___Registrar—class schedule
___Bursar—bring checkbook if not prepaid
___Course assignments
___Bookstore
___Parking Sticker
___Locker
___ID photo
___Law school tour
___Find out who is "The Dean"
___Nearby food
___Library carrel (if available)

First Classes

Unlike classes in undergraduate school, the first classes in law school are generally real classes. The professor may simply walk in and call on a student for the first case. She may give a short speech on what will be expected of you in her course before turning to the cases. Or she may provide a background lecture for most of the first hour. It is likely that the professor will not simply say, "Hello, I'm Professor Jones. Your assignment for Tuesday will be to read the first 30 pages in the book. I'll see you Tuesday." During the first class, the professor may present certain special rules such as the maximum number of class cuts you are allowed, the number of times you may be unprepared before being dropped from the course, what the final exam will be like, what her office hours will be, what outside materials (hornbooks, treatises, etc.) you should read. Such information is important to know.

Such works as *One L* and *The Paper Chase* probably have instilled a sense of fear in the minds of many beginning law students. In reality, not all law professors are as intimidating as Professor Kingsfield, although the terror and alienation described there are very accurate.

You will find yourself in a lecture hall with roughly one hundred more or less equally frightened souls. Your sense of anonymity and privacy will be invaded by the seemingly all-knowing professor armed with a seating chart and an uncanny ability to identify the least prepared student in the class to discuss the case at hand.

During the first week of classes, you will learn the ground rules. Let there be no doubt about it: This is the lions versus the Christians, and regardless of your religious affiliation, you and your classmates are the Christians.

Also, during the first week, you will be introduced to the subject matter to be covered in each course, the professor's unique philosophy of legal education, a new language called legalese, and those ponderous, pictureless tomes called casebooks.

You will also begin to get acquainted with your fellow law students. You may meet a few individuals whom you come to know as real people. Most of your classmates will fall into one of two groups: the nameless faces who fill the classroom and the ones who, by virtue of having been called on or volunteered to speak in class, are identified by name (as in "Mr. Simon, who sits in the first row in Torts"). Custom dictates that you use last names to identify students (as in "Ms. Miller" or "Mr. Musser") and you refer to the teacher as "Professor" or "Dean" as appropriate.

You may encounter some upperclass students who offer with a certain patronizing smugness to teach you the tricks of the trade. A healthy sense of skepticism about the value or motives of such advice is a good sign that you will eventually become a successful lawyer.

Routine

After the first week of classes, you will begin to establish a pattern in each course, and a timetable for your entire life. The reading will average between 10 and 30 pages per night, per class. You may find that the progress in some of the classes is painfully slow, with the professor covering only a portion of the assigned reading each time. Some classes may move along at an almost military clip of three to four cases per class, no matter what. During the first few weeks, you will find yourself spending an inordinate amount of time briefing cases, attempting to fathom the classroom discussion, and wondering secretly if someone in the admissions office hadn't screwed up by sending you an acceptance letter. You will wonder with increasing frequency whether you screwed up in deciding to come to law school. During this phase of school, you may wonder why everyone else in the class but you seems to know what is going on.

When I was in law school, there was a guy named Holtzman, and although Holtzman was only three or four years older than most of the rest of us, it seemed that in every class he had some personal experience relating to the case. If the case involved shoes, he had been in the shoe business; if the case involved clothes, he had been in the clothing business; if the case involved doctors, he had been in the medical business.

Other students will amaze you with their seeming ability to converse freely with the professor in legalese, whereas you find yourself stuck at the *Bonjour Jean* stage. But you will derive hope from the fact that some students' comments will seem totally inane to you, reassuring you that you must be smarter than *someone* in the class. And you will find a wicked satisfaction in seeing a handful of students whose hands are always in the air given their comeuppance by the professor. In every class, there will be at least one individual who, no matter how bloodied by the fray, will keep coming back for more. A pack psychology will come to dominate the class and seek to drive out the weak or the deviant. By mid-semester, the fear of embarrassment in front of the class will inhibit all but the most fearless souls from making rash statements. This mentality is typified by graffito on a bathroom stall at one law school: "After the sixth week of class, if you don't know who the class jerk is, it's you."

These pressures to conform may dissuade some students from ever participating in class discussions unless specifically required to do so by the professor. By laughing at a fellow student, you help to create an environment where one day others may laugh at you.

As the semester wears on, the professor comes to be viewed not so much as a god, but as a common enemy. You learn that the classroom routine is a game the teacher always wins. You learn that the stupidest answers have some value, and you begin to recognize that even the most articulate students really don't know much more than you do. When you come to this realization, you will have reached another milestone in your law school journey.

The Wall

Somewhere between the tenth and twelfth week of classes you will hit the wall. It is during this period that some students actually drop out of school; virtually every student at least contemplates that possibility. By this time in the semester, your work is piling up, final exams are just around the corner, and you still don't have a clue what you need to know. At this point, when your psychological and physical resources are drained, you will wonder if you can possibly survive for two and a half or three and a half more years. It is critical when you hit the wall to press on. It may help during this period to talk to a sympathetic professor, mentor, or counselor. Family and loved ones, who up until now have been totally supportive, will seem to become part of the problem. Prelaw school friends may find that you have changed, and you may find yourself increasingly irritated that they never see the issue.

Panic

By about the thirteenth week of the semester, you will have no time to worry about such self-indulgent psychological concerns, because finals will be upon you. Some professors, in what is variously perceived as a last minute attempt to catch up with the syllabus or a final effort to break your backs, will increase the reading assignments to two or three times what they were at the beginning of the semester. A full-scale panic attack may threaten to debilitate you before the first test. Somehow, you will survive.

First Semester Finals

At last, final examinations will arrive. As a rule, law school exams average one hour of exam for each credit hour of class. The amount of material you will have to study will be immense. Whole parts of some courses may be incomprehensible when you go back to review them. When you walk out of these exams, your head will feel as if Evander Holyfield had used it as a punching bag. You will have no idea how well you did, but if you thought the test was easy, you probably missed something really big.

Semester Break

Semester break is the time when you regroup. Immediately after your last exam, your impulse will be to engage in the most hedonistic activity possible. Many will actually succumb to this impulse. Next, you will sleep for two days. Then, you will engage in mindless activity such as watching soap operas or football games, reading trashy novels, attending holiday parties, or vegging out with your family. If you are an evening student, you may not have the luxury of all of this R & R. However, to the extent possible, you should try to get away from both school and work for a while.

Toward the end of semester break, you will begin to think about law school again. You may do some reading for class. You may reflect about how you will avoid making the same mistakes you did the first semester. You will rush madly to clear up loose ends in your personal life, in order to give yourself time to devote your full attention to law school.

Renewed Hope

The second semester is better in some ways, and worse in others. It is better in that you know the ropes. You have a better picture of what to expect. You have a clearer idea of what it will take to succeed. On the other hand, the workload will pick up even more. The professors will take off at the same pace they ended the previous semester. In addition, at many schools a required moot court problem will swallow the bulk of your free time.

The January Blues

During January (and sometimes February or March) first semester grades will be posted. The wait for grades may be agonizing. The actual knowledge of your grades may be worse. Most students are disappointed in some or all of their marks. You learn how fast the track really is. Unfortunately, many students do not handle this experience well. They go into a depression from which they do not escape until after the bar exam. Although there is no grade for it, your grade point average may depend on your ability to bounce back psychologically and to learn from this experience.

Falling Behind

In all but the warmest climates, the arrival of spring will bring the last great temptation of the school year. When the flowers begin to bloom and warm winds touch the land, sitting in a law school classroom will not be your first choice of activities. Spring break may help but chances are good that you will fall behind in your reading and studying. If you are not careful, you could find yourself in the proverbial hot water.

The Mad Rush

As March dissolves into April, you will once again find yourself staring at final exams. If you have been diligent, you will simply experience anxiety about finishing the year on a high note; if you find yourself hopelessly behind your schedule, you will be working feverishly to catch up. The last two weeks of school will pass quickly, and your first year will be almost over.

Finals Again

Final exams in the spring will probably not seem as daunting. The experience will be the same as in the fall, but this time you will be more prepared for it mentally. The amount of work you cover in these exams will be more prodigious than in the fall. But the skills you have developed during the course of the year will make the load seem more manageable. This time, when finals are over, you will just go home, have dinner with friends, and go on about your business.

Over a period of 36 weeks, more or less, you will have been transformed from an ordinary person into a budding lawyer. Whether you want it or not, like it or not, or need it or not, you will never be the same again. The process is in some ways like marine boot camp, taking apart whatever you were before you arrived and rebuilding it into a new person. Whatever other criticisms of law school one might make, it certainly cannot be said that the program does not work.

LAW SCHOOL COURSES

The curricula at most American law schools are comparable. In fact, the first year law school curriculum has not changed appreciably in the past one hundred years. At the same time, there are minor variations in course offerings from school to school, reflecting differences in educational philosophy and institutional tradition.

Most law school courses are offered as 2-, 3-, or 4-semester-hour courses. Full-time first year students take five or six courses for a total of 15-16 credit hours; part-time students generally take one or two fewer courses and 10-11 hours. At some schools, grades are based on an entire year's work for 4- to 6-hour courses. You will study some, if not all, of the following courses during the first year of law school. Some schools will defer certain courses until the second year or not require them at all.

Torts

The word tort comes from an old French term meaning wrong. Torts as a law school subject area refers to a series of legal actions and remedies against wrongdoers for injuries sustained.

Torts fall into three broad groups: *intentional torts* where an actor intends conduct that causes injury to another; *negligence torts* where an actor owing a duty to act with reasonable care toward another breaches that duty and causes injury resulting in damages; and *strict liability torts* where an actor causes injury to another without fault or intent but is held liable for policy reasons. You will study a number of distinct tort actions, including assault, battery, false imprisonment, and intentional infliction of emotional distress; negligence actions; misrepresentation; defamation; products liability; and privacy.

Property

The Property course deals with the rights associated with the ownership of property. In the beginning of the course you will probably discuss the origins of property rights in Anglo-American law. You will study such tantalizing questions as who owns the rights to the meteorite: the farmer in whose field it fell or the guy walking down the road who saw it fall? Some of us are still trying to figure that one out. A small portion of the course is devoted to the law of personal property, but the bulk of the year will involve issues relating to real property, or land. In the first semester, you will devote considerable time to basic concepts such as estates in land, transferability of land, and title. Some time during the year you will learn about future interests, those medieval devices for controlling the ownership of land beyond the life of the owner. In the second semester, you will deal with more modern concepts such as easements, zoning, and land use planning.

Contracts

Contracts involves the study of the body of law governing the making and breaking of agreements. You will learn what it takes to create a binding contract with another party. You will spend considerable time discussing what happens when one of the parties breaks its promises, or breaches the contract. You will learn about liquidated damages, specific performance, express and implied warranties, and unilateral contracts. Much of the course will deal with the development of contracts in the commercial setting, including the "battle of forms" and substitution of statutory law in the form of the Uniform Commercial Code for the common law in many situations.

Civil Procedure

Civil Procedure refers to the rules by which the civil courts operate. Most Civ Pro instructors utilize the Federal Rules of Civil Procedure in teaching their courses. Some of the course may touch upon historical material, such as the evolution of the English forms of action into the rules of procedure of today. Most of your time will be spent looking at such concepts as jurisdiction (including subject matter, personal, and diversity), standing, discovery, pleading, appeal, summary judgments, and numerous other provisions of the Rules. A substantial part of the course will address the Erie problem. The case of *Erie Railroad v. Tompkins* held that the federal courts, while applying federal procedural rules, must apply the substantive common law of the state. The ripples from this seemingly simple rule have extended far beyond the original case and have engrossed generations of judges, law professors, legal writers, and students (perhaps *engrossed* is too strong a word for the student response).

Constitutional Law

Many law schools require Constitutional Law during the first year. As the name suggests, Con Law deals with the enforcement of rights and duties established under the United States Constitution. Because there are so many constitutional issues, no two professors will emphasize exactly the same topics. You will look at some fundamental problems such as jurisdiction and standing, separation of powers, the commerce clause, and the privileges and immunities clause. You will deal with cases arising under the first, fifth, and fourteenth amendments as well as others. Perhaps most importantly, you will study the decision-making process in the United States Supreme Court from Chief Justice Marshall's power grab of judicial review in *Marbury v. Madison* to Chief Justice Rehnquist's reshaping the direction of the court in the 1980s.

Criminal Law

Criminal Law is the law of crimes. For a good portion of this course, you will grapple with concepts such as intent, *mens rea,* and lesser included offenses. You will learn the basic elements of crimes you have known about all your life, and a few you have never heard of before. You will study such issues as the right to trial by jury, double jeopardy, the state's burden of proof, and conspiracy.

Professional Responsibility

Although most law schools offer Professional Responsibility during the last year of law school, some require it during the second year, and a few the first. Professional Responsibility deals with the ethical obligations of the lawyer in representing clients. A few of the subjects you will cover in this course are: lawyer/client confidentiality, conflicts of interest, legal fees, advertising and solicitation of business, fitness to practice law, lawyer discipline, and candor to the tribunal. In a broader sense, however, professional responsibility addresses the role of the legal profession in society. What is a lawyer anyway? Are there limits on his or her conduct? Is law a business, a profession, or both? What is the role of the Bar Association? Can one be a good lawyer and a good person at the same time?

Legal Writing

At every law school, there is a course known by a variety of names, but with a general aim of teaching you how to conduct legal research, draft legal briefs and memoranda, prepare and make oral arguments, and gain an understanding of a legal system. These courses are often much maligned by first-year students, but revered by lawyers who come to know the value of the skills they learned in that course. Legal Writing frequently requires a time commitment out of proportion with the amount of credit received. An important consideration during the course of the school year will be your ability to allocate time to Legal Writing in accordance with its relative importance and credit weight, and not to set aside work in other classes for research, writing, and advocacy projects.

THE PROFESSORS

Law students develop a special relationship with their first year teachers. It is not uncommon to experience a love/hate relationship with these professors. Later in law school you will wonder how you placed some of these individuals on such high pedestals. During the first semester of law school they will be like gods—not necessarily in their perfection of appearance, but in their seeming knowledge and omnipotence.

Many of those who become law teachers attained their positions by having done very well academically in law school. Additionally, many of them enter the profession after having served as judicial clerks for the United States Supreme Court or other prestigious tribunals. Increasingly, today, law teachers have some experience in the practice of law. They come from large law firms, corporations, and government agencies. All of them have made an affirmative decision to pursue a career in education, rather than one in a traditional area of law practice. Professors who worked in large law firms or possess more than a few years of experience probably have taken a considerable cut in pay to enter the teaching field. Although law professors as a group have a higher median income than the average of all lawyers, they probably could make more money doing something else.

THE STUDENTS

Classmates

Your classmates can be allies as well as foes during your struggle to master the first year of law school. They can help you to cope in a number of different ways. First, they can help you with assignments. If you happen to miss a class, you need to find someone whose notes you can review. If your own notes have gaps, you may be able to fill them with the help of someone else. If reading assignments or case citations are unclear, you should identify one or more people to call. Even though law school is a competitive environment, most students are willing to help out in this way, as long as their generosity is not abused.

You may study with one of more other students from time to time. Informal small group discussions are common even among students who do not organize formal study groups. In law school, a great amount of learning takes place outside the classroom, and to the extent that your out-of-class conversations are discussions begun during class, the learning process will continue.

If you have ever been to the zoo, you may recall watching a pride of lions or other large cats. The young ones will tussle and play endlessly. Sometimes Mom or Dad will play too, letting the kittens attack and snarl and slap. You know that the older cat can send the kittens flying with a flick of the paw, but they play along until they get bored. You know that the kittens are learning skills they will need as adults in the wild, and the big cats are helping in the process. You also know that the kittens learn from their mock battles with each other just as they do from Mom and Dad. In law school, the professors take on the role of the big cats, and you as kittens should learn from them. However, you should remember that you learn from the rest of the litter as well.

Your classmates can provide an outlet from the pressures of law school. Whether it involves coffee in the morning, eating lunch or dinner, exercising or working out, or partying, you need to socialize from time to time. Those of you who are married to people unconnected with the legal profession, and those who have jobs in nonlegal settings may find it less difficult to break away from law school psychologically. On the other hand, it may be more difficult to find the time to get to know your classmates socially. If you don't want your families and coworkers to despise you because you talk about law all the time, you should try to make some time to get to know your fellow law students in a social setting.

There is an insidious downside to developing relationships with your classmates. Several caveats are in order. Law school is very competitive. Some students will help no one. Some students will promise help, but fail to deliver. Some will take far more than they give. Always remember that the admissions committee did not pick the first year class on the basis of integrity. Although you will meet some of the most honest and honorable people you could hope to know, you may also encounter others who would stoop to any depth to get ahead, and use any means to reach a desired end. Most of you will conclude that you are unwilling to lie, cheat, and steal in order to succeed in law school. Do not be so naive as to believe that everyone feels the same. Beware of the snakes in the grass, and pick your friends carefully.

Your classmates can exert considerable pressure not to succeed. A collective striving for mediocrity may seem to be the norm. Those who study too much, talk too often in class, or don't get into the law school social scene may be branded as outsiders. You have had to deal with similar peer pressure since grade school. The point here is that the pressure to conform does not end in law school. You may have seen the gopher game at the boardwalk or midway. In this game, the gopher pops his head out of one of the number of round holes while the player, wielding a mallet, tries to knock him back into the hole again. If you imagine that the class is the midway player ready to knock down any gopher who has the audacity to stick his head up above the crowd, you get the picture.

One way the group may push you toward mediocrity is by encouraging you to socialize. Although occasional social activity is beneficial, too much can be the kiss of death. When study sessions deteriorate into bull sessions like you had when you were a freshman in college, when quick lunches extend into afternoon shopping trips, when an occasional class party becomes an evening ritual, then you will know you have exceeded the bounds of moderation.

Some semblance of self-discipline in the area of time management is absolutely essential. You must decide how much time you are willing to devote to personal and social activities, and live with that decision.

Socializing with other students can take on a more serious note: emotional involvement through love and dependency. Guess what? Law students fall in love. They fall in love with each other and with nonlaw students. It would be futile to say: "Don't fall in love." However, if you do, you will find yourself in turmoil. When you fall in love, your lover tends to become (at least during early stages of infatuation) all-important in your life. Unfortunately, so does law school. Justice Holmes once remarked that the law is a jealous mistress. This conflict appears in the play *Phantom of the Opera*. Christine, the heroine, is torn between her physical relationship with the Vicomte de Chegny and her passion to excel in her career represented by her relationship with the Phantom. It is interesting to note that the author of the book, Gaston Leroux, was himself a lawyer and may have understood the conflict in terms of the law.

A second dangerous emotional involvement is to buy into someone else's problems to the detriment of your own studies. Law students are not immune from the vagaries of life. Some of your friends will have serious problems while they are in school. The stress of law school may compound their anxiety. Some may turn to you to serve as an emotional crutch. In fact, some students are like magnets for those with problems. Lest your friend's difficulties drag you down, the best thing you can do is to get them to go to someone who can really help.

Upperclass Students

When you arrive at law school, you will find a place already populated by students who have gone before you. These upperclass students will be ready and willing to regale you with tales of their own experiences in the first year, to give you the inside scoop on all the profs, and to share the definitive answers on what you need to do to get ahead. Some of them will want you to join their organizations, come to their parties, or buy their old books. They may seem like the smug but grizzled veterans joined in the field by some new recruits in the standard war movie: "Don't worry, kid; I'll show you what you need to do to get out of this place alive." Of course, in the movies, the guy who says that always seems to get killed.

The lesson to learn is to take everything you hear with a grain of salt. You will find out information that is useful. Every law school has a grapevine, and the news, if not always accurate, is at least entertaining. Some of your sources may prove better than others. So use what you can and discard the rest.

Consider the motivation of the upperclass student who offers advice. Is this someone who just likes being a big shot? Someone who needs reaffirmation for his or her own decisions in law school (even if those choices have produced a record of mediocrity)? Someone who would like to ask you out? (Yes, this goes on in law school like everywhere else!) Someone who wants to sell you something (bar reviews, books, bar association memberships)? You do not have to shun all these people, just remember that they want something in return for their information. (In the words of Hannibal Lecter from *The Silence of the Lambs,* "Quid pro quo, Clarice.")

While casual advice should be approached with skepticism, it might be valuable to look for an upperclass mentor. Such a person might well be someone who has similar interests, career aspirations, problems, or background. For example, a first year student with young children at home might encounter an upperclass student who has gone through the same experience and survived. A mentor might be someone you happen to meet and become friendly with during the course of the year. Some schools even offer programs that assign upperclass mentors to first year students. However it occurs that a true mentoring relationship develops, take advantage of it.

A mentor can help to guide you through the law school maze, talk to you when you are down, share your joy when you are flush with success, and set an example for you to follow. Mentoring relationships are built upon a foundation of common interest, molded by walls of trust, and covered by a protective roof of the experience of the mentor for the student. Mentoring relationships are common in the legal profession, not only in law school but in practice as well. To the extent that you find a good mentor, you will discover that the law school experience is a more palatable one.

THE LAW SCHOOL CULTURE

Rules and Procedures

Law school culture is unique, created in part by the intense experience of those involved, and in part by the insular setting of the law school itself. Because most law students did not attend undergraduate school at the university where they attend law school, they tend to have limited interaction with the university community generally. The law school on many campuses is set apart on the edge of campus or on a separate campus altogether. Some law schools are not connected with an undergraduate university at all. There are advantages and disadvantages to attending an independent law school. Such a school can devote all its resources to the law students, but may lack the rich culture of a university setting.

There may be other differences about the physical location or layout of the law building(s) that make the law school environment unique. Does the law school share its campus with undergrads or graduate students? Does the law school share space with other departments? Are law school facilities located in one building or several? The presence or absence of a nonlegal academic community affects not only the type and extent of extracurricular programs and activities, but also the sense of the law school as an insular institution.

In one sense, every law school is different, but in another sense, every law school is the same. Regardless of the idiosyncrasies of different law schools, the process of legal education is similar everywhere.

In this environment, a distinct law school culture has evolved. Law schools have their own student government (the Student Bar Association or SBA), activities, social events, intramurals, and newspapers. Some law schools even have their own yearbooks. At many law schools, the students put on an annual comedy show, generally making fun of the faculty in a singular effort to even the score for a year's worth of abuse.

Within the law school culture, there are several common elements worth noting: First, rules and procedures take on a distinctly legal flavor. Announcements and information may be posted by the registrar, the Dean's Office, or teachers. You will be deemed to know what is in these notices by virtue of the doctrine of constructive notice. The upshot of this concept is that you have to watch out for announcements that pertain to you. The first example of constructive notice during your law school tenure will be the posting of class assignments on a wall or bulletin board prior to the beginning of classes. You will find very little hand-holding by law school teachers and administrators. Students who graduated from small intimate colleges may find this somewhat of a shock.

A second concept that permeates the rules and procedures is the notion of due process. Lawyers, more than those who are not trained in the law, tend to be aware of individual rights to hearings, representation, confrontation of accusers, and appeal. Most law schools operate under some code of conduct for dealing with academic dishonesty, as well as a code of academic standards to cover issues involving academic performance. Both sets of rules tend to focus heavily on due process and protection of the individual.

Another aspect of the law school culture is that it is a small world. The largest law school in the country has around 2,000 students; at most law schools the enrollment is no more than several hundred. The small size of the student body, combined with the nature of the educational process, means that students know much more about each other, law school affairs, and their professors than they did in all but the smallest undergraduate schools. Unlike your high school or college acquaintances, you will tend to maintain contact with many of your law school classmates throughout your career. At every law school there is a student grapevine, laden with information about everything from what courses to take, which firms to interview, to who is sleeping with whom. The old adage, "Believe a tenth of what you hear and half of what you see," is apropos.

Socializing and Breaks

You will find an abundance of opportunities for escape from law school studies in the form of parties and school-sponsored social events. During the year, there will be several receptions, mixers, and even a dance or two sponsored by the SBA. Many student organizations offer periodic social events for their members. And informal groups of students organize their own parties as a break from the grind of law school or meet at a local bar for drinks after class.

In fact, if you are interested, you can find a party almost every night. Unfortunately, partying leads you down a certain path of self-destruction in law school. Everyone needs an occasional break from study; however, the occasional break can easily become a regular habit. The party scene can become an escape from law school pressures generally, and may shift your values away from learning.

If you were a party animal in college, it may be difficult to break out of old patterns. Unfortunately, most of us cannot get by with the same antics we did in undergraduate school. In law school one all-nighter will not save a semester of neglect.

Law school provides abundant breaks between and during semesters. You will probably have two weeks or more between the end of first semester exams and the start of spring semester classes. Most schools provide a spring break midway through the second semester. And, of course, summers are open.

Students usually use breaks during the year either to get away for a vacation or to get ahead in their work. Sometimes you may not have a choice. If you decide to vacation, leave your guilt at home. If you take your books with you, plan and make time to study. If you have no time to study, do not make a pretense of it by surrounding yourself with symbols of law school while doing nothing to further your cause.

Summer vacation is another matter. Here are 12 to 14 weeks that you can utilize in a variety of different ways. How you choose to spend your summer vacation will have an impact, one way or the other, on your legal education.

A large percentage of law students work for legal employers during the summer. Although it is harder for them to find positions, many first year students take this option, even if they have to work for free. For some students, it is necessary to work in high paying nonlegal jobs in order to earn enough to come back to school the next year.

Many students go to summer school, at their institution or abroad. You may find, however, that you are so burned out that you simply want to relax. And some students do just that after the first year. If you want to travel, this might be the time to do it, before you take your first job.

Competition

A final note about the law school culture is that it is competitive. Entrance to law school was competitive; law school itself is competitive; and law practice by its nature is competitive. Your relationships with other students will be colored by competition. Ironically, many students try to deny the competitive nature of the process. They will say to each other that grades don't matter. They will ostracize fellow students who appear too competitive. They may deny to other students that they study as much as they do. On the other hand, competitiveness can go too far. In all likelihood, before you graduate from law school, you will hear about at least one cheating incident at your school. You will see other examples, such as library books being misshelved by unscrupulous students. If you should be tempted, it's not worth it. In the 1988 presidential campaign, a law school indiscretion may have cost one candidate the nomination for the presidency of the United States.

Excerpted from *How to Succeed in Law School,* by Gary A. Munneke, Barron's Educational Series, Inc. 1994, 1989.

CHAPTER 8

What Are the Career Opportunities in Law?

Although it may seem quite early to begin to think about employment after law school, many prelaw students ask themselves whether they will find employment after investing thousands of dollars in a legal education. Some students understand that the choice of law schools has an impact on the career choices they ultimately make. The school's reputation, geographic location, substantive curriculum, and many other factors go into determining what opportunities are most likely to be available to its graduates. For instance, law schools in the Washington, DC area typically have more graduates go to work for the federal government than law schools in other areas. Law schools with specialty programs may have a disproportionate number of graduates pursue careers in the specialty field.

First year law students are often surprised to discover that after spending considerable time and energy making a career choice to go to law school, they are now called upon to make additional career choices about what to do with their law degree. Law is practiced in many different ways and many different settings. Some legally trained individuals never practice law at all, but use their legal training in a variety of other fields.

A career counselor at your law school will be able to help you make decisions about your legal career. Although career services for law students may vary from school to school, most law schools employ full-time professionals who possess either a counseling or law degree (or both) to work with law students in developing career plans. Law professors may be able to help, not only with advising, but also with information about contacts and recommendations. The chart beginning on page 62 provides an overview of the career planning and placement services of the law schools included in this guide. For a more extensive discussion of the career opportunities for law graduates and the career planning process, see Gary A. Munneke, *The Legal Career Gude: From Law Student to Lawyer,* American Bar Association (2002). You cannot begin too early to start reflecting on career issues.

WORK DURING LAW SCHOOL

Many law students work in legal or law-related jobs while they are in law school. Still others will work in nonlegal jobs that lead them to legal jobs in the area of business where they were working, or into a totally alternative career. Many law students work in law firms, corporate law departments, or government law offices. These positions may be full-time or part-time, and they may be summer jobs, work during the school year, or permanent positions.

Many larger firms, government agencies, and corporate legal departments offer summer internship or clerkship programs as part of a formal recruiting process. These positions tend to be highly competitive, and hiring for them may be heavily influenced by academic performance in law school and the prestige of the law school attended. Many of the organizations that sponsor these summer programs use them as a tool to help make permanent hiring decisions.

Even in law firms and other employers that do not regularly recruit on campus for summer clerks or permanent associates, it is common for students who work in these organizations during law school to accept positions there when they graduate. Even if they do not ultimately stay with the organization where they have worked, the experience they gain is very likely to impress other employers with whom they apply. This kind of hands-on training is an excellent counterbalance to the more esoteric experience of law school.

Types of Employment

The largest segment of the population of law school graduates each year goes to work in private law firms. These firms provide legal services to clients for profit. The owners of the firm may be individual lawyers or partners in multi-lawyer partnerships of several hundred partners, or anything in between. In addition to the partners/owners, law firms also employ salaried junior lawyers or associates. Some of these associates may eventually become partners in the firm; some may remain as permanent associates or staff attorneys; and some may leave the firm to find other employment or start their own practices. The percentage of lawyers in private practice has decreased from around 80 percent in 1950 to around 60 percent today. Additionally, the vast majority of private practitioners in 1950 were solo practitioners, while less than half of them are now. Whereas in 1950, there were only a few law firms with over ten lawyers (partners and associates combined), today there are hundreds of firms with more than one hundred lawyers.

Still, the largest law firm in the United States (with slightly over one thousand lawyers and perhaps twice as many support staff) is small compared to business entities in many other fields. There is no big five of law firms like there is in accounting. There is no legal equivalent of Microsoft or General Motors. The reality is that most lawyers will engage in the private practice of law at some point during their careers, but most of these will be in solo practices or small firms. No more than 15 percent of the population of private practitioners work in the largest five hundred law firms in the country.

If six out of ten lawyers work in private practice, the remaining four are employed in a variety of different endeavors. The largest of these other groups are corporations (including both in-house counsel and other corporate positions) and government service in federal, state, and local agencies. Government service also includes work as prosecutors and public defenders in the criminal justice system. Judicial administration is usually listed as a separate category, because of the unique nature of the work performed. While many government lawyers practice law like lawyers in firms (the big difference being that the government is their employer), judges, court administrators, and law clerks engage in a very different kind of activity—running the justice system. Other lawyers work for political action or public interest organizations, serve in legislatures as representatives, or aides, and participate in political parties, campaigns, and other related activities.

Many lawyers go into other lines of work outside the practice of law altogether, having never gone into law, or having left the practice at some time during their careers. Some of these people may simply want a law degree to supplement other qualifications they have. Others may become enticed by personal dreams or business deals along the way. Some, unfortunately, discover after going to law school and practicing law that they are not happy with the career choices they have made, and leave the practice of law for greener pastures. The ranks of these legal expatriates are filled with entrepreneurs, athletes, writers, correspondents, inventors, entertainers, restaurateurs, and even a prominent wine critic. A list of well-known personalities who are also lawyers would surprise most people. For more information, see Gary A. Munneke and William D. Henslee, *Nonlegal Careers for Lawyers,* American Bar Association (2002).

Each year, the National Association for Law Placement, an organization comprised of representatives of the nation's law schools and legal employers, conducts an employment report and salary survey. (See *Jobs and JDs: Employment and Salaries of New Law School Graduates,* National Association for Law Placement, 2001.) The most recent class on which data are available suggests that law graduates go into positions in the percentages not too different from the makeup of the legal profession as a whole. The breakdowns for private practice, corporate, government, and judicial categories are similar to the breakdown for lawyers as a whole, although NALP reported that 57.8 percent of the law school graduates in 2001 entered private practice, down from a high of 64.3 percent ten years earlier. A very small percentage of law students actually open their own law offices, a practice euphemistically referred to as "hanging out a shingle." More law graduates go to work in law offices of less than 100 lawyers than accept positions in large offices. The judicial cohort is made up of judicial clerks rather than judges and courts administrators for obvious reasons. The largest area of government practice for recent graduates is work in a prosecutor's office. Another area, often listed as a separate category, is the military, which recruits lawyers for the judge advocate generals corps for the service branches, as well as individuals who have completed law school before fulfilling other military obligations. Very few law school graduates go into teaching—particularly law school teaching—directly out of law school, but

(*go to page 86*)

THE JOB OUTLOOK

SCHOOL	CAREER SERVICES														PLACEMENT RECORD												
	FACILITIES		SERVICES													PERCENTAGE BREAKDOWN OF TYPE OF EMPLOYER											
	LAW PLACEMENT OFFICE	UNIVERSITY PLACEMENT OFFICE	EMPLOYMENT COUNSELING	JOB OPENINGS INFORMATION	SOLO PRACTICE ADVICE	RESUME PREPARATION	INTERVIEW COUNSELING	EMPLOYMENT PLANNING	JOB INTERVIEWS ARRANGEMENT	LAW, CORPORATE, AND GOVERNMENT CONTACT	ALUMNI CONTACTS	PART-TIME/SUMMER EMPLOYMENT	INTERNSHIPS	ALUMNI PLACEMENT	PLACEMENT WITHIN 6 TO 9 MONTHS	PRIVATE PRACTICE 2-10 ATTORNEYS	PRIVATE PRACTICE 11-25 ATTORNEYS	PRIVATE PRACTICE 26-50 ATTORNEYS	PRIVATE PRACTICE 51-100 ATTORNEYS	JUDICIAL CLERKSHIPS	GOVERNMENT	BUSINESS/INDUSTRY	PUBLIC INTEREST	MILITARY	ACADEMIC	OTHER	AVERAGE STARTING SALARY
Albany Law School 80 New Scotland Avenue Albany, NY 12208 518-445-2326 Fax: 518-445-2369 *admissions@mail.als.edu*	•		•	•	•	•	•	•	•	•	•	•	•	•	96%	26	12	5	7	6	26	13	2	1	2		$31,000-$125,000
American University (Washington College of Law) 4801 Massachusetts Avenue, N.W. Washington, DC 20016-8186 202-274-4101 Fax: 202-274-4107 *wcladmit@wcl.american.edu*	•		•	•		•	•	•	•	•	•	•	•	•	97%	7	4	2	4	10	19	11	5	2	1	32	$35,000-$125,000
Appalachian School of Law P.O. Box 2825 Grundy, VA 24614 276-935-4349 Fax: 276-935-8261 *vkeene@asl.edu*			•	•		•	•	•	•		•	•	•	•	82%	53	3			7	10	7			3	17	$29,000-$60,000
Arizona State University (College of Law/Armstrong Hall) Box 877906 Tempe, AZ 85287-7906 480-965-1474 Fax: 480-727-7930 *chitra.damania@asu.edu*	•		•	•	•	•	•		•	•	•	•	•	•	95%	25	6	9	5	12	16	7	2		4	14	$24,600-$152,000
Baylor University (School of Law) P.O. Box 97288 Waco, TX 76798-7288 254-710-1911 Fax: 254-710-2316 *becky-beck@baylor.edu*	•	•	•	•	•	•	•	•	•	•	•	•	•	•	96%	30	15	7	6	8	8	5	3	14	4		$38,346-$73,455
Boston College (Law School) 885 Centre Street Newton, MA 02459 617-552-4351 Fax: 617-552-2917 *bclawadm@bc.edu*	•		•	•	•	•	•	•	•	•	•	•	•	•	98%	4	4	6	5	13	8	6	3				$40,000-$100,000
Boston University (School of Law) 765 Commonwealth Avenue Boston, MA 02215 617-353-3100 *bulawadm@bu.edu*	•		•	•	•	•	•	•	•	•	•	•	•	•	100%	6	6	7	52	9	5	4	1		1	9	$58,000-$125,000

Brigham Young University (J. Reuben Clark Law School) 342 JRCB Brigham Young University Provo, UT 84602 801-378-4277 Fax: 801-378-5897 *wilcock@lawgate.byu.edu*	•		•	•	•	•	•	•	•	•	•	•	•	•	98%	16	8	5	5	18	8	19	2	1	2	15	$22,000-$90,000
Brooklyn Law School 250 Joralemon Street Brooklyn, NY 11201 718-780-7906 Fax: 718-780-0395 *admitq@brooklaw.edu*	•		•	•	•	•	•	•	•	•	•	•	•	•	97%	31	9	5	9	8	18	16	2		2		$50,000-$100,000
California Western School of Law 225 Cedar Street San Diego, CA 92101-3046 619-525-1401 Fax: 619-615-1401 *admissions@cwsl.edu*	•		•	•	•	•	•	•	•	•	•	•	•	•	95%	24	5	12	2	3	21	12	2	2	2	15	$20,000-$135,000
Campbell University (Norman Adrian Wiggins School of Law) P.O. Box 158 Buies Creek, NC 27506 910-893-1754 Fax: 910-893-1780 *culaw@webster.campbell.edu*	•		•	•	•	•	•	•	•	•	•	•	•	•	97%	86				4	2	4	4				
Capital University (Law School) 303 East Broad Street Columbus, OH 43215-3200 614-236-6500 Fax: 614-236-6972 *admissions@law.capital.edu*	•		•	•	•	•	•	•	•	•	•	•	•	•	92%	26	10	3	6	5	12	8	1	2	4	23	$40,000-$150,000
Case Western Reserve University (School of Law) 11075 East Boulevard Cleveland, OH 44106 216-368-3600 Fax: 216-368-6144 *lawadmissions@po.cwru.edu* or *lawmoney@po.cwru.edu*	•		•	•	•	•	•	•	•	•	•	•	•	•	97%	7	8	6	7	3	9	11	3	2	1	4	$28,000-$135,000
Catholic University of America (Columbus School of Law) Cardinal Station Washington, DC 20064 (202) 319-5151 Fax: (202) 319-6285 *admission@law.edu*	•		•	•	•	•	•	•	•	•	•	•	•	•	100%	38				18	23	14	2			5	$22,000-$88,000
Catholic University of Puerto Rico (School of Law) Avenida Las Americas-Station 6 Ponce, PR 00732 809-841-2000	•		•	•						•	•														50	50	$14,000-$24,000
Chapman University (School of Law) One University Drive Orange, CA 92866 714-628-2500 Fax: 714-628-2501 *heyer@chapman.edu*	•		•	•	•	•	•	•	•	•	•	•	•	•	89%	19	13	3	3		3	44			9	6	$24,000-$150,000

SCHOOL	CAREER SERVICES														PLACEMENT RECORD												
	FACILITIES		SERVICES													PERCENTAGE BREAKDOWN OF TYPE OF EMPLOYER											
	LAW PLACEMENT OFFICE	UNIVERSITY PLACEMENT OFFICE	EMPLOYMENT COUNSELING	JOB OPENINGS INFORMATION	SOLO PRACTICE ADVICE	RESUME PREPARATION	INTERVIEW COUNSELING	EMPLOYMENT PLANNING	JOB INTERVIEWS ARRANGEMENT	LAW, CORPORATE, AND GOVERNMENT CONTACT	ALUMNI CONTACTS	PART-TIME/SUMMER EMPLOYMENT	INTERNSHIPS	ALUMNI PLACEMENT	PLACEMENT WITHIN 6 TO 9 MONTHS	PRIVATE PRACTICE 2-10 ATTORNEYS	PRIVATE PRACTICE 11-25 ATTORNEYS	PRIVATE PRACTICE 26-50 ATTORNEYS	PRIVATE PRACTICE 51-100 ATTORNEYS	JUDICIAL CLERKSHIPS	GOVERNMENT	BUSINESS/INDUSTRY	PUBLIC INTEREST	MILITARY	ACADEMIC	OTHER	AVERAGE STARTING SALARY
City University of New York at Queens College (School of Law) 65-21 Main Street Flushing, NY 11367-1300 718-340-4210 Fax: 718-340-4435 *admissions@mail.law.cuny.edu*	•		•	•	•	•	•	•	•			•	•	•	84%					5	20	13	26			36	$22,000-$42,000
Cleveland State University (Cleveland-Marshall College of Law) 1801 Euclid Avenue Cleveland, OH 44115 216-687-2304 Fax: 216-687-6881	•		•	•	•	•	•	•	•	•	•	•	•	•	96%	25	4	6	12	5	25	18	2		1	1	$27,500-$127,000
College of William & Mary (William & Mary Law School) P.O. Box 8795 Williamsburg, VA 23187-8795 757-221-3785 Fax: 757-221-3261 *lawadm@.wm.edu*	•		•	•	•	•	•	•	•	•	•	•	•	•	99%	9	5	4	10	18	7	10	1	5	1	30	$26,000-$135,000
Columbia University (School of Law) 435 West 116th Street New York, NY 10027 212-854-2670 Fax: 212-854-1109 *admissions@law.columbia.edu*	•		•	•		•	•	•	•	•	•	•	•	•	99%				2	19	2	3	4			70	$37,500-$200,000
Cornell University (Law School) Myron Taylor Hall Ithaca, NY 14853-4901 607-255-5141 Fax: 607-255-7193 *lawadmit@postoffice.law.cornell.edu*	•		•	•	•	•	•	•	•	•	•	•	•	•	99%		4	5	11	12	2	4	2	1	1	57	$36,000-$140,000
Creighton University (School of Law) 2500 California Plaza Omaha, NE 68178 402-280-2872 Fax: 402-280-3161 *admit@culaw.creighton.edu*	•		•	•	•	•	•	•	•	•	•	•	•	•	97%	26	7	5	1	6	13	22	2	4	3	6	$43,013

De Paul University **(College of Law)** 25 East Jackson Boulevard Chicago, IL 60604 312-362-6831 Fax: 312-362-5280 *lawinfo@wppost.depaul.edu*	•	•	•	•	•	•	•	•	•	•	•	•	•	•	93%	19	7	4	4	3	15	18	2	1	1	16	$24,000-$140,000
Drake University **(Law School)** 2507 University Avenue Des Moines, IA 50311 515-271-2782 Fax: 515-271-1990 *lawadmit@drake.edu*	•		•	•	•	•	•	•	•	•	•	•	•	•	93%	13	9	4	2	18	15	13	4		1	18	$22,000-$85,000
Duke University **(School of Law)** Science and Towerview Drive, Box 90393 Durham, NC 27708 919-613-7020 Fax: 919-613-7257 *admissions@law.duke.edu*	•		•	•	•	•	•	•	•	•	•	•	•	•	99%		1	2	72	17	2		1	2	1	2	$35,000-$95,000
Duquesne University **(School of Law)** 900 Locust Street, Hanley Hall Pittsburgh, PA 15282 412-396-6296 *campion@duq.edu*	•		•	•	•	•	•	•	•	•	•	•	•	•	95%					11	8	16	3		1	61	$30,000-$90,000
Emory University **(School of Law)** Gambrell Hall Atlanta, GA 30322 404-727-6801 Fax: 404-727-2477 *jbalej@law.emory.edu*	•		•	•	•	•	•	•	•	•	•	•	•	•	95%	11	7	6	8	7	9	11	3		1	37	$28,000-$128,000
Florida Coastal School of Law 7555 Beach Boulevard Jacksonville, FL 32216 904-680-7710 Fax: 904-680-7776 *admissions@fcsl.edu*	•		•	•	•	•	•	•	•	•	•	•	•	•	82%	27	4	6	4	4	26	24		2	2		$37,241-$58,684
Florida State University **(College of Law)** 425 W. Jefferson St. Tallahassee, FL 32306-1601 850-644-3787 Fax: 850-644-7284 *admissions@law.fsu.edu*	•	•	•	•	•	•	•	•	•	•	•	•	•	•	95%	15	10	4	2	7	28	3	3	4		8	$24,000-$110,000
Fordham University **(School of Law)** 140 West 62nd Street New York, NY 10023 212-626-6810	•		•	•	•	•	•	•	•	•	•	•	•	•	99%	6	4	2	6	4	13	8	3		1	43	$60,000-$140,000
Franklin Pierce Law Center 2 White Street Concord, NH 03301 603-228-9217 Fax: 603-228-1074 *admissions@fplc.edu*	•		•	•	•	•	•	•	•	•	•	•	•	•	97%	15	12	2	17	3	5	13	4			27	$37,150-$115,000

SCHOOL	CAREER SERVICES — Facilities: Law Placement Office	Facilities: University Placement Office	Services: Employment Counseling	Services: Job Openings Information	Services: Solo Practice Advice	Services: Resume Preparation	Services: Interview Counseling	Services: Employment Planning	Services: Job Interviews Arrangement	Services: Law, Corporate, and Government Contact	Services: Alumni Contacts	Services: Part-Time/Summer Employment	Services: Internships	Services: Alumni Placement	PLACEMENT RECORD — Placement within 6 to 9 Months	Percentage Breakdown of Type of Employer: Private Practice 2-10 Attorneys	Private Practice 11-25 Attorneys	Private Practice 26-50 Attorneys	Private Practice 51-100 Attorneys	Judicial Clerkships	Government	Business/Industry	Public Interest	Military	Academic	Other	Average Starting Salary
George Mason University (School of Law) 3301 North Fairfax Drive Arlington, VA 22201-4426 703-993-8010 Fax: 703-993-8260 *arichar5@gmu.edu*	•		•	•	•	•	•	•	•	•	•	•	•	•	98%					11	19	18	2	4	1		$39,000-$88,000
George Washington University (Law School) 2000 H Street, N.W. Washington, DC 20052 202-739-0648 *jd@main.n/c.gwu.edu*	•		•	•	•	•	•	•	•	•	•	•	•	•	97%					11	10	5	4			57	$86,880
Georgetown University (Law Center) 600 New Jersey Avenue, N.W. Washington, DC 20001 202-662-9010 Fax: 202-662-9439 *admis@law.georgetown.edu*	•		•	•	•	•	•	•	•	•	•	•	•	•	98%	2	2	3	4	11	12	5	3		1	56	$43,000-$125,000
Georgia State University (College of Law) P.O. Box 4037 Atlanta, GA 30302-4037 404-651-2048 Fax: (404) 651-2048 *cjjackson@gsu.edu*	•		•	•	•	•	•	•	•	•	•	•	•	•	95%	25	5	3	6	6	9	21	1	1	2	21	$29,000-$170,000
Golden Gate University (School of Law) 536 Mission Street San Francisco, CA 94105-2968 415-442-6630	•		•	•		•	•			•	•	•	•	•	84%	25	11	1	16	3	16	15	6		2	5	$52,000
Gonzaga University (School of Law) Box 3528 Spokane, WA 99220-3528 509-323-5532 Fax: 509-323-5744 *admissions@lawschool.gonzaga.edu*	•		•	•	•	•	•	•	•	•	•	•	•	•	92%	31	6	6	1	7	19	14	4	2	2	8	$22,000-$110,000
Hamline University (School of Law) 1536 Hewitt Avenue St. Paul, MN 55104-1284 651-523-2461 Fax: 651-523-3064 *lawadm@gw.hamline.edu*	•		•	•	•	•	•	•	•	•	•	•	•	•	99%	14	7	3	1	26	4	24	4			17	$26,000-$121,000

Harvard University (Harvard Law School) Cambridge, MA 02138 617-495-3179 *jdadmiss@law.harvard.edu*	•		•	•	•	•	•	•	•	•	•	•	•	•	100%	1	1	2	4	18	1	6	4		1	36	
Hofstra University (School of Law) 121 Hofstra University Hempstead, NY 11549 516-463-5916 Fax: 516-463-6264 *lawpts@hofstra.edu*	•		•	•	•	•	•	•	•	•	•	•	•	•	98%	13	4	6	4	5	10	18	3		1	12	$30,000-$150,000
Howard University 2900 Van Ness Street, N.W. Washington, DC 20008 202-806-8008 Fax: 202-806-8162 *admissions@law.howard.edu*	•		•	•	•	•	•	•	•	•	•	•	•	•	91%	5	1	3	3	16	30	19	3		1	1	$30,000-$150,000
Illinois Institute of Technology (Chicago-Kent College of Law) 565 West Adams Street Chicago, IL 60661 312-906-5020 Fax: 312-906-5274 *admit@kentlaw.edu*	•		•	•	•	•	•	•	•	•	•	•	•	•	95%	12	8	5	5	2	19	21	1		1	1	$23,000-$140,000
Indiana University at Bloomington (School of Law) 211 S. Indiana Avenue Bloomington, IN 47405-1001 812-855-4765 Fax: 812-855-0555 *Lawadmis@indiana.edu*	•		•	•	•	•	•	•	•	•	•	•	•	•	96%	19	5	9	9	9	12	11	5	1	3	80	$19,000-$185,000
Indiana University-Purdue University at Indianapolis (Indiana University School of Law-Indianapolis) 530 West New York Street Indianapolis, IN 46202-3225 317-274-2459 Fax: 317-274-3955 *khmiller@iupui.edu*	•		•	•	•	•	•			•	•	•	•		93%					6	19	19	2	1	1	52	$30,000-$81,000
Inter-American University of Puerto Rico (School of Law) P.O. Box 70351 San Juan, PR 00936-8351 787-751-1912, ext. 2013			•	•		•	•	•	•	•	•	•	•	•	98%												$28,000-$68,000
John Marshall Law School 315 South Plymouth Court Chicago, IL 60604 312-987-1406 Fax: 312-427-5136 *admission@jmls.edu*	•		•	•	•	•	•	•	•	•	•	•	•	•	90%	23	7	6	4	4	12	21	1			6	$48,900
Lewis and Clark College (Northwestern School of Law) 10015 Southwest Terwilliger Boulevard Portland, OR 97219 503-768-6613 Fax: 503-768-6850 *lawadmss@lclark.edu*	•		•	•	•	•	•	•	•	•	•	•	•	•	97%	14	5	5	2	13	12	12	9	2			$35,000-$50,000

SCHOOL	CAREER SERVICES														PLACEMENT RECORD													
	FACILITIES		SERVICES													PERCENTAGE BREAKDOWN OF TYPE OF EMPLOYER												
	LAW PLACEMENT OFFICE	UNIVERSITY PLACEMENT OFFICE	EMPLOYMENT COUNSELING	JOB OPENINGS INFORMATION	SOLO PRACTICE ADVICE	RESUME PREPARATION	INTERVIEW COUNSELING	EMPLOYMENT PLANNING	JOB INTERVIEWS ARRANGEMENT	LAW, CORPORATE, AND GOVERNMENT CONTACT	ALUMNI CONTACTS	PART-TIME/SUMMER EMPLOYMENT	INTERNSHIPS	ALUMNI PLACEMENT	PLACEMENT WITHIN 6 TO 9 MONTHS	PRIVATE PRACTICE 2-10 ATTORNEYS	PRIVATE PRACTICE 11-25 ATTORNEYS	PRIVATE PRACTICE 26-50 ATTORNEYS	PRIVATE PRACTICE 51-100 ATTORNEYS	JUDICIAL CLERKSHIPS	GOVERNMENT	BUSINESS/INDUSTRY	PUBLIC INTEREST	MILITARY	ACADEMIC	OTHER	AVERAGE STARTING SALARY
Louisiana State University (Paul M. Hebert Law Center) Baton Rouge, LA 70803 225-578-8646 Fax: 225-578-8647 *mforbe1@lsu.edu*	•		•	•	•	•	•	•	•	•	•	•	•	•	99%	29	1	11	6	25	6	3			1	8	$24,500-$111,500
Loyola Marymount University (Loyola Law School) 919 S. Albany Street Los Angeles, CA 90015 213-736-1180 *admissions@lls.edu*	•		•	•	•	•	•	•	•	•	•	•	•	•	94%	17	9	5	25	2	13	21	2		2	4	$55,000-$120,000
Loyola University of Chicago (School of Law) One East Pearson Street Chicago, IL 60611 312-915-7170 Fax: 312-915-7906 *law-admissions@luc.edu*	•		•	•	•	•	•	•	•	•	•	•	•	•	95%	10	9	5	4	5	18	18	5		1	24	$19,000-$140,000
Loyola University of New Orleans (School of Law) 7214 St. Charles Avenue New Orleans, LA 70118 504-861-5575 Fax: 504-861-5772 *ladmit@loyno.edu*	•	•	•	•	•	•	•	•	•	•	•	•	•	•	100%					14	9	13	1		1	54	$32,600-$125,000
Marquette University (Law School) Office of Admissions, Sensenbrenner Hall, P.O. Box 1881 Milwaukee, WI 53201-1881 414-288-6767 Fax: 414-288-0676 *law.admission@marquette.edu*	•		•	•	•	•	•	•	•	•	•	•	•	•	95%	40	20	4	4	7	11	12	1		1		$24,750-$125,000
Mercer University (Walter F. George School of Law) 1021 Georgia Ave. Macon, GA 31207 478-301-2605 Fax: 478-301-2989 *Sutton_me@mercer.edu*	•		•	•	•	•	•	•	•	•	•	•	•	•	94%	26	4	2	2	17	13	7	2	3		3	$26,000-$100,000

Michigan State University (Detroit College of Law) 316 Law College Bldg. East Lansing, MI 48824-1300 517-432-0222 Fax: 517-432-0098 *heatleya@pilot.msu.edu*	•		•	•	•	•	•	•	•	•	•	•	•	•	86%	32	6	2	3	3	14	15	7		5	13	$30,000-$64,000
Mississippi College (School of Law) 151 E. Griffith Street Jackson, MS 39201 601-925-7150 *pevans@mc.edu*	•		•	•	•	•	•	•	•	•	•	•	•	•	90%	30	25	10		20	10	3		2			$35,000-$48,000
New England School of Law 154 Stuart Street Boston, MA 02116 617-422-7210 Fax: 617-422-7200 *admit@admin.nesl.edu*	•		•	•	•	•	•	•	•	•	•	•	•	•	99%	23	3	3	3	8	17	24	2	1	1	7	$32,000-$100,000
New York Law School 57 Worth Street New York, NY 10013-2960 212-431-2888 Fax: 212-966-1522 *admissions@nyls.edu*	•		•	•	•	•	•	•	•	•	•	•	•	•	93%	45				6	20	16	3		2	8	$39,500-$62,500
New York University (School of Law) 110 West Third Street New York, NY 10012 212-998-6060 Fax: 212-995-4527	•		•	•	•	•	•	•	•	•	•	•	•	•	100%					15	2	4	7			72	$38,881-$120,017
North Carolina Central University (School of Law) 1512 S. Alston Avenue Durham, NC 27707 919-560-6333 Fax: 919-560-6339 *jfaucett@wpo.nccu.edu*	•		•	•	•	•	•	•	•	•	•	•	•	•	89%					5	18	5	6	2	2	43	$25,000-$101,000
Northeastern University (School of Law) 400 Huntington Avenue Boston, MA 02115 617-373-2395 Fax: 617-373-8865 *m.knoll@neu.edu*	•		•	•	•	•	•	•	•	•	•	•	•	•	95%	8	4	2	4	25	12	5	9			7	$26,000-$150,000
Northern Illinois University (College of Law) Swen Parson Hall De Kalb, IL 60115-2890 815-753-1420 Fax: 815-753-4501 *lawadm@niu.edu*	•	•	•	•	•	•	•	•	•	•	•	•	•	•	90%	43	4	3	4	7	25	9	3		2		$31,000-$80,000
Northern Kentucky University (Salmon P. Chase College of Law) Louie B. Nunn Hall Highland Heights, KY 41099 859-572-6476 Fax: 859-572-6081 *brayg@nku.edu*	•	•	•	•	•	•	•	•	•	•	•	•	•	•	94%	33	5	1		8	18	26	1		1	1	$20,000-$100,000

SCHOOL	CAREER SERVICES														PLACEMENT RECORD												
	FACILITIES		SERVICES													PERCENTAGE BREAKDOWN OF TYPE OF EMPLOYER											
	LAW PLACEMENT OFFICE	UNIVERSITY PLACEMENT OFFICE	EMPLOYMENT COUNSELING	JOB OPENINGS INFORMATION	SOLO PRACTICE ADVICE	RESUME PREPARATION	INTERVIEW COUNSELING	EMPLOYMENT PLANNING	JOB INTERVIEWS ARRANGEMENT	LAW, CORPORATE, AND GOVERNMENT CONTACT	ALUMNI CONTACTS	PART-TIME/SUMMER EMPLOYMENT	INTERNSHIPS	ALUMNI PLACEMENT	PLACEMENT WITHIN 6 TO 9 MONTHS	PRIVATE PRACTICE 2-10 ATTORNEYS	PRIVATE PRACTICE 11-25 ATTORNEYS	PRIVATE PRACTICE 26-50 ATTORNEYS	PRIVATE PRACTICE 51-100 ATTORNEYS	JUDICIAL CLERKSHIPS	GOVERNMENT	BUSINESS/INDUSTRY	PUBLIC INTEREST	MILITARY	ACADEMIC	OTHER	AVERAGE STARTING SALARY
Northwestern University (School of Law) 357 East Chicago Avenue Chicago, IL 60611 312-503-8465 Fax: 312-503-0178 *nulawadm@law.northwestern.edu*	•		•	•	•	•	•	•	•	•	•	•	•	•	100%				88	7	1		3		1		$34,200-$125,000
Nova Southeastern University (Shepard Broad Law Center) 3305 College Avenue Fort Lauderdale, FL 33314-7721 954-262-6117 Fax: 954-262-3844 *admission@nsu.law.nova.edu*	•		•	•	•	•	•	•	•	•	•	•	•	•	86%	28	12	4	4	3	22	15	2	1	1	8	$29,914-$38,747
Ohio Northern University (Claude W. Pettit College of Law) 525 South Main Street Ada, OH 45810 419-772-2211 Fax: 419-772-1487 *l-english@onu.edu*	•		•	•	•	•	•	•	•	•	•	•	•	•	91%	22	15	6	12	3	16	7	5	1	2	11	$32,000-$75,000
Ohio State University (Michael E. Moritz College of Law) 55 West 12th Avenue, John Deaver Drinko Hall Columbus, OH 43210-1391 614-292-8810 Fax: 614-292-1383 *lawadmit@osu.edu*	•		•	•	•	•	•	•	•	•	•	•	•	•	97%	52				10	14	13	3	4	2	2	$40,000-$90,000
Oklahoma City University (School of Law) 2501 North Blackwelder Oklahoma City, OK 73106-1493 405-521-5354 Fax: 405-521-5802 *lawadmit@okcu.edu*	•		•	•	•	•	•	•	•	•	•	•	•	•	86%	27	7	4	1	6		12	2		4	1	$27,500-$42,000
Pace University (School of Law) 78 North Broadway White Plains, NY 10603 914-422-4210 Fax: 914-422-4010 *calexander@law.pace.edu*	•		•	•	•	•	•	•	•	•	•	•	•	•	92%	37	8	8	3	8	11	14	3		1	9	$25,000-$150,000

Pennsylvania State University (Dickinson School of Law) 150 South College Street Carlisle, PA 17013 717-240-5207 Fax: 717-241-3503 *dsladmit@psu.edu*	•		•	•	•	•	•	•	•	•	•	•	•	•	91%	20	10	6	17	30	10	3	1	2		1	$28,985-$95,340
Pepperdine University (School of Law) 24255 Pacific Coast Highway Malibu, CA 90263 310-506-4631 Fax: 310-506-7668 *soladmis@pepperdine.edu*			•	•	•	•	•	•	•	•		•		•	92%												
Quinnipiac University (School of Law) 275 Mt. Carmel Avenue Hamden, CT 06518-1948 203-582-3400 Fax: 203-582-3339 *ladm@quinnipiac.edu*	•		•	•	•	•	•	•		•	•	•	•	•	95%	45	8	4	4	11	5	13	1		3	6	$38,000-$62,500
Regent University (School of Law) 1000 Regent University Drive Virginia Beach, VA 23464-9800 757-226-4584 Fax: 757-226-4139 *lawschool@regent.edu*	•		•	•	•	•	•	•	•	•	•	•	•	•	79%	44	6	2		1	10	14	6	3	8	6	
Roger Williams University (Ralph R. Papitto School of Law) Ten Metacom Avenue Bristol, RI 02809-5171 401-254-4555 Fax: 401-254-4516 *admissions@law.rwu.edu*	•		•	•	•	•	•	•	•	•	•	•	•	•	82%	27	3	2	2	13	10	15	3		2	19	$25,000-$105,000
Rutgers University/Camden (School of Law) Fifth and Penn Streets Camden, NJ 08102 856-225-6102 Fax: 856-225-6537	•		•	•	•	•	•	•	•	•	•	•	•	•	98%	4	5	5	5	54	8	8	1	3	1	6	$45,000-$110,000
Rutgers University/Newark (School of Law) Center for Law and Justice, 123 Washington St. Newark, NJ 07102 973-353-5557/5554 Fax: 973-353-3459 *awalton@andromeda.rutgers.edu*	•		•	•	•	•	•	•	•	•	•	•	•	•	98%					24	9	20	5		2	40	$25,000-$85,000
Saint John's University (School of Law) 8000 Utopia Parkway Jamaica, NY 11439 718-990-6474 *rsvp@stjohns.edu*	•		•	•	•	•	•	•	•	•	•	•	•	•	99%	15	5	2	5	6	18	15		2	2	17	$30,000-$160,000
Saint Louis University (School of Law) 3700 Lindell Boulevard St. Louis, MO 63108 314-977-2800 Fax: 314-977-1464 *admissions@law.slu.edu*	•		•	•	•	•	•	•	•	•	•	•	•	•	95%	59				6	11	16	2	1	1	5	$58,605

SCHOOL	CAREER SERVICES														PLACEMENT RECORD												
	FACILITIES		SERVICES													PERCENTAGE BREAKDOWN OF TYPE OF EMPLOYER											
	LAW PLACEMENT OFFICE	UNIVERSITY PLACEMENT OFFICE	EMPLOYMENT COUNSELING	JOB OPENINGS INFORMATION	SOLO PRACTICE ADVICE	RESUME PREPARATION	INTERVIEW COUNSELING	EMPLOYMENT PLANNING	JOB INTERVIEWS ARRANGEMENT	LAW, CORPORATE, AND GOVERNMENT CONTACT	ALUMNI CONTACTS	PART-TIME/SUMMER EMPLOYMENT	INTERNSHIPS	ALUMNI PLACEMENT	PLACEMENT WITHIN 6 TO 9 MONTHS	PRIVATE PRACTICE 2-10 ATTORNEYS	PRIVATE PRACTICE 11-25 ATTORNEYS	PRIVATE PRACTICE 26-50 ATTORNEYS	PRIVATE PRACTICE 51-100 ATTORNEYS	JUDICIAL CLERKSHIPS	GOVERNMENT	BUSINESS/INDUSTRY	PUBLIC INTEREST	MILITARY	ACADEMIC	OTHER	AVERAGE STARTING SALARY
Saint Mary's University (School of Law) One Camino Santa Maria San Antonio, TX 78228-8601 210-436-3523 Fax: 210-431-4202 *meryc@law.stmarytx.edu*	•		•	•	•	•	•	•	•	•	•	•	•	•	92%	35	13	13	6	4	9	5	3	1	1		$40,000-$60,000
Samford University (Cumberland School of Law) 800 Lakeshore Drive Birmingham, AL 35229 205-726-2702 Fax: 205-726-2057 *law.admissions@samford.edu*	•		•	•	•	•	•	•	•	•	•	•	•	•	96%	43	9	6	2	11	8	8	1	2	2	5	$26,000-$150,000
Santa Clara University (School of Law) 500 EL Camino Real Santa Clara, CA 95053 408-554-4800 Fax: 408-554-7897 *lawadmissions@scu.edu*	•		•	•	•	•	•	•	•	•	•	•	•	•	95%	60				1	8	28	2				$86,825
Seattle University (School of Law) 900 Broadway Seattle, WA 98122-4340 206-398-4200 Fax: 206-398-4058 *lawadmis@seattleu.edu*	•		•	•	•	•	•	•	•	•	•	•	•	•	88%	24	3	2	12	6	17	12	2	1		21	$35,000-$125,000
Seton Hall University (School of Law) One Newark Center Newark, NJ 07102-5210 973-642-8747 Fax: 973-642-8876 *admitme@shu.edu*	•		•	•	•	•	•	•	•	•	•	•	•	•	96%	39				36	6	6	3		1	9	$60,000-$70,000
South Texas College of Law 1303 San Jacinto Street Houston, TX 77002-7000 713-646-1810 Fax: 713-646-2906 *admissions@stcl.edu*	•		•	•	•	•	•	•	•	•	•	•	•	•	90%	25	9	5	7	5	10	19	1	1	1	17	$40,000-$65,000
Southern Illinois University (School of Law) Lesar Law Building, Mail Code 6804 Carbondale, IL 62901-6804 618-453-8767 Fax: 618-453-8769 *lawadmit@siu.edu*	•		•	•	•	•	•	•	•	•	•	•	•	•	94%	25	6	2	2	12	31	10	3	3	3	3	$35,000-$40,000

Southern Methodist University (School of Law) Office of Admissions, P.O. Box 750110 Dallas, TX 75275-0110 214-768-2550 Fax: 214-768-2549 *lawadmit@mail.smu.edu*	•		•	•	•	•	•	•	•	•	•	•	•	•	95%				69	3	8	15	1			5	$66,000
Southern University and A & M College (Law Center) Post Office Box 9294 Baton Rouge, LA 70813-9294 225-771-5340 Fax: 225-771-2121 *vwilkerson@sus.edu*	•		•	•		•	•	•	•	•	•	•	•	•	10%	33	2		3	21	13	8		2	2	8	$28,000-$53,000
Southwestern University (School of Law) 675 South Westmoreland Avenue Los Angeles, CA 90005-3992 213-738-6717 Fax: 213-383-1688 *admissions@swlaw.edu*			•	•	•	•	•	•	•	•	•	•	•	•	84%	15	11	10	11	2	11	23	1		3	13	$54,680
St. Thomas University (School of Law) 16400 N.W. 32nd Avenue Miami, FL 33054 305-623-2310 *lamy@stu.edu*	•		•	•	•	•	•	•	•	•	•	•	•	•	85%	27	8	3	6		16	25	3			9	$38,000-$40,000
Stanford University (Stanford Law School) Crown Quadrangle Stanford, CA 94305-8610 650-723-4985 Fax: 650-723-0838 *law.admissions@forsythe.stanford.edu/*	•		•	•		•	•	•	•	•	•	•	•	•	98%		4	1	5	33	3	9	3		1	41	$45,000-$153,500
State University of New York at Buffalo (Law School) O'Brian Hall Buffalo, NY 14260 716-645-2907 Fax: 716-645-6676 *coxublaw@buffalo.edu*	•	•	•	•	•	•	•	•	•	•	•	•	•	•	97%	17	5	5	21	8	14	13	5	1	8	3	$18,000-$125,000
Stetson University (College of Law) 1401 61st Street South St. Petersburg, FL 33707 727-562-7802 Fax: 727-343-0136 *lawadmit@hermes.law.stetson.edu*	•		•	•	•	•	•	•	•	•	•	•	•	•	97%	26	18	10	5	5	24	3	2	2	4	1	$30,000-$150,000
Suffolk University (Law School) 120 Tremont Street Boston, MA 02108-4977 617-573-8144 Fax: 617-523-1367	•		•	•		•	•	•	•	•	•	•	•	•	94%	12	15	10	3	9	17	28	1	1	3	1	$22,000-$60,000
Syracuse University (College of Law) Office of Admissions and Financial Aid Syracuse, NY 13244-1030 315-443-1962 Fax: 315-443-9568	•		•	•	•	•	•	•	•	•	•	•	•	•	93%	14	7	7	22	11	16	13	1		1	8	$28,000-$150,000

SCHOOL	CAREER SERVICES														PLACEMENT RECORD											
	FACILITIES		SERVICES													PERCENTAGE BREAKDOWN OF TYPE OF EMPLOYER										
	LAW PLACEMENT OFFICE	UNIVERSITY PLACEMENT OFFICE	EMPLOYMENT COUNSELING	JOB OPENINGS INFORMATION	SOLO PRACTICE ADVICE	RESUME PREPARATION	INTERVIEW COUNSELING	EMPLOYMENT PLANNING	JOB INTERVIEWS ARRANGEMENT	LAW, CORPORATE, AND GOVERNMENT CONTACT	ALUMNI CONTACTS	PART-TIME/SUMMER EMPLOYMENT	INTERNSHIPS	ALUMNI PLACEMENT	PLACEMENT WITHIN 6 TO 9 MONTHS	PRIVATE PRACTICE 2-10 ATTORNEYS	PRIVATE PRACTICE 11-25 ATTORNEYS	PRIVATE PRACTICE 26-50 ATTORNEYS	PRIVATE PRACTICE 51-100 ATTORNEYS	JUDICIAL CLERKSHIPS	GOVERNMENT	BUSINESS/INDUSTRY	PUBLIC INTEREST	MILITARY	ACADEMIC	OTHER	AVERAGE STARTING SALARY
Temple University (James E. Beasley School of Law) 1719 N. Broad Street Philadelphia, PA 19122 215-204-8925 Fax: 215-204-1185 *lawadmis@blue.temple.edu*	•		•	•	•	•	•	•	•	•	•	•	•	•	93%	11	3	3	27	13	17	18	6		2		$20,000-$75,000
Texas Southern University (Thurgood Marshall School of Law) 3100 Cleburne Avenue Houston, TX 77004 713-313-7114 Fax: 713-313-1049 *cgardner@tsulaw.edu*	•		•	•	•	•	•	•	•	•	•	•	•	•	72%	88					7	4	2				$47,000
Texas Tech University (School of Law) 1802 Hartford Lubbock, TX 79409 806-742-3990, ext. 273 Fax: 806-742-1629 *donna.williams@ttu.edu*	•		•	•	•	•	•	•	•	•	•	•	•	•	97%	12	18	34	17	6	11	1	1				$40,000-$110,000
Texas Wesleyan University (School of Law) 1515 Commerce Street Fort Worth, TX 76102 817-212-4040 Fax: 817-212-4002 *law-admissions@law.txwes.edu*	•		•	•	•	•	•		•	•	•	•	•	•	83%	56	9	4		3	14	12	1		1		$33,000-$80,000
Thomas Jefferson School of Law 2121 San Diego Avenue San Diego, CA 92110 619-297-9700 Fax: 619-294-4713 *adm@tjsl.edu*	•		•	•	•	•	•	•	•	•	•	•	•	•	94%	26	8	5		7	14	24	1	4		11	$28,000-$160,000
Thomas M. Cooley Law School 300 South Capitol Avenue Lansing, MI 48901 517-371-5140 Fax: 517-334-5718 *admissions@cooley.edu*	•		•	•	•	•	•	•	•	•	•	•	•	•	84%	40	9	3	4	6	22	11	3		2		$10,400-$150,000
Touro College (Jacob D. Fuchsberg Law Center) 300 Nassau Road Huntington, NY 11743 631-421-2244 ext. 312 Fax: 631-421-9708 *admissions@tourolaw.edu*	•		•	•	•	•	•	•	•	•	•	•	•	•	89%	26	7	3	6	3	19	18	4	1	1	3	$37,500-$67,500

Tulane University (Law School) Weinmann Hall, 6329 Freret Street New Orleans, LA 70118 504-865-5930 Fax: 504-865-6710 *admissions@law.tulane.edu*	•		•	•	•	•	•	•	•	•	•	•	•	•	92%					16	12	10	2		2	48	$33,189-$125,000
University of Akron (School of Law) Corner of Wolf Ledges and University Avenue Akron, OH 44325-2901 330-972-7331 Fax: 330-258-2343 *lawadmissions@uakron.edu*	•	•	•	•	•	•	•	•	•	•	•	•	•	•	90%	28	8	2	5	9	17	17			3	4	$18,000-$150,000
University of Alabama (School of Law) Box 870382 Tuscaloosa, AL 35487-0382 205-348-5440 Fax: 205-348-3917 *admissions@law.ua.edu*	•		•	•	•	•	•	•	•	•	•	•	•	•	99%	25	11	4	4	17	10	10	4		3	2	$26,000-$125,000
University of Arizona (James E. Rogers College of Law) Mountain and Speedway P.O. Box 210176 Tucson, AZ 85721-0176 520-621-3477 Fax: 520-621-9140 *admissions@law.arizona.edu*	•		•	•	•	•	•	•	•	•	•	•	•	•	94%	5	8	20	18	19	15	4	2	2	4	3	$39,818-$79,652
University of Arkansas (School of Law) Robert A. Leflar Law Center, Waterman Hall Fayetteville, AR 72701 501-575-3102	•	•	•	•	•	•	•	•	•		•	•	•	•	95%	32	9		3	9	14	21	2		2		$18,000-$82,000
University of Arkansas at Little Rock (UALR William H. Bowen School of Law) 1201 McMath Avenue Little Rock, AR 72202-5142 501-324-9439 Fax: 501-324-9433 *lawadm@ualr.edu*	•		•	•	•	•	•	•	•		•	•	•	•	95%	31	6	3	3	11	20	13	3	1	1	8	$18,480-$100,000
University of Baltimore (School of Law) 1420 North Charles Street Baltimore, MD 21201-5779 410-837-4459 Fax: 410-837-4450 *lwadmiss@ubmail.ubalt.edu*	•		•	•	•	•	•	•	•	•	•	•	•	•	88%	15	6	3	4	26	22	16	2			6	$44,577
University of California (Hastings College of the Law) 200 McAllister Street San Francisco, CA 94102 415-565-4623 Fax: 415-565-4863 *admiss@uchastings.edu*	•		•	•	•	•	•	•	•	•	•	•	•	•	95%	15	4	5	8	7	10	13	3		1	24	$26,000-$90,000
University of California at Berkeley (Boalt Hall) 5 Boalt Hall Berkeley, CA 94720 510-642-2274 Fax: 510-643-6222	•	•	•	•	•	•	•	•	•	•	•	•	•	•	98%	1	2	1	7	14	6	3	4		1	58	$25,000-$145,000

SCHOOL	CAREER SERVICES														PLACEMENT RECORD												
	FACILITIES		SERVICES													PERCENTAGE BREAKDOWN OF TYPE OF EMPLOYER											
	LAW PLACEMENT OFFICE	UNIVERSITY PLACEMENT OFFICE	EMPLOYMENT COUNSELING	JOB OPENINGS INFORMATION	SOLO PRACTICE ADVICE	RESUME PREPARATION	INTERVIEW COUNSELING	EMPLOYMENT PLANNING	JOB INTERVIEWS ARRANGEMENT	LAW, CORPORATE, AND GOVERNMENT CONTACT	ALUMNI CONTACTS	PART-TIME/SUMMER EMPLOYMENT	INTERNSHIPS	ALUMNI PLACEMENT	PLACEMENT WITHIN 6 TO 9 MONTHS	PRIVATE PRACTICE 2-10 ATTORNEYS	PRIVATE PRACTICE 11-25 ATTORNEYS	PRIVATE PRACTICE 26-50 ATTORNEYS	PRIVATE PRACTICE 51-100 ATTORNEYS	JUDICIAL CLERKSHIPS	GOVERNMENT	BUSINESS/INDUSTRY	PUBLIC INTEREST	MILITARY	ACADEMIC	OTHER	AVERAGE STARTING SALARY
University of California at Davis (School of Law) Martin Luther King, Jr. Hall - 400 Mrak Hall Drive Davis, CA 95616-5201 530-752-6477 *lawadmissions@ucdavis.edu*	•		•	•	•	•	•	•	•	•	•	•	•	•	99%	13	9	6	4	7	15	12	5		1	25	$30,000-$200,000
University of California at Los Angeles (School of Law) P.O. Box 951445 Los Angeles, CA 90095-1445 310-825-2080 Fax: 310-825-9450 *admissions@law.ucla.edu*	•		•	•	•	•	•	•	•	•	•	•	•	•	98%	8	6	4	7	8	4	7	3		1	1	$30,000-$180,000
University of Chicago (Law School) 1111 East 60th Street Chicago, IL 60637 773-702-9484 Fax: 773-834-0942 *admissions@law.uchicago.edu*	•		•	•	•	•	•	•	•	•	•	•	•	•	100%					28	2	2	1		1	66	$15,000-$165,000
University of Cincinnati (College of Law) P.O. Box 210040 Cincinnati, OH 45221-0040 513-556-6805 *admissions@law.uc.edu*	•		•	•	•	•	•	•	•	•	•	•	•	•	94%	11	8	5	4	10	3	10	4		3	23	$24,500-$140,000
University of Colorado (School of Law) Campus Box 403 Boulder, CO 80309-0403 303-492-7203	•		•	•	•	•	•	•	•	•	•	•	•	•	97%	17	5	4	18	19	9	9	5	1	1	13	$27,000-$125,000
University of Connecticut (School of Law) 55 Elizabeth Street Hartford, CT 06105 860-570-5159 Fax: 860-570-5153 *admit@law.uconn.edu*	•		•	•	•	•	•	•	•	•	•	•	•	•	95%					8	13	13	4	1	3	58	$28,000-$101,000
University of Dayton (School of Law) 300 College Park Dayton, OH 45469-2760 937-229-3555 Fax: 937-229-4194 *lawinfo@udayton.edu*	•		•	•	•	•	•	•	•	•	•	•	•	•	92%	25	8	7	4	7	14	20	1	2	4	1	$23,000-$115,000

University of Denver (College of Law) 7039 E. 18th Avenue Denver, CO 80220 303-871-6135 Fax: 303-871-6100 *khigganb@law.du.edu*	•		•	•	•	•	•	•	•	•	•	•	•	•	93%	17	5	3	2	6	12	30	3	2		14	$20,000-$125,000
University of Detroit Mercy (School of Law) 651 East Jefferson Avenue Detroit, MI 48226 313-596-0264 Fax: 313-596-0280 *udmlawao@udmercy.edu*	•		•	•	•	•	•	•	•	•	•	•	•	•	85%	18	5	2	3	9	20	20	3		3		$41,000
University of Florida (College of Law) 325 Holland Hall P.O. Box 117622 Gainesville, FL 32611-7622 352-392-2087 Fax: 352-392-2087 *patrick@law.ufl.edu*	•		•	•	•	•	•	•	•	•	•	•	•	•	85%	9	7	5	5	6	19	6	1				$28,000-$75,000
University of Georgia (School of Law) Hirsch Hall, 225 Herty Drive Athens, GA 30602-6012 706-542-7060 *ugajd@arches.uga.edu*	•		•	•	•	•	•	•	•	•	•	•	•	•	96%	22	11	6	4	16	6	14	4			13	$20,000-$82,000
University of Hawaii at Manoa (William S. Richardson School of Law) 2515 Dole Street Honolulu, HI 96822 808-956-7966 Fax: 808-956-3813 *lawadm@hawaii.educ*	•		•	•		•	•	•	•	•	•	•	•	•	96%	13	8	7	8	36	15	12	3				$24,000-$70,000
University of Houston (Law Center) 100 Law Center Houston, TX 77204-6060 713-743-2280 Fax: 713-743-2194 *admission@www.law.uh.edu*	•		•	•	•	•	•	•	•	•	•	•	•	•	93%	27	15	9	3	4	13	19	1			9	$45,000-$78,000
University of Idaho (College of Law) P.O. Box 442321 Moscow, ID 83844-2321 208-885-6423 Fax: 208-885-5709 *erickl@uidaho.edu*	•		•	•	•	•	•	•	•	•	•	•	•	•	93%	25	5	1	4	23	18	5	2		1	13	$35,385-$49,677
University of Illinois (College of Law) 504 East Pennsylvania Avenue Champaign, IL 61820 217-244-6415 Fax: 217-244-1478 *admissions@law.uiuc.edu*	•	•	•	•	•	•	•	•	•	•	•	•	•	•	96%	11	13	6	12	19	16	21	2				$19,000-$148,000
University of Iowa (College of Law) 276 Boyd Law Building, Melrose at Byington Street Iowa City, IA 52242 319-335-9095 or 319-335-9142 Fax: 319-335-9019 *law-admissions@uiowa.edu*	•		•	•	•	•	•	•	•	•	•	•	•	•	100%	16	6	5	3	16	8	13	1		2	28	$40,213-$170,000

SCHOOL	CAREER SERVICES														PLACEMENT RECORD												
	FACILITIES		SERVICES													PERCENTAGE BREAKDOWN OF TYPE OF EMPLOYER											
	LAW PLACEMENT OFFICE	UNIVERSITY PLACEMENT OFFICE	EMPLOYMENT COUNSELING	JOB OPENINGS INFORMATION	SOLO PRACTICE ADVICE	RESUME PREPARATION	INTERVIEW COUNSELING	EMPLOYMENT PLANNING	JOB INTERVIEWS ARRANGEMENT	LAW, CORPORATE, AND GOVERNMENT CONTACT	ALUMNI CONTACTS	PART-TIME/SUMMER EMPLOYMENT	INTERNSHIPS	ALUMNI PLACEMENT	PLACEMENT WITHIN 6 TO 9 MONTHS	PRIVATE PRACTICE 2-10 ATTORNEYS	PRIVATE PRACTICE 11-25 ATTORNEYS	PRIVATE PRACTICE 26-50 ATTORNEYS	PRIVATE PRACTICE 51-100 ATTORNEYS	JUDICIAL CLERKSHIPS	GOVERNMENT	BUSINESS/INDUSTRY	PUBLIC INTEREST	MILITARY	ACADEMIC	OTHER	AVERAGE STARTING SALARY
University of Kansas (School of Law) 205 Green Hall Lawrence, KS 66045 785-864-4378 Fax: 785-864-5054 *reitz@law.wpo.ukans.edu*	•		•	•	•	•	•	•	•	•	•	•	•	•	94%	26	14	6	11	7	2	26	4	2	2		$23,000-$52,000
University of Kentucky (College of Law) 209 Law Building Lexington, KY 40506-0048 606-257-7938 Fax: n/av *dbakert@uky.edu*	•		•	•	•	•	•	•	•	•	•	•	•	•	100%	22	7	10	20	17	10	9	2	2		1	$23,000-$127,000
University of Louisville (Louis D. Brandeis School of Law) University of Louisville Belknap Campus-Wilson W. Wyatt Hall Louisville, KY 40292 502-852-6364 Fax: 502-852-0862 *lawadmissions@louisville.edu*	•		•	•	•	•	•	•	•	•	•	•	•	•	96%	31	10	9	15	2	13	15	3	1	1		$23,500-$85,000
University of Maine (School of Law) 246 Deering Avenue Portland, ME 04102 207-780-4341 *mainelaw@usm.maine.edu*	•		•	•	•	•	•	•	•	•	•	•	•	•	80%	37				19	15	15	3			9	$20,000-$50,000
University of Maryland (School of Law) 500 West Baltimore Street Baltimore, MD 21201 410-706-3492 Fax: 410-706-4045 *admissions@law.umaryland.edu*	•		•	•	•	•	•	•	•	•	•	•	•	•	97%	10	3	1	3	24	17	15	4	1	4	15	$45,000-$75,000
University of Memphis (Cecil C. Humphreys School of Law) 207 Humphreys Law School Memphis, TN 38152-3140 901-678-5403 Fax: 901-678-5210 *lawadmissions@spc75.law.memphis.edu*	•		•	•	•	•	•	•	•	•	•	•	•	•	96%	42	7	4	1	8	12	12	1	5	1	7	$24,000-$140,000

University of Miami (School of Law) P.O. Box 248087, 1311 Miller Drive Coral Gables, FL 33124-8087 305-284-2523 *admissions@law.miami.edu*	•	•	•	•	•	•	•	•	•	•	•	•	•	•	91%				62	3	14	8	4	1	1	7	$29,000- $250,000
University of Michigan (Law School) 625 South State Street Ann Arbor, MI 48109-1215 734-764-0537 Fax: 734-647-3218 *law.jd.admissions@umich.edu*	•		•	•	•	•	•	•	•	•	•	•	•	•	99%					16	2	4	1		1	76	$41,834- $155,000
University of Minnesota (Law School) 229 19th Avenue S. Minneapolis, MN 55455 612-625-3487 Fax: 612-626-1874	•		•	•	•	•	•	•	•	•	•	•	•	•	99%	8	7	3	8	24	9	5	5	2	1	29	$28,100- $150,000
University of Mississippi (L.Q.C. Lamar Hall) Grove Loop University, MS 38677 601-915-6910 Fax: 601-915-1289 *bvinson@olemiss.edu*	•		•	•		•	•	•	•	•	•	•	•	•	98%	35	5	6	7	14	5	9	3	3	1	5	$30,000- $115,000
University of Missouri-Columbia (School of Law) 103 Hulston Hall Columbia, MO 65211 573-882-6042 Fax: 573-882-9625 *CatheyA@missouri.edu*	•	•	•	•	•	•	•	•	•	•	•	•	•	•	92%	24	8	1	15	14	22	13	1		1	1	$25,000- $140,000
University of Missouri-Kansas City (School of Law) 500 East 52nd Street Kansas City, MO 64110-2499 816-235-1644 Fax: 816-235-5276 *brooksdv@umkc.edu*	•		•	•	•	•	•	•	•	•	•	•	•	•	89%	18	5	2	3	3	29	16	1	3	2	13	$24,960- $100,000
University of Montana (School of Law) Missoula, MT 59812 406-243-2698 *lawadmis@selway.umt.edu*	•		•	•	•	•	•	•	•	•	•	•	•	•	96%	44				24	17	6			1	4	$33,750
University of Nebraska (College of Law) P.O. Box 830902 Lincoln, NE 68583-0902 402-472-2161 Fax: 402-472-5185 *lawadm@unl.edu*	•		•	•	•	•	•	•	•	•	•	•	•	•	98%	26	8	3	4	8	19	11	1	3	3	11	$20,000- $110,000
University of Nevada, Las Vegas (William S. Boyd School of Law) 4505 Maryland Parkway, Box 451003 Las Vegas, NV 89154-1003 702-895-3671 Fax: 702-895-1095 *request@law.unlv.edu*	•		•	•	•	•	•	•	•	•		•	•	•													

SCHOOL	CAREER SERVICES: Facilities: LAW PLACEMENT OFFICE	UNIVERSITY PLACEMENT OFFICE	Services: EMPLOYMENT COUNSELING	JOB OPENINGS INFORMATION	SOLO PRACTICE ADVICE	RESUME PREPARATION	INTERVIEW COUNSELING	EMPLOYMENT PLANNING	JOB INTERVIEWS ARRANGEMENT	LAW, CORPORATE, AND GOVERNMENT CONTACT	ALUMNI CONTACTS	PART-TIME/SUMMER EMPLOYMENT	INTERNSHIPS	ALUMNI PLACEMENT	PLACEMENT RECORD: PLACEMENT WITHIN 6 TO 9 MONTHS	Percentage Breakdown of Type of Employer: PRIVATE PRACTICE 2-10 ATTORNEYS	PRIVATE PRACTICE 11-25 ATTORNEYS	PRIVATE PRACTICE 26-50 ATTORNEYS	PRIVATE PRACTICE 51-100 ATTORNEYS	JUDICIAL CLERKSHIPS	GOVERNMENT	BUSINESS/INDUSTRY	PUBLIC INTEREST	MILITARY	ACADEMIC	OTHER	AVERAGE STARTING SALARY
University of New Mexico (School of Law) 1117 Stanford Drive N.E. Albuquerque, NM 87131-1431 505-277-0572 Fax: 505-277-9958	•	•	•	•	•	•	•		•	•	•	•	•	•	87%	31	4	4	1	11	30	6	4	1		5	$18,000-$100,000
University of North Carolina at Chapel Hill (School of Law) Campus Box 3380, 101 Van Hecke-Wettach Hall Chapel Hill, NC 27599-3380 919-962-5109 Fax: 919-843-7939 *law_admission@unc.edu*	•	•	•	•	•	•	•	•	•	•	•	•	•	•	98%	15	4	4	4	10	11	10	6	1	1		$23,000-$100,000
University of North Dakota (School of Law) Box 9003 Grand Forks, ND 58202 701-777-2104 Fax: 701-777-2217 *linda.kohoutek@thor.law.und.nodak.edu*	•		•	•	•	•	•	•	•	•	•	•	•	•	100%	32	3	2		35	10	14		4			$19,000-$70,000
University of Notre Dame (Notre Dame Law School) P.O. Box R Notre Dame, IN 46556-0780 574-631-6626 Fax: 574-631-5474 *lawadmit@nd.edu*	•		•	•	•	•	•	•	•	•	•	•	•	•	99%	5	6	3	6	7	5		4		1	63	$75,000-$125,000
University of Oklahoma (College of Law) 300 Timberdell Road Norman, OK 73019 405-325-4726 Fax: 405-325-0502 *kmadden@ou.edu*	•		•	•	•	•	•	•	•	•	•	•	•	•	97%	27	9	4	5	5	21	12	4	1	4	8	$20,000-$80,000
University of Oregon (School of Law, William W. Knight Law Center) 1515 Agate Street Eugene, OR 97403-1221 541-346-1553 Fax: 541-346-3984 *admissions@law.uoregon.edu*	•		•	•	•	•	•	•	•	•	•	•	•	•	92%												$40,000-$80,000

University of Pennsylvania (Law School) 3400 Chestnut Street Philadelphia, PA 19104-6204 215-898-7400 *admissions@oyez.law.upenn.edu*	•		•	•	•	•	•	•	•	•	•	•	•	•	100%			1	70	19	1	5	3			1	$30,000-$100,000
University of Pittsburgh (School of Law) 3900 Forbes Avenue Pittsburgh, PA 15260 412-648-1400 Fax: 412-648-2647 *admissions@law.pitt.edu*	•		•	•	•	•	•	•	•	•	•	•	•	•	99%	32	8	2	24	4	1	6	2	2		19	$26,000-$125,000
University of Puerto Rico (School of Law) P.O. Box 23349, UPR Station Rio Piedras, PR 00931-3349 787-772-1472 Fax: 787-764-4360 *wandi_perez@hotmail.com*	•		•	•		•	•	•	•	•	•	•		•		9	13	15	16	10		1	1			35	$28,000-$35,000
University of Richmond (The T.C. Williams School of Law) University of Richmond, VA 23173 804-289-8189 *admissions@uofrlaw.richmond.edu*	•	•	•	•		•	•	•	•	•	•	•	•	•	100%	25	3	5	8	21	10	13	1	1	1	12	$30,000-$130,000
University of San Diego (School of Law) 5998 Alcala Park San Diego, CA 92110 619-260-4528 Fax: 619-260-2218 *jdinfo@sandiego.edu*	•		•	•	•	•	•	•	•	•	•	•	•	•	89%	29	14	9	11	2	17	15	1	1	1		$30,000-$85,000
University of San Francisco (School of Law) 2130 Fulton Street San Francisco, CA 94117-1080 415-422-6586 Fax: 415-422-6433	•		•	•	•	•	•	•		•	•	•	•	•	94%	60				5	7	15	5		1	7	$60,000-$107,500
University of South Carolina (School of Law) Main and Greene Streets Columbia, SC 29208 803-777-6605 Fax: 803-777-7751 *usclaw@law.law.sc.edu*	•		•	•	•	•	•	•	•	•	•	•	•	•	94%	25	6	4	5	25	13	8	1	1	1	11	$19,500-$105,000
University of South Dakota (School of Law) 414 East Clark Street Vermillion, SD 57069-2390 605-677-5443 Fax: 605-677-5417 *lawreq@usd.edu*	•	•	•	•	•	•	•	•	•	•	•	•	•	•	90%	23	3		1	35	18	8	4	1		7	$33,600-$39,500
University of Southern California (Law School) Los Angeles, CA 90089-0074 213-740-2523	•		•	•	•	•	•	•	•	•	•	•	•	•	96%	5	5	1	2	8	3	12	2		1	61	$75,000-$125,000

SCHOOL	CAREER SERVICES														PLACEMENT RECORD												
	FACILITIES		SERVICES													PERCENTAGE BREAKDOWN OF TYPE OF EMPLOYER											
	LAW PLACEMENT OFFICE	UNIVERSITY PLACEMENT OFFICE	EMPLOYMENT COUNSELING	JOB OPENINGS INFORMATION	SOLO PRACTICE ADVICE	RESUME PREPARATION	INTERVIEW COUNSELING	EMPLOYMENT PLANNING	JOB INTERVIEWS ARRANGEMENT	LAW, CORPORATE, AND GOVERNMENT CONTACT	ALUMNI CONTACTS	PART-TIME/SUMMER EMPLOYMENT	INTERNSHIPS	ALUMNI PLACEMENT	PLACEMENT WITHIN 6 TO 9 MONTHS	PRIVATE PRACTICE 2-10 ATTORNEYS	PRIVATE PRACTICE 11-25 ATTORNEYS	PRIVATE PRACTICE 26-50 ATTORNEYS	PRIVATE PRACTICE 51-100 ATTORNEYS	JUDICIAL CLERKSHIPS	GOVERNMENT	BUSINESS/INDUSTRY	PUBLIC INTEREST	MILITARY	ACADEMIC	OTHER	AVERAGE STARTING SALARY
University of Tennessee (College of Law) 1505 W. Cumberland Avenue Knoxville, TN 37996-1810 865-974-4131 Fax: 865-974-1572 *lawadmit@libra.law.utk.edu*	•		•	•	•	•	•	•	•	•	•	•	•	•	89%	28	11	5	4	15	12	8	2	1	1	13	$29,400-$125,000
University of Texas at Austin (School of Law) 727 East Dean Keeton Street Austin, TX 78705 512-232-1200 Fax: 512-471-6988 *admissions@mail.law.utexas.edu*	•		•	•	•	•	•	•	•	•	•	•	•	•	100%	5	4	3	6	13	7	10	2	2	2	35	$33,000-$100,946
University of the District of Columbia (David A. Clarke School of Law) 4200 Connecticut Avenue, N.W. Washington, DC 20008 202-274-7341 Fax: 202-274-5583 *vcanty@law.udc.edu*	•		•	•	•	•	•	•	•	•	•	•	•	•	85%	30	5			5	30	10	10	2	2	5	$27,000-$102,000
University of the Pacific (McGeorge School of Law) 3200 Fifth Avenue Sacramento, CA 95817 916-739-7105 Fax: 916-739-7134 *admissionsmcgeorge@uop.edu*	•		•	•	•	•	•	•	•	•	•	•	•	•	87%	56				4	20	13	2	2	1	2	$25,000-$135,000
University of Toledo (College of Law) 2801 West Bancroft Street Toledo, OH 43606-3390 419-530-4131 Fax: 419-530-4345 *law.utoledo.edu*	•		•	•	•	•	•	•	•	•	•	•	•	•	95%	25	4	4	1	3	18	22	6	1	5	11	$18,000-$125,000
University of Tulsa (College of Law) 3120 East Fourth Place Tulsa, OK 74104-2499 918-631-2709 Fax: 918-631-3630 *george-justice@utulsa.edu*	•	•	•	•	•	•	•	•	•	•	•	•	•	•	81%	40	4	2	1	2	11	25	4	2		9	$42,000

University of Utah (College of Law) 332 South 1400 East Front Room 101 Salt Lake City, UT 84112 801-581-7479 Fax: 801-581-6897 *aguilarr@law.utah.edu*	•		•	•	•	•	•	•	•	•	•	•	•	•	96%	9	22	16	6	16	17	10	2	1	1		$19,000-$150,000
University of Virginia (School of Law) 580 Massie Road Charlottesville, VA 22903-1789 804-924-7351 Fax: 804-982-2128 *lawadmit@virginia.edu*	•		•	•	•	•	•	•	•	•	•	•	•	•	100%					17	2	2	1	2		76	$32,000-$145,000
University of Washington (School of Law) 1100 Northeast Campus Parkway Seattle, WA 98105-6617 206-543-4078 *admissions@law.washington.edu*	•		•	•	•	•	•	•	•	•	•	•	•	•	96%	6	6	7	7	16	19	7	6	1	1	20	$35,000-$80,000
University of Wisconsin (Law School) 975 Bascom Mall Madison, WI 53706 608-262-5914 Fax: 608-262-5485 *admissions@law.wisc.educ*	•		•	•	•	•	•	•	•	•	•	•	•	•	100%	21	6	8	4	8	8	7	5	2	2	27	$24,000-$130,000
University of Wyoming (College of Law) P.O. Box 3035 Laramie, WY 82071 307-766-6416 *lawadmis@uwyo.edu*	•	•	•	•	•	•	•	•	•	•	•	•	•	•	93%					14	22	12	2			50	$18,000-$110,000
Valparaiso University (School of Law) Wesemann Hall Valparaiso, IN 46383-6493 219-465-7829 Fax: 219-465-7808 *marilyn.olson@valpo.edu*	•		•	•	•	•	•	•	•	•	•	•	•	•	95%	38	11	7	2	7	12	5	2	2	3	11	$34,000-$105,000
Vanderbilt University (Law School) 131 21st Avenue South Nashville, TN 37203 615-322-6452 Fax: 615-322-1531	•		•	•		•	•	•	•	•	•	•	•	•	98%	3	8	15	45	20	4	2	1		2		$62,000
Vermont Law School P.O. Box 96, Chelsea Street South Royalton, VT 05068-0096 802-763-8303 Fax: 802-763-7071 *admiss@vermontlaw.edu*	•		•	•	•	•	•	•	•	•	•	•	•	•	83%	20	7	9	6	15	20	7	9	2	2	3	$33,088-$46,369
Villanova University (School of Law) Garey Hall Villanova, PA 19085 610-519-7010 Fax: 610-519-6291 *admissions@law.vill.edu*	•		•	•	•	•	•	•	•	•	•	•	•	•	94%	12	10	10	6	17	10	5	1		6	23	$23,000-$140,000

SCHOOL	CAREER SERVICES														PLACEMENT RECORD												
	FACILITIES		SERVICES													PERCENTAGE BREAKDOWN OF TYPE OF EMPLOYER											
	LAW PLACEMENT OFFICE	UNIVERSITY PLACEMENT OFFICE	EMPLOYMENT COUNSELING	JOB OPENINGS INFORMATION	SOLO PRACTICE ADVICE	RESUME PREPARATION	INTERVIEW COUNSELING	EMPLOYMENT PLANNING	JOB INTERVIEWS ARRANGEMENT	LAW, CORPORATE, AND GOVERNMENT CONTACT	ALUMNI CONTACTS	PART-TIME/SUMMER EMPLOYMENT	INTERNSHIPS	ALUMNI PLACEMENT	PLACEMENT WITHIN 6 TO 9 MONTHS	PRIVATE PRACTICE 2-10 ATTORNEYS	PRIVATE PRACTICE 11-25 ATTORNEYS	PRIVATE PRACTICE 26-50 ATTORNEYS	PRIVATE PRACTICE 51-100 ATTORNEYS	JUDICIAL CLERKSHIPS	GOVERNMENT	BUSINESS/INDUSTRY	PUBLIC INTEREST	MILITARY	ACADEMIC	OTHER	AVERAGE STARTING SALARY
Wake Forest University (School of Law) P.O. Box 7206, Reynolda Station Winston-Salem, NC 27109 336-758-5437	•		•	•	•	•	•	•	•	•	•	•	•	•	99%	17	9	6	5	20	9	11	1	3	1	18	
Washburn University (School of Law) 1700 College Topeka, KS 66621 785-231-1185 Fax: 785-232-8087 *admissions@washburnlaw.edu*	•		•	•	•	•	•	•	•	•	•	•	•	•	96%	35	4	1	6		34	14	4		2		$22,000-$74,000
Washington and Lee University (School of Law) Lewis Hall Lexington, VA 24450 540-463-8504 Fax: 540-463-8586 *lawadm@wlu.edu*	•		•	•	•	•	•	•	•	•	•	•	•	•	98%	10	7	10	5	27	4	4	3	1		24	$25,000-$125,000
Washington University in St. Louis (School of Law) Box 1120, One Brookings Drive St. Louis, MO 63130 314-935-4525 Fax: 314-935-6959 *admiss@walaw.wash.edu*	•		•	•	•	•	•	•	•	•	•	•	•	•	98%	17		25		8	11	12	4	1	3	19	$23,000-$100,000
Wayne State University (Law School) 471 W. Palmer Detroit, MI 48202 313-577-3937 Fax: 313-577-6000 *linda.sims@wayne.edu*	•		•	•		•	•		•	•	•	•	•	•	94%					5	12	18	3		1	56	$15,000-$130,000
West Virginia University (College of Law) P.O. Box 6130 Morgantown, WV 26506 304-293-5304 Fax: 304-293-6891 *lawaply@wvu.edu*	•	•	•	•	•	•	•	•	•	•	•	•	•	•	90%	39	10	7	6	4	18	11	4		1		$36,610-$72,000
Western New England College (School of Law) 1215 Wilbraham Road Springfield, MA 01119 413-782-1406 Fax: 413-796-2067 *lawadmis@wnec.edu*	•		•	•	•	•	•	•	•	•	•	•	•	•	89%	21	2	2	2	12	21	25	4	3	3	4	$18,000-$106,000

Western State University (College of Law) 1111 North State College Blvd Fullerton, CA 92831 714-738-1000, ext. 2600 Fax: 714-441-1748 *paulb@wsulaw.edu*	•		•	•	•	•	•	•	•	•	•	•	•	•	88%	17	12	5	5	1	18	28	1	1	5	6	$41,000-$175,000
Whittier College (School of Law) 3333 Harbor Blvd. Costa Mesa, CA 92626 714-444-4141, ext. 121 Fax: 714-444-0250 *info@law.whittier.edu*	•		•	•	•	•	•	•	•	•	•	•	•	•	79%	41	3	4	4	4	6	25	1		4	8	$35,000-$250,000
Widener University (School of Law) 4601 Concord Pike, P.O. Box 7474 Wilmington, DE 19803, 302-477-2162 (DE); 717-541-3903 (PA) Fax: 302-477-2224 (DE); 717-541-3999 (PA) *law.admissions@law.widener.edu*	•		•	•	•	•	•	•	•	•	•	•	•	•	89%	14	5	2	2	16	14	22	1		1	22	$20,000-$350,000
Willamette University (College of Law) 245 Winter Street S.E. Salem, OR 97301 503-370-6282 Fax: 503-370-6375 *law-admission@willamette.edu*	•		•	•	•	•	•	•	•	•	•	•	•	•	84%	24	8	5	2	10	30	12	3	3		3	$22,880-$112,500
William Mitchell College of Law 875 Summit Avenue St. Paul, MN 55105-3076 651-290-6476 Fax: 651-290-6414 *admissions@wmitchell.edu*	•		•	•	•	•	•	•	•	•	•	•	•	•	94%	20	4	4	3	17	10	24	2	1	2	12	$20,800-$260,000
Yale University (Yale Law School) P.O. Box 208329 New Haven, CT 06520-8329 203-432-4995 *admissions.law@yale.edu*	•		•	•	•	•	•	•	•	•	•	•	•	•	96%	36				45	2	7	7		3		
Yeshiva University (Benjamin N. Cardozo School of Law) 55 Fifth Avenue New York, NY 10003 212-790-0274 Fax: 212-790-0482 *lawinfo@ymail.yu.edu*	•		•	•	•	•	•	•	•	•	•	•	•	•	99%	5	9	7	9	5	15	13	7		1	27	$37,500-$150,000

an appreciable number pursue advanced degrees both in law and other fields.

The 2001 NALP survey accounts for approximately 90 percent of the graduating class, leaving the employment status of 10 percent unknown. Of those whose employment status was known, 90 percent were employed and the remainder unemployed or enrolled in advanced degree programs at the time of the NALP survey, approximately nine months after graduation. These numbers have remained fairly consistent over a period of more than twenty-five years, during which NALP has surveyed law school graduates. Not surprisingly, the employment picture is slightly better in years when the general economy is strong, and slightly worse in years with recession. The NALP survey does support the observation that the legal job market is fairly stable and predictable. Competition for the most prestigious and desirable jobs can be fierce, although most people who want jobs as lawyers will eventually get them.

Geographic Locations

Lawyers work almost everywhere. More lawyers are concentrated in the largest population centers, because of the high volume of commercial activity that occurs in those areas. Lawyers are also concentrated in the seats of government, from Washington, DC, to state capitals, to county seats, throughout the United States. Even in rural areas, lawyers can be found with offices close to the clients they serve. An increasing number of U.S. lawyers work outside the boundaries of the United States. With the increasing internationalization of business, lawyers have become a new kind of export.

The NALP statistics for the employment of law school graduates parallel the demographic patterns for lawyers as a whole. The greatest number of legal jobs are found in the largest cities, but law graduates are disbursed to a wide variety of places throughout the country. There is some correlation between law school attended and location of first employment, suggesting that people either choose their law school because of the geographic area or become attached to the area while they are in law school.

The bar exam represents a hurdle to entry into the practice of law, because for most legal positions, it is necessary to pass the bar exam in the state where the lawyer will be working prior to beginning to serve clients. The majority of law graduates take only one bar exam, and are thus limited to the jurisdiction where they become licensed. If graduates have employment in a jurisdiction where they do not pass the bar exam, they will lose those jobs. If they take the exam before they have a job, they will be limited in their job search to positions where they become licensed. Applicants to law school should be aware of these jurisdictional requirements, and investigate the possibilities as appropriate.

Salaries

Lawyers' salaries are reported by various bar associations and consultant surveys, as well as the U.S. Bureau of Labor Statistics and NALP. All of these surveys seem to show that there is a wide range of income among lawyers. Some lawyers, particularly in the rural areas, may not have enough business to sustain a full-time practice. Lawyers in certain metropolitan areas with high lawyer population may find competition for clients to be intense. Some of these lawyers may discover that even after years of practice they do not make a good living practicing law. On the other end of the spectrum are lawyers whose income is in the seven figure range.

Different surveys show discrepancies in reported results that may reflect more on their sampling techniques than actual differences, but most seem to point to an average income for all lawyers of between $100,000 and $150,000. This figure includes not only law firm partners, but also semi-retired senior lawyers and brand new associates as well. It includes not only private practice, but also lower paying government service positions. Within private practice it is generally the case that lawyers in larger firms make more money than lawyers in smaller firms. It is also the case that some areas of practice, notably corporate and tax work, show better returns than other areas, such as criminal law and domestic relations.

Starting salaries nationally range from less than $20,000 to more than $140,000. The NALP's *Jobs and JDs* indicates that the median for all graduates is more than $50,000. In most cities, the largest firms will pay a standard rate for new associates, and smaller firms will offer salaries somewhat less than the salary leaders. Small firms often pay at or below the median for all graduates. (Remember: a median means that half the scores fall below the midpoint.)

CHAPTER 9

What Trends Are Affecting the Practice of Law?

Like other businesses and professions, the practice of law has changed dramatically in recent years. A revolution in technology has swept the business world. Computers have altered the way law is practiced in countless ways, including how lawyers relate to their clients. Technology has even altered the dynamics of how lawyers relate to each other in organizations.

During the first half of the twentieth century, most lawyers practiced alone. Since World War II, however, more and more lawyers have gone to work in ever-larger law firms. In these firms, partners hired junior lawyers—associates—to assist them in the delivery of legal services. The development of these large law firms paralleled the growth of corporations, which fueled an increase in the need for legal services, and for large firms.

During the same period of time the demographics of the U.S. population were also changing. More and more people were living in large cities or metropolitan areas. Waves of immigrants were producing an increasingly diverse society. Global conflict and worldwide depression illustrated the futility of American isolation on the world stage.

The end of World War II brought new challenges to the legal profession in America. As large numbers of veterans attended law school on the GI bill, there was a rapid increase in the number of lawyers graduating from law school. This growth paralleled a dramatic rise in business opportunity, fueled by post-war prosperity.

In the early 1960s, most lawyers were particularly ill-prepared for the dramatic changes in the practice of law that subsequently occurred in the last half of the twentieth century. Evolution is a good word to use to describe these developments, because they produced a kind of economic Darwinism, in which the fittest adapt and survive, and the less competitive individuals and forms of practice become extinct.

As someone who is thinking about going to law school, you should understand that this evolution is continuing and is likely to continue for the foreseeable future. You should recognize that the changes that have transformed other segments of business and industry have had an impact on the practice of law as well. You should know that some people will succeed in these times and some will not. Law, far from being a refuge from a competitive workplace, is subject to risks like most other fields of endeavor.

What you can do to improve the likelihood that you will be successful in this environment is seek to understand the changes that have occurred and that are likely to take place in the future. Of course, it is impossible to predict the future, but sensitivity to trends and insightful analysis of events can help you to adapt. Several areas are worth watching:

GLOBALIZATION

Electronic communication, air transportation, and global migration have produced a world that is inevitably interconnected. It is possible to know the local news almost anywhere in the world. The distribution of products and services transcends international boundaries, producing at the same time tremendous variety in the marketplace and increased homogeneity in availability. English has increasingly become the default language of world commerce. Stock markets in Asia, wars in Africa, and mergers in Europe all have an impact on business in America. Lawyers increasingly will be called upon to represent clients who have interests outside the United States, or who come from outside the United States and need a lawyer's assistance here. Lawyers themselves will face competition from foreign law firms, and even from organizations that provide law-related services that would be viewed as unauthorized practice of law in the United States.

TECHNOLOGY

The information revolution has transformed the way law is practiced. Today, most lawyers have a computer on their desktop with access to the Internet, legal databases, and software applications. Technology allows lawyers and law firms to practice more efficiently. These new resources also place additional demands on practitioners, particularly older lawyers, who grew up in an era when the most advanced technology needed to practice law was an Underwood typewriter. Technological advancements force lawyers to find new ways to ply their services, and to communicate with clients who are increasingly wired and connected themselves. As legal information and forms become increasingly available on the Internet and other electronic formats, the role of the lawyer shifts to one of information provider, interpreter, and advisor.

DEMOGRAPHICS

After a century of urbanization, there appear to be signs that the American population is disbursing again to the countryside. Unlike the nineteenth century migration westward, which was fueled by farmers and ranchers, this movement is led by lifestyle pioneers, who seek to get away from the pressure of big city life. It is supported by electronic access to goods, services, and entertainment that negate the effects of isolation sometimes associated with country life. A system of good roads and a web of transportation connections mean that no place is more than a few hours from all the cultural attractions that cities have to offer. Yet telecommuting makes it possible for people to do their jobs not only hundreds of miles away, but halfway around the world. Lawyers benefit from this trend as well, because they can remain connected to their offices and their clients. They can commute great distances from homes and can stay in touch while they are out of the office—even on vacation—and can deal with client matters in distant jurisdictions.

A second demographic trend that has had a significant impact on lawyers is the entrance of large numbers of women into the workforce. Until the 1960s, only a handful of women entered the legal profession, and law firms were often an exclusively male domain. Women who did go to work in law firms were often relegated to secretarial and other low-paying jobs. Over the past three decades, the legal profession has experienced a dramatic increase in the number of women lawyers. Today, half of all law students are women, and the percentage of women in the profession as a whole increases each year. This change not only produces more opportunities for women in the practice of law, but it also puts pressure on law firms and other organizations that employ lawyers to assure that these opportunities are meaningful ones.

A related issue is the advent of the two-career family. Since the 1960s, more and more families have become dual-career households, where both spouses either choose to work or have to work in order to sustain a desired lifestyle. When one or both of the people in such a family is a lawyer, there can be a variety of interesting problems, from conflicts of interest between the two lawyers' firms, to employment in different cities, to questions about allocating responsibility for child care and housework.

Since divorce hits one out of two American families, single parents are often forced to raise children without a partner. The problem of single parenting impacts not only the lawyers but also the support staff in law firms. The upheaval can be disruptive to organizations that are trying to provide quality legal services to clients. For law firms, most of which are very small organizations compared to nonlegal businesses, it can be difficult to accommodate the needs of employees in our complex society.

LIFESTYLES

Many young lawyers must face fundamental lifestyle issues, enhanced in part by the great variety of choices available to them. Do they have children or not? If so, when? Who will stay at home with young children and for how long? What kind of childcare and early education will children receive? What kind of geographical setting is most compatible with their interests, hobbies, and professional needs? The beach? The mountains? The big city? A rural county seat? How many hours a week do you and your spouse/partner want to put into the practice of law? Forty? Sixty? Eighty? One hundred? Where do you see yourself in ten or twenty years as your practice matures? And family? Do you want the people you grew up with to be close at hand, or will you be satisfied to see them once or twice a year? Is the type of law that you hope to practice likely to be available in the geographic locale where you would like to live?

CHANGE

One common thread that cuts through all the trends described above is change. The world is changing in unprecedented ways, and will continue to change throughout the professional lives of those students entering law school in the coming years. The changes that we are experiencing are profound; they are transforming. Author Tom Peters, at a 1999 conference on the future of the legal profession, said that humankind may be in the midst of the biggest revolution in the way people live since we came in off the savannahs to live in permanent villages—a 10,000-year sea change. Other observers might not go as far as Peters does, but virtually everyone who has thought about the future believes that we are in the midst of something really big.

It should come as no surprise that the legal profession is undergoing dramatic change in the way legal services are delivered. Just as the industrial base of America has shifted to Third World countries, and the medical profession has endured the rise of managed care, lawyers face an increasingly competitive environment and pressures to deliver better services more economically. Although the number of law school graduates continues to climb, more and more lawyers opt to work in settings outside of private practice (i.e., law firms). An increasing number of graduates accept positions in corporations, government service, private associations, accounting or professional services firms, banks, group legal services, private associations, and a variety of other organizations. Other lawyers start out in law firms, but move to some other type of organization, often one that has been a client of the firm. Some lawyers may abandon the law completely, but the vast majority of them continue to utilize their legal skills and "practice law" in a new environment.

Someone contemplating a career in law should appreciate the fact that the opportunities for lawyers are changing as the world around them changes. All this change creates tremendous challenges and risks, but it also generates unusual opportunities. It will be important for you to stay attuned to how society and the practice of law continue to evolve in order to maximize your opportunities and achieve your goals in the coming years.

These are not simple questions, and there are no easy answers. But both lawyers and applicants to law school will have to face these issues at some time or other. It makes sense to think now about how lifestyle questions will affect the career choices that you make as a lawyer, and try to make decisions that are consistent with your long-term personal needs.

SUBSTANTIVE PRACTICE AREAS

People often ask what are the growing practice areas in the law? There is probably no consensus answer to this question, and many pundits have attempted to predict substantive trends in the law—many with great imprecision. Understanding the risks inherent in such predictions, this author will offer insights into a number of practice areas that are likely to experience growth in the coming decade:

- **Environmental law.** Global environmental issues are protracted; resources are limited. It is inevitable that a world population of six billion will have to confront issues like global warming, extinction of animal species, resource allocation, and sustainable development. Lawyers involved in this process are likely to have their hands full for the foreseeable future.

- **Health care.** In the United States there have been dramatic changes in the way health care services are delivered. The availability of medical treatment, risks associated with scientific advancement, and issues involving death and dying all present health care issues. Decisions about treatment are no longer limited to the patient and provider, but often involve a hospital and/or other corporate employer, and an insurance company or HMO. With a population that is graying demographically, health care issues can be expected to increase during the early part of the twenty-first century.

- **Elder law.** In addition to health care, older citizens have a variety of other issues that they must confront, from increased leisure associated with retirement to legal issues like estate planning, to a variety of other unique problems. An increasing number of lawyers are defining their practice in terms of these clients under the heading of Elder Law. The number of Americans age 55 and older continues to grow, not only because baby boomers are reaching their golden years, but also because Americans are living longer.

- **International business.** The growing international interdependence of countries, particularly in the delivery of goods and services, will continue to produce a high level of complex legal work. Lawyers from this country and others around the world will be involved in solving the legal problems that these commercial transactions create. From the European community to the Pacific Rim, from the former eastern bloc to Central and South America, American lawyers will find opportunities in all these areas.

- **Communications and technology.** The Internet, satellite communications, cable, and other legal problems associated with computers and electronic technology will continue to evolve in the near future. Many of the concepts of common law from copyright to theft must be redefined in the electronic environment. From the antitrust questions confronting Microsoft Corporation to the privacy rights of office workers, without a doubt this area of law will be booming.

- **Leisure law.** Sports and entertainment law, travel law, and related subject areas will experience a period of growth in the coming years, as people have more and more free time. Even those who work long hours will be seeking leisure opportunities during their vacation periods. Many workers will be retiring earlier and looking for leisure activities to fill their time. Although this is a fairly small field of practice today, it is likely to grow in the coming decades.

- **Preventive law.** Estate planning, business planning, tax planning, and other areas where lawyers can advise individuals and businesses on how to avoid legal problems, rather than trying to help once things have fallen apart, will experience considerable growth. This will be not only because lawyers will be seeking these markets, but also because a more sophisticated client base will seek to have this kind of legal help more readily available.

- **Mediation and other forms of alternative dispute resolution.** More and more legal cases will be resolved without going to court, through mediation and alternative dispute resolution processes. Lawyers will be involved in these practice areas as well, because their legal skills of negotiation, persuasion, analysis, and organization will work well to help clients solve problems in a variety of different ways.

- **Employment law.** The proliferation of state and federal law governing the workplace has created a growing practice in employment law. Practice settings in private firms range from small and large law firms devoted exclusively to this area of practice to more general practice firms in which fewer than all of the lawyers specialize in this area. With the growth in business generally, and with large corporate mergers, there will continue to be a need for lawyers to advise clients on employee matters, such as ERISA and pension benefits, to train clients and their employees on prevention (e.g., harassment training) and to litigate or mediate employee complaints and claims arising under the many laws in this area.

- **Intellectual property law.** The growth in certain specialized businesses, particularly in the health care and computer technology industries, will require lawyers who have technological or scientific backgrounds to assist clients in protecting the new technologies they develop. While patent law and copyright law are not new, continued innovations, particularly those triggered by the Internet, and growing technological sophistication, have created an increase in demand for lawyers to help clients secure patents and to help clients protect their intellectual property.

Although the areas of practice described above represent fields where growth can be inferred from a variety of factual indicia, many other specialized or "boutique" practice areas will blossom in the coming years. Because virtually every form of human endeavor has legal implications, it follows that very little in life can be conducted outside the law. This means that there is a substantive practice area for almost anything you can imagine, and if you can imagine it, you can bet that somewhere there is a lawyer practicing in that field. Lawyers today are increasingly becoming specialists, who concentrate their practice in a narrow field of expertise. The general practitioner is a dying breed in law, just as in medicine. And as in medicine, the more complex society becomes, the more specialties emerge.

CONCLUSION

For someone about to enter law school, it should be clear that choosing to become a lawyer is just the beginning of a long path of career choices. Not only will law school graduates have to choose from a variety of practice settings, they will have to decide among an almost infinite array of substantive fields within the law. On top of all this, they will have to be astute enough to understand that the underpinnings of their decisions will be undergoing continual change. The element of change will be a factor in every facet of life, whether you decide to attend law school or not, but if you do elect to go to law school, do not imagine that you will be immune from the forces that are transforming the rest of the world. If you remember that society and the practice of law are both changing, and continually reflect upon how these changes will affect you, you will improve your chances of achieving success professionally and personally.

PART II

Taking the LSAT

CHAPTER 10

The LSAT and the Admissions Process

The Law School Admission Test (LSAT) is required for all law school applicants. Although law school admissions committees consider a variety of criteria, there is little doubt that the LSAT plays a significant role in the selection process.

Preparation for the LSAT is the rule rather than the exception. This section is an introduction to the LSAT preparation process.

ANSWERS TO SOME COMMONLY ASKED QUESTIONS

What does the LSAT measure?

The LSAT is designed to measure a range of mental abilities related to the study of law; therefore, it is used by most law schools to evaluate their applicants.

Will any special knowledge of the law raise my score on the LSAT?

The LSAT is designed so that candidates from a particular academic background are given no advantage. The questions measure reading comprehension, logical reasoning, and analytical reasoning, drawing from a variety of verbal and analytical material.

Does a high score on the LSAT predict success in law school or in the practice of law?

Success on the LSAT demonstrates your ability to read with understanding and to reason clearly under pressure; surely these strengths are important to both the study and the practice of law, as is the ability to write well, measured by the LSAT Writing Sample. To say that success on the LSAT *predicts* success in law school may overstate the case, however, because success in law school also involves skills that are not measured by the LSAT.

When is the LSAT administered?

The regular administration of the test occurs nationwide four times each year, around the beginning of the fall, winter, spring, and summer seasons. Except for the summer month, the test is usually administered on a Saturday morning from 8:30 A.M. to about 1:00 P.M. For the past few years, the *summer exam* has been given on a Monday afternoon. Dates are announced annually by the Law School Admission Council in Newtown, Pennsylvania.

What if I cannot take the test on a Saturday?

Some special arrangements are possible: Check the LSAS General Information Booklet in your registration packet. Those who must take the exam at a time when the regular administration occurs on Saturday, but who cannot participate on Saturday for religious reasons, may arrange for a special Monday administration.

How early should I register?

Regular registration closes about one month before the exam date. Late registration is available up to three weeks prior to the exam date. There is an additional fee for late registration.

Is walk-in registration available?

For security reasons, walk-in registration is no longer permitted. Students may register by telephone by the telephone deadline. The Law School Admission Services (LSAS) will not permit walk-ins the day of the test. Be sure to read very carefully the General Information Booklet section on "registering to take the LSAT."

What is the LSDAS?

The LSDAS (Law School Data Assembly Service) compiles a report about each subscribing applicant. The report contains LSAT results, a summary of the applicant's academic work, and copies of college transcripts. A report is sent to each law school that the applicant designates. Thus, if you register for the LSDAS, you will not need to mail a separate transcript to each of your prospective law schools. REMINDER: You can register for the Candidate Referral Service only at the same time you register for the LSDAS.

How is the LSAT used?

Your LSAT score is one common denominator by which a law school compares you to other applicants. Other factors also determine your acceptance to law school: a law school may consider your personal qualities, grade-point average, extracurricular achievements, and letters of recommendation. Requirements for admission vary widely from school to school, so you are wise to contact the law school of your choice for specific information.

How do I obtain registration forms?

The registration form covering both the LSAT and the LSDAS is available in the LSAT/LSDAS REGISTRATION PACKET. Copies of the packet are available at the admissions offices of most law schools and the testing offices at most undergraduate universities and colleges. You may also obtain the packet by writing to LAW SCHOOL ADMISSION SERVICES, Box 2000, Newtown, PA 18940.

What is the structure of the LSAT?

The LSAT contains five 35-minute multiple-choice sections followed by a 30-minute Writing Sample. The Writing Sample does not count as part of your LSAT score. The common question types that do count toward your score are Logical Reasoning (two sections), Analytical Reasoning (one section), and Reading Comprehension (one section). In addition to these four sections, one experimental or pretest section will appear. This experimental or pretest section, which will probably be a repeat of one of the common question types, will not count in your score.

How is the LSAT scored?

The score for the objective portion of the test ranges from 120 to 180, and there is no penalty for wrong answers. The Writing Sample is unscored, but copies are sent to the law schools of your choice for evaluation.

What about question structure and value?

All LSAT questions, apart from the Writing Sample, are multiple-choice with five choices. All questions within a section are of equal value, regardless of difficulty.

Should I guess?

There is no penalty for guessing on the LSAT. Therefore, before you move on to the next question, at least take a guess. You should fill in guess answers for those you have left blank or did not get to, before time is called for that section. If you can eliminate one or more choices as incorrect, your chances for a correct guess increase.

How often can I take the LSAT?

You may take the LSAT more than once if you wish. But keep in mind that any report sent to you or to law schools will contain scores for any exams taken over the past few years, along with an average score for those exams. The law school receiving your scores will decide which score is the best estimate of your ability; many law schools rely on the average score as a figure.

Is it at all possible to cancel my LSAT score?

You may cancel your score only within five days after taking the test.

How early should I arrive at the test center, and what should I bring?

Arrive at the test center 15 to 30 minutes before the time designated on your admission ticket. Bring three or four sharpened No. 2 pencils, an eraser, and a watch, as well as your LSAT Admission Ticket and proper identification as described in the LSAT Registration/Information Booklet.

Can I prepare for the LSAT?

Yes. Reading skills and test-taking strategies should be the focus of your preparation for the test as a whole. Success on the more specialized analytical sections of the test depends on your thorough familiarity with the types of problems you are likely to encounter and the reasoning process involved. For maximum preparation, work through this book and practice the strategies and techniques outlined in each section.

BASIC FORMAT OF THE LSAT AND SCORING

THE *ORDER* OF THE FOLLOWING MULTIPLE-CHOICE SECTIONS *WILL* VARY. The Experimental Section is not necessarily the last section.

	Section	*Number of Questions*	*Minutes*
I.	Logical Reasoning	24-26	35
II.	Analytical Reasoning	22-24 (4 sets)	35
III.	Reading Comprehension	26-28 (4 passages)	35
IV.	Logical Reasoning	24-26	35
V.	Experimental Section	varies	35
	Writing Sample	1 essay	30
TOTALS		118-132 questions (only 96-104 count toward your score)	205 minutes or 3 hours 25 minutes

NOTE: For your convenience, this Barron's text labels each section of this Model Test (e.g., Reading Comprehension, Logical Reasoning, etc.). In contrast, sections of the actual LSAT exam are not usually labeled.

The LSAT is scored on a 120 to 180 scale.

The following simple chart will give you a very general approximation of the LSAT scoring system. It shows the approximate percentage of right answers necessary on the LSAT to be in a certain score range.

Approximate % of right answers	*Approximate Score Range*
Between 75% and 100%	160-180
Between 50% and 75%	145-159
Between 25% and 50%	130-144
Between 0% and 25%	120-129

Note that this chart is meant to give you an *approximate* score range.

A Closer Look at the Timing—What It Really Means

Although the LSAT is comprised of five 35-minute multiple-choice sections and a 30-minute unscored essay, it is important to understand the timing breakdown and what it means. The test is actually broken down as follows:

105 min. { Section I 35 minutes
Section II 35 minutes
Section III 35 minutes

Short break—usually 5-10 minutes

70 min. { Section IV 35 minutes
Section V 35 minutes

Very, very short break—usually 1 or 2 minutes

30 min. { Writing Sample (Essay)—30 minutes

Notice that you are given three multiple-choice sections with no breaks in between. When they say "stop" at the end of 35 minutes they will immediately say something like, "Turn to the next section, make sure that you are in the right section, ready, begin." So, in essence, you are working three sections back to back to back. This means that when you practice you should be sure to practice testing for 1 hour and 45 minutes without a break.

After the short break, when you may get up, get a drink, and go to the restroom, you are back for two more back-to-back multiple-choice sections.

For the final 30-minute writing sample you will be given a pen and scratch paper to do your prewriting or outlining.

Keep in mind that there will be some time taken before the exam and after the exam for clerical-type paperwork—distributing and picking up paperwork, filling out test forms, and so on.

Important Reminders

- At least half of your test will contain Logic Reasoning questions; prepare accordingly. Make sure that you are good at Logical Reasoning!
- The experimental or pretest section will usually repeat other sections and can appear in different places on the exam. At the time of the exam, you will not know which section is experimental. Take the test as if all of the sections count.
- Scoring will be from 120-180. This is the score, and the percentile rank that goes with it is what the law schools look at and are referring to in their discussions.
- All questions in a section are of equal value, so do not get stuck on any one question. The scores are determined by totaling all of your right answers on the test and then scaling.
- There is NO PENALTY for guessing, so at least take a guess before you move to the next question.
- The 30-minute Writing Sample will not be scored, but copies will be forwarded to the law schools to which you apply. Scratch paper and a pen will be provided for the Writing Sample only.
- Keep in mind that regardless of the format of your exam, two sections of Logical Reasoning, one section of Analytical Reasoning, and one section of Reading Comprehension always count toward your score.

SOME WORDS TO THE WISE

Ask a Few Questions

Before you actually start your study plan there are four basic questions that you should ask the law schools to which you are applying:

1. Considering my GPA and other qualifications, what score do you think I need to get into your law school?
2. When do you need to get my score reports? Or, When should I take the test to meet your deadlines?
3. What do you do if I take the LSAT more than once? Remember that when the law school receives your score report it will see a score for each time you've taken the test *and* an average of the scores. It is up to the law schools and their governing bodies as to what score(s) they will consider. Try to do your best on the first try and take the LSAT only once, if possible.
4. What do you do with my Writing Sample? Is it used as a tiebreaker? Do you score it yourself? Is it just another piece of the process?

Knowing the answers to most of these questions before you start your study will help you understand what is expected and will help you get mentally ready for the task ahead.

Excerpted from *How to Prepare for the LSAT,* by Jerry Bobrow, Ph.D., Barron's Educational Series, Inc., 1996.

ANSWER SHEET—MODEL TEST
LAW SCHOOL ADMISSION TEST (LSAT)

Section I: Reading Comprehension

1. Ⓐ Ⓑ Ⓒ Ⓓ Ⓔ
2. Ⓐ Ⓑ Ⓒ Ⓓ Ⓔ
3. Ⓐ Ⓑ Ⓒ Ⓓ Ⓔ
4. Ⓐ Ⓑ Ⓒ Ⓓ Ⓔ
5. Ⓐ Ⓑ Ⓒ Ⓓ Ⓔ
6. Ⓐ Ⓑ Ⓒ Ⓓ Ⓔ
7. Ⓐ Ⓑ Ⓒ Ⓓ Ⓔ
8. Ⓐ Ⓑ Ⓒ Ⓓ Ⓔ
9. Ⓐ Ⓑ Ⓒ Ⓓ Ⓔ
10. Ⓐ Ⓑ Ⓒ Ⓓ Ⓔ
11. Ⓐ Ⓑ Ⓒ Ⓓ Ⓔ
12. Ⓐ Ⓑ Ⓒ Ⓓ Ⓔ
13. Ⓐ Ⓑ Ⓒ Ⓓ Ⓔ
14. Ⓐ Ⓑ Ⓒ Ⓓ Ⓔ
15. Ⓐ Ⓑ Ⓒ Ⓓ Ⓔ
16. Ⓐ Ⓑ Ⓒ Ⓓ Ⓔ
17. Ⓐ Ⓑ Ⓒ Ⓓ Ⓔ
18. Ⓐ Ⓑ Ⓒ Ⓓ Ⓔ
19. Ⓐ Ⓑ Ⓒ Ⓓ Ⓔ
20. Ⓐ Ⓑ Ⓒ Ⓓ Ⓔ
21. Ⓐ Ⓑ Ⓒ Ⓓ Ⓔ
22. Ⓐ Ⓑ Ⓒ Ⓓ Ⓔ
23. Ⓐ Ⓑ Ⓒ Ⓓ Ⓔ
24. Ⓐ Ⓑ Ⓒ Ⓓ Ⓔ
25. Ⓐ Ⓑ Ⓒ Ⓓ Ⓔ
26. Ⓐ Ⓑ Ⓒ Ⓓ Ⓔ
27. Ⓐ Ⓑ Ⓒ Ⓓ Ⓔ
28. Ⓐ Ⓑ Ⓒ Ⓓ Ⓔ

Section II: Analytical Reasoning

1. Ⓐ Ⓑ Ⓒ Ⓓ Ⓔ
2. Ⓐ Ⓑ Ⓒ Ⓓ Ⓔ
3. Ⓐ Ⓑ Ⓒ Ⓓ Ⓔ
4. Ⓐ Ⓑ Ⓒ Ⓓ Ⓔ
5. Ⓐ Ⓑ Ⓒ Ⓓ Ⓔ
6. Ⓐ Ⓑ Ⓒ Ⓓ Ⓔ
7. Ⓐ Ⓑ Ⓒ Ⓓ Ⓔ
8. Ⓐ Ⓑ Ⓒ Ⓓ Ⓔ
9. Ⓐ Ⓑ Ⓒ Ⓓ Ⓔ
10. Ⓐ Ⓑ Ⓒ Ⓓ Ⓔ
11. Ⓐ Ⓑ Ⓒ Ⓓ Ⓔ
12. Ⓐ Ⓑ Ⓒ Ⓓ Ⓔ
13. Ⓐ Ⓑ Ⓒ Ⓓ Ⓔ
14. Ⓐ Ⓑ Ⓒ Ⓓ Ⓔ
15. Ⓐ Ⓑ Ⓒ Ⓓ Ⓔ
16. Ⓐ Ⓑ Ⓒ Ⓓ Ⓔ
17. Ⓐ Ⓑ Ⓒ Ⓓ Ⓔ
18. Ⓐ Ⓑ Ⓒ Ⓓ Ⓔ
19. Ⓐ Ⓑ Ⓒ Ⓓ Ⓔ
20. Ⓐ Ⓑ Ⓒ Ⓓ Ⓔ
21. Ⓐ Ⓑ Ⓒ Ⓓ Ⓔ
22. Ⓐ Ⓑ Ⓒ Ⓓ Ⓔ
23. Ⓐ Ⓑ Ⓒ Ⓓ Ⓔ
24. Ⓐ Ⓑ Ⓒ Ⓓ Ⓔ

Section III: Logical Reasoning

1. Ⓐ Ⓑ Ⓒ Ⓓ Ⓔ
2. Ⓐ Ⓑ Ⓒ Ⓓ Ⓔ
3. Ⓐ Ⓑ Ⓒ Ⓓ Ⓔ
4. Ⓐ Ⓑ Ⓒ Ⓓ Ⓔ
5. Ⓐ Ⓑ Ⓒ Ⓓ Ⓔ
6. Ⓐ Ⓑ Ⓒ Ⓓ Ⓔ
7. Ⓐ Ⓑ Ⓒ Ⓓ Ⓔ
8. Ⓐ Ⓑ Ⓒ Ⓓ Ⓔ
9. Ⓐ Ⓑ Ⓒ Ⓓ Ⓔ
10. Ⓐ Ⓑ Ⓒ Ⓓ Ⓔ
11. Ⓐ Ⓑ Ⓒ Ⓓ Ⓔ
12. Ⓐ Ⓑ Ⓒ Ⓓ Ⓔ
13. Ⓐ Ⓑ Ⓒ Ⓓ Ⓔ
14. Ⓐ Ⓑ Ⓒ Ⓓ Ⓔ
15. Ⓐ Ⓑ Ⓒ Ⓓ Ⓔ
16. Ⓐ Ⓑ Ⓒ Ⓓ Ⓔ
17. Ⓐ Ⓑ Ⓒ Ⓓ Ⓔ
18. Ⓐ Ⓑ Ⓒ Ⓓ Ⓔ
19. Ⓐ Ⓑ Ⓒ Ⓓ Ⓔ
20. Ⓐ Ⓑ Ⓒ Ⓓ Ⓔ
21. Ⓐ Ⓑ Ⓒ Ⓓ Ⓔ
22. Ⓐ Ⓑ Ⓒ Ⓓ Ⓔ
23. Ⓐ Ⓑ Ⓒ Ⓓ Ⓔ
24. Ⓐ Ⓑ Ⓒ Ⓓ Ⓔ
25. Ⓐ Ⓑ Ⓒ Ⓓ Ⓔ
26. Ⓐ Ⓑ Ⓒ Ⓓ Ⓔ

✂ To remove, cut along dotted line.

ANSWER SHEET—MODEL TEST
LAW SCHOOL ADMISSION TEST (LSAT)

Section IV:
Analytical Reasoning

1. Ⓐ Ⓑ Ⓒ Ⓓ Ⓔ
2. Ⓐ Ⓑ Ⓒ Ⓓ Ⓔ
3. Ⓐ Ⓑ Ⓒ Ⓓ Ⓔ
4. Ⓐ Ⓑ Ⓒ Ⓓ Ⓔ
5. Ⓐ Ⓑ Ⓒ Ⓓ Ⓔ
6. Ⓐ Ⓑ Ⓒ Ⓓ Ⓔ
7. Ⓐ Ⓑ Ⓒ Ⓓ Ⓔ
8. Ⓐ Ⓑ Ⓒ Ⓓ Ⓔ
9. Ⓐ Ⓑ Ⓒ Ⓓ Ⓔ
10. Ⓐ Ⓑ Ⓒ Ⓓ Ⓔ
11. Ⓐ Ⓑ Ⓒ Ⓓ Ⓔ
12. Ⓐ Ⓑ Ⓒ Ⓓ Ⓔ
13. Ⓐ Ⓑ Ⓒ Ⓓ Ⓔ
14. Ⓐ Ⓑ Ⓒ Ⓓ Ⓔ
15. Ⓐ Ⓑ Ⓒ Ⓓ Ⓔ
16. Ⓐ Ⓑ Ⓒ Ⓓ Ⓔ
17. Ⓐ Ⓑ Ⓒ Ⓓ Ⓔ
18. Ⓐ Ⓑ Ⓒ Ⓓ Ⓔ
19. Ⓐ Ⓑ Ⓒ Ⓓ Ⓔ
20. Ⓐ Ⓑ Ⓒ Ⓓ Ⓔ
21. Ⓐ Ⓑ Ⓒ Ⓓ Ⓔ
22. Ⓐ Ⓑ Ⓒ Ⓓ Ⓔ
23. Ⓐ Ⓑ Ⓒ Ⓓ Ⓔ
24. Ⓐ Ⓑ Ⓒ Ⓓ Ⓔ

Section V:
Logical Reasoning

1. Ⓐ Ⓑ Ⓒ Ⓓ Ⓔ
2. Ⓐ Ⓑ Ⓒ Ⓓ Ⓔ
3. Ⓐ Ⓑ Ⓒ Ⓓ Ⓔ
4. Ⓐ Ⓑ Ⓒ Ⓓ Ⓔ
5. Ⓐ Ⓑ Ⓒ Ⓓ Ⓔ
6. Ⓐ Ⓑ Ⓒ Ⓓ Ⓔ
7. Ⓐ Ⓑ Ⓒ Ⓓ Ⓔ
8. Ⓐ Ⓑ Ⓒ Ⓓ Ⓔ
9. Ⓐ Ⓑ Ⓒ Ⓓ Ⓔ
10. Ⓐ Ⓑ Ⓒ Ⓓ Ⓔ
11. Ⓐ Ⓑ Ⓒ Ⓓ Ⓔ
12. Ⓐ Ⓑ Ⓒ Ⓓ Ⓔ
13. Ⓐ Ⓑ Ⓒ Ⓓ Ⓔ
14. Ⓐ Ⓑ Ⓒ Ⓓ Ⓔ
15. Ⓐ Ⓑ Ⓒ Ⓓ Ⓔ
16. Ⓐ Ⓑ Ⓒ Ⓓ Ⓔ
17. Ⓐ Ⓑ Ⓒ Ⓓ Ⓔ
18. Ⓐ Ⓑ Ⓒ Ⓓ Ⓔ
19. Ⓐ Ⓑ Ⓒ Ⓓ Ⓔ
20. Ⓐ Ⓑ Ⓒ Ⓓ Ⓔ
21. Ⓐ Ⓑ Ⓒ Ⓓ Ⓔ
22. Ⓐ Ⓑ Ⓒ Ⓓ Ⓔ
23. Ⓐ Ⓑ Ⓒ Ⓓ Ⓔ
24. Ⓐ Ⓑ Ⓒ Ⓓ Ⓔ
25. Ⓐ Ⓑ Ⓒ Ⓓ Ⓔ

✂ To remove, cut along dotted line.

CHAPTER 11

A Model LSAT

This chapter contains a full-length Model Test. It is geared to the format of the LSAT and it is complete with answers and explanations. It is equivalent to the LSAT in question structure, number of questions, level of difficulty, and time allotments. (The questions used are not taken directly from the LSAT, as those questions are copyrighted and may not be reproduced.)

The Model Test should be taken under strict test conditions. The test ends with a 30-minute Writing Sample, which is not scored.

Section	Description	Number of Questions	Time Allowed
I	Reading Comprehension	28	35 minutes
II	Analytical Reasoning	24	35 minutes
III	Logical Reasoning	26	35 minutes
IV	Analytical Reasoning	24	35 minutes
V	Logical Reasoning	25	35 minutes
	Writing Sample		30 minutes
TOTALS:		127	3 hours 25 minutes

Now please turn to the next page, remove your answer sheets, and begin the Model Test.

1 1 1 1 1

SECTION I

TIME — 35 MINUTES
28 QUESTIONS

Directions: Read the passages and answer the questions following each passage by blackening the appropriate space on the answer sheet. You may refer back to the passages when answering the questions. Answer all questions on the basis of what is stated or implied.

Although statutory law (a law enacted by the legislature) expressly forbids strikes by government workers, the constitutional validity of these laws as well as their interpretative applications have been under attack in various cases, the most publicized case being that of the federal government air traffic controllers.

The First Amendment to the United States Constitution guarantees the right of free speech. The constitutional issue to be resolved therefore is whether strikes are a form of "symbolic speech" or "symbolic conduct" that should be accorded the same degree of First Amendment protection as verbal communications. In a case that involved private rather than public employees, a Texas Court held that picketing as an incident to a labor dispute is a proper exercise of freedom of speech. The court went on to say that only a "clear and present danger of substantive evil will justify an abridgement of the right to picket." Later, the New Jersey state court concluded that even though picketing is protected by freedom of speech, this does not mean that statutes prohibiting strikes are constitutionally invalid. This case involved a constitutional interpretation of the New Jersey statute. The court stated that the justification of this statute is based on the ground of "clear and present danger" that would result to the state if the performance of functions of a public utility was ceased or impaired by a strike. Those in favor of no-strike clauses seem to concede that strikes are a form of symbolic speech that should be accorded the same degree of First Amendment protection as verbal speech. Their justification for upholding these clauses is the "clear and present danger" doctrine. They tend to believe that strikes by government employees automatically present a "clear and present danger of substantive evil." However, according to the U.S. Supreme Court, legislatures cannot be relied upon to make a determination of what constitutes a "clear and present danger." In effect this is what happened when President Reagan ordered the firing of the air traffic controllers, based on the antistrike clause pronounced by Congress. The Supreme Court held that courts themselves must determine what constitutes a clear and present danger. The Supreme Court went on to say that mere public inconvenience or annoyance is not enough to constitute a clear and present danger. Thus, the public inconvenience and annoyance created by the curtailment of air traffic as a result of the controllers' strike may not be sufficient to constitute such a danger. The argument that a clear and present danger resulted from the emergency staffing of control towers by military and supervisory personnel is invalidated by the fact that the airlines have run safely since the strike.

This is not to suggest that every employee should automatically have the right to strike. However, constitutional consideration of due process and freedom of speech should bar denying government workers, as a class, the right to strike. A close look should be taken at what actually constitutes a "clear and present danger of substantive evil." It is an evasion for courts to allow legislatures to prejudge all government services to be different for "strike" purposes than those provided by the private sector. The court itself should look at such factors as the nature of the service in determining whether particular no-strike clauses are constitutionally valid. The nature of the provider of the service (i.e., government v. private) is not a compelling justification for upholding no-strike clauses.

GO ON TO THE NEXT PAGE ➤

1. According to the passage, strikes by government workers are

(A) constitutionally invalid
(B) forbidden by statutory law
(C) permissible when there is no danger of substantial evil
(D) permissible when there is no public inconvenience or annoyance
(E) permissible when there is no danger to national security and safety

2. If government workers as a class are denied the right to strike, it can be argued that they have been denied all of the following EXCEPT

(A) due process
(B) freedom of speech
(C) the clear and present danger doctrine
(D) redress from abnormally dangerous working conditions
(E) an abridgment of the right to picket

3. According to the passage, the "clear and present danger" justification of forbidding a strike has been misapplied for all of the following reasons EXCEPT

(A) the dangers were determined by the executive branch
(B) the dangers are often merely inconveniences
(C) the dangers were determined by the courts
(D) strikes by government workers do not automatically present dangers
(E) the inconvenience caused by the air traffic controllers may not have been a danger

4. The fact that there was no rise in the number of airline accidents in the first six months after the firing and replacement of the striking air traffic controllers undermines the

(A) government's argument that a strike would present a danger to the public
(B) argument that the no-strike clause violates first amendment rights
(C) argument that a strike is a form of symbolic speech
(D) air traffic controllers' argument that they left their jobs because of dangerous working conditions
(E) argument that no-strike clauses discourage more highly qualified individuals from applying for positions

5. The author of the passage objects to the current situation in which

(A) all employees equally have the right to strike
(B) the government regards national security more important than an individual's freedom
(C) the Supreme Court avoids taking a position in its dealing with regret-to-strike cases
(D) an unfair burden of proof is placed upon workers who leave jobs they believe to have unsafe working conditions
(E) a false distinction is made between workers doing similar jobs for the government and private employees

6. Which one of the following might the author cite to exemplify another of the harmful effects of the no-strike rule?

(A) It deters the highly skilled from taking government jobs.
(B) It can be used as a precedent in the private sector.
(C) It places too much power in the hands of the judicial branch of the government.
(D) It encourages the courts to determine whether or not particular no-strike clauses are valid.
(E) It protects some workers from abnormally dangerous working conditions.

GO ON TO THE NEXT PAGE ➤

Virginia Woolf's development as a novelist was deeply influenced by her struggle to reconcile feminism and art. Long before the aesthetic creed of Bloomsbury came into being she had learned from her father that a work of literature is no better than the morality which it is intended to express—a lesson she never forgot. Virginia Woolf was a passionate moralist, though she directed all her fervor into one narrow channel. The impulse to write *Three Guineas* possessed her for years, "violently . . . persistently, pressingly, compulsorily," until she carried it into action. This moral fervor was not contained within the limits of her tracts, nor could it have been. Feminism is implicit in her novels. The novels are not, of course, didactic in the narrow sense of pleading for specific reforms, but they illustrate the dangers of one-sidedness and celebrate the androgynous mind.

Virginia Woolf's main emphasis in her feminist writings, as in the novels, was on self-reform, and on art as a means to that end. Novels and tracts alike grew out of a preoccupation with her own spiritual dilemma. Fiction was the medium within which Virginia Woolf controlled and directed this intense self-absorption. When she deserted art for propaganda, as in *Three Guineas*, her self-absorption got the upper hand. Thus, paradoxically, she was truer to her feminist ideas as a novelist than as a pamphleteer. Her social conscience and her aesthetic vision were mutually dependent. She could express her feminism only by means of her art; but her art owed its character to her feminism.

The contract between Virginia Woolf's failure in *Three Guineas* and her triumph in The Years confirms this impression. In the first, confining herself to political and social controversy, she lost her grasp of reality and ended up talking to herself. In the second, striving, as she said, "to give the whole of the present society . . . facts as well as the vision," she transcended purely personal preoccupations and created a lasting work of art. Virginia Woolf's direct attack on social evil is too shrill and self-indulgent to succeed, even as propaganda. On the other hand, her symbolic representation of the Wasteland—pollution, faithlessness, remorse—has a lucid objectivity that forces the reader to see through her eyes. The tract, with all its talk of reform, is one-sided. The novel is whole.

In Virginia Woolf's case, the myth of the artist as more or less helpless agent of his own creative drive seems to have a foundation in fact. She needed the discipline of art, because it permitted her to express her intense moral indignation, while at the same time controlling the disintegrating effects of that indignation upon her personality. Art produced feelings of release and harmony, such as she associated with the androgynous mind. When she avoided that discipline, as in *Three Guineas*, her writing tended to become morbid. In relation to the radiance of Virginia Woolf's artistic successes, therefore, *Three Guineas* represents a kind of negative definition. Through it we can glance into the heart of her darkness.

7. According to the passage, Woolf's father influenced her
   (A) choice of writing as a career
   (B) belief in the importance of self-reform
   (C) belief that literature should have a moral base
   (D) desire to write tracts and pamphlets
   (E) views on the equality of men and women

GO ON TO THE NEXT PAGE ➤

8. We can infer from the passage that the "spiritual dilemma" mentioned in line 29 refers to a
   (A) need to transcend one-sidedness and encompass both the masculine and feminine
   (B) desire to retire from the world rather than participate actively in society
   (C) need to choose between artistic endeavors and social work
   (D) desire to pursue a writing career and a desire to raise a family
   (E) need to transcend lucid objectivity and express passion in her work

9. According to the passage, which one of the following best characterizes Woolf's feminism?
   (A) a faith in feminine creativity and intuition
   (B) an integration of the masculine and the feminine
   (C) an indignation toward social institutions
   (D) an emphasis on social equality
   (E) a morbid preoccupation with self

10. The function of the third paragraph of the passage is to provide a
   (A) concrete example of the points made in paragraph 2
   (B) view contrasting with the one presented in paragraph 1
   (C) transition between paragraphs 2 and 4
   (D) subtopic to the main topic of paragraph 1
   (E) exegesis of the works introduced in paragraph 1

11. Which one of the following oppositions does the author principally address in the passage?
   (A) Woolf's aesthetic creed and the aesthetic creed of the Bloomsbury group
   (B) Woolf's novels of social reform and Woolf's novels of individual soul-searching
   (C) masculinity and femininity
   (D) social injustice and self-reform
   (E) Woolf's propaganda and Woolf's art

12. From the passage we can infer that the author
   (A) questions the validity of the Bloomsbury aesthetic creed
   (B) approves of symbolism only when used for social reform
   (C) finds Woolf's fiction more successful than her nonfiction
   (D) believes Woolf's social concerns are trivial
   (E) dislikes literature written in the cause of social reform

13. Which one of the following would be the best title for this passage?
   (A) *Three Guineas* and *The Years:* A Study
   (B) Virginia Woolf's Success
   (C) Virginia Woolf: Problems with Nonfiction
   (D) Virginia Woolf: Reconciling Feminism and Art
   (E) Masculine vs. Feminine: A Study of Virginia Woolf

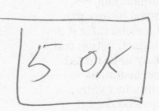

GO ON TO THE NEXT PAGE ➤

1 1 1 1 1

Much as they may deplore the fact, historians have no monopoly on the past and no franchise as its privileged interpreters to the public. It may have been different once, but there can no longer be any doubt about the relegation of the historian to a back seat. Far surpassing works of history, as measured by the size of their public and the influence they exert, are the novel, works for the stage, the screen, and television. It is mainly from these sources that millions who never open a history book derive such conceptions, interpretations, convictions, or fantasies as they have about the past. Whatever gives shape to popular conceptions of the past is of concern to historians, and this surely includes fiction.

Broadly speaking, two types of fiction deal with the past—historical fiction and fictional history. The more common of the two is historical fiction, which places fictional characters and events in a more or less authentic historical background. Examples range from *War and Peace* to *Gone With the Wind.* Since all but a few novelists must place their fictional characters in some period, nearly all fiction can be thought of as in some degree historical. But the term is applied as a rule only to novels in which historical events figure prominently. Fictional history, on the other hand, portrays and focuses attention upon real historical figures and events, but with the license of the novelist to imagine and invent. It has yet to produce anything approaching Tolstoy's masterpiece. Some fictional history makes use of invented characters and events, and historical fiction at times mixes up fictional and nonfictional characters. As a result the two genres overlap sometimes, but not often enough to make the distinction unimportant.

Of the two, it is fictional history that is the greater source of mischief, for it is here that fabrication and fact, fiction and nonfiction, are most likely to be mixed and confused. Of course, historians themselves sometimes mix fact with fancy, but it is a rare one who does it consciously or deliberately, and he knows very well that if discovered he stands convicted of betraying his calling. The writer of fictional history, on the other hand, does this as a matter of course and with no compunction whatever. The production and consumption of fictional history appear to be growing of late. Part of the explanation of this is probably the fragmentation of history by professionals, their retreat into specializations, their abandonment of the narrative style, and with it the traditional patronage of lay readers. Fictional history has expanded to fill the gap thus created but has at the same time gone further to create a much larger readership than history books ever had.

14. We can infer from the passage that the author is probably

(A) a historian
(B) a historical novelist
(C) a literary critic
(D) a social commentator
(E) a literary historian

15. According to the passage, which one of the following is likely to have contributed to the increasing popularity of fictional history?

(A) a change in the demographics of lay readers of history
(B) an increase in the audience for movies and television
(C) a decline in historians' use of a storytelling style
(D) an increase in historians' mixing fact and fancy
(E) a decline in the writing ability of professional historians

GO ON TO THE NEXT PAGE ➤

16. The author's attitude toward fictional history can best be summarized in which one of the following statements?
    (A) Masterpieces such as *War and Peace* and *Gone With the Wind* could not be created in the fictional history genre.
    (B) Fictional history is responsible for leading the reading public away from traditional historical works.
    (C) Fictional history provides a useful service by filling the gap for readers not interested in traditional history.
    (D) Writers of fictional history should not mix historical figures with fictional characters.
    (E) Fictional history can mislead readers about actual historical events.

17. Of the following, which one would the author consider most likely to cause a reader to confuse fact and fiction?
    (A) a book about the Watergate scandal with fictionalized dialogue between President Nixon and his attorney general, John Mitchell
    (B) a book about a fictional platoon in Vietnam during the last days of the war
    (C) a fictional account of the adventures of a group of servants in the White House under Eisenhower, Kennedy, Johnson, and Nixon
    (D) an account of the assassination of President Kennedy as viewed by a Texas adolescent on the parade route
    (E) a book based on newspaper accounts about the reaction to the Cuban missile crisis in the United States, the U.S.S.R., and Western Europe

18. The function of the second paragraph of the passage is to
    (A) reinforce the argument about fictionalized history presented in the first paragraph
    (B) define and contrast fictional history and historical fiction
    (C) emphasize the superiority of historical fiction to fictional history
    (D) provide context for the analysis in the third paragraph
    (E) clarify the difference between history and fiction

19. According to the passage, the author would agree with all of the following statements EXCEPT
    (A) historical fiction and fictional history are of concern to the professional historian
    (B) the works of today's professional historians tend to be more specialized than historical works of the past
    (C) professional historians understand that they should not mix fact and fiction in their works
    (D) a historical event presented as a TV miniseries is likely to be accepted as true by many people
    (E) fictional history has succeeded because of a failure of the academic history curriculum

20. The author's attitude about the issue of fiction and history is presented most clearly in
    (A) paragraph 1, lines 1-7
    (B) paragraph 1, lines 17-20
    (C) paragraph 2, lines 35-41
    (D) paragraph 3, lines 49-53
    (E) paragraph 3, lines 62-64

21. The tone of this passage could best be described as
    (A) hostile and didactic
    (B) moderate and concerned
    (C) pedantic and detached
    (D) ironic and condescending
    (E) philosophical and enlightened

GO ON TO THE NEXT PAGE ➤

Most of our knowledge about how the brain links memory and emotion has been gleaned through the study of so-called classical fear conditioning. In this process the subject, usually a rat, hears a noise or sees a flashing light that is paired with a brief, mild electric shock to its feet. After a few such experiences, the rat responds automatically to the sound or light even in the absence of the shock. Its reactions are typical to any threatening situation: the animal freezes, its blood pressure and heart rate increase, and it startles easily. In the language of such experiments, the noise or flash is a conditioned stimulus, the foot shock is an unconditioned stimulus, and the rat's reaction is a conditioned response, which consists of readily measured behavioral and physiological changes.

Conditioning of this kind happens quickly in rats—indeed, it takes place as rapidly as it does in humans. A single pairing of the shock to the sound or sight can bring on the conditioned effect. Once established, the fearful reaction is relatively permanent. If the noise or light is administered many times without an accompanying electric shock, the rat's response diminishes. This change is called extinction. But considerable evidence suggests that this behavioral alteration is the result of the brain's controlling the fear response rather than the elimination of the emotional memory. For example, an apparently extinguished fear response can recover spontaneously or can be reinstated by an irrelevant stressful experience. Similarly, stress can cause the reappearance of phobias in people who have been successfully treated. This resurrection demonstrates that the emotional memory underlying the phobia was rendered dormant rather than erased by treatment.

Fear conditioning has proved an ideal starting point for studies of emotional memory for several reasons. First, it occurs in nearly every animal group in which it has been examined: fruit flies, snails, birds, lizards, fish, rabbits, rats, monkeys, and people. Although no one claims that the mechanisms are precisely the same in all these creatures, it seems clear from studies to date that the pathways are very similar in mammals and possibly in all vertebrates. We therefore are confident in believing that many of the findings in animals apply to humans. In addition, the kinds of stimuli most commonly used in this type of conditioning are not signals that rats—or humans, for that matter—encounter in their daily lives. The novelty and irrelevance of these lights and sounds help to ensure that the animals have not already developed strong emotional reactions to them. So researchers are clearly observing learning and memory at work. At the same time, such cues do not require complicated cognitive processing from the brain. Consequently, the stimuli permit us to study emotional mechanisms relatively directly. Finally, our extensive knowledge of the neural pathways involved in processing acoustic and visual information serves as an excellent starting point for examining the neurological foundations of fear elicited by such stimuli.

22. Which one of the following best states the main idea of the passage?

(A) Fear conditioning in animals and humans proves the direct link between emotion and memory.
(B) The mechanisms for linking memory and emotion are the same in mammals and possibly all vertebrates.
(C) Fear conditioning is a helpful starting point to use in studying emotional memory.
(D) Fearful reactions created by a conditioned stimulus are relatively permanent in both animals and humans.
(E) Fear conditioning in rats and other mammals is similar to the creation of phobias in humans.

wrong

0 ok

1 1 1 1 1

23. Which one of the following statements is best supported by information presented in the passage?

(A) Fear conditioning requires that the conditioned and unconditioned stimuli are paired on many occasions.
(B) Emotional mechanisms in the brain are linked to complicated cognitive processing.
(C) The recurrence of human phobias under stress may be compared to the spontaneous recovery of the fear response in rats.
(D) A conditioned response is weakened in times of stress provided emotion and memory have been successfully linked.
(E) A rat's conditioned response to the pairing of conditioned and unconditioned stimuli diminishes over time.

OK

24. A rat is exposed to a buzzer and an electric shock. After pairing the two stimuli 50 times, the rat exhibits a fear response when the buzzer alone is administered. The buzzer is then sounded *without* the shock an additional 200 times. According to the passage, the rat will probably

(A) continue to exhibit the fear response to the buzzer alone
(B) initially exhibit the fear response to the buzzer alone but then entirely lose the response
(C) initially exhibit the fear response to the buzzer alone, then appear to lose the response, then after the buzzer and shock are paired one additional time, exhibit it again to the buzzer alone
(D) initially exhibit the fear response to the buzzer alone, then appear to lose the response, then exhibit it again after a cat is introduced into the area
(E) initially exhibit the fear response to the buzzer alone, then begin to exhibit the response erratically, then lose the response entirely

wrong

25. The author contends that an apparently extinguished fear response that is recovered under stress indicates

(A) learning and memory
(B) complex cognitive processing
(C) previous strong emotional response to stimuli
(D) inadequate pairing of conditioned/unconditioned stimuli
(E) lack of control by the brain

OK

26. The passage lists the nine specific animal groups for which fear conditioning studies have been performed in order to

(A) suggest the neural basis of the fear response
(B) show in how wide a range of animals fear conditioning is exhibited
(C) show the developmental link from fruit flies to people
(D) raise the question of the role of complex cognitive processes in fear conditioning
(E) show that emotions are present in simple as well as complex creatures

OK

27. We can infer that the immediate goal of research described in the passage is to understand

(A) the neural basis of fear
(B) the relationship between cognition and emotion
(C) the mechanism of conditioning
(D) the effects of acoustic and visual stimuli
(E) the similarities among mammalian cognitive processes

wrong

3 OK

GO ON TO THE NEXT PAGE ➤

28. Which one of the following best describes the relationship of the third paragraph to the passage as a whole?

    (A) It completes the definition of the method begun by the author in the first paragraph and elaborated upon in the second paragraph.
    (B) It presents qualifications to the points made in the first and second paragraphs and suggests other possible approaches.
    (C) It summarizes the evidence and conclusions described in detail in the second paragraph.
    (D) It presents further applications of the method explained in the first and second paragraphs.
    (E) It justifies the use of the method explained in the first and second paragraphs.

STOP

IF YOU FINISH BEFORE THE TIME IS UP, CHECK YOUR WORK ON THIS SECTION OF THE TEST ONLY. DO NOT GO ON TO THE NEXT SECTION OF THE TEST UNTIL TIME IS UP FOR THIS SECTION.

SECTION II

TIME — 35 MINUTES
24 QUESTIONS

Directions: In this section you will be given groups of questions based on different sets of conditions. Drawing a simple diagram may be helpful in answering some of the questions. You are to choose the best answer and mark the corresponding space on your answer sheet.

Questions 1-6

The Bell Canyon Condominium is a four-story building with a single penthouse apartment on the fourth floor. There are two apartments on each of the three other floors. The apartments are owned by A, B, C, D, E, F, and G.

A's apartment is on one of the floors higher than B's.
C's apartment is on one of the floors lower than D's.
C's apartment is on one of the floors lower than E's.
F and G's apartments are on the same floor.

1. Which one of the following could be the owner of the penthouse?

(A) B
(B) C
(C) E
(D) F
(E) G

2. If F's apartment is on the second floor, which one of the following must be true?

(A) C's apartment is on the first floor.
(B) D's apartment is on the third floor.
(C) A's apartment is on the fourth floor.
(D) G's apartment is on the first floor.
(E) B's apartment is on the third floor.

3. If D owns the penthouse apartment, on which floor or floors could G's apartment be located?

(A) the first floor only
(B) the second floor only
(C) the third floor only
(D) the second or the third floor
(E) the first, second, or third floor

4. If D's and E's apartments are on the same floor, which one of the following must be true?

(A) D and E are on the third floor.
(B) D and E are on the second floor.
(C) A is on the fourth floor.
(D) B and C are on the first floor.
(E) F and G are on the second floor.

5. If C's apartment is on the first floor, and A is the owner of the penthouse, which one of the following must be true?

(A) G's apartment is on the third floor.
(B) D's apartment is on the second floor.
(C) E's apartment is on the second floor.
(D) B's apartment is on the first floor.
(E) F's apartment is on the second floor.

6. Which one of the following is possible?

(A) A and C are on the same floor.
(B) A and E are on the same floor.
(C) A is on the first floor.
(D) D is on the first floor.
(E) C is on the fourth floor.

Questions 7-12

A new bank has decided to stay open only on weekends—all day Saturday and Sunday—and no other days. The bank has hired two managers (U and V), four tellers (W, X, Y, and Z), and two operations officers (S and T), for a total of exactly eight full-time employees. No part-time employees are hired. Each employee works a complete day when working.

A manager must be on duty each day.
The managers cannot work on the same day.
At least two tellers must be working on the same day.
W and X will not work on the same day.
S and Z will only work on Saturday.
No employee can work on consecutive days, but each employee must work on Saturday or Sunday.

7. Which one of the following could be false?

(A) If U works on Saturday, then V works on Sunday.
(B) If X works on Saturday, then W works on Sunday.
(C) T can work either day.
(D) If W works on Saturday and Y works on Sunday, then X works on Sunday.
(E) If U works on Sunday, then X works on Saturday.

8. Which one of the following is an acceptable group of employees that could work on Saturday?

(A) ZWYST
(B) UVWYZS
(C) VWXZT
(D) UZST
(E) VWZS

9. What is the greatest number of employees that can work on Saturday?

(A) 2
(B) 3
(C) 4
(D) 5
(E) 6

10. If W works on Sunday, then which one of the following must be true?

(A) X works on Saturday.
(B) Y works on Saturday.
(C) T works on Sunday.
(D) Z works on Sunday.
(E) U works on Saturday.

11. Which one of the following must be true?

(A) T always works the same day as Y.
(B) S never works the same day as U.
(C) Z never works the same day as X.
(D) If W works on Sunday, then Y always works on Saturday.
(E) Only two tellers work on Saturday.

12. Which one of the following is a complete and accurate list of the employees who have the possibility of working on Sunday?

(A) UWYZ
(B) UWYS
(C) UVWXT
(D) UVWXYT
(E) UVWXYTS

GO ON TO THE NEXT PAGE ➤

2 2 2 2 2

Questions 13-19

Three division office managers, Fred, Al, and Cynthia, draw office assistants each day from the clerical and typing pools available to them. The clerical pool consists of Lyndia, Jim, Dennis, and Sylvia. The typing pool consists of Edra, Gene, and Helen. The office assistants are selected according to the following conditions:

Fred always needs at least one typist, but never more than two assistants.
Al always needs at least two assistants, but never more than three.
Sylvia or Gene and one other assistant always work for Cynthia.
Gene and Lyndia always work together.
Dennis and Edra will not work together.
No more than two typists work for the same manager, but all three typists must work each day.

13. If Gene works for Fred and all of the assistants work, then which one of the following must be FALSE?

(A) Jim works for Cynthia.
(B) Sylvia works for Cynthia.
(C) Lyndia works for Fred.
(D) Dennis works for Al.
(E) Edra works for Al.

14. If Sylvia doesn't work for Cynthia, then which one of the following must be true?

(A) Edra works for Fred.
(B) Gene works for Al.
(C) Lyndia works for Cynthia.
(D) Dennis works for Al.
(E) Helen works for Cynthia.

15. Assume that Lyndia and Jim work for Al. Which one of the following must be true?

(A) Gene works for Al.
(B) Edra works for Cynthia.
(C) Helen works for Fred.
(D) Edra works for Fred.
(E) Helen works for Cynthia.

16. Assume that Sylvia and Jim work for Al. If all of the assistants work, then which one of the following must be true?

(A) Edra works for Al.
(B) Gene works for Fred.
(C) Lyndia works for Al.
(D) Helen works for Fred.
(E) Dennis works for Fred.

17. Which one of the following must be FALSE?

(A) Helen and Edra never work for Cynthia on the same day.
(B) Edra can work for Cynthia.
(C) Dennis and Gene never work for Fred on the same day.
(D) Jim and Sylvia never work for Fred on the same day.
(E) Lyndia and Sylvia can work for Al on the same day.

18. If Jim works for Cynthia and all of the assistants work, then

(A) Dennis works for Al.
(B) Edra works for Al.
(C) Helen works for Al.
(D) Lyndia works for Al.
(E) Sylvia works for Fred.

19. Assume that Al needs only two assistants and Fred needs only one assistant. If Helen works for Fred, then which one of the following must be true?

(A) Jim works for Al.
(B) Sylvia doesn't work.
(C) Dennis doesn't work.
(D) Edra works for Al.
(E) Edra works for Cynthia.

2 2 2 2 2

Questions 20-24

Four teams (Red, Blue, Green, and Yellow) participate in the Junior Olympics, in which there are five events. In each event participants place either 1st, 2nd, 3rd, or 4th. First place is awarded a gold medal, 2nd place is awarded a silver medal, and 3rd place is awarded a bronze medal. There are no ties and each team enters one contestant in each event. All contestants finish each event.

The results of the Junior Olympics are:

No team wins gold medals in two consecutive events.

No team fails to win a medal within two consecutive events.

The Blue team wins only two medals, neither of them gold.

The Red team only wins three gold medals, and no other medals.

20. If the green team wins only one gold medal, then which one of the following must be true?

(A) The yellow team wins two gold medals.
(B) The red team wins only two bronze medals.
(C) The yellow team wins only one gold medal.
(D) The yellow team wins only silver medals.
(E) The green team wins only bronze medals.

21. Which one of the following must be true?

(A) The yellow team wins only bronze and gold medals.
(B) The yellow team wins five medals.
(C) The green team cannot win a silver medal.
(D) The yellow team cannot win a bronze medal.
(E) The green team wins exactly three medals.

22. If the yellow team wins five silver medals, then the green team must win

(A) more silver than gold
(B) more gold than bronze
(C) two gold, two bronze, one silver
(D) two gold, three bronze
(E) six medals

23. All of the following must be true EXCEPT

(A) the green team wins five medals
(B) the yellow team wins five medals
(C) if the green team wins one gold medal, the yellow team wins one gold medal
(D) if the green team wins only one silver medal, the yellow team wins only one silver medal
(E) if the yellow team wins only silver medals, the green team cannot win a silver medal

24. If a fifth team, Orange, enters all events and wins only three consecutive silver medals, which one of the following must be true?

(A) If green wins a gold in the 2nd event, it also wins a bronze in the 3rd event.
(B) If green wins a gold in the 2nd event, it also wins a silver in the 4th event.
(C) If yellow wins a gold in the 2nd event, green wins a bronze in the 3rd event.
(D) If yellow wins a gold in the 2nd event, blue wins a silver in the 3rd event.
(E) If red wins a gold in the 1st event, orange wins a silver in the last event.

STOP

IF YOU FINISH BEFORE THE TIME IS UP, CHECK YOUR WORK ON THIS SECTION OF THE TEST ONLY. DO NOT GO ON TO THE NEXT SECTION OF THE TEST UNTIL TIME IS UP FOR THIS SECTION.

3 3 3 3 3

SECTION III

TIME — 35 MINUTES
26 QUESTIONS

Directions: In this section you will be given brief statements or passages and will be required to evaluate the reasoning involved. In some instances, more than one choice will appear to be a possible answer. You are to choose the *best* answer. Use common sense and reasonableness in making your selection; then mark the proper space on the answer sheet.

1. Though the benefits of the hot tub and the Jacuzzis have been well publicized by their manufacturers, there are also some less widely-known dangers. Young children, of course, cannot be left unattended near a hot tub, and even adults have fallen asleep and drowned. Warm water can cause the blood vessels to dilate and the resulting drop in blood pressure can make people liable to fainting, especially when they stand up quickly to get out. Improperly maintained water can promote the growth of bacteria that can cause folliculitis.

   The main point of this passage is that

   (A) the benefits of the hot tub and the Jacuzzi have been overrated
   (B) the dangers of the hot tub and Jacuzzi outweigh their potential publicized benefits
   (C) users of hot tubs and Jacuzzis should be aware of the dangers connected with their use
   (D) the hot tub and Jacuzzi are dangerous only when improperly maintained
   (E) the hot tub is potentially beneficial in the treatment of high blood pressure

2. *Chariots of Fire* may have caught some professional critics off guard in 1982 as the Motion Picture Academy's choice for an Oscar as the year's best film, but it won wide audience approval as superb entertainment.

   Refreshingly, *Chariots of Fire* features an exciting story, enchanting English and Scottish scenery, a beautiful musical score, and appropriate costumes. All of these attractions are added to a theme that extols traditional religious values—without a shred of offensive sex, violence, or profanity.

   Too good to be true? See *Chariots of Fire* and judge for yourself.

   Those who condemn the motion picture industry for producing so many objectionable films can do their part by patronizing wholesome ones, thereby encouraging future Academy Award judges to recognize and reward decency.

   Which one of the following is a basic assumption underlying the final sentence of the passage?

   (A) Academy judges are not decent people.
   (B) The popularity of a film influences academy judges.
   (C) Future academy judges will be better than past ones.
   (D) There are those who condemn the motion picture industry.
   (E) *Chariots of Fire* is a patronizing film.

3. *Andy:* All teachers are mean.
Bob: That is not true. I know some doctors who are mean too.

Bob's answer demonstrates that he thought Andy to mean that

(A) all teachers are mean
(B) some teachers are mean
(C) doctors are meaner than teachers
(D) teachers are meaner than doctors
(E) only teachers are mean

4. Theodore Roosevelt was a great hunter. He was the mighty Nimrod of his generation. He had the physical aptitude and adventurous spirit of the true frontiersman. "There is delight," he said, "in the hardy life of the open; in long rides, rifle in hand; in the thrill of the fight with dangerous game." But he was more than a marksman and tracker of beasts, for he brought to his sport the intellectual curiosity and patient observation of the natural scientist.

Which one of the following would most weaken the author's concluding contention?

(A) Theodore Roosevelt never studied natural science.
(B) Actually, Theodore Roosevelt's sharpshooting prowess was highly exaggerated.
(C) Theodore Roosevelt always used native guides when tracking game.
(D) Theodore Roosevelt was known to leave safaris if their first few days were unproductive.
(E) Theodore Roosevelt's powers of observation were significantly hampered by his nearsightedness.

5. The following is an excerpt from a letter sent to a law school applicant:

"Thank you for considering our school to further your education. Your application for admission was received well before the deadline and was processed with your admission test score and undergraduate grade report.

"We regret to inform you that you cannot be admitted for the fall semester. We have had to refuse admission to many outstanding candidates because of the recent cut in state funding of our program.

"Thank you for your interest in our school and we wish you success in your future endeavors."

Which one of the following can be deduced from the above letter?

(A) The recipient of the letter did not have a sufficiently high grade point average to warrant admission to this graduate program.
(B) The recipient of the letter was being seriously considered for a place in the evening class.
(C) The law school sending the letter could not fill all the places in its entering class due to a funding problem.
(D) Criteria other than test scores and grade reports were used in determining the size of the entering class.
(E) The school sending the letter is suffering severe financial difficulties.

GO ON TO THE NEXT PAGE ➤

Questions 6-7

At birth we have no self-image. We cannot distinguish anything from the confusion of light and sound around us. From this beginning of no-dimension, we gradually begin to differentiate our body from our environment and develop a sense of identity, with the realization that we are a separate and independent human being. We then begin to develop a conscience, the sense of right and wrong. Further, we develop social consciousness, where we become aware that we live with other people. Finally, we develop a sense of values, which is our overall estimation of our worth in the world.

6. Which one of the following would be the best completion of this passage?

(A) The sum total of all these developments we call the self-image or the self-concept.
(B) This estimation of worth is only relative to our value system.
(C) Therefore, our social consciousness is dependent on our sense of values.
(D) Therefore, our conscience keeps our sense of values in perspective.
(E) The sum total of living with other people and developing a sense of values makes us a total person.

7. The author of this passage would most likely agree with which one of the following?

(A) Children have no self-dimension.
(B) Having a conscience necessitates the ability to differentiate between right and wrong.
(C) Social consciousness is our most important awareness.
(D) Heredity is predominant over environment in development.
(E) The ability to distinguish the difference between moral issues depends on the overall dimension of self-development.

8. *Editorial:* A previously undisclosed transcript has revealed that Richard Nixon's secret White House slush fund that was used to silence the Watergate burglars came from illegally donated campaign money. After Nixon resigned, his successor, Gerald Ford, pardoned him. The same Gerald Ford has joined Presidents Carter and Bush in urging campaign funding reforms. Recent hearings have shown all too clearly that both parties have been guilty of highly questionable fund-raising practices. Unless the laws are changed, the shoddy practices of the last thirty years will undoubtedly continue.

Which one of the following most accurately states the main point of the argument?

(A) It is hypocritical of Gerald Ford to urge campaign reform after his pardon of Richard Nixon.
(B) Both the Democrats and the Republicans have been guilty of unethical campaign fund-raising practices.
(C) The laws governing campaign fund-raising must be reformed.
(D) Reform of campaign fund-raising has been supported by former presidents of both parties.
(E) We cannot expect that those who benefit from a problem will wish to take steps to solve it.

3 3 3 3 3

Questions 9-10

In a report released last week, a government-funded institute concluded that there is "overwhelming" evidence that violence on television leads to criminal behavior by children and teenagers.

The report based on an extensive review of several hundred research studies conducted during the 1970s, is an update of a 1972 Surgeon General's report that came to similar conclusions.

9. Which one of the following is the most convincing statement in support of the argument in the first paragraph above?

(A) A 50-state survey of the viewing habits of prison inmates concluded that every inmate watches at least 2 hours of violent programming each day.
(B) A 50-state survey of the viewing habits of convicted adolescents shows that each of them had watched at least 2 hours of violent programming daily since the age of 5.
(C) One juvenile committed a murder that closely resembled a crime portrayed on a network series.
(D) The 1972 Surgeon General's report was not nearly as extensive as this more recent study.
(E) Ghetto residents who are burglarized most often report the theft of a television set.

10. The argument above is most weakened by its vague use of the word

(A) violence
(B) government
(C) extensive
(D) update
(E) overwhelming

Questions 11-12

Violence against racial and religious minority groups increased sharply throughout the county last year, despite a slight decline in statewide figures. Compiling incidents from police departments and private watchdog groups, the County Human Relations Committee reported almost 500 hate crimes in the year, up from only 200 last year. It was the first increase since the committee began to report a yearly figure six years ago. The lower statewide figures are probably in error due to underreporting in other counties; underreporting is the major problem that state surveyors face each year.

11. All of the following, if true, would support the conclusion or the explanation of the discrepancy in the state and county figures EXCEPT

(A) the number of hate crimes and those resulting in fatalities has increased in neighboring states
(B) anti-immigration sentiment was fanned this year by an anti-immigration ballot referendum
(C) funding for police departments throughout the state has decreased
(D) many law-abiding members of minority groups are fearful or distrustful of the police
(E) all of the counties in the state have active private watchdog groups that carefully monitor hate crimes

12. The author of this passage makes his case by

(A) establishing the likelihood of an event by ruling out several other possibilities
(B) combining several pieces of apparently unrelated evidence to build support for a conclusion
(C) contrasting a single certain case with several others with less evidence in their support
(D) assuming that what is only probable is certain
(E) using a general rule to explain a specific case

GO ON TO THE NEXT PAGE ➤

3 3 3 3 3

13. The study of village communities has become one of the fundamental methods of discussing the ancient history of institutions. It would be out of the question here to range over the whole field of human society in search for communal arrangements of rural life. It will be sufficient to confine the present inquiry to the varieties presented by nations of Aryan race, not because greater importance is to be attached to these nations than to other branches of humankind, although this view might also be reasonably urged, but principally because the Aryan race in its history has gone through all sorts of experiences, and the data gathered from its historical life can be tolerably well ascertained. Should the road be sufficiently cleared in this particular direction, it will not be difficult to connect the results with similar researches in other racial surroundings.

    Which one of the following, if true, most weakens the author's conclusion?

    (A) Information about the Aryan race is no more conclusive than information about any other ethnic group.
    (B) The experiences and lifestyle of Aryans are uniquely different from those of other cultures.
    (C) The Aryan race is no more important than any other race.
    (D) The historical life of the Aryans dates back only 12 centuries.
    (E) Aryans lived predominantly in villages, while today 90 percent of the world population live predominantly in or around major cities.

14. Although any reasonable modern citizen of the world must abhor war and condemn senseless killing, we must also agree that honor is more valuable than life. Life, after all, is transient, but honor is ____.

    Which one of the following most logically completes the passage above?

    (A) sensible
    (B) real
    (C) eternal
    (D) of present value
    (E) priceless

Questions 15-16

Bill said, "All dogs bark. This animal does not bark. Therefore it is not a dog."

15. Which one of the following most closely parallels the logic of this statement?

    (A) All rocks are hard. This lump is hard. Therefore, it may be a rock.
    (B) All foreign language tests are difficult. This is not a foreign language test. Therefore, it is not difficult.
    (C) All Blunder automobiles are poorly built. Every auto sold by Joe was poorly built. Therefore, Joe sells Blunder automobiles.
    (D) Rocks beat scissors, scissors beat paper, and paper beats rocks. Therefore, it is best to choose paper.
    (E) All paint smells. This liquid does not smell. Therefore, it is not paint.

16. Which one of the following would weaken Bill's argument the most?

    (A) Animals other than dogs bark.
    (B) Some dogs cannot bark.
    (C) Dogs bark more than cockatiels.
    (D) You can train a dog not to bark.
    (E) You can train birds to bark.

GO ON TO THE NEXT PAGE ➤

17. In the last three years the number of arrests for burglary and robbery in Sandy Beach has declined by more than 30 percent. At the same time, the city has reduced the size of its police force by 25 percent.

    Which one of the following helps to resolve an apparent discrepancy in the information above?

    (A) Neighborhood Watch programs have always been active in Sandy Beach.
    (B) The number of reported burglaries and robberies in Sandy Beach has increased in the last three years.
    (C) Compared to other cities in the state, Sandy Beach has one of the lowest crime rates.
    (D) By using motorcycles rather than foot patrols, the police are able to cover larger areas of the city using fewer officers.
    (E) Many of the residents of Sandy Beach have installed expensive security systems in their homes.

Questions 18-19

California and Nevada officials have questioned the impartiality of the board of scientists from the National Academy of Science who assess the safety of proposed nuclear dumping sites. They claim that the panels are heavily weighted in favor of the nuclear power companies that have been lobbying for the creation of nuclear dump sites in the deserts of the Southwest. At least ten members of the panels are or have been employees of the Department of Energy, but none is associated with any environmental organization. Environmentalists fear that long-lived nuclear wastes may leach into the groundwater and ultimately into the waters of the Colorado River. They also point out that 90 percent of the budget of the National Academy's Radioactive Waste Management Board is provided by the Department of Energy. The inventory of radioactive waste has been growing larger and larger in temporary storage places, but so far there has been virtually no agreement about a permanent dump site.

18. The officials who question the impartiality of the Management Board assume that the Department of Energy

    (A) supports the activities of the nuclear power industry
    (B) supports the activities of environmental groups
    (C) wishes to delay the selection of permanent nuclear waste dumping sites for as long as possible
    (D) is indifferent to the growing mass of nuclear wastes in temporary storage sites
    (E) has declined to take a stand for or against the use of nuclear power

19. The Nuclear Waste Management Board could best allay doubt of its impartiality if it were to

    (A) publish the results of its studies of the feasibility of locating nuclear waste dumps in the deserts of the Southwest
    (B) add one or two environmentalists to the panels that assess locations for nuclear dump sites
    (C) make public the sources of all its funding
    (D) recommend desert sites at a greater distance from the Colorado River
    (E) base decisions on feasibility studies by scientists with no connection to the National Academy

---

20. The law of parsimony urges a strict economy upon us; it requires that we can never make a guess with two or three assumptions in it if we can make sense with one.

    Which one of the following is the main point of the author's statement?

    (A) Complications arise from economy.
    (B) Simplify terminology whenever possible.
    (C) Don't complicate a simple issue.
    (D) Assumptions are necessarily simple in nature.
    (E) Excess assumptions never clarify the situation.

GO ON TO THE NEXT PAGE ➤

3 3 3 3 3

21. You can use a bottle opener to open the new beer bottles. You do not need to use a bottle opener to open the new beer bottles.

Which one of the following most closely parallels the logic of these statements?

(A) You must turn on the switch to light the lamp. If you turn on the switch, the lamp may not light.
(B) A cornered rattlesnake will strike, so do not corner a rattlesnake.
(C) If you do not study you will fail the test. If you do study, you may fail the test.
(D) Every candidate I voted for in the election lost his race. I must learn to vote better.
(E) I can move the sofa with my brother's help. If my brother is not available, I'll get a neighbor to help me.

22. To be admitted to Bigshot University, you must have a 3.5 grade-point average (GPA) and a score of 800 on the admissions test, a 3.0 GPA and a score of 1000 on the admissions test, or a 2.5 GPA and a score of 1200 on the admissions test. A sliding scale exists for other scores and GPAs.

Which one of the following is inconsistent with the above?

(A) The higher the GPA, the lower the admissions test score needed for admission.
(B) Joe was admitted with a 2.7 GPA and a score of 1100 on the admissions test.
(C) No student with a score of less than 800 on the admissions test and a 3.4 GPA will be admitted.
(D) More applicants had a GPA of 3.5 than had a GPA of 2.5.
(E) Some students with a score of less than 1200 on the admissions test and a GPA of less than 2.5 were admitted.

23. The Census Bureau's family portrait of America may remind us of the problems we face as a nation, but it also gives us reason to take heart in our ability to solve them in an enlightened way. The 1980 census was the first in history to show that the majority of the population in every state has completed high school. And the percentage of our people with at least 4 years of college rose from 11 percent in 1970 to 16.3 percent in 1980. That's progress—where it really counts.

Which one of the following assumptions underlies the author's conclusion in the above passage?

(A) Greater numbers of high school and college degrees coincide with other firsts in the 1980 census.
(B) Greater numbers of high school and college degrees coincide with greater numbers of well-educated people.
(C) Greater numbers of high school and college degrees coincide with a great commitment to social progress.
(D) Greater numbers of high school and college degrees coincide with a better chance to avoid national catastrophe.
(E) Greater numbers of high school and college degrees coincide with the 1980 census.

24. Add No-NOCK to your car and watch its performance soar. No-NOCK will give it more get-up-and-go and keep it running longer. Ask for No-NOCK when you want better mileage!

According to the advertisement above, No-NOCK claims to do everything EXCEPT

(A) improve your car's performance
(B) increase your car's life
(C) improve your car's miles per gallon
(D) cause fewer breakdowns
(E) stop the engine from knocking

GO ON TO THE NEXT PAGE ➤

25. So many arrogant and ill-tempered young men have dominated the tennis courts of late that we had begun to fear those characteristics were prerequisites for championship tennis.

    Tennis used to be a gentleman's game. What is sad is not just that the game has changed. With so much importance placed on success, it may be that something has gone out of the American character—such things as gentleness and graciousness.

    Which one of the following statements, if true, would most weaken the above argument?

    (A) The American character is a result of American goals.
    (B) Tennis has only recently become a professional sport.
    (C) Some ill-tempered tennis players are unsuccessful.
    (D) The "gentlemen" of early tennis often dueled to the death off the court.
    (E) Some even-tempered tennis players are successful.

26. *Dolores:* To preserve the peace, we must be prepared to go to war with any nation at any time, using either conventional or nuclear weapons.
    Fran: Which shall it be, conventional weapons or nuclear weapons?

    Fran mistakenly concludes that the "either or" phrase in Dolores's statement indicates

    (A) fear
    (B) indecision
    (C) a choice
    (D) a question
    (E) a refusal

STOP

IF YOU FINISH BEFORE THE TIME IS UP, CHECK YOUR WORK ON THIS SECTION OF THE TEST ONLY. DO NOT GO ON TO THE NEXT SECTION OF THE TEST UNTIL TIME IS UP FOR THIS SECTION.

SECTION IV

TIME — 35 MINUTES
24 QUESTIONS

Directions: In this section you will be given groups of questions based on different sets of conditions. Drawing a simple diagram may be helpful in answering some of the questions. You are to choose the best answer and mark the corresponding space on your answer sheet.

Questions 1-6

A group of tourists is planning to visit a cluster of islands—U, V, W, X, Y, and Z, connected by bridges. The tourists must stay on each island visited for exactly three days and three nights. Each bridge takes one hour to cross, may be crossed in either direction, and can be crossed only in the morning to give the tourists a full day on the island.

The islands are connected by bridges only as indicated below:

U is connected to W, X, and Y
V is connected to Y and Z
X is connected to Z and W
Y is connected to X and Z

1. If the group visits island W first, eight days later it could NOT be at which one of the following islands?

(A) U
(B) V
(C) X
(D) Y
(E) Z

2. If the group stays on island X for three nights, it CANNOT spend the next three days and nights on island.

(A) U
(B) V
(C) W
(D) Y
(E) Z

3. Which one of the following is a possible order of islands visited in 12 days and nights?

(A) UWYZ
(B) UVYZ
(C) UYVX
(D) UXZV
(E) UWYX

4. If the group visits island W first and can visit an island more than once, but does not use a bridge more than once, what is the greatest number of visits it can make?

(A) 5
(B) 6
(C) 7
(D) 8
(E) 9

5. Assume the group visits island X first, and does not use a bridge more than once. Assume also that the group does stay at island Y twice. What is the greatest number of different islands the group can visit?

(A) 3
(B) 4
(C) 5
(D) 6
(E) 7

6. Assume another island, T, is added to the tour. Assume also that T is connected only to U. Which one of the following statements must be true?

(A) On the eighth day of a tour, starting its visit at island T, the group could be on island V.
(B) On the fifth day of a tour, starting its visit at island T, the group could be on island X.
(C) On the seventh day of a tour, starting its visit at island T, the group could be on island U.
(D) On the eighth day of a tour, starting its visit at island V, the group could be on island T.
(E) On the tenth day of a tour, starting its visit at island Z, the tour group could be on island T.

Questions 7-13

Teams A and B play a series of 9 games. To win the series, a team must win the most games, but must also win a minimum of 3 games.

There are no ties in the first 3 games.

Team A wins more of the last 3 games than team B.

Team B wins more of the last 5 games than team A.

The last game is a tie.

Games 1 and 3 are won by the same team.

7. Which one of the following must be true?

(A) One team must win 5 games to win the series.
(B) There are no ties.
(C) One team wins at least 2 of the first 3 games.
(D) The same team wins the last 5 games.
(E) The last three games are won by one team.

8. Considering all of the conditions mentioned above, game 6

(A) could be won by team A
(B) could be won by team B
(C) could be a tie
(D) must be won by team A
(E) must be won by team B

9. If game 7 is won by team A, then

(A) game 8 is a tie
(B) game 2 is a tie
(C) game 4 is won by team A
(D) game 5 is a tie
(E) game 6 is won by team A

10. Which one of the following must be true?

(A) There is only 1 tie in the last 5 games.
(B) Team A wins 2 of the first 3 games.
(C) Team B can win 3 of the last 5 games.
(D) Game 4 is a tie.
(E) Team A can win only 1 of the last 5 games.

11. If team A wins game 1 and game 4, then which one of the following must be FALSE?

(A) Team A wins game 3.
(B) Team A wins game 2.
(C) Team B wins game 2.
(D) Team A wins the series.
(E) Team B wins the series.

12. Assume that game 4 is won by the winner of game 5. If game 2 is not won by the winner of game 3, then which one of the following must be true?

(A) Team A wins game 7.
(B) Team B is the winner of the series.
(C) Team A wins game 2.
(D) Team B wins game 1.
(E) Team A wins game 3.

13. Which one of the following must be true?

(A) For team A to win the series, team A must win exactly two of the first four games.
(B) For team B to win the series, team B must win exactly one of the first four games.
(C) For team A to win the series, team A must win only three of the first seven games.
(D) For team B to win the series, team B must win at least three of the first four games.
(E) For team A to win the series, team A must win two consecutive games.

4 4 4 4 4

Questions 14-18

Eight busts of American Presidents are to be arranged on two shelves, left to right. Each shelf accommodates exactly four busts. One shelf is directly above the other shelf. The busts are of John Adams, George Washington, Abraham Lincoln, Thomas Jefferson, James Monroe, John Kennedy, Theodore Roosevelt and Franklin Delano Roosevelt.

The Roosevelt busts may not be directly one above the other.

The bust of Kennedy must be adjacent to the bust of a Roosevelt.

The bust of Jefferson must be directly above the bust of John Adams.

The busts of Monroe, Adams, Kennedy and Franklin Delano Roosevelt must be on the bottom shelf.

The bust of Monroe must be third from the left.

14. If the bust of Theodore Roosevelt is second from the left on one shelf, which one of the following must be true?

(A) The bust of Adams must be first on a shelf.
(B) The bust of Adams must be third on a shelf.
(C) The bust of Kennedy must be first on a shelf.
(D) The bust of Kennedy must be second on a shelf.
(E) The bust of Kennedy must be third on a shelf.

15. Which one of the following must be true about the bust of Monroe?

(A) It is next to the bust of Adams.
(B) It is next to the bust of Kennedy.
(C) It is next to the bust of Franklin Delano Roosevelt.
(D) It is directly under the bust of Lincoln.
(E) It is directly under the bust of Theodore Roosevelt.

16. If the bust of Washington is first, directly above Kennedy's, all of the following must be true EXCEPT

(A) the bust of Jefferson is fourth
(B) the bust of Theodore Roosevelt is third
(C) the bust of Franklin Delano Roosevelt is second
(D) the bust of Lincoln is third
(E) the bust of Adams is fourth

17. Which one of the following is <u>not</u> a possible order for the busts on either shelf?

(A) Washington, Lincoln, Theodore Roosevelt, Jefferson
(B) Franklin Delano Roosevelt, Kennedy, Monroe, Adams
(C) Theodore Roosevelt, Lincoln, Washington, Jefferson
(D) Lincoln, Theodore Roosevelt, Washington, Jefferson
(E) Kennedy, Adams, Monroe, Franklin Delano Roosevelt

18. If the bust of Lincoln is next to the bust of Jefferson, all of the following are true EXCEPT

(A) if the bust of Kennedy is first, the bust of Theodore Roosevelt is also first
(B) if the bust of Washington is first, the bust of Franklin Delano Roosevelt is also first
(C) if the bust of Washington is second, the bust of Kennedy is also second
(D) if the bust of Kennedy is second, the bust of Theodore Roosevelt is also second
(E) if the bust of Washington is second, the bust of Franklin Delano Roosevelt is also second

Questions 19-24

For a dinner party, a hostess needs several different three-bean salads.

Each salad is to contain three types of beans, chosen from garbanzos, chili beans, wax beans, lima beans, and kidney beans.

Chili beans and lima beans do not taste good together and therefore are never used in the same salad.

Lima beans and kidney beans do not look good together and therefore are never used in the same salad.

19. How many different salads (using the above ingredients) could the hostess serve that contain lima beans?

(A) 0
(B) 1
(C) 2
(D) 3
(E) 4

20. How many different salads could she serve that do not contain chili beans?

(A) 0
(B) 1
(C) 2
(D) 3
(E) 4

21. How many different salad combinations could she serve at the party?

(A) 4
(B) 5
(C) 6
(D) 7
(E) 8

22. Which beans will occur most often in the salad combinations that could be served at the party?

(A) chili and garbanzos
(B) chili and limas
(C) limas and wax beans
(D) kidney and limas
(E) garbanzos and wax beans

23. If there are only enough wax beans to go into two salads, what is the total number of salads that can be served?

(A) 1
(B) 2
(C) 3
(D) 4
(E) 5

24. If the hostess discovers the garbanzos have gone bad, how many three-bean combinations can she serve without using the rotten garbanzos?

(A) 0
(B) 1
(C) 2
(D) 3
(E) 4

STOP

IF YOU FINISH BEFORE THE TIME IS UP, CHECK YOUR WORK ON THIS SECTION OF THE TEST ONLY. DO NOT GO ON TO THE NEXT SECTION OF THE TEST UNTIL TIME IS UP FOR THIS SECTION.

SECTION V

TIME—35 MINUTES
25 QUESTIONS

Directions: In this section you will be given brief statements or passages and will be required to evaluate the reasoning involved. In some instances, more than one choice will appear to be a possible answer. You are to choose the best answer. Use common sense and reasonableness in making your selection; then mark the proper space on the answer sheet.

1. Chrysanthemums that have not been fertilized in July will normally not blossom in October. In October, the chrysanthemums did not blossom.

   With the premises given above, which one of the following would logically complete an argument?

   (A) Therefore, the chrysanthemums were not fertilized in July.
   (B) Therefore, the chrysanthemums may not have been fertilized in July.
   (C) Therefore, the chrysanthemums may blossom later in the fall.
   (D) Therefore, the chrysanthemums will blossom in the fall.
   (E) Therefore, the chrysanthemums will not blossom later in the fall.

2. When asked about the danger to public health from the spraying of pesticides by helicopters throughout the county, the County Supervisor replied, "The real danger to the public is the possibility of an infestation of harmful fruit-flies, which this spraying will prevent. Such an infestation would drive up the cost of fruits and vegetables by 15 percent."

   Which one of the following is the most serious weakness in the Supervisor's reply to the question?

   (A) He depends upon the ambiguity in the word "danger."
   (B) His response contains a self-contradiction.
   (C) He fails to support his argument concretely.
   (D) He fails to answer the question that has been asked.
   (E) His chief concern is the economic consequences of spraying.

3. So far this year researchers have reported the following:

   Heavy coffee consumption can increase the risk of heart attacks.

   Drinking a cup of coffee in the morning increases feelings of well-being and alertness.

   Boiled coffee increases blood cholesterol levels.

   Coffee may protect against cancer of the colon.

   If all these statements are true, which one of the following conclusions can be drawn from this information?

   (A) Reducing coffee consumption will make people healthier.
   (B) Reducing coffee consumption will make people feel better.
   (C) People at risk for heart attack should limit their coffee drinking.
   (D) Percolated coffee will not affect cholesterol levels.
   (E) People at risk for cancer should reduce their coffee consumption.

GO ON TO THE NEXT PAGE ➤

4. Compared with children in other states, infants born in California weigh more, survive the first years in greater numbers, and live longer. The hysteria about the danger of pesticides in California has attracted attention simply because a few Hollywood stars have appeared on television talk shows. Pesticides are the responsibility of the California Department of Food and Agriculture, and we can be sure its members are doing their job.

   The argument of this paragraph would be weakened if all of the following were shown to be true EXCEPT

   (A) rates of melanoma and some forms of leukemia in California are above national norms
   (B) the three highest positions at the California Department of Food and Agriculture are held by farm owners
   (C) synthetic pesticide residues in food cause more cancer than do "natural pesticides" that the plants themselves produce
   (D) more Californians suffer the consequences of air pollution than do the citizens in any other state
   (E) children of farm workers are three times more likely to suffer childhood cancers than children of urban parents

5. Should we allow the Fire Department to continue to underpay its women officers by using policies of promotion that favor men?

   The question above most closely resembles which one of the following in terms of its logical features?

   (A) Should the excessive tax on cigarettes, liquor, and luxury goods be unfairly increased again this year?
   (B) Should corrupt politicians be subject to the same sentencing laws as blue-collar felons?
   (C) Should the police chief be chosen by examination score regardless of gender or seniority?
   (D) Should the religious right be allowed to determine the censorship laws for all of society?
   (E) Are liberal political values an appropriate basis for all of the social values in this state?

6. If airline fares have risen, then either the cost of fuel has risen or there are no fare wars among competing companies. If there are no fare wars among competing companies, the number of airline passengers is larger than it was last year.

   According to the passage above, if there has been a rise in airline fares this month, which one of the following CANNOT be true?

   (A) There are no fare wars among competing airlines.
   (B) The cost of fuel has risen, and the number of passengers is the same as last year.
   (C) The cost of fuel has risen, there are no fare wars, and the number of passengers is larger than it was last year.
   (D) There are no fare wars, and the number of passengers is larger than it was last year.
   (E) The cost of fuel has risen, there are no fare wars, and the number of passengers is smaller than it was last year.

7. Only 75 years ago, the best fishing in the world was the Grand Banks of the North Atlantic. But now overfishing and man's pollution have decimated the area. There will be no fishing industry in the Americas in a very few years. The waters off Newfoundland now yield less than half the catch of five years ago, and less than one quarter of the total of ten years ago. The cod has almost disappeared. The number of fishermen in Newfoundland and New England has declined, and their yearly earnings are now at an all-time low. Yet radar has made fishing methods more efficient than ever.

Which one of the following identifies most clearly a faulty assumption in the reasoning of this passage?

(A) Ten years is too short a time period to use to draw conclusions about the natural world.
(B) The argument assumes that the waters off Newfoundland are representative of all the American oceans.
(C) The pollution of the sea may have been caused by natural as well as by human forces.
(D) The argument does not allow for the possibility that the catch may increase in size in the next five years.
(E) The argument fails to consider that the decline in the catch may be due to factors other than pollution.

8. A cigarette advertisement in a magazine asks, "What do gremlins, the Loch Ness monster, and a filter cigarette claiming 'great taste' have in common?" The answer is "You've heard of all of them, but don't really believe they exist." The advertisement contains no pictures, and no additional text except the words Gold Star Cigarettes and the Surgeon General's warning in a box in the lower corner.

Which one of the following conclusions can be drawn from the information given above?

(A) Cigarette advertising depends upon visual appeal to create images for specific brands.
(B) All cigarette advertising depends on praising a specific brand.
(C) Gold Star Cigarettes are non-filters.
(D) The writers of this advertisement do not believe in advertising.
(E) The writers of this advertisement do not believe the Surgeon General's warning is true.

9. The traffic on the Imperial Highway has always been slowed by the dangerous curves in the road. It was built when cars were much smaller and less powerful, and very few drivers traveled between Imperial City and Fremont. All this has changed. The cost of widening and straightening the road would now be many times greater than building the proposed new toll road on the borders of the Imperial Wetlands reserve. Environmentalists fear the construction noise and waste will harm the wildlife in the reserve, and have urged that the toll road not be constructed.

   Which one of the following, if true, would most strengthen the case of the environmentalists?

   (A) None of the animals living in the Imperial Wetlands is on the list of endangered species.
   (B) The traffic congestion on the Imperial Highway increases each year.
   (C) The cost of building the new road will be amortized in ten years by the tolls collected.
   (D) There are several less direct routes the toll road could take between Fremont and Imperial City.
   (E) The environmentalists threaten to bring a lawsuit in federal court to halt construction of the road.

10. Despite the very large increase in the federal tax on luxury items, the value of the stock of Harry Evans, Inc., seller of the world's most expensive jewelry, continues to rise. Six months after the introduction of the tax, Evans's stock is at an all-time high. Moreover, sales in the United States continue to increase. In other countries, where Evans does 30 percent of its business, there have been no rises in excise taxes and the company will open new stores in Tokyo, Monte Carlo, and Singapore. According to a company spokesperson, ____.

    Which one of the following most logically completes this paragraph?

    (A) American customers who can afford to shop at Evans are not likely to be deterred by a rise in luxury taxes
    (B) American customers are expected to spend far less at Evans because of the tax rise
    (C) American sales are not significant enough to affect the overall profits of the firm
    (D) the company will probably be forced to close most of its stores in America
    (E) state taxes are more likely to influence jewelry sales than federal taxes

11. A recent study of cigarette smokers has shown that, of cancer patients who are heavy smokers of unfiltered cigarettes, 40 percent will die of the disease. For cancer patients who are light smokers of filter cigarettes, the percentage is 25 percent.

    Which one of the following conclusions can be drawn from the information above?

    (A) There are more heavy smokers of unfiltered cigarettes than light smokers of filter cigarettes.
    (B) More heavy smokers of unfiltered cigarettes die of cancer than light smokers of filter cigarettes.
    (C) A heavy smoker of unfiltered cigarettes who has cancer is more likely to die than a light smoker of unfiltered cigarettes.
    (D) A heavy smoker of unfiltered cigarettes who has cancer may be more likely to die than a light smoker of unfiltered cigarettes.
    (E) A heavy smoker of unfiltered cigarettes who has cancer is more likely to die than a light smoker of filtered cigarettes who has cancer.

<u>Questions 12–13</u>

Archeologists have come to the support of Arctic anthropologists. A small minority of anthropologists assert that Stone-Age tribes of the Arctic domesticated wolves and trained them to haul sleds. Excavations have recently found evidence to support this claim. Archeologists have found wolf bones near the site of a Stone-Age village. They have also found walrus bones that might have been used on primitive sleds. The small minority of anthropologists believe that their theories have been proved.

12. Which one of the following is true of the evidence cited in the paragraph above?

    (A) It is not relevant to the anthropologists' conclusions.
    (B) It conclusively contradicts the anthropologists' conclusions.
    (C) It neither supports nor refutes the anthropologists' conclusions positively.
    (D) It supports the anthropologists' conclusions authoritatively.
    (E) It conclusively supports only a part of the anthropologists' conclusions.

13. Which one of the following, if true, would best support the theory of the anthropologists?

    (A) Wolves are known to have fed upon the garbage of villages in northern Europe.
    (B) Wolves as a species are easily domesticated and trained.
    (C) Almost all Stone-Age Arctic tools were made of walrus bone.
    (D) Stone-Age villages were located on the migration routes of the caribou herds upon which wolves preyed.
    (E) The earliest sled part found in the Arctic was made one thousand years after the Stone Age.

GO ON TO THE NEXT PAGE ➤

5 5 5 5 5

Questions 14–15

The following criticism of a self-portrait by Vincent van Gogh appeared in a magazine in 1917:

"Here we have a work of art which is so self-evidently a degenerate work by a degenerate artist that we need not say anything about the inept creation. It is safe to say that if we were to meet in our dreams such a villainous looking jailbird with such a deformed Neanderthal skull, degenerate ears, hobo beard and insane glare, it would certainly give us a nightmare."

14. The author of this passage makes his point by using

(A) invective
(B) analogy
(C) citation of authority
(D) paradox
(E) example

15. In relation to the first sentence of the quotation, the second sentence is

(A) an example of an effect following a cause
(B) a specific derived from a general principle
(C) a logical conclusion
(D) a contradiction
(E) a personal experience in support of a generalization

16. A company called Popcorn Packaging is promoting the use of popcorn as a cushioning material in packing. Unlike the commonly used Styrofoam beads or chips, popcorn can be recycled as a food for birds or squirrels and can serve as a garden mulch. Used out of doors, popcorn disappears almost overnight, while the Styrofoam beads may be in the environment for centuries. Even before we became ecology conscious, popcorn was used in packing in the 1940s. Since it now costs less to produce than Styrofoam, there is every reason to return to wide-scale use of packaging by popcorn.

Which one of the following, if true, would most seriously weaken the author's argument?

(A) A package using popcorn as a cushioning material will weigh less than a package using Styrofoam beads.
(B) Popcorn may attract rodents and insects.
(C) A large number of squirrels can damage a garden by consuming flowering bulbs.
(D) Less than 1 percent of the material now used for package cushioning is recycled.
(E) Styrofoam replaced popcorn in the early 1950s because it was cheaper to produce.

17. This produce stand sells fruits and vegetables. All fruits are delicious, and all vegetables are rich in vitamins. Every food that is vitamin-rich is delicious, so everything sold at this stand is delicious.

Which one of the following assumptions is necessary to make the conclusion in the argument above logically correct?

(A) The stand sells many fruits and vegetables.
(B) This produce stand sells only fruits and vegetables.
(C) Something cannot be both vitamin-rich and delicious.
(D) Some stands sell fruits that are not delicious.
(E) Some vegetables are delicious.

5 ◇5◇ ◇5◇ ◇5◇ 5

18. Voter turnout in primary elections has declined steadily from 1982 to 1990. In 1990, more than 80 percent of the Americans eligible to vote failed to do so. Only 11.9 percent of the Democrats and 7.7 percent of the Republicans went to the polls. The largest number of voters turned out for elections in the District of Columbia (28 percent) and in Massachusetts, where the 32 percent total was the highest since 1962. In each of the twenty-four other states holding elections, the number of voters was smaller than it had been in 1986 and 1982.

    Based on the information in this passage, which one of the following must be true?

    (A) The turnout in the District of Columbia was affected by favorable weather conditions.
    (B) Fewer than 20 percent of the eligible major-party voters voted in the 24 states other than Massachusetts.
    (C) The voter turnout in Massachusetts is always higher than the turnouts in other states.
    (D) The voter turnout decline is a signal of a nationwide voter rebellion.
    (E) More voters cast their votes in general elections than in primary elections.

19. Each year the number of schools that no longer allow smoking on school property grows larger. Four states, New Jersey, Kansas, Utah, and New Hampshire, now require tobacco-free schools. The Tobacco Institute has fought against regulations restricting smoking everywhere from airlines to restaurants on the grounds that they trample on the rights of smokers, but is conspicuously absent from school board lobbyists. Tobacco industry spokesmen have denounced the rules treating teachers like children, but have said they will not go on record to defend policies that affect children.

    Which one of the following, if true, best accounts for the Tobacco Institute's behavior?

    (A) The tobacco industry is presently fighting the charge that it attempts to recruit new smokers among minors.
    (B) The tobacco industry can depend on continued high profits from overseas operations, where restrictions do not exist.
    (C) Most tobacco companies are highly diversified corporations whose profits no longer depend wholly on tobacco products.
    (D) The tobacco industry believes the rights of children to be equal to the rights of adults.
    (E) The tobacco industry agrees with the schools that have rules against tobacco.

Questions 20–21

A number of lawsuits have been brought against popular singing groups charging that suicidal themes in their songs have led to teenage suicides. So far, the courts have found that the lyrics are protected by the First Amendment. But what if this should change, and a court decides that suicidal themes in popular songs are dangerous? In fact, the songs that have been charged so far are antisuicide; they present sardonically the self-destructive behavior of drinking, drugs, and escape by death. They describe a pitiful state of mind, but they do not endorse it.

Blaming suicide on the arts is nothing new. In the late eighteenth century, Goethe's popular novel *Werther* was said to be the cause of a rash of suicides in imitation of the novel's hero. If we begin to hold suicide in books or music responsible for suicides in real life, the operas of Verdi and Puccini will have to go, and *Romeo and Juliet* and *Julius Caesar* will disappear from high school reading lists.

20. The author of this passage argues by

(A) providing examples to support two opposing positions
(B) using an observation to undermine a theoretical principle
(C) disputing an interpretation of evidence cited by those with an opposing view
(D) predicting personal experience from a general principle
(E) accusing the opposing side of using inaccurate statistical information

21. Which one of the following is an assumption necessary to the author's argument?

(A) A lyric presenting suicide in a favorable light should not have First Amendment protection.
(B) Literature or music cannot directly influence human behavior.
(C) Many record albums already carry labels warning purchasers of their dangerous contents.
(D) The audience, not the performer, is responsible for the audience's actions.
(E) Freedom of speech is the most threatened of our personal freedoms.

---

22. Haven't you at some time had a favorite song or book or film that was not well known but later became popular? And didn't you feel somehow betrayed and resentful when what you had thought was unique became commonplace? On a larger scale, the same thing happens to novelists or film makers who have enjoyed critical esteem without popular success. Let them become public sensations, and the critics who praised their work will attack them virulently.

This paragraph most likely introduces an article on a film maker who has made a

(A) series of commercially successful films
(B) series of commercially unsuccessful films
(C) single film, a commercial success
(D) single film, a commercial failure
(E) critical success and a commercial success

GO ON TO THE NEXT PAGE ➤

23. Studies of the effects of drinking four or more cups of coffee per day have shown that coffee consumption increases work efficiency by improving the ability to process information. People who drink two cups of coffee in the morning are more alert and feel better than those who do not. But there are other factors to be considered.

Which one of the following sentences would provide the most logical continuation of this paragraph?

(A) Contrary to popular belief, drinking coffee cannot erase the effect of alcohol.
(B) Some studies suggest that coffee drinking will protect against cancer of the colon.
(C) Combined with the stress of heavy exercise, coffee drinking may be the cause of higher blood pressure.
(D) Drinking two or more cups of coffee per day increases the risk of heart attacks in men.
(E) Many people cannot distinguish between the taste of decaffeinated and that of regular coffee.

24. All of the members of the chorus will sing in the performance of the oratorio *Messiah*. Some of these are highly trained professionals, some are gifted amateurs, and some are singers of mediocre ability.

If the statements above are true, which one of the following must also be true?

(A) *Messiah* will be performed by highly trained professionals, gifted amateurs, and some singers of mediocre ability.
(B) Some of the members of the chorus are not highly trained professionals, gifted amateurs, or singers of mediocre ability.
(C) *Messiah* will be performed by some highly trained professionals, but not all of them are in the chorus.
(D) Not all of those in the chorus who are gifted amateurs will perform in the oratorio.
(E) All of those who will perform *Messiah* are members of the chorus.

25. The passage of laws that limit elected officials to one or two terms in office is an admission that voters are civic fools, unable to tell good lawmakers from bad ones. To ban all the politicians when the real intention is to get rid of the corrupt ones is to burn the house down to get rid of the vermin.

The author of this passage makes his point chiefly by

(A) defining a key term
(B) exposing a self-contradiction
(C) drawing an analogy
(D) questioning the evidence of his opponents
(E) citing an example

STOP

IF YOU FINISH BEFORE THE TIME IS UP, CHECK YOUR WORK ON THIS SECTION OF THE TEST ONLY. DO NOT GO ON TO THE NEXT SECTION OF THE TEST UNTIL TIME IS UP FOR THIS SECTION.

Writing Sample

Directions: You have 30 minutes to write an essay in response to a given topic. Take a few minutes to plan your work before you begin writing. DO NOT WRITE ON A TOPIC OF YOUR OWN CHOICE. ESSAYS THAT DO NOT ADDRESS THE GIVEN TOPIC ARE UNACCEPTABLE.

The quality of your writing is more important than the length of your response or the content. Pay attention to organization, appropriate diction, and correct usage. You will not be expected to display any specialized knowledge in your response, nor will you be expected to write a "perfect" essay; law schools understand that you are writing under a time constraint, and will allow for the minor lapses in writing ability that might occur under this circumstance.

Only the lined area in your booklet will be reproduced for the law schools, so do not write outside this space. *Do not* skip lines or use wide margins. These precautions, along with careful planning and legible handwriting that is not unduly large, will keep you within the allowed space.

Sample Topic

ead the following descriptions of Jackson and Brown. *Then, in the space provided, write an argument for deciding which of the two should e assigned the responsibility of hiring teachers for the Hapsville School System.* The following criteria are relevant to your decision:

- The taxpayers want educators who can instill in students the desire to learn and an excitement for knowledge, something that has been lacking in their schools.
- A majority of students' parents believe that their children should be equipped, upon graduation, to earn a living, and thus favor a more trade-oriented (rather than academic) approach to schooling.

JACKSON was appointed as Superintendent of Schools by the Hapsville School Board, which was elected by the community's tax-ayers. As a 30-year resident of Hapsville (population 45,000), Jackson is unique in that he holds not only a doctorate in administration, ut also a master's degree in education. He taught in the Hapsville schools for 16 years until he served on the state Commission on Edu-ation. He has always favored a progressive approach to education, although it may not always have been popular with the town's popu-ation. Through the years he has brought many fine teachers to the faculty, because of his willingness to encourage new classroom tech-ques.

BROWN is a 52-year resident of Hapsville, having been born in the same house in which he now lives. He was elected to the School oard 13 years ago, and continues to win nearly unanimous reelection every two years. As the foremost developer in the Four Counties rea, Mr. Brown has had the opportunity to build hundreds of new homes in the six housing developments he's planned and actualized, nd, in the interim, has employed hundreds of Hapsville residents as carpenters, electricians, plumbers, architects, landscapers, roundskeepers, etc. As such, he is held in high esteem by most of the town, not only for his providing livelihoods for many, but also for is fair and realistic outlook on life. Mr. Brown feels strongly that the key to life is having a marketable skill.

Answer Key

Section I: Reading Comprehension

1. **B**	6. **A**	11. **E**	16. **E**	21. **B**	26. **B**
2. **C**	7. **C**	12. **C**	17. **A**	22. **C**	27. **A**
3. **A**	8. **A**	13. **D**	18. **B**	23. **C**	28. **E**
4. **A**	9. **B**	14. **A**	19. **E**	24. **D**	
5. **E**	10. **A**	15. **C**	20. **D**	25. **A**	

Section II: Analytical Reasoning

1. **C**	5. **D**	9. **D**	13. **A**	17. **E**	21. **B**
2. **A**	6. **B**	10. **A**	14. **C**	18. **D**	22. **D**
3. **E**	7. **E**	11. **E**	15. **A**	19. **C**	23. **D**
4. **C**	8. **E**	12. **D**	16. **D**	20. **C**	24. **C**

Section III: Logical Reasoning

1. **C**	6. **A**	11. **E**	16. **B**	21. **E**	26. **B**
2. **B**	7. **B**	12. **C**	17. **B**	22. **E**	
3. **E**	8. **C**	13. **B**	18. **A**	23. **B**	
4. **D**	9. **B**	14. **C**	19. **E**	24. **E**	
5. **D**	10. **E**	15. **E**	20. **C**	25. **D**	

Section IV: Analytical Reasoning

1. **B**	5. **D**	9. **A**	13. **E**	17. **E**	21. **B**
2. **B**	6. **E**	10. **E**	14. **D**	18. **C**	22. **E**
3. **D**	7. **C**	11. **E**	15. **A**	19. **B**	23. **C**
4. **E**	8. **E**	12. **B**	16. **D**	20. **C**	24. **B**

Section V: Logical Reasoning

1. **B**	6. **E**	11. **E**	16. **B**	21. **D**
2. **D**	7. **B**	12. **C**	17. **B**	22. **E**
3. **C**	8. **C**	13. **B**	18. **B**	23. **D**
4. **D**	9. **D**	14. **A**	19. **A**	24. **A**
5. **A**	10. **A**	15. **D**	20. **C**	25. **C**

MODEL TEST ANALYSIS

Doing a model exam and understanding the explanations afterwards are of course important in acquainting you with typical LSAT question types and successful approaches to the questions. However, another benefit of carefully analyzing these model tests is to understand the kinds of errors you are making and thus work to minimize them. For instance, if a very high percentage of your incorrect answers is due to "careless error" or "misread problem" then perhaps you are working much too fast and should slow your pace accordingly. If your incorrect answers are due primarily to "lack of knowledge," then a careful rereading and reworking of the appropriate question-type chapter may be in order. Or if you find that you aren't completing a large number of questions because of lack of time, you may need to either increase your speed or learn to use the "one-check, two-check" technique more effectively.

This kind of analysis of the model test will enable you to identify your particular weaknesses and thus remedy them.

Model Test Analysis

Section	Total Number of Questions	Number Correct	Number Incorrect	Number Unanswered*
I. Reading Comprehension	28			
II. Analytical Reasoning	24			
III. Logical Reasoning	26			
IV. Analytical Reasoning	24			
V. Logical Reasoning	25			
TOTALS:	127			

*At this stage in your preparation, you should not be leaving any blank answer spaces. At least fill in a guess, as there is no penalty for a wrong answer.

Reasons for Incorrect Answers

You may wish to evaluate the explanations before completing this chart.

Section	Total Number Incorrect	Lack of Knowledge	Misread Problem	Careless Error	Unanswered or Wrong Guess
I. Reading Comprehension					
II. Analytical Reasoning					
III. Logical Reasoning					
IV. Analytical Reasoning					
V. Logical Reasoning					
TOTALS:					

Explanation of Answers

Section I

Passage 1

1. **B** The first sentence of the passage makes it clear that government workers are forbidden to strike by statutory law.

2. **C** If strikes are a form of symbolic speech, the denial of the right to strike is arguably a denial of free speech. It also can be argued that it denies due process, the right to picket, and the right to avoid abnormally dangerous working conditions.

3. **A** The courts, not the legislative or the executive branches, must determine the "clear and present danger," according to the Supreme Court decision described in the second paragraph.

4. **A** Because the firing of the controllers had the same effect as a strike, it appears that there was no danger to the public.

5. **E** The author points out that workers in government who do that same job as workers in private industry cannot strike. The passage argues that the nature of the service should determine the right to strike, not the employer.

6. **A** It is possible that the "highly qualified" may seek employment outside of government, because of the no-strike clause. Choices (B), (C), (D), (E) are not plausible weaknesses of the no-strike rule.

Passage 2

7. **C** See lines 4–9. Her father also may have influenced her in the ways suggested in (A), (B), (D), and (E), but these answers are not suggested by the passage itself.

8. A We can infer from lines 19–24 that this was Woolf's dilemma, particularly because in lines 25–28 we learn that the emphasis in her feminism was self-reform. E is incorrect; "lucid objectivity" is cited as a strength of her novel *The Years*, not something that needed to be overcome. C is not supported by the passage because there is nothing to suggest that Virginia Woolf wished to pursue "social work." Similarly, (B) and (D) are not supported by any information in the passage.

9. **B** In the passage, the integration of masculine and feminine (the androgynous mind) and the danger of one-sidedness (lines 18–24) describe Woolf's feminism. Although C and D might also characterize her feminism, the passage emphasizes a need for wholeness. A is not supported by the passage. E might be suggested in lines 30–35 and lines 77–80 but it is *not* presented as a characterization of her feminism.

10. **A** Paragraph two is concerned with the superiority of Woolf's novels to her tracts in dealing with her feminist concerns. Paragraph three contrasts a tract and a novel to illustrate this point. Paragraph three doesn't present a contrast to or a subtopic of paragraph one (B, D), nor does it act as a transition (C). (In fact, the passage could move smoothly from paragraph two to paragraph four even if paragraph three were missing. What would be missing would be a concrete example—i.e., answer A.) Paragraph two does not present an exegesis (E).

11. **E** This opposition is at the heart of the passage—see paragraphs two, three, and four. Different types of novels are *not* contrasted (B), nor is Woolf's aesthetic creed contrasted to the aesthetic creed of the Bloomsbury group (A). (A contrast is suggested in lines 4–9, but it is minor, and not explained or developed.) C is incorrect; the passage explicitly addresses Woolf's *avoidance* of such a contrast and her belief in the androgynous mind. D is unclear and inaccurate.

12. **C** See paragraph four. Although the author does say that Woolf's primary emphasis was on self-reform, he does not suggest that her social concerns were trivial (D). Nothing in the passage suggests that the author is criticizing the Bloomsbury aesthetic creed (A). Similarly, although the author finds Woolf's novels more successful than her tracts, it is a giant leap to infer that he dislikes social reform literature in general (E). (B) is clearly incorrect.

13. **D** The passage states this idea in the first line and then continues throughout to develop the subject of the importance of both feminism and art in Woolf's writing. See lines 37–43. (A) is too limited; these two works are used to illustrate the main point of the passage. (B) is broad and imprecise. (C) is also imprecise. (E) is incorrect; opposition of masculine and feminine is not part of the passage.

Passage 3

14. **A** The author is obviously most concerned with the work of historians and the current state of written history, which is what prompts his discussion of fiction in relation to history. See lines 4–7, 17–20, 53–59, 64–70. Literature and literary concerns (answer C) are secondary.

15. **C** See lines 68–69: ". . . their abandonment of the narrative style." A decline in the writing *ability* of historians (E) is not implied. And although the author does mention the movies and television, he does not attribute the growth of fictional history to an increase in their audiences (B).

16. **E** This attitude is clearly stated in lines 49–53. B may seem correct, but the author does not say that fictional history on its own has won the audience away from traditional history. On the contrary, he suggests that professional historians themselves may be partly responsible for the growth of fictional history (lines 64–68).

17. **A** This book would most clearly fit the definition of fictional history given in lines 35–39. According to the author, it is fictional history that causes the greatest confusion (lines 49–53). (B) and (C) would be classified as historical fiction according to the author's definitions, and (D) and (E) as nonfiction.

18. **B** The second paragraph is devoted to defining and contrasting the two terms. (D) might be considered a possible answer but is less clear and specific. The other answers are simply inaccurate.

19. **E** Nothing in the passage suggests a judgment of history taught in the schools. The other statements are all supported in the passage: (A)—lines 17–20; (B)—lines 64–68; (C)—lines 53–59; (D)—lines 12–16.

20. **D** Throughout the passage the author is most concerned with the growth of fictional history and its effects. None of the other answers present his *attitude* as clearly, though (C) does define fictional history.

21. **B** The author is obviously concerned with the "mischief" that the mixture of history with fiction can cause. However, he presents his concern in a moderate fashion. He is not hostile, he does not preach, he is not pedantic, nor does he display irony. (E) suggests an elevated tone not present in the passage

Passage 4

22. **C** (C) is the best answer because the author explains fear conditioning in order to show how it is a good method for studying emotional memory. (A) is incorrect; the passage "proves" nothing. (B) is also incorrect. The fact that the mechanisms in mammals and vertebrates may be similar is not the main point of the passage; also, the passage does not state that the mechanisms are "the same." (D) is only a supporting point—not the main point—of the passage. (E) is incorrect; the way that phobias are initially created in humans is not addressed in the passage.

23. **C** The passage makes this connection in lines 37–43. (A) is incorrect—see lines 27–28. (B) is also incorrect; lines 72–75 specifically state that cues to which subjects respond fearfully are not linked to complicated cognitive processing. (D) is incorrect because the passage states that stress, rather than *weakening* a response, may cause its recurrence. (E) is not the right choice. See lines 27–28. The rat's conditioned response diminishes only when the conditioned stimulus is administered many times without the unconditioned stimulus. As long as the shock and conditioned stimulus are paired, the rat's response to the conditioned stimulus will remain.

24. **D** The passage states than an extinguished fear response can recover spontaneously or can be reinstated by an irrelevant stressful experience (lines 37–41). We can assume that for a rat, introduction of a cat could be an "irrelevant stressful experience." (A) and (B) are incorrect; both are contradicted by information in the passage (lines 28–32 and lines 32–37). (C) and (E) are not supported by information in the passage.

25. **A** This answer is directly supported in lines 70–72. According to lines 27–28, the response is not related to complex cognitive processing. Therefore, (B) is incorrect. (C) and (D) are not supported by any information presented in the passage. (E) is incorrect; in lines 32–37, the brain's control, rather than lack of control, is cited.

26. **B** The author cites the nine animals to show the wide range of animal groups in which fear conditioning occurs. This supports his point that fear conditioning is an ideal starting point for studies of emotional memory. Although fear conditioning occurring in so many animal groups may support (A) (that the fear response is neural), this is not the primary reason for citing them. See lines 48–52. There is no suggestion of a developmental link between the animal groups listed, making (C) an incorrect choice. (D) and (E) are also incorrect; the author's listing of the nine animals is not connected in the passage to the role of the brain, nor is any point made about the emotions of fruit flies, snails, and so on.

27. **A** The last line of the passage states that the object of the research is to examine the "neurological foundations of fear." (B) and (E) are incorrect; the primary object of the research is not "cognition" nor how mammals are similar. (C) is also incorrect; conditioning is the *method* to be used to study the neurological basis of fear, not the object of the research itself. (D) should be ruled out because the effects of acoustic and visual stimuli are a small part of the research, not its main object.

28. **E** The third paragraph is devoted to reasons that fear conditioning is an "ideal starting point" for research of emotional memory, i.e., it occurs in many animal groups, the signals are not the type to which subjects have preexisting strong emotional reactions, and so on. (A) is incorrect because the definition is completed in paragraphs 1 and 2. (B) is incorrect because the author presents no qualifications or reservations about fear conditioning. (C) is not a good choice because the passage adds new information (i.e., reasons or justifications) and does not summarize. Finally, (D) is not correct because the passage does not present any applications other than the study of emotion and memory for the fear conditioning method.

Section II

Answers 1–6

From the information given, you could have made the following diagram:

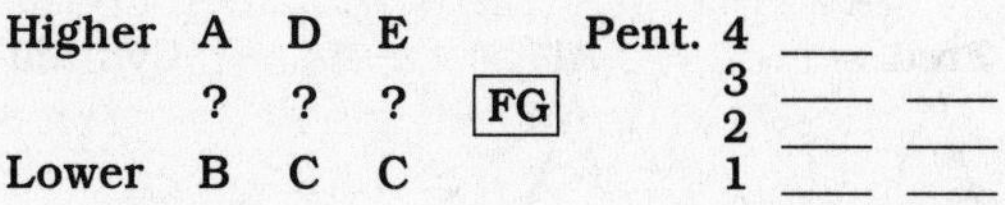

1. **C** Since F and G are on the same floor, they can't be on 4. Since B and C are below A or D/E, they can't be on 4; therefore only A, D, or E can be on 4.

2. **A** If F's apartment is on 2, so is G's. For B and C to be below A, D, and E, B and C must be on 1 and A, D, and E on 3 and 4, but we don't know exactly where on 3/4.

3. **E** If D is on 4, G (and F) *can* be on 3, 2, or 1.

D	D	D
FG	AE	AE
AE	FG	BC
BC	BC	FG

4. **C** If D and E are on the same floor, A must be on 4. All the other answers are possible but *not* certain.

5. **D** If A is on 4 or C on 1, the arrangement must be either

A		A
FG	or	DE
DE		FG
BC		BC

6. **B** A and E can be on the same floor if D is on 4.

D		D
AE	or	AE
FG		BC
BC		FG

Answers 7–12

From the information given, you may have constructed a simple grouping display of information similar to this:

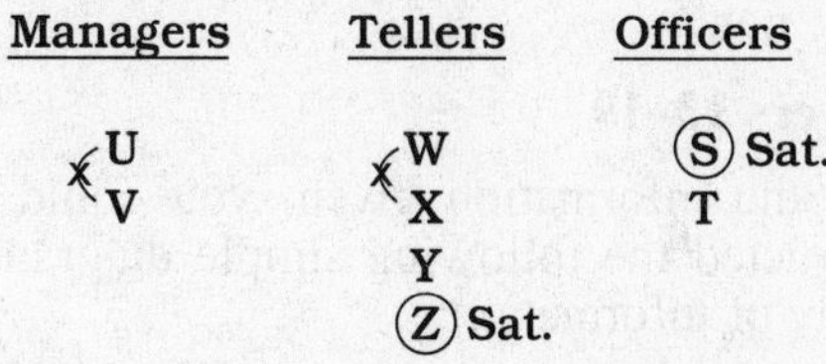

Another possible display might look like this:

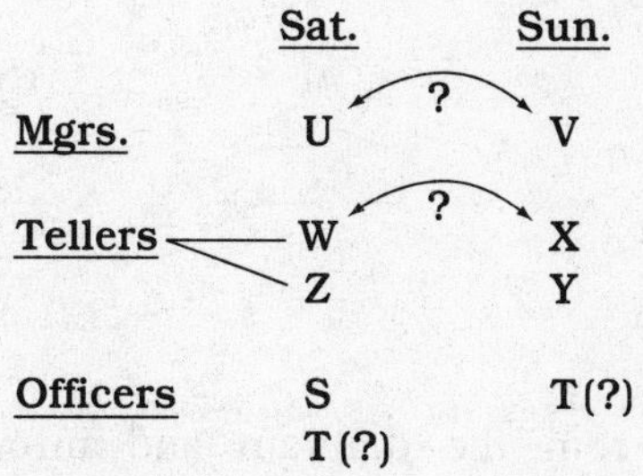

7. **E** From the original information, a manager must be on duty each day and the managers cannot work on the same day. Therefore (A) must be true. (E) does not have to be true, since U's schedule has no bearing on X's schedule. Since W and X will not work on the same day, (B) must also be true. There is no restriction placed on T.

8. **E** V, W, Z, S can work on Saturday without breaking any of the conditions given. Choice (A) is missing a manager. Choice (B) has two managers working on the same day. Choices (C) and (D) have W and X working on the same day.

9. **D** Five employees, U or V, X or W, Z, S, and T are the greatest number to work on Saturday.

10. **A** Since W and X will not work on the same day, (A) must be true. (B) is false since Y must work on Sunday. (C) could be true. Since W's schedule has no effect on Z and U, (D) and (E) may be true or false.

11. **E** Since no employee can work on consecutive days, and there are four tellers, then two must work on Saturday.

12. **D** U, V, W, X, Y, Z, and T have the possibility of working on Sunday; S and Z do not.

Answers 13–19

From the information given, you could have constructed the following simple diagram and display of information:

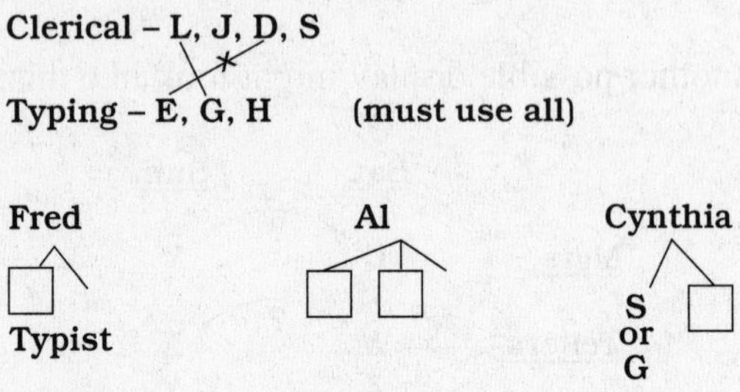

13. **A** From the diagram and information above, if Gene works for Fred, then Lyndia also works for Fred, and Sylvia must work for Cynthia. Since Dennis and Edra will not work together, one of them must work for Cynthia; therefore choice (A) must be false. Jim cannot work for Cynthia.

14. **C** Using the diagram, if Sylvia doesn't work for Cynthia, then Gene must work for Cynthia. If Gene works for Cynthia, then Lyndia must also work for Cynthia, since Gene and Lyndia always work together.

15. **A** If Lyndia and Jim work for Al, then Gene must also work for Al, and Sylvia must work for Cynthia. The diagram would look like this:

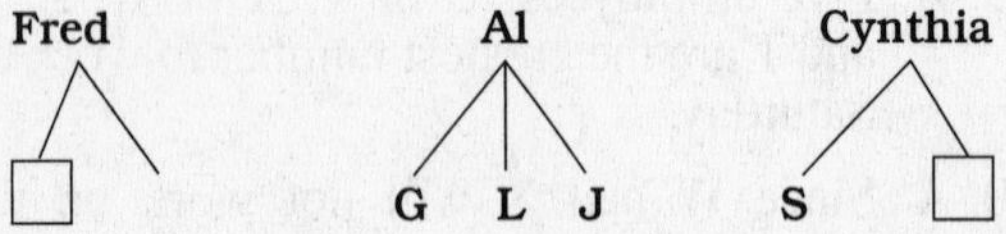

First, (A) is true since Gene and Lyndia always work together. Stop there. Go no further. Edra could work for Cynthia or Fred, and also Helen could work for Cynthia or Fred.

16. **D** If Sylvia and Jim work for Al, then Gene and Lyndia must work for Cynthia. Since Dennis and Edra cannot work together, one of them must work for Fred and the other for Al. The diagram would now look like this:

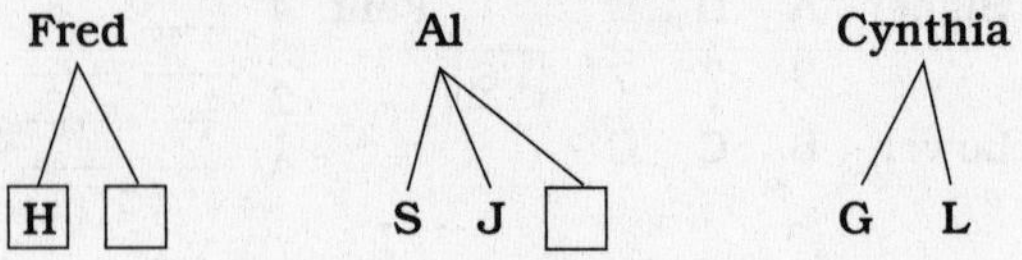

Therefore, only (D) is true.

17. **E** From the diagram, if Lyndia and Sylvia work for Al, then Gene also must work for Al. But either Sylvia or Gene must work for Cynthia. Therefore (E) must be false.

18. **D** From the diagram, if Jim works for Cynthia, then Sylvia must also work for Cynthia, since Gene and Lyndia must work together. Gene and Lyndia cannot work for Fred, because then Dennis and Edra (who cannot work together) would work for Al. Therefore, Lyndia must work for Al. The diagram would look like this:

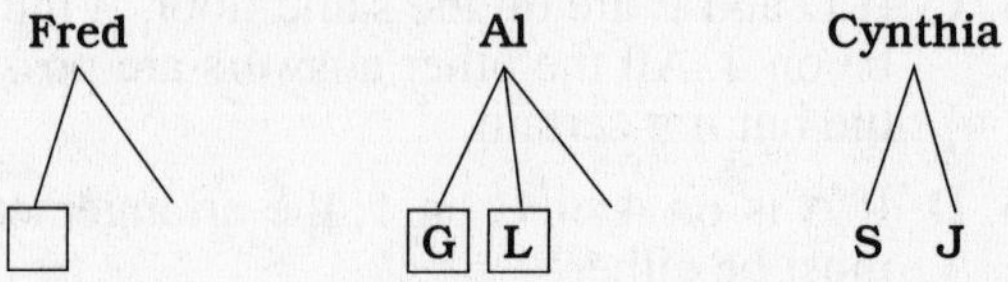

19. **C** If Al needs only two assistants and Fred needs only one, and if Helen works for Fred, then the diagram would look like this:

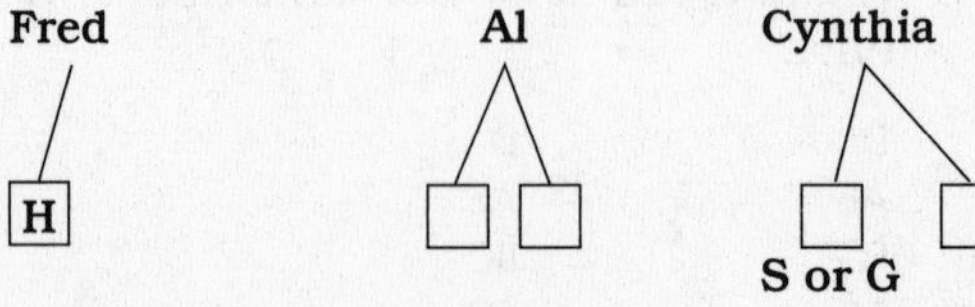

Since Gene and Lyndia must work together, they can work for either Al or Cynthia. Since Edra (typist) must work and Dennis and Edra cannot work together, then Dennis doesn't work. Otherwise, Dennis and Edra would work together. Statements A, B, D, and E *could* be true.

Answers 20–24

Drawing a diagram, below, will help answer the questions.

	EVENTS				
	1	2	3	4	5
RED	G	—	G	—	G
BLUE	—	B/S	—	B/S	—
GREEN					
YELLOW					

Since the red team wins only 3 gold medals, it must win gold medals in events 1, 3, and 5, since no team wins gold medals in consecutive events. Also, note that since blue wins only two medals (neither of them gold), it must have won medals in events 2 and 4, so that it didn't fail to win a medal within two consecutive events. Be aware then that green and yellow, therefore, must each have won medals in all five events.

20. **C** If the green team wins only one gold medal, there remains only one gold medal, which the yellow team must win.

21. **B** Since three medals are given for each event, and, according to our diagram from the facts, red and blue already account for their total awards with one medal in each event, the other two medals in each event must go to yellow and green. Thus, yellow and green will each be awarded five medals.

22. **D** By completing the chart such that the yellow team wins five silver medals, we can see that green must win two gold and three bronze medals.

	1	2	3	4	5
RED	G	—	G	—	G
BLUE	—	B/S	—	B/S	—
GREEN					
YELLOW	S	S	S	S	S

23. **D** We know choices (A) and (B) are both true: both the green and yellow teams each must win five medals. Therefore (E) is also true. Choice (C) is true because three of the gold medals are already won by the red team; since blue doesn't win gold, if green wins one gold, yellow wins the remaining gold medal. Choice (D) is not true: if the green team wins only one silver medal, the yellow team must win at least two silver medals.

24. **C** If a fifth team enters all events and wins only three consecutive silver medals, it must win the silver in events 2, 3, and 4, so that it does not fail to win a medal within two consecutive events. Therefore our diagram would look like this:

	1	2	3	4	5
RED	G	—	G	—	G
BLUE	—	B	—	B	—
GREEN					
YELLOW					
ORANGE	—	S	S	S	—

Therefore, if yellow wins a gold in the 2nd event, green must win a medal in the 3rd event (since no team fails to win a medal within two consecutive events). Thus, green must win a bronze in the 3rd event.

Section III

1. **C** The passage is more restrained in its criticism than (A) or (B), while (D) and (E) are only elements of the paragraph, not its main point.

2. **B** By urging moviegoers to patronize films *in order to* influence academy judges, the author reveals his assumption that the academy will be influenced by the number of people paying to see a movie.

3. **E** Bob's answer shows that he thinks that people other than teachers are mean. His thought was that Andy meant otherwise.

4. **D** The author's concluding contention is that Roosevelt was not only a good marksman, but also an intellectually curious and patient man. If Roosevelt was known to leave safaris which were not immediately productive, this fact would substantially weaken the author's contention about Roosevelt's "patient observation."

5. **D** The words "because of a recent cut in state funding of our program" indicate that another criterion was used in determining entering class size besides candidates' scores and grades, namely, the financial situation of the college. The words *seriously* in choice (B) and *severe* in choice (E) are not necessarily supported by the passage, and thus make those choices incorrect. Since grade point average is only one of several criteria for admission, we cannot deduce (A) with certainty.

6. **A** This sentence not only fits well stylistically but completes the thought of the passage by tying it into the opening statement.

7. **B** The author of this passage actually defines conscience as the ability to sense right and wrong.

8. **C** The main point of the paragraph is the need for campaign reform. Choice (D) supports the argument, while the other three choices are assumptions that might arise, but these are not the main point of the paragraph.

9. **B** This choice offers the most thorough and comprehensive evidence that the viewing of violent television precedes criminal behavior. (A) is not the best choice because it describes viewing habits that follow rather than precede criminal behavior.

10. **E** The use of "overwhelming" leaves the evidence unspecified, thus opening to challenge the extent and nature of the report's data.

11. **E** All of the first four statements can be used to explain the underreporting. In D, for example, if the size of police departments has declined, they would have less manpower available to gather and report information. E is a reason against underreporting rather than an explanation for it.

12. **C** The argument uses the case of the county to call the state figures into question. The underreported figures are "less evidence."

13. **B** If the experiences and lifestyle of the Aryan race are uniquely different from those of other cultures, it would seriously weaken the author's conclusion that studying the Aryan race will be helpful in understanding the experiences and life styles of other races. That its communal arrangements are *unique* would make comparison between the Aryan race and other cultures impossible.

14. **C** The author presents a *contrast* between life and honor: in particular, the final sentence suggests that life and honor have opposite qualities. Of the choices, the only opposite of *transient* is *eternal*.

15. **E** The logic of this statement goes from the general absolute ("all") to the specific ("this animal"), concluding with specific to specific. Symbolically, if *P* implies *Q*, then *not Q* implies *not P*. (E) goes from general absolute ("all") to specific ("this liquid"), concluding with specific to specific. Notice how and where the inverse ("not") is inserted. Using symbols, we have that, if *P* implies *Q*, then *not Q* implies *not P*.

16. **B** This is a close one. (B) and (D) both weaken the argument by pointing out that all dogs do not always bark, but (B) is absolute. (D) is tentative, since a dog trained not to bark might do so by accident.

17. **B** The apparent discrepancy in the paragraph is why should arrests decline when there are fewer policemen to arrest the criminals? One explanation is that though the number of arrests has declined, the number of crimes has risen, and because there are fewer police officers, more crimes are unsolved.

18. **A** The complaint about ex-employees of the Department of Energy on the board, and the financial tie of the National Academy Board to the Energy Department indicate the officials' belief that the Department of Energy supports the nuclear power industry against the views of environmentalists.

19. **E** Though adding one or two environmentalists might help, they would still be outnumbered by the ten panel members with ties to the Department of Energy. Of the five choices, E offers the best hope of impartiality.

20. **C** (A) contradicts the statement's urging of economy. (B) introduces an irrelevant word, "terminology." (D) and (E) are *absolute* statements about assumptions, but the statement itself is *relative,* urging us only to simplify our assumptions *if one such simplification is possible; in other words, "If an issue is simple, don't complicate it."*

21. **E** The question demonstrates a solution and the fact that an alternative exists.

22. **E** (A) is obviously true. (B) also satisfies the conditions. (C) is correct, since 3.5 was required with a score of 800. (D) is correct, since we do not know anything about numbers of applicants. (E) is inconsistent, since a score of 1200 is required with a GPA of 2.5. (E) specifies a score *less than* 1200. Therefore, a GPA greater than (*not less than*) 2.5 would be required for admittance.

23. **B** To speak in positive terms about the increase in school degrees, the author must assume that the degrees indicate what they are supposed to indicate, that is, well-educated individuals. (A) and (E) are empty statements; (C) and (D) are altogether unsubstantiated by either expressed or implied information.

24. **E** Although the brand name is No-NOCK, the advertisement makes no claim to stop the engine from knocking. All the other claims are contained in the advertisement.

25. **D** The choice repudiates the suggestion that gentleness and graciousness were once part of the American character. (B), another choice worth considering, is not best because it does not address the temperament of tennis players as directly as does (D).

26. **B** By asking Dolores to choose between conventional and nuclear weapons, Fran has concluded that Dolores's statement calls for a decision. (C), worth considering, is not best because Fran supposes that Dolores has *not* made a choice—hence her question.

Section IV

Answers 1–6

From the information given, you should have constructed a diagram similar to this:

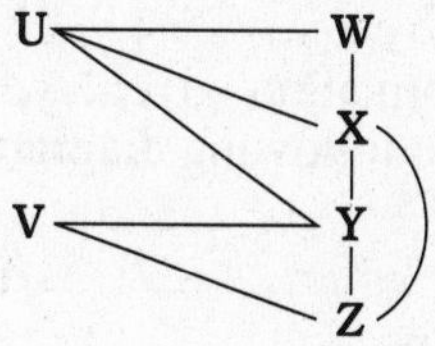

1. **B** From the diagram, if the group begins on island W, it could not reach island V in the eight days. Remember three days would have to be spent on W and three on X.

2. **B** From the diagram, if the group stays on island X for three nights, then the group cannot get to island V on the next visit.

3. **D** To answer this question, you must try each answer choice and eliminate the ones that do not connect. From the diagram, the only possible order listed would be U X Z V.

4. **E** From the diagram, if the group visits island W first, it could go to X to Y to Z, back to X, to U back to Y, to V and back to Z. A total of 9 visits. You could work from the choices, but remember to start from the highest number.

5. **D** From the diagram, the group could go from X to W to U to Y to V to Z to Y. This would be 6 different islands.

6. **E** Adding island T to the diagram connected only to U could look like this:

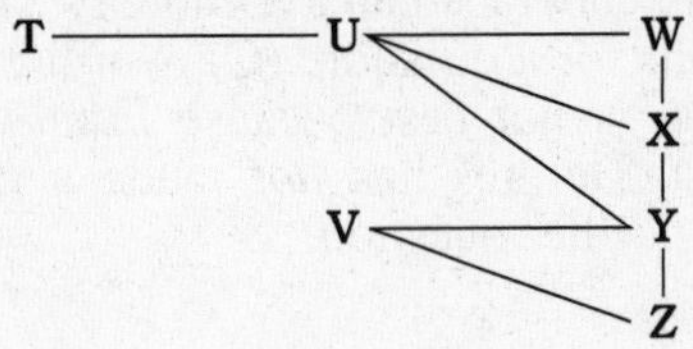

From this revised diagram, only (E) must be true. On the tenth day of a tour starting on Z, the tour group could be on island T. It would go from Z to Y to U to T or Z to X to U to T.

Answers 7–13

From the information given, you could have constructed the following diagram:

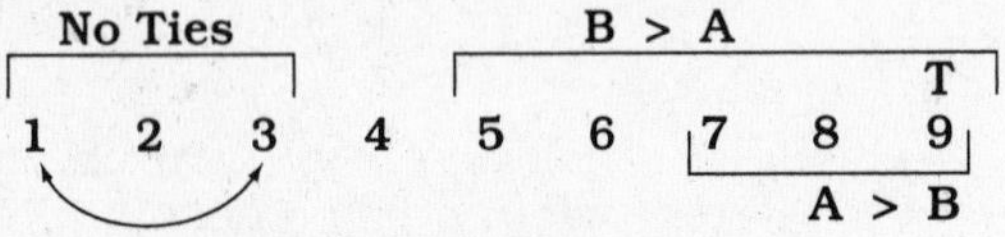

Notice the simple markings to show:

There are no ties in the first 3 games.
Team A wins more of the last 3 games than team B.
Team B wins more of the last 5 games than team A.
The last game is a tie.
Games 1 and 3 are won by the same team.

From this information you could deduce that team A wins either game 7 or 8, but not both, and team B cannot win any of the last 3 games. (If team A won both, team B could not win more of the last 5 games.) If team A wins game 7, then 8 is a tie, and if team A wins game 8, then 7 is a tie.

You could also deduce that team B must win games 5 and 6. Your diagram now looks like this:

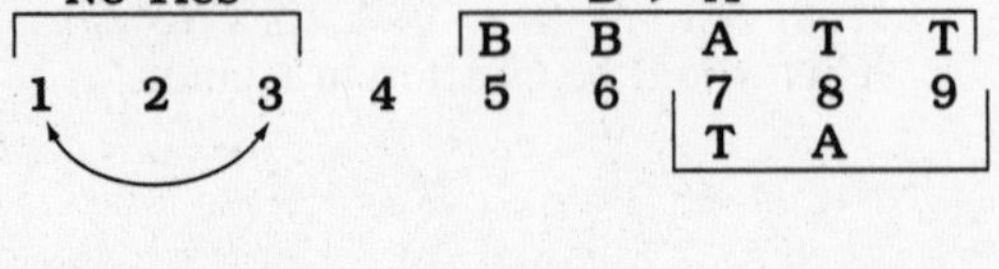

7. **C** From the information given, since games 1 and 3 are won by the same team, then one team wins at least 2 of the first 3 games.

8. **E** From the diagram, game 6 must be won by team B.

9. **A** From the diagram, if game 7 is won by team A, then game 8 must be a tie.

10. **E** From the diagram, you can see that (E) must be true.

11. **E** If team A wins games 1 and 4, then it must also win game 3. This would give team A four wins total, and team B could only win three, therefore team B could not win the series. For this question, the diagram would now look like this:

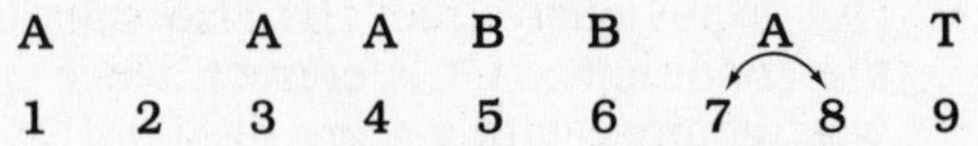

12. **B** If game 4 is won by the winner of game 5, then team B wins game 4. If game 2 is not won by the winner of game 3, then team B wins either game 2 or 3. This gives team B at least four wins and team A only a possible three wins, therefore B is the winner of the series.

13. **E** From the original diagram, team A must win either games 1, 2, and 3, or games 1, 3, and 4 to win the series. [This also eliminates choice (A).] If team B wins exactly one of the first four games [choice (B)], then team B cannot win the series as team A will win at least three games. If team A wins only three of the first seven games [choice (C)], then team A could still lose the series as team B could win games 2, 4, 5, and 6, with team A winning only games 1, 3, and 7. Team B could win the series by winning two of the first four games, eliminating choice (D).

Answers 14–18

Drawing a simple diagram, below, will help answer the questions.

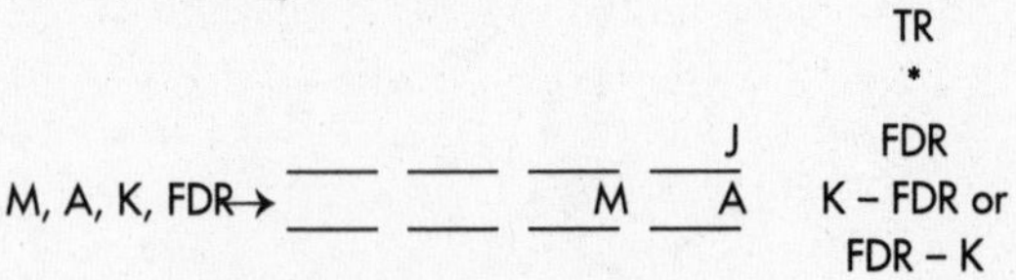

Note that, once Madison is placed in position 3 on the bottom, Adams must go in position 4 in order to leave spots for Kennedy to be adjacent to Franklin Delano Roosevelt.

14. **D** If Theodore Roosevelt is second from the left (on top), then Franklin Delano Roosevelt must be first on the bottom since one Roosevelt may not be above the other. Therefore, Kennedy must be second on the bottom.

15. **A** Adams must go to the far right on the bottom to allow Kennedy to be adjacent to Franklin Delano Roosevelt.

16. **D** If Washington and Kennedy are both first on their shelves, then Franklin Delano Roosevelt must be second on the lower shelf. Therefore, Theodore Roosevelt cannot be second on the top shelf and therefore must be third. Thus, statement D cannot be true.

17. **E** Since Adams must be on the right in the second row, only (E) is not possible.

18. **C** If Lincoln is next to Jefferson, that leaves Theodore Roosevelt and Washington for the first two positions on the top shelf. All of the choices are therefore true except (C) because that choice would place one Roosevelt above the other, which is not permitted.

Answers 19–24

19. **B** Since lima beans will not go with kidney beans or chili beans, they can go only with wax beans and garbanzos. Therefore, there is only one salad (limas + wax + garbanzos) that contains limas and that may be served at the party.

20. **C** The combinations of salads without chili beans are as follows:

1. garbanzos + wax + limas
2. garbanzos + limas + kidneys
3. garbanzos + wax + kidneys
4. wax + limas + kidneys

But remember that the *servable* salads may not include limas with kidneys or chili beans, thus reducing the number to two: garbanzos + wax + kidneys, and garbanzos + wax + limas.

21. **B** Without any restrictions there are 10 possible ways to choose three ingredients from a total of five:

CGW	GWL	WLK
CGL	GLK	
CGK	GWK	
CWL		
CWK		
CLK		

However, the imposed restrictions (lima beans do not go with kidney beans or chili beans) narrow the servable salads down to five:

CGW	GWL	~~WLK~~
~~CGL~~	~~GLK~~	
CGK	GWK	
~~CWL~~		
CWK		
~~CLK~~		

22. **E** From the chart above, we can see that garbanzos and wax beans appear more times in the servable salads. The other ingredients do not appear as often.

23. **C** From our chart we can see that having only enough wax beans for two salads will eliminate two of the four wax bean salads. Therefore, instead of five servable salads, there will now be only three.

24. **B** Again from our chart, if we eliminate the servable salads with garbanzos, we are left with only one servable salad: chili + wax + kidneys.

Section V

1. **B** The correct answer must use both premises. The first qualifies the assertion with "normally," so (A) will not follow, but (B) (with the qualifier "may") will. (C) may or may not be true, but it is not a logical conclusion based on the two premises. (D) and (E), like (A), do not use both premises.

2. **D** The question asked concerns the danger to public health, but the reply does not deal with this issue at all. It changes the subject.

3. **C** Reducing coffee consumption in general will not guarantee a healthier population (A) if "heavy" consumers do not reduce their coffee intake. Reducing coffee consumption would make those who drink a morning cup of coffee feel less well (B). (C) is a logical conclusion since heavy consumption increases heart attack risk. There is no information in the passage to justify the assertion about percolated coffee (D). If coffee may protect against colon cancer, (E) is not true.

4. **D** The issue of the danger of pesticides is addressed by (A), (C), and (E), while (B) calls into question the objectivity of the Food and Agriculture Department. But (D) deals with a different issue: air pollution. And if air pollution is a cause of illness, pesticides may be less to blame.

5. **A** The question contains its own prior judgment (underpay, unfair promotion policies) on what it asks, regardless of a "yes" or "no" answer. Similarly, the adjective "excessive" and the adverb "unfairly" prejudge any answer in choice (A).

6. **E** Since fares have risen, the cost of fuel has risen or there are no fare wars. And if there are no fare wars, the number of passengers is larger. Only (E) cannot be true. (B) is possible if fuel costs have risen, and there are fare wars.

7. **B** Though the argument for a decline in fishing off Newfoundland is convincing, the generalization that the "fishing industry in the Americas" will disappear is here based only on information about the Atlantic waters off Canada. It is possible that other areas have not been so affected.

8. **C** The advertisement asserts filter cigarettes cannot have great taste. A reasonable inference is that Gold Star is not a filter cigarette. (A) is contradicted by this ad without visual appeal. (B) is contradicted by this ad, which does not specifically praise a brand. (D) is illogical given the existence of this ad. Nothing in the ad supports (E).

9. **D** Choices (A), (B), and (C) strengthen the case for building the toll road. The environmentalists may be able to make their case for one of the other possible routes that, if less direct, would not disturb the reserve. With the information we have, the value of (E) is indeterminable.

10. **A** There is nothing in the paragraph to support (E), and there are details that contradict (B), (C), and (D). That "sales in the United States continue to increase" supports (A).

11. **E** The passage does not give the information that would lead to the conclusion in (A), (B), or (C). (E) is a better answer than (D), the odds against the heavy smoker being 40 in 100 as opposed to 25 in 100 for the light smoker.

12. **C** The presence of wolf bones and walrus bones near a village is not evidence that wolves were trained to haul sleds; it does not disprove the theory, however.

13. **B** Choices (A), (C), (D), and (E) would undermine the theory. But if wolves were easily domesticated and trained, it would make the theory of their domestication by Stone-Age tribes more plausible.

14. **A** The author makes his point by invective, an abrasive verbal attack.

15. **D** The first sentence asserts the needlessness of commenting on the picture; the second nonetheless makes a detailed criticism.

16. **B** If popcorn attracts rodents and insects, warehouses where packages using popcorn are stored would have vermin problems.

17. **B** Only (B) is a necessary assumption. It must be assumed that no other items (for example dressings, recipes, spices, etc.) are sold at the stand in order to conclude definitively that everything sold there is delicious.

18. **B** Though (E) is probably true, it is not a conclusion based on the information in the passage. But the passage does assert that only 19.67 percent (11.9 plus 7.7) of the eligible voters in the Democratic and Republican parties went to the polls.

19. **A** Choices (B) and (C), although true, are not relevant, while (D) and (E) are probably untrue. That it is only in the schools that the tobacco spokesmen are silent supports the inference of (A).

20. **C** In both paragraphs, the author disputes the interpretations of his opponents.

21. **D** The author assumes that an audience is able to evaluate a work and determine its own course of action.

22. **E** The opening lines describe esteem without popularity, later followed by popular success.

23. **D** The "But" introducing the last sentence suggests that a contrast, a disadvantage of coffee, is to follow. Either (C) or (D) is possible, but since exercise has not been an issue, (D) is the better choice.

24. **A** Only choice (A) must be true. There may be other performers as well as the chorus members (the orchestra, for example) in the performance, so (E) is incorrect.

25. **C** The passage draws an analogy comparing corrupt politicians to vermin.

ANALYZING YOUR LSAT SCORE: A BROAD RANGE SCORE APPROXIMATOR

The chart that follows is designed to give you a *general approximation* of the number of questions you need to get right to fall into a general score range and percentile rank on your LSAT. It should help you see if you are in the "ballpark" of the score you need. This range approximator is *not* designed to give you an exact score or to predict your LSAT score. The actual LSAT will have questions that are similar to the ones encountered in this book, but some questions may be either easier or more difficult. The variance in difficulty levels and testing conditions can affect your score range.

Obtaining Your Approximate Score Range

Although the LSAT uses a very precise formula to convert raw scores to scaled scores, for the purpose of this broad range approximation simply total the number of questions you answered correctly. Next divide the total number of correct answers by the total number of questions on the sample test. This will give you the percent correct. Now look at the following chart to see the approximate percent you need to get right to get into your score range. Remember, on the actual test one of the sections is experimental and, therefore, doesn't count toward your score.

On the actual LSAT, the percent of correct answers to get certain scores will vary slightly from test to test, depending on the number of problems and level of difficulty of that particular exam.

An average score is approximately 151.

If you are not in the range that you wish to achieve, check the approximate percent of correct answers that you need to achieve that range. Carefully analyze the types of errors you are making and continue practicing and analyzing. Remember, in trying to approximate a score range, you must take the complete sample test under strict time and test conditions.

Approximate Scaled Score Range	*Approx. % of Correct Answers Necessary*	*Approx. Score Percentile for Test-takers (Est. % below)*
171–180	93% and up	98–99.9
161–170	79%–92%	86–97
151–160	62%–78%	52–83
141–150	44%–61%	17–48
131–140	30%–43%	3–15
121–130	20%–29%	0–2

PART III

Profiles of Law Schools

CHAPTER 12

Overview of ABA-Approved Law Schools

There are currently 186 law schools approved by the American Bar Association (including the U.S. Army Judge Advocate General's School, which is not profiled here). The ABA is the largest organization of lawyers in the world, and its members come from every state in the United States. Because the ABA is a voluntary bar association, its members are not required to join in order to practice law, although nearly 40 percent of all American lawyers are currently members.

The power to grant individuals a license to practice law resides in the highest court of each state; thus, every jurisdiction administers its own bar examination, character and fitness inquiry, and licensing procedures for admission to the bar. The states also administer the disciplinary process for sanctioning lawyers who violate ethics rules of professional conduct. Because each state adopts its own rules establishing who is eligible to take the bar examination, some states require all candidates to be graduates of ABA-approved law schools, while others do not (see Chapter 14 for a discussion of non-ABA-approved law schools).

Authority to approve the right of educational institutions to grant degrees has been delegated by Congress to the U.S. Department of Education, which in turn delegates the responsibility for approving degree programs to designated accrediting agencies. In the case of law schools, the agency that has been given this power is the American Bar Association. Within the ABA, accreditation matters are handled by the Accreditation Committee of the Section of Legal Education and Admissions to the Bar with the support of a Consultant on Legal Education. The standards of approval themselves are promulgated by the ABA's governing body, the House of Delegates, upon recommendation of the Section of Legal Education. The Accreditation Committee is charged with the inspection and evaluation of law schools and law school programs, not only when a school or program is started, but also periodically during the life of the institution. The purpose of the accreditation process is to assure that every law school in the United States meets a common set of quality standards, and that every degree awarded confers the same benefit on recipients as comparable degrees at other ABA-approved law schools.

The imprimatur of the ABA carries great weight with state bar admission authorities, and every state allows graduates of any ABA law school to sit for the bar exam. From an applicant's standpoint, graduating from an ABA-approved law school is like a stamp of approval, a ticket to seek admission to practice law anywhere in the country. From the point of view of a law student, ABA approval is a guarantee that certain basic educational requirements have been met, and that the education they receive will be comparable to the education at any other ABA-approved law school. Additional information on the accreditation process and law schools generally may be obtained by writing the ABA Section of Legal Education and Admissions to the Bar, 750 North Lake Shore Drive, Chicago, IL 60611.

This does not mean that law schools are all the same. As this Guide demonstrates, law schools come in many shapes and sizes. Some are more difficult to get into than others. Some offer special programs that set them apart from other schools. Some serve special audiences that others do not. Some are rated more highly than others. Neither the ABA nor this Guide attempts to rank law schools. The ABA certifies that approved schools meet minimum standards, but encourages them to seek to exceed those standards. Barron's *Guide to Law Schools* provides a wealth of information to help applicants make the difficult decision about which law school is best for them. Implicit in this approach is the notion that different schools are right for different people, and that no single school is best for everyone.

The ranking of law schools by some publications may provide interesting reading, and may reflect the relative prestige of law schools as filtered through the eyes of the publication's editors, but the uncritical use of such rankings without looking at the facts and figures behind them can distort the process of selecting a law school. The real question should be: What are the top ten schools for you personally? The question is not: What are the top ten schools for some faceless editor at some magazine or publishing house?

During 1995 and into 1996, the American Bar Association conducted a thorough review of the standards for approval of law school. A revised set of standards was adopted by the ABA House of Delegates in August, 1996. The impetus for this review came in part from criticism of the standards both inside and outside the ABA, as well as recognition by leaders in the Section of Legal Education and Admissions to the Bar that legal education is changing, particularly in the area of skills education, such as teaching students the practice skills they will need to be successful practitioners, not just the legal theory and analysis characteristic of traditional legal education. These changes to the standards will eventually be integrated into the fabric of the law schools that seek ABA accreditation or reaccreditation.

The following table provides information about the tuition, programs, and academic community at the schools that have been approved by the American Bar Association. This is designed to provide a quick overview of the schools, and should be used in conjunction with the detailed profiles of the individual schools that can be found in Chapter 13.

Most of the information on these charts should be self-explanatory. If you are uncertain about the significance of any item, consult the profile of the school for additional information or explanation.

In several sections of the table, a check (✓) indicates "yes" and a blank indicates "no." For example, under Calendar, the possibilities are Fall, Winter, Spring, and Summer. At any given school, you can begin your law studies only at those times indicated by a check.

Since most law schools operate on a semester basis, information about credits and required courses is given in terms of semester hours. If a school operates on the quarter system, the abbreviation *qh* is added.

Similarly, tuition is generally given for a full year. When part-time tuition is given per credit, this refers to semester courses unless the abbreviation *qh* is used.

Where a category does not apply to a school or when information was not available, the cell is left blank.

INSTITUTION		APPLICATIONS			TUITION		CALENDAR				PROGRAMS							ENROLLED	STUDENT BODY				FACULTY	LIBRARY	
	Profile Page	Fee	Deadline	Deadline Financial Aid	In State Full Time (Part Time)	Out of State Full Time (Part Time)	Fall	Winter	Spring	Summer	Day	Evening	Credits for JD	Required Creits for Courses	Transferable Summer Courses	Joint Degree	Graduate Law Degree	Full Time (Part Time)	Average Age First Year	% Women	% Minority	Attrition Rate %	Full Time (Part Time)	Volumes	Microforms
Albany Law School 80 New Scotland Avenue Albany, NY 12208 518-445-2326 Fax: 518-445-2369 *admissions@mail.als.edu*	188	$50	March 15	$22,250 rolling	$22,250 ($16,688)	($16,688)	✓				✓		87	31	✓	✓	711 ✓	(60)	27	53	20	43 10	(34)	260,380	1,583,827
American University (Washington College of Law) 4801 Massachusetts Avenue, N.W. Washington, DC 20016-8186 202-274-4101 Fax: 202-274-4107 *wcladmit@wcl.american.edu*	190	$55	March 1	March 1	$26,050 ($18,335)	$26,050 ($18,335)	✓				✓	✓	86	34	✓	✓	✓	996 (310)	24	62	27	1	77 (202)	479,412	
Appalachian School of Law P.O. Box 2825 Grundy, VA 24614 276-935-4349 Fax: 276-935-8261 *vkeene@asl.edu*	192	$40	rolling	rolling	$1,600		✓				✓		90				✓	238	29	43	10		15 (8)	76,275	87,651
Arizona State University (College of Law/Armstrong Hall) Box 877906 Tempe, AZ 85287-7906 480-965-1474 Fax: 480-727-7930 *chitra.damania@asu.edu*	194	$45	March 1	rolling	$5,162	$13,028	✓				✓	✓	87	37	✓	✓		534	27	50	29	3	37 (40)	394,805	131,321
Baylor University (School of Law) P.O. Box 97288 Waco, TX 76798-7288 254-710-1911 Fax: 254-710-2316 *becky-beck@baylor.edu*	196	$40	March 1	May 1	$16,716	$16,716	✓		✓	✓	✓		126	79	✓	✓		425	24	40	12	5	21 (34)	194,429	101,287
Boston College (Law School) 885 Centre Street Newton, MA 02459 617-552-4351 Fax: 617-552-2917 *bclawadm@bc.edu*	198	$65	March 1	March 15	$25,854	$25,854	✓				✓		85	38		✓		805	24	51	18	1	48 (41)	403,537	1,031,218
Boston University (School of Law) 765 Commonwealth Avenue Boston, MA 02215 617-353-3100 *bulawadm@bu.edu*	200	$60	March 1	March 1	$25,872	$25,872	✓				✓	✓	84	33		✓	✓	837	23	53	22	4	69 (24)	586,557	258,428
Brigham Young University (J. Reuben Clark Law School) 342 JRCB Brigham Young University Provo, UT 84602 801-378-4277 Fax: 801-378-5897 *wilcock@lawgate.byu.edu*	202	$50	Feb 1	March 1	$6,140	$9,210	✓				✓		90	36		✓	✓	480	26	37	14	1	38 (32)	441,860	149,367

INSTITUTION	Profile Page	APPLICATIONS: Fee	APPLICATIONS: Deadline	APPLICATIONS: Deadline Financial Aid	TUITION: In State Full Time (Part Time)	TUITION: Out of State Full Time (Part Time)	CALENDAR: Fall	CALENDAR: Winter	CALENDAR: Spring	CALENDAR: Summer	PROGRAMS: Day	PROGRAMS: Evening	PROGRAMS: Credits for JD	PROGRAMS: Required Creits for Courses	PROGRAMS: Transferable Summer Courses	PROGRAMS: Joint Degree	PROGRAMS: Graduate Law Degree	ENROLLED: Full Time (Part Time)	STUDENT BODY: Average Age First Year	STUDENT BODY: % Women	STUDENT BODY: % Minority	STUDENT BODY: Attrition Rate %	FACULTY: Full Time (Part Time)	LIBRARY: Volumes	LIBRARY: Microforms
Brooklyn Law School 250 Joralemon Street Brooklyn, NY 11201 718-780-7906 Fax: 718-780-0395 *admitq@brooklaw.edu*	204	$60	April 1	March 15	$26,745 ($20,100)	$26,745 ($20,100)	✓				✓	✓	86	35	✓	✓	✓	1072 (443)	25	51	22	3	67 (97)	511,570	1,195,345
California Western School of Law 225 Cedar Street San Diego, CA 92101-3046 619-525-1401 Fax: 619-615-1401 *admissions@cwsl.edu*	206	$45	April 1	March 16	$23,420 ($17,090)	$23,420 ($17,090)	✓		✓		✓		89	43	✓	✓	✓	692 (98)	27	55	31	19	38 (55)	287,445	715,738
Campbell University **(Norman Adrian Wiggins School of Law)** P.O. Box 158 Buies Creek, NC 27506 910-893-1754 Fax: 910-893-1780 *culaw@webster.campbell.edu*	208	$50	open	open	$19,988	$19,988	✓				✓	✓	90 sem.	73		✓	✓	311	26	47	7	10	20 (17)	177,493	56,998
Capital University **(Law School)** 303 East Broad Street Columbus, OH 43215-3200 614-236-6500 Fax: 614-236-6972 *admissions@law.capital.edu*	210	$35	April 1	April 1	$18,009 ($11,178)	$18,009 ($11,178)	✓				✓	✓	86	44	✓	✓	✓	409 (353)	28	48	12	8	30 (83)	246,619	42,753
Case Western Reserve University **(School of Law)** 11075 East Boulevard Cleveland, OH 44106 216-368-3600 Fax: 216-368-6144 *lawadmissions@po.cwru.edu* or/ *awmoney@po.cwru.edu*	212	$40	April 1	May 1	$23,300 ($971/hr)	$23,300 ($971/hr)	✓				✓		88	33	✓	✓	✓	618 (12)	24			3	47 (88)	378,317	474,557
Catholic University of America **(Columbus School of Law)** Cardinal Station Washington, DC 20064 (202) 319-5151 Fax: (202) 319-6285 *admission@law.edu*	214	$55	March 1	March 1	$25,092 ($18,937)	$25,092 ($18,937)	✓				✓	✓	84	33	✓	✓		654 (278)	23	52	22	4	46 (87)	322,816	52,864
Catholic University of Puerto Rico **(School of Law)** Avenida Las Americas-Station 6 Ponce, PR 00732 809-841-2000	216		Check	Check			✓				✓	✓	94	82		✓	✓	220 (220)	24	50		11	14 (18)	135,000	15,000
Chapman University **(School of Law)** One University Drive Orange, CA 92866 714-628-2500 Fax: 714-628-2501 *heyer@chapman.edu*	218	$50	open	April 1	$23,200 ($15,950)	$23,200 ($15,950)	✓				✓	✓	88	51 to 52	✓	✓		206 (105)	28	48	26	12	21 (43)	249,764	184,488

City University of New York at Queens College (School of Law) 65-21 Main Street Flushing, NY 11367-1300 718-340-4210 Fax: 718-340-4435 *admissions@mail.law.cuny.edu*	220	$40	March 15	May 15	$5,700	$8,930	✓				✓		91	60	✓			442	29	60	42	10	37 (18)	267,244	34,653
Cleveland State University (Cleveland-Marshall College of Law) 1801 Euclid Avenue Cleveland, OH 44115 216-687-2304 Fax: 216-687-6881	222	$35	April 1	March 1	$8,899 ($6,846)	$17,798 ($13,792)	✓				✓	✓	90	43	✓	✓	✓	520 (307)	27	47	11	10	44 (27)	479,214	58,129
College of William & Mary (William & Mary Law School) P.O. Box 8795 Williamsburg, VA 23187-8795 757-221-3785 Fax: 757-221-3261 *lawadm@.wm.edu*	224	$40	March 1	Feb 15	$10,400	$19,750	✓				✓		86	35	✓	✓	✓	666	25	42	16	3	33 (49)	379,000	840,000
Columbia University (School of Law) 435 West 116th Street New York, NY 10027 212-854-2670 Fax: 212-854-1109 *admissions@law.columbia.edu*	226	$65	Feb 15	March 1	$30,868	$30,868	✓				✓		83	35		✓	✓	1139	24	51	32		91 (52)	1,020,000	737,500
Cornell University (Law School) Myron Taylor Hall Ithaca, NY 14853-4901 607-255-5141 Fax: 607-255-7193 *lawadmit@postoffice.law.cornell.edu*	228	$65	Feb 1	March 15	$29,200	$29,200	✓				✓		84	36	✓	✓	✓	552	25	48	26	1	40 (10)	641,000	5,500
Creighton University (School of Law) 2500 California Plaza Omaha, NE 68178 402-280-2872 Fax: 402-280-3161 *admit@culaw.creighton.edu*	230	$45	May 1	July 1	$18,506 ($620/hr)	$18,506 ($620/hr)	✓				✓	✓	94	40	✓	✓		444 (23)	26	42	12		29 (45)	278,917	120,733
De Paul University (College of Law) 25 East Jackson Boulevard Chicago, IL 60604 312-362-6831 Fax: 312-362-5280 *lawinfo@wppost.depaul.edu*	232	$50	April 1	March 1	$23,900 ($15,500)	$23,900 ($15,500)	✓				✓	✓	86	37	✓	✓	✓	671 (264)	24	54	29	3	49 (85)	356,525	998,028
Drake University (Law School) 2507 University Avenue Des Moines, IA 50311 515-271-2782 Fax: 515-271-1990 *lawadmit@drake.edu*	234	$40	April 1	March 1	$18,800 ($625/hr)	$18,800 ($625/hr)	✓			✓	✓		90	41	✓	✓		384 (14)	25	50	11	8	30 (22)	300,000	100,000
Duke University (School of Law) Science and Towerview Drive, Box 90393 Durham, NC 27708 919-613-7020 Fax: 919-613-7257 *admissions@law.duke.edu*	236	$65	Jan 1	March 15	$28,250	$28,250	✓			✓	✓		84	30		✓	✓	660	24	43	25	1	36 (42)	535,000	71,000

INSTITUTION	Profile Page	APPLICATIONS: Fee	APPLICATIONS: Deadline	APPLICATIONS: Deadline Financial Aid	TUITION: In State Full Time (Part Time)	TUITION: Out of State Full Time (Part Time)	CALENDAR: Fall	CALENDAR: Winter	CALENDAR: Spring	CALENDAR: Summer	PROGRAMS: Day	PROGRAMS: Evening	PROGRAMS: Credits for JD	PROGRAMS: Required Creits for Courses	PROGRAMS: Transferable Summer Courses	PROGRAMS: Joint Degree	PROGRAMS: Graduate Law Degree	ENROLLED: Full Time (Part Time)	STUDENT BODY: Average Age First Year	STUDENT BODY: % Women	STUDENT BODY: % Minority	STUDENT BODY: Attrition Rate %	FACULTY: Full Time (Part Time)	LIBRARY: Volumes	LIBRARY: Microforms
Duquesne University (School of Law) 900 Locust Street, Hanley Hall Pittsburgh, PA 15282 412-396-6296 *campion@duq.edu*	238	$50	April 1	May 31	$18,124 ($13,928)	$18,124 ($13,928)	✓				✓	✓	86	33	✓	✓		351 (295)	25	48		2	24 (45)	265,195	210,000
Emory University (School of Law) Gambrell Hall Atlanta, GA 30322 404-727-6801 Fax: 404-727-2477 *jbalej@law.emory.edu*	240	$65	March 1	March 1	$26,318	$26,318	✓				✓	✓	90	45		✓	✓	638	24	54	22	3	49 (54)	368,000	71,734
Florida Coastal School of Law 7555 Beach Boulevard Jacksonville, FL 32216 904-680-7710 Fax: 904-680-7776 *admissions@fcsl.edu*	242	$50	open		$19,340 ($15,470)	$19,340 ($15,470)	✓		✓		✓	✓	87	56	✓			248 (204)	28	47	21	8	27 (31)	207,870	439,452
Florida State University (College of Law) 425 W. Jefferson St. Tallahassee, FL 32306-1601 850-644-3787 Fax: 850-644-7284 *admissions@law.fsu.edu*	244	$20	Feb 15	April 1	$5,286	$17,585	✓				✓	✓	88	35	✓	✓		714	25	46	21	1	49 (15)	432,878	911,330
Fordham University (School of Law) 140 West 62nd Street New York, NY 10023 212-626-6810	246	$60	March 1	May 15	$28,100 ($21,075)	$28,100 ($21,075)	✓				✓	✓	83	39	✓	✓	✓	1109 (350)	24	50	24	2	68 (257)	578,718	1,379,151
Franklin Pierce Law Center 2 White Street Concord, NH 03301 603-228-9217 Fax: 603-228-1074 *admissions@fplc.edu*	248	$55	May 1	open	$19,962 ($14,972)		✓				✓	✓	84	39	✓	✓	✓	381 (8)	28	36	12	10	24 (37)	143,418	507,000
George Mason University (School of Law) 3301 North Fairfax Drive Arlington, VA 22201-4426 703-993-8010 Fax: 703-993-8260 *arichar5@gmu.edu*	250	$35	March 15		$8,092 ($6,358)	$18,704 ($14,696)	✓				✓	✓	84	43	✓			371 (361)	27	42	10	3	37 (89)	400,000	886,000
George Washington University (Law School) 2000 H Street, N.W. Washington, DC 20052 202-739-0648 *jd@main.n/c.gwu.edu*	252	$65	March 1		$28,045 ($987/hr)	$28,045 ($987/hr)	✓				✓	✓	84	34	✓	✓	✓	1233 (256)	24	47	32	1	67 (211)	563,509	1,223,445

Georgetown University (Law Center) 600 New Jersey Avenue, N.W. Washington, DC 20001 202-662-9010 Fax: 202-662-9439 *admis@law.georgetown.edu*	254	$65	Feb 1	March 1	$28,040 ($22,000)	$28,040 ($22,000)	✓				✓	✓	83	31	✓	✓	✓	1603 (426)	24	52	26	1	102 (100)	1,028,658	2,331,239
Georgia State University (College of Law) P.O. Box 4037 Atlanta, GA 30302-4037 404-651-2048 Fax: (404) 651-2048 *cjjackson@gsu.edu*	256	$30	March 15	April 1	$3,696 ($154/hr)	$14,784 ($616/hr)	✓				✓	✓	90	43	✓	✓		452 (192)	29	51	15	11	42 (28)	145,617	623,675
Golden Gate University (School of Law) 536 Mission Street San Francisco, CA 94105-2968 415-442-6630	258	$40	April 15	March 1	$22,910 ($15,800)	$22,910 ($15,800)	✓		✓		✓	✓	88	54	✓	✓	✓	418 (334)	26	57	28	17	39 (121)	117,371	126,112
Gonzaga University (School of Law) Box 3528 Spokane, WA 99220-3528 509-323-5532 Fax: 509-323-5744 *admissions@lawschool.gonzaga.edu*	260	$40	April 1	Feb 1	$20,340 ($678/hr)	$20,340 ($678/hr)	✓				✓		90	59	✓	✓		480 (21)	27	48	15	10	33 (36)	152,933	109,870
Hamline University (School of Law) 1536 Hewitt Avenue St. Paul, MN 55104-1284 651-523-2461 Fax: 651-523-3064 *lawadm@gw.hamline.edu*	262	$40	April 1	rolling	$19,090 ($13,720)	$19,090 ($13,720)	✓				✓	✓	88	33	✓	✓	✓	473 (80)	25	56	12	6	30 (52)	150,135	110,923
Harvard University (Harvard Law School) Cambridge, MA 02138 617-495-3179 *jdadmiss@law.harvard.edu*	264	$70	Feb 1		$27,500		✓				✓		82	30		✓	✓	1673	24	45	28	1	80 (90)	2,039,000	187,600
Hofstra University (School of Law) 121 Hofstra University Hempstead, NY 11549 516-463-5916 Fax: 516-463-6264 *lawpts@hofstra.edu*	266	$60	April 15	June 1	$25,752 ($19,314)	$25,752 ($19,314)	✓				✓		87	39	✓	✓	✓	712 (107)	26	47	19	11	40 (59)	516,621	1,758,120
Howard University (Howard University) 2900 Van Ness Street, N.W. Washington, DC 20008 202-806-8008 Fax: 202-806-8162 *admissions@law.howard.edu*	268	$60	March 31	April 1	$13,030		✓		✓		✓	✓	88	n/av	✓	✓	✓	412 (3)	25	60	94	5	33 (23)	283,000	54,000
Illinois Institute of Technology (Chicago-Kent College of Law) 565 West Adams Street Chicago, IL 60661 312-906-5020 Fax: 312-906-5274 *admit@kentlaw.edu*	270	$45	March 1	March 15	$24,220 ($17,770)	$24,220 ($17,770)	✓				✓	✓	87	42	✓	✓	✓	708 (259)	25	48	13	10	63 (105)	560,000	139,045

INSTITUTION		APPLICATIONS			TUITION		CALENDAR				PROGRAMS							ENROLLED	STUDENT BODY				FACULTY	LIBRARY	
	Profile Page	Fee	Deadline	Deadline Financial Aid	In State Full Time (Part Time)	Out of State Full Time (Part Time)	Fall	Winter	Spring	Summer	Day	Evening	Credits for JD	Required Creits for Courses	Transferable Summer Courses	Joint Degree	Graduate Law Degree	Full Time (Part Time)	Average Age First Year	% Women	% Minority	Attrition Rate %	Full Time (Part Time)	Volumes	Microforms
Indiana University at Bloomington (School of Law) 211 S. Indiana Avenue Bloomington, IN 47405-1001 812-855-4765 Fax: 812-855-0555 *Lawadmis@indiana.edu*	272	$35	open	March 1	$6,850	$17,568	✓			✓	✓		86	36	✓	✓	✓	608 (4)	24	43	20	3	38 (16)	591,504	1,138,543
Indiana University-Purdue University at Indianapolis (Indiana University School of Law-Indianapolis) 530 West New York Street Indianapolis, IN 46202-3225 317-274-2459 Fax: 317-274-3955 *khmiller@iupui.edu*	274	$35	March 1	March 1	$8,568 ($5,528)	$19,696 ($12,707)	✓				✓	✓	90	37	✓	✓	✓	550 (291)	27	47	13	3	47 (40)	530,267	60,524
Inter-American University of Puerto Rico (School of Law) P.O. Box 70351 San Juan, PR 00936-8351 787-751-1912, ext. 2013	276		March		$12,000 ($9,600)	$12,000 ($9,600)	✓				✓	✓	92	62				373 (350)	24	47		8	20 (16)	160,098	139,963
John Marshall Law School 315 South Plymouth Court Chicago, IL 60604 312-987-1406 Fax: 312-427-5136 *admission@jmls.edu*	278		March 1	Check	$21,000 ($700/hr)	$700/hr ($700/hr)	✓		✓		✓	✓	90	52	✓	✓	✓	719 (433)	25	43	17	5	56 (138)	353,737	55,710
Lewis and Clark College (Northwestern School of Law) 10015 Southwest Terwilliger Boulevard Portland, OR 97219 503-768-6613 Fax: 503-768-6850 *lawadmss@lclark.edu*	280	$50	March 15	March 1	$22,090 ($16,570)	$22,090 ($16,570)	✓				✓	✓	86	28-35			✓	486 (189)	28	49	16	7	38 (54)	465,803	268,075
Louisiana State University (Paul M. Hebert Law Center) Baton Rouge, LA 70803 225-578-8646 Fax: 225-578-8647 *mforbe1@lsu.edu*	282	$25	Feb 1	April 1	$6,711 ($4,891)	$12,552 ($9,149)	✓				✓		97	62	✓	✓	✓	637	25	46	13	18	42 (35)	406,308	890,000
Loyola Marymount University (Loyola Law School) 919 S. Albany Street Los Angeles, CA 90015 213-736-1180 *admissions@lls.edu*	284	$50	Feb 1	March 1	$24,924 ($16,666)	$24,924 ($16,666)	✓				✓	✓	87	41	✓	✓	✓	1012 (341)	24	52	37	5	66 (69)	533,799	1,256,026

Loyola University of Chicago (School of Law) One East Pearson Street Chicago, IL 60611 312-915-7170 Fax: 312-915-7906 *law-admissions@luc.edu*	286	$50	April 1	March 1	$24,370 ($18,278)	$24,370 ($18,278)	✓			✓	✓	86	46	✓	✓	✓	511 (220)	25	60	20	3	32 (108)	172,165	196,710
Loyola University of New Orleans (School of Law) 7214 St. Charles Avenue New Orleans, LA 70118 504-861-5575 Fax: 504-861-5772 *ladmit@loyno.edu*	288	$40	April 1		$22,568 ($15,288)	$22,568 ($15,288)	✓					90	50	✓	✓	✓	557 (209)	26	52	20	12	28 (57)	300,000	119,380
Marquette University (Law School) Office of Admissions, Sensenbrenner Hall, P.O. Box 1881 Milwaukee, WI 53201-1881 414-288-6767 Fax: 414-288-0676 *law.admission@marquette.edu*	290	$40	April 1	April 1	$21,550 ($895/hr)	$21,550 ($895/hr)	✓			✓	✓	90	34	✓	✓	✓	616 (169)	25	45	11	2	35 (65)	159,238	133,167
Mercer University (Walter F. George School of Law) 1021 Georgia Ave. Macon, GA 31207 478-301-2605 Fax: 478-301-2989 *Sutton_me@mercer.edu*	292	$45	March 15	April 1	$21,190	$21,190	✓			✓		91	65	✓	✓		432 (3)	25	49	15	5	27 (27)	304,497	
Michigan State University (Detroit College of Law) 316 Law College Bldg. East Lansing, MI 48824-1300 517-432-0222 Fax: 517-432-0098 *heatleya@pilot.msu.edu*	294	$50	April 15	July 2	$19,227 ($15,912)	$19,227 ($15,912)	✓			✓	✓	88	56	✓	✓		596 (184)	28	40	14	6	28 (37)	118,631	91,094
Mississippi College (School of Law) 151 E. Griffith Street Jackson, MS 39201 601-925-7150 *pevans@mc.edu*	296	$40	May 1		$15,600	$15,600	✓			✓		90	36	✓	✓		375	26	44	10	7	18 (18)	253,000	540,000
New England School of Law 154 Stuart Street Boston, MA 02116 617-422-7210 Fax: 617-422-7200 *admit@admin.nesl.edu*	298	$50	March 15	April 17	$18,560 ($13,920)	$18,560 ($13,920)	✓			✓	✓	84	43	✓			611 (345)	28	55	18	13	33 (69)	322,506	715,067
New York Law School 57 Worth Street New York, NY 10013-2960 212-431-2888 Fax: 212-966-1522 *admissions@nyls.edu*	300	$50	April 1	April 15	$23,268 ($16,588)	$23,268 ($16,588)	✓			✓	✓	86	38		✓		921 (453)	27	48	24	3	53 (82)	475,188	981,917
New York University (School of Law) 110 West Third Street New York, NY 10012 212-998-6060 Fax: 212-995-4527	302	$70	Feb 1	April 15	$30,650	$30,650	✓			✓	✓	82	44		✓	✓	1296	25	50	24	1	94 (75)	1,012,051	138,600

INSTITUTION		APPLICATIONS			TUITION		CALENDAR				PROGRAMS							ENROLLED	STUDENT BODY				FACULTY	LIBRARY	
	Profile Page	Fee	Deadline	Deadline Financial Aid	In State Full Time (Part Time)	Out of State Full Time (Part Time)	Fall	Winter	Spring	Summer	Day	Evening	Credits for JD	Required Creits for Courses	Transferable Summer Courses	Joint Degree	Graduate Law Degree	Full Time (Part Time)	Average Age First Year	% Women	% Minority	Attrition Rate %	Full Time (Part Time)	Volumes	Microforms
North Carolina Central University (School of Law) 1512 S. Alston Avenue Durham, NC 27707 919-560-6333 Fax: 919-560-6339 *jfaucett@wpo.nccu.edu*	304	$30	April 15	Feb 1	$2,288 ($2,288)	$11,392 ($11,392)	✓				✓	✓	88	65	✓	✓		255 (107)		56	53		23 (9)	284,115	639,314
Northeastern University (School of Law) 400 Huntington Avenue Boston, MA 02115 617-373-2395 Fax: 617-373-8865 *m.knoll@neu.edu*	306	$65	March 1	Feb 15	$26,820	$26,820	✓				✓		103	50	✓	✓		588	25	58	22	2	33 (18)	251,000	113,535
Northern Illinois University (College of Law) Swen Parson Hall De Kalb, IL 60115-2890 815-753-1420 Fax: 815-753-4501 *lawadm@niu.edu*	308	$40	May 15	March 1	$6,360	$12,720	✓				✓		90	36	✓	✓		287 (21)	27	46	21	9	26 (16)	222,774	477,561
Northern Kentucky University (Salmon P. Chase College of Law) Louie B. Nunn Hall Highland Heights, KY 41099 859-572-6476 Fax: 859-572-6081 *brayg@nku.edu*	310	$30	March 1	April 1	$6,408 ($4,806)	$14,004 ($10,512)	✓				✓	✓	90	42	✓	✓	✓	203 (173)	29	45	6	19	27 (33)	33,117	861
Northwestern University (School of Law) 357 East Chicago Avenue Chicago, IL 60611 312-503-8465 Fax: 312-503-0178 *nulawadm@law.northwestern.edu*	312	$70	Feb 15	March 1	$30,226	$30,226	✓				✓		86	32		✓	✓	657	25	49	30	1	59 (149)	656,775	209,977
Nova Southeastern University (Shepard Broad Law Center) 3305 College Avenue Fort Lauderdale, FL 33314-7721 954-262-6117 Fax: 954-262-3844 *admission@nsu.law.nova.edu*	314	$50	March 1	March 1	$19,970 ($14,980)	$19,970 ($14,980)	✓				✓	✓	90	44	✓	✓		726 (212)		49	29	8	45 (64)	314,036	137,029
Ohio Northern University (Claude W. Pettit College of Law) 525 South Main Street Ada, OH 45810 419-772-2211 Fax: 419-772-1487 *l-english@onu.edu*	316	$40		April 3	$19,740	$19,740	✓				✓		88	37	✓		✓	273	26	40	12	6	23 (12)	295,639	84,999

Ohio State University (Michael E. Moritz College of Law) 55 West 12th Avenue, John Deaver Drinko Hall Columbus, OH 43210-1391 614-292-8810 Fax: 614-292-1383 *lawadmit@osu.edu*	318		March 15	Check	$10,826	$21,702	✓				✓		88	37	✓	✓		661	22	44	16	1	41 (26)	653,399	880,049
Oklahoma City University (School of Law) 2501 North Blackwelder Oklahoma City, OK 73106-1493 405-521-5354 Fax: 405-521-5802 *lawadmit@okcu.edu*	320	$35	Aug 1	March 1	$17,700 ($11,800)	$17,700 ($11,800)	✓						90	46	✓	✓		371 (133)	30	41	15	8	32 (17)	271,739	618,909
Pace University (School of Law) 78 North Broadway White Plains, NY 10603 914-422-4210 Fax: 914-422-4010 *calexander@law.pace.edu*	322	$55	Feb 15	Feb 1	$25,294 ($18,996)	$25,294 ($18,996)	✓				✓	✓	84	36	✓	✓	✓	408 (315)	25	57	16	6	48 (62)	352,130	62,001
Pennsylvania State University (Dickinson School of Law) 150 South College Street Carlisle, PA 17013 717-240-5207 Fax: 717-241-3503 *dsladmit@psu.edu*	324	$50	March 1	Feb 15	$18,446	$18,446	✓				✓	✓	88	40	✓	✓	✓	535 (1)	25	46	10	7	35 (57)	454,000	1,055,000
Pepperdine University (School of Law) 24255 Pacific Coast Highway Malibu, CA 90263 310-506-4631 Fax: 310-506-7668 *soladmis@pepperdine.edu*	326	$50	March 1	Check	$26,070		✓				✓		88	57	✓	✓	✓	631	23	47	17	5	29	342,450	87,000
Quinnipiac University (School of Law) 275 Mt. Carmel Avenue Hamden, CT 06518-1948 203-582-3400 Fax: 203-582-3339 *ladm@quinnipiac.edu*	328	$40	rolling	May 1	$26,550 ($16,815)	$26,550 ($16,815)	✓				✓	✓	86	53	✓	✓		412 (283)	27	46	13	4	35 (32)	362,618	196,886
Regent University (School of Law) 1000 Regent University Drive Virginia Beach, VA 23464-9800 757-226-4584 Fax: 757-226-4139 *lawschool@regent.edu*	330	$40	June 1	March 1	$16,480 ($515/hr)	$16,480 ($515/hr)	✓				✓	✓	90	66		✓	✓	413 (78)	27	45	18	7	22 (37)	316,000	900,000
Roger Williams University (Ralph R. Papitto School of Law) Ten Metacom Avenue Bristol, RI 02809-5171 401-254-4555 Fax: 401-254-4516 *admissions@law.rwu.edu*	332	$60	May 15	March 15	$22,200 ($17,020)	$22,200 ($17,020)	✓				✓	✓	90	48	✓	✓		338 (132)	27	51	10		25 (22)	261,666	940,773
Rutgers University/Camden (School of Law) Fifth and Penn Streets Camden, NJ 08102 856-225-6102 Fax: 856-225-6537	334	$50	March 1	March 1	$11,394 ($472/hr)	$16,600 ($691/hr)	✓				✓	✓	84	34	✓	✓		551 (202)	26	46	17	3	51 (70)	419,058	120,658

INSTITUTION	Profile Page	APPLICATIONS: Fee	APPLICATIONS: Deadline	APPLICATIONS: Deadline Financial Aid	TUITION: In State Full Time (Part Time)	TUITION: Out of State Full Time (Part Time)	CALENDAR: Fall	CALENDAR: Winter	CALENDAR: Spring	CALENDAR: Summer	PROGRAMS: Day	PROGRAMS: Evening	PROGRAMS: Credits for JD	PROGRAMS: Required Creits for Courses	PROGRAMS: Transferable Summer Courses	PROGRAMS: Joint Degree	PROGRAMS: Graduate Law Degree	ENROLLED: Full Time (Part Time)	STUDENT BODY: Average Age First Year	STUDENT BODY: % Women	STUDENT BODY: % Minority	STUDENT BODY: Attrition Rate %	FACULTY: Full Time (Part Time)	LIBRARY: Volumes	LIBRARY: Microforms
Rutgers University/Newark (School of Law) Center for Law and Justice, 123 Washington St. Newark, NJ 07102 973-353-5557/5554 Fax: 973-353-3459 *awalton@andromeda.rutgers.edu*	336	$50	March 15	March 1	$11,394 ($472/hr)	$16,600 ($691/hr)	✓				✓	✓	84	31 to 32	✓	✓		560 (177)	28	49	41	5	54 (57)	412,542	144,376
Saint John's University (School of Law) 8000 Utopia Parkway Jamaica, NY 11439 718-990-6474 *rsvp@stjohns.edu*	338	$60	April 1	Feb 1	$24,900 ($18,680)	$24,900 ($18,680)	✓		✓		✓	✓	85	53	✓	✓	✓	720 (214)	23	45	19		48 (49)	466,306	1,250,000
Saint Louis University (School of Law) 3700 Lindell Boulevard St. Louis, MO 63108 314-977-2800 Fax: 314-977-1464 *admissions@law.slu.edu*	340	$55	March 1	June 1	$23,300 ($17,000)	$23,300 ($17,000)	✓				✓	✓	88	37	✓	✓	✓	542 (207)	26	48	13	8	34 (31)	581,638	58,692
Saint Mary's University (School of Law) One Camino Santa Maria San Antonio, TX 78228-8601 210-436-3523 Fax: 210-431-4202 *meryc@law.stmarytx.edu*	342	$45	March 1	April 1	$17,970	$17,970	✓				✓		90	46	✓	✓	✓	704		48	46	3	36 (53)	320,000	633,117
Samford University (Cumberland School of Law) 800 Lakeshore Drive Birmingham, AL 35229 205-726-2702 Fax: 205-726-2057 *law.admissions@samford.edu*	344	$40	Feb 28	March 1	$20,528 ($5,544)	$20,528 ($6,237)	✓				✓		90	51	✓	✓	✓	509 (2)	23	42	6	2	22 (9)	268,048	84,676
Santa Clara University (School of Law) 500 El Camino Real Santa Clara, CA 95053 408-554-4800 Fax: 408-554-7897 *lawadmissions@scu.edu*	346	$60	March 1	Feb 1	$25,560 ($17,892)	$25,560 ($17,892)	✓				✓	✓	86	43	✓	✓	✓	677 (214)	26	52	37	16	36 (21)	302,875	883,580
Seattle University (School of Law) 900 Broadway Seattle, WA 98122-4340 206-398-4200 Fax: 206-398-4058 *lawadmis@seattleu.edu*	348	$50	April 1	March 1	$21,210 ($17,675)	$21,210 ($17,675)	✓			✓	✓	✓	90	44	✓	✓	✓	765 (245)	28	53	23	5	36 (79)	332,145	979,998

Seton Hall University (School of Law) One Newark Center Newark, NJ 07102-5210 973-642-8747 Fax: 973-642-8876 *admitme@shu.edu*	350	$50	April 1	April 15	$22,680 ($16,200)	$22,680 ($16,200)	✓				✓	✓	85	44	✓	✓	✓	784 (372)	26	48	15	10	58 (84)	425,509	495,570
South Texas College of Law 1303 San Jacinto Street Houston, TX 77002-7000 713-646-1810 Fax: 713-646-2906 *admissions@stcl.edu*	352	$50	Feb 25	May 1	$17,100 ($11,400)	$17,100 ($11,400)	✓		✓		✓	✓	90	44	✓			831 (419)	28	49	25	11	55 (38)	214,935	1,202,508
Southern Illinois University (School of Law) Lesar Law Building, Mail Code 6804 Carbondale, IL 62901-6804 618-453-8767 Fax: 618-453-8769 *lawadmit@siu.edu*	354	$40	March 1	April 1	$5,178	$15,534	✓				✓		90	48	✓	✓		347 (3)	26	45	8	7	27 (9)	367,614	854,156
Southern Methodist University (School of Law) Office of Admissions, P.O. Box 750110 Dallas, TX 75275-0110 214-768-2550 Fax: 214-768-2549 *lawadmit@mail.smu.edu*	356	$50	Feb 1	June 1	$23,000	$23,000	✓				✓		90	37		✓	✓	773 (13)	24	38	13	3	42 (100)	480,000	75,217
Southern University and A & M College (Law Center) Post Office Box 9294 Baton Rouge, LA 70813-9294 225-771-5340 Fax: 225-771-2121 *vwilkerson@sus.edu*	358	$25	March 31	April 15	$3,684 ($1,828)	$3,684 ($1,828)	✓				✓		96	75	✓	✓		365 (7)	27	49	62	10	30 (14)	415,208	7,867
Southwestern University (School of Law) 675 South Westmoreland Avenue Los Angeles, CA 90005-3992 213-738-6717 Fax: 213-383-1688 *admissions@swlaw.edu*	360	$50	June 30	June 1	$24,840 ($15,732)	$24,840 ($15,732)	✓				✓	✓	87	52	✓			597 (282)	26	52	38	20	50 (38)	428,947	59,459
St. Thomas University (School of Law) 16400 N.W. 32nd Avenue Miami, FL 33054 305-623-2310 *lamy@stu.edu*	362	$40	April 30	May 1	$22,400	$22,400	✓		✓		✓	✓	87	62	✓	✓	✓	466 (1)	27	48	46	32	26 (21)	301,971	1,032,585
Stanford University (Stanford Law School) Crown Quadrangle Stanford, CA 94305-8610 650-723-4985 Fax: 650-723-0838 *law.admissions@forsythe.stanford.edu/*	364	$65	Feb 1		$29,398	$29,398	✓				✓		86	27		✓	✓	559	24	48	32		52	440,000	480,000
State University of New York at Buffalo (Law School) O'Brian Hall Buffalo, NY 14260 716-645-2907 Fax: 716-645-6676 *coxublaw@buffalo.edu*	366	$50	March 15	March 1	$9,900	$15,450	✓				✓	✓	90	35	✓	✓	✓	703	24	49	16	2	55 (101)	301,692	1,983,759

INSTITUTION	Profile Page	APPLICATIONS			TUITION		CALENDAR				PROGRAMS							ENROLLED	STUDENT BODY				FACULTY	LIBRARY	
		Fee	Deadline	Deadline Financial Aid	In State Full Time (Part Time)	Out of State Full Time (Part Time)	Fall	Winter	Spring	Summer	Day	Evening	Credits for JD	Required Creits for Courses	Transferable Summer Courses	Joint Degree	Graduate Law Degree	Full Time (Part Time)	Average Age First Year	% Women	% Minority	Attrition Rate %	Full Time (Part Time)	Volumes	Microforms
Stetson University (College of Law) 1401 61st Street South St. Petersburg, FL 33707 727-562-7802 Fax: 727-343-0136 *lawadmit@hermes.law.stetson.edu*	368	$50	Feb 15		$21,905	$21,905	✓		✓	✓	✓	✓	88	48	✓	✓	✓	711 (12)	24	54	18	4	41 (54)	367,000	769,000
Suffolk University (Law School) 120 Tremont Street Boston, MA 02108-4977 617-573-8144 Fax: 617-523-1367	370	$50	March 1	March 1	$24,870 ($18,652)		✓				✓	✓	84	58	✓	✓	✓	1000 (715)	26	50	10	8	60 (114)	318,000	801,693
Syracuse University (College of Law) Office of Admissions and Financial Aid Syracuse, NY 13244-1030 315-443-1962 Fax: 315-443-9568	372	$50	April 1	Feb 1	$25,940	$25,940	✓				✓		87	40	✓	✓		756 (7)	25	47	22		46 (50)	400,000	
Temple University (James E. Beasley School of Law) 1719 N. Broad Street Philadelphia, PA 19122 215-204-8925 Fax: 215-204-1185 *lawadmis@blue.temple.edu*	374	$50	March 1	March 1	$10,308 ($8,246)	$17,864 ($14,292)	✓				✓	✓	87	39		✓	✓	783 (291)	26	49	19	3	61 (155)	529,695	733,797
Texas Southern University (Thurgood Marshall School of Law) 3100 Cleburne Avenue Houston, TX 77004 713-313-7114 Fax: 713-313-1049 *cgardner@tsulaw.edu*	376		April 1	Check	$5,144	$9,024	✓				✓		90	70	✓			632	27	46	80	35	34 (19)	229,464	100,536
Texas Tech University (School of Law) 1802 Hartford Lubbock, TX 79409 806-742-3990, ext. 273 Fax: 806-742-1629 *donna.williams@ttu.edu*	378	$50	Feb 1	March	$7,134	$12,204	✓				✓		90	55	✓	✓		663	25	46	13	13	26 (18)	179,368	522,434
Texas Wesleyan University (School of Law) 1515 Commerce Street Fort Worth, TX 76102 817-212-4040 Fax: 817-212-4002 *law-admissions@law.txwes.edu*	380	$75	open	Check	$7,800 ($5,720)	$8,000	✓				✓	✓	88	50	✓			339 (283)	30	52	19	15	26 (28)	186,000	441,501
Thomas Jefferson School of Law 2121 San Diego Avenue San Diego, CA 92110 619-297-9700 Fax: 619-294-4713 *adm@tjsl.edu*	382	$35	open	Feb 15	$22,180 ($13,140)	$22,180 ($13,140)	✓		✓		✓	✓	88	55	✓			423 (188)	28	42	22		26 (30)	231,301	124,905

Thomas M. Cooley Law School 300 South Capitol Avenue Lansing, MI 48901 517-371-5140 Fax: 517-334-5718 *admissions@cooley.edu*	384		rolling	rolling	$18,648 ($13,320)	$18,648 ($13,320)	✓	✓	✓				90	63	✓	✓		389 (1431)	29	49	37	30	62 (100)	429,735	117,732
Touro College (Jacob D. Fuchsberg Law Center) 300 Nassau Road Huntington, NY 11743 631-421-2244 ext. 312 Fax: 631-421-9708 *admissions@tourolaw.edu*	386	$50	rolling	April 15	$22,410 ($17,380)	$22,410 ($17,380)	✓				✓	✓	87	55 to 56	✓	✓	✓	329 (298)	29	49	26	5	37 (30)	400,000	
Tulane University (Law School) Weinmann Hall, 6329 Freret Street New Orleans, LA 70118 504-865-5930 Fax: 504-865-6710 *admissions@law.tulane.edu*	388	$50	May 1	Feb 15	$24,676	$24,676	✓				✓		88	31	✓	✓	✓	963 (4)	24	52	24	5	50 (49)	500,000	
University of Akron (School of Law) Corner of Wolf Ledges and University Avenue Akron, OH 44325-2901 330-972-7331 Fax: 330-258-2343 *lawadmissions@uakron.edu*	390	$35	March 1	May 1	$9,386 ($7,541)	$14,801 ($11,873)	✓				✓	✓	88	44	✓	✓		363 (227)	26	47	12	20	30 (42)	267,581	385,300
University of Alabama (School of Law) Box 870382 Tuscaloosa, AL 35487-0382 205-348-5440 Fax: 205-348-3917 *admissions@law.ua.edu*	392	$25	March 1	March 1	$5,111	$10,222	✓				✓		90	36		✓	✓	523	25	41	12	2	38 (42)	395,318	122,762
University of Arizona (James E. Rogers College of Law) Mountain and Speedway P.O. Box 210176 Tucson, AZ 85721-0176 520-621-3477 Fax: 520-621-9140 *admissions@law.arizona.edu*	394	$50	March 1	March 1	$5,240	$13,106	✓				✓		85	39	✓	✓	✓	503	26	51	24	1	30 (55)	380,000	426,000
University of Arkansas (School of Law) Robert A. Leflar Law Center, Waterman Hall Fayetteville, AR 72701 501-575-3102	396		April 1	April 1	$3,362	$7,779	✓				✓		90	43	✓	✓	✓	372	26	44	10		35 (5)	243,962	43,584
University of Arkansas at Little Rock (UALR William H. Bowen School of Law) 1201 McMath Avenue Little Rock, AR 72202-5142 501-324-9439 Fax: 501-324-9433 *lawadm@ualr.edu*	398	$40	May 1	March 1	$5,880 ($3,528)	$13,200 ($7,920)	✓						90	48	✓	✓		234 (140)	28	46	10	1	28 (29)	168,938	534,284
University of Baltimore (School of Law) 1420 North Charles Street Baltimore, MD 21201-5779 410-837-4459 Fax: 410-837-4450 *lwadmiss@ubmail.ubalt.edu*	400	$35	April 1	April 1	$9,942	$17,760	✓				✓	✓	90	39	✓	✓	✓	602 (302)	28	49	19	2	46 (79)	320,526	561,053

INSTITUTION		APPLICATIONS			TUITION		CALENDAR				PROGRAMS							ENROLLED	STUDENT BODY				FACULTY	LIBRARY	
	Profile Page	Fee	Deadline	Deadline Financial Aid	In State Full Time (Part Time)	Out of State Full Time (Part Time)	Fall	Winter	Spring	Summer	Day	Evening	Credits for JD	Required Creits for Courses	Transferable Summer Courses	Joint Degree	Graduate Law Degree	Full Time (Part Time)	Average Age First Year	% Women	% Minority	Attrition Rate %	Full Time (Part Time)	Volumes	Microforms
University of California (Hastings College of the Law) 200 McAllister Street San Francisco, CA 94102 415-565-4623 Fax: 415-565-4863 *admiss@uchastings.edu*	402	$60	March 1	March 1	$11,409	$20,895	✓				✓		86	34		✓	✓	1237	24	52	32	5	46 (88)	653,988	1,322,970
University of California at Berkeley (Boalt Hall) 5 Boalt Hall Berkeley, CA 94720 510-642-2274 Fax: 510-643-6222	404	$65	Feb 1	March 2	$10,945	$21,649	✓				✓		85	30		✓	✓	958	24	50	31		61 (102)	680,000	660,000
University of California at Davis (School of Law) Martin Luther King, Jr. Hall 400 Mrak Hall Drive Davis, CA 95616-5201 530-752-6477 *lawadmissions@ucdavis.edu*	406	$70	Feb 1	March 2	$11,424	$22,128	✓				✓		88	33		✓	✓	540	25	57	19	6	30 (20)	282,566	676,254
University of California at Los Angeles (School of Law) P.O. Box 951445 Los Angeles, CA 90095-1445 310-825-2080 Fax: 310-825-9450 *admissions@law.ucla.edu*	408	$70	Feb 1	Check	$11,156	$21,860	✓				✓		87	35		✓	✓	969	25	52	28	1	83 (26)	512,769	403,651
University of Chicago (Law School) 1111 East 60th Street Chicago, IL 60637 773-702-9484 Fax: 773-834-0942 *admissions@law.uchicago.edu*	410	$65	Feb 1	March 1	$29,112	$29,112	✓				✓		105	40			✓	649	24	40	23	1	50 (21)	651,822	64,007
University of Cincinnati (College of Law) P.O. Box 210040 Cincinnati, OH 45221-0040 513-556-6805 *admissions@law.uc.edu*	412	$35	April 1	March 1	$9,622	$18,336	✓				✓		90	35	✓	✓		366	24	55	18	1	24	394,852	783,306
University of Colorado (School of Law) Campus Box 403 Boulder, CO 80309-0403 303-492-7203	414	$55	Feb 15	March 1	$6,352	$19,510	✓				✓		89	43	✓	✓		485	26	54	19	5	40 (30)	383,000	725,704
University of Connecticut (School of Law) 55 Elizabeth Street Hartford, CT 06105 860-570-5159 Fax: 860-570-5153 *admit@law.uconn.edu*	416	$30	March 15	March 15	$11,374 ($397/hr)	$23,992 ($837/hr)	✓				✓	✓	86	36	✓	✓	✓		25	50	18	1	52 (74)	471,556	976,556

University of Dayton (School of Law) 300 College Park Dayton, OH 45469-2760 937-229-3555 Fax: 937-229-4194 *lawinfo@udayton.edu*	418	$50	May 1	March 1	$21,766	$21,766	✓				✓	✓	87	36	✓	✓	✓	426	25	41	16	6	28 (32)	283,994	700,794
University of Denver (College of Law) 7039 E. 18th Avenue Denver, CO 80220 303-871-6135 Fax: 303-871-6100 *khigganb@law.du.edu*	420	$45	none	Feb 15	$22,723 ($14,660)	$22,723 ($14,660)	✓				✓	✓	90	44	✓	✓	✓	859 (326)	25	52	9	4	49 (66)	274,284	48,685
University of Detroit Mercy (School of Law) 651 East Jefferson Avenue Detroit, MI 48226 313-596-0264 Fax: 313-596-0280 *udmlawao@udmercy.edu*	422	$50	April 15	April 1	$17,360 ($12,400)	$17,360 ($12,400)	✓				✓	✓	90	49	✓	✓		220 (144)	27	52	16	10	19 (20)	307,767	94,430
University of Florida (College of Law) 325 Holland Hall P.O. Box 117622 Gainesville, FL 32611-7622 352-392-2087 Fax: 352-392-2087 *patrick@law.ufl.edu*	424	$20	Feb 1	April 1	$4,836	$16,109	✓		✓		✓		88	34	✓	✓	✓	1145	25	48	26	4	69 (18)	592,000	200,000
University of Georgia (School of Law) Hirsch Hall, 225 Herty Drive Athens, GA 30602-6012 706-542-7060 *ugajd@arches.uga.edu*	426	$30	March 1		$5,272	$18,730	✓				✓		88	33	✓	✓	✓	670	24	46	11	5	48 (36)	360,950	504,653
University of Hawaii at Manoa (William S. Richardson School of Law) 2515 Dole Street Honolulu, HI 96822 808-956-7966 Fax: 808-956-3813 *lawadm@hawaii.educ*	428	$45	March 1	Check	$9,624	$16,512	✓						89	42		✓		233	27	52	72	5	19 (29)	248,838	875,305
University of Houston (Law Center) 100 Law Center Houston, TX 77204-6060 713-743-2280 Fax: 713-743-2194 *admission@www.law.uh.edu*	430	$50	Feb 15	April 1	$5,600 ($4,000)	$9,520 ($6,800)	✓				✓	✓	90	35	✓	✓	✓	750 (181)	25	47	19	3	46 (67)	460,569	911,626
University of Idaho (College of Law) P.O. Box 442321 Moscow, ID 83844-2321 208-885-6423 Fax: 208-885-5709 *erickl@uidaho.edu*	432	$40	Feb 1	Feb 15	$5,160	$11,160	✓				✓		88	37		✓		304	28	38	7	9	16 (1)	180,892	
University of Illinois (College of Law) 504 East Pennsylvania Avenue Champaign, IL 61820 217-244-6415 Fax: 217-244-1478 *admissions@law.uiuc.edu*	434	$40	March 15	March 15	$9,872	$21,770	✓				✓		90	34		✓	✓	672	24	40	27	1	45 (33)	565,660	775,212

INSTITUTION		APPLICATIONS			TUITION		CALENDAR				PROGRAMS							ENROLLED	STUDENT BODY				FACULTY	LIBRARY	
	Profile Page	Fee	Deadline	Deadline Financial Aid	In State Full Time (Part Time)	Out of State Full Time (Part Time)	Fall	Winter	Spring	Summer	Day	Evening	Credits for JD	Required Creits for Courses	Transferable Summer Courses	Joint Degree	Graduate Law Degree	Full Time (Part Time)	Average Age First Year	% Women	% Minority	Attrition Rate %	Full Time (Part Time)	Volumes	Microforms
University of Iowa **(College of Law)** 276 Boyd Law Building, Melrose at Byington Street Iowa City, IA 52242 319-335-9095 or 319-335-9142 Fax: 319-335-9019 *law-admissions@uiowa.edu*	436	$30	March 1		$8,152	$20,274	✓			✓	✓		90	35	✓	✓	✓	707	25	47	14	3	51 (29)	678,130	317,212
University of Kansas **(School of Law)** 205 Green Hall Lawrence, KS 66045 785-864-4378 Fax: 785-864-5054 *reitz@law.wpo.ukans.edu*	438	$40	March 15	March 1	$6,402	$13,733	✓			✓	✓		90	43 to 45	✓	✓		522	23	42	11	3	34 (7)	325,000	333,169
University of Kentucky **(College of Law)** 209 Law Building Lexington, KY 40506-0048 606-257-7938 Fax: n/av *dbakert@uky.edu*	440	$35	March 1	April 1	$6,250	$16,064	✓				✓		90	34	✓	✓		373	23	45	7	6	28 (20)	437,233	195,875
University of Louisville **(Louis D. Brandeis School of Law)** University of Louisville Belknap Campus- Wilson W. Wyatt Hall Louisville, KY 40292 502-852-6364 Fax: 502-852-0862 *lawadmissions@louisville.edu*	442	$40	March 1	June 1	$6,882 ($5,840)	$17,710 ($14,880)	✓				✓	✓	90	44	✓	✓		281 (102)	24	48	84		33 (8)	385,367	8,461
University of Maine **(School of Law)** 246 Deering Avenue Portland, ME 04102 207-780-4341 *mainelaw@usm.maine.edu*	444	$50	Feb 15	Feb 1	$10,200 ($340/hr)	$18,150 ($605/hr)	✓				✓		89	40	✓	✓		221 (9)	29	53	5	3	16 (3)	336,000	16,300
University of Maryland **(School of Law)** 500 West Baltimore Street Baltimore, MD 21201 410-706-3492 Fax: 410-706-4045 *admissions@law.umaryland.edu*	446	$60	March 1	March 1	$10,692 ($8,051)	$19,639 ($14,759)	✓						85	36 to 38	✓	✓	✓	719 (239)	26	56	23	1	58 (98)	283,743	106,876
University of Memphis **(Cecil C. Humphreys School of Law)** 207 Humphreys Law School Memphis, TN 38152-3140 901-678-5403 Fax: 901-678-5210 *lawadmissions@spc75.law.memphis.edu*	448	$25	Feb 15	April 1	$6,290 ($5,422)	$17,546 ($14,638)	✓				✓		90	56	✓	✓		387 (34)	26	47	15	8	23 (34)	273,360	602,670
University of Miami **(School of Law)** P.O. Box 248087, 1311 Miller Drive Coral Gables, FL 33124-8087 305-284-2523 *admissions@law.miami.edu*	450	$50	March 8	March 1	$24,876 ($18,658)	$24,876 ($18,658)	✓				✓	✓	88	73	✓	✓	✓	1047 (136)	26	46	30	5	57 (103)	368,011	846,350

University of Michigan (Law School) 625 South State Street Ann Arbor, MI 48109-1215 734-764-0537 Fax: 734-647-3218 *law.jd.admissions@umich.edu*	452	$60	Feb 15		$23,164	$29,164	✓			✓	✓		80	32		✓	✓	1098	24	43	23	1	72 (50)	876,822	1,245,320
University of Minnesota (Law School) 229 19th Avenue S. Minneapolis, MN 55455 612-625-3487 Fax: 612-626-1874	454	$50	March 1	March 15	$10,954	$18,624	✓				✓		88	32	✓	✓	✓	693	25	49	18	4	43 (112)	923,000	304,000
University of Mississippi (L.Q.C. Lamar Hall) Grove Loop University, MS 38677 601-915-6910 Fax: 601-915-1289 *bvinson@olemiss.edu*	456	$25	March 1	March 1	$5,654	$11,142	✓			✓	✓		90	54 to 57	✓	✓		480	24	41	12	9	32 (17)	314,929	155,585
University of Missouri-Columbia (School of Law) 103 Hulston Hall Columbia, MO 65211 573-882-6042 Fax: 573-882-9625 *CatheyA@missouri.edu*	458	$40	March 1	March 1	$9,738	$18,846	✓				✓		89	57	✓	✓	✓	553	23	39	11	3	36 (15)	331,663	444,865
University of Missouri-Kansas City (School of Law) 500 East 52nd Street Kansas City, MO 64110-2499 816-235-1644 Fax: 816-235-5276 *brooksdv@umkc.edu*	460	$25	April 1	Check	$10,433 ($660/hr)	$20,192 ($660/hr)	✓				✓	✓	91	52		✓	✓	456 (59)	25	47	8	12	28 (42)	202,809	89,195
University of Montana (School of Law) Missoula, MT 59812 406-243-2698 *lawadmis@selway.umt.edu*	462	$60	March 1	March 1	$7,550	$14,142	✓				✓		90	56		✓		234	28	41	7	1	19 (16)	108,599	57,584
University of Nebraska (College of Law) P.O. Box 830902 Lincoln, NE 68583-0902 402-472-2161 Fax: 402-472-5185 *lawadm@unl.edu*	464	$25	March 1	March 1	$4,743	$12,717	✓				✓		96	45	✓	✓	✓	396	24	46	8	8	28 (28)	217,729	158,056
University of Nevada, Las Vegas (William S. Boyd School of Law) 4505 Maryland Parkway, Box 451003 Las Vegas, NV 89154-1003 702-895-3671 Fax: 702-895-1095 *request@law.unlv.edu*	466	$40	March 15	Feb 1	$7,000 ($4,500)	$14,000 ($9,000)	✓				✓	✓	86	44	✓			241 (197)	30	49	19		31 (13)	202,277	138,618
University of New Mexico (School of Law) 1117 Stanford Drive N.E. Albuquerque, NM 87131-1431 505-277-0572 Fax: 505-277-9958	468	$40	Feb 15	March 1	$5,544	$18,520	✓				✓		86	41		✓		330	27	59	35		34 (29)	412,694	31,691
University of North Carolina at Chapel Hill (School of Law) Campus Box 3380, 101 Van Hecke-Wettach Hall Chapel Hill, NC 27599-3380 919-962-5109 Fax: 919-843-7939 *law_admission@unc.edu*	470		Feb 1	Check	$3,602	$15,702	✓				✓		86	33		✓		683	23	49	21	1	44 (35)	447,320	11,302

INSTITUTION	Profile Page	APPLICATIONS: Fee	APPLICATIONS: Deadline	APPLICATIONS: Deadline Financial Aid	TUITION: In State Full Time (Part Time)	TUITION: Out of State Full Time (Part Time)	CALENDAR: Fall	CALENDAR: Winter	CALENDAR: Spring	CALENDAR: Summer	PROGRAMS: Day	PROGRAMS: Evening	PROGRAMS: Credits for JD	PROGRAMS: Required Creits for Courses	PROGRAMS: Transferable Summer Courses	PROGRAMS: Joint Degree	PROGRAMS: Graduate Law Degree	ENROLLED: Full Time (Part Time)	STUDENT BODY: Average Age First Year	STUDENT BODY: % Women	STUDENT BODY: % Minority	STUDENT BODY: Attrition Rate %	FACULTY: Full Time (Part Time)	LIBRARY: Volumes	LIBRARY: Microforms
University of North Dakota (School of Law) Box 9003 Grand Forks, ND 58202 701-777-2104 Fax: 701-777-2217 *linda.kohoutek@thor.law.und.nodak.edu*	472		April 1	Check	$4,376	$9,220	✓				✓		90	34	✓	✓		188	26	39	5	6	14 (9)	251,320	129,554
University of Notre Dame (Notre Dame Law School) P.O. Box R Notre Dame, IN 46556-0780 574-631-6626 Fax: 574-631-5474 *lawadmit@nd.edu*	474	$55	March 1	March 1	$24,920	$24,920	✓				✓		90	42	✓	✓	✓	528	24	42	19	1	35 (29)	563,174	1,548,800
University of Oklahoma (College of Law) 300 Timberdell Road Norman, OK 73019 405-325-4726 Fax: 405-325-0502 *kmadden@ou.edu*	476	$50	March 15	March 1	$5,259	$14,285	✓				✓		90	42	✓	✓		513	24	45	15	4	33 (20)	331,510	80,970
University of Oregon (School of Law, William W. Knight Law Center) 1515 Agate Street Eugene, OR 97403-1221 541-346-1553 Fax: 541-346-3984 *admissions@law.uoregon.edu*	478	$50	Feb 15	Check	$12,552	$17,130	✓				✓		85	37	✓	✓		535	25	48	16	2	32 (11)	177,409	169,187
University of Pennsylvania (Law School) 3400 Chestnut Street Philadelphia, PA 19104-6204 215-898-7400 *admissions@oyez.law.upenn.edu*	480	$70	March 1	March 1	$27,960	$27,960	✓				✓	✓	89	28		✓	✓	751	24	50	26	1	65 (52)	742,009	940,251
University of Pittsburgh (School of Law) 3900 Forbes Avenue Pittsburgh, PA 15260 412-648-1400 Fax: 412-648-2647 *admissions@law.pitt.edu*	482	$50	March 1	March 1	$14,560	$22,434	✓				✓		88	34		✓	✓	766	24	45	9	3	42 (38)	379,723	
University of Puerto Rico (School of Law) P.O. Box 23349, UPR Station Rio Piedras, PR 00931-3349 787-772-1472 Fax: 787-764-4360 *wandi_perez@hotmail.com*	484	$15	Feb 15	May 1	$2,250 ($1,050)	$5,750	✓				✓	✓	92	46		✓	✓	366 (186)	23	56		5	35 (29)	223,000	152,000

University of Richmond (The T.C. Williams School of Law) University of Richmond, VA 23173 804-289-8189 *admissions@uofrlaw.richmond.edu*	486	$35	Jan 15	Feb 25	$21,770 ($1,090/hr)	$21,770 ($1,090/hr)	✓			✓	✓		86	38	✓	✓		478 (1)	25	47	9	1	30 (69)	311,084	126,941
University of San Diego (School of Law) 5998 Alcala Park San Diego, CA 92110 619-260-4528 Fax: 619-260-2218 *jdinfo@sandiego.edu*	488	$40	Feb 1	March 2	$24,880 ($17,660)	$24,880 ($17,660)	✓				✓	✓	85	48	✓	✓	✓	711 (280)	24	49	27	16	61 (56)	453,301	1,415,092
University of San Francisco (School of Law) 2130 Fulton Street San Francisco, CA 94117-1080 415-422-6586 Fax: 415-422-6433	490	$60	Feb 1	rolling	$26,282 ($21,643)		✓				✓	✓	86	48	✓	✓	✓	527 (110)	25	56	28	9	33 (63)	295,317	161,252
University of South Carolina (School of Law) Main and Greene Streets Columbia, SC 29208 803-777-6605 Fax: 803-777-7751 *usclaw@law.law.sc.edu*	492	$40	Feb 15	April 15	$8,820	$18,250	✓				✓		90	46	✓	✓		706	23	43	9	3	43 (26)	330,000	2,718
University of South Dakota (School of Law) 414 East Clark Street Vermillion, SD 57069-2390 605-677-5443 Fax: 605-677-5417 *lawreq@usd.edu*	494	$35	March 1	Check	$3,432 ($1,602)	$9,948 ($4,642)	✓				✓		90	43	✓	✓		181 (3)	27	51	9	8	15 (2)	192,397	12,052
University of Southern California (Law School) Los Angeles, CA 90089-0074 213-740-2523	496	$60	Feb 1	Feb 15	$29,454	$29,454	✓				✓		88	33		✓		628	24	51	40	1	48 (54)	381,032	89,917
University of Tennessee (College of Law) 1505 W. Cumberland Avenue Knoxville, TN 37996-1810 865-974-4131 Fax: 865-974-1572 *lawadmit@libra.law.utk.edu*	498	$15	Feb 15	March 1	$6,118	$17,580	✓				✓		89	46	✓	✓		467	25	48	15	3	30 (26)	498,656	1,216,308
University of Texas at Austin (School of Law) 727 East Dean Keeton Street Austin, TX 78705 512-232-1200 Fax: 512-471-6988 *admissions@mail.law.utexas.edu*	500	$65	Feb 1	March 31	$8,960	$17,960	✓				✓		86	38	✓	✓	✓	1453	23	49	19	1	73 (102)	992,745	766,572
University of the District of Columbia (David A. Clarke School of Law) 4200 Connecticut Avenue, N.W. Washington, DC 20008 202-274-7341 Fax: 202-274-5583 *vcanty@law.udc.edu*	502	$35	April 1	May 1	$7,000	$14,000	✓				✓	✓	90	66	✓			133	30	65	71	15	18 (18)	205,000	90
University of the Pacific (McGeorge School of Law) 3200 Fifth Avenue Sacramento, CA 95817 916-739-7105 Fax: 916-739-7134 *admissionsmcgeorge@uop.edu*	504	$40	May 1	open	$24,104 ($16,024)	$24,104 ($16,024)	✓				✓	✓	88	58	✓	✓	✓	635 (301)	24	49	24	26	44 (64)	454,775	1,189,824

INSTITUTION		APPLICATIONS			TUITION		CALENDAR				PROGRAMS							ENROLLED	STUDENT BODY				FACULTY	LIBRARY	
	Profile Page	Fee	Deadline	Deadline Financial Aid	In State Full Time (Part Time)	Out of State Full Time (Part Time)	Fall	Winter	Spring	Summer	Day	Evening	Credits for JD	Required Creits for Courses	Transferable Summer Courses	Joint Degree	Graduate Law Degree	Full Time (Part Time)	Average Age First Year	% Women	% Minority	Attrition Rate %	Full Time (Part Time)	Volumes	Microforms
University of Toledo (College of Law) 2801 West Bancroft Street Toledo, OH 43606-3390 419-530-4131 Fax: 419-530-4345 *law.utoledo.edu*	506	$30	June 1	July 1	$7,860 ($6,550)	$16,330 ($13,608)	✓				✓	✓	89	42	✓	✓		326 (124)	26	46	6	5	33 (29)	327,663	128,622
University of Tulsa (College of Law) 3120 East Fourth Place Tulsa, OK 74104-2499 918-631-2709 Fax: 918-631-3630 *george-justice@utulsa.edu*	508	$30	open	open	$18,500 ($12,067)	$18,500 ($12,067)	✓		✓		✓	✓	88	42	✓	✓	✓	397 (129)	27	35	13	2	27 (28)	290,669	688,772
University of Utah (College of Law) 332 South 1400 East Front Room 101 Salt Lake City, UT 84112 801-581-7479 Fax: 801-581-6897 *aguilarr@law.utah.edu*	510	$50	Feb 1	March 15	$6,761	$14,500	✓				✓		88	40	✓	✓	✓	375	28	43	13	3	28 (32)	300,000	98,000
University of Virginia (School of Law) 580 Massie Road Charlottesville, VA 22903-1789 804-924-7351 Fax: 804-982-2128 *lawadmit@virginia.edu*	512	$65	Jan 15	Feb 15	$16,866	$24,092	✓				✓		86 quar-ter	27		✓	✓	1068	24	45	15		70 (59)	827,768	1,174,043
University of Washington (School of Law) 1100 Northeast Campus Parkway Seattle, WA 98105-6617 206-543-4078 *admissions@law.washington.edu*	514	$50	Jan 15	Feb 28	$6,911	$17,114	✓				✓		135		✓	✓	✓	485	25	51	27	2	43	539,771	163,030
University of Wisconsin (Law School) 975 Bascom Mall Madison, WI 53706 608-262-5914 Fax: 608-262-5485 *admissions@law.wisc.educ*	516	$45	Feb 1	Feb 1	$8,180 ($342/hr)	$22,484 ($938/hr)	✓				✓	✓	90	30 to 31	✓	✓	✓	796 (34)	26	47	25	1	48	513,573	812,276
University of Wyoming (College of Law) P.O. Box 3035 Laramie, WY 82071 307-766-6416 *lawadmis@uwyo.edu*	518	$35	March 15	Feb 1	$4,890	$10,362	✓				✓		88	51		✓	✓	233	27	45	10	9	14	274,178	137,574
Valparaiso University (School of Law) Wesemann Hall Valparaiso, IN 46383-6493 219-465-7829 Fax: 219-465-7808 *marilyn.olson@valpo.edu*	520	$30	April 15	March 15	$19,950 ($780/hr)	$19,950 ($780/hr)	✓				✓	✓	90	46	✓	✓	✓	397 (39)	25	47	8	10	27 (37)	283,803	774,186

Vanderbilt University (Law School) 131 21st Avenue South Nashville, TN 37203 615-322-6452 Fax: 615-322-1531	522	$50	March 1	Feb 15	$26,960	$26,960	✓				✓		88	37		✓	✓	574	24	48	22	2	42 (39)	541,321	403,590
Vermont Law School P.O. Box 96, Chelsea Street South Royalton, VT 05068-0096 802-763-8303 Fax: 802-763-7071 *admiss@vermontlaw.edu*	524	$50	Feb 1	Feb 15	$22,164		✓				✓		84	44	✓	✓	✓	510	26	46	13	8	36 (36)	215,000	95,000
Villanova University (School of Law) Garey Hall Villanova, PA 19085 610-519-7010 Fax: 610-519-6291 *admissions@law.vill.edu*	526	$75	March 1		$22,340		✓				✓		87	44		✓	✓	737	23	47	11	1	44 (46)	315,575	902,755
Wake Forest University (School of Law) P.O. Box 7206, Reynolda Station Winston-Salem, NC 27109 336-758-5437	528	$60	March 15	May 1	$22,950	$22,950	✓				✓		89	41	✓	✓	✓	473 (9)	25	48	10	2	39 (38)	355,000	800,000
Washburn University (School of Law) 1700 College Topeka, KS 66621 785-231-1185 Fax: 785-232-8087 *admissions@washburnlaw.edu*	530	$30	March 15	April 1	$8,870	$14,160	✓		✓		✓		90	37	✓			393	27	35	13	7	29 (36)	321,470	141,744
Washington and Lee University (School of Law) Lewis Hall Lexington, VA 24450 540-463-8504 Fax: 540-463-8586 *lawadm@wlu.edu*	532	$50	Feb 1	Feb 15	$20,020	$20,020	✓				✓		85	37				355	24	42	9	1	33 (19)	372,675	808,493
Washington University in St. Louis (School of Law) Box 1120, One Brookings Drive St. Louis, MO 63130 314-935-4525 Fax: 314-935-6959 *admiss@walaw.wash.edu*	534	$60	March 1	March 1	$27,100	$27,100	✓				✓		85	7	✓	✓	✓	773 (42)	24	43	20	7	47 (50)	563,292	847,000
Wayne State University (Law School) 471 W. Palmer Detroit, MI 48202 313-577-3937 Fax: 313-577-6000 *linda.sims@wayne.edu*	536	$20	March 15	April 30	$8,592 ($6,138)	$18,676 ($13,850)	✓				✓	✓	86	36	✓	✓	✓	503 (244)	26	47		11	33 (48)	388,390	199,607
West Virginia University (College of Law) P.O. Box 6130 Morgantown, WV 26506 304-293-5304 Fax: 304-293-6891 *lawaply@wvu.edu*	538		March 1		$5,200 ($650/hr)	$12,300 ($650/hr)	✓				✓		93	52		✓		436 (10)	26	42	7		26 (11)	246,532	355,617

INSTITUTION		APPLICATIONS			TUITION		CALENDAR				PROGRAMS							ENROLLED	STUDENT BODY				FACULTY	LIBRARY	
	Profile Page	Fee	Deadline	Deadline Financial Aid	In State Full Time (Part Time)	Out of State Full Time (Part Time)	Fall	Winter	Spring	Summer	Day	Evening	Credits for JD	Required Creits for Courses	Transferable Summer Courses	Joint Degree	Graduate Law Degree	Full Time (Part Time)	Average Age First Year	% Women	% Minority	Attrition Rate %	Full Time (Part Time)	Volumes	Microforms
Western New England College (School of Law) 1215 Wilbraham Road Springfield, MA 01119 413-782-1406 Fax: 413-796-2067 *lawadmis@wnec.edu*	540	$45	open	rolling	$21,866 ($16,398)	$21,866 ($16,398)	✓				✓	✓	88 units	46		✓		260 (231)	27	53	13	9	33 (34)	360,000	169,000
Western State University (College of Law) 1111 North State College Blvd Fullerton, CA 92831 714-738-1000, ext. 2600 Fax: 714-441-1748 *paulb@wsulaw.edu*	542	$50	open	March 1	$22,168 ($14,920)	$22,168 ($14,920)	✓		✓		✓	✓	88	58	✓			225 (235)	28	49	42	35	21 (50)	174,569	44,237
Whittier College (School of Law) 3333 Harbor Blvd. Costa Mesa, CA 92626 714-444-4141, ext. 121 Fax: 714-444-0250 *info@law.whittier.edu*	544	$50	March 15	June 1	$24,064 ($14,452)	$24,064 ($14,452)	✓		✓		✓	✓	87	40	✓		✓	373 (280)	25	57	42	30	28 (43)	356,086	168,765
Widener University (School of Law) 4601 Concord Pike, P.O. Box 7474 Wilmington, DE 19803, 302-477-2162 (DE); 717-541-3903 (PA) Fax: 302-477-2224 (DE); 717-541-3999 (PA) *law.admissions@law.widener.edu*	546	$60	May 15	open	$21,200 ($15,850)	$21,200 ($15,850)	✓		✓		✓	✓	87	64	✓	✓	✓	862 (574)	25	48	12	8	80 (110)	322,141	293,021
Willamette University (College of Law) 245 Winter Street S.E. Salem, OR 97301 503-370-6282 Fax: 503-370-6375 *law-admission@willamette.edu*	548	$50	April 1	Feb 1	$20,850	$20,850	✓				✓		92	39	✓	✓	✓	418 (4)	26	45	10	9	24 (5)	272,000	866,000
William Mitchell College of Law 875 Summit Avenue St. Paul, MN 55105-3076 651-290-6476 Fax: 651-290-6414 *admissions@wmitchell.edu*	550	$45	June 28	March 15	$20,040 ($14,630)	$20,040 ($14,630)	✓				✓	✓	86	46	✓	✓		537 (478)	29	54	10	2	36 (160)	313,093	139,351
Yale University (Yale Law School) P.O. Box 208329 New Haven, CT 06520-8329 203-432-4995 *admissions.law@yale.edu*	552	$55	Feb 15	March 15	$29,800	$29,800	✓				✓		82	19		✓	✓	588	25	47	29		67 (39)	798,200	2,583
Yeshiva University (Benjamin N. Cardozo School of Law) 55 Fifth Avenue New York, NY 10003 212-790-0274 Fax: 212-790-0482 *lawinfo@ymail.yu.edu*	554	$60	April 1	April 15	$26,700	$26,700				✓	✓		84	38		✓	✓	880 (51)	24	50	20	4	44 (52)	465,353	1,178,352

Regional Maps Locating ABA-Approved Law Schools

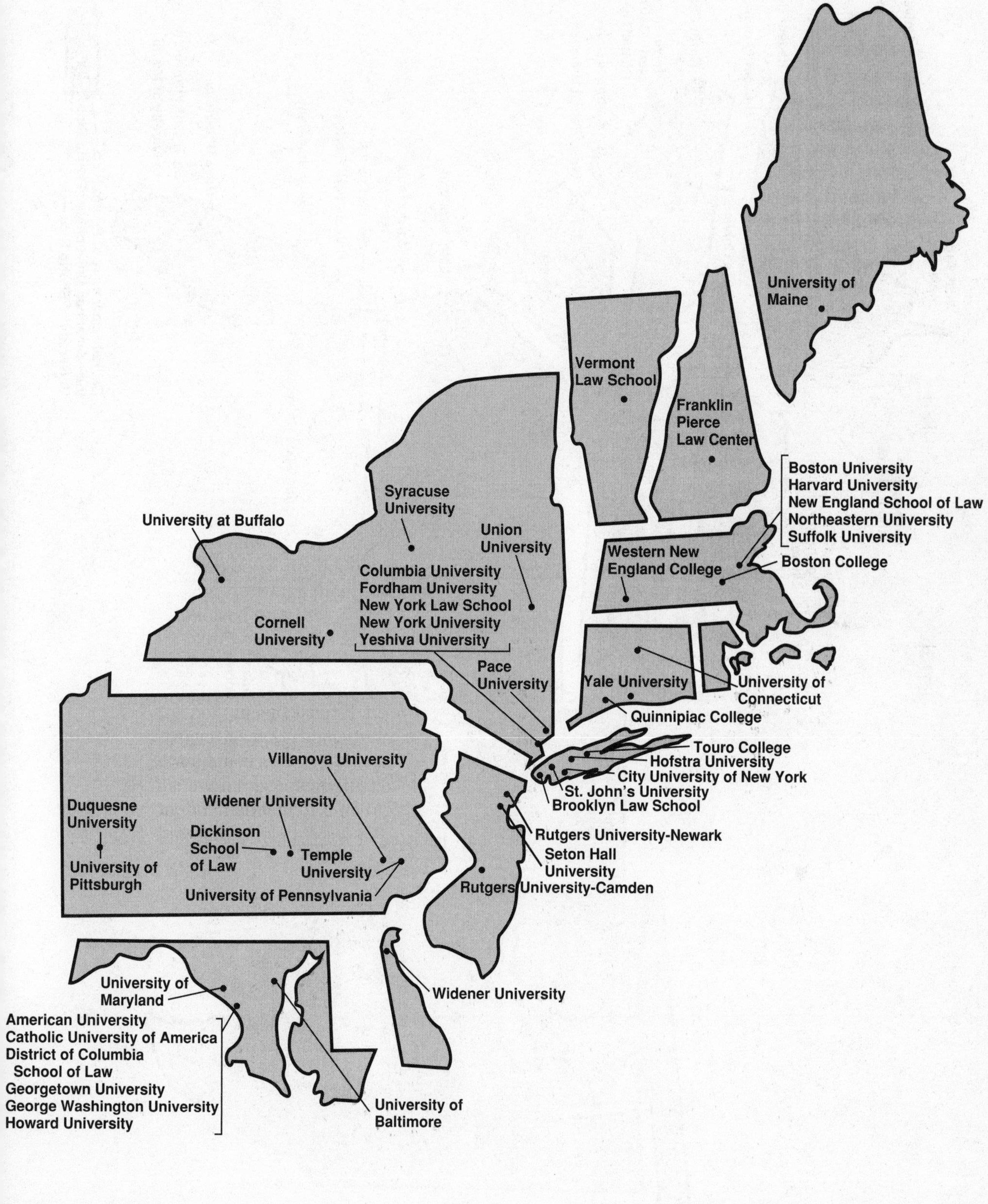
University of Maine
Vermont Law School
Franklin Pierce Law Center
Boston University
Harvard University
New England School of Law
Northeastern University
Suffolk University
Boston College
Western New England College
Syracuse University
University at Buffalo
Union University
Columbia University
Fordham University
New York Law School
New York University
Yeshiva University
Cornell University
Pace University
Yale University
University of Connecticut
Quinnipiac College
Touro College
Hofstra University
City University of New York
St. John's University
Brooklyn Law School
Villanova University
Duquesne University
Widener University
Dickinson School of Law
Temple University
University of Pittsburgh
University of Pennsylvania
Rutgers University-Newark
Seton Hall University
Rutgers University-Camden
Widener University
University of Maryland
American University
Catholic University of America
District of Columbia School of Law
Georgetown University
George Washington University
Howard University
University of Baltimore

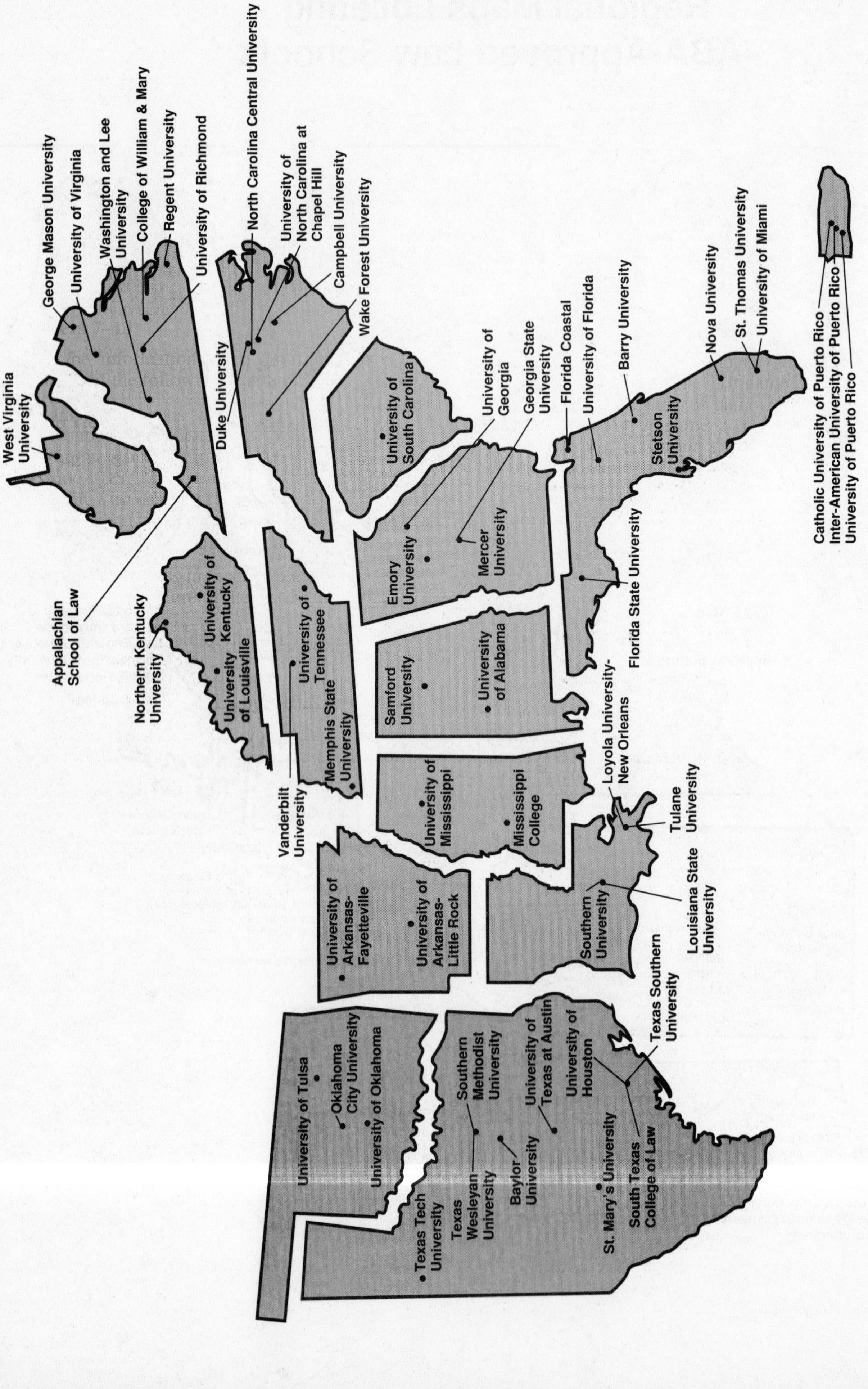
West Virginia University
Appalachian School of Law
George Mason University
University of Virginia
Washington and Lee University
College of William & Mary
Regent University
University of Richmond
North Carolina Central University
University of North Carolina at Chapel Hill
Campbell University
Wake Forest University
Duke University
University of South Carolina
Northern Kentucky University
University of Kentucky
University of Louisville
University of Tennessee
Memphis State University
Vanderbilt University
University of Georgia
Georgia State University
Emory University
Mercer University
Florida Coastal
University of Florida
Barry University
Stetson University
Nova University
St. Thomas University
University of Miami
Florida State University
Catholic University of Puerto Rico
Inter-American University of Puerto Rico
University of Puerto Rico
Samford University
University of Alabama
University of Mississippi
Mississippi College
Loyola University-New Orleans
Tulane University
Louisiana State University
Southern University
University of Arkansas-Fayetteville
University of Arkansas-Little Rock
University of Tulsa
Oklahoma City University
University of Oklahoma
Texas Tech University
Texas Wesleyan University
Southern Methodist University
Baylor University
University of Texas at Austin
University of Houston
St. Mary's University
South Texas College of Law
Texas Southern University

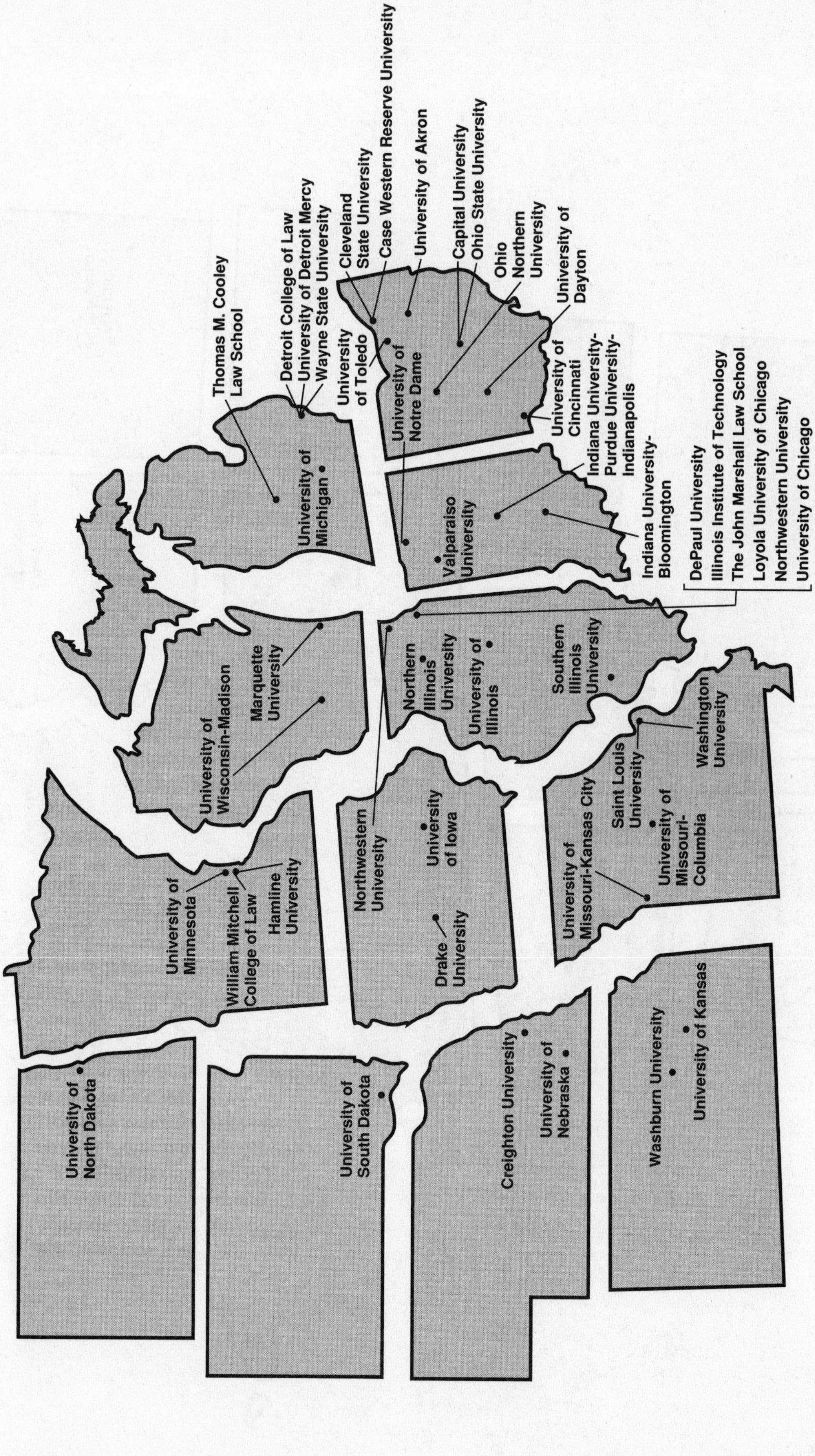

Thomas M. Cooley
Law School
Detroit College of Law
University of Detroit Mercy
Wayne State University
University of Michigan
University
of Toledo
Cleveland
State University
Case Western Reserve University
University of Akron
Capital University
Ohio State University
Ohio
Northern
University
University of
Dayton
University of
Cincinnati
University of
Notre Dame
Indiana University-
Purdue University-
Indianapolis
Indiana University-
Bloomington
Valparaiso
University
DePaul University
Illinois Institute of Technology
The John Marshall Law School
Loyola University of Chicago
Northwestern University
University of Chicago
Northern
Illinois
University
University of
Illinois
Southern
Illinois
University
Marquette
University
University of
Wisconsin-Madison
Washington
University
Saint Louis
University
University of
Missouri-
Columbia
University of
Missouri-Kansas City
Northwestern
University
University
of Iowa
Drake
University
University of
Minnesota
William Mitchell
College of Law
Hamline
University
University of
North Dakota
University of
South Dakota
Creighton University
University of
Nebraska
Washburn University
University of Kansas

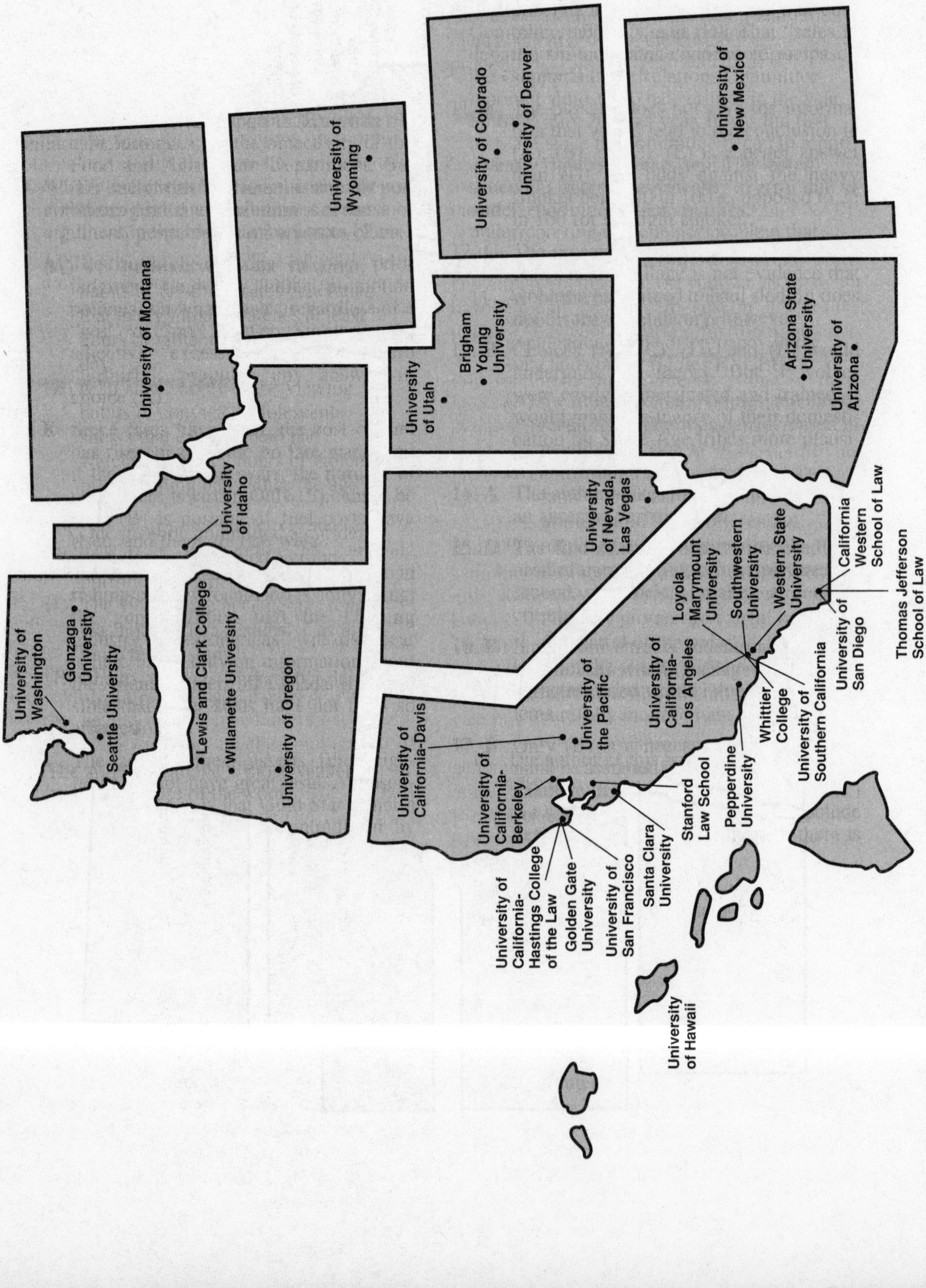
University of Washington
Gonzaga University
Seattle University
University of Montana
University of Idaho
Lewis and Clark College
Willamette University
University of Oregon
University of Wyoming
University of Colorado
University of Denver
University of New Mexico
University of Utah
Brigham Young University
Arizona State University
University of Arizona
University of Nevada, Las Vegas
University of California-Davis
University of the Pacific
University of California-Berkeley
University of California-Hastings College of the Law
Golden Gate University
University of San Francisco
Santa Clara University
Stanford Law School
Pepperdine University
University of California-Los Angeles
Loyola Marymount University
Southwestern University
Whittier College
Western State University
University of Southern California
University of San Diego
California Western School of Law
Thomas Jefferson School of Law
University of Hawaii

CHAPTER 13

Profiles of ABA-Approved Law Schools

The school profiles included in Barron's *Guide to Law Schools* comprise the listing of 185 law schools that are fully or provisionally approved by the American Bar Association and grant the J.D. degree. (One ABA-approved law school, the Judge Advocate General's School, located in Charlottesville, Virginia, and associated with the U.S. Army, is not included in our listings because it offers post-J.D. programs only.) The schools are arranged in alphabetical order by the name of the institution to which they are attached or, for independent law schools, by the name of the school. Also included for your convenience is a listing of the law schools by state.

So that you may use the profiles to best advantage, an explanation of the entries follows.

THE HEADING

The first-page heading of each profile presents the official name of the parent college or university (if any) and of the law school and the law school mailing address. The page two heading of each entry contains phone and fax numbers, followed by e-mail and WWW addresses; names and phone numbers of admissions and financial aid contacts; and a map showing the location within the respective state of each school.

THE CAPSULE

The capsule of each profile provides basic information about the law school. Wherever *n/av* is used in the capsule, it means the information was not available. Wherever *none* or *n/app* is used in the capsule, it means the category was not applicable to the law school.

Application filing dates and fees lead off the capsule.

Accrediting agencies, and **degrees granted** fill out this section of the capsule.

Accreditation Every school profiled is fully or provisionally approved by the American Bar Association. This means that the law school has met the educational standards set by the ABA regarding faculty, curricula, facilities, and other matters to qualify its graduates for admission to the Bar. In addition, membership in the Association of American Law Schools (AALS) is also indicated. Schools are not eligible for AALS membership until they have graduated three classes and have been in operation for five years. AALS membership is complementary to, but *not* competitive with, ABA approval.

Degrees Granted Law schools today offer the J.D. (Juris Doctor) degree, rather than the traditional LL.B. This recognizes the fact that virtually all law schools now require a B.A. for admission and that the curriculum of the law school represents graduate-level work. Law schools offering post-law school graduate work leading to such degrees as the LL.M. (Master of Laws), M.C.L. (Master of Comparative Law), and J.S.D. (Doctor of the Science of Law) degrees are noted.

These data are followed by **enrollment** figures for men, women, and minorities, and out-of-state students in the first-year class. Actual figures and percentages are both given.

This section also includes the number of applicants, accepted candidates, and enrolled first-year students.

The current **class profile** includes LSAT scoring and passing-the-bar information.

Finally, **tuition and fees** are graphically displayed for both in- and out-of-state applicants, showing comparisons with average nationwide figures. It is important to remember that tuition costs generally change at least yearly, and that changes can be substantial. Students are therefore urged to contact individual law schools for the most current tuition figures.

Also shown in this section is the percentage of current law students receiving **financial aid.**

Admissions The **admissions** section leads off the law school's descriptive passages, where some of the capsule information is reinforced.

The subsection *Requirements* includes whether a bachelor's degree is an absolute necessity and lists the factors considered in the admissions decision, such as LSAT percentile, GPA, and any nonacademic requirements. Virtually all of the law schools require the LSAT and a bachelor's degree, although some schools admit students without a bachelor's degree in exceptional cases. Very few schools require specific undergraduate courses or degrees or an admissions interview. Although not actual requirements, there are some qualities that schools seek in their applicants, such as preferred LSAT percentiles and GPAs. Where available, these preferred qualities also are given.

The subsection *Procedure* lists the application deadlines for various sessions, when the LSAT should be taken, the application fee, and when students are notified of the admissions decision. If a school makes admissions decisions on a rolling basis, it decides on each application as soon as possible after the file is complete and does not specify a notification deadline. As a general rule, it is best to submit applications as early as possible. Many schools require a tuition deposit to hold a place in the class. In some cases the deposit is refundable; in some, it is partially refundable; and in some, it is nonrefundable. Most schools participate in the Law School Data Assembly Service (LSDAS); if the school uses this application service, it is noted in this section.

The subsection *Special* describes admissions programs and includes information on special recruiting procedures and considerations for minority and disadvantaged students; whether the school's requirements for out-of-state students differ and whether transfer students are admitted. Although requirements for transfer with advanced standing differ from school to school, in general the applicant must have been in good standing at the school he or she is transferring from and must have completed a minimum of one year of law school study. Preadmissions courses offered by the school are also described.

Costs As noted in the explanation for the capsule, costs change from year to year; therefore, students are urged to contact the individual law schools for the most current figures. This section gives costs for tuition, additional fees, room and board, and books and supplies.

Financial Aid This section describes the availability of financial aid. It includes the percentage of students who receive aid; the types and sources of aid available, such as scholarships, grants, loans, part-time jobs, and assistantships; and the criteria for aid awards. The size of the average scholarship or grant is noted. Information on aid application deadlines and notification dates is also provided.

THE GENERAL DESCRIPTION

About the Law School This paragraph indicates, in general, whether the law school is part of a university or college, when it was founded, whether it is public or private, and its religious affiliation, if any. The school's educational philosophy, primary goals, and major characteristics are noted. Because law school programs often make use of law-related institutions, such as courts, jails, and public defenders' offices, the school's proximity to such institutions is noted. There is also information on the law school's facilities: the campus (its size, the type of area in which it is located, and its proximity to a large city); whether housing is available on campus; and whether the housing office helps students find off-campus accommodations. This section also describes the percentage of the campus accessible to physically disabled persons.

Calendar This section describes whether courses are offered for full-time and/or part-time students and whether they are offered during the day and/or evening. It also describes the minimum and maximum lengths of time allowed for completion of the program, when new students may enter the program, the availability of summer sessions, and the availability of transferable summer credits.

Programs Entries list the degrees granted, including graduate law degrees and joint degrees.

The subsection *Required* describes the number of credits needed for the J.D. and the minimum grade point average that must be maintained. The specific mandatory course requirements are listed, as well as any additional requirements for graduation. At some law schools required courses make up a major portion of the curriculum, whereas at others there are fewer required courses, allowing more room for electives. The majority of schools have a fairly even mix of mandatory and elective courses, although in most cases first-year courses are prescribed. Many law schools permit students to take a limited number of relevant graduate courses offered by other schools or departments of the institution.

Special programs are described in the subsection *Electives.* Clinical training programs offer a wide range of activities allied with, but separate from, traditional classroom studies. They cover such areas as working with legal aid societies and antipoverty groups; doing research for consumer-protection agencies; working with public defender programs or as interns in federal, district, or county attorneys' offices; and engaging in a multitude of legal or quasilegal activities. Some law schools offer a variety of programs and special activities, which allow all students to participate in some way. Other law schools have narrow or limited programs, or limit the number of students who may participate. Some schools have special or unusual seminars; some have programs involving study abroad; and some allow students to pursue independent study, usually under the supervision of a member of the law school faculty. Some schools also have tutorial or remedial programs. The most widely taken electives are listed here.

The subsection *Graduation Requirements* describes the minimum grade point average a student must maintain, whether or not there is an upper-division writing requirement, and what other requirements must be fulfilled.

Organizations Virtually all law schools have student-edited law reviews; some law schools publish more than one law review and some publish other types of legal journals and newspapers as well. Students selected to work on these publications gain valuable research, writing, and editing experience. Most schools also have moot court programs and engage in intramural and interschool competitions. Other campus activities and organizations, such as special interest or academic clubs and sororities and fraternities, are also listed in this section.

Library This section lists the resources of the law library, such as the total number of hard-copy volumes, the number of microform volume equivalents, the number of serial publications, and special collections or depositories. Computerized legal-research databases, such as LEXIS and WESTLAW, are noted, as well as the ratio of library volumes to faculty and to students, and the ratio of seats in the library to students. Recent improvements to the library are also described.

Faculty The number of full-time and part-time faculty members is given here. The percentage of full-time faculty members with a graduate law degree is noted. The ratio of full-time students to full-time faculty in an average class and in a clinic are noted here. In addition to regular classroom lectures, those law schools that have a regular program of inviting legal scholars, attorneys, and other notable speakers to campus to lecture on law-related topics are indicated. If the school has a chapter of the Order of the Coif, a national law school honor society, this is also noted here; the number of faculty who are members as well as the number of recent graduates who became members are sometimes given. Only students who are in the top 10 percent of their class are eligible for membership.

Students This paragraph gives an idea of the mix of backgrounds at a school. It includes, where available, data on the geographic distribution of the student body and on how many students enter directly from undergraduate school, have a graduate degree, or have full-time work experience. The average age of entering students is given, as is the age range. The attrition rate and reasons for discontinuing law study are noted.

The **Placement** sidebar is the final section offered for each school entry. Displayed here is information concerning the number of J.D.s awarded the previous academic year, followed by a listing of the placement services and special features available to students. Statistics relating to job interviews and job placement (and average starting salaries) follow. Finally, a breakdown of placement history is presented.

INDEX BY STATE OF ABA-APPROVED LAW SCHOOLS

MISSOURI
Saint Louis University
University of Missouri-Columbia
University of Missouri-Kansas City
Washington University in St. Louis

MONTANA
University of Montana

NEBRASKA
Creighton University
University of Nebraska

NEVADA
University of Nevada, Las Vegas

NEW HAMPSHIRE
Franklin Pierce Law Center

NEW JERSEY
Rutgers University/Camden
Rutgers University/Newark
Seton Hall University

NEW MEXICO
University of New Mexico

NEW YORK
Brooklyn Law School
City University of New York at Queens College
Columbia University
Cornell University
Fordham University
Hofstra University
New York Law School
New York University
Pace University
Saint John's University
State University of New York at Buffalo
Syracuse University
Touro College
Union University
Yeshiva University

NORTH CAROLINA
Campbell University
Duke University
North Carolina Central University
University of North Carolina at Chapel Hill
Wake Forest University

NORTH DAKOTA
University of North Dakota

OHIO
Capital University
Case Western Reserve University
Cleveland State University
Ohio Northern University
Ohio State University
University of Akron
University of Cincinnati
University of Dayton
University of Toledo

OKLAHOMA
Oklahoma City University
University of Oklahoma
University of Tulsa

OREGON
Lewis and Clark College
University of Oregon
Willamette University

PENNSYLVANIA
Duquesne University
Pennsylvania State University
Temple University
University of Pennsylvania
University of Pittsburgh
Villanova University

PUERTO RICO
Catholic University of Puerto Rico
Inter-American University of Puerto Rico
University of Puerto Rico

RHODE ISLAND
Roger Williams University

SOUTH CAROLINA
University of South Carolina

SOUTH DAKOTA
University of South Dakota

TENNESSEE
University of Memphis
University of Tennessee
Vanderbilt University

TEXAS
Baylor University
Saint Mary's University
South Texas College of Law
Southern Methodist University
Texas Southern University
Texas Tech University
Texas Wesleyan University
University of Houston
University of Texas at Austin

UTAH
Brigham Young University
University of Utah

VERMONT
Vermont Law School

VIRGINIA
Appalachian School of Law
College of William & Mary
George Mason University
Regent University
University of Richmond
University of Virginia
Washington and Lee University

WASHINGTON
Gonzaga University
Seattle University
University of Washington

WEST VIRGINIA
West Virginia University

WISCONSIN
Marquette University
University of Wisconsin

WYOMING
University of Wyoming

ALBANY LAW SCHOOL

80 New Scotland Avenue
Albany, NY 12208

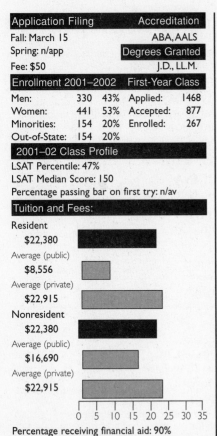

Application Filing	Accreditation
Fall: March 15	ABA, AALS
Spring: n/app	**Degrees Granted**
Fee: $50	J.D., LL.M.

Enrollment 2001–2002			First-Year Class	
Men:	330	43%	Applied:	1468
Women:	441	53%	Accepted:	877
Minorities:	154	20%	Enrolled:	267
Out-of-State:	154	20%		

2001–02 Class Profile

LSAT Percentile: 47%
LSAT Median Score: 150
Percentage passing bar on first try: n/av

Tuition and Fees:

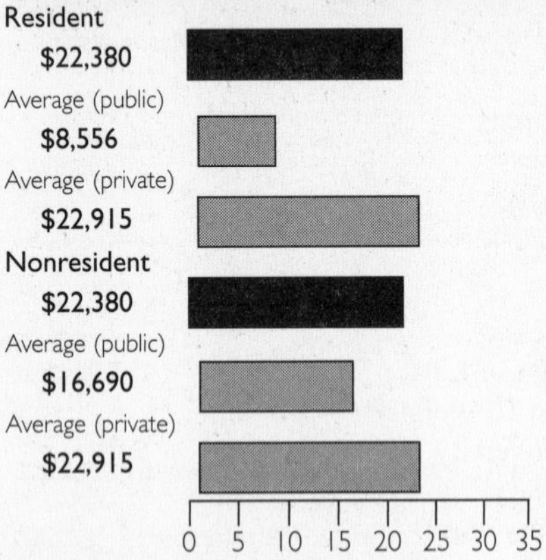

Percentage receiving financial aid: 90%

ADMISSIONS

In the fall 2001 first-year class, 1468 applied, 877 were accepted, and 267 enrolled. Four transfers enrolled. The median LSAT percentile of the most recent first-year class was 47; the median GPA was 3.24 on a scale of 4.0. The lowest LSAT percentile accepted was 13; the highest was 96.

Requirements

In general, applicants must have a bachelor's degree and take the LSAT. Students without a baccalaureate degree are admitted only with exceptional undergraduate credentials. The most important admission factors include academic achievement, LSAT results, and general background. No specific undergraduate courses are required. Candidates are not interviewed.

Procedure

The application deadline for fall entry is March 15. Applicants should submit an application form, LSAT results, transcripts, a nonrefundable application fee of $50, and 2 letters of recommendation. Notification of the admissions decision is on a rolling basis. The latest acceptable LSAT test date for fall entry is February. The law school uses the LSDAS.

Special

The law school recruits minority and disadvantaged students through current minority students who assist the Admissions Office by recruiting at colleges and universities with large minority populations and by offering tuition scholarships and grants that are awarded to more than half of the accepted minority applicants. Requirements are not different for out-of-state students. Transfer students must have one year of credit and have attended an ABA-approved law school.

Costs

Tuition and fees for the 2001-2002 academic year are $22,380 for all full-time students. Tuition for part-time students is $16,818 per year. Books and supplies run about $695 annually.

Financial Aid

About 90% of current law students receive some form of aid. The average annual amount of aid from all sources combined, including scholarships, loans, and work contracts, is $26,000; maximum, $34,000. Awards are based on need and merit, along with and diversity. The required financial statement is the FAFSA. The aid application deadline for fall entry is rolling. Special funds for minority or disadvantaged students include diversity scholarships and full- or partial-tuition waivers. First-year students are notified about their financial aid application at the time of acceptance.

About the Law School

Union University Albany Law School was established in 1851 and is an independent institution. The 6-acre campus is in an urban area 150 miles north of New York City. The primary mission of the law school is to provide students with a quality education in accordance with ethical principles and professional standards. The curriculum is traditional, yet innovative, and stresses legal knowledge, professional skills, thought habits, and contemporary techniques and technologies. Students have access to federal, state, county, city, and local agencies, courts, correctional facilities, law firms, and legal aid organizations in the Albany area. The school is located in Albany, the state capital. Facilities of special interest to law students are the Government Law Center, Science and Technology Law Center, and Moot Court Program. Housing for students is available and inexpensive off campus. About 98% of the law school facilities are accessible to the physically disabled.

Calendar

The law school operates on a traditional semester basis. Courses for full-time students are offered days only and must be completed within 3 years. For part-time students, courses are offered days only and must be completed within 4 years. New full- and part-time students are admitted in the fall. There is a 7-week summer session. Transferable summer courses are offered.

Programs

In addition to the J.D., the law school offers the LL.M. and Master of Science in legal studies. Students may take relevant courses in other programs and apply credit toward the J.D.; a maximum of 4 credits may be applied. The following joint degrees may be earned: J.D./M.B.A. (Juris Doctor/Master of Business Administration), J.D./M.P.A. (Juris Doctor/Master of Public Administration), J.D./M.R.P. (Juris Doctor/Master of Regional Planning), and J.D./M.S.W. (Juris Doctor/ Master of Social Work).

Required

To earn the J.D., candidates must complete 87 total credits, of which 31 are for required courses. They must maintain a minimum GPA of 1.7 in the required courses. The following first-year courses are required of all students: Contracts, Constitutional Law, Criminal Law, Introduction to Civil Procedure, Introduction to Lawyering, Property I and II, Torts, and Legal Methods. Required upper-level courses consist of an upper-class writing requirement and The Legal Professional/Professional Responsibility seminar. The required orientation program for first-year students is a week long program that includes a 1 credit "Legal Methods" class, social activities, and administrative activities.

Phone: 518-445-2326
Fax: 518-445-2369
E-mail: *admissions@mail.als.edu*
Web: *www.als.edu*

Contact

Dawn M. Chamberlaine, Assistant Dean, 518-445-2326 for general inquiries and financial aid information.

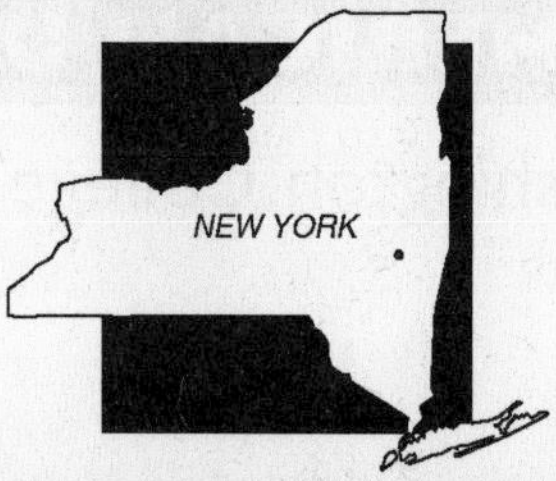

Electives

Students must take 24 credits in their area of concentration. The Albany Law School offers concentrations in corporate law, criminal law, environmental law, family law, international law, labor law, litigation, securities law, tax law, and commercial law, constitutional law, civil procedure, health law, estate law, government administration and regulation, court administration, intellectual property, and perspectives on law and legal systems. In addition, a clinical program enables upper-level students to obtain practical experience in a public law office. A classroom component is available; students may earn 12 credits, 2 to 6 each semester. Clinics include Civil Rights and Disabilities Law Clinic, AIDS Law Clinic, Civil Litigation Clinic, Domestic Violence Clinic, and Taxpayer Clinic. Seminars, worth 2 or 3 credits each semester, and research assistantships are open to upper-level students. Internships in government agencies are offered through the Government Law Center, and externships in public law offices are arranged through the Placement Clinic. Annual special lectures include the Justice Jackson and the Edward L. Swobota Memorial Lecture Series. Study abroad may be arranged through other ABA-accredited law schools for upper-level students. Albany and Tulane Law Schools jointly operate an ABA-approved summer school focusing on international commerical lawyering at McGill University in Montreal, Canada. The Lewis A. Swyer Academic Success Program provides small groups and individual instruction in legal reasoning, case analysis and synthesis, writing, and study skills. Entering students who have been out of the academic environment for several years, those whose academic backgrounds differ substantially, and those with language, physical, or emotional handicaps, are eligible to participate in the program. Minority programs are offered through student organizations, faculty, the administration, and alumni. Several societies offer lectures, symposia, and other events, including the International Law Society and Environmental Law Society. The most widely taken electives are Business Organizations, Evidence, and New York Practice.

Graduation Requirements

In order to graduate, candidates must have a GPA of 2.0 and have completed the upper-division writing requirement.

Organizations

Students edit the *Albany Law Review, Albany Law Journal of Science and Technology*, the student newspaper *The Issue*, the yearbook *The Verdict*, the *Literary Review*, and *Environmental Outlook*. Intraschool moot court competitions include the Domenick L. Gabrielli Appellate Advocacy Competition, the Karen C. McGovern Senior Prize Trials, and the Donna Jo Morse Client Counseling Competition. Other interschool competitions include ABA Client Counseling, ABA Negotiations, ABA National Applellate Advocacy, First Amendment, Products Liability, Civil Rights, Constitutional, Criminal Procedure, Entertainment, Environmental law, Evidence, Health Law, International, Labor, National Security, Privacy, and Securities Law. Campus clubs include the People's Law Project, International Law Society, and Intellectual Property Law Society. There are local chapters of Phi Alpha Delta, the National Lawyers Guild, and the Lambda Law Students Association. Other organizations are the Nontraditional Students Association, Black Law Students Association, and Latino Law Students Association.

Library

The law library contains 260,380 hardcopy volumes and 1,583,827 microform volume equivalents, and subscribes to 1496 serial publications. Such on-line databases and networks as CALI, CIS Universe, DIALOG, Infotrac, Legal-Trac, LEXIS, Mathew Bender, NEXIS, WESTLAW, New York Legislature Retrieval System, Court of Appeals on-line information service, Internet, and NELLCO Intranet are available to law students for research. Special library collections include a U.S. government documents depository, New York State documents research repository, and a New York Court of Appeals oral argument videotape repository. The ratio of library volumes to faculty is 6055 to 1 and to students, 338 to 1. The ratio of seats in the library to students is 1 to 2.

Faculty

The law school has 43 full-time and 34 part-time faculty members, of whom 28 are women. According to AAUP standards for Category I institutions, faculty salaries are well above average. About 21% of full-time faculty have a graduate law degree in addition to the J.D.; about 9% of part-time faculty have one. The ratio of full-time students to full-time faculty in an average class is 17 to 1; in a clinic, 8 to 1. The law school has a regular program of bringing visiting professors and other distinguished lecturers and visitors to campus.

Placement

J.D.s awarded: 203

Services available through: a separate law school placement center

Services: off-campus Interview programs in selected cities; job fairs; recruitment programs for full-time, summer, and part-time employment opportunities; judicial clerkship, fellowship, and internship assistance; resume and cover letter writing assistance; job search workshops; career panel; employment reports listing summer and full-time employers; job listing newsletters for alumni and recent graduates; Public Service Law Net Worldwide (PS LawNet); and computer services for job searches

Special features: career planning staff of 6 committed to personalized service; quarterly career bulletin; career education seminars featuring alumni and faculty members; Career Advisory Network; and videotape mock interviews with alumni practitioners.

Full-time job interviews:	150 employers
Summer job interviews:	150 employers
Placement by graduation:	96% of class
Placement within 9 months:	96% of class
Average starting salary:	$31,000 to $125,000

Areas of placement:

Private practice 2-10 attorneys	26%
Private practice 11-25 attorneys	12%
Private practice 26-50 attorneys	5%
Private practice 51-100 attorneys	7%
Government	26%
Business/industry	13%
Judicial clerkships	6%
Public interest	2%
Academic	2%
Military	1%

Students

About 53% of the student body are women; 20%, minorities; 8%, African American; 6%, Asian American; and 5%, Hispanic. The majority of students come from New York (80%). The average age of entering students is 27; age range is 19 to 60. About 50% of students enter directly from undergraduate school. About 10% drop out after the first year for academic or personal reasons; 90% remain to receive a law degree.

AMERICAN UNIVERSITY

Washington College of Law

4801 Massachusetts Avenue, N.W.
Washington, DC 20016-8186

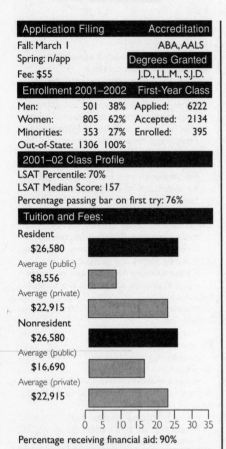

Application Filing		Accreditation
Fall: March 1		ABA, AALS
Spring: n/app		**Degrees Granted**
Fee: $55		J.D., LL.M., S.J.D.

Enrollment 2001–2002			First-Year Class	
Men:	501	38%	Applied:	6222
Women:	805	62%	Accepted:	2134
Minorities:	353	27%	Enrolled:	395
Out-of-State:	1306	100%		

2001–02 Class Profile

LSAT Percentile: 70%
LSAT Median Score: 157
Percentage passing bar on first try: 76%

Tuition and Fees:

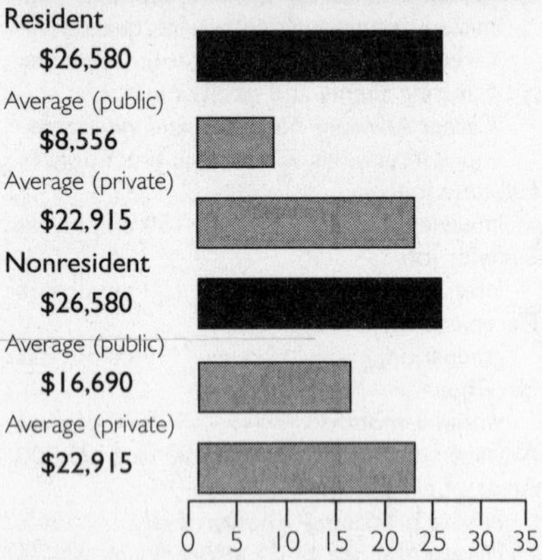

Percentage receiving financial aid: 90%

ADMISSIONS

In the fall 2001 first-year class, 6222 applied, 2134 were accepted, and 395 enrolled. Twenty-three transfers enrolled. The median LSAT percentile of the most recent first-year class was 70; the median GPA was 3.4 on a scale of 4.0.

Requirements

Applicants must have a bachelor's degree and take the LSAT. The most important admission factors include GPA, LSAT results, and college attended. No specific undergraduate courses are required. Candidates are not interviewed.

Procedure

The application deadline for fall entry is March 1. Applicants should submit an application form, LSAT results, transcripts, a nonrefundable application fee of $55, 1 letter of recommendation, and a personal statement. Notification of the admissions decision begins February 1. The latest acceptable LSAT test date for fall entry is February. The law school uses the LSDAS.

Special

The law school recruits minority and disadvantaged students in collaboration with the Office of Admissions and Office of Diversity Services. Every effort is made to attend recruiting events that are targeted to enroll the most diverse class possible. Requirements are not different for out-of-state students. Transfer students must have one year of credit, have attended an ABA-approved law school, and should be in the top 20% of the present law school class.

Costs

Tuition and fees for the 2001-2002 academic year are $26,580 for all full-time students. Tuition for part-time students is $18,645 per year. Books and supplies run about $830 annually.

Financial Aid

About 90% of current law students receive some form of aid. The average annual amount of aid from all sources combined, including scholarships, loans, and work contracts, is $27,511; maximum, is the cost of attendance. Awards are based on need and merit. Required financial statements are the FAFSA and Need Access Application. The aid application deadline for fall entry is March 1. Special funds for minority or disadvantaged students consists of need-based grants and donor-restricted scholarships. First-year students are notified about their financial aid application approximately 2 weeks following acceptance if the application deadline is met.

About the Law School

American University Washington College of Law was established in 1896 and is a private institution. The campus is in an urban area 3 miles northwest of downtown Washington. The primary mission of the law school is to provide an individualized, high-quality legal education by engaging the community, the nation, and the world through a vision that integrates theory and practice, doctrine and experiential learning, and skills and values, all in a diverse and demanding environment. Students have access to federal, state, county, city, and local agencies, courts, correctional facilities, law firms, legal aid organizations in the Washington area, U.S. Congress, U.S. Supreme Court, Library of Congress, IMF, World Bank, and other NGOs. The law school is located in a residential area of the city where many apartment buildings and rental houses are located. All law school facilities are accessible to the physically disabled.

Calendar

The law school operates on a traditional semester basis. Courses for full-time students are offered both day and evening and must be completed within 3 years. For part-time students, courses are offered both day and evening and must be completed within 4 years. New full- and part-time students are admitted in the fall. There is a 9-week summer session. Transferable summer courses are offered.

Programs

In addition to the J.D., the law school offers the LL.M. and S.J.D. Students may take relevant courses in other programs and apply credit toward the J.D.; a maximum of 6 credits may be applied. The following joint degrees may be earned: J.D./M.A. (Juris Doctor/Master of Arts in international affairs), J.D./M.B.A. (Juris Doctor/Master of Business Administration), and J.D./M.S. (Juris Doctor/Master of Science in law, justice, and society).

Required

To earn the J.D., candidates must complete 86 total credits, of which 34 are for required courses. They must maintain a minimum GPA of 2.0 in the required courses. The following first-year courses are required of all students: Torts, Contracts, Property I and II, Civil Procedure I and II, Criminal Law, Legal Rhetoric I and II, and Constitutional Law. Required upper-level courses consist of Criminal Procedure I and Legal Ethics. The required orientation program for first-year students is 2 days and includes a financial aid entrance interview, registration, dean's and faculty welcome, academic orientation, school/alumni reception, and Student Bar Association social activities.

Phone: 202-274-4101
Fax: 202-274-4107
E-mail: *wcladmit@wcl.american.edu*
Web: *www.wcl.american.edu*

Contact
Admissions Office, 202-274-4101 for general inquiries; Financial Aid Office, 202-274-4040 for financial aid information.

Electives
The Washington College of Law offers concentrations in corporate law, criminal law, environmental law, family law, international law, juvenile law, litigation, securities law, tax law, and torts and insurance. In addition, clinical experiences offered to students include the Public Interest Clinic for 14 credits, Appellate Advocacy Clinic for 12 credits, and D.C. Litigation Clinic for 7 credits. Internships, available with government agencies and nonprofit entities, are under faculty supervision. The Independent Study Program permits directed research under faculty supervision. The Field Component Program offers field work with the Securities and Exchange Commission and the Commodities Futures Trading Commission. Special lecture series include an extensive series of conferences and speaker series that deal with topics of contemporary interest. In addition, student organizations sponsor lectures and panel discussions on a range of topics. Study abroad consists of summer programs in Chile (study involving legal structures in Latin America); Paris/Geneva (international business, human rights, and environmental law); a semester exchange: Paris-X Nanterre, France; Hong Kong Exchange; and the NAFTA County Exchange. Upper-level students counsel other law students in academic subjects and law school adjustment matters in the Peer Counseling Program. The Office of Minority Affairs offers minority programs and advisory services. The most widely taken electives are Evidence, Business Associations, and Administrative Law.

Graduation Requirements
In order to graduate, candidates must have a GPA of 2.0 and have completed the upper-division writing requirement.

Organizations
Students edit the *American University Law Review, Administrative Law Review,* (ABA Section Publication), *American University International Law Review, American University Journal of Gender, Social Policy and the Law,* and the newspaper *American Jurist.* The school hosts 3 nationally/internationally recognized programs: 1) Burton D. Wechsler First Amendment Moot Court Competition; 2) "We the Students" National Moot Court Tournament; and 3) the Inter-American Moot Court Competition (in Spanish and English). Intra-school moot court competitions include the Alvira Reckman Myers competition for first-year students, and the Upper Class Moot Court Competition for second- and third-year students. Law student organizations include Equal Justice Foundation, Black Law Students Association, and Law and Government Society. There are local chapters of National Lawyers Guild, Federalist Society, and Phi Delta Phi.

Library
The law library contains 479,412 hard-copy volumes, and subscribes to 6462 serial publications. Such on-line databases and networks as CALI, CIS Universe, DIALOG, Infotrac, Legal-Trac, LEXIS, LOIS, NEXIS, OCLC First Search, WESTLAW, and Wilsonline Indexes are available to law students for research. Special library collections include European Community and U.S. government depositories as well as the Baxter Collection in international law and a National Equal Justice Library. The library occupies 55,700 net square feet in a state-of-the-art facility. There are 677 seats with electric outlets, and 342 of the seats also have data ports that have broad band access to the Internet and networks. The computer laboratory seats 40 and there are 4 group-study rooms. The ratio of library volumes to faculty is 6226 to 1 and to students is 367 to 1. The ratio of seats in the library to students is 1 to 2.

Faculty
The law school has 77 full-time and 202 part-time faculty members, of whom 86 are women. According to AAUP standards for Category I institutions, faculty salaries are above average. About 25% of full-time faculty have a graduate law degree in addition to the J.D.; about 20% of part-time faculty have one. The ratio of full-time students to full-time faculty in an average class is 8 to 1; in a clinic, 10 to 1. The law school has a regular program of bringing visiting professors and other distinguished lecturers and visitors to campus.

Placement	
J.D.s awarded:	344
Services available through: a separate law school placement center	
Services: practice interviews with alumni and 2 web-based job-posting systems for students and alumni	
Full-time job interviews:	134 employers
Summer job interviews:	134 employers
Placement by graduation:	80% of class
Placement within 9 months:	97% of class
Average starting salary:	$35,000 to $125,000
Areas of placement:	
Private practice 2-10 attorneys	7%
Private practice 11-25 attorneys	4%
Private practice 26-50 attorneys	2%
Private practice 51-100 attorneys	4%
Private practice 101+ attorneys	25%
Government	19%
Business/industry	11%
Judicial clerkships	10%
Public interest	5%
Military	2%
Academic	1%
Unknown	10%

Students
About 62% of the student body are women; 27%, minorities; 8%, African American; 12%, Asian American; 6%, Hispanic; and 1%, Native American. Most students come from the Northeast (54%). The average age of entering students is 24; age range is 20 to 45. About 13% of students have a graduate degree. About 1% drop out after the first year for academic or personal reasons; 95% remain to receive a law degree.

APPALACHIAN SCHOOL OF LAW

P.O. Box 2825
Grundy, VA 24614

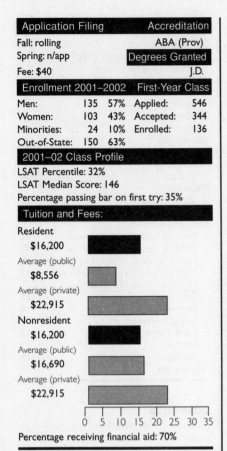

Application Filing		Accreditation
Fall: rolling		ABA (Prov)
Spring: n/app		**Degrees Granted**
Fee: $40		J.D.

Enrollment 2001–2002			First-Year Class	
Men:	135	57%	Applied:	546
Women:	103	43%	Accepted:	344
Minorities:	24	10%	Enrolled:	136
Out-of-State:	150	63%		

2001–02 Class Profile

LSAT Percentile: 32%
LSAT Median Score: 146
Percentage passing bar on first try: 35%

Tuition and Fees:

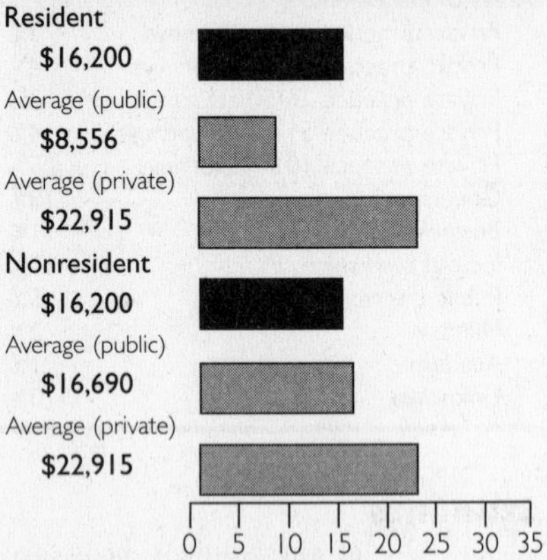

Percentage receiving financial aid: 70%

ADMISSIONS

In the fall 2001 first-year class, 546 applied, 344 were accepted, and 136 enrolled. Two transfers enrolled. The median LSAT percentile of the most recent first-year class was 32; the median GPA was 2.86 on a scale of 4.0.

Requirements

Applicants must have a bachelor's degree and take the LSAT. The most important admission factors include GPA, LSAT results, and academic achievement. No specific undergraduate courses are required. Candidates are not interviewed.

Procedure

The application deadline for fall entry is rolling. Applicants should submit an application form, LSAT results, transcripts, TOEFL for international students, a nonrefundable application fee of $40, 2 letters of recommendation, and a personal statement. Notification of the admissions decision is 3 to 4 weeks after the file is completed. The latest acceptable LSAT test date for fall entry is February. The law school uses the LSDAS.

Special

The law school recruits minority and disadvantaged students by attending events at schools with minority student populations. Requirements are not different for out-of-state students. Transfer students must have a 2.0 GPA at an ABA-approved or state-approved law school. Preadmissions courses consist of a 4-week Pre-Admission Summer Opportunity program.

Costs

Tuition and fees for the 2001-2002 academic year are $16,200 for full-time in-state students. Books and supplies run about $600 annually.

Financial Aid

About 70% of current law students receive some form of aid. The average annual amount of aid from all sources combined, including scholarships, loans, and work contracts, is $29,000; maximum, $31,031. Awards are based on need and merit. Required financial statement is the FAFSA. The aid application deadline for fall entry is rolling. First-year students are notified about their financial aid application at time of acceptance.

About the Law School

Appalachian School of Law was established in 1997 and is a private, independent institution not affiliated with a university. The 3.2-acre campus is in a small town. The primary mission of the law school is to train lawyers to be community leaders. Students have access to federal, state, county, city, and local agencies, courts, correctional facilities, law firms, and legal aid organizations in the Grundy area. Housing for students consists of rental housing in the surrounding community. All law school facilities are accessible to the physically disabled.

Calendar

The law school operates on a traditional semester basis. Courses for full-time students are offered days only and must be completed within 5 years. There is no part-time program. New students are admitted in the fall.

Phone: 276-935-4349
800-895-7411
Fax: 276-935-8261
E-mail: *vkeene@asl.edu*
Web: *www.asl.edu*

Contact

Vickie Keene, Director of Student Services, 800-895-7411 for general inquiries; Christopher Clifton, Admissions and Financial Aid Assistant, 800-895-7411 for financial aid information.

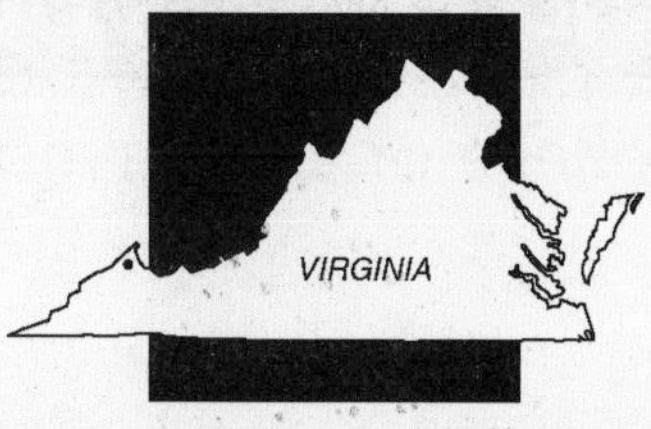

Programs

The law school offers the J.D.

Required

To earn the J.D., candidates must complete 90 total credits. They must maintain a minimum GPA of 2.0 in the required courses. The following first-year courses are required of all students: Contracts I and II, Civil Procedure I and II, Property I and II, Torts, Criminal Law, Legal Process I and II, and Introduction to Law. Required upper-level courses consist of a seminar, 2 practicum courses, Constitutional Law I and II, Dispute Resolution, Criminal Procedure, Legal Process III, Evidence, Federal Income Taxation, Estates and Trust, Professional Responsibility, Payment Systems, and an externship. The required orientation program for first-year students is 2 weeks, covering skills needed to be a successful law student, core issues of professionalism, and an introduction to Central Appalachia.

Electives

All students take a 2-credit seminar in their third year. The seminars include Administrative Law, International Law, and Juvenile Law. Students also participate in a 3-credit internship during the summer after their first year. Judicial chambers, prosecutors' offices, legal and organizational positions are typical placements. Remedial programs consist of an Academic Success Program. The most widely taken electives are Secured Transactions, Trial Advocacy, and Natural Resources.

Graduation Requirements

In order to graduate, candidates must have a GPA of 2.0 and have completed the upper-division writing requirement.

Organizations

The primary law review is the *Appalachian Journal of Law*. The student newspaper is the *Res Ipsa/Ipse Dixit*. There is a National Appellate Advocacy Competition, ATLA Student Trial Advocacy Competition, ABA Client Counseling Competition, and ABA Negotiation Competition. Law student organizations include the Black Law Students Association, and NAPIL. There are local chapters of Phi Alpha Delta, ATLA, and The Federalist Society. Campus clubs and other organizations include Democratic Society, Republican Law Students Association, and Appalachian Women in Law.

Library

The law library contains 76,275 hardcopy volumes and 87,651 microform volume equivalents, and subscribes to 2940 serial publications. Such on-line databases and networks as CALI, CIS Universe, DIALOG, Infotrac, Legal-Trac, LEXIS, LOIS, Mathew Bender, NEXIS, OCLC First Search, and WESTLAW are available to law students for research. Special library collections include Appalachian collection, government document depository, and 4th Circuit briefs. The ratio of library volumes to faculty is 5085 to 1 and to students is 320 to 1. The ratio of seats in the library to students is 1 to 1.

Faculty

The law school has 15 full-time and 8 part-time faculty members, of whom 9 are women. About 47% of full-time faculty have a graduate law degree in addition to the J.D. The ratio of full-time students to full-time faculty in an average class is 43 to 1.

Students

About 43% of the student body are women; 10%, minorities; 7%, African American; 2%, Asian American; and 1%, Hispanic. The majority of students come from the South (54%). The average age of entering students is 29; age range is 20 to 60.

Placement

J.D.s awarded:	33
Services available through: Null	
Special features: placement in academic externships after first year of law school.	
Full-time job interviews:	n/av
Summer job interviews:	n/av
Placement by graduation:	29% of class
Placement within 9 months:	82% of class
Average starting salary:	$29,000 to $60,000
Areas of placement:	
Private practice 2-10 attorneys	53%
Private practice 11-25 attorneys	3%
Solo practice	17%
Government	10%
Judicial clerkships	7%
Business/industry	7%
Academic	3%

ARIZONA STATE UNIVERSITY

College of Law/Armstrong Hall

Box 877906
Tempe, AZ 85287-7906

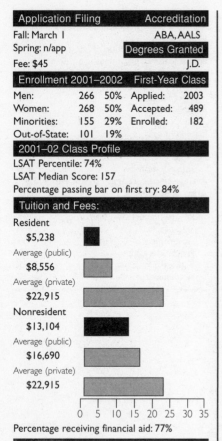

Application Filing		Accreditation
Fall: March 1		ABA, AALS
Spring: n/app		**Degrees Granted**
Fee: $45		J.D.

Enrollment 2001–2002			First-Year Class	
Men:	266	50%	Applied:	2003
Women:	268	50%	Accepted:	489
Minorities:	155	29%	Enrolled:	182
Out-of-State:	101	19%		

2001–02 Class Profile

LSAT Percentile: 74%
LSAT Median Score: 157
Percentage passing bar on first try: 84%

Tuition and Fees:

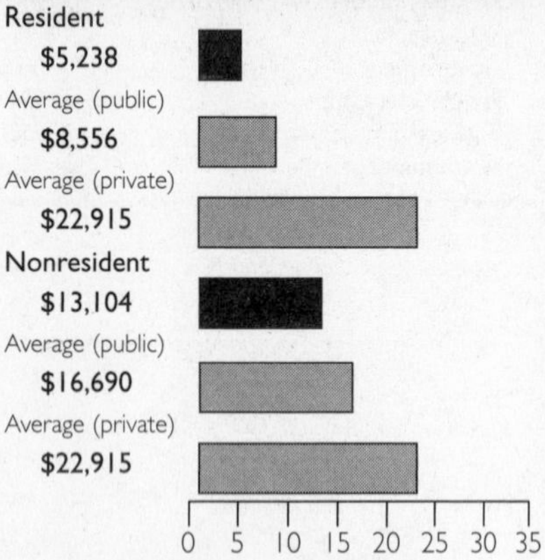

Percentage receiving financial aid: 77%

ADMISSIONS

In the fall 2001 first-year class, 2003 applied, 489 were accepted, and 182 enrolled. Four transfers enrolled. The median LSAT percentile of the most recent first-year class was 74; the median GPA was 3.4 on a scale of 4.0.

Requirements

Applicants must have a bachelor's degree and take the LSAT. No specific undergraduate courses are required. Candidates are not interviewed.

Procedure

The application deadline for fall entry is March 1. Applicants should submit an application form, LSAT results, transcripts, TOEFL (for international students), a nonrefundable application fee of $45, 2 letters of recommendation, and a personal statement no longer than 3 typed pages. Notification of the admissions decision is by mid-April on a rolling basis. The latest acceptable LSAT test date for fall entry is February. The law school uses the LSDAS.

Special

The law school recruits minority and disadvantaged students by means of special mailings, personal contact, and the involvement of current students and alumni. Requirements are not different for out-of-state students. Transfer students must have one year of credit, have attended an ABA-approved law school, and in general, be in the top 10% of their law school class.

Costs

Tuition and fees for the 2001-2002 academic year are $5238 for full-time in-state students and $13,104 for out-of-state students. Room and board costs about $7026 annually; books and supplies run $726.

Financial Aid

About 77% of current law students receive some form of aid. The average annual amount of aid from all sources combined, including scholarships, loans, and work contracts, is $14,841; maximum, $39,729. Awards are based on need and merit. Required financial statement is the FAFSA. The aid application deadline for fall entry is on a rolling basis. Special funds for minority or disadvantaged students include Graduate College Mentor Program funds; Bureau of Reclamation funds for Native American attorneys; scholarships from several Native American tribes; Federal Direct Stafford loans; Federal Perkins loans; scholarships; private alternative loans, and bar exam loans. First-year students are notified about their financial aid application on a rolling basis, depending on when the application is received.

About the Law School

Arizona State University College of Law/Armstrong Hall was established in 1967 and is a public institution. The 700-acre campus is in a suburban area 5 miles east of Phoenix, Arizona's capital. The primary mission of the law school is to provide the highest quality professional legal education; to engage in legal research, scholarship, and education; and to contribute to the local, regional, and national communities through its public service activities. Students have access to federal, state, county, city, and local agencies, courts, correctional facilities, law firms, and legal aid organizations in the Tempe area. Many opportunities, including externships, are available in the capital area. Facilities of special interest to law students are concentrated in Phoenix, the sixth largest city in the U.S. and the largest state capital. It is home to the Chief Judge of the 9th Circuit Court of Appeals, a federal courthouse, the Arizona Supreme Court, Arizona Court of Appeals, and the Arizona legislature. Externship opportunities abound. On-campus housing for students is limited and is designated specifically for graduate and/or law students. Adequate housing is found off campus. All law school facilities are accessible to the physically disabled.

Calendar

The law school operates on a traditional semester basis. Courses for full-time students are offered both day and evening and must be completed within 5 years. There is no part-time program. New students are admitted in the fall. In the summer, there are 2 5-week, an 8-week, and a 10-week session. Transferable summer courses are offered.

Programs

Students may take relevant courses in other programs and apply credit toward the J.D.; a maximum of 6 credits may be applied. The following joint degrees may be earned: J.D./M.B.A. (Juris Doctor/Master of Business Administration), J.D./M.H.S.A. (Juris Doctor/Master of Health Science Services Administration), and J.D./Ph.D. (Juris Doctor/Ph.D. Justice Studies).

Phone: 480-965-1474
Fax: 480-727-7930
E-mail: *chitra.damania@asu.edu*
Web: *www.law.asu.edu*

Contact

Chitra Damania, Admissions Officer, 480-965-1474 for general inquiries; Eileen Hanson, 480-965-6925 for financial aid information.

Required

To earn the J.D., candidates must complete 87 total credits, of which 37 are for required courses. They must maintain a minimum grade average of 70 in the required courses. The following first-year courses are required of all students: Contracts I and II, Criminal Law, Torts I and II, Civil Procedure I and II, Property I and II, Constitutional Law I, and Legal Research and Writing I and II. Required upper-level courses consist of Legal Profession, and either Constitutional Law II or Advanced Criminal Procedure. The required orientation program for first-year students is a program lasting several days that introduces students to legal professionalism and to the practicalities of legal study.

Electives

The College of Law/Armstrong Hall offers concentrations in environmental law and Certificate in Indian Law; Certificate in Law, Science & Technology with choice of concentration in Intellectual Property, Environmental Law, or Health Law. In addition, there is a Criminal Practice Clinic, a Civil Practice Clinic, and a Public Defender Clinic, each worth 6 credit hours, and a Mediation Clinic, worth 4 credits. Final year students are given preference for clinics and seminars; 10 to 15 seminars per semester are offered (worth 2 to 3 credit hours). Externships and field work allow upper-level students to earn 12 credits while working at 1 of the 49 participating agencies and courts. Numerous research opportunities are available. Professor Joe Feller's Natural Resources Field Seminar is held in northern Arizona, and gives students the opportunity to visit the places and resources discussed in the Water Law and Natural Resources Law courses, other environmentally sensitive locations, and meet with federal and state resource managers and scientists to discuss the application and implementation of environmental laws. Numerous lecture series and symposia are sponsored yearly. Study abroad is possible through a semester exchange program with Universidad Torcuato Di Tella in Buenos Aires. Career Services offers a minority Legal Intern Writing Program with a number of Phoenix firms. The most widely taken electives are Evidence, Business Associations, and Federal Courts.

Graduation Requirements

In order to graduate, candidates must have a grade average of 70, have completed the upper-division writing requirement, and 87 credit hours including the required courses and the writing requirement.

Organizations

The primary law review is the *Arizona State Law Journal*. Students also edit the *Jurimetrics Journal of Law, Science and Technology* (the official scholarly journal of the ABA Section on Law, Science and Technology). The school participates yearly in the National Moot Court, Environmental Moot Court, and Jenkes competitions. Other competitions include National NALSA Moot Court (Native American Law Students), ABA Section of Dispute Resolution's "Representation in Mediation" Competition, and various writing competitions. Law student organizations include Corporate and Business Law Student Society, Family Law Students Association, and Law & Science Student Association. Local chapters of national associations include ABA Law Student Division, Native American Law Student Association, and The Federalist Society. Campus clubs include technology, women, and Asian.

Library

The law library contains 394,805 hard-copy volumes and 131,321 microform volume equivalents, and subscribes to 3862 serial publications. Such on-line databases and networks as CALI, CIS Universe, Legal-Trac, LEXIS, LOIS, OCLC First Search, WESTLAW, and Academic Universe are available to law students for research. Special library collections include Anglo-American case reports and statutes and special collections of Indian law, Mexican law, and law and technology. Recently, the library added a building, which provides seating for approximately 490, has 179 study carrels, a 30 station computer laboratory, and LEXIS and WESTLAW rooms containing 10 stations each, and 27 study/meeting rooms. The ratio of library volumes to faculty is 10,670 to 1 and to students is 739 to 1. The ratio of seats in the library to students is 1 to 1.

Placement

J.D.s awarded:	153
Services available through: a separate law school placement center	
Special features: personal individualized service for students and grads.	
Full-time job interviews:	50 employers
Summer job interviews:	12 employers
Placement by graduation:	n/av
Placement within 9 months:	95% of class
Average starting salary:	$24,600 to $152,000
Areas of placement:	
Private practice 2-10 attorneys	25%
Private practice 11-25 attorneys	6%
Private practice 26-50 attorneys	9%
Private practice 51-100 attorneys	5%
Private practice 101-500 attorneys	14%
Government	16%
Judicial clerkships	12%
Business/industry	7%
Academic	4%
Public interest	2%

Faculty

The law school has 37 full-time and 40 part-time faculty members, of whom 11 are women. According to AAUP standards for Category I institutions, faculty salaries are above average. About 1% of full-time faculty have a graduate law degree in addition to the J.D.; about 5% of part-time faculty have one. The ratio of full-time students to full-time faculty in an average clinic is 6 to 1. The law school has a regular program of bringing visiting professors and other distinguished lecturers and visitors to campus. There is a chapter of the Order of the Coif; 224 graduates are members.

Students

About 50% of the student body are women; 29%, minorities; 5%, African American; 4%, Asian American; 13%, Hispanic; and 7%, Native American. The majority of students come from Arizona (81%). The average age of entering students is 27; age range is 20 to 73. About 27% of students enter directly from undergraduate school and 9% have a graduate degree. About 3% drop out after the first year for academic or personal reasons.

BAYLOR UNIVERSITY

School of Law

P.O. Box 97288
Waco, TX 76798-7288

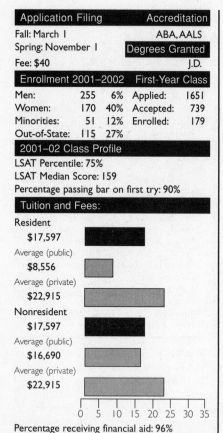

Application Filing		Accreditation
Fall: March 1		ABA, AALS
Spring: November 1		**Degrees Granted**
Fee: $40		J.D.

Enrollment 2001–2002			First-Year Class	
Men:	255	6%	Applied:	1651
Women:	170	40%	Accepted:	739
Minorities:	51	12%	Enrolled:	179
Out-of-State:	115	27%		

2001–02 Class Profile

LSAT Percentile: 75%
LSAT Median Score: 159
Percentage passing bar on first try: 90%

Tuition and Fees:

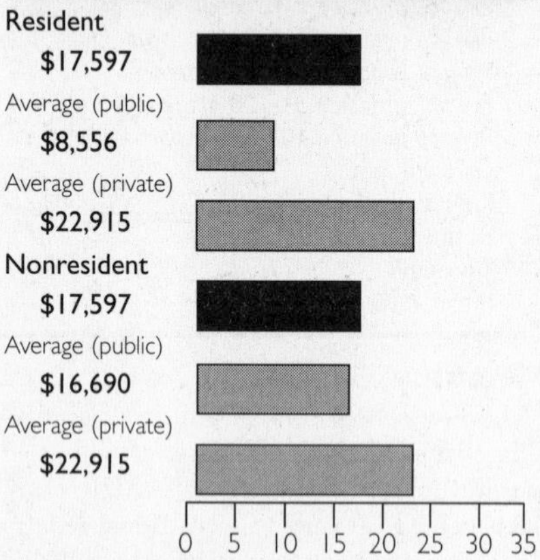

Percentage receiving financial aid: 96%

ADMISSIONS

In the fall 2001 first-year class, 1651 applied, 739 were accepted, and 179 enrolled. Four transfers enrolled. The median LSAT percentile of the most recent first-year class was 75; the median GPA was 3.65 on a scale of 4.0. The lowest LSAT percentile accepted was 52; the highest was 98.

Requirements

Applicants must have a bachelor's degree and take the LSAT. The most important admission factors include LSAT results, GPA, and general background. No specific undergraduate courses are required. Candidates are not interviewed.

Procedure

The application deadline for fall entry is March 1. Applicants should submit an application form, LSAT results, transcripts, LSDAS, a nonrefundable application fee of $40, 2 letters of recommendation, and a personal statement. Notification of the admissions decision is 4 to 6 weeks after the application deadline. The latest acceptable LSAT test date for fall entry is December. The law school uses the LSDAS.

Special

The law school recruits minority and disadvantaged students the same as nonminority students. A member of the Law School faculty serves as the Minority Law Student Adviser. Requirements are not different for out-of-state students. Transfer students must have one year of credit, have a minimum GPA of 3.0, and have attended an ABA-approved law school. To be competitive with the applicant pool, the applicants should be in the top 15% to 20% of their class at a comparable law school.

Costs

Tuition and fees for the 2001-2002 academic year are $17,597 for all full-time students. On-campus room and board costs about $9972 annually; books and supplies run $600.

Financial Aid

About 96% of current law students receive some form of aid. The average annual amount of aid from all sources combined, including scholarships, loans, and work contracts, is $21,798; maximum, $46,759. Awards are based on need and merit. Required financial statement is the CSS Profile. The aid application deadline for fall entry is May 1. There are special funds for minority or disadvantaged students, including a limited number of scholarships ranging from one-third to one-half of tuition for students who have overcome educational and/or emotional disadvantages or other personal hardship experiences. First-year students are notified about their financial aid application before enrollment.

About the Law School

Baylor University School of Law was established in 1849 and is a private institution. The 432-acre campus is in an urban area 92 miles south of Dallas. The primary mission of the law school is to train students in all facets of the law, including theoretical analysis, practical application, legal writing and advocacy, negotiation, and counseling skills, in order to equip them to practice effectively in any area of the law. Students have access to federal, state, county, city, and local agencies, courts, correctional facilities, law firms, and legal aid organizations in the Waco area. Facilities of special interest to law students include a $30 million, state-of-the-art 128,000 square foot facility. Housing for students consists of private and university rental housing, including numerous rooms and condominiums near the Baylor campus and other properties throughout the city of Waco. Families with children may choose to live further away from the campus if they have an automobile. All law school facilities are accessible to the physically disabled.

Calendar

The law school operates on a quarter basis. Courses for full-time students are offered days only and must be completed within 5 years. For part-time students, courses are offered days only and must be completed within 5 years. New students are admitted in the fall, spring, and summer. There is an 11-week summer session. Transferable summer courses are offered.

Programs

Students may take relevant courses in other programs and apply credit toward the J.D.; a maximum of 12 credits may be applied. The following joint degrees may be earned: J.D./M.B.A. (Juris Doctor/Master of Business Administration), J.D./M.Tax (Juris Doctor/Master of Taxation), and J.D/M.P.P.A. (Juris Doctor/ Master of Public Policy Administration).

Required

To earn the J.D., candidates must complete 126 total credits, of which 79 are for required courses. They must maintain a minimum GPA of 2.0 in the required courses. The following first-year courses are required of all students: Legal Analysis, Research, and Communication I, II, and III, Criminal Law, Civil Procedure, Contracts I and II, Property I and II, Torts I and II, Criminal Procedure, and Legislative and Administrative Process and Procedure. Required upper-level courses consist of Evidence, Constitutional Law, Practice Court I and II, Professional Responsibility, Federal Income

Phone: 254-710-1911
800-BAYLOR
Fax: 254-710-2316
E-mail: *becky-beck@baylor.edu*
Web: *law.baylor.edu*

Contact

Becky L. Beck, Admissions Director, 254-710-1911 for general inquiries; Office of Financial Aid, Baylor University, 254-710-2611 for financial aid information.

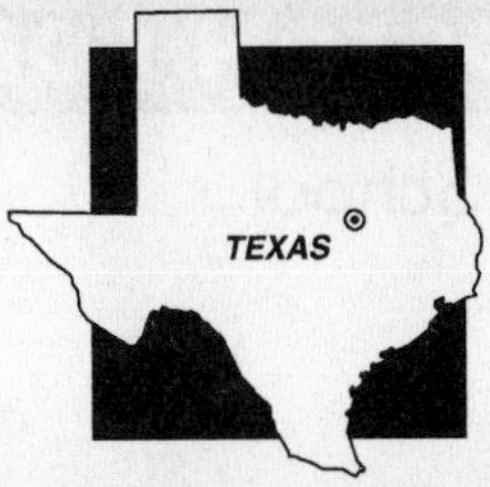

Taxation, Business Organization I, Consumer Protection, and Trusts and Estates I. All students must take clinical courses. The required orientation program for first-year students is a 2-day program that covers case analysis, statutory interpretation, and judicial processes.

Electives

The School of Law offers concentrations in criminal law, litigation, business transactions, administrative law, estate planning, and business litigation. In addition, a practice court clinic is required in the third year and includes rigorous hands-on training. Students are required to complete at least 4 mini trials and 1 large trial along with several other exercises. There are real-life client opportunities for pro bono divorce cases and other client opportunities for penalty cases. Seminars are available in the area of Supreme Court. Internships are available in the District Attorney's Office, U.S. Attorney's Office, U.S. District Court, U.S. Bankruptcy Court, Texas Attorney General's Office-Child Support Division, Legal Services Office, and others for 2 hours of credit, and the Texas Supreme Court and Court of Criminal Appeals for 5 hours of credit. Independent studies for 1 or 2 hours of credit are available for second- and third-year students under faculty supervision. Field work opportunities are available in a number of offices such as General Counsel for Hillcrest Hospital. Special lecture series include the Frank Wilson Memorial, W.R. White Memorial, R. Matt Dawson Lecture Series, and the John William Minton and Florence Dean Minton Endowed Law School Lecture Series. Students may study in Guadalajara, Mexico and earn up to 5 credits during a 2-week program in August. A faculty-conducted tutorial program is available for students placed on academic probation as well as for other interested students. There is a designated faculty Minority Student Adviser and a Minority Law Students Association. Special interest group programs include an Environmental Law program once a year and various speakers throughout the year. The most widely taken electives are Family Law, Alternative Dispute Resolution, Advanced Texas Criminal Procedure, Administration of Estates, Appellate Procedure, Trusts and Estates II, Secured Transactions.

Graduation Requirements

In order to graduate, candidates must have a GPA of 2.0.

Organizations

The primary law review is the *Baylor Law Review*. Moot court competitions include the Dawson and Sodd Fall Moot Court and the Strasburger and Price Spring Moot Court. Another intrascholastic competition is the Naman, Howell, Smith and Lee Client Counseling Competition. Interscholastic competitions include the National Trial, National Moot Court, National Appellate Advocacy, Texas Young Lawyers Moot Court, National Negotiations, and National Client Counseling. Law student organizations include the Baylor University Student Bar Association, Minority Student Association, and Civil Rights Society. Local chapters of national associations include the R.E.B. Baylor Chapter of Phi Alpha Delta, James P. Alexander Senate of Delta Phi, and the Hemphill Inn Chapter of Phi Delta Phi.

Library

The law library contains 194,429 hard-copy volumes and 101,287 microform volume equivalents, and subscribes to 4135 serial publications. Such on-line databases and networks as DIALOG, LEXIS, NEXIS, WESTLAW, and NEXIS are available to law students for research. Special library collections include the Frank M. Wilson Rare Book Room Collection, which contains first editions and rare printings of legal writings, novels, and research titles relating to law. Recently, the library moved into a spacious facility with a state-of-the-art computer laboratory and wireless connectivity throughout and a view of the Brazos River. The ratio of library volumes to faculty is 9259 to 1 and to students is 457 to 1. The ratio of seats in the library to students is 1 to 77.

Faculty

The law school has 21 full-time and 34 part-time faculty members, of whom 9 are women. According to AAUP standards for Category I institutions, faculty salaries are below average. About 25% of full-time faculty have a graduate law degree in addition to the J.D.; about 3% of part-time faculty have one. The ratio of full-time students to full-time faculty in an average class is 25 to 1; in a clinic, 2 to 1. The law school has a regular program of bringing visiting professors and other distinguished lecturers and visitors to campus.

Placement

J.D.s awarded:	128
Services available through: a separate law school placement center, the university placement center; reciprocity may be requested from other law schools.	
Services: resource library; use of telephone/fax/typewriter for job search purposes	
Special features: the Direct Contact Program, Resume Collection Program, job search skills programs, mock interviews, guest speaker panel discussions, and participation in various job fairs in Texas as well as out of state.	
Full-time job interviews:	31 employers
Summer job interviews:	127 employers
Placement by graduation:	66% of class
Placement within 9 months:	96% of class
Average starting salary:	$38,346 to $73,455
Areas of placement:	
Private practice 2-10 attorneys	30%
Private practice 11-25 attorneys	15%
Private practice 26-50 attorneys	7%
Private practice 51-100 attorneys	6%
Military	14%
Judicial clerkships	8%
Government	8%
Business/industry	5%
Academic	4%
Public interest	3%

Students

About 40% of the student body are women; 12%, minorities; 1%, African American; 2%, Asian American; and 9%, Hispanic. The majority of students come from Texas (73%). The average age of entering students is 24; age range is 21 to 55. About 76% of students enter directly from undergraduate school, 11% have a graduate degree, and 24% have worked full-time prior to entering law school. About 5% drop out after the first year for academic or personal reasons; 95% remain to receive a law degree.

BOSTON COLLEGE

Law School

885 Centre Street
Newton, MA 02459

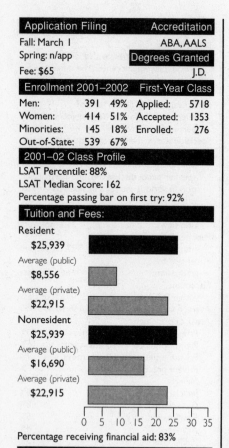

Application Filing

Fall: March 1
Spring: n/app
Fee: $65

Accreditation

ABA, AALS

Degrees Granted

J.D.

Enrollment 2001–2002			First-Year Class	
Men:	391	49%	Applied:	5718
Women:	414	51%	Accepted:	1353
Minorities:	145	18%	Enrolled:	276
Out-of-State:	539	67%		

2001–02 Class Profile

LSAT Percentile: 88%
LSAT Median Score: 162
Percentage passing bar on first try: 92%

Tuition and Fees:

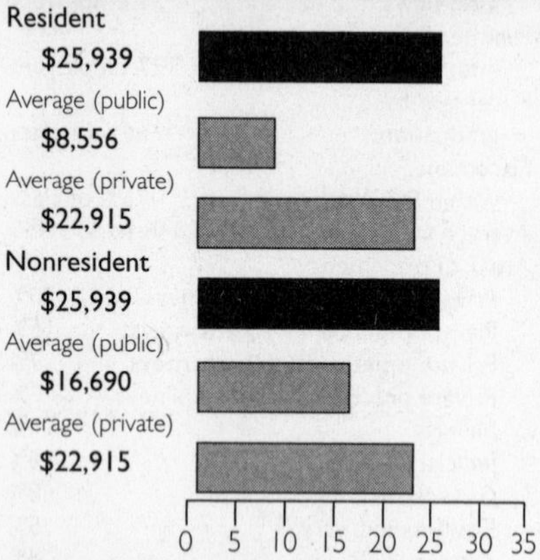

Percentage receiving financial aid: 83%

ADMISSIONS

In the fall 2001 first-year class, 5718 applied, 1353 were accepted, and 276 enrolled. Nine transfers enrolled. The median LSAT percentile of the most recent first-year class was 88; the median GPA was 3.5 on a scale of 4.0.

Requirements

Applicants must have a bachelor's degree and take the LSAT. Minimum acceptable GPA is 2.0 on a scale of 4.0. The most important admission factors include academic achievement, character, personality, and undergraduate curriculum. No specific undergraduate courses are required. Candidates are not interviewed.

Procedure

The application deadline for fall entry is March 1. Applicants should submit an application form, LSAT results, a nonrefundable application fee of $65, 2 letters of recommendation, and the LSDAS report. Notification of the admissions decision is on a rolling basis. The latest acceptable LSAT test date for fall entry is February. The law school uses the LSDAS.

Special

The law school recruits minority and disadvantaged students through a program of active outreach by the Admissions Committee and minority student organizations. Requirements are not different for out-of-state students. Transfer students must have one year of credit and have attended an ABA-approved law school. Applicants are considered on a space-available basis.

Costs

Tuition and fees for the 2001-2002 academic year are $25,939 for all full-time students. Books and supplies run about $800 annually.

Financial Aid

About 83% of current law students received some form of aid in a recent year. The average annual amount of aid from all sources combined, including scholarships, loans, and work contracts, was $29,850; maximum, $38,045. Awards are based on need and merit. Required financial statements are the CSS Profile and the FAFSA. The Need Access application may be submitted instead of the CSS Profile. The aid application deadline for fall entry is March 15. Special funds for minority or disadvantaged students consist of additional tuition remission. First-year students are notified about their financial aid application some time before the first deposit is due, if the aid application is timely.

About the Law School

Boston College Law School was established in 1929 and is a private institution. The 40-acre campus is in a suburban area 8 miles west of downtown Boston. The primary mission of the law school is to provide a quality legal education in the Jesuit, Catholic tradition to a highly qualified and diverse group of men and women in order to prepare them to serve their communities and serve as leaders in the profession. Students have access to federal, state, county, city, and local agencies, courts, correctional facilities, law firms, and legal aid organizations in the Newton area. Facilities of special interest to law students include a $16 million library, a $13 million classroom building with state-of-the-art audiovisual and computing capabilities, and a Career Resources Center. Housing for students is extensive; there is ample rental housing in Newton and the surrounding communities, and the College's off-campus Housing Office assists students in finding accommodations. All law school facilities are accessible to the physically disabled.

Calendar

The law school operates on a traditional semester basis. Courses for full-time students are offered days only and must be completed within 4 years. There is no part-time program. New students are admitted in the fall. There is no summer session. Transferable summer courses are not offered.

Phone: 617-552-4351
Fax: 617-552-2917
E-mail: *bclawadm@bc.edu*
Web: *www.bc.edu/lawschool*

Contact

Elizabeth A. Rosselot, Director of Admissions and Financial Aid, 617-552-4351 for general inquiries and financial aid information.

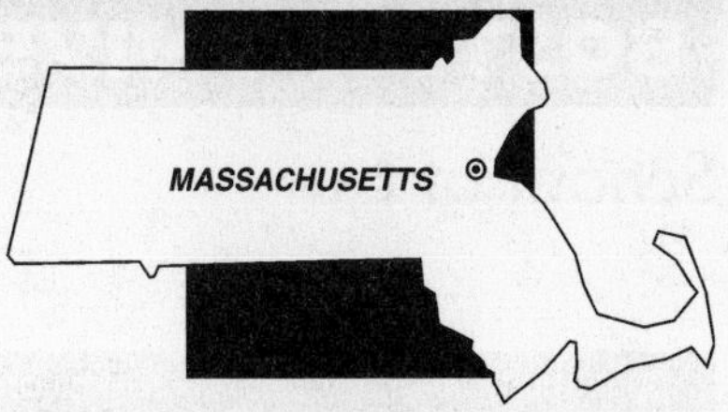

Programs

Students may take relevant courses in other programs and apply credit toward the J.D.; a maximum of 12 credits may be applied. The following joint degrees may be earned: J.D./M.A. (Juris Doctor/Master of Arts in education), J.D./M.B.A. (Juris Doctor/Master of Business Administration), J.D./M.Ed. (Juris Doctor/Master of Education), and J.D./M.S.W. (Juris Doctor/Master of Social Work).

Required

To earn the J.D., candidates must complete 85 total credits, of which 38 are for required courses. They must maintain a minimum GPA of 2.0 in the required courses. The following first-year courses are required of all students: Torts, Property, Civil Procedure, Contracts, Constitutional Law, Legal Research and Writing, and Introduction to Lawyering and Professional Responsibility. Required upper-level courses consist of Constitutional Law II and Professional Responsibility. The required orientation program for first-year students is 1 day followed by a 3-day Fundamentals of Legal Process course.

Electives

The Law School offers concentrations in corporate law, criminal law, entertainment law, environmental law, family law, international law, juvenile law, litigation, securities law, sports law, tax law, and torts and insurance. Clinics include Civil Litigation Clinic for 7 credits, Women and the Law Clinic for 7 credits, and the Criminal Justice Clinic for 7 credits. Internships include the ULL Externship Program and the Attorney General's Program. A London program is offered to second-and third-year students for 13 credits. Students in the program complete course work in international and comparative law, and serve as legal interns in a range of British organizations. Tutorial programs are available to students who require them. Programming for minority students is sponsored by student groups. Minority students are actively recruited. The most widely taken electives are Taxation, Corporations, and Commercial Law.

Graduation Requirements

In order to graduate, candidates must have a GPA of 2.0.

Organizations

Students edit the *Boston College Law Review, Boston College Environmental Affairs Law Review, Boston College International and Comparative Law Review, Boston College Third World Law Journal*, and the *Uniform Commercial Code Reporter Digest*. Moot court competitions include the Wendell F. Grimes Moot Court, Jessup International Moot Court, and National Moot Court competitions. Other competitions are the Mock Trial, Negotiations, Client Counseling, and Administrative Law Moot Court. Law student organizations include the Law Students Association, Board of Student Advisers, and the Public Interest Law Foundation. There are local chapters of the ABA-Law Student Division, Black Law Students Association, and Latino Law Students Association.

Library

The law library contains 403,537 hard-copy volumes and 1,031,218 microform volume equivalents, and subscribes to 6608 serial publications. Such on-line databases and networks as DIALOG, LEXIS, and WESTLAW are available to law students for research. The ratio of library volumes to faculty is 8407 to 1 and to students is 501 to 1. The ratio of seats in the library to students is 1 to .8.

Faculty

The law school has 48 full-time and 41 part-time faculty members, of whom 29 are women. According to AAUP standards for Category I institutions, faculty salaries are above average. About 21% of full-time faculty have a graduate law degree in addition to the J.D. The ratio of full-time students to full-time faculty in an average class is 30 to 1; in a clinic, 8 to 1. The law school has a regular program of bringing visiting professors and other distinguished lecturers and visitors to campus. There is a chapter of the Order of the Coif; 22 faculty and 830 graduates are members.

Placement

Placement	
J.D.s awarded:	272
Services available through: a separate law school placement center	
Special features: extensive skills workshops and career panels featuring alumni and a Career Resource Library that includes books, directories, periodicals, and videotapes. There are on-campus and off-campus recruitment programs.	
Full-time job interviews:	474 employers
Summer job interviews:	n/av
Placement by graduation:	n/av
Placement within 9 months:	98% of class
Average starting salary:	$40,000 to $100,000
Areas of placement:	
Private practice 2-10 attorneys	4%
Private practice 11-25 attorneys	4%
Private practice 26-50 attorneys	6%
Private practice 51-100 attorneys	5%
Judicial clerkships	13%
Government	8%
Business/industry	6%
Public interest	3%
Unknown	51%

Students

About 51% of the student body are women; 18%, minorities; 5%, African American; 8%, Asian American; 5%, Hispanic; and 1%, Native American. The majority of students come from Massachusetts (33%). The average age of entering students is 24; age range is 21 to 48. About 40% of students enter directly from undergraduate school, 10% have a graduate degree, and 60% have worked full-time prior to entering law school. About 1% drop out after the first year for academic or personal reasons; 99% remain to receive a law degree.

BOSTON UNIVERSITY

School of Law

765 Commonwealth Avenue
Boston, MA 02215

Application Filing		Accreditation
Fall: March 1		ABA, AALS
Spring: n/app		**Degrees Granted**
Fee: $60		J.D., LL.M.

Enrollment 2001–2002			First-Year Class	
Men:	391	47%	Applied:	5171
Women:	446	53%	Accepted:	1310
Minorities:	184	22%	Enrolled:	246
Out-of-State:	519	62%		

2001–02 Class Profile

LSAT Percentile: 90%
LSAT Median Score: 163
Percentage passing bar on first try: 86%

Tuition and Fees:

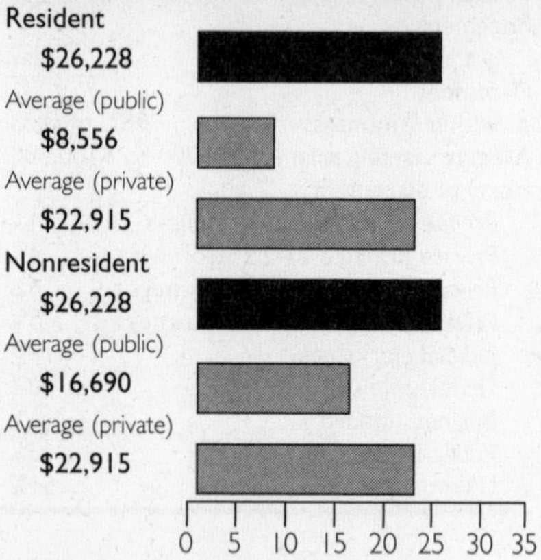

Percentage receiving financial aid: 83%

ADMISSIONS

In the fall 2001 first-year class, 5171 applied, 1310 were accepted, and 246 enrolled. Six transfers enrolled. The median LSAT percentile of the most recent first-year class was 90; the median GPA was 3.4 on a scale of 4.0. The lowest LSAT percentile accepted was 20; the highest was 99.

Requirements

Applicants must have a bachelor's degree and take the LSAT. The most important admission factors include GPA, LSAT results, and academic achievement. Social and economic obstacles and undergraduate study are considered. Specific undergraduate courses and interviews are not required.

Procedure

The application deadline for fall entry is March 1. Applicants should submit an application form, LSAT results, transcripts, TOEFL for international students only, a nonrefundable application fee of $60, 2 letters of recommendation, a dean's letter of certification, and a personal statement. Notification of the admissions decision is on a rolling basis. The latest acceptable LSAT test date for fall entry is February. The law school uses the LSDAS.

Special

The law school recruits minority and disadvantaged students by means of the Candidate Referral Service, LSAC forums, active minority groups on campus, alumni contacts, and the Legal Defense Fund Latino Day in New York City. Requirements are not different for out-of-state students. Transfer students must have one year of credit, have attended an ABA-approved law school, and must submit a regular application, but indicate that it is for a transfer.

Costs

Tuition and fees for the 2001-2002 academic year are $26,228 for all full-time students. On-campus room and board costs about $9795 annually; books and supplies run $1056.

Financial Aid

About 83% of current law students receive some form of aid. The average annual amount of aid from all sources combined, including scholarships, loans, and work contracts, is $25,428; maximum, $40,575. Awards are based on need and merit. Required financial statements are the CSS Profile, the FAFSA, and institutional form. The aid application deadline for fall entry is March 1. Special funds for minority or disadvantaged students consist of Martin Luther King Jr., Whitney Young, Norbert Simmons, and Barbara Jordan fellowships and scholarships. First-year students are notified about their financial aid application within 2 weeks after acceptance.

About the Law School

Boston University School of Law was established in 1872 and is a private institution. The 132-acre campus is in an urban area in Boston. The primary mission of the law school is to teach its students to understand the nature of the law, to provide them with training in legal principles and professional techniques, and to equip them to succeed in a rapidly changing world. Students have access to federal, state, county, city, and local agencies, courts, correctional facilities, law firms, and legal aid organizations in the Boston area. The school hosts the American Society for Law, Medicine, and Ethics, the Morin Center for Banking and Financial Law Studies, and the Pike Institute of Law and Disability. Facilities of special interest to law students are the Case Center for athletics, the university's Concert Series, the Tsai Performance Center, boating on campus, and all the amenities of Boston, such as the Boston Symphony, opera, theater, and sports. Housing for students is available as apartment units within walking distance of the school or as suburban accommodations easily reached by mass transportation lines. About 98% of the law school facilities are accessible to the physically disabled.

Calendar

The law school operates on a traditional semester basis. Courses for full-time students are offered days only and must be completed within 3 years. For part-time students, courses are offered both day and evening. Graduate studies are offered part-time. New full- and part-time students are admitted in the fall. There is no summer session. Transferable summer courses are not offered.

Programs

In addition to the J.D., the law school offers the LL.M. Students may take relevant courses in other programs and apply credit toward the J.D.; a maximum of 12 credits may be applied. The following joint degrees may be earned: J.D./LL.M. (Juris Doctor/Master of Laws in taxation and in banking and financial law), J.D./M.A. (Juris Doctor/Master of Arts in international relations, preservation studies, and philosophy), J.D./M.B.A. (Juris Doctor/Master of Business Administration in law and health care), J.D./M.P.H. (Juris Doctor/Master of Public Health), J.D./M.S. (Juris Doctor/Master of Science in mass communication), and J.D./M.S.W. (Juris Doctor/Master of Social Work).

Required

To earn the J.D., candidates must complete 84 total credits, of which 33 are for required courses. They must maintain a minimum GPA of 2.0 in the required courses. The following first-year courses are required of all students: Contracts, Torts, Civil Procedure, Property, Legal Writing and Research, Criminal Law, and Constitutional Law. Required upper-level courses consist of Legal Ethics. All students choose from voluntary clinical programs that include a Legal Externship program, Legislative Services, Criminal Trial Advocacy, judicial internships, Legal Aid, and Student Defenders and Prosecutors.The required orientation

Phone: 617-353-3100
E-mail: *bulawadm@bu.edu*
Web: *http://www.bu.edu/LAW*

Contact

Joan Horgan, Director of Admissions and Financial Aid, 617-353-3100 for general inquiries; Joan Horgan, Director of Admissions and Financial Aid, 617-353-3160 for financial aid information.

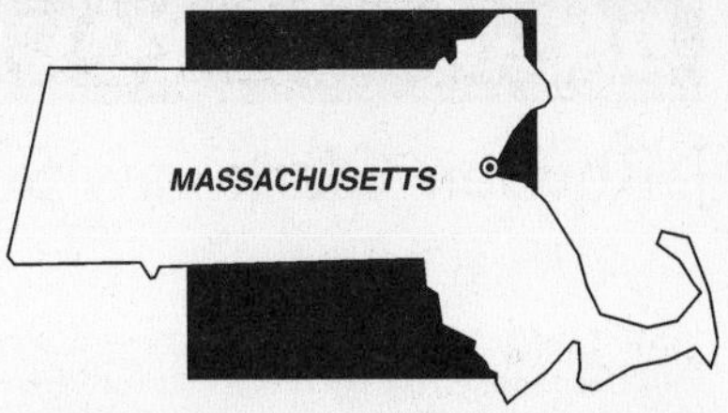

program for first-year students is a 1½-day program including building tours and panel discussions.

Electives

The School of Law offers concentrations in corporate law, international law, litigation, and health law, and intellectual property. In addition, clinics for upper-level students include Legislative Services, Criminal Trial Advocacy, and Civil Litigation Clinic. Credit varies from 3 to 8 hours. More than 50 seminars for varying credit are open to upper-level students. A judicial internship is worth 3 credits and a variety of externships, geared toward individual student interest, is offered for 6 credits. Independent Study with a faculty member is offered to upper-level students for 1 to 3 credits. Special lecture series include the Distinguished Speaker Series, Shapiro Lecture, and Legal History Lectures. The school offers 8 overseas study programs: in Lyon, France; Paris; Oxford, England; Tel Aviv, Israel; Leiden, the Netherlands; Buenos Aires, Argentina; Florence, Italy; and Hong Kong. There is a Voluntary Academic Support Program for first-year students whose first-semester grades indicate that they need assistance. The program is offered in the second semester of the first year for no credit. The law school has an Academic Support Program for second- and third-year students whose GPA ranges from 2.0 to 2.7. There is an orientation program for incoming minority students. Minority law student organizations include APALSA (Asian-Pacific American students); BLSA (Black students); LALSA (Latin American students); and SALSA (South Asian American students). A Student Organization Activities Fair introduces students to school organizations and groups. The most widely taken electives are Corporations, Evidence, and Federal Income Taxation.

Graduation Requirements

In order to graduate, candidates must have a GPA of 2.0, have completed the upper-division writing requirement, and have researched and written a major paper on a topic of their choice. The paper is faculty supervised and evaluated.

Organizations

Students edit the *Boston University Law Review, American Journal of Law and Medicine, Annual Review of Banking Law, Boston University International Law Journal, Public Interest Law Journal,* and *Journal of Science and Technology Law.* All first-year students participate in the intramural J. Newton Esdaile Moot Court program during the spring semester. Second-year students may participate in the Edward C. Stone Appellate Moot Court Competition in the fall; the top advocates from the Stone Competition advance to the Homer Albers Prize Moot Court Competition during the spring semester of their second year. Teams of third-year students are sent to national intramural competitions such as National Moot Court and National Appellate Advocacy. Students may participate in the Association of Trial Lawyers of America National Student Trial Advocacy Competition and the ABA Negotiation and Client Counseling competitions. Student organizations include Student Bar Association; Women's Law Association; and Corporate Law Society. There are local chapters of The Federalist Society, Phi Alpha Delta, and Phi Delta Phi.

Library

The law library contains 586,557 hard-copy volumes and 258,428 microform volume equivalents, and subscribes to 5896 serial publications. Such on-line databases and networks as CALI, CIS Universe, DIALOG, Dow-Jones, Infotrac, Legal-Trac, LEXIS, NEXIS, OCLC First Search, RLIN, WESTLAW, Wilsonline Indexes, and more than 100 electronic data bases are available to law students for research. Special library collections include a U.S. government selected depository, and intellectual property, banking law, health law, human rights, tax law, and international law collections. Recently, the library installed a wireless network. The ratio of library volumes to faculty is 8501 to 1 and to students is 701 to 1. The ratio of seats in the library to students is 1 to 1.

Faculty

The law school has 69 full-time and 24 part-time faculty members, of whom 29 are women. About 19% of full-time faculty have a graduate law degree in addition to the J.D.; about 13% of part-time faculty have one. The ratio of full-time students to full-time faculty in an average class is 37 to 1; in a clinic, 11 to 1. The law school has a regular program of bringing visiting professors and other distinguished lecturers and visitors to campus.

Placement

J.D.s awarded: 292

Services available through: a separate law school placement center

Services: extensive off-campus interview programs in 8 cities and numerous specialty job fairs; job search strategy and interview workshops; numerous presentations on areas of practice and law-related careers featuring alumni

Special features: There are 4 staff counselors, 3 of whom are also attorneys. One counselor specializes in public interest and government positions. The school also employs a recruitment and marketing manager, a recruitment coordinator, and a program coordinator. Additionally, there is an extensive Internet-based computer data base of legal employers, on-line interview selectors and job listings, and numerous publications, directories, manuals, and periodicals on private, public, in-house, judicial clerkships, nontraditional, and academic careers. The school also provides information on domestic and international fellowships. The Career Assistance Program (CAP) matches students with alumni contacts who assist in the job search nationwide.

Full-time job interviews:	384 employers
Summer job interviews:	n/av
Placement by graduation:	88% of class
Placement within 9 months:	100% of class
Average starting salary:	$58,000 to $125,000
Areas of placement:	
Private practice 2-10 attorneys	6%
Private practice 11-25 attorneys	6%
Private practice 26-50 attorneys	7%
Private practice 51-100 attorneys	52%
Judicial clerkships	9%
Government	5%
Business/industry	4%
Public interest	1%
Academic	1%

Students

About 53% of the student body are women; 22%, minorities; 3%, African American; 10%, Asian American; and 8%, Hispanic. Most students come from Massachusetts (38%). The average age of entering students is 23; age range is 20 to 36. About 40% of students enter directly from undergraduate school and 3% have a graduate degree. About 4% drop out after the first year for academic or personal reasons; 93% remain to receive a law degree.

BRIGHAM YOUNG UNIVERSITY

J. Reuben Clark Law School

342 JRCB Brigham Young University
Provo, UT 84602

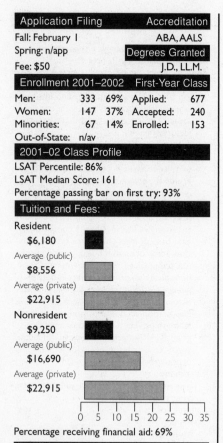

Application Filing		Accreditation
Fall: February 1		ABA, AALS
Spring: n/app		**Degrees Granted**
Fee: $50		J.D., LL.M.

Enrollment 2001–2002			First-Year Class	
Men:	333	69%	Applied:	677
Women:	147	37%	Accepted:	240
Minorities:	67	14%	Enrolled:	153
Out-of-State:	n/av			

2001–02 Class Profile

LSAT Percentile: 86%
LSAT Median Score: 161
Percentage passing bar on first try: 93%

Tuition and Fees:

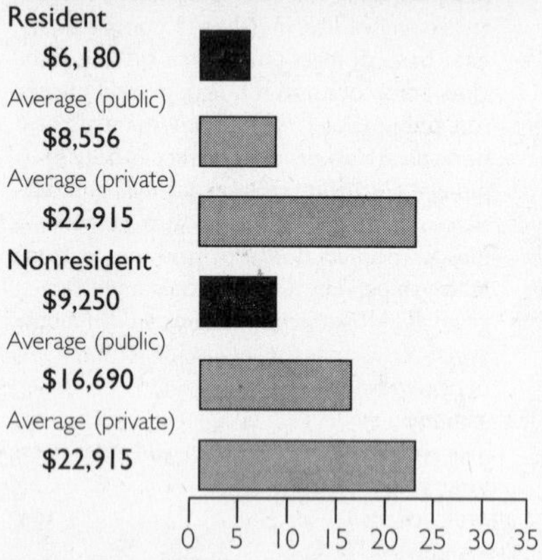

Percentage receiving financial aid: 69%

ADMISSIONS

In the fall 2001 first-year class, 677 applied, 240 were accepted, and 153 enrolled. Five transfers enrolled. The median LSAT percentile of the most recent first-year class was 86; the median GPA was 3.67 on a scale of 4.0. The highest LSAT percentile was 99.

Requirements

Applicants must have a bachelor's degree and take the LSAT. The most important admission factors include GPA and LSAT results. No specific undergraduate courses are required. Candidates are not interviewed.

Procedure

The application deadline for fall entry is February 1. Applicants should submit an application form, LSAT results, transcripts, a nonrefundable application fee of $50, 3 letters of recommendation, and a personal statement. Notification of the admissions decision is no later than March 30. The latest acceptable LSAT test date for fall entry is December. The law school uses the LSDAS.

Special

The law school recruits minority and disadvantaged students by direct mail, law forums, visiting undergraduate institutions, and personal contact from students, alumni, and friends of the law school. The school works closely with the Minority Law Students Association in recruiting minority students. Requirements are not different for out-of-state students. Transfer students must have one year of credit, have attended an ABA-approved law school, and must be in the top third of the class in their prior school.

Costs

Tuition and fees for the 2001-2002 academic year are $6180 for full-time in-state students and $9250 for out-of-state students. On-campus room and board costs about $6100 annually; books and supplies run $1230.

Financial Aid

About 69% of current law students receive some form of aid. The average annual amount of aid from all sources combined, including scholarships, loans, and work contracts, is $10,000; maximum, $17,000. Awards are based on need and merit. Required financial statements are the CSS Profile and the FAFSA. The aid application deadline for fall entry is March 1. Special funds for minority or disadvantaged students are available. First-year students are notified about their financial aid application at time of acceptance.

About the Law School

Brigham Young University J. Reuben Clark Law School was established in 1973 and is a private institution. The 544-acre campus is in a suburban area 50 miles south of Salt Lake City. The primary mission of the law school is to affirm the strength brought to the law by a student's personal religious conviction. The school encourages public service and professional excellence and the promotion of fairness and virtue founded upon the rule of law. Students have access to federal, state, county, city, and local agencies, courts, correctional facilities, law firms, and legal aid organizations in the Provo area. The World Family Policy Center and the International Center for Law and Religion Studies afford opportunities for international involvement with issues of global importance. The school provides each student with a personal study carrel within the law library, which is wired to the Internet, Lexis and Westlaw where books and personal effects may be secured. Individual study rooms and family support rooms (wired to classrooms for audio and video) are located in the library. Housing for single and married students is available within easy access of the school. All law school facilities are accessible to the physically disabled.

Calendar

The law school operates on a traditional semester basis. Courses for full-time students are offered days only and must be completed within 3 years. There is no part-time program. New students are admitted in the fall. There is no summer session. Transferable summer courses are not offered.

Programs

In addition to the J.D., the law school offers the LL.M. Students may take relevant courses in other programs and apply credit toward the J.D.; a maximum of 9 credits may be applied. The following joint degrees may be earned: J.D./Ed.D. (Juris Doctor/Doctor of Education), J.D./M.Acc. (Juris Doctor/Master of Accountancy), J.D./M.B.A. (Juris Doctor/Master of Business Administration), J.D./M.Ed. (Juris Doctor/Master of Education), and J.D./M.P.A. (Juris Doctor/Master of Public Administration).

Required

To earn the J.D., candidates must complete 90 total credits, of which 36 are for required courses. They must maintain a minimum GPA of 2.7 in the required courses. The following first-year courses are required of all students: Criminal Law, Introduction to Advocacy I and II, Contracts, Property, Torts, Structures of the Constitution, Perspectives on Law, and Civil Procedure. Required upper-level courses consist of Professional Responsibility, a substantial paper, and Advanced Legal Research. The required orientation program for first-year students is a 4-day program that includes an introduction to the study of law and legal research.

Phone: 801-378-4277
Fax: 801-378-5897
E-mail: *wilcock@lawgate.byu.edu*
Web: *law.byu.edu*

Contact

Lola K. Wilcock, Admissions Director, 801-378-4277 for general inquiries; Douglas Young, 801-378-6425 for financial aid information.

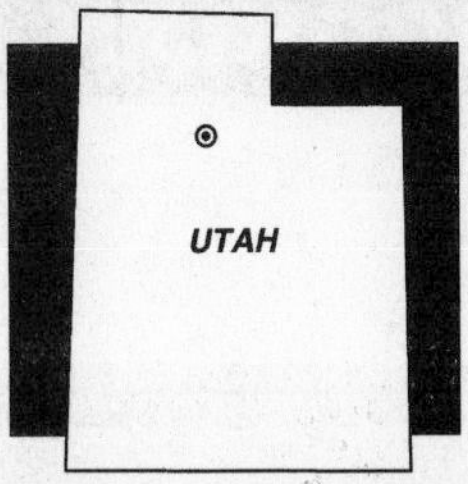

Electives

The law school has LawHelp seminars in which students provide legal services to clients under the direction of an attorney. Second- and third-year students may earn up to 15 credits in externships, LawHelp seminars, internships, or field work. Each first-year student has 1 class taught in seminar/small section form; 41 seminars are available for second- and third-year students. Students are allowed up to 15 credit hours for judicial, prosecutorial, governmental, private law firm, and public interest internships; 2 credit hours for research programs; and 15 for field work. The Career Services Office offers a weekly lecture series course, which features guest speakers from practice area specialties. There are professional seminars for first-year students. Student organizations sponsor speakers on topics ranging from practical lawyering skills to jurisprudential theory. Students interested in study abroad programs sponsored by other law schools may transfer credit. Each first-year course has a weekly tutorial. Additionally, the Academic Success Program includes (1) a series of 6 workshops providing instruction related to law school study skills, (2) assigning individual tutors to students when professors and the Assistant Dean feel it is needed, and (3) office hours for students to meet 1-on-1 with tutors. The Assistant Dean meets with students in academic jeopardy to design study plans and identify resources. Minority recruiting is very important at BYU and includes the Minority Law School night, the Diversity Job Fair, and outreach to the multi-cultural offices at many undergraduate institutions. A joint student/faculty Law School Discovery Committee is geared to expanding the school's diversity. The most widely taken electives are Constitutional Law, Secured Transactions, and Wills and Estates.

Graduation Requirements

In order to graduate, candidates must have a GPA of 2.7 and have completed the upper-division writing requirement. The grading scale is a 1.6 to 4.0 scale.

Organizations

Students edit the *Brigham Young University Law Review*, *Journal of Public Law*, *Education and Law Journal*, and the newspaper *Reuby's RegisterJ*. The *Clark Memorandum* is a semi-annual Law Society and alumni magazine. *BYU Law News* is constantly updated on-line. The school sends teams to the Jessup International Moot Court Competition and 5 other competitions annually. All first-year students participate in a competitive moot court program as part of the mandatory legal research and writing course. Other competitions include the John Welch Award for Outstanding Writing, the A.H. Christensen Advocacy Award, the Woody Deem Trial Advocacy Competition, BYU Research and Writing Award, LeBoeuf Bankruptcy Scholar Award, Utah State Bar Business Writing Award, and Utah Bar Foundation Public Interest Award. Law student organizations include Minority Law Student Association, Women's Law Forum, and Government and Politics Legal Society. Local chapters of national associations include Public Interest Law Foundation (NAPIL), Federalist Society, and Phi Delta Phi. Campus clubs and other organizations include the Student Intellectual Property Association (SIPLA), International and Comparative Law Society, and Sports and Entertainment Law Society (SPENT).

Library

The law library contains 441,860 hard-copy volumes and 149,367 microform volume equivalents, and subscribes to 5616 serial publications. Such on-line databases and networks as CIS Universe, DIALOG, Dow-Jones, Infotrac, LegalTrac, LEXIS, LOIS, NEXIS, RLIN, WESTLAW, Wilsonline Indexes, and state gateway access to catalogs that are shared databases, LAN access to databases at the main library, and 64 CD-ROM databases are available to law students for research. Special library collections include U.S. government documents and Utah State documents depositories, American Indian Law Collection, and Canadian and UK Collections. Recently, the library adopted and installed the SIRS/integrated library system. The ratio of library volumes to full-time faculty is 11,628 to 1 and to students is 920 to 1. The ratio of seats in the library to students is 1 to 1.

Faculty

The law school has 38 full-time and 32 part-time faculty members, of whom 18 are women. About 4% of full-time faculty have a graduate law degree in addition to the J.D.; about 4% of part-time faculty have one. The ratio of full-time students to full-time faculty in an average class is 16 to 1. The law school has a regular program of bringing visiting professors and other distinguished lecturers and visitors to campus. There is a chapter of the Order of the Coif; 27 faculty and 297 graduates are members.

Placement

J.D.s awarded:	156
Services available through: a separate law school placement center	
Services: weekly lecture series course that features attorneys speaking on different areas of practice, resume review service, and workshops	
Special features: networking groups, practice area, tutorials, a professional development skills training course, satellite interviewing programs, attorney mock interviewing programs, video interviews, a judicial clerkship handbook, a job hunt handbook, a legal career planning handbook, and alumni receptions.	
Full-time job interviews:	62 employers
Summer job interviews:	72 employers
Placement by graduation:	85% of class
Placement within 9 months:	98% of class
Average starting salary:	$22,000 to $90,000
Areas of placement:	
Private practice 2-10 attorneys	16%
Private practice 11-25 attorneys	8%
Private practice 26-50 attorneys	5%
Private practice 51-100 attorneys	5%
Private practice 101+ attorneys	15%
Solo Practice	1%
Business/industry	19%
Judicial clerkships	18%
Government	8%
Public interest	2%
Academic	2%
Military	1%

Students

About 37% of the student body are women; 14%, minorities; 1%, African American; 5%, Asian American; 5%, Hispanic; 1%, Native American; and 1%, foreign nationals. The average age of entering students is 26; age range is 20 to 53. About 85% of students enter directly from undergraduate school. Less than 1% drop out after the first year for academic or personal reasons; 99% remain to receive a law degree.

BROOKLYN LAW SCHOOL

250 Joralemon Street
Brooklyn, NY 11201

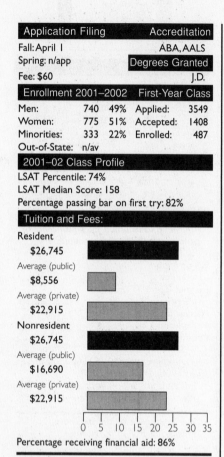

Application Filing		Accreditation
Fall: April 1		ABA, AALS
Spring: n/app		**Degrees Granted**
Fee: $60		J.D.

Enrollment 2001–2002			First-Year Class	
Men:	740	49%	Applied:	3549
Women:	775	51%	Accepted:	1408
Minorities:	333	22%	Enrolled:	487
Out-of-State:	n/av			

2001–02 Class Profile

LSAT Percentile: 74%
LSAT Median Score: 158
Percentage passing bar on first try: 82%

Tuition and Fees:

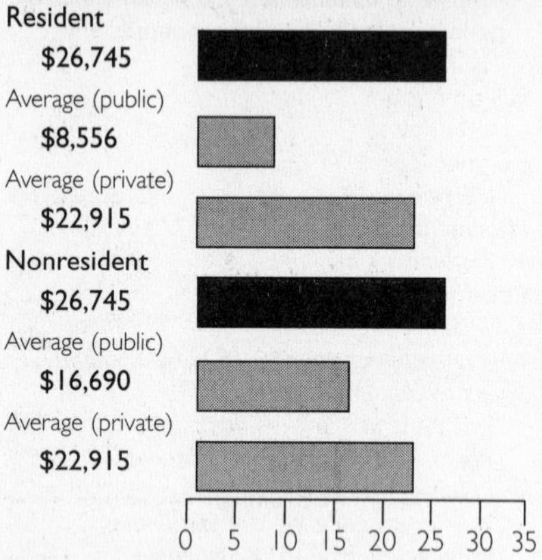

Percentage receiving financial aid: 86%

ADMISSIONS

In the fall 2001 first-year class, 3549 applied, 1408 were accepted, and 487 enrolled. Eighteen transfers enrolled. The median LSAT percentile of the most recent first-year class was 74; the median GPA was 3.4 on a scale of 4.0. The lowest LSAT percentile accepted was 43; the highest was 99.

Requirements

Applicants must have a bachelor's degree and take the LSAT. The most important admission factors include college attended, GPA, and academic achievement. No specific undergraduate courses are required. Candidates are not interviewed.

Procedure

The application deadline for fall entry is April 1. Applicants should submit an application form, LSAT results, transcripts, a nonrefundable application fee of $60, transcripts (via LSDAS) and Dean's Certification Form. Letters of recommendation are optional, but encouraged. Notification of the admissions decision begins in December. The latest acceptable LSAT date for fall entry is June. The law school uses the LSDAS.

Special

The law school recruits minority and disadvantaged students by means of recruitment visits to historically black colleges and universities; various minority law career days and professional school forums; assistance from school chapters of Asian, Black, and Latin American Law Student Associations; an annual on-campus Minority Student Recruitment event; the LSDAS Candidate Referral Service (CRS); and a series of orientation programs for prospective students. Requirements are not different for out-of-state students. Transfer students must have a minimum GPA of approximately 3.0, have attended an ABA-approved law school, and have a letter of good standing from the dean of the current school. The law school must be a member of AALS; 33 credits are the maximum allowable.

Costs

Tuition and fees for the 2001-2002 academic year are $26,745 for all full-time students. Tuition for part-time students is $20,100 per year. Books and supplies run about $1200 annually.

Financial Aid

About 86% of current law students receive some form of aid. The average annual amount of aid from all sources combined, including scholarships, loans, and work contracts, is $25,325. Awards are based on need and merit. Aid takes the form of grants, loans, and work-study. Required financial statements are the FAFSA, Need Access Form, and the IRS Form 1040 for the applicant as well as their parents' 1040 Forms. Also required are the school's financial assistance application forms. No application is required for merit-based awards. The aid application deadline for fall entry is March 15. Special funds for minority or disadvantaged students include the Geraldo Rivera Scholarship; MLK, Jr. Scholarship, and others. First-year students are notified at time of acceptance for merit scholarships. Need-based award notification is sent late spring or early summer prior to enrollment.

About the Law School

Brooklyn Law School was established in 1901 and is an independent institution. The 1-acre campus is in an urban area in New York City. The primary mission of the law school is not only to train practicing attorneys, but also to help students develop the intellectual capacity required to succeed whether they choose to practice law or pursue an alternative career with a legal background. Students have access to federal, state, county, city, and local agencies, courts, correctional facilities, law firms, and legal aid organizations in the Brooklyn area. Nearby are the U.S. district court, appellate division court, state supreme and family courts, city civil and criminal courts, U.S. attorney's office, and Legal Aid Society. Facilities of special interest to law students include a technologically advanced library and fully-wired classrooms with more than 1400 Internet connections available throughout the facility. Housing is available for 140 students in 7 residence halls located in the Brooklyn Heights Historic District; the Office of Administrative and Student Services publishes housing information. All law school facilities are accessible to the physically disabled.

Calendar

The law school operates on a traditional semester basis. Courses for full-time students are offered both day and evening and must be completed within 4 years. Electives may be taken in the evening division. For part-time students, courses are offered both day and evening and must be completed within 5 years. New full- and part-time students are admitted in the fall. There is a 6-week summer session. Transferable summer courses are offered.

Programs

In addition to the J.D., the law school offers the Foreign Trained Lawyers Certificate Program. The following joint degrees may be earned: J.D./M.A. (Juris Doctor/Master of Arts in law and in political science), J.D./M.B.A. (Juris Doctor/Master of Business Administration), J.D./M.P.A. (Juris Doctor/Master of Public Administration), J.D./M.S. (Juris Doctor/Master of Science in library and information science), J.D./M.S. (Juris Doctor/Master of Science in planning), and J.D./M.U.P. (Juris Doctor/Master of Urban Planning).

Phone: 718-780-7906
Fax: 718-780-0395
E-mail: *admitq@brooklaw.edu*
Web: *brooklaw.edu*

Contact

Dean of Admissions and Financial Aid, 718-780-7906 for general inquiries; Gerard Anderson, Financial Aid Director, 718-780-7915 for financial aid information.

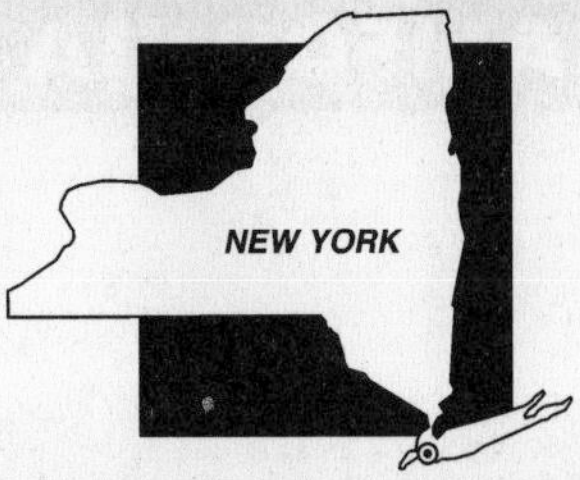

Required

To earn the J.D., candidates must complete 86 total credits, of which 35 are for required courses. They must maintain a minimum GPA of 2.0 in the required courses. The following first-year courses are required of all students: Civil Procedure, Constitutional Law, Contracts, Criminal Law, Legal Process, Legal Writing, Property, and Torts. Required upper-level courses consist of Legal Profession and upper-class writing requirement. The required orientation program for first-year students is a week before classes begin and consists of services; students receive faculty and student advisers, start the Legal Process course and the First-Year Legal Writing Program, and participate in workshops.

Electives

The Brooklyn Law School offers concentrations in corporate law, criminal law, entertainment law, family law, international law, litigation, securities law, sports law, tax law, torts and insurance, intellectual property, international business law, public interest, and international human rights. Any student who has completed the first year of study may take clinics in legal services for the elderly, criminal practice, federal civil litigation, immigration law, mediation, not-for-profit corporations, and bankruptcy. Seminars range from 4 to 6 credits. All students who have completed their first year of study may enroll in internships with judges, criminal justice agencies, and a wide range of organizations in areas such as environmental law, children's rights, business regulation, and arts/entertainment. Up to 3 credits may be earned by any upper-level student who, under the supervision of a faculty member, researches and writes a paper of publishable quality. The Media and Society Lecture Series brings new members from around the country to address current issues involving the media. Summer study in Bologna, Italy and Beijing, China is available. Upper-level students may also pursue study abroad through other law schools if they demonstrate, in writing, special needs and obtain the written approval of the Associate Dean for Academic Affairs. First-year students may take advantage of year-long support services offered through the Academic Success Program. A summer legal process course and various tutorial programs specifically target affirmative action students. The most widely taken electives are New York Civil Practice, Commercial Paper, Criminal Procedure, and Debtor-Creditor Rights.

Graduation Requirements

In order to graduate, candidates must have a GPA of 2.0, have completed the upper-division writing requirement, and pass the Legal Profession course.

Organizations

Students edit the *Brooklyn Law Review*, *Brooklyn Journal of International Law*, and *Journal of Law and Public Policy*, and the newspapers *Justinian* and *The Docket*. Moot court teams annually compete in 15 to 18 tournaments including the ABA's National Moot Court Competition; the International Law Students Association's Phillip C. Jessup International Law Competition; and the National First Amendment Competition. Law student organizations include the Student Bar Association; Asian, Black, and Latin American Law Student associations, local chapters of the Association of Trial Lawyers of America, the National Lawyers Guild, and Legal Association of Women.

Library

The law library contains 511,570 hardcopy volumes and 1,195,345 microform volume equivalents, and subscribes to 1000 serial publications. Such on-line databases and networks as CALI, CIS Universe, DIALOG, Legal-Trac, LEXIS, LOIS, OCLC First Search, WESTLAW, CCH Tax Service, CIS Statistical Universe, IndexMaster, Hein on Line, LawPro, UN Access, UN Treaty Database, NBER, and Chronicle of Higher Education are available to law students for research. Special library collections include a selective U.S. government depository, a selective New York depository, and international law and women in the law collections. Recently, the library completed construction of a library facility. The 78,000 square foot building offers multiple reading rooms, and more than 20 group study and conference rooms. Most areas of the library have network connections to accommodate student or library-provided laptops. A computer lab offers 35 workstations. The ratio of library volumes to faculty is 7635 to 1 and to students is 338 to 1. The ratio of seats in the library to students is 1 to 2.

Placement	
J.D.s awarded:	454
Services available through: a separate law school placement center	
Services: on-line job listings; specialized public interest counseling	
Special features: a network of 15,000 alumni, mandatory first-semester individual counseling for first-year students, and professional and support staff.	
Full-time job interviews:	53 employers
Summer job interviews:	69 employers
Placement by graduation:	75% of class
Placement within 9 months:	97% of class
Average starting salary:	$50,000 to $100,000
Areas of placement:	
Private practice 2-10 attorneys	31%
Private practice 11-25 attorneys	9%
Private practice 26-50 attorneys	5%
Private practice 51-100 attorneys	9%
Government	18%
Business/industry	16%
Judicial clerkships	8%
Public interest	2%
Academic	2%

Faculty

The law school has 67 full-time and 97 part-time faculty members, of whom 50 are women. About 25% of full-time faculty have a graduate law degree in addition to the J.D.; about 28% of part-time faculty have one. The ratio of full-time students to full-time faculty in an average class is 16 to 1; in a clinic, 8 to 1. The law school has a regular program of bringing visiting professors and other distinguished lecturers and visitors to campus.

Students

About 51% of the student body are women; 22%, minorities; 5%, African American; 11%, Asian American; and 6%, Hispanic. The average age of entering students is 25; age range is 19 to 56. More than 75% of students are from the New York-New Jersey area. About 34% of students enter directly from undergraduate school, 7% have a graduate degree, and 66% have worked full-time prior to entering law school. About 3% drop out after the first year for academic or personal reasons; 97% remain to receive a law degree.

CALIFORNIA WESTERN SCHOOL OF LAW

225 Cedar Street
San Diego, CA 92101-3046

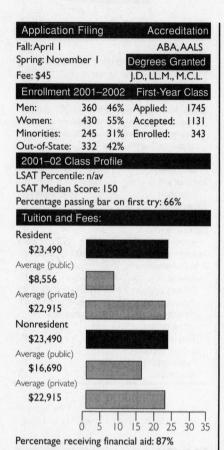

Application Filing		Accreditation
Fall: April 1		ABA, AALS
Spring: November 1		**Degrees Granted**
Fee: $45		J.D., LL.M., M.C.L.

Enrollment 2001–2002			First-Year Class	
Men:	360	46%	Applied:	1745
Women:	430	55%	Accepted:	1131
Minorities:	245	31%	Enrolled:	343
Out-of-State:	332	42%		

2001–02 Class Profile

LSAT Percentile: n/av
LSAT Median Score: 150
Percentage passing bar on first try: 66%

Tuition and Fees:

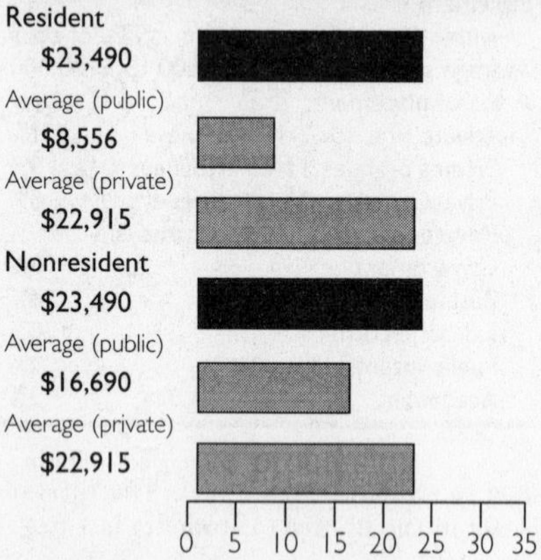

Percentage receiving financial aid: 87%

ADMISSIONS

In the fall 2001 first-year class, 1745 applied, 1131 were accepted, and 343 enrolled. Seventeen transfers enrolled. The median GPA of the most recent first-year class was 3.09. The lowest LSAT percentile accepted was 25; the highest was 75.

Requirements

Applicants must have a bachelor's degree and take the LSAT. The most important admission factors include LSAT results, GPA, and college attended. No specific undergraduate courses are required. Candidates are not interviewed.

Procedure

The application deadline for fall entry is April 1. Applicants should submit an application form, LSAT results, transcripts, a nonrefundable application fee of $45, 2 letters of recommendation, a personal statement, and a resume. Notification of the admissions decision is on a rolling basis. The latest acceptable LSAT test date for fall entry is February. The law school uses the LSDAS.

Special

The Office of Diversity Services coordinates the ethnic diversity recruitment program and maintains working relationships with law firms, alumni, professional and community organizations, and college administrators who provide valuable resources for minority students. Requirements are not different for out-of-state students. Transfer students must have one year of credit, have attended an ABA-approved law school, and submit an official transcript and 2 letters of recommendation, preferably from a law school dean or professors. Preadmissions courses consist of the 6-week Summer Enrichment Program, a 3-credit course, which is an introduction to law school and the American legal system.

Costs

Tuition and fees for the 2001-2002 academic year are $23,490 for all full-time students. Tuition for part-time students is $17,160 per year. Books and supplies run about $780 annually.

Financial Aid

About 87% of current law students receive some form of aid. The average annual amount of aid from all sources combined, including scholarships, loans, and work contracts, is $27,000; maximum, $37,000. Awards are based on need. Required financial statements are the FAFSA and California Western School of Law financial aid application. The aid application deadline for fall entry is March 16. Special funds for minority or disadvantaged students consist of scholarships. First-year students are notified about their financial aid application at time of acceptance.

About the Law School

California Western School of Law was established in 1924 and is a private, independent institution not affiliated with a university. The 199,970 square-foot campus is in an urban area in San Diego. The primary mission of the law school is to educate lawyers to be creative problem-solvers who will contribute to improving the lives of their clients and the quality of justice in society. Students have access to federal, state, county, city, and local agencies, courts, correctional facilities, law firms, and legal aid organizations in the San Diego area. The San Diego Law Library is nearby. Facilities of special interest to law students are within walking distance and include courts, law firms, city, state, and federal agencies, and a county law library. Housing for students is off campus. The school has a housing coordinator to assist students. Most students live within 5 to 10 minutes of school. About 95% of the law school facilities are accessible to the physically disabled.

Calendar

The law school operates on a trimester basis. Courses for full-time students are offered days only and must be completed within 5 years. For part-time students, courses are offered days only and must be completed within 6 years. New full- and part-time students are admitted in the fall and spring. There is a 15-week summer session. Transferable summer courses are offered.

Programs

In addition to the J.D., the law school offers the LL.M. and M.C.L. Students may take relevant courses in other programs and apply credit toward the J.D.; a maximum of 12 credits may be applied. The following joint degrees may be earned: J.D./M.B.A. (Juris Doctor/Master of Business Administration), J.D./M.S.W. (Juris Doctor/Master of Social Work), J.D./Ph.D. (Juris Doctor/Ph.D. in political science or history), LL.M. (Master of Laws in trial advocacy), and LL.M./M.C.L. (Master of Laws/Master of Comparative Law).

Phone: 619-525-1401
800-255-4252
Fax: 619-615-1401
E-mail: *admissions@cwsl.edu*
Web: *www.californiawestern.edu*

Contact

Jean Whalen, Assistant Director Admissions, 619-525-1401 for general inquiries; Kyle Poston, Executive Director of Financial Aid, 619-525-7060 for financial aid information.

Required

To earn the J.D., candidates must complete 89 total credits, of which 43 are for required courses. They must maintain a minimum grade average of 74 in the required courses. The following first-year courses are required of all students: Legal Skills I and II, Property I and II, Contracts I and II, Torts I, Criminal Law, and Civil Procedure I and II. Required upper-level courses consist of Constitutional Law I, Criminal Procedure, Evidence, Professional Responsibility, Legal Skills III, and Torts II. The required orientation program for first-year students is a mandatory 1-day general orientation. There is also an optional 2-week academic success program for culturally disadvantaged students.

Electives

California Western School of Law offers concentrations in corporate law, criminal law, entertainment law, environmental law, family law, international law, labor law, litigation, sports law, tax law, real estate law, telecommunication law, biotechnology law, and creative problem solving. In addition, there are a wide variety of specialized seminar courses open to upper-level students. The school has an internship program open to upper-level students; students may take up to 10 credit hours and will receive 1 credit hour for a weekly seminar. Students may assist faculty as research assistants. Special lecture series include the Faculty Speakers Series, the Scholar in Residence Series and S. Houston Lay International Law and Relations Series. Students may participate in any ABA-approved study-abroad program and transfer up to 8 credit hours of work. California Western sponsors study-abroad programs in New Zealand, Malta, England (London), and Ireland (Galway). Tutorial programs include the Academic Success Program. The Office of Diversity Services administers a 2-week orientation program prior to the fall trimester, coordinates a mentor program for students with local minority lawyers, and sponsors tutorials. The school sponsors more than 30 student organizations that cover a wide range of interests and topics. The most widely taken electives are International Law, Litigation and Advocacy, and Sports and Entertainment Law.

Graduation Requirements

In order to graduate, candidates must have a grade average of 74, have completed the upper-division writing requirement, and a practicum course.

Organizations

Students edit the *California Western Law Review*, the *California Western International Law Journal*, and the student newspaper the *Commentary*. Moot court competitions include the National Appellate Advocacy, Roger J. Traynor Moot Court, and Phillip C. Jessup International Law. Student organizations include Entertainment Sports Law, International Law Society, and Family Law Society. There are local chapters of Public Interest Law Foundation, Phi Alpha Delta, and Student Bar Association. Other organizations include La Raza Law Students Association, Parents in Law School, and Black Law Students Association.

Library

The law library contains 287,445 hard-copy volumes and 715,738 microform volume equivalents, and subscribes to 3867 serial publications. Such on-line databases and networks as CALI, CIS Universe, DIALOG, Dow-Jones, Legal-Trac, LEXIS, LOIS, Mathew Bender, NEXIS, WESTLAW, and Wilsonline Indexes are available to law students for research. Special library collections include collections on creative problem solving, constitutional and human rights law, military law, and international law. California Western is a partial California Depository Library. Recently, the law school built a library facility. The ratio of library volumes to faculty is 7564 to 1 and to students is 364 to 1. The ratio of seats in the library to students is 1 to 1.

Faculty

The law school has 38 full-time and 55 part-time faculty members, of whom 37 are women. About 22% of full-time faculty have a graduate law degree in addition to the J.D. The ratio of full-time students to full-time faculty in an average class is 21 to 1; in a clinic, 1 to 1. The law school has a regular program of bringing visiting professors and other distinguished lecturers and visitors to campus.

Placement

J.D.s awarded:	215
Services available through: a separate law school placement center	
Services: nonlegal career alternatives, judicial clerkships, and decision-making counseling.	
Special features: intensive individual planning and counseling, Alumni Career Advisor/mentor program, minority career development program, government legal careers job fair, public interest job fair, 3 career counselors on staff, a Pro Bono Program, and practice area/career option panels.	
Full-time job interviews:	21 employers
Summer job interviews:	48 employers
Placement by graduation:	n/av
Placement within 9 months:	95% of class
Average starting salary:	$20,000 to $135,000
Areas of placement:	
Private practice 2-10 attorneys	24%
Private practice 11-25 attorneys	5%
Private practice 26-50 attorneys	12%
Private practice 51-100 attorneys	2%
Private practice 100+ attorneys	15%
Government	21%
Business/industry	12%
Judicial clerkships	3%
Public interest	2%
Military	2%
Academic	2%

Students

About 55% of the student body are women; 31%, minorities; 3%, African American; 10%, Asian American; 10%, Hispanic; 1%, Native American; and 7%, Middle Eastern, East Indian, Iraqi, Pakistani, Iranian, Assyrian, multiracial. The majority of students come from California (58%). The average age of entering students is 27; age range is 20 to 59. About 4% of students have a graduate degree. About 19% drop out after the first year for academic or personal reasons; 73% remain to receive a law degree.

CAMPBELL UNIVERSITY

Norman Adrian Wiggins School of Law

P.O. Box 158
Buies Creek, NC 27506

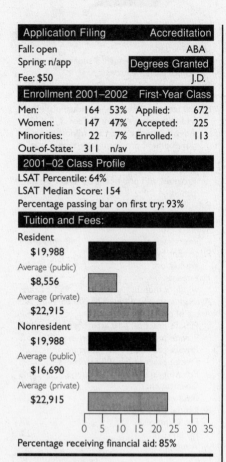

Application Filing		Accreditation
Fall: open		ABA
Spring: n/app		**Degrees Granted**
Fee: $50		J.D.

Enrollment 2001–2002			First-Year Class	
Men:	164	53%	Applied:	672
Women:	147	47%	Accepted:	225
Minorities:	22	7%	Enrolled:	113
Out-of-State:	311	n/av		

2001–02 Class Profile

LSAT Percentile: 64%
LSAT Median Score: 154
Percentage passing bar on first try: 93%

Tuition and Fees:

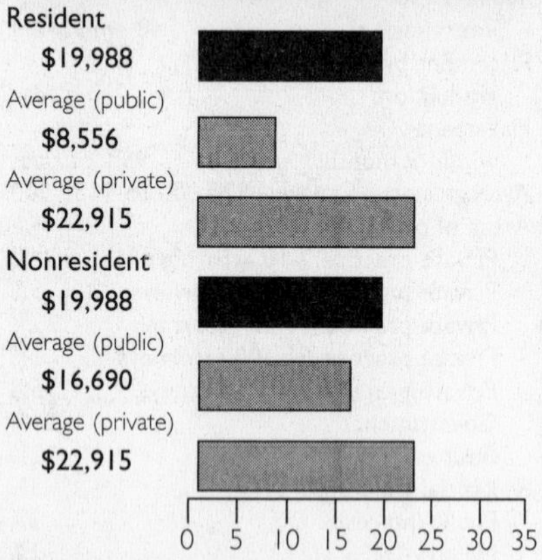

Percentage receiving financial aid: 85%

ADMISSIONS

In the fall 2001 first-year class, 672 applied, 225 were accepted, and 113 enrolled. Five transfers enrolled. The median LSAT percentile of the most recent first-year class was 64; the median GPA was 3.3 on a scale of 4.0.

Requirements

Applicants must have a bachelor's degree and take the LSAT. The most important admission factors include LSAT results, GPA, and personal interview. No specific undergraduate courses are required. Candidates are interviewed.

Procedure

The application deadline for fall entry is open; the priority deadline is March 31. Applicants should submit an application form, LSAT results, transcripts, a nonrefundable application fee of $50, and 2 letters of recommendation. Notification of the admissions decision is on a rolling basis. The latest acceptable LSAT test date for fall entry is February. The law school uses the LSDAS.

Special

The law school recruits minority and disadvantaged students by visiting minority schools and through alumni efforts. Requirements are not different for out-of-state students. Transfer students must have one year of credit and have attended an ABA-approved law school. The school conducts a summer Performance Based Admission Program. Students admitted to this program take 2 law courses over 7 weeks. Their performance on the examinations in these courses determines whether they are offered admission to the fall program.

Costs

Tuition and fees for the 2001-2002 academic year are $19,988 for all full-time students. On-campus room and board costs about $8608 annually; books and supplies run $750.

Financial Aid

About 85% of current law students receive some form of aid. Awards are based on need and merit. Required financial statement is the FAFSA. The aid application deadline for fall entry is open; the priority deadline is April 15. First-year students are notified about their financial aid application at time of acceptance.

About the Law School

Campbell University Norman Adrian Wiggins School of Law was established in 1976 and is a private institution. The 875-acre campus is in a rural area 30 miles from Raleigh and Fayetteville. The primary mission of the law school is to equip men and women for the practice of law, while fostering a sound philosophical and ethical foundation for a legal career, and instilling in students a sense of professional responsibility. Students have access to federal, state, county, city, and local agencies, courts, correctional facilities, law firms, and legal aid organizations in the Buies Creek area. The district and superior courts, which are the trial courts of North Carolina, sit in Lillington, approximately 5 miles from the law school. The North Carolina Supreme Court and Court of Appeals, and the U.S. District Court for the Eastern District of North Carolina sit in Raleigh, 30 miles away. The Governor's office, the General Assembly, and various executive agencies sit in Raleigh, the state capital. Housing for students is available for single students in the dormitories. The University has a limited number of apartments available for married students. Off-campus apartments in the towns surrounding the law school are also available. All law school facilities are accessible to the physically disabled.

Calendar

The law school operates on a traditional semester basis. Courses for full-time students are offered both day and evening and must be completed within 5 years. There is no part-time program. New students are admitted in the fall. There is a 7-week summer session. Transferable summer courses are not offered.

Programs

The following joint degrees may be earned: J.D./M.B.A. (Juris Doctor/Master of Business Administration).

Phone: 910-893-1754
334-4111, ext. 1754
Fax: 910-893-1780
E-mail: *culaw@webster.campbell.edu*
Web: *webster.campbell.edu/culawsch.htm*

Contact

Alan D. Woodlief, Associate Dean for Admissions, 910-893-1753 for general inquiries; Nancy Beasley, Director, 910-893-1310 for financial aid information.

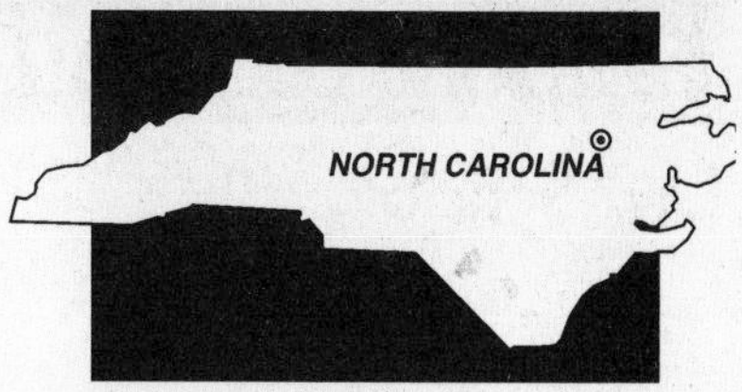

Required

To earn the J.D., candidates must complete 90 total credits, of which 73 are for required courses. They must maintain a minimum grade average of 75 in the required courses. The following first-year courses are required of all students: Contracts I and II, Civil Procedure I and II, Criminal Law, Legal Method and Research, Appellate Advocacy, Torts I and II, Property I and II, Elementary Jurisprudence, Constitutional Law: Federal Powers and Fourteenth Amendment, Professional Responsibility Lecture Series, and Practical Skills and Values. Required upper-level courses consist of Constitutional Law: First Amendment, Wills and Trusts, Criminal Procedure, Commercial Law I and II, Income Taxation, Evidence, Trial Advocacy, Pre-Trial Litigation or Advanced Trial Advocacy, Business Associations, Professional Responsibility and Ethics, Alternate Dispute Resolution, Mediation and Conciliation, Law Office Operation and Management, and Perspectives on Professionalism and Leadership or Perspectives. All students must take clinical courses. The required orientation program for first-year students is a 6-day session that includes both lectures and small group meetings on legal analysis, case analysis and synthesis, and legal research.

Electives

In addition, Trial Advocacy is a required "simulated" clinic offering 7 credit hours over 2 semesters. Seminars include Environmental Law, Insurance Law, and Intellectual Property. Public-service internships are available to second- and third-year students with a maximum of 2 hours credit. The Professional Responsibility Lecture Series is required of all first-year students. Special interest group programs include Law Students Civil Rights Research Council. The most widely taken electives are Family Law, Remedies, and Workers' Compensation.

Graduation Requirements

In order to graduate, candidates must have a grade average of 75.

Organizations

Students edit the *Campbell Law Review* and the newspaper *Campbell Law Observer*. Moot court competitions entered by students are the ABA National Appellate Advocacy, National Moot Court, and John Marshall Privacy and International Law Moot Court Competition. Other competitions are the National Trial, American Trial Lawyers Association, National Student Trial Advocacy, ABA Client Counseling, and NITA Tournament of Champions Trial Competition. Law student organizations include the Student Bar Association, ABA-Law Student Division, and Black Law Students Association. Local chapters of national associations include Delta Theta Phi-Bryan Senate and Phi Alpha Delta fraternities. Campus clubs and other organizations include the Christian Legal Society, Project for Older Prisoners, and Women in Law.

Library

The law library contains 177,493 hard-copy volumes and 56,998 microform volume equivalents, and subscribes to 2559 serial publications. Such on-line databases and networks as CALI, DIALOG, Infotrac, LEXIS, NEXIS, WESTLAW, and Current Index to Legal Periodicals are available to law students for research. Special library collections are in the areas of trial advocacy, ethics and jurisprudence, public interest law, church-state resources, and federal taxation. Recently, the library updated 3 computer laboratories: 1 for teaching, 1 for on-line research, and 1 for research and writing; all have Internet access. In addition, several library study carrels have Internet access. The ratio of library volumes to faculty is 8875 to 1 and to students is 571 to 1. The ratio of seats in the library to students is 1 to 1.

Faculty

The law school has 20 full-time and 17 part-time faculty members, of whom 7 are women. About 25% of full-time faculty have a graduate law degree in addition to the J.D.; about 5% of part-time faculty have one. The ratio of full-time students to full-time faculty in an average class is 15 to 1.

Placement	
J.D.s awarded:	89
Services available through: a separate law school placement center	
Services: in- and out-of-state job fairs	
Special features: targeted mailings sent to regions of North Carolina, press releases issued on student activities, alumni assistance in specific areas of job search, a separate placement resource center and library, a mentor program matching law students with Campbell alumni, and a North Carolina job fair.	
Full-time job interviews:	n/av
Summer job interviews:	n/av
Placement by graduation:	74% of class
Placement within 9 months:	97% of class
Average starting salary:	n/av
Areas of placement:	
Private practice 2-100 attorneys	86%
Judicial clerkships	4%
Business/industry	4%
Public interest	4%
Government	2%

Students

About 47% of the student body are women; 7%, minorities; 3%, African American; 2%, Asian American; 2%, Hispanic; and 1%, Native American. The average age of entering students is 26; age range is 21 to 47. About 10% drop out after the first year for academic or personal reasons; 90% remain to receive a law degree.

Law School

303 East Broad Street
Columbus, OH 43215-3200

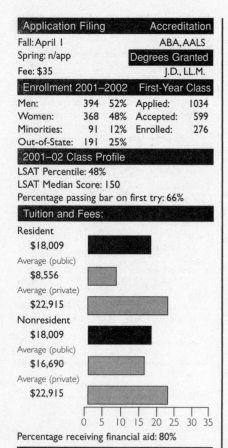

Application Filing		Accreditation
Fall: April 1		ABA, AALS
Spring: n/app		**Degrees Granted**
Fee: $35		J.D., LL.M.

Enrollment 2001–2002			First-Year Class	
Men:	394	52%	Applied:	1034
Women:	368	48%	Accepted:	599
Minorities:	91	12%	Enrolled:	276
Out-of-State:	191	25%		

2001–02 Class Profile

LSAT Percentile: 48%
LSAT Median Score: 150
Percentage passing bar on first try: 66%

Tuition and Fees:

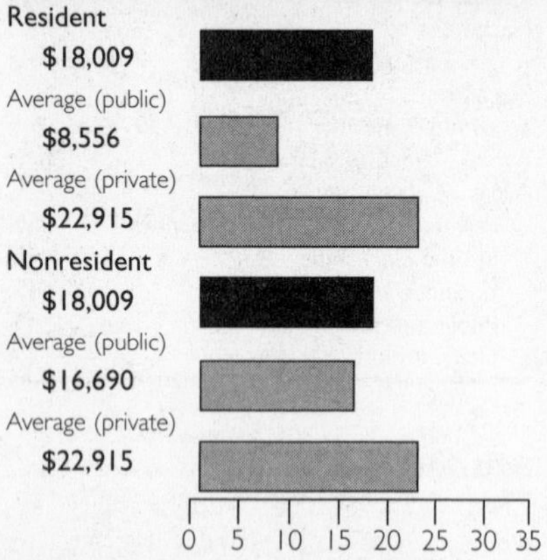

Percentage receiving financial aid: 80%

ADMISSIONS

In the fall 2001 first-year class, 1034 applied, 599 were accepted, and 276 enrolled. Six transfers enrolled. The median LSAT percentile of the most recent first-year class was 48; the median GPA was 3.14 on a scale of 4.0. The lowest LSAT percentile accepted was 36; the highest was 98.

Requirements

Applicants must have a bachelor's degree and take the LSAT. Minimum acceptable GPA is 2.0 on a scale of 4.0. The most important admission factors include academic achievement, LSAT results, and faculty recommendation. No specific undergraduate courses are required. Candidates are not interviewed.

Procedure

The application deadline for fall entry is April 1. Applicants should submit an application form, LSAT results, transcripts, a nonrefundable application fee of $35, 2 letters of recommendation, an essay or personal statement, and a $100 tuition deposit for accepted students; a second $100 seat deposit is due by June 14. Notification of the admissions decision is on a rolling basis. The latest acceptable LSAT test date for fall entry is February. The law school uses the LSDAS.

Special

The law school recruits minority and disadvantaged students by means of an annual Black Law Students Association open house, targeted mailings, use of minority students, faculty, and alumni in the recruitment process, financial assistance programs, and participation in the Academic Success Program. Requirements are not different for out-of-state students. Transfer students must have one year of credit and have attended an ABA-approved law school.

Costs

Tuition and fees for the 2001-2002 academic year are $18,009 for all full-time students. Tuition for part-time students is $11,178 per year. Books and supplies run about $887 annually.

Financial Aid

About 80% of current law students receive some form of aid. The average annual amount of aid from all sources combined, including scholarships, loans, and work contracts, is $21,396; maximum, $28,737. Awards are based on need and merit. Required financial statement is the FAFSA. The aid application deadline for fall entry is April 1. Special funds for minority or disadvantaged students include teaching and research assistantships, grants and scholarships, work-study awards, low-interest student loans, and endowed scholarships. First-year students are notified about their financial aid application at time of acceptance.

About the Law School

Capital University Law School was established in 1903 and is a private institution. The campus is in an urban area in the Discovery District of downtown Columbus. The primary mission of the law school is to provide a solid legal education to the next generation of leaders in the legal profession through student-centered teaching, cutting-edge academic programs, service to the legal profession, commitment to diversity, and to improving our legal system. Students have access to federal, state, county, city, and local agencies, courts, correctional facilities, law firms, and legal aid organizations in the Columbus area. There are extensive externship and mentoring programs. Facilities of special interest to law students include Capital's family advocacy clinic, general legal clinic, and Dave Thomas Center for Adoption Law. Housing for students is available off campus; the university helps students find suitable housing. All law school facilities are accessible to the physically disabled.

Calendar

The law school operates on a traditional semester basis. Courses for both full-time and part-time students are offered both day and evening and must be completed within 6 years. New full- and part-time students are admitted in the fall. There is a 10-week summer session. Transferable summer courses are offered.

Programs

In addition to the J.D., the law school offers the LL.M. and Master of Taxation. Students may take relevant courses in other programs and apply credit toward the J.D.; a maximum of 9 credits may be applied. The following joint degrees may be earned: J.D./LL.M. (Juris Doctor/Master of Laws in taxation), J.D./M.B.A. (Juris Doctor/Master of Business Administration), J.D./M.S.A. (Juris Doctor/Master of Sports Administration), and J.D./M.S.N. (Juris Doctor/Master of Science in Nursing).

Phone: 614-236-6500
Fax: 614-236-6972
E-mail: *admissions@law.capital.edu*
Web: *law.capital.edu*

Contact

Assistant Dean of Admission and Financial Aid, 614-236-6310 for general inquiries; Samantha Stalnaker, Assistant Director, 614-236-6350 for financial aid information.

Required

To earn the J.D., candidates must complete 86 semester total credits, of which 44 are for required courses. They must maintain a minimum GPA of 2.0 in the required courses. The following first-year courses are required of all students: Contracts I and II, Torts I and II, Property I and II, Constitutional Law I, Legal Writing I and II, Criminal Law, and Civil Prodedure I. Required upper-level courses consist of Evidence, Professional Responsibility, Civil Procedure II, a writing or research requirement, Constitutional Law II, and Federal Personal Income Tax. The required orientation program for first-year students lasts 2½ days and includes a mock classroom discussion and meetings with faculty and peer advisers. An extended orientation provides study skills, time and stress management, and exam-taking seminars.

Electives

Students must take 11 credits in their area of concentration. The Law School offers concentrations in environmental law, family law, labor law, tax law, governmental affairs, labor and employment, publicly held companies, small business entities, and alternative dispute resolution. In addition, clinics in general, civil, and criminal litigation are available to students who have qualified as legal interns. Several seminars are offered each year in a variety of subjects. Externships are available through the local, state, and federal courts and through several government agencies and nonprofit organizations. Students may serve as research assistants for law professors or enroll in independent studies. All students must satisfy an upper-class scholarship requirement. Field work may be done through the Externship Programs, as well as clinics, and the Alternative Dispute Resolution-Night Prosecutor's Program. Special lecture series include the Sullivan Lectures. There is the Greece International Law Student Program, Passau, Germany Summer Program, and sister-school relationships with law schools in Passau, Germany, Glasgow, Scotland, and Saskatchewan, Canada. Tutorial programs include the Academic Success Programs, available to students with lower entering credentials. The law school's office of minority affairs offers programs for minority students. Special interest group programs include the Dave Thomas Center for Adoption Law, Center for Dispute Resolution, and graduate tax and business law programs. The most widely taken electives are Business Associations I and II, Commercial Paper, and Commercial Transactions.

Graduation Requirements

In order to graduate, candidates must have a GPA of 2.0 and have completed the upper-division writing requirement.

Organizations

Students edit *The Capital University Law Review*, the newspaper *Res Ipsa Loquitur*, and the *Adoption Law News Summary*. Moot court competitions include National Moot Court, Sports Law, and Labor Law competitions. Other competitions include Negotiation, First Year Moot Court, Environmental Law, and Frederick Douglass. Student organizations include the ABA-Law Student Division, Women's Law Student Association, and Capital Public Interest Law Foundation. There are local chapters of Delta Theta Phi, Phi Delta Phi, and Phi Alpha Delta. Other law student organizations include Student Bar Association, The Federalist Society, and Black Law Student Association.

Library

The law library contains 246,619 hard-copy volumes and 42,753 microform volume equivalents, and subscribes to 2640 serial publications. Such on-line databases and networks as CALI, CIS Universe, DIALOG, LEXIS, NEXIS, OCLC First Search, WESTLAW, Wilsonline Indexes, OhioLink, Jstor, Hein Online, and CCH Tax are available to law students for research. Special library collections include American Law of Taxation and American Constitutional Law. Recently, the library added a computer lab. The ratio of library volumes to faculty is 8221 to 1 and to students is 324 to 1. The ratio of seats in the library to students is 1 to 1.5.

Placement

J.D.s awarded:	220
Services available through: a separate law school placement center	
Special features: a career library, recruiting conferences, an alumni network and newsletter, on-campus interviews, and on-line access to postings from 7/9 Ohio law schools.	
Full-time job interviews:	n/av
Summer job interviews:	34 employers
Placement by graduation:	n/av
Placement within 9 months:	92% of class
Average starting salary:	$40,000 to $150,000
Areas of placement:	
Private practice 2-10 attorneys	26%
Private practice 11-25 attorneys	10%
Private practice 26-50 attorneys	3%
Private practice 51-100 attorneys	6%
Private practice 101+ attorneys, solo and other	23%
Government	12%
Business/industry	8%
Judicial clerkships	5%
Academic	4%
Military	2%
Public interest	1%

Faculty

The law school has 30 full-time and 83 part-time faculty members, of whom 16 are women. According to AAUP standards for Category IIA institutions, faculty salaries are average. About 48% of full-time faculty have a graduate law degree in addition to the J.D. The ratio of full-time students to full-time faculty in an average class is 23 to 1; in a clinic, 8 to 1.

Students

About 48% of the student body are women; 12%, minorities; 8%, African American; 2%, Asian American; and 2%, Hispanic. The majority of students come from Ohio (75%). The average age of entering students is 28; age range is 21 to 62. About 30% of students enter directly from undergraduate school and 12% have a graduate degree. About 8% drop out after the first year for academic or personal reasons; 92% remain to receive a law degree.

CASE WESTERN RESERVE UNIVERSITY

School of Law

11075 East Boulevard
Cleveland, OH 44106

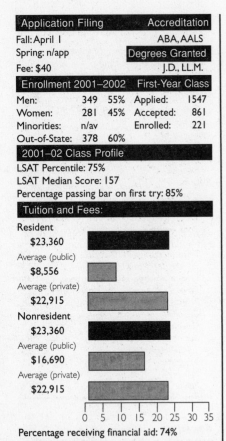

Application Filing		Accreditation
Fall: April 1		ABA, AALS
Spring: n/app		**Degrees Granted**
Fee: $40		J.D., LL.M.

Enrollment 2001–2002			First-Year Class	
Men:	349	55%	Applied:	1547
Women:	281	45%	Accepted:	861
Minorities:	n/av		Enrolled:	221
Out-of-State:	378	60%		

2001–02 Class Profile

LSAT Percentile: 75%
LSAT Median Score: 157
Percentage passing bar on first try: 85%

Tuition and Fees:

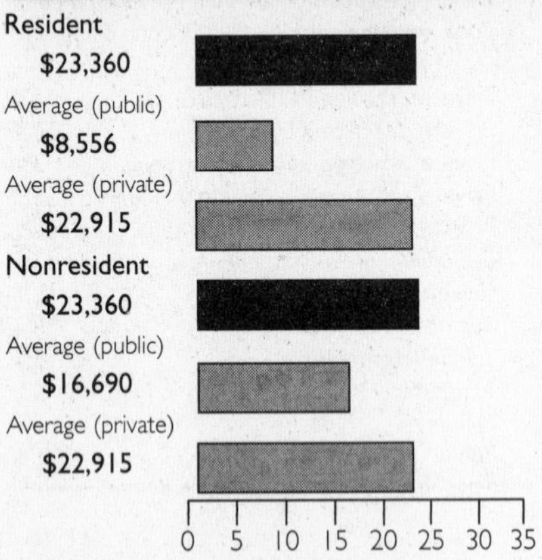

Percentage receiving financial aid: 74%

ADMISSIONS

In the fall 2001 first-year class, 1547 applied, 861 were accepted, and 221 enrolled. The median LSAT percentile of the most recent first-year class was 75; the median GPA was 3.24 on a scale of 4.0.

Requirements

Applicants must have a bachelor's degree and take the LSAT. The most important admission factors include LSAT results, GPA, and writing ability. No specific undergraduate courses are required. Candidates are not interviewed.

Procedure

The application deadline for fall entry is April 1. Applicants should submit an application form, a nonrefundable application fee of $40, and a personal statement. Notification of the admissions decision is between January 1 and May 1. The latest acceptable LSAT test date for fall entry is February. The law school uses the LSDAS.

Special

The law school recruits minority and disadvantaged students by means of attendance at law school fairs likely to be attended by minority and disadvantaged students, financial assistance, the Pre-Law Conference for People of Color, and co-sponsoring of the Midwest Minority Recruitment Fair. Requirements are not different for out-of-state students. Transfer students must have one year of credit, have attended an ABA-approved law school, and have performed very well at the school from which they are transferring.

Costs

Tuition and fees for the 2001-2002 academic year are $23,360 for all full-time students. Books and supplies run about $950 annually.

Financial Aid

About 74% of current law students receive some form of aid. The average annual amount of aid from all sources combined, including scholarships, loans, and work contracts, is $29,100; maximum, $36,775. Awards are based on merit. Required financial statements are the FAFSA and either copies of the student's previous year's federal tax return or a student's statement of income (if the student was not required to file a tax return). The aid application deadline for fall entry is May 1. Diversity leadership grants may be offered to candidates with outstanding academic credentials. First-year students are notified about their financial aid application approximately 4 weeks after the aid application is complete and the student has been admitted.

About the Law School

Case Western Reserve University School of Law was established in 1892 and is a private institution. The 128-acre campus is in an urban area 3 miles east of downtown Cleveland. The primary mission of the law school is to prepare leaders in the practice of law, public and community service, and commerce; to provide enlightenment to the legal profession and the larger society; and to foster an accessible, fair, and reliable system of justice. Students have access to federal, state, county, city, and local agencies, courts, correctional facilities, law firms, and legal aid organizations in the Cleveland area. Home to 4 of the nation's top 50 law firms, Greater Cleveland ranks fourth in the nation for the number of Fortune 500 company headquarters. Facilities of special interest to law students are the state-of-the-art computer laboratory and moot court room, along with a legal clinic that operates as a law firm within the law school setting. Most students live in apartments in nearby Cleveland Heights. All law school facilities are accessible to the physically disabled.

Calendar

The law school operates on a traditional semester basis. Courses for full-time students are offered days only and must be completed within 3 years. For part-time students, courses are offered days only and must be completed within 6 years. New full- and part-time students are admitted in the fall. There is a 6-week summer session. Transferable summer courses are offered.

Programs

In addition to the J.D., the law school offers the LL.M. in taxation and in U.S. legal studies. Students may take relevant courses in other programs and apply credit toward the J.D.; a maximum of 9 credits may be applied. The following joint degrees may be earned: J.D./M.A. (Juris Doctor/Master of Arts in legal history), J.D./M.B. (Juris Doctor/Master of Bioethics), J.D./M.B.A. (Juris Doctor/Master of Business Administration), J.D./M.D. (Juris Doctor/Doctor of Medicine), J.D./M.N.M. (Juris Doctor/Master of Nonprofit Management), J.D./M.P.H. (Juris Doctor/Master of Public Health), J.D./M.S.M.-I.S. (Juris Doctor/Master of Science in management and information systems), and J.D./M.S.S.A. (Juris Doctor/Master of Science in Social Administration).

Required

To earn the J.D., candidates must complete 88 total credits, of which 33 are for required courses. They must maintain a minimum GPA of 1.67 in the required courses. The following first-year courses are required of all students: Contracts, Criminal Law, Torts, Research, Analysis, and Writing, Constitutional Law, Civil Procedure, Property, and perspectives. Required upper-level courses consist of Professional Responsibility and a sub-

Phone: 216-368-3600
800-756-0036
Fax: 216-368-6144
E-mail: *lawadmissions@po.cwru.edu* or *lawmoney@po.cwru.edu*
Web: *www.law.cwru.edu*

Contact

Barbara Andelman, Associate Dean for Student Services, Enrollment Planning, and Special Projects, 216-368-3600 for general inquiries; Jay Ruffner, Student Finances Administrator, 216-368-3602 for financial aid information.

stantial research paper. The required orientation program for first-year students is 3 days, during which students are welcomed into the law school community, oriented to the facilities and the library, and introduced to ethics and professionalism. They meet often with their first-year writing instructors and become acquainted with school and university administrators.

Electives

Students must take 15 credits in their area of concentration. The School of Law offers an optional concentration program in corporate law, criminal law, international law, litigation, securities law, tax law, health law, intellectual property, and public law. In addition, clinical courses, offered for either a half- or full-year, provide students with the opportunity to sit first chair, representing clients in a variety of real life experiences. Students provide legal representation each year to 250 indigent clients. A wide range of seminars is limited to 12 students and range from Bioethics and Law to Contemporary International Legal Problems. Judicial externships with federal district and circuit court judges are available to selected students for 3 credits. Supervised research with faculty is worth 2 credit hours, and is offered to second- and third-year students. Field work is available for credit through dual-degree programs and the law school's judicial externship program. Special lecture series include the Sumner Canary Memorial Lectureship, the Klatsky Seminar in Human Rights, the Frederick K. Cox International Law Center Lecture Series, the Jonathan M. Ault Symposium, the Rush McKnight Labor Law Lecture, Arthur W. Fiske Memorial Lectureship, and the Distinguished Intellectual Property Lecture. A study-abroad program is created for any student in the country of choice, in addition to the already established programs at the University of Western Ontario and at universities in Mexico and French Canada. Academic exchange arrangements have been made with numerous overseas universities. An academic assistance program offers tutorial assistance to first- and second-year students, primarily on exam technique and general writing skills. Moreover, the school is actively involved in the recruitment of students who will enhance the diversity of the student body and legal profession. An annual Pre-Law Conference for People of Color is held and the school participates in the annual BLSA Midwest Minority Recruitment Fair. Scholarship opportunities are significant. The most widely taken electives are Evidence, Business Associations and Trial Tactics, and Wills, Trusts, and Future Interests.

Graduation Requirements

In order to graduate, candidates must have a GPA of 2.0 and have completed the upper-division writing requirement.

Organizations

Students edit the *Case Western Reserve Law Review, Health Matrix: The Journal of Law-Medicine, Journal of International Law, Canada-United States Law Journal, The Internet Law Journal*, and the newspaper *The Docket*. Students compete in the local Dean Dunmore Moot Court competition; the National Moot Court, held regionally and in New York; Niagara, Canada-U.S. relations; and the local Jessup competition sponsored by the International Law Society. Other competitions include the Jonathan M. Ault Mock Trial in Houston. Law student organizations include Big Buddies, the Student Intellectual Property Law Association, and the Student Health Law Association. There are local chapters of Phi Delta Phi and Phi Alpha Theta.

Library

The law library contains 378,317 hard-copy volumes and 474,557 microform volume equivalents, and subscribes to 4834 serial publications. Such on-line databases and networks as CALI, CIS Universe, Dow-Jones, Infotrac, Legal-Trac, LEXIS, LOIS, Mathew Bender, NEXIS, OCLC First Search, RLIN, WESTLAW, Wilsonline Indexes, Academic Universe, Hein Online, JSTOR, and NetLibrary are available to law students for research. Special library collections include a U.S. government documents depository and a Canadian government documents depository. Recently, the library upgraded physical facilities and network connections. The ratio of library volumes to faculty is 7276 to 1 and to students is 600 to 1. The ratio of seats in the library to students is 1 to 1.

Faculty

The law school has 47 full-time and 88 part-time faculty members, of whom 33 are women. According to AAUP standards for Category I institutions, faculty salaries are above average. About 15% of full-time faculty have a graduate law degree in addition to the J.D. The ratio of full-time students to full-time faculty in an average class is 14 to 1; in a clinic, 8 to 1. The law school has a regular program of bringing visiting professors and other distinguished lecturers and visitors to campus. There is a chapter of the Order of the Coif; 100 faculty and 10 graduates are members.

Students

Most students come from Ohio (40%). The average age of entering students is 24; age range is 20 to 50. About 45% of students enter directly from undergraduate school, 23% have a graduate degree, and 55% have worked full-time prior to entering law school. About 3% drop out after the first year for academic or personal reasons; 90% remain to receive a law degree.

Placement

J.D.s awarded:	186
Services available through: a separate law school placement center	
Services: videotaped mock interviews	
Special features: speakers, panels, and programs on a wide range of career options. Also, firms, corporations, and agencies are visited and an annual Midwest Minority Recruitment Conference is hosted. The school has an extensive recruitment program that includes both on-campus and out-of-state recruitment programs, as well as Resume Direct and Resume Collect.	
Full-time job interviews:	65 employers
Summer job interviews:	36 employers
Placement by graduation:	69% of class
Placement within 9 months:	97% of class
Average starting salary:	$28,000 to $135,000
Areas of placement:	
Private practice 2-10 attorneys	7%
Private practice 11-25 attorneys	8%
Private practice 26-50 attorneys	6%
Private practice 51-100 attorneys	7%
Business/industry	11%
Government	9%
Unknown	39%
Judicial clerkships	3%
Public interest	3%
Military	2%
Academic	1%

CATHOLIC UNIVERSITY OF AMERICA

Columbus School of Law

Cardinal Station
Washington, DC 20064

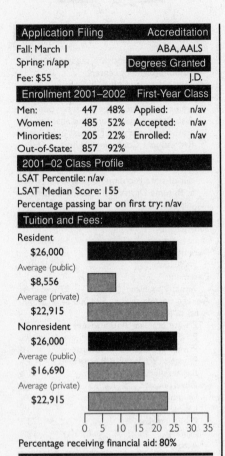

Application Filing		Accreditation
Fall: March 1		ABA, AALS
Spring: n/app		**Degrees Granted**
Fee: $55		J.D.

Enrollment 2001–2002			First-Year Class	
Men:	447	48%	Applied:	n/av
Women:	485	52%	Accepted:	n/av
Minorities:	205	22%	Enrolled:	n/av
Out-of-State:	857	92%		

2001–02 Class Profile

LSAT Percentile: n/av
LSAT Median Score: 155
Percentage passing bar on first try: n/av

Tuition and Fees:

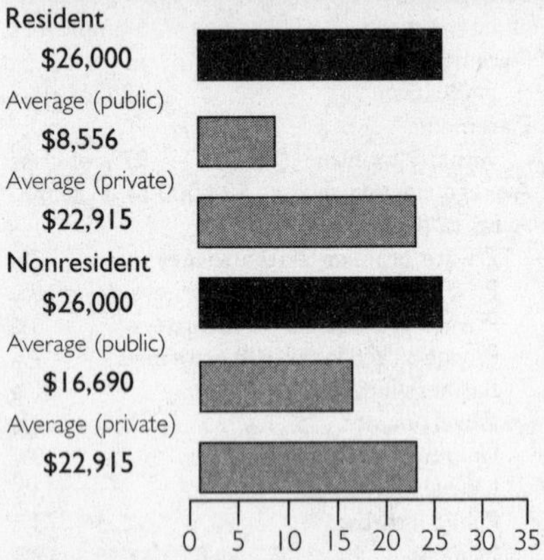

Percentage receiving financial aid: 80%

ADMISSIONS

Information in the above capsule is from an earlier year. In a recent class, nineteen transfers enrolled. The median GPA of a recent first-year class was 3.1. The lowest LSAT percentile accepted was 23; the highest was 99.

Requirements

Applicants must have a bachelor's degree and take the LSAT. The most important admission factors include LSAT results, GPA, and letter of recommendation. No specific undergraduate courses are required. Candidates are not interviewed.

Procedure

Check with the school for current application deadlines and fee. Applicants should submit an application form, LSAT results, transcripts, a nonrefundable application fee, and 2 letters of recommendation. Notification of the admissions decision is on a rolling basis. The law school uses the LSDAS.

Special

The law school recruits minority and disadvantaged students by visiting colleges and geographical areas with large minority populations. Minority applicants are encouraged to write brief background statements as part of the admissions process. Requirements are not different for out-of-state students. Transfer students must have one year of credit, have attended an ABA-approved law school, be in good standing, and be competitive in class rank.

Costs

Tuition and fees for the academic year are approximately $26,000 for all full-time students. Tuition for part-time students is approximately $19,000 per year. On-campus room and board costs about $6800 annually; books and supplies run $790.

Financial Aid

About 80% of law students receive some form of aid. The maximum annual amount of aid from all sources combined, including scholarships, loans, and work contracts, is about $40,000. Awards are based on need and merit, along with community service in conjunction with other considerations. Required financial statement is the FAFSA. Special funds for minority or disadvantaged students consist of scholarships that are merit based. First-year students are notified about their financial aid application after acceptance when the financial aid file is complete, beginning in March. Check with the school for current deadlines.

About the Law School

Catholic University of America Columbus School of Law was established in 1898 and is a private institution. The 154-acre campus is in an urban area in a noncommercial area, accessible by public transportation. The primary mission of the law school is to provide a small, diverse student body with a quality legal education and to prepare students for the ethical practice of law. Students have access to federal, state, county, city, and local agencies, courts, correctional facilities, law firms, and legal aid organizations in the Washington, D.C. area including the nearby Library of Congress and the U.S. Supreme Court. Facilities of special interest to law students consist of a law school facility completed in 1994, that houses all components of the school. Law students also have access to the university's athletic complex, including a pool, Nautilus equipment, sauna, tennis courts, and a track. Housing for students is available in 2 dormitories as single and double rooms. A variety of apartments and private rooms is within easy traveling distance. All law school facilities are accessible to the physically disabled.

Calendar

The law school operates on a traditional semester basis. Courses for full-time students are offered days only and must be completed within 5 years. For part-time students, courses are offered evenings only and must be completed within 6 years. New full- and part-time students are admitted in the fall. There is a 7- to 8-week summer session. Transferable summer courses are offered.

Programs

Students may take relevant courses in other programs and apply credit toward the J.D. If the student is not a joint degree candidate, 3 courses may be applied. The following joint degrees may be earned: J.D./J.C.L. (Juris Doctor/Licentiate of Canon Law), J.D./M.A. (Juris Doctor/Master of Arts in accounting, philosophy, psychology), J.D./M.L.S. (Juris Doctor/Master of Library Science), and J.D./M.S.W. (Juris Doctor/Master of Social Work).

Phone: (202) 319-5151
Fax: (202) 319-6285
E-mail: *admission@law.edu*
Web: *www.law.edu*

Contact

George Braxton, Admissions Director, 202-319-5151 for general inquiries; Gretchen Bonfardine, 202-319-5143 for financial aid information.

Required

To earn the J.D., candidates must complete 84 total credits, of which 33 are for required courses. They must maintain a minimum grade average of 70 (2.0) in the required courses. The following first-year courses are required of all students: Lawyering Skills, Contracts, Constitutional Law, Property, Criminal Law, Torts, and Civil Procedure. Required upper-level courses consist of Professional Reponsibility. The required orientation program for first-year students occurs during the first week and consists of the beginning of the Lawyering Skills course, a general introduction to the law library and the law school, study skills, and social activities.

Electives

The Columbus School of Law offers concentrations in corporate law, criminal law, family law, international law, labor law, litigation, media law, securities law, tax law, and public policy and law and religion. In addition, 7 clinical programs emphasize client representation. Two others involve legislative, administrative, and policy-making processes. Courses are open to upper-level students and credit varies. Seminars are also open only to upper-level students. Internships are available in a variety of legal settings and are supervised by practicing attorneys. Students may serve as research assistants to law faculty members. Special lecture series are the Pope John XXIII Lectures, the Brendan F. Brown Distinguished Lectures and Scholars-in-Residence, and the Mirror of Justice Lectures. There is a 6-week summer program at the Jagiellonian University in Cracow, Poland. Student groups and individual faculty members conduct informal tutorial sessions. A 2-week early start program is offered to entering students whose numerical credentials indicate that it would be especially beneficial. The most widely taken electives are Evidence, Corporations, and Family Law.

Graduation Requirements

In order to graduate, candidates must have a minimum grade average of 70 (or 2.0) and have completed the upper-division writing requirement.

Organizations

Student-edited publications are *The Catholic University of America Law Review, The Journal of Contemporary Health Law and Policy, CommLaw Conspectus: Journal of Communications Law and Policy*, and the newspaper *Judicial Notice*. Moot Court teams compete in the Wagner Cup in Labor Law, Environmental Law, and Polsky Criminal Law. Student organizations include student divisions of the ABA and the American Society of International Law, Communications Law Students, and Evening Law Students. There is a local chapter of Thurgood Marshall American Inn of Court. Other organizations include the Graduate Student Association.

Library

The law library contains 322,816 hardcopy volumes and 52,864 microform volume equivalents, and subscribes to 5334 serial publications. Such on-line databases and networks as DIALOG, LEXIS, and WESTLAW are available to law students for research. Special library collections include a partial U.S. government depository and United Nations documents, which may be accessed through hard-bound, on-line, and CD-ROM indices or by the Internet. A recently constructed law building features a 3-level library wing with 3 videotape viewing rooms, spacious tables and computer-equipped carrels with task lights, classic scholar reading rooms, and 2 computer laboratories that also serve as training centers. The ratio of library volumes to faculty is 7173 to 1 and to students is 347 to 1. The ratio of seats in the library to students is 1 to 2.

Faculty

The law school has approximately 46 full-time and 87 part-time faculty members, of whom 34 are women. According to AAUP standards for Category I institutions, faculty salaries are average. About 20% of full-time faculty have a graduate law degree in addition to the J.D. The ratio of full-time students to full-time faculty in an average class is 14 to 1; in a clinic, 8 to 1. The law school has a regular program of bringing visiting professors and other distinguished lecturers and visitors to campus.

Placement

J.D.s awarded:	291
Services available through: a separate law school placement center	
Special features: individual consultations, on-campus interviewing, consortium interviewing conferences, resume collection service, workshops on planning and executing a job search, writing resumes and cover letters, developing interviewing skills, building legal credentials, understanding the legal job market, and videotapes of alumni discussing specialties.	
Full-time job interviews:	53 employers
Summer job interviews:	53 employers
Placement by graduation:	89% of class
Placement within 9 months:	100% of class
Average starting salary:	$22,000 to $88,000
Areas of placement:	
Private practice 2-10 attorneys	38%
Government	23%
Judicial clerkships	18%
Business/industry	14%
unknown	5%
Public interest	2%

Students

About 52% of the student body are women; 22%, minorities; 13%, African American; 4%, Asian American; and 5%, Hispanic. The majority of students come from the Northeast (55%). The average age of entering students is 23; age range is 20 to 51. About 37% of students enter directly from undergraduate school and 7% have a graduate degree. About 4% drop out after the first year for academic or personal reasons; 95% remain to receive a law degree.

CATHOLIC UNIVERSITY OF PUERTO RICO

School of Law

Avenida Las Americas-Station 6
Ponce, PR 00732

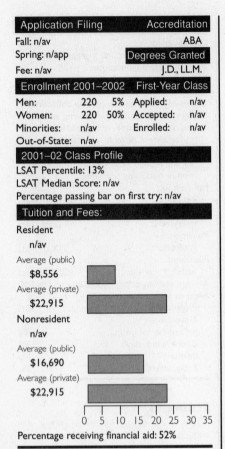

Application Filing		Accreditation
Fall: n/av		ABA
Spring: n/app		**Degrees Granted**
Fee: n/av		J.D., LL.M.

Enrollment 2001–2002			First-Year Class	
Men:	220	5%	Applied:	n/av
Women:	220	50%	Accepted:	n/av
Minorities:	n/av		Enrolled:	n/av
Out-of-State:	n/av			

2001–02 Class Profile

LSAT Percentile: 13%
LSAT Median Score: n/av
Percentage passing bar on first try: n/av

Tuition and Fees:

Resident
n/av
Average (public)
$8,556
Average (private)
$22,915
Nonresident
n/av
Average (public)
$16,690
Average (private)
$22,915

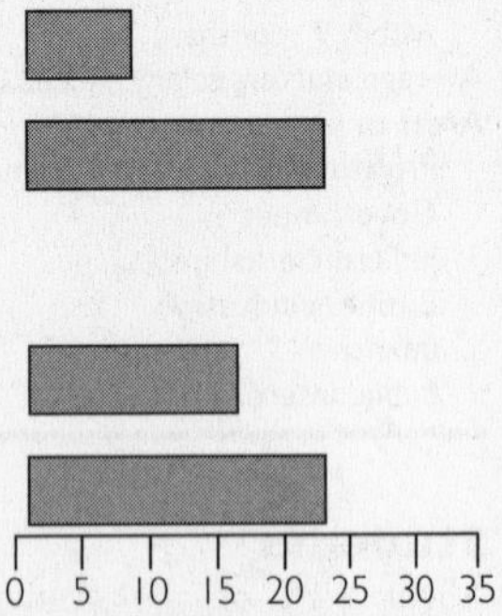

Percentage receiving financial aid: 52%

ADMISSIONS

Information in the above capsule is from an earlier year. The median LSAT percentile of a recent first-year class was 13; the median GPA was 2.9 on a scale of 4.0.

Requirements

Applicants must have a bachelor's degree and take the LSAT. Minimum acceptable GPA is 2.5 on a scale of 4.0. The most important admission factors include GPA, LSAT and PAEG results, and general background. No specific undergraduate courses are required. Candidates are not interviewed.

Procedure

Check with the school for current deadlines and fee. Applicants should submit an application form, transcripts, and PAEG. The law school uses the LSDAS.

Special

Requirements are not different for out-of-state students. Transfer students must have a minimum GPA of 2. Preadmissions courses consist of allowing students with an undergraduate GPA of lower than 2.5 or who don't achieve adequate scores on the admissions exam to enroll in special remedial courses and then be admitted conditionally.

Costs

Check with the school for current tuition and fees.

Financial Aid

About 52% of law students receive some form of aid. The average annual amount of aid from all sources combined, including scholarships, loans, and work contracts, is about $2000. Awards are based on need and merit. Check with the school for current application deadlines.

About the Law School

Catholic University of Puerto Rico School of Law was established in 1961 and is a private institution. The 92-acre campus is in an urban area 60 miles from San Juan. The primary mission of the law school is to develop lawyers with a thorough training in the law and a practical mastery of legal techniques within the context of Catholic teachings. Students have access to federal, state, county, city, and local agencies, courts, correctional facilities, law firms, and legal aid organizations in the Ponce area. Housing for students is available.

Calendar

The law school operates on a traditional semester basis. Courses for full-time and part-time students are offered both day and evening. New full- and part-time students are admitted in the fall. There is a summer session. Transferable summer courses are not offered.

Phone: 809-841-2000

Contact

Maurice Luciano, Associate Dean, (787) 841-2000, ext. 341 for general inquiries; Maria Izquierdo de Whitaker, Director of Student Aid, (787) 841-2000 for financial aid information.

Programs

In addition to the J.D., the law school offers the LL.M. Students may take relevant courses in other programs and apply credit toward the J.D.The following joint degrees may be earned: J.D./M.B.A. (Juris Doctor/Master of Business Administration).

Required

To earn the J.D., candidates must complete 94 total credits, of which 82 are for required courses. The following first-year courses are required of all students: Introduction to Law, Legal Bibliography and Writing, Constitutional Law, Property Law, Moral and Dogmatic Theory, Family Law, Criminal Procedure, Obligations, and Logic and Redaction. Required upper-level courses consist of Special Contracts, Civil Procedure I and II, Torts, Corporations, Successions and Donations, Evidence, Notarial Law, Mercantile law, Mortgages, Legal Ethics, Legal Clinics, Administrative Law, Appellate Practice, Negotiable Instruments, Federal Jurisdiction, Special Logical Procedures, and Advanced Logical Analysis.

Electives

Clinical training is provided through the school's downtown Ponce Legal Aid Clinic for indigent clients and through judicial clerkships in superior and federal district courts and placements with district attorneys' offices. The Center for Legal and Social Investigations allows for research under the supervision of a faculty director.

Organizations

The primary law review is the *Revista de Derecho Puertorriqueno*, which is edited by a student board. Law student organizations include the Law Student Division of the American Bar Association, National Law Students of Puerto Rico, and the Women's Rights Organization. Local chapters of national associations are Delta Theta Phi and Phi Alpha Delta.

Library

The law library contains 135,000 hardcopy volumes and 15,000 microform volume equivalents. Special library collections include deposits of U.S. government and United Nations documents.

Faculty

The law school has approximately 14 full-time and 18 part-time faculty members. About 50% of full-time faculty have a graduate law degree in addition to the J.D. The ratio of full-time students to full-time faculty in an average class is 12 to 1.

Students

About 50% of the student body are women. The average age of entering students is 24; age range is 21 to 51. About 50% of students enter directly from undergraduate school. About 11% drop out after the first year for academic or personal reasons.

Placement	
J.D.s awarded:	n/av
Services available through: a separate law school placement center	
Full-time job interviews:	n/av
Summer job interviews:	n/av
Placement by graduation:	n/av
Placement within 9 months:	n/av
Average starting salary:	$14,000 to $24,000
Areas of placement:	
Academic	50%
Unknown	50%

CHAPMAN UNIVERSITY

School of Law

One University Drive
Orange, CA 92866

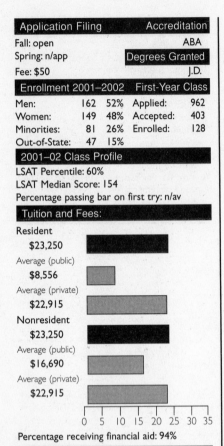

Application Filing		Accreditation
Fall: open		ABA
Spring: n/app		**Degrees Granted**
Fee: $50		J.D.

Enrollment 2001–2002			First-Year Class	
Men:	162	52%	Applied:	962
Women:	149	48%	Accepted:	403
Minorities:	81	26%	Enrolled:	128
Out-of-State:	47	15%		

2001–02 Class Profile

LSAT Percentile: 60%
LSAT Median Score: 154
Percentage passing bar on first try: n/av

Tuition and Fees:

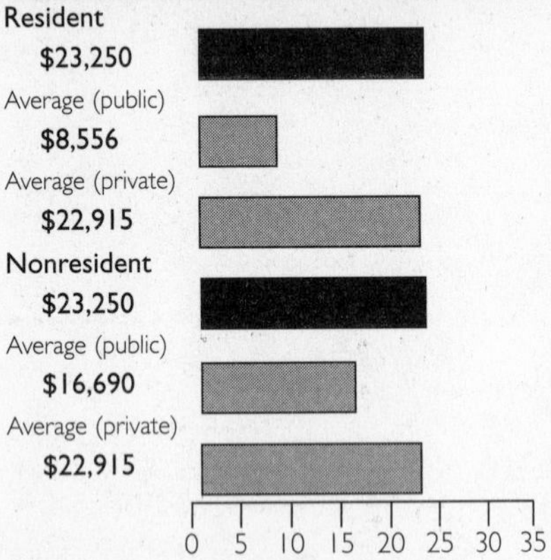

Percentage receiving financial aid: 94%

ADMISSIONS

In the fall 2001 first-year class, 962 applied, 403 were accepted, and 128 enrolled. Twelve transfers enrolled. The median LSAT percentile of the most recent first-year class was 60; the median GPA was 3.13 on a scale of 4.0. The lowest LSAT percentile accepted was 24; the highest was 99.

Requirements

Applicants must have a bachelor's degree and take the LSAT. Minimum acceptable GPA is 2.0 on a scale of 4.0. The most important admission factors include LSAT results, GPA, and personal interview. No specific undergraduate courses are required. Candidates are not interviewed.

Procedure

The application deadline for fall entry is open. Applicants should submit an application form, LSAT results, TOEFL, where indicated, a nonrefundable application fee of $50, 2 letters of recommendation submitted to LSDAS, a personal statement, and LSDAS report. Notification of the admissions decision is usually within two weeks after file is complete. The latest acceptable LSAT test date for fall entry is June. The law school uses the LSDAS.

Special

The law school recruits minority and disadvantaged students by recruiting at colleges and universities that have a high percentage of minority students, by advertising in and supporting publications reaching the various ethnic communities, and by hosting special events. Requirements are not different for out-of-state students. Transfer students must have one year of credit and 2 letters of recommendation (one from a law professor), an official law transcript, letter of good standing, and an LSDAS Report.

Costs

Tuition and fees for the 2001-2002 academic year are $23,250 for all full-time students. Tuition for part-time students is $16,000 per year. On-campus room and board costs about $10,017 annually; books and supplies run $810.

Financial Aid

About 94% of current law students receive some form of aid. The average annual amount of aid from all sources combined, including scholarships, loans, and work contracts, is $23,500; maximum, $37,000. Awards are based on need and merit. Required financial statement is the FAFSA. The aid application deadline for fall entry is April 1. Students get an estimate of aid when an offer of admission is made. The actual financial aid offer is made after the student accepts the admit offer and makes a deposit.

About the Law School

Chapman University School of Law was established in 1995 and is a private institution. The 52-acre campus is in a suburban area in Orange, California. The primary mission of the law school is to provide personalized education in a challenging academic environment that stimulates intellectual inquiry, embraces diverse ideas and viewpoints, and fosters competent, ethical lawyering that enhances the capacity of legal institutions to provide justice. Students have access to federal, state, county, city, and local agencies, courts, correctional facilities, law firms, and legal aid organizations in the Orange area. Facilities of special interest to law students include a state-of-the-art law building, with drop ports throughout, digital document cameras, touch screen computers at podiums, electronic court rooms, assisted-listening devices, and an outstanding law library. Limited university-owned housing is available for law school students. Various apartment complexes are within proximity of the law school. All law school facilities are accessible to the physically disabled.

Calendar

The law school operates on a traditional semester basis. Courses for full-time students are offered both day and evening and must be completed within 5 years. For part-time students, courses are offered both day and evening and must be completed within 6 years. New full- and part-time students are admitted in the fall. There is a 7-week summer session. Transferable summer courses are offered.

Programs

Students may take relevant courses in other programs and apply credit toward the J.D.; a maximum of 6 credits may be applied. The following joint degrees may be earned: J.D./M.B.A. (Juris Doctor/ Master of Business Administration).

Phone: 714-628-2500
877-Chaplaw
Fax: 714-628-2501
E-mail: *heyer@chapman.edu*
Web: *chapman.edu/law*

Contact

Diann Heyer, Assistant Director of Admissions, 714-628-2515 for general inquiries; Kathleen Clark, Assistant Director of Financial Aid, 714-628-2510 for financial aid information.

Required

To earn the J.D., candidates must complete 88 total credits, of which 51 to 52 are for required courses. They must maintain a minimum GPA of 2.0 in the required courses. The following first-year courses are required of all students: Civil Procedure I and II, Property I and II, Torts I and II, Contracts I and II, Criminal Law, and Legal Research and Writing I and II. Required upper-level courses consist of Professional Responsibility, Constitutional Law I and II, Federal Income Tax, Evidence, writing requirement, Corporations, and Lawyering Skills. The required orientation program for first-year students lasts approximately 4 days and includes an introduction to the process of legal education and analysis, professionalism, legal education in practice, as well as informal, social events and information sessions on navigating through the Law School experience.

Electives

Students must take 11 to 14 credits in their area of concentration. The School of Law offers concentrations in corporate law, environmental law, tax law, land use/real estate, advocacy, and dispute resolution. In addition, a U.S. Tax Court Clinic, Elder Law Clinic, and Bankruptcy Clinic are available for students for varying academic credit. A variety of seminar-type courses for upperclassmen is offered, ranging from 2 to 4 credits. Various externship opportunities, including judicial externships, are available to students in good standing; credits vary with a maximum of 8 total. Special lecture series include the Distinguished Jurist in Residence Program, open to all students for no credit. The Academic Support Program offers lectures and workshops, individualized tutoring for students, and referrals to university or outside programs or support services designed to meet identified special student needs. The most widely taken electives are Externship, clinical coursework, and Wills and Trusts.

Graduation Requirements

In order to graduate, candidates must have a GPA of 2.0, have completed the upper-division writing requirement, and have satisfied ABA residency requirements.

Organizations

Students edit *The Chapman Law Review, Nexus*, and *A Journal of Opinion*. Moot court competitions include Giles Rich Moot Court, Traynor Moot Court, and Jessup International Moot Court. Other competitions include Negotiation Competition, American Trial Lawyers Competition, International Arbitration Competition, Vis International Commercial Competition, Client Counseling Competition, and National Environmental Competition. Student organizations include the Student Bar Association, Honor Council, and Women's Law Forum. There are local chapters of the Public Interest Law Forum (NAPIL), Phi Alpha Delta, and ABA-LSD. Other organizations include the Land Resources Society, Tax Law Society, and Technology and Intellectual Property Law Society.

Library

The law library contains 249,764 hardcopy volumes and 184,488 microform volume equivalents, and subscribes to 577 serial publications. Such on-line databases and networks as CALI, LEXIS, LOIS, WESTLAW, and Wilsonline Indexes are available to law students for research. The library maintains special collections to support the financial aid and placement areas of the law school. Recently, the library upgraded its on-line catalog (Innopac) to a Windows-based system (Millenium). The law library catalog has merged with the University Library Catalog. The ratio of library volumes to faculty is 11,894 to 1 and to students is 806 to 1. The ratio of seats in the library to students is 1 to 1.

Faculty

The law school has 21 full-time and 43 part-time faculty members, of whom 28 are women. According to AAUP standards for Category IIA institutions, faculty salaries are well above average. About 33% of full-time faculty have a graduate law degree in addition to the J.D. The ratio of full-time students to full-time faculty in an average class is 13 to 1; in a clinic, 8 to 1. The law school has a regular program of bringing visiting professors and other distinguished lecturers and visitors to campus.

Placement

J.D.s awarded:	34
Services available through: a separate law school placement center	
Services: information sessions, panels, law firm nights, mock interviews, and a mentor program	
Special features: n/av	
Full-time job interviews:	5 employers
Summer job interviews:	8 employers
Placement by graduation:	30% of class
Placement within 9 months:	89% of class
Average starting salary:	$24,000 to $150,000
Areas of placement:	
Private practice 2-10 attorneys	19%
Private practice 11-25 attorneys	13%
Private practice 26-50 attorneys	3%
Private practice 51-100 attorneys	3%
Business/industry	44%
Academic	9%
Unknown	6%
Government	3%

Students

About 48% of the student body are women; 26%, minorities; 2%, African American; 11%, Asian American; 12%, Hispanic; and 1%, Native American. The majority of students come from California (85%). The average age of entering students is 28; age range is 20 to 56. About 34% of students enter directly from undergraduate school, 13% have a graduate degree, and 66% have worked full-time prior to entering law school. About 12% drop out after the first year for academic or personal reasons; 82% remain to receive a law degree.

City University of New York School of Law at Queens Collegee

65-21 Main Street
Flushing, NY 11367-1300

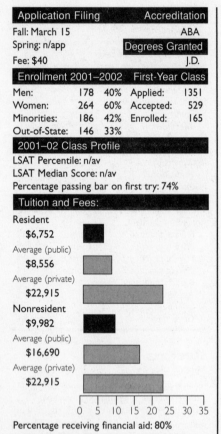

Application Filing		Accreditation
Fall: March 15		ABA
Spring: n/app		**Degrees Granted**
Fee: $40		J.D.

Enrollment 2001–2002			First-Year Class	
Men:	178	40%	Applied:	1351
Women:	264	60%	Accepted:	529
Minorities:	186	42%	Enrolled:	165
Out-of-State:	146	33%		

2001–02 Class Profile

LSAT Percentile: n/av
LSAT Median Score: n/av
Percentage passing bar on first try: 74%

Tuition and Fees:

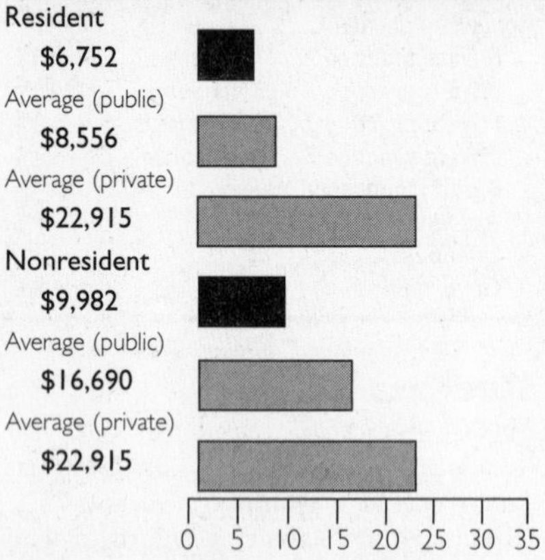

Percentage receiving financial aid: 80%

ADMISSIONS

In the fall 2001 first-year class, 1351 applied, 529 were accepted, and 165 enrolled. Five transfers enrolled.

Requirements

Applicants must have a bachelor's degree and take the LSAT. The most important admission factors include a letter of recommendation, academic achievement, and a demonstrated commitment to public interest/public service. No specific undergraduate courses are required. Candidates are not interviewed.

Procedure

The application deadline for fall entry is March 15. Applicants should submit an application form, LSAT results, transcripts, a nonrefundable application fee of $40, 2 letters of recommendation, a personal statement, and the LSDAS. Notification of the admissions decision begins in January. The latest acceptable LSAT test date for fall entry is February. The law school uses the LSDAS.

Special

The law school recruits minority and disadvantaged students through programs similar to those used by most other law schools. Requirements are not different for out-of-state students. Transfer students must have one year of credit, have attended an ABA-approved law school, and have demonstrated a commitment to public interest/public service.

Costs

Tuition and fees for the 2001-2002 academic year are $6752 for full-time in-state students and $9982 for out-of-state students. Books and supplies run about $550 annually.

Financial Aid

About 80% of current law students receive some form of aid. The maximum annual amount of aid from all sources combined, including scholarships, loans, and work contracts, is $20,669. Awards are based on need. Required financial statement is the FAFSA. The aid application deadline for fall entry is May 15. Special funds for minority or disadvantaged students include the Professional Opportunity Scholarship, CLEO, and various other scholarships. First-year students are notified about their financial aid application on a rolling basis.

About the Law School

City University of New York at Queens College School of Law was established in 1983 and is a public institution. The campus is in an urban area in the New York City borough of Queens. The primary mission of the law school is to emphasize clinical education, legal theory, and professional responsibility by integrating these elements into the curriculum, and to develop special relationships and work opportunities with the city's courts, agencies, advocacy groups, and law firms. The school aims to prepare students for careers in public service and public interest law. Students have access to federal, state, county, city, and local agencies, courts, correctional facilities, law firms, and legal aid organizations in the Flushing area. There are several notable in-house clinical programs. Facilities of special interest to law students include a 3-story building adjacent to the Queens College campus, which houses classrooms, the library, lounge, administrative offices, day-care center, and cafeteria. Housing for students is available off campus. About 99% of the law school facilities are accessible to the physically disabled.

Calendar

The law school operates on a traditional semester basis. Courses for full-time students are offered days only and must be completed within 5 years. There is no part-time program, but in exceptional cases upon approval, some day classes may be offered. New students are admitted in the fall. There is a 6-week summer session. Transferable summer courses are offered.

Programs

Students may take relevant courses in other programs and apply credit toward the J.D.; a maximum of 6 credits may be applied.

Required

To earn the J.D., candidates must complete 91 total credits, of which 60 are for required courses. They must maintain a minimum GPA of 2.0 in the required courses. The following first-year courses are required of all students: Liberty, Equality, and Due Process, Law and Family Relations, Legal Research I and II, Law and a Market Economy I and II: Contracts, Lawyering Seminar: Work of a Lawyer I and II, Responsibility for Injurious Conduct I and II: Torts and Criminal law, and Civil Procedure I. Required upper-level courses consist of Public Institutions and Law, Constitutional Structures and the Law, Lawyering and the Public Interest I: Evidence, Law and a Market Economy III: Proper-

Phone: 718-340-4210
Fax: 718-340-4435
E-mail: *admissions@mail.law.cuny.edu*
Web: *www.law.cuny.edu*

Contact

Yvonne Cherena-Pacheco, Asst Dean for Enrollment, 718-340-4210 for general inquiries; Angela Joseph, Director of Financial Aid, 718-340-4292 for financial aid information.

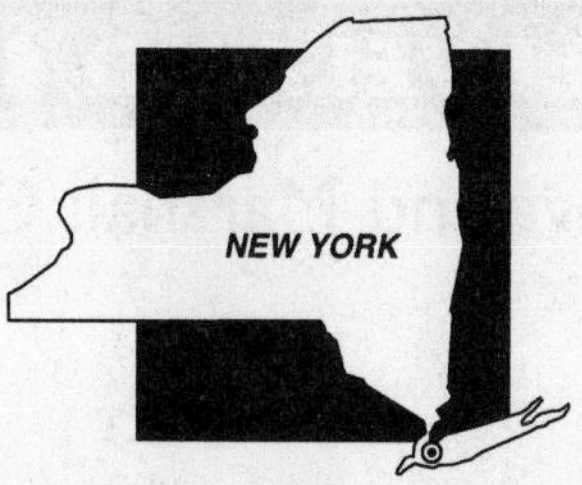

ty, Lawyering Seminar III, and a clinic or concentration. All students must take clinical courses. The required orientation program for first-year students is a 1-week academic, skills, and social program, including court visits.

Electives

The School of Law offers concentrations in criminal law, environmental law, family law, international law, juvenile law, labor law, litigation, and health, mediation, domestic violence, elder law, immigration, human rights, and civil rights. All students must enroll in a clinic (12 to 16 credits) or a concentration (12 credit internship). Current clinic offerings include Immigrant and Refugee Rights, Elder Law, Battered Women, Defenders Clinic, International Women's Human Rights, and Mediation Clinic. Each first-year student takes 2 4-credit Lawyering Seminars. Limited to 24 students, these seminars imbed lawyering skills such as legal analysis, legal research, legal writing, interviewing, counseling, and negotiating in doctrine taught in first-year courses. Second-year students choose a Lawyering Seminar in an area of interest. Recent Lawyering Seminar offerings include Trial Advocacy, Appellate Advocacy, Labor: Collective Bargaining and Arbitration, Mediation, Complex Litigation, Criminal Defense and Defense of Juveniles. In addition, at least 4 upper-division classes are taught in a 20:1 ratio. Internships are available in connection with the concentration program in placements related to specially-designed courses. Current areas are civil rights/discrimination and health law. Students spend 2 full days in the field and 8 hours in class. Field work is connected to concentrations and to a 3-credit summer school course—Public Interest/Public Service. Special lecture series are sponsored by various student organizations. A selective summer program in Comparative Law is offered in Havana, Cuba. A professional skills center and a writing center are available to students who are encountering academic difficulty. Special offerings are also available to 2nd and 3rd semester students who are experiencing difficulty. The most widely taken electives are NY Practice, Criminal Procedure, and Business Associations.

Graduation Requirements

In order to graduate, candidates must have a GPA of 2.0, have completed the upper-division writing requirement, and clinic/concentration.

Organizations

Students edit the *New York Law Review* and a student newspaper, *The Brief*, and participate in the annual National Moot Court Competition and Carl A. Stickel Cybercrimes National Competition. Student organizations include the Black Law Students Association, Public Interest Law Association, and Domestic Violence Coalition. Local chapters of national associations include the American Civil Liberties Union, National Lawyers Guild, and Phi Alpha Delta. Other organizations include the Entertainment Law Society, Children's Rights Association, and Environmental Law Students Association.

Library

The law library contains 267,244 hard-copy volumes and 34,653 microform volume equivalents, and subscribes to 2955 serial publications. Such on-line databases and networks as CALI, DIALOG, Dow-Jones, Legal-Trac, LEXIS, LOIS, NEXIS, OCLC First Search, and WESTLAW are available to law students for research. Special library collections include a U.S. Government Printing Office depository; the school is a member of the New York Joint International Law Program Consortium. The library maintains a large number of student access computer terminals, microform readers, and microform reader-printers. The ratio of library volumes to faculty is 7223 to 1 and to students is 605 to 1. The ratio of seats in the library to students is 1 to 1.

Faculty

The law school has 37 full-time and 18 part-time faculty members, of whom 32 are women. About 22% of full-time faculty have a graduate law degree in addition to the J.D. The ratio of full-time students to full-time faculty in an average class is 13 to 1. The law school has a regular program of bringing visiting professors and other distinguished lecturers and visitors to campus.

Placement

J.D.s awarded:	97
Services available through: a separate law school placement center	
Services: counseling, seminars, workshops, and panels with local practitioners, faculty, and alumni	
Special features: The Career Planning Office is responsibile for helping students find meaningful work. Special focus is placed on public interest careers.	
Full-time job interviews:	6 employers
Summer job interviews:	3 employers
Placement by graduation:	n/av
Placement within 9 months:	84% of class
Average starting salary:	$22,000 to $42,000
Areas of placement:	
Private practice	36%
Public interest	26%
Government	20%
Business/industry	13%
Judicial clerkships	5%

Students

About 60% of the student body are women; 42%, minorities; 16%, African American; 11%, Asian American; 14%, Hispanic; and 1%, Native American. The majority of students come from New York (67%). The average age of entering students is 29; age range is 20 to 66. About 20% of students enter directly from undergraduate school, 25% have a graduate degree, and 60% have worked full-time prior to entering law school. About 10% drop out after the first year for academic or personal reasons; 85% remain to receive a law degree.

CLEVELAND STATE UNIVERSITY

Cleveland-Marshall College of Law

1801 Euclid Avenue
Cleveland, OH 44115

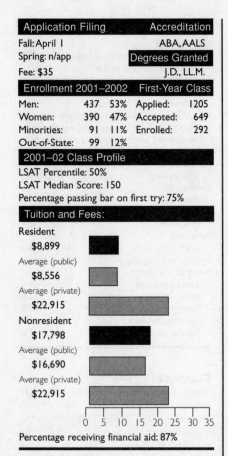

Application Filing		Accreditation
Fall: April 1		ABA, AALS
Spring: n/app		**Degrees Granted**
Fee: $35		J.D., LL.M.

Enrollment 2001–2002			First-Year Class	
Men:	437	53%	Applied:	1205
Women:	390	47%	Accepted:	649
Minorities:	91	11%	Enrolled:	292
Out-of-State:	99	12%		

2001–02 Class Profile

LSAT Percentile: 50%
LSAT Median Score: 150
Percentage passing bar on first try: 75%

Tuition and Fees:

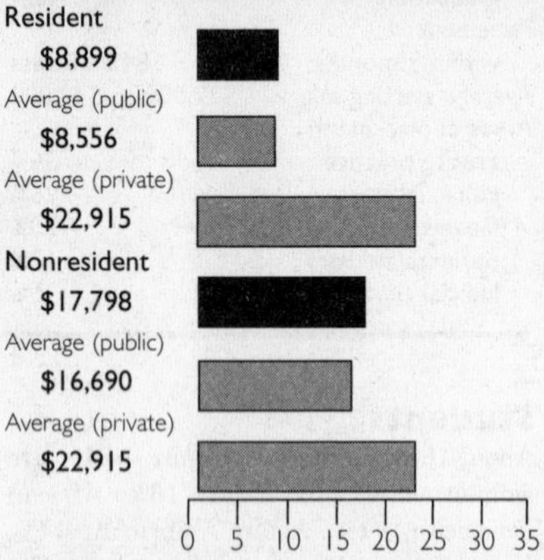

Percentage receiving financial aid: 87%

ADMISSIONS

In the fall 2001 first-year class, 1205 applied, 649 were accepted, and 292 enrolled. Fourteen transfers enrolled. The median LSAT percentile of the most recent first-year class was 50; the median GPA was 3.0 on a scale of 4.0. The lowest LSAT percentile accepted was 5; the highest was 95.

Requirements

Applicants must have a bachelor's degree and take the LSAT. Minimum acceptable GPA is 2.0 on a scale of 4.0. The most important admission factors include academic achievement, LSAT results, and ethnic background. No specific undergraduate courses are required. Candidates are not interviewed.

Procedure

The application deadline for fall entry is April 1. Applicants should submit an application form, LSAT results, transcripts, a nonrefundable application fee of $35, 2 letters of recommendation, and a personal statement. Notification of the admissions decision is on a rolling basis. The latest acceptable LSAT test date for fall entry is February. The law school uses the LSDAS.

Special

The law school recruits minority and disadvantaged students by means of the Legal Career Opportunities Program, a special admissions program for applicants whose background and experience deserve special consideration. The Admissions Committee invites applicants whose test scores or academic records are not strong but whose skills, accomplishments, and other qualifications merit consideration. The Admissions Committee seeks to admit candidates who have encountered adversity but have a record of accomplishment, either academic or professional. LCOP, an evening program, begins in the early part of June and continues through mid-July; students earn 2 or 3 semester credits, depending on the summer course that is offered, and credit is applied to the J.D. degree program. Requirements are not different for out-of-state students. Transfer students must have one year of credit, have a minimum GPA of 3.0, and have attended an ABA-approved law school.

Costs

Tuition and fees for the 2001-2002 academic year are $8899 for full-time in-state students and $17,798 for out-of-state students. Tuition for part-time students is $6846 in-state and $13,792 out-of-state. On-campus room and board costs about $6452 annually; books and supplies run $700.

Financial Aid

About 87% of current law students receive some form of aid. The average annual amount of aid from all sources combined, including scholarships, loans, and work contracts, is $13,100; maximum, $29,404. Awards are based on need and merit. Required financial statements are the FAFSA and Institutional Application. The aid application deadline for fall entry is March 1. A variety of funds is available for students of color or those who are disadvantaged. Students who complete the admissions and financial aid materials are considered for these funds. First-year students are notified about their financial aid application at time of acceptance.

About the Law School

Cleveland State University/Cleveland-Marshall College of Law was established in 1897 and is a public institution. The campus is in an urban area in downtown Cleveland. The primary mission of the law school is to prepare students to enter a learned profession and to provide them with an understanding of the legal profession and system and of their responsibility to maintain and improve the legal system to serve society. Students have access to federal, state, county, city, and local agencies, courts, correctional facilities, law firms, and legal aid organizations in the Cleveland area. Facilities of special interest to law students are the intramural competition, student health services, library, student social center, Cleveland Public Library, physical education facilities, University Circle Cultural Arts Center, Playhouse Square, and student counseling services. Housing for students is available on campus and in nearby suburbs, many within a 20-minute commuting distance. All law school facilities are accessible to the physically disabled.

Calendar

The law school operates on a traditional semester basis. Courses for full-time students are offered days only and must be completed within 6 years. For part-time students, courses are offered both day and evening and must be completed within 6 years. New full- and part-time students are admitted in the fall. There is a 7½-week summer session. Transferable summer courses are offered.

Programs

In addition to the J.D., the law school offers the LL.M. Students may take relevant courses in other programs and apply credit toward the J.D.; a maximum of 8 credits may be applied. The following joint degrees may be earned: J.D./M.B.A. (Juris Doctor/Master of

Phone: 216-687-2304
Fax: 216-687-6881

Contact

Margaret A. McNally, Assistant Dean for Admissions, 216-687-2304 for general inquiries; Catherine Buzanski, Financial Aid Administrator, 216-687-2317 for financial aid information.

Business Administration), J.D./M.P.A. (Juris Doctor/Master of Public Administration), and J.D/M.U.P.D.D. (Juris Doctor/Master of Urban Planning, Design, and Development).

Required

To earn the J.D., candidates must complete 90 total credits, of which 43 are for required courses. They must maintain a minimum GPA of 2.0 in the required courses. The following first-year courses are required of all students: Contracts, Criminal Law, Legal Writing, Property, Torts, a perspective elective, and Civil Procedure I. Required upper-level courses consist of Constitutional Law, Evidence, Legal Profession, and Civil Procedure II. The required orientation program for first-year students is 5 days and includes social activities, introductory classes in case briefing, library tours, and peer adviser meetings.

Electives

Students must take 18 to 20 credits in their area of concentration. The Cleveland-Marshall College of Law offers concentrations in criminal law and tax law. In addition, the Employment Law Clinic offers from 6 to 10 credits, the Community Advocacy Clinic offers from 2 to 10 credits, and the Fair Housing Clinic offers from 2 to 8 credits. Upper-level students may take seminars and up to 3 hours of independent research; seminar papers fulfill the upper-level writing requirement. A judicial externship is worth 6 credits; students work 24 hours a week in a federal or state appellate court. A U.S. Attorney externship is worth 4 credits; students are placed in a civil or criminal U.S. Attorney's office. There are independent/public service externships worth 4 to 6 hours. Special lecture series include the Cleveland-Marshall Lecture Series. Students may participate in study-abroad programs run by ABA/AALS-approved law schools. Cleveland-Marshall also runs an ABA/AALS summer program in St. Petersburg, Russia. First-year students admitted to the Legal Career Opportunities Program are offered tutorials. Cleveland-Marshall has a Director of Minority Affairs who oversees minority programs. A variety of special interest group programs is available. The most widely taken electives are Advocacy, Business, and Tax.

Graduation Requirements

In order to graduate, candidates must have a GPA of 2.0, have completed the upper-division writing requirement, and have completed a course with an administrative component of law, evidence, and legal professions. A perspective course and upper-division writing requires a third semester of Legal Writing and a research paper.

Organizations

Students edit the *Cleveland State Law Review, Journal of Law and Health*, and the newspaper *The Gavel*. The college sends teams to some 41 competitions, including the National Appellate Advocacy and the National Moot Court. Law student organizations include the Student Bar Association, Women's Legal Caucus, and Lawyers Guild. There are local chapters of the NBA-Law School Division and the ABA-Law School Division.

Library

The law library contains 479,214 hard-copy volumes and 58,129 microform volume equivalents, and subscribes to 1516 serial publications. Such on-line databases and networks as DIALOG, LEXIS, WESTLAW, the Internet, SCHOLAR, VuTExt, Datatimes, BRS, RLIN, Compuserve, Gongwer, EPIC, OCLC, Hannah, and MF-DIS are available to law students for research. Special library collections include federal government documents. Recently, the library added a 4-story structure with 85,000 square feet, including a 50-seat computer laboratory, 207 student carrels, and 17 group-study rooms. The ratio of library volumes to faculty is 10,891 to 1 and to students is 580 to 1. The ratio of seats in the library to students is 1 to 2.

Faculty

The law school has 44 full-time and 27 part-time faculty members, of whom 29 are women. According to AAUP standards for Category 1 institutions, faculty salaries are below average. About 20% of full-time faculty have a graduate law degree in addition to the J.D. The ratio of full-time students to full-time faculty in an average class is 20 to 1; in a clinic, 4 to 1. The law school has a regular program of bringing visiting professors and other distinguished lecturers and visitors to campus.

Placement

J.D.s awarded:	228
Services available through: a separate law school placement center	
Services: practice interviews, matching students with local attorneys for interest interviews, and career-related workshops.	
Special features: There is individualized counseling, cover letter development, a skills bank, first-year orientation program, mock interviews, and references and resources containing more than 1000 employment opportunities annually.	
Full-time job interviews:	27 employers
Summer job interviews:	36 employers
Placement by graduation:	65% of class
Placement within 9 months:	96% of class
Average starting salary:	$27,500 to $127,000
Areas of placement:	
Private practice 2-10 attorneys	25%
Private practice 11-25 attorneys	4%
Private practice 26-50 attorneys	6%
Private practice 51-100 attorneys	12%
Government	25%
Business/industry	18%
Judicial clerkships	5%
Public interest	2%
Academic	1%
Pursuing additional full-time degree	1%

Students

About 47% of the student body are women; 11%, minorities; 8%, African American; 1%, Asian American; and 2%, Hispanic. The majority of students come from the Midwest (93%). The average age of entering students is 27; age range is 21 to 64. About 10% of students enter directly from undergraduate school and 12% have a graduate degree. About 10% drop out after the first year for academic or personal reasons; 89% remain to receive a law degree.

COLLEGE OF WILLIAM & MARY

William & Mary Law School

P.O. Box 8795
Williamsburg, VA 23187-8795

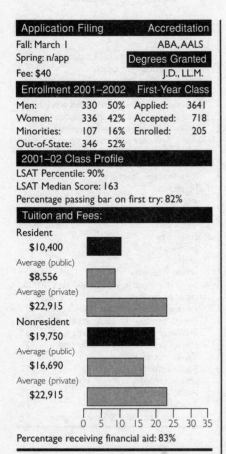

Application Filing		Accreditation
Fall: March 1		ABA, AALS
Spring: n/app		**Degrees Granted**
Fee: $40		J.D., LL.M.

Enrollment 2001–2002			First-Year Class	
Men:	330	50%	Applied:	3641
Women:	336	42%	Accepted:	718
Minorities:	107	16%	Enrolled:	205
Out-of-State:	346	52%		

2001–02 Class Profile

LSAT Percentile: 90%
LSAT Median Score: 163
Percentage passing bar on first try: 82%

Tuition and Fees:

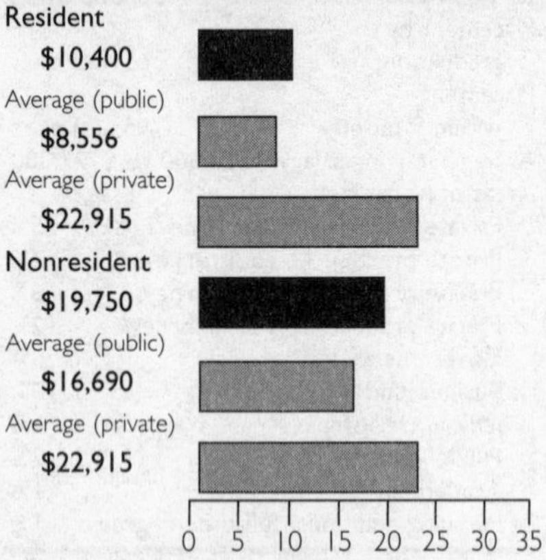

Percentage receiving financial aid: 83%

ADMISSIONS

In the fall 2001 first-year class, 3641 applied, 718 were accepted, and 205 enrolled. Two transfers enrolled. The median LSAT percentile of the most recent first-year class was 90; the median GPA was 3.4 on a scale of 4.0. The lowest LSAT percentile accepted was 26; the highest was 99.

Requirements

Applicants must have a bachelor's degree and take the LSAT. Minimum acceptable GPA is 2.0 on a scale of 4.0. No specific undergraduate courses are required. Candidates are interviewed.

Procedure

The application deadline for fall entry is March 1. Applicants should submit an application form, LSAT results, transcripts, a nonrefundable application fee of $40, 2 letters of recommendation, and a personal statement. Notification of the admissions decision is from January through April. The latest acceptable LSAT test date for fall entry is February. The law school uses the LSDAS.

Special

The law school recruits minority and disadvantaged students by means of on- and off-campus recruitment, brochures, grant proposals, LSDAS Candidate Referral Services, BLSA Programs, and financial aid. Requirements are not different for out-of-state students. Transfer students must have attended an ABA-approved law school.

Costs

Tuition and fees for the 2001-2002 academic year are $10,400 for full-time in-state students and $19,750 for out-of-state students. On-campus room and board costs about $6300 annually; books and supplies run $1000.

Financial Aid

About 83% of current law students receive some form of aid. The average annual amount of aid from all sources combined, including scholarships, loans, and work contracts, is $21,322; maximum, $32,628. Awards are based on need and merit. Required financial statement is the FAFSA. The aid application deadline for fall entry is February 15. Diversity is considered as a factor in the packaging of aid. First-year students are notified about their financial aid application in February and March.

About the Law School

College of William & Mary/William & Mary Law School was established in 1779 and is a public institution. The 1200-acre campus is in a small town 45 miles west of Norfolk, and 45 miles east of Richmond. The primary mission of the law school is to provide students with a superior legal education in a close-knit collegial environment and to offer the opportunity to confront the demands of constructive citizenship and leadership. Students have access to federal, state, county, city, and local agencies, courts, correctional facilities, law firms, legal aid organizations in the Williamsburg area, the National Center for State Courts, and Colonial Williamsburg. Facilities of special interest to law students include the Courtroom 21 Project, the world center for courtroom technology research, housed within the McGlothlin Courtroom, the world's most technologically advanced courtroom. The project has an extensive student staff, trains all second-year students in hands-on courtroom technology use, and supports the Law School activities and courses, such as the legal technology seminar and technology augmented trial advocacy. Housing for students is available on-campus in graduate apartments located next to the law school building. Commercial apartments, townhouses, and other area housing are available as well. About 90% of the law school facilities are accessible to the physically disabled.

Calendar

The law school operates on a traditional semester basis. Courses for full-time students are offered days only and must be completed within 3 years. There is no part-time program. New students are admitted in the fall. There is a 6-week summer session. Transferable summer courses are offered.

Programs

In addition to the J.D., the law school offers the LL.M. Students may take relevant courses in other programs and apply credit toward the J.D.; a maximum of 6 credits may be applied. The following joint degrees may be earned: J.D./M.A. (Juris Doctor/Master of Arts in American studies), J.D./M.B.A. (Juris Doctor/Master of Business Administration), and J.D./M.P.P. (Juris Doctor/Master of Public Policy).

Required

To earn the J.D., candidates must complete 86 total credits, of which 35 are for required courses. They must maintain a minimum GPA of 2.0 in the required courses. The following first-year courses are required of all students: Civil Procedure, Contracts, Property, Torts, Constitutional Law, Legal Skills I and II, and Criminal Law. Required upper-level courses consist of Legal Skills III, IV, and V. All student clinics are elective courses that provide students actual contact with legal cases, clients, and/or courts. There are a limited number of places in each clinic and students can enroll in only 1 clinic while at law school.The required orientation program for first-year students is a 1-week program designed to introduce incoming first-year law students to legal analysis, legal

Phone: 757-221-3785
Fax: 757-221-3261
E-mail: *lawadm@wm.edu*
Web: *http://www.wm.edu*

Contact

Faye F. Shealy, Associate Dean, 757-221-3785 for general inquiries; Ed Irish, Director of Student Financial Aid, 757-221-2420 for financial aid information.

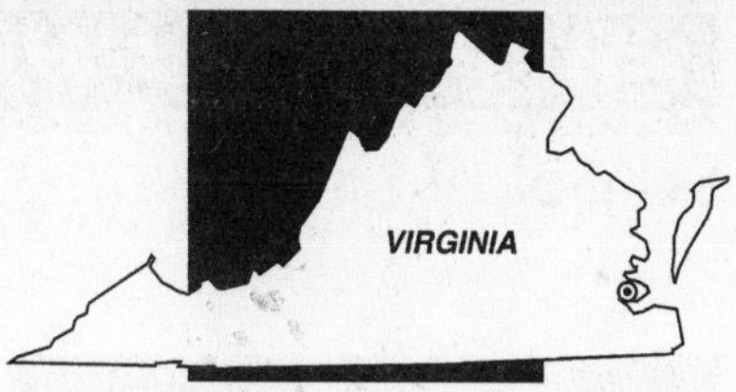

vocabulary, legal teaching methods, legal writing, and the law firm structure of the Legal Skills Program.

Electives

Clinics, worth 3 credits each and limited to third-year students, include Attorney General Practice, Department of Employment Dispute Resolution, and Virginia Court of Appeals. Seminars, worth 3 credits, are open to both second- and third-year students (size limited to 15 to 25 students) and include civil rights, constitutional decision making, and legal technology. Internships, worth 2 to 3 credits, marry a classroom component with supervised work in an office setting and include domestic violence, legal aid, and federal tax practice. Research programs, worth 1 to 2 credits, include independent research, advance research, and tax research, and are open to second- and third-year students; these must be completed in conjunction with a supervising professor. Field work is offered through a clerking program open to second- and third-year students for 1 to 2 credits, involving 40 hours with a law firm or judge, writing a synopsis of work done, and receiving an evaluation letter from the attorney or judge. Special lectures include the Institute of Bill of Rights Law, Cutler Lectures, and George Wythe Lectures. Study abroad is available during the summer in Madrid, Spain, with most classes worth 2 credits and open to any second- or third-year student who applies from an ABA-accredited law school. Tutorial programs are available to any first-year student under the direction of the Assistant Dean for Programs. Minority programs are arranged by minority student organizations. Special interest group programs are arranged by individual student organizations. The most widely taken electives are business, evidence, and corporations.

Graduation Requirements

In order to graduate, candidates must have a GPA of 2.0 and have completed the upper-division writing requirement.

Organizations

Students edit the *William & Mary Law Review, William & Mary Bill of Rights Journal, William & Mary Journal of Women and the Law, William & Mary Environmental Law and Policy Review,* and the newspaper *Amicus Curiae.* Ten teams compete each year at competitions such as the National Tournament, ABA Tournament, and Jessup International Tournament. Each year the school sponsors the National Trial Team competitions and the Bushrod T. Washington Moot Court Tournament, which is open to second-year students only, with the top 32 students earning the right to compete on one of the moot court teams in their third year. The William B. Spong, Jr. Invitational Moot Court Tournament attracts approximately 20 to 22 teams from throughout the nation annually. Law Student organizations include the Black Law Student Association, Christian Legal Society, and the Public Service Fund. Campus clubs and other organizations include the Institute of Bill of Rights Law-Student Division, Law Students Involved in the Community, and Lesbian and Gay Law Student Association.

Library

The law library contains 379,000 hard-copy volumes and 840,000 microform volume equivalents, and subscribes to 4500 serial publications. Such on-line databases and networks as CALI, CIS Universe, DIALOG, Dow-Jones, Infotrac, Legal-Trac, LEXIS, LOIS, Mathew Bender, NEXIS, OCLC First Search, WESTLAW, Wilsonline Indexes, First Search, and VIVA are available to law students for research. Special library collections include Thomas Jefferson law collection, environmental law, Roman law, constitutional law, jurisprudence, intellectual property, and taxation. Recently, the library installed 2 computer laboratories with 32 stations. The ratio of library volumes to faculty is 11,484 to 1 and to students is 569 to 1. The ratio of seats in the library to students is 1 to 1.3.

Faculty

The law school has 33 full-time and 49 part-time faculty members, of whom 25 are women. According to AAUP standards for Category I institutions, faculty salaries are above average. About 11% of full-time faculty have a graduate law degree in addition to the J.D.; about 5% of part-time faculty have one. The ratio of full-time students to full-time faculty in an average class is 35 to 1; in a clinic, 6 to 1. The law school has a regular program of bringing visiting professors and other distinguished lecturers and visitors to campus. There is a chapter of the Order of the Coif; 15 faculty and 337 graduates are members.

Placement

J.D.s awarded:	180
Services available through: a separate law school placement center. Students also have access to the College's other career services offices.	
Services: career planning/counseling, 7 summer public service funding programs, 18 off-campus job fairs, and assistance with judicial clerkships	
Special features: professional staff includes 2 attorneys who, together, have significant experience in career counseling, practicing law, and lawyer recruiting and hiring. The emphasis is on individualized career planning for students with extensive programs and resources designed to enable them to make informed career choices. Students interested in public service work may utilize funding programs which, during the summer of 2001, provided approximately $140,000 for internships throughout the world.	
Full-time job interviews:	110 employers
Summer job interviews:	168 employers
Placement by graduation:	82% of class
Placement within 9 months:	99% of class
Average starting salary:	$26,000 to $135,000
Areas of placement:	
Private practice 2-10 attorneys	9%
Private practice 11-25 attorneys	5%
Private practice 26-50 attorneys	4%
Private practice 51-100 attorneys	10%
Private practice 101+ attorneys	27%
Judicial clerkships	18%
Business/industry	10%
Government	7%
Military	5%
Public interest	1%

Students

About 42% of the student body are women; 16%, minorities; 9%, African American; 4%, Asian American; 2%, Hispanic; 1%, Native American; and 7%, unknown. Most students come from Virginia (48%). The average age of entering students is 25; age range is 20 to 54. About 42% of students enter directly from undergraduate school, 10% have a graduate degree, and 58% have worked full-time prior to entering law school. About 3% drop out after the first year for academic or personal reasons; 97% remain to receive a law degree.

COLUMBIA UNIVERSITY

School of Law

435 West 116th Street
New York, NY 10027

Application Filing	Accreditation
Fall: February 15	ABA, AALS
Spring: n/app	**Degrees Granted**
Fee: $65	J.D., LL.M., S.J.D.

Enrollment 2001–2002			First-Year Class	
Men:	563	49%	Applied:	6614
Women:	576	51%	Accepted:	1157
Minorities:	364	32%	Enrolled:	356
Out-of-State:	1139	100%		

2001–02 Class Profile

LSAT Percentile: 98%
LSAT Median Score: 169
Percentage passing bar on first try: 94%

Tuition and Fees:

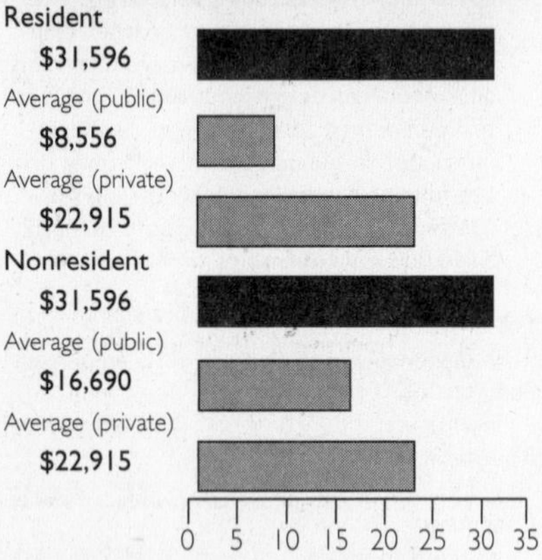

Percentage receiving financial aid: 75%

ADMISSIONS

In the fall 2001 first-year class, 6614 applied, 1157 were accepted, and 356 enrolled. One-hundred-three transfers enrolled. The median LSAT percentile of the most recent first-year class was 98; the median GPA was 3.64 on a scale of 4.0. The highest LSAT percentile was 99.

Requirements

Applicants must have a bachelor's degree and take the LSAT. Specific undergraduate courses and interviews are not required.

Procedure

The application deadline for fall entry is February 15. Applicants should submit an application form, LSAT results, transcripts, a nonrefundable application fee of $65, and 3 letters of recommendation. Notification of the admissions decision is in March and April. The latest acceptable LSAT test date for fall entry is December. The law school uses the LSDAS.

Special

The law school recruits minority and disadvantaged students through outreach efforts, counseling initiatives, and national database searches with invitations to apply. Requirements are not different for out-of-state students. Transfer students must have one year of credit, have attended an ABA-approved law school, and have completed the first year with distinction at an ABA-approved law school or at an accredited Canadian law school.

Costs

Tuition and fees for the 2001-2002 academic year are $31,596 for all full-time students. On-campus room and board costs about $14,700 annually; books and supplies run $915.

Financial Aid

About 75% of current law students receive some form of aid. The average annual amount of aid from all sources combined, including scholarships, loans, and work contracts, is $38,000; maximum, $48,500. Awards are based on need, as are financial aid grants; a small number of merit-based awards are also offered. Required financial statements are the FAFSA and Need Access application. The aid application deadline for fall entry is March 1. First-year students are notified about their application following admission, but prior to the deadline for a student's acceptance of the offer.

About the Law School

Columbia University School of Law was established in 1858 and is a private institution. The 36-acre campus is in the Morningside Heights section of northwest Manhattan. The primary mission of the law school is to serve as a leading center of research and scholarship regarding law and its role in society. Students have access to federal, state, county, city, and local agencies, courts, correctional facilities, law firms, and legal aid organizations in the New York City area. The Law School is nearing completion of a $75 million physical expansion and renewal project, begun in 1996. The Law School's main building, Greene Hall, has undergone significant expansion and improvements. Across the street from Greene Hall is William C. Warren Hall, home to the *Columbia Law Review*, Morningside Heights Legal Services, and the Center for Public Interest Law. Housing for students includes on-campus apartments, available to both single students and couples; the Off-Campus Housing Office (OCHA) helps students find off-campus housing. About 98% of the law school facilities are accessible to the physically disabled.

Calendar

The law school operates on a traditional semester basis. Courses for full-time students are offered days only and must be completed within 6 semesters (or up to 9 semesters for students with disabilities or with responsibilities for small children). There is no part-time program. New students are admitted in the fall. There is no summer session. Transferable summer courses are not offered.

Programs

In addition to the J.D., the law school offers the LL.M. and S.J.D. Students may take relevant courses in other programs and apply credit toward the J.D.; a maximum of 10 credits may be applied. These joint degrees are offered: J.D./M.B.A. (Juris Doctor/Master of Business Administration), J.D./M.A., M.Phil., or Ph.D. (Juris Doctor/Master of Arts or Doctor of Philosophy in history, philosophy, economics, anthropology, psychology, religious studies, or sociology), J.D./M.F.A. (Juris Doctor/Master of Arts in theater arts), J.D./M.I.A. (Juris Doctor/Master of International Affairs), J.D./M.P.A. (Juris Doctor/Master of Public Administration with Princeton's Woodrow Wilson School), J.D./M.P.A. (Juris Doctor/Master of Public Affairs (Columbia)), and J.D./M.S. (Juris Doctor/Master of Science in journalism, urban planning, and social work).

Required

To earn the J.D., candidates must complete 83 total credits, of which 35 are for required courses. The following first-year courses are required of all students: Legal Methods and Legal Writing and Research, Constitutional Law or Property, Contracts, Torts, Civil Procedure, Criminal Law, Foundations of the Regulatory State, Foundation Year Moot Court, and Perspectives on Legal Thought. Required upper-level courses consist of Profession of Law, a minimum of 2 writing credits, and a pro bono service requirement (40 hours in second and third years). Clinics are electives. The required orientation program for first-year students lasts 2 days and starts before Legal Methods course begins. Topics covered include student services, law school and university administrative matters, computer training, and financial aid information.

Phone: 212-854-2670
Fax: 212-854-1109
E-mail: *admissions@law.columbia.edu*
Web: *www.law.columbia.edu*

Contact

Admissions Office, 212-854-2670 for general inquiries; Alice Rigas, Financial Aid Director, 212-854-6522 for financial aid information.

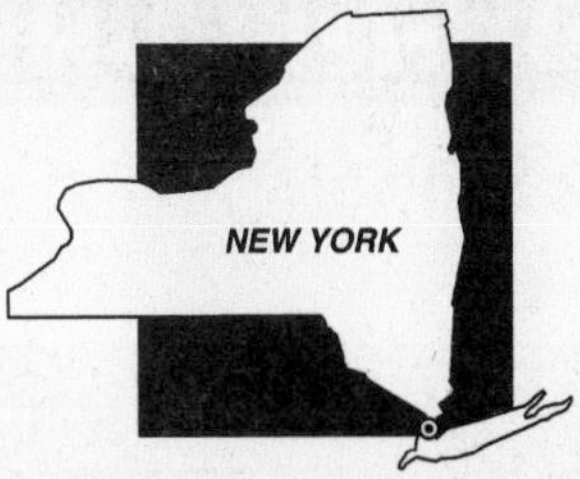

Electives

The School of Law offers concentrations in corporate law, criminal law, entertainment law, environmental law, family law, international law, labor law, litigation, media law, securities law, sports law, tax law, torts and insurance, constitutional law, human rights law, labor law, history and philosophy of law, health care and the law, and education law. In addition, clinics such as the Mediation Clinic, Child Advocacy Clinic, and Human Rights Clinic offer client-based experiences to upper-class students for 5 to 7 points. Seminars are offered in such areas as Constitutional Law, Corporate Law, and Human Rights for 2 points (generally). Admission to a seminar is by lottery. Additional training through internships is available through arrangements with city agencies and consumer advocacy groups; clerkships with criminal, appellate, and federal court judges; and the pro bono service requirement. Research may be done as part of the legal writing requirement. Law school lectures regularly bring leading figures from business, politics, entertainment, and areas of the law and judiciary to Columbia. Columbia established a Dean's Breakfast Series in which distinguished alumni from the law school come and meet informally with small groups of students. There is a 4-year double degree program with the University of Paris, giving students a J.D. and Maitrise en Droit, a 4-year program with the University of London, giving students a J.D. and LL.B, and a 3-year program with the University of London where students receive a Columbia J.D. and University of London LL.M. The most widely taken electives are Corporations, Federal Income Taxation, and Evidence.

Graduation Requirements

In order to graduate, candidates must have completed the upper-division writing requirement and satisfied degree requirements (including pro bono service).

Organizations

Students edit the *Columbia Law Review, Columbia Journal of Environmental Law, Columbia Human Rights Law Review*, and *Columbia Journal of Law and Social Problems*. Other law reviews include *Columbia Journal-VLA Journal of Law and the Arts, Columbia Business Law Review, Columbia Journal of Gender and the Law, Columbia Journal of East European Law, Columbia Journal of European Law, Columbia Science and Technology Law Review*, and *National Black Law Journal*. Students also edit the newspaper *Columbia Law School News* and the yearbook *Pegasus*. The Moot Court Committee sponsors the Harlan Fiske Stone Honor Competition and the Jerome Michael Jury Trials. Students also participate, with distinction, in the Jessup International Moot Court Competition. Other competitions include the Frederick Douglass National Competition and Native American Law Students Moot Court Competition. Law student organizations include the Civil Rights Society, Environmental Law Society, and Columbia Society of International Law. There are local chapters of the American Civil Liberties Union, Federalist Society, National Lawyers Guild, and BALSA.

Library

The law library contains 1,020,000 hardcopy volumes and 737,500 microform volume equivalents, and subscribes to 7314 serial publications. Such on-line databases and networks as CALI, DIALOG, Legal-Trac, LEXIS, LOIS, NEXIS, OCLC First Search, RLIN, WESTLAW, Jutastat, CCH, PLC Global, UN Optical Disk, and TIARA TREATIES are available to law students for research. Special library collections include a notable collection on foreign law, Roman law, and a large rare book collection, Perlin/Rosenberg Papers, as well as papers from the Nuremberg Trials and the South African Treason Trials, and a gift of the papers of Telford Taylor, who was the main U.S. prosecutor at the Nuremberg Trials. Local Area Network (LAN) connections are available for laptops. The school received a $7 million gift for improvements to the law library. The school restructured the library organization to provide more reference staff for direct user support. Moreover, the school added 1 additional reference librarian, a large number of foreign and international law databases, and table of contents information to bibliography records. The ratio of library volumes to faculty is 11,209 to 1 and to students is 896 to 1.

Placement

J.D.s awarded:	381
Services available through: a separate law school placement center	
Services: extensive judicial clerkship counseling; international internship opportunities	
Special features: resource library, web-based newsletter, career adviser program, a public interest program, extensive web-based resource database, e-mail of all position listings, and one of the largest on-campus recruiting programs in the country.	
Full-time job interviews:	500 employers
Summer job interviews:	500 employers
Placement by graduation:	97% of class
Placement within 9 months:	99% of class
Average starting salary:	$37,500 to $200,000
Areas of placement:	
Private practice 51-100 attorneys	2%
Private practice 100-500 attorneys	70%
Judicial clerkships	19%
Public interest	4%
Business/industry	3%
Government	2%

Faculty

The law school has 91 full-time and 52 part-time faculty members, of whom 33 are women. According to AAUP standards for Category I institutions, faculty salaries are well above average. About 15% of full-time faculty have a graduate law degree in addition to the J.D.; about 10% of part-time faculty have one. The ratio of full-time students to full-time faculty in an average class is 14 to 1; in a clinic, 8 to 1. The law school has a regular program of bringing visiting professors and other distinguished lecturers and visitors to campus.

Students

About 51% of the student body are women; 32%, minorities; 9%, African American; 14%, Asian American; 8%, Hispanic; 1%, Native American; and 7%, foreign nationals. Most students come from the West (18%). The average age of entering students is 24; age range is 20 to 47. About 34% of students enter directly from undergraduate school, 15% have a graduate degree, and 65% have worked full-time prior to entering law school. No students drop out after the first year for academic or personal reasons; all remain to receive a law degree.

CORNELL UNIVERSITY

Law School

Myron Taylor Hall
Ithaca, NY 14853-4901

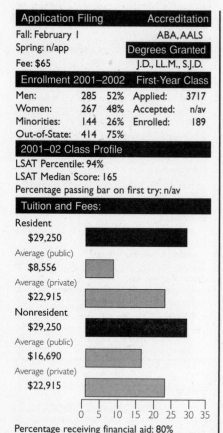

Application Filing		Accreditation
Fall: February 1		ABA, AALS
Spring: n/app		**Degrees Granted**
Fee: $65		J.D., LL.M., S.J.D.

Enrollment 2001–2002			First-Year Class	
Men:	285	52%	Applied:	3717
Women:	267	48%	Accepted:	n/av
Minorities:	144	26%	Enrolled:	189
Out-of-State:	414	75%		

2001–02 Class Profile

LSAT Percentile: 94%
LSAT Median Score: 165
Percentage passing bar on first try: n/av

Tuition and Fees:

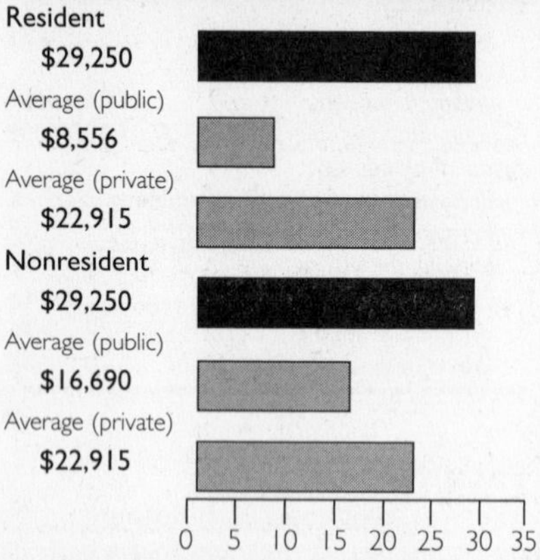

Percentage receiving financial aid: 80%

ADMISSIONS

In the fall 2001 first-year class, 3717 applied and 189 enrolled. Ten to 15 transfers enrolled. The median LSAT percentile of the most recent first-year class was 94; the median GPA was 3.6 on a scale of 4.0.

Requirements

Applicants must have a bachelor's degree and take the LSAT. No specific undergraduate courses are required. Candidates are not interviewed.

Procedure

The application deadline for fall entry is February 1. Applicants should submit an application form, LSAT results, a nonrefundable application fee of $65, 3 letters of recommendation, and a personal statement. Transcripts must be sent via the LSDAS. Notification of the admissions decision is from January through April. The latest acceptable LSAT test date for fall entry is December. The law school uses the LSDAS.

Special

The law school recruits minority and disadvantaged students by aggressively encouraging them to apply. In addition, a student's minority or disadvantaged status is considered to be a positive part of the application; offers of financial aid are also made. Requirements are not different for out-of-state students. Transfer students must have one year of credit, have attended an ABA-approved law school, and must be in the top 10% of the class.

Costs

Tuition and fees for the 2001-2002 academic year are $29,250 for all full-time students. On-campus room and board costs about $7870 annually; books and supplies run $760.

Financial Aid

About 80% of current law students receive some form of aid. The average annual amount of aid from all sources combined, including scholarships, loans, and work contracts, is $29,100; maximum, $37,880. Awards are based on need and merit. Required financial statements are the FAFSA and Need Access. Special funds for minority or disadvantaged students consist of need-based enhanced grants. First-year students are notified about their financial aid application shortly after acceptance.

About the Law School

Cornell University Law School was established in 1888 and is a private institution. The 745-acre campus is in a small town 250 miles northwest of New York City. The primary mission of the law school is to teach law within the context of humanity. Students have access to federal, state, county, city, and local agencies, courts, correctional facilities, law firms, and legal aid organizations in the Ithaca area. A full range of opportunities consistent with a small city is available to students. Facilities of special interest to law students are the Legal Aid Clinic, international legal studies program, and the Legal Information Institute. Housing for students is ample both on and off campus. About 90% of the law school facilities are accessible to the physically disabled.

Calendar

The law school operates on a traditional semester basis. Courses for full-time students are offered days only and must be completed within 3 years. There is no part-time program. New students are admitted in the fall. There is a 4-week summer session. Transferable summer courses are offered.

Programs

In addition to the J.D., the law school offers the LL.M. and S.J.D. Students may take relevant courses in other programs and apply credit toward the J.D.; a maximum of 12 credits may be applied. The following joint degrees may be earned: J.D./LL.M. (in international and comparative law), J.D./M.A., Ph.D. (Ph.D. Juris Doctor/Master of Arts in Philosophy or Doctor of Philosophy), J.D./M.B.A. (Juris Doctor/Master of Business Administration), J.D./M.I.L.R. (Juris Doctor/Master of Industrial and Labor Relations), J.D./M.L.L.P. (Juris Doctor/Master of German and European Law and Legal Practice), J.D./M.P.A. (Juris Doctor/Master of Public Administration), and J.D./M.R.P. (Juris Doctor/Master of Regional Planning).

Phone: 607-255-5141
Fax: 607-255-7193
E-mail: *lawadmit@postoffice.law.cornell.edu*
Web: *www.lawschool.cornell.edu*

Contact

Admissions Office, 607-255-5141 for general inquiries; Financial Aid Office, 607-255-6292 for financial aid information.

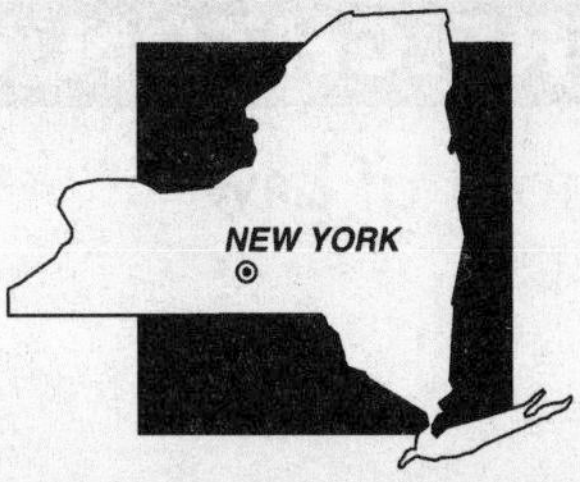

Required

To earn the J.D., candidates must complete 84 total credits, of which 36 are for required courses. They must maintain a minimum GPA of 2.3 in the required courses. The following first-year courses are required of all students: Civil Procedure, Constitutional Law, Contracts, Legal Methods, Criminal Law, Property, and Torts. Required upper-level courses consist of a writing requirement (2 writing courses) and Professional Responsibility course. The required orientation program for first-year students is a 2-day introduction to the school.

Electives

Students must take 14 credits in their area of concentration. The Law School offers concentrations in advocacy, business law and regulation, general practice, and public law. In addition, clinics, worth 4 to 6 credits, include the Legal Aid Clinic, Women and the Law Clinic, and Youth Law Clinic. Multiple seminars in the upper division are open to a maximum of 16 students per semester. Internships include the judicial externship, Neighborhood Legal Services, Criminal Justice, and legislative. Full term externships are worth 12 credits at approved sites. Special lecture series are the International Lecture Series, the Robert S. Stevens Lecture Series, Henry Korn Lecture Series, Bernard S. Yadowitz Lecture Series, and the Berger Program in International Law. Study abroad may be done through the Paris Institute, exchange programs (Sydney and Humboldt), and individual ABA-approved programs. An academic support coordinator program and Minorities-in-the-Law Conference are held. The most widely taken electives are Corporations, Evidence, and Federal Income Taxation.

Graduation Requirements

In order to graduate, candidates must have a GPA of 2.3, have completed the upper-division writing requirement, and first-year Legal Methods Writing Program, and Professional Responsibility course.

Organizations

Students edit the *Cornell Law Review, Cornell Journal of Law and Public Policy, Cornell International Law Journal,* LII Bulletin-NY, LII Bulletin-Patent, the student newspaper *Tower*, and the *Cornell Law Forum*. A variety of moot court competitions, such as the Cuccia Cup, Jessup, and Niagara CISG, is held, mostly at the school. Law student organizations include the Herbert W. Briggs Society of International Law, Cornell Law Students Association, and Environment Law. There are local chapters of National Lawyers Guild, Phi Delta Phi, and Order of the Coif.

Library

The law library contains 641,000 hard-copy volumes and 5500 microform volume equivalents, and subscribes to 6387 serial publications. Such on-line databases and networks as CALI, CIS Universe, DIALOG, Dow-Jones, Infotrac, Legal-Trac, LEXIS, LOIS, Mathew Bender, NEXIS, OCLC First Search, RLIN, WESTLAW, and Wilsonline Indexes are available to law students for research. Special library collections include international and foreign law, a U.S. government documents depository, the Bennett Collection of Statutory Materials, and rare books. The ratio of library volumes to faculty is 12,820 to 1 and to students, 1161 to 1. The ratio of seats in the library to students is 1 to 1.

Faculty

The law school has 40 full-time and 10 part-time faculty members, of whom 13 are women. According to AAUP standards for Category I institutions, faculty salaries are well above average. About 16% of full-time faculty have a graduate law degree in addition to the J.D.; about 9% of part-time faculty have one. The ratio of full-time students to full-time faculty in an average class is 13 to 1; in a clinic, 8 to 1. The law school has a regular program of bringing visiting professors and other distinguished lecturers and visitors to campus. There is a chapter of the Order of the Coif; 30 faculty and 18 graduates are members.

Placement

J.D.s awarded:	186
Services available through: a separate law school placement center	
Services: off-campus job fairs in major U.S. cities	
Special features: The Public Interest Low Income Protection Plan for loan forgiveness and moderate payback plans program is for students who intend to work in the public or nonprofit sector. Public Interest Foundation and work-study grants are available for summer public interest work.	
Full-time job interviews:	221 employers
Summer job interviews:	325 employers
Placement by graduation:	94% of class
Placement within 9 months:	99% of class
Average starting salary:	$36,000 to $140,000
Areas of placement:	
Private practice 11-25 attorneys	4%
Private practice 26-50 attorneys	5%
Private practice 51-100 attorneys	11%
Private practice 100+ attorneys	57%
Judicial clerkships	12%
Business/industry	4%
Government	2%
Public interest	2%
Military	1%
Academic	1%

Students

About 48% of the student body are women; 26%, minorities; 6%, African American; 15%, Asian American; 4%, Hispanic; and 1%, Native American. The majority of students come from the Northeast (55%). The average age of entering students is 25; age range is 20 to 40. About 38% of students enter directly from undergraduate school, 17% have a graduate degree, and 62% have worked full-time prior to entering law school. About 1% drop out after the first year for academic or personal reasons; 99% remain to receive a law degree.

CREIGHTON UNIVERSITY

School of Law

2500 California Plaza
Omaha, NE 68178

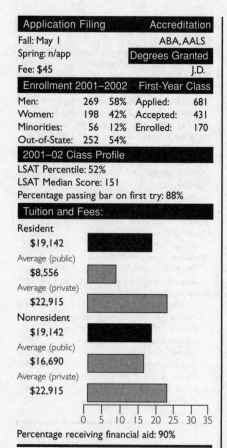

Application Filing	Accreditation
Fall: May 1	ABA, AALS
Spring: n/app	**Degrees Granted**
Fee: $45	J.D.

Enrollment 2001–2002			First-Year Class	
Men:	269	58%	Applied:	681
Women:	198	42%	Accepted:	431
Minorities:	56	12%	Enrolled:	170
Out-of-State:	252	54%		

2001–02 Class Profile

LSAT Percentile: 52%
LSAT Median Score: 151
Percentage passing bar on first try: 88%

Tuition and Fees:

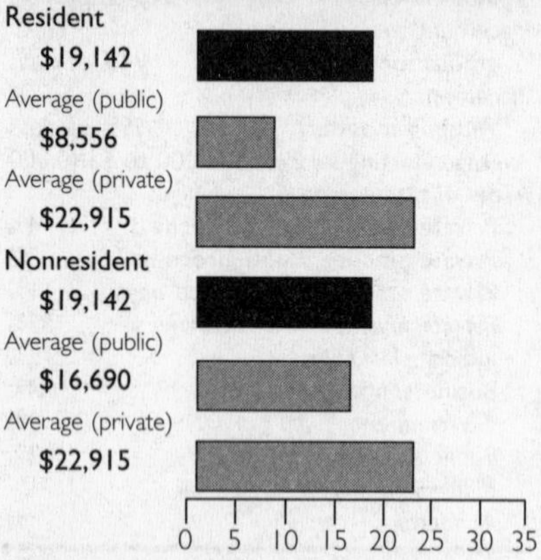

Percentage receiving financial aid: 90%

ADMISSIONS

In the fall 2001 first-year class, 681 applied, 431 were accepted, and 170 enrolled. Twelve transfers enrolled. The median LSAT percentile of the most recent first-year class was 52; the median GPA was 3.23 on a scale of 4.0. The lowest LSAT percentile accepted was 21; the highest was 99.

Requirements

Applicants must have a bachelor's degree and take the LSAT. The most important admission factors include LSAT results, GPA, and general background. No specific undergraduate courses are required. Candidates are not interviewed.

Procedure

The application deadline for fall entry is May 1. Applicants should submit an application form, LSAT results, transcripts, a nonrefundable application fee of $45, and 2 letters of recommendation. Notification of the admissions decision is on a rolling basis. The latest acceptable LSAT test date for fall entry is February. The law school uses the LSDAS.

Special

The law school recruits minority and disadvantaged students by means of a substantial Minority Scholarship Program. Requirements are not different for out-of-state students. Transfer students must have one year of credit and have attended an ABA-approved law school.

Costs

Tuition and fees for the 2001-2002 academic year are $19,142 for all full-time students. On-campus room and board costs about $10350 annually; books and supplies run $1120.

Financial Aid

About 90% of current law students receive some form of aid. The average annual amount of aid from all sources combined, including scholarships, loans, and work contracts, is $20,000; maximum, $33,362. Awards are based on need and merit. Loans are need based, whereas scholarships are merit based. The required financial statement is the FAFSA. Special funds for minority or disadvantaged students consist of a substantial scholarship program for Native American, African American, and Hispanic applicants. First-year students are notified about their financial aid application at time of acceptance.

About the Law School

Creighton University School of Law was established in 1904 and is a private institution. The 93.5-acre campus is in an urban area near downtown Omaha. The primary mission of the law school is to train lawyers to practice in every jurisdiction in the United States and to prepare men and women to render morally responsible services in all phases of the administration of justice. Students have access to federal, state, county, city, and local agencies, courts, correctional facilities, law firms, and legal aid organizations in the Omaha area. The state's capital and legislature are 45 minutes away by car. The law center houses all functions of the law school under one roof. The library has been expanded, allowing for more individual and group study spaces. Housing for students is available in a university-owned high-rise apartment complex exclusively for use by professional students and families. About 99% of the law school facilities are accessible to the physically disabled.

Calendar

The law school operates on a traditional semester basis. Courses for full-time students are offered both day and evening and must be completed within 3 years. For part-time students, courses are offered both day and evening and must be completed within 6 years. New full- and part-time students are admitted in the fall. There is a 5- to 6-week summer session. Transferable summer courses are offered.

Programs

Students may take relevant courses in other programs and apply credit toward the J.D.; a maximum of 6 credits may be applied. The following joint degrees may be earned: J.D./M.B.A. (Juris Doctor/Master of Business Administration) and J.D./M.S. (Juris Doctor/Master of Science in electronic commerce).

Phone: 402-280-2872
800-282-5835
Fax: 402-280-3161
E-mail: *admit@culaw.creighton.edu*
Web: *http://culaw.creighton.edu*

Contact

Andrea D. Bashara, Assistant Dean, 402-280-2872 for general inquiries; Dean Obenauer, Associate Director, 402-280-2731 for financial aid information.

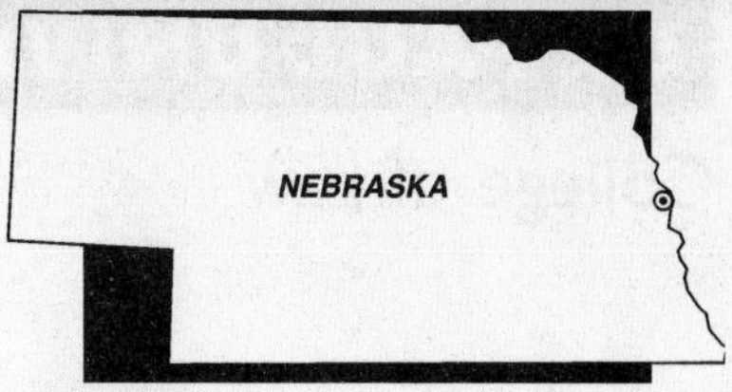

Required
To earn the J.D., candidates must complete 94 total credits, of which 40 are for required courses. They must maintain a minimum grade average of 57 (on a scale of 50 to 100) in the required courses. The following first-year courses are required of all students: Constitutional Law I and II, Contracts I and II, Torts I and II, Legal Research, Property I and II, Civil Procedure I and II, and Legal Writing and Lawyering Skills I. Required upper-level courses consist of Professional Responsibility and Legal Writing and Lawyering Skills II. The required orientation program for first-year students is 2 days of general orientation, including an introduction to briefing cases and the Socratic method.

Electives
Students must take 24 credits in their area of concentration. The School of Law offers concentrations in corporate law, criminal law, litigation, tax law, business, taxation, and commercial transactions. In addition, the Milton R. Abrahams Legal Clinic is open to all students who have completed all required courses and are classified as third-year students. The Clinic accepts a variety of civil matters that vary in complexity. Clinic participants earn 4 credit hours. Seminars, worth 2 and 3 credits, include the Securities Practice Seminar, Advanced Writing Seminar, and Mediation Seminar. Many electives have fewer than 20 students and are taught in seminar fashion. Internships are offered to eligible upper-level students in many different city, county, and federal offices and legal aid offices. Participants serve as law clerks to the various attorneys and judges, for 3 nonclassroom hours. Students may select research topics and write papers for credit under the guidance of a faculty member. Special lecture series include the annual TePoel Lecture Series and Lane Foundation Lectures. Students may study abroad in ABA-accredited programs and transfer up to 6 credit hours. The Black Law Students Association and Latino Law Students Association offer tutorial programs to minority members. The most widely taken electives are Evidence, Business Associations, and Trusts and Estates I.

Graduation Requirements
In order to graduate, candidates must have a minimum grade average of 65% and have completed the upper-division writing requirement.

Organizations

Students edit the *Creighton Law Review*. The student newspaper is *The Praetor*. Moot Court opportunites include the second-year intramural ABA regional, national, and international tournaments as well as invitational tournaments. Other competitions include the Negotiation Competition, Client Counseling, ABA National Criminal Justice Trial Advocacy Competition, and essay competitions. Student organizations include the Law Society, Environmental Law Society, and Law Partners. There are local chapters of Phi Alpha Delta, Phi Delta Phi, and the Student Bar Association. Other student organizations include the Public Interest Law Forum, Women's Law Student Association, and Law Ambassadors.

Library

The law library contains 278,917 hard-copy volumes and 120,733 microform volume equivalents, and subscribes to 1496 serial publications. Such on-line databases and networks as CALI, CIS Universe, Legal-Trac, LEXIS, LOIS, Mathew Bender, NEXIS, OCLC First Search, WESTLAW, Hein Online, CCH Tax Research Network, United Nations Treaty Collection, and Academic Universe are available to law students for research. The law library is a selective U.S. government depository consisting of a complete Congressional Information Service Legislative History service from 1970 to the present, Nebraska Appellate and Supreme Court briefs, and a rare book collection containing approximately 750 British and American legal texts from the 15th through the 19th centuries. Recently, the library was remodeled and a new lower level was constructed. This project nearly doubled the size of the library, and added 7 new group study rooms, a 24-station computer classroom, and multiple data lines for network access. The ratio of library volumes to faculty is 12,678 to 1 and to students, 619 to 1. The ratio of seats in the library to students is 1 to 2.

Placement	
J.D.s awarded:	132
Services available through: a separate law school placement center	
Services: n/av	
Special features: Web page (job postings are password protected).	
Full-time job interviews:	30 employers
Summer job interviews:	n/av
Placement by graduation:	46% of class
Placement within 9 months:	97% of class
Average starting salary:	$43,013
Areas of placement:	
Private practice 2-10 attorneys	26%
Private practice 11-25 attorneys	7%
Private practice 26-50 attorneys	5%
Private practice 51-100 attorneys	1%
Private practice 101+ attorneys	6%
Business/industry	22%
Government	13%
Judicial clerkships	6%
Military	4%
Academic	3%
Public interest	2%

Faculty

The law school has 29 full-time and 45 part-time faculty members, of whom 21 are women. According to AAUP standards for Category IIA institutions, faculty salaries are above average. About 38% of full-time faculty have a graduate law degree in addition to the J.D. The ratio of full-time students to full-time faculty in an average class is 16 to 1; in a clinic, 6 to 1. The law school has a regular program of bringing visiting professors and other distinguished lecturers and visitors to campus.

Students

About 42% of the student body are women; 12%, minorities; 4%, African American; 2%, Asian American; 5%, Hispanic; and 1%, Native American. The majority of students come from Nebraska (46%). The average age of entering students is 26; age range is 21 to 48. About 45% of students enter directly from undergraduate school.

DE PAUL UNIVERSITY

College of Law

25 East Jackson Boulevard
Chicago, IL 60604

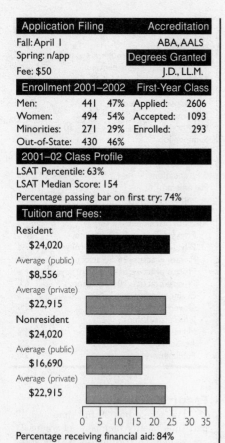

Application Filing	Accreditation
Fall: April 1	ABA, AALS
Spring: n/app	**Degrees Granted**
Fee: $50	J.D., LL.M.

Enrollment 2001–2002			First-Year Class	
Men:	441	47%	Applied:	2606
Women:	494	54%	Accepted:	1093
Minorities:	271	29%	Enrolled:	293
Out-of-State:	430	46%		

2001–02 Class Profile

LSAT Percentile: 63%
LSAT Median Score: 154
Percentage passing bar on first try: 74%

Tuition and Fees:

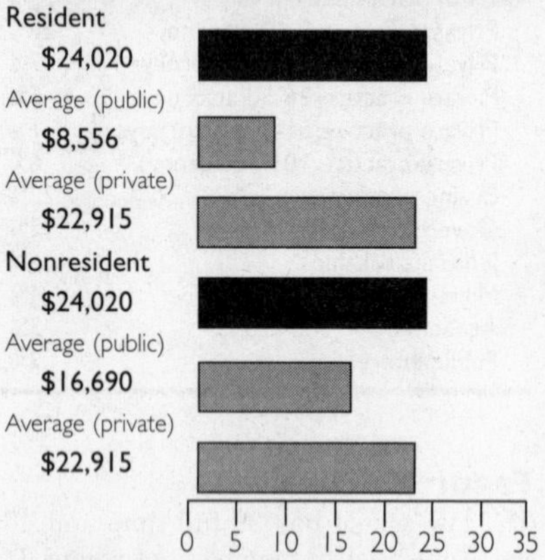

Percentage receiving financial aid: 84%

ADMISSIONS

In the fall 2001 first-year class, 2606 applied, 1093 were accepted, and 293 enrolled. Twenty-five transfers enrolled. The median LSAT percentile of the most recent first-year class was 63; the median GPA was 3.27 on a scale of 4.0. The lowest LSAT percentile accepted was 33; the highest was 99.

Requirements

Applicants must have a bachelor's degree and take the LSAT. No specific undergraduate courses are required. Candidates are not interviewed.

Procedure

The application deadline for fall entry is April 1. Applicants should submit an application form, LSAT results, transcripts, a nonrefundable application fee of $50, 1 letters of recommendation, and Accepted students must pay $200; another deposit is required upon registration in June. Notification of the admissions decision is on a rolling basis. The latest acceptable LSAT test date for fall entry is February. The law school uses the LSDAS.

Special

The law school recruits minority and disadvantaged students through office appointments, direct mail, and a number of on-campus programs. In addition, merit scholarships are awarded. Requirements are not different for out-of-state students. Transfer students must have one year of credit, have attended an ABA-approved law school, and submit their LSDAS reports, law school transcripts, and letters of good standing by August 1.

Costs

Tuition and fees for the 2001-2002 academic year are $24,020 for all full-time students. Tuition for part-time students is $15,620 per year. On-campus room and board costs about $900 annually.

Financial Aid

About 84% of current law students receive some form of aid. The average annual amount of aid from all sources combined, including scholarships, loans, and work contracts, is $4253; maximum, $23,900. Awards are based on need and merit. Required financial statement is the FAFSA. The aid application deadline for fall entry is March 1. Special funds for minority or disadvantaged students Merit awards are available to minority or disadvantaged students. First-year students are notified about their financial aid application within 4 weeks after the financial aid file is complete.

About the Law School

De Paul University College of Law was established in 1898 and is a private institution. The campus is in an urban area in downtown Chicago. The primary mission of the law school is to train and educate men and women who will ethically and competently represent the legal profession in urban and international settings and in private practice, business, or government. Students have access to federal, state, county, city, and local agencies, courts, correctional facilities, law firms, and legal aid organizations in the Chicago area. Extensive clinical and externship opportunities are available. Facilities of special interest to law students include amphitheater-style video-equipped classrooms, a state-of-the-art moot court room, a legal clinic, and the law library. Housing for students is available off campus. The Office of Admission assists students in locating apartments and studios. About half of the student body is from out of state. All law school facilities are accessible to the physically disabled.

Calendar

The law school operates on a traditional semester basis. Courses for full- and part-time students are offered both day and evening and must be completed within 5 years. Part-time students may take some upper-level day courses. New full- and part-time students are admitted in the fall. There is a 6-week summer session. Transferable summer courses are offered.

Programs

In addition to the J.D., the law school offers the LL.M. in Taxation and in Health Law. Students may take relevant courses in other programs and apply credit toward the J.D. The following joint degrees may be earned: J.D./M.A. (Juris Doctor/Master in International Studies), J.D./M.B.A. (Juris Doctor/Master of Business Administration), and J.D./M.S. (Juris Doctor/Master of Public Service Management).

Required

To earn the J.D., candidates must complete 86 total credits, of which 37 are for required courses. They must maintain a minimum GPA of 2.0 in the required courses. The following first-year courses are required of all students: Civil Procedure, Contracts I and II, Torts, Legal Writing I and II, Constitutional Process I and II, Criminal Law, and Property. Required upper-level courses consist of Criminal Procedure, a senior seminar with a research paper, and Legal Profession. The required orientation program for first-year students is a 2-day program for full-time students and a 3-night program for part-time students.

Phone: 312-362-6831
428-7453
Fax: 312-362-5280
E-mail: *lawinfo@wppost.depaul.edu*
Web: *law.depaul.edu*

Contact

Priscilla Miller, Assistant Director, 312-362-6831 for general inquiries; Office of Financial Aid, 312-362-8091 for financial aid information.

Electives

The College of Law offers concentrations in corporate law, criminal law, entertainment law, environmental law, family law, international law, juvenile law, labor law, litigation, media law, securities law, sports law, tax law, torts and insurance, health law, and international human rights law. In addition, upper-level students may enroll in the following clinics: Technology and Intellectual Property Clinic, Immigration and Asylum Law, Community Development, and Disability Rights. Each clinic is worth 3 hours of credit. DePaul has 2 unique programs for first-year students: Family Law and Intellectual Property, and legal writing programs with summer internships. Seminars are 3-credit hour courses taken during the last year of legal studies. The school also offers externships. Students work with a government agency (such as the State Attorney's Office, the Public Defender's Office, or the judiciary) or other organizations. Students may undertake an independent study project in which they develop in-depth, publishable research paper under guidance of a professor. Courses with field work are offered in Health Law, International Human Rights, and Mediation, as well as a legal clinic. An annual Visiting Scholar program is offered. Students may study abroad in an exchange program in conjunction with University College in Dublin, Ireland. An extensive Academic Support Program under the supervision of the Assistant Dean for Educational Services is offered. A wide range of services and activities for minorities are provided by DePaul's Black, Latino, and Asian student associations. An Assistant Dean of Multi-Cultural Affairs is on the staff of the Law School. Special interest programs include the Women's Law Caucus, Public Interest Law Association, Human Rights Bar Association, Environmental Law Society, Labor Law Society, International Law Society, and Gay and Lesbian Society. The College also sponsors the following institutes: Health Law Institute, Intellectual Property and Information Technology Institute, Family Law Center, International Human Rights Law Institute, Center for Justice in Capital Cases, and the Center for Law and Science. The most widely taken electives are Litigation Strategies, Alternate Dispute Resolution, and Corporate Law.

Graduation Requirements

In order to graduate, candidates must have a GPA of 2.0, and have completed the upper-division writing requirement and a required seminar.

Organizations

Students edit the *De Paul Law Review, Journal of Health Care Law, De Paul Business Journal, De Paul/LCA Journal of Arts and Entertainment Law, Environmental Law Digest*, and the *International Law Digest*. The *Cause of Action* is the student newspaper. Students participate in an annual international moot court competition. The Moot Court Society enters national and international competitions. Negotiations, Client Counseling, and Jessup International Moot Court competitions are held annually. Law student organizations include the Women's Law Caucus, the National Lawyers Guild, and Computer Law Society. There are local chapters of the Federalist Society, International Law Society, and Justinian Society of Lawyers. Other organizations include Phi Alpha Delta, Delta Theta Phi, and Decalogoe Society.

Library

The law library contains 356,525 hardcopy volumes and 998,028 microform volume equivalents, and subscribes to 5059 serial publications. Such on-line databases and networks as CALI, CIS Universe, Legal-Trac, LEXIS, NEXIS, OCLC First Search, WESTLAW, and Wilsonline Indexes are available to law students for research. Special library collections include an official U.S. government depository, and tax law, health law, and human rights law collections. Recently, a total renovation of the 3-floor library was completed. The ratio of library volumes to faculty is 7276 to 1 and to students, 381 to 1. The ratio of seats in the library to students is 1 to 1.

Faculty

The law school has 49 full-time and 85 part-time faculty members, of whom 55 are women. According to AAUP standards for Category I institutions, faculty salaries are average. About 30% of full-time faculty have a graduate law degree in addition to the J.D.; about 10% of part-time faculty have one. The ratio of full-time students to full-time faculty in an average class is 15 to 1; in a clinic, 6 to 1. The law school has a regular program of bringing visiting professors and other distinguished lecturers and visitors to campus. There is a chapter of the Order of the Coif; 50 faculty and 198 graduates are members.

Students

About 54% of the student body are women; 29%, minorities; 8%, African American; 10%, Asian American; 10%, Hispanic; 1%, Native American; and 1%, foreign nationals. The majority of students come from Illinois (54%). The average age of entering students is 24; age range is 21 to 49. About 44% of students enter directly from undergraduate school, 10% have a graduate degree, and 62% have worked full-time prior to entering law school. About 3% drop out after the first year for academic or personal reasons; 97% remain to receive a law degree.

Placement

J.D.s awarded: 311

Services available through: a separate law school placement center and the university placement center

Services: career and advisory programs are available as well as an Alumni Job Newsletter, in-office fax and copier, and Network, Internet, LEXIS, and WESTLAW capabilities.

Special features: The De Paul College of Law Alumni Board is very active in career planning and placement programs, and supports a proactive approach to students and alumni career development.

Full-time job interviews:	38 employers
Summer job interviews:	65 employers
Placement by graduation:	54% of class
Placement within 9 months:	93% of class
Average starting salary:	$12,000 to $140,000
Areas of placement:	
Private practice 2-10 attorneys	19%
Private practice 11-25 attorneys	7%
Private practice 26-50 attorneys	4%
Private practice 51-100 attorneys	4%
Private practice 100+ attorneys	16%
Business/industry	18%
Government	15%
Judicial clerkships	3%
Public interest	2%
Military	1%
Academic	1%

DRAKE UNIVERSITY

Law School

2507 University Avenue
Des Moines, IA 50311

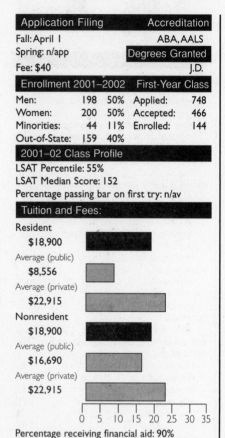

Application Filing		Accreditation
Fall: April 1		ABA, AALS
Spring: n/app		**Degrees Granted**
Fee: $40		J.D.

Enrollment 2001–2002			First-Year Class	
Men:	198	50%	Applied:	748
Women:	200	50%	Accepted:	466
Minorities:	44	11%	Enrolled:	144
Out-of-State:	159	40%		

2001–02 Class Profile

LSAT Percentile: 55%
LSAT Median Score: 152
Percentage passing bar on first try: n/av

Tuition and Fees:

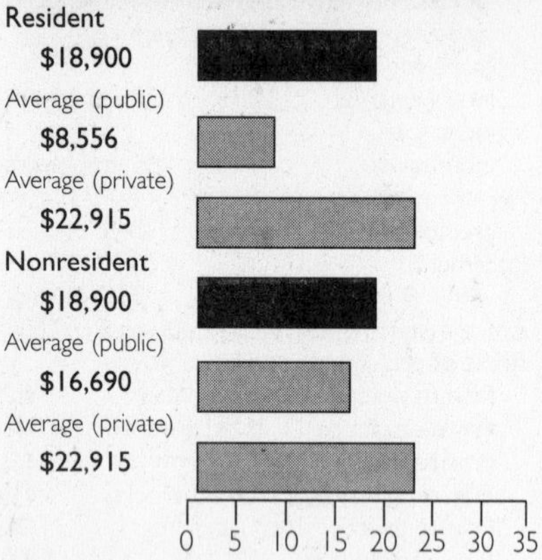

Percentage receiving financial aid: 90%

ADMISSIONS

In the fall 2001 first-year class, 748 applied, 466 were accepted, and 144 enrolled. Four transfers enrolled. The median LSAT percentile of the most recent first-year class was 55; the median GPA was 3.28 on a scale of 4.0. The lowest LSAT percentile accepted was 14; the highest was 96.

Requirements

Applicants must have a bachelor's degree and take the LSAT. The most important admission factors include LSAT results, GPA, and undergraduate curriculum. No specific undergraduate courses are required. Candidates are not interviewed.

Procedure

The application deadline for fall entry is April 1. Applicants should submit an application form, LSAT results, transcripts, TOEFL (for international students), a nonrefundable application fee of $40, 2 recommended letters of recommendation, and a personal statement. Notification of the admissions decision is within 4 to 6 weeks after the file is complete. The latest acceptable LSAT test date for fall entry is June. The law school uses the LSDAS.

Special

The law school recruits minority and disadvantaged students by means of targeted efforts at nationally identified feeder schools for students of color, the use of the Candidate Referral Service (CRS), and a February recruitment event during National Minority Law School Recruitment Month. Requirements are not different for out-of-state students. Transfer students must have one year of credit, and have attended an ABA-approved law school. Generally, students must rank in the upper half of their current law school class and have certification of good academic standing and eligibility to re-enroll at that school.

Costs

Tuition and fees for the 2001-2002 academic year are $18,900 for all full-time students. On-campus room and board costs about $7100 annually; books and supplies run $1100.

Financial Aid

About 90% of current law students receive some form of aid. The average annual amount of aid from all sources combined, including scholarships, loans, and work contracts, is $22,945; maximum, $30,475. Awards are based on need and merit. Loans are offered on the basis of need. The school offers numerous scholarships, some based on merit; some on merit and need. The required financial statement is the FAFSA. The aid application deadline for fall entry is March 1. Special funds for minority or disadvantaged students consist of the Law Opportunity scholarships, which are awards for entering students from educationally or economically disadvantaged backgrounds who demonstrate need. First-year students are notified about their financial aid application some time after admission and before a seat deposit is required.

About the Law School

Drake University Law School was established in 1865 and is a private institution. The 120-acre campus is in an urban area 5 miles northwest of downtown Des Moines. The primary mission of the law school is to provide students with the opportunities to benefit from hands-on learning experiences and to gain the skills needed to be successful in whatever career path they choose in any geographic location. Students have access to federal, state, county, city, and local agencies, courts, correctional facilities, law firms, and legal aid organizations in the Des Moines area, as well as legal clinics, insurance companies, corporate offices, and internships. Facilities of special interest to law students are the Constitutional Law Resource Center, Agricultural Law Center, Neal and Bea Smith Law Center, the school's legal clinic, a national training center for public service attorneys, and the Legislative Practice Center. Housing for students consist of university-owned and privately-owned apartments located within walking distance of the campus; housing is also available in city suburbs just 15 minutes from the campus. About 99% of the law school facilities are accessible to the physically disabled.

Calendar

The law school operates on a traditional semester basis. Courses for full- and part-time students are offered days only and must be completed within 6 years. New full- and part-time students are admitted in the fall and summer. There is a 7-week summer session. Transferable summer courses are offered.

Programs

Students may take relevant courses in other programs and apply credit toward the J.D.; a maximum of 6 credits may be applied. The following joint degrees may be earned: J.D./M.A. (Juris Doctor/Master of Arts in political science), J.D./M.B.A. (Juris Doctor/ Master of Business Administration), J.D./M.P.A. (Juris Doctor/ Master of Public Administration), J.D./M.S. (Juris Doctor/ Master of Science in agricultural economics), J.D./M.S.W. (Juris Doctor/ Master of Social Work), and J.D./Pharm.D. (Juris Doctor/ Pharmacy Doctorate).

Required

To earn the J.D., candidates must complete 90 total credits, of which 41 are for required courses. They must maintain a minimum GPA of 2.0 in the required courses. The following first-year courses are required of all students: Torts; Property; Criminal Law; Civil Procedure I and II; Contracts I and II; Legal Research, Writing, and Appellate Practice; and Constitutional Law I. Required upper-level courses consist of Legal Ethics and Professional Responsibility, Advanced Legal Writing, Constitutional Law II, and Evidence. All students who have completed 45 hours of class may

Phone: 515-271-2782
800-44-DRAKE, ext. 2782
Fax: 515-271-1990
E-mail: *lawadmit@drake.edu*
Web: *www.lawdrake.edu*

Contact

Office of Admission and Financial Aid, 515-271-2782; 800-44-DRAKE, ext. 2782 for general inquiries; Kara Blanchard, Admissions and Financial Aid, 515-271-2782; 800-44-DRAKE, ext. 2782 for financial aid information.

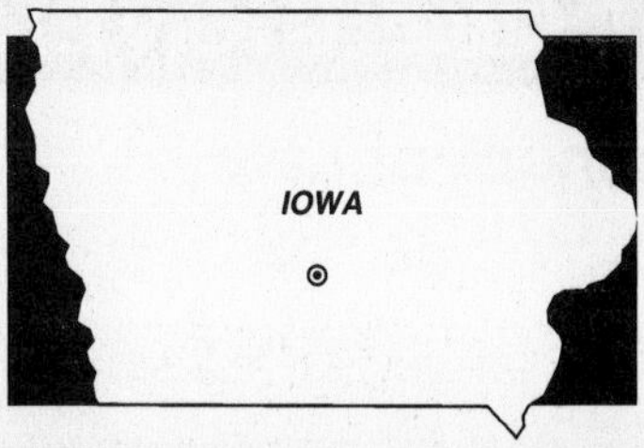

take the clinical courses as electives.The required orientation program for first-year students is 3 days and includes registration instructions, law school tour, fee payment session, small group meetings, computer training, sessions on professionalism, and the noncredit Introduction to Law course.

Electives

The Law School offers concentrations in corporate law, criminal law, environmental law, family law, international law, labor law, litigation, securities law, tax law, torts and insurance, agricultural law, constitutional law, and public interest law. In addition, the Law School's clinical programs provide students with the opportunity to represent clients through the General Civil Practice Clinic, Criminal Defense Clinic, Elder Law Clinic or the Middleton Children's Rights Clinic. Generally, students must have completed 45 hours of classroom credit prior to enrolling; however, prerequisites vary. To enroll in seminars, students must have completed 30 hours with a 2.0 GPA; to enroll in more than one seminar, a student must have completed 45 hours with a cumulative GPA of 2.5. Generally, 1 to 3 hours of credit may be granted for a seminar course. Internships are available in administrative law, the legislature, the judiciary, insurance, environmental law, securities, probate, and health law. Internships with the prosecutor, the county attorney, the U.S. Attorney's Office, and the Civil Rights Commission are also available. Credit varies from 1 to 4 credit hours and prerequisites vary. Independent research may be undertaken for 1 to 3 credit hours and is graded on a credit/no credit basis. A Public Law Externship worth 10 credit hours is offered. Special lecture series include the Constitutional Law Resource Center Speaker Series and the Dwight D. Opperman Lecture in Consitutional Law. Drake offers a 4-week summer abroad program in Nantes, France worth up to 6 credits; credit may also be accepted from programs offered by other law schools. Special interest group programs include the Summer Institute in Constitutional Law and the Summer Institute in Agricultural Law. The most widely taken electives are Trial Advocacy, Client Representation and Litigation, and Advanced Client Representation and Litigation.

Graduation Requirements

In order to graduate, candidates must have a GPA of 2.0, have completed the upper-division writing requirement, have completed 6 semesters for residence credit and 90 hours for academic credit, and have satisfied the advanced writing requirement through either independent study or course work.

Organizations

Students edit the *Drake Law Review*, the *Drake Journal of Agricultural Law*, and the student newspaper *The Gavel*. Moot court teams are sent to the C. Edwin Moore Appellate Advocacy, National Moot Court, and National Appellate Advocacy competitions. Student organizations include the Student Bar Association, Drake Law Women, and International Law Society. There are local chapters of the Order of Barristers, American Trial Lawyers Association, and Delta Theta Phi.

Library

The law library contains 300,000 hard-copy volumes and 100,000 microform volume equivalents, and subscribes to 3100 serial publications. Such on-line databases and networks as CALI, CIS Universe, DIALOG, Infotrac, Legal-Trac, LEXIS, LOIS, NEXIS, OCLC First Search, and WESTLAW are available to law students for research. Special library collections include a government depository, and agricultural, tax, computer, and constitutional law collections. Recently, the library completed a new $8.5 million, 70,000 square foot library. In addition to the on-line catalog and automated circulation system, the library provides computer access with several computer laboratories and Ethernet connections throughout the library, at carrels, tables, and study rooms, including Internet access from any student workstation in the library. A wireless network is accessible throughout the library and law school. The ratio of library volumes to faculty is 12,000 to 1 and to students, 781 to 1. The ratio of seats in the library to students is 1 to 1.

Faculty

The law school has 30 full-time and 22 part-time faculty members, of whom 19 are women. According to AAUP standards for Category IIA institutions, faculty salaries are above average. About 33% of full-time faculty have a graduate law degree in addition to the J.D. The ratio of full-time students to full-time faculty in an average class is 16 to 1; in a clinic, 20 to 1. The law school has a regular program of bringing visiting professors and other distinguished lecturers and visitors to campus. There is a chapter of the Order of the Coif; 12 faculty and 586 graduates are members.

Students

About 50% of the student body are women; 11%, minorities; 5%, African American; 4%, Asian American; 2%, Hispanic; and 1%, foreign nationals. The majority of students come from the Midwest (81%). The average age of entering students is 25; age range is 21 to 50. About 41% of students enter directly from undergraduate school and 7% have a graduate degree. About 8% drop out after the first year for academic or personal reasons; 92% remain to receive a law degree.

Placement

J.D.s awarded:	116
Services available through: a separate law school placement center	
Services: provides seminars	
Special features: a nationwide network of alumni in specific geographic and practice areas that has been developed to assist students with employment opportunities; additionally, students are assisted by 2 full-time staff..	
Full-time job interviews:	22 employers
Summer job interviews:	22 employers
Placement by graduation:	56% of class
Placement within 9 months:	93% of class
Average starting salary:	$22,000 to $85,000
Areas of placement:	
Private practice 2-10 attorneys	13%
Private practice 11-25 attorneys	9%
Private practice 26-50 attorneys	4%
Private practice 51-100 attorneys	2%
Judicial clerkships	18%
Unknown	18%
Government	15%
Business/industry	13%
Public interest	4%
Academic	1%

DUKE UNIVERSITY

School of Law

Science and Towerview Drive,
Box 90393
Durham, NC 27708

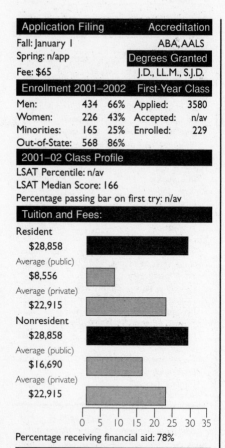

Application Filing	Accreditation
Fall: January 1	ABA, AALS
Spring: n/app	**Degrees Granted**
Fee: $65	J.D., LL.M., S.J.D.

Enrollment 2001–2002			First-Year Class	
Men:	434	66%	Applied:	3580
Women:	226	43%	Accepted:	n/av
Minorities:	165	25%	Enrolled:	229
Out-of-State:	568	86%		

2001–02 Class Profile

LSAT Percentile: n/av
LSAT Median Score: 166
Percentage passing bar on first try: n/av

Tuition and Fees:

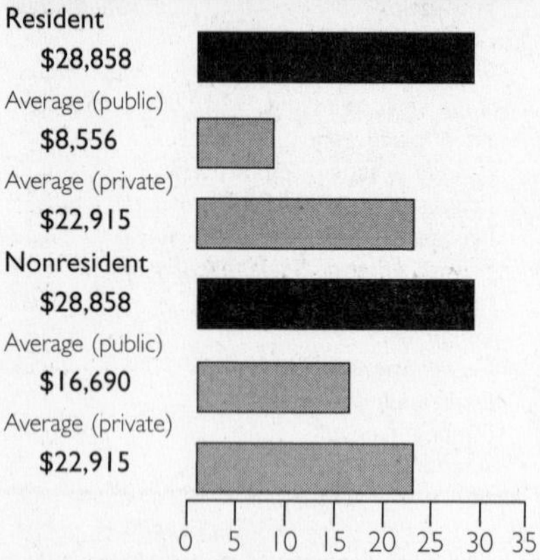

Percentage receiving financial aid: 78%

ADMISSIONS

In the fall 2001 first-year class, 3580 applied and 229 enrolled. Eleven transfers enrolled. The median GPA of the most recent first-year class was 3.5 on a scale of 4.0. The highest LSAT percentile was 99.

Requirements

Applicants must have a bachelor's degree and take the LSAT. No specific undergraduate courses are required. Candidates are not interviewed.

Procedure

The application deadline for fall and summer entry is January 1. Applicants should submit an application form, LSAT results, transcripts, a nonrefundable application fee of $65, 2 academic letters of recommendation, and 1 certification from an academic dean. Notification of the admissions decision is on a rolling basis. The latest acceptable LSAT test date for fall entry is December. The law school uses the LSDAS.

Special

The law school invites admitted minority applicants to visit the school and meet with faculty and other minority students. Minority student organizations work with the Admissions Office to contact and recruit minority candidates. Requirements are not different for out-of-state students. Transfer students must have one year of credit, have attended an ABA-approved law school, and must be eligible to re-enroll and otherwise be in good standing at the current law school.

Costs

Tuition and fees for the 2001-2002 academic year are $28,858 for all full-time students. On-campus room and board costs about $4350 annually; books and supplies run $1200.

Financial Aid

About 78% of current law students receive some form of aid. The average annual amount of aid from all sources combined, including scholarships, loans, and work contracts, is $31,700; maximum, $42,388. Awards are based on need and merit. The required financial statement is the FAFSA. The aid application deadline for fall and summer entry is March 15. Special funds for minority or disadvantaged students consist of a scholarship for minority students established by the national law firm of Baker and McKenzie. First-year students are notified about their financial aid application some time shortly after acceptance.

About the Law School

Duke University School of Law was established in 1930 and is a private institution. The campus is in an urban area in Durham. The primary mission of the law school is to prepare students for responsible and productive lives in the legal profession. The law school also provides leadership at both national and international levels to improve the law and legal institutions through teaching, research, and other forms of public service. Students have access to federal, state, county, city, and local agencies, courts, correctional facilities, law firms, and legal aid organizations in the Durham area. The law school is an integral part of Duke University, so students have access to all the resources of a major research university. Facilities of special interest to law students include the Private Adjudication Center; Pro Bono Project; Center for Law, Ethics, and National Security; Center for the Study of Congress; and Center for the Study of Global Information Technologies. Housing for students is limited on campus, but there are ample rental units in the surrounding area. All law school facilities are accessible to the physically disabled.

Calendar

The law school operates on a traditional semester basis. Courses for full-time students are offered days only and must be completed within 3 years. There is no part-time program. New students are admitted in the fall and summer. There is a 10-week summer session. Transferable summer courses are not offered.

Programs

In addition to the J.D., the law school offers the LL.M. and S.J.D. Students may take relevant courses in other programs and apply credit toward the J.D.; a maximum of 3 credits may be applied. The following joint degrees may be earned: J.D./LL.M. (Juris Doctor/Master of Laws in comparative and international law), J.D./M.A. (Juris Doctor/Master of Arts in cultural anthropology, English, environmental studies, history, humanities, mechanical engineering, philosophy, political science, psychology, public policy studies, or romance studies), J.D./M.B.A. (Juris Doctor/Master of Business Administration), J.D./M.D.

Phone: 919-613-7020
Fax: 919-613-7257
E-mail: *admissions@law.duke.edu*
Web: *http://admissions.law.duke.edu*

Contact
Admissions Staff, 919-613-7020 for general inquiries; Kim Overton, Assistant Director of Financial Aid, 919-613-7025 for financial aid information.

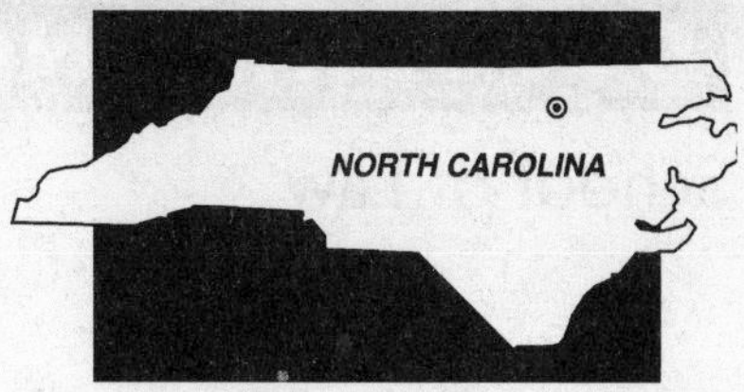

(Juris Doctor/Master of Medicine), J.D./M.E.M. (Juris Doctor/Master of Environmental Management), J.D./M.P.P. (Juris Doctor/Master of Public Policy), J.D./M.S. (Juris Doctor/Master of Science in mechanical engineering), J.D./M.T.S. (Juris Doctor/Master of Theological Studies), and J.D./Ph.D. (Juris Doctor/Doctor of Philosophy in political science).

Required
To earn the J.D., candidates must complete 84 total credits, of which 30 are for required courses. They must maintain a minimum GPA of 2.1 in the required courses. The following first-year courses are required of all students: Constitutional Law, Contracts, Civil Procedure, Criminal Law, Legal Research and Writing, Property, Torts, and Professional Responsibility. Clinical courses are available as elective course work for upper-class students.The required orientation program for first-year students lasts 4 days immediately prior to the start of classes.

Electives
Students who have met the prerequisites may take clinics. Credit hours are dependent on the particular course. Many students gain clinical experience by providing volunteer legal services in areas of individual interest through pro bono work, which, if taken as independent study, is worth academic credit. Students can take seminars, worth 2 to 3 credit hours each. International law internships are offered to upper-class students for 14 credit hours. One to 3 credit hours may be granted for directed independent research with the permission of supervising faculty. Through the Pro Bono Project, students provide volunteer legal services in areas of individual interest. Special lectures include the Annual Brainerd Currie Memorial Lecture Series. Study abroad is possible through the Summer Institute in Transnational Law in Geneva or Hong Kong. This program is required of J.D./LL.M. students. Up to 6 hours of academic credit is offered and is available to all J.D. students. Tutorial assistance is provided as needed. The most widely taken electives are Business, Evidence, and International Law.

Graduation Requirements
In order to graduate, candidates must have a GPA of 2.1.

Organizations
Students edit the *Duke Law Journal, Law and Contemporary Problems, Alaska Law Review, Duke Journal of Comparative and International Law*, and the newspaper the *Herald*. Other publications include interdisciplinary magazines such as the *Duke Environmental Law and Public Policy Forum* and the *Duke Journal of Gender Law and Policy*. Moot court competitions include the National Moot Court in Richmond, Virginia; Jessup International Law Moot Court; and the J. Braxton Craven, Jr. Memorial Moot Court at the University of North Carolina. Law student organizations include the Duke Bar Association, Moot Court Board, and International Law Society. Local chapters of national associations include the ABA-Law Student Division, Amnesty International, and American Civil Liberties Union.

Library
The law library contains 535,000 hard-copy volumes and 71,000 microform volume equivalents, and subscribes to 6998 serial publications. Such on-line databases and networks as DIALOG, LEXIS, and WESTLAW are available to law students for research. Special library collections include federal government documents, the Christie Collection of jurisprudence, and the Riddick Collection of autographed senatorial papers. Recently, the library completed a major renovation and expansion that enlarged the law library to more than 65,000 square feet and is designed to accommodate both the traditional and rapidly changing needs of the law school community. The ratio of library volumes to faculty is 14,861 to 1 and to students, 811 to 1. The ratio of seats in the library to students is 1 to 4.

Placement	
J.D.s awarded:	203
Services available through: a separate law school placement center	
Special features: The staff of the Office of Career Planning and Placement makes a special effort to get to know all the students and to offer personal attention and assistance whenever possible..	
Full-time job interviews:	450 employers
Summer job interviews:	n/av
Placement by graduation:	94% of class
Placement within 9 months:	99% of class
Average starting salary:	$35,000 to $95,000
Areas of placement:	
Private practice 11-25 attorneys	1%
Private practice 26-50 attorneys	2%
Private practice 51-100 attorneys	72%
Judicial clerkships	17%
Government	2%
Military	2%
Unknown	2%
Public interest	1%
Academic	1%

Faculty
The law school has 36 full-time and 42 part-time faculty members, of whom 22 are women. According to AAUP standards for Category 1 institutions, faculty salaries are well above average. About 19% of full-time faculty have a graduate law degree in addition to the J.D.; about 4% of part-time faculty have one. The ratio of full-time students to full-time faculty in an average class is 16 to 1; in a clinic, 12 to 1. There is a chapter of the Order of the Coif; 10 graduates are members.

Students
About 43% of the student body are women; 25%, minorities; 9%, African American; 8%, Asian American; 5%, Hispanic; and 1%, Native American. Most students come from the Northeast (47%). The average age of entering students is 24. About 42% of students enter directly from undergraduate school. About 1% drop out after the first year for academic or personal reasons; 99% remain to receive a law degree.

DUQUESNE UNIVERSITY

School of Law

900 Locust Street, Hanley Hall
Pittsburgh, PA 15282

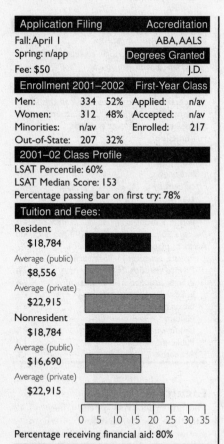

Application Filing		Accreditation
Fall: April 1		ABA, AALS
Spring: n/app		**Degrees Granted**
Fee: $50		J.D.

Enrollment 2001–2002			First-Year Class	
Men:	334	52%	Applied:	n/av
Women:	312	48%	Accepted:	n/av
Minorities:	n/av		Enrolled:	217
Out-of-State:	207	32%		

2001–02 Class Profile

LSAT Percentile: 60%
LSAT Median Score: 153
Percentage passing bar on first try: 78%

Tuition and Fees:

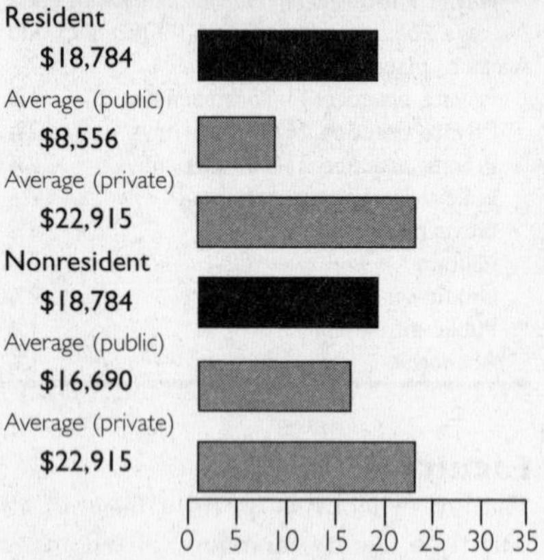

Percentage receiving financial aid: 80%

ADMISSIONS

In the fall 2001 first-year class, 217 enrolled. The median LSAT percentile of the most recent first-year class was 60; the median GPA was 3.25 on a scale of 4.0.

Requirements

Applicants must have a bachelor's degree and take the LSAT. The most important admission factors include academic achievement, LSAT results, and life experience. No specific undergraduate courses are required. Candidates are not interviewed.

Procedure

The application deadline for fall entry is April 1. Applicants should submit an application form, LSAT results, transcripts, TOEFL for foreign students, a nonrefundable application fee of $50, and 2 letters of recommendation. Notification of the admissions decision is on a rolling basis. The latest acceptable LSAT test date for fall entry is December for day students. The law school uses the LSDAS.

Special

The law school recruits minority and disadvantaged students by means of Candidate Referral Service minority search, law fairs, contact with minority coordinators, and assistance with scholarships and grants. Requirements are not different for out-of-state students. Transfer students must have one year of credit and have attended an ABA-approved law school. Admission depends on space availability.

Costs

Tuition and fees for the 2001-2002 academic year are $18,784 for all full-time students. Tuition for part-time students is $14,588 per year. Books and supplies run about $800 annually.

Financial Aid

About 80% of current law students receive some form of aid. Awards are based on need and merit, along with minority status. Required financial statements are the FFS, the CSS Profile, and the FAFSA. The aid application deadline for fall entry is May 31. Special funds for minority or disadvantaged students consist of scholarships and grants. First-year students are notified about their financial aid application at time of acceptance.

About the Law School

Duquesne University School of Law was established in 1911 and is a private institution. The 43-acre campus is in an urban area in Pittsburgh. The primary mission of the law school is to educate students in the fundamental principles of law, to assist students in forming sound judgment, and to develop facility in legal research and writing. Students have access to federal, state, county, city, and local agencies, courts, correctional facilities, law firms, and legal aid organizations in the Pittsburgh area. Varied clinical programs supervised by the school allow students to gain practical experience. Facilities of special interest to law students are the District Attorney's Office Clinical Program, the Department of Environmental Resources Clinical Program, in-house Economic and Community Development Clinic, Neighborhood Legal Services Clinic, and Civil and Family Justice. Housing for students is available off campus. All law school facilities are accessible to the physically disabled.

Calendar

The law school operates on a traditional semester basis. Courses for full-time students are offered days only and must be completed within 4 years. For part-time students, courses are offered both day and evening and must be completed within 5 years. New full- and part-time students are admitted in the fall. There is a 5-week summer session. Transferable summer courses are offered.

Programs

Students may take relevant courses in other programs and apply credit toward the J.D.; the maximum number of credits that may be applied varies. The following joint degrees may be earned: J.D./M.B.A. (Juris Doctor/Master of Business Administration), J.D./M.Div. (Juris Doctor/Master of Divinity in conjunction with Pittsburgh Theological Seminary), J.D./M.S. (Juris Doctor/Master of Science in taxation), and J.D./M.S.E.S.M. (Juris Doctor/Master of Science in Environmental Science and Management).

Phone: 412-396-6296
E-mail: *campion@duq.edu*
Web: *www.law.duq.edu*

Contact

Jospeh P. Campion, Jr., Director of Admissions, 412-396-6296 for general inquiries; Frank Dutkovich, Financial Aid Director, 412-396-6607 for financial aid information.

Required

To earn the J.D., candidates must complete 86 total credits, of which 33 are for required courses. They must maintain a minimum GPA of 3.0 in the required courses. The following first-year courses are required of all students: Contracts, Torts, Property (second year for evening students), Legal Process and Procedure, Criminal Law and Procedure (second year for evening students), Civil Procedure I, and Legal Research and Writing. Required upper-level courses consist of Professional Responsibility. The required orientation program for first-year students consists of 1-½ days of sessions on requirements in the first year and handling stress. The students meet with their faculty adviser and student mentors.

Electives

The School of Law offers concentrations in corporate law, criminal law, environmental law, family law, international law, labor law, litigation, securities law, tax law, and torts and insurance. In addition, clinics, which are considered all upper-division classes worth 3 credits, include the U.S. Attorney's Program, District Attorney's Program, and Pennsylvania Department of Environmental Resources Program. Also open to upper-division students are internships and seminars, both worth 2 to 3 credits. Seminar topics include labor arbitration, collective bargaining, and trial tactics. Upper-division students are eligible to serve as faculty research assistants. Special lectures are given by the guest speakers who visit the school throughout the year. Law students may request permission to participate in study-abroad programs offered by other ABA-approved law schools. There are summer study-abroad programs in China, Ireland, and Russia. The Black Law Students Association sponsors a tutoring program. Special interest programs are offered by the Public Interest Law Association, Health Care Law Association, Law Review, *Juris* Magazine, Black Law Students Association, Corporate Law Society, and Women's Law Association. The most widely taken electives are Constitutional Law, Taxation, and Evidence.

Graduation Requirements

In order to graduate, candidates must have a GPA of 3.0 and have completed the upper-division writing requirement.

Organizations

Students edit the *Duquesne Law Review*; *Juris*, a newsmagazine; and the *Duquesne Business Law Journal*. Moot courts include a trial moot court, an appellate moot court, a corporate moot court, and a tax moot court. Law student organizations include the Student Bar Association and Corporate Law Association. Campus clubs and other organizations include the Environmental Law Association, The Federalist Society, and Health Care Law Association. There are local chapters of Phi Alpha Delta, Association of Trial Lawyers of America, and ABA - Law Student Division.

Library

The law library contains 265,195 hardcopy volumes and 210,000 microform volume equivalents, and subscribes to 2400 serial publications. Such on-line databases and networks as DIALOG, LEXIS, WESTLAW, INNOVACQ, and OCLC are available to law students for research. Special library collections include audiovisual tapes and U.S. government documents. Recently, the library installed the INNOVACQ computer system, an audiovisual center, and West CD-ROM Library. The ratio of library volumes to faculty is 11,050 to 1 and to students is 411 to 1. The ratio of seats in the library to students is 1 to 2.

Faculty

The law school has 24 full-time and 45 part-time faculty members, of whom 13 are women. According to AAUP standards for Category IIA institutions, faculty salaries are above average. About 32% of full-time faculty have a graduate law degree in addition to the J.D.; about 10% of part-time faculty have one. The ratio of full-time students to full-time faculty in an average class is 14 to 1. The law school has a regular program of bringing visiting professors and other distinguished lecturers and visitors to campus.

Placement

J.D.s awarded:	190
Services available through: a separate law school placement center and a full-time Career Services Office for law students	
Special features: individual counseling for students, videotaped mock interviews, and focus groups for nontraditional students.	
Full-time job interviews:	47 employers
Summer job interviews:	32 employers
Placement by graduation:	50% of class
Placement within 9 months:	95% of class
Average starting salary:	$30,000 to $90,000
Areas of placement:	
Private practice 2-100 attorneys	61%
Business/industry	16%
Judicial clerkships	11%
Government	8%
Public interest	3%
Academic	1%

Students

About 48% of the student body are women; 3%, African American; 2%, Asian American; and 1%, Hispanic. The majority of students come from Pennsylvania (68%). The average age of entering students is 25; age range is 21 to 55. About 70% of students have worked full-time prior to entering law school. About 2% drop out after the first year for academic or personal reasons; 95% remain to receive a law degree.

EMORY UNIVERSITY

School of Law

Gambrell Hall
Atlanta, GA 30322

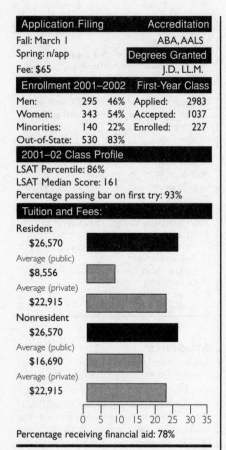

Application Filing	Accreditation
Fall: March 1	ABA, AALS
Spring: n/app	**Degrees Granted**
Fee: $65	J.D., LL.M.

Enrollment 2001–2002			First-Year Class	
Men:	295	46%	Applied:	2983
Women:	343	54%	Accepted:	1037
Minorities:	140	22%	Enrolled:	227
Out-of-State:	530	83%		

2001–02 Class Profile

LSAT Percentile: 86%
LSAT Median Score: 161
Percentage passing bar on first try: 93%

Tuition and Fees:

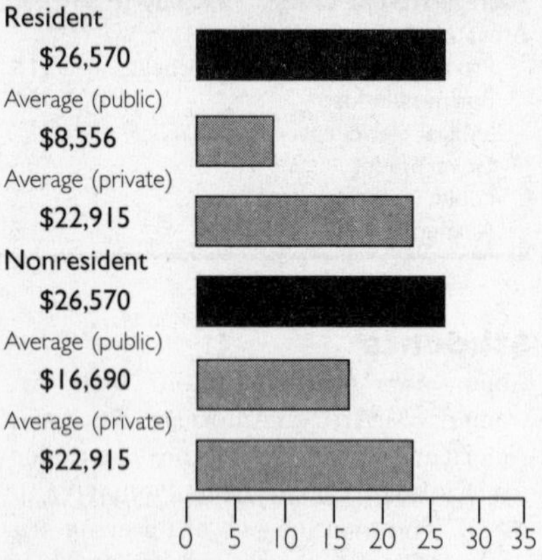

Percentage receiving financial aid: 78%

ADMISSIONS

In the fall 2001 first-year class, 2983 applied, 1037 were accepted, and 227 enrolled. Ten transfers enrolled. The median LSAT percentile of the most recent first-year class was 86; the median GPA was 3.52 on a scale of 4.0. The lowest LSAT percentile accepted was 43; the highest was 97.

Requirements

Applicants must have a bachelor's degree and take the LSAT. The most important admission factors include LSAT results, GPA, and academic achievement. No specific undergraduate courses are required. Candidates are not interviewed.

Procedure

The application deadline for fall entry is March 1. Applicants should submit an application form,LSAT results, transcripts, TOEFL for foreign applicants, a nonrefundable application fee of $65, 2 letters of recommendation, and a personal statement, resume, or list of extracurricular activities. Notification of the admissions decision is from January to May. The latest acceptable LSAT test date for fall entry is February. The law school uses the LSDAS.

Special

The law school recruits minority and disadvantaged students by visiting historically black colleges, attending college law fairs in the fall, sending mailings to minority students, and hosting several special on-site visits throughout the year. Requirements are not different for out-of-state students. Transfer students must have one year of credit, have attended an ABA-approved law school, and have a ranking of at least the top 50% of the class, although the top 20% to 25% is preferred. Preadmissions courses consist of the occasional CLEO summer institutes. Also, a small program sponsored by the Georgia Legislature for minority students and students from disadvantaged backgrounds. Four students are chosen by Emory to participate in summer law classes held at the University of Georgia. Passing grades in the courses allow them to enroll at Emory Law School in the fall.

Costs

Tuition and fees for the 2001-2002 academic year are $26,570 for all full-time students. On-campus room and board costs about $11,480 annually; books and supplies run $1374.

Financial Aid

About 78% of current law students receive some form of aid. The maximum annual amount of aid from all sources combined, including scholarships, loans, and work contracts, is $39,424. Scholarships are based on both merit and need; loans are either need or non-need, depending on the loan. Required financial statements are the CSS Profile and FAFSA. The aid application deadline for fall entry is March 1. Special funds for minority or disadvantaged students consist of scholarships based on merit and need. First-year students are notified about their financial aid application sometime shortly after students are accepted, but before a tuition deposit is required.

About the Law School

Emory University School of Law was established in 1923 and is a private institution. The 600-acre campus is in an urban area 6 miles northeast of Atlanta. The primary mission of the law school is to educate law students from both a professional and ethical standpoint as they prepare to enter the profession while emphasizing the role of attorney as public servant. Commitment to service underlies both classroom and extracurricular experiences. Students have access to federal, state, county, city, and local agencies, courts, correctional facilities, law firms, and legal aid organizations in the Atlanta area. Students have access to national and regional businesses as well. Facilities of special interest to law students are the more than 45 clinics with federal agencies, judges, public interest offices, and businesses. Housing for students is available both as university-owned and privately operated housing, both of which are readily available in the immediate area. All law school facilities are accessible to the physically disabled.

Calendar

The law school operates on a traditional semester basis. Courses for full-time students are offered both day and evening and must be completed within 3 years. There is no part-time program. New students are admitted in the fall. There is no summer session. Transferable summer courses are not offered.

Programs

In addition to the J.D., the law school offers the LL.M. Students may take relevant courses in other programs and apply credit toward the J.D.; a maximum of 6 credit hours credits may be applied. The following joint degrees may be earned: J.D./M.A. (Juris Doctor/Master of Arts in Judaic studies), J.D./M.B.A. (Juris Doctor/Master of Business Administration), J.D./M.Div. (Juris Doctor/

Phone: 404-727-6801
Fax: 404-727-2477
E-mail: *jbalej@law.emory.edu*
Web: *www.law.emory.edu*

Contact

Janet E. Balej, Assistant Director of Admission, 404-727-6802 for general inquiries; Brenda Hill, Associate Director of Financial Aid, 404-727-6039 for financial aid information.

Master of Divinity), J.D./M.P.H. (Juris Doctor/Master of Public Health), J.D./M.T.S. (Juris Doctor/Master of Theological Studies), J.D./Ph.D. in religion (Juris Doctor/Doctor of Philosophy in religion), and J.D./REES (Juris Doctor/Russian East European Studies Certificate).

Required

To earn the J.D., candidates must complete 90 total credits, of which 45 are for required courses. They must maintain a minimum GPA of 2.25 in the required courses. The following first-year courses are required of all students: Contracts, Torts, Civil Procedure I and II, Criminal Law, Property, Legal Methods, Constitutional Law, and Legal Writing, Research and Appellate Advocacy. Required upper-level courses consist of Evidence, Legal Profession, Trial Techniques, and Business Associations. The required orientation program for first-year students is a 2-day period prior to registration that introduces students to the university and the law school communities. Students also attend a small section class during orientation.

Electives

The School of Law offers concentrations in corporate law, environmental law, international law, litigation, tax law, and law and religion. In addition, clinics are available to second- and third-year students for 2 credits, generally. Seminars are also open to second- and third-year students for 2 hours of academic credit. During the summer, most students have paid internships with firms, businesses, government offices, or public interest agencies. A small number of students may be offered research assistantships. Special lectures in law and public policy and law and medicine are open to the public. Students may take advantage of ABA accredited law school study abroad programs. Tutorials are offered to all students by professors on an individual basis. Special consideration is given to minority students in the admissions process; scholarships are offered to minority students based on merit and need.

Graduation Requirements

In order to graduate, candidates must have a GPA of 2.25 and have completed the upper-division writing requirement.

Organizations

Student-edited publications are the *Emory Law Journal, Emory International Law Review*, and *Emory Bankruptcy Developments Journal*. Annually, moot court teams participate in internal competitions and the Georgia Intra-State, National Moot Court, and Jessup Moot Court competitions. Law student organizations include the Student Bar Association, Moot Court Society, and Emory Law Outreach. Local chapters of national associations are Phi Alpha Delta, Black Law Students Association, and Phi Delta Phi. Other on-campus organizations are the Emory intramural teams and clubs.

Library

The law library contains 368,000 hard-copy volumes and 71,734 microform volume equivalents, and subscribes to 6000 serial publications. Such on-line databases and networks as DIALOG, LEXIS, WESTLAW, NEXIS, OCLC, RUN, and RLIN are available to law students for research. Special library collections include a European Union depository and a federal depository. Recently, the library automated circulation. The ratio of library volumes to faculty is 7510 to 1 and to students, 577 to 1. The ratio of seats in the library to students is 1 to 1.3.

Faculty

The law school has 49 full-time and 54 part-time faculty members, of whom 31 are women. According to AAUP standards for Category I institutions, faculty salaries are well above average. About 20% of full-time faculty have a graduate law degree in addition to the J.D. The ratio of full-time students to full-time faculty in an average class is 13 to 1; in a clinic, 2 to 1. The law school has a regular program of bringing visiting professors and other distinguished lecturers and visitors to campus. There is a chapter of the Order of the Coif; 38 faculty are members.

Placement	
J.D.s awarded:	233
Services available through: a separate law school placement center	
Services: n/av	
Special features: personal advising and programming designed to assist students, specific advising in public interest law by the Associate Director of Career Services, and off-campus job fairs in New York and Washington, D.C., among others.	
Full-time job interviews:	129 employers
Summer job interviews:	n/av
Placement by graduation:	67% of class
Placement within 9 months:	95% of class
Average starting salary:	$28,000 to $128,000
Areas of placement:	
Private practice 2-10 attorneys	11%
Private practice 11-25 attorneys	7%
Private practice 26-50 attorneys	6%
Private practice 51-100 attorneys	8%
Private practice 101+ attorneys	37%
Business/industry	11%
Government	9%
Judicial clerkships	7%
Public interest	3%
Academic	1%

Students

About 54% of the student body are women; 22%, minorities; 9%, African American; 9%, Asian American; 4%, Hispanic; 1%, Native American; and 1%, Foreign. The majority of students come from the South (47%). The average age of entering students is 24; age range is 20 to 50. About 45% of students enter directly from undergraduate school, 9% have a graduate degree, and 50% have worked full-time prior to entering law school. About 3% drop out after the first year for academic or personal reasons; 95% remain to receive a law degree.

FLORIDA COASTAL SCHOOL OF LAW

7555 Beach Boulevard
Jacksonville, FL 32216

Application Filing		Accreditation
Fall: open		ABA
Spring: open		**Degrees Granted**
Fee: $50		J.D.

Enrollment 2001–2002			First-Year Class	
Men:	241	53%	Applied:	2156
Women:	211	47%	Accepted:	585
Minorities:	95	21%	Enrolled:	165
Out-of-State:	212	47%		

2001–02 Class Profile

LSAT Percentile: 50%
LSAT Median Score: 150
Percentage passing bar on first try: 75%

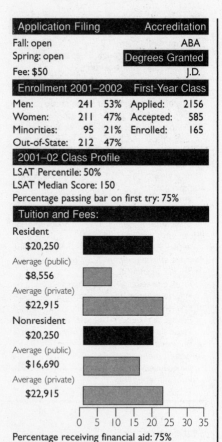

Tuition and Fees:

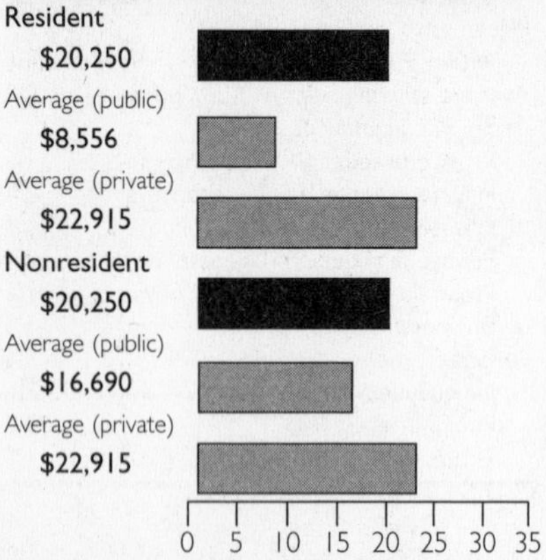

Percentage receiving financial aid: 75%

ADMISSIONS

In the fall 2001 first-year class, 2156 applied, 585 were accepted, and 165 enrolled. Fifteen transfers enrolled. The median LSAT percentile of the most recent first-year class was 50; the median GPA was 2.9 on a scale of 4.0. The lowest LSAT percentile accepted was 15; the highest was 93.

Requirements

Applicants must have a bachelor's degree and take the LSAT. Minimum acceptable GPA is 2.0 on a scale of 4.0. The most important admission factors include LSAT results, GPA, and life experience. No specific undergraduate courses are required. Candidates are not interviewed.

Procedure

The application deadline for fall entry is open. Applicants should submit an application form, LSAT results, a nonrefundable application fee of $50, and 2 letters of recommendation. Notification of the admissions decision is on a rolling basis. The latest acceptable LSAT test date for fall entry is June. The law school uses the LSDAS.

Special

Requirements are not different for out-of-state students. Transfer students must have a minimum GPA of 2.0 and have attended an ABA-approved law school.

Costs

Tuition and fees for the 2001-2002 academic year are $20,250 for all full-time students. Tuition for part-time students is $16,380 per year. Books and supplies run about $1000 annually.

Financial Aid

About 75% of current law students receive some form of aid. The average annual amount of aid from all sources combined, including scholarships, loans, and work contracts, is $18,500; maximum, $33,000. Awards are based on need and merit. The required financial statement is the FAFSA. Check with the school for current application deadlines. First-year students are notified about their financial aid application at time of acceptance.

About the Law School

Florida Coastal School of Law was established in 1994 and is independent, not affiliated with a university. The 5-acre campus is in a suburban area near downtown Jacksonville and the beach. The primary mission of the law school is to distinguish itself as a forward-looking, globally interactive, and culturally diverse institution dedicated to having a positive impact on its students, the community, the legal profession, and the justice system. Students have access to federal, state, county, city, and local agencies, courts, correctional facilities, law firms, and legal aid organizations in the Jacksonville area. Facilities of special interest to law students include the Information Resources and Technology Division; the Center for Strategic Governance and Information Initiatives, and an on-campus teen court. Housing for students includes a large variety of close and affordable off-campus apartments and houses. All law school facilities are accessible to the physically disabled.

Calendar

The law school operates on a traditional semester basis. Courses for full-time students are offered both day and evening and must be completed within 5 years. For part-time students, courses are offered both day and evening and must be completed within 6 years. New full- and part-time students are admitted in the fall and spring. There is an 8-week summer session. Transferable summer courses are offered.

Programs

Students may take relevant courses in other programs and apply credit toward the J.D.; a maximum of 6 credits may be applied.

Required

To earn the J.D., candidates must complete 87 total credits, of which 56 are for required courses. They must maintain a minimum GPA of 2.0 in the required courses. The following first-year courses are required of all students: Torts I, Torts II, Paths of the Law, Civil Dispute Resolution, Lawyering Process I, Contracts I, Constitutional Law, Criminal Law, Lawyering Process II, and Contracts II. Required upper-level courses consist of Business Associations, Evidence, Professional Responsibility, Advanced Constitutional Law, Criminal Procedure, Family Law, Property, Commercial Law, and an advanced writing requirement. All students must take clinical courses. The required orientation program for first-year students is 2 days and includes interactions with faculty, staff, and students; the role of the lawyer and professionalism; the responsibilities of the future lawyer and student ethics; Academic Success programs; and a reception.

Phone: 904-680-7710
877-210-2591
Fax: 904-680-7776
E-mail: *admissions@fcsl.edu*
Web: *fcsl.edu*

Contact

Office of Admissions, 904-680-7710 for general inquiries and financial aid information.

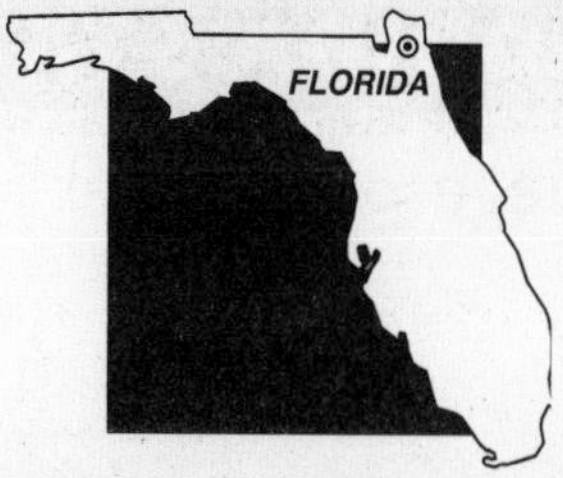

Electives

Third-year clinics include Criminal, Civil, Municipal, Domestic Violence, and Caribbean Law Clinic. Students may earn up to 6 credits in each clinic. Seminars are available to upper-division students only. These include Environmental Law, Sports Law, Appellate Advocacy, and Maritime Law, each worth 3 credit hours each. Other seminars may be offered periodically depending upon the interest of students and faculty. Internships with federal and state court judges can be taken for 3 or 4 credit hours. Students must have completed Professional Responsibility, Evidence, and Constitutional Law. Advanced Legal Research, worth 2 credit hours, is open to upper-division students. Independent study with a full-time faculty member is also available for up to 2 credit hours. The School of Law invites practitioners, judges, and other public figures to speak on a variety of topics, including legal practice, legal education, and jurisprudence. An Academic Success program is aimed at serving two groups of students: (1) incoming students considered at risk because of low LSAT scores or low GPA; (2) or students who are re-entering school after a long absence; and (3) current students who are at risk or on academic probation. The program consists of workshops on a variety of topics, including case briefing, study aids, and exam-taking. In addition, the School of Law has tutors for all first-year classes. Students may also meet with the program director to deal with individual problem issues. The most widely taken electives are Remedies, Trusts and Estates, and Florida Practice and Procedure.

Graduation Requirements

In order to graduate, candidates must have a GPA of 2.0 and have completed the upper-division writing requirement.

Organizations

Students edit the *Florida Coastal School of Law Review*, the *Weekly Leader*, and the newspaper, *Coastal Tidings*. Moot court competitions include the Robert Orseck Memorial Moot Court and the E. Earl Zehemer Memorial Moot Court. Law student organizations include the Student Bar Association, Black American Law Students Association, and NAPIL. There is a local chapter of ABA-Law Students Division, Phi Alpha Delta, and Law and Technology Society. Other organizations include the Environmental and Land Use Club, Hispanic American Law Students Association, and Christian Legal Society.

Library

The law library contains 207,870 hard-copy volumes and 439,452 microform volume equivalents, and subscribes to 2617 serial publications. Such on-line databases and networks as CALI, Legal-Trac, LEXIS, LOIS, Mathew Bender, NEXIS, OCLC First Search, WESTLAW, and CCH Internet Tax and Business Networks are available to law students for research. Recently, the library provided access to more on-line resources and dedicated a WESTLAW connection and WESTLAW and LEXIS printers in all computer laboratories. The ratio of library volumes to faculty is 8315 to 1 and to students, 972 to 1. The ratio of seats in the library to students is 1 to 1.

Faculty

The law school has 27 full-time and 31 part-time faculty members, of whom 15 are women. The ratio of full-time students to full-time faculty in an average class is 14 to 1; in a clinic, 13 to 1. The law school has a regular program of bringing visiting professors and other distinguished lecturers and visitors to campus.

Placement

J.D.s awarded:	110
Services available through: a separate law school placement center	
Services: job opportunity list service, job fairs	
Special features: extensive programming on a variety of career development topics including practice areas, work environments, alternative careers, and transition from school to the work force.	
Full-time job interviews:	6 employers
Summer job interviews:	n/av
Placement by graduation:	n/av
Placement within 9 months:	82% of class
Average starting salary:	$37,241 to $58,684
Areas of placement:	
Private practice 2-10 attorneys	27%
Private practice 11-25 attorneys	4%
Private practice 26-50 attorneys	6%
Private practice 51-100 attorneys	4%
Government	26%
Business/industry	24%
Judicial clerkships	4%
Military	2%
Academic	2%

Students

About 47% of the student body are women; 21%, minorities; 12%, African American; 4%, Asian American; 4%, Hispanic; and 1%, Native American. The majority of students come from Florida (53%). The average age of entering students is 28; age range is 21 to 64. About 50% of students enter directly from undergraduate school, 20% have a graduate degree, and 50% have worked full-time prior to entering law school. About 8% drop out after the first year for academic or personal reasons; 92% remain to receive a law degree.

FLORIDA STATE UNIVERSITY

College of Law

425 W. Jefferson St.
Tallahassee, FL 32306-1601

Application Filing		Accreditation
Fall: February 15		ABA, AALS
Spring: n/app		**Degrees Granted**
Fee: $20		J.D.

Enrollment 2001–2002			First-Year Class	
Men:	383	54%	Applied:	2209
Women:	331	46%	Accepted:	765
Minorities:	150	21%	Enrolled:	215
Out-of-State:	207	29%		

2001–02 Class Profile

LSAT Percentile: 68%
LSAT Median Score: 155
Percentage passing bar on first try: 87%

Tuition and Fees:

Resident
$5,286
Average (public)
$8,556
Average (private)
$22,915
Nonresident
$17,585
Average (public)
$16,690
Average (private)
$22,915

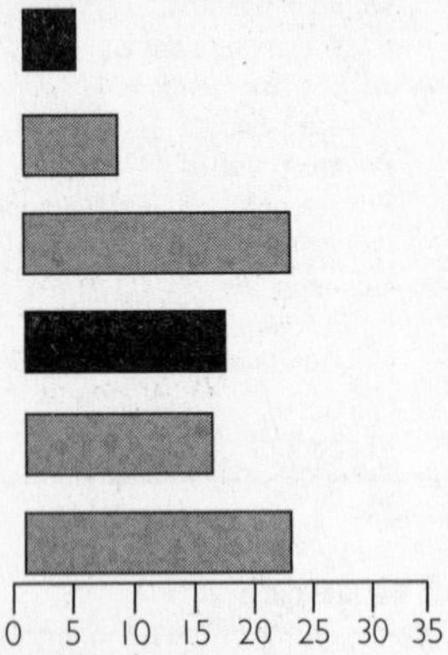

Percentage receiving financial aid: 75%

ADMISSIONS

In the fall 2001 first-year class, 2209 applied, 765 were accepted, and 215 enrolled. Seven transfers enrolled. The median LSAT percentile of the most recent first-year class was 68; the median GPA was 3.32 on a scale of 4.0. The highest LSAT percentile was 99.

Requirements

Applicants must have a bachelor's degree and take the LSAT. The most important admission factors include academic achievement and LSAT results. No specific undergraduate courses are required. Candidates are not interviewed.

Procedure

The application deadline for fall entry is February 15. Applicants should submit an application form, LSAT results, transcripts, a nonrefundable application fee of $20, 2 letters of recommendation, and a personal statement. Notification of the admissions decision is on a rolling basis. The latest acceptable LSAT test date for fall entry is February. The law school uses the LSDAS.

Special

The law school recruits minority and disadvantaged students through the LSDAS-CRS, by sponsoring special programs throughout the year, and by recruiting at colleges and universities. Requirements are different for out-of-state students in that LSAT scores and GPA requirements are generally higher for nonresidents. Transfer students must have one year of credit and be in the top third of their class.

Costs

Tuition and fees for the 2001-2002 academic year are $5286 for full-time in-state students and $17,585 for out-of-state students. On-campus room and board costs about $9000 annually; books and supplies run $1000.

Financial Aid

About 75% of current law students receive some form of aid. The maximum annual amount of aid from all sources combined, including scholarships, loans, and work contracts, is $18,500. Awards are based on need and merit. Fellowships of up to $15,000 per year also are available. About 1% of the students serve as research assistants to faculty members. The required financial statement is the FAFSA. Special funds for minority or disadvantaged students include a stipend for attending a summer orientation program. Other scholarships and aid are available. The average amount is $14,500. First-year students are notified about their financial aid application on a rolling basis.

About the Law School

Florida State University College of Law was established in 1966 and is a public institution. The 1200-acre campus is in a suburban area in Tallahassee, the state capital. The primary mission of the law school is to prepare students to practice law in a changing, pluralistic society by offering a curriculum that includes strong internship and joint-degree programs. Students have access to federal, state, county, city, and local agencies, courts, correctional facilities, law firms, and legal aid organizations in the Tallahassee area. The College of Law is located 1 block from the Florida Supreme Court building and within 5 blocks of federal, state, district, county, and bankruptcy courts, the State Legislature, and the State and Supreme Court law libraries. Housing for students is available in dormitories for single students and apartments for both single and married students. A housing office helps students find off-campus accommodations.

Calendar

The law school operates on a traditional semester basis. Courses for full-time students are offered both day and evening and must be completed within 3-years. There is no part-time program. New students are admitted in the fall. There is a 7-week summer session. Transferable summer courses are offered.

Programs

Students may take relevant courses in other programs and apply credit toward the J.D.; a maximum of 6 credits may be applied. The following joint degrees may be earned: J.D./M.B.A. (Juris Doctor/Master of Business Administration), J.D./M.P.A. (Juris Doctor/Master of Public Administration), J.D./M.S. (Juris Doctor/Master of Science in economics or international), J.D./M.S. (Juris Doctor/Master of Science in international affairs), J.D./M.S. L.I.S. (Juris Doctor/Master of Science in library information studies), J.D./M.S.P. (Juris Doctor/Master of Science in Urban and Regional Planning), and J.D./M.S.W. (Juris Doctor/Master of Social Work).

Phone: 850-644-3787
Fax: 850-644-7284
E-mail: *admissions@law.fsu.edu*

Contact

Sharon Booker, Director of Admissions and Records, 850-644-3787 for general inquiries; Joanne Clark, Financial Aid Office, 850-644-5871 for financial aid information.

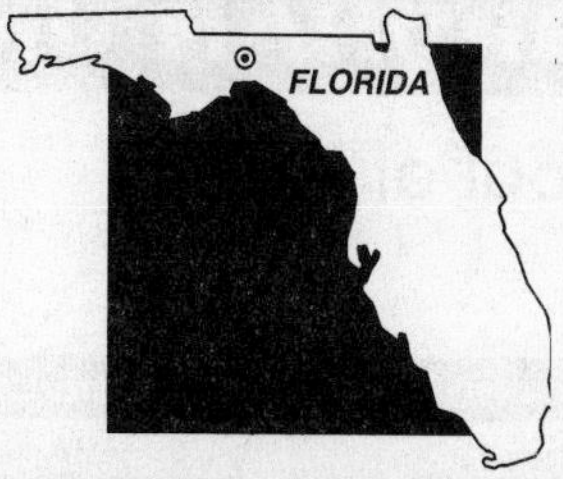

Required

To earn the J.D., candidates must complete 88 total credits, of which 35 are for required courses. They must maintain a minimum grade average of 67 or better in the required courses. The following first-year courses are required of all students: Civil Procedure, Torts, Contracts I and II, Property I and II, Legal Writing and Research I and II, Criminal Law, and Constitutional Law I. Required upper-level courses consist of Constitutional Law II, Professional Responsibility, and a writing requirement course. All students must complete 20 hours of civil pro bono work.The required orientation program for first-year students is a 3-day program that includes an introduction to legal education, research and writing, and ethics.

Electives

The College of Law offers concentrations in environmental law, international law, and mediation. In addition, the college offers more than 60 externship programs, either full- or part-time, encompassing judicial placements, administrative agency placements, and many civil and criminal lawyering programs. A variety of seminars is offered, such as legal ethics and bankruptcy. There are the Brown Bag Lecture Series and the Mason Ladd Memorial Lectures. Study abroad is available during summer terms at Oxford University in England and the University of West Indies in Barbados. The Academic Support Program is open to all interested first-year students. The most widely taken electives are Evidence, Business Associations, and Income Tax.

Graduation Requirements

In order to graduate, candidates must have a minimum grade average of 67, have completed the upper-division writing requirement, 20 hours of pro bono work, and the 6-semester residency requirement.

Organizations

The primary law review is the *Florida State University Law Review*. Other law journals include the *Journal of Land Use and Environmental Law*, begun in 1983 and the state's first and only student publication in environmental and land law use. Students also edit the *Journal of Transnational Law and Policy*. The college's moot court team participates in about 10 regional and national competitions each year, including the Florida Bar Robert Orseck Moot Court Competition, Juvenile Law National Moot Court Competition, and the John Gibbons National Constitutional Criminal Law Moot Court Competition. The college also takes part in 3 mock trial competitions each year. Law student associations include the Student Bar Association and chapters of the American Civil Liberties Union and the American Trial Lawyers Association.

Library

The law library contains 432,878 hardcopy volumes and 911,330 microform volume equivalents, and subscribes to 5101 serial publications. Such on-line databases and networks as CALI, CIS Universe, Infotrac, Legal-Trac, LEXIS, Mathew Bender, NEXIS, OCLC First Search, RLIN, WESTLAW, Wilsonline Indexes, and more than 100 databases are available to law students for research. Special library collections include rare English, American, and Floridian legal materials, including a first edition of Blackstone's Commentaries, and videotapes of oral arguments before the Florida Supreme Court of cases since 1985. The library also makes the full text of Florida Supreme Court briefs and opinions available on the Web. The ratio of library volumes to faculty is 8834 to 1 and to students, 606 to 1. The ratio of seats in the library to students is 1 to 48.

Faculty

The law school has 49 full-time and 15 part-time faculty members, of whom 18 are women. According to AAUP standards for Category I institutions, faculty salaries are below average. About 13% of full-time faculty have a graduate law degree in addition to the J.D. The ratio of full-time students to full-time faculty in an average class is 14 to 1; in a clinic, 13 to 1. The law school has a regular program of bringing visiting professors and other distinguished lecturers and visitors to campus. There is a chapter of the Order of the Coif; 36 faculty and 319 graduates are members.

Placement	
J.D.s awarded:	226
Services available through: a separate law school placement center and the university placement center	
Services: various workshops/lectures on specific placement topics such as Internet job hunting, judicial clerkships, and job searches beyond OCI and practice area panels	
Special features: a monthly job notice bulletin for alumni; e-mail notification of job opportunities for students and alumni.	
Full-time job interviews:	60 employers
Summer job interviews:	63 employers
Placement by graduation:	64% of class
Placement within 9 months:	95% of class
Average starting salary:	$24,000 to $110,000
Areas of placement:	
Private practice 2-10 attorneys	15%
Private practice 11-25 attorneys	10%
Private practice 26-50 attorneys	4%
Private practice 51-100 attorneys	2%
Private practice 101+ attorneys	8%
Government	28%
Judicial clerkships	7%
Military	4%
Business/industry	3%
Public interest	3%

Students

About 46% of the student body are women; 21%, minorities; 8%, African American; 2%, Asian American; 9%, Hispanic; and 1%, Native American. The majority of students come from Florida (71%). The average age of entering students is 25; age range is 20 to 58. About 1% drop out after the first year for academic or personal reasons; 99% remain to receive a law degree.

FORDHAM UNIVERSITY

School of Law

140 West 62nd Street
New York, NY 10023

Application Filing		Accreditation
Fall: March 1		ABA, AALS
Spring: n/app		**Degrees Granted**
Fee: $60		J.D., LL.M.

Enrollment 2001–2002			First-Year Class	
Men:	727	50%	Applied:	5177
Women:	732	50%	Accepted:	1486
Minorities:	350	24%	Enrolled:	510
Out-of-State:	598	41%		

2001–02 Class Profile

LSAT Percentile: 92%
LSAT Median Score: 164
Percentage passing bar on first try: 83%

Tuition and Fees:

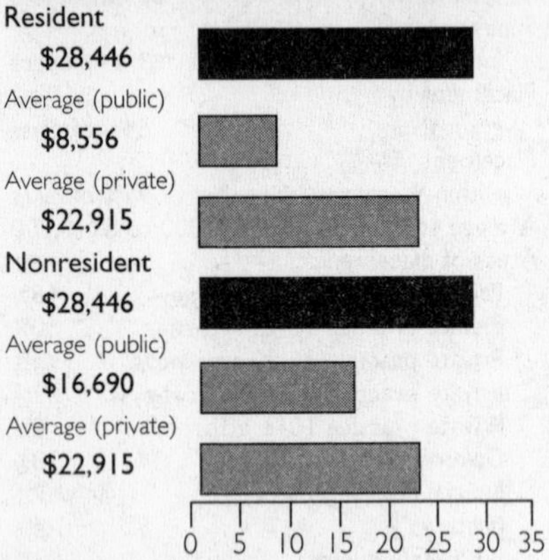

Percentage receiving financial aid: 76%

ADMISSIONS

In the fall 2001 first-year class, 5177 applied, 1486 were accepted, and 510 enrolled. Twenty-seven transfers enrolled. The median LSAT percentile of the most recent first-year class was 92; the median GPA was 3.5 on a scale of 4.0. The lowest LSAT percentile accepted was 48; the highest was 99.

Requirements

Applicants must have a bachelor's degree and take the LSAT. The most important admission factors include LSAT results, GPA, and general background. Specific undergraduate courses and interviews are not required.

Procedure

The application deadline for fall entry is March 1. Applicants should submit an application form, LSAT results, transcripts, TOEFL, a nonrefundable application fee of $60, a personal statement, LSAT results, and transcripts submitted through LSDAS. Notification of the admissions decision is 6 to 8 weeks after application is complete. The latest LSAT test date for fall entry is February. The law school uses the LSDAS.

Special

The law school recruits minority and disadvantaged students by means of attendance at forums and law fairs, LSDAS Candidate Referral Service, alumni assistance, and current minority students contacting accepted minority applicants. Requirements are not different for out-of-state students. Transfer students must have a minimum GPA of 3, have attended an ABA-approved law school, and fulfill a 2-year residency requirement at Fordham.

Costs

Tuition and fees for the 2001-2002 academic year are $28,446 for all full-time students. Tuition for part-time students is $21,365 per year. On-campus room and board costs about $13,400 annually; books and supplies run $800.

Financial Aid

About 76% of current law students receive some form of aid. The average annual amount of aid from all sources combined, including scholarships, loans, and work contracts, is $28,575; maximum, $47,000. Awards are based on need along with with approximately 10% based on merit. Required financial statement is the FAFSA. The aid application deadline for fall entry is May 15. Special funds for minority or disadvantaged students consist of funds contributed by benefactors of the school. Also, some school funds are specifically allocated to assist these groups. First-year students are notified about their financial aid application after acceptance when their file is complete.

About the Law School

Fordham University School of Law was established in 1905 and is a private institution. The 8-acre campus is in an urban area in the Lincoln Center area of New York City. The primary mission of the law school is to provide students with an understanding of legal doctrine and a solid foundation of analytical reasoning, lawyering skills, and professional values that they will be able to use in law practice or law-related professions; to contribute to the development of the law and legal education; and to serve the wider community. Students have access to federal, state, county, city, and local agencies, courts, correctional facilities, law firms, and legal aid organizations in the New York area. Lincoln Center is across the street; the midtown area, home of the media, law firms, corporate headquarters, and nonprofit organizations, is a few blocks away; there is also convenient transportation to the courts. Facilities of special interest to law students include the law school and attached buildings, which include a 250-seat amphitheater, 2 cafeterias, student activities center, student journal offices, counseling center, bookstore, 2 computer centers, and a chapel. Housing for students is available in a 250-bed, 20-story university residence hall connected to the law school; there is some student housing in the neighborhood; many students commute from other parts of the city or the metropolitan area. About 95% of the law school facilities are accessible to the physically disabled.

Calendar

The law school operates on a traditional semester basis. Courses for full-time students are offered both day and evening and must be completed within 3 years. For part-time students, courses are offered both day and evening and must be completed within 4 years. New students are admitted in the fall. There is an 8-week summer session. Transferable summer courses are offered.

Programs

In addition to the J.D., the law school offers the LL.M. Students may take relevant courses in other programs and apply credit toward the J.D.; a maximum of 13 credits may be applied. The following joint degrees may be earned: J.D./M.A. (Juris Doctor/Master of Arts (International Political Economy and Development), J.D./M.B.A. (Juris Doctor/Master of Business Administration), and J.D./M.S.W. (Juris Doctor/Master of Social Work).

Required

To earn the J.D., candidates must complete 83 total credits, of which 39 are for required courses. They must maintain a minimum GPA of 1.9 in the required courses. The following first-year courses are required of all students: Contracts, Criminal Justice, Civil Procedure, Property, Torts, Constitutional Law, Legal Process, and Legal Writing and Research. Required upper-level courses consist of Corporations and Partnerships and Professional Responsibility. The required orientation program for first-

Phone: 212-626-6810
Web: www.fordham.edu

Contact

Kevin Downey, Assistant Dean, Admissions, 212-636-6810 for general inquiries; Stephen G. Brown, Financial Aid Director, 212-636-6815 for financial aid information.

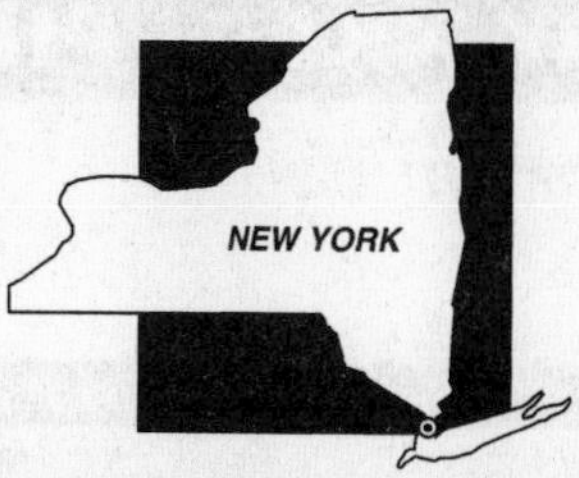

year students is a 1-day program and a 1-week legal process course. There are separate programs for legal writing, library use, career planning, university resources, and clinical programs.

Electives

The School of Law offers concentrations in corporate law, criminal law, entertainment law, environmental law, family law, international law, labor law, litigation, maritime law, media law, securities law, sports law, tax law, torts and insurance, European Community law, trial advocacy, public interest law, consumer law, professional responsibility, evidence, banking and finance antitrust and economic regulation, and commercial law. Clinics include Litigation Skills, Comprehensive Lawyering Skills, and Civil Rights. Seminars include Advanced Bankruptcy and Advanced Copyright Law. After the first year, students may participate in a broad range of actual practice settings in federal and state courts, administrative agencies, prosecutors' and defenders' offices, and nonprofit agencies for 2 credits. In a typical year, more than 250 students participate. Research is done through the Stein Institute of Law and Ethics Research fellowships and the MCI/Fordham Travel Abroad Fellowship. Also, many students serve as research assistants to faculty. Field work may be undertaken in the noncredit Pro Bono program, where students assist in preparing cases under the direction of attorneys from the Legal Aid Society and various public agencies and nonprofit organizations. Special lecture series include John F. Sonnett Lectures by distinguished judges and litagators; Stein Lectures in ethics and professional responsibility, and others. Anyone may study abroad for up to 1 year for up to 24 credits in approved subjects with the MCI/Fordham Travel Abroad Fellowship. The Law School operates a summer program in Dublin and Belfast. The noncredit Academic Enrichment Program provides training in briefing cases, study strategies, and exam-taking techniques. The school contributes to the CLEO program. Public service programs include a nonlegal community service project; advocacy projects for battered women, low-income tenants, and unemployed individuals; and student-funded fellowships for summer work at public interest organizations. The most widely taken electives are Income Taxation, New York Practice, and Evidence.

Graduation Requirements

In order to graduate, candidates must have a GPA of 1.9 and have completed the upper-division writing requirement.

Organizations

Students edit the *Fordham Law Review*, *Fordham Urban Law Journal*, *Fordham International Law Journal*, the newspaper, *The Advocate*, and the yearbook *In Summation*. Moot court competitions include the intramural William Hughes Mulligan, the I. Maurice Wormser, and the interschool Irving R. Kaufman Securities Law Competition. Teams also compete at the National Moot Court, Jessup International Law, and other competitions. Student organizations include Student Bar Association, Stein Scholars, and Fordham Law Women. The university has the largest student-run radio station in the country. There are local chapters of the Federalist Society, National Lawyers Guild, and Phi Alpha Delta. Campus clubs include Habitat for Humanity, National Association of Public Interest Law, and the Sports Law Association.

Library

The law library contains 578,718 hard-copy volumes and 1,379,151 microform volume equivalents, and subscribes to 7315 serial publications. Such on-line databases and networks as CALI, CIS Universe, DIALOG, Dow-Jones, Infotrac, Legal-Trac, LEXIS, LOIS, NEXIS, OCLC First Search, RLIN, WESTLAW, and Wilsonline Indexes are available to law students for research. Special library collections include an EEC collection and a federal documents depository. Recently, the library acquired the INNOPACQ on-line catalog system and an Automated Circulation System. There is a LAN for computers and the computer classroom and laboratory. Many additional carrels and tables were wired for data use. The ratio of library volumes to faculty is 8511 to 1 and to students is 397 to 1. The ratio of seats in the library to students is 1 to 3.

Faculty

The law school has 68 full-time and 257 part-time faculty members, of whom 102 are women. According to AAUP standards for Category I institutions, faculty salaries are above average. About 45% of full-time faculty have a graduate law degree in addition to the J.D.; about 8% of part-time faculty have one. The ratio of full-time students to full-time faculty in an average class is 50 to 1; in a clinic, 8 to 1. The law school has a regular program of bringing visiting professors and other distinguished lecturers and visitors to campus. There is a chapter of the Order of the Coif.

Placement

J.D.s awarded:	446
Services available through: a separate law school placement center	
Services: self-assessment seminars, mock interviews, and networking/job prospecting workshops	
Special features: The school designs its own programs to ensure that students have opportunites to interact with alumni and employers.	
Full-time job interviews:	340 employers
Summer job interviews:	310 employers
Placement by graduation:	90% of class
Placement within 9 months:	99% of class
Average starting salary:	$60,000 to $140,000
Areas of placement:	
Private practice 2-10 attorneys	6%
Private practice 11-25 attorneys	4%
Private practice 26-50 attorneys	2%
Private practice 51-100 attorneys	6%
Private practice 100+ attorneys	43%
Government	13%
Business/industry	8%
Judicial clerkships	4%
Public interest	3%
Academic	1%

Students

About 50% of the student body are women; 24%, minorities; 8%, African American; 8%, Asian American; and 8%, Hispanic. The majority of students come from the Northeast (80%). The average age of entering students is 24; age range is 20 to 53. About 35% of students enter directly from undergraduate school, 7% have a graduate degree, and 66% have worked full-time prior to entering law school. About 2% drop out after the first year for academic or personal reasons.

FRANKLIN PIERCE LAW CENTER

2 White Street
Concord, NH 03301

Application Filing	Accreditation
Fall: May 1	ABA
Spring: n/app	**Degrees Granted**
Fee: $55	J.D., LL.M.

Enrollment 2001–2002			First-Year Class	
Men:	220	57%	Applied:	916
Women:	169	36%	Accepted:	532
Minorities:	47	12%	Enrolled:	128
Out-of-State:	315	81%		

2001–02 Class Profile

LSAT Percentile: n/av
LSAT Median Score: 151
Percentage passing bar on first try: 70%

Tuition and Fees:

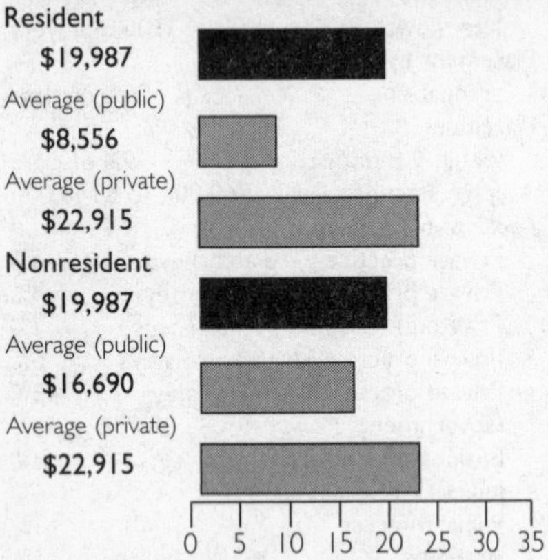

Percentage receiving financial aid: 76%

ADMISSIONS

In the fall 2001 first-year class, 916 applied, 532 were accepted, and 128 enrolled. The median GPA of the most recent first-year class was 3.0 on a scale of 4.3.

Requirements

Applicants must have a bachelor's degree and take the LSAT. The most important admission factors include academic achievement, motivation, and writing ability. No specific undergraduate courses are required. Candidates are interviewed.

Procedure

The application deadline for fall entry is May 1. Applicants should submit an application form, LSAT results, transcripts, a nonrefundable application fee of $55, 2 letters of recommendation, and a personal statement. Notification of the admissions decision is on a rolling basis. The latest acceptable LSAT test date for fall entry is June. The law school uses the LSDAS.

Special

The law school recruits minority and disadvantaged students by participating in minority programs such as the Council on Legal Education Opportunity and the Puerto Rican Legal Defense Fund, actively recruiting self-identified minorities through the Law School Admission Council, and offering diversity scholarships. Students are also invited to submit a supplemental statement addressing their challenges and achievements. Requirements are not different for out-of-state students. Transfer students must have one year of credit, have a minimum GPA of 3, and have attended an ABA-approved law school.

Costs

Tuition and fees for the 2001-2002 academic year are $19,987 for all full-time students. Tuition for all part-time students is $14,997. Books and supplies run about $600 annually.

Financial Aid

About 76% of current law students receive some form of aid. The average annual amount of aid from all sources combined, including scholarships, loans, and work contracts, is $2815. Awards are based on need and merit. Required financial statement is the FAFSA. The aid application deadline for fall entry is open. Special funds for minority or disadvantaged students consist of diversity scholarships that are available to members of groups currently underrepresented in the law center community. They are awarded based on academic and community involvement factors.

About the Law School

Franklin Pierce Law Center was established in 1973 and is a private institution. The 1-acre campus is in a small town 70 miles north of Boston, Massachusetts. The primary mission of the law school is to encourage innovation in legal education. Self-reliant students who know their strengths, objectives, and motivations are able to shape individualized programs from the array of educational opportunities. Students have access to federal, state, county, city, and local agencies, courts, correctional facilities, law firms, and legal aid organizations in the Concord area. Many students find paid employment, work as volunteers, or have externships in all these facilities situated in Concord, the state capital. Facilities of special interest to law students consist of the attorney general offices and city, state, and federal court clerkships. Housing for students is available around the law center's residential setting. About 95% of the law school facilities are accessible to the physically disabled.

Calendar

The law school operates on a traditional semester basis. Courses for full-time students are offered both day and evening and must be completed within 3 years. There is no part-time program. New students are admitted in the fall. There is a 14-week summer session. Transferable summer courses are offered.

Programs

In addition to the J.D., the law school offers the LL.M. and M.E.L.—Master of Education Law, M.I.P.—Master of Intellectual Property. Students may take relevant courses in other programs and apply credit toward the J.D.; a maximum of 8 credits may be applied. The following joint degrees may be earned: J.D./M.E.L. (Juris Doctor/Master of Education Law) and J.D./M.I.P. (Juris Doctor/Master of Intellectual Property).

Required

To earn the J.D., candidates must complete 84 total credits, of which 39 are for required courses. They must maintain a minimum GPA of 2.0 in the required courses. The following first-year courses are required of all students: Torts, Property, Constitutional Law, Contracts I and II, Civil Procedure, Legal Writing, 1 legal perspective course, and Legal Research. Required upper-level courses consist of Criminal Procedure I, Administrative Law, and Professional Responsibility. The required orientation program for first-year students is a 4-day orientation program that includes an introduction to the Career Services Center and student organizations, a demonstration of briefing cases, service as a juror for a mock trial, and social events such as an evening with a faculty host at their home.

Electives

The Franklin Pierce Law Center offers concentrations in corporate law, criminal law, entertainment law, family law, international law, juvenile law, litigation, tax law, health law, intellectual property, legal services, regulatory and administrative law, and education law. In addition, Pierce Law operates 5 clinics in offices designed to emulate a state-of-the-art law office. Clinics include the Civil Practice

Phone: 603-228-9217
Fax: 603-228-1074
E-mail: *admissions@fplc.edu*
Web: *fplc.edu*

Contact

Lory Attalla, 603-228-9217 for general inquiries; Clinton A. Hanson, Director of Financial Aid, 603-228-1541, ext. 104 for financial aid information.

Clinic where students represent actual clients in a range of civil matters in state, federal, and bankruptcy courts. The Children's Advocacy Clinic offers students the opportunity to represent children either as the attorney for the child or as *Guardian ad Litem*. In the Appellate Defender program students review trial transcripts, research, and write appellate briefs to the New Hampshire Supreme Court. Students in the Mediation Clinic undergo classroom training in the techniques and ethics of alternative dispute resolution, followed by actual experience conducting mediations for local district courts in civil cases involving less than $5000. Students in the Criminal Practice Clinic represent clients in misdemeanor and felony cases before District and Superior Courts. Before all significant court appearances, students practice moot court exercises in our in-house courtroom. This clinic is open to second and third year students who are eligible to appear in New Hampshire state and federal courts under Supreme Court Rule 36. Second- and third-year students may take independent study with a faculty member for a maximum of 4 credits. Research seminars are offered in medical decision making, Supreme Court issues, and advanced legal research. Speakers are invited to lecture on a wide variety of subjects, including civil rights, health law, patent law, and coporate law. Study abroad is available through programs at ABA-approved schools. Computer tutorial programs are offered to all students. Faculty will work with individuals needing remediation. Teaching assistants are available for individual consultation; all first-year courses have teaching assistants for discussion and explanation. Various student organizations bring in speakers, special programs, and conferences annually. Externships are available to students after their third semester. Externships are part time for 4 credits or full time for 12 credits. The school has a large number of regular placements and students may design their own externship as long as it is appropriate for the number of credits and with an experienced pactitioner who has committed to educating the student. The most widely taken electives are Evidence and Copyright and Trademarks.

Graduation Requirements

In order to graduate, candidates must have a GPA of 2.0 and have completed 84 credits, have 6 full-time semesters of residency, offset all credits below C- with an equal number of credits of B- or above, have satisfied any terms of academic probation or financial obligation, and not be the subject of an alleged Honor Code violation.

Organizations

Student-edited publications are *IDEA: The Journal Of Law and Technology* and *RISK: Issues of Health, Safety and Environment. The Annual Survey of New Hampshire Law*, which publishes articles focusing on recent opinions of the New Hampshire Supreme Court, is a 4-credit, 2-semester course in which second-year students write articles and a third-year student serves as editor. Moot court competitions include the required appellate argument for second semester first-year students. Students annually enter the Giles Sutherland Rich Intellectual Property Moot Court, Saul Lefkowitz Moot Court Competition, National Health Law Competition, Association of Trial Lawyers of America, and Student Trial Advocacy Competition. Students enter legal essay writing contests on a volunteer basis. Law student organizations include the Student Intellectual Property Association, Cyber Law Group, and Women's Law Students Association. Local chapters of national associations include Phi Alpha Delta, Licensing Executives Society, and Association of Trial Lawyers of America.

Library

The law library contains 143,418 hard-copy volumes and 507,000 microform volume equivalents, and subscribes to 1044 serial publications. Such on-line databases and networks as CALI, DIALOG, Legal-Trac, LEXIS, LOIS, NEXIS, and WESTLAW are available to law students for research. Special library collections include an intellectual property special collection, a repository for the World Intellectual Property Organization (WIPO), a federal GPO selective depository, and an education law special collection. Recently, the library renovated the ground floor with carpeting and lighting. The ratio of library volumes to faculty is 5976 to 1 and to students is 369 to 1. The ratio of seats in the library to students is 1 to 2.

Placement

J.D.s awarded: 119

Services available through: a separate law school placement center

Services: video interviews and playbacks; workshops on information interviewing; career planning for students interested in intellectual property, business, public interest, and general practice; externships for academic credit

Special features: individual and personal service to its students, with emphasis on helping students network; and nationwide academic externship opportunities.

Full-time job interviews:	56 employers
Summer job interviews:	56 employers
Placement by graduation:	66% of class
Placement within 9 months:	97% of class
Average starting salary:	$37,150 to $115,000
Areas of placement:	
Private practice 2-10 attorneys	15%
Private practice 11-25 attorneys	12%
Private practice 26-50 attorneys	2%
Private practice 51-100 attorneys	17%
private practice 100+ attorneys	27%
Business/industry	13%
Government	5%
Public interest	4%
Judicial clerkships	3%
Academic	2%

Faculty

The law school has 24 full-time and 37 part-time faculty members, of whom 16 are women. According to AAUP standards for Category IIA institutions, faculty salaries are well above average. About 17% of full-time faculty have a graduate law degree in addition to the J.D. The ratio of full-time students to full-time faculty in an average class is 16 to 1; in a clinic, 1 to 1.

Students

About 36% of the student body are women; 12%, minorities; 2%, African American; 3%, Asian American; 2%, Hispanic; and 1%, Native American. The majority of students come from the Northeast (42%). The average age of entering students is 28; age range is 20 to 45. About 20% of students enter directly from undergraduate school, 20% have a graduate degree, and 80% have worked full-time prior to entering law school. About 10% drop out after the first year for academic or personal reasons; 90% remain to receive a law degree.

GEORGE MASON UNIVERSITY

School of Law

3301 North Fairfax Drive
Arlington, VA 22201-4426

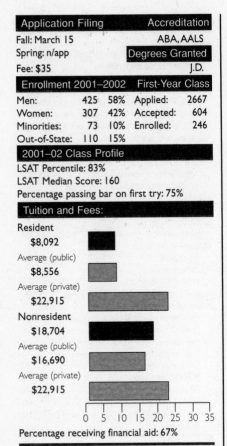

Application Filing		Accreditation
Fall: March 15		ABA, AALS
Spring: n/app		**Degrees Granted**
Fee: $35		J.D.

Enrollment 2001–2002			First-Year Class	
Men:	425	58%	Applied:	2667
Women:	307	42%	Accepted:	604
Minorities:	73	10%	Enrolled:	246
Out-of-State:	110	15%		

2001–02 Class Profile

LSAT Percentile: 83%
LSAT Median Score: 160
Percentage passing bar on first try: 75%

Tuition and Fees:

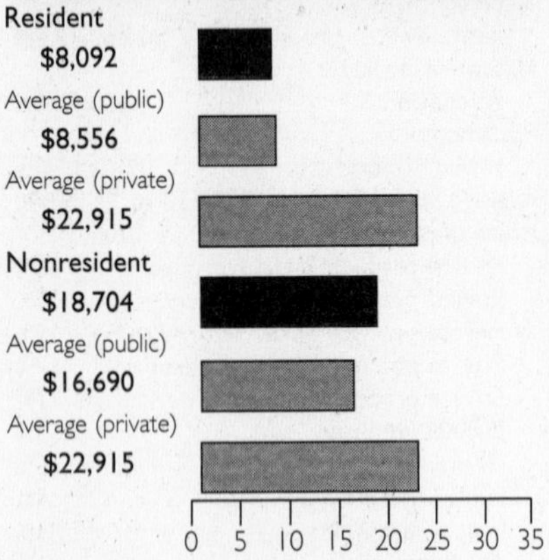

Percentage receiving financial aid: 67%

ADMISSIONS

In the fall 2001 first-year class, 2667 applied, 604 were accepted, and 246 enrolled. Thirty-five transfers enrolled. The median LSAT percentile of the most recent first-year class was 83; the median GPA was 3.35 on a scale of 4.0.

Requirements

Applicants must have a bachelor's degree and take the LSAT. The most important admission factors include LSAT results, class rank, and GPA. No specific undergraduate courses are required. Candidates are not interviewed.

Procedure

The application deadline for fall entry is March 15. Applicants should submit an application form, LSAT results, LSDAS Report, a nonrefundable application fee of $35, 2 letters of recommendation, and 500-word personal statement. Notification of the admissions decision is approximately from December 1 to the end of June on a rolling basis. The latest acceptable LSAT test date for fall entry is February. The law school uses the LSDAS.

Special

The law school recruits minority and disadvantaged students through the Law Services' Candidate Referral Service, Law School Forums, regional law fairs, and CLEO. Requirements are not different for out-of-state students. Transfer students must have one year of credit, have a minimum GPA of 3, and have attended an ABA-approved law school.

Costs

Tuition and fees for the 2001-2002 academic year are $8092 for full-time in-state students and $18,704 for out-of-state students. Tuition for part-time students is $6358 in-state and $14,696 out-of-state.

Financial Aid

About 67% of current law students receive some form of aid. The average annual amount of aid from all sources combined, including scholarships, loans, and work contracts, is $14,315. Awards are based on merit. Required financial statement is the FAFSA. The deadline for aid applications for fall entry is open. First-year students are notified about their financial aid application between the time of acceptance and the first day of school.

About the Law School

George Mason University School of Law was established in 1979 and is a public institution. The 1-acre campus is in a suburban area 2 miles south of Washington, D.C. The primary mission of the law school is to provide superior legal education programs leading to the first professional degree in law, the Juris Doctor. The school stresses the case method. Students have access to federal, state, county, city, and local agencies, courts, correctional facilities, law firms, and legal aid organizations in the Arlington area. Housing for students is not available on the metro campus. All law school facilities are accessible to the physically disabled.

Calendar

The law school operates on a traditional semester basis. Courses for full-time students are offered days only and must be completed within 3 years. For part-time students, courses are offered evenings only and must be completed within 4 years. New full- and part-time students are admitted in the fall. There is an 8-week summer session. Transferable summer courses are offered.

Phone: 703-993-8010
Fax: 703-993-8260
E-mail: *arichar5@gmu.edu*
Web: *www.gmu.edu*

Contact

Anne M. Richard, Director of Admissions, 703-993-8010 for general inquiries; Office of Financial Aid, 703-993-2353 for financial aid information.

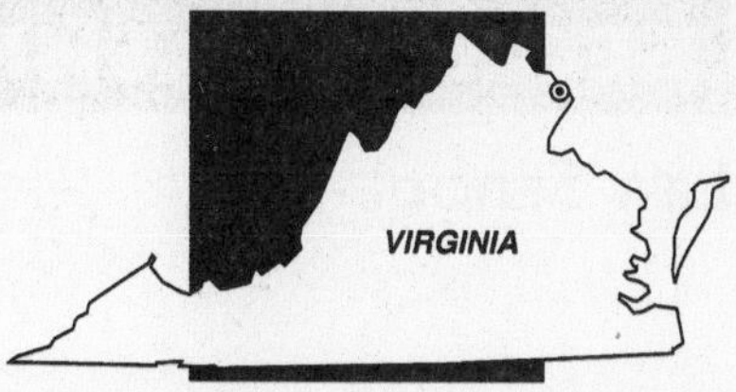

Programs

Required

To earn the J.D., candidates must complete 84 total credits, of which 43 are for required courses. They must maintain a minimum GPA of 2.15 in the required courses. The following first-year courses are required of all students: Property, Legal Research, Writing, and Analysis I and II, Contracts I and II, Civil Procedure, Criminal Law, Economic Foundations of Legal Studies, and Torts I + II. Required upper-level courses consist of Professional Responsibility, Constitutional Law, Administrative Law, Legal Research, Writing, and Analysis III and IV, and a minimum of 2 upper-level courses in which substantial papers are required. The required orientation program for first-year students is presented during the first week of school. The program lasts 1 to 3 days and consists of presentations by the administration, legal writing classes, small group meetings with faculty and student advisers, and a reception with representatives of student organizations.

Electives

The School of Law offers concentrations in corporate law, criminal law, international business law, litigation, securities law, tax law, patent law, regulatory law, technology law, legal and economic theory, and personal law. In addition, clinics are limited to upper-level students, and are worth 3 credits. Seminars, taken in the second, third, or fourth year, consist of a minimum of 2 upper-level courses in which substantial papers are required or there is a satisfaction of track thesis requirement. Internships are limited to upper-level students and are worth 2 to 3 credits, up to a maximum of 4 credits. The Law and Economics Center administers a series of interdisciplinary symposia, lectures, and conferences devoted to current topics in law and economics. The most widely taken electives are Virginia Practice, Domestic Relations, and Business Associations.

Graduation Requirements

In order to graduate, candidates must have a GPA of 2.15 and have completed the upper-division writing requirement.

Organizations

Students edit the *George Mason University Law Review*, the *Civil Rights Law Journal*, the *Journal of International Legal Studies, Federal Circuit Bar Journal*, and the newspaper *The Docket*. The school sponsors several in-house competitions each year, and sends teams to numerous national and regional competitions. Law student organizations include the Student Bar Association, Business Law Society, and Association for Public Interest Law. There are local chapters of the ABA-Law Student Division, Phi Delta Phi (Lewis Powell Inn), and Phi Alpha Delta (George Mason Chapter).

Library

The law library contains 400,000 hard-copy volumes and 886,000 microform volume equivalents, and subscribes to 5400 serial publications. Such on-line databases and networks as ALADIN, CALI, Legal-Trac, LEXIS, LOIS, TWEN, VIVA, and WESTLAW are available to law students for research. Special library collections include business, economic theory and history, ethics and philosophy, banking, patent law, international law, law and economics, and tax sections. The school is also a participant in the Federal Government Documents Depository. Recently, the library added 2 computer laboratories with 50 PCs providing access to the Internet, LEXIS, WESTLAW, and university network facilities. The ratio of library volumes to faculty is 10,810 to 1 and to students is 546 to 1. The ratio of seats in the library to students is 1 to 2.

Faculty

The law school has 37 full-time and 89 part-time faculty members, of whom 27 are women. According to AAUP standards for Category I institutions, faculty salaries are above average. About 42% of full-time faculty have a graduate law degree in addition to the J.D.; about 3% of part-time faculty have one. The ratio of full-time students to full-time faculty in an average class is 16 to 1.

Placement	
J.D.s awarded:	208
Services available through: a separate law school placement center	
Services: mock interview program, mentoring program	
Special features: participation in the D.C. Public Interest Job Fair, and the BLSA Regional Job Fair.	
Full-time job interviews:	190 employers
Summer job interviews:	n/av
Placement by graduation:	92% of class
Placement within 9 months:	98% of class
Average starting salary:	$39,000 to $88,000
Areas of placement:	
Private practice: 2-100 attorneys	45%
Government	19%
Business/industry	18%
Judicial clerkships	11%
Military	4%
Public interest	2%
Academic	1%

Students

About 42% of the student body are women; 10%, minorities; 1%, African American; 6%, Asian American; and 2%, Hispanic. The majority of students come from Virginia (85%). The average age of entering students is 27; age range is 20 to 50. About 26% of students enter directly from undergraduate school, 17% have a graduate degree, and 70% have worked full-time prior to entering law school. About 3% drop out after the first year for academic or personal reasons.

GEORGE WASHINGTON UNIVERSITY

Law School

2000 H Street, N.W.
Washington, DC 20052

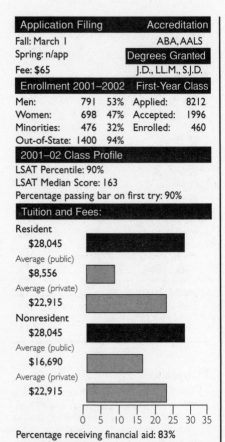

Application Filing		Accreditation
Fall: March 1		ABA, AALS
Spring: n/app		**Degrees Granted**
Fee: $65		J.D., LL.M., S.J.D.

Enrollment 2001–2002			First-Year Class	
Men:	791	53%	Applied:	8212
Women:	698	47%	Accepted:	1996
Minorities:	476	32%	Enrolled:	460
Out-of-State:	1400	94%		

2001–02 Class Profile

LSAT Percentile: 90%
LSAT Median Score: 163
Percentage passing bar on first try: 90%

Tuition and Fees:

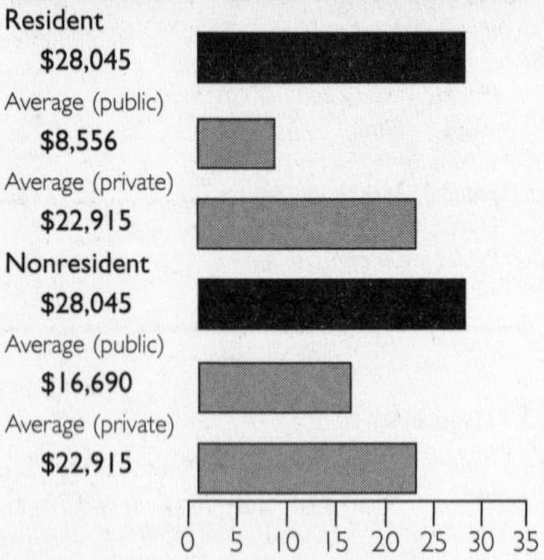

Percentage receiving financial aid: 83%

ADMISSIONS

In the fall 2001 first-year class, 8212 applied, 1996 were accepted, and 460 enrolled. Thirty-three transfers enrolled. The median LSAT percentile of the most recent first-year class was 90; the median GPA was 3.4 on a scale of 4.0. The lowest LSAT percentile accepted was 37; the highest was 100.

Requirements

Applicants must have a bachelor's degree and take the LSAT. The most important admission factors include academic achievement, LSAT results, and writing ability. No specific undergraduate courses are required. Candidates are not interviewed.

Procedure

The application deadline for fall entry is March 1. Applicants should submit an application form, LSAT results, transcripts, a nonrefundable application fee of $65. Two letters of recommendation are recommended, but not required. Notification of the admissions decision is as soon as a decision is made. The latest acceptable LSAT test date for fall entry is February, but only in certain cases. The law school uses the LSDAS.

Special

The law school recruits minority and disadvantaged students by participating in law forums throughout the country and visiting schools with large minority populations. In addition, each admitted applicant is contacted by a currently enrolled student. Requirements are not different for out-of-state students. Transfer students must have one year of credit and have attended an ABA-approved law school; admissions decisions are based on the applicant's law school record and the amount of space available.

Costs

Tuition and fees for the 2001-2002 academic year are $28,045 for all full-time students. Books and supplies run about $840 annually.

Financial Aid

About 83% of current law students receive some form of aid. The average annual amount of aid from all sources combined, including scholarships, loans, and work contracts, is $28,867; maximum, $40,122. Awards are based on need and merit. Required financial statements are the CSS Profile and FAFSA. First-year students are notified about their financial aid application some time after admission, providing all files are complete.

About the Law School

George Washington University Law School was established in 1865 and is a private institution. The campus is in an urban area in downtown Washington, D.C. The primary mission of the law school is to offer students the opportunity to study and observe lawmaking at its source, by combining a wide variety of courses in public law with the traditional fields of law. Students have access to federal, state, county, city, and local agencies, courts, correctional facilities, law firms, and legal aid organizations in the Washington area. Extensive clinical opportunities exist in the nation's capital. Housing for students consists of a limited number of spaces available on campus in efficiency, 1- and 2-bedroom apartments.

Calendar

The law school operates on a traditional semester basis. Courses for full-time students are offered both day and evening and must be completed within 3 years. For part-time students, courses are offered both day and evening and must be completed within 4 years. New full- and part-time students are admitted in the fall. There is a 7-week summer session. Transferable summer courses are offered.

Programs

In addition to the J.D., the law school offers the LL.M. and S.J.D. Students may take relevant courses in other programs and apply credit toward the J.D.; a maximum of 6 credits may be applied. The following joint degrees may be earned: J.D./M.A. (Juris Doctor/Master of Arts in international affairs or), J.D./M.B.A. (Juris Doctor/Master of Business Administration), J.D./M.P.A. (Juris Doctor/Master of Public Administration), J.D./M.P.H. (Juris Doctor/Master of Public Health), and J.D./M.P.P. (Juris Doctor/Master of Public Policy).

Phone: 202-739-0648
E-mail: *jd@main.n/c.gwu.edu*
Web: *www.law.gwu.edu*

Contact

Office of Law Admissions, 202-739-0648 for general inquiries; Law Financial Aid Office, 202-739-0641 for financial aid information.

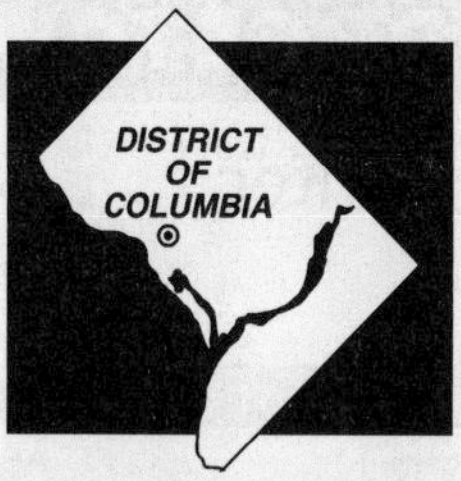

Required

To earn the J.D., candidates must complete 84 total credits, of which 34 are for required courses. They must maintain a minimum GPA of 1.67 in the required courses. The following first-year courses are required of all students: Contracts I and II, Criminal Law, Torts, Civil Procedure I and II, Property, Constitutional Law I, Legal Researching and Writing, and Introduction to Advocacy. Required upper-level courses consist of Professional Responsibility and Ethics. All clinics are optional. The required orientation program for first-year students is a 3-day program that includes registration.

Electives

The Law School offers concentrations in corporate law, criminal law, environmental law, family law, international law, labor law, litigation, securities law, tax law, torts and insurance, government contracts, intellectual property, and constitutional law. In addition, clinics and internships are open to all students; the amount of credit awarded depends on each student's time commitment. Seminars are available to students who have completed all prerequisites, and generally are worth 2 credits. Research programs are open to students through legal writing programs. Credit hours vary according to the paper produced. Field work is offered to students through clinical programs. Credits vary according to each student's time commitment. Through the Enrichment Program, speakers are brought to the law school for lectures and informal seminars that are open to all students. A study-abroad program in international human rights is offered with Oxford University. Tutors can be arranged if needed. Minority programs are sponsored by groups such as the Black Law Students Association, Hispanic Law Students Association, Movimiento Legal Latino, and Asian/Pacific American Law Student Association. Special interest groups include the Law Association for Women, Christian Law Society, Law Students for the Arts, International Law Society, and politically-oriented groups. The most widely taken electives are Federal Income Taxation, Evidence, and Corporations.

Graduation Requirements

In order to graduate, candidates must have a GPA of 1.67, and have completed the upper-division writing requirement and the required curriculum.

Organizations

Students edit the *George Washington Law Review, Journal of International Law and Economics, Environmental Lawyer*, and the newspaper, *Nota Bene*. The *American Intellectual Property Law Association Quarterly Journal*, a publication of the AIPLA, is housed at the law school. The Moot Court Board sponsors the Van Vleck Appellate Moot Court competition, the Jessup Cup competition in international law, and the Giles S. Rich competition in patent law. Teams participate in other moot court competitions around the country. Student organizations include the Student Bar Association, Legal Support Group, Black Law Students Association, and Environmental Law Society. Local chapters of national associations include Phi Alpha Delta, Phi Delta Phi, and the Federalist Society.

Library

The law library contains 563,509 hardcopy volumes and 1,223,445 microform volume equivalents, and subscribes to 5675 serial publications. Such on-line databases and networks as CALI, CIS Universe, DIALOG, Legal-Trac, LEXIS, LOIS, Mathew Bender, NEXIS, OCLC First Search, RLIN, WESTLAW, and Wilsonline Indexes are available to law students for research. Special library collections include a government documents collection and an extensive treatise library; particularly strong collections in environmental, intellectual property, international, and government procurement law. Recently, the library built a copy center and expanded computer laboratories. The ratio of library volumes to faculty is 8410 to 1 and to students is 378 to 1. The ratio of seats in the library to students is 1 to 7.

Placement	
J.D.s awarded:	468
Services available through: a separate law school placement center	
Services: n/av	
Special features: on-line job listings and evening student counselor	
Full-time job interviews:	433 employers
Summer job interviews:	433 employers
Placement by graduation:	92% of class
Placement within 9 months:	97% of class
Average starting salary:	$86,880
Areas of placement:	
Private practice	57%
Judicial clerkships	11%
Government	10%
Business/industry	5%
Public interest	4%

Faculty

The law school has 67 full-time and 211 part-time faculty members, of whom 79 are women. According to AAUP standards for Category I institutions, faculty salaries are well above average. The ratio of full-time students to full-time faculty in an average class is 15 to 1; in a clinic, 8 to 1. The law school has a regular program of bringing visiting professors and other distinguished lecturers and visitors to campus. There is a chapter of the Order of the Coif.

Students

About 47% of the student body are women; 32%, minorities; 13%, African American; 10%, Asian American; and 9%, Hispanic. The majority of students come from the South (32%). The average age of entering students is 24; age range is 19 to 48. About 34% of students enter directly from undergraduate school, 33% have a graduate degree, and 66% have worked full-time prior to entering law school. About 1% drop out after the first year for academic or personal reasons; 99% remain to receive a law degree.

GEORGETOWN UNIVERSITY

Law Center

600 New Jersey Avenue, N.W.
Washington, DC 20001

Application Filing		Accreditation
Fall: February 1		ABA, AALS
Spring: n/app		**Degrees Granted**
Fee: $65		J.D., LL.M., S.J.D.

Enrollment 2001–2002			First-Year Class	
Men:	982	48%	Applied:	9557
Women:	1047	52%	Accepted:	2299
Minorities:	528	26%	Enrolled:	656
Out-of-State:	2029	100%		

2001–02 Class Profile

LSAT Percentile: 96%
LSAT Median Score: 167
Percentage passing bar on first try: n/av

Tuition and Fees:

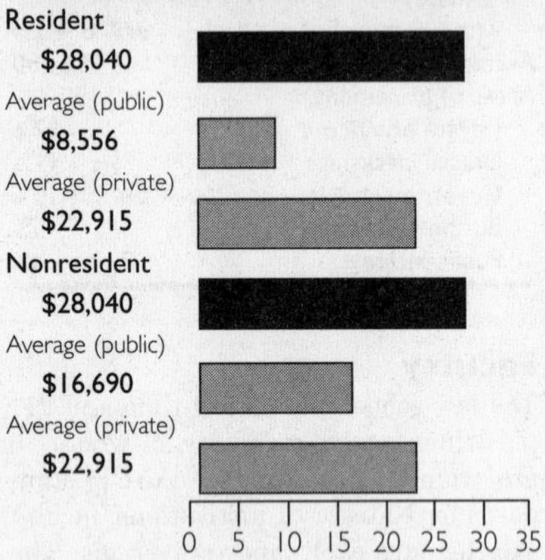

Percentage receiving financial aid: 84%

ADMISSIONS

In the fall 2001 first-year class, 9557 applied, 2299 were accepted, and 656 enrolled. Fifty transfers enrolled. The median LSAT percentile of the most recent first-year class was 96; the median GPA was 3.64 on a scale of 4.0. The lowest LSAT percentile accepted was 37; the highest was 99.

Requirements

Applicants must have a bachelor's degree and take the LSAT. The most important admission factors include academic achievement, LSAT results, and life experience. No specific undergraduate courses or interviews are required.

Procedure

The application deadline for fall entry is February 1. Applicants should submit an application, LSAT results, a nonrefundable application fee of $65, and 1 letter of recommendation; transcripts must be received through the LSDAS. Notification of the admissions decision is within 6 to 14 weeks. The latest acceptable LSAT test date for fall entry is February.

Special

The law school recruits minority and disadvantaged students by encouraging qualified minority and disadvantaged students to apply. Requirements are not different for out-of-state students. Transfer students must have one year of credit and have attended an ABA-approved law school.

Costs

Tuition and fees for the 2001-2002 academic year are $28,040 for all full-time students. Tuition for part-time students is $22,000 per year. On-campus room and board costs about $15,770 annually; books and supplies run $690.

Financial Aid

About 84% of current law students receive some form of aid. The average annual amount of aid from all sources combined, including scholarships, loans, and work contracts, is $31,105; maximum, $44,500. Awards are based on need. Required financial statements are CSS Profile, FAFSA, and Need Access Diskette. The aid application deadline is March 1. First-year students are notified after acceptance and completion of financial aid requirements. Awards are given on a rolling basis.

About the Law School

Georgetown University Law Center was established in 1870 and is a private institution. The 1-acre campus is in an urban area in Washington, D.C. The primary mission of the law school is to prepare graduates to excel in legal careers ranging from private practice to teaching to public service. Students have access to federal, state, county, city, and local agencies, courts, correctional facilities, law firms, and legal aid organizations in the Washington area. Other resources include the U.S. Supreme Court, federal courts, U.S. Congress, and major federal departments and agencies, many of which are within walking distance. Facilities of special interest to law students are the Law Center's 3-building campus, which includes McDonough Hall, Williams Library, and the Gewirz Student Center, with fitness, child care, and student health facilities. Housing is available in the Gewirz Student Center. Law students are also supported through a variety of other housing programs. About 99% of the facilities are accessible to the physically disabled.

Calendar

The law school operates on a traditional semester basis. Courses for full-time students are offered both day and evening and must be completed within 5 years. For part-time students, courses are offered in the evening only and must be completed within 6 years. New full- and part-time students are admitted in the fall. There is an 8-week summer session with transferable summer courses.

Programs

In addition to the J.D., the law school offers the LL.M., S.J.D., and LL.M. concentrations in international legal studies, taxation, securities and financial regulation, as well as individual study. Students may take relevant courses in other programs and apply credit toward the J.D.; a maximum of 6 credits may be applied. The following joint degrees may be earned: J.D./Govt. (Juris Doctor/Ph.D. in government), J.D./M.B.A. (Juris Doctor/Master of Business Administration), J.D./M.P.P. (Juris Doctor/Master in Public Policy), J.D./M.S.F.S. (Juris Doctor/Master of Foreign Service), J.D./Phil. (Juris Doctor/Master in Arts or Ph.D. in philosophy), and J.D/.M.P.H. (Juris Doctor/Master in Public Health).

Required

To earn the J.D., candidates must complete 83 total credits, of which 31 are for required courses. Some required first-year courses are: Legal Process and Society; Civil Procedure; Constitutional Law I; Contracts; Criminal Justice; and Legal Research and Writing. Required upper-level courses consist of Professional Responsibility and a legal writing seminar. The optional orientation program is 4 days and includes a review of academic services and student activities, and an introduction to first-year course work.

Electives

The Law Center offers concentrations in corporate law, criminal law, entertainment law, environmental law, family law, international law, juvenile law, labor law, litigation, maritime law, media law, securities law, sports law, tax law, torts and insurance, commercial law, constitutional law and government, administrative law and government regulation, jurisprudence, public interest law, alternative dispute resolution, negotiations, trial practice, health law, and intellectual property law. In addition, the Law

Phone: 202-662-9010
Fax: 202-662-9439
E-mail: *admis@law.georgetown.edu*
Web: *www.law.georgetown.edu*

Contact

Andrew Cornblatt, Assistant Dean of Admissions, 202-662-9010 for general inquiries; Ruth Lammert-Reeves, Assistant Dean for Financial Aid, 202-662-9210 for financial aid information.

Center offers 15 in-house clinical courses. Credits earned range from 3 to 12 per semester and clinics are either 1 or 2 semesters. Students represent real clients in practice areas such as appellate advocacy, criminal defense, civil rights, and environmental justice. More than 150 seminars are offered on such topics as environmental law, intellectual property law, international law, constitutional law and government, and corporate law and securities. Many students pursue internships with government agencies, judges, and other organizations. Research projects may be undertaken with faculty guidance. Some courses involve field work, such as the Public School Reform seminar, in which students work with the D.C. school board. Several lecture series held each year bring prominent legal scholars, judges, lawyers, and business executives to the Law Center. There is a 4-week summer study-abroad program in Florence, Italy for up to 6 credits and a 3-week study abroad course in London for up to 4 credits. Both programs are open to students and graduates of accredited law and European law schools. Tutorials are open to all students but are primarily designed for first-year students. These programs provide academic support, but are not remedial. A diversity clerkship program is offered and other educational programs are sponsored by the Career Services Office and minority student groups. The Law Center participates in minority recruiting programs sponsored by outside groups. The Law Center's Loan Repayment Assistance Program (LRAP), one of the strongest in the country, assists graduates in public interest and government jobs with their law school loans. In addition, the Public Interest Law Scholars Program (PILS) provides scholarships and other assistance to 8 members of each entering class, and the student-run Equal Justice Foundation provides stipends to students accepting unpaid summer internships with nonprofit or government organizations. The most widely taken electives are Constitutional Law, Corporations, and Evidence.

Graduation Requirements

In order to graduate, candidates must have a GPA of 2.0, have completed the upper-division writing requirement, and the Professional Responsibility course.

Organizations

Student-edited publications include the *Georgetown Law Journal, American Criminal Law Review, Georgetown Journal of Gender and the Law, Georgetown Immigration Law Journal,* and the newspaper *Law Weekly*. Georgetown competes in 12 moot court competitions, including Jessup International, Cardozo Entertainment, and Wechsler First Amendment competitions. The Law Center sponsors the Beaudry Cup Moot Court (first-year students), Leahy Prize Moot Court (upper-class students), and the William W. Greenhalgh Trial Advocacy competitions (all students). There are 60 student organizations, including the Association of Trial Lawyers of America, Federalist Society, and Phi Alpha Delta. There are local chapters of Alternative Dispute Resolution Society, Equal Justice Foundation, and the Society of Law, Health, and Bioethics.

Library

The law library contains 1,028,658 hardcopy volumes and 2,331,239 microform volume equivalents, and subscribes to 11,755 serial publications. Such on-line databases and networks as CALI, CIS Universe, DIALOG, LEXIS, Mathew Bender, OCLC First Search, and WESTLAW are available. Special library collections include rare books and international law and tax collections. Recently, the library wired carrels for network access by laptops. Numerous database subscriptions are available for access from home. The ratio of library volumes to faculty is 10,085 to 1 and to students, 507 to 1.

Faculty

The law school has 102 full-time and 100 part-time faculty members, of whom 55 are women. According to AAUP standards for Category I institutions, faculty salaries are well above average. About 17% of full-time faculty have a graduate law degree in addition to the J.D.; about 10% of part-time faculty have one. The ratio of full-time students to full-time faculty in an average class is 15 to 1; in a clinic, 7 to 1. The law school has a regular program of bringing visiting professors and other distinguished lecturers and visitors to campus. There is a chapter of the Order of the Coif.

Placement

J.D.s awarded: 629

Services available through: a separate law school placement center, on-line services, and the Office of Public Interest and Community Service

Services: public interest organizations, small firm job fairs, regional job fairs in cities nationwide, and a large international internship program.

Special features: multiple programs for students interested in international as well as traditional private practice settings; extensive print and database career services library. In addition, the Law Center's Office of Public Interest and Community Service (OPICS) provides specialty career advising for legal careers in public interest or government. OPICS conducts individual and group counseling, skills workshops, job fairs, and other programs.

Full-time job interviews:	200 employers
Summer job interviews:	600 employers
Placement by graduation:	94% of class
Placement within 9 months:	98% of class
Average starting salary:	$43,000 to $125,000
Areas of placement:	
Private practice 2-10 attorneys	2%
Private practice 11-25 attorneys	2%
Private practice 26-50 attorneys	3%
Private practice 51-100 attorneys	4%
Private practice 101+ attorneys	56%
Government	12%
Judicial clerkships	11%
Business/industry	5%
Public interest	3%
Academic	1%

Students

About 52% of the student body are women; 26%, minorities; 11%, African American; 10%, Asian American; 5%, Hispanic; 1%, Native American; and 3%, foreign nationals. The average age of entering students is 24; age range is 20 to 54. About 44% of students enter directly from undergraduate school, 12% have a graduate degree, and 52% have worked full-time prior to entering law school. About 1% drop out after the first year for academic or personal reasons; 97% remain to receive a law degree.

GEORGIA STATE UNIVERSITY

College of Law

P.O. Box 4037
Atlanta, GA 30302-4037

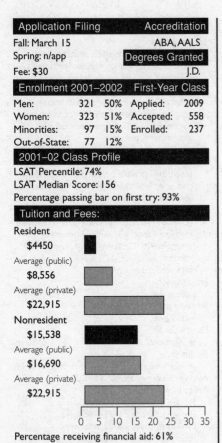

Application Filing		Accreditation
Fall: March 15		ABA, AALS
Spring: n/app		**Degrees Granted**
Fee: $30		J.D.

Enrollment 2001–2002			First-Year Class	
Men:	321	50%	Applied:	2009
Women:	323	51%	Accepted:	558
Minorities:	97	15%	Enrolled:	237
Out-of-State:	77	12%		

2001–02 Class Profile

LSAT Percentile: 74%
LSAT Median Score: 156
Percentage passing bar on first try: 93%

Tuition and Fees:

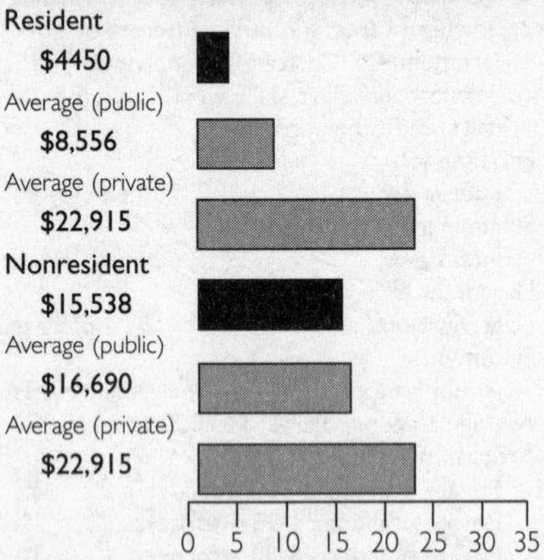

Percentage receiving financial aid: 61%

ADMISSIONS

In the fall 2001 first-year class, 2009 applied, 558 were accepted, and 237 enrolled. Eight transfers enrolled. The median LSAT percentile of the most recent first-year class was 74; the median GPA was 3.2 on a scale of 4.0. The lowest LSAT percentile accepted was 33; the highest was 99.

Requirements

Applicants must have a bachelor's degree and take the LSAT. The most important admission factors include academic achievement, LSAT results, and GPA. No specific undergraduate courses are required. Candidates are not interviewed.

Procedure

The application deadline for fall entry is March 15. Applicants should submit an application form, LSAT results, transcripts, LSDAS report, TOEFL for applicants whose native language is not English, a nonrefundable application fee of $30, 2 letters of recommendation, and a personal statement in support of the applicant's admission. This gives the applicant an opportunity to add information about abilities and interests. Notification of the admissions decision begins in January. The latest acceptable LSAT test date for fall entry is February. The law school uses the LSDAS.

Special

The law school recruits minority and disadvantaged students by means of visiting other colleges and universities during graduate and professional program days, speaking to prelaw clubs and classes, and recruiting at schools with large minority student populations. The law school also conducts high school visits. Requirements are not different for out-of-state students. Transfer students must have one year of credit, have attended an ABA-approved law school, and have a letter from the dean of the student's previous law school stating that the student is in good standing and is eligible to return to the school, and stating the student's class ranking.

Costs

Tuition and fees for the 2001-2002 academic year are $4450 for full-time in-state students and $15,538 for out-of-state students. Books and supplies run about $1146 annually.

Financial Aid

About 61% of current law students receive some form of aid. The average annual amount of aid from all sources combined, including scholarships, loans, and work contracts, is $2225; maximum, $3500. Awards are based on need and merit. There are also loans that are need- and non-need-based. The required financial statement is the FAFSA. Special funds for minority or disadvantaged students consist of scholarships. First-year students are notified about their financial aid application at time of acceptance.

About the Law School

Georgia State University College of Law was established in 1982 and is a public institution. The 25-acre campus is in an urban area in the city of Atlanta. The primary mission of the law school is to provide both part- and full-time programs that are designed for students wishing to gain a knowledge of the law, of legal institutions, and of legal processes. The college is equally committed to part- and full-time legal studies. Students have access to federal, state, county, city, and local agencies, courts, correctional facilities, law firms, and legal aid organizations in the Atlanta area. A variety of institutions and law-related agencies are located in the metropolitan area. Facilities of special interest to law students include the Richard B. Russell Federal Building; Federal Reserve Bank; state capitol building; state legislature; federal, state and local court systems; and offices of the U.S. Attorney, state Attorney General, and county and city District Attorneys. Housing for students is on a first-come, first-served basis in the Olympic Village, which accommodates 2000 students in modern apartments. All law school facilities are accessible to the physically disabled.

Calendar

The law school operates on a traditional semester basis. Courses for full- and part-time students are offered both day and evening and must be completed within 6 years. New full- and part-time students are admitted in the fall. There is a 7-week summer session. Transferable summer courses are offered.

Programs

Students may take relevant courses in other programs and apply credit toward the J.D.; a maximum of 14 semester hours credits may be applied. The following joint degrees may be earned: J.D./M.A. (Juris Doctor/Master of Arts in philosophy), J.D./M.B.A. (Juris Doctor/Master of Business Administration), and J.D./M.P.A. (Juris Doctor/Master of Public Administration).

Required

To earn the J.D., candidates must complete 90 total credits, of which 43 are for required courses. They must maintain a minimum grade average of 73 in the required courses. The following first-year courses are required of all students: Civil Procedure I and II, Property I and II, Contracts I and II, Legal Method, Research Writing and Advocacy I and II,

Phone: 404-651-2048
Fax: (404) 651-2048
E-mail: *cjjackson@gsu.edu*
Web: *www.law.gsu.edu*

Contact

Cheryl Jester Jackson, Director of Admissions, 404-651-2048 for general inquiries; Dave Bledsoe, Interim Director of Financial Aid, 404-651-2227 for financial aid information.

Legal Bibliography, Criminal Law, and Torts I and II. Required upper-level courses consist of Constitutional Law, Evidence, Litigation, and Professional Responsibility. The required orientation program for first-year students occurs in the first week of the fall semester and is designed to introduce some of the first-year required courses, college personnel, and facilities, and to familiarize students with procedures.

Electives

Students must take 47 hours credits in their area of concentration. The College of Law offers concentrations in corporate law, criminal law, environmental law, family law, international law, labor law, litigation, tax law, and torts and insurance. In addition, second- and third-year students may earn 3 or 6 semester hours by enrolling in the Tax Clinic, which permits students to assist individual clients in preparing their cases for presentation before the Small Claims Division of the U.S. Tax Court and the administrative appeals offices of the IRS. Seminars are offered to students who have completed the prerequisites and are normally worth 2 semester hours. Internships include working for local district attorneys, solicitors, and defenders; clerking for county, state, and federal judges; and placement in a variety of other governmental or public interest organizations. Independent research for 1 to 2 semester hours credit may be selected by third-year students upon approval by a faculty adviser and the administration. Special lecture series include the Henry J. Miller Distinguised Lecture Series. The college does not sponsor a regular study-abroad program, but some elective summer courses are offered that include trips to Europe. The administration offers an academic enrichment program for students who need or desire additional help in required courses. Minority and special interest programs are usually sponsored by student organizations and/or faculty members. The most widely taken electives are Basic Tax; Wills, Trusts, and Estates; and Criminal Procedure.

Graduation Requirements

In order to graduate, candidates must have a grade average of 73 and have completed the upper-division writing requirement.

Organizations

The primary law review is the *Georgia State University Law Review*. Students edit *The Docket, The Black Letter Law* and *The Federalist*. The Moot Court Society competes 7 or 8 times a year. Other competitions include the National Moot Court Competition, sponsored by the Association of the Bar of New York City and the National Appellate Advocacy Competition, sponsored by the ABA. Student organizations include the Christian Legal Society, Lesbian and Gay Law Student Association, and Federalist Society. Local chapters of national associations include the Association of Women Law Students, Black Law Students Association, and Environmental Law Society. Other groups include Delta Theta Phi, Phi Alpha Delta, and Phi Delta Phi law fraternities.

Library

The law library contains 145,617 hard-copy volumes and 623,675 microform volume equivalents, and subscribes to 3504 serial publications. Such on-line databases and networks as CALI, DIALOG, Legal-Trac, LEXIS, LOIS, NEXIS, WESTLAW, and SMARTCILP, Ingenta Indexmaster, HEIN, Tax Research Net., Galileo, and Business and Finance Net are available to law students for research. Special library collections include a U.S. depository and collections in tax, labor, health law, and international law. Recently, the library upgraded computer systems in the computer laboratory and installed GIL by Endeavor, an automation system; upgraded electric compact shelving; installed wired carrels; and obtained remote storage. The ratio of library volumes to faculty is 3467 to 1 and to students, 226 to 1. The ratio of seats in the library to students is 1 to 2.

Faculty

The law school has 42 full-time and 28 part-time faculty members, of whom 26 are women. According to AAUP standards for Category I institutions, faculty salaries are average. About 17% of full-time faculty have a graduate law degree in addition to the J.D.; about 11% of part-time faculty have one. The ratio of full-time students to full-time faculty in an average class is 16 to 1. The law school has a regular program of bringing visiting professors and other distinguished lecturers and visitors to campus.

Placement

J.D.s awarded:	163

Services available through: a separate law school placement center

Services: programming and counseling on career options for lawyers, and participating in national and regional job fairs

Special features: state-of-the-art Internet-based job listings service for students and alumni. Personalized, one-on-one job search planning sessions for first-year, second-year, and third-year students in addition to alumni transitioning into other practice areas and legal related or alternative careers.

Full-time job interviews:	n/av
Summer job interviews:	n/av
Placement by graduation:	n/av
Placement within 9 months:	95% of class
Average starting salary:	$29,000 to $170,000
Areas of placement:	
Private practice 2-10 attorneys	25%
Private practice 11-25 attorneys	5%
Private practice 26-50 attorneys	3%
Private practice 51-100 attorneys	6%
Private practice 100+ attorneys	21%
Business/industry	21%
Government	9%
Judicial clerkships	6%
Academic	2%
Public interest	1%
Military	1%

Students

About 51% of the student body are women; 15%, minorities; 11%, African American; 3%, Asian American; 1%, Hispanic; and 7%, other. Students may select multi-racial as an ethnic classification. The majority of students come from Georgia (88%). The average age of entering students is 29; age range is 21 to 61. About 21% of students enter directly from undergraduate school and 19% have a graduate degree. About 11% drop out after the first year for academic or personal reasons; 89% remain to receive a law degree.

GOLDEN GATE UNIVERSITY

School of Law

536 Mission Street
San Francisco, CA 94105-2968

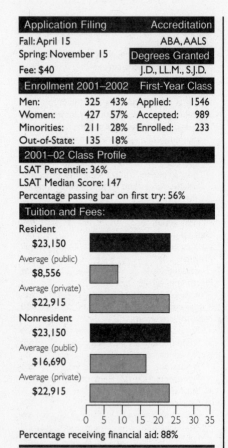

Application Filing	Accreditation
Fall: April 15	ABA, AALS
Spring: November 15	**Degrees Granted**
Fee: $40	J.D., LL.M., S.J.D.

Enrollment 2001–2002			First-Year Class	
Men:	325	43%	Applied:	1546
Women:	427	57%	Accepted:	989
Minorities:	211	28%	Enrolled:	233
Out-of-State:	135	18%		

2001–02 Class Profile

LSAT Percentile: 36%
LSAT Median Score: 147
Percentage passing bar on first try: 56%

Tuition and Fees:

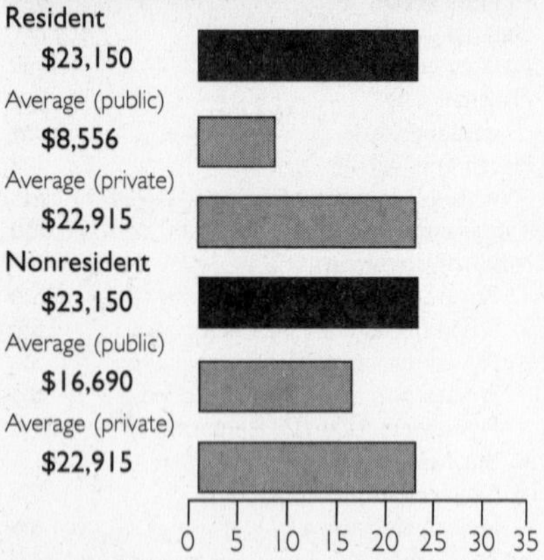

Percentage receiving financial aid: 88%

ADMISSIONS

In the fall 2001 first-year class, 1546 applied, 989 were accepted, and 233 enrolled. Ten transfers enrolled. The median LSAT percentile of the most recent first-year class was 36; the median GPA was 3.1 on a scale of 4.0.

Requirements

Applicants must have a bachelor's degree and take the LSAT. The most important admission factors include LSAT results, GPA, and life experience. No specific undergraduate courses are required. Candidates are not interviewed.

Procedure

The application deadline for fall entry is April 15. Applicants should submit an application form, LSAT results, transcripts, a nonrefundable application fee of $40, 1 letter of recommendation, and a personal statement. Notification of the admissions decision is 4 to 5 weeks after material is submitted. The latest acceptable LSAT test date for fall entry is February. The law school uses the LSDAS.

Special

The law school recruits minority and disadvantaged students by targeting recruiting to underrepresented communities, supporting the CLEO program, and the law school's minority scholarship program. Requirements are not different for out-of-state students. Transfer students must have one year of credit, have attended an ABA-approved law school, and are subject to the availability of seats, the personal statement, and a competitive review of the students' academic record from the first year of law school.

Costs

Tuition and fees for the 2001-2002 academic year are $23,150 for all full-time students. Tuition for part-time students is $16,040 per year. Books and supplies run about $870 annually.

Financial Aid

About 88% of current law students receive some form of aid. The average annual amount of aid from all sources combined, including scholarships, loans, and work contracts, is $32,000; maximum, $45,000. Awards are based on need and merit. Required financial statement is the FAFSA. The aid application deadline for fall entry is March 1. Special funds for minority or disadvantaged students include a scholarship fund reserved for minority students or those from disadvantaged backgrounds. First-year students are notified about their financial aid application at time of acceptance.

About the Law School

Golden Gate University School of Law was established in 1901 and is a private institution. The campus is in an urban area in the financial district in downtown San Francisco. The primary mission of the law school is to educate lawyers in a humanistic yet rigorous environment through a balance of traditional legal theory courses and clinical experiences. Students have access to federal, state, county, city, and local agencies, courts, correctional facilities, law firms, and legal aid organizations in the San Francisco area. Facilities of special interest to law students include the law school, which occupies an architecturally acclaimed building that includes classrooms, a moot court room, student computer laboratories, and a law library. Housing for students is not available on campus, but the housing office helps students find accommodations off campus. All law school facilities are accessible to the physically disabled.

Calendar

The law school operates on a traditional semester basis. Courses for full-time students are offered days only and must be completed within 3-years. For part-time students, courses are offered both day and evening and must be completed within 4-years. New full- and part-time students are admitted in the fall and spring. There is an 8-week summer session. Transferable summer courses are offered.

Programs

In addition to the J.D., the law school offers the LL.M. and S.J.D. Students may take relevant courses in other programs and apply credit toward the J.D.The following joint degrees may be earned: J.D./M.B.A. (Juris Doctor/Master of Business Administration in law) and J.D./Ph.D. (J.D./Ph.D. in Clinical Psychology with the Pacific Graduate School of Psychology).

Required

To earn the J.D., candidates must complete 88 total credits, of which 54 are for required courses. They must maintain a minimum GPA of 2.05 in the required courses. The following first-year courses are required of all students: Civil Procedure I and II, Contracts, Property, Torts,

Phone: 415-442-6630
800-GGU-4YOU

Contact

Admissions Office, 415-442-6630 for general inquiries; Tracy Simmons, Assistant Dean of Admissions and Financial Aid, 415-442-6635 for financial aid information.

Criminal Law, Writing and Research, and Constitutional Law I. Required upper-level courses consist of Appellate Advocacy, Constitutional Law II, Corporations, Criminal Procedure I, Evidence, Solving Legal Problems, Professional Responsibility, and Wills and Trusts. Students are encouraged to enroll in our many clinics. The required orientation program for first-year students is a 4-day program held before class begins. In addition, enrolled and prospective students may participate in a 3-week Introduction to Law School summer program.

Electives

The School of Law offers concentrations in corporate law, criminal law, environmental law, international law, labor law, litigation, intellectual property law, real estate, and public interest law. In addition, the school offers 8 clinics, worth from 2 to 5 credits. Clinics include Constitutional Law, Criminal Litigation, Environmental Law and Justice, Women's Employment Rights, Civil Practice, and Public Interest/Government. Seminars are worth 2 credits and prerequisites vary. Topics include Asian Pacific Trade, Bankruptcy Litigation, and Disability Rights. Full- and part-time internships with law firms, government agencies, and judges are offered. There is also an Honors Lawyering Program through which students spend 2 semesters working full-time in legal settings. Students may pursue independent research under the direction of faculty members. Summer study abroad is possible in Bangkok, Thailand. An Academic Assistance Program develops skills in legal analysis and exam writing. Through the Public Interest/Government Clinic, students may work in public interest law firms in preparation to become public interest lawyers. A major part of professional skills training are the Litigation and Advocacy courses, which deal with civil and criminal law, pretrial litigation, mock trial, and other areas. The most widely taken electives are Tax, Remedies, and Intellectual Property.

Graduation Requirements

In order to graduate, candidates must have a GPA of 2.0 and have completed the upper-division writing requirement. Students take writing courses in each of their 3 years in law school.

Organizations

Students edit the *Golden Gate University Law Review*, and the *Annual Survey of International and Comparative Law*. Teams attend various national and international contests, including the Jessup Moot Court Competition. Other competitions attended are the National Mock Trial Competition, Association of Trial Lawyers of America Competition, and the ABA's Criminal Justice Trial Competition, among others. Law student organizations include LEGALS (Lesbian, Gay, Bisexual, and Transgender), Black Law Students Association, and Golden Gate Association of International Lawyers. Local chapters of national associations include the Student Bar Association, Intellectual Property Law Association, and Latino Law Students Association. Campus clubs include the International Law Association, Environmental Law Society, and Association of Trial Lawyers of America.

Library

The law library contains 117,371 hardcopy volumes and 126,112 microform volume equivalents, and subscribes to 3424 serial publications. Such on-line databases and networks as CALI, DIALOG, Dow-Jones, Infotrac, Legal-Trac, LEXIS, LOIS, Mathew Bender, NEXIS, and WESTLAW are available to law students for research. Special library collections include a depository for both California and federal documents and the archives of the National Educational Foundation. Its collections emphasize taxation, real estate, land use, and individual rights. Recently, the library installed furniture and computers. The ratio of library volumes to faculty is 3010 to 1 and to students is 156 to 1. The ratio of seats in the library to students is 1 to 2.

Faculty

The law school has 39 full-time and 121 part-time faculty members, of whom 66 are women. About 11% of full-time faculty have a graduate law degree in addition to the J.D.; about 8% of part-time faculty have one. The ratio of full-time students to full-time faculty in an average class is 14 to 1; in a clinic, 5 to 1. The law school has a regular program of bringing visiting professors and other distinguished lecturers and visitors to campus.

Placement

J.D.s awarded:	158
Services available through: a separate law school placement center	
Services: encourages private firms and public agencies to list job opportunities, solicits on-campus interviews.	
Special features: computer-assisted job search through WESTLAW and eAttorney.	
Full-time job interviews:	21 employers
Summer job interviews:	n/av
Placement by graduation:	n/av
Placement within 9 months:	84% of class
Average starting salary:	$52,000
Areas of placement:	
Private practice 2-10 attorneys	25%
Private practice 11-25 attorneys	11%
Private practice 26-50 attorneys	1%
Private practice 51-100 attorneys	16%
Government	16%
Business/industry	15%
Public interest	6%
Solo practice or unknown	5%
Judicial clerkships	3%
Academic	2%

Students

About 57% of the student body are women; 28%, minorities; 7%, African American; 14%, Asian American; 6%, Hispanic; and 1%, Native American. The majority of students come from California (82%). The average age of entering students is 26; age range is 20 to 59. About 57% of students enter directly from undergraduate school, 7% have a graduate degree, and 43% have worked full-time prior to entering law school. About 17% drop out after the first year for academic or personal reasons; 83% remain to receive a law degree.

GONZAGA UNIVERSITY

School of Law

Box 3528
Spokane, WA 99220-3528

Application Filing	Accreditation
Fall: April 1	ABA, AALS
Spring: n/app	**Degrees Granted**
Fee: $40	J.D.

Enrollment 2001–2002			First-Year Class	
Men:	262	52%	Applied:	943
Women:	239	48%	Accepted:	568
Minorities:	75	15%	Enrolled:	209
Out-of-State:	235	47%		

2001–02 Class Profile

LSAT Percentile: 52%
LSAT Median Score: 152
Percentage passing bar on first try: 67%

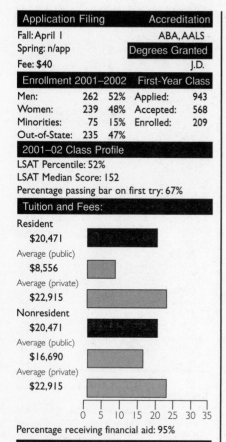

Tuition and Fees:

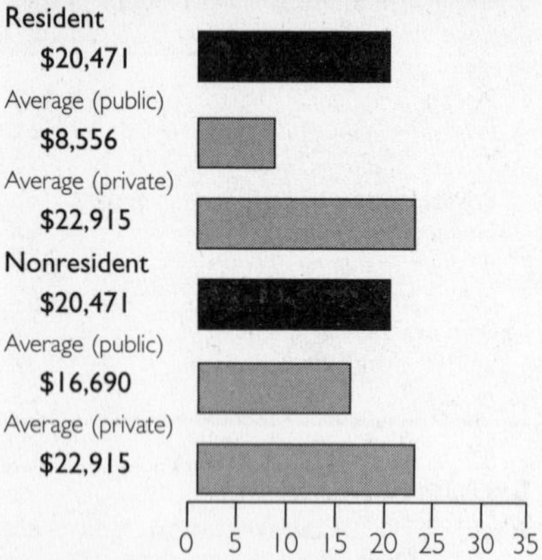

Percentage receiving financial aid: 95%

ADMISSIONS

In the fall 2001 first-year class, 943 applied, 568 were accepted, and 209 enrolled. Two transfers enrolled. The median LSAT percentile of the most recent first-year class was 52; the median GPA was 3.13 on a scale of 4.0. The lowest LSAT percentile accepted was 15; the highest was 98.

Requirements

Applicants must have a bachelor's degree and take the LSAT. The most important admission factors include LSAT results, GPA, and letter of recommendation. No specific undergraduate courses are required. Candidates are not interviewed.

Procedure

The application deadline for fall entry is April 1. Applicants should submit an application form, TOEFL for international applicants, and a nonrefundable application fee of $40. Recommendations are not required, but if submitted, there should be no more than 3. A resume and LSDAS report are required. Notification of the admissions decision is after January 1, based on the date received. The latest acceptable LSAT test date for fall entry is February. The law school uses the LSDAS.

Special

The law school recruits minority and disadvantaged students by means of CRS mailings, alumni referrals, scholarships, prelaw advisers, campus visits, and law school forums. Requirements are not different for out-of-state students. Transfer students must have one year of credit, have a minimum GPA of 2.4, and have attended an ABA-approved law school. Transfer students are accepted on a space-available basis and must be in good standing and eligible to return to their previous law school.

Costs

Tuition and fees for the 2001-2002 academic year are $20,471 for all full-time students. On-campus room and board costs about $7375 annually; books and supplies run $900.

Financial Aid

About 95% of current law students receive some form of aid. The average annual amount of aid from all sources combined, including scholarships, loans, and work contracts, is $33,090 (maximum). Awards are based on need and merit. Required financial statement is the FAFSA. The aid application deadline for fall entry is February 1. Special funds for minority or disadvantaged students consist of diversity scholarships. First-year students are notified about their financial aid application within one month of acceptance if FAFSA is complete.

About the Law School

Gonzaga University School of Law was established in 1912 and is a private institution. The 94-acre campus is in an urban area 1½ miles from downtown Spokane. The primary mission of the law school is to preserve and develop a humanistic, Catholic, and Jesuit legal education. Students have access to federal, state, county, city, and local agencies, courts, correctional facilities, law firms, and legal aid organizations in the Spokane area. Facilities of special interest to law students include the law library, the Martin Athletic Center, the Foley Center, and a computer laboratory. Apartments are available, often within a 10-block radius of the law school. About 90% of the law school facilities are accessible to the physically disabled.

Calendar

The law school operates on a traditional semester basis. Courses for full-time and part-time students are offered days only and must be completed within 5 years. New full- and part-time students are admitted in the fall. There are 2 5-week summer sessions. Transferable summer courses are offered.

Programs

The following joint degrees may be earned: J.D./M.Acc. (Juris Doctor/Master of Accounting) and J.D./M.B.A. (Juris Doctor/Master of Business Administration).

Required

To earn the J.D., candidates must complete 90 total credits, of which 59 are for required courses. They must maintain a minimum GPA of 2.2 in the required courses. The following first-year courses are required of all students: Contracts I and II, Legal Research Writing I and II, Civil Procedure I and II, Property I and II, Torts I and II, Criminal Law, and Constitutional Law I. Required upper-level courses consist of Professional Responsibility, Evidence, Constitutional Law II, Administrative Law, Business Associations, Creditors' Rights, writing

Phone: 509-323-5532
800-793-1710
Fax: 509-323-5744
E-mail: *admissions@lawschool.gonzaga.edu*
Web: *www.law.gonzaga.edu*

Contact

Tamara Martinez, Assistant Dean for Admissions, 509-323-5532 or (800) 793-1710 for general inquiries; Joan Henning, Coordinator of Financial Services, 509-323-3859 for financial aid information.

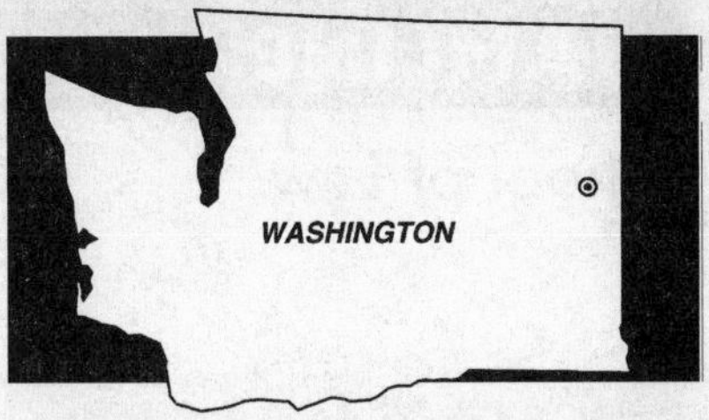

requirement, Legal Writing and Research III and IV, Criminal Procedure, Remedies, Law Office Management workshop, Family Law, Litigation and Dispute Resolution or Trial Advocacy, and a public service requirement. The required orientation program for first-year students consists of 3 days of introduction to the legal system, introduction to the law, and information regarding Gonzaga.

Electives

The School of Law offers concentrations in corporate law, environmental law, and public interest law. In addition, upper-level students, who have completed 60 academic hours, may participate in both in-house and outplacement clinics. Second-year students may take mini-clinics for 2 credits. Various 2-credit seminars are offered, including those on the First Amendment, privacy law, and aviation law. Internships are available when 60 academic hours have been completed. Research programs, worth 1 or 2 credits, must be supervised by a faculty member. Special lecture series include the William O. Douglas, Lewis H. Orland, Paul Luvera, Themis Film Series, Public Issues and the Law Forum, and the Dr. Martin Luther King Jr. Committee Series. Tutorial programs are available at a student's request. The Academic Resource Program provides tutorial assistance to participating first-year students. The Student Bar Association sponsors large-group tutorials for all first-year courses. Minority programs are sponsored by the Multicultural Law Caucus, Hawaii Club, JANALA, and BLSA. Special interest group programs include the Public Interest Law Project, Street Law, Property Law Interest Group, and Criminal Defense Law Caucus. The most widely taken electives are Environmental Law, Tax Law, and International Law.

Graduation Requirements

In order to graduate, candidates must have a GPA of 2.2, have completed the upper-division writing requirement, and have 90 credit hours and 90 weeks in residence.

Organizations

Students edit the *Gonzaga Law Review* and the newspaper *Bill of Particulars*. *Across Borders* is a World Wide Web-based journal specializing in international law, business, political, and socioeconomic issues. The web site is *http://www.law.gonzaga.edu/borders/borders.html*. Moot court competitions include the National Appellate Advocacy, Jessup Cup, and National Moot Court. Teams also take part in the Negotiation, National Trial, and Client Counseling competitions. Law student organizations include the Student Bar Association, Public Interest Law Project, and Environmental Law Caucus. There are local chapters of Phi Alpha Delta, Phi Delta Phi, and Alpha Sigma Nu. Campus clubs and other organizations include the Women's Law Caucus, International Law Society, and Christian Legal Society.

Library

The law library contains 152,933 hardcopy volumes and 109,870 microform volume equivalents, and subscribes to 2605 serial publications. Such on-line databases and networks as CALI, DIALOG, Infotrac, LEXIS, NEXIS, OCLC First Search, WESTLAW, CARL, OGLC, and the Internet are available to law students for research. Special library collections include ABA Archives; American Indian Selected Publications; Canon Law Materials; Federal Legislative Histories; Hein's American Law Institution Publications; Hein's Legal Thesis and Dissertations; Karol Llewellyn Papers; Scrapbooks of the Honorable Richard Guy; and selected Nineteenth Century treatises. Recently, the library was moved to a facility containing 41,843 square feet of space with 442 seats for patrons. The facility is part of the law school building completed early in 2000. The ratio of library volumes to faculty is 4634 to 1 and to students is 305 to 1. The ratio of seats in the library to students is 1 to 1.

Placement	
J.D.s awarded:	148
Services available through: a separate law school placement center	
Services: on-campus interviews, workshops, spring Career Fest, Judicial Clerkship Committee Participation, minority Career Fairs, Public Interest Career Fair	
Special features: counseling on employment and mock videotaped interviews.	
Full-time job interviews:	35 employers
Summer job interviews:	50 employers
Placement by graduation:	48% of class
Placement within 9 months:	92% of class
Average starting salary:	$22,000 to $110,000
Areas of placement:	
Private practice 2-10 attorneys	31%
Private practice 11-25 attorneys	6%
Private practice 26-50 attorneys	6%
Private practice 51-100 attorneys	1%
Government	19%
Business/industry	14%
Firms of other sizes	8%
Judicial clerkships	7%
Public interest	4%
Military	2%
Academic	2%

Faculty

The law school has 33 full-time and 36 part-time faculty members, of whom 21 are women. About 18% of full-time faculty have a graduate law degree in addition to the J.D. The ratio of full-time students to full-time faculty in an average class is 27 to 1; in a clinic, 15 to 1.

Students

About 48% of the student body are women; 15%, minorities; 2%, African American; 6%, Asian American; 5%, Hispanic; and 2%, Native American. Most students come from Washington (53%). The average age of entering students is 27; age range is 21 to 53. About 51% of students enter directly from undergraduate school and 7% have a graduate degree. About 10% drop out after the first year for academic or personal reasons; 90% remain to receive a law degree.

HAMLINE UNIVERSITY

School of Law

1536 Hewitt Avenue
St. Paul, MN 55104-1284

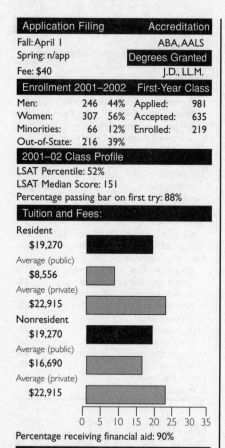

Application Filing		Accreditation
Fall: April 1		ABA, AALS
Spring: n/app		**Degrees Granted**
Fee: $40		J.D., LL.M.

Enrollment 2001–2002			First-Year Class	
Men:	246	44%	Applied:	981
Women:	307	56%	Accepted:	635
Minorities:	66	12%	Enrolled:	219
Out-of-State:	216	39%		

2001–02 Class Profile

LSAT Percentile: 52%
LSAT Median Score: 151
Percentage passing bar on first try: 88%

Tuition and Fees:

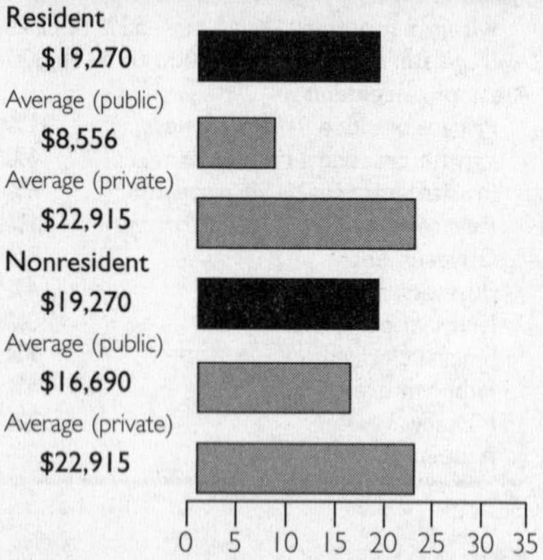

Percentage receiving financial aid: 90%

ADMISSIONS

In the fall 2001 first-year class, 981 applied, 635 were accepted, and 219 enrolled. Three transfers enrolled. The median LSAT percentile of the most recent first-year class was 52; the median GPA was 3.2 on a scale of 4.0. The lowest LSAT percentile accepted was 5; the highest was 99.

Requirements

Applicants must have a bachelor's degree and take the LSAT. No specific undergraduate courses are required. Candidates are not interviewed.

Procedure

The application deadline for fall entry is April 1. Applicants should submit an application form, LSAT results, transcripts, a nonrefundable application fee of $40, and 2 or 3 letters of recommendation, which are strongly recommended but not required. Notification of the admissions decision is 2 to 6 weeks after file is completed. The latest acceptable LSAT test date for fall entry is February. The law school uses the LSDAS.

Special

The law school recruits minority and disadvantaged students through special consideration in the admissions process and by annually hosting an admissions program geared specifically for minority students. The school also participates in CLEO. Requirements are not different for out-of-state students. Transfer students must have one year of credit, have attended an ABA-approved law school, and submit a letter of good standing and a transcript from the previous institution. Preadmissions courses consist of a summer conditional program, Acceptance by Performance (ABP), in which students selected by the Admissions Committee take 2 courses over a 6-week period. If they pass these courses, they are offered admission.

Costs

Tuition and fees for the 2001-2002 academic year are $19,270 for all full-time students. Tuition for part-time students is $13,900 per year. On-campus room and board costs about $8186 annually; books and supplies run $500.

Financial Aid

About 90% of recent law students receive some form of aid. The average recent annual amount of aid from all sources combined, including scholarships, loans, and work contracts, was $20,000; maximum, $28,000. Awards are based on need and merit. Required financial statement is the FAFSA. The aid application deadline for fall entry is rolling. Special funds for minority or disadvantaged students include the equivalent of 8 ½ full-tuition scholarships. First-year students are notified about their financial aid application at time of acceptance.

About the Law School

Hamline University School of Law was established in 1972 and is a private institution. The 50-acre campus is in a suburban area located between St. Paul and Minneapolis. The primary mission of the law school is to provide socially responsible education with extensive offerings in public law and to integrate analysis, lawyering skills, and ethics. Students have access to federal, state, county, city, and local agencies, courts, correctional facilities, law firms, and legal aid organizations in the St. Paul area. The state capital is minutes away from the campus in St. Paul. Facilities of special interest to law students include an expanded Law Center designed for interaction, with a moot court room as a focal point. The library addition provides increased study space. Housing for students is readily available, both on and off campus. All law school facilities are accessible to the physically disabled.

Calendar

The law school operates on a traditional semester basis. Courses for full-time students are offered both day and evening and must be completed within 5 years. For part-time students, courses are offered both day and evening but first-year students attend days only. A weekend part-time option is now available. The degree must be completed within 6 years. New full- and part-time students are admitted in the fall. There is an 8-week summer session. Transferable summer courses are offered.

Programs

In addition to the J.D., the law school offers the LL.M. Students may take relevant courses in other programs and apply credit toward the J.D.; a maximum of 12 credits may be applied. The following joint degrees may be earned: J.D./A.M.B.A. (Juris Doctor/Accounting Master of Business Administration), J.D./M.A.M. (Juris Doctor/Master of Arts in Management), J.D./M.A.P.A. (Juris Doctor/ Master of Arts in Public Administration), J.D./M.A.N.M. (Juris Doctor/Master of Arts in Nonprofit Management), and J.D./M.B.A. (Juris Doctor/ Master of Business Administration).

Phone: 651-523-2461
800-388-3688
Fax: 651-523-3064
E-mail: *lawadm@gw.hamline.edu*
Web: *www.hamline.edu/law*

Contact

Office of Admissions, 651-523-2461 or 800-388-3688 for general inquiries; Lynette Wahl, Associate Director of Financial Aid, 651-523-2280 for financial aid information.

Required

To earn the J.D., candidates must complete 88 total credits, of which 33 are for required courses. They must maintain a minimum GPA of 2.0 in the required courses. The following first-year courses are required of all students: Civil Procedure, Contracts, Criminal Law, Torts I, Property I, Legal Research and Writing, and Constitutional Law I. Required upper-level courses consist of Professional Responsibility, seminar course, and legal perspectives course. The required orientation program for first-year students is 1 day and consists of processing administrative requirements.

Electives

The number of credits students must take in their area of concentration varies from 18 to 24.The School of Law offers concentrations in corporate law, criminal law, international law, juvenile law, labor law, civil dispute resolution, commercial law, government and regulatory affairs, and intellectual property. In addition, 3- or 4-credit clinics provide upper-level students with practical experience in family law and child advocacy, immigration law, public interest law, unemployment compensation law, and alternative dispute resolution. In seminars, 15 upper-level students per semester engage in an in-depth study of a selected topic for 3 credits. Internships for 3 credits offer upper-level students the opportunity to work with expert practitioners in various types of legal practice. Upper-level students may be research assistants for professors. Credit is given only if research assistance is structured as an independent study. Opportunities for study abroad consist of summer programs at the University of Bergen (Norway), Hebrew University (Jerusalem), University of Modena (Italy), and Central European University (Budapest, Hungary). A legal writing tutorial is available to students with a GPA below 2.0 after the first semester or on the recommendation of the legal writing professors. The Academic Success Program, which includes legal writing tutors and substantive review of courses, is offered to students who need remedial assistance. Other offerings include special scholarships and student organizations for minority students. There is a variety of special interest group programs. The most widely taken electives are Corporations Dispute Resolution Practices and Family Law.

Graduation Requirements

In order to graduate, candidates must have a GPA of 2.0, have completed the upper-division writing requirement, and have completed the Professional Responsibility course.

Organizations

Students edit the *Hamline Law Review*, the *Hamline Journal of Public Law and Policy*, the *Journal of Law and Religion*, and the newspaper, *The Appellate Review*. There are many moot court competitions, including the National Moot Court, the Frederick Douglass, and the Rich Intellectual Property competition. Other competitions include Client Couseling and Negotiation. Law student organizations include the Student Bar Association, Nontraditional Students Association, and Multicultural Law Students Association. There are local chapters of the Business Law Association, International Law Society, and Environmental Law Society. Other organizations include Delta Theta Phi, Phi Alpha Delta, and ABA Law School Division.

Library

The law library contains 150,135 hard-copy volumes and 110,923 microform volume equivalents, and subscribes to 2709 serial publications. Such on-line databases and networks as DIALOG, LEXIS, and WESTLAW are available to law students for research. Special library collections include a U.S. government selective depository collection. Recently, the library implemented a computer library expansion and upgrade, CD-ROM facilities, an automated circulation system, new offices, and improved lighting. The ratio of library volumes to faculty is 6040 to 1 and to students is 18 to 1. The ratio of seats in the library to students is 1 to 2.

Faculty

The law school has 30 full-time and 52 part-time faculty members, of whom 26 are women. According to AAUP standards for Category IIB institutions, faculty salaries are above average. About 26% of full-time faculty have a graduate law degree in addition to the J.D. The ratio of full-time students to full-time faculty in an average class is 26 to 1; in a clinic, 8 to 1.

Placement	
J.D.s awarded:	161
Services available through: a separate law school placement center	
Special features: extensive career programming.	
Full-time job interviews:	41 employers
Summer job interviews:	48 employers
Placement by graduation:	69% of class
Placement within 9 months:	99% of class
Average starting salary:	$26,000 to $121,000
Areas of placement:	
Private practice 2-10 attorneys	14%
Private practice 11-25 attorneys	7%
Private practice 26-50 attorneys	3%
Private practice 51-100 attorneys	1%
Private practice 100+ attorneys	3%
Private practice solo	4%
Private practice unknown size	10%
Judicial clerkships	26%
Business/industry	24%
Government	4%
Public interest	4%

Students

About 56% of the student body are women; 12%, minorities; 5%, African American; 5%, Asian American; 1%, Hispanic; and 1%, Native American. The majority of students come from the Midwest (90%). The average age of entering students is 25; age range is 21 to 58. About 20% of students enter directly from undergraduate school, 10% have a graduate degree, and 70% have worked full-time prior to entering law school. About 6% drop out after the first year for academic or personal reasons; 92% remain to receive a law degree.

Harvard Law School

Cambridge, MA 02138

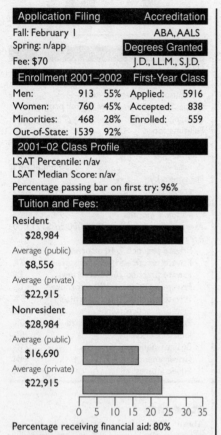

Application Filing		Accreditation
Fall: February 1		ABA, AALS
Spring: n/app		**Degrees Granted**
Fee: $70		J.D., LL.M., S.J.D.

Enrollment 2001–2002			First-Year Class	
Men:	913	55%	Applied:	5916
Women:	760	45%	Accepted:	838
Minorities:	468	28%	Enrolled:	559
Out-of-State:	1539	92%		

2001–02 Class Profile

LSAT Percentile: n/av
LSAT Median Score: n/av
Percentage passing bar on first try: 96%

Tuition and Fees:

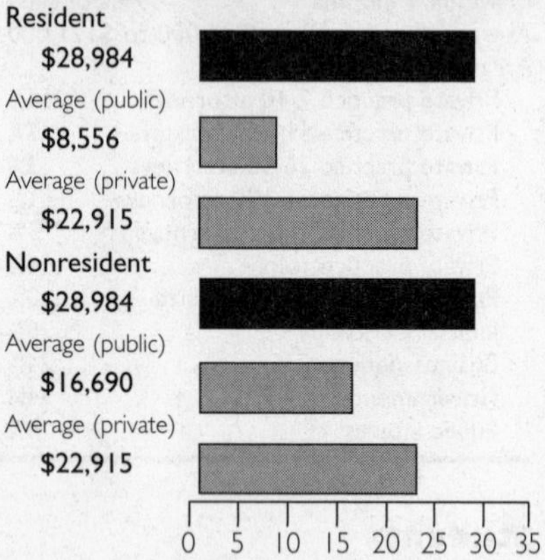

Percentage receiving financial aid: 80%

ADMISSIONS

In the fall 2001 first-year class, 5916 applied, 838 were accepted, and 559 enrolled. Eleven transfers enrolled.

Requirements
Applicants must have a bachelor's degree and take the LSAT. No specific undergraduate courses are required. Candidates are not interviewed.

Procedure
The application deadline for fall entry is February 1. Applicants should submit an application form, LSAT results, transcripts, a nonrefundable application fee of $70, and 2 letters of recommendation. Students are urged to visit the school. A personal statement and a college certification form are required. Accepted students must make a deposit of $500. Notification of the admissions decision is on a rolling basis. The latest acceptable LSAT test date for fall entry is December. The law school uses the LSDAS.

Special
The law school recruits minority and disadvantaged students by encouraging all who would like to study law at Harvard to apply. Requirements are not different for out-of-state students. Transfer students must have one year of credit, have attended an ABA-approved law school, and have outstanding records in college and in the first year of law school.

Costs

Tuition and fees for the 2001-2002 academic year are $28,984 for full-time in-state students. On-campus room and board costs about $13,127 annually; books and supplies run $930.

Financial Aid

About 80% of current law students received some form of aid in a recent year. Awards are based on need. Required financial statements are the CSS Profile or the FAFSA. First-year students are notified about their financial aid application some time after admission. Assuming a timely aid application, students are not required to submit a deposit to reserve a place in the class until a financial aid decision has been made.

About the Law School

Harvard University/Harvard Law School was established in 1817 and is a private institution. The campus is in an urban area within Cambridge. The primary mission of the law school is to stress an understanding of the principles of law and a mastery of such skills as oral advocacy, research, and legal writing, and to educate lawyers to be capable of addressing new legal problems in a changing society. Students have access to federal, state, county, city, and local agencies, courts, correctional facilities, law firms, legal aid organizations in the Cambridge area, and externship clinical practice sites. Facilities of special interest to law students are the 21 buildings for classrooms, dormitories, student activities, libraries, and the Hale and Dorr Legal Services Center in Jamaica Plain. Housing for students consists of law school dormitories, Harvard-affiliated housing, and off-campus housing. There is housing for single and married students. All law school facilities are accessible to the physically disabled.

Calendar

The law school operates on a traditional semester basis. Courses for full-time students are offered days only and must be completed within 3 years. There is no part-time program. New students are admitted in the fall. There is no summer session. Transferable summer courses are not offered.

Programs

In addition to the J.D., the law school offers the LL.M. and S.J.D. Students may take relevant courses in other programs and apply credit toward the J.D.; a maximum of 10 credits through cross credits may be applied. The following joint degrees may be earned: J.D./M.A. (Juris Doctor/Master of Arts), J.D./M.A.L.D. (Juris Doctor/Master of Arts in Law and Diplomacy with Tufts), J.D./M.B.A. (Juris Doctor/Master of Business Administration), J.D./M.P.A. (Juris Doctor/Master of Public Administration), J.D./M.P.P. (Juris Doctor/Master of Public Policy), and J.D./Ph.D. (Juris Doctor/Doctor of Philosophy).

Required
To earn the J.D., candidates must complete 82 total credits, of which 30 are for required courses. The following first-year courses are required of all students: Torts, Contracts, Property, Civil Procedure, Criminal Law, an elective, and Lawyering. Required upper-level courses consist of a professional responsibility requirement and a written work requirement. Harvard offers one of the most extensive clinical programs in the country with more than 20 courses offering clinical placements. In addition, several student practice organizations offer clinical placements.The required orientation program for first-year students lasts 2 days and is described as comprehensive.

Electives
The Law School has no formal program of offering concentrations in particular specialties. However, because the curriculum is so extensive, it allows for many different paths of study. Students are encouraged to discuss their plans with faculty members involved in relevant areas of study and are encouraged to take courses in a number of different fields, as well as in other parts of the University. The School offers a broad array of clinical opportunities to students. Through Harvard's Hale and Dorr Legal Services Center, students can focus on a number of practice areas, including the Community Enterprise Project, Medical and Legal Services Unit, Family and Children's Law Practice, Immigration Law, Housing Law and Litigation, and the General

Phone: 617-495-3179
E-mail: *jdadmiss@law.harvard.edu*
Web: *law.harvard.edu*

Contact

Admissions Office, 617-495-3109, fax 617-436-7290 for general inquiries.

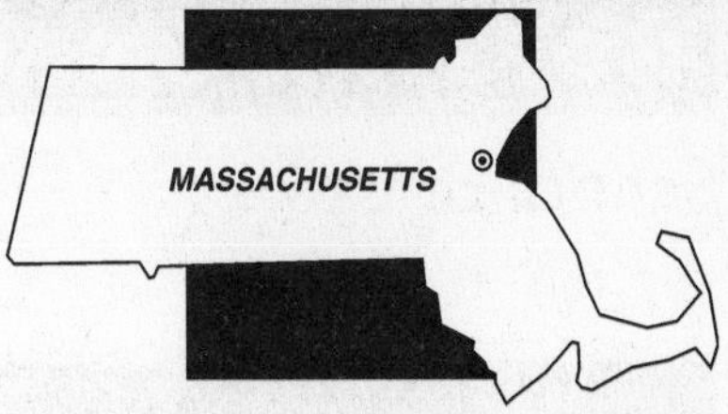

Practice Unit. The Criminal Justice institute is Harvard Law School's curriculum-based clinical program in criminal law. The Harvard Defenders is a student-operated organization dedicated to providing quality legal representation to people with low income in criminal show-cause hearings and welfare fraud. The Harvard Legal Aid Bureau is a student-run legal services office dedicated to providing legal assistance to low-income people and to creating a clinical education environment in which its members learn from legal practice. The Harvard Mediation Program (HMP) works to resolve disputes both in and out of the courts in the Boston area. Students can participate also in a wide variety of externships for credit, including the Harvard Immigration and Refugee Clinic, Office of Attorney General, U.S. and District Attorneys' offices as well as numerous government agencies and nonprofit organizations. More than 30 courses offer clinical field work experience and more than 2 others include simulated exercises. There are 57 seminars, including those on affirmative action, the federal budgetary process, and corporate theory. Internships are available for credit. Research programs may be conducted with the Center for Criminal Justice, Human Rights Program, East Asian Legal Studies, International Tax Program, Program on International Financial Systems, European Law Research Center, Program in Law and Economics, Program on the Legal Profession, Program on Negotiation, International and Comparative Legal Studies, International Tax Program, and Islamic Legal Studies. Field work is available in business, civil and criminal, mediation, and environmental law. A number of courses provide students with field work in local courts and government agencies, and others provide instruction in aspects of legal practice through simulated casework and a problem-oriented approach. Special lecture series include the BSA Speaker Series, the DSAC Brown-Bag Lunch Discussion Series, East Asian Legal Studies Speaker Program, HLS Forum, Human Rights Program Speaker Series, and Introduction to the World of Law. The Saturday School, in an effort to increase dialog between faculty and students, offers a series of informal lectures by individuals from diverse backgrounds and careers such as law professors, judges, former prison inmates, writers, artists, government and law enforcement officials, and health care providers. The most widely taken electives are Constitutional Law, Taxation, and Corporations.

Graduation Requirements

In order to graduate, candidates must have completed the upper-division writing requirement.

Organizations

Students edit the *Harvard Law Review, Blackletter Law Journal, Civil Rights-Civil Liberties Law Review, Human Rights Journal, Journal of Law and Public Policy, Journal of Law and Technology, Journal on Legislation, Women's Law Journal, International Law Journal, Environmental Law Review, Latino Law Review, Negotiation Law Review,* the student newspaper, the *Harvard Law Record*, and a yearbook. Moot court opportunities include the Ames Competition, which offers moot court competitions for first-year and upper-class students. The school also participates in interschool contests, including the Williston Legislative Drafting Competition and the Jessup International Law Moot Court Competition. Students may choose to participate in more than 70 student organizations and 14 publications. Campus clubs and other organizations include various language tables that offer informal lunch/dinners and sometimes invite speakers and other guests.

Library

The law library contains 2,039,000 hardcopy volumes and 187,600 microform volume equivalents, and subscribes to 15,336 serial publications. Such on-line databases and networks as CALI, DIALOG, LEXIS, LOIS, NEXIS, WESTLAW, Harvard On-Line Library Information System (HOLLIS), RUN, Vu/Text, Dow Jones News Retrieval, and Legi-Slate are available to law students for research. Special library collections include a comprehensive collection of Anglo American reports and treatises, and a special collection on international law as well as rare books and a 30,000-item art collection. The Law School Library was completely renovated during 1996-1997 to accommodate present and future technology needs of library users. The ratio of library volumes to faculty is 25,488 to 1 and to students is 1219 to 1.

Placement

J.D.s awarded:	540
Services available through: a separate law school placement center and and separate Office of Public Interest Advising	
Services: on-campus interviews for first, second- and third-year students	
Full-time job interviews:	704 employers
Summer job interviews:	n/av
Placement by graduation:	100% of class
Placement within 9 months:	100% of class
Average starting salary:	n/av
Areas of placement:	
Private practice 2-10 attorneys	1%
Private practice 11-25 attorneys	1%
Private practice 26-50 attorneys	2%
Private practice 51-100 attorneys	4%
Private practice 101-250 attorneys	18%
Private practice 251-500 attorneys	36%
Private practice 500+ attorneys	11%
Judicial clerkships	18%
Business/industry	6%
Public interest	4%
Government	1%

Faculty

The law school has 80 full-time and 90 part-time faculty members, of whom 41 are women. According to AAUP standards for Category I institutions, faculty salaries are well above average. About 7% of full-time faculty have a graduate law degree in addition to the J.D.; about 11% of part-time faculty have one. The ratio of full-time students to full-time faculty in an average class is 14 to 1. The law school has a regular program of bringing visiting professors and other distinguished lecturers and visitors to campus.

Students

About 45% of the student body are women; 28%, minorities; 10%, African American; 11%, Asian American; 6%, Hispanic; and 1%, Native American. Most students come from the Northeast (34%). The average age of entering students is 24; age range is 19 to 47. About 41% of students enter directly from undergraduate school, 15% have a graduate degree, and 60% have worked full-time prior to entering law school. About 1% drop out after the first year for academic or personal reasons; 99% remain to receive a law degree.

School of Law

121 Hofstra University
Hempstead, NY 11549

Application Filing		Accreditation
Fall: April 15		ABA, AALS
Spring: n/app		**Degrees Granted**
Fee: $60		J.D., LL.M.

Enrollment 2001–2002			First-Year Class	
Men:	428	52%	Applied:	3066
Women:	391	47%	Accepted:	1073
Minorities:	156	19%	Enrolled:	306
Out-of-State:	819	100%		

2001–02 Class Profile

LSAT Percentile: 71%
LSAT Median Score: 156
Percentage passing bar on first try: n/av

Tuition and Fees:

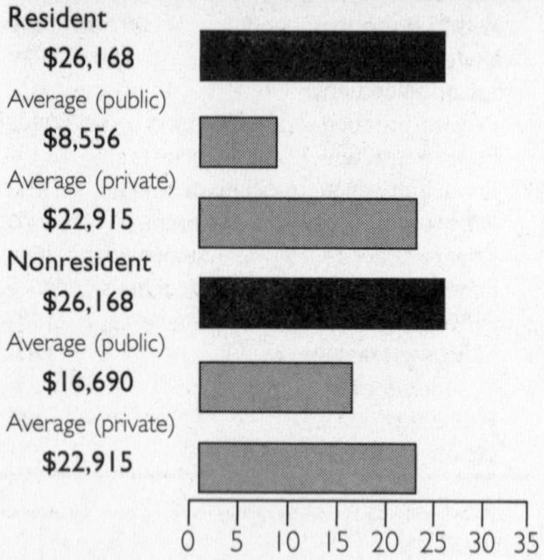

Percentage receiving financial aid: 75%

ADMISSIONS

In the fall 2001 first-year class, 3066 applied, 1073 were accepted, and 306 enrolled. Twenty-four transfers enrolled. The median LSAT percentile of the most recent first-year class was 71; the median GPA was 3.3 on a scale of 4.0. The lowest LSAT percentile accepted was 8; the highest was 99.

Requirements

Applicants must have a bachelor's degree and take the LSAT. The most important admission factors include academic achievement, LSAT results, and general background. No specific undergraduate courses are required. Candidates are not interviewed.

Procedure

The application deadline for fall entry is April 15. Applicants should submit an application form, LSAT results, transcripts, a nonrefundable application fee of $60, and 1 letter of recommendation. Notification of the admissions decision is on a rolling basis. The latest acceptable LSAT test date for fall entry is February, generally. The law school uses the LSDAS.

Special

The law school recruits minority and disadvantaged students by means of student, faculty, graduate, and administrator visits to a diverse range of institutions to increase the number of law students from traditionally excluded groups. Requirements are not different for out-of-state students. Transfer students must have one year of credit and have attended an ABA-approved law school.

Costs

Tuition and fees for the 2001-2002 academic year are $26,168 for all full-time students. Tuition for part-time students is $19,624 per year. On-campus room and board costs about $8350 annually; books and supplies run $900.

Financial Aid

About 75% of current law students receive some form of aid. The average annual amount of aid from all sources combined, including scholarships, loans, and work contracts, is $20,000; maximum, $40,418. Awards are based on need and merit. Required financial statement is the FAFSA. The aid application deadline for fall entry is June 1. First-year students are notified about their financial aid application upon acceptance if the financial aid application is complete, or at the time of completion of the financial aid application.

About the Law School

Hofstra University School of Law was established in 1970 and is a private institution. The 240-acre campus is in a suburban area 25 miles east of New York City. The primary mission of the law school is to prepare students for success in the practice of law by combining rigorous intellectual discussion with hands-on training in the skills required to excel in today's competitive legal environment. Students have access to federal, state, county, city, and local agencies, courts, correctional facilities, law firms, and legal aid organizations in the Hempstead area. Students have special access to the federal courthouse located on campus. Facilities of special interest to law students are all university facilities, including the university library center, athletic facilities, cultural programs, and social events. Housing for students is provided by the university in townhouses and high-rise residence halls. Many law students rent houses or apartments within a short commuting distance from the university. All law school facilities are accessible to the physically disabled.

Calendar

The law school operates on a traditional semester basis. Courses for full-time students are offered days only and must be completed within 3 years. For part-time students, courses are offered days only and must be completed within 4 years. New full- and part-time students are admitted in the fall. There is a 7-week summer session. Transferable summer courses are offered.

Programs

In addition to the J.D., the law school offers the LL.M. The following joint degrees may be earned: J.D./M.B.A. (Juris Doctor/Master of Business Administration).

Required

To earn the J.D., candidates must complete 87 total credits, of which 39 are for required courses. They must maintain a minimum GPA of 2.0 in the required courses. The following first-year courses are required of all students: Civil Procedure I and II, Contracts I and II, Criminal Law, Lawmaking Institutions, Legal Writing and Research, Property I and II, and Torts I and II. Required upper-level courses consist of Appellate Advocacy, Constitutional Law I and II, Legal Ethics, and upper-class writing requirements I and II. The required orientation program for first-year students is a 3-day program that includes legal method classes taught by faculty members, general lectures, panels concerning student services, and social activities.

Electives

The School of Law offers concentrations in corporate law, criminal law, environmental law, family law, international law, juvenile law, labor law, litigation, securities law, tax law, torts and insurance, constitutional law, and health law. In addition, students may enroll in the Housing Rights Clinic, the Criminal Justice Clinic, or the Child Advocacy Clinic for 6 credits each. Upper-class students may choose from a large number of 2- to 3-credit seminars. First-year students take 1 course in a small section of 25 to 30 students. Students may enroll in the Externship Program for 3 credits; they

Phone: 516-463-5916
Fax: 516-463-6264
E-mail: *lawpts@hofstra.edu*

Contact

Peter T. Sylver, Senior Assistant Dean for Admissions, 516-463-5916 for general inquiries; Nancy Modell, Assistant Dean for Financial Aid, 516-463-5929 for financial aid information.

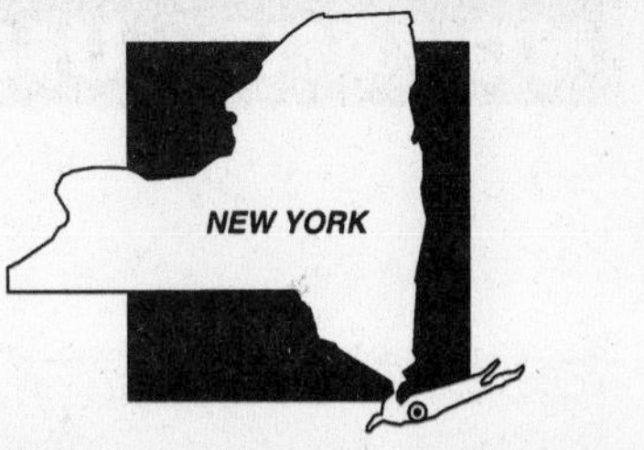

may work for judges or in nonprofit or government agencies, dealing with civil and criminal matters. Faculty-supervised independent study is worth from 2 to 6 credits. The law school offers special problems seminars, in which 3 to 5 students work closely with a professor in a tutorial setting on a topic of current interest. In addition, the law school offers an extensive Pro Bono Student Volunteer Program, in which more than 400 students have donated their efforts to assist attorneys and other agencies with cases. Through the Unemployment Action Center, students provide assistance to unemployed persons seeking benefits. A Visiting Scholar Program brings to the law school a distinguished scholar for a visit of 3 to 4 days; the visiting scholar teaches classes, gives a lecture, and meets informally with students and faculty. Annually scheduled lectures involve experts in bankruptcy law, family law, legal ethics, and health law, and feature distinguished jurists, scholars, and practitioners. The law school offers a summer program in Nice, France in cooperation with the University of Nice Law School, and one in Sydney, Australia in cooperation with the University of New South Wales Faculty of Law. Incoming students may be selected by the tutorial committee to participate in a voluntary enhancement program taught by faculty. The Director of Multicultural Student Affairs is responsible for minority student affairs, minority recruitment and admissions, the coordination of the law school's Enhancement Program and the coordination of the Dwight L. Greene Scholarship Program. Specific initiatives to support students of color include: an Open House for minority applicants, Law Day for admitted students of color, a Minority Student Orientation Program for incoming students, a first-year reception, mentoring programs, and other programs throughout the year. The most widely taken electives are Business Organizations, Criminal Procedure, and Wills, Trusts, and Estates.

Graduation Requirements

In order to graduate, candidates must have a GPA of 2.0, have completed the upper-division writing requirement, and completed 2 upper-level writing requirements.

Organizations

Students edit the *Hofstra Law Review, Hofstra Labor and Employment Law Journal, Family Court Review, Hofstra Law and Policy Symposium*, and the law school student newspaper, *Conscience.* Teams compete annually in the following national competition; the National Moot Court Competition, the Robert F. Wagner, Jr. Labor & Employment Law Competition, the Conrad L. Duberstein Competition and the Phillip Jessup International Law Competition. Students also participate in the Nassau County Bar Association's Long Island Moot Court Competition sponsored by the Nassau Academy of Law and also intramural competitions sponsored by the Hofstra Law School Moot Court Association. Law student organizations include the Corporate Law Society, Hofstra Law Women, and The International Law Society. There are local chapters of Asian-Pacific American Law Student Association, Black American Law Student Association, Latino American Law Student Association, and Phi Alpha Delta. Hofstra University supports more than 100 student cultural, media, sports, creative, service, and politically and socially active clubs.

Library

The law library contains 516,621 hardcopy volumes and 1,758,120 microform volume equivalents, and subscribes to 1300 serial publications. Such on-line databases and networks as CALI, CIS Universe, DIALOG, Infotrac, Legal-Trac, LEXIS, LOIS, WESTLAW, NEXIS, and the Internet are available to law students for research. Special library collections include records and briefs of U.S. Supreme Court cases (1832 to the present) and of the New York Court of Appeals and Appellate Division; federal depository materials; and all U.N. documents (1976 to the present) on microfiche. Additional microfiche holdings are the ABA archival collection (1878 to the present) and the archival collection of the American Law Institute. Recently, the library installed a wireless network with network cards available for checkout. The ratio of library volumes to faculty is 12,916 to 1 and to students is 631 to 1. The ratio of seats in the library to students is 2 to 3.

Placement

J.D.s awarded:	230
Services available through: a separate law school placement center	
Special features: one-on-one videotaped interview skills training programs, 24-hour resume and cover letter review, computerized employer databases, and Rapid Research program.	
Full-time job interviews:	54 employers
Summer job interviews:	52 employers
Placement by graduation:	n/av
Placement within 9 months:	98% of class
Average starting salary:	$30,000 to $150,000
Areas of placement:	
Private practice 2-10 attorneys	13%
Private practice 11-25 attorneys	4%
Private practice 26-50 attorneys	6%
Private practice 51-100 attorneys	4%
Private practice 101 - 500 attorneys	12%
Business/industry	18%
Government	10%
Judicial clerkships	5%
Public interest	3%
Academic	1%

Faculty

The law school has 40 full-time and 59 part-time faculty members, of whom 24 are women. According to AAUP standards for Category I institutions, faculty salaries are above average. About 25% of full-time faculty have a graduate law degree in addition to the J.D.; about 7% of part-time faculty have one. The ratio of full-time students to full-time faculty in an average class is 21 to 1; in a clinic, 10 to 1. The law school has a regular program of bringing visiting professors and other distinguished lecturers and visitors to campus.

Students

About 47% of the student body are women; 19%, minorities; 7%, African American; 6%, Asian American; and 6%, Hispanic. The average age of entering students is 26; age range is 20 to 70. About 53% of students enter directly from undergraduate school, 8% have a graduate degree, and 46% have worked full-time prior to entering law school. About 11% drop out after the first year for academic or personal reasons; 89% remain to receive a law degree.

HOWARD UNIVERSITY

2900 Van Ness Street, N.W.
Washington, DC 20008

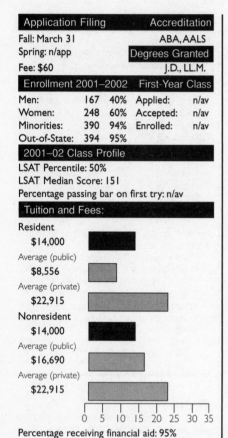

Application Filing		Accreditation
Fall: March 31		ABA, AALS
Spring: n/app		**Degrees Granted**
Fee: $60		J.D., LL.M.

Enrollment 2001–2002			First-Year Class	
Men:	167	40%	Applied:	n/av
Women:	248	60%	Accepted:	n/av
Minorities:	390	94%	Enrolled:	n/av
Out-of-State:	394	95%		

2001–02 Class Profile

LSAT Percentile: 50%
LSAT Median Score: 151
Percentage passing bar on first try: n/av

Tuition and Fees:

Resident
$14,000
Average (public)
$8,556
Average (private)
$22,915
Nonresident
$14,000
Average (public)
$16,690
Average (private)
$22,915

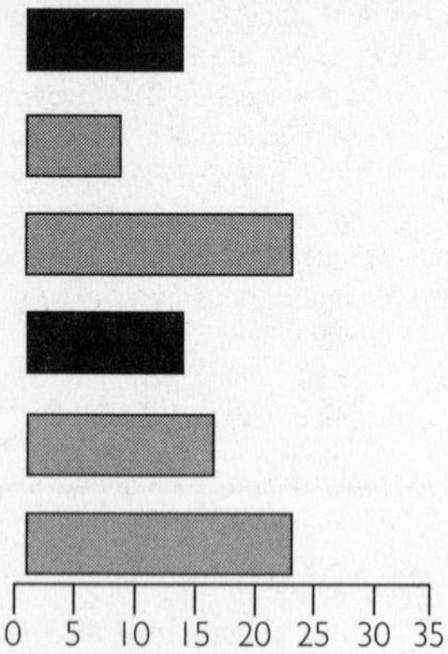

Percentage receiving financial aid: 95%

ADMISSIONS

Information in the above capsule is from an earlier year. In a recent first-year class, ten transfers enrolled. The median LSAT percentile of a recent first-year class was 50; the median GPA was 2.9 on a scale of 4.0.

Requirements

Applicants must have a bachelor's degree and take the LSAT. Minimum acceptable LSAT percentile is 35 and minimum acceptable GPA is 3.0 on a scale of 4.0. The most important admission factors include general background, GPA, and LSAT results. No specific undergraduate courses are required. Candidates are not interviewed.

Procedure

Check with the school for current application deadlines and fee. Applicants should submit an application form, LSAT results, transcripts, a nonrefundable application fee, 2 letters of recommendation, a personal statement, and the Dean's survey. Notification of the admissions decision is on a rolling basis. The law school uses the LSDAS.

Special

Requirements are not different for out-of-state students. Transfer students must have one year of credit, have attended an ABA-approved law school, and be ranked in the upper quarter to one-third of their class.

Costs

Tuition and fees for the academic year are approximately $14,000 for full-time in-state students. On-campus room and board costs about $13,000 annually; books and supplies run about $1100.

Financial Aid

About 95% of current law students receive some form of aid. The average annual amount of aid from all sources combined, including scholarships, loans, and work contracts, is about $18,000; maximum, $27,600. Awards are based on merit. Required financial statement is the FAFSA. First-year students are notified about their financial aid application at time of acceptance. Check with the school for current deadlines.

About the Law School

Howard University was established in 1869 and is a private institution. The 22-acre campus is in an urban area in northwest Washington, D.C. The mission of Howard University School of Law includes the provision of quality education for any student, with emphasis on the educational opportunities for those students who may not otherwise have them. Students have access to federal, state, county, city, and local agencies, courts, correctional facilities, law firms, and legal aid organizations in the Washington, D.C. area, including the Washington Consortium of Law Libraries, which offers use of all law libraries in the D.C. metropolitan area. Facilities of special interest to law students include the superior moot court room. Housing for students is limited on campus; most students live off campus. All law school facilities are accessible to the physically disabled.

Calendar

The law school operates on a traditional semester basis. Courses for full-time students are offered both day and evening and must be completed within 5 years. For part-time students, courses are offered both day and evening. New students are admitted in the fall and spring. There is no summer session. Transferable summer courses are offered.

Programs

In addition to the J.D., the law school offers the LL.M. and master's specialization in international law and comparative law. Students may take relevant courses in other programs and apply credit toward the J.D.; a maximum of 30 credits may be applied. The following joint degrees may be earned: J.D./M.B.A. (Juris Doctor/Master of Business Administration).

Phone: 202-806-8008
Fax: 202-806-8162
E-mail: *admissions@law.howard.edu*
Web: *www.law.howard.edu*

Required
To earn the J.D., candidates must complete 88 total credits. They must maintain a minimum grade average of 72 in the required courses. The following first-year courses are required of all students: Torts I & II, Property, Contracts, Civil Procedure, Criminal Law, Legal Method, Legal Research and Writing, and Constitutional Law I. Required upper-level courses consist of Legal Writing II, Constitutional Law II, Professional Responsibility, Evidence, Skills, and Legal Writing III. The required orientation program for first-year students is two weeks long and includes an introduction to legal methods.

Electives
In addition, clinics in a wide range of areas are available to third-year students; 4 to 12 credits are offered for each clinic. Second and third-year students may take seminars for 3 credits. Internships are available to third-year students for 3 credits. Third-year students may also participate in research for 2 credits. All students may attend tutorials, and special lectures for no credit. After the first year of study, students may undertake a study-abroad program. ABA-approved courses worth 2 credits each are offered at HUSL/University of Western Capetown, South Africa. The most widely taken electives are Federal Tax; Wills, Trusts, and Estates; and Administrative Law.

Graduation Requirements
In order to graduate, candidates must have completed the upper-division writing requirement.

Organizations
Students edit the *Howard Law Journal* and the newspaper *Barrister*. Moot court competitions include ABA National Appellate Advocacy-Northeast Regional, Jessup International, and Frederick Douglass National. Law student organizations include the Student Bar Association, International Law Society, and Entertainment Law Association. There are local chapters of Black Law Students Association, Public Interest Law Society, and the ABA.

Contact
Kim Gray, Assistant Director of Admissions, 202-806-8008 for general inquiries; Norman James, Financial Aid Officer, 202-806-8005 for financial aid information.

Library
The law library contains 283,000 hard-copy volumes and 54,000 microform volume equivalents, and subscribes to 1643 serial publications. Such on-line databases and networks as DIALOG, LEXIS, WESTLAW, and the Internet are available to law students for research. Special library collections include Fats Waller Litigation Files and a civil rights collection. Recently, the library implemented a web-based library catalog, developed library home-page research tools, and distributed CD-ROM materials for the library LAN. The ratio of library volumes to faculty is 8333 to 1 and to students is 555 to 1. The ratio of seats in the library to students is 1 to 3.

Faculty
The law school has approximately 33 full-time and 23 part-time faculty members, of whom 19 are women. About 2% of full-time faculty have a graduate law degree in addition to the J.D.; about 4% of part-time faculty have one. The ratio of full-time students to full-time faculty in an average class is 40 to 1; in a clinic, 8 to 1. The law school has a regular program of bringing visiting professors and other distinguished lecturers and visitors to campus.

Students
About 60% of the student body are women; 94%, minorities; 87%, African American; 4%, Asian American; 4%, Hispanic; and 5%, Caucasian. Most students come from the Northeast (39%). The average age of entering students is 25; age range is 21 to 48. About 80% of students enter directly from undergraduate school, 7% have a graduate degree, and 20% have worked full-time prior to entering law school. About 5% drop out after the first year for academic or personal reasons; 94% remain to receive a law degree.

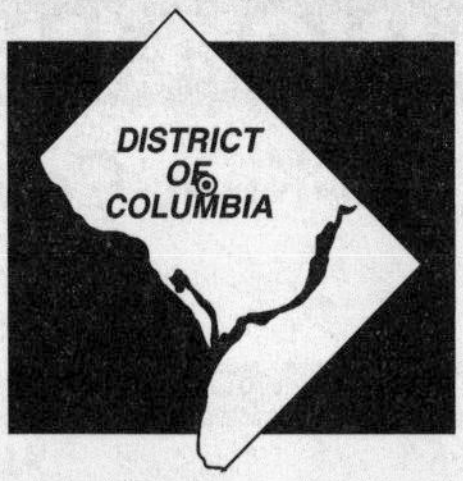

Placement

J.D.s awarded:	118
Services available through: a separate law school placement center	
Special features: Summer Clerkship Program (for the summer following a student's first year) and workshops and seminars featuring Howard Law alumni and other practitioners regarding legal career settings, practice specialties, and employment trends; first-year summer clerkship program (through partnerships with major law firms and corporations; summer associate training program; workshops and seminars on job search skills, legal career settings and practice specialties, and employment trends.	
Full-time job interviews:	109 employers
Summer job interviews:	169 employers
Placement by graduation:	60% of class
Placement within 9 months:	91% of class
Average starting salary:	$30,000 to $150,000
Areas of placement:	
Private practice 2-10 attorneys	5%
Private practice 11-25 attorneys	1%
Private practice 26-50 attorneys	3%
Private practice 51-100 attorneys	3%
Government	30%
Business/industry	19%
Judicial clerkships	16%
Public interest	3%
Academic	1%
Unknown	1%

Chicago-Kent College of Law

565 West Adams Street
Chicago, IL 60661

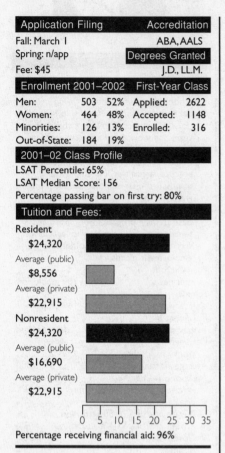

Application Filing		Accreditation
Fall: March 1		ABA, AALS
Spring: n/app		**Degrees Granted**
Fee: $45		J.D., LL.M.

Enrollment 2001–2002			First-Year Class	
Men:	503	52%	Applied:	2622
Women:	464	48%	Accepted:	1148
Minorities:	126	13%	Enrolled:	316
Out-of-State:	184	19%		

2001–02 Class Profile

LSAT Percentile: 65%
LSAT Median Score: 156
Percentage passing bar on first try: 80%

Tuition and Fees:

Resident
$24,320
Average (public)
$8,556
Average (private)
$22,915
Nonresident
$24,320
Average (public)
$16,690
Average (private)
$22,915

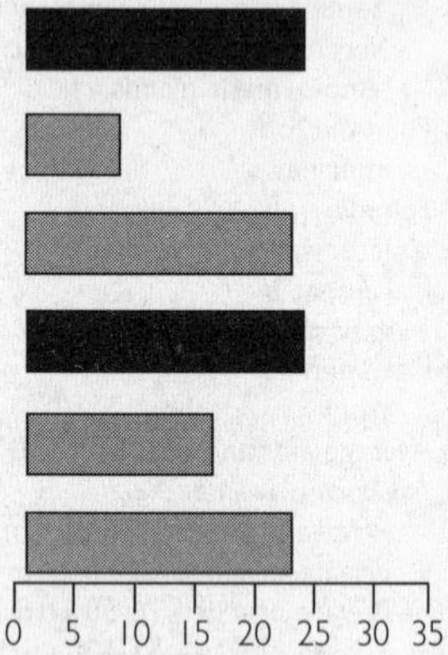

Percentage receiving financial aid: 96%

ADMISSIONS

In the fall 2001 first-year class, 2622 applied, 1148 were accepted, and 316 enrolled. Twelve transfers enrolled. The median LSAT percentile of the most recent first-year class was 65; the median GPA was 3.27 on a scale of 4.0. The highest LSAT percentile was 99.

Requirements

Applicants must have a bachelor's degree and take the LSAT. No specific undergraduate courses are required. Candidates are not interviewed.

Procedure

The application deadline for fall entry is March 1. Applicants should submit an application form, LSAT results, transcripts, a nonrefundable application fee of $45, 1 letter of recommendation (academic preferred), and a personal statement. Admitted applicants must submit a nonrefundable seat deposit, payable in 2 installments in April and June. Notification of the admissions decision is on a rolling basis. The latest acceptable LSAT test date for fall entry is February. The law school uses the LSDAS.

Special

The law school recruits minority and disadvantaged students through minority student law days, direct mail, and events sponsored by minority law student groups. Requirements are not different for out-of-state students. Transfer students must have one year of credit, have attended an ABA-approved law school, and present a letter of good standing from the dean of their law school and 1 letter of recommendation.

Costs

Tuition and fees for the 2001-2002 academic year are $24,320 for all full-time students. Tuition for part-time students is $17,870 per year. On-campus room and board costs about $6144 annually; books and supplies run $610.

Financial Aid

About 96% of current law students receive some form of aid. The average annual amount of aid from all sources combined, including scholarships, loans, and work contracts, is $27,479; maximum, $57,572. Awards are based on need and merit. Required financial statement is the FAFSA. The aid application deadline for fall entry is March 15. Special funds for minority or disadvantaged students are available. First-year students are notified about their financial aid application at time of acceptance.

About the Law School

Illinois Institute of Technology/Chicago-Kent College of Law was established in 1888 and is a private institution. The campus is in an urban area in downtown Chicago. The primary mission of the law school is to provide students with a solid grounding in legal theory and ethics, along with innovative approaches to teaching and skills training. Students have access to federal, state, county, city, and local agencies, courts, correctional facilities, law firms, and legal aid organizations in the Chicago area. The college is located in the Loop, Chicago's central business district, providing access to federal, state, county, and city agencies, courts, and law firms. Facilities of special interest to law students include a 10-story law building, built in 1992, which houses the law school. The majority of classrooms and seminar rooms have power and data ports at each seat for connection to the computer network. There is also a state-of-the-art courtroom. Housing is available in nearby urban and suburban neighborhoods and on-campus housing is available in the Law House on the university's main campus. All law school facilities are accessible to the physically disabled.

Calendar

The law school operates on a traditional semester basis. Courses for full-time students are offered both day and evening and must be completed within 5 years. For part-time students, courses are offered both day and evening and must be completed within 6 years. New full- and part-time students are admitted in the fall. There is an 8-week summer session. Transferable summer courses are offered.

Programs

In addition to the J.D., the law school offers the LL.M. Students may take relevant courses in other programs and apply credit toward the J.D.; a maximum of 12 credits may be applied. The following joint degrees may be earned: J.D./LL.M. (Juris Doctor/Master of Laws in taxation or financial services), J.D./M.B.A. (Juris Doctor/Master of Business Administration), J.D./M.E.M. (Juris Doctor/Master of Science in environmental management), J.D./M.P.A. (Juris Doctor/Master of Public Administration), J.D./M.P.H. (Juris Doctor/Master of Public Health), and J.D./M.S. (Juris Doctor/Master of Science in financial markets and trading).

Required

To earn the J.D., candidates must complete 87 total credits, of which 42 are for required courses. They must maintain a minimum GPA of 2.1 in the required courses. The following first-year courses are required of all students: Torts, Contracts, Property, Criminal Law, Civil Procedure, Legal Writing I and II, and Justice and the Legal System. Required upper-level courses consist of Professional Responsibility, Constitutional Law, Seminar, Advanced Research, and Legal Drafting. The required orientation program for first-year students is a 1-week program combining introductory programs, library tours, computer training, legal research and writing, and small sessions with current students and faculty.

Electives

Students must take 14 credits in their area of concentration. The Chicago-Kent

Phone: 312-906-5020
Fax: 312-906-5274
E-mail: *admit@kentlaw.edu*
Web: *www.kentlaw.edu*

Contact

Assistant Dean for Admissions, 312-906-5020 for general inquiries; Ada Chin, Director of Financial Aid, 312-906-5180 for financial aid information.

College of Law offers concentrations in corporate law, criminal law, entertainment law, environmental law, international law, labor law, litigation, securities law, tax law, torts and insurance, intellectual property, public interest, real estate, dispute resolution, and litigation. A certificate program for J.D. students in environmental and energy law includes a series of electives in land use, energy, and environmental law, as well as interdisciplinary classes in the scientific and economic analysis of environmental problems. Similar certificate programs exist in international and comparative law, litigation and alternative dispute resolution, intellectual property law, and labor and employment law. In addition, students may take clinical work in criminal, civil, mediation, health, or tax areas through the Chicago-Kent-Law Offices. One seminar of 2 hours credit is required of all students. An Advanced Externship Program places students with public agencies and teaching attorneys. A Judicial Externship program places students in clerkships with federal judges. Students can take Individual Research for 1 credit per semester, working under the supervision of a professor. Special lecture series include the Morris Lecture in International and Comparative Law and the Piper Lecture in Labor Law. Study abroad is possible through the London Consortium. The Academic Empowerment Program is offered to students based on factors including LSAT score, undergraduate and graduate GPA, socioeconomic background, years out of school, native language, and disabilities. Student groups, such as BLSA, HLSA, and APALSA sponsor and co-sponsor minority programs. Certificate programs include environmental and energy law, international and comparative law, litigation and alternative dispute resolution, intellectual property law, and labor and employment law. The most widely taken electives are Evidence, Remedies, and Business Organizations.

Graduation Requirements

In order to graduate, candidates must have a GPA of 2.1, have completed the upper-division writing requirement, required courses, Professional Responsibility, and a seminar. Attendance at Professionalism Day is also required.

Organizations

Students edit the *Chicago-Kent Law Review*, which is published 3 times a year, *The Journal of International and Comparative Law*, *The Journal of Intellectual Property*, and the *Employee Rights and Employment Policy Journal*. The student newspaper is the *Kent Commentator*. The Moot Court Honor Society, which enters its members in 10 intercollegiate competitions annually, sponsors the Ilana Diamond Rovner Appellate Advocacy Competition for upper-class students who are members of the Society. First-year students compete in the Charles Evans Hughes Moot Court Competition. The College of Law's 43 law student organizations include the Environmental Law Society, International Law Society, the Intellectual Property Law Society, and the Society of Women in Law. There are local chapters of the Asian-American, Black, and Hispanic Law Students Associations. Local chapters exist of the Kent Association of Trial Lawyers of America, Phi Alpha Delta, and National Lawyers Guild.

Library

The law library contains 560,000 hardcopy volumes and 139,045 microform volume equivalents, and subscribes to 9093 serial publications. Such on-line databases and networks as CALI, DIALOG, Dow-Jones, Infotrac, Legal-Trac, LEXIS, LOIS, NEXIS, OCLC First Search, RLIN, WESTLAW, Wilsonline Indexes, and the Internet are available for research. Special library collections include a depository of federal documents, a special collection on law and the aging, as well as international organization documents (UN, EU, and GATT, among others). The library offers interlibrary loan to all students for materials that the library doesn't own. A current awareness reading area, housing 25 to 30 current subscriptions to news magazines and newspapers is available. The ratio of library volumes to faculty is 8889 to 1 and to students is 579 to 1.

Faculty

The law school has 63 full-time and 105 part-time faculty, of whom 45 are women. According to AAUP standards for Category I institutions, faculty salaries are average. About 16% of full-time faculty have a graduate law degree in addition to the J.D.; about 7% of part-time faculty have one. The ratio of full-time students to full-time faculty in an average class is 37 to 1; in a clinic, 9 to 1. The law school has a regular program of bringing visiting professors and lecturers to campus. There is a chapter of the Order of the Coif; 46 faculty and 465 graduates are members.

Placement

J.D.s awarded:	342
Services available through: a separate law school placement center	
Special features: 1 part-time plus 6 full-time staff members, including 4 counselors; a resource center with reference materials and computers for resume printing and database searches, and participation in various job fairs including: 4 minority job fairs, 2 public interest career conferences, the Patent Law Interview Program, the Cyber Law Career Fair, and the NYU Job Fair for foreign LLM students.	
Full-time job interviews:	27 employers
Summer job interviews:	53 employers
Placement by graduation:	n/av
Placement within 9 months:	95% of class
Average starting salary:	$23,000 to $140,000
Areas of placement:	
Private practice 2-10 attorneys	12%
Private practice 11-25 attorneys	8%
Private practice 26-50 attorneys	5%
Private practice 51-100 attorneys	5%
Private practive 100+ attorneys	13%
Private practice, solo	1%
Private practice, firm size unknown	12%
Business/industry	21%
Government	19%
Judicial clerkships	2%
Public interest	1%

Students

About 48% of the student body are women; 13%, minorities; 6%, African American; 4%, Asian American; 2%, Hispanic; and 1%, Native American. The majority of students come from the Midwest (89%). The average age of entering students is 25; age range is 21 to 46. About 49% of students enter directly from undergraduate school, 6% have a graduate degree, and 51% have worked full-time prior to entering law school. About 10% drop out after the first year for academic or personal reasons; 90% remain to receive a law degree.

INDIANA UNIVERSITY AT BLOOMINGTON

School of Law

211 S. Indiana Avenue
Bloomington, IN 47405-1001

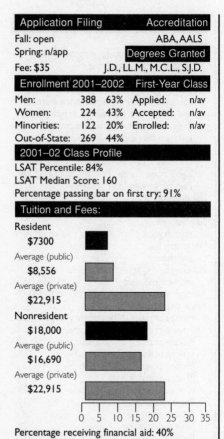

Application Filing		Accreditation
Fall: open		ABA, AALS
Spring: n/app		**Degrees Granted**
Fee: $35		J.D., LL.M., M.C.L., S.J.D.

Enrollment 2001–2002			First-Year Class	
Men:	388	63%	Applied:	n/av
Women:	224	43%	Accepted:	n/av
Minorities:	122	20%	Enrolled:	n/av
Out-of-State:	269	44%		

2001–02 Class Profile

LSAT Percentile: 84%
LSAT Median Score: 160
Percentage passing bar on first try: 91%

Tuition and Fees:

Resident
$7300
Average (public)
$8,556
Average (private)
$22,915
Nonresident
$18,000
Average (public)
$16,690
Average (private)
$22,915

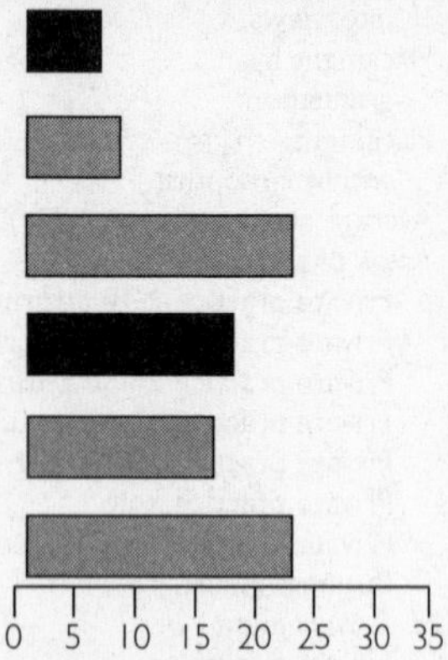

Percentage receiving financial aid: 40%

ADMISSIONS

Information in the above capsule is from an earlier year. In a recent first-year class, nineteen transfers enrolled. The median LSAT percentile of a recent first-year class was 84; the median GPA was 3.4 on a scale of 4.0. The highest LSAT percentile was 99.

Requirements
Applicants must have a bachelor's degree and take the LSAT. The most important admission factors include academic achievement, GPA, and undergraduate curriculum. No specific undergraduate courses are required. Candidates are not interviewed.

Procedure
Check with the school for current application deadline and fee. Applicants should submit an application form, LSAT results, transcripts, a nonrefundable application fee, and a personal statement (recommended). Notification of the admissions decision is in the beginning of December, prior to matriculation. The law school uses the LSDAS.

Special
The law school recruits minority and disadvantaged students by recruiting at minority colleges and universities in major urban areas; by hosting a Minority Law Day for interested students and prelaw advisers, and by providing fellowships. Requirements are not different for out-of-state students. Transfer students must have one year of credit, have attended an ABA-approved law school, and have a superior law school record, have credentials comparable to the class in which they wish to transfer (in terms of LSAT score and GPA), and provide reasons for transfer. Space availabilty is also a factor in the acceptance decision.

Costs

Tuition and fees for the academic year are approximately $7300 for full-time in-state students and $18,000 for out-of-state students. On-campus room and board costs about $6200 annually; books and supplies run about $1050.

Financial Aid

About 40% of law students receive some form of aid. The average annual amount of aid from all sources combined, including scholarships, loans, and work contracts, is about $17,500; maximum, $31,000. Awards are based on need and merit. Required financial statement is the FAFSA. Check with the school for current deadlines. Special funds for minority or disadvantaged students consist of Education Opportunity Fellowships and Graduate Minority Fellowships (through the University's Research and Graduate School). First-year students are notified about their financial aid application beginning mid-March for scholarships; summer for loan packages..

About the Law School

Indiana University at Bloomington School of Law was established in 1842 and is a public institution. The 1855-acre campus is in a small town 50 miles south of Indianapolis. The primary mission of the law school is to prepare graduates for the many roles lawyers may play throughout the world; to stress the development and discipline of analytical reasoning, clear writing skills, and a deep understanding of the basic principles of a variety of substantive areas of the law; to prepare global professionals for leadership roles in the 21st century. Students have access to federal, state, county, city, and local agencies, courts, correctional facilities, law firms, and legal aid organizations in the Bloomington area. The school has been completely remodeled, including classrooms; trial and appellate courtrooms; a student lounge and canteen; offices for student groups; and a computer center and laptop room, both of which are located in the law library. On-campus graduate student housing is available in several units (total: approximately 395,338 square feet); off-campus housing options include apartments, condominiums, and houses for rent throughout the community. All law school facilities are accessible to the physically disabled.

Calendar

The law school operates on a traditional semester basis. Courses for full-time students are offered days only and must be completed within 3 years. There is no part-time program. New students are admitted in the fall and summer. There are several summer sessions. Transferable summer courses are offered.

Programs

In addition to the J.D., the law school offers the LL.M., M.C.L., and S.J.D. Students may take relevant courses in other programs and apply credit toward the J.D.; a maximum of 6 credits may be applied. The following joint degrees may be earned: J.D./M.A. or J.D./M.S. (Juris Doctor/Master of Arts or Juris Doctor/Master of Science), J.D./M.B.A. (Juris Doctor/Master of Business Administration), J.D./M.L.S. (Juris Doctor/Master of Library Science), J.D./M.P.A. (Juris Doctor/Master of Public Affairs), and J.D./M.S.E.S. (Juris Doctor/Master of Science in Environmental Science).

Required
To earn the J.D., candidates must complete 86 total credits, of which 36 are for required courses. They must maintain a minimum GPA of 2.3 in the required courses. The following first-year courses are required of all students: Criminal

Phone: 812-855-4765
Fax: 812-855-0555
E-mail: *Lawadmis@indiana.edu*
Web: *www.law.indiana.edu*

Contact

Patricia Clark, Director of Admissions, 812-855-4765 for general inquiries; Patricia S. Clark, Admissions Coordinator, 812-855-2704 for financial aid information.

Law, Civil Procedure I and II, Contracts I and II, Torts, Property, Constitutional Law I, and Legal Research and Writing I and II. The school holds a 2-day orientation program immediately preceding the beginning of classes. Law School policies and procedures, academic regulations, course requirements, and special services (career planning, educational assistance) are discussed.

Electives

The School of Law offers concentrations in corporate law, criminal law, entertainment law, environmental law, family law, international law, juvenile law, labor law, litigation, maritime law, media law, securities law, sports law, tax law, torts and insurance, communications law, law and society. Clinics include the Community Legal Clinic, which assists area residents with family law issues; the Child Advocacy Clinic, which provides students with for-credit legal experiences in pending custody, visitation, and guardianship cases; and the Federal Courts Clinic, in which students work with a federal judge in Indianapolis for one day each week and receive academic credit. Each year the school offers 10 to 14 seminars that involve intensive analysis of one or more legal issues and submission of a substantive research paper. Internships are available in all 3 years of law study with a variety of public agencies, nonprofit organizations, and public interest groups, and may be arranged for credit. Students must demonstrate proficiency in legal research and writing by the execution of a complex research project involving problem definition, research, and completion of a substantial written product. Credit ranges from 1 to 3 credits. Second- and third-year students may arrange supervised clinical projects under the direction of a faculty member who specializes in the relevant area of law. A number of prominent judges and lawyers visit the school each year, including Chief Justice Rehnquist and Judge Ginsberg. The school participates in a consortium that holds a semester-long program in London each spring. All first-year students take small group instruction in a year-long course designed to teach students to research and write about legal issues. Remedial programs include a voluntary Educational Assistance Program. The school hosts a Minority Law Day each year for prospective students and prelaw advisers and participates in the state bar Minority Clerkship Program and in the state-run Legal Education Opportunities Program. Special interest group programs include the Jurist-in-Residence and Practitioner-in-Residence programs. The most widely taken electives are Business, communications/intellectual property, and environmental law.

Graduation Requirements

In order to graduate, candidates must have a GPA of 2.3, have completed the upper-division writing requirement, and must be in residence in an approved law school for 6 semesters of full-time study.

Organizations

Students edit the *Indiana Law Journal, Federal Communications Law Journal,* and the *Indiana Journal of Global Legal Studies.* Annual competitions include the ABA National Appellate Advocacy Competition, Jessup International Competition, the Trial Practice Competition, and the Negotiations Competition. The school hosts its own internal Sherman Minton Moot Court Competition. Law student organizations include the Moot Court Board, Black Law Students Association, and Christian Legal Society. There are local chapters of Delta Theta Phi, Phi Alpha Delta, and Phi Delta Phi.

Library

The law library contains 591,504 hard-copy volumes and 1,138,543 microform volume equivalents, and subscribes to 7584 serial publications. Such on-line databases and networks as DIALOG, LEXIS, WESTLAW, NEXIS, OCLC, GPO Access, and the Internet are available to law students for research. The law library is a depository for records and briefs of the U.S. Supreme Court, Indiana Court of Appeals, Indiana Supreme Court, and Seventh Circuit Court of Appeals; a selective depository for U.S. government publications; and houses a rare books and archives collection. The library recently added a laptop room where students can bring their own laptops and connect to the university's network. Network cards may be checked out for students who need them. The ratio of library volumes to faculty is 18,485 to 1 and to students is 911 to 1. The ratio of seats in the library to students is 1 to 1.

Placement

J.D.s awarded: 215

Services available through: a separate law school placement center

Services: job fairs and career planning seminars, videotaped mock interview program, minority clerkship program

Special features: office staffed by two experienced attorneys; extensive resource collection and handout series on career options and job search strategies; an alumni career network; weekly career seminars; and an employer visitation program.

Full-time job interviews:	n/av
Summer job interviews:	117 employers
Placement by graduation:	65% of class
Placement within 9 months:	96% of class
Average starting salary:	$19,000 to $185,000

Areas of placement:

Private practice 2-10 attorneys	19%
Private practice 11-25 attorneys	5%
Private practice 26-50 attorneys	9%
Private practice 51-100 attorneys	9%
Private practice 101-250 attorneys	6%
Government	12%
Unknown	12%
Business/Industry	11%
Judicial clerkships	9%
Public interest	5%
Academic	3%
Military	1%

Faculty

The law school has approximately 38 full-time and 16 part-time faculty members, of whom 17 are women. According to AAUP standards for Category I institutions, faculty salaries are average. About 41% of full-time faculty have a graduate law degree in addition to the J.D.; about 13% of part-time faculty have one. The ratio of full-time students to full-time faculty in an average class is 18 to 1; in a clinic, 5 to 1. There is a chapter of the Order of the Coif; 16 faculty are members.

Students

About 43% of the student body are women; 20%, minorities; 8%, African American; 5%, Asian American; and 4%, Hispanic. Most students come from Indiana (56%). The average age of entering students is 24; age range is 18 to 52. About 50% of students enter directly from undergraduate school, 10% have a graduate degree, and 50% have worked full-time prior to entering law school. About 3% drop out after the first year for academic or personal reasons; 97% remain to receive a law degree.

INDIANA UNIVERSITY-PURDUE UNIVERSITY

University School of Law-Indianapolis

530 West New York Street
Indianapolis, IN 46202-3225

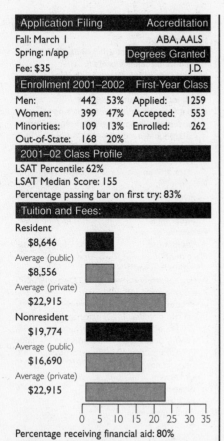

Application Filing		Accreditation
Fall: March 1		ABA, AALS
Spring: n/app		**Degrees Granted**
Fee: $35		J.D.

Enrollment 2001–2002			First-Year Class	
Men:	442	53%	Applied:	1259
Women:	399	47%	Accepted:	553
Minorities:	109	13%	Enrolled:	262
Out-of-State:	168	20%		

2001–02 Class Profile

LSAT Percentile: 62%
LSAT Median Score: 155
Percentage passing bar on first try: 83%

Tuition and Fees:

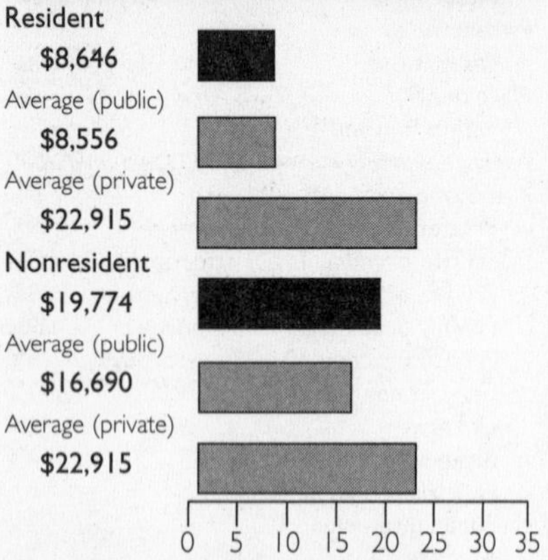

Percentage receiving financial aid: 80%

ADMISSIONS

In the fall 2001 first-year class, 1259 applied, 553 were accepted, and 262 enrolled. Thirty-three transfers enrolled. The median LSAT percentile of the most recent first-year class was 62; the median GPA was 3.3 on a scale of 4.0. The lowest LSAT percentile accepted was 6; the highest was 97.

Requirements

Applicants must have a bachelor's degree and take the LSAT. Minimum acceptable LSAT percentile is 20 and minimum acceptable GPA is 2.5 on a scale of 4.0. The most important admission factors include GPA, LSAT results, and academic achievement. No specific undergraduate courses are required. Candidates are not interviewed.

Procedure

The application deadline for fall entry is March 1. Applicants should submit an application form, LSAT results, transcripts, a nonrefundable application fee of $35, 3 letters of recommendation (optional, but encouraged), and a personal statement. Notification of the admissions decision is on a rolling basis. The latest acceptable LSAT test date for fall entry is February. The law school uses the LSDAS.

Special

The law school recruits minority and disadvantaged students by means of Minority Law Day visits to historically black colleges and universities, CLEO, ICLEO, and LSASS candidate referral search. Requirements are not different for out-of-state students. Transfer students must have one year of credit and have attended an ABA-approved law school. Acceptance also depends on space availability.

Costs

Tuition and fees for the 2001-2002 academic year are $8646 for full-time in-state students and $19,774 for out-of-state students. Tuition for part-time students is $5606 in-state and $12,785 out-of-state. On-campus room and board costs about $8000 annually; books and supplies run $500.

Financial Aid

About 80% of current law students receive some form of aid. The average annual amount of aid from all sources combined, including scholarships, loans, and work contracts, is $11,000; maximum, $18,500. Awards are based on need and merit; if awards are from a private donor, requirements differ. Required financial statements are the CSS Profile and the law school's financial aid application. The aid application deadline for fall entry is March 1. Special funds for minority or disadvantaged students consist of awards from private donors and the National Labor Relations Board, Region 25, as well as Indiana CLEO for under-represented groups in the legal field. First-year students are notified about their financial aid application at time of acceptance.

About the Law School

Indiana University-Purdue University at Indianapolis School of Law was established in 1895 and is a public institution. The campus is in an urban area in Indianapolis. The primary mission of the law school is to provide a legal education that will equip graduates with highly refined analytical and problem-solving skills, compassion, and ethics. Students have access to federal, state, county, city, and local agencies, courts, correctional facilities, law firms, and legal aid organizations in the Indianapolis area. Facilities of special interest to law students include the Municipal Court House where some classes are held and the National Institute of Fitness and Sports. Housing for students is available for single and married students in university-owned housing, but that housing is in short supply. Most students live in off-campus apartments.

Calendar

The law school operates on a traditional semester basis. Courses for full-time students are offered days only and must be completed within 60 months. For part-time students, courses are offered evenings only and must be completed within 60 months. New full- and part-time students are admitted in the fall. There is an 8-week summer session. Transferable summer courses are offered.

Programs

In addition to the J.D., the law school offers the LL.B. and the LL.M. for foreign students. The following joint degrees may be earned: J.D./M.B.A. (Juris Doctor/Master of Business Administration), J.D./M.H.A. (Juris Doctor/Master of Health Administration), J.D./M.P.A. (Juris Doctor/Master of Public Affairs), and J.D./M.P.H. (Master of Public Health).

Phone: 317-274-2459
Fax: 317-274-3955
E-mail: *khmiller@iupui.edu*
Web: *indylaw.indiana.edu*

Contact

Angela Espada, Assistant Dean for Admissions, 317-274-2459 for general inquiries; Financial Aid Office, 317-278-4723 for financial aid information.

Required

To earn the J.D., candidates must complete 90 total credits, of which 37 are for required courses. They must maintain a minimum GPA of 2.3 in the required courses. The following first-year courses are required of all students: Civil Procedure I and II, Contracts I and II, Legal Writing I and II, Property I and II, Torts I and II, and Criminal Law. Required upper-level courses consist of Constitutional Law I and Professional Responsibility. The required orientation program for first-year students is 2 days in the fall, which covers case briefing, outlining, library use, and basic computer use.

Electives

The Indiana University School of Law-Indianapolis offers concentrations in corporate law, criminal law, international law, litigation, tax law, health law, international human rights, and state and local government law. In addition, halfway through their studies, students may take clinics in Civil Practice, Disability, and Criminal Defense. Clients are represented by students under the supervision of faculty. Seminars are available for 2 credits in areas such as evidence, agricultural law, and American Legal history. Internships for students are offered in banking (trust division); commercial, environmental, immigration, international, and local government law; with the federal court; with the Indiana Civil Liberties Union; with a public defender; and for noncredit opportunities. Credit varies from none to 2 hours. A special lecture series is active at the law school with various speakers and topics of interest. Study abroad is available through the Annual Summer China and France programs as well as the International Human Rights program. Tutorial assistance is offered through the Dean's Tutorial Society, led by students, and the Tutorial Study group, led by a faculty member. There is a summer program for first-year students prior to fall classes. A Minority Law Day is held for prospective students. Indiana CLEO is available for under-represented groups in the legal profession. Special interest group programs are Law and Medicine and the Colloquim on Environmental Law. The most widely taken electives are Environmental Law and Family Law.

Graduation Requirements

In order to graduate, candidates must have a GPA of 2.3 and have completed the upper-division writing requirement.

Organizations

Students edit the *Indiana Law Review*, the *Indiana International and Comparative Law Review*, and the student newspaper, *The Dictum*. Moot court teams are sent annually to the ABA-National Appellate Advocacy Competition, the Privacy Competition in Chicago, Illinois, and the Philip C. Jessup International Law Competition. Teams also compete in the Client Counseling Competition. Law student organizations include the Black Law Students Association, Women's Caucus, and Phi Alpha Delta. Other organizations include the Health Law Society, the Law and Technology Association, and the Wendell Wilkie International Law Society. Campus clubs include Students Against Capital Punishment, LAMBDA, and Sports and Entertainment Law Association.

Library

The law library contains 530,267 hardcopy volumes and 60,524 microform volume equivalents, and subscribes to 7229 serial publications. Such on-line databases and networks as LEXIS and WESTLAW are available to law students for research. Special library collections include United States government and United Nations publications. Recently, the library increased library space in another building. The ratio of library volumes to faculty is 11,282 to 1 and to students is 666 to 1. The ratio of seats in the library to students is 1 to 1.

Faculty

The law school has 47 full-time and 40 part-time faculty members, of whom 27 are women. According to AAUP standards for Category IIA institutions, faculty salaries are above average. About 39% of full-time faculty have a graduate law degree in addition to the J.D.; about 16% of part-time faculty have one. The ratio of full-time students to full-time faculty in an average class is 16 to 1; in a clinic, 10 to 1. The law school has a regular program of bringing visiting professors and other distinguished lecturers and visitors to campus.

Placement

J.D.s awarded: 262
Services available through: a separate law school placement center
Services: mock interviews and a 24-hour resume service
Special features: panel discussions on alternative and nontraditional careers. The "A day in the life" series highlights the judiciary, corporate law, clerkships, and public interest careers, among others.
Full-time job interviews: 43 employers
Summer job interviews: n/av
Placement by graduation: 70% of class
Placement within 9 months: 93% of class
Average starting salary: $30,000 to $81,000
Areas of placement:

Private practice 2-100 attorneys	52%
Government	19%
Business/industry	19%
Judicial clerkships	6%
Public interest	2%
Military	1%
Academic	1%

Students

About 47% of the student body are women; 13%, minorities; 10%, African American; 3%, Asian American; 1%, Hispanic; and 1%, Native American. The majority of students come from Indiana (80%). The average age of entering students is 27; age range is 21 to 53. About 25% of students enter directly from undergraduate school, 14% have a graduate degree, and 74% have worked full-time prior to entering law school. About 3% drop out after the first year for academic or personal reasons; 97% remain to receive a law degree.

INTER-AMERICAN UNIVERSITY OF PUERTO RICO

School of Law

P.O. Box 70351
San Juan, PR 00936-8351

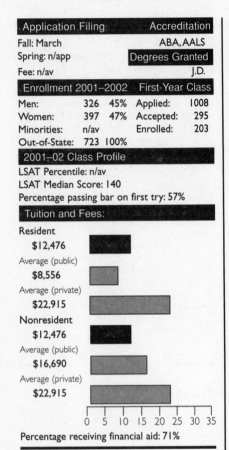

Application Filing

Fall: March
Spring: n/app
Fee: n/av

Accreditation

ABA, AALS

Degrees Granted

J.D.

Enrollment 2001–2002		
Men:	326	45%
Women:	397	47%
Minorities:	n/av	
Out-of-State:	723	100%

First-Year Class	
Applied:	1008
Accepted:	295
Enrolled:	203

2001–02 Class Profile

LSAT Percentile: n/av
LSAT Median Score: 140
Percentage passing bar on first try: 57%

Tuition and Fees:

Resident
$12,476
Average (public)
$8,556
Average (private)
$22,915
Nonresident
$12,476
Average (public)
$16,690
Average (private)
$22,915

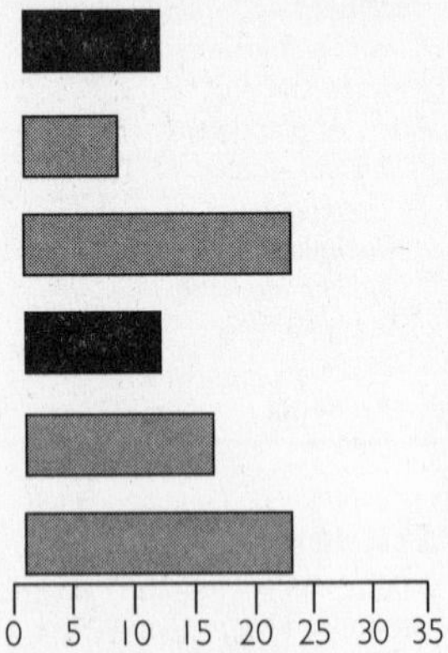

Percentage receiving financial aid: 71%

ADMISSIONS

In the fall 2001 first-year class, 1008 applied, 295 were accepted, and 203 enrolled. The median GPA of a recent first-year class was 3.1. The lowest LSAT percentile accepted was 2; the highest was 86.

Requirements

Applicants must have a bachelor's degree and take the LSAT. Minimum acceptable GPA is 2.5 on a scale of 4.0. No specific undergraduate courses are required. Candidates are not interviewed.

Procedure

The application deadline for fall entry is March. Applicants should submit an application form, LSAT results, transcripts, PAEG scores, and have a proficiency in Spanish. Accepted students must pay a $125 seat deposit. Notification of the admissions decision is by May 20. The latest acceptable LSAT test date for fall entry is February. The law school uses the LSDAS.

Special

Requirements are different for out-of-state students in that foreign students are required to submit evidence of their authorization to study in Puerto Rico, as well as the documents required by the Immigration and Naturalization Office of the U.S. Department of Justice. Transfer students must have a minimum GPA of 2.5 and have attended an ABA-approved law school. They are admitted for fall, spring, or summer session. The School offers a compulsory 3-week summer preparation course for students admitted to the J.D. program.

Costs

Tuition and fees for the 2001-2002 academic year are $12,476 for all full-time students. Tuition for part-time students is $10,076 per year. Books and supplies run about $600 annually.

Financial Aid

About 71% of current law students receive some form of aid. The average annual amount of aid from all sources combined, including scholarships, loans, and work contracts, is $8466. Awards are based on need and merit. Although law students do not qualify for BEOG awards, the FAFSA is required. Required financial statement is the FAFSA. First-year students are notified about their financial aid application at time of acceptance.

About the Law School

Inter-American University of Puerto Rico School of Law was established in 1961 and is a private institution. The campus is in an urban area in metropolitan San Juan. The primary mission of the law school is to train professionals competent for public and private practice through a broad background in the history and development of the law, particulary how it affects contemporary Puerto Rican legal issues and institutions; and also to promote legal research and continued legal education of its alumni and others in the legal profession. Students have access to federal, state, county, city, and local agencies, courts, correctional facilities, law firms, and legal aid organizations in the San Juan area. The school's location grants students access to additional resources such as the University of Puerto Rico Law School and the Puerto Rico Bar Association. Facilities of special interest to law students are the moot courtroom and law library. Housing for students is available in the neighborhood for those students who reside outside the metropolitan area. The school does not provide housing facilities.

Calendar

The law school operates on a traditional semester basis. Courses for full-time students are offered both day and evening and must be completed within from 3 to 6 years. For part-time students, courses are offered both day and evening and must be completed within from 4 to 8 years. New full- and part-time students are admitted in the fall. There is a summer session. Transferable summer courses are not offered.

Phone: 787-751-1912, ext. 2013
Web: *www.inter.edu/derecho.html*

Contact

Marilucy Gonzalez, Dean of Students, 787-751-1912, ext. 2011 for general inquiries; Ricardo Crespo, Director of Financial Aid, 787-751-1912, ext. 2014 for financial aid information.

Programs

Required

To earn the J.D., candidates must complete 92 total credits, of which 62 are for required courses. They must maintain a minimum GPA of 2.0 in the required courses. The following first-year courses are required of all students: Introduction to Law, Research Analysis and Writing, Family Law, Criminal Law, Property Law, Constitutional Law I, General Theory of Obligations and Contracts, and Criminal Procedure. Required upper-level courses consist of Constitutional Law II, History of Puerto Rican Law, Administrative Law, Civil Procedure—Successions, Evidence, Torts, Ethics of the Legal Professional, Mortgage Law, and Litigation: Theory, Doctrine, and Practice. All students must take clinical courses. The required orientation program for first-year students is a summer introductory course and a program during the week preceding the fall semester.

Electives

The Legal Aid Clinic involves students in offering legal advice, handling cases before courts and administrative agencies, and drafting legal documents for 4 credits. Seminars provide in-depth study in various areas of law and are worth 3 credits each. The most widely taken electives are Labor Law, Employment Law, Commercial Law, Corporate Law, Federal Jurisdiction, and Notarial Practice.

Graduation Requirements

In order to graduate, candidates must have a GPA of 2.0 and have completed the upper-division writing requirement.

Organizations

The primary law review is the *Revista Juridica de la Universidad Interamerica de Puerto Rico*, which is edited by students, professors, and scholars. The student newspaper is the *Student Council Bulletin*. Other publications include *AD REM*. Student council members serve on law school committees. There are local chapters of the ABA-Law Student Division, National Law Students Association, Phi Alpha Delta-Luis Munoz Morales chapter, and the National Hispanic Bar Association—Law Student Division. Other organizations include the Students' Cooperative Bookstore.

Library

The law library contains 160,098 hard-copy volumes and 139,963 microform volume equivalents, and subscribes to 2329 serial publications. Such on-line databases and networks as LEXIS and Internet, LIBIS (the university's library), and MICROJURIS (Puerto Rican Law Data Base) are available to law students for research. Special library collections include Domingo Toledo Alamo, Jose Ramon Velez Torres, and Hipolito Marcano. Also, 3 private collections of civil law books include rare books. Recently, the library had main library services that were fully computerized (circulation, acquisition, and an on-line catalog with bilingual subject headings—English and Spanish) and a building was constructed. The ratio of library volumes to faculty is 4447 to 1 and to students is 270 to 1. The ratio of seats in the library to students is 1 to 2.

Faculty

The law school has 20 full-time and 16 part-time faculty members, of whom 11 are women. About 70% of full-time faculty have a graduate law degree in addition to the J.D.; about 37% of part-time faculty have one. The ratio of full-time students to full-time faculty in an average class is 13 to 1; in a clinic, 4 to 1.

Students

About 47% of the student body are women. The average age of entering students is 24; age range is 21 to 50. About 90% of students enter directly from undergraduate school and 10% have a graduate degree. About 8% drop out after the first year for academic or personal reasons; 92% remain to receive a law degree.

Placement	
J.D.s awarded:	n/av
Services available through:	Office of the Dean of Students
Full-time job interviews:	n/av
Summer job interviews:	n/av
Placement by graduation:	20% of class
Placement within 9 months:	98% of class
Average starting salary:	$28,000 to $68,000
Areas of placement:	n/av

JOHN MARSHALL LAW SCHOOL

315 South Plymouth Court
Chicago, IL 60604

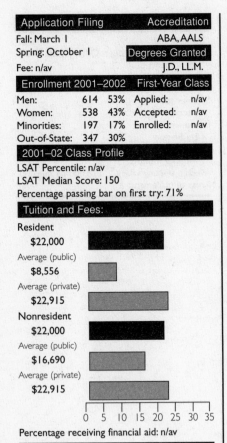

Application Filing | **Accreditation**
Fall: March 1 | ABA, AALS
Spring: October 1
Fee: n/av

Degrees Granted
J.D., LL.M.

Enrollment 2001–2002			First-Year Class	
Men:	614	53%	Applied:	n/av
Women:	538	43%	Accepted:	n/av
Minorities:	197	17%	Enrolled:	n/av
Out-of-State:	347	30%		

2001–02 Class Profile
LSAT Percentile: n/av
LSAT Median Score: 150
Percentage passing bar on first try: 71%

Tuition and Fees:

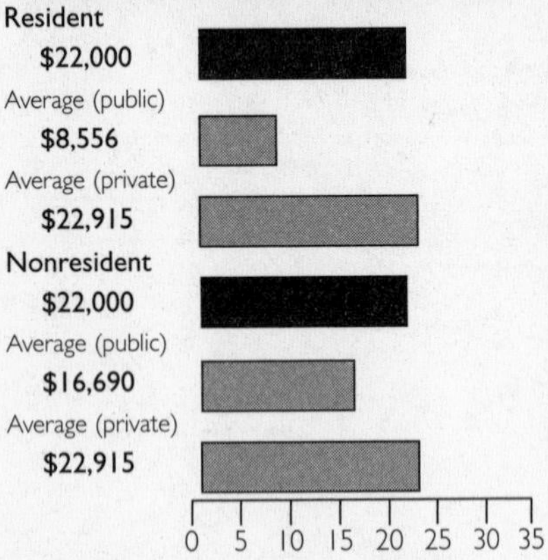

Percentage receiving financial aid: n/av

ADMISSIONS

Information in the above capsule is from an earlier year. In a recent first-year class, fifteen transfers enrolled. The median GPA of a recent first-year class was 3.4.

Requirements

Applicants must have a bachelor's degree and take the LSAT. The most important admission factors include character, personality, GPA, and LSAT results. No specific undergraduate courses are required. Candidates are not interviewed.

Procedure

Check with the school for current application deadlines and fee. Applicants should submit an application form, TOEFL or TWE if applicable, 2 to 3 letters of recommendation, and LSDAS report. Notification of the admissions decision is 2 to 5 weeks after their file is complete. The law school uses the LSDAS.

Special

Requirements are not different for out-of-state students. Transfer students must have a minimum GPA of 2.5 and have attended an ABA-approved law school.

Costs

Tuition and fees for the academic year are approximately $22,000 for full-time in-state students. Books and supplies run about $780.

Financial Aid

The maximum annual amount of aid from all sources combined, including scholarships, loans, and work contracts, is about $32,000. Awards are based on need and merit. Required financial statement is the FAFSA. Check with the school for current application deadlines. First-year students are notified about their financial aid application at time of acceptance.

About the Law School

John Marshall Law School was established in 1899 is independent. The campus is in an urban area in Chicago. The primary mission of the law school is to provide students with an intellectually challenging foundation in legal principles and a rigorous background in lawyering skills. Students have access to federal, state, county, city, and local agencies, courts, correctional facilities, law firms, and legal aid organizations in the Chicago area. Housing for students is readily available and assistance is provided through the admissions office. All law school facilities are accessible to the physically disabled.

Calendar

The law school operates on a traditional semester basis. Courses for full-time students are offered both day and evening and must be completed within 5 years. For part-time students, courses are offered both day and evening and Saturdays and must be completed within 6 years. New full- and part-time students are admitted in the fall and spring. There is an 8-week summer session. Transferable summer courses are offered.

Programs

In addition to the J.D., the law school offers the LL.M. in intellectual property, taxation, and real estate. The following joint degrees may be earned: J.D./M.B.A. (Juris Doctor/Master of Business Administration).

Phone: 312-987-1406
537-4280
Fax: 312-427-5136
E-mail: *admission@jmls.edu*
Web: *www.jmls.edu*

Contact
Admissions and Student Affairs, 312-987-1406 for general inquiries; Susan Bogart, Assistant Director, 312-427-2737, ext. 510 for financial aid information.

Required
To earn the J.D., candidates must complete 90 total credits, of which 52 are for required courses. They must maintain a minimum GPA of 2.0 in the required courses. The following first-year courses are required of all students: Contracts I and II, Property I and II, Criminal Law, Torts I and II, Civil Procedure I and II, Lawyering Skills I and II, and Constitutional Law I and II. Required upper-level courses consist of Evidence, Trial Advocacy, and Lawyering Skills III and IV. All students must take clinical courses. The required orientation program for first-year students is 1 day for day students and 2 evenings for evening students entering with the August class, and 2 evenings for day and evening students entering with the January class.

Electives
The John Marshall Law School offers concentrations in international law, tax law, and advocacy and dispute resolution, business, estate planning, general practice, informatics, intellectual property, and real estate. In addition, clinics are open to students with at least 53 hours and prior approval. Clinics offer from 1 to 3 credits and are with the Chicago Corporation Counsel, Fair Housing, Legal Aid Bureau, Illinois Attorney General, intellectual property law, judicial and legislative clerkships, Legal Aid Bureau, Public Defender, State's Attorney of Cook County, Travelers and Immigrants Aid, and the U.S. Attorney, Northern District of Illinois. Seminars are worth 2 to 3 credits, and are in the areas of banking, business planning, computers, constitutional law, counseling and negotiating, estate planning, information law, rights of prisoners, scientific evidence, intellectual property, taxation, and trial advocacy. Research programs, worth 1 to 2 credits, are open to students who have at least 59 hours. A scholarly paper must be produced from research supervised by a faculty member. Special interest groups are the Center for Informatics Law, Center for Intellectual Property Law, Center for Forensic Science, Fair Housing Legal Support Center, and the International Law Program. The most widely taken electives are Corporations, Remedies, and Negotiable Instruments.

Graduation Requirements
In order to graduate, candidates must have a GPA of 2.0 and have completed 4 semesters of Lawyering Skills.

Organizations
Student-edited publications are *The John Marshall Law Review*, the *Journal of Computer and Information Law*, and the student newspaper *Decisive Utterance*. Teams are sent annually to more than 20 interscholastic moot court competitions. Law student organizations include the Student Bar Association, Illinois State Bar Association-Law Student Division, and ABA-Law Student Division.

Library
The law library contains 353,737 hard-copy volumes and 55,710 microform volume equivalents, and subscribes to 5011 serial publications. Such on-line databases and networks as DIALOG, LEXIS, WESTLAW, NEXIS, CCALI, InfoTrac, Wilsondisc, OCLC, and DOLLY, the school's on-line catalog are available to law students for research. Special library collections include a U.S. goverment documents depository. The ratio of library volumes to faculty is 6317 to 1 and to students is 326 to 1. The ratio of seats in the library to students is 1 to 2.

Faculty
The law school has approximately 56 full-time and 138 part-time faculty members, of whom 43 are women. About 25% of full-time faculty have a graduate law degree in addition to the J.D. The ratio of full-time students to full-time faculty in an average class is 23 to 1.

Students
About 43% of the student body are women; 17%, minorities; 6%, African American; 5%, Asian American; 5%, Hispanic; and 1%, Native American. The majority of students come from Illinois (70%). The average age of entering students is 25; age range is 20 to 69. About 14% of students have a graduate degree and 40% have worked full-time prior to entering law school. About 5% drop out after the first year for academic or personal reasons.

Placement

J.D.s awarded:	313
Services available through: a separate law school placement center and career services office	
Special features: the Law Practice Management Program, an 8-week course offered free to recent graduates interested in starting their own practice.	
Full-time job interviews:	35 employers
Summer job interviews:	35 employers
Placement by graduation:	52% of class
Placement within 9 months:	90% of class
Average starting salary:	$48,900
Areas of placement:	
Private practice 2-10 attorneys	23%
Private practice 11-25 attorneys	7%
Private practice 26-50 attorneys	6%
Private practice 51-100 attorneys	4%
Private practice 100+ attorneys; 6% unknown	6%
Business/industry	21%
Government	12%
Judicial clerkships	4%
Public interest	1%

LEWIS AND CLARK COLLEGE

Northwestern School of Law

10015 Southwest Terwilliger Boulevard
Portland, OR 97219

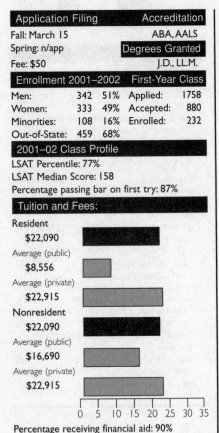

Application Filing
Fall: March 15
Spring: n/app
Fee: $50

Accreditation
ABA, AALS

Degrees Granted
J.D., LL.M.

Enrollment 2001–2002

Men:	342	51%
Women:	333	49%
Minorities:	108	16%
Out-of-State:	459	68%

First-Year Class

Applied:	1758
Accepted:	880
Enrolled:	232

2001–02 Class Profile
LSAT Percentile: 77%
LSAT Median Score: 158
Percentage passing bar on first try: 87%

Tuition and Fees:
Resident
$22,090
Average (public)
$8,556
Average (private)
$22,915
Nonresident
$22,090
Average (public)
$16,690
Average (private)
$22,915

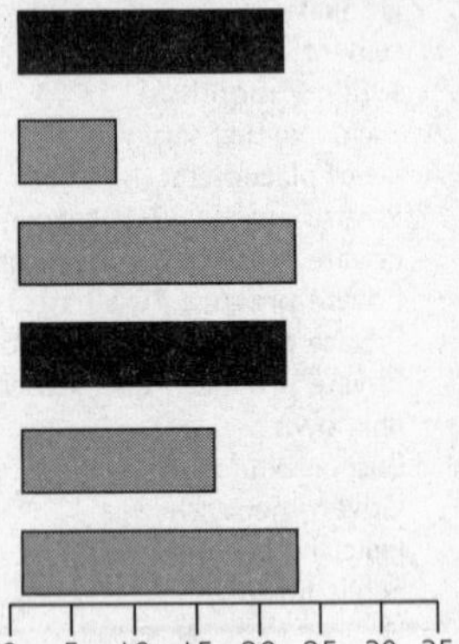

Percentage receiving financial aid: 90%

ADMISSIONS

In the fall 2001 first-year class, 1758 applied, 880 were accepted, and 232 enrolled. Thirty transfers enrolled. The median LSAT percentile of the most recent first-year class was 77; the median GPA was 3.27 on a scale of 4.0. The lowest LSAT percentile accepted was 11; the highest was 99.

Requirements
Applicants must have a bachelor's degree and take the LSAT. The most important admission factors include LSAT results, GPA, and writing ability. No specific undergraduate courses are required. Candidates are not interviewed.

Procedure
The application deadline for fall entry is March 15. Applicants should submit an application form, LSAT results, transcripts, a nonrefundable application fee of $50, 1 or 2 letters of recommendation, an essay, resume, LSDAS report of undergraduate work, and optional statements on extracurricular activities or special circumstances. Notification of the admissions decision is on a rolling basis. The latest acceptable LSAT test date for fall entry is February. The law school uses the LSDAS.

Special
The law school recruits minority and disadvantaged students by having law school representatives visit undergraduate institutions with significant ethnic enrollment; by offering scholarships to ethnic minority admits through funds provided by the law school, by inviting prelaw advisers from undergraduate schools with large ethnic minority populations to visit the campus; by partnering with the Oregon State Bar to attract and retain ethnic minority students in Oregon; and by contacting ethnic minority candidates who take the LSAT. Requirements are not different for out-of-state students. Transfer students must have one year of credit, have attended an ABA-approved law school, and achieved strong academic standing at the school from which the student is transferring, and present a compelling reason for wishing to transfer to Lewis and Clark.

Costs

Tuition and fees for the 2001-2002 academic year are $22,090 for all full-time students. Tuition for part-time students is $16,570 per year. Books and supplies run about $800 annually.

Financial Aid

About 90% of current law students receive some form of aid. The average annual amount of aid from all sources combined, including scholarships, loans, and work contracts, is $26,982; maximum, $33,794. Awards are based on need and merit. Required financial statement is the FAFSA. The aid application deadline for fall entry is March 1. Special funds for minority or disadvantaged students consist of scholarship monies from the school, Oregon State Bar funds, and a special Native American Scholarship. Loans are determined shortly after admittance; scholarships are granted with the offer of admission.

About the Law School

Lewis and Clark College Northwestern School of Law was established in 1884 and is a private institution. The 31-acre campus is in a suburban area within Portland. The primary mission of the law school is to train and educate students about the law and about being ethical, well-rounded professionals. The school also strives to advance the knowledge, skills, and professionalism of legal practitioners. Students have access to federal, state, county, city, and local agencies, courts, correctional facilities, law firms, and legal aid organizations in the Portland area. The American Inns of Court; clinical internship seminars; externships, and the Oregon student appearance rule, which allows students to appear in court, are available to students. Housing for students consists of a wide variety of off-campus apartments and houses that students share at reasonable rents. Campus-owned houses are also available for law students to rent. All law school facilities are accessible to the physically disabled.

Calendar

The law school operates on a traditional semester basis. Courses for full-time students are offered both day and evening and must be completed within 5 years. For part-time students, courses are offered both day and evening and must be completed within 6 years. New students are admitted in the fall. There are 2 5-week summer sessions. Transferable summer courses are not offered.

Programs

In addition to the J.D., the law school offers the LL.M.

Required
To earn the J.D., candidates must complete 86 total credits, of which 28-35 are for required courses. They must maintain a minimum GPA of 1.7 (first year) in the required courses. The following first-year courses are required of all students: Criminal Law (full-time students), Civil Procedure, Contracts, Property, Torts, Legal Analysis and Writing, and Constitutional Law I. Required upper-level courses consist of Constitutional Law II, Seminar, Professionalism, and Criminal Law (part-time students). The required orientation program for first-year students is a 2-day program consisting of registration on the first day and legal analysis introduction on the second day.

Electives
The Northwestern School of Law offers concentrations in corporate law, criminal law, environmental law, family law, international law, labor law, litigation, tax law, torts and insurance, intellectual property, and employment law. In addi-

Phone: 503-768-6613
800-303-4860
Fax: 503-768-6850
E-mail: *lawadmss@lclark.edu*
Web: *www.lclark.edu/LAW*

Contact

Admissions Office, 503-768-6613 for general inquiries; Diana Meyer, Assistant Director of Financial Services, 503-768-7090 for financial aid information.

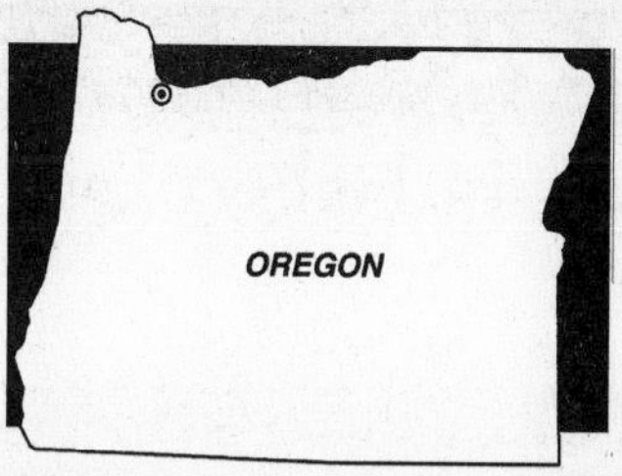

tion, the law school operates a clinic in downtown Portland that serves indigent clients and performs civil work in the areas of consumer, landlord-tenant, employment, and tax law. It is available to all upper-division students for 4 credits; qualified students may make court appearances. Other opportunities include the Pacific Environmental Advocacy Center, the International Environmental Law Project, and clinical internship seminars. Seminars are available in a variety of subjects and are limited to 20 students and usually require a paper. Each upper-division student must take 1 seminar to graduate. A 3-hour seminar is offered in conjunction with a 10-hour per week placement in the areas of criminal law, natural resources, intellectual property, in-house corporate counsel, and legal services for the disabled. The school also offers full semester or summer externships, which require a substantial paper in addition to working full time in an approved placement with significant faculty supervision. Students may work as research assistants to faculty members, write for the law reviews, and perform independent research projects for credit with faculty. Internship placements are available with the federal judiciary and state supreme court in areas such as tax law and endangered species. Externships are available in Oregon and throughout the world. The Higgins Visitor consists of a 2-week long visit from a distinguished attorney or professor who lectures in classes and to the school at large, and who meets with students in small groups. The school also hosts distinguished visitors each year in the area of natural resources and intellectual property. Students participate in study abroad at ABA law schools and apply these credits at Lewis and Clark. An academic support program is available to first-year ethnic minority students and to any upper-division student in academic difficulty, or to students who have overcome significant challenges and show exceptional promise. Students may begin the first year of school 1 week early, take a mini-class, and learn about exams and study skills. This is followed by seminars and workshops during the academic year. Students may participate in a wide variety of student organizations including, but not limited to the Student Bar Association, Public Interest Law Project, and Business Law Society. The most widely taken electives are Business/Corporate Law, Environmental, and Intellectual Property.

Graduation Requirements

In order to graduate, candidates must have a GPA of 2.0 and have completed the upper-division writing requirement.

Organizations

The primary law review is the *Environmental Law Review*. Other student-edited publications include *Journal of Small and Emerging Business Law, International Legal Perspectives*, and *Animal Law*. Moot Court competitions consist of a negotiation competition, environmental law, and tax law. A writing competition for the best paper in the area of international law is sponsored by the law firm of Ragen, Davis, and Wright. Law student organizations include Student Bar Association, Public Interest Law Project, and Minority Law Student Association. There are also local chapters of National Lawyers Guild, Phi Delta Phi, and the Student Animal Legal Defense Fund. The Softball League, Intellectual Property Society, and Women's Law Caucus are among clubs and organizations on campus.

Library

The law library contains 465,803 hard-copy volumes and 268,075 microform volume equivalents, and subscribes to 4879 serial publications. Such on-line databases and networks as CALI, CIS Universe, Legal-Trac, LEXIS, LOIS, and NEXIS, among others are available. Special library collections include the Milton Pearl Environmental Law Collection, Tax/Estate Planning Collection, and others. Recently, the library was completely remodeled to add 17,200 square feet of space in a building, increased the number of group study rooms, and networked all library seats (375). The ratio of library volumes to faculty is 12,258 to 1 and to students is 690 to 1. The ratio of seats in the library to students is 1 to 2.

Faculty

The law school has 38 full-time and 54 part-time faculty members, of whom 33 are women. About 26% of full-time faculty have a graduate law degree in addition to the J.D. The ratio of full-time students to full-time faculty in an average class is 14 to 1; in a clinic, 4 to 1. The law school has a regular program of bringing visiting professors and other distinguished lecturers and visitors to campus.

Placement

J.D.s awarded: 218

Services available through: a separate law school placement center

Services: extensive resource library, 2 mentor programs, a video mock interview program, monthly jobs newsletter, a comprehensive web site with links, on-campus interview program, and public interest/pro bono honors program.

Special features: Regular information panels given by alumni and other Portland practitioners, a public-interest career information fair, breakfast with judges, clerking opportunities available throughout the year; pro bono honors program, an alumni network around the country, law firm receptions for first-year students, mandatory first year classes, and comprehensive handbook.

Full-time job interviews:	32 employers
Summer job interviews:	46 employers
Placement by graduation:	49% of class
Placement within 9 months:	97% of class
Average starting salary:	$35,000 to $50,000

Areas of placement:

Private practice 2-10 attorneys	14%
Private practice 11-25 attorneys	5%
Private practice 26-50 attorneys	5%
Private practice 51-100 attorneys	2%
Private practice 101+ attorneys	11%
Private practice—solo	6%
Private practice—firm size unknown	6%
Judicial clerkships	13%
Government	12%
Business/industry	12%
Public interest	9%
Academic	3%

Students

About 49% of the student body are women; 16%, minorities; 3%, African American; 7%, Asian American; 5%, Hispanic; 2%, Native American; and 3%, international students (all); 9% race/ethnicity unknown. 32% of students come from Oregon. The average age of entering students is 28; age range is 22 to 54. About 7% drop out after the first year for academic or personal reasons; 91% remain to receive a law degree.

LOUISIANA STATE UNIVERSITY

Paul M. Hebert Law Center

Baton Rouge, LA 70803

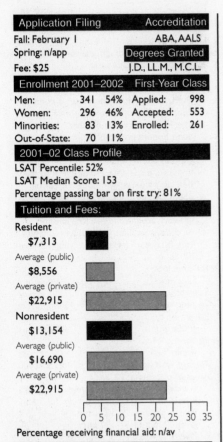

Application Filing		Accreditation
Fall: February 1		ABA, AALS
Spring: n/app		**Degrees Granted**
Fee: $25		J.D., LL.M., M.C.L.

Enrollment 2001–2002			First-Year Class	
Men:	341	54%	Applied:	998
Women:	296	46%	Accepted:	553
Minorities:	83	13%	Enrolled:	261
Out-of-State:	70	11%		

2001–02 Class Profile

LSAT Percentile: 52%

LSAT Median Score: 153

Percentage passing bar on first try: 81%

Tuition and Fees:

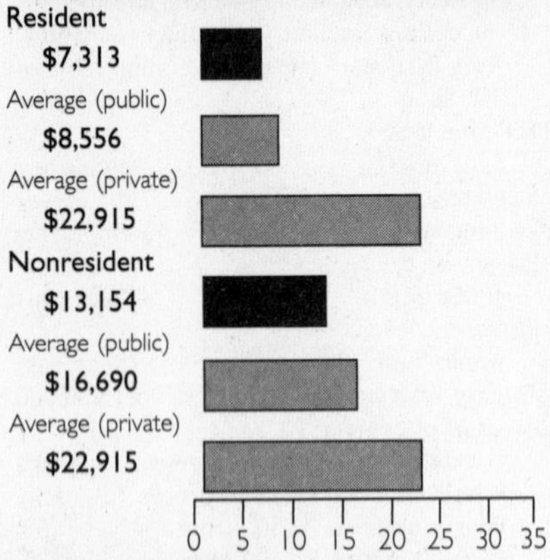

Percentage receiving financial aid: n/av

ADMISSIONS

In the fall 2001 first-year class, 998 applied, 553 were accepted, and 261 enrolled. One transfer enrolled. The median LSAT percentile of the most recent first-year class was 52; the median GPA was 3.28 on a scale of 4.0. The lowest LSAT percentile accepted was 7; the highest was 98.

Requirements

Applicants must have a bachelor's degree and take the LSAT. The most important admission factors include academic achievement and LSAT results. No specific undergraduate courses are required. Candidates are not interviewed.

Procedure

The application deadline for fall entry is February 1. Applicants should submit an application form, LSAT results, transcripts, a nonrefundable application fee of $25, 2 letters of recommendation, and a $500 seat deposit credited toward tuition. Notification of the admissions decision is on a rolling basis. The latest acceptable LSAT test date for fall entry is February. The law school uses the LSDAS.

Special

The law school recruits minority and disadvantaged students by means of an active recruiting program that identifies students through test scores and information received through the Law Services Candidate Referral Program. Requirements are different for out-of-state students in that credentials are usually higher than for in-state applicants, due to a 10% limit on out-of-state students. Transfer students must have one year of credit, have attended an ABA-approved law school, have reasons for seeking a transfer, and provide information on their overall first-year academic performance.

Costs

Tuition and fees for the 2001-2002 academic year are $7313 for full-time in-state students and $13,154 for out-of-state students. Tuition for part-time students is $5020 in-state and $9278 out-of-state. On-campus room and board costs about $10550 annually; books and supplies run $500.

Financial Aid

Required financial statement is the FFS. The aid application deadline for fall entry is April 1. First-year students are notified about their financial aid application shortly after applying.

About the Law School

Louisiana State University Paul M. Hebert Law Center was established in 1906 and is a public institution. The campus is in an urban area in Baton Rouge. The primary mission of the law school is to develop to the highest level the intellectual and professional capabilities of Louisiana citizens through resident instruction while enriching instruction and establishing new frontiers of knowledge through research and scholarly activity. Students have access to federal, state, county, city, and local agencies, courts, correctional facilities, law firms, and legal aid organizations in the Baton Rouge area. Legislative and executive branches of state government are also accessible to students. Housing for students is available in residence hall accommodations, as well as rooms and apartments in privately-owned facilities and university facilities.

Calendar

The law school operates on a traditional semester basis. Courses for full-time students are offered days only and must be completed within 4 years. There is no part-time program. New students are admitted in the fall. There is a 7-week summer session. Transferable summer courses are offered.

Programs

In addition to the J.D., the law school offers the LL.M. and M.C.L. Students may take relevant courses in other programs and apply credit toward the J.D.; a maximum of 12 hours of credits may be applied. The following joint degrees may be earned: J.D./B.C.L. (Juris Doctor/Bachelor of Civil Law), M.B.A./J.D. (Master of Business Administration/Juris Doctor), and M.P.A./J.D. (Master of Public Administration/Juris Doctor).

Phone: 225-578-8646
Fax: 225-578-8647
E-mail: *mforbe1@lsu.edu*
Web: *law.lsu.edu*

Contact

Michele Forbes, Director of Admissions and Student Affairs, 225-578-8646 for general inquiries; Kathy Sciacchetano, Director, 225-578-3103 for financial aid information.

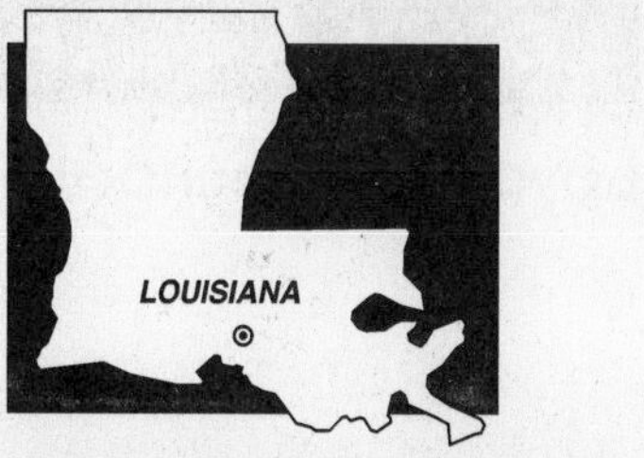

Required

To earn the J.D., candidates must complete 97 total credits, of which 62 are for required courses. They must maintain a minimum GPA of 1.0 in the required courses. The following first-year courses are required of all students: Administration of Criminal Justice I, Civil Law Property, Contracts, Basic Civil Procedure I, Constitutional Law I, Criminal Law, Torts, Obligations, Legal Traditions and Systems, Basic Civil Procedure II, and Legal Research and Writing. Required upper-level courses consist of Legal Profession, Evidence, Appellate Advocacy, and Trial Advocacy. All students must take clinical courses including Trial Advocacy and Appellate Advocacy. The required orientation program for first-year students provides some 2 hours with students, about 1 hour with faculty, and a 2-hour Professionalism Program sponsored by the Louisiana State Bar Association.

Electives

The Paul M. Hebert Law Center offers concentrations in corporate law, criminal law, environmental law, family law, international law, juvenile law, labor law, litigation, maritime law, media law, securities law, tax law, and torts and insurance. In addition, third-year students may take clinical courses in preparing for trials and oral arguments, generally worth 2 credits. Seminars are offered for 2 hours of credit. Special lecture series are the Edward Douglass White Lectures, the James J. Bailey Lectures, and the John H. Tucker, Jr. Lectures. Students may study for 6 weeks during the summer in Aix-en-Provence, France. Freshman tutorial programs are available. Minority students may take advantage of the summer conditional admit program. Students must pass the program to enroll in the fall semester. There are externships whereby 5 students may be selected to work under the supervision of any agency and the instructor in certain courses.

Graduation Requirements

In order to graduate, candidates must have a GPA of 2.0, and have completed the upper-division writing requirement by taking a seminar in which they must submit a paper.

Organizations

Students edit the *Louisiana Law Review* and the newspaper *Civilian*. Moot court competitions include the Tullis Moot Court at the Law Center and at the regional and national Jessup Moot Court and National Moot Court competitions. Teams also participate in the F. Lee Bailey, Frederick Douglass, and Entertainment Law moot courts, and the American Trial Lawyers and Louisiana State Bar Association, Young Lawyers Division, Mock Trial competitions. Law student organizations include the Student Bar Association, Flory Trial Club, and the Moot Court Board.

Library

The law library contains 406,308 hardcopy volumes and 890,000 microform volume equivalents, and subscribes to 3001 serial publications. Such on-line databases and networks as DIALOG, LEXIS, LOIS, and WESTLAW are available to law students for research. Special library collections include a U.S. government document depository, a depository for Louisiana Supreme Court and Court of Appeals briefs and records, and international, comparative, and foreign law collections, which include Roman Law. Recently, the library updated 3 computer laboratories. The ratio of library volumes to faculty is 12,974 to 1 and to students is 629 to 1. The ratio of seats in the library to students is 1 to 1.

Faculty

The law school has 42 full-time and 35 part-time faculty members, of whom 11 are women. According to AAUP standards for Category I institutions, faculty salaries are below average. About 24% of full-time faculty have a graduate law degree in addition to the J.D.; about 14% of part-time faculty have one. The ratio of full-time students to full-time faculty in an average class is 60 to 1; in a clinic, 20 to 1. There is a chapter of the Order of the Coif.

Placement

J.D.s awarded:	172
Services available through: a separate law school placement center and Law Center Career Services	
Special features: resume quick check, mock interviews for students, individual counseling, guest speakers, and special programs.	
Full-time job interviews:	47 employers
Summer job interviews:	67 employers
Placement by graduation:	75% of class
Placement within 9 months:	99% of class
Average starting salary:	$24,500 to $111,500
Areas of placement:	
Private practice 2-10 attorneys	29%
Private practice 11-25 attorneys	1%
Private practice 26-50 attorneys	11%
Private practice 51-100 attorneys	6%
Private practice 101-501 attorneys	8%
Judicial clerkships	25%
Government	6%
Business/industry	3%
Academic	1%

Students

About 46% of the student body are women; 13%, minorities; 10%, African American; 1%, Asian American; and 2%, Hispanic. The majority of students come from Louisiana (89%). The average age of entering students is 25; age range is 20 to 54. About 18% drop out after the first year for academic or personal reasons; 82% remain to receive a law degree.

LOYOLA MARYMOUNT UNIVERSITY

Loyola Law School

919 S. Albany Street
Los Angeles, CA 90015

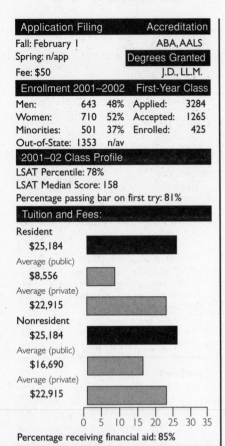

Application Filing	Accreditation
Fall: February 1	ABA, AALS
Spring: n/app	**Degrees Granted**
Fee: $50	J.D., LL.M.

Enrollment 2001–2002			First-Year Class	
Men:	643	48%	Applied:	3284
Women:	710	52%	Accepted:	1265
Minorities:	501	37%	Enrolled:	425
Out-of-State:	1353	n/av		

2001–02 Class Profile

LSAT Percentile: 78%
LSAT Median Score: 158
Percentage passing bar on first try: 81%

Tuition and Fees:

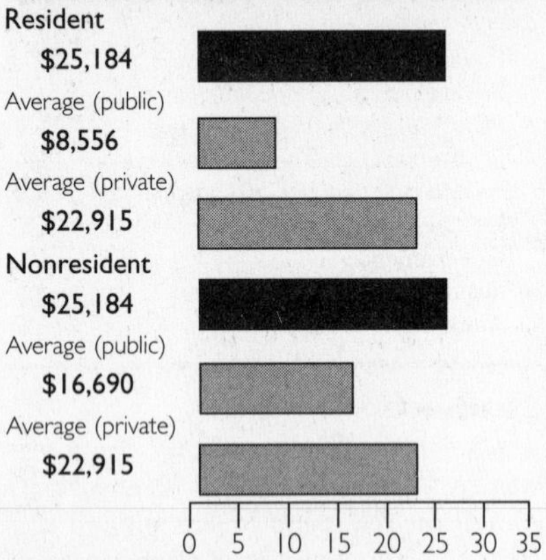

Percentage receiving financial aid: 85%

ADMISSIONS

In the fall 2001 first-year class, 3284 applied, 1265 were accepted, and 425 enrolled. Thirty-seven transfers enrolled. The median LSAT percentile of the most recent first-year class was 78; the median GPA was 3.34 on a scale of 4.0. The lowest LSAT percentile accepted was 23; the highest was 99.

Requirements

Applicants must have a bachelor's degree and take the LSAT. The most important admission factors include academic achievement, LSAT results, and general background. No specific undergraduate courses are required. Candidates are not interviewed.

Procedure

The application deadline for fall entry is February 1 (day program) and April 15 (evening program). Applicants should submit an application form, TOEFL (where applicable), a nonrefundable application fee of $50, 1 letter of recommendation, and a personal statement. Notification of the admissions decision is December through June. The latest acceptable LSAT test date for fall entry is February. The law school uses the LSDAS.

Special

The law school recruits minority and disadvantaged students with programs such as the Open House, campus visits by faculty, and financial support for outstanding minority applicants. Additionally, there is a Summer Institute program for students who need additional preparation prior to law school. Requirements are not different for out-of-state students. Transfer students must have one year of credit, have attended an ABA-approved law school, and have above average performance at prior law school.

Costs

Tuition and fees for the 2001-2002 academic year are $25,184 for all full-time students. Tuition for part-time students is $16,906 per year. Books and supplies run about $683 annually.

Financial Aid

About 85% of current law students receive some form of aid. The average annual amount of aid from all sources combined, including scholarships, loans, and work contracts, is $31,005; maximum, $40,763. Awards are based on need and merit. Required financial statement is the FAFSA. The aid application deadline for fall entry is March 1. Special funds for minority or disadvantaged students consist of scholarships. First-year students are notified about their financial aid application at time of acceptance.

About the Law School

Loyola Marymount University Loyola Law School was established in 1920 and is a private institution. The 2.5-acre campus is in an urban area ½ mile west of downtown Los Angeles. The primary mission of the law school is to educate men and women who will be leaders of both the legal profession and society, demonstrating in their practice of law and public service the highest standards of personal integrity, professional ethics, and a deep concern for social justice in the Jesuit Marymount tradition. Students have access to federal, state, county, city, and local agencies, courts, correctional facilities, law firms, and legal aid organizations in the Los Angeles area. Facilities of special interest to law students are the federal and municipal courts that are the regional head offices of major law firms and companies that comprise the financial center of the Pacific Rim countries. Housing for students is not available on campus, but there is a housing referral service. All law school facilities are accessible to the physically disabled.

Calendar

The law school operates on a traditional semester basis. Courses for full-time students are offered both day and evening and must be completed within 5 years. For part-time students, courses are offered both day and evening and must be completed within 5 years. New full- and part-time students are admitted in the fall. There is a 7 ½-week summer session. Transferable summer courses are offered.

Programs

In addition to the J.D., the law school offers the LL.M. Students may take relevant courses in other programs and apply credit toward the J.D.; a maximum of 6 credits may be applied. The following joint degrees may be earned: J.D./M.B.A. (Juris Doctor/Master of Business Administration).

Required

To earn the J.D., candidates must complete 87 total credits, of which 41 are for required courses. They must maintain a minimum grade average of 70 in the required courses. The following first-year courses are required of all students:

Phone: 213-736-1180
E-mail: *admissions@lls.edu*
Web: *www.lls.edu*

Contact

Cynthia Belevick, Assistant Director of Admissions, 213-736-1180 for general inquiries; John Hoyt, Director of Financial Aid, 212-736-1140 for financial aid information.

Criminal Law, Civil Procedure, Constitutional Law I, Contracts, Legal Research and Writing, Property, and Torts. Required upper-level courses consist of Constitutional Law II, Ethical Lawyering, Evidence, and a writing course. The required orientation program for first-year students is 2 to 3 days.

Electives

The Loyola Law School offers concentrations in corporate law, criminal law, entertainment law, environmental law, family law, international law, juvenile law, labor law, litigation, maritime law, media law, securities law, sports law, tax law, and torts and insurance. In addition, clinics are open to advanced students in good academic standing for a maximum of 14 clinical credits. Seminars and research programs are open to advanced students; these students are also eligible for internships, field work, and study-abroad programs. Seminars are generally worth 2 units each. The Fritz B. Burns Lecture Series brings nationally known legal scholars to the law school for debate and discourse. The law school offers 3 study abroad programs: Costa Rica (worth 4 units); Bologna, Italy (worth 2 to 4 units); and Beijing China (worth 3 units). Tutorials are available to students with academic need. The most widely taken electives are Copyright Law, Sports Law, and Marital Property.

Graduation Requirements

In order to graduate, candidates must have a grade average of 75, have completed the upper-division writing requirement, and 58 resident credits in addition to 40 hours of community service work.

Organizations

The primary student-edited law review is *Loyola of Los Angeles Law Review*. Other student-edited law reviews are the *Loyola of Los Angeles International and Comparative Law Review*, the *Loyola Entertainment Law Review*, and the campus electronic newsletter "In Brief." Annual moot court competitions include the Jessup, National, and Traynor competitions. Other competitions include the Byrne Trial Advocacy Competition, which includes on- and off-campus competitions in the fall and spring, the Black Law Students Association (BLSA) Moot Court Competition, the Hispanic National Bar Association (HWBA) Moot Court Competition, the White Collar Crime Competition, and the Patent Law Competition. Law student organizations include the Entertainment and Sports Law Society, the Criminal Law Society, and the St. Thomas More Honor Society. Local chapters of national associations include Phi Alpha Delta, National Lawyers Guild, and Public Interest Law Association. Campus clubs and other organizations include the Women's Law Association, the Asian Pacific American Law Student's Association (APALSA), and the Corporate and Business Law Association.

Library

The law library contains 533,799 hard-copy volumes and 1,256,026 microform volume equivalents, and subscribes to 7231 serial publications. Such on-line databases and networks as CALI, CIS Universe, Infotrac, Legal-Trac, LEXIS, LOIS, Mathew Bender, NEXIS, RLIN, WESTLAW, Wilsonline Indexes, Congressional Masterfile I and II, Congressional Universe, Dow Jones, State Net, RLIN, ORION, CALI, and LUCY (the library's on-line catalog) are available to law students for research. Special library collections include federal and state depositories and foreign collections of selected European, Latin American, and Pacific Rim countries. A complete U.S. legislative history from 1970 to the present includes all available records and briefs of the U.S. Supreme Court. There is also a complete collection of United Nations documents, law and popular culture, and a CBS News O.J. Simpson archive. Recently, the library was renovated and expanded. The renovated library features generous study carrels with electrical outlets, comfortable lounge seating, 24 group study rooms and 6 multi-media rooms. The library's Computer Resource Center offers 89 workstations and 461 Internet accessible ports througout the library for laptop computer connections. The ratio of library volumes to faculty is 8088 to 1 and to students is 395 to 1. The ratio of seats in the library to students is 1 to 2.

Faculty

The law school has 66 full-time and 69 part-time faculty members, of whom 47 are women. According to AAUP standards for Category IIA institutions, faculty salaries are well above average. About 10% of full-time faculty have a graduate law degree in addition to the J.D.; about 1% of part-time faculty have one. The ratio of full-time students to full-time faculty in an average class is 20 to 1; in a clinic, 7 to 1. The law school has a regular program of bringing visiting professors and other distinguished lecturers and visitors to campus. There is a chapter of the Order of the Coif; 24 faculty and 500 graduates are members.

Placement

J.D.s awarded: 408

Services available through: a separate law school placement center

Services: information on practice areas, computer-assisted job search, and on-campus interview programs

Special features: numerous workshops and panel discussions, an extensive resource library, special programs for students interested in pursuing government or public interest careers, and programs promoting issues of diversity and minority recruitment and hiring.

Full-time job interviews:	56 employers
Summer job interviews:	46 employers
Placement by graduation:	58% of class
Placement within 9 months:	94% of class
Average starting salary:	$55,000 to $120,000

Areas of placement:

Private practice 2-10 attorneys	17%
Private practice 11-25 attorneys	9%
Private practice 26-50 attorneys	5%
Private practice 51-100 attorneys	25%
Business/industry	21%
Government	13%
Unknown	4%
Judicial clerkships	2%
Public interest	2%
Academic	2%

Students

About 52% of the student body are women; 37%, minorities; 5%, African American; 20%, Asian American; 11%, Hispanic; and 1%, Native American. The average age of entering students is 24; age range is 20 to 64. About 35% of students enter directly from undergraduate school. About 5% drop out after the first year for academic or personal reasons; 95% remain to receive a law degree.

LOYOLA UNIVERSITY OF CHICAGO

School of Law

One East Pearson Street
Chicago, IL 60611

Application Filing		Accreditation
Fall: April 1		ABA, AALS
Spring: n/app		**Degrees Granted**
Fee: $50		J.D., LL.M., S.J.D.

Enrollment 2001–2002			First-Year Class	
Men:	293	40%	Applied:	2461
Women:	438	60%	Accepted:	938
Minorities:	146	20%	Enrolled:	263
Out-of-State:	278	38%		

2001–02 Class Profile

LSAT Percentile: 78%
LSAT Median Score: 158
Percentage passing bar on first try: 93%

Tuition and Fees:

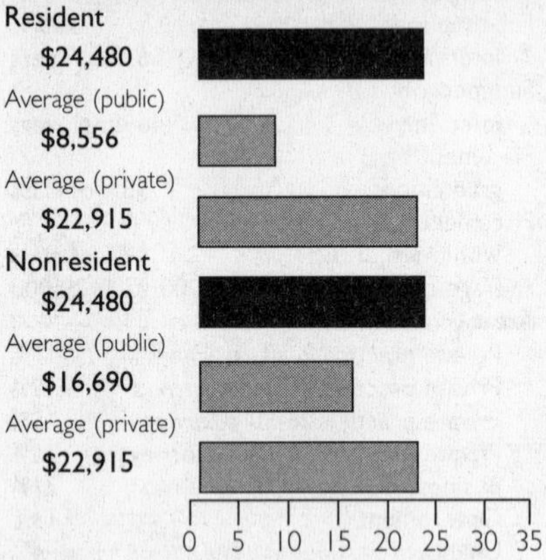

Percentage receiving financial aid: 85%

ADMISSIONS

In the fall 2001 first-year class, 2461 applied, 938 were accepted, and 263 enrolled. Six transfers enrolled. The median LSAT percentile of the most recent first-year class was 78; the median GPA was 3.3 on a scale of 4.0. The lowest LSAT percentile accepted was 36; the highest was 98.

Requirements

Applicants must have a bachelor's degree and take the LSAT. The most important admission factors include academic achievement, GPA, and LSAT results. No specific undergraduate courses are required. Candidates are not interviewed.

Procedure

The application deadline for fall entry is April 1. Applicants should submit an application form, LSAT results, transcripts, a nonrefundable application fee of $50, and 2 academic letters of recommendation. Notification of the admissions decision is within 4 weeks of receipt of completed application file. The latest acceptable LSAT test date for fall entry is February. The law school uses the LSDAS.

Special

The law school recruits minority and disadvantaged students through national law forums and university-sponsored law days. Requirements are not different for out-of-state students. Transfer students must have one year of credit, have a minimum GPA of 3, and have attended an ABA-approved law school.

Costs

Tuition and fees for the 2001-2002 academic year are $24,480 for all full-time students. Tuition for part-time students is $18,388 per year. Books and supplies run about $900 annually.

Financial Aid

About 85% of current law students receive some form of aid. The average annual amount of aid from all sources combined, including scholarships, loans, and work contracts, is $26,000; maximum, $39,260. Awards are based on need and merit. Required financial statement is the FAFSA. The aid application deadline for fall entry is March 1. Special funds for minority or disadvantaged students consist of 2 renewable full-tuition scholarships and 2 partial tuition scholarships. First-year students are notified about their financial aid application 2 to 3 weeks after the law school receives results of the FAFSA.

About the Law School

Loyola University of Chicago School of Law was established in 1908 and is a private institution. The campus is in an urban area in Chicago. The primary mission of the law school is to encourage the development of a sense of professional responsibility and respect for the judicial process, and an understanding of the social, moral, and ethical values inherent in the practice of law. Students have access to federal, state, county, city, and local agencies, courts, correctional facilities, law firms, and legal aid organizations in the Chicago area. Facilities of special interest to law students consist of the Water Tower campus, housing a gymnasium, cafeteria, coffee shop, and bookstore. Loyola also has a campus in Rome, Italy. The law school is in the heart of Chicago's North Michigan Avenue shopping/tourist district, within blocks of Lake Michigan and cultural attractions including the Museum of Contemporary Art. Housing for students is available in apartments within walking distance of the law school and in various Chicago neighborhoods. All law school facilities are accessible to the physically disabled.

Calendar

The law school operates on a traditional semester basis. Courses for full-time students are offered both day and evening and must be completed within 4 years. For part-time students, courses are offered both day and evening and must be completed within 6 years. New full- and part-time students are admitted in the fall. There is a summer session. Transferable summer courses are offered.

Programs

In addition to the J.D., the law school offers the LL.M., S.J.D., and M.J. (Master of Jurisprudence in health law, child and family law, and business law). Students may take relevant courses in other programs and apply credit toward the J.D.; a maximum of 9 credits may be applied. The following joint degrees may be earned: J.D./M.A. (Juris Doctor/ Master of Arts in political science), J.D./M.B.A. (Juris Doctor/ Master of Business Administration), J.D./M.S.W. (Juris Doctor/ Master of Social Work), and JD/M.S.I.R. (Juris Doctor/ Master of Human Resources and Industrial Relations).

Required

To earn the J.D., candidates must complete 86 total credits, of which 46 are for required courses. They must maintain a minimum GPA of 2.0 in the required courses. The following first-year courses are required of all students: Civil Procedure I and II, Contracts, Criminal Law, Property I and II, Torts, Legal Research, Legal Writing I and II, Fundamentals of American Legal System, and Constitutional Law I. Required upper-level courses consist of Federal Income Tax, Professional Responsibility, Constitutional Law II, Advocacy, and Business Organizations. The required orientation program for first-year students is a 2- to 3-day program that acquaints students with school regulations, facilities, and program requirements; during orientation, a writing evaluation is conducted.

Electives

The School of Law offers concentrations in corporate law, criminal law, family law, international law, juvenile law, labor law, litigation, tax law, and health law, and public interest law. With the exceptions of health law, tax law, and child law, none

Phone: 312-915-7170
800-545-5744
Fax: 312-915-7906
E-mail: *law-admissions@luc.edu*
Web: *www.luc.edu/schools/law*

Contact

Law Admission and Financial Assistance, 312-915-7170 for general inquiries; Michael Minnice, Assistant Director of Financial Assistance, 312-915-7170 for financial aid information.

of the concentrations is formalized. In addition, clinical legal experience is gained through the Loyola University Community Law Center, where students provide legal assistance to area residents who cannot afford private legal representation. The Federal Tax Clinic is staffed by law students who are trained in tax law and handle a wide range of legal matters related to federal income tax law before the IRS and the Tax Court. The Child Law Clinic has been established for students interested in representing abused or neglected children. Moreover, the Business Law Clinic offers legal representation at low cost to small businesses and community-based organizations. Seminars, of which there are a variety, are offered for 2 to 3 credit hours. Second- and third-year law students receive 3 hours credit for teaching a course called Street Law in Chicago-area high schools. Law students attend weekly seminars in which they study Illinois law and educational methodology. Externships are available every semester; supervised experience is offered in judicial, criminal, corporate, health law, child law, and government for 2 or 3 credit hours. Individualized research projects, under the supervision of a faculty member, are available every semester for 1 to 2 hours credit. Special lecture series include the Baker McKenzie Lecture on professionalism, the Wing-Tat Lee Lecture on international and comparative law, the Dooley Lecture on the judiciary, and the Law and Literature Lecture. Study-abroad programs include the Rome Program and the Oxford Program (European Union). Rome and Oxford are each 5-week summer programs offering 4 or 5 elective courses for 2 credits each. Loyola's Academic Enhancement Program is conducted during the spring semester. The voluntary program provides extensive tutoring and faculty mentors to students who fall within the lower 20% of the first-year class. The Child Advocacy Program utilizes interdisciplinary instruction and field experience to train students to become child advocates. The Public Interest Law Program provides law students with opportunities to explore public interest law through the legal clinic. The most widely taken electives are Evidence, Sales, and Secured Transactions.

Graduation Requirements

In order to graduate, candidates must have a GPA of 2.0 and 86 hours that fulfill all required courses.

Organizations

Student-edited publications include the *Loyola Law Journal, Loyola Consumer Law Review, Annals of Health Law, Public Interest Law Reporter, Children's Legal Rights Journal, the International Forum*, the newspaper, *Blackacre*, and a weekly SBA newsletter. A bi-weekly newsletter, *The Bulletin*, is published by the law school administration with student assistance. Moot Court competitions include the National Moot Court, Jessup Competition, and Wagner (labor law). Other competitions include the National Mock Trial Competition and the Client Counseling Competition and Negotiations Competition, both sponsored by the ABA. Loyola also participates annually in the Intra-school Moot Court Competition, Chicago Bar, Illinois Bar, Niagara, Sutherland Rich (intellectual property), National Juvenile Law, National Health Law, ABA, Hispanic Bar, Frederick Douglass, Willem Vis, and Thomas Tang. Student organizations include the Student Bar Association, Decalogue Society, and National Lawyers Guild. There are local chapters of the Black Law Students Association, American Society of International Law, and Latin American Law Student Association. Other organizations include Health Law Society, Child Law Society, and Phi Alpha Delta Legal Fraternity.

Library

The law library contains 172,165 hardcopy volumes and 196,710 microform volume equivalents, and subscribes to 3790 serial publications. Such on-line databases and networks as DIALOG, LEXIS, and WESTLAW are available to law students for research. Special library collections include a G.P.O. depository, an Illinois depository, and a collection on medical jurisprudence. The ratio of library volumes to faculty is 5380 to 1 and to students is 262 to 1. The ratio of seats in the library to students is 1 to 2.

Faculty

The law school has 32 full-time and 108 part-time faculty members, of whom 60 are women. According to AAUP standards for Category I institutions, faculty salaries are average. About 18% of full-time faculty have a graduate law degree in addition to the J.D. The ratio of full-time students to full-time faculty in an average class is 18 to 1; in a clinic, 9 to 1. The law school has a regular program of bringing visiting professors and other distinguished lecturers and visitors to campus.

Placement

J.D.s awarded:	226
Services available through: a separate law school placement center	
Services: alumni may be contacted through research conducted on Martindale-Hubbell, LEXIS, and WESTLAW.	
Special features: mock interviews, minority job fairs, the Patent Law Interview Program, the Midwest Public Interest Law Career Conference, biweekly student newsletter, 3 computer terminals and printer for resume and cover letter production and career research, a Public Service Law Center, and the Public Service Law Network Worldwide Internet database.	
Full-time job interviews:	110 employers
Summer job interviews:	220 employers
Placement by graduation:	81% of class
Placement within 9 months:	95% of class
Average starting salary:	$19,000 to $140,000
Areas of placement:	
Private practice 2-10 attorneys	10%
Private practice 11-25 attorneys	9%
Private practice 26-50 attorneys	5%
Private practice 51-100 attorneys	4%
Private practice 100+ attorneys	24%
Private practice—firm size unknown	1%
Government	18%
Business/industry	18%
Judicial clerkships	5%
Public interest	5%
Academic	1%

Students

About 60% of the student body are women; 20%, minorities; 4%, African American; 6%, Asian American; 5%, Hispanic; and 5%, foreign national. The majority of students come from Illinois (62%). The average age of entering students is 25; age range is 21 to 56. About 35% of students enter directly from undergraduate school and 14% have a graduate degree. About 3% drop out after the first year for academic or personal reasons; 90% remain to receive a law degree.

LOYOLA UNIVERSITY OF NEW ORLEANS

School of Law

7214 St. Charles Avenue
New Orleans, LA 70118

Application Filing		Accreditation
Fall: April 1		ABA, AALS
Spring: n/app		**Degrees Granted**
Fee: $40		J.D.

Enrollment 2001–2002			First-Year Class	
Men:	365	48%	Applied:	1518
Women:	401	52%	Accepted:	839
Minorities:	153	20%	Enrolled:	313
Out-of-State:	276	36%		

2001–02 Class Profile

LSAT Percentile: 48%
LSAT Median Score: 150
Percentage passing bar on first try: n/av

Tuition and Fees:

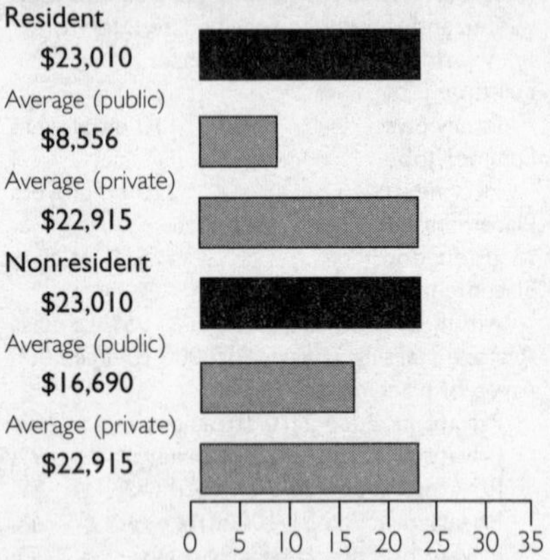

Percentage receiving financial aid: 82%

ADMISSIONS

In the fall 2001 first-year class, 1518 applied, 839 were accepted, and 313 enrolled. Sixteen transfers enrolled. The median LSAT percentile of the most recent first-year class was 48; the median GPA was 3 on a scale of 4.0. The lowest LSAT percentile accepted was 22; the highest was 96.

Requirements

Applicants must take the LSAT. Most do have a bachelor's degree, but some are accepted through the early admit program with three-fourths of a bachelor's degree completed. Minimum acceptable LSAT percentile is 22 and minimum acceptable GPA is 2.0 on a scale of 4.0. The most important admission factors include LSAT results, GPA, and academic achievement. No specific undergraduate courses are required. Candidates are interviewed at the request of the applicant, for informational purposes only.

Procedure

The priority application deadline for fall entry is April 1. Applicants should submit an application form, LSAT results, transcripts, a nonrefundable application fee of $40, 3 letters of recommendation (suggested, but not required), and a personal statement and resume (both suggested, but not required). Notification of the admissions decision is 4 to 6 weeks after the file is complete. The latest acceptable LSAT test date for fall entry is generally February. The law school uses the LSDAS.

Special

The law school recruits minority and disadvantaged students through alumni involvement, recruitment at institutions with traditionally minority-dominated enrollment, the use of CLEO, and the Black Law Students Association and Spanish-American Law Student Association. Requirements are not different for out-of-state students. Transfer students must have one year of credit, have attended an ABA-approved law school, and have entering LSAT and undergraduate GPA eligible for acceptance at Loyola and above average law school GPA.

Costs

Tuition and fees for the 2001-2002 academic year are $23,010 for all full-time students. Tuition for part-time students is $15,730 per year. On-campus room and board costs about $8359 annually; books and supplies run $950.

Financial Aid

About 82% of current law students receive some form of aid. The average annual amount of aid from all sources combined, including scholarships, loans, and work contracts, is approximately $27,000; maximum, $36,247. Awards are based on need and merit. Required financial statement is the FAFSA. Special funds for minority or disadvantaged students consist of scholarships and grants based on academic merit alone. Scholarship/grant notification is sent with the acceptance letter. Loan notification begins in March and is sent as acceptance is made and complete FAFSA is received.

About the Law School

Loyola University of New Orleans School of Law was established in 1914 and is a private institution. The 4.2-acre campus is in an urban area. The primary mission of the law school is to educate future members of the bar to be skilled advocates and sensitive counselors-at-law committed to ethical standards in pursuit of human dignity for all. Students have access to federal, state, county, city, and local agencies, courts, correctional facilities, law firms, and legal aid organizations in the New Orleans area. Facilities of special interest to law students include the U.S. Court of Appeals for the Fifth Circuit, the Supreme Court of the State of Louisiana, and the U.S. Court for the Eastern District of Louisiana. Housing for students is available in a dorm located directly across the street from the law school building; there is no married student housing on campus. All law school facilities are accessible to the physically disabled.

Calendar

The law school operates on a traditional semester basis. Required courses for full-time students are offered day only; electives, day and evening and must be completed within 5 years. For part-time students, required courses are offered evenings only; electives, day and evening and must be completed within 5 years. New full- and part-time students are admitted in the fall. There is an 8-week summer session. Transferable summer courses are offered.

Programs

Students may take relevant courses in other programs and apply credit toward the J.D.; a maximum of 9 credits may be applied. The following joint degrees may be earned: J.D./M.A. (Juris Doctor/Master of Arts in communications), J.D./M.A. (Juris Doctor/Master of Arts in religious studies), J.D./M.B.A. (Juris Doctor/Master of Business Administration), J.D./M.P.A. (Juris Doctor/Master of Public Administration), and J.D./M.U.R.P. (Juris Doctor/Master of Urban and Regional Planning).

Required

To earn the J.D., candidates must complete 90 total credits, of which 50 are for required courses (56 for Civil Law Division). They must maintain a minimum GPA of 2.0 in the required courses. The following first-year courses are required of all students: Civil Procedure I and II, Moot Court, Legal Profession, Criminal Law, Legal Research and Writing, Civil Law Property or Common Law Property I, Conventional Obligations or Contracts I, Sales and Leases or Common Law Property II, Torts I and II, and Common Law Contracts for Civil Law Students or Contracts II. Required upper-level courses consist of Successions or Trusts and

Phone: 504-861-5575
Fax: 504-861-5772
E-mail: *ladmit@loyno.edu*
Web: *law.loyno.edu*

Contact

K. Michele Allison-Davis, Assistant Dean of Admissions, 504-861-5575 for general inquiries; Nadine Lewis, Assistant Director of Financial Aid, 504-861-5551 for financial aid information.

Estates, Evidence, Administration of Criminal Justice I, Law and Poverty, Constitutional Law I, Business Organizations I, Security Rights, and Donations or Civil Law of Persons or Security Rights or Community Property. (Civil law students are only required to take 2 of these courses.) Loyola has a mandatory skills curriculum; courses that students must take for 8 skills points are drawn from the following categories: office practice, trial practice, appellate practice, and pro bono practice.The required orientation program for first-year students is held for 3 days prior to the beginning of classes. Students complete requirements for registration, receive welcoming remarks from university officials, meet professors, and meet with upper-level students. There is also an optional academic orientation that is 8 days long. It includes mock classes, brief writing, outlining, and exam preparation.

Electives

The School of Law offers concentrations in corporate law, criminal law, family law, international law, litigation, maritime law, tax law, torts and insurance, civil law, and public interest law. In addition, there are 2 clinics for third-year students who may earn a total of 9 credit hours for 3 semesters (including the summer semester). At the Public Law Center, students participate in legislative and administrative advocacy, and at the Loyola Law Clinic, students participate in a clinical setting, working on both civil and criminal cases. Seminars are offered as part of the regular curriculum. Credit is usually 2 hours. Second- and third-year law students in the upper third of their class may participate in externship programs. Students devote at least 12 hours a week to various assignments for a total of 4 credits earned over 2 semesters. Independent research projects may be undertaken under the supervision of a professor for 1 or 2 credit hours, depending on the project. A Street Law course is available. Loyola offers several lecture series that promote the legal profession. No credit is given and attendance is voluntary. There are study-abroad programs in Cuernavaca, Mexico; Brazil or Costa Rica; Moscow and St. Petersburg, Russia; Budapest, Hungary; and Vienna, Austria. All programs are open to second- and third-year students who may earn a total of 6 to 8 credits. Second- and third-year students may serve as Teacher Assistants (T.A.) in the Legal Research and Writing and Moot Court programs. The Academic Success Program is maintained for first-year students who need assistance with organizing and preparing for classes and exams. Minority grants based on merit are available. The most widely taken electives are Mediation, Family Law, and Negotiable Instruments.

Graduation Requirements

In order to graduate, candidates must have a GPA of 2.0, have completed the upper-division writing requirement, and have fulfilled the Perspective requirement by taking 1 of 3 possible courses that give a philosophical and historical perspective on law.

Organizations

Students edit the *Loyola Law Review, Loyola Journal of Public Interest Law, Maritime Law Journal, Loyola Intellectual Property and High Technology Law Journal*, and the newspaper, *The Code.* Moot court competitions include the National Moot Court Competition, Stetson International Environment Moot Court Competition, and National Mardi Gras Invitational Competition. Other competitions include the Frederick Douglass Moot Court Competition (participation by the Black Law Students Association) and the Thomas Tang Competition (participation by the Asian Pacific American Law Student Association). Law student organizations include the Student Bar Association, Black Law Students Association, and Spanish-American Law Students Association. Delta Theta Phi, Phi Delta Phi, and National Lawyers Guild have local chapters. Campus clubs and other organizations include Communications Law Society, JD/MBA Society, and Loyola Environmental Law Society.

Library

The law library contains 300,000 hard-copy volumes and 119,380 microform volume equivalents, and subscribes to 3400 serial publications. Such on-line databases and networks as CALI, CIS Universe, DIALOG, Legal-Trac, LEXIS, NEXIS, OCLC First Search, WESTLAW, and Wilsonline Indexes are available to law students for research. Special library collections include French, Quebec, and Scottish law; U.S. government documents and Louisiana state documents; and GATT depository. Recently, the library added a computer laboratory with more than 45 computers and an on-line catalog. The ratio of library volumes to faculty is 10,714 to 1 and to students is 392 to 1. The ratio of seats in the library to students is 1 to 1.

Placement	
J.D.s awarded:	194
Services available through: a separate law school placement center and the university placement center	
Services: such as coordination of speakers for various employment opportunities, a student news and job information monthly newsletter, and a resume bank.	
Full-time job interviews:	70 employers
Summer job interviews:	n/av
Placement by graduation:	94% of class
Placement within 9 months:	100% of class
Average starting salary:	$32,600 to $125,000
Areas of placement:	
Private practice all size firms	54%
Judicial clerkships	14%
Business/industry	13%
Government	9%
Unknown	8%
Public interest	1%
Academic	1%

Faculty

The law school has 28 full-time and 57 part-time faculty members, of whom 21 are women. According to AAUP standards for Category IIA institutions, faculty salaries are above average. About 39% of full-time faculty have a graduate law degree in addition to the J.D. The ratio of full-time students to full-time faculty in an average class is 21 to 1; in a clinic, 10 to 1. The law school has a regular program of bringing visiting professors and other distinguished lecturers and visitors to campus.

Students

About 52% of the student body are women; 20%, minorities; 11%, African American; 2%, Asian American; 6%, Hispanic; and 1%, Native American. The majority of students come from Louisiana (64%). The average age of entering students is 26; age range is 20 to 57. About 12% drop out after the first year for academic or personal reasons; 88% remain to receive a law degree.

MARQUETTE UNIVERSITY

Law School

Office of Admissions, Sensenbrenner Hall, P.O. Box 1881
Milwaukee, WI 53201-1881

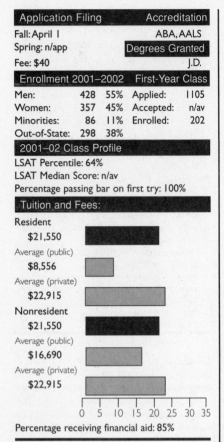

Application Filing		Accreditation
Fall: April 1		ABA, AALS
Spring: n/app		**Degrees Granted**
Fee: $40		J.D.

Enrollment 2001–2002			First-Year Class	
Men:	428	55%	Applied:	1105
Women:	357	45%	Accepted:	n/av
Minorities:	86	11%	Enrolled:	202
Out-of-State:	298	38%		

2001–02 Class Profile

LSAT Percentile: 64%
LSAT Median Score: n/av
Percentage passing bar on first try: 100%

Tuition and Fees:

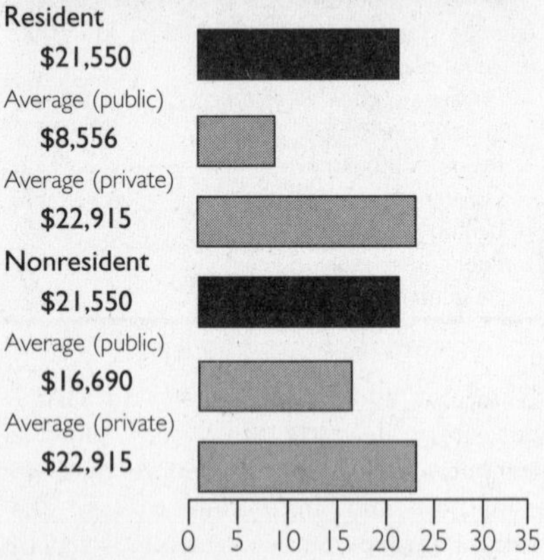

Percentage receiving financial aid: 85%

ADMISSIONS

In the fall 2001 first-year class, 1105 applied and 202 enrolled. Twenty-one transfers enrolled. The median LSAT percentile of the most recent first-year class was 64; the median GPA was 3.33 on a scale of 4.0.

Requirements

Applicants must have a bachelor's degree and take the LSAT. The most important admission factors include character, personality, GPA, and LSAT results. No specific undergraduate courses are required. Candidates are not interviewed.

Procedure

The application deadline for fall entry is April 1. Applicants should submit an application form, LSAT results, transcripts, TOEFL for students from non-English speaking countries, a nonrefundable application fee of $40, and 2 letters of recommendation. Accepted students must pay a nonrefundable $250 first tuition deposit and a $250 second tuition deposit in June; both are applied to the first semester tuition. Notification of the admissions decision is on a rolling basis. The latest acceptable LSAT test date for fall entry is February. The law school uses the LSDAS.

Special

The law school recruits minority and disadvantaged students through CRS, minority open houses, and targeted recruitment. Requirements are not different for out-of-state students. Transfer students must have one year of credit, have a minimum GPA of 2.5, have attended an ABA-approved law school, and must complete 54 credits at Marquette.

Costs

Tuition for the 2001-2002 academic year is $21,550 for all full-time students. On-campus room and board costs about $8290 annually; books and supplies run $1065.

Financial Aid

About 85% of current law students receive some form of aid. Awards are based on need and merit. Required financial statement is the FAFSA. The aid application deadline for fall entry is April 1. Special funds for minority or disadvantaged students are available. First-year students are notified about their financial aid application after acceptance, but prior to enrollment if financial aid forms are filed in a timely manner.

About the Law School

Marquette University Law School was established in 1892 and is a private institution. The 80-acre campus is in an urban area adjacent to downtown Milwaukee. The primary mission of the law school is to offer a balanced curriculum noted for its comprehensive teaching of both the theory and practice of law and to instill in students a sense of professional responsibility. Marquette graduates are admitted to the Wisconsin bar without taking the bar exam. Students have access to federal, state, county, city, and local agencies, courts, correctional facilities, law firms, and legal aid organizations in the Milwaukee area. The federal and municipal courthouses are located 2 blocks away. Facilities of special interest to law students include the Legal Research Center, Sensenbrenner Hall, and fitness and recreation centers. Housing for students consists of on-campus and campus area apartments. The Office of Residence Life assists students with off-campus accommodations. About 99% of the law school facilities are accessible to the physically disabled.

Calendar

The law school operates on a traditional semester basis. Courses for full-time students are offered both day and evening and must be completed within 4 years. For part-time students, courses are offered both day and evening and must be completed within 6 years. New full- and part-time students are admitted in the fall. There is a summer session. Transferable summer courses are offered.

Programs

Students may take relevant courses in other programs and apply credit toward the J.D.; a maximum of 9 credits may be applied. The following joint degrees may be earned: J.D./M.A. (Juris Doctor/Master of Arts in bioethics), J.D./M.A. (Juris Doctor/Master of Arts in international affairs), J.D./M.A. (Juris Doctor/Master of Arts in political science), and J.D./M.B.A. (Juris Doctor/Master of Business Administration).

Phone: 414-288-6767
Fax: 414-288-0676
E-mail: *law.admission@marquette.edu*
Web: *www.mu.edu/law*

Contact

Assistant Dean for Admissions, 414-288-6767 for general inquiries; Office of Student Financial Aid, 414-288-0200 for financial aid information.

Required

To earn the J.D., candidates must complete 90 total credits, of which 34 are for required courses. They must maintain a minimum GPA of 2.0 in the required courses. The following first-year courses are required of all students: Civil Procedure, Contracts, Property, Constitutional Law, Legal Writing and Research, Criminal Law, Law and the Ethics of Lawyering, and Torts. Required upper-level courses consist of a Perspectives course, a workshop course, Law and the Ethics of Lawyering, Advanced Legal Research, Trusts and Estates, Evidence, a process elective, a public law elective, and a seminar. The required orientation program for first-year students takes place 1 week prior to the start of the semester and includes all aspects of law school. Students meet with professors in small groups; discussions include classes in The Lawyer in American Society.

Electives

The Law School offers concentrations in corporate law, criminal law, environmental law, family law, international law, juvenile law, labor law, litigation, sports law, tax law, torts and insurance, and constitutional law and intellectual property. Clinical training is available through the Prosecutor Clinic, Defender Clinic, and Legal Aid Society. Small enrollment courses provide students with an opportunity to work intensely under faculty supervision and are generally worth 2 credits. Internships are available in both appellate and trial courts, including the Wisconsin Supreme Court and the U.S. Court of Appeals for the Seventh Circuit, and with the Municipal Ordinance Defense Clinics. Research programs provide students with an appreciation of the relationship of law to other disciplines, and an understanding of the process through which legal doctrine is formed as well as comparisons of the American legal system with other legal systems. A supervised field-work program provides students with the opportunity to intern with a variety of governmental and public service agencies such as the Equal Employment Opportunity Commission, Internal Revenue Service, Centro Legal, Juvenile Law-Children's Court, and the U.S. Attorney's Office. Study abroad is available through the T.C. Beirne School of Law, the University of Queensland, and the Brisbane (Australia) Program in International, Comparative, and Foreign Law. There is an Academic Support Program for first-year students. The school actively recruits minority students. The most widely taken electives are Trial Advocacy, Criminal Procedure, and Sports Law courses.

Graduation Requirements

In order to graduate, candidates must have a GPA of 2.0 and have completed the upper-division writing requirement.

Organizations

Students edit the *Marquette Law Review, Marquette Sports Law Review, Marquette Intellectual Property Law Review*, and the *Federation of Insurance and Corporate Counsel Quarterly*. Moot court competitions include patent law, sports law, and alternative dispute resolution competitions. National competitions include the National Moot Court, Philip C. Jessup International, Giles Rich Intellectual Property, and Sports Law Moot Court. Law student organizations include the Student Bar Association, Health Law Society, Environmental Law Society, Public Interest Law Society, Sports Law Society, and Black Law Students Association. There are local chapters of Delta Theta Phi, Phi Alpha Delta, and Phi Delta Phi.

Library

The law library contains 159,238 hard-copy volumes and 133,167 microform volume equivalents, and subscribes to 3439 serial publications. Such on-line databases and networks as CALI, CIS Universe, DIALOG, Infotrac, Legal-Trac, LEXIS, LOIS, Mathew Bender, NEXIS, OCLC First Search, WESTLAW, and Wilsonline Indexes are available to law students for research. Special library collections include a federal depository. Recently, the library upgraded the computer laboratory. The ratio of library volumes to faculty is 4550 to 1 and to students is 203 to 1. The ratio of seats in the library to students is 1 to 5.

Placement

J.D.s awarded: 188

Services available through: a separate law school placement center

Services: mock interviews

Special features: personal counseling with students, access to a computer and a laser printer in the office to prepare resumes and cover letters, and access to an on-line WESTLAW database of lawyers and judicial clerkships.

Full-time job interviews:	75 employers
Summer job interviews:	n/av
Placement by graduation:	73% of class
Placement within 9 months:	95% of class
Average starting salary:	$24,750 to $125,000
Areas of placement:	
Private practice 2-10 attorneys	40%
Private practice 11-25 attorneys	20%
Private practice 26-50 attorneys	4%
Private practice 51-100 attorneys	4%
Business/industry	12%
Government	11%
Judicial clerkships	7%
Public interest	1%
Academic	1%

Faculty

The law school has 35 full-time and 65 part-time faculty members, of whom 32 are women. According to AAUP standards for Category I institutions, faculty salaries are below average. About 20% of full-time faculty have a graduate law degree in addition to the J.D. The ratio of full-time students to full-time faculty in an average class is 15 to 1. The law school has a regular program of bringing visiting professors and other distinguished lecturers and visitors to campus.

Students

About 45% of the student body are women; 11%, minorities; 3%, African American; 3%, Asian American; 2%, Hispanic; and 1%, Native American. The majority of students come from Wisconsin (62%). The average age of entering students is 25; age range is 21 to 72. About 62% of students enter directly from undergraduate school, 10% have a graduate degree, and 27% have worked full-time prior to entering law school. About 2% drop out after the first year for academic or personal reasons; 98% remain to receive a law degree.

MERCER UNIVERSITY

Walter F. George School of Law

1021 Georgia Ave.
Macon, GA 31207

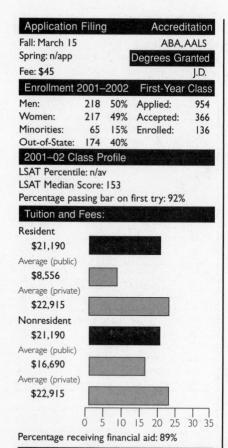

Application Filing	Accreditation
Fall: March 15	ABA, AALS
Spring: n/app	
Fee: $45	

Degrees Granted
J.D.

Enrollment 2001–2002			First-Year Class	
Men:	218	50%	Applied:	954
Women:	217	49%	Accepted:	366
Minorities:	65	15%	Enrolled:	136
Out-of-State:	174	40%		

2001–02 Class Profile

LSAT Percentile: n/av
LSAT Median Score: 153
Percentage passing bar on first try: 92%

Tuition and Fees:

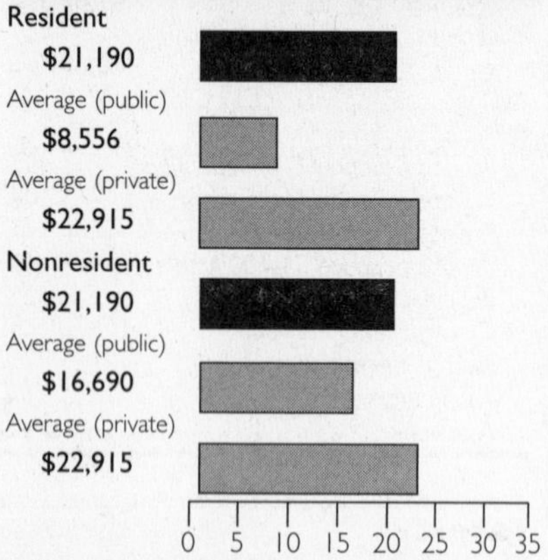

Percentage receiving financial aid: 89%

ADMISSIONS

In the fall 2001 first-year class, 954 applied, 366 were accepted, and 136 enrolled. Ten transfers enrolled. The median GPA of the most recent first-year class was 3.32. The lowest LSAT percentile accepted was 25; the highest was 75.

Requirements

Applicants must have a bachelor's degree and take the LSAT. The most important admission factors include LSAT results and GPA. No specific undergraduate courses are required. Candidates are not interviewed.

Procedure

The application deadline for fall entry is March 15. Applicants should submit an application form, LSAT results, transcripts, a nonrefundable application fee of $45, 2 letters of recommendation, and a personal statement to be used as a writing sample. Notification of the admissions decision is on the day of the decision. The latest acceptable LSAT test date for fall entry is February. The law school uses the LSDAS.

Special

The law school recruits minority and disadvantaged students by visiting colleges that are traditionally minority schools and by using the Candidate Referral Service of Law Services to identify qualified minority students. Requirements are not different for out-of-state students. Transfer students must have one year of credit, have attended an ABA-approved law school, be in top 50% of their class, submit a letter of good standing from their dean, have 2 letters of recommendation from their professors, subscribe to LSDAS and submit a current transcript of all law schools attended to Mercer.

Costs

Tuition and fees for the 2001-2002 academic year are $21,190 for all full-time students. On-campus room and board costs about $11,900 annually; books and supplies run $600.

Financial Aid

About 89% of current law students receive some form of aid. The average annual amount of aid from all sources combined, including scholarships, loans, and work contracts, is $25,400; maximum, $33,690. Awards are based on need and merit. Students are awarded merit scholarships and need- and non-need based loans. Required financial statements are the FAFSA and institutional application. The aid application deadline for fall entry is April 1. Mercer participates in the National and Georgia CLEO programs. First-year students are notified about their financial aid application at the time of application to law school.

About the Law School

Mercer University Walter F. George School of Law was established in 1873 and is a private institution. The 130-acre campus is in an urban area 80 miles south of Atlanta, Georgia. The primary mission of the law school is to prepare students for high-quality general practice of law, and to do so in a learning environment that is strongly supportive and consistently professional. Mercer seeks to produce genuinely good lawyers in an ethical as well as a pragmatic sense. Students have access to federal, state, county, city, and local agencies, courts, correctional facilities, law firms, and legal aid organizations in the Macon area. Facilities of special interest to law students include the 3-story law building located in Macon's historical district, overlooking downtown Macon. It was built as a partial replica of Philadelphia's Independence Hall. Housing for students consists of privately owned and university owned apartments available within walking distance of the school, and multiple apartment complexes throughout the city. All law school facilities are accessible to the physically disabled.

Calendar

The law school operates on a traditional semester basis. Courses for full-time students are offered days only and must be completed within 3 years; summer classes are offered in the evening. For part-time students, courses are offered days only and must be completed within 5 years. New full- and part-time students are admitted in the fall. There is a 7-week summer session. Transferable summer courses are offered.

Programs

The following joint degrees may be earned: J.D./M.B.A. (Juris Doctor/Master of Business Administration).

Phone: 478-301-2605
800-637-2378
Fax: 478-301-2989
E-mail: *Sutton_me@mercer.edu*
Web: *www.Law.Mercer.edu*

Contact

Marilyn E. Sutton, Assistant Dean of Admissions and Financial Aid, 478-301-2605 for general inquiries and financial aid information.

Required

To earn the J.D., candidates must complete 91 total credits, of which 65 are for required courses. The following first-year courses are required of all students: Contracts, Criminal Law, Property, Torts, American Constitutional System, Jurisdiction and Judgments, Sales, Statutory Law and Analysis, Introduction to Legal Research, and Legal Writing I. Required upper-level courses consist of Civil Lawsuits, Legal Writing II, Income Taxation, Evidence, Remedies, and Law of Lawyering. All students must take clinical courses. The required orientation program for first-year students is a 1-week course, Introduction to Law Study, taught before the start of regular first-year courses. It carries 1 hour of credit, has an exam, and is graded. Additional information is offered in a 3-day session before the start of classes.

Electives

The Walter F. George School of Law offers concentrations in corporate law, criminal law, environmental law, family law, international law, juvenile law, labor law, litigation, media law, securities law, sports law, tax law, and torts and insurance. No concentrations are formally recognized; all areas are offered as electives. In addition, all students must elect at least 1 advanced skills course of 2 credit hours that simulates law practice tasks. Most students also enroll in a trial practice course. Each student must also elect at least 1 seminar in the third year, of 2 credit hours. Approximately 12 seminars are offered each year on a range of subjects from legal ethics to mass media. Supervised internships of 1 to 3 credit hours may be arranged under the Public Interest Practicum Program. Faculty-supervised research and writing projects, of 1 to 3 credit hours, may be pursued after the first year. Three lecture series bring speakers to the school annually. A limited number of students are selected annually to voluntarily tutor deserving first-year students. An academic tutorial program offers one-on-one mentoring to students in academic difficulty. Minority programs include a local BALSA chapter and a local Hispanic Students Association. The most widely taken electives are Business Associations, Criminal Procedure, and Decedents' Estates and Trusts.

Organizations

Students edit the *Mercer Law Review*, the *Journal of Southern Legal History*, published by the law school, and the student newspaper, *The Janus Chronicle*. National moot court competitions held annually are the National Moot Court, Gabrielli National Family Law, and Gibbons National Criminal Procedure. Other competitions include the National Client Counseling Competition, Florida Worker's Compensation, Georgia Intrastate, Vale National Corporate Law, National Negotiation, National Civil Rights, Evans Constitutional Law, and Southeast Regional Client Counseling. Law student organizations include the Association of Women Law Students, the Black Law Students Association, and the ABA-Law Student Division. There are local chapters of Phi Alpha Delta—William Hansell Fish chapter, and Phi Delta Phi—George Inn. Other campus organizations include the American Trial Lawyers Association, the Environmental Law Society, and the National Association of Criminal Defense Lawyers.

Library

The law library contains 304,497 hard-copy volumes, and subscribes to 1050 serial publications. Such on-line databases and networks as CALI, CIS Universe, Legal-Trac, LEXIS, LOIS, NEXIS, OCLC First Search, WESTLAW, and CCH Internet Tax Research Network, and Hein Online are available to law students for research. Special library collections include Georgia legal research materials and a federal depository library. Recently, the library updated carpeting and paint, and wiring for laptop computers. The ratio of library volumes to faculty is 11,278 to 1 and to students is 700 to 1. The ratio of seats in the library to students is 1 to 1.

Faculty

The law school has 27 full-time and 27 part-time faculty members, of whom 10 are women. According to AAUP standards for Category IIA institutions, faculty salaries are above average. About 22% of full-time faculty have a graduate law degree in addition to the J.D.; about 18% of part-time faculty have one. The ratio of full-time students to full-time faculty in an average class is 15 to 1. The law school has a regular program of bringing visiting professors and other distinguished lecturers and visitors to campus.

Graduation Requirements

In order to graduate, candidates must have a grade average of 76 and have completed the upper-division writing requirement.

Placement

J.D.s awarded:	116
Services available through: a separate law school placement center	
Special features: videotaped practice interviews and critiques, job fairs and consortia, and seminars and educational panels on types of practice and interviewing.	
Full-time job interviews:	27 employers
Summer job interviews:	44 employers
Placement by graduation:	57% of class
Placement within 9 months:	94% of class
Average starting salary:	$26,000 to $100,000
Areas of placement:	
Private practice 2-10 attorneys	28%
Private practice 11-25 attorneys	5%
Private practice 26-50 attorneys	3%
Private practice 51-100 attorneys	3%
Private practice 101-250 attorneys	4%
Private pratice, size unknown	7%
Judicial clerkships	17%
Government	13%
Self-employed	8%
Business/industry	7%
Military	3%
Public interest	2%

Students

About 49% of the student body are women; 15%, minorities; 9%, African American; 2%, Asian American; 1%, Hispanic; 1%, Native American; and 1%, Puerto Rican/Mexican American. The majority of students come from the South (95%). The average age of entering students is 25; age range is 20 to 50. About 5% drop out after the first year for academic or personal reasons; 95% remain to receive a law degree.

MICHIGAN STATE UNIVERSITY

Detroit College of Law

316 Law College Bldg.
East Lansing, MI 48824-1300

Application Filing		Accreditation
Fall: April 15		ABA, AALS
Spring: n/app		**Degrees Granted**
Fee: $50		J.D.

Enrollment 2001–2002			First-Year Class	
Men:	436	56%	Applied:	1200
Women:	344	40%	Accepted:	720
Minorities:	109	14%	Enrolled:	250
Out-of-State:	179	23%		

2001–02 Class Profile

LSAT Percentile: 50%
LSAT Median Score: 152
Percentage passing bar on first try: 64%

Tuition and Fees:

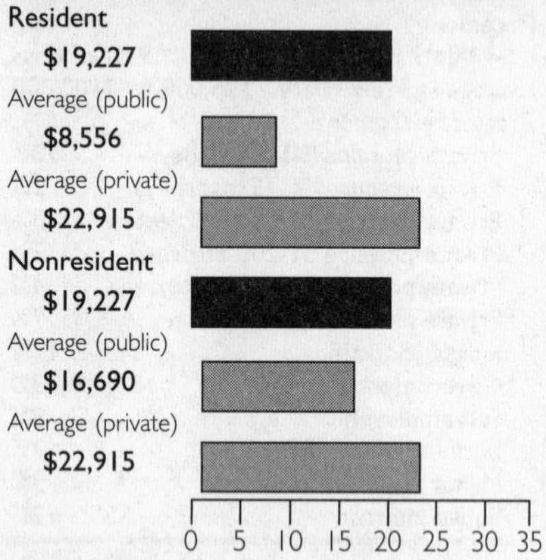

Percentage receiving financial aid: 85%

ADMISSIONS

In the fall 2001 first-year class, 1200 applied, 720 were accepted, and 250 enrolled. Thirty-five transfers enrolled. The median LSAT percentile of the most recent first-year class was 50; the median GPA was 3.2 on a scale of 4.0. The lowest LSAT percentile accepted was 21; the highest was 93.

Requirements

Applicants must have a bachelor's degree and take the LSAT. The most important admission factors include GPA, LSAT results, and academic achievement. No specific undergraduate courses are required. Candidates are interviewed.

Procedure

The application deadline for fall entry is April 15. Applicants should submit an application form, LSAT results, transcripts, ACT, SAT I, GRE, and GMAT scores, and a nonrefundable application fee of $50. Letters of recommendation are recommended but not required. Accepted students must submit a nonrefundable tuition deposit of $200, which is credited toward tuition. Notification of the admissions decision is on a rolling basis, as early as possible after the file is completed. The latest acceptable LSAT test date for fall entry is February. The law school uses the LSDAS.

Special

The law school recruits minority and disadvantaged students by means of conducting special interviews for acceptance purposes, awarding half- and full-tuition scholarships, and sponsoring an annual Minority Recruitment Conference and an Enhance Your Future Conference. Requirements are not different for out-of-state students. Transfer students must have one year of credit, have a minimum GPA of 3.0, have attended an ABA-approved law school, be in good academic standing, and be eligible to return to the law school they currently attend.

Costs

Tuition and fees for the 2001-2002 academic year are $19,227 for all full-time students. Tuition for part-time students is $15,912 per year. On-campus room and board costs about $6624 annually; books and supplies run $992.

Financial Aid

About 85% of current law students receive some form of aid. The average annual amount of aid from all sources combined, including scholarships, loans, and work contracts, is $18,500 (maximum). Awards are based on need and merit. Required financial statement is the FAFSA. The aid application deadline for fall entry is July 2. Special funds for minority or disadvantaged students are available on the basis of academic promise as evidenced by LSAT scores and undergraduate curriculum and performance. First-year students are notified about their financial aid application at the time of the application's submission.

About the Law School

Michigan State University Detroit College of Law was established in 1891 and is a private institution. The 5000+ acre campus is in a suburban area just outside the state capital. The primary mission of the law school is to provide outstanding educational training and opportunities for qualified applicants seeking to enter the legal profession. Students have access to federal, state, county, city, and local agencies, courts, correctional facilities, law firms, and legal aid organizations in the East Lansing area. Through the externship programs, a number of local courts are used officially as training forums for students. Facilities of special interest to law students include the college's expanded operations and law library, classrooms, offices for faculty, administrators and student organizations, study and lounge facilities, the Moot Court, the expanded computer laboratory, and the Career Services Office. Housing for students is available both on and off campus. On-campus housing includes both residence halls and apartments. All law school facilities are accessible to the physically disabled.

Calendar

The law school operates on a traditional semester basis. Courses for full-time students are offered both day and evening and must be completed within 3 years. For part-time students, courses are offered both day and evening and must be completed within 4 or 5 years. New full- and part-time students are admitted in the fall. There is an 8-week summer session. Transferable summer courses are offered.

Programs

Students may take relevant courses in other programs and apply credit toward the J.D.; a maximum of 6 credits may be applied. The following joint degrees may be earned: J.D./M.A. (Juris Doctor/Master of Arts), J.D./M.B.A. (Juris Doctor/Master of Business Administration), J.D./M.L.R.H.R. (Juris Doctor/Master of Labor Relations & Human Resources), J.D./M.P.A. (Juris Doctor/Master of Public Administration), and J.D./M.S. (Juris Doctor/Master of Science).

Required

To earn the J.D., candidates must complete 88 total credits, of which 56 are for required courses. They must maintain a minimum GPA of 2.0 in the required courses. The following first-year courses are required of all students: Contracts I and II, Property, Civil Procedure I and II, Torts, Research, Writing, Advocacy I and II, and Constitutional Law I. Required upper-level courses consist of Basic Income Taxation, Decendents' Estates and Trusts, Criminal Law, Constitutional Law II, Corporations, Agency and Partnership, Commercial Transactions, Secured Transactions, Small Business Enterprises, Evidence, and Legal Profession. Clinical courses are electives.The required orientation program for first-year students consists of a social event and 3 days of intensive study in research and writing. Students are taught

Phone: 517-432-0222
844-9352
Fax: 517-432-0098
E-mail: *heatleya@pilot.msu.edu*
Web: *www.dcl.edu*

Contact

Lorae Hamilton, Assistant Director of Admissions, 517-432-0222 for general inquiries; Financial aid officers, 517-432-6810 for financial aid information.

research skills, use of library techniques, how to brief a case, and how to write an exam. Students receive a reading assignment prior to entry and are expected to be prepared at orientation.

Electives

Students must take 14 credits in their area of concentration. The Detroit College of Law offers concentrations in corporate law, environmental law, international law, litigation, tax law, health law, and certificate in law and social work. MSU-DCL is home of the Geoffrey Fieger Trial Practice Institute. In addition, clinical programs and externships offer students practical experience in criminal and civil law through work with the Women's Justice Center, Misdemeanor Defender's Clinic, Landlord-Tenant Clinic, Wayne County Circuit Court, Juvenile Defender's Office, and federal and local prosecutors' offices. Approximately 30 seminars in specialized areas are offered each year, allowing students to explore areas of interest in depth with expert faculty members. Students may intern as judicial clerks in the federal courts. The Centre for Canadian-United States Law offers courses on Canadian law and Canadian-American relations and sponsors summer internships in Ottawa and Montreal. In the Legal Drafting Program, students prepare legislative documents and develop explanations of their applications. Advanced legal research is offered to support in-depth exploration of a topic and to foster strong research skills. In addition, students may enroll in directed studies. Students combine class participation (civil law topics such as landlord/tenant, housing law, family law, rights and liberties, and consumer law) with performance in local high schools in a course entitled Street Law. There are student-, faculty-, and alumni-sponsored lecture series featuring experts on current matters of law. The Law College offers a cooperative study program with the University of Ottawa and is developing a joint J.D./LL.B. program as well. Through the Canadian summer program, students participate in internships in the Houses of Parliament in Ottawa and Montreal. Students, with permission, are allowed to study abroad through other ABA-approved law programs. The Law College also sponsors a summer-abroad study program in Guadalajara, Mexico. Minorities are active in the Wolverine Student Bar Association and sponsor tutorial programs in regular courses as well as in exam-writing techniques. The most widely taken electives are Environmental Law, Intellectual Property, and Sports Law.

Graduation Requirements

In order to graduate, candidates must have a GPA of 2.0 and have completed the upper-division writing requirement.

Organizations

Students edit the *Detroit College of Law Review*, the *Journal of International Law and Practice*, and *The Journal of Medicine and Law*. Other student publications are a Sixth Circuit Survey publication and an issue publishing the results of the National Labor Law Writing Competition. The student newspapers are *The Brief Case, Eco-Voice on Environmental Law*, and *Res Ipsa Loquitor*. A Moot Court Board offers intramural competitions. The college participates in regional, national, and international moot court competitions, including the National Moot Court, William F. Starr Insurance Law, and Chicago Bar Association Moot Court. The College also hosts the National Trial Advocacy Competition, which attracts 12 to 14 competing school teams each fall. Law student organizations include the Wolverine Student Bar Association, Student Bar Association, and Sports and Entertainment Law Society. Campus clubs and other organizations include the Women's Law Caucus, Jewish Legal Society, and Christian Legal Society. Local chapters of national associations include Phi Alpha Delta, ABA-Student Division, and the Wolverine Student Bar Association.

Library

The law library contains 118,631 hardcopy volumes and 91,094 microform volume equivalents, and subscribes to 3687 serial publications. Such on-line databases and networks as CALI, CIS Universe, Infotrac, Legal-Trac, LEXIS, LOIS, NEXIS, OCLC First Search, WESTLAW, Wilsonline Indexes, and the Internet are available to law students for research. Special library collections include international, labor, and taxation; there is a Government Printing Office depository. The library contains a 24-station computer laboratory on Novell providing access to the Internet, word processing, and other networks, and provides laptop access throughout the law library and the building. The ratio of library volumes to faculty is 4237 to 1 and to students is 152 to 1. The ratio of seats in the library to students is 1 to 2.

Placement

J.D.s awarded:	181
Services available through: a separate law school placement center	
Special features: On-line job listing service, J.D. JobNet	
Full-time job interviews:	13 employers
Summer job interviews:	21 employers
Placement by graduation:	n/av
Placement within 9 months:	86% of class
Average starting salary:	$30,000 to $64,000
Areas of placement:	
Private practice 2-10 attorneys	32%
Private practice 11-25 attorneys	6%
Private practice 26-50 attorneys	2%
Private practice 51-100 attorneys	3%
Business/industry	15%
Government	14%
Unknown	13%
Public interest	7%
Academic	5%
Judicial clerkships	3%

Faculty

The law school has 28 full-time and 37 part-time faculty members, of whom 22 are women. According to AAUP standards for Category I institutions, faculty salaries are above average. About 39% of full-time faculty have a graduate law degree in addition to the J.D.; about 20% of part-time faculty have one. The ratio of full-time students to full-time faculty in an average class is 21 to 1; in a clinic, 5 to 1. The law school has a regular program of bringing visiting professors and other distinguished lecturers and visitors to campus.

Students

About 40% of the student body are women; 14%, minorities; 6%, African American; 6%, Asian American; 2%, Hispanic; and 1%, Native American. The majority of students come from Michigan (77%). The average age of entering students is 28; age range is 22 to 51. About 42% of students enter directly from undergraduate school. About 6% drop out after the first year for academic or personal reasons; 92% remain to receive a law degree.

MISSISSIPPI COLLEGE

School of Law

151 E. Griffith Street
Jackson, MS 39201

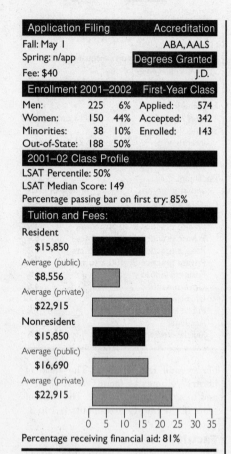

Application Filing		Accreditation
Fall: May 1		ABA, AALS
Spring: n/app		**Degrees Granted**
Fee: $40		J.D.

Enrollment 2001–2002			First-Year Class	
Men:	225	6%	Applied:	574
Women:	150	44%	Accepted:	342
Minorities:	38	10%	Enrolled:	143
Out-of-State:	188	50%		

2001–02 Class Profile

LSAT Percentile: 50%
LSAT Median Score: 149
Percentage passing bar on first try: 85%

Tuition and Fees:

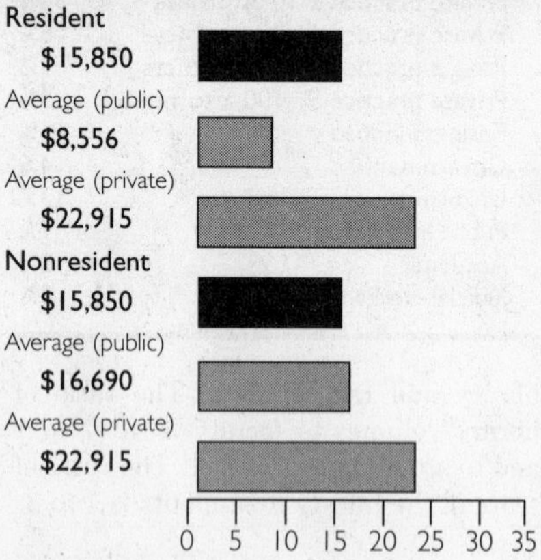

Percentage receiving financial aid: 81%

ADMISSIONS

In the fall 2001 first-year class, 574 applied, 342 were accepted, and 143 enrolled. Enrollment figures in the above capsule are approximate. Two transfers enrolled. The median LSAT percentile of the most recent first-year class was 50; the median GPA was 3 on a scale of 4.0. The highest LSAT percentile was 93.

Requirements

Applicants must have a bachelor's degree and take the LSAT. Minimum acceptable LSAT percentile is 38. The most important admission factors include LSAT results, GPA, and academic achievement. No specific undergraduate courses are required. Candidates are not interviewed.

Procedure

The application deadline for fall entry is May 1. Applicants should submit an application form, LSAT results, transcripts, and a nonrefundable application fee of $40. Notification of the admissions decision is on a rolling basis. The latest acceptable LSAT test date for fall entry is February. The law school uses the LSDAS.

Special

The law school recruits minority and disadvantaged students by means of recruiting at historically black institutions. Scholarship and stipends are designated for tuition for minority students. Requirements are not different for out-of-state students. Transfer students must have one year of credit, have a minimum GPA of 2, have attended an ABA-approved law school, and submit an LSDAS report and 2 letters of recommendation from their current law school dean.

Costs

Tuition and fees for the 2001-2002 academic year are $15,850 for all full-time students. Books and supplies run about $850 annually.

Financial Aid

About 81% of current law students receive some form of aid. The average annual amount of aid from all sources combined, including scholarships, loans, and work contracts, is $16,000; maximum, $20,938. Awards are based on merit. Required financial statement is the FAFSA. Special funds for minority or disadvantaged students consist of minority scholarships. First-year students are notified about their financial aid application when financial aid papers are completed, which may occur before acceptance.

About the Law School

Mississippi College School of Law was established in 1975 and is a private institution. The campus is in an urban area in Jackson. The primary mission of the law school is to impart to its students quality education within the context of a Christian institution and to instill in them the highest degree of professional proficiency and integrity. Students have access to federal, state, county, city, and local agencies, courts, correctional facilities, law firms, and legal aid organizations in the Jackson area. Housing for students is available off campus. Some on-campus housing at the Clinton campus may be available. All law school facilities are accessible to the physically disabled.

Calendar

The law school operates on a traditional semester basis. Courses for full-time students are offered days only and must be completed within 3 years. There is no part-time program. New students are admitted in the fall. There is a 9-week summer session. Transferable summer courses are offered.

Programs

The following joint degrees may be earned: J.D./M.B.A. (Juris Doctor/Master of Business Administration).

Required

To earn the J.D., candidates must complete 90 total credits, of which 36 are for required courses. They must maintain a minimum GPA of 2.0 in the required courses. The following first-year courses are required of all students: Torts, Contracts I and II, Property I and II, Civil Procedure I and II, Criminal Law, Legal Research and Legal Writing, and Legal Analysis. Required upper-level courses consist of Professional Responsibility and Ethics, Appellate Advocacy, a writing requirement, and Constitutional Law. The required orientation program for first-year students is a 3-day program that includes how to brief a case, an introduction to basic legal methods, and the development of the Anglo-American legal system.

Phone: 601-925-7150
800-738-1236
E-mail: *pevans@mc.edu*
Web: *http://law.mc.edu*

Contact

Patricia H. Evans, Director of Admissions, 601-925-7150 for general inquiries; Jackie Banes, 601-925-7110 for financial aid information.

Electives

The School of Law offers concentrations in corporate law, family law, litigation, and general and government related areas. In addition, seminars are open to all upper-class students and are usually worth 2 credit hours. The externship program is a small, select program that provides closely supervised externships with legal/judicial offices and governmental agencies; 2 credit hours are generally given. Legal research and writing programs provide an opportunity to work directly with a faculty member on a topic of the student's choice for 2 credit hours. Field work is possible through the extern program, which is open to upper-class students. Placement is with government and nonprofit entities for 1 to 3 hours during a semester to provide hands-on training. A remedial writing workshop is offered to first-year students exhibiting need based upon a written submission; no credit is offered. A 3 credit-hour special interest program, Comparative Legal Systems: Civil Law and Common Law, is offered to students interested in Louisiana law. The most widely taken electives are Trial Practice, Pretrial Practice, and Counseling and Negotiations.

Graduation Requirements

In order to graduate, candidates must have a GPA of 2.0 and have completed the upper-division writing requirement.

Organizations

Students edit the *Mississippi College Law Review* and the student paper, *Legal Eye*. The moot court board conducts the appellate competitions. Law student organizations include the Law Student Association, Women's Student Bar Association, and Environmental Club. There are local chapters of Phi Alpha Delta, Delta Theta Phi, and Phi Delta Phi.

Library

The law library contains 253,000 hard-copy volumes and 540,000 microform volume equivalents, and subscribes to 3100 serial publications. Such on-line databases and networks as DIALOG, LEXIS, and WESTLAW are available to law students for research. Special library collections include a partial government printing office depository for U.S. government documents. Recently, the library became a member of CALI; the computer laboratory was made available to students. The ratio of library volumes to faculty is 14,055 to 1 and to students is 675 to 1. The ratio of seats in the library to students is 1 to 1.

Faculty

The law school has 18 full-time and 18 part-time faculty members, of whom 8 are women. About 38% of full-time faculty have a graduate law degree in addition to the J.D. The ratio of full-time students to full-time faculty in an average class is 24 to 1; in a clinic, 24 to 1. The law school has a regular program of bringing visiting professors and other distinguished lecturers and visitors to campus.

Students

About 44% of the student body are women; 10%, minorities; 9%, African American; 1%, Asian American; and 1%, Hispanic. Half of the students come from Mississippi. The average age of entering students is 26; age range is 21 to 53. About 70% of students enter directly from undergraduate school, 10% have a graduate degree, and 20% have worked full-time prior to entering law school. About 7% drop out after the first year for academic or personal reasons; 93% remain to receive a law degree.

Placement	
J.D.s awarded:	105
Services available through: a separate law school placement center	
Full-time job interviews:	32 employers
Summer job interviews:	32 employers
Placement by graduation:	63% of class
Placement within 9 months:	90% of class
Average starting salary:	$35,000 to $48,000
Areas of placement:	
Private practice 2-10 attorneys	30%
Private practice 11-25 attorneys	25%
Private practice 26-50 attorneys	10%
Judicial clerkships	20%
Government	10%
Business/industry	3%
Military	2%

154 Stuart Street
Boston, MA 02116

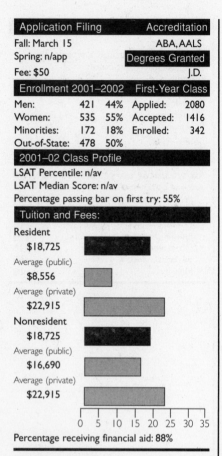

Application Filing		Accreditation
Fall: March 15		ABA, AALS
Spring: n/app		**Degrees Granted**
Fee: $50		J.D.

Enrollment 2001–2002			First-Year Class	
Men:	421	44%	Applied:	2080
Women:	535	55%	Accepted:	1416
Minorities:	172	18%	Enrolled:	342
Out-of-State:	478	50%		

2001–02 Class Profile

LSAT Percentile: n/av
LSAT Median Score: n/av
Percentage passing bar on first try: 55%

Tuition and Fees:

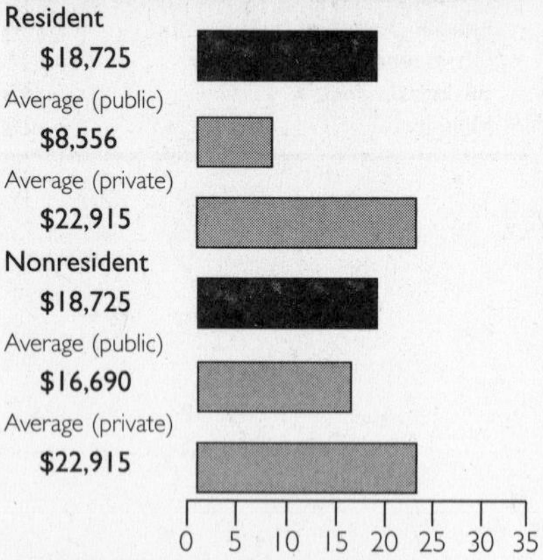

Percentage receiving financial aid: 88%

ADMISSIONS

In the fall 2001 first-year class, 2080 applied, 1416 were accepted, and 342 enrolled. Twenty-nine transfers enrolled.

Requirements

Applicants must have a bachelor's degree and take the LSAT. The most important admission factors include LSAT results, GPA, and motivation. No specific undergraduate courses are required. Candidates are not interviewed.

Procedure

The application deadline for fall entry is March 15. Applicants should submit an application form, LSAT results, transcripts, a nonrefundable application fee of $50, 2 letters of recommendation, a personal statement, and the LSDAS Report. Notification of the admissions decision is on a rolling basis. The latest acceptable LSAT test date for fall entry is February. The law school uses the LSDAS.

Special

The law school recruits minority and disadvantaged students by means of attendance at minority recruitment fairs, a Minority Outreach Recruitment Program geared toward institutions with large minority populations, and participation in CLEO and CRS searches. Requirements are not different for out-of-state students. Transfer students must have one year of credit, a minimum average of C+, and have a dean's letter of good standing.

Costs

Tuition and fees for the 2001-2002 academic year are $18,725 for all full-time students. Tuition for part-time students is $14,085 per year. Books and supplies cost about $950 annually.

Financial Aid

About 88% of current law students receive some form of aid. The average annual amount of aid from all sources combined, including scholarships, loans, and work contracts, is $22,746; maximum, $34,290. Awards are based on need and merit. Required financial statements are the FAFSA, the institutional application, and federal tax returns. The aid application deadline for fall entry is April 17. Special funds for minority or disadvantaged students consist of the Maclean Grant for disadvantaged students and the Jacqueline Lloyd Grant for minority students. First-year students are notified about their financial aid application at time of acceptance.

About the Law School

New England School of Law was established in 1908 and is a private institution. The campus is in an urban area in Boston. The primary mission of the law school is to provide the opportunity for quality legal education and ethical training to men and women, especially those who might otherwise not have that opportunity. Students have access to federal, state, county, city, and local agencies, courts, correctional facilities, law firms, and legal aid organizations in the Boston area. Boston is the state capital, and as such offers many opportunities to law students. Facilities of special interest to law students are the Clinical Law Office, a school-sponsored neighborhood law office that provides clinical training and assists low-income litigants, and other clinical programs with the attorney general, Massachusetts Revenue Department, and other agencies. Housing for students is not available on campus; however, assistance is provided for finding housing and roommates. About 98% of the law school facilities are accessible to the physically disabled.

Calendar

The law school operates on a traditional semester basis. Courses for full-time students are offered both day and evening and must be completed within 5 years. For part-time students, courses are offered both day and evening and must be completed within 6 years. New full- and part-time students are admitted in the fall. There is an 8-week summer session. Transferable summer courses are offered.

Programs

Students may take relevant courses in other programs and apply credit toward the J.D.; a maximum of 6 credits may be applied.

Phone: 617-422-7210
Fax: 617-422-7200
E-mail: *admit@admin.nesi.edu*
Web: *www.nesi.edu*

Contact

Pamela Jorgensen, Director of Admissions, 617-422-7210 for general inquiries; Douglas Leman, Director of Financial Aid, 617-451-0010, ext. 298 for financial aid information.

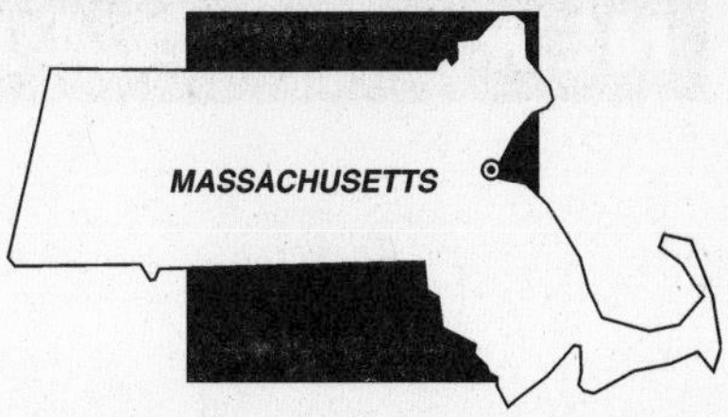

Required

To earn the J.D., candidates must complete 84 total credits, of which 43 are for required courses. They must maintain a minimum GPA of 2.0 in the required courses. The following first-year courses are required of all students: Civil Procedure, Constitutional Law, Contracts, Property, Torts, and Legal Methods. Required upper-level courses consist of Criminal Law, Evidence, Criminal Procedure I, and Law and Ethics of Lawyering. The required orientation program for first-year students is a 1-week program with panel discussions on legal issues and lectures on the legal process, how to brief a case, and the procedures of a civil case.

Electives

The New England School of Law offers concentrations in corporate law, criminal law, environmental law, family law, international law, litigation, and tax law. In addition, clinics are available to second- and third-year day division students and third- and fourth-year evening division students for 2 to 6 credits. All upper-class students may take electives for 2 to 3 credits. Final-year students may undertake research programs for a 2-credit maximum per year. Special lecture series are available to all students for no credit. Up to 6 credits may be transferred from another school's ABA-approved study-abroad program. In addition, the New England School of Law, in cooperation with 3 other law schools, sponsors 3 summer-abroad programs and 2 semester-abroad programs. Students may spend a summer studying in Galway, Ireland; London; or Malta. Students may also spend a semester studying in New Zealand or the Netherlands, and at the University of Paris X in Nanterre through the New England School of Law student exchange program. The school will accept credit for courses taken in any summer-abroad program approved by the American Bar Association. In recent years, students have attended programs in Canada, the United Kingdom, France, Japan, China, and Argentina. A noncredit remedial research and writing program is open to first-year students. Noncredit minority programs are open to all students. The most widely taken electives are Wills, Estates, and Trusts, and Business Organization.

Graduation Requirements

In order to graduate, candidates must have a GPA of 2.0 and have completed the upper-division writing requirement.

Organizations

Students edit the *New England Law Review*, the *New England Journal on Criminal and Civil Confinement*, and the student newspaper, *Due Process*. Other publications include the *International and Comparative Law Annual*. Students participate in an annual in-house Honors Moot Court Competition and Trial Competition. Other competitions include the National Moot Court Competition, National Trial Competition, National Tax Moot Court, Jessup International Moot Court, and occasionally the ABA Appellate Advocacy Competition. Student organizations include the Student Bar Association, International Law Society, and Environmental Law Society. There are local chapters of the ABA-Law Student Division and Phi Alpha Delta law fraternity.

Library

The law library contains 322,506 hard-copy volumes and 715,067 microform volume equivalents, and subscribes to 3181 serial publications. Such on-line databases and networks as CALI, CIS Universe, DIALOG, Dow-Jones, Infotrac, Legal-Trac, LEXIS, LOIS, Mathew Bender, NEXIS, OCLC First Search, RLIN, WESTLAW, Wilsonline Indexes, CD-ROMs, and the Internet are available to law students for research. Special library collections include women and the law, Portia Law School archives, a Massachusetts continuing legal education depository, Massachusetts and New England-area publications, media, and all standard legal research materials such as court reports, statutes, treatises, restatements, and legal periodicals. Recently, the library made available 12 laptops for checkout, wireless access throughout the library, and 87 workstations. The ratio of library volumes to faculty is 9773 to 1 and to students is 337 to 1. The ratio of seats in the library to students is 1 to 2.

Placement

J.D.s awarded:	279
Services available through: a separate law school placement center	
Services: computerized job search resources and assistance with judicial clerkships	
Special features: individual and group counseling services as well as strong alumni contacts.	
Full-time job interviews:	20 employers
Summer job interviews:	20 employers
Placement by graduation:	47% of class
Placement within 9 months:	99% of class
Average starting salary:	$32,000 to $100,000
Areas of placement:	
Private practice 2-10 attorneys	23%
Private practice 11-25 attorneys	3%
Private practice 26-50 attorneys	3%
Private practice 51-100 attorneys	3%
Private practice size unknown	7%
Business/industry	24%
Government	17%
Judicial clerkships	8%
Public interest	2%
Military	1%
Academic	1%

Faculty

The law school has 33 full-time and 69 part-time faculty members, of whom 23 are women. According to AAUP standards for Category IIA institutions, faculty salaries are well above average. About 22% of full-time faculty have a graduate law degree in addition to the J.D.; about 23% of part-time faculty have one. The ratio of full-time students to full-time faculty in an average class is 26 to 1; in a clinic, 10 to 1. The law school has a regular program of bringing visiting professors and other distinguished lecturers and visitors to campus.

Students

About 55% of the student body are women; 18%, minorities; 4%, African American; 4%, Asian American; 8%, Hispanic; and 1%, Native American. Most students come from Massachusetts (50%). The average age of entering students is 28; age range is 19 to 57. About 13% drop out after the first year for academic or personal reasons; 87% remain to receive a law degree.

NEW YORK LAW SCHOOL

57 Worth Street
New York, NY 10013-2960

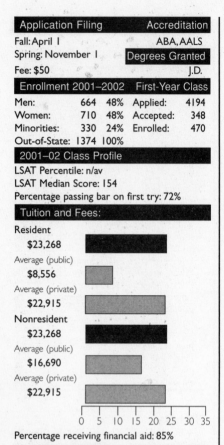

Application Filing		Accreditation
Fall: April 1		ABA, AALS
Spring: November 1		**Degrees Granted**
Fee: $50		J.D.

Enrollment 2001–2002			First-Year Class	
Men:	664	48%	Applied:	4194
Women:	710	48%	Accepted:	348
Minorities:	330	24%	Enrolled:	470
Out-of-State:	1374	100%		

2001–02 Class Profile

LSAT Percentile: n/av
LSAT Median Score: 154
Percentage passing bar on first try: 72%

Tuition and Fees:

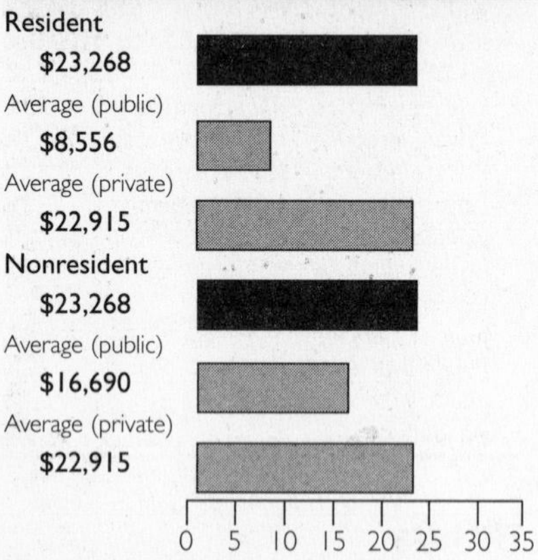

Percentage receiving financial aid: 85%

ADMISSIONS

Figures in the above capsule are from an earlier year. In the fall 2001 first-year class, 4194 applied, 348 were accepted, and 470 enrolled. Nineteen transfers enrolled. The median GPA of the most recent first-year class was 3.1.

Requirements

Applicants must have a bachelor's degree and take the LSAT. Minimum acceptable GPA is 2.0 on a scale of 4.0. No specific undergraduate courses are required. Candidates are not interviewed.

Procedure

The application deadline for fall entry is April 1. Applicants should submit an application form, LSAT results, a nonrefundable application fee of $50, and Accepted students must submit a $250 deposit by April 1, which is applied toward tuition upon registration, and a $500 deposit by June 1. Notification of the admissions decision is on a rolling basis. The latest acceptable LSAT test date for fall entry is February. The law school uses the LSDAS.

Special

The law school recruits minority and disadvantaged students through diversity recruitment efforts initiated by the minority recruitment coordinator in the Admissions Office. Requirements are not different for out-of-state students. Transfer students must have one year of credit, have a minimum GPA of 3, have attended an ABA-approved law school, and have a bachelor's degree from an accredited college or university. Preadmissions courses consist of .

Costs

Tuition and fees for the 2001-2002 academic year are $23,268 for all full-time students. Tuition for part-time students is $16,588 per year. On-campus room and board costs about $9945 annually; books and supplies run $800.

Financial Aid

About 85% of current law students receive some form of aid. The average annual amount of aid from all sources combined, including scholarships, loans, and work contracts, is $18,500; maximum, $33,975. Awards are based on need Scholarships are awarded on the basis of merit. NYLS need-based grants are awarded on the basis of financial need. Required financial statement is the FAFSA. The aid application deadline for fall entry is April 15. Special funds for minority or disadvantaged students are available through scholarship funds. First-year students are notified about their financial aid application contingent upon its completion.

About the Law School

New York Law School was established in 1891 and is independent. The campus is in an urban area on 4 contiguous city blocks in the historic TriBeca district of New York City. The primary mission of the law school is to deliver a sense of public service in law students, melding the theoretical and the practical to provide a strong foundation of legal knowledge as well as diverse perspectives. Students have access to federal, state, county, city, and local agencies, courts, correctional facilities, law firms, and legal aid organizations in the New York City area. Facilities of special interest to law students include the Communications Media Center, which promotes learning about mass communications law; the Center for New York City Law, which focuses on urban governmental and legal processes; and the Center for International Law, which supports teaching and research in that field. Housing for students consists of dormitory rooms in a renovated facility 15 minutes from the school. Additional apartments and roommate referrals are available through the Housing Office. All law school facilities are accessible to the physically disabled.

Calendar

The law school operates on a traditional semester basis. Courses for full-time students are offered both day and evening and must be completed within 3 years. For part-time students, courses are offered both day and evening and must be completed within 4 years. New full- and part-time students are admitted in the fall. There is an 8-week summer session. Transferable summer courses are not offered.

Programs

Students may take relevant courses in other programs and apply credit toward the J.D.; a maximum of 10 credits from the new School for Social Research may be applied. The following joint degrees may be earned: J.D./M.B.A. (Juris Doctor/Master of Business Administration (in association with Baruch College).

Required

To earn the J.D., candidates must complete 86 total credits, of which 38 are for required courses. They must maintain a minimum GPA of 2.0 in the required courses. The following first-year courses are required of all students: Civil Procedure, Contracts I and II, Lawyering, Legal Reasoning, Writing and Research, Torts, Criminal Law, Property, Written and Oral Advocacy, and Evidence. Required upper-level courses consist of The Legal Profession, a writing requirement, and Constitutional Law I and II. The required orientation program for first-year students is a week-long and is designed to ease the anxieties of incom-

Phone: 212-431-2888
877-YES-NYLS
Fax: 212-966-1522
E-mail: *admissions@nyls.edu*
Web: *www.nyls.edu*

Contact

Thomas Antonio Matos, Director of Admissions, 212-431-2888 for general inquiries; Toby White, Director of Financial Aid, 212-431-2828 for financial aid information.

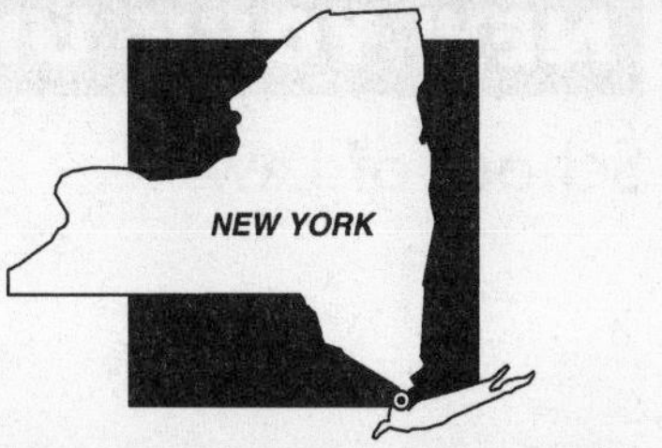

ing students by having them meet informally with professors and fellow students at planned social events as well as introducing them to the rigors of law studies.

Electives

The New York Law School offers concentrations in corporate law, criminal law, entertainment law, environmental law, family law, international law, labor law, litigation, media law, securities law, tax law, torts and insurance, business and commercial law, constitutional law, procedure and evidence, property and real estate, public interest law, administrative law and practice, and immigration law. Students in the Civil and Human Rights Clinic have assisted with racial discrimination cases in federal court as well as housing cases and related banking and discrimination matters, Social Security cases, and nonlitigation representation and counseling of not-for-profit corporations. Students gain additional legal practice experience through workshop courses. These courses link a seminar in a specialized body of law to field placements in offices and agencies practicing in that area of the law. Externships and judicial internships provide opportunities to do actual legal work, in private or public law offices or in judges' chambers, while being supervised by a practitioner at the placement site and meeting with a faculty member at the school. Special lecture series include the Steifel Symposium, Fall Executive Speakers Series, New York City Law Breakfasts, Solomon Lecture, Professional Development Seminar, Faculty Lecture Series, Dean's Roundtable, and Spotlight on Women. Independent study programs are available. The Academic Support Program consists of a condensed introductory course in legal methods in the summer followed by weekly tutorial meetings with second- and third-year teaching fellows through the first academic year. The Admissions Office has an Assistant Director with specific responsibility for minority recruitment and enrollment initiatives. In conjunction with the Office of Student Life, the Asian American Law Students Association, Black Law Students Association, and the Latino Law Students Association offer support to minority students. Special interest group programs include Media Law Project, Domestic Violence Project, New York Law School Civil Liberties Union, Public Interest Coalition, and Trial Lawyers Association. The most widely taken electives are Commercial Transactions; Corporations; and Wills, Trusts, and Future Interests.

Graduation Requirements

In order to graduate, candidates must have a GPA of 2.0 and have completed the upper-division writing requirement.

Organizations

Students edit the *New York Law School Law Review, New York Law School Journal of Human Rights, New York Law School Journal of International and Comparative Law*, and the newspaper *The L.* Students may participate in the Froessel Moot Court intramural competition. Students become members of the Moot Court Association by invitation and may represent the school in intramural competitions held at law schools nationwide. The Robert F. Wagner National Labor Law Moot Court competition is hosted by the school each spring. Law student organizations include Business Law Society, International Law Society, and Legal Association for Women. There are local chapters of Phi Alpha Delta, Phi Delta Phi, and Amnesty International.

Library

The law library contains 475,188 hardcopy volumes and 981,917 microform volume equivalents, and subscribes to 5329 serial publications. Such on-line databases and networks as DIALOG, LEXIS, WESTLAW, Legal-Trac, WILSON DISC, CIS Masterfile I and II, CD-ROM, NEXIS, OCLC, Wilsonline, Law Schools On-line, Index to UN documents, and 25 other CD-ROM databases are available to law students for research. Special library collections include the U.S. government documents depository and special collections in communications rights law, alternative dispute resolution, and labor law. Recently, the library added the INNOPAC On-line Catalog, with dial-in access to the library's holdings and electronic access to the Index of Legal Periodicals. A CD-ROM tower workstation is available. The ratio of library volumes to faculty is 8966 to 1 and to students is 346 to 1. The ratio of seats in the library to students is 1 to 1.

Placement

J.D.s awarded:	403
Services available through: a separate law school placement center	
Services: more than 200 law firms participated in the 1999 recruitment programs	
Special features: a resource library, which contains a collection of job search and career planning materials, information on law firms, corporations, government agencies, the judiciary, public interest organizations, a computerized database; and an alumni network.	
Full-time job interviews:	n/av
Summer job interviews:	n/av
Placement by graduation:	n/av
Placement within 9 months:	93% of class
Average starting salary:	$39,500 to $62,500
Areas of placement:	
Private practice 2-100 attorneys	45%
Government	20%
Business/industry	16%
Unknown	8%
Judicial clerkships	6%
Public interest	3%
Academic	2%

Faculty

The law school has 53 full-time and 82 part-time faculty members, of whom 42 are women. About 36% of full-time faculty have a graduate law degree in addition to the J.D.; about 19% of part-time faculty have one. The ratio of full-time students to full-time faculty in an average class is 22 to 1; in a clinic, 6 to 1. The law school has a regular program of bringing visiting professors and other distinguished lecturers and visitors to campus. There is a chapter of the Order of the Coif.

Students

About 48% of the student body are women; 24%, minorities; 10%, African American; 6%, Asian American; 7%, Hispanic; and 3%, mixed race/ethnicity. The average age of entering students is 27; age range is 21 to 58. About 3% drop out after the first year for academic or personal reasons; 85% remain to receive a law degree.

NEW YORK UNIVERSITY

School of Law

110 West Third Street
New York, NY 10012

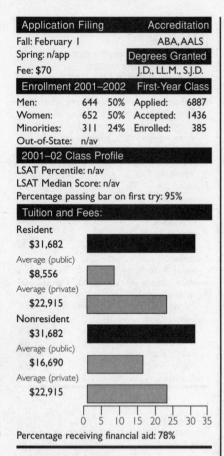

Application Filing		Accreditation
Fall: February 1		ABA, AALS
Spring: n/app		**Degrees Granted**
Fee: $70		J.D., LL.M., S.J.D.

Enrollment 2001–2002			First-Year Class	
Men:	644	50%	Applied:	6887
Women:	652	50%	Accepted:	1436
Minorities:	311	24%	Enrolled:	385
Out-of-State:	n/av			

2001–02 Class Profile

LSAT Percentile: n/av
LSAT Median Score: n/av
Percentage passing bar on first try: 95%

Tuition and Fees:

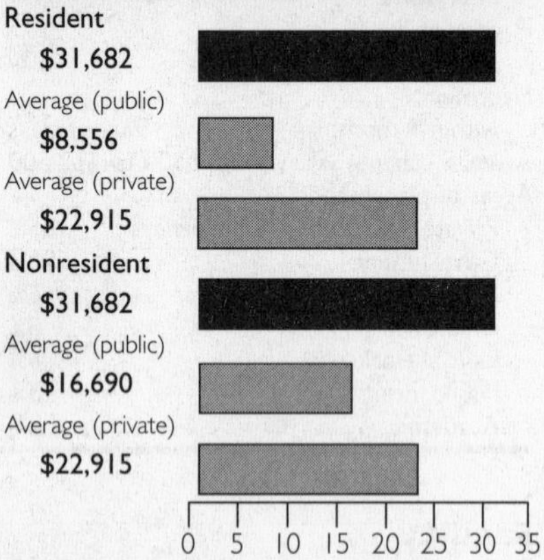

Percentage receiving financial aid: 78%

ADMISSIONS

In the fall 2001 first-year class, 6887 applied, 1436 were accepted, and 385 enrolled. Forty-three transfers enrolled.

Requirements

Applicants must have a bachelor's degree, be at least 18 years old, and take the LSAT. No specific undergraduate courses are required. Candidates are not interviewed.

Procedure

The application deadline for fall entry is February 1; early action deadline is October 15. Applicants should submit an application form, LSAT results, transcripts, a nonrefundable application fee of $70, 1 letter of recommendation, and a personal statement. Notification of the admissions decision is by mid-April. The latest acceptable LSAT test date for fall entry is December. The law school uses the LSDAS.

Special

The law school recruits minority and disadvantaged students by paying special attention to application information other than the GPA and LSAT results. Requirements are not different for out-of-state students. Transfer students must have one year of credit, have attended an ABA-approved law school, submit all college and law school transcripts, LSAT scores, a letter of recommendation from a law school professor, and a statement of good standing from a dean. The school attended must be a member of the AALS or be approved by the Section on Legal Education of the ABA.

Costs

Tuition and fees for the 2001-2002 academic year are $31,682 for all full-time students. On-campus room and board costs about $17,330 annually; books and supplies run $680.

Financial Aid

About 78% of current law students receive some form of aid. Awards are based on need and merit. Required financial statement is the FAFSA. The aid application deadline for fall entry is April 15. First-year students are notified about their financial aid application at time of acceptance.

About the Law School

New York University School of Law was established in 1835 and is a private institution. The campus is in an urban area in New York City. The primary mission of the law school is to produce men and women who are leaders of the bar, public and private, in a world that operates across national boundaries. Students have access to federal, state, county, city, and local agencies, courts, correctional facilities, law firms, and legal aid organizations in the New York area. In addition, the many and varied resources of New York City are available. Facilities of special interest to law students include Vanderbilt Hall, which contains classrooms, faculty and administrative offices, and the library; D'Agostino and Mercer Student residences, with meeting rooms, student journal offices, and a conference center. Housing for students is available for virtually all who request it, including couples and families; 2 law school-owned apartment buildings are within 4 blocks of the campus. About 95% of the law school facilities are accessible to the physically disabled.

Calendar

The law school operates on a traditional semester basis. Courses for full-time students are offered both day and evening, but classes are primarily during the day and must be completed within 6 semesters. There is no part-time program. New students are admitted in the fall. There is no summer session. Transferable summer courses are not offered.

Programs

In addition to the J.D., the law school offers the LL.M. and S.J.D. Students may take relevant courses in other programs and apply credit toward the J.D.; a maximum of 10 credits may be applied. The following joint degrees may be earned: J.D./LL.M. (Juris Doctor/Master of Laws in taxation), J.D./M.A. (Juris Doctor/ Master of Arts in economics, philosophy, etc.), J.D./M.B.A. (Juris Doctor/Master of Business Administration), J.D./M.I.A. (Juris Doctor/Master of International and Public Affairs), J.D./M.P.A. (Juris Doctor/Master of Public Administration), J.D./M.S.W. (Juris Doctor/Master of Social Work), and J.D./M.U.P. (Juris Doctor/Master of Urban Planning).

Required

To earn the J.D., candidates must complete 82 total credits, of which 44 are for required courses. The following first-year courses are required of all students: Contracts I and II, Criminal Law, Civil Procedure I and II, Property, Torts, and Lawyering. Required upper-level courses consist of Constitutional Law, Professional Responsibility, the Legal Institutions requirement, and 2 upper-level writing requirements. The required orientation program for first-year students is a 2-day academic and social orientation period before the start of classes, followed by a series of optional weekly programs during the first term.

Phone: 212-998-6060
Fax: 212-995-4527
Web: *www.nyu.edu/law*

Contact

Assistant Dean for Admissions, 212-998-6060 for general inquiries; John Kelly, Associate Director of Financial Aid, 212-998-6050 for financial aid information.

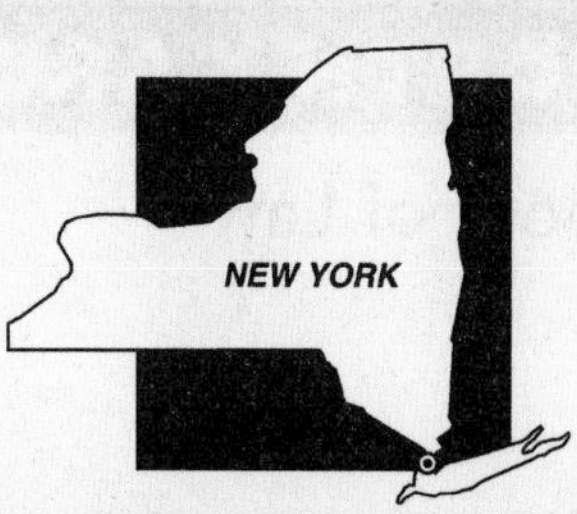

Electives

The School of Law offers concentrations in corporate law, criminal law, entertainment law, environmental law, family law, international law, juvenile law, labor law, litigation, securities law, tax law, torts and insurance, global law, public interest law, and real estate law. In addition, clinics provide simulated and actual trial experience; clinics include the Capital Defender Clinic, Civil Rights Clinic, and International Human Rights Clinic. Seminars are offered in areas such as constitutional law, corporate and commercial law, and criminal justice. The school provides financial assistance for summer internships for 245 first-and second year students committed to public interest law. These summer internships are with public interest organizations worldwide. Additionally, Root-Tilden-Kern Scholars participate in a 10-week internship in public interest law. Students may arrange with faculty to conduct research; the Directed Writing Project requires a substantial paper that may fulfill part of the upper-level writing requirement. Research is also part of the Hays Civil Liberties Program, open to selected third-year students; the Boudin and Blaustein Fellowships in human rights; and junior fellowships in international legal studies. Among others, special lecture series include the Root-Tilden-Kern Speakers Program, Legal, Political, and Moral Philosophy Colloquium, Innovation Policy Colloquium, the National Center on Philanthropy and the Law, and the Legal History Colloquium. Study abroad is possible through a 1-semester exchange program with universities in Belgium, Italy, Australia, Paris, Amsterdam, and Copenhagen. The most widely taken electives are Colloquia (faculty-student discussions); all 16 clinical program and advocacy courses; and seminars.

Graduation Requirements

In order to graduate, candidates must have completed the upper-division writing requirement and attend 6 semesters of classes.

Organizations

Students edit the *New York University Law Review, Annual Survey of American Law* , *Journal of International Law and Politics, Environmental Law Journal, Review of Law and Social Change, Journal of Legislation and Public Policy, Tax Law Review, Clinical Law Review, Eastern European Constitutional Review*, the newspaper, *The Commentator*, and the *Moot Court Board Casebook*. Members of the Moot Court Board enter intraschool and nationwide competitions, as well as develop moot court cases for use in nationwide competition. There are more than 60 funded law student groups on campus, including the Student Bar Association. For a full listing of student organizations, please refer to the school's web site at *www.law.nyu.edu/studentlife/*.

Library

The law library contains 1,012,051 hard-copy volumes and 138,600 microform volume equivalents, and subscribes to 6885 serial publications. Such on-line databases and networks as CALI, CIS Universe, DIALOG, Dow-Jones, Legal-Trac, LEXIS, OCLC First Search, RLIN, and WESTLAW and many international Internet databases are available to law students for research. Special library collections include Anglo-American materials; international law; Jewish law; tax law; patent, trademark, and copyright law; and securities and finance law. The library's seating capacity is 799. Recently, the library has been wired for approximately 100 public access terminals connected to the Internet, as well as plug-in capacity for student laptops. Concurrently, students have access to electronic sources from a hard-wired Resnet in the 2 law school dorms. The Global Law Program and a $500,000 grant from the Starr Foundation have increased the library's focus on foreign, comparative, and international law. The ratio of library volumes to faculty is 10,767 to 1 and to students is 781 to 1. The ratio of seats in the library to students is 1 to 2.

Placement

J.D.s awarded:	454
Services available through: a separate law school placement center	
Services: hosting 35 legal career panel discussions with 150 lawyers each year, and sending judicial clerkship letters of recommendation.	
Special features: Early Interview Week each August, public interest and government and international job fairs, and off-campus recruitment programs in Washington, D.C., Chicago, Los Angeles, and San Francisco.	
Full-time job interviews:	500 employers
Summer job interviews:	n/av
Placement by graduation:	97% of class
Placement within 9 months:	100% of class
Average starting salary:	$38,881 to $120,017
Areas of placement:	
Private practice 2-100 attorneys	72%
Judicial clerkships	15%
Public interest	7%
Business/industry	4%
Government	2%

Faculty

The law school has 94 full-time and 75 part-time faculty members, of whom 52 are women. According to AAUP standards for Category I institutions, faculty salaries are well above average. The ratio of full-time students to full-time faculty in an average class is 12 to 1; in a clinic, 8 to 1. The law school has a regular program of bringing visiting professors and other distinguished lecturers and visitors to campus. There is a chapter of the Order of the Coif.

Students

About 50% of the student body are women; 24%, minorities; 6%, African American; 11%, Asian American; and 6%, Hispanic. The average age of entering students is 25. About 36% of students enter directly from undergraduate school and 10% have a graduate degree. About 1% drop out after the first year for academic or personal reasons.

NORTH CAROLINA CENTRAL UNIVERSITY

School of Law

1512 S. Alston Avenue
Durham, NC 27707

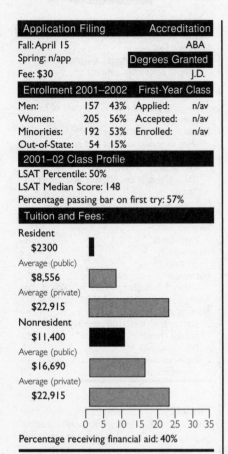

Application Filing		Accreditation
Fall: April 15		ABA
Spring: n/app		**Degrees Granted**
Fee: $30		J.D.

Enrollment 2001–2002			First-Year Class	
Men:	157	43%	Applied:	n/av
Women:	205	56%	Accepted:	n/av
Minorities:	192	53%	Enrolled:	n/av
Out-of-State:	54	15%		

2001–02 Class Profile

LSAT Percentile: 50%
LSAT Median Score: 148
Percentage passing bar on first try: 57%

Tuition and Fees:

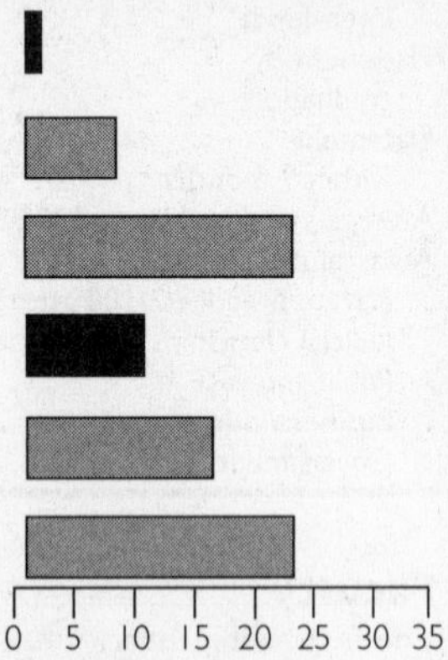

Resident
$2300
Average (public)
$8,556
Average (private)
$22,915
Nonresident
$11,400
Average (public)
$16,690
Average (private)
$22,915

Percentage receiving financial aid: 40%

ADMISSIONS

Information in the above capsule is from an earlier year. In a recent first-year class, one transfer enrolled. The median LSAT percentile of a recent first-year class was 50; the median GPA was 3.1 on a scale of 4.0. The lowest LSAT percentile accepted was 143; the highest was 152.

Requirements

Applicants must have a bachelor's degree and take the LSAT. No specific undergraduate courses are required. Candidates are not interviewed.

Procedure

Check with the school for current application deadlines and fee. Applicants should submit an application form, LSAT results, transcripts, a nonrefundable application fee, and 2 letters of recommendation. Accepted students who intend to enroll must submit a nonrefundable $100 tuition deposit, which is applied to the student's first tuition payment. Notification of the admissions decision is on a rolling basis. The law school uses the LSDAS.

Special

The law school recruits minority and disadvantaged students by means of the Performance-Based Admissions Program, which is designed to identify applicants who have the potential to succeed in law school, but whose undergraduate transcripts and LSAT scores do not meet traditional standards. Requirements are not different for out-of-state students. Transfer students must have a minimum GPA of 2, have attended an ABA-approved law school, have 1 year of residence at the School of Law, and be in good standing at the previous law school.

Costs

Tuition and fees for the academic year are approximately $2300 for full-time in-state students and $11,400 for out-of-state students. Tuition for part-time students is about $2300 in-state and $11,400 out-of-state. On-campus room and board costs about $4300 annually.

Financial Aid

About 40% of law students receive some form of aid. The average annual amount of aid from all sources combined, including scholarships, loans, and work contracts, is about $400. Awards are based on need and merit. Required financial statement is the FAFSA. Special funds for minority or disadvantaged students are available through fellowships and national associations. The Council on Legal Education Opportunity (CLEO) is a federally funded program for disadvantaged students. Check with the school for current deadlines.

About the Law School

North Carolina Central University School of Law was established in 1939 and is a public institution. The 105-acre campus is in an urban area 20 miles from Raleigh, 5 miles from Research Triangle Park. The primary mission of the law school is to provide a challenging and broad-based educational program designed to stimulate intellectual inquiry, and foster in each student a sense of community service, professional responsibility, and personal integrity. The law school student body is diverse in terms of gender, ethnicity, and economic and experiential backgrounds. Students have access to federal, state, county, city, and local agencies, courts, correctional facilities, law firms, and legal aid organizations in the Durham area. Facilities of special interest to law students include a modern law library, computer laboratory, academic support programs, and individual offices for student organizations. Some on-campus housing is available for single students, but married students must live off campus. About 90% of the law school facilities are accessible to the physically disabled.

Calendar

The law school operates on a traditional semester basis. Courses for full-time students are offered days only. (Some special elective classes may meet in the evening and must be completed within 3 years.) For part-time students, courses are offered evenings only and must be completed within 4 years. New full- and part-time students are admitted in the fall. There are two 5 ½-week summer sessions. Transferable summer courses are offered.

Programs

Students may take relevant courses in other programs and apply credit toward the J.D.; a maximum of 6 hours may be applied. The following joint degrees may be earned: J.D./M.B.A. (Juris Doctor/Master of Business Administration) and J.D./M.L.S. (Juris Doctor/Master of Library and Information Services).

Phone: 919-560-6333
Fax: 919-560-6339
E-mail: *jfaucett@wpo.nccu.edu*
Web: *www.nccu.edu/law*

Contact

Admissions Coordinator, 919-530-5243 for general inquiries; Office of Scholarships and Student Aid, 919-560-6202/919-530-6365 for financial aid information.

Required

To earn the J.D., candidates must complete 88 total credits, of which 65 are for required courses. They must maintain a minimum GPA of 2.0 in the required courses. The following first-year courses are required of all students: Contracts I, Civil Procedure I, Property I, Legal Method I, Torts I, Legal Bibliography, Contracts II, Civil Procedure II, Property II, Legal Method II, and Criminal Law. Required upper-level courses consist of Advanced Legal Writing I and II (Senior Writing Evening Program), Appellate Advocacy I, Business Associations (Corporations Evening Program), Constitutional Law I and II, Decedents' Estates and Trusts I, Evidence, Professional Responsibility, Sales and Secured Transactions, Statutory Interpretation, and Taxation. Although not required, students are encouraged to enroll in the clinical program. There is a model law office that houses clinical facilities. The required orientation program for first-year students lasts 2 days and includes pre-enrollment seminars.

Electives

The Clinical Experience Program consists of preliminary courses in the rules of evidence and trial practice with mock trials and oral arguments. Students work with law enforcement officials, legal services agencies, and attorneys in North Carolina. Seminars include the Land Loss Prevention Project (LLPP), which assists limited-resource landholders to preserve their lands and livelihoods; the Civil Rights Project, an in-depth study of special problems involved in litigating federal civil rights actions; and Women in the Law. The school is a member of an interinstitutional enrollment program that includes Duke University School of Law and University of North Carolina School of Law. An academic support program is available to students for assistance with specific academic needs, problems, and adjustment expectations. Tutorials in each first-year substantive course and selected upper-level courses are open to all interested students. In addition, the school offers a noncredit writing laboratory for 1 hour every week in the fall and spring semesters. The Pro Bono Clinic offers many opportunities for second- and third-year students to volunteer in local special interest agencies and organizations. The most widely taken electives are the Clinical Program, Criminal Procedure, and Trial Practice.

Graduation Requirements

In order to graduate, candidates must have a GPA of 2.0 and have completed the upper-division writing requirement.

Organizations

Students edit the *North Carolina Central Law Journal* and the newspaper *The Barrister*. Moot Court competitions include the J. Braxton Craven, Jr. Memorial Moot Court Competition; Saul Lefkowitz Moot Court Competition; and Ernest B. Fullwood Moot Court Competition. Other competitions include Trial Advocacy Competition, National Trial Competition, and Association of Trial Lawyers of America (ATLA) Trial Competition. Law student organizations include the Student Bar Association, Intellectual Property Society, and Entertainment and Sports Law Association. There are local chapters of Phi Alpha Delta, Phi Delta Phi, and Delta Theta Phi. Other organizations include Alpha Kappa Alpha Sorority, Delta Sigma Theta Sorority, and Omega Psi Phi Fraternity.

Library

The law library contains 284,115 hardcopy volumes and 639,314 microform volume equivalents, and subscribes to 2370 serial publications. Such on-line databases and networks as DIALOG, LEXIS, and WESTLAW are available to law students for research. Special library collections include a depository for U.S. government documents. The ratio of library volumes to faculty is 4420 to 1 and to students is 363 to 1. The ratio of seats in the library to students is 1 to 1.

Placement	
J.D.s awarded:	95
Services available through: a separate law school placement center	
Services: workshop sessions on various practice areas; mock interviews; and participation in job fairs.	
Special features: placement programs that bring in recruiters from government, private firms, legal services, and corporations.	
Full-time job interviews:	7 employers
Summer job interviews:	18 employers
Placement by graduation:	49% of class
Placement within 9 months:	89% of class
Average starting salary:	$25,000 to $101,000
Areas of placement:	
Private practice 2-100 attorneys	43%
Government	18%
Public interest	6%
Judicial clerkships	5%
Business/industry	5%
Military	2%
Academic	2%

Faculty

The law school has approximately 23 full-time and 9 part-time faculty members, of whom 15 are women. According to AAUP standards for Category IIA institutions, faculty salaries are above average. About 49% of full-time faculty have a graduate law degree in addition to the J.D.; about 5% of part-time faculty have one. The ratio of full-time students to full-time faculty in an average class is 15 to 1. The law school has a regular program of bringing visiting professors and other distinguished lecturers and visitors to campus.

Students

About 56% of the student body are women; 53%, minorities; 49%, African American; 1%, Asian American; 2%, Hispanic; and 1%, Native American. The majority of students come from North Carolina (85%).

NORTHEASTERN UNIVERSITY

School of Law

400 Huntington Avenue
Boston, MA 02115

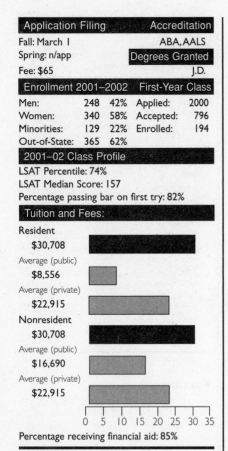

Application Filing		Accreditation
Fall: March 1		ABA, AALS
Spring: n/app		**Degrees Granted**
Fee: $65		J.D.

Enrollment 2001–2002			First-Year Class	
Men:	248	42%	Applied:	2000
Women:	340	58%	Accepted:	796
Minorities:	129	22%	Enrolled:	194
Out-of-State:	365	62%		

2001–02 Class Profile

LSAT Percentile: 74%
LSAT Median Score: 157
Percentage passing bar on first try: 82%

Tuition and Fees:

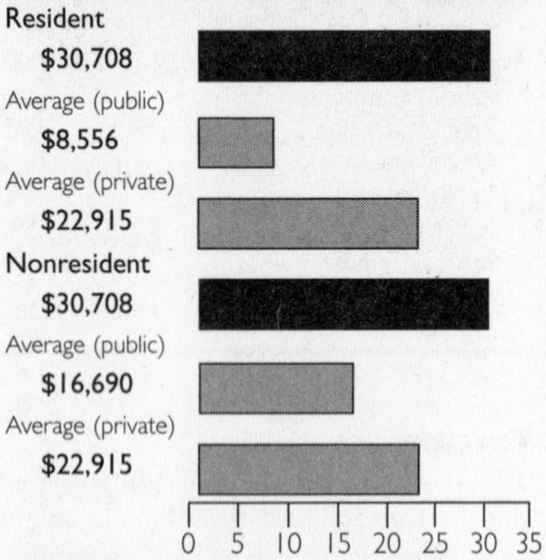

Percentage receiving financial aid: 85%

ADMISSIONS

In the fall 2001 first-year class, 2000 applied, 796 were accepted, and 194 enrolled. Five transfers enrolled. The median LSAT percentile of the most recent first-year class was 74; the median GPA was 3.3 on a scale of 4.0. The lowest LSAT percentile accepted was 10; the highest was 97.

Requirements

Applicants must have a bachelor's degree and take the LSAT. The most important admission factors include work experience, academic achievement, and LSAT results. No specific undergraduate courses are required. Candidates are not interviewed.

Procedure

The application deadline for fall entry is March 1. Applicants should submit an application form, LSAT results, transcripts, TOEFL, if indicated, a nonrefundable application fee of $65, 2 letters of recommendation, and a personal statement. Notification of the admissions decision is on a modified rolling basis. The latest acceptable LSAT test date for fall entry is October and December. The law school uses the LSDAS.

Special

The law school recruits minority and disadvantaged students by targeting historically black colleges and universities, providing scholarships, and being a member of CLEO. Requirements are not different for out-of-state students. Transfer students must have one year of credit, have attended an ABA-approved law school, and must submit 1 recommendation from the dean of their current law school attesting to their good standing and eligibility, and at least 1 letter from a first-year law professor.

Costs

Tuition and fees for the 2001-2002 academic year are $30,708 for all full-time students. On-campus room and board costs about $12,150 annually; books and supplies run $1200.

Financial Aid

About 85% of current law students receive some form of aid. The average annual amount of aid from all sources combined, including scholarships, loans, and work contracts, is $33,000; maximum, $41,463. Awards are based on merit and need and merit combined. Required financial statements are the FAFSA, institutional application, and federal tax returns. The aid application deadline for fall entry is February 15. First-year students are notified about their financial aid application at time of acceptance and upon completion of financial aid information.

About the Law School

Northeastern University School of Law was established in 1898 and is a private institution. The 5556-acre campus is in an urban area in Boston. The primary mission of the law school is to fuse theory and practice with ethical and social justice ideals so that students understand what it is that lawyers do, how they do it, and the difference they can make in the lives of others. Students have access to federal, state, county, city, and local agencies, courts, correctional facilities, law firms, and legal aid organizations in the Boston area. Housing for students is available on campus. All law school facilities are accessible to the physically disabled.

Calendar

The law school operates on a quarter basis. Courses for full-time students are offered days only and must be completed within 3 years. There is no part-time program. New students are admitted in the fall. There is a 12 week summer session that is part of the full-year required curriculum. Transferable summer courses are offered.

Programs

Students may take relevant courses in other programs and apply credit toward the J.D.; a maximum of 6 credits may be applied. The following joint degrees may be earned: J.D./M.B.A. (Juris Doctor/Master of Business Administration), J.D./M.P.H. (Juris Doctor/Master of Public Health), and J.D./M.S. (Juris Doctor/Master of Science in accounting).

Required

To earn the J.D., candidates must complete 103 total credits, of which 50 are for required courses. The following first-year courses are required of all students: Torts, Property, Contracts, Constitutional Issues, Criminal Justice, Civil Procedure, Legal Practice, and Law, Culture, and Difference. A required upper-level course is Professional Responsibility. Students are required to complete 4 supervised legal internships under the

Phone: 617-373-2395
Fax: 617-373-8865
E-mail: *m.knoll@neu.edu*
Web: *www.slaw.neu.edu*

Contact

M.J. Knoll, Assistant Dean and Director, 617-373-2395 for general inquiries; Lori Moore, Director of Financial Aid, 617-373-4620 for financial aid information.

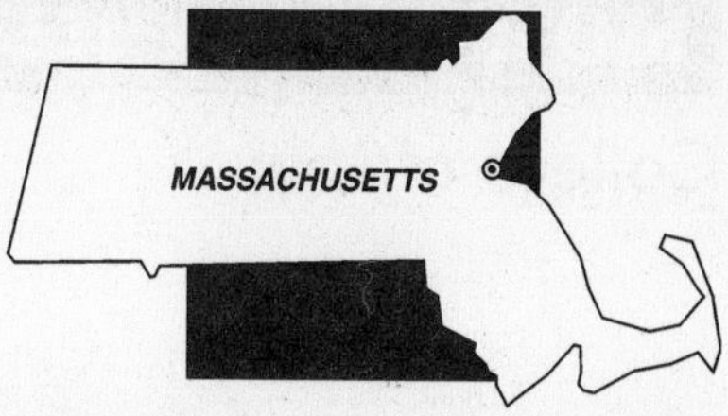

school's program of cooperative legal education. In the second and third year of school, students alternate every 3 months between full-time class work and full-time co-op work. The school also offers traditional clinical courses as electives for upper-level students.The required orientation program for first-year students is 1 to 2 days and introduces students to the first-year curriculum, faculty, law school, and university services.

Electives

The School of Law offers concentrations in corporate law, criminal law, environmental law, family law, international law, labor law, public interest, and advocacy. In addition, clinical courses include Certiorari Clinic/Criminal Appeals for 3 credits, Criminal Advocacy for 7 credits, and Poverty Law and Practice for 6 credits. Seminars include an Advanced Writing Seminar, Health Law Seminar, and Racism and American Law Seminar. Research assistantships are available with individual professors. For field work, students are required to complete 4 distinct cooperative legal education quarters during the second and third year of school, alternating every 3 months between full-time classes and full-time work. Study abroad is possible through international co-ops available on a limited basis. There are many academic support programs, including the Legal Writing Workshop, Legal Analysis Workshop, and Analytical Skills Workshop. Upper-level courses include Advanced Writing, Legal Reasoning, Advanced Legal Research, and a not-for-credit Bar preparation course. Minority students may take advantage of the Legal Analysis Workshop and tutorial programs, which are targeted to students of color. Special interest group programs include the Environmental Law Forum, Tobacco Products Liability Project, Prisoner's Assistance Project, Domestic Violence Institute, and the Urban Law Institute. The most widely taken electives are Evidence, Corporations, Federal Courts, the Federal System, and Trusts and Estates.

Graduation Requirements

In order to graduate, candidates must the complete cooperative education requirement and a public interest requirement.

Organizations

Students frequently participate in moot court competitions nationwide. Student organizations include the National Lawyers Guild, Queer Caucus, and Jewish Law Students Association. There are local chapters of the Black Law Students Association, Asian Pacific Law Students Association, and LaTinoa Law Students Association. Other organizations include Jewish Law Students, Environmental Law Forum, and International Law Society.

Library

The law library contains 251,000 hard-copy volumes and 113,535 microform volume equivalents, and subscribes to 3325 serial publications. Such on-line databases and networks as CALI, CIS Universe, DIALOG, Infotrac, Legal-Trac, LEXIS, LOIS, NEXIS, OCLC First Search, WESTLAW, the Internet, and Social Law Library's on-line database are available to law students for research. Special library collections include the Sara Ehrmann Collection on the death penalty and the Pappas Public Interest Law Collection. Recently, the library upgraded the library's on-line catalog: Acquired Innovative Interfaces' Millennium Integrated Library System. The ratio of library volumes to faculty is 7606 to 1 and to students is 427 to 1. The ratio of seats in the library to students is 1 to 1.

Faculty

The law school has 33 full-time and 18 part-time faculty members, of whom 27 are women. According to AAUP standards for Category I institutions, faculty salaries are average. About 12% of full-time faculty have a graduate law degree in addition to the J.D. The ratio of full-time students to full-time faculty in an average class is 20 to 1; in a clinic, 9 to 1. The law school has a regular program of bringing visiting professors and other distinguished lecturers and visitors to campus.

Placement

J.D.s awarded:	171
Services available through: a separate law school placement center and Career Counseling, Career Resource Library, written materials prepared by the office on career related topics, on-campus interview programs and participation in numerous job fairs, informational programs on all types of public and private interest legal practice options, as well as programs targeted to specific areas of student interest. The Law School also posts job listings on its web page.	
Services: career development and self-assessment workshops and counseling, a Career Resource Library, materials prepared by the Office of Career Services or Self-Assessment, interviewing skills, resume writing, networking, job search strategies, and judicial clerkships.	
Full-time job interviews:	20 employers
Summer job interviews:	33 employers
Placement by graduation:	n/av
Placement within 9 months:	95% of class
Average starting salary:	$26,000 to $150,000
Areas of placement:	
Private practice 2-10 attorneys	8%
Private practice 11-25 attorneys	4%
Private practice 26-50 attorneys	2%
Private practice 51-100 attorneys	4%
Judicial clerkships	25%
Unknown	12%2
Government	12%
Business/industry	12%
Public interest	9%

Students

About 58% of the student body are women; 22%, minorities; 6%, African American; 7%, Asian American; 7%, Hispanic; 1%, Native American; and 2%, International Students. 38% of students come from Massachusetts. The average age of entering students is 25; age range is 21 to 57. About 28% of students enter directly from undergraduate school, 11% have a graduate degree, and 72% have worked full-time prior to entering law school. About 2% drop out after the first year for academic or personal reasons; 98% remain to receive a law degree.

NORTHERN ILLINOIS UNIVERSITY

College of Law

Swen Parson Hall
De Kalb, IL 60115-2890

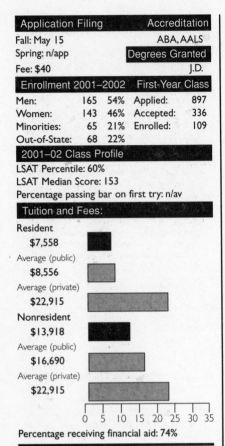

Application Filing		Accreditation
Fall: May 15		ABA, AALS
Spring: n/app		**Degrees Granted**
Fee: $40		J.D.

Enrollment 2001–2002			First-Year Class	
Men:	165	54%	Applied:	897
Women:	143	46%	Accepted:	336
Minorities:	65	21%	Enrolled:	109
Out-of-State:	68	22%		

2001–02 Class Profile

LSAT Percentile: 60%
LSAT Median Score: 153
Percentage passing bar on first try: n/av

Tuition and Fees:

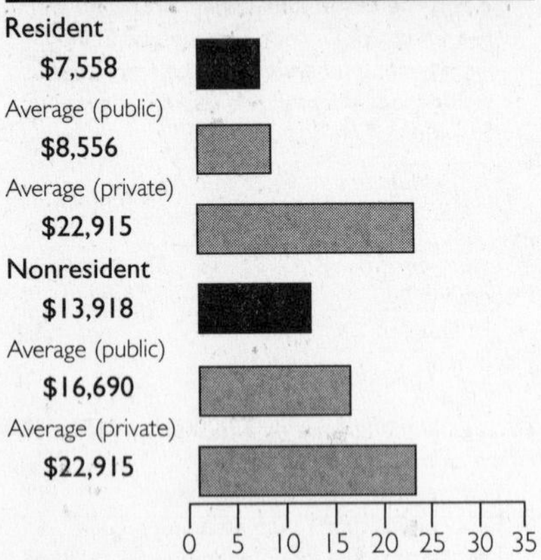

Percentage receiving financial aid: 74%

ADMISSIONS

In the fall 2001 first-year class, 897 applied, 336 were accepted, and 109 enrolled. Three transfers enrolled. The median LSAT percentile of the most recent first-year class was 60; the median GPA was 3.1 on a scale of 4.0. The highest LSAT percentile was 95.

Requirements

Applicants must have a bachelor's degree and take the LSAT. The most important admission factors include academic achievement, LSAT results, and letter of recommendation. No specific undergraduate courses are required. Candidates are not interviewed.

Procedure

The application deadline for fall entry is May 15. Applicants should submit an application form, LSAT results, a nonrefundable application fee of $40, 2 letters of recommendation, a personal statement, and LSDAS report. Notification of the admissions decision is as early as possible. The latest acceptable LSAT test date for fall entry is June. The law school uses the LSDAS.

Special

The law school recruits minority and disadvantaged students by encouraging all students who are underrepresented ethnically or culturally, or who are financially disadvantaged, to apply. The BLSA, HLSA, ALSN, and the Women's Law Caucus work closely with the Admissions Office to increase the student body's diversity. Requirements are not different for out-of-state students. Transfer students must have one year of credit and have attended an ABA-approved law school.

Costs

Tuition and fees for the 2001-2002 academic year are $7558 for full-time in-state students and $13,918 for out-of-state students. On-campus room and board costs about $5396 annually; books and supplies run $1500.

Financial Aid

About 74% of current law students receive some form of aid. The average annual amount of aid from all sources combined, including scholarships, loans, and work contracts, is $14,000; maximum, $15,460. Awards are based on need and merit combined. Required financial statements are the FAFSA and in-house financial aid verification form. The aid application deadline for fall entry is March 1. Special funds for minority or disadvantaged students consist of scholarships for partial- or full-tuition waivers (some with stipends) available to culturally and/or financially disadvantaged individuals. First-year students are notified about their financial aid application at time of application.

About the Law School

Northern Illinois University College of Law was established in 1974 and is a public institution. The 755-acre campus is in a small town 65 miles west of Chicago. The primary mission of the law school is to prepare its graduates not only for the traditional role of lawyers, but for the nontraditional tasks that may be assumed by the law-trained in the future. Students have access to federal, state, county, city, and local agencies, courts, correctional facilities, law firms, and legal aid organizations in the De Kalb area. Facilities of special interest to law students include a full service law library, adjacent to the main university library; a computer laboratory for law students as well as other laboratories on campus; and a moot court room equipped with voice-activated cameras as well as a movable wall to create classroom space. Housing for students includes Neptune Hall, one block away from the law school, whose first floor is designated and equipped for law students. There are also affordable apartment options surrounding the campus. All law school facilities are accessible to the physically disabled.

Calendar

The law school operates on a traditional semester basis. Courses for full-time students are offered primarily during the day, but there are some upper-division courses taught in the evening, and must be completed within 3 years. For part-time students, courses are offered days only and must be completed within 5 years. New full- and part-time students are admitted in the fall. There is a 6-week summer session. Transferable summer courses are offered.

Programs

Students may take relevant courses in other programs and apply credit toward the J.D.; a maximum of 6 credits may be applied. The following joint degrees may be earned: J.D./M.B.A. (Juris Doctor/Master of Business Administration) and J.D./M.P.A. (Juris Doctor/Master of Public Administration).

Phone: 815-753-1420
892-3050
Fax: 815-753-4501
E-mail: *lawadm@niu.edu*
Web: *niu.edu/col*

Contact

Special Assistant to the Director of Admissions, 815-753-8559 for general inquiries; Assistant to the Director of Admission, 815-753-9485 for financial aid information.

Required

To earn the J.D., candidates must complete 90 total credits, of which 36 are for required courses. They must maintain a minimum GPA of 2.0 in the required courses. The following first-year courses are required of all students: Criminal Law, Torts I and II, Civil Procedure, Property, Contracts I and II, Constitutional Law I, Legal Writing and Advocacy I and II, and Basic Legal Research I and II. Required upper-level courses consist of Constitutional Law II and Professional Responsibility. The required orientation program for first-year students is a week-long introduction to the law school, briefing skills, the courts, and the university.

Electives

The College of Law offers concentrations in corporate law, criminal law, environmental law, family law, international law, juvenile law, labor law, litigation, maritime law, sports law, tax law, torts and insurance, and public interest. In addition, There is an Appellate Defender Clinical program for 3 credit hours for students who work under the supervision of a staff attorney at the Illinois Appellate Defender Office. The Zeke Giorgi Legal Clinic affords students practical legal experience. All students must complete a 3-hour seminar in their fourth or fifth semester. Externships are offered in the Judicial Externship Program, which places students with state and federal judges; civil and criminal externships are also available with state criminal prosecutors, public defenders, and civil legal services for the needy. There is the annual Riley Lecture Series on Professionalism and the annual Land Use Symposium. Study abroad in Agen, France is available for law students as well as other options through the International Program Office. Tutors are available to first-year students upon request. The Academic Support Program is available for students who may need additional support during the first year of law school. Peer and faculty support programs are available for minorities. Speakers on a variety of topics are sponsored by the Women's Law Caucus, International Law Society, BLSA, LLSA, ACLU, and Federalist Society. The most widely taken electives are Evidence, and Trust and Estates.

Graduation Requirements

In order to graduate, candidates must have a GPA of 2.0.

Organizations

The *Northern Illinois University Law Review* and *The Advocate* are student-edited publications. Teams compete at the National Moot Court, the Chicago Bar Association, and the National Trial Advocacy competitions. Other competitions include the ABA Client Counseling, the ABA National Appellate Advocacy, and International Law Jessup Cup competitions. Student organizations include the International Law Society, Women's Law Caucus, and the Public Interest Law Society. There are local chapters of Phi Alpha Delta, Delta Theta Phi, and the American Civil Liberties Union. Other organizations include the BLSA, LLSA, and Business Law Society.

Library

The law library contains 222,774 hard-copy volumes and 477,561 microform volume equivalents, and subscribes to 3331 serial publications. Such on-line databases and networks as CALI, CIS Universe, DIALOG, Legal-Trac, LEXIS, LOIS, NEXIS, OCLC First Search, WESTLAW, Wilsonline Indexes, and EBSCO are available to law students for research. Special library collections include a federal document selective depository. Recently, the library added network connections for student laptop access to the Internet. The ratio of library volumes to faculty is 8568 to 1 and to students is 723 to 1. The ratio of seats in the library to students is 1 to 1.

Faculty

The law school has 26 full-time and 16 part-time faculty members, of whom 13 are women. According to AAUP standards for Category I institutions, faculty salaries are below average. About 36% of full-time faculty have a graduate law degree in addition to the J.D.; about 15% of part-time faculty have one. The ratio of full-time students to full-time faculty in an average class is 14 to 1. The law school has a regular program of bringing visiting professors and other distinguished lecturers and visitors to campus.

Placement

J.D.s awarded:	102
Services available through: a separate law school placement center and the university placement center	
Services: participating in regional and national job fairs.	
Special features: individual career counseling for students and alumni about traditional and nontraditional jobs for law graduates.	
Full-time job interviews:	12 employers
Summer job interviews:	10 employers
Placement by graduation:	38% of class
Placement within 9 months:	90% of class
Average starting salary:	$31,000 to $80,000
Areas of placement:	
Private practice 2-10 attorneys	43%
Private practice 11-25 attorneys	4%
Private practice 26-50 attorneys	3%
Private practice 51-100 attorneys	4%
Government	25%
Business/industry	9%
Judicial clerkships	7%
Public interest	3%
Academic	2%

Students

About 46% of the student body are women; 21%, minorities; 7%, African American; 6%, Asian American; 7%, Hispanic; and 1%, Native American. The majority of students come from Illinois (78%). The average age of entering students is 27; age range is 22 to 58. About 9% drop out after the first year for academic or personal reasons.

Salmon P. Chase College of Law

Louie B. Nunn Hall
Highland Heights, KY 41099

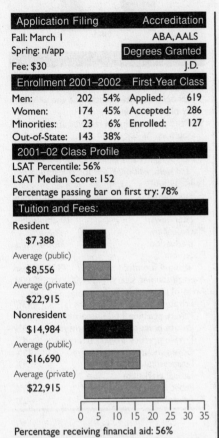

Application Filing		Accreditation
Fall: March 1		ABA, AALS
Spring: n/app		**Degrees Granted**
Fee: $30		J.D.

Enrollment 2001–2002			First-Year Class	
Men:	202	54%	Applied:	619
Women:	174	45%	Accepted:	286
Minorities:	23	6%	Enrolled:	127
Out-of-State:	143	38%		

2001–02 Class Profile

LSAT Percentile: 56%
LSAT Median Score: 152
Percentage passing bar on first try: 78%

Tuition and Fees:

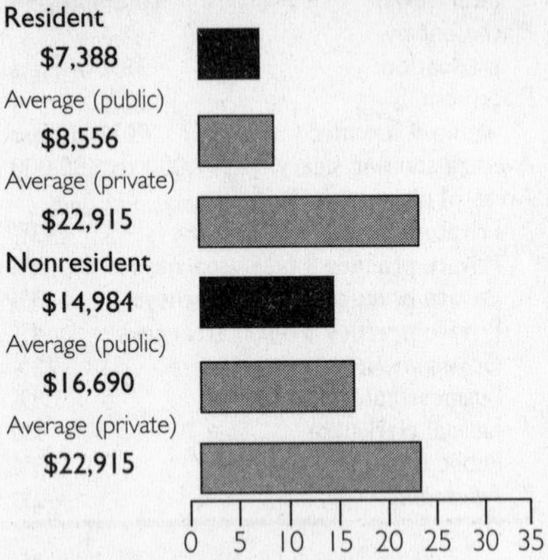

Percentage receiving financial aid: 56%

ADMISSIONS

In the fall 2001 first-year class, 619 applied, 286 were accepted, and 127 enrolled. Twelve transfers enrolled. The median LSAT percentile of the most recent first-year class was 56; the median GPA was 3.1 on a scale of 4.0. The lowest LSAT percentile accepted was 18; the highest was 98.

Requirements

Applicants must have a bachelor's degree and take the LSAT. The most important admission factors include LSAT results, GPA, and writing ability. No specific undergraduate courses are required. Candidates are not interviewed.

Procedure

The application deadline for fall entry is March 1. Applicants should submit an application form, LSAT results, transcripts, a nonrefundable application fee of $30, 2 letters of recommendation, and essay questions. Transcripts must be submitted through the LSDAS. A $150 acceptance deposit must be submitted to reserve a place after an offer is made, and a $300 registration deposit is required preceding enrollment. Notification of the admissions decision is on a rolling basis. The latest acceptable LSAT test date for fall entry is February. The law school uses the LSDAS.

Special

The law school recruits minority and disadvantaged students through minority career days, contacts with members of the school's Black American Law Students Association and through the Law Services CRS search. Requirements are different for out-of-state students in that admissions are more selective. Transfer students must have a minimum GPA of 3, have attended an ABA-approved law school, and must be in good standing and eligible to continue study at their current school, and must provide an official transcript documenting acceptably high-quality performance.

Costs

Tuition and fees for the 2001-2002 academic year are $7388 for full-time in-state students and $14,984 for out-of-state students. Tuition for part-time students is $5436 in-state and $11,142 out-of-state. On-campus room and board costs about $13,526 annually; books and supplies run $1000.

Financial Aid

About 56% of current law students receive some form of aid. The average annual amount of aid from all sources combined, including scholarships, loans, and work contracts, is $16,888; maximum, $18,500. Awards are based on need and merit; a number of scholarships based on merit, need, or a combination of both are available. Required financial statement is the FAFSA. The aid application deadline for fall entry is April 1. Special funds for minority or disadvantaged students include scholarship funds for minority and disadvantaged students. First-year students are notified about their financial aid application at time of acceptance, but after the processing of the aid application.

About the Law School

Northern Kentucky University Salmon P. Chase College of Law was established in 1893 and is a public institution. The 300-acre campus is in a suburban area 7 miles southeast of Cincinnati. The primary mission of the law school is to train competent lawyers and to enable students to gain proficiency in specific areas of law. Students have access to federal, state, county, city, and local agencies, courts, correctional facilities, law firms, and legal aid organizations in the Highland Heights area. The school is located in a major metropolitan area that provides a wide variety of opportunities for law students. Housing for students is available on campus in the Residential Village, including suites and apartments, computer rooms, a store, a dining hall, dormitories, and numerous apartments close to campus. About 95% of the law school facilities are accessible to the physically disabled.

Calendar

The law school operates on a traditional semester basis. Courses for full-time students are offered days only and with some electives being offered on Saturdays and must be completed within 3 ½ years. For part-time students, courses are offered both day and evening and on Saturdays and must be completed within 4 ½ years. New full- and part-time students are admitted in the fall. There is a 7-week summer session. Transferable summer courses are offered.

Programs

The following joint degrees may be earned: J.D./M.B.A. (Juris Doctor/Master of Business Administration).

Required

To earn the J.D., candidates must complete 90 total credits, of which 42 are for required courses. They must maintain a minimum GPA of 2.15 in the required courses. The following first-year courses are required of all students: Contracts I and II, Torts I and II, Property I and II, Introduction to Legal Studies, Civil Procedure I and II, and Basic Legal Skills I and II. Required upper-level courses consist of Constitutional Law I and II, Criminal Law, Criminal Procedure, Evidence, Federal Taxation 1A, and Professional Responsibility. The required orientation program for first-year students consists of an extensive combination of voluntary and required orientation programs: 1.) Spring Orientation — a voluntary half-day program in May focusing on what entering students can do over the summer to prepare; 2.) Summer Program for legal analysis — a voluntary 2-week program offered at no charge twice during July, focusing on developing essential case-reading skills; 3.) Orientation – a required half-day orientation in August

Phone: 859-572-6476
Fax: 859-572-6081
E-mail: *brayg@nku.edu*
Web: *www.nku.edu/~@chase*

Contact

Gina Bray, Admissions Specialist, 859-572-5384 for general inquiries; Financial Aid Office, Bob Sprauge, Director, 859-572-6437 for financial aid information.

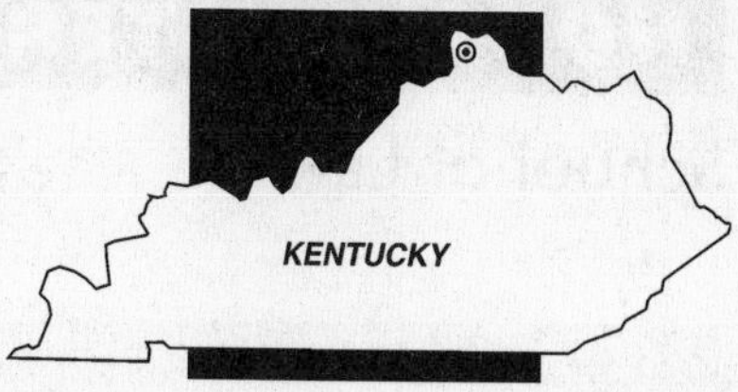

to the programs and services available at the College of Law and the university; 4.) Introduction to Legal Studies — a required 2-week, 1 credit hour course in August designed especially to introduce students to their first year of legal studies; 5.) Professionalism Workshop — a required half-day program presented in conjunction with the Kentucky Bar Association to sensitize students to ethical concerns.

Electives

In addition, clinics offered include the in-house Local Government Law Center Clinic and specialized clinical externships with federal trial judges, the Children's Law Center, the IRS tax center, and state and local government agencies, as well as a wide variety of more general clinical externships. All clinical opportunities are 2 or 3 credits per semester. Seminars include Business, Technology, and Regulation, Constitutional Law Seminar, and Criminal Law/Justice Seminar. Chase has IOLTA Public Interest Fellowships that provide financial remuneration (rather than credit) to students interning part time during the academic year and full time in the summer with public interest organizations in the Commonwealth. An active supervised independent research program is offered. Public policy research opportunities are available through the in-house Local Government Law Center and in conjunction with the Children's Law Center. The *Law Review* sponsors a major national symposium annually. Special academic development programs (all at no cost) for first-year students include a 2-week summer program in Legal Analysis in July before entry; Academic Development program workshops and tutorials on Saturdays in the fall semester; an exam writing seminar and follow-up tutorials on Saturdays in the spring semester, and additional individual tutoring help available through the Chase Academic Learning and Development Center. Special "early bird" Bar preparation programs are provided for graduating students, again at no cost. First-year students with less developed writing skills are placed in small, specially enriched legal writing sections. For second-year students in difficulty, special tutorials are available in conjunction with the required Criminal Law course and additional remedial writing instruction is available in conjunction with the Legal Drafting course. Professional and social activities, as well as special tutorial assistance, are available in conjunction with the Black Lawyers Association of Cincinnati (BLAC) and the Cincinnati Bar Association/BLAC Lawyers' Association Roundtable. A variety of programs throughout the year is sponsored by the Appalachian Law Society, Environmental Law Organization, International Law Society, Women's Law Caucus, and several law fraternities. Chase offers a wide range of both required and optional academic support programs to help its students prepare for law school. Chase also offers a wide range of legal skills offerings—writing, counseling, negotiating, litigating, and oral advocacy courses—to help students prepare for legal practice. The most widely taken electives are Wills and Trusts, Corporations, and Trial Advocacy.

Graduation Requirements

In order to graduate, candidates must have a GPA of 2.0 and have completed the upper-division writing requirement.

Organizations

Students edit the *Northern Kentucky Law Review*. Students participate in a variety of moot court competitions at numerous locations, including the New York Bar Association, National Moot Court, and Grosse competitions. Law student organizations include the Chase Association of Trial Lawyers, Christian Law Students, Environmental Law Society, International Law Society, Legal Volunteers Society, and local chapters of the Young Democrats, Young Republicans, and the ABA-Law Student Division. Other law student organizations include Student Government, Student Ambassadors, and PBL Leadership Organization.

Library

The law library contains 33,117 hard-copy volumes and 861 microform volume equivalents, and subscribes to 1936 serial publications. Such on-line databases and networks as CALI, DIALOG, LegalTrac, LEXIS, WESTLAW, and Kentucky Virtual Library are available to law students for research. Special library collections include the Harold J. Siebenthaler Rare Book Room. Recently, the library instituted a program permitting law students physical access to the law library 24 hours a day, 7 days a week. The ratio of library volumes to faculty is 1227 to 1 and to students is 88 to 1.

Placement	
J.D.s awarded:	112
Services available through: a separate law school placement center and the university placement center	
Special features: workshops and job fairs, including the Minority Access Program at the University of Cincinnati, Federal Job Options Program, Local Government/Public Interest Job Fair, Alumni Legal Career Options Day, and Bridge the Gap Program.	
Full-time job interviews:	14 employers
Summer job interviews:	20 employers
Placement by graduation:	50% of class
Placement within 9 months:	94% of class
Average starting salary:	$20,000 to $100,000
Areas of placement:	
Private practice 2-10 attorneys	33%
Private practice 11-25 attorneys	5%
Private practice 26-50 attorneys	1%
Private Practice 101-250 attorneys	1%
Business/industry	26%
Government	18%
Judicial clerkships	8%
Unknown	6%
Public interest	1%
Academic	1%

Faculty

The law school has 27 full-time and 33 part-time faculty members, of whom 18 are women. According to AAUP standards for Category IIA institutions, faculty salaries are well below average. About 28% of full-time faculty have a graduate law degree in addition to the J.D. The ratio of full-time students to full-time faculty in an average class is 7 to 1.

Students

About 45% of the student body are women; 6%, minorities; 4%, African American; 1%, Asian American; 1%, Hispanic; and 1%, Native American. The majority of students come from Kentucky (62%). The average age of entering students is 29; age range is 21 to 55. About 14% of students have a graduate degree. About 19% drop out after the first year for academic or personal reasons.

NORTHWESTERN UNIVERSITY

School of Law

357 East Chicago Avenue
Chicago, IL 60611

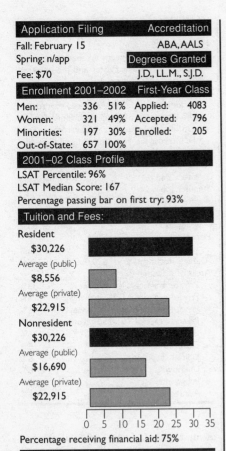

Application Filing		Accreditation
Fall: February 15		ABA, AALS
Spring: n/app		**Degrees Granted**
Fee: $70		J.D., LL.M., S.J.D.

Enrollment 2001–2002			First-Year Class	
Men:	336	51%	Applied:	4083
Women:	321	49%	Accepted:	796
Minorities:	197	30%	Enrolled:	205
Out-of-State:	657	100%		

2001–02 Class Profile

LSAT Percentile: 96%
LSAT Median Score: 167
Percentage passing bar on first try: 93%

Tuition and Fees:

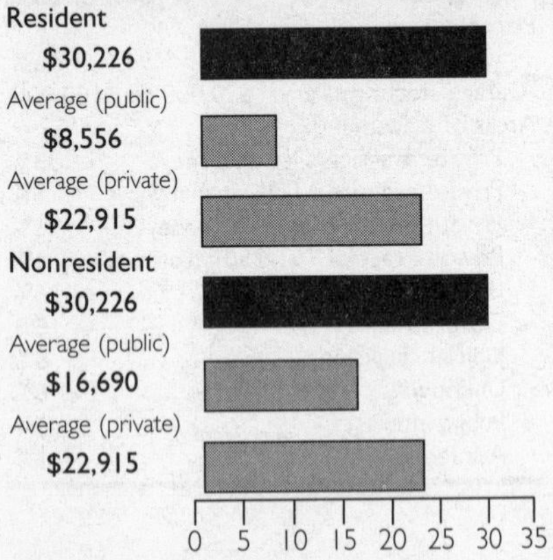

Percentage receiving financial aid: 75%

ADMISSIONS

In the fall 2001 first-year class, 4083 applied, 796 were accepted, and 205 enrolled. Twenty-eight transfers enrolled. The median LSAT percentile of the most recent first-year class was 96; the median GPA was 3.6 on a scale of 4.0. The lowest LSAT percentile accepted was 45; the highest was 99.

Requirements

Applicants must have a bachelor's degree and take the LSAT. The most important admission factors include character, personality, life experience, and academic achievement. No specific undergraduate courses are required. Candidates are interviewed.

Procedure

The application deadline for fall entry is February 15. Applicants should submit an application form, LSAT results, transcripts, a nonrefundable application fee of $70, 2 letters of recommendation, and a personal statement and resume. Registration with LSDAS is required. Interviews are strongly encouraged. Notification of the admissions decision is by May 1. The latest acceptable LSAT test date for fall entry is February. The law school uses the LSDAS.

Special

The law school recruits minority and disadvantaged students through the efforts of the Director of Minority Affairs. Requirements are not different for out-of-state students. Transfer students must have one year of credit, have attended an ABA-approved law school, and have earned a minimum of 30 credit hours.

Costs

Tuition and fees for the 2001-2002 academic year are $30,226 for all full-time students. On-campus room and board costs about $1300 annually; books and supplies run $11,448.

Financial Aid

About 75% of current law students receive some form of aid. Awards are based on need and merit. Required financial statements are the FAFSA and Institutional Financial Aid Application Form. The aid application deadline for fall entry is March 1. First-year students are notified about their financial aid application before May 1 if all required documents are received by the Office of Admission and Financial Aid before the March 15 deadline.

About the Law School

Northwestern University School of Law was established in 1859 and is a private institution. The 20-acre campus is in an urban area in Chicago. The primary mission of the law school is to advance the understanding of law and legal institutions and to produce graduates who are prepared to lead and succeed in a rapidly changing world. Students have access to federal, state, county, city, and local agencies, courts, correctional facilities, law firms, and legal aid organizations in the Chicago area. The Arthur Rubloff Building, an addition to the school, houses the national headquarters of the American Bar Association, American Bar Foundation, and American Bar Endowment. Facilities of special interest to law students consist of 2 fully equipped, modern courtrooms. Computer terminals are available for use in the library and a computer laboratory provides computers and printers for word processing. Housing for students is available in 2 residence buildings located within 1 block of the school. There are more than 750 rooms, including some 1-bedroom and efficiency apartments for married students. About 90% of the law school facilities are accessible to the physically disabled.

Calendar

The law school operates on a traditional semester basis. Courses for full-time students are offered days only and must be completed within 3 years. There is no part-time program. New students are admitted in the fall. Transferable summer courses are not offered.

Programs

In addition to the J.D., the law school offers the LL.M., S.J.D., and LL.M. with a certificate in management; LL.M. in Taxation. Students may take relevant courses in other programs and apply credit toward the J.D.; a maximum of 6 credits may be applied. The following joint degrees may be earned: J.D./M.B.A. (Juris Doctor/Master of Business Administration) and J.D./Ph.D. (Juris Doctor/Doctor of Philosophy).

Required

To earn the J.D., candidates must complete 86 total credits, of which 32 are for required courses. They must maintain a minimum GPA of 2.25 in the required courses. The following first-year courses are required of all students: Contracts, Torts, Civil Procedure, Criminal Law, Property, Constitutional Law, and Communication and Legal Reasoning. Required upper-level courses consist of Legal Ethics and a writing requirement that may be fulfilled with either a 2-semester Senior Research project or several upper-level electives with significant writing requirement. The required orientation program for first-year students is 1 week before classes begin. First-year students register and receive class assignments, meet with their faculty advisers, tour the school, and attend social functions.

Phone: 312-503-8465
Fax: 312-503-0178
E-mail: *nulawadm@law.northwestern.edu*
Web: *www.law.northwestern.edu*

Contact

Donald Rebstock, Associate Dean of Enrollment Management, 312-503-8465 for general inquiries; Donald Rebstock, 312-503-8465 for financial aid information.

Electives

The School of Law offers concentrations in corporate law, international law, litigation, health law, dispute resolution, and law and social policy. Clinics are open to second- and third-year students. A sequence of simulation-based courses are offered in the second year, Clinical Trial Advocacy and Pre-Trial Litigation, as well as case-based instruction. Students also take clinically based Evidence, which presents the principles of evidence in the context of simulated cases. Course credits vary between 3 to 4 hours. Students can represent clients through the Children's and Family Justice Center, Small Business Opportunity Clinic, and Center for International Human Rights. Seminars are offered in legal history, civil law, civil rights litigation, arbitration, race relations, computers and the law, nonprofit organizations, criminal evidence, entertainment law, jurisprudence, health law, and other areas. A third-year student may earn up to 14 credits for advanced research under the personal supervision of 1 or more faculty members. Completion of this project fulfills the writing requirement. Professional Responsibility Practicums consist of a 10 to 12 hours per week field work component, and a weekly 2-hour seminar. Annually, the Rosenthal Lecture Series brings preeminent figures in law and related fields to the school. The Pope and John Lecture on Professionalism deals with ethics and professional responsibility. The Howard J. Trienens Visiting Judicial Scholar Program brings leading jurists to the school to lecture on legal issues and to meet informally with students. Study abroad opportunities include Catholic University of Leuven, Belgium; Free University of Amsterdam, The Netherlands; Tel Aviv University, Israel; Universidad Torcuato Di Tella in Argentina; and Bond University, Australia. Tutorial programs are offered through the Dean of Students on an individual basis. The Director of Minority Affairs provides academic admission, placement counseling, and other supportive services. The most widely taken electives are Real Estate, Commercial Transactions, and International Law.

Graduation Requirements

In order to graduate, candidates must have a GPA of 2.2 and have completed the upper-division writing requirement.

Organizations

Student-edited publications include the *Northwestern University Law Review*, *The Journal of Criminal Law and Criminology*, *The Northwestern Journal of International Law and Business*, the newspaper *Hoops*, and the student newspaper, *The Pleader*. Annual moot court competitions are the Arlyn Miner First-Year Moot Court Program, the Julius H. Miner Moot Court, and the Philip C. Jessup International Law Moot Court. Other competitions are the John Paul Stevens Prize for academic excellence, Lowden-Wigmore Prizes for best contributions to journals and best Julius Miner Moot Court performances, Barnet and Scott Hodes Prize for best student paper in international law, Arlyn Miner Book Award for the best brief by a first-year student, Harold D. Shapiro Prize for best student in an international economics relations class, the West Publishing Company Awards for scholastic achievement, and the Nathan Burkhan Memorial Competition for best paper on copyright law. Student organizations include Amnesty International, Feminists for Social Change, and Northwestern Law Students for the Homeless. There are local chapters of the National Lawyers Guild, The Federalist Society, and the ABA-Law Student Division. Other organizations are the Cabrini Green Youth Program and HORIZONS; and Wigmore Follies, and annual student-run variety show.

Library

The law library contains 656,775 hard-copy volumes and 209,977 microform volume equivalents, and subscribes to 8258 serial publications. Such on-line databases and networks as DIALOG, LEXIS, WESTLAW, and CCH Access, and NEXIS are available to law students for research. Special library collections include a large international collection and the Hodes Rare Book Room. The ratio of library volumes to faculty is 11,132 to 1 and to students is 1000 to 1. The ratio of seats in the library to students is 1 to 1.

Placement	
J.D.s awarded:	222
Services available through: a separate law school placement center	
Services: arrangement of job fairs for off-campus interviews	
Full-time job interviews:	325 employers
Summer job interviews:	325 employers
Placement by graduation:	99% of class
Placement within 9 months:	100% of class
Average starting salary:	$34,200 to $125,000
Areas of placement:	
Private practice 51-100 attorneys	88%
Judicial clerkships	7%
Public interest	3%
Government	1%
Academic	1%

Faculty

The law school has 59 full-time and 149 part-time faculty members, of whom 51 are women. According to AAUP standards for Category I institutions, faculty salaries are well above average. About 99% of full-time faculty have a graduate law degree in addition to the J.D.; nearly all of the part-time faculty have one. The ratio of full-time students to full-time faculty in an average class is 12 to 1; in a clinic, 8 to 1. The law school has a regular program of bringing visiting professors and other distinguished lecturers and visitors to campus. There is a chapter of the Order of the Coif; 40 faculty and 20 graduates are members.

Students

About 49% of the student body are women; 30%, minorities; 7%, African American; 14%, Asian American; 8%, Hispanic; and 1%, Native American. The majority of students come from the Midwest (32%). The average age of entering students is 25; age range is 21 to 44. About 20% of students enter directly from undergraduate school, 8% have a graduate degree, and 80% have worked full-time prior to entering law school. About 1% drop out after the first year for academic or personal reasons; 99% remain to receive a law degree.

NOVA SOUTHEASTERN UNIVERSITY

Shepard Broad Law Center

3305 College Avenue
Fort Lauderdale, FL 33314-7721

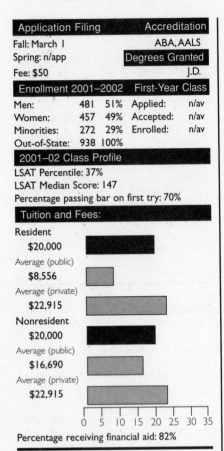

Application Filing		Accreditation
Fall: March 1		ABA, AALS
Spring: n/app		**Degrees Granted**
Fee: $50		J.D.

Enrollment 2001–2002			First-Year Class	
Men:	481	51%	Applied:	n/av
Women:	457	49%	Accepted:	n/av
Minorities:	272	29%	Enrolled:	n/av
Out-of-State:	938	100%		

2001–02 Class Profile

LSAT Percentile: 37%
LSAT Median Score: 147
Percentage passing bar on first try: 70%

Tuition and Fees:

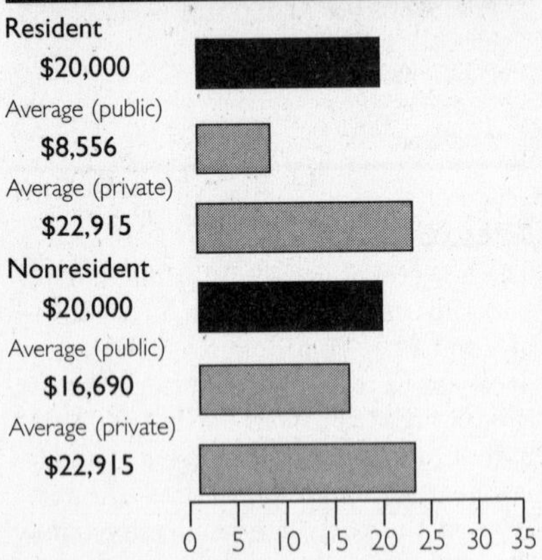

Percentage receiving financial aid: 82%

ADMISSIONS

Information in the above capsule is from an earlier year. In a recent first-year class, twenty-three transfers enrolled. The median LSAT percentile of a recent first-year class was 37; the median GPA was 2.8 on a scale of 4.0. The lowest LSAT percentile accepted was 3; the highest was 99.

Requirements

Applicants must have a bachelor's degree and take the LSAT. The most important admission factors include undergraduate curriculum, life experience, and academic achievement. No specific undergraduate courses are required. Candidates are not interviewed.

Procedure

Check with the school for current application deadlines and fee. Applicants should submit an application form, LSAT results, transcripts, a nonrefundable application fee, and 2 letters of recommendation (suggested). Notification of the admissions decision is on a rolling basis. The law school uses the LSDAS.

Special

The law school recruits minority and disadvantaged students by means of on-campus minority programs, attendance at historically black college fairs, and participation in and maintenance of a good relationship with the CLEO program. Requirements are not different for out-of-state students. Transfer students must have one year of credit, have attended an ABA-approved law school, have no grade below C in required courses, and provide a letter of good standing from the current dean. Foreign attorneys are also admitted. Preadmissions courses consist of summer conditional admissions programs where students must earn at least a C+ average for 2 courses.

Costs

Tuition and fees for the academic year are approximately $20,000 for all full-time students. Tuition for part-time students is about $15,000 per year. On-campus room and board costs about $6700 annually; books and supplies run about $1480.

Financial Aid

About 82% of law students receive some form of aid. The maximum annual amount of aid from all sources combined, including scholarships, loans, and work contracts, is about $36,000. Loans are need-based; most scholarships are merit-based; some scholarships are need- and merit-based. Required financial statement is the FAFSA. No statements are required for merit-based aid. Check with the school for current deadline. Special funds for minority or disadvantaged students are scholarship funds. First-year students are notified about their financial aid application when the application for aid is complete.

About the Law School

Nova Southeastern University Shepard Broad Law Center was established in 1974 and is a private institution. The 232-acre campus is in a suburban area 3 miles west of Fort Lauderdale, Florida. The primary mission of the law school is to allow students to reach their potential as ethical, competent, and caring advocates in a supportive environment stressing lawyering skills and values. Students have access to federal, state, county, city, and local agencies, courts, correctional facilities, law firms, and legal aid organizations in the Fort Lauderdale area. Of special interest to law students is the law center's building, the Leo C. Goodwin, Sr., Hall. All students can access computing facilities from anywhere in the building using wireless technology. Housing for students is in 4 university-owned apartment buildings; there are also numerous apartments available near the campus. All law school facilities are accessible to the physically disabled.

Calendar

The law school operates on a traditional semester basis. Courses for full-time students are offered both day and evening and must be completed within 5 years. For part-time students, courses are offered evenings only, but some day classes are available, and must be completed within 6 years. New full- and part-time students are admitted in the fall. There is a 7-week summer session. Transferable summer courses are offered.

Programs

Students may take relevant courses in other programs and apply credit toward the J.D.; a maximum of 4 (8 in joint-degree programs) credits may be applied. The following joint degrees may be earned: J.D./M.B.A. (Juris Doctor/Master of Business Administration), J.D./M.S. (Juris Doctor/Master of Science in dispute resolution), J.D./M.S. (Juris Doctor/Master of Science in psychology), and J.D./M.U.R.P. (Juris Doctor/Masters of Urban and Regional Planning).

Phone: 954-262-6117
800-986-6529
Fax: 954-262-3844
E-mail: *admission@nsu.law.nova.edu*
Web: *www.nsu.law.nova.edu*

Contact

Nancy Kelly Sanguigni, Director, 954-262-6117 for general inquiries; Lynn Acosta, Counselor, Financial Aid Office, 800-522-3243 for financial aid information.

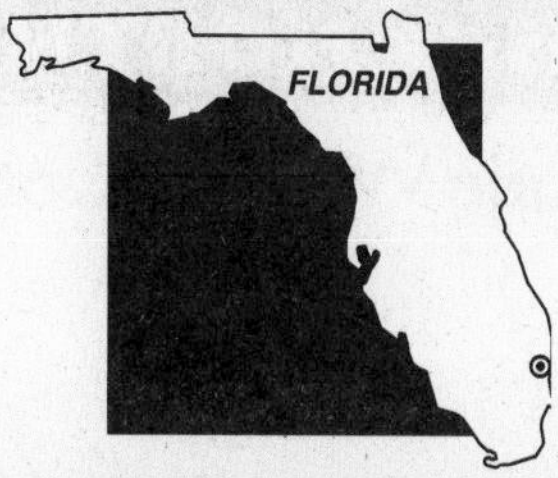

Required

To earn the J.D., candidates must complete 90 total credits, of which 44 are for required courses. The following first-year courses are required of all students: Contracts, Torts, Criminal Law, Property, Civil Procedure, Constitutional Law I, and Lawyering Skills and Values I and II. Required upper-level courses consist of Professional Responsibility, an upper-class writing requirement, Constitutional Law II, Evidence or Corporations, and Lawyering Skills and Values III and IV. All students are guaranteed a clinical semester. The required orientation program for first-year students includes an introduction to the law school experience before classes begin; other sessions are held during the semester.

Electives

The Shepard Broad Law Center offers concentrations in corporate law, criminal law, environmental law, international law, torts and insurance, and children and family. In addition, the clinics offer 12 credits to students who work with families and children, an environmental group, an international agency, a prosecutor or public defender, a corporation or business firm, a personal injury firm, or a mediation program. The mediation program is worth 8 credits. Upper-level students may take seminars for 2 to 3 credits. As interns, students earn 2 credits researching for a judge or serving as a guardian ad litem. The Career Development Office sponsors lecture series on various types of law practices. The office also offers lawyering skills courses in its Career Development Academy. ABA-approved summer programs in Caracas, Venezuela, and Cambridge, England are available. The Law Center is seeking ABA acquiescence for programs in Costa Rica and Israel. Tutorial programs consist of the Academic Resource Program, including a writing program taught by an English professor who holds a J.D. Special interest group programs are the Individuals with Disabilities Project and Guardian ad Litem. Both offer credit for working to protect the rights of the disabled and children. The most widely taken electives are Family Law, Evidence, and Wills and Trusts.

Graduation Requirements

In order to graduate, candidates must have a GPA of 2.0, have completed the upper-division writing requirement, and passed all required courses.

Organizations

Students edit the *Nova Law Review*, the *Journal of International and Comparative Law*, and the newspaper, *Broadly Speaking*. Intramural moot court competitions are held in the fall for upper-class students and in the winter for first-year students; the Round Robin Moot Court Competition is hosted by NSU each February. A team competes in the American Trial Lawyers Association trial competition as well as other trial and moot court competitions. Law student organizations include the International Law Society, Entertainment and Sports Law Society, and the Student Bar Association. Local chapters of national associations include the ABA-Law Student Division, Phi Alpha Delta, and Phi Delta Phi. Campus clubs and other organizations include Yearbook, Young Democrats, and Young Republicans.

Library

The law library contains 314,036 hard-copy volumes and 137,029 microform volume equivalents, and subscribes to 1213 serial publications. Such on-line databases and networks as DIALOG, LEXIS, WESTLAW, Wilsonline, NEXIS, OCLC, Seflink, and First Search are available to law students for research. Special library collections include state, federal, and United Nations depositories and collections in tax, criminal law, international law, children/family, jurisprudence, admiralty, trial practice, and law and popular culture. Recently, the library expanded the computer laboratory and permanent learning center facilities, including interactive video, CD-ROM, and computer-assisted instruction stations. The ratio of library volumes to faculty is 6976 to 1 and to students is 334 to 1. The ratio of seats in the library to students is 1 to 6.

Placement	
J.D.s awarded:	290
Services available through: a separate law school placement center	
Services: Southeast Minority Job Fair, Mid-Florida Job Fair	
Special features: the Alumni Job-Line, and a monthly alumni job bulletin.	
Full-time job interviews:	22 employers
Summer job interviews:	25 employers
Placement by graduation:	n/av
Placement within 9 months:	86% of class
Average starting salary:	$29,914 to $38,747
Areas of placement:	
Private practice 2-10 attorneys	28%
Private practice 11-25 attorneys	12%
Private practice 26-50 attorneys	4%
Private practice 51-100 attorneys	4%
Government	22%
Business/industry	15%
Unknown	8%
Judicial clerkships	3%
Public interest	2%
Military	1%
Academic	1%

Faculty

The law school has approximately 45 full-time and 64 part-time faculty members, of whom 38 are women. About 40% of full-time faculty have a graduate law degree in addition to the J.D.; about 14% of part-time faculty have one. The ratio of full-time students to full-time faculty in an average class is 50 to 1; in a clinic, 20 to 1. The law school has a regular program of bringing visiting professors and other distinguished lecturers and visitors to campus. There is a chapter of the Order of the Coif; 5 faculty are members.

Students

About 49% of the student body are women; 29%, minorities; 8%, African American; 2%, Asian American; and 19%, Hispanic. The age range of entering students is 22 to 85. About 8% drop out after the first year for academic or personal reasons; 83% remain to receive a law degree.

OHIO NORTHERN UNIVERSITY

Claude W. Pettit College of Law

525 South Main Street
Ada, OH 45810

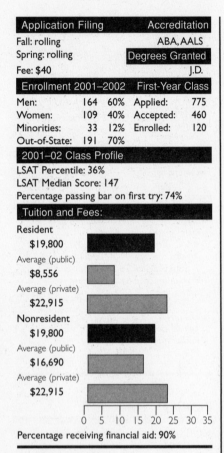

Application Filing		Accreditation
Fall: rolling		ABA, AALS
Spring: rolling		**Degrees Granted**
Fee: $40		J.D.

Enrollment 2001–2002			First-Year Class	
Men:	164	60%	Applied:	775
Women:	109	40%	Accepted:	460
Minorities:	33	12%	Enrolled:	120
Out-of-State:	191	70%		

2001–02 Class Profile

LSAT Percentile: 36%
LSAT Median Score: 147
Percentage passing bar on first try: 74%

Tuition and Fees:

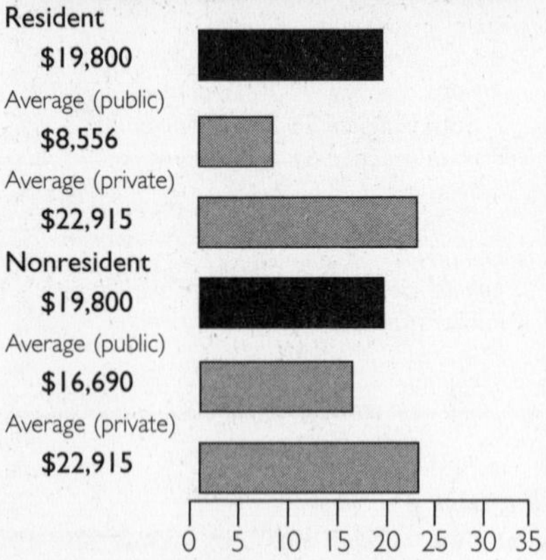

Percentage receiving financial aid: 90%

ADMISSIONS

In the fall 2001 first-year class, 775 applied, 460 were accepted, and 120 enrolled. One transfer enrolled. The median LSAT percentile of the most recent first-year class was 36; the median GPA was 3.22 on a scale of 4.0.

Requirements

Applicants must have a bachelor's degree and take the LSAT. Minimum acceptable GPA is 2.0 on a scale of 4.0. The most important admission factors include LSAT results, GPA, and college attended. All credentials in application materials are considered. No specific undergraduate courses are required. Candidates are not interviewed.

Procedure

Applicants should submit an application form, transcripts, a nonrefundable application fee of $40 (waived if applying online), maximum of 3 letters of recommendation, a resume, a personal statement, and the LSDAS report. Notification of the admissions decision is on a rolling basis. The latest acceptable LSAT test date for fall entry is June. The law school uses the LSDAS.

Special

The law school recruits minority and disadvantaged students by means of on-site college recruitment, CLEO, CRS mailings, and campus visit days. Requirements are not different for out-of-state students. Transfer students must have attended an ABA-approved law school and provide a letter of good standing, a transcript of law school work, undergraduate transcripts, and the LSDAS report.

Costs

Tuition and fees for the 2001-2002 academic year are $19,800 for all full-time students. On-campus room and board costs about $6210 annually; books and supplies run $700.

Financial Aid

About 90% of current law students receive some form of aid. The average annual amount of aid from all sources combined, including scholarships, loans, and work contracts, is $23,785. The maximum varies. Awards are based on need and merit. Required financial statements are the FAFSA and the school's financial aid application. The aid application deadline for fall entry is April 3. Special funds for minority or disadvantaged students include special funds for students to enhance cultural and ethnic diversity. First-year students are notified about their financial aid application at time of acceptance.

About the Law School

Ohio Northern University Claude W. Pettit College of Law was established in 1885 and is a private institution. The 280-acre campus is in a small town 70 miles south of Toledo. The primary mission of the law school is to educate and train students from diverse backgrounds to become responsible and successful practitioners capable of exemplary legal service in roles throughout society. Students have access to federal, state, county, city, and local agencies, courts, correctional facilities, law firms, and legal aid organizations in the Ada area. Facilities of special interest to law students include the Lima Legal Aid Office, ONU Legal Aid Clinic, and Legal Services of Northern Ohio. Housing for students is available on campus and reasonable off-campus housing is also available. About 90% of the law school facilities are accessible to the physically disabled.

Calendar

The law school operates on a traditional semester basis. Courses for full-time students are offered days only and must be completed within 5 years. There is no part-time program. New students are admitted in the fall. There is an 8-week summer session. Transferable summer courses are offered.

Programs

Required

To earn the J.D., candidates must complete 87 total credits, of which 57 are for required courses. They must maintain a minimum GPA of 2.0 in the required courses. The following first-year courses are required of all students: Contracts I and II, Torts I and II, Property I and II, Civil Procedure I and II, Criminal Law, and Legal Research and Writing I and II. Required upper-level courses consist of Evidence, Federal Income Tax, Business Organizations I, Constitutional Law I, Legal Profession, and writing seminar. All students must take clinical courses. L-2s and L-3s are required, as are 10 hours of skill courses, which can include clinical hours. The required orientation program for first-year students comprises a 2-day introduction to university and law school procedures and the instructional approach followed by 4 special continuing orientation programs.

Phone: 419-772-2211
Fax: 419-772-1487
E-mail: *l-english@onu.edu*
Web: *www.law.onu.edu*

Contact

Linda English, Director of Law Admissions, 419-772-2211 for general inquiries; Financial Aid Director, 419-772-2272 for financial aid information.

Electives

The Claude W. Pettit College of Law offers concentrations in criminal law, international law, and tax law. In addition, clinics include Legal Aid, Bankruptcy, and Criminal Law. Seminars are open to second- and third-year students and include Criminal Law, International Legal Issues, and Environmental Law. There is a Civil Internship Program. Students are required to do a major research project, worth 2 credits, as part of the seminar requirement. Field work includes judicial externships with state and federal courts, criminal externships, and governmental-legislative externships. The Annual Kormendy Lecture Series sponsors prominent national legal figures. Recent lecturers have included Justice Clarence Thomas and Professor Deborah Rhode, Stanford School of Law. The college will give credit for ABA-approved law schools' study-abroad programs with prior approval. There is an Icelandic Study Exchange Program. The Academic Support Program offers a fully staffed office. Minority students benefit from the Black Law Students Association-sponsored study groups and the EXCEL-Academic Success Program. The Asian-Pacific-American Law Student Association also sponsors special programs. Special interest groups include International Law Society, Legal Association of Women, and Environmental Law Society. The most widely taken electives are Criminal Procedure, Decendents' Estates and Trusts, and Commercial Transactions.

Graduation Requirements

In order to graduate, candidates must have a GPA of 2.0 and have completed the upper-division writing requirement.

Organizations

Students edit the *Ohio Northern University Law Review*. Teams compete in the New York Bar Association's Annual National Moot Court, ABA Negotiations, and Jessup International Law competitions. Local chapters of national associations include the Student Bar Association, Legal Association of Women, and Black Law Students Association. Law student organizations include Street Law, International Law Society, and Christian Legal Society. Campus clubs include Habitat for Humanity, Wilderness Society, and Italian American Legal Society.

Library

The law library contains 295,639 hard-copy volumes and 84,999 microform volume equivalents, and subscribes to 3023 serial publications. Such on-line databases and networks as CALI, CIS Universe, DIALOG, Infotrac, Legal-Trac, LEXIS, LOIS, Mathew Bender, NEXIS, OCLC First Search, WESTLAW, and Wilsonline Indexes are available to law students for research. Special library collections include a federal government depository. Recently, the library upgraded the computer laboratory. The ratio of library volumes to faculty is 12,854 to 1 and to students is 1083 to 1. The ratio of seats in the library to students is 1 to 1.

Faculty

The law school has 23 full-time and 12 part-time faculty members, of whom 12 are women. According to AAUP standards for Category IIB institutions, faculty salaries are well above average. About 22% of full-time faculty have a graduate law degree in addition to the J.D. The ratio of full-time students to full-time faculty in an average class is 14 to 1; in a clinic, 10 to 1. The law school has a regular program of bringing visiting professors and other distinguished lecturers and visitors to campus.

Placement

J.D.s awarded:	100
Services available through: a separate law school placement center	
Services: Spring Recruiting Conference and Spring Public Interest Career Fair	
Special features: An active membership in NALP and the Ohio Law Placement Consortium (OLPC), through which the college participates in a variety of joint recruiting projects throughout the year.	
Full-time job interviews:	8 employers
Summer job interviews:	8 employers
Placement by graduation:	31% of class
Placement within 9 months:	91% of class
Average starting salary:	$32,000 to $75,000
Areas of placement:	
Private practice 2-10 attorneys	22%
Private practice 11-25 attorneys	15%
Private practice 26-50 attorneys	6%
Private practice 51-100 attorneys	12%
Solo practice and other	11%
Government	16%
Business/industry	7%
Public interest	5%
Judicial clerkships	3%
Academic	2%
Military	1%

Students

About 40% of the student body are women; 12%, minorities; 8%, African American; 1%, Asian American; 2%, Hispanic; and 1%, Native American. Most students come from Ohio (30%). The average age of entering students is 26; age range is 20 to 68. About 50% of students enter directly from undergraduate school. About 6% drop out after the first year for academic or personal reasons; 85% remain to receive a law degree.

OHIO STATE UNIVERSITY

Michael E. Moritz College of Law

55 West 12th Avenue,
John Deaver Drinko Hall
Columbus, OH 43210-1391

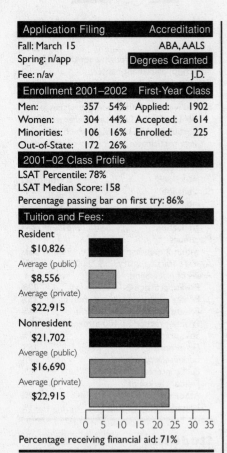

Application Filing		Accreditation
Fall: March 15		ABA, AALS
Spring: n/app		**Degrees Granted**
Fee: n/av		J.D.

Enrollment 2001–2002			First-Year Class	
Men:	357	54%	Applied:	1902
Women:	304	44%	Accepted:	614
Minorities:	106	16%	Enrolled:	225
Out-of-State:	172	26%		

2001–02 Class Profile

LSAT Percentile: 78%
LSAT Median Score: 158
Percentage passing bar on first try: 86%

Tuition and Fees:

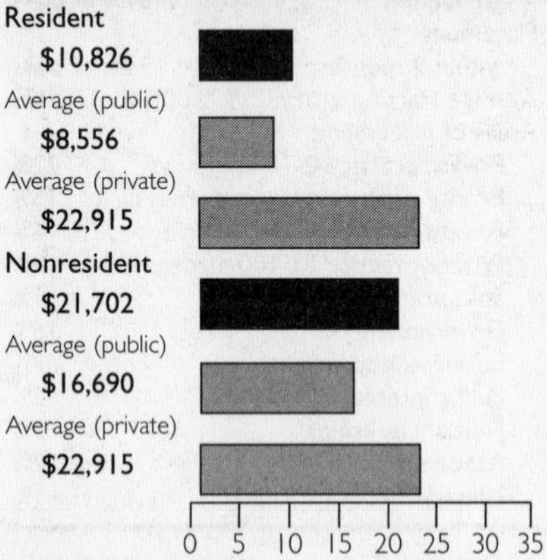

Percentage receiving financial aid: 71%

ADMISSIONS

In the fall 2001 first-year class, 1902 applied, 614 were accepted, and 225 enrolled. Ten transfers enrolled. The median LSAT percentile of the most recent first-year class was 78; the median GPA was 3.6 on a scale of 4.0. The highest LSAT percentile was 99.

Requirements

Applicants must have a bachelor's degree and take the LSAT. The most important admission factors include academic achievement, undergraduate curriculum, and life experience. No specific undergraduate courses are required. Candidates are not interviewed.

Procedure

The application deadline for fall entry is March 15. Applicants should submit an application form, LSAT results, transcripts, 2 letters of recommendation, and the Academic Records Office Evaluation from undergraduate school. Notification of the admissions decision is on a rolling basis. The latest acceptable LSAT test date for fall entry is February. The law school uses the LSDAS.

Special

The law school recruits minority and disadvantaged students through participation in CLEO and as a part of the overall recruitment program. Requirements are not different for out-of-state students. Transfer students must have one year of credit and have attended an ABA-approved law school.

Costs

Tuition and fees for the 2001-2002 academic year are $10,826 for full-time in-state students and $21,702 for out-of-state students. On-campus room and board costs about $7326 annually; books and supplies run $2715.

Financial Aid

About 71% of current law students receive some form of aid. The average annual amount of aid from all sources combined, including scholarships, loans, and work contracts, is $16,929; maximum, $26,259. Awards are based on need and merit. Required financial statement is the FAFSA. Check with the school for current application deadlines. There are special funds for minority or disadvantaged students including CLEO participation. First-year students are notified about their financial aid application shortly after acceptance.

About the Law School

Ohio State University Michael E. Moritz College of Law was established in 1891 and is a public institution. The 3200-acre campus is in an urban area 2 miles north of downtown Columbus. The primary mission of the law school is to produce lawyers from a base of scholarship, education, and service; the approach is broad-based and academically oriented. Students have access to federal, state, county, city, and local agencies, courts, correctional facilities, law firms, and legal aid organizations in the Columbus area. Facilities of special interest to law students are the state legislature and the state supreme court. Housing for students is available in 3 campus dormitories reserved for graduate and professional students; there are off-campus housing facilities sufficient for all students. All law school facilities are accessible to the physically disabled.

Calendar

The law school operates on a traditional semester basis. Courses for full-time students are offered days only and must be completed within 5 years. There is no part-time program. New students are admitted in the fall. There is an 8-week summer session. Transferable summer courses are offered.

Programs

Students may take relevant courses in other programs and apply credit toward the J.D.; a maximum of 5 credits may be applied. The following joint degrees may be earned: (Individually designed programs with all graduate departments a), J.D./M.B.A. (Juris Doctor/Master of Business Administration), J.D./M.H.A. (Juris Doctor/Master of Health and Hospital Administration), and J.D./M.P.A. (Juris Doctor/Master of Public Administration).

Phone: 614-292-8810
Fax: 614-292-1383
E-mail: *lawadmit@osu.edu*
Web: *www.osu.edu/units/law*

Contact

Kathy S. Northern, Associate Dean, 614-292-8810 for general inquiries; Robert L. Solomon, Assistant Dean, 614-292-8807 for financial aid information.

Required

To earn the J.D., candidates must complete 88 total credits, of which 37 are for required courses. They must maintain a minimum GPA of 2.0 in the required courses. The following first-year courses are required of all students: Contracts, Torts, Property, Civil Procedure, Constitutional Law, Legal Research, Legislation, Writing and Analysis, and Criminal Law. Required upper-level courses consist of Professional Responsibility, 2 courses with a writing component, and Appellate Practice. The required orientation program for first-year students is a day long and covers case briefing, professional responsibility, and college policies and offices.

Electives

The Michael E. Moritz College of Law offers concentrations in corporate law, criminal law, entertainment law, environmental law, family law, international law, juvenile law, labor law, litigation, media law, securities law, sports law, tax law, torts and insurance, and alternative dispute resolution. In addition, second- and third-year students may take clinics. Second-year students take simulation clinics such as pretrial litigation, negotiation, and client counseling. Third-year students may act as legal interns representing clients under faculty supervision. At least one seminar must be taken by second- or third-year students; seminars range from creative and constitutional aspects of law to those devoted to a student's research of a specific legal area. Internships are available with certain federal and state judges. Research programs include opportunities for independent study. There are field work opportunities to work for the public and private sector; opportunities to do volunteer work, such as the Volunteer Income Tax Assistance (VITA) program. Special lectures are supported by the Ohio State Law Forum, which invites distinguished academicians, jurists, and practitioners; speakers are also invited by faculty and student groups. Study abroad is possible through the Oxford Summer Program and is open to students from the college and all other accredited law schools. Students can earn 3 or 6 hours of credit during the summer. A legal methods program, designed to help certain first-year students who may need more time and attention adapting to law school, is available. The Black Law Students Association, Hispanic Law Students Association, and Asian Law Students Association sponsor various events and programs. Special interest groups include the sports and entertainment law society, pro bono research group, public interest law forum, women's law caucus, and health law society. The most widely taken electives are those that are directly bar-related (Evidence, Corporations), international law offerings, and alternative dispute resolution offerings.

Graduation Requirements

In order to graduate, candidates must have a GPA of 2.0 and have completed the upper-division writing requirement and an ethics course.

Organizations

Students edit the *Ohio State Law Journal, Journal on Dispute Resolution*, and the newspaper *Hearsay*. Appellate Practice is the first moot court experience required of all students. The college has 12 separate moot court teams. There are also several national trial competition teams and 2 negotiation teams. There are also intraschool Moot Court, Negotiation, and Trial Competitions. Law student organizations include the Student Bar Association, the Pro Bono Research Group, and International Law Society. There are local chapters of legal fraternities, as well as a student section of the American Bar Association. Other organizations include Hillel, Ski Club, and the Ballroom Dance Association.

Library

The law library contains 653,399 hard-copy volumes and 880,049 microform volume equivalents, and subscribes to 7722 serial publications. Such on-line databases and networks as DIALOG, LEXIS, WESTLAW, and LCS and OCLC are available to law students for research. Special library collections include a government depository, a large foreign law collection, and materials on dispute resolution. Recently, the library added 64,000 square feet to the existing library space, which accomodates 12 study rooms with 300 carrels and 40 word processors. The ratio of library volumes to faculty is 19,799 to 1 and to students is 972 to 1. The ratio of seats in the library to students is 1 to 1.

Placement

J.D.s awarded:	195
Services available through: a separate law school placement center	
Services: practice interviews with local attorneys and job search workshops	
Special features: encouragement to do judicial clerkships.	
Full-time job interviews:	52 employers
Summer job interviews:	89 employers
Placement by graduation:	67% of class
Placement within 9 months:	97% of class
Average starting salary:	$40,000 to $90,000
Areas of placement:	
Private practice 2-10 attorneys	52%
Government	14%
Business/industry	13%
Judicial clerkships	10%
Military	4%
Public interest	3%
Academic	2%
unknown	2%

Faculty

The law school has 41 full-time and 26 part-time faculty members, of whom 24 are women. According to AAUP standards for Category I institutions, faculty salaries are above average. The ratio of full-time students to full-time faculty in an average class is 20 to 1; in a clinic, 15 to 1. There is a chapter of the Order of the Coif.

Students

About 44% of the student body are women; 16%, minorities; 7%, African American; 6%, Asian American; and 2%, Hispanic. The majority of students come from Ohio (74%). The average age of entering students is 22; age range is 21 to 47. About 12% of students have a graduate degree. About 1% drop out after the first year for academic or personal reasons; 99% remain to receive a law degree.

OKLAHOMA CITY UNIVERSITY

School of Law

2501 North Blackwelder
Oklahoma City, OK 73106-1493

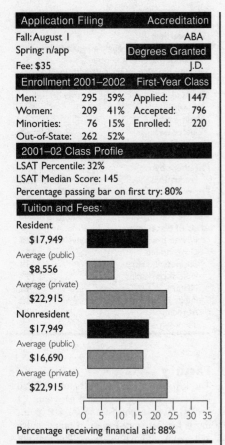

Application Filing		Accreditation
Fall: August 1		ABA
Spring: n/app		**Degrees Granted**
Fee: $35		J.D.

Enrollment 2001–2002			First-Year Class	
Men:	295	59%	Applied:	1447
Women:	209	41%	Accepted:	796
Minorities:	76	15%	Enrolled:	220
Out-of-State:	262	52%		

2001–02 Class Profile

LSAT Percentile: 32%
LSAT Median Score: 145
Percentage passing bar on first try: 80%

Tuition and Fees:

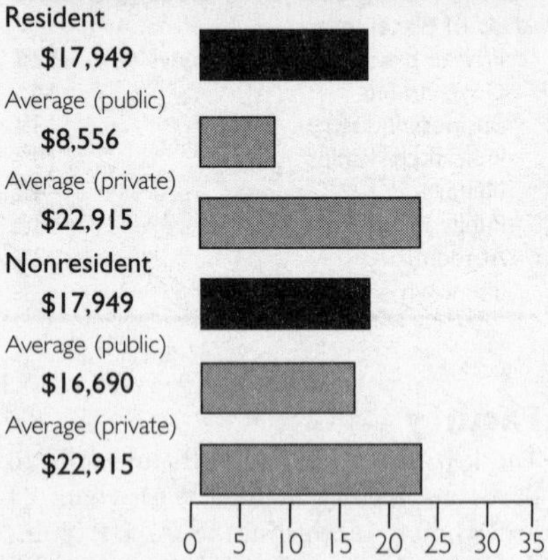

Percentage receiving financial aid: 88%

ADMISSIONS

In the fall 2001 first-year class, 1447 applied, 796 were accepted, and 220 enrolled. Six transfers enrolled. The median LSAT percentile of the most recent first-year class was 32; the median GPA was 2.9 on a scale of 4.0. The lowest LSAT percentile accepted was 10; the highest was 92.

Requirements

Applicants must have a bachelor's degree and take the LSAT. Minimum acceptable GPA is 2.0 on a scale of 4.0. The most important admission factors include LSAT results, GPA, and undergraduate curriculum. No specific undergraduate courses are required. Candidates are not interviewed.

Procedure

The application deadline for fall entry is August 1. Applicants should submit an application form, LSAT results, a nonrefundable application fee of $35, and 2 letters of recommendation. Notification of the admissions decision is as soon as a decision has been made. The latest acceptable LSAT test date for fall entry is June. The law school uses the LSDAS.

Special

The law school recruits minority and disadvantaged students through the Alternate Summer Admissions Program, which is designed for applicants from disadvantaged backgrounds whose LSAT scores and GPAs do not qualify them for regular admission. Requirements are not different for out-of-state students. Transfer students must have attended an ABA-approved law school and complete their last 45 hours at the school, be in good standing at their former law school, and submit a letter from the dean along with official transcripts.

Costs

Tuition and fees for the 2001-2002 academic year are $17,949 for all full-time students. Tuition for part-time students is $12,045 per year. On-campus room and board costs about $4200 annually; books and supplies run $750.

Financial Aid

About 88% of current law students receive some form of aid. The average annual amount of aid from all sources combined, including scholarships, loans, and work contracts, is $20,968; maximum, $32,500. Awards are based on need. Required financial statement is the FAFSA. The aid application deadline for fall entry is March 1. First-year students are notified about their financial aid application approximately 2 to 6 weeks after their financial file is completed.

About the Law School

Oklahoma City University School of Law was established in 1907 and is a private institution. The 68-acre campus is in an urban area in Oklahoma City, approximately 3 miles from the state capital. The primary mission of the law school is to prepare students to become responsible professionals in the legal and leadership roles assumed by lawyers today and that may be assumed in the future. Students have access to federal, state, county, city, and local agencies, courts, correctional facilities, law firms, and legal aid organizations in the Oklahoma City area. Oklahoma City, as the state capital, is a major center for law, business, and banking in the region. Facilities of special interest to law students include the state capitol complex, which contains the Supreme Court, the Court of Criminal Appeals, the Court of Appeals, the state legislature, and various state administrative and regulatory agencies. It is also near the U.S. District Court and numerous other federal and state entities, law firms, and business institutions. Housing for students is in on-campus dormitories and an on-campus apartment complex. No on-campus housing is available for married students, but many private apartments are available in the metro area. All law school facilities are accessible to the physically disabled.

Calendar

The law school operates on a traditional semester basis. Required courses for full-time students are offered during the day and must be completed within 4 years. For part-time students, required courses are offered during the evening and must be completed within 5 years. New full- and part-time students are admitted in the fall. There is a 7½-week summer session. Transferable summer courses are offered.

Programs

The following joint degrees may be earned: J.D./M.B.A. (Juris Doctor/Master of Business Administration) and J.D./M.Div. (Juris Doctor/Master of Divinity).

Required

To earn the J.D., candidates must complete 90 total credits, of which 46 are for required courses. They must maintain a minimum GPA of 4.5 on a scale of 12 in the required courses. The following first-year courses are required of all students: Civil Procedure I and II, Contracts I and II, Criminal Law, Legal Research and Writing I and II, Property I, Torts I and II, and Legal Analysis. Required upper-level courses consist of Constitutional Law I, Criminal Procedure I, Evidence, Legal Profession, and Property II. The required orientation program for first-year students consists of both large-group presentations and smaller "break-out" sessions in which students discuss

Phone: 405-521-5354
800-633-7242
Fax: 405-521-5802
E-mail: *lawadmit@okcu.edu*
Web: *www.okcu.edu/law*

Contact

Peter Storandt, Director of Admissions, 405-521-5354 for general inquiries; Molly Roberts, Director, 405-521-5211 for financial aid information.

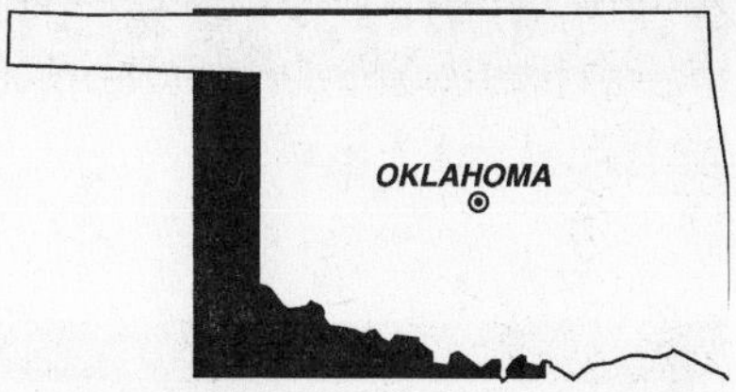

with professors issues such as studying, exams, and stress management.

Electives

A 2-credit Native American Legal Assistance Clinic is available to 15 students each semester. They work 7 hours a week and meet 1 hour a week in class, under the direction of the clinic's director and supervising attorneys. An externship in criminal law is available for 2 credits, and a Federal Court externship is available for 1 credit hour. Six to eight 2-hour seminars are offered each semester on selected advanced topics. Recent seminars include Bioethics, Native American Economic Development, and selected topics in Oil and Gas. As part of an internship, students who meet requirements and have a sponsoring attorney may appear in court alone in certain matters. With a supervising attorney present, they may handle any court proceeding. Students may conduct research through seminars, advanced reading courses, supervised papers, or directed research projects. They may also assist faculty as research assistants. The annual Quinlan Lecture series presents a nationally preeminent legal scholar or jurist. The annual Brennan Lecture series presents a nationally prominent scholar or jurist in the field of state constitutional law. An academic support program is available for first-year students and for second-year students on academic probation. Students with writing problems may seek help at the University Writing Center. The academic support program offers tutoring by upper-level students. Minority programs include the Native American Legal Resource Center. The most widely taken electives are Wills and Estates, Bankruptcy, and Corporations.

Graduation Requirements

In order to graduate, candidates must have a GPA of 4.5 on a scale of 12, have completed the upper-division writing requirement, and have 6 or 8 residency semesters, depending on whether the student is enrolled full- or part-time, respectively.

Organizations

The Oklahoma City University Law Review publishes 3 issues annually. The Student Bar Association publishes *The Verdict*, a monthly newsletter. The law school has an annual Intramural Moot Court Competition. It also fields teams for the ABA Moot Court and the Jessup International Law Moot Court. There is also an Energy Law Writing Competition. Law student organizations include Law Partners, Environmental Law Association, and Federalist Society. There are local chapters of Hand Inn (Phi Delta Phi) and The Vaught Chapter (Phi Alpha Delta). In addition, two Inns of Court (William J. Holloway, Jr. Inn and Ruth Bader Ginsburg Inn) are affiliated with the school. Other law student organizations include Sports and Entertainment Law Association, Constitution Society, and the Federalist Society.

Library

The law library contains 271,739 hard-copy volumes and 618,909 microform volume equivalents, and subscribes to 3972 serial publications. Such on-line databases and networks as DIALOG, LEXIS, and WESTLAW are available to law students for research. Special library collections include the Native American collections and the Real Property Title Standards Collection. Recently, the library gained a 25-workstation computer lab that also has Macs. A 12-workstation lab, with a screen and whiteboard, is used for teaching small groups. Each law student has an e-mail address. Students have home access through the web to CALI, a collection of more than 90 interactive computer exercises covering 22 legal education subjects. The law school and library web pages provide links to career services, current job information, course descriptions, admissions information, web subscriptions, such as the Matthew Bender Authority and CIS Congressional Universe, and the university and law library on-line catalog (OLIB). Study rooms and carrels on the lower level are wired to the law library and campus networks, while on-line workstations are available on all floors. The ratio of library volumes to faculty is 8492 to 1 and to students is 539 to 1. The ratio of seats in the library to students is 1 to 2.

Faculty

The law school has 32 full-time and 17 part-time faculty members, of whom 17 are women. According to AAUP standards for Category IIA institutions, faculty salaries are below average. About 29% of full-time faculty have a graduate law degree in addition to the J.D. The ratio of full-time students to full-time faculty in an average class is 19 to 1; in a clinic, 10 to 1. The law school has a regular program of bringing visiting professors and other distinguished lecturers and visitors to campus.

Placement	
J.D.s awarded:	142
Services available through: a separate law school placement center	
Services: Sunbelt Minority Job Fair, Patent Job Fair, Chicago, Illinois, and Southeastern Minority Job Fair, National Association Public Interest in Washington D.C.	
Special features: 2.5 full-time career services personnel who help students find employment; resource center materials, including monthly employment listings in a publication exchanged with approximately 85 ABA-approved law schools nationwide; and a Graduate Mentor Program.	
Full-time job interviews:	9 employers
Summer job interviews:	9 employers
Placement by graduation:	n/av
Placement within 9 months:	86% of class
Average starting salary:	$27,500 to $42,000
Areas of placement:	
Private practice 2-10 attorneys	27%
Private practice 11-25 attorneys	7%
Private practice 26-50 attorneys	4%
Private practice 51-100 attorneys	1%
Private practice 250+ attorneys	1%
Unknown	31%
Business/industry	12%
Judicial clerkships	6%
Solo practice	5%
Academic	4%
Public interest	2%

Students

About 41% of the student body are women; 15%, minorities; 6%, African American; 4%, Asian American; 5%, Native American; and 4%, other Hispanic American. Most students come from Oklahoma (48%). The average age of entering students is 30; age range is 21 to 56. About 8% drop out after the first year for academic or personal reasons; 92% remain to receive a law degree.

PACE UNIVERSITY

School of Law

78 North Broadway
White Plains, NY 10603

Application Filing		Accreditation
Fall: February 15		ABA, AALS
Spring: n/app		**Degrees Granted**
Fee: $55		J.D., LL.M., S.J.D.

Enrollment 2001–2002			First-Year Class	
Men:	309	43%	Applied:	1802
Women:	414	57%	Accepted:	819
Minorities:	116	16%	Enrolled:	230
Out-of-State:	268	37%		

2001–02 Class Profile

LSAT Percentile: 52%
LSAT Median Score: 152
Percentage passing bar on first try: n/av

Tuition and Fees:

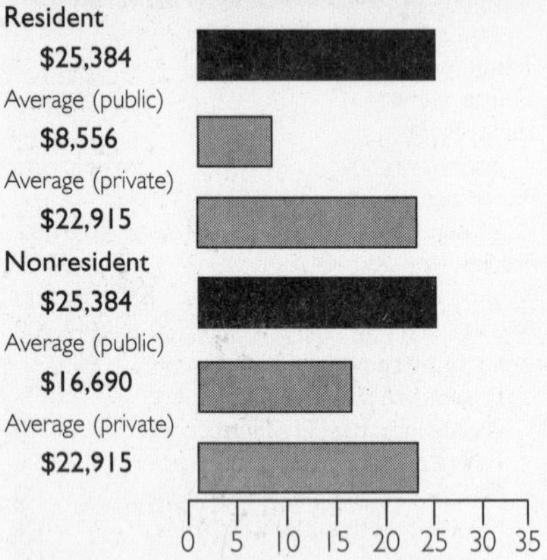

Percentage receiving financial aid: 85%

ADMISSIONS

In the fall 2001 first-year class, 1802 applied, 819 were accepted, and 230 enrolled. The median LSAT percentile of the most recent first-year class was 52; the median GPA was 3.2 on a scale of 4.0.

Requirements

Applicants must have a bachelor's degree and take the LSAT. Minimum acceptable GPA is 2.0 on a scale of 4.0. The most important admission factors include LSAT results, GPA, and letter of recommendation. Specific undergraduate courses and interviews are not required.

Procedure

The application deadline for fall entry is February 15. Applicants should submit an application form, LSAT results, transcripts, a nonrefundable application fee of $55, 2 letters of recommendation, a personal statement, and TOEFL or TWE test scores, if applicable. Notification of the admissions decision is on a rolling basis. The latest acceptable LSAT test date for fall entry is February. The law school uses the LSDAS.

Special

The law school recruits minority and disadvantaged students by hosting a Law Day for minority students each year and visiting historically black colleges. From 1999 to 2001, Pace co-hosted the Puerto Rican Legal Defense and Education Fund Program. Requirements are not different for out-of-state students. Transfer students must have one year of credit, have attended an ABA-approved law school, and have a maximum of 30 transfer credits from state-approved law schools.

Costs

Tuition and fees for the 2000-2001 academic year were $25,384 for all full-time students. Tuition for part-time students was $19,066 per year. On-campus room and board costs about $8000 annually; books and supplies run $1000.

Financial Aid

About 85% of current law students receive some form of aid. The average annual amount of aid from all sources combined, including scholarships, loans, and work contracts, is $23,218; maximum, $38,274. Awards are based on need and merit. Required financial statement is the FAFSA. The aid application deadline for fall entry is February 1. First-year students are notified about their application at time of acceptance from March 15 through August 30.

About the Law School

Pace University School of Law was established in 1976 and is a private institution. The 12-acre campus is in a suburban area in White Plains. The primary mission of the law school is to permit students the flexibility to build their own program of legal study on the foundation of basic legal principles and skills. Students have access to federal, state, county, city, and local agencies, courts, correctional facilities, law firms, and legal aid organizations in the White Plains area. Major state courts for the New York State Ninth Judicial District, county courts, county government, and the district attorney's office are within walking distance. The Judicial Institute of the State of New York, an innovative center for judicial education, will be housed in a state-of-the-art facility at Pace. Housing for students includes an on-campus residence hall, providing single rooms. The university also assists students in locating off-campus accommodations close to campus. All law school facilities are accessible to the physically disabled.

Calendar

The law school operates on a traditional semester basis. Courses for full-time students are offered days only during the first year and must be completed in a minimum of 3 years. For part-time students, courses are offered both day and evening and must be completed in a minimum of 4 years. New full- and part-time students are admitted in the fall. There is a 7-week summer session. Transferable summer courses are offered.

Programs

In addition to the J.D., the law school offers the LL.M., S.J.D., and Environmental Law/LLM Comparative Law. Students may take relevant courses in other programs and apply credit toward the J.D.; a maximum of 10 credits may be applied. The following joint degrees may be earned: J.D./M.B.A. (Juris Doctor/Master of Business Administration), J.D./M.E.M. (Juris Doctor/Master of Environmental Management with Yale University), and J.D./M.P.A. (Juris Doctor/Master of Public Administration with a concentration in government, not-for-profit, and health care administration).

Required

To earn the J.D., candidates must complete 84 total credits, of which 36 are for required courses. They must maintain a minimum GPA of 2.3 in the required courses. The following first-year courses are required of all students: Civil Procedure, Contracts, Property I, Torts, Constitutional Law, Legal Analysis and Writing I and II (combined with Criminal Law), and Professional Responsibility. Required upper-level courses consist of Federal Income Tax I, electives from 18 course programs of more than 70 courses, and an upper-level writing requirement. Students can register for a maximum of 13 clinical credit hours if they wish to test for the New York bar exam.The required orientation program for first-year students consists of a full week prior to the beginning of classes, with substantive law courses that emphasize briefing techniques and lectures.

Electives

Students must take 12 credits in their area of concentration. The School of Law offers concentrations in corporate law, criminal law, environmental law, family

Phone: 914-422-4210
Fax: 914-422-4010
E-mail: *calexander@law.pace.edu*
Web: *www.law.pace.edu*

Contact

Cathy M. Alexander, Director of Admissions, Office of Admissions, 914-422-4210 for general inquiries; Virgil Villani, Associate Director, Financial Aid, 914-422-4050 for financial aid information.

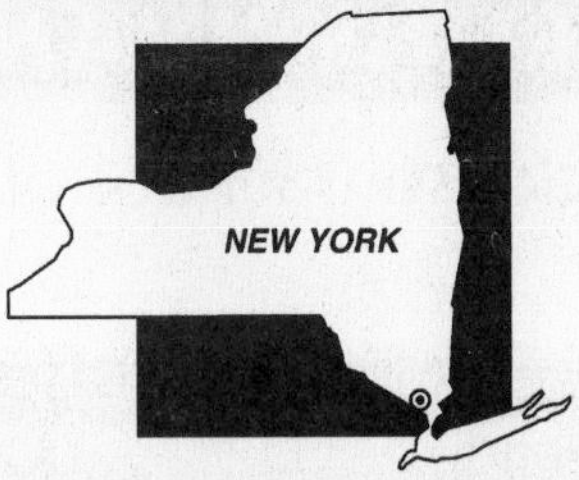

law, international law, and health. In addition, the Criminal Defense Clinic (6 credit hours over 2 semesters) offers actual representation of clients in criminal court; an intensive seminar in criminal practice; and representation of post-conviction "innocence cases." The Environmental Litigation Clinic (6 credits) represents public interest environmental groups bringing citizen enforcement actions in state and federal courts on a variety of environmental and land use issues. In addition to the casework, 2 weekly seminars focus on substantive environmental law and on lawyering skills encountered in major civil litigation. The clinic, developed by Professor Robert F. Kennedy, Jr., has been a model for other environmental clinics across the country. The Securities Arbitration Clinic (2 credit hours over 2 semesters) helps small investors whose financial losses are not significant enough for representation by the private bar. Student lawyers prepare and conduct arbitrations before the New York Stock Exchange or the National Association of Securities Dealers and try to negotiate fair settlements for their clients. Seminars include Advanced Family Law, International Human Rights, and In-House Counsel. Students may work as interns in prosecutors' or public defenders' offices or municipal attorney's offices, or may help income taxpayers in cases involving the Internal Revenue Service. A Judicial Administration Internship course allows students to do field research on problems in the criminal justice system. Outstanding third-year students may be eligible for clerkships with federal and state judges. Research assistant positions are available for students. The school hosts 3 academic lectures each year: Dyson Lecture, Garrison Lecture in Environmental, and Blank Lecture on Ethics. A semester at the University of London's Faculty of Laws is available each spring for second- and third-year students as well as visiting students from other ABA-accredited institutions. Tutorial programs include the Academic Support Program and the Dean's Scholar Program. The most widely taken electives are Family Law, Environmental Law, and International Law.

Graduation Requirements

In order to graduate, candidates must have a GPA of 2.3 and have completed the upper-division writing requirement.

Organizations

Students edit the *Pace Law Review*, the *Pace Environmental Law Review*, the *Pace International Law Review*, and the student newspaper *Hearsay*. The Moot Court Committee sponsors the required competition for first-year students and an advanced competition for second- and third-year students, and sends teams to national and international competitions. Internal competitions include the National Environmental Moot Court, Jessup International Moot Court, and Willem C. Vis International Commercial Arbitration moot competitions. Other competitions include Client Counseling, sponsored by the American Bar Association, Environmental Law, National Moot Court, Unified Moot Court, Frederick Douglass Moot, International Environmental Moot, and Pace/Gray's Inn Moot competitions. Student organizations include the Student Bar Association, Women's Association of Law Students, and the Environmental Law Society. Phi Alpha Delta has a local chapter.

Library

The law library contains 352,130 hard-copy volumes and 62,001 microform volume equivalents, and subscribes to 1372 serial publications. Such on-line databases and networks as CALI, CIS Universe, DIALOG, Infotrac, Legal-Trac, LEXIS, LOIS, NEXIS, RLIN, and WESTLAW are available. Special library collections include collections on environmental law, international law with an emphasis on international environmental law, human rights law, and international trade and business law, and a selective U.S. government depository. Recently, the library improved seating, upgraded computers, wired carrels for laptop access, and enhanced access to audiovisual materials. The ratio of library volumes to faculty is 7336 to 1 and to students is 487 to 1. The ratio of seats in the library to students is 1 to 3.

Faculty

The law school has 48 full-time and 62 part-time faculty members, of whom 40 are women. According to AAUP standards for Category I institutions, faculty salaries are well above average. About 19% of full-time faculty have a graduate law degree in addition to the J.D.; about 13% of part-time faculty have one. The ratio of full-time students to full-time faculty in an average class is 16 to 1; in a clinic, 8 to 1. The law school has a regular program of bringing visiting professors and other distinguished lecturers and visitors to campus.

Placement

J.D.s awarded:	214
Services available through: a separate law school placement center	
Services: seminars and workshops, on-line job listings for students and alumni, databases for judicial clerkships, and private and public sector employment opportunities.	
Special features: videotaped mock interviews, Alumni Adviser and Westchester Bar Association Mentor programs, the Alumni Mentor Program for first years, and a career newsletter, and annual bulletin of career information.	
Full-time job interviews:	55 employers
Summer job interviews:	55 employers
Placement by graduation:	60% of class
Placement within 9 months:	92% of class
Average starting salary:	$25,000 to $150,000
Areas of placement:	
Private practice 2-10 attorneys	37%
Private practice 11-25 attorneys	8%
Private practice 26-50 attorneys	8%
Private practice 51-100 attorneys	3%
Private practice 101-500+ attorneys	9%
Business/industry	14%
Government	11%
Judicial clerkships	8%
Public interest	3%
Academic	1%

Students

About 57% of the student body are women; 16%, minorities; 6%, African American; 4%, Asian American; 6%, Hispanic; and 1%, Mexican American. The majority of students come from the Northeast (87%). The average age of entering students is 25; age range is 18 to 60. About 28% of students enter directly from undergraduate school, 16% have a graduate degree, and 60% have worked full-time prior to entering law school. About 6% drop out after the first year for academic or personal reasons; 84% remain to receive a law degree.

Dickinson School of Law

150 South College Street
Carlisle, PA 17013

Application Filing		Accreditation
Fall: March 1		ABA, AALS
Spring: n/app		**Degrees Granted**
Fee: $50		J.D., LL.M.

Enrollment 2001–2002			First-Year Class	
Men:	288	54%	Applied:	1718
Women:	248	46%	Accepted:	824
Minorities:	54	10%	Enrolled:	181
Out-of-State:	172	32%		

2001–02 Class Profile

LSAT Percentile: 59%
LSAT Median Score: 153
Percentage passing bar on first try: 87%

Tuition and Fees:

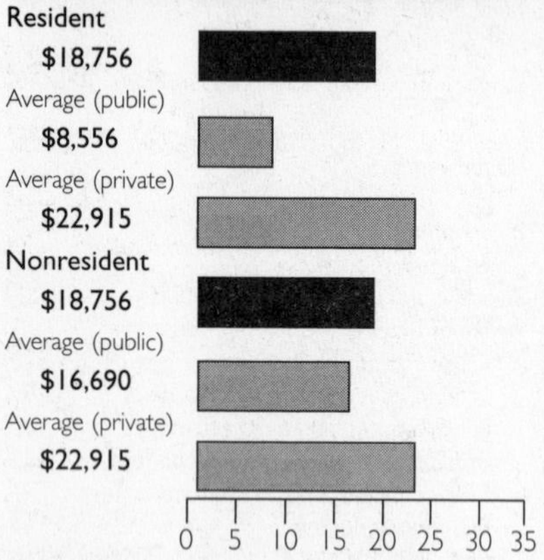

Percentage receiving financial aid: 84%

ADMISSIONS

In the fall 2001 first-year class, 1718 applied, 824 were accepted, and 181 enrolled. Ten transfers enrolled. The median LSAT percentile of the most recent first-year class was 59; the median GPA was 3.3 on a scale of 4.0. The lowest LSAT percentile accepted was 19; the highest was 93.

Requirements

Applicants must have a bachelor's degree and take the LSAT. The most important admission factors include LSAT results, GPA, and academic achievement. No specific undergraduate courses are required. Candidates are not interviewed.

Procedure

The application deadline for fall entry is March 1. Applicants should submit an application form, LSAT results, transcripts, a nonrefundable application fee of $50, 2 (preferably academic) letters of recommendation, a record of work experience, and a 1-page personal statement. Notification of the admissions decision is on a rolling basis. The latest acceptable LSAT test date for fall entry is February. The law school uses the LSDAS.

Special

The law school recruits minority and disadvantaged students by means of minority forums such as the LSAT Candidate Referral Service, recruitment outreach to historically black colleges, and outreach by current minority students and minorty alumni. Requirements are not different for out-of-state students. Transfer students must have one year of credit, have attended an ABA-approved law school, and be in the top 25% of the previous law school in order to be competitive for available space.

Costs

Tuition and fees for the 2001-2002 academic year are $18,756 for all full-time students. On-campus room and board costs about $6200 annually; books and supplies run $900.

Financial Aid

About 84% of current law students receive some form of aid. The average annual amount of aid from all sources combined, including scholarships, loans, and work contracts, is $25,986; maximum, $32,331. Awards are based on need and merit. The required financial statements are the FAFSA and Access Form. The aid application deadline for fall entry is February 15. First-year students are notified about their financial aid application at time of acceptance if required forms are received.

About the Law School

Pennsylvania State University Dickinson School of Law was established in 1834 and is a public institution. The 5-acre campus is in a small town 18 miles west of Harrisburg, Pennsylvania. The school has 11 additional acres at another location. The primary mission of the law school is to offer a balanced program of study that lays the foundation for careers in leadership positions as lawyers, judges, legislators, public officials, and community leaders by fostering development of sound analytical skills, judgment, and communication skills. Students have access to federal, state, county, city, and local agencies, courts, correctional facilities, law firms, and legal aid organizations in the Carlisle area. Facilities of special interest to law students include the Dale F. Shughart Community Law Center, located a few blocks from the Law School. It houses the Family and Disability law clinics. The building's law library and proximity to county courts and offices create an environment identical to that of many private law offices. In addition, an office building and warehouse occupy an 11-acre site housing Alumni, Development, and Communications offices and library storage. The Levinson Curtilage provides single dormitory rooms for approximately 14% of the students. There is also affordable housing within walking distance. About 95% of the law school facilities are accessible to the physically disabled.

Calendar

The law school operates on a traditional semester basis. Courses for full-time students are offered both day and evening and must be completed within 4.5 years. There is no part-time program. New students are admitted in the fall. There are 2 4-week summer sessions. Transferable summer courses are offered.

Programs

In addition to the J.D., the law school offers the LL.M. and LL.M. in comparative law for foreign lawyers. Students may take relevant courses in other programs and apply credit toward the J.D.; a maximum of 6 credits may be applied. The following joint degrees may be earned: J.D./M.B.A. (Juris Doctor/Master of Business Administration), J.D./M.E.P.C. (Juris Doctor/Master of Environmental Pollution Control), J.D./M.Eng. (Juris Doctor/Master of Engineering in environmental pollution), J.D./M.P.A. (Juris Doctor/Master of Public Administration), J.D./M.S.E.P.C. (Juris Doctor/Master of Science in environmental pollution control), and J.D./M.S.I.S. (Juris Doctor/Master of Science in Information Systems).

Required

To earn the J.D., candidates must complete 88 total credits, of which 40 are for required courses. They must maintain a minimum grade average of 70 in the required courses. The following first-year courses are required of all students: Civil Procedure, Contracts, Property, Torts, Lawyering Skills I and II, Criminal Procedure, Criminal Law, Constitutional Law, and Legislative and Administrative Interpretation and Process. Required upper-level courses consist of Professional Responsibility, Appellate Practice, Basic Federal Income Tax, Evidence, and one of the following: Sales, Secured Transactions, or Payment Systems. The required orientation program for first-year students is a 2-day process during which students are introduced to faculty

Phone: 717-240-5207
800-840-1122
Fax: 717-241-3503
E-mail: *dsladmit@psu.edu*
Web: *www.dsl.psu.edu*

Contact

Barbara W. Guillaume, Director of Admissions Services, 717-240-5207 for general inquiries; Joyce James, Financial Aid Director, 717-240-5256 for financial aid information.

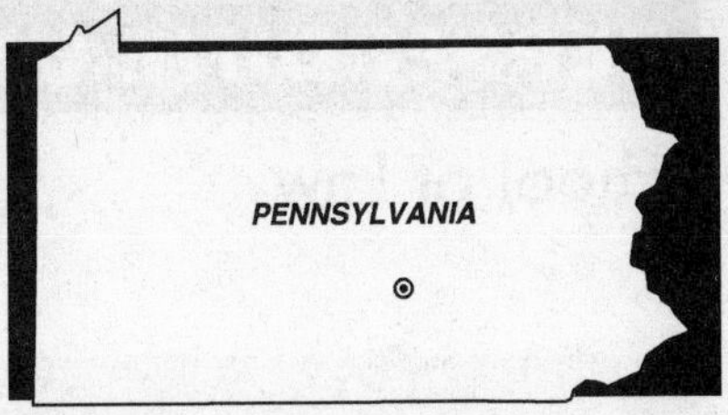

and staff of the law school as well as the structure of the court system, the anatomy of a case, and basic case briefing.

Electives

The Dickinson School of Law offers concentrations in corporate law, criminal law, entertainment law, environmental law, family law, international law, litigation, tax law, and torts and insurance. In addition, In-house clinics are Elder Law, Family Law, Art, Sports, and Entertainment Law and Disability Law for second- and third-year students. Enrollment in any clinic is limited to 2 semesters. A student may earn up to 9 credits for clinics, but may not enroll in more than 1 clinic concurrently. Seminars include Elder Law; Comparative Law; Race, Racism and American Law; and Anglo-American Legal History. Seminars are designed to develop and test students' research and writing skills. Grading is based on class participation and attendance in addition to the quality of the papers submitted. A small number of students can earn up to 3 credits during a summer, working without compensation in a government or public setting, similar to the field-placement clinic settings. These students also attend an orientation meeting before beginning their service and a review session at the end of the summer. Research programs (independent study) may be arranged with full-time professors. Any second- or third-year student may elect one independent study for 2 credits. More than one-third of the Law School's students obtain clinical credit in either an in-house clinic or field-placement clinic. Field-placement settings include several state agencies and the FCC, state and federal judges, local government offices, public prosecutor and public defender offices at the state and federal levels, and legal services offices. Students earn up to 6 credits for 2 semesters' work. Special lecture series include the Dean's Forum, Polisher Lecture, Senior Speakers' Dinner, Speakers Trust Fund, and Faculty Development and Oxford Series. Study abroad consists of 2 4-week summer credit programs: 1 in Florence, Italy; the other in Vienna; Strasbourg; Oxford; and Brussels in the areas of international law and comparative legal systems. Student-to-student tutoring is provided when requested by individual students, particularly those experiencing academic difficulty. Students who do not perform well after first-semester, first-year examinations are offered the opportunity to receive one-on-one assistance from a full-time faculty member as part of the school's Academic Support Program. First-year students who do not perform well in their Lawyering Skills class are offered the opportunity to receive one-on-one assistance from a writing specialist. All first-year students who are members of the Minority Law Students Association may participate in a voluntary tutoring program. The most widely taken electives are Advocacy I, Sales, and Trusts and Estates.

Graduation Requirements

In order to graduate, candidates must have a minimum grade average of 70 and have completed the upper-division writing requirement. In addition, each student must successfully complete a seminar and the Appellate Practice course, which requires preparation of an appellate brief.

Organizations

The primary law review is the *Dickinson Law Review*. Other law reviews include the *Dickinson Journal of International Law* and the *Dickinson Journal of Environmental Law and Policy*. *Res Ipsa Loquitur* is the student yearbook. The school generally fields as many as 10 teams in various interscholastic moot court competitions. The competitions include Jessup International, National Appellate, and National Trial. Other competitions include an ABA client counseling competition, an environmental law competition, and a labor law competition. Law student organizations include PILF, International Law Society, and Federalist Society. There are local chapters of ABA-Law Student Divison, Amnesty International, and Association of Trial Lawyers of America. Campus clubs and other organizations include Corpus Juris Society, Women's Law Caucus, and Dickinson Lesbian and Gay Law Association.

Library

The law library contains 454,000 hard-copy volumes and 1,055,000 microform volume equivalents, and subscribes to 1200 serial publications. Such on-line databases and networks as DIALOG, LEXIS, WESTLAW, and LIAS are available to law students for research. Special library collections include a U.S. government depository, European Community and United Nations documents, and Pennsylvania briefs and records. Recently, the library renovated a lounge/study area and added 90 carrels. The ratio of library volumes to faculty is 12,971 to 1 and to students, 847 to 1. The ratio of seats in the library to students is 1 to 1.2.

Placement

J.D.s awarded:	168
Services available through: a separate law school placement center	
Services: videotaped practice interview	
Special features: a very personalized emphasis, which is available due to limited enrollment.	
Full-time job interviews:	38 employers
Summer job interviews:	50 employers
Placement by graduation:	56% of class
Placement within 9 months:	91% of class
Average starting salary:	$28,985 to $95,340
Areas of placement:	
Private practice 2-10 attorneys	20%
Private practice 11-25 attorneys	10%
Private practice 26-50 attorneys	6%
Private practice 51-100 attorneys	17%
Judicial clerkships	30%
Government	10%
Business/industry	3%
Military	2%
Public interest	1%
Unknown	1%

Faculty

The law school has 35 full-time and 57 part-time faculty members, of whom 21 are women. About 43% of full-time faculty have a graduate law degree in addition to the J.D.; about 14% of part-time faculty have one. The ratio of full-time students to full-time faculty in an average class is 21 to 1; in a clinic, 4 to 1. The law school has a regular program of bringing visiting professors and other distinguished lecturers and visitors to campus.

Students

About 46% of the student body are women; 10%, minorities; 2%, African American; 1%, Asian American; 6%, Hispanic; and 1%, Native American. The majority of students come from Pennsylvania (68%). The average age of entering students is 25; age range is 20 to 48. About 31% of students have worked full-time prior to entering law school. About 7% drop out after the first year for academic or personal reasons; 93% remain to receive a law degree.

PEPPERDINE UNIVERSITY

School of Law

24255 Pacific Coast Highway
Malibu, CA 90263

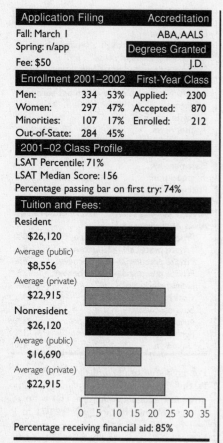

Application Filing		Accreditation
Fall: March 1		ABA, AALS
Spring: n/app		**Degrees Granted**
Fee: $50		J.D.

Enrollment 2001–2002			First-Year Class	
Men:	334	53%	Applied:	2300
Women:	297	47%	Accepted:	870
Minorities:	107	17%	Enrolled:	212
Out-of-State:	284	45%		

2001–02 Class Profile

LSAT Percentile: 71%
LSAT Median Score: 156
Percentage passing bar on first try: 74%

Tuition and Fees:

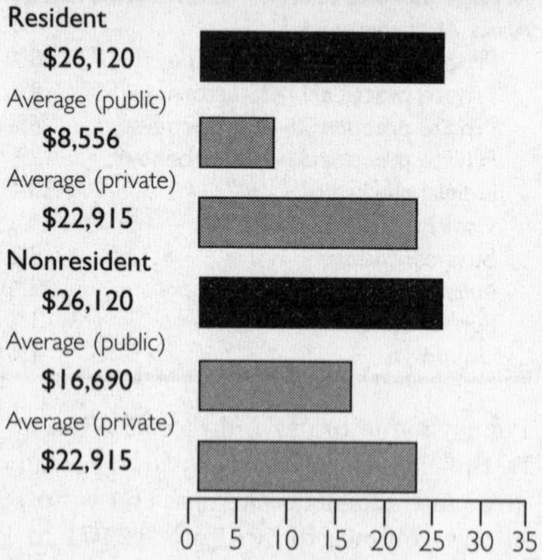

Percentage receiving financial aid: 85%

ADMISSIONS

In the fall 2001 first-year class, 2300 applied, 870 were accepted, and 212 enrolled. Thirty transfers enrolled. The median LSAT percentile of the most recent first-year class was 71; the median GPA was 3.3 on a scale of 4.0.

Requirements

Applicants must have a bachelor's degree and take the LSAT. No specific undergraduate courses are required. Candidates are not interviewed.

Procedure

The application deadline for fall entry is March 1. Applicants should submit an application form, a nonrefundable application fee of $50, 2 letters of recommendation, and a seat deposit. Notification of the admissions decision is on a rolling basis. The latest acceptable LSAT test date for fall entry is February. The law school uses the LSDAS.

Special

The law school recruits minority and disadvantaged students by actively encouraging applications from ethnic minorities. Requirements are not different for out-of-state students. Transfer students must have one year of credit, have attended an ABA-approved law school, submit an official law school transcript, a letter from the dean indicating the student's eligibility to continue his or her studies and indicating the student's class rank, and supply a photocopy of the current school's LSDAS report. The student must rank in the top 30% of the first-year law class.

Costs

Tuition and fees for the 2001-2002 academic year are $26,120 for all full-time students. On-campus room and board costs about $15,378 annually; books and supplies run $700.

Financial Aid

About 85% of current law students receive some form of aid. The maximum annual amount of aid from all sources combined, including scholarships, loans, and work contracts, is $37,084. Awards are based on need and merit. Need-based financial aid awards are generally a combination of grants, loans, and work-study employment. The required financial statement is the FAFSA. Check with the school for current application deadlines. Special funds for minority or disadvantaged students consist of the Diversity Scholarship, based on academic and personal achievement. First-year students are notified about their financial aid application 2 weeks after acceptance notification, if completed.

About the Law School

Pepperdine University School of Law was established in 1969 and is a private institution. The 830-acre campus is in a small town 30 miles north of Los Angeles, California. The primary mission of the law school is to provide highly qualified students with a distinctive and solid legal education. The school maintains a Christian emphasis. Students have access to federal, state, county, city, and local agencies, courts, correctional facilities, law firms, and legal aid organizations in the Malibu area. Facilities of special interest to law students include the Odell McConnell Law Center, which overlooks the Pacific Ocean; the facility contains an auditorium-classroom, law library, classrooms, an atrium, an appellate courtroom, a trial courtroom, cafeteria, lounges, and student services offices. Housing for students is limited on campus; on-campus apartments house 4 students in each of the 36 apartments. All law school facilities are accessible to the physically disabled.

Calendar

The law school operates on a traditional semester basis. Courses for full-time students are offered days only. There is no part-time program. New students are admitted in the fall. There is a 7 1/2-week summer session. Transferable summer courses are offered.

Phone: 310-506-4631
Fax: 310-506-7668
E-mail: *soladmis@pepperdine.edu*
Web: *http://law.pepperdine.edu*

Contact

Shannon Phillips, Director of Admissions and Records, 310-506-4631 for general inquiries; Janet Lockhart, Director of Financial Aid, 310-506-4633 for financial aid information.

Programs

In addition to the J.D., the law school offers the Master of Dispute Resolution. The following joint degrees may be earned: J.D./M.B.A. (Juris Doctor/Master of Business Administration), J.D./M.D.R. (Juris Doctor/Master of Dispute Resolution), and J.D./M.P.P. (Juris Doctor/Master of Public Policy).

Required

To earn the J.D., candidates must complete 88 total credits, of which 57 are for required courses. They must maintain a minimum grade average of 72 in the required courses. The following first-year courses are required of all students: Civil Pleadings and Procedure I and II, Contracts I and II, Criminal Law, Legal Research and Writing I and II, Real Property I and II, Torts I and II, and Criminal Procedure. Required upper-level courses consist of Legal Ethics, Constitutional Law I and II, Corporations, Evidence, Federal Income Taxation, Remedies, and Wills and Trusts. The required orientation program for first-year students is a 4-day program that includes introduction to legal ethics, the socratic method, case briefing, note taking, outlining, and legal research and writing.

Electives

The School of Law offers concentrations in corporate law, criminal law, entertainment law, environmental law, family law, international law, labor law, tax law, tort law, property law, intellectual property law, advocacy and dispute resolution, public interest, technology and entrepreneurship, and constitutional law. In addition, clinical opportunities are available with the District Attorney's Office of Los Angeles and Ventura counties, and with state and federal court judges in Los Angeles and Ventura counties. Also, smaller programs offer training in corporate and securities law, tax law, juvenile law, domestic arbitration, labor law, consumer protection, trade regulation, and with various media industries. Second- and third-year students may study in the London Law Program during the fall and summer semesters. Courses are taught by British and American faculty. The most widely taken electives are the London Law Program, entertainment and sports law courses, and technology and entrepreneurship.

Graduation Requirements

In order to graduate, candidates must have a grade average of 72.

Organizations

Students edit the *Pepperdine Law Review, National Association of Administrative Law Journal*, and *Dispute Resolution Journal*. First-year students participate in an appellate advocacy experience. Upper-level students compete for places on teams that attend the National Moot Court and other competitions. Each spring there is the Dalsimer Moot Court intraschool competition. Law student organizations are the Student Bar Association, Asian Pacific American Law Students Association, and Black Law Students Association. There are local chapters of Delta Theta Phi, Phi Alpha Delta, and Phi Delta Phi.

Library

The law library contains 342,450 hard-copy volumes and 87,000 microform volume equivalents, and subscribes to 1300 serial publications. Such on-line databases and networks as DIALOG, LEXIS, and WESTLAW are available to law students for research. Recently, the library installed 49 computer workstations and 70 open network connections. The ratio of library volumes to faculty is 11,809 to 1 and to students is 543 to 1.

Faculty

The law school has 29 full-time faculty members, of whom 6 are women. According to AAUP standards for Category IIA institutions, faculty salaries are well above average. The law school has a regular program of bringing visiting professors and other distinguished lecturers and visitors to campus.

Students

About 47% of the student body are women; 17%, minorities; 5%, African American; 6%, Asian American; 5%, Hispanic; and 1%, Native American. Most students come from California (55%). The average age of entering students is 23; age range is 20 to 55. About 6% of students have a graduate degree. About 5% drop out after the first year for academic or personal reasons.

Placement

J.D.s awarded:	225
Services available through: the school's Career Services Center	
Services: co-sponsor workshops on practice specialties	
Special features: seminars to assist students in preparing resumes and improving job search and interviewing skills, counseling expertise in practice areas and alternative careers.	
Full-time job interviews:	220 employers
Summer job interviews:	n/av
Placement by graduation:	65% of class
Placement within 9 months:	92% of class
Average starting salary:	n/av
Areas of placement:	n/av

QUINNIPIAC UNIVERSITY

School of Law

275 Mt. Carmel Avenue
Hamden, CT 06518-1948

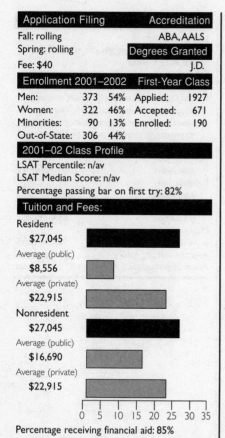

Application Filing		Accreditation
Fall: rolling		ABA, AALS
Spring: rolling		**Degrees Granted**
Fee: $40		J.D.

Enrollment 2001–2002			First-Year Class	
Men:	373	54%	Applied:	1927
Women:	322	46%	Accepted:	671
Minorities:	90	13%	Enrolled:	190
Out-of-State:	306	44%		

2001–02 Class Profile

LSAT Percentile: n/av
LSAT Median Score: n/av
Percentage passing bar on first try: 82%

Tuition and Fees:

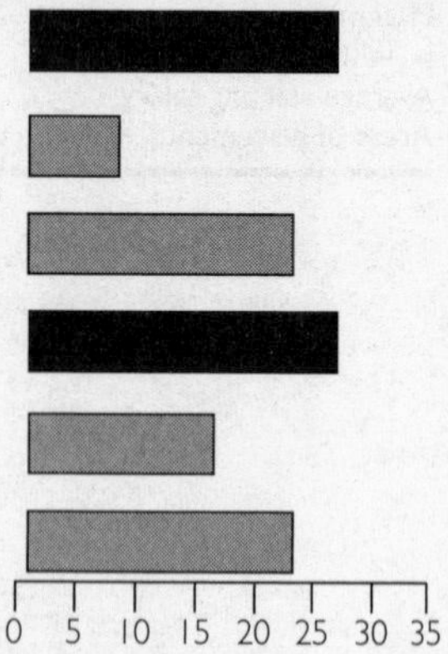

Resident
$27,045
Average (public)
$8,556
Average (private)
$22,915
Nonresident
$27,045
Average (public)
$16,690
Average (private)
$22,915

Percentage receiving financial aid: 85%

ADMISSIONS

In the fall 2001 first-year class, 1927 applied, 671 were accepted, and 190 enrolled. One transfer enrolled. The median GPA of the most recent first-year class was 3.0 on a 4.0 scale.

Requirements

Applicants must have a bachelor's degree and take the LSAT. The most important admission factors include LSAT results, GPA, and academic achievement. No specific undergraduate courses are required. Candidates are interviewed.

Procedure

The application deadline for fall entry is rolling. Applicants should submit an application form, LSAT results, transcripts, a nonrefundable application fee of $40, 2 letters of recommendation, and an admissions essay. Notification of the admissions decision is on a rolling basis so decisions are continuously rendered as files are completed. The latest acceptable LSAT test date for fall entry is June. The law school uses the LSDAS.

Special

The law school recruits minority and disadvantaged students by means of student search, community outreach programs, the CLEO program, minority days on campus, and attendance at various minority programs. Requirements are not different for out-of-state students. Transfer students must have one year of credit, have attended an ABA-approved law school, and a letter of good standing from the dean of the law school from which the student is transferring. A 7-week summer conditional acceptance program is taught by a full professor. Upon successful completion, the student is admitted into the part-time evening program in the fall. The law faculty decides each April if the program is to be offered that summer.

Costs

Tuition and fees for the 2001-2002 academic year are $27,045 for all full-time students. Tuition for part-time students is $17,310 per year. Books and supplies run about $1000 annually.

Financial Aid

About 85% of current law students receive some form of aid. The average annual amount of aid from all sources combined, including scholarships, loans, and work contracts, is $18,617; maximum, $40,535. Awards are based on need and merit. The required financial statement is the FAFSA. The aid application deadline for fall entry is May 1. The deadline for spring is December 1. Special funds for minority or disadvantaged students consist of a diversity scholarship and grant program. First-year students are notified about their financial aid application at the time of acceptance.

About the Law School

Quinnipiac University School of Law was established in 1978 and is a private institution. The 300-acre campus is in a suburban area 90 miles north of New York City. The primary mission of the law school is to provide an education in the nature and the function of law and the skills of legal practice. Students have access to federal, state, county, city, and local agencies, courts, correctional facilities, law firms, and legal aid organizations in the Hamden area. Facilities of special interest to law students include the School of Law Library, Student Activities Center, and Grand Courtroom. Housing for students is available off-campus in the area; the Office of Residential Life and Admissions Office assists students with housing opportunities. All law school facilities are accessible to the physically disabled.

Calendar

The law school operates on a traditional semester basis. Courses for full- and part-time students are offered both day and evening and must be completed within 6 years. New full-time students are admitted in the fall; part-time, fall and spring. There is a 7-week summer session. Transferable summer courses are offered.

Programs

The following joint degrees may be earned: J.D./M.B.A. (Juris Doctor/Master of Business Administration) and J.D./M.H.A. (Juris Doctor/Master of Health Administration).

Phone: 203-582-3400
800-462-1944
Fax: 203-582-3339
E-mail: *ladm@quinnipiac.edu*
Web: *http://www.quinnipiac.edu/academics/law.asp*

Contact

John J. Noonan, Dean of Admissions, 203-582-3400 for general inquiries; Anne Traverso, Director of Financial Aid, 203-582-3405 for financial aid information.

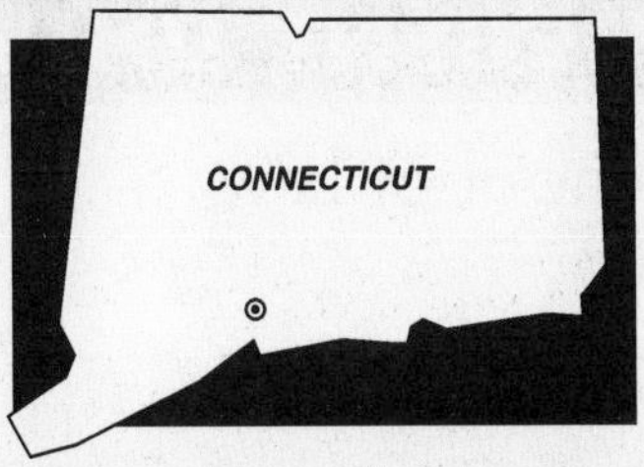

Required

To earn the J.D., candidates must complete 86 total credits, of which 53 are for required courses. They must maintain a minimum GPA of 2.0 in the required courses. The following first-year courses are required of all students: Legal Skills I and II, Criminal Law, Civil Procedure I and II, Contracts I and II, Property, Constitutional Law, and Torts. Required upper-level courses consist of Federal Income Tax, Business Organizations, Evidence, Commercial Law, Trusts and Estates, Administrative Law, and Lawyer's Professional Responsibility. The required orientation program for first-year students is a 2-day general introductory program to the school, the faculty, the administration, and the students. There is also a continuing program in the first semester covering professional responsibility and ethics.

Electives

The School of Law offers concentrations in corporate law, criminal law, environmental law, family law, international law, juvenile law, labor law, litigation, tax law, and health law. In addition, students may participate in a Civil Clinic for 8 credits, a Criminal Justice Clinic for 7 credits, and a Tax Clinic for 8 credits. Seminars are varied. The internship program includes 5 courses, and students receive variable credits for the internship. Areas are public interest, corporate counsel, judicial, legislative, and municipal counsel. Research programs are varied. A summer program in Ireland with Trinity College (Dublin), as well as independent study-abroad programs are available. An academic support program and writing program are available to students at the law school. A bar review class is taught by a law professor. There is a special minority recruitment and information day at the school, with the Thurgood Marshall Awards Dinner in the evening recognizing individual achievement and service to the school. The most widely taken electives are Criminal Procedure, Family Law, and Advanced Constitutional Law.

Graduation Requirements

In order to graduate, candidates must have a GPA of 2.0 and have completed the upper-division writing requirement.

Organizations

Students edit the *Quinnipiac College Law Review*, *Quinnipiac Probate Law Journal*, *Quinnipiac Health Law Journal*, and the student newspaper, *The Quinnipiac Legal Times*. Moot court competitions are the National Appellate Advocacy Competition, Albert Mugel Tax Moot Court Competition, and Dean Jerome Prince Evidence Competition. The Mock Trial Society competes in American Trial Lawyers Competition, Texas Young Lawyers Association Competition, and the American Bar Association Competition. Student organizations include the Student Bar Association, Women's Law Association, and the Black Law Students Association. There are local chapters of Phi Alpha Delta and Phi Delta Phi on campus.

Library

The law library contains 362,618 hard-copy volumes and 196,886 microform volume equivalents, and subscribes to 2487 serial publications. Such on-line databases and networks as CALI, CIS Universe, DIALOG, Infotrac, Legal-Trac, LEXIS, LOIS, NEXIS, OCLC First Search, WESTLAW, and Wilsonline Indexes are available to law students for research. Special library collections include a federal government depository library collection, a tax collection, and a Connecticut collection. The ratio of library volumes to faculty is 10,361 to 1 and to students, 522 to 1. The ratio of seats in the library to students is 1 to 1.

Faculty

The law school has 35 full-time and 32 part-time faculty members, of whom 20 are women. According to AAUP standards for Category IIA institutions, faculty salaries are well above average. About 50% of full-time faculty have a graduate law degree in addition to the J.D. The ratio of full-time students to full-time faculty in an average class is 20 to 1; in a clinic, 8 to 1. The law school has a regular program of bringing visiting professors and other distinguished lecturers and visitors to campus.

Placement

J.D.s awarded: 226

Services available through: a separate law school placement center

Services: counseling on cover letter preparation, mock interviews, educational and informational programs, and membership in law placement consortia.

Special features: staff members with J.D. degrees counsel students and develop employment opportunities for students and graduates.

Full-time job interviews:	n/av
Summer job interviews:	n/av
Placement by graduation:	n/av
Placement within 9 months:	95% of class
Average starting salary:	$38,000 to $62,500
Areas of placement:	
Private practice 2-10 attorneys	45%
Private practice 11-25 attorneys	8%
Private practice 26-50 attorneys	4%
Private practice 51-100 attorneys	4%
Business/industry	13%
Judicial clerkships	11%
Unknown	6%
Government	5%
Academic	3%
Public interest	1%

Students

About 46% of the student body are women; 13%, minorities; 6%, African American; 1%, Asian American; and 5%, Hispanic. Most students come from Connecticut (56%). The average age of entering students is 27; age range is 20 to 71. About 22% of students enter directly from undergraduate school and 9% have a graduate degree. About 4% drop out after the first year for academic or personal reasons; 96% remain to receive a law degree.

REGENT UNIVERSITY

School of Law

1000 Regent University Drive
Virginia Beach, VA 23464-9800

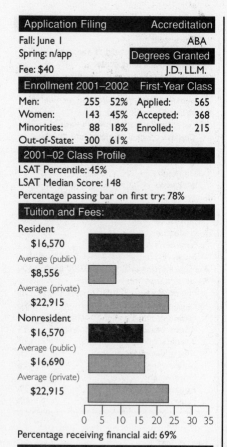

Application Filing		Accreditation
Fall: June 1		ABA
Spring: n/app		**Degrees Granted**
Fee: $40		J.D., LL.M.

Enrollment 2001–2002			First-Year Class	
Men:	255	52%	Applied:	565
Women:	143	45%	Accepted:	368
Minorities:	88	18%	Enrolled:	215
Out-of-State:	300	61%		

2001–02 Class Profile

LSAT Percentile: 45%
LSAT Median Score: 148
Percentage passing bar on first try: 78%

Tuition and Fees:

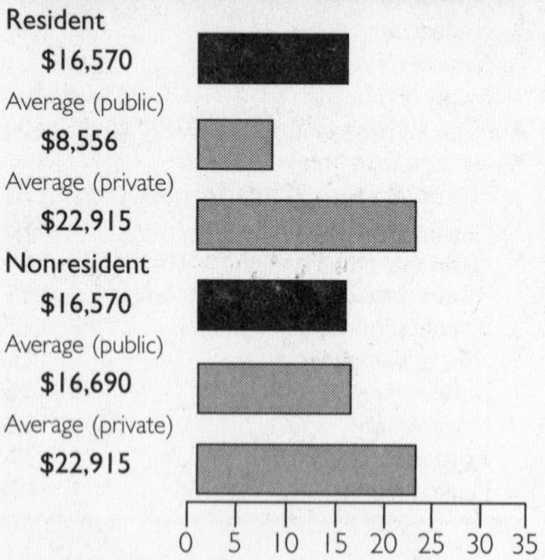

Percentage receiving financial aid: 69%

ADMISSIONS

Information in the above capsule is from an earlier year. In a recent year first-year class, 565 applied, 368 were accepted, and 215 enrolled. Thirteen transfers enrolled. The median LSAT percentile of a recent first-year class was 45; the median GPA was 3.1 on a scale of 4.0. The lowest LSAT percentile accepted was 18; the highest was 97.

Requirements

Applicants must have a bachelor's degree and take the LSAT. Minimum acceptable GPA is 2.0 on a scale of 4.0. The most important admission factors include academic achievement, character, personality, and general background. No specific undergraduate courses are required. Candidates are not interviewed.

Procedure

The application deadline for fall entry is June 1. Applicants should submit an application form, LSAT results, transcripts, a nonrefundable application fee of $40, and 3 letters of recommendation. Check with the school for current application deadlines and fee. Notification of the admissions decision is on a rolling basis. The latest acceptable LSAT test date for fall entry is June. The law school uses the LSDAS.

Special

The law school recruits minority and disadvantaged students through recruitment travel, referrals, CRS mailings, and special scholarships. Requirements are not different for out-of-state students. Transfer students must have one year of credit, have a minimum GPA of 2.0, and have attended an ABA-approved law school.

Costs

Tuition and fees for the a recent academic year were $16,570 for all full-time students. On-campus room and board costs about $6150 annually; books and supplies run about $1000.

Financial Aid

About 69% of current law students receive some form of aid. In a recent year, the average annual amount of aid from all sources combined, including scholarships, loans, and work contracts, was $3250; maximum, $15,345. Awards are based on need and merit, along with leadership and public interest awards. Required financial statement is the FAFSA. Check with the school for current application deadline. Special funds for minority or disadvantaged students include 2 scholarship categories for individuals called to serve the minority community. First-year students are notified about their financial aid application at time of acceptance.

About the Law School

Regent University School of Law was established in 1986 and is a private institution. The 80-acre campus is in a suburban area 7 miles southeast of Norfolk, Virginia. The primary mission of the law school is to train lawyers to participate effectively and professionally in the private and public sectors of this nation while affirming their understanding of the relationship between Christian principles and the practice of law. Students have access to federal, state, county, city, and local agencies, courts, correctional facilities, law firms, and legal aid organizations in the Virginia Beach area. Facilities of special interest to law students include a 134,000-square foot law center equipped with the latest technology in audiovisual equipment, such as cameras for simultaneous broadcasting. There is also a 350-seat moot court/city council chamber. Housing for students consists of university-owned and operated two- and three-bedroom apartments (224 units). All law school facilities are accessible to the physically disabled.

Calendar

The law school operates on a traditional semester basis. Courses for full-time students are offered both day and evening and must be completed within 5 years. For part-time students, courses are offered evenings only and some Saturdays. New full- and part-time students are admitted in the fall. There is a 9-week summer session. Transferable summer courses are not offered.

Programs

In addition to the J.D., the law school offers the LL.M. and M.I.T. (Master of International Taxation). Students may take relevant courses in other programs and apply credit toward the J.D.; a maximum of 6 credits may be applied. The following joint degrees may be earned: J.D./M.A. (Juris Doctor/Master of Arts in government, management, and communications) and J.D./M.B.A. (Juris Doctor/Master of Business Administration).

Phone: 757-226-4584
Fax: 757-226-4139
E-mail: *lawschool@regent.edu*
Web: *www.regent.edu/law/admissions*

Contact

Charles W. Roboski, Director of Law Admissions, 757-226-4584 for general inquiries; Bonnie Creef, 757-226-4584 for financial aid information.

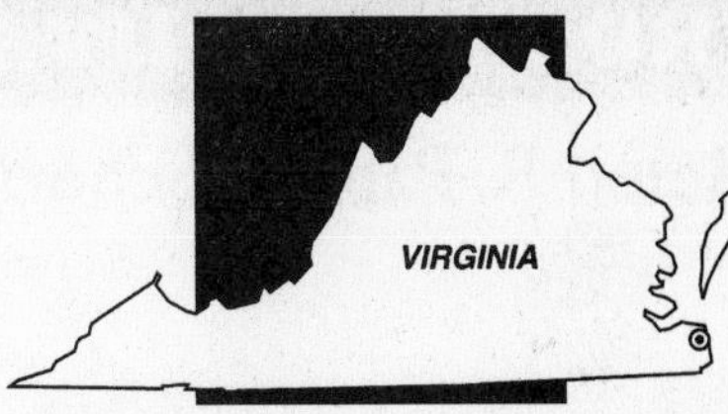

Required

To earn the J.D., candidates must complete 90 total credits, of which 66 are for required courses. They must maintain a minimum GPA of 2.0 in the required courses. The following first-year courses are required of all students: Common Law, Contracts I and II, Criminal Law, Torts I and II, Civil Procedure I and II, Legal Research and Writing I and II, and Property I and II. Required upper-level courses consist of Constitutional Law, Evidence, Individual Federal Income Taxation, and Law and Professional Responsibility. The optional orientation program for first-year students is a 2-day program including a legal study skills workshop covering preparation for class, case briefing, outlining, and study skills. There is also an orientation for electronic legal education using a laptop computer.

Electives

The School of Law offers concentrations in family law and litigation. Seminars include Human Life and Death, Crime and Punishment, Inalienable Rights, Environmental Law, Charitable Trusts, Constitutional Litigation, Jurisprudence, Legal History, and Advanced Family Law. Internships are available as research assistants or law clerks for a public interest law firm. Research programs include Advanced Legal Research, a special project, and Independent Studies, which may be undertaken for 1 to 3 hours of credit each. Practical experience may also be gained through externships (up to a maximum of 4 hours of credit) in an approved study program with a practicing attorney or judicial officer, or with a federal/state prosecutor or defender. Study abroad includes a summer session in Strasbourg, France that emphasizes international human rights and jurisprudence. A mandatory summer assistance program is offered to select admits. Part of the program is for credit and part is not. The most widely taken electives are Remedies, Bankruptcy, and Drafting of Contracts.

Graduation Requirements

In order to graduate, candidates must have a GPA of 2.0 and have completed the upper-division writing requirement.

Organizations

Students edit the *Regent University Law Review* and the student newspaper *Class Action*. Moot court competitions for students include the Jessup International, sponsored by the Grotius International Law Society; National Juvenile Law Competition, and Spong Cup Moot Court. Other competitions include the ABA Negotiation, sponsored by the ABA-Law Student Division, and the Robert Merhige, Jr. National Environmental Law, sponsored by the University of Richmond. Student organizations include the Student Bar Association, Moot Court Board, and Alternative Dispute and Client Counseling Board. There are local chapters of the Christian Legal Society, Federalist Society, and The American Inns of Court. Other organizations include Regent Students for Life, Catholic Law Student Organization, and Sports and Entertainment Law Society.

Library

The law library contains 316,000 hard-copy volumes and 900,000 microform volume equivalents, and subscribes to 920 serial publications. Such on-line databases and networks as DIALOG, LEXIS, WESTLAW, Legal-Trac, NEXIS, and First-Search are available to law students for research. Special library collections include an essentially complete set of CIS microfiche, and the Transylvania Collection from former Transylvania University Law School (Kentucky) with materials dating from the 1700s. Recently, the library was remodeled and expanded to about 35,000 feet. The ratio of library volumes to faculty is 12,153 to 1 and to students is 638 to 1. The ratio of seats in the library to students is 1 to 2.

Faculty

The law school has approximately 22 full-time and 37 part-time faculty members, of whom 9 are women. About 23% of full-time faculty have a graduate law degree in addition to the J.D.; about 16% of part-time faculty have one. The ratio of full-time students to full-time faculty in an average class is 17 to 1.

Placement	
J.D.s awarded:	130
Services available through: a separate law school placement center	
Special features: extensive career planning and professional development seminars, participation in career planning programs, panel discussions and mock interviews, as well as one-to-one counseling of law students with the director. Examples of fall programs include topics such as Interview Skills Workshop, Resume Preparation, Focusing on a Litigation Career, Solo Practice, and What Being a Lawyer is Really Like.	
Full-time job interviews:	14 employers
Summer job interviews:	n/av
Placement by graduation:	n/av
Placement within 9 months:	79% of class
Average starting salary:	n/av
Areas of placement:	
Private practice 2-10 attorneys	44%
Private practice 11-25 attorneys	6%
Private practice 26-50 attorneys	2%
Business/industry	14%
Government	10%
Academic	8%
Public interest	6%
Unknown	6%
Military	3%
Judicial clerkships	1%

Students

About 45% of the student body are women; 18%, minorities; 4%, African American; 1%, Asian American; 2%, Hispanic; and 2%, foreign national. Most students come from Virginia (39%). The average age of entering students is 27; age range is 50 to 20. About 28% of students enter directly from undergraduate school, 6% have a graduate degree, and 72% have worked full-time prior to entering law school. About 7% drop out after the first year for academic or personal reasons; 91% remain to receive a law degree.

ROGER WILLIAMS UNIVERSITY

Ralph R. Papitto School of Law

Ten Metacom Avenue
Bristol, RI 02809-5171

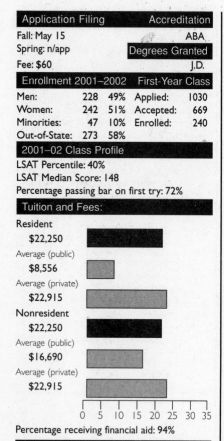

Application Filing	Accreditation
Fall: May 15	ABA
Spring: n/app	**Degrees Granted**
Fee: $60	J.D.

Enrollment 2001–2002			First-Year Class	
Men:	228	49%	Applied:	1030
Women:	242	51%	Accepted:	669
Minorities:	47	10%	Enrolled:	240
Out-of-State:	273	58%		

2001–02 Class Profile

LSAT Percentile: 40%

LSAT Median Score: 148

Percentage passing bar on first try: 72%

Tuition and Fees:

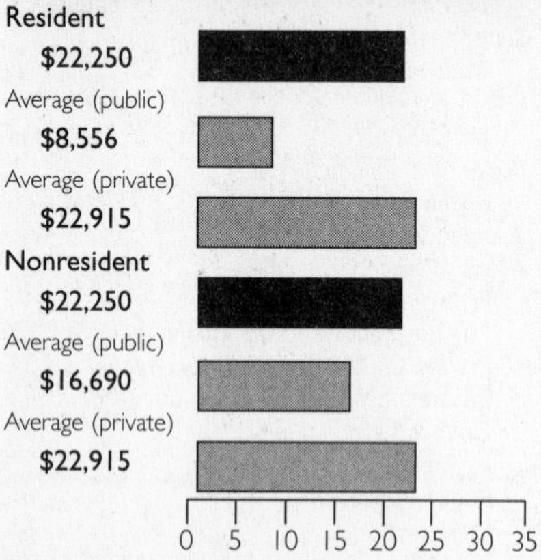

Percentage receiving financial aid: 94%

ADMISSIONS

In the fall 2001 first-year class, 1030 applied, 669 were accepted, and 240 enrolled. Ten transfers enrolled. The median LSAT percentile of the most recent first-year class was 40; the median GPA was 3.04 on a scale of 4.0.

Requirements

Applicants must have a bachelor's degree and take the LSAT. Minimum acceptable GPA is 2.0 on a scale of 4.0. The most important admission factors include LSAT results, GPA, and academic achievement. No specific undergraduate courses are required. Candidates are not interviewed.

Procedure

The application deadline for fall entry is May 15. Applicants should submit an application form, LSAT results, transcripts, TOEFL for students who are citizens of a foreign country and whose native language is not English, a nonrefundable application fee of $60 (recommended, not required) letters of recommendation, and a personal statement. Notification of the admissions decision is on a rolling basis. The latest acceptable LSAT test date for fall entry is June. The law school uses the LSDAS.

Special

The law school recruits minority and disadvantaged students by visiting historically black and Hispanic colleges and universities. Requirements are not different for out-of-state students. Transfer students must have a minimum GPA of 2.0, have attended an ABA-approved law school, and a letter of good standing from their prior law school.

Costs

Tuition and fees for the 2001-2002 academic year are $22,250 for all full-time students. Tuition for part-time students is $17,070 per year. Books and supplies run about $1000 annually.

Financial Aid

About 94% of current law students receive some form of aid. The average annual amount of aid from all sources combined, including scholarships, loans, and work contracts, is $29,270; maximum, $36,720. Awards are based on need and merit. The required financial statement is the FAFSA. The aid application deadline for fall entry is March 15. First-year students are notified about their financial aid application once they are accepted and the necessary financial aid paperwork has been completed.

About the Law School

Roger Williams University Ralph R. Papitto School of Law was established in 1992 and is a private institution. The 140-acre campus is in a small town on a peninsula in the historic seacoast town of Bristol. The primary mission of the law school is to prepare students for the competent and ethical practice of law. Students have access to federal, state, county, city, and local agencies, courts, correctional facilities, law firms, and legal aid organizations in the Bristol area. There are also state library archives and libraries at Brown University, University of Rhode Island, Providence College, and at the Rhode Island Historical Society. Facilities of special interest to law students include the Criminal Defense and Disability Law clinics located in Providence. Housing for students is available in 1-bedroom apartments and townhouses 2 miles from campus. Nearby Bristol and Warren have numerous apartments available in private homes and apartment complexes. All law school facilities are accessible to the physically disabled.

Calendar

The law school operates on a traditional semester basis. Courses for full-time students are offered both day and evening and must be completed within 3 years. Day students are required to take at least 12 day credits. For part-time students, courses are offered both day and evening and must be completed within 4 years. Extended division students are required to take at least 6 evening credits. New full- and part-time students are admitted in the fall. There is a 7-week summer session. Transferable summer courses are offered.

Programs

The following joint degrees may be earned: J.D./M.C.P. (Juris Doctor/Master of Community Planning), J.D./M.M.A. (Juris Doctor/Master of Marine Affairs), and J.D./M.S. (Juris Doctor/Master of Science in Labor Relations and Human Resources).

Phone: 401-254-4555
633-2727
Fax: 401-254-4516
E-mail: *admissions@law.rwu.edu*
Web: *http:\\law.rwu.edu*

Contact

Christel L. Ertez, Dean of Admissions, 401-254-4555 for general inquiries; Amanda Cicciarella, Assistant Director, Financial Aid, 401-254-4510 for financial aid information.

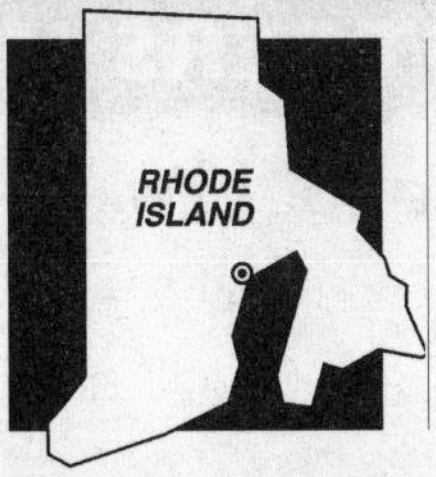

Required

To earn the J.D., candidates must complete 90 total credits, of which 48 are for required courses. They must maintain a minimum GPA of 2.0 in the required courses. The following first-year courses are required of all students: Torts I and II, Property I and II, Contracts I and II, Civil Procedure I and II, Legal Methods I and II, and Criminal Procedure. Required upper-level courses consist of Criminal Law, Upper Level Legal Methods, Constitutional Law I and II, Professional Responsibility, and Evidence. The required orientation program for first-year students is held 3 1/2 days prior to the first day of classes, includes an introduction to the judicial system and the study of law, case briefing, exam-taking techniques, professionalism, meetings with academic advisers, student services introduction, and social events.

Electives

In addition, third-year students participate in the Criminal Defense Clinic or the Disability Law Clinic for 6 credits. Seminars, available to second- and third-year students, include Domestic Violence, Marine Pollution, Ocean and Coastal Law, and Judicial Process. They are worth 2 credits each. Internships for third-year students consist of judicial clerkships worth 3 credits and public interest clerkships with such placements as the Rhode Island Attorney General's Office, Public Defenders Office, and Legal Services. There is faculty-supervised directed research for 1 or 2 credits. Students are required to perform 20 hours of public service before graduation. A special lecture series includes topics on Maritime, Public Interest, and Intellectual Property Law. Study abroad is available through the London Summer Program and the Lisbon, Summer Program. There are workshops on studying, briefing, course outlining, and exam taking. Minority programs include a mentor program sponsored by the Multicultural Law Students Association that matches students of color with Rhode Island attorneys. The most widely taken electives are Wills and Trusts, Family Law, and First Amendment.

Graduation Requirements

In order to graduate, candidates must have a GPA of 2.0 and have completed the upper-division writing requirement.

Organizations

Students edit the *Roger Williams University Law Review* and the newspaper *The Docket*. Moot court competitions include the Roger Williams University School of Law Moot Court, the National Moot Court Competition, and the John R. Brown Admiralty Moot Court Competition. Law student organizations include the Marine Affairs Society, Student Bar Association, and Environmental Law Society. Local chapters of national organizations include the American Trial Lawyers Association, ABA, and National Association of Public Interest Lawyers. Other campus organizations include the Multicultural Law Students Association, Women's Law Caucus, and Justinian Law Society.

Library

The law library contains 261,666 hard-copy volumes and 940,773 microform volume equivalents, and subscribes to 3385 serial publications. Such on-line databases and networks as CALI, CIS Universe, Legal-Trac, LEXIS, LOIS, NEXIS, OCLC First Search, RLIN, WESTLAW, Wilsonline Indexes, BNA, IndexMaster, HeinOnline, AccessUN, and LawTel are available to law students for research. Special library collections include Rhode Island law, the State Justice Institute depository, Maritime Law, and Portuguese-American Comparative Law. Recently, the library upgraded computers in 2 training laboratories and created space for the Portuguese-American Comparative Law Center collection. The ratio of library volumes to faculty is 10,467 to 1 and to students, 557 to 1. The ratio of seats in the library to students is 1 to 1.

Placement

J.D.s awarded:	118
Services available through: a separate law school placement center	
Special features: Rhode Island State Government Internship Program, extensive one-on-one counseling sessions, symposiums, and coordinated programs with the Rhode Island Bar Association, and a student research pool for project-based assignments with local attorneys	
Full-time job interviews:	7 employers
Summer job interviews:	7 employers
Placement by graduation:	n/av
Placement within 9 months:	82% of class
Average starting salary:	$25,000 to $105,000
Areas of placement:	
Private practice 2-10 attorneys	27%
Private practice 11-25 attorneys	3%
Private practice 26-50 attorneys	2%
Private practice 51-100 attorneys	2%
Unknown	19%
Business/industry	15%
Judicial clerkships	13%
Government	10%
Public interest	3%
Academic	2%

Faculty

The law school has 25 full-time and 22 part-time faculty members, of whom 16 are women. About 33% of full-time faculty have a graduate law degree in addition to the J.D.; about 8% of part-time faculty have one. The ratio of full-time students to full-time faculty in an average class is 14 to 1; in a clinic, 10 to 1. The law school has a regular program of bringing visiting professors and other distinguished lecturers and visitors to campus.

Students

About 51% of the student body are women; 10%, minorities; 5%, African American; 3%, Asian American; and 2%, Hispanic. Most students come from Rhode Island (42%). The average age of entering students is 27; age range is 20 to 55.

RUTGERS UNIVERSITY/CAMDEN

School of Law

Fifth and Penn Streets
Camden, NJ 08102

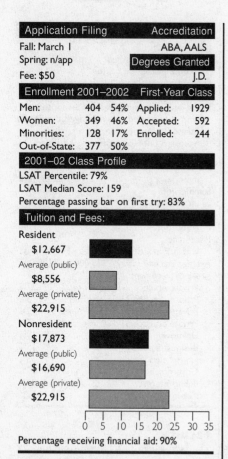

Application Filing		Accreditation
Fall: March 1		ABA, AALS
Spring: n/app		**Degrees Granted**
Fee: $50		J.D.

Enrollment 2001–2002			First-Year Class	
Men:	404	54%	Applied:	1929
Women:	349	46%	Accepted:	592
Minorities:	128	17%	Enrolled:	244
Out-of-State:	377	50%		

2001–02 Class Profile

LSAT Percentile: 79%
LSAT Median Score: 159
Percentage passing bar on first try: 83%

Tuition and Fees:

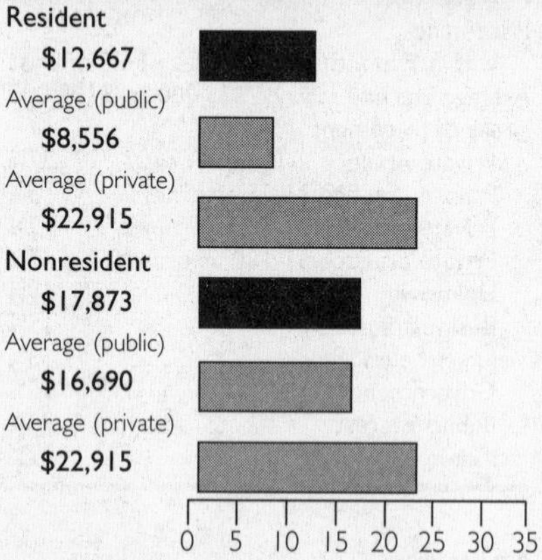

Percentage receiving financial aid: 90%

ADMISSIONS

In the fall 2001 first-year class, 1929 applied, 592 were accepted, and 244 enrolled. Seventy-five transfers enrolled. The median LSAT percentile of the most recent first-year class was 79; the median GPA was 3.2 on a scale of 4.0. The highest LSAT percentile was 98.

Requirements

Applicants must have a bachelor's degree and take the LSAT. The most important admission factors include LSAT results, GPA, and general background. No specific undergraduate courses are required. Candidates are not interviewed.

Procedure

The application deadline for fall entry is March 1, but rolling. Applicants should submit an application form, LSAT results, transcripts, a nonrefundable application fee of $50, and 2 letters of recommendation. Notification of the admissions decision is on a rolling basis. The latest acceptable LSAT test date for fall entry is June. The law school uses the LSDAS.

Special

The law school recruits minority and disadvantaged students by means of mail, student organizations, interviews, campus visits, and law forums. Requirements are not different for out-of-state students. Transfer students must have one year of credit and have attended an ABA-approved law school.

Costs

Tuition and fees for the 2001-2002 academic year are $12,667 for full-time in-state students and $17,873 for out-of-state students. On-campus room and board costs about $4796 annually; books and supplies run $1000.

Financial Aid

About 90% of current law students receive some form of aid. The average annual amount of aid from all sources combined, including scholarships, loans, and work contracts, is $19,000. Awards are based on need and merit. The required financial statements are the FAFSA. The aid application deadline for fall entry is March 1. The aid deadline for spring is January 1. Special funds for minority or disadvantaged students consist of funds that are available from state, university, and school programs. First-year students are notified about their financial aid application at the time of acceptance.

About the Law School

Rutgers University/Camden School of Law was established in 1926 and is a public institution. The 25-acre campus is in an urban area adjacent to Center City district of Philadelphia. The primary mission of the law school is to provide a dynamic program of professional training, distinguished legal scholarship, and service to the bar and community. Students have access to federal, state, county, city, and local agencies, courts, correctional facilities, law firms, and legal aid organizations in the Camden area. Facilities of special interest to law students include computer laboratories, e-mail accounts, Internet connections, and on-line legal research. Housing for students is available in a 6-story apartment complex that houses 248 students in 62 graduate apartments. About 90% of the law school facilities are accessible to the physically disabled.

Calendar

The law school operates on a traditional semester basis. Courses for full- and part-time students are offered both day and evening and must be completed within 5 years. New full- and part-time students are admitted in the fall. There is a 7-week summer session. Transferable summer courses are offered.

Programs

Students may take relevant courses in other programs and apply credit toward the J.D.; a maximum of 6 credits may be applied. The following joint degrees may be earned: J.D./D.O. (Juris Doctor/Doctor of Osteopathic Medicine), J.D./M.B.A. (Juris Doctor/Master of Business Administration), J.D./M.C.R.P. (Juris Doctor/Master of City and Regional Planning), J.D./M.D. (Juris Doctor/Doctor of Medicine), J.D./M.P.A. (Juris Doctor/Master of Public Administration), J.D./M.P.A.P. (Juris Doctor/Master of Public Affairs and Politics), and J.D./M.S.W. (Juris Doctor/Master of Social Work).

Required

To earn the J.D., candidates must complete 84 total credits, of which 34 are for required courses. They must maintain a minimum GPA of 2.0 in the required courses. The following first-year courses are required of all students: Civil Procedure, Contracts, Torts, Legal Research and Writing, Constitutional Law, Criminal Law, Property, and Moot Court I. Required upper-level courses consist of Professional Responsibility, elective courses with writing components, and Introduction to Federal Income Taxation. The required orientation program for first-year students is 2 days prior to the start of classes; there is a briefing on reading and analyzing cases, library usage, legal writing, professional responsibility, and general study techniques, as well as an introduction to computer usage and student organizations and social events.

Phone: 856-225-6102
800-466-7561
Fax: 856-225-6537

Contact

Maureen B. O'Boyle, Associate Director of Admissions, 856-225-6102 for general inquiries; Richard Woodland, Financial Aid Director, 856-225-6039 for financial aid information.

Electives

The School of Law offers concentrations in corporate law, criminal law, environmental law, family law, international law, labor law, litigation, tax law, health law, and public interest law. In addition, clinics include a Small Business Counseling Clinic and a Gender-Equity in Education Clinic, each worth 3 credits, and a Civil Practice Clinic. The Pro Bono/Public Interest program enables students to represent clients, under the supervision of attorneys, in domestic violence, immigration, and bankruptcy cases, and to conduct mediations in local courts. All students take at least 1 course each semester with a significant writing component to complete the advanced writing requirement. The school conducts an extensive externship program, worth 6 credits, for third-year students in good academic standing with members of the judiciary and various public agencies. Third-year students may take independent study for 1 to 2 credits in each of their last 2 semesters, under the supervision of a faculty member. The annual state Constitution Law Lecture and Corman Distinguished Lecture bring nationally known scholars and jurists to the law school. Students can also attend other law schools' study-abroad programs. No-credit tutorial programs are offered on an individual basis for students in need. Workshops on study techniques, test taking, and individual subject review are available for all students. An extensive Academic Success Program is also available. Programming for minority students is sponsored by student groups and supported by the administration and faculty. The most widely taken electives are Evidence, Commercial Law, and Business Organizations.

Graduation Requirements

In order to graduate, candidates must have a GPA of 2.0 and have completed the upper-division writing requirement.

Organizations

Students edit the *Rutgers Law Journal* and the *Rutgers Journal of Law and Religion*. A highlight of the upper-level curriculum is the Judge James A. Hunter III Advanced Moot Court Program. Other moot court competitions include the National Moot Court Competition and Jessup International Moot Court Competition. Other competitions include the Gibbons National Criminal Procedure Moot Court Competition, Admiralty Moot Court Competition, National Black Law Students Association Frederick Douglass Competition, National Latino Law Students Association Moot Court Competition, and the Environmental Moot Court Competition. Law student organizations include the Student Bar Association, Association for Public Interest Law, and the Francis Deak International Law Society. There are local chapters and clubs of all major national law student organizations, including Phi Alpha Delta law fraternity, Women's Law Caucus, Black Law Students Association, Hispanic Students Association, Student Bar Association, Latino Law Students Association, and Asian/Pacific American Student Association.

Library

The law library contains 419,058 hard-copy volumes and 120,658 microform volume equivalents, and subscribes to 1886 serial publications. Such on-line databases and networks as LEXIS, NEXIS, and WESTLAW are available to law students for research. Special library collections include a historical collection of Soviet and Eastern European legal matters and a U.S. government depository library. Recently, the library added a computer room and court web sites (the only access in New Jersey for New Jersey administrative court cases). The ratio of library volumes to faculty is 8217 to 1 and to students, 557 to 1. The ratio of seats in the library to students is 1 to 2.

Faculty

The law school has 51 full-time and 70 part-time faculty members, of whom 37 are women. According to AAUP standards for Category IIA institutions, faculty salaries are well above average. About 43% of full-time faculty have a graduate law degree in addition to the J.D.; about 28% of part-time faculty have one. The ratio of full-time students to full-time faculty in an average class is 15 to 1; in a clinic, 8 to 1. The law school has a regular program of bringing visiting professors and other distinguished lecturers and visitors to campus.

Placement

J.D.s awarded: 273

Services available through: a separate law school placement center and Law School Placement Center and University Career Services Center for joint degree candidates

Services: assistance with LEXIS, WESTLAW, and the Internet career searches; fall and spring on-campus interview programs

Special features: interview workshops, on-campus interview programs, career forums, resource library, and participation in a consortium with the law schools of the University of Pennsylvania, Temple, and Villanova; full service Career Services Office with 3 full-time professional career services staff members in addition to 1 full-time pro bono coordinator and public interest adviser; videotaped mock interviews, individualized and small group career workshops, career panels, and several alumni and attorney mentoring programs.

Full-time job interviews:	150 employers
Summer job interviews:	150 employers
Placement by graduation:	75% of class
Placement within 9 months:	98% of class
Average starting salary:	$45,000 to $110,000
Areas of placement:	
Private practice 2-10 attorneys	4%
Private practice 11-25 attorneys	5%
Private practice 26-50 attorneys	5%
Private practice 51-100 attorneys	5%
Private practice firm size unknown	6%
Judicial clerkships	54%
Government	8%
Business/industry	8%
Military	3%
Public interest	1%
Academic	1%

Students

About 46% of the student body are women; 17%, minorities; 6%, African American; 5%, Asian American; 5%, Hispanic; 1%, Native American; and 1%, foreign. Most students come from New Jersey (50%). The average age of entering students is 26; age range is 20 to 55. About 42% of students enter directly from undergraduate school, 8% have a graduate degree, and 56% have worked full-time prior to entering law school. About 3% drop out after the first year for academic or personal reasons; 96% remain to receive a law degree.

RUTGERS UNIVERSITY/NEWARK

School of Law

Center for Law and Justice,
123 Washington St.
Newark, NJ 07102

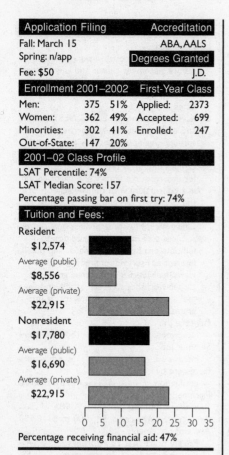

Application Filing		Accreditation
Fall: March 15		ABA, AALS
Spring: n/app		**Degrees Granted**
Fee: $50		J.D.

Enrollment 2001–2002			First-Year Class	
Men:	375	51%	Applied:	2373
Women:	362	49%	Accepted:	699
Minorities:	302	41%	Enrolled:	247
Out-of-State:	147	20%		

2001–02 Class Profile

LSAT Percentile: 74%
LSAT Median Score: 157
Percentage passing bar on first try: 74%

Tuition and Fees:

Resident
$12,574
Average (public)
$8,556
Average (private)
$22,915
Nonresident
$17,780
Average (public)
$16,690
Average (private)
$22,915

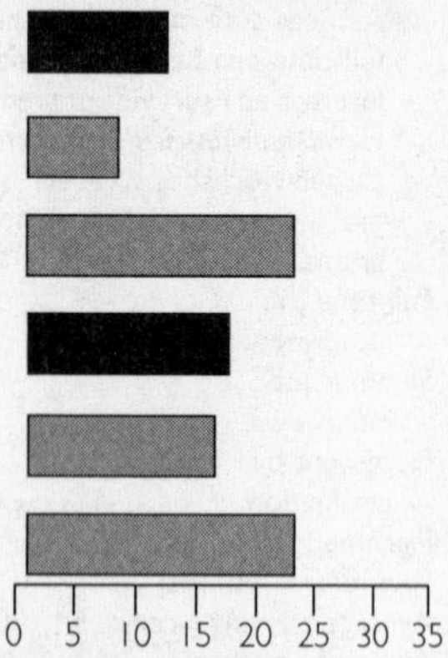

Percentage receiving financial aid: 47%

ADMISSIONS

In the fall 2001 first-year class, 2373 applied, 699 were accepted, and 247 enrolled. Twenty-three transfers enrolled. The median LSAT percentile of the most recent first-year class was 74; the median GPA was 3.3 on a scale of 4.0. The highest LSAT percentile was 99.

Requirements

Applicants must have a bachelor's degree and take the LSAT. However, applicants may be considered with three-quarters of their undergraduate work completed. The most important admission factors include academic achievement, LSAT results, and GPA. No specific undergraduate courses are required. Candidates are not interviewed.

Procedure

The application deadline for fall entry is March 15. Applicants should submit an application form, LSAT results, transcripts, a nonrefundable application fee of $50, and 1 letter of recommendation. LSAT results and transcripts are sent through the LSDAS. Notification of the admissions decision is on a rolling basis. The latest acceptable LSAT test date for fall entry is February. The law school uses the LSDAS.

Special

The law school recruits minority and disadvantaged students through participation in LSAC forums, participation in Puerto Rican Legal Defense Fund Law Day, visits to historically black colleges, black, Latino, and Asian law days, and contact with high school and college students. The Minority Student Program is open to disadvantaged students of all races. Requirements are not different for out-of-state students. Transfer students must have one year of credit, have a minimum GPA of 3, have attended an ABA-approved law school, and have a letter of good standing.

Costs

Tuition and fees for the 2001-2002 academic year are $12,574 for full-time in-state students and $17,780 for out-of-state students. On-campus room and board costs about $9000 annually; books and supplies run $1500.

Financial Aid

About 47% of current law students receive some form of aid. The average annual amount of aid from all sources combined, including scholarships, loans, and work contracts, is $15,000; maximum, $22,000. Awards are based on need and merit, although most financial aid and scholarships are awarded on the basis of need. Limited merit scholarships and a number of need and merit (combined) scholarships are also available. Required financial statement is the FAFSA. The aid application deadline for fall entry is March 1. Special funds for minority or disadvantaged students consist of the Ralph Bunche Fellowships, which yield tuition remission and a stipend; the C. Clyde Ferguson Scholarships, which yield full in-state tuition and housing for New Jersey residents; Marie Slocum Scholarship; Judge Herbert Tate, Sr. Scholarship; Judge John Dios Scholarship; and other scholarships. First-year students are notified about their financial aid application several weeks after an offer of admission.

About the Law School

Rutgers University/Newark School of Law was established in 1908 and is a public institution. The 11-acre campus is in an urban area in the city of Newark, 8 miles southwest of New York City. The primary mission of the law school is to prepare students for professional practice by offering high-quality education in all fields of law, as well as to preserve and expand knowledge as part of a national community of legal scholars, and to serve the public by working to achieve social justice through law. Students have access to federal, state, county, city, and local agencies, courts, correctional facilities, law firms, and legal aid organizations in the Newark area. Also nearby are the American Civil Liberties Union and public interest organizations. Facilities of special interest to law students are the federal courts and county and state court complexes, which are located in downtown Newark, the Newark Museum and Public Library, and the New Jersey Performing Arts Center, which is located just a few blocks away. The Center For Law and Justice is a technologically advanced building. Housing for students is available on campus—a third of students live on campus. Most students live in nearby communities, however. All law school facilities are accessible to the physically disabled.

Calendar

The law school operates on a traditional semester basis. Courses for full-time students are offered both day and evening and must be completed within 3½ years. For part-time students, courses are offered both day and evening and must be completed within 4½ years. New full- and part-time students are admitted in the fall. There is a 7-week summer session. Transferable summer courses are offered.

Programs

Students may take relevant courses in other programs and apply credit toward the J.D.; a maximum of 12 credits may be applied. The following joint degrees may be earned: J.D./M.A. (Juris Doctor/Master of Arts in criminal justice, political science), J.D./M.B.A. (Juris Doctor/Master of Business Administration), J.D./M.C.R.P. (Juris Doctor/Master in City and Regional Planning), and J.D./M.S.W. (Juris Doctor/Master of Social Work).

Phone: 973-353-5557/5554
Fax: 973-353-3459
E-mail: *awalton@andromeda.rutgers.edu*
Web: *www.rutgers-newark.rutgers.edu/law*

Contact

Anita Walton, Director of Admissions, 973-353-5557/5554 for general inquiries; Nicky Fornarotto, Coordinator for Financial Aid, 973-353-1702 for financial aid information.

Required

To earn the J.D., candidates must complete 84 total credits, of which 31 to 32 are for required courses. They must maintain a minimum GPA of 1.67 in the required courses. The following first-year courses are required of all students: Contracts, Torts, Property, Criminal Law, Constitutional Law, Civil Procedure, Legal Research and Writing I and II, and a required freshman elective. Required upper-level courses consist of Professional Responsibility and an upper-level writing requirement. The required orientation program for first-year students is 2 days and covers registration, student services, health and safety issues, an Introduction to Legal Research course, and provides opportunities to meet upper-class students and all student organization representatives.

Electives

The School of Law offers concentrations in corporate law, criminal law, entertainment law, environmental law, family law, international law, juvenile law, labor law, litigation, media law, securities law, sports law, tax law, torts and insurance, and constitutional law, health law, and intellectual property. In addition, students can earn up to 8 credits per semester for clinics. Clinics are open only to upper-level students, and some require students to be in their final year. Clinics are Constitutional Rights, Women's Rights, Environmental Law, Urban Legal, Special Education, Women and Aids, Domestic Violence, Child Advocacy Project, and Federal Tax Law. Some 20 seminars are offered each semester. They are open to all upper-level students and offer the opportunity to write a substantial legal paper that meets the writing requirement. Each seminar carries 2 credits. Students may engage in internships with state or federal magistrates, justices, judges, the attorney general's office, or the National Labor Relations Board. These carry 3 credits and are open to all upper-level students with grades of B- or better and are supported by a weekly in-house seminar. Students may assist full-time faculty members in their research for 2 or 3 credits. Independent research may be undertaken by upper-level students for 2 or 3 credits with faculty permission. Special lecture series include Pfizer, Stoffer, and Weintraub lectureships, which are given annually. Students may enroll for up to 12 credits in an ABA/AALS sponsored semester-abroad program. Approximately 25 students engage in this study, from China to Greece and at the University of Leiden-Holland. First-year students are tutored by upper-level students with good grades; tutors may earn 2 credits. The Minority Student Program is dependent on socio-economic status, regardless of race. The school also has programs on behalf of women, minority groups, and gay and lesbian groups. The most widely taken electives are Evidence, Commercial Law I and II, Business Associations, and Copyright.

Graduation Requirements

In order to graduate, candidates must have a GPA of 2.0 and have completed the upper-division writing requirement.

Organizations

Students edit the *The Rutgers Law Review, Computer and Technology Law Journal, Women's Rights Law Reporter, Race and the Law Review*, and *The Rutgers Law Record*. Students compete in the Nathan Baker Mock Trial, David Cohn Moot Court, and the ABA Negotiations competitions. Students are also invited to participate in approximately 25 to 30 writing competitions, among them the Nathan Burkan Copyright Competition. Law student organizations include Student Bar Association, Public Interest Law Foundation, and Federalist Society. There are local chapters of Student Lawyers Guild, Jackson chapter of Phi Alpha Delta, and ABA-Law Students Division. Other campus groups include Medicine and Health Law Society, Women's Law Forum, and International Law Students Society.

Library

The law library contains 412,542 hard-copy volumes and 144,376 microform volume equivalents, and subscribes to 3073 serial publications. Such on-line databases and networks as DIALOG, LEXIS, and WESTLAW are available to law students for research. Special library collections include depositories for U.S. and New Jersey documents. Recently, the library installed INNOPAC, an automated serials and acquisition system and online public access catalog. The ratio of library volumes to faculty is 7640 to 1 and to students is 560 to 1. The ratio of seats in the library to students is 1 to 2.

Placement

J.D.s awarded:	191
Services available through: a separate law school placement center	
Services: extensive on-campus interviewing program as well as co-sponsorship of off-campus job fairs; career panels on specific practice areas, judicial clerkships, networking and job search skills	
Special features: with stress placed on individual counseling, the alumni/ae job hotline, updated daily, and videotaped mock interviews.	
Full-time job interviews:	59 employers
Summer job interviews:	68 employers
Placement by graduation:	n/av
Placement within 9 months:	98% of class
Average starting salary:	$25,000 to $85,000
Areas of placement:	
Unknown	40%
Judicial clerkships	24%
Business/industry	20%
Government	9%
Public interest	5%
Academic	2%

Faculty

The law school has 54 full-time and 57 part-time faculty members, of whom 41 are women. According to AAUP standards for Category I institutions, faculty salaries are well above average. About 6% of full-time faculty have a graduate law degree in addition to the J.D. The ratio of full-time students to full-time faculty in an average class is 29 to 1; in a clinic, 8 to 1. There is a chapter of the Order of the Coif; 35 faculty and 123 graduates are members.

Students

About 49% of the student body are women; 41%, minorities; 15%, African American; 14%, Asian American; and 11%, Hispanic. The majority of students come from the Northeast (91%). The average age of entering students is 28; age range is 20 to 59. About 40% of students enter directly from undergraduate school, 21% have a graduate degree, and 34% have worked full-time prior to entering law school. About 5% drop out after the first year for academic or personal reasons; 95% remain to receive a law degree.

SAINT JOHN'S UNIVERSITY

School of Law

8000 Utopia Parkway
Jamaica, NY 11439

Application Filing		Accreditation
Fall: April 1		ABA, AALS
Spring: December 1		**Degrees Granted**
Fee: $60		J.D., LL.M.

Enrollment 2001–2002			First-Year Class	
Men:	518	55%	Applied:	2534
Women:	416	45%	Accepted:	900
Minorities:	177	19%	Enrolled:	300
Out-of-State:	934	100%		

2001–02 Class Profile

LSAT Percentile: 71%
LSAT Median Score: 156
Percentage passing bar on first try: 82%

Tuition and Fees:

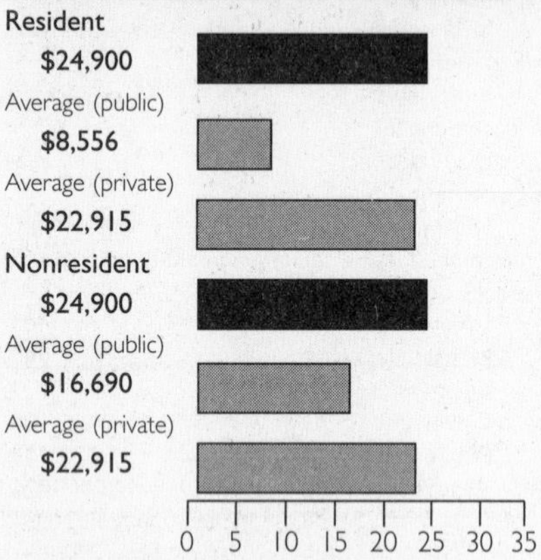

Percentage receiving financial aid: 88%

ADMISSIONS

In the fall 2001 first-year class, 2534 applied, 900 were accepted, and 300 enrolled. Thirteen transfers enrolled. The median LSAT percentile of the most recent first-year class was 71; the median GPA was 3.28 on a scale of 4.0.

Requirements
Applicants must have a bachelor's degree and take the LSAT. No specific undergraduate courses are required. Candidates are not interviewed. (An interview is not required, but a visit to the law school is recommended.)

Procedure
The application deadline for fall entry is April 1. Applicants should submit an application form, LSAT results, transcripts, and a nonrefundable application fee of $60. Notification of the admissions decision is on a rolling basis. The latest acceptable LSAT test date for fall entry is February. The law school uses the LSDAS.

Special
The law school recruits minority and disadvantaged students through special visits to historically black colleges and universities, open houses, and need-based and academic scholarships to improve diversity. Requirements are not different for out-of-state students. Preadmissions courses consist of the Summer Institute, a special educational program for individuals who have suffered the effects of discrimination, chronic financial hardship, and/or other social, educational, or physical disadvantages to such an extent that their undergraduate performance or LSAT score cannot otherwise warrant unconditional acceptance into the entering class.

Costs

Tuition and fees for the 2001-2002 academic year are $24,900 for all full-time students. Tuition for all part-time students is $18,680 per year. On-campus room and board costs about $9330 annually; books and supplies run $1000.

Financial Aid

About 88% of current law students receive some form of aid. The average annual amount of aid from all sources combined, including scholarships, loans, and work contracts, is $25,618; maximum, $39,585. Awards are based on need and merit. Required financial statement is the FAFSA. The aid application deadline for fall entry is February 1. Special funds for minority or disadvantaged students are available. First-year students are notified about their financial aid application at time of acceptance.

About the Law School

Saint John's University School of Law was established in 1925 and is a private institution. The 100-acre campus is in a suburban area in New York City (suburban Queens county), 10 miles east of Manhattan. The primary mission of the law school is to ensure the School of Law is recognized as a premier law school, preparing an ever-widening range of students to enter the legal profession with excellent lawyering skills and a commitment to high principles of professionalism and community service. Students have access to federal, state, county, city, and local agencies, courts, correctional facilities, law firms, and legal aid organizations in the Jamaica area, and a variety of year-long programs at the law school, including clinics, externships, colloquia, and trial and appellate experiences. Facilities of special interest to law students include a renovated moot court room and adjoining classrooms, providing faculty and students with state-of-the-art learning spaces. There is state-of-the-art technology in most classrooms, including wireless capability throughout the law school. Housing for students is available in campus residence halls. The residential complex around a grassy quadrangle includes suites with singles and doubles, bathrooms, a common area with a microwave and refrigerator in the living area. Each unit is fully wired for personal computers and laptops. Each of the residence halls have chapels, study lounges, and laundry facilities. All law school facilities are accessible to the physically disabled.

Calendar

The law school operates on a traditional semester basis. Courses for full-time students are offered both day and evening and must be completed within 3 years. For part-time students, courses are offered both day and evening and must be completed within 4 years. New full-time students are admitted in the fall and spring; part-time, fall. There is an 8-week summer session. Transferable summer courses are offered.

Programs

In addition to the J.D., the law school offers the LL.M. Students may take relevant courses in other programs and apply credit toward the J.D.; a maximum of 3 credits may be applied. The following joint degrees may be earned: J.D./B.A.-B.S. (Juris Doctor/Bachelor of Arts and/or Bachelor of Science), J.D./M.A. (Juris Doctor/Master of Arts in government and politics), and J.D./M.B.A. (Juris Doctor/Master of Business Administration).

Required
To earn the J.D., candidates must complete 85 total credits, of which 53 are for required courses. They must maintain a minimum GPA of 2.0 in the required courses. The following first-year courses are required of all students: Contracts I and II (6 credits), Criminal Law (3 credits), Introduction to Civil Procedure (3 credits), Legal Research and Writing (3 credits), Property I and II (6 credits), and Introduction to the Law and the Legal Profession (3 credits). Required upper-level courses consist of Basic Income Tax (3 credits), Business Organizations (4 credits), Constitutional Law I and II (6

Phone: 718-990-6474
E-mail: *rsvp@stjohns.edu*
Web: *www.law.stjohns.edu*

Contact

Admissions Office, 718-990-6474 for general inquiries; Jorge Rodriguez, Assistant Vice President, 718-990-6403 for financial aid information.

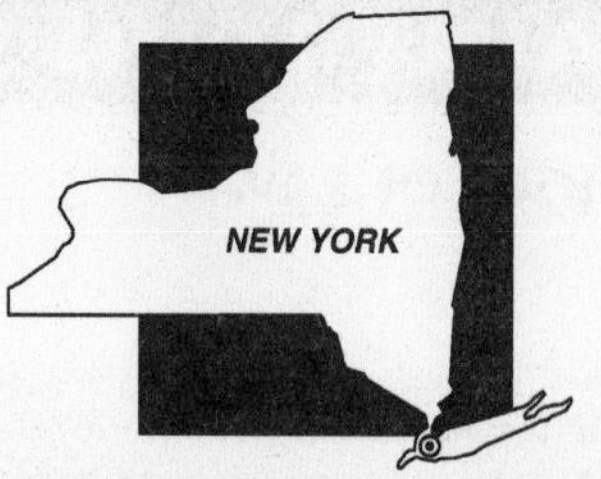

credits), Evidence (4 credits), Professional Responsibility (3 credits), and Trusts and Estates (4 credits). The required orientation program for first-year students is a 1-day program describing the program of study, rules and regulations of the law school, support services, tutorial programs, and career development with panels on professionalism and the law school experience.

Electives

The School of Law offers concentrations in corporate law, criminal law, entertainment law, environmental law, family law, international law, labor law, litigation, maritime law, securities law, tax law, intellectual property, estate administration, and real estate (property). In addition, the Elder Law Clinic is a 1-semester course where students receive 4 credits for their participation. Student interns represent Queens low income senior citizens in the areas of consumer law including consumer fraud, predatory lending practices, and public benefits law. The Domestic Violence Litigation Clinic gives students the opportunity to serve as attorneys of record on behalf of battered women. Seminars include the Civil Practice Seminar, Constitutional Rights Seminar, and Race and the Law Seminar. In the Criminal Clinical Externship, students work with mentor attorneys representing both sides of criminal cases doing research, preparing motions to suppress, and so on. In the Civil Clinical Externship, students, under the guidance of carefully selected mentor-attorneys, perform a variety of legal assignments, including research and preparation of legal documents, appearances in court, interviews with clients, interactions with opposing counsel, and participation in negotiations and settlements. Working over a semester, students in the Judicial Clinical Externship are placed in the chambers of administrative, city, state, and federal judges. In that capacity, they research the statutory and case law relevant to motions filed by litigants, assist law clerks in drafting decisions, and sit in on settlement discussions and trial proceedings. Research programs include the St. Thomas More Institute for Legal Research. Each year the school hosts guest speakers, Judge-in-Residence and Scholar-in-Residence programs, and various other symposia. Tutorial programs include academic support programs and the Writing Center. The most widely taken electives are New York Practice, Criminal Procedure I, and Family Law.

Graduation Requirements

In order to graduate, candidates must have a GPA of 2.0 and have completed the upper-division writing requirement. The Advanced Writing requirement is intended to ensure that all students have the opportunity after the first year to compose at least 1 scholarly writing for which they must analyze, synthesize, organize, and present substantive material.

Organizations

The primary law review is the *St. John's Law Review*. Other law reviews include the *Journal of Legal Commentary, The Catholic Lawyer, New York International Law Review, American Bankruptcy Institute Law Review* and *N.Y. Litigator*. The student newspaper is *The Forum* and the yearbook is *Res Gestae*. Moot court competitions include John J. Gibbons National Criminal Procedure Moot Court, Sutherland Cup Moot Court, and Domenick L. Gabrielli National Moot Court competitions. Other competitions include the Intra-School, First Year Trial, Client Counseling, Criminal Law Institute, and Civil Trial Institute competitions. Law student organizations include BALLSA (Black, Asian, and Latino Law Students Association), Student Bar Association, Labor Relations and Employment Law Society, and Environmental Law Society. There are local chapters of Delta Theta Phi, Phi Alpha Delta, and Phi Delta Phi. Campus clubs and other organizations include The Corporate and Securities Law Society, Admiralty Law Society, and Family Law Society.

Library

The law library contains 466,306 hard-copy volumes and 1,250,000 microform volume equivalents, and subscribes to 5757 serial publications. Such on-line databases and networks as CALI, CIS Universe, DIALOG, Infotrac, Legal-Trac, LEXIS, LOIS, NEXIS, WESTLAW, Wilsonline Indexes, and SUNY/OCLC are available to law students for research. Special library collections include the United Nations Depository, New York State Depository, Civil Rights, and Bankruptcy. Recently, the library added a wireless network, web site, casual seating area, and renovated a computer laboratory. The ratio of library volumes to faculty is 9715 to 1 and to students is 499 to 1. The ratio of seats in the library to students is 1 to 2.

Placement	
J.D.s awarded:	274
Services available through: a separate law school placement center	
Services: n/av	
Full-time job interviews:	52 employers
Summer job interviews:	71 employers
Placement by graduation:	80% of class
Placement within 9 months:	99% of class
Average starting salary:	$30,000 to $160,000
Areas of placement:	
Private practice 2-10 attorneys	15%
Private practice 11-25 attorneys	5%
Private practice 26-50 attorneys	2%
Private practice 51-100 attorneys	5%
Private practice 101 - 500+ attorneys	17%
Government	18%
Business/industry	15%
Judicial clerkships	6%
Military	2%
Academic	2%

Faculty

The law school has 48 full-time and 49 part-time faculty members, of whom 22 are women. According to AAUP standards for Category I institutions, faculty salaries are above average. About 44% of full-time faculty have a graduate law degree in addition to the J.D.; about 10% of part-time faculty have one. The ratio of full-time students to full-time faculty in an average class is 19 to 1; in a clinic, 8 to 1. The law school has a regular program of bringing visiting professors and other distinguished lecturers and visitors to campus.

Students

About 45% of the student body are women; 19%, minorities; 6%, African American; 7%, Asian American; and 6%, Hispanic. The average age of entering students is 23; age range is 20 to 49.

SAINT LOUIS UNIVERSITY

School of Law

3700 Lindell Boulevard
St. Louis, MO 63108

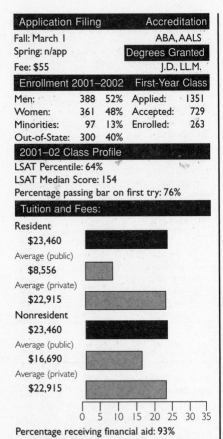

Application Filing	Accreditation
Fall: March 1	ABA, AALS
Spring: n/app	**Degrees Granted**
Fee: $55	J.D., LL.M.

Enrollment 2001–2002			First-Year Class	
Men:	388	52%	Applied:	1351
Women:	361	48%	Accepted:	729
Minorities:	97	13%	Enrolled:	263
Out-of-State:	300	40%		

2001–02 Class Profile

LSAT Percentile: 64%

LSAT Median Score: 154

Percentage passing bar on first try: 76%

Tuition and Fees:

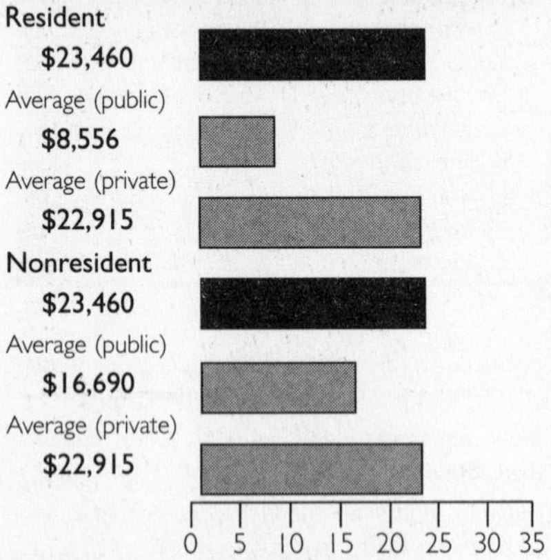

Percentage receiving financial aid: 93%

ADMISSIONS

In the fall 2001 first-year class, 1351 applied, 729 were accepted, and 263 enrolled. Four transfers enrolled. The median LSAT percentile of the most recent first-year class was 64; the median GPA was 3.34 on a scale of 4.0. The lowest LSAT percentile accepted was 13; the highest was 97.

Requirements

Applicants must have a bachelor's degree and take the LSAT. The most important admission factors include LSAT results, GPA, and a personal statement. No specific undergraduate courses are required. Candidates are not interviewed.

Procedure

The application deadline for fall entry is March 1 (scholarship deadline). Applicants should submit an application form, LSAT results, transcripts, TOEFL where applicable, a nonrefundable application fee of $55, and 2 letters of recommendation. Accepted students must pay a $100 deposit to reserve a place and a $200 final deposit to confirm attendance. Notification of the admissions decision is on a rolling basis. The latest acceptable LSAT test date for fall entry is February. The law school uses the LSDAS.

Special

The law school recruits minority and disadvantaged students actively through the Special Admission Summer Institute, scholarships for diversity, active BLSA and Latin American Society, the Minority Clerkship Program, and by recruiting at colleges and universities throughout the United States. Requirements are not different for out-of-state students. Transfer students must have one year of credit, have attended an ABA-approved law school, and rank in the top third of the law class.

Costs

Tuition and fees for the 2001-2002 academic year are $23,460 for all full-time students. Tuition for part-time students is $17,110 per year. Books and supplies run about $1000 annually.

Financial Aid

About 93% of current law students receive some form of aid. Awards are based on need and merit. Required financial statements are the FAFSA and Financial Aid Award Letter. The aid application deadline for fall entry is June 1. Special funds for minority or disadvantaged students consist of scholarships and grants up to full tuition. Awards are based on merit, and the average award is $8000. First-year students are notified about their financial aid application some time after acceptance.

About the Law School

Saint Louis University School of Law was established in 1843 and is a private institution. The 50-acre campus is in an urban area within St. Louis. The primary mission of the law school is to advance the understanding and the development of law, and prepare students to achieve professional success and personal satisfaction through leadership and service to others. The School of Law is guided by the Jesuit tradition of academic excellence, freedom of inquiry, and respect for individual differences. Students have access to federal, state, county, city, and local agencies, courts, correctional facilities, law firms, and legal aid organizations in the St. Louis area. Housing for students consists of off-campus housing, which is readily available and affordable. Limited on-campus housing is also available. All law school facilities are accessible to the physically disabled.

Calendar

The law school operates on a traditional semester basis. Courses for full-time students are offered both day and evening and must be completed within 3 years. For part-time students, courses are offered both day and evening and must be completed within 5 years (4 year plan includes summer classes). New full- and part-time students are admitted in the fall. There is an 8-week summer session. Transferable summer courses are offered.

Programs

In addition to the J.D., the law school offers the LL.M. in Health Law and the LL.M. for Foreign Lawyers. Students may take relevant courses in other programs and apply credit toward the J.D.; a maximum of 6 credits may be applied. The following joint degrees may be earned: J.D./M.A. (Juris Doctor/Master of Arts in public administration), J.D./M.A. (Juris Doctor/Master of Arts in urban affairs), J.D./M.B.A. (Juris Doctor/Master of Business Administration), J.D./M.H.A. (Juris Doctor/Master of Health Care Administration), and J.D./M.P.H. (Juris Doctor/Master of Public Health). Others are available through the graduate school.

Phone: 314-977-2800
Fax: 314-977-1464
E-mail: *admissions@law.slu.edu*
Web: *www.law.slu.edu*

Contact

Assistant Dean and Director of Admissions, 314-977-2800 for general inquiries; Kristina Bryan, Financial Aid Coordinator, 314-977-3369 for financial aid information.

Required

To earn the J.D., candidates must complete 88 total credits, of which 37 are for required courses. They must maintain a minimum GPA of 2.0 in the required courses. The following first-year courses are required of all students: Contracts I and II, Torts, Property, Civil Procedure I and II, Legal Research and Writing I and II, Constitutional Law I, and Criminal Law. Required upper-level courses consist of Legal Profession (Professional Ethics), a seminar, and a humanistic requirement. The required orientation program for first-year students is 2 days.

Electives

The School of Law offers concentrations in international law, labor law, and health law. In addition, clinical training includes the Civil Clinic, Criminal Clinic, Judicial Process Clinic, and the Corporate General Counsel Externship Program. An average of 10 seminars are offered each semester. Internships are available through clinical programs. Special lecture series include the Melvin Dubinsky Visiting Lecture, the Richard Childress Memorial Lecture Series, the Terence K. McCormack Memorial Lecture, the Sanford Sarasohn Memorial Lecture, and the James Millstone Lecture. Summer study abroad is available in Brussels, Belgium, at Ruhr University in Bochum, Germany, and in Madrid. All students are offered an academic support adviser, and have access to an Office of Academic Support. The Summer Institute includes students with some educational disadvantage, such as students with English as a second language or those with a learning disability. There is also a Minority Clerkship Program. Special interest group programs include the William C. Wefel Center for Employment Law, the Center for Health Law Studies, and the Center for International and Comparative Law. The most widely taken electives are Health Law, Employment Law/Business, and International Law.

Graduation Requirements

In order to graduate, candidates must have a GPA of 2.0.

Organizations

Students edit the *Saint Louis University Law Journal, Public Law Review, Saint Louis-Warsaw Transatlantic Law Journal*, and *Journal of Health Law*. Students may participate in the Jessup International Moot Court Program, numerous writing competitions, and a client counseling competition. Student organizations include the Student Bar Association, ABA-Law Student Division, the Health Law Association, and the Women's Law Student Association. There are local chapters of Phi Alpha Delta, Delta Theta Phi, and Phi Delta Phi.

Library

The law library contains 581,638 hard-copy volumes and 58,692 microform volume equivalents, and subscribes to 6400 serial publications. Such on-line databases and networks as DIALOG, LEXIS, and WESTLAW are available to law students for research. Special library collections include the Leonor K. Sullivan Congressional Papers, the Leo C. Brown Arbitration Papers, the Irish Law Collection, the Jewish Law Collection, and the Polish Law Collection. Recently, the library installed a specially equipped PC for those with reading disabilties. The ratio of library volumes to faculty is 17,107 to 1 and to students is 777 to 1. The ratio of seats in the library to students is 1 to 2.

Faculty

The law school has 34 full-time and 31 part-time faculty members, of whom 15 are women. According to AAUP standards for Category I institutions, faculty salaries are below average. About 51% of full-time faculty have a graduate law degree in addition to the J.D. The ratio of full-time students to full-time faculty in an average class is 16 to 1; in a clinic, 3 to 1. The law school has a regular program of bringing visiting professors and other distinguished lecturers and visitors to campus.

Placement

J.D.s awarded:	219
Services available through: a separate law school placement center	
Services: special programs on various areas of practice, such as health law, international, corporate, government, public interest, and judicial clerkships.	
Special features: an extensive career library with a computer search service.	
Full-time job interviews:	40 employers
Summer job interviews:	55 employers
Placement by graduation:	65% of class
Placement within 9 months:	95% of class
Average starting salary:	n/av
Areas of placement:	
Private practice 2-100 attorneys	59%
Private practice 100+ attorneys	5%
Business/industry	16%
Government	11%
Judicial clerkships	6%
Public interest	2%
Military	1%
Academic	1%

Students

About 48% of the student body are women; 13%, minorities; 7%, African American; 1%, Asian American; and 2%, Hispanic. The majority of students come from the Midwest (70%). The average age of entering students is 26; age range is 20 to 55. About 42% of students enter directly from undergraduate school, 13% have a graduate degree, and 58% have worked full-time prior to entering law school. About 8% drop out after the first year for academic or personal reasons; 90% remain to receive a law degree.

SAINT MARY'S UNIVERSITY

School of Law

One Camino Santa Maria
San Antonio, TX 78228-8601

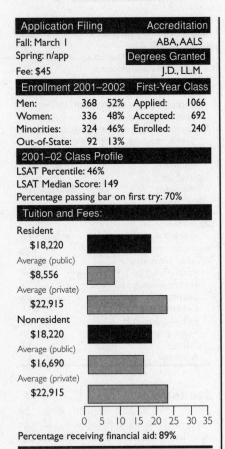

Application Filing		Accreditation
Fall: March 1		ABA, AALS
Spring: n/app		**Degrees Granted**
Fee: $45		J.D., LL.M.

Enrollment 2001–2002			First-Year Class	
Men:	368	52%	Applied:	1066
Women:	336	48%	Accepted:	692
Minorities:	324	46%	Enrolled:	240
Out-of-State:	92	13%		

2001–02 Class Profile

LSAT Percentile: 46%
LSAT Median Score: 149
Percentage passing bar on first try: 70%

Tuition and Fees:

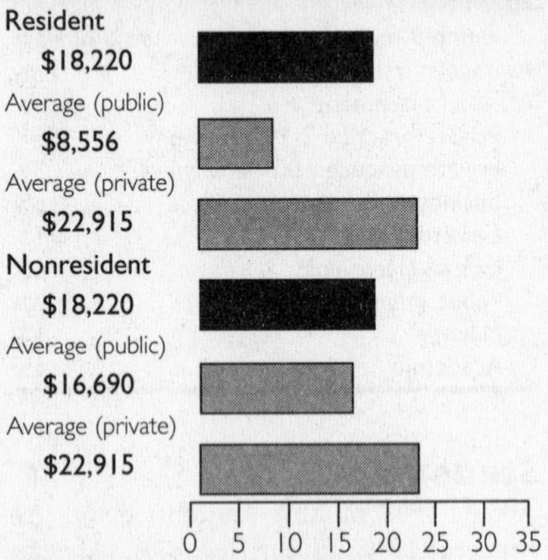

Percentage receiving financial aid: 89%

ADMISSIONS

In the fall 2001 first-year class, 1066 applied, 692 were accepted, and 240 enrolled. Seven transfers enrolled. The median LSAT percentile of the most recent first-year class was 46; the median GPA was 3 on a scale of 4.0. The lowest LSAT percentile accepted was 25; the highest was 75.

Requirements

Applicants must have a bachelor's degree and take the LSAT. All admission factors are considered by the admissions staff. Minimum acceptable GPA is 2.0 on a scale of 4.0. No specific undergraduate courses are required. Candidates are not interviewed.

Procedure

The application deadline for fall entry is March 1. Applicants should submit an application form, a nonrefundable application fee of $45, 2 letters of recommendation, but as many as 5 may be accepted. Notification of the admissions decision is after May 1. The latest acceptable LSAT test date for fall entry is February. The law school uses the LSDAS.

Special

Admissions requirements are not different for out-of-state students. Transfer students must have one year of credit, have a minimum GPA of 2.5, and have attended an ABA-approved law school.

Costs

Tuition and fees for the 2001-2002 academic year are $18,220 for all full-time students. On-campus room and board costs about $2500 annually; books and supplies run $1100.

Financial Aid

About 89% of current law students receive some form of aid. The average annual amount of aid from all sources combined, including scholarships, loans, and work contracts, is $18,500; maximum, $20,000. Awards are based on need. Required financial statement is the FAFSA. The aid application deadline for fall entry is April 1. Special funds for minority or disadvantaged students are available based on need. First-year students are notified about their financial aid application at time of acceptance.

About the Law School

Saint Mary's University School of Law was established in 1948 and is a private institution. The 135-acre campus is in a suburban area in San Antonio, Texas. The primary mission of the law school is to offer a solid curriculum of traditional legal studies and to teach students the practical skills and habits necessary to practice effective public service advocacy. Students have access to federal, state, county, city, and local agencies, courts, correctional facilities, law firms, and legal aid organizations in the San Antonio area. A joint program with the Universidad de Monterrey (Mexico) allows attorneys to represent clients with business in Mexico. Housing for students is available in on-campus resident dormitory facilities for single students only. Information and application forms may be obtained from the Director of Housing. All law school facilities are accessible to the physically disabled.

Calendar

The law school operates on a traditional semester basis. Courses for full-time students are offered days only and must be completed within 5 years. There is no part-time program. New students are admitted in the fall. There is a 5 1/2-week summer session. Transferable summer courses are offered.

Programs

In addition to the J.D., the law school offers the LL.M. The following joint degrees may be earned: J.D./M.A. (Juris Doctor/Master of Arts in theology), J.D./M.B.A. (Juris Doctor/Master of Business Administration), J.D./M.Econ (Juris Doctor/Master of Economics), J.D./M.P.A. (Juris Doctor/Master of Public Administration), and J.D./M.S. (Juris Doctor/Master of Science in engineering).

Required

To earn the J.D., candidates must complete 90 total credits, of which 46 are for required courses. They must maintain a minimum GPA of 2.0 in the required courses. The following first-year courses are required of all students: Constitutional Law, Contracts I and II, Criminal Law, Procedure I, Property I and II, Torts I and II, Legal Research and Writing II, and Legal Writing I. Required upper-level courses consist of Professional Responsibility, Texas Civil Procedure, Evidence, a perspective course, and a research paper that fulfills the writing requirement, and Evidence. Although not required, law students are urged to participate in clinics for credit in the third year or as volunteers in the first and second years.The required orientation program for first-year students consists of a 2-day orientation session during which first-year law students discuss their expectations regarding law school and the law profession.

Electives

The School of Law offers concentrations in corporate law, criminal law, environmental law, family law, international law, juvenile law, labor law, litigation, maritime law, securities law, tax law, and torts and insurance. In addition, 3 clinics—Civil Justice Clinic, Criminal Justice Clinic, and Immigration and Human

Phone: 210-436-3523
866-639-5831
Fax: 210-431-4202
E-mail: *meryc@law.stmarytx.edu*
Web: *http://stmarylaw.stmarytx.edu*

Contact

Catherine L. Mery, Admissions Officer, 210-436-3523 for general inquiries; Diana Perez, 210-431-6743 for financial aid information.

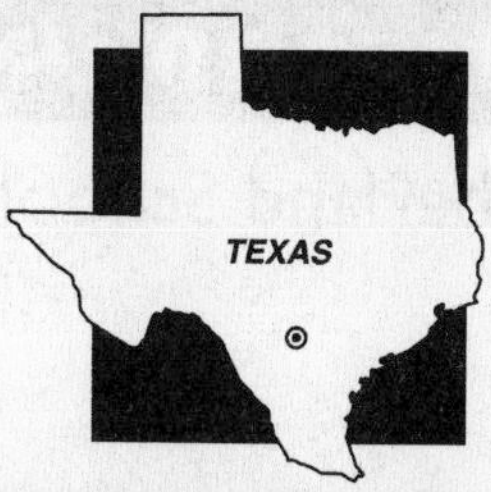

Rights Clinic—are open to second- and third-year students. Limited to an enrollment of 12 students, seminars are opportunities for research and discussion on advanced or special issues. Past seminars have included Natural Resource Protection Law; Doing Business with Mexico; International Law; Mediation; Health Care Crisis; First Amendment/Reporter Privilege; and International Arbitration. Two judicial internships, with the Texas Supreme Court and with the Court of Appeals, Third District of Texas, both located in Austin, Texas, are offered. Students earn 4 hours of credit for the internship and may enroll at the University of Texas Law School for additional credits. Students are required to do field work in the clinical programs. Students in the judicial internships spend a semester at the court, and students may seek independent study credit for worthwhile projects taken with the approval and supervision of a faculty member. St. Mary's sponsors conferences and symposia on such diverse topics as United Nations Law and Legal Research, Human Rights in the Americas, and Legal Aspects of Doing Business with Mexico. The school also presents lectures by renowned legal scholars. St. Mary's Institute on World Legal Problems is conducted 5 weeks each summer, during July and August, at the University of Innsbruck, Austria. Beginning in the second semester of the first year, students who scored poorly in their first-semester examinations are required to attend small-group tutorials. The tutorials are conducted by upper-class students under professional supervision. Each year, 20 students are accepted into the Law Skills Enhancement Program, a 5-week summer program that provides intensive writing instruction, and instruction on how to read, analyze, and brief cases. The Minority Law Students Association, the Black Allied Law Students Association, and the Asian-Pacific American Law Students Association offer tutorials to first-year students who are members. Special-interest groups include the Society of Legal Entrepreneurs, Education Law Association, Environmental Law Society, Criminal Law Association, and Family Law Association. Several student groups, including the Environmental Law Society, the Women's Bar Association, and the Minority Law Students Association, have developed mentor relationships with local bar associations. The most widely taken electives are Wills and Estates, Trusts, and Business Associations.

Graduation Requirements

In order to graduate, candidates must have a GPA of 2.0 and have completed the upper-division writing requirement.

Organizations

Students edit the *St. Mary's University School of Law Law Journal* and the *Hispanic Law Review*. Moot court competitions include the Norvell Moot Court Competition, involving all Texas schools, the Walker Moot Court, held on campus, and the National ABA Regional Moot Court competition. Other competitions include the Shannon Thurmond Giltner Novice Mock Trial, National Mock Trial, and the ABA Client-Counseling. Law student organizations are the Student Bar Association, Family Law Association, and William Sessions American Inn of Court. Local chapters of national associations are Delta Theta Phi, Delta Alpha Delta, and Harlan Society. Campus clubs and other organizations include the Student Aggie Bar Association, the Longhorn Bar Association, and Hispanic Law Association.

Library

The law library contains 320,000 hard-copy volumes and 633,117 microform volume equivalents, and subscribes to 3804 serial publications. Such on-line databases and networks as CALI, CIS Universe, DIALOG, Infotrac, Legal-Trac, LEXIS, LOIS, NEXIS, OCLC First Search, WESTLAW, IndexMaster, ELibrary Classic, and Netlibrary are available to law students for research. Special library collections include Mexican legal materials, microtext of records and briefs of the United States Supreme Court, and legal documents from the United Nations and from American, British, Canadian, and international law. The library is a depository for U.S. government documents. The ratio of library volumes to faculty is 8889 to 1 and to students is 455 to 1. The ratio of seats in the library to students is 1 to 3.

Placement	
J.D.s awarded:	249
Services available through: a separate law school placement center	
Services: individual strategy sessions and a weekly job newsletter.	
Special features: The Office of Career Counseling and Services arranges seminars throughout the year to assist students in career planning and job searches. Alumni mentors are available, and a Student Resource Center has been established.	
Full-time job interviews:	35 employers
Summer job interviews:	n/av
Placement by graduation:	77% of class
Placement within 9 months:	92% of class
Average starting salary:	$40,000 to $60,000
Areas of placement:	
Private practice 2-10 attorneys	35%
Private practice 11-25 attorneys	13%
Private practice 26-50 attorneys	13%
Private practice 51-100 attorneys	6%
Government	9%
Unknown	8%
Business/industry	5%
Judicial clerkships	4%
Public interest	3%
Self-employed	2%
Military	1%
Academic	1%

Faculty

The law school has 36 full-time and 53 part-time faculty members, of whom 29 are women. According to AAUP standards for Category IIA institutions, faculty salaries are above average. About 44% of full-time faculty have a graduate law degree in addition to the J.D. The ratio of full-time students to full-time faculty in an average class is 21 to 1; in a clinic, 4 to 1. The law school has a regular program of bringing visiting professors and other distinguished lecturers and visitors to campus.

Students

About 48% of the student body are women; 46%, minorities; 4%, African American; 3%, Asian American; 39%, Hispanic; and 1%, Native American. The majority of students come from Texas (87%). The age range of entering students is 23 to 65. About 3% drop out after the first year for academic or personal reasons; 88% remain to receive a law degree.

SAMFORD UNIVERSITY

Cumberland School of Law

800 Lakeshore Drive
Birmingham, AL 35229

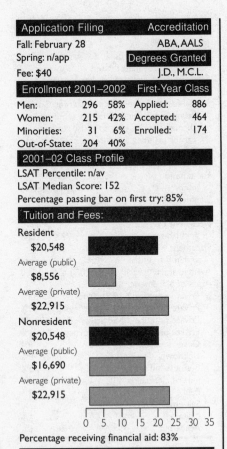

Application Filing		Accreditation
Fall: February 28		ABA, AALS
Spring: n/app		**Degrees Granted**
Fee: $40		J.D., M.C.L.

Enrollment 2001–2002			First-Year Class	
Men:	296	58%	Applied:	886
Women:	215	42%	Accepted:	464
Minorities:	31	6%	Enrolled:	174
Out-of-State:	204	40%		

2001–02 Class Profile

LSAT Percentile: n/av
LSAT Median Score: 152
Percentage passing bar on first try: 85%

Tuition and Fees:

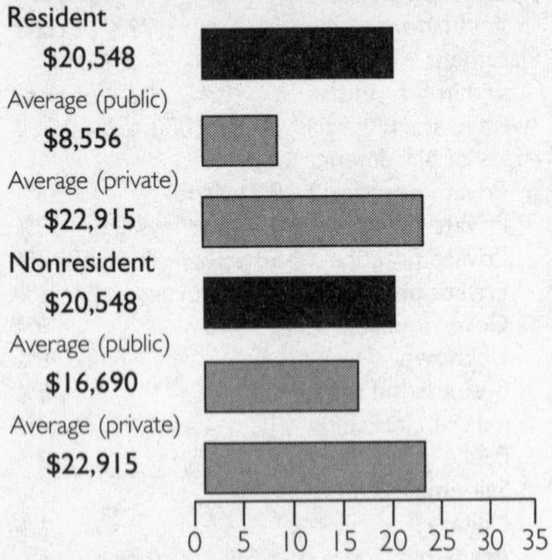

Percentage receiving financial aid: 83%

ADMISSIONS

In the fall 2001 first-year class, 886 applied, 464 were accepted, and 174 enrolled. Six transfers enrolled. The median GPA of the most recent first-year class was 3.1.

Requirements

Applicants must have a bachelor's degree and take the LSAT. The most important admission factors include LSAT results, GPA, and academic achievement. No specific undergraduate courses are required. Candidates are not interviewed.

Procedure

The application deadline for fall entry is February 28. Applicants should submit an application form, a nonrefundable application fee of $40, 2 letters of recommendation, and LSAT results. Transcripts, test results, and letters of recommendation must come from LSDAS. Notification of the admissions decision is on a rolling basis. The latest acceptable LSAT test date for fall entry is February. The law school uses the LSDAS.

Special

The law school recruits minority and disadvantaged students by means of recruiting at historically black colleges and universities. The Black Law Students Association is active in on-campus recruiting and has special events for minority students during the school's Black Law Student Recruitment Day. Requirements are not different for out-of-state students. Transfer students must have one year of credit, have a minimum GPA of 3, have attended an ABA-approved law school, and have attended an AALS-and ABA-approved school, and have a letter of good standing from the dean of the former law school.

Costs

Tuition and fees for the 2001-2002 academic year are $20,548 for all full-time students. Tuition for all part-time flex program students is $693 per credit. Books and supplies run about $1200 annually.

Financial Aid

About 83% of current law students receive some form of aid. The average annual amount of aid from all sources combined, including scholarships, loans, and work contracts, is $22,000; maximum, $29,000. Awards are based on need and merit. Required financial statement is the FAFSA. The aid application deadline for fall entry is March 1. Special funds for minority or disadvantaged students consist of full or partial tuition scholarships. First-year students are notified about their financial aid application at time of acceptance.

About the Law School

Samford University Cumberland School of Law was established in 1847 and is a private institution. The 300-acre campus is in a suburban area 6 miles from downtown Birmingham. The primary mission of the law school is to educate students to be responsible lawyers, trained to exercise their professional skills competently with sensitivity to the needs and concerns of their clients, and to act in strict accord with the highest ethical standards. Students have access to federal, state, county, city, and local agencies, courts, correctional facilities, law firms, and legal aid organizations in the Birmingham area. Facilities of special interest to law students include an $8.4 million, 61,000-square-foot freestanding library connected to the Law School building by a covered breezeway on the second floor, easily accessible to physically disabled students. Housing for students is available off campus in any number of nearby neighborhoods. Assistance in obtaining apartment rental information is provided by the Student Bar Association, which also provides a roommate referral service. About 95% of the law school facilities are accessible to the physically disabled.

Calendar

The law school operates on a traditional semester basis. Courses for full-time students are offered days only and must be completed within 4 years. For part-time students, courses are offered days only and must be completed within 5 years. New full- and part-time students are admitted in the fall. There is a 9-week summer session. Transferable summer courses are offered.

Programs

In addition to the J.D., the law school offers the M.C.L. and LL.M./S.J.D. in Law, Religion, and Culture. Students may take relevant courses in other programs and apply credit toward the J.D.; a maximum of 12 credits may be applied. The following joint degrees may be earned: J.D./M.Acc. (Juris Doctor/Master of Accounting), J.D./M.B.A. (Juris Doctor/Master of Business Administration), J.D./M.Div. (Juris Doctor/Master of Divinity), J.D./M.P.A. (Juris Doctor/Master of Public Administration), J.D./

Phone: 205-726-2702
800-888-7213
Fax: 205-726-2057
E-mail: *law.admissions@samford.edu*
Web: *http://cumberland.samford.edu*

Contact

Mitzi S. Davis, Assistant Dean, 800-888-7213 for general inquiries; Ann Waller, Director of Financial Aid, 800-888-7245 for financial aid information.

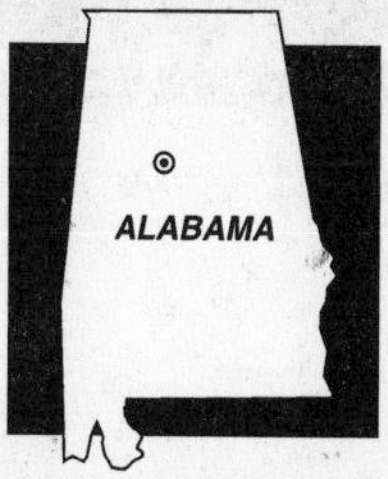

M.P.H. (Juris Doctor/Master of Public Health), and J.D./M.S. (Juris Doctor/ Master of Science in environmental management).

Required

To earn the J.D., candidates must complete 90 total credits, of which 51 are for required courses. They must maintain a minimum GPA of 2.0 in the required courses. The following first-year courses are required of all students: Contracts I and II, Criminal Law, Civil Procedure I and II, Evidence, Torts, Real Property, and Lawyering Skills and Legal Reasoning I and II. Required upper-level courses consist of Constitutional Law I and II, Business Organizations, Decedents' Estate and Trusts, Professional Responsibility, Taxation, and Commercial Law (Payment Systems or Secured Transactions). The required orientation program for first-year students is designed to introduce new students to the school, the faculty, and the curriculum. Entering students begin the required Lawyering and Legal Reasoning course and receive instruction on the briefing of cases and demonstration of law school teaching methods. This 6-credit hour, 2 semester course provides students with intensive hands-on experience in practical lawyering skills.

Electives

The Center for Advocacy and Clinical Education offers upper-level students clinical courses for 1 to 2 credit hours and internships for 2 to 3 credit hours. Seminars are offered for 2 credit hours. Research programs are directed by individual professors and are aimed at upper-level students. Field work placement is available with government agencies, judges, legal services, and corporations. Special lecture series include the Cordell Hull Speakers Forum, a student-run organization; the Ray Rushton Distinguished Lecturer Series; the Cumberland Colloquium on Law, Religion, and Culture, a faculty-run organization; the Thurgood Marshall Speakers' Forum, a student-sponsored event; and a faculty colloquium on American Legal History. Study-abroad programs include international and comparative law at the University of Durham in England; the University of Victoria in British Columbia and at the faculdade de Direito da Universidade de Sao Paulo, the Sao Paulo University Law School. A writing laboratory is available for students who need additional coaching in this critical skill. The Black Law Students Association sponsors a tutorial program, a mentor program, a speakers forum, special recognition events, and Black Law Student Recruitment Day. The most widely taken electives are Mediation, Basic Skills, and Law Office Practice and Management.

Graduation Requirements

In order to graduate, candidates must have a GPA of 2.0 and have completed the upper-division writing requirement.

Organizations

Students edit the *Cumberland Law Review, American Journal of Trial Advocacy*, and the newspaper *Pro Confesso.* Moot court competitions include the Justice Janie Shores Moot Court; Gordon T. Saad, which is held in conjunction with the Appellate Advocacy course; and the Robert Donworth Freshman Competition. Other competitions include Mock Trial, Herbert W. Peterson Senior, Judge James O. Haley Federal Court, Parham H. Williams Freshman Mock Trial, Albert P. Brewer Client Counseling, and Negotiation. Student organizations include the Association of Trial Lawyers of America, ABA-Student Division, and Federalist Society. Local chapters of national organizations include Delta Theta Phi, Phi Alpha Delta, and Phi Delta Phi. Other organizations include the State Student Bar Associations of Alabama, Florida, Georgia, Mississippi, North Carolina, South Carolina, Tennessee, and Virginia.

Library

The law library contains 268,048 hard-copy volumes and 84,676 microform volume equivalents, and subscribes to 2448 serial publications. Such on-line databases and networks as LEXIS and WESTLAW are available to law students for research. Special library collections include the Brantley collection. Recently, the library added the Lucille Stewart Beeson Law Library. The ratio of library volumes to faculty is 12,184 to 1 and to students is 525 to 1. The ratio of seats in the library to students is 1 to 1.

Placement

J.D.s awarded:	192
Services available through: a separate law school placement center	
Services: national and regional law fairs	
Special features: interviewing and job search skills workshops, pictorial directory, alumni job placement newsletter, and speakers' forum on legal career specialties.	
Full-time job interviews:	72 employers
Summer job interviews:	72 employers
Placement by graduation:	51% of class
Placement within 9 months:	96% of class
Average starting salary:	$26,000 to $150,000
Areas of placement:	
Private practice 2-10 attorneys	43%
Private practice 11-25 attorneys	9%
Private practice 26-50 attorneys	6%
Private practice 51-100 attorneys	2%
Private practice 101-250 attorneys	5%
Judicial clerkships	11%
Government	8%
Business/industry	8%
Self-Employed	3%
Military	2%
Academic	2%
Public interest	1%

Faculty

The law school has 22 full-time and 9 part-time faculty members, of whom 7 are women. According to AAUP standards for Category IIA institutions, faculty salaries are above average. About 21% of full-time faculty have a graduate law degree in addition to the J.D.; about 13% of part-time faculty have one. The ratio of full-time students to full-time faculty in an average class is 19 to 1; in a clinic, 10 to 1.

Students

About 42% of the student body are women; 6%, minorities; 4%, African American; 1%, Asian American; 1%, Hispanic; and 1%, Native American. The majority of students come from Alabama (60%). The average age of entering students is 23; age range is 21 to 42. About 2% drop out after the first year for academic or personal reasons; 91% remain to receive a law degree.

School of Law

500 EL Camino Real
Santa Clara, CA 95053

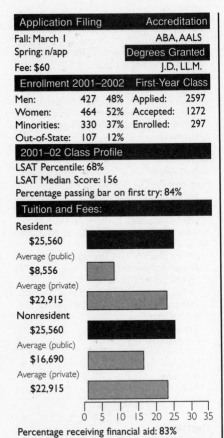

Application Filing		Accreditation
Fall: March 1		ABA, AALS
Spring: n/app		**Degrees Granted**
Fee: $60		J.D., LL.M.

Enrollment 2001–2002			First-Year Class	
Men:	427	48%	Applied:	2597
Women:	464	52%	Accepted:	1272
Minorities:	330	37%	Enrolled:	297
Out-of-State:	107	12%		

2001–02 Class Profile

LSAT Percentile: 68%
LSAT Median Score: 156
Percentage passing bar on first try: 84%

Tuition and Fees:

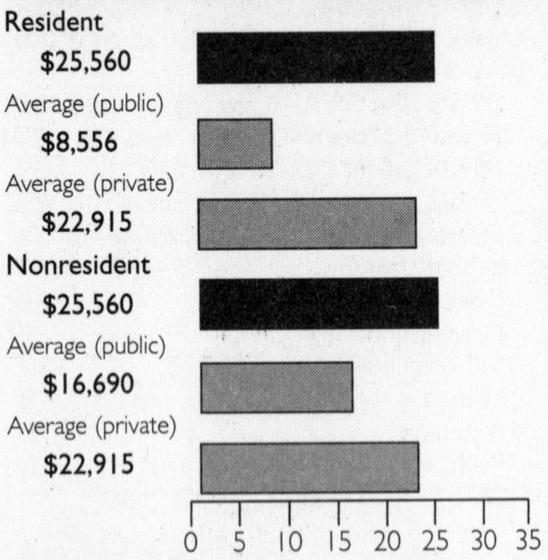

Percentage receiving financial aid: 83%

ADMISSIONS

In the fall 2001 first-year class, 2597 applied, 1272 were accepted, and 297 enrolled. Forty-three transfers enrolled. The median LSAT percentile of the most recent first-year class was 68; the median GPA was 3.27 on a scale of 4.0.

Requirements

Applicants must have a bachelor's degree and take the LSAT. The most important admission factors include LSAT results, undergraduate curriculum, and GPA. No specific undergraduate courses are required. Candidates are not interviewed.

Procedure

The application deadline for fall entry is March 1. Applicants should submit an application form, LSAT results, transcripts, a nonrefundable application fee of $60, and optional letters of recommendation. Notification of the admissions decision is January through May. The latest acceptable LSAT test date for fall entry is February. The law school uses the LSDAS.

Special

The law school recruits minority and disadvantaged students by means of ethnic student organizations that advise the faculty admissions committee and by providing substantial financial assistance. Requirements are not different for out-of-state students. Transfer students must have one year of credit, have attended an ABA-approved law school, and have a letter of good standing from their prior school.

Costs

Tuition and fees for the 2001-2002 academic year are $25,560 for all full-time students. Tuition for part-time students is $17,892 per year. On-campus room and board costs about $11,822 annually; books and supplies run $1304.

Financial Aid

About 83% of current law students receive some form of aid. The average annual amount of aid from all sources combined, including scholarships, loans, and work contracts, is $25,896; maximum, $44,752. Awards are based on need and merit. Required financial statement is the FAFSA. The aid application deadline for fall entry is February 1. Special funds for minority or disadvantaged students consist of the Law Faculty Scholarship. First-year students are notified about their financial aid application at time of acceptance for scholarships; other aid decisions are made known upon completion of financial aid applications.

About the Law School

Santa Clara University School of Law was established in 1912 and is a private institution. The 104-acre campus is in a suburban area less than 1 mile west of San Jose and 45 miles south of San Francisco. The primary mission of the law school is wholly consistent with the Jesuit purpose in professional education: to train men and women of competence, conscience, and compassion. Students have access to federal, state, county, city, and local agencies, courts, correctional facilities, law firms, and legal aid organizations in the Santa Clara area. The area is widely known as Silicon Valley. Local law firms have specialties that serve the needs of the high-tech industry and advise the school. Facilities of special interest to law students are Heafey Law Library; Bergin Hall faculty office building; Law Clinic; Law House and Bannan Hall, which houses classrooms and the law student lounge; law review offices at Benton street; and the East San Jose Community Law Center. Housing for students is limited on campus to 20 2- or 3-person apartments and 20 studio apartments; housing of all types is readily available off campus. About 97% of the law school facilities are accessible to the physically disabled.

Calendar

The law school operates on a traditional semester basis. Courses for all full-time and part-time students are offered both day and evening and must be completed within 5 years. New full- and part-time students are admitted in the fall. There is a 7 ½-week summer session. Transferable summer courses are offered.

Programs

In addition to the J.D., the law school offers the LL.M. for foreign lawyers. Students may take relevant courses in other programs and apply credit toward the J.D.; a maximum of 12 credits may be applied. The following joint degrees may be earned: J.D./M.B.A. (Juris Doctor/Master of Business Administration) and J.D./M.S.T. (Juris Doctor/Master of Science in Taxation).

Required

To earn the J.D., candidates must complete 86 total credits, of which 43 are for required courses. They must maintain a minimum GPA of 2.33 in the required courses. The following first-year courses are required of all students: Legal Research and Writing, Torts, Contracts, Property, Criminal Law, and Pleading and Civil Procedure. Required upper-level courses consist of Constitutional Law I and II, Evidence, and The Legal Profession. The required orientation program for first-year students is a 3-day introduction to the legal system and the study of law.

Phone: 408-554-4800
Fax: 408-554-7897
E-mail: *lawadmissions@scu.edu*
Web: *scu.edu/law*

Contact

Jeanette Leach, Associate Director, 408-554-4800 for general inquiries; Bryan Hinkle, Financial Aid Counselor, 408-554-4800 for financial aid information.

Electives

The School of Law offers concentrations in corporate law, criminal law, environmental law, family law, international law, labor law, litigation, tax law, high tech law, and public interest law. In addition, through the on-campus Law Clinic Office, upper-division students practice law under the supervision of faculty. Students participate in all phases of a case, from the initial client interview through trial and may receive 3 to 6 units. The focus of the Criminal Law Clinic is the North California Innocence Project. Fifteen to 20 seminars are offered each year in areas such as social justice and public interest law, sports law, and drug abuse law. Internships are in civil practice and the criminal justice system. Judicial externships are offered with the California Supreme Court and other state and federal courts. Faculty members engage students as research assistants for a variety of projects. During the academic year, students have access to the courts and legal community of the San Francisco Bay Area. The voluntary Pro Bono Project matches students and alumni for work on pro bono cases. The school hosts lectures on topics ranging from intellectual property issues to current events in international law. The Institute of International and Comparative Law sponsors Summer Law study-abroad programs in Strasbourg, France; Geneva, Switzerland; Oxford, England; Hong Kong; Singapore; Seoul, Korea; Bangkok, Thailand; Tokyo, Japan; Beijing, P.R.C; Ho Chi Minh City, Vietnam; Kuala Lumpur, Malaysia; and Munich, Germany. The Academic Success Program offers personal and tutorial support to minority students, students identified through the admission process as needing academic support, and students recommended by their first-year instructors. Tutorial support emphasizes legal analysis and uses the writing of briefs, outlines, and exams to develop this skill. The Director of Admissions and Diversity Services acts as a mentor to students of color. The minority alumni network actively supports current students. Students may earn a certificate in public interest law by taking 14 units, plus a unit of Public Interest Seminar, and completing a practicum. Certificates are also offered in international law and high-technology law with varying requirements. The most widely taken electives are Community Property, Wills and Trusts, and Remedies.

Graduation Requirements

In order to graduate, candidates must have a GPA of 2.33, have completed the upper-division writing requirement, and have fulfilled a residency requirement of 3 academic years in the full-time division or 4 academic years in the part-time division.

Organizations

Students edit the *Santa Clara Law Review* and the *Computer and High Technology Law Journal*. The student newspaper is *The Advocate*. Moot court competitions include the Jessup International Moot Court, Traynor Moot Court, and the Giles Rich Moot Court. Other competitions include ABA Client Counseling Competition, ABA National Trial Competition, and the Negotiation Competition. Student organizations include Intellectual Property Association, Public Interest Coalition, and the International Law Society. There are local chapters of Phi Alpha Delta, Phi Delta Phi, and ACLU. Other campus organizations include the Student Bar Association, BALSA, and Women in Law.

Library

The law library contains 302,875 hard-copy volumes and 883,580 microform volume equivalents, and subscribes to 3748 serial publications. Such on-line databases and networks as CALI, CIS Universe, DIALOG, Dow-Jones, Infotrac, Legal-Trac, LEXIS, NEXIS, OCLC First Search, RLIN, WESTLAW, Wilsonline Indexes, Link+ Indexmaster, Hein Online, CIAO, CCH Internet Research, JSTOR, and UN Readex are available to law students for research. Special library collections include the proceedings of the House Judiciary Committee on the Watergate Hearings. Recently, the library installed an integrated library automation system, beginning with OPAC; upgraded student computer laboratories with Pentiums; networked some carrels; and remodeled the reference area. The ratio of library volumes to faculty is 8413 to 1 and to students is 340 to 1. The ratio of seats in the library to students is 1 to 2.

Placement

J.D.s awarded:	254
Services available through: a separate law school placement center and Law Career Services	
Special features: fall and spring on-campus interview programs, career-oriented workshops and events, web site with current listings and job search tips, extensive resource library, and reciprocity with other Bay area and ABA-accredited law schools.	
Full-time job interviews:	30 employers
Summer job interviews:	60 employers
Placement by graduation:	65% of class
Placement within 9 months:	95% of class
Average starting salary:	n/av
Areas of placement:	
Private practice 2-100 attorneys	60%
Business/industry	28%
Government	8%
Public interest	2%
Judicial clerkships	1%

Faculty

The law school has 36 full-time and 21 part-time faculty members, of whom 19 are women. According to AAUP standards for Category IIA institutions, faculty salaries are well above average. The ratio of full-time students to full-time faculty in an average class is 30 to 1; in a clinic, 12 to 1. The law school has a regular program of bringing visiting professors and other distinguished lecturers and visitors to campus.

Students

About 52% of the student body are women; 37%, minorities; 3%, African American; 25%, Asian American; 9%, Hispanic; and 1%, Native American. The majority of students come from California (88%). The average age of entering students is 26; age range is 21 to 53. About 35% of students enter directly from undergraduate school and 13% have a graduate degree. About 16% drop out after the first year for academic or personal reasons; 99% remain to receive a law degree.

SEATTLE UNIVERSITY

School of Law

900 Broadway
Seattle, WA 98122-4340

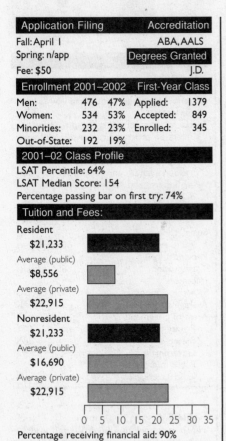

Application Filing		Accreditation
Fall: April 1		ABA, AALS
Spring: n/app		**Degrees Granted**
Fee: $50		J.D.

Enrollment 2001–2002			First-Year Class	
Men:	476	47%	Applied:	1379
Women:	534	53%	Accepted:	849
Minorities:	232	23%	Enrolled:	345
Out-of-State:	192	19%		

2001–02 Class Profile

LSAT Percentile: 64%
LSAT Median Score: 154
Percentage passing bar on first try: 74%

Tuition and Fees:

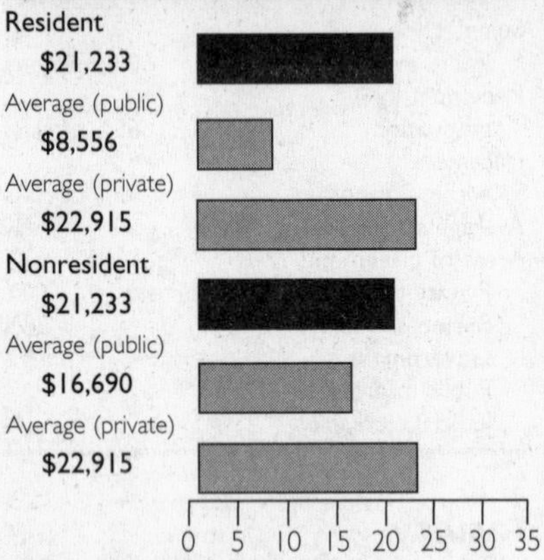

Percentage receiving financial aid: 90%

ADMISSIONS

In the fall 2001 first-year class, 1379 applied, 849 were accepted, and 345 enrolled. Eleven transfers enrolled. The median LSAT percentile of the most recent first-year class was 64. The lowest LSAT percentile accepted was 11; the highest was 99.

Requirements

Applicants must have a bachelor's degree and take the LSAT. The most important admission factors include GPA, LSAT results, and character, personality. No specific undergraduate courses are required. Candidates are not interviewed.

Procedure

The application deadline for fall entry is April 1. Applicants should submit an application form, LSAT results, transcripts, a nonrefundable application fee of $50, 2 letters of recommendation, personal statement, and a resume. Notification of the admissions decision is February 1 to May 1. The latest acceptable LSAT test date for fall entry is June on a limited basis. The law school uses the LSDAS.

Special

The law school recruits minority and disadvantaged students through admission officer visits, minority community service organizations, minority prelaw and bar associations, candidate referral services, prelaw adviser mailings, and a fee waiver program. Requirements are not different for out-of-state students. Transfer students must have one year of credit, have attended an ABA-approved law school, be in good academic standing and in the top half of their class.

Costs

Tuition and fees for the 2001-2002 academic year are $21,233 for all full-time students. Tuition for part-time students is $17,691 per year. Books and supplies run about $903 annually.

Financial Aid

About 90% of current law students receive some form of aid. The average annual amount of aid from all sources combined, including scholarships, loans, and work contracts, is $26,492; maximum, $38,117. Awards are based on need and merit. Required financial statement is the FAFSA. The aid application deadline for fall entry is March 1. Special funds for minority or disadvantaged students range from $2500 to $12,500 and may be renewable, with conditions, for the full term of legal studies. First-year students are notified about their financial aid application within 3 weeks of the offer of admission.

About the Law School

Seattle University School of Law was established in 1972 and is a private institution. The 56-acre campus is in an urban area on Seattle's First Hill. The primary mission of the law school is to prepare students to practice law with competence and honor. Students have access to federal, state, county, city, and local agencies, courts, correctional facilities, law firms, and legal aid organizations in the Seattle area. Facilities of special interest to law students Sullivan Hall which contains classrooms and seminar spaces equipped with data ports for each seat and desk space large enough to accommodate a laptop computer for every student. The entire building is wired for the use of on-line legal research services such as Westlaw and other Internet uses. There is also an on-line electronic teaching laboratory. The Archbishop Thomas Murphy Apartments are designed for single students seeking an environment conducive to academic pursuits. They include furnished private studios, private and shared 1-bedrooms, shared 2-bedroom townhouses, and shared 4-bedroom apartments. All apartments feature controlled access, appliances, and mircowaves. Rents range from $620 to $739 per month. All law school facilities are accessible to the physically disabled.

Calendar

The law school operates on a traditional semester basis. Courses for full-time students are offered both day and evening and must be completed within 5 years. For part-time students, courses are offered both day and evening and must be completed within 6 years. New full- and part-time students are admitted in the fall and summer. There is a 6- to 8-week summer session. Transferable summer courses are offered.

Programs

Students may take relevant courses in other programs and apply credit toward the J.D.; a maximum of 4 credits may be applied. The following joint degrees may be earned: J.D./M.B.A. (Juris Doctor/Master of Business Administration), J.D./M.I.B (Juris Doctor/Master of International Business), and J.D./M.S. (Juris Doctor/Master of Science in finance).

Required

To earn the J.D., candidates must complete 90 total credits, of which 44 are for required courses. They must maintain a minimum GPA of 2.0 in the required courses. The following first-year courses are required of all students: Criminal Law, Civil Procedure, Contracts, Property, Torts, and Legal Writing. Required upper-level courses consist of Constitutional Law, Legal Writing II, Evidence, and Professional Responsibility. The required orientation program for first-year students consists of a 2-day series of workshops and, throughout the year, seminars on both academic and non-academic issues.

Electives

Students must take a minimum of 3 courses in their area of concentration. The School of Law offers concentrations in corporate law, criminal law, environmental law, international law, labor law, litigation, securities law, tax law, torts

Phone: 206-398-4200
Fax: 206-398-4058
E-mail: *lawadmis@seattleu.edu*
Web: *www.law.seattleu.edu*

Contact

Carol Cochran, Associate Director of Admission, 206-398-4200 for general inquiries; Kathleen Koch, Director of Financial Aid, 206-398-4250 for financial aid information.

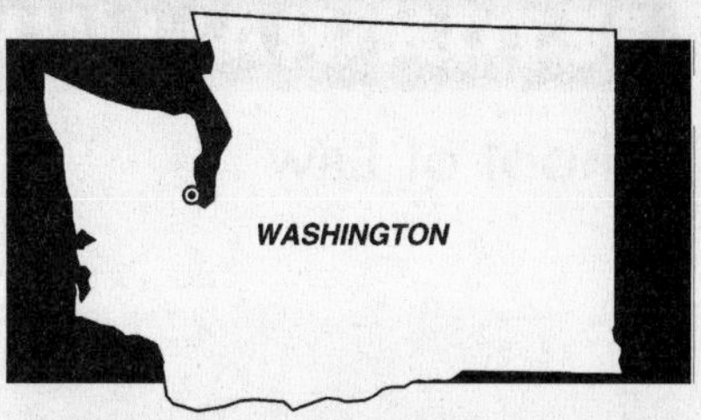

and insurance, health and medicine, commercial law, estate planning, and intellectual property and law. In addition, clinics include Law Practice, a 4- to 6-credit course in which 30 third-year students, supervised by faculty members, represent clients in civil cases and the state in criminal misdemeanor cases. Seminars are available in 15 limited-enrollment advanced classes, worth 2 to 4 credits, with subjects ranging from Constitutional Adjudication and Corporate Finance to Human Rights. Part-time externships, worth 3 to 4 credits, are available for students in the judiciary and with several preapproved agencies and governmental organizations. Full-time judicial externships, worth 15 credits, are also available. Research programs include work with faculty members conducting research in subjects such as involuntary commitment of mentally ill, and freedom of the press and the First Amendment; independent study on topics of student interest are also encouraged. More than 80% of students are employed in law-related field work positions each year with corporate firms, partnerships, federal, state, and local public agencies, and nonprofit associations. The Alumni/ae Lecture Series brings distinguished scholars, jurists, and practitioners to campus to comment on compelling legal issues. Students may participate in study-abroad programs sponsored by other ABA law schools and receive up to 6 credits. The Academic Resource Center, staffed by a full-time J.D. alumna, offers tutorial services as well as group workshops and seminars. The Alternative Admission Program, designed for historically disadvantaged, physically challenged, and older applicants (limited to 30 students a year), is an intensive program integrating first-year classes with group instruction. Minority programs are conducted through the Black Law Student Association, Latino Law Student Society, and Asian/Pacific Islander Law Student Association. Special interest group programs include activities by the Environmental Law Society, International Law Society, and Entertainment/Sports Law Society. The most widely taken electives are Administrative Law, UCC Sales, and Secured Transactions.

Graduation Requirements

In order to graduate, candidates must have a GPA of 2.0 and have completed the upper-division writing requirement.

Organizations

Students edit the *Seattle University Law Review, The Seattle Journal of Social Justice*, and the newspaper *The Prolific Reporter*. Moot court competitions include Jessup International Law, Giles S. Rich Patent Law, and Frederick Douglass. Other competitions include National Mock Trial, Association of Trial Lawyers of America, Client Counseling, and Alternative Dispute Resolution. Law student organizations include the Student Bar Association, Public Interest Law Foundation, and St. Thomas More Society. Other organizations include Amnesty International, Christian Legal Society, and Black Law Student Association. There are local chapters of American Trial Lawyers Association, Phi Alpha Delta, and Phi Delta Phi.

Library

The law library contains 332,145 hard-copy volumes and 979,998 microform volume equivalents, and subscribes to 3790 serial publications. Such on-line databases and networks as CALI, DIALOG, LEXIS, LOIS, NEXIS, OCLC First Search, and WESTLAW are available to law students for research. Special library collections include a U.S. government documents depository. Virtually every library carrel, table, and study area provides Internet access. Extensive compact shelving ensures onsite access to all library materials. A Document Delivery Center offers students printing and photocopying services. The ratio of library volumes to faculty is 9226 to 1 and to students is 329 to 1. The ratio of seats in the library to students is 1 to 3.

Faculty

The law school has 36 full-time and 79 part-time faculty members, of whom 42 are women. According to AAUP standards for Category IIA institutions, faculty salaries are above average. About 15% of full-time faculty have a graduate law degree in addition to the J.D.; about 15% of part-time faculty have one. The ratio of full-time students to full-time faculty in an average class is 21 to 1; in a clinic, 10 to 1. The law school has a regular program of bringing visiting professors and other distinguished lecturers and visitors to campus.

Placement

J.D.s awarded:	261
Services available through: a separate law school placement center.	
Services: comprehensive lists of judges, courts, and application requirements for judicial clerkships.	
Special features: daily postings of student and alumni job openings; jobs posted on a web site; a "Job Board" newsletter sent to all graduates for free for 1 year; a "Hotline" available 24 hours daily for weekly listing of jobs; and videotaped workshops so evening students and others can have access to information on interviewing techniques, resume writing, and job search strategies. Printed material is also available.	
Full-time job interviews:	27 employers
Summer job interviews:	60 employers
Placement by graduation:	51% of class
Placement within 9 months:	88% of class
Average starting salary:	$35,000 to $125,000
Areas of placement:	
Private practice 2-10 attorneys	24%
Private practice 11-25 attorneys	3%
Private practice 26-50 attorneys	2%
Private practice 51-100 attorneys	12%
Unknown	21%
Government	17%
Business/industry	12%
Judicial clerkships	6%
Public interest	2%
Military	1%

Students

About 53% of the student body are women; 23%, minorities; 3%, African American; 11%, Asian American; 4%, Hispanic; 1%, Native American; and 4%, multi-cultural. The majority of students come from Washington (81%). The average age of entering students is 28; age range is 20 to 60. About 27% of students enter directly from undergraduate school, 12% have a graduate degree, and 79% have worked full-time prior to entering law school. About 5% drop out after the first year for academic or personal reasons; 86% remain to receive a law degree.

SETON HALL UNIVERSITY

School of Law

One Newark Center
Newark, NJ 07102-5210

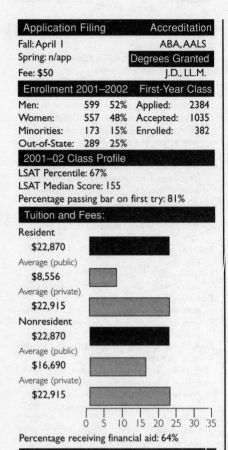

Application Filing		Accreditation
Fall: April 1		ABA, AALS
Spring: n/app		**Degrees Granted**
Fee: $50		J.D., LL.M.

Enrollment 2001–2002			First-Year Class	
Men:	599	52%	Applied:	2384
Women:	557	48%	Accepted:	1035
Minorities:	173	15%	Enrolled:	382
Out-of-State:	289	25%		

2001–02 Class Profile

LSAT Percentile: 67%
LSAT Median Score: 155
Percentage passing bar on first try: 81%

Tuition and Fees:

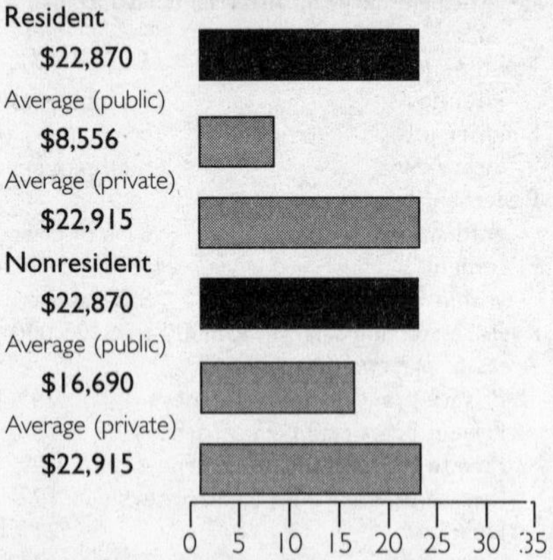

Percentage receiving financial aid: 64%

ADMISSIONS

In the fall 2001 first-year class, 2384 applied, 1035 were accepted, and 382 enrolled. Ten transfers enrolled. The median LSAT percentile of the most recent first-year class was 67; the median GPA was 3.2 on a scale of 4.0. The lowest LSAT percentile accepted was 50; the highest was 95.

Requirements

Applicants must have a bachelor's degree and take the LSAT. Minimum acceptable GPA is 2.5 on a scale of 4.0. The most important admission factors include LSAT results, GPA, and undergraduate curriculum. No specific undergraduate courses are required. Candidates are not interviewed.

Procedure

The application deadline for fall entry is April 1. Applicants should submit an application form, LSAT results, transcripts, TOEFL for non-English speaking applicants, a nonrefundable application fee of $50, 2 letters of recommendation, and a personal statement. Notification of the admissions decision is January to May. The latest acceptable LSAT test date for fall entry is February. The law school uses the LSDAS.

Special

The law school recruits minority and disadvantaged students through Legal Education Opportunities for educationally disadvantaged applicants, Minority Law Day, the Pre-Legal Institute, the Mentor Program, Candidate Referral Service, and campus visits. Requirements are not different for out-of-state students. Transfer students must have one year of credit, have attended an ABA-approved law school, and be in the top 15% of the law class. Preadmissions courses consist of the Pre-Legal Institute, the Mentor Program, and the Legal Education Opportunities program for admission to law school for the educationally disadvantaged.

Costs

Tuition and fees for the 2001-2002 academic year are $22,870 for all full-time students. Tuition for part-time students is $16,290 per year. Books and supplies run about $850 annually.

Financial Aid

About 64% of current law students receive some form of aid. The average annual amount of aid from all sources combined, including scholarships, loans, and work contracts, is $8000. Awards are based on need and merit. Required financial statement is the FAFSA. The aid application deadline for fall entry is April 15. Special funds for minority or disadvantaged students are set aside from overall aid funds. First-year students are notified about their financial aid application on a rolling basis.

About the Law School

Seton Hall University School of Law was established in 1951 and is a private institution. The 2-acre campus is in an urban area in Newark. The primary mission of the law school is to synthesize a strong traditional approach to legal training with a commitment to community involvement. Students are encouraged to excel and to appreciate key values: integrity, responsibility, ethics, and service. Students have access to federal, state, county, city, and local agencies, courts, correctional facilities, law firms, and legal aid organizations in the Newark area. All legal resources are blocks away from the school. The resources of New York City are 20 minutes away. Facilities of special interest to law students include a modern 200,000 square foot law center with a state-of-the-art computer, library, classrooms, and moot courts. Housing for students is available as rental housing in the vicinity and university housing on the South Orange campus, 5 miles away. All law school facilities are accessible to the physically disabled.

Calendar

The law school operates on a traditional semester basis. Courses for full-time students are offered both day and evening and must be completed within 6 years. For part-time students, courses are offered both day and evening and must be completed within 6 years. New full- and part-time students are admitted in the fall. There is a 6- to 8-week summer session. Transferable summer courses are offered.

Programs

In addition to the J.D., the law school offers the LL.M. and M.S.J. The following joint degrees may be earned: J.D./M.A. (Juris Doctor/Master of Arts in diplomacy), J.D./M.B.A. (Juris Doctor/Master of Business Administration), and J.D./M.D. (Juris Doctor/Doctor of Medicine).

Phone: 973-642-8747
888-415-7271
Fax: 973-642-8876
E-mail: *admitme@shu.edu*
Web: *law.shu.edu*

Contact

Dean of Admissions and Financial Resource Management, 973-642-8747 or 888-415-7271 for general inquiries; Sharon Williams, Director of Financial Aid, 973-642-8744 for financial aid information.

Required

To earn the J.D., candidates must complete 85 total credits, of which 44 are for required courses. The following first-year courses are required of all students: Civil Procedure, Constitutional Law, Contracts, Criminal Law, Torts, Property, and Legal Research and Legal Writing. Required upper-level courses consist of Business Associations, Appellate Advocacy, Evidence, Professional Responsibility, and Federal Income Taxation. All students must take clinical courses. The required orientation program for first-year students is a day-long program commencing immediately before the start of classes with activities continuing into the first week of classes.

Electives

The School of Law offers concentrations in corporate law, criminal law, entertainment law, environmental law, family law, international law, juvenile law, labor law, litigation, tax law, health law, property and estates, and public law. All clinics are live client clinics and include Preventive Law, a voluntary pro bono proram with juvenile counseling, 5 community service placements, and Legal Services. Seminars are offered in all major areas for upper-level students. Internships include Judicial, U.S. Bankruptcy Trustee, Environmental Protection Administration, Internal Revenue Service, European Court of Justice, Health, NLRB, and U.S. Attorney. Research opportunities include an independent research course, many seminars, and the opportunity to serve as a faculty research assistant. There are lectures in sports law, environmental law, legislative topics, health law, and from nearly all student organizations. There are summer study-abroad programs in Parma and Milan, Italy as well as Cairo, Egypt. Tutorial assistance is available for all first-year courses. Special programs for minority students are the Mentor Program for high school students and the Legal Education Opportunities Admissions program. Special interest group programs are available through various religious and ethnic-based organizations. The most widely taken electives are Criminal Procedure, Decedents' Estates and Trusts, and Remedies.

Graduation Requirements

In order to graduate, candidates must have a GPA of 2.0, have completed the upper-division writing requirement, and have no more than 10 credits of D or D+ and no more than 95 credits.

Organizations

Students edit the *Seton Hall Law Review*, *Legislative Journal*, *Sports Law Journal*, *Constitutional Law Journal*, and the newspaper *Res Ipsa Loquitur*. Second-year students compete in the Appellate Advocacy Moot Court Competition; teams are selected from intraschool competitions held for credit during the fall semester. Teams also compete in the National Moot Court Competition and competitions in corporate, constitutional, and family law. Law student organizations include the Health Law Society, Environmental Law Society, and Women's Law Forum. There are local chapters of Phi Alpha Delta and Black Law Students Association.

Library

The law library contains 425,509 hardcopy volumes and 495,570 microform volume equivalents, and subscribes to 6614 serial publications. Such on-line databases and networks as DIALOG, LEXIS, WESTLAW, NEXIS, and the Internet are available to law students for research. Special library collections include the Rodino Papers and depositories for federal and New Jersey state documents. Recently, the library completed a 65,000 square-foot, 3-level facility with electronic classroom and 235 computer workstations. The ratio of library volumes to faculty is 7336 to 1 and to students is 368 to 1. The ratio of seats in the library to students is 1 to 2.

Faculty

The law school has 58 full-time and 84 part-time faculty members, of whom 44 are women. About 25% of full-time faculty have a graduate law degree in addition to the J.D.; about 10% of part-time faculty have one. The ratio of full-time students to full-time faculty in an average class is 20 to 1; in a clinic, 5 to 1. The law school has a regular program of bringing visiting professors and other distinguished lecturers and visitors to campus.

Placement

J.D.s awarded: 320

Services available through: a separate law school placement center

Services: mentor programs, attorney writing sample review

Special features: an evening placement counselor, on-site meeting rooms, newsletters, on-line services, extensive placement library.

Full-time job interviews:	100 employers
Summer job interviews:	100 employers
Placement by graduation:	95% of class
Placement within 9 months:	96% of class
Average starting salary:	$60,000 to $70,000
Areas of placement:	
Private practice 2-100 attorneys	39%
Judicial clerkships	36%
Unknown	9%
Government	6%
Business/industry	6%
Public interest	3%
Academic	1%

Students

About 48% of the student body are women; 15%, minorities; 6%, African American; 8%, Asian American; 8%, Hispanic; and 1%, Native American. The majority of students come from New Jersey (75%). The average age of entering students is 26; age range is 21 to 52. About 39% of students enter directly from undergraduate school. About 10% drop out after the first year for academic or personal reasons; 90% remain to receive a law degree.

SOUTH TEXAS COLLEGE OF LAW

1303 San Jacinto Street
Houston, TX 77002-7000

Application Filing		Accreditation
Fall: February 25		ABA, AALS
Spring: October 1		**Degrees Granted**
Fee: $50		J.D.

Enrollment 2001–2002			First-Year Class	
Men:	636	51%	Applied:	1394
Women:	614	49%	Accepted:	934
Minorities:	313	25%	Enrolled:	436
Out-of-State:	63	5%		

2001–02 Class Profile

LSAT Percentile: 43%
LSAT Median Score: 149
Percentage passing bar on first try: 78%

Tuition and Fees:

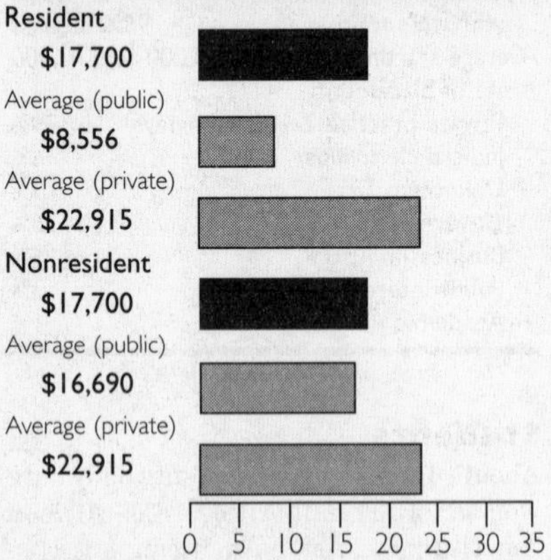

Percentage receiving financial aid: 90%

ADMISSIONS

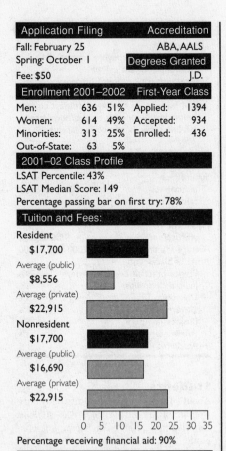

In the fall 2001 first-year class, 1394 applied, 934 were accepted, and 436 enrolled. Six transfers enrolled. The median LSAT percentile of the most recent first-year class was 43; the median GPA was 2.95 on a scale of 4.0. The lowest LSAT percentile accepted was 15; the highest was 92.

Requirements

Applicants must have a bachelor's degree and take the LSAT. The most important admission factors include LSAT results, GPA, and life experience. No specific undergraduate courses are required. Candidates are not interviewed.

Procedure

The application deadline for fall entry is February 25. Applicants should submit an application form, a nonrefundable application fee of $50, 2 required letters of recommendation, a personal statement, and a resume. Notification of the admissions decision is ongoing following the deadline. The latest acceptable LSAT test date for fall entry is February. The law school uses the LSDAS.

Special

The law school recruits minority and disadvantaged students by offering application-fee waivers for those with documented need. South Texas considers ethnicity and disadvantaged backgrounds in the admissions process and offers scholarships to those who qualify. Requirements are not different for out-of-state students. Transfer students must have one year of credit, have attended an ABA-approved law school, and be ranked in the upper 10% of the current law school class, and be able to provide a letter of good standing.

Costs

Tuition and fees for the 2001-2002 academic year are $17,700 for all full-time students. Tuition for part-time students is $12,000 per year. Books and supplies run about $912 annually.

Financial Aid

About 90% of current law students receive some form of aid. The average annual amount of aid from all sources combined, including scholarships, loans, and work contracts, is $21,523; maximum, $40,463. Awards are based on need and merit. Required financial statement is the FAFSA. The aid application deadline for fall entry is May 1. Special funds for minority or disadvantaged students are available through Enhancement Scholarships for continuing students. First-year students are notified about their financial aid application at time of application.

About the Law School

South Texas College of Law was established in 1923 is independent. The campus is in an urban area in downtown Houston. The primary mission of the law school is to develop highly ethical lawyers from all segments of society who are committed to promoting equal and accessible justice for all. Students have access to federal, state, county, city, and local agencies, courts, correctional facilities, law firms, and legal aid organizations in the Houston area. South Texas is the only American law school to house on its premises two appellate courts on a permanent basis. The Law Institute for Medical Studies is a forum for interdiciplinary dialogue and education on health care topics with special legal concerns. The Center for Legal Responsibility involves students in managing conflict, resolving disputes, and devising settlement strategies. Both institutes are actively involved in community outreach and publication. On-campus housing is not available. However, high-rise apartments are within walking distance of the campus. Apartment locators are available, usually at no cost. All law school facilities are accessible to the physically disabled.

Calendar

The law school operates on a traditional semester basis. Courses for full-time students are offered both day and evening and must be completed within 6 years. For part-time students, courses are offered both day and evening and must be completed within 6 years. New full- and part-time students are admitted in the fall and spring. There is an 8-week summer session. Transferable summer courses are offered.

Programs

Required

To earn the J.D., candidates must complete 90 total credits, of which 44 are for required courses. They must maintain a minimum GPA of 2.0 in the required courses. The following first-year courses are required of all students: Torts I and II, Contracts I and II, Property I, Civil Procedure, Legal Research and Writing I and II, Criminal Law, and Constitutional Law. Required upper-level courses consist of Property II, Federal Income

Phone: 713-646-1810
Fax: 713-646-2906
E-mail: *admissions@stcl.edu*
Web: *www.stcl.edu*

Contact

Alicia Cramer, Director of Admissions, 713-646-1810 for general inquiries; Sergio Gonzalez, Director of Financial Aid, 713-646-1820 for financial aid information.

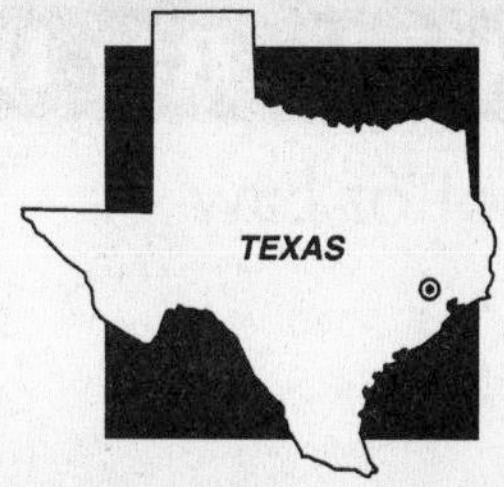

Tax, Evidence, and Professional Responsibility, and a substantial research paper. The required 3- or 4-day orientation is generally scheduled the week prior to the beginning of classes, formatted to accommodate both full- and part-time students.

Electives

The South Texas College of Law offers concentrations in environmental law, international law, Advocacy, Health Law, and Alternative Dispute Resolution. In addition, the college offers both on- and off-site clinics where upper-level students are eligible to earn a maximum of 6 semester hours of credit during their law school career by representing clients in a variety of cases in state and federal courts and administrative agencies.To qualify for enrollment in a seminar, a student must have completed 45 hours and usually a required paper. A limit of 3 seminar courses may be applied toward graduation. Seminars are offered for 2 hours credit. Externships are normally offered during the fall, spring, and summer and are limited to a maximum of 6 credit hours. After completion of certain prerequisites, upper-level students are eligible to enroll in the Criminal Process Clinic, Judicial Process Clinic, Public and Governmental Interest Clinic, or the Hospital Law Externship Program. South Texas co-sponsors a number of ABA-approved summer abroad programs, in addition to 3 cooperative semester abroad programs. Students may apply to study abroad as transient students, and all approved credit hours earned will be applied toward graduation. South Texas also administers an academic assistance program to help students achieve their scholastic endeavors. The program includes individual counseling and study skills seminars on the outlining process, as well as preparing for and taking exams. The program also provides eligible students with weekly group sessions focusing on study skills and legal analysis. The college is committed to affirmative action programs. The most widely taken electives are Marital Property, Family Law, and Texas Pretrial Procedure.

Graduation Requirements

In order to graduate, candidates must have a GPA of 2.0 and have completed the upper-division writing requirement.

Organizations

Students edit the *South Texas Law Review, Corporate Counsel Review, Currents: International Trade Law Journal*, and the newspaper, *Annotations*. Students enrolled in the Moot Court Competition course are selected to participate among the 24 national moot court and mock trial competitons held annually. South Texas has more than 25 registered organizations in which students can participate. There are local chapters of Phi Delta Phi, Phi Alpha Delta, and Delta Theta Phi. Campus clubs and other organizations include the Student Bar Association, the Order of the Lytae, and the Order of Barristers.

Library

The law library contains 214,935 hard-copy volumes and 1,202,508 microform volume equivalents, and subscribes to 4427 serial publications. Such on-line databases and networks as CALI, CIS Universe, Infotrac, Legal-Trac, LEXIS, LOIS, Mathew Bender, NEXIS, OCLC First Search, and WESTLAW are available to law students for research. Special library collections include a U.S. government selective depository and a rare books collection, college archives, and various manuscript collections. Recently, the library completed construction on The Fred Parks Law Library. Floors 1 to 5 of the building are comprised of classrooms, seminar and conference rooms with additional carrel space, 2-person study rooms, faculty study rooms, and soft seating. The 6th floor is a flexible combination of classroom and ceremonial space with an adjoining outdoor terrace. The ratio of library volumes to faculty is 3908 to 1 and to students is 172 to 1. The ratio of seats in the library to students is 1 to 7.

Faculty

The law school has 55 full-time and 38 part-time faculty members, of whom 24 are women. About 31% of full-time faculty have a graduate law degree in addition to the J.D. The ratio of full-time students to full-time faculty in an average class is 20 to 1; in a clinic, 16 to 1. The law school has a regular program of bringing visiting professors and other distinguished lecturers and visitors to campus.

Placement

J.D.s awarded:	334
Services available through: a separate law school placement center. The Career Services Office publicizes various job fairs and maintains a library of placement opportunities.	
Special features: seminars and speaker programs, skills training workshops, alumni mentor program, tours and visits to local and out-of-city courts, area corporations and law firms, networking breakfasts, 6 to 8 job fairs each year, and coordination of campus interviews.	
Full-time job interviews:	25 employers
Summer job interviews:	44 employers
Placement by graduation:	n/av
Placement within 9 months:	90% of class
Average starting salary:	$40,000 to $65,000
Areas of placement:	
Private practice 2-10 attorneys	25%
Private practice 11-25 attorneys	9%
Private practice 26-50 attorneys	5%
Private practice 51-100 attorneys	7%
Business/industry	19%
Unknown	12%
Government	10%
Judicial clerkships	5%
Self-employed	3%
Graduate Students	2%
Public interest	1%
Military	1%

Students

About 49% of the student body are women; 25%, minorities; 6%, African American; 6%, Asian American; 12%, Hispanic; 1%, Native American; and 75%, white. The majority of students come from Texas (95%). The average age of entering students is 28; age range is 21 to 60. About 11% drop out after the first year for academic or personal reasons; 89% remain to receive a law degree.

SOUTHERN ILLINOIS UNIVERSITY

School of Law

Lesar Law Building, Mail Code 6804
Carbondale, IL 62901-6804

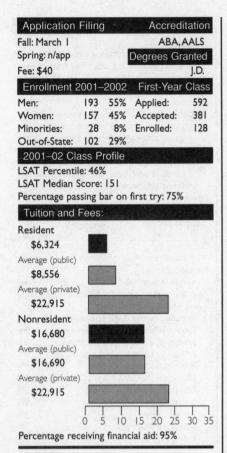

Application Filing	Accreditation
Fall: March 1	ABA, AALS
Spring: n/app	**Degrees Granted**
Fee: $40	J.D.

Enrollment 2001–2002			First-Year Class	
Men:	193	55%	Applied:	592
Women:	157	45%	Accepted:	381
Minorities:	28	8%	Enrolled:	128
Out-of-State:	102	29%		

2001–02 Class Profile

LSAT Percentile: 46%
LSAT Median Score: 151
Percentage passing bar on first try: 75%

Tuition and Fees:

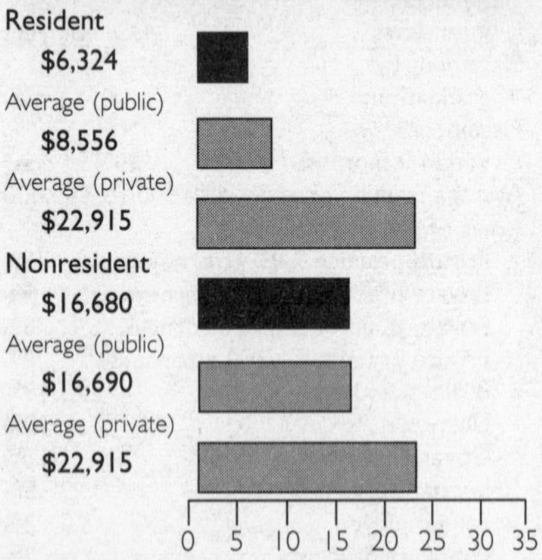

Percentage receiving financial aid: 95%

ADMISSIONS

In the fall 2001 first-year class, 592 applied, 381 were accepted, and 128 enrolled. Six transfers enrolled. The median LSAT percentile of the most recent first-year class was 46; the median GPA was 3.17 on a scale of 4.0. The lowest LSAT percentile accepted was 24; the highest was 89.

Requirements

Applicants must have a bachelor's degree and take the LSAT. Minimum acceptable LSAT percentile is 24. The most important admission factors include LSAT results, GPA, and writing ability. No specific undergraduate courses are required. Candidates are not interviewed.

Procedure

The application deadline for fall entry is March 1. Applicants should submit an application form, LSAT results, transcripts, a nonrefundable application fee of $40, 2 recommended letters of recommendation, and a personal statement. Notification of the admissions decision is as early as possible. The latest acceptable LSAT test date for fall entry is February. The law school uses the LSDAS.

Special

The law school recruits minority and disadvantaged students by means of the Candidate Referral Service; special programs at the School of Law, including an Open House for admitted minority applicants; networking; and contacting institutions that serve minority and disadvantaged students. Requirements are not different for out-of-state students. Transfer students must have one year of credit and have attended an ABA-approved law school. Applicants may be admitted if it appears likely that they will successfully complete the School of Law curriculum. Factors considered include, among other things, the applicant's law school record, class rank, law school attended, LSAT, and GPA.

Costs

Tuition and fees for the 2001-2002 academic year are $6324 for full-time in-state students and $16,680 for out-of-state students. On-campus room and board costs about $6086 annually; books and supplies run $870.

Financial Aid

About 95% of current law students receive some form of aid. The average annual amount of aid from all sources combined, including scholarships, loans, and work contracts, is $14,240; maximum, $18,500. Awards are based on need and merit. The required financial statement is the FAFSA. The aid application deadline for fall entry is April 1. Special funds for minority or disadvantaged students include scholarships. First-year students are notified about their financial aid application at time of acceptance.

About the Law School

Southern Illinois University School of Law was established in 1973 and is a public institution. The 3290-acre campus is in a rural area 100 miles southeast of St. Louis, Missouri. The primary mission of the law school is to train lawyers who will be competent to practice law now and in the future, exhibit leadership, and adhere to the ethical standards of the legal profession. Students have access to federal, state, county, city, and local agencies, courts, correctional facilities, law firms, and legal aid organizations in the Carbondale area. Facilities of special interest to law students consist of numerous law firms, state, local, (and federal law offices, nonprofit organizations), and courts in southern Illinois where students can get legal experience and training. Housing for students is available in dorms across the street from the law school. There is also plenty of off-campus housing available within 10 minutes of the law school. All law school facilities are accessible to the physically disabled.

Calendar

The law school operates on a traditional semester basis. Courses for full-time students are offered days only and must be completed within 5 years. There is no part-time program. New full-time students are admitted in the fall. There is an 8-week summer session. Transferable summer courses are offered.

Programs

Students may take relevant courses in other programs and apply credit toward the J.D.; a maximum of 6 credits may be applied. The following joint degrees may be earned: J.D./M. Acct. (Juris Doctor/Master of Accounting), J.D./M.B.A. (Juris Doctor/Master of Business Administration), J.D./M.D. (Juris Doctor/Doctor of Medicine), J.D./M.P.A. (Juris Doctor/Master of Public Administration), J.D./M.S.W. (Juris Doctor/Master of Social Work), and J.D./Ph.D. (Juris Doctor/Doctor of Philosophy in political science).

Phone: 618-453-8767
800-739-9187
Fax: 618-453-8769
E-mail: *lawadmit@siu.edu*
Web: *www.lawsiu.edu*

Contact

Assistant Dean for Admissions and Student Affairs, 618-453-8768 or 800-739-9187 for general inquiries; Financial Aid Office Coordinator (Rick Steudel), 618-453-4334 for financial aid information.

Required

To earn the J.D., candidates must complete 90 total credits, of which 48 are for required courses. They must maintain a minimum GPA of 2.0 in the required courses. The following first-year courses are required of all students: Torts, Contracts I and II, Property I and II, Lawyering Skills I and II, Legislative and Administrative Process, Civil Procedure I, and Criminal Law. Required upper-level courses consist of Civil Procedure II, Evidence, Legal Profession, Constitutional Law, and a writing requirement. All students must take clinical courses. The required orientation program for first-year students extends over a 3-day period and consists of small group discussions, tours, a mock class, an ethics lecture, and a full day of academic content.

Electives

The School of Law offers concentrations in international law, litigation, tax law, and health law. In addition, 3 in-house clinics are offered to senior law students for up to 6 hours of credit: the elder law clinic, the alternative dispute resolution clinic, and the domestic violence clinic. Third-year students, except editors of the *Southern Illinois University Law Journal*, are required to take a senior writing seminar for 3 credit hours. Senior law students may enroll for up to 6 hours in externships; credit is earned by working public interest or legal services agency for local prosecutors and public defenders, for local judges, or for local and state agencies. Independent research and a writing credit is allowed under certain conditions. Each year the law school hosts the Lesar Lecture Series and the Dr. Arthur Grayson Distinguished Lecture (Law and Medicine). A voluntary tutorial program is available for first-year students. An academic enhancement course is available to students who need extra assistance during their first year. The school makes individual accommodations to the needs of its disabled students. The most widely taken electives are Criminal Procedure, Introduction to Commercial Law, and Remedies.

Graduation Requirements

In order to graduate, candidates must have a GPA of 2.0, have completed the upper-division writing requirement, and must maintain a 2.0 GPA for courses taken during the third year of law school.

Organizations

Students edit the *Southern Illinois University Law Journal* and the *Journal of Legal Medicine*. The Moot Court Board sends teams to numerous competitions, including the ABA Appellate Advocacy Competition, Jessup International Moot Court Competition, and Illinois Moot Court Competition. The student division of the ABA holds an annual intraschool Client, Interviewing and Counseling Competition as well as a Negotiation Competition. Student organizations include the Student Bar Association, Environmental Law Society, and Christian Legal Society. There are local chapters of the Black Law Students Association, Lesbian and Gay Law Students Association, and Women's Law Forum. Other organizations include Amnesty International, Federalist Society, and the ABA/Law School Division.

Library

The law library contains 367,614 hard-copy volumes and 854,156 microform volume equivalents, and subscribes to 4324 serial publications. Such on-line databases and networks as CALI, CIS Universe, Infotrac, Legal-Trac, LEXIS, LOIS, NEXIS, OCLC First Search, WESTLAW, Wilsonline Indexes, Access UN, CCH Tax, CILP, Global Newsbank, Hein-Online, News Illinois, PDR, Shepard's Citation Service, Britannica, BNA U.S. Law Week, and ABA/BNA Lawyers Manual on Professional Conduct are available to law students for research. Special library collections include a federal government selective depository library and Illinois state comprehensive document depository. Recently, the library installed new carpeting, painted, and added public computer stations. The ratio of library volumes to faculty is 13,615 to 1 and to students, 1050 to 1. The ratio of seats in the library to students is 1 to 1.

Placement

J.D.s awarded:	116
Services available through: a separate law school placement center	
Full-time job interviews:	28 employers
Summer job interviews:	28 employers
Placement by graduation:	n/av
Placement within 9 months:	94% of class
Average starting salary:	$35,000 to $40,000
Areas of placement:	
Private practice 2-10 attorneys	25%
Private practice 11-25 attorneys	6%
Private practice 26-50 attorneys	2%
Private practice 51-100 attorneys	2%
Government	31%
Judicial clerkships	12%
Business/industry	10%
Public interest	3%
Military	3%
Academic	3%
Unknown	3%

Faculty

The law school has 27 full-time and 9 part-time faculty members, of whom 14 are women. According to AAUP standards for Category I institutions, faculty salaries are well below average. About 30% of full-time faculty have a graduate law degree in addition to the J.D. The ratio of full-time students to full-time faculty in an average class is 34 to 1; in a clinic, 4 to 1. The law school has a regular program of bringing visiting professors and other distinguished lecturers and visitors to campus.

Students

About 45% of the student body are women; 8%, minorities; 3%, African American; 3%, Asian American; and 2%, Hispanic. The majority of students come from the Midwest (84%). The average age of entering students is 26. About 7% drop out after the first year for academic or personal reasons; 93% remain to receive a law degree.

SOUTHERN METHODIST UNIVERSITY

School of Law

Office of Admissions, P.O. Box 750110
Dallas, TX 75275-0110

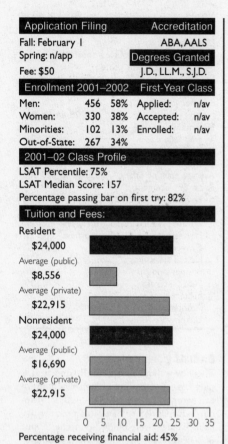

Application Filing	Accreditation
Fall: February 1	ABA, AALS
Spring: n/app	**Degrees Granted**
Fee: $50	J.D., LL.M., S.J.D.

Enrollment 2001–2002			First-Year Class	
Men:	456	58%	Applied:	n/av
Women:	330	38%	Accepted:	n/av
Minorities:	102	13%	Enrolled:	n/av
Out-of-State:	267	34%		

2001–02 Class Profile

LSAT Percentile: 75%
LSAT Median Score: 157
Percentage passing bar on first try: 82%

Tuition and Fees:

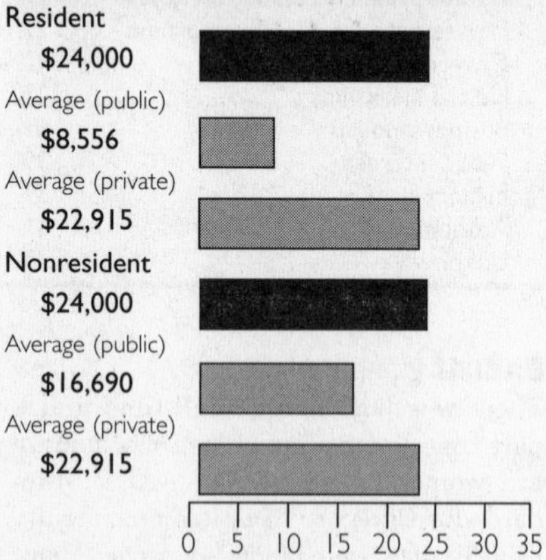

Percentage receiving financial aid: 45%

ADMISSIONS

Information in the above capsule is from an earlier year. In a recent first-year class, seventeen transfers enrolled. The median LSAT percentile of a recent first-year class was 75; the median GPA was 3.3 on a scale of 4.0. The highest LSAT percentile was 99.

Requirements

Applicants must have a bachelor's degree and take the LSAT. Minimum acceptable GPA is 2.0 on a scale of 4.0. The most important admission factors include academic achievement, LSAT results, and writing ability. No specific undergraduate courses are required. Candidates are not interviewed.

Procedure

Check with the school for current application deadlines and fee. Applicants should submit an application form, LSAT results, a nonrefundable application fee, 2 letters of recommendation, a personal statement, and a resume. Notification of the admissions decision is rolling, beginning December 15. The law school uses the LSDAS.

Special

The law school recruits minority and disadvantaged students by means of school visitations and special mailings and telethons. Requirements are not different for out-of-state students. Transfer students must have one year of credit and have attended an ABA-approved law school. Admission for transfers is described as highly competitive and very restrictive.

Costs

Tuition and fees for the academic year are approximately $24,000 for all full-time students. On-campus room and board costs about $8400 annually; books and supplies run about $1300.

Financial Aid

About 45% of law students receive some form of aid. The average annual amount of aid from all sources combined, including scholarships, loans, and work contracts, is about $6000; maximum, $24,800. Awards are based on need and merit. Required financial statements are the FAFSA and others, depending on the type of scholarship being sought. Check with the school for current deadlines. Special funds for minority or disadvantaged students are provided through scholarships, which are available on a need and merit basis and are designed to promote the diversity of the student body and the legal profession, and to assist those who have had fewer academic opportunities. First-year students are notified about their financial aid application at time of acceptance.

About the Law School

Southern Methodist University School of Law was established in 1925 and is a private institution. The campus is in a suburban area 5 miles north of downtown Dallas. The primary mission of the law school is to prepare students for the competent and ethical practice of law through a curriculum that combines training in the science and method of law, knowledge of the substance and procedure of law, understanding of the role of law in an international society, and practical experience in handling professional problems. Students have access to federal, state, county, city, and local agencies, courts, correctional facilities, law firms, and legal aid organizations in the Dallas area. Facilities of special interest to law students are the fully computerized Underwood Law Library, and remodeled Collins Hall, which houses expanded admissions and career services offices, a large career services resource center, student lounges, and state-of-the art seminar rooms. Housing for students, consisting of both single- and married-student housing, is available on campus on a first-come, first-served basis.

Calendar

The law school operates on a traditional semester basis. Courses for full-time students are offered days with a few evening courses, and must be completed within 5 years. There is no part-time program. New students are admitted in the fall. There is an 8-week summer session. Transferable summer courses are not offered.

Programs

In addition to the J.D., the law school offers the LL.M. and S.J.D. Students may take relevant courses in other programs and apply credit toward the J.D.; a maximum of 6 credits may be applied. The following joint degrees may be earned: J.D./M.A. (Juris Doctor/Master of Arts in applied economics) and J.D./M.B.A. (Juris Doctor/Master of Business Administration).

Phone: 214-768-2550
Fax: 214-768-2549
E-mail: *lawadmit@mail.smu.edu*
Web: *law.smu.edu*

Contact

Lynn Bozalis, Assistant Dean of Admissions, 214-768-2550 for general inquiries; Financial Aid Counselor, 214-768-3417 for financial aid information.

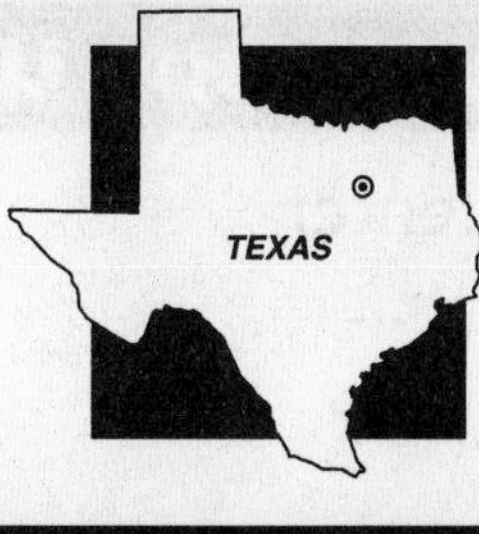

Required

To earn the J.D., candidates must complete 90 total credits, of which 37 are for required courses. They must maintain a minimum GPA of 2.0 in the required courses. The following first-year courses are required of all students: Contracts, Property, Torts, Civil Procedure, Criminal Law and Procedure, Legal Research, Analysis, and Writing, Lawyering, and Constitutional Law. Required upper-level courses consist of a writing requirement, an edited writing seminar, and Professional Responsibility. The required orientation program for first-year students consists of a 2-day introduction to the study of law.

Electives

The School of Law offers concentrations in corporate law, criminal law, environmental law, family law, international law, litigation, securities law, and tax law. In addition, Civil, Criminal, and Tax clinics may be taken by second- or third-year students who meet prerequisites. Seminars include such topics as Advanced Commercial Law, Antitrust, and Civil Rights. Directed Research is worth a maximum of 3 hours. Field work may be done through Directed Studies, and is worth 1 to 2 hours. A mandatory 30 hours of pro bono work is required for graduation. The special lecture series includes the Murrah Lecture and the Tate Lecture. A summer program at Oxford University is provided for students who wish to study abroad. The Academic Support Tutorial program is available by invitation only. The non-credit Student Tutorial program is available for all first-year law students. Minority programs include Minority Law Day, the Diversity Clerkship Program, Southeastern Minority Job Fair, Sunbelt Minority Job Fair, and the Black/Hispanic/Asian Law Students Associations. Special interest group programs include the Board of Advocates and law student groups.

Graduation Requirements

In order to graduate, candidates must have a GPA of 2.0, have completed the upper-division writing requirement, and a 30-hour pro bono work requirement.

Organizations

Students edit the *SMU Law Review, Journal of Air Law and Commerce, The International Lawyer, Computer Section Reporter, NAFTA: Law and Business Review of the Americas*, and the newspaper *Advocate*. Moot court competitions include the Jackson and Walker, National Frederick Douglass, and Jessup Moot Court competitions. Other competitions include the Client Counseling, ABA Mock Trial, ATLA Mock Trial, and the Geary, Glast, and Middleton Mock Trial. Law student organizations include Barristers, LEGALS, and Student Bar Association. Local chapters of national associations include Delta Theta Phi, Phi Alpha Delta, and Phi Delta Phi.

Library

The law library contains 480,000 hardcopy volumes and 75,217 microform volume equivalents, and subscribes to 2000 serial publications. Such on-line databases and networks as DIALOG, LEXIS, WESTLAW, and NEXIS are available to law students for research. Special library collections include a rare book room. Recently, the library was refurbished with chairs, tables, carpet, and paint. The ratio of library volumes to faculty is 9792 to 1 and to students is 500 to 1. The ratio of seats in the library to students is 1 to 1.

Faculty

The law school has approximately 42 full-time and 100 part-time faculty members. According to AAUP standards for Category I institutions, faculty salaries are above average. About 40% of full-time faculty have a graduate law degree in addition to the J.D. The ratio of full-time students to full-time faculty in an average class is 20 to 1; in a clinic, 8 to 1. The law school has a regular program of bringing visiting professors and other distinguished lecturers and visitors to campus. There is a chapter of the Order of the Coif; 5 faculty and 10 graduates are members.

Placement

J.D.s awarded:	n/av
Services available through: a separate law school placement center	
Full-time job interviews:	n/av
Summer job interviews:	n/av
Placement by graduation:	68% of class
Placement within 9 months:	95% of class
Average starting salary:	$66,000
Areas of placement:	
Private practice 51-100 attorneys	69%
Business/industry	15%
Government	8%
unknown	5%
Judicial clerkships	3%
Public interest	1%

Students

About 38% of the student body are women and 13% are minorities. The majority of students come from Texas (66%). The average age of entering students is 24; age range is 20 to 51. About 3% drop out after the first year for academic or personal reasons; 90% remain to receive a law degree.

SOUTHERN UNIVERSITY AND A & M COLLEGE

Law Center

Post Office Box 9294
Baton Rouge, LA 70813-9294

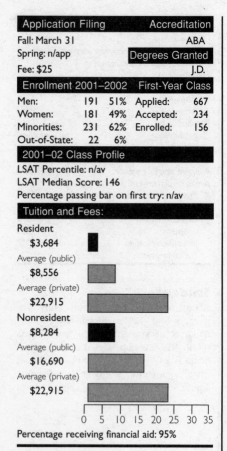

Application Filing		Accreditation
Fall: March 31		ABA
Spring: n/app		**Degrees Granted**
Fee: $25		J.D.

Enrollment 2001–2002			First-Year Class	
Men:	191	51%	Applied:	667
Women:	181	49%	Accepted:	234
Minorities:	231	62%	Enrolled:	156
Out-of-State:	22	6%		

2001–02 Class Profile

LSAT Percentile: n/av
LSAT Median Score: 146
Percentage passing bar on first try: n/av

Tuition and Fees:

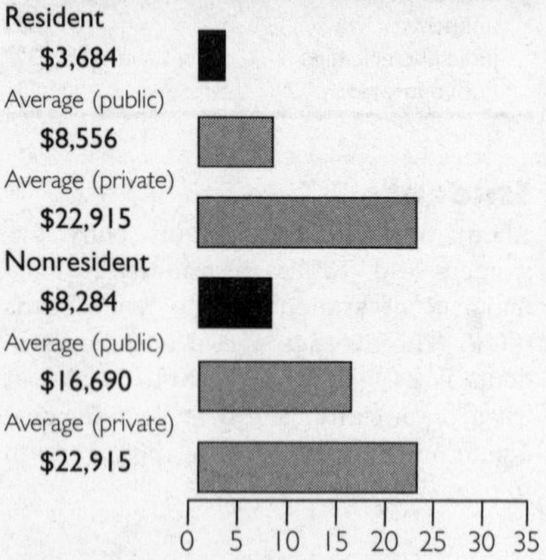

Percentage receiving financial aid: 95%

ADMISSIONS

In the fall 2001 first-year class, 667 applied, 234 were accepted, and 156 enrolled. The median GPA of the most recent first-year class was 2.8 on a scale of 4.0.

Requirements

Applicants must have a bachelor's degree and take the LSAT. Minimum acceptable GPA is 2.0 on a scale of 4.0. The most important admission factors include LSAT results, GPA, and academic achievement. No specific undergraduate courses are required. Candidates are not interviewed.

Procedure

The application deadline for fall entry is March 31. Applicants should submit an application form, LSAT results, transcripts, a nonrefundable application fee of $25, 2 letters of recommendation, and a personal statement. Notification of the admissions decision is from April 15 to July 30. The latest acceptable LSAT test date for fall entry is February. The law school uses the LSDAS.

Special

The law school recruits minority and disadvantaged students by participating in various programs at minority feeder schools. Requirements are not different for out-of-state students. Transfer students must have one year of credit, have a minimum GPA of 2.5, have attended an ABA-approved law school, and matriculate at least 1 year at the law center if transferring from a Louisiana law school, and 2 if from others.

Costs

Tuition and fees for the 2001-2002 academic year are $3684 for full-time in-state students and $8284 for out-of-state students. Tuition for part-time students is $1828 in-state and $6428 out-of-state. On-campus room and board costs about $5375 annually; books and supplies run $1800.

Financial Aid

About 95% of current law students receive some form of aid. The average annual amount of aid from all sources combined, including scholarships, loans, and work contracts, is $15,363; maximum, $19,963. Awards are based on need and merit. The required financial statement is the FAFSA. The aid application deadline for fall entry is April 15. First-year students are notified about their financial aid application at the time of application to the law school.

About the Law School

Southern University and A & M College Law Center was established in 1947 and is a public institution. The campus is in an urban area in Baton Rouge. The primary mission of the law school is to prepare students for the practice of law with specific emphasis upon minorities and the disadvantaged; the program of study is designed to give students a comprehensive knowledge of both the civil law and common law and knowledge of a lawyer's ethics and responsibility to society. Students have access to federal, state, county, city, and local agencies, courts, correctional facilities, law firms, and legal aid organizations in the Baton Rouge area. Facilities of special interest to law students are the WESTLAW and LEXIS Laboratory, the Law Review, and the computer laboratory. Housing for students is convenient and ample. About 90% of the law school facilities are accessible to the physically disabled.

Calendar

The law school operates on a traditional semester basis. Courses for full-time students are offered days only and must be completed within 5 years. There is no part-time program. New students are admitted in the fall. There is a 6-week summer session. Transferable summer courses are offered.

Phone: 225-771-5340
800-537-1135
Fax: 225-771-2121
E-mail: *vwilkerson@sus.edu*
Web: *sulc.edu*

Contact

Velma Wilkerson, Admissions Coordinator, 225-771-5340 for general inquiries; Jerome Harris, Director of Financial Aid, 225-771-2141 for financial aid information.

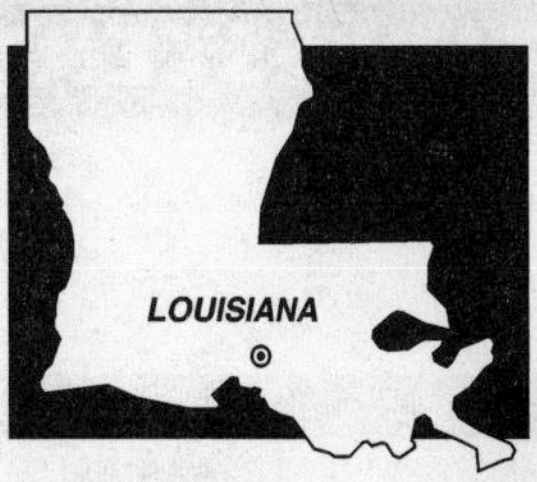

Programs

The following joint degrees may be earned: J.D./M.P.A. (Juris Doctor/Master of Public Administration).

Required

To earn the J.D., candidates must complete 96 total credits, of which 75 are for required courses. They must maintain a minimum GPA of 2.0 in the required courses. The following first-year courses are required of all students: Basic Civil Procedure, Legal Writing I and II, Legal Research, Torts I and II, Contracts, Civil Law Property, Constitutional Law I, Obligations, Family Law, and Criminal Law. Required upper-level courses consist of Evidence, Civil Procedure I and II, Sales and Leases, Criminal Procedure, Trial Advocacy, Agency and Partnership, Corporations, Successions and Donations, Federal Jurisdiction and Procedure, Commercial Papers, Professional Responsibility, Conflict of Laws, Security Devices, Constitutional Law II, and Advanced Legal Writing I and II. The required orientation program for first-year students is a 1- or 2-day program, with emphasis on analysis, reading comprehension, case briefing, and communication skills.

Electives

Administrative, Juvenile, Criminal, and Elderly Law clinics are limited to third-year students who may earn 6 credit hours. Seminars are available in various subject areas for second- and third-year students. Individual student research projects are available for 1 credit hour under the supervision of a professor. Nationally recognized legal scholars are invited each semester to lecture on current issues. At least 3 lectures are scheduled during the school year. Freshman students are required to participate in 1 monthly session and tutorial programs 2 times a week. The most widely taken electives are Civil Rights, Law Office Practice, and Workers Compensation.

Graduation Requirements

In order to graduate, candidates must have a GPA of 2.0 and complete a residency requirement (6 semesters).

Organizations

Students edit the *Southern University Law Review* and the student newspaper, *The Public Defender*. Moot court competitions include the annual National Moot Court competition, the In-House Round Robin, and Thurgood Marshall competitions. Student organizations include Student Bar Association, Black Law Students Association, and Student Trial Lawyers Association. Local chapters of national associations include Phi Alpha Delta, Delta Theta Phi, and ABA-Law Student Division. Other organizations include the Environmental Law Society, Women in Law, and Sports and Entertainment Legal Association.

Library

The law library contains 415,208 hard-copy volumes and 7867 microform volume equivalents, and subscribes to 670 serial publications. Such on-line databases and networks as CALI, DIALOG, Legal-Trac, LEXIS, LOIS, NEXIS, and WESTLAW are available to law students for research. Special library collections include civil rights and civil law collections, and state and federal depositories. Recently, the library added a computer laboratory with 25 terminals and on-line terminals for federal documents. The ratio of library volumes to faculty is 13,840 to 1 and to students, 1116 to 1. The ratio of seats in the library to students is 1 to 89.

Faculty

The law school has 30 full-time and 14 part-time faculty members, of whom 12 are women. According to AAUP standards for Category IIA institutions, faculty salaries are well below average. About 20% of full-time faculty have a graduate law degree in addition to the J.D.; about 15% of part-time faculty have one. The ratio of full-time students to full-time faculty in an average class is 14 to 1; in a clinic, 11 to 1. The law school has a regular program of bringing visiting professors and other distinguished lecturers and visitors to campus.

Placement	
J.D.s awarded:	86
Services available through: a separate law school placement center	
Special features: web site information on job opportunities and newsletters from other campuses.	
Full-time job interviews:	6 employers
Summer job interviews:	18 employers
Placement by graduation:	90% of class
Placement within 9 months:	10% of class
Average starting salary:	$28,000 to $53,000
Areas of placement:	
Private practice 2-10 attorneys	33%
Private practice 11-25 attorneys	2%
Private practice 51-100 attorneys	3%
Solo practice	8%
Judicial clerkships	21%
Government	13%
Business/industry	8%
Unknown	8%
Military	2%
Academic	2%

Students

About 49% of the student body are women; 62%, minorities; 60%, African American; 1%, Asian American; 1%, Hispanic; and 38%, Caucasian. The majority of students come from the South (96%). The average age of entering students is 27; age range is 21 to 58. About 60% of students enter directly from undergraduate school, 20% have a graduate degree, and 40% have worked full-time prior to entering law school. About 10% drop out after the first year for academic or personal reasons; 90% remain to receive a law degree.

SOUTHWESTERN UNIVERSITY

School of Law

675 South Westmoreland Avenue
Los Angeles, CA 90005-3992

Application Filing		Accreditation
Fall: June 30		ABA, AALS
Spring: n/app		**Degrees Granted**
Fee: $50		J.D.

Enrollment 2001–2002			First-Year Class	
Men:	418	48%	Applied:	2143
Women:	461	52%	Accepted:	1007
Minorities:	334	38%	Enrolled:	380
Out-of-State:	132	15%		

2001–02 Class Profile

LSAT Percentile: n/av
LSAT Median Score: n/av
Percentage passing bar on first try: n/av

Tuition and Fees:

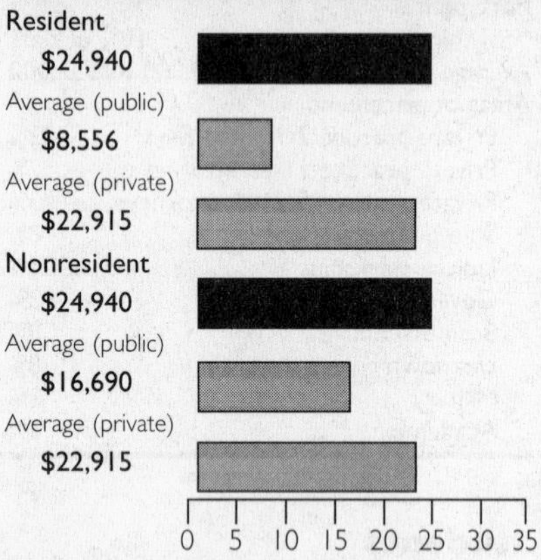

Percentage receiving financial aid: 80%

ADMISSIONS

In the fall 2001 first-year class, 2143 applied, 1007 were accepted, and 380 enrolled. Eighteen transfers enrolled.

Requirements

Applicants must have a bachelor's degree and take the LSAT. The most important admission factors include LSAT results, GPA, and academic achievement. No specific undergraduate courses are required. Candidates are not interviewed.

Procedure

The application deadline for fall entry is June 30. Applicants should submit an application form, LSAT results, transcripts, a nonrefundable application fee of $50, and a personal statement; up to 3 letters of recommendation are strongly recommended. Notification of the admissions decision is on a rolling basis. The latest acceptable LSAT test date for fall entry is February, although June may be acceptable for some candidates. The law school uses the LSDAS.

Special

The law school recruits minority and disadvantaged students by means of participation by admissions staff in minority recruitment programs at undergraduate campuses around the country, a Law Day program held at the law school for minority junior college and university students, admissions receptions on campus, public service announcements in print and broadcast media, scholarship programs, and programs for prospective students sponsored by minority student organizations at the law school. Requirements are not different for out-of-state students. Transfer students must have one year of credit, have a minimum GPA of 2.0, have attended an ABA-approved law school, and have a maximum of 43 transferable semester units; they must also submit a letter of good standing from that school's dean. Preadmissions courses consist of Introduction to Legal Writing: a Seminar for Pre-Law Students, a 4-week, noncredit course that provides a foundation in specialized legal writing skills. An academic support program is also offered for 2 weeks before the start of school.

Costs

Tuition and fees for the 2001-2002 academic year are $24,940 for all full-time students. Tuition for part-time students is $15,832 per year. Books and supplies run about $620 annually.

Financial Aid

About 80% of current law students receive some form of aid. The average annual amount of aid from all sources combined, including scholarships, loans, and work contracts, is $21,500; maximum, $37,000. Awards are based on need and merit. The required financial statements are the FAFSA and the school's financial aid application. The aid application deadline for fall entry is June 1. Special funds for minority or disadvantaged students consist of approximately a dozen different scholarship funds, the most significant of which is the John J. Schumacher Minority Leadership Scholarship Program for outstanding academic and leadership potential. First-year students are notified about their financial aid application within 2 weeks of acceptance.

About the Law School

Southwestern University School of Law was established in 1911 and is a private institution. The 2-acre campus is in an urban area in Los Angeles. The primary mission of the law school is to offer, through an excellent and committed faculty, full-time, part-time, traditional, and nontraditional Juris Doctorate programs that prepare students with diverse backgrounds and interests to assume positions of responsiblity and trust within the legal profession and the greater community. Students have access to federal, state, county, city, and local agencies, courts, correctional facilities, law firms, and legal aid organizations in the Los Angeles area. Facilities of special interest to law students include the renovated historic Bullocks Wilshire building, which accommodates the Law Library and features state-of-the-art computer laboratories, research training classrooms, and study rooms. Ample parking for students is available on campus. Housing for students is not available on campus; however, apartments and homes are located nearby. About 99% of the law school facilities are accessible to the physically disabled.

Calendar

The law school operates on a traditional semester basis. Courses for full-time students are offered days only and with some evening electives available and must be completed within 5 years. For part-time students, courses are offered both day and evening and must be completed within 5 years. New full- and part-time students are admitted in the fall. There is an 8-week summer session. Transferable summer courses are offered.

Programs

Required

To earn the J.D., candidates must complete 87 total credits, of which 52 are for required courses. They must maintain a minimum GPA of 2.0 in the required courses. The following first-year courses are required of all students: Civil Procedure I and II, Contracts I and II, Criminal Law, Legal Process, Legal Research and Writing I and II, Property I and II, Torts I and II, and Legal Profession. Required upper-level courses consist of Business Associations, Constitutional Law I and II, Evidence, Remedies, a seminar that satisfies a writing requirement, and Constitutional Criminal Procedure. Simulation training is part of required courses such as Legal Research and Writing and electives such as Civil Pre-Trial Practice; Interviewing, Counseling and Negotiating; and Trial Advocacy. The required orientation program for first-year students is a 3-day program featuring formal presentations by deans and faculty, a Legal Process

Phone: 213-738-6717
Fax: 213-383-1688
E-mail: *admissions@swlaw.edu*

Contact

Anne Wilson, Admissions Director, 213-738-6717 for general inquiries; Wayne Mahoney, Financial Aid Director, 213-738-6719 for financial aid information.

course, and a luncheon/dinner for students and faculty members.

Electives

The School of Law offers concentrations in corporate law, criminal law, entertainment law, environmental law, family law, international law, litigation, media law, tax law, and health law. In addition, a simulated clinical experience is available through courses such as Legal Research and Writing; Interviewing, Counseling, and Negotiating; and Trial Advocacy. Seminars offered for 2 units require in-depth research, analysis, and writing. Titles encompass many areas of the law, including intellectual property, international law, and private and public sector administrative issues. Practical experience may be gained through more than 100 part- and full-time externships available in the judiciary; public interest law firms; federal, state, and local government offices; and entertainment industry settings. Two to ten units per externship placement may be earned on a credit/no credit basis. A limited number of judicial externships in Argentine courts is also available through the Summer Program in Buenos Aires. Paid faculty research assistant positions are available. Special lecture series include the Law Review Distinguished Lecture Series, Faculty Speakers Committee Lecture Series, Alumni Judges Lecture Series, Career Development Panels, and a variety of speakers presented by student organizations. The law review and law journal also sponsor scholarly symposia. Study-abroad programs featuring international and comparative law courses taught by school faculty and other international legal experts are offered in Vancouver, British Columbia, Canada, Buenos Aires, Argentina, and Guanajuato, Mexico. Formal tutorial programs for first-year students and all students on academic probation are offered. Student organizations and faculty members sponsor research and exam-writing tutorials, and librarians conduct tutorials for new law clerks. The Academic Support Program is available for a selected number of entering students. Programs offered especially for minority students include a Minority Career Development seminar, other panel presentations by minority attorneys and judges, and job search skills reviews sponsored by the Placement Office in conjunction with minority bar and law student associations. A Diversity Day for prospective students provides information on admissions and financial aid processes. More than 35 special-interest student organizations offer lectures, seminars, and workshops to students. The most widely taken electives are Administrative Law, Community Property, and Federal Courts.

Graduation Requirements

In order to graduate, candidates must have a GPA of 2.0 and have completed the upper-division writing requirement.

Organizations

Students edit the *Southwestern University Law Review*, the *Southwestern Journal of Law and Trade in the Americas*, a law journal devoted to the legal and economic issues of North, Central, and South America, and the newspaper *The Commentator*. The annual moot court competition for first-year students consists of successive rounds held on campus, at the Los Angeles Superior Court, and the U.S. Court of Appeals. Moot Court Honors Program members compete in 12 to 15 regional and national interscholastic competitions annually. A formal Interscholastic Trial Advocacy Program fields several teams at competitions around the country. Teams also compete in the Interscholastic Client Counseling and the Interscholastic Negotiation competitions. Law student organizations include the ABA-Law Student Division, Criminal Law Society, and Entertainment and Sports Law Society. There are local chapters of American Society of International Law, Association of Trial Lawyers of America, and the Federalist Society. Graduate student organizations include the Alumni Association, Friends of the Library, and the Dean's Circle.

Library

The law library contains 428,947 hardcopy volumes and 59,459 microform volume equivalents, and subscribes to 4626 serial publications. Such on-line databases and networks as DIALOG, LEXIS, WESTLAW, NEXIS and Wilsonline (ILP) are available to law students for research. Special library collections include U.S. and California depositories, a trial practice collection, and collections in taxation, constitutional law, and entertainment law. Recently, the library added comprehensive LEXIS and WESTLAW training centers and installed the Innopac automated cataloging system. The ratio of library volumes to faculty is 8579 to 1 and to students, 488 to 1. The ratio of seats in the library to students is 1 to 2.

Placement

J.D.s awarded:	207
Services available through: the school's placement center	
Services: videotaped mock interviews conducted by alumni practitioners	
Special features: career seminars, panel presentations on various areas of law practice, workshops on job search techniques and interview strategies, joint Career Day and interview programs with other law schools, a comprehensive career resource library, and on-campus interview programs in the fall and spring.	
Full-time job interviews:	n/av
Summer job interviews:	n/av
Placement by graduation:	64% of class
Placement within 9 months:	84% of class
Average starting salary:	$54,680
Areas of placement:	
Private practice 2-10 attorneys	15%
Private practice 11-25 attorneys	11%
Private practice 26-50 attorneys	10%
Private practice 51-100 attorneys	11%
Business/industry	23%
Unknown	13%
Government	11%
Academic	3%
Judicial clerkships	2%
Public interest	1%

Faculty

The law school has 50 full-time and 38 part-time faculty members, of whom 29 are women. About 20% of full-time faculty have a graduate law degree in addition to the J.D. The ratio of full-time students to full-time faculty in an average class is 16 to 1; in a clinic, 16 to 1.

Students

About 52% of the student body are women; 38%, minorities; 7%, African American; 18%, Asian American; 12%, Hispanic; and 1%, Native American. The majority of students come from California (85%). The average age of entering students is 26; age range is 20 to 55. About 30% of students enter directly from undergraduate school, 12% have a graduate degree, and 50% have worked full-time prior to entering law school. About 20% drop out after the first year for academic or personal reasons; 80% remain to receive a law degree.

ST. THOMAS UNIVERSITY

School of Law

16400 N.W. 32nd Avenue
Miami, FL 33054

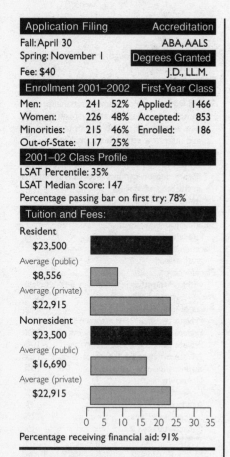

Application Filing		Accreditation
Fall: April 30		ABA, AALS
Spring: November 1		**Degrees Granted**
Fee: $40		J.D., LL.M.

Enrollment 2001–2002			First-Year Class	
Men:	241	52%	Applied:	1466
Women:	226	48%	Accepted:	853
Minorities:	215	46%	Enrolled:	186
Out-of-State:	117	25%		

2001–02 Class Profile

LSAT Percentile: 35%
LSAT Median Score: 147
Percentage passing bar on first try: 78%

Tuition and Fees:

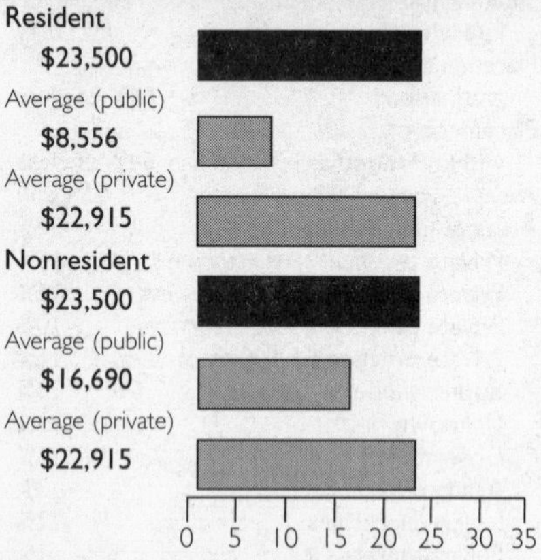

Percentage receiving financial aid: 91%

ADMISSIONS

In the fall 2001 first-year class, 1466 applied, 853 were accepted, and 186 enrolled. Four transfers enrolled. The median LSAT percentile of the most recent first-year class was 35; the median GPA was 2.8 on a scale of 4.0. The lowest LSAT percentile accepted was 16; the highest was 96.

Requirements

Applicants must have a bachelor's degree and take the LSAT. Minimum acceptable LSAT percentile is 15 and minimum acceptable GPA is 2.0 on a scale of 4.0. The most important admission factors include LSAT results, academic achievement, and general background. No specific undergraduate courses are required. Candidates are not interviewed.

Procedure

The application deadline for fall entry is April 30. Applicants should submit an application form, LSAT results, transcripts, a nonrefundable application fee of $40, 1 letter of recommendation, and a personal statement. Notification of the admissions decision is on a rolling basis. The latest acceptable LSAT test date for fall entry is June. The law school uses the LSDAS.

Special

The law school recruits minority and disadvantaged students by means of recruiting at various historically black colleges and universities, and direct mail to target populations using Candidate Referral Service (CRS). Requirements are not different for out-of-state students. Transfer students must have one year of credit, a minimum GPA of 2.7, have attended an ABA-approved law school, and have a letter of good standing.

Costs

Tuition and fees for the 2001-2002 academic year are $23,500 for all full-time students. On-campus room and board costs about $7900 annually; books and supplies run $1000.

Financial Aid

About 91% of current law students receive some form of aid. The average annual amount of aid from all sources combined, including scholarships, loans, and work contracts, is $25,570; maximum, $38,830. Awards are based on need and merit. Required financial statement is the FAFSA. The aid application deadline for fall entry is May 1. First-year students are notified about their financial aid application at time of acceptance.

About the Law School

St. Thomas University School of Law was established in 1984 and is a private institution. The campus is in a suburban area 15 miles northwest of downtown Miami. The primary mission of the law school is to provide a personalized, value-oriented legal education to a diverse student body, including those from groups traditionally underrepresented by and within the legal profession. Students have access to federal, state, county, city, and local agencies, courts, correctional facilities, law firms, and legal aid organizations in the Miami area. Housing for students include on-campus dormitories and a variety of off-campus housing, located within a few miles of the campus. All law school facilities are accessible to the physically disabled.

Calendar

The law school operates on a traditional semester basis. Courses for full-time students are offered both day and evening and must be completed within 5 years. There is no part-time program. New students are admitted in the fall and spring. There is an 8-week summer session. Transferable summer courses are offered.

Programs

In addition to the J.D., the law school offers the LL.M. The following joint degrees may be earned: J.D./M.B.A. (Juris Doctor/Master of Business Administration in accounting and international business) and J.D./M.S. (Juris Doctor/ Master of Science in marriage and family counseling and sports administration).

Required

To earn the J.D., candidates must complete 87 total credits, of which 62 are for required courses. They must maintain a minimum GPA of 2.0 in the required courses. The following first-year courses are required of all students: Civil Procedure I and II, Contracts I and II, Torts I and II, Criminal Law, Legal Analysis, Writing, and Research, Appellate Advocacy, and Perspectives on Legal Thought. Required upper-level courses consist of Property I and II, Constitutional Law II, Advanced Legal Research and Writing, Evidence, Criminal Procedure I, Profes-

Phone: 305-623-2310
800-245-4569
E-mail: *lamy@stu.edu*

Contact

Lydia Amy, Assistant Dean for Enrollment/Career Services, 305-623-2384 for general inquiries; Office of Financial Aid, 305-628-6547 for financial aid information.

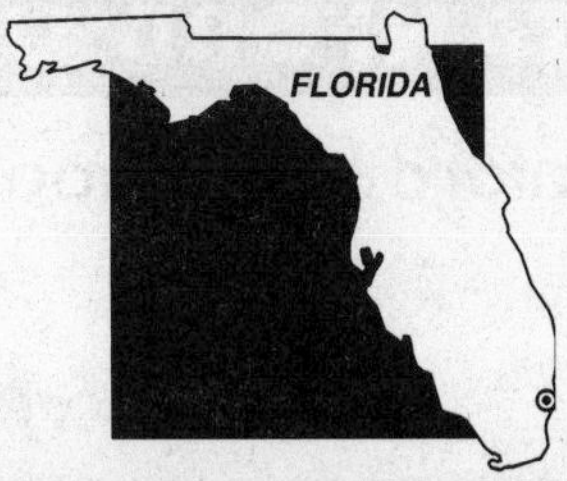

sional Responsibility, senior writing requirement, Agency and Partnership, Corporations, and Wills and Trusts. The required orientation program for first-year students is a 2-day program during which students register, are introduced to legal research and writing, learn how to brief a case, meet faculty, administration, and staff, and learn about student organizations.

Electives

The law school sponsors an immigration clinic, a bankruptcy clinic, a family court clinic, and a tax clinic. Clinics are 4 credits per semester, including a separate summer clinic. A wide range of 2-credit seminars are available to upper-class students, including, for example, Church and State, Health Law and Policy, and Women and the Law. Independent research projects may be undertaken by upper-class students for 2 credits. An 8-credit, year-long clinical field placement program is available to upper-class students and features placement in civil and criminal government agencies. A lecture series every fall offers presentations primarily geared to first-year students on effective note taking, time management and study strategies, stress management, the importance of writing well, and effective exam preparation. St. Thomas sponsors a month-long summer-abroad program in Spain. In addition, upper-class students may take up to 7 credits in an ABA-accredited summer-abroad program sponsored by law schools other than St. Thomas. Students are provided with a high-ranking upper-class tutor upon request. Second- and third-year black students serve as mentors for first-year black law students in a Big Brother/Big Sister program. Legal fraternities and other student organizations offer lecture series, mentoring programs, and other projects. The most widely taken electives are Family Law, Alternative Dispute Resolution, and Real Estate Transactions.

Graduation Requirements

In order to graduate, candidates must have a GPA of 2.5, have completed the upper-division writing requirement, study law in residence for 96 weeks, and pursue the entire study of law as a full-time student for 6 semesters or the equivalent, the last 2 of which must be at St. Thomas. They must also complete 40 hours of pro bono work and pass a competency exam.

Organizations

Students edit the *St. Thomas Law Review* and the newspaper *Opinio Juris.* Moot court competitions include the Philip C. Jessup International Law Moot Court, National Entertainment Law Moot Court, and the National Labor Law Moot Court. Other competitions include the American Bar Association National Trial Tournament, The American Trial Lawyers Association National Trial Tournament, the National Trial Advocacy Competition, and the Frederick Douglass Trial Competition. Law student organizations include American Bar Association/Law Student Division, Black Law Student Association, and Catholic Student Lawyers Guild. Local chapters of national organizations include the Entertainment and Sports Law Society, the Florida Association for Women Lawyers, and Phi Delta Phi - Spellman Inn.

Library

The law library contains 301,971 hardcopy volumes and 1,032,585 microform volume equivalents, and subscribes to 2976 serial publications. Such on-line databases and networks as CALI, CIS Universe, DIALOG, Legal-Trac, LEXIS, Mathew Bender, NEXIS, OCLC First Search, WESTLAW, and NEXIS are available to law students for research. Recently, the library made available a wireless network with capacity for 1054 connections. The ratio of library volumes to faculty is 11,614 to 1 and to students is 647 to 1. The ratio of seats in the library to students is 1 to 80.

Faculty

The law school has 26 full-time and 21 part-time faculty members, of whom 15 are women. About 38% of full-time faculty have a graduate law degree in addition to the J.D.; about 9% of part-time faculty have one. The ratio of full-time students to full-time faculty in an average class is 22 to 1; in a clinic, 8 to 1. The law school has a regular program of bringing visiting professors and other distinguished lecturers and visitors to campus.

Placement

J.D.s awarded: 141

Services available through: a separate law school placement center

Services: providing monthly newsletter for students, monthly job listings for alumni, written guides on aspects of job search and career planning, conducting workshops and seminars, participating in southeastern job fairs, sponsoring guest speakers on areas of legal practice, judicial clerkships, and alternative careers, participating in minority opportunity programs and mentoring programs with alumni, the Florida Bar Association, and the Broward and Dade County Bar Associations.

Special features: individualized attention for all students. The Office conducts mandatory individual meetings with first-year students, sets aside 4 hours daily for appointments with advanced and graduating students, and schedules exit interviews.

Full-time job interviews:	22 employers
Summer job interviews:	30 employers
Placement by graduation:	23% of class
Placement within 9 months:	85% of class
Average starting salary:	$38,000 to $40,000
Areas of placement:	
Private practice 2-10 attorneys	27%
Private practice 11-25 attorneys	8%
Private practice 26-50 attorneys	3%
Private practice 51-100 attorneys	6%
Private practice solo	9%
Business/industry	25%
Government	16%
Public interest	3%

Students

About 48% of the student body are women; 46%, minorities; 13%, African American; 2%, Asian American; 31%, Hispanic; 1%, Native American; and 6%, international students and those from an unknown ethnic group. The majority of students come from Florida (75%). The average age of entering students is 27; age range is 21 to 55. About 94% of students enter directly from undergraduate school, 6% have a graduate degree, and 5% have worked full-time prior to entering law school. About 32% drop out after the first year for academic or personal reasons; 68% remain to receive a law degree.

STANFORD UNIVERSITY

Stanford Law School

Crown Quadrangle
Stanford, CA 94305-8610

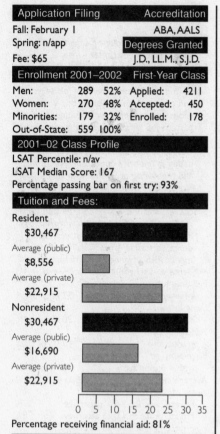

Application Filing		Accreditation
Fall: February 1		ABA, AALS
Spring: n/app		**Degrees Granted**
Fee: $65		J.D., LL.M., S.J.D.

Enrollment 2001–2002			First-Year Class	
Men:	289	52%	Applied:	4211
Women:	270	48%	Accepted:	450
Minorities:	179	32%	Enrolled:	178
Out-of-State:	559	100%		

2001–02 Class Profile

LSAT Percentile: n/av
LSAT Median Score: 167
Percentage passing bar on first try: 93%

Tuition and Fees:

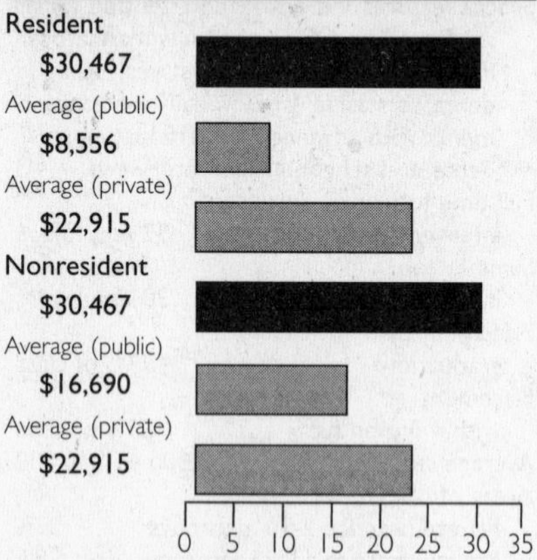

Percentage receiving financial aid: 81%

ADMISSIONS

In the fall 2001 first-year class, 4211 applied, 450 were accepted, and 178 enrolled. Eight transfers enrolled. The median GPA of the most recent first-year class was 3.83 on a scale of 4.0.

Requirements

Applicants must have a bachelor's degree and take the LSAT. No specific undergraduate courses are required. Candidates are not interviewed.

Procedure

The application deadline for fall entry is February 1. Applicants should submit an application form, LSAT results, transcripts, a nonrefundable application fee of $65, 2 letters of recommendation, and a statement of good standing from the undergraduate dean. Notification of the admissions decision is on a rolling basis. The latest acceptable LSAT test date for fall entry is December. The law school uses the LSDAS.

Special

The law school recruits minority and disadvantaged students by attending law forums and Law Days, and making individual school visits. Requirements are not different for out-of-state students. Transfer students must have one year of credit and have attended an ABA-approved law school.

Costs

Tuition and fees for the 2001-2002 academic year are $30,467 for full-time students. On-campus room and board costs about $12,705 annually; books and supplies run $1360.

Financial Aid

About 81% of current law students receive some form of aid. The average annual amount of aid from all sources combined, including scholarships, loans, and work contracts, is $34,701; maximum, $52,339. Awards are based on need. The required financial statements are the FAFSA and Need Access Form. First-year students are notified about their financial aid application upon receipt of the Need Access and FAFSA analyses.

About the Law School

Stanford University Stanford Law School was established in 1893 and is a private institution. The 6109-acre campus is in a suburban area 35 miles south of San Francisco. The primary mission of the law school is to be a national and world leader in the education of lawyers and in the expansion of legal knowledge through research with the ultimate aim of improving the legal orders of the domestic and global communities. Students have access to federal, state, county, city, and local agencies, courts, correctional facilities, law firms, and legal aid organizations in the Stanford area. Housing for students is guaranteed to all new students who apply for housing by a specified date and are willing to live anywhere on campus. Law students are given priority for Crothers Hall. All law school facilities are accessible to the physically disabled.

Calendar

The law school operates on a traditional semester basis. Courses for full-time students are offered days only and must be completed within 7 semesters. There is no part-time program. New students are admitted in the fall. There is no summer session. Transferable summer courses are not offered.

Programs

In addition to the J.D., the law school offers the LL.M., S.J.D., and M.L.S. Students may take relevant courses in other programs and apply credit toward the J.D.; a maximum of 11 credits may be applied. The following joint degrees may be earned: J.D./M.A. (Juris Doctor/Master of Arts with Johns Hopkins) and J.D./M.P.A. (Juris Doctor/Master of Public Administration with Princeton University).

Required

To earn the J.D., candidates must complete 86 total credits, of which 27 are for required courses. The following first-year courses are required of all students: Civil Procedure, Contracts, Criminal Law, Torts, Research and Legal Writing, Constitutional Law, and Property. The required orientation program for first-year students is a 2-day program that includes an introduction to legal institutions and work on case briefings.

Phone: 650-723-4985
Fax: 650-723-0838
E-mail: *law.admissions@forsythe.stanford.edu/*

Contact

Office of Admissions, 650-723-4985 for general inquiries; Office of Financial Aid, 650-723-9247 for financial aid information.

Electives

The Law School offers courses with clinical components from 2 to 4 units of credit in a variety of areas. A variety of seminars, worth 2 to 3 units, is offered to upper-level students each year. Externships, from 4 to 10 units of credit, are offered to upper-level students each year. The Law School offers directed research. This is an opportunity for students beyond the first-year program in law to research problems in any field of law. A wide variety of lecture series is sponsored by the Law School and student organizations.

Graduation Requirements

In order to graduate, candidates must have completed the upper-division writing requirement and at least one advanced course that contains one or more units of ethics instruction.

Organizations

Students edit the *Stanford Law Review, Environmental Law Journal, Stanford Journal of International Law, Stanford Law and Policy Review, Stanford Journal of Law, Business and Finance, Stanford Agora: An Online Journal of Legal Perspectives,* and *Stanford Technology Law Review*. The Kirkwood Moot Court Competition is held in May each year. All first year students participate in a noncompetitive moot court program in the spring semester as part of their mandatory legal research and writing course. The Law School also offers a variety of writing competitions. The Law School has more than 30 separate student organizations, including Asian and Pacific Islander Law Students Association, Black Law Students Association, and Stanford Latino Law Students Association. There are local chapters of the American Constitution Society, Federalist Society, and the National Lawyers Guild.

Library

The law library contains 440,000 hardcopy volumes and 480,000 microform volume equivalents, and subscribes to 7924 serial publications. Such on-line databases and networks as CIS Universe, DIALOG, Infotrac, Legal-Trac, LEXIS, LOIS, NEXIS, OCLC First Search, RLIN, WESTLAW, and NEXIS, plus extensive other sources via local and national networks, are available to law students for research. Special library collections include U.S. government documents and California state documents. Recently, the library added additional computer facilities, systems, and databases. The ratio of library volumes to faculty is 8461 to 1 and to students, 787 to 1. The ratio of seats in the library to students is 1 to 1.

Faculty

The law school has 52 full-time faculty members, of whom 11 are women. According to AAUP standards for Category I institutions, faculty salaries are well above average. About 11% of full-time faculty have a graduate law degree in addition to the J.D. The ratio of full-time students to full-time faculty in an average class is 12.5 to 1. The law school has a regular program of bringing visiting professors and other distinguished lecturers and visitors to campus. There is a chapter of the Order of the Coif.

Students

About 48% of the student body are women; 32%, minorities; 8%, African American; 9%, Asian American; 14%, Hispanic; and 1%, Native American. The average age of entering students is 24; age range is 20 to 36. About 30% of students enter directly from undergraduate school and 21% have a graduate degree.

Placement	
J.D.s awarded:	178
Services available through: a separate law school placement center	
Services: Externships are coordinated through the Director of Public Interest Programs	
Special features: counseling and advising students regarding job search, career decisions, and public service.	
Full-time job interviews:	337 employers
Summer job interviews:	337 employers
Placement by graduation:	97% of class
Placement within 9 months:	98% of class
Average starting salary:	$45,000 to $153,500
Areas of placement:	
Private practice 11-25 attorneys	4%
Private practice 26-50 attorneys	1%
Private practice 51-100 attorneys	5%
Private practice 101+ attorneys	41%
Judicial clerkships	33%
Business/industry	9%
Government	3%
Public interest	3%
Academic	1%

STATE UNIVERSITY OF NEW YORK AT BUFFALO

Law School

O'Brian Hall
Buffalo, NY 14260

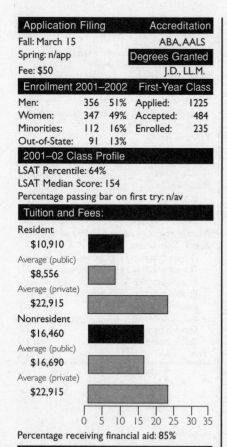

Application Filing	Accreditation
Fall: March 15	ABA, AALS
Spring: n/app	**Degrees Granted**
Fee: $50	J.D., LL.M.

Enrollment 2001–2002			First-Year Class	
Men:	356	51%	Applied:	1225
Women:	347	49%	Accepted:	484
Minorities:	112	16%	Enrolled:	235
Out-of-State:	91	13%		

2001–02 Class Profile

LSAT Percentile: 64%
LSAT Median Score: 154
Percentage passing bar on first try: n/av

Tuition and Fees:

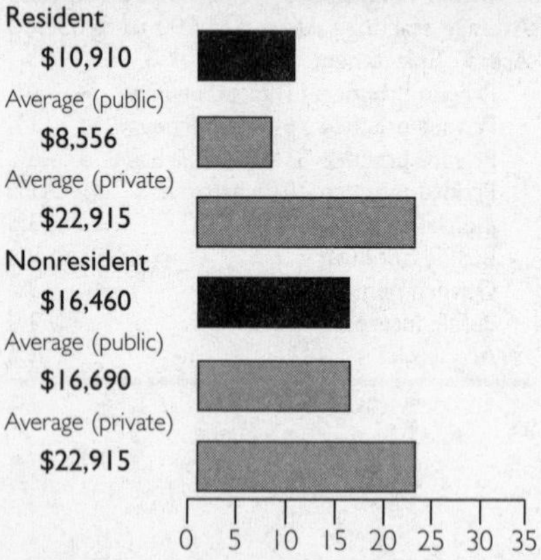

Percentage receiving financial aid: 85%

ADMISSIONS

In the fall 2001 first-year class, 1225 applied, 484 were accepted, and 235 enrolled. Seventeen transfers enrolled. The median LSAT percentile of the most recent first-year class was 64; the median GPA was 3.36 on a scale of 4.0. The lowest LSAT percentile accepted was 17; the highest was 96.

Requirements

Applicants must have a bachelor's degree and take the LSAT. Minimum acceptable LSAT percentile is 15 and minimum acceptable GPA is 2.0 on a scale of 4.0. The most important admission factors include academic achievement, LSAT results, and writing ability. No specific undergraduate courses are required. Candidates are not interviewed.

Procedure

The application deadline for fall entry is March 15. Applicants should submit an application form, LSAT results, transcripts, TOEFL for international applicants, a nonrefundable application fee of $50, and 2 letters of recommendation. Notification of the admissions decision is as early as January. The latest acceptable LSAT test date for fall entry is February. The law school uses the LSDAS.

Special

The law school recruits minority and disadvantaged students through targeted recruitment efforts at colleges with significant minority student populations and participation in a tuition waiver program for EOP, HEOP, and SEEK students. Requirements are not different for out-of-state students. Transfer students must have one year of credit, have attended an ABA-approved law school, and have submitted 2 letters of reference from law professors, a letter of good standing from the initial law school, the first page of the LSDAS report, an official law school transcript, and the $50 application fee. There are no preadmissions courses.

Costs

Tuition and fees for the 2001-2002 academic year are $10,910 for full-time in-state students and $16,460 for out-of-state students. On-campus room and board costs about $7433 annually; books and supplies run $1323.

Financial Aid

About 85% of current law students receive some form of aid. The average annual amount of aid from all sources combined, including scholarships, loans, and work contracts, is $12,800; maximum, $18,500. Awards are based on need. Required financial statement is the FAFSA. The aid application deadline for fall entry is March 1. Special funds for minority or disadvantaged students consist of state and federal tuition fellowship programs. First-year students are notified about their financial aid application at time of acceptance.

About the Law School

State University of New York at Buffalo Law School was established in 1887 and is a public institution. The 154-acre campus is in a suburban area 3 miles north of Buffalo in Amherst, New York. The primary mission of the law school is to provide an excellent professional education while emphasizing the role of law and lawyers within the broader context of American society. Students have access to federal, state, county, city, and local agencies, courts, correctional facilities, law firms, and legal aid organizations in the Buffalo area. The University at Buffalo undergraduate and graduate schools and libraries are also available to students. Facilities of special interest to law students include the nation's only fully functioning state court housed on a university campus. Housing for students is available in apartment-style on-campus housing, as well as ample graduate student housing. All law school facilities are accessible to the physically disabled.

Calendar

The law school operates on a traditional semester, 4-1-4 modified semester, and 3-1-3 basis. Courses for full-time students are offered during the day with occasional evening classes and must be completed within 3 to 4 years. There is no part-time program. New students are admitted in the fall. There is a 7-week summer session. Transferable summer courses are offered.

Programs

In addition to the J.D., the law school offers the LL.M. Students may take relevant courses in other programs and apply credit toward the J.D.; a maximum of 9 credits may be applied. The following joint degrees may be earned: J.D./M.B.A. (Juris Doctor/Master of Business Administration), J.D./M.L.S. (Juris Doctor/collaborative Program in Law and Library Studies), J.D./M.P.H. (Juris Doctor/Interdisciplinary Program in Law and Public Health), J.D./M.S.W. (Juris Doctor/Master of Social Work), and J.D./Ph.D. (Juris Doctor/Doctor of Philosophy in selected disciplines).

Required

To earn the J.D., candidates must complete 90 total credits, of which 35 are for required courses. The following first-year courses are required of all students: Civil Procedure, Constitutional Law, Contracts, Criminal law, Research and Writing (2 semesters), Property, Torts, intensive bridge course (taught during the month of January), and Legal Profession and Ethics. Required upper-level courses consist of seminars. The required orientation program for first-

Phone: 716-645-2907
Fax: 716-645-6676
E-mail: *coxublaw@buffalo.edu*
Web: *www.buffalo.edu/law*

Contact

Jack Cox, Associate Dean for Admissions, 716-645-6233 for general inquiries; Brezetta Stevenson, Financial Aid/Scheduling Coordinator, 716-645-7324 for financial aid information.

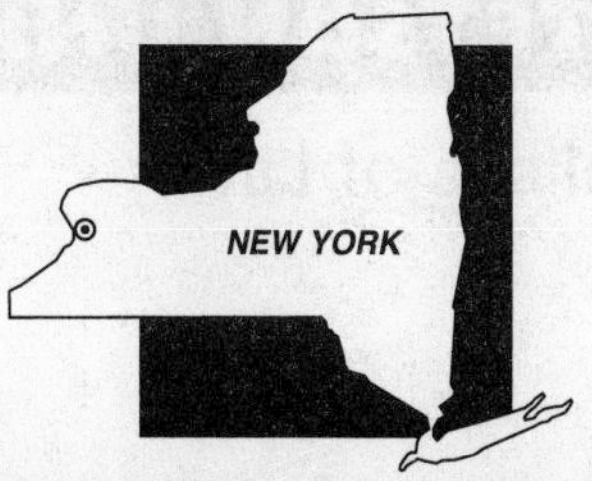

year students lasts 1 week and includes an introduction to faculty, administrators, and student organizations, as well as an introductory course on legal methods, reasoning, argument, and legal institutions and the profession.

Electives

The Law School offers concentrations in corporate law, criminal law, environmental law, family law, international law, labor law, litigation, tax law, and health law; state and local government; technology and intellectual property; law and social justice; affordable housing; and community economic development. In addition, upper-division students may take clinical courses for 3 to 4 credit hours each semester for up to 4 semesters after the first year of law school. Topics include affordable housing, education law, elder law, community economic development, family violence, securities law, and environmental law. Upper-division students must take at least 1 seminar for 3 credit hours. Numerous seminars are offered, and students may enroll in multiple seminars. Field placements are associated with various courses, including child welfare, criminal law, legislative internships, and judicial clerkships. Upper-division students may take independent research for 3 to 6 credit hours, and may participate in any of several law school research centers. Internships are available in public interest, governmental, and international settings. Special lecture series include the Mitchell and Baldy Center Lecture Series and the Baldy Center "short courses." There are summer internships abroad with leading human rights organizations through the Buffalo Human Rights Center. Academic support is available to students in need. Special interest group programs include the Buffalo Public Interest Law Program, Domestic Violence Task Force, and Prison Task Force. The most widely taken electives are Gratuitous Transfers, Sales-Secured Transactions, and Commercial Paper.

Graduation Requirements

In order to graduate, candidates must have completed the upper-division writing requirement and 90 credit hours. Grades of A, B, or C must be earned in at least 80 hours. A seminar is also required.

Organizations

Students edit the *Buffalo Law Review, Buffalo Environmental Law Journal, Buffalo Human Rights Law Review, Buffalo Criminal Law Review, Buffalo Women's Law Journal, Buffalo Intellectual Property Law Journal, Buffalo Public Interest*, and the newspaper, *The Opinion*. Other publications include the *Buffalo Journal of Public Interest Law*, and the *ABA Journal of Affordable Housing and Community Development Law*. Moot court competitions include the Desmond Intramural held in November, the National Mugal Tax held in the spring, and the Herbert Wechsler Criminal Moot Court. Law student organizations include the Entertainment and Sports Law Society, Buffalo Environmental Law Society, and the Labor and Employment Law Association. There are local chapters of the Association of Trial Lawyers of America, National Lawyers Guild, and Phi Alpha Delta. Other law student organizations include the Asian American Law Students Association, Black Law Students Association, and Latin American Law Students Association.

Library

The law library contains 301,692 hard-copy volumes and 1,983,759 microform volume equivalents, and subscribes to 964 serial publications. Such on-line databases and networks as DIALOG, LEXIS, WESTLAW, and NEXIS are available to law students for research. Special library collections include a U.S. government document depository; the Morris L. Cohen Rare Book collection; the papers of John Lord O'Brian; Berman Human Rights Collections, and a substantial United Nations documents collection. Recently, the library added a CD-ROM network, 75 Internet ports, and an electronic classroom. The ratio of library volumes to faculty is 5485 to 1 and to students is 429 to 1. The ratio of seats in the library to students is 1 to 2.

Faculty

The law school has 55 full-time and 101 part-time faculty members, of whom 47 are women. According to AAUP standards for Category I institutions, faculty salaries are above average. About 26% of full-time faculty have a graduate law degree in addition to the J.D.; about 4% of part-time faculty have one. The ratio of full-time students to full-time faculty in an average class is 21 to 1; in a clinic, 10 to 1. The law school has a regular program of bringing visiting professors and other distinguished lecturers and visitors to campus.

Placement

Placement	
J.D.s awarded:	220
Services available through: a separate law school placement center and the university placement center	
Services: alumni mentoring program, alumni career panels, training and skills-building programs that devise networking opportunities.	
Special features: an employment bulletin that is sent free for 18 months to graduates, a unique mock interview program, and required individual career counseling for ILS.	
Full-time job interviews:	25 employers
Summer job interviews:	30 employers
Placement by graduation:	64% of class
Placement within 9 months:	97% of class
Average starting salary:	$18,000 to $125,000
Areas of placement:	
Private practice 2-10 attorneys	17%
Private practice 11-25 attorneys	5%
Private practice 26-50 attorneys	5%
Private practice 51-100 attorneys	21%
Government	14%
Business/industry	13%
Judicial clerkships	8%
Academic	8%
Public interest	5%
Unknown	2%
Military	1%

Students

About 49% of the student body are women; 16%, minorities; 8%, African American; 4%, Asian American; 4%, Hispanic; and 1%, Native American. The majority of students come from New York (87%). The average age of entering students is 24; age range is 20 to 53. About 33% of students enter directly from undergraduate school, 15% have a graduate degree, and 30% have worked full-time prior to entering law school. About 2% drop out after the first year for academic or personal reasons; 96% remain to receive a law degree.

STETSON UNIVERSITY

College of Law

1401 61st Street South
St. Petersburg, FL 33707

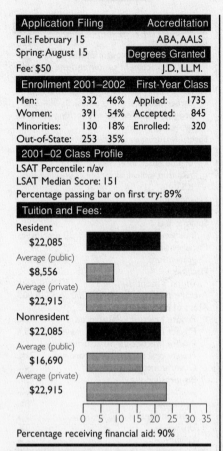

Application Filing		Accreditation
Fall: February 15		ABA, AALS
Spring: August 15		**Degrees Granted**
Fee: $50		J.D., LL.M.

Enrollment 2001–2002			First-Year Class	
Men:	332	46%	Applied:	1735
Women:	391	54%	Accepted:	845
Minorities:	130	18%	Enrolled:	320
Out-of-State:	253	35%		

2001–02 Class Profile

LSAT Percentile: n/av
LSAT Median Score: 151
Percentage passing bar on first try: 89%

Tuition and Fees:

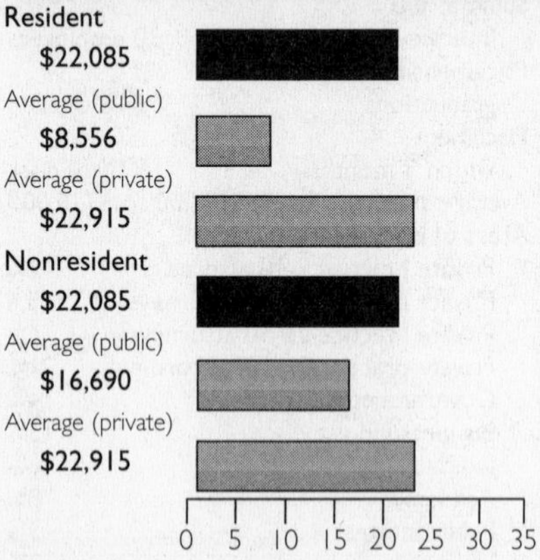

Percentage receiving financial aid: 90%

ADMISSIONS

In the fall 2001 first-year class, 1735 applied, 845 were accepted, and 320 enrolled. Ten transfers enrolled. The median GPA of the most recent first-year class was 3.24.

Requirements
Applicants must have a bachelor's degree and take the LSAT. The most important admission factors include LSAT results and GPA. No specific undergraduate courses are required. Candidates are not interviewed.

Procedure
The application deadline for fall entry is February 15. Applicants should submit an application form, a nonrefundable application fee of $50, a personal statement, and the college questionnaire. Three letters of recommendation are suggested, but optional. Notification of the admissions decision is on a rolling basis. The latest acceptable LSAT test date for fall entry is December. The law school uses the LSDAS.

Special
The law school recruits minority and disadvantaged students by means of CRS mailings, CLEO, law school forums, and college campus visits. Requirements are not different for out-of-state students. Transfer students must have one year of credit, have attended an ABA-approved law school, and must be ranked in the top 20% of their first-year class. There are no preadmissions courses.

Costs

Tuition and fees for the 2001-2002 academic year are $22,085 for all full-time students. On-campus room and board costs about $7250 annually; books and supplies run $1200.

Financial Aid

About 90% of current law students receive some form of aid. The average annual amount of aid from all sources combined, including scholarships, loans, and work contracts, is $21,000; maximum, $36,735. Awards are based on need and merit. Required financial statements are the FAFSA, supplemental application for Stetson grant, and a copy of an income tax return. Special funds for minority or disadvantaged students include the Florida Minority Participation in Legal Education Scholarships program and Stetson minority scholarships. First-year students are notified about their financial aid application between the time of acceptance and the due date of the confirmation deposit.

About the Law School

Stetson University College of Law was established in 1900 and is a private institution. The 21-acre campus is in a suburban area 20 miles southwest of Tampa. The primary mission of the law school is to educate men and women who will ethically and competently serve the state, the region, and the nation as members of the legal profession in private practice, business, and government. Students have access to federal, state, county, city, and local agencies, courts, correctional facilities, law firms, and legal aid organizations in the St. Petersburg area. Facilities of special interest to law students include 4 on-campus courtrooms available for skills training. Housing for students is available in residence halls, 2-bedroom apartments, and school-owned houses for single and married students; also, housing options are available in the community. All law school facilities are accessible to the physically disabled.

Calendar

The law school operates on a traditional semester basis. Courses for full-time students are offered both day and evening and must be completed within 2 1/2 to 3 years. For part-time students, courses are offered evenings only and must be completed within 4 years. New full-time students are admitted in the fall, spring, and summer; part-time, fall. There is an 8-week summer session. Transferable summer courses are offered.

Programs

In addition to the J.D., the law school offers the LL.M. Students may take relevant courses in other programs and apply credit toward the J.D.; a maximum of 12 credits may be applied. The following joint degrees may be earned: J.D./M.B.A. (Juris Doctor/Master of Business Administration).

Required
To earn the J.D., candidates must complete 88 total credits, of which 48 are for required courses. They must maintain a minimum GPA of 2.0 in the required courses. The following first-year courses are required of all students: Contracts I and II, Criminal Law, Real Property I

Phone: 727-562-7802
Fax: 727-343-0136
E-mail: *lawadmit@hermes.law.stetson.edu*
Web: *www.law.stetson.edu*

Contact

Pamela Coleman, Assistant Dean of Admissions, 727-562-7802 for general inquiries; Emily Schmidt, Director of Financial Aid, 727-562-7813 for financial aid information.

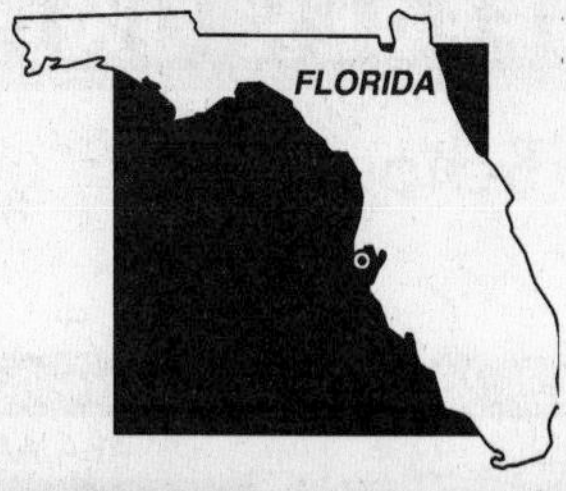

and II, Research and Writing I and II, Civil Procedure, Torts, and Agencies and Unincorporated Associations. Required upper-level courses consist of Constitutional Law, Evidence, Professional Responsibility, skills area, code area, writing, and Administrative Law requiremenst. The required orientation program for first-year students is a 3-day program that consists of general orientation and an academic orientation led by full-time faculty members that focus on analytical skills.

Electives

Students must take 18 hours in their area of concentration. The College of Law offers concentrations in international law, litigation, health law, and elder law. In addition, clinic programs, available to third-year students, include the Alternative Dispute Resolution Clinic, Local Government Clinic, and Civil Property Law Clinic. Most clinics are for 5 credit hours. Many seminars for second- and third-year students are offered each year. Internships with federal and state court judges are available for upper-level students for 4 credit hours. Practicum programs are available with state and federal agencies. Inns of Court programs, featuring prominent speakers, are held every year. Other programs are also sponsored by faculty and student organizations of the law school. Second- and third-year students may participate in study-abroad programs offered through Stetson and other law schools. Stetson sponsors summer-abroad programs in Grenada, Spain and Tallian, Estonia. Individual tutors are available for students. Stetson has a comprehensive Academic Success Program and an Academic Advising Program. Special interest group programs include an honors program for top students, environmental law society, elder law study group, and health law associations. The most widely taken electives are Trial Advocacy, Alternative Dispute Resolution, and Criminal Procedure.

Graduation Requirements

In order to graduate, candidates must have a GPA of 2.0, have completed the upper-division writing requirement, and 20 hours of public service.

Organizations

Students edit the *Stetson Law Review* and *Stetson Law Forum*. Annually, students compete in many competitions, including the National Moot Court, National Appellate Advocacy, and Jessup International Moot Court competitions. Other competitions include regional and national client counseling competitions; state, regional and national mock trial competitions; regional and national mediation competitions; and regional and national negotiation competitions. Law student organizations include the Student Bar Association; ABA-Law Student Division; and ACLU. Other organizations include Maritime Law Society; Business Law Society; and Sports, Entertainment and Art Law Society. Local chapters of national associations include Delta Theta Phi, Phi Alpha Delta, and Phi Delta Phi.

Library

The law library contains 367,000 hard-copy volumes and 769,000 microform volume equivalents, and subscribes to 5086 serial publications. Such on-line databases and networks as CALI, CIS Universe, DIALOG, Infotrac, Legal-Trac, LEXIS, LOIS, Mathew Bender, NEXIS, and WESTLAW are available to law students for research. Special library collections include a depository for selected U.S. Government publications. Recently a newly constructed library opened. The ratio of library volumes to faculty is 8951 to 1 and to students is 508 to 1. The ratio of seats in the library to students is 1 to 3.

Faculty

The law school has 41 full-time and 54 part-time faculty members, of whom 32 are women. According to AAUP standards for Category IIA institutions, faculty salaries are above average. About 50% of full-time faculty have a graduate law degree in addition to the J.D.; about 30% of part-time faculty have one. The ratio of full-time students to full-time faculty in an average class is 17 to 1; in a clinic, 10 to 1. The law school has a regular program of bringing visiting professors and other distinguished lecturers and visitors to campus.

Placement

Placement	
J.D.s awarded:	215
Services available through: a separate law school placement center	
Services: on-campus interviewing programs in the fall and spring semesters	
Special features: office equipment for student use, including computers for job searches on LEXIS and WESTLAW, a fax machine, and a laser printer for resume and cover letter production.	
Full-time job interviews:	42 employers
Summer job interviews:	48 employers
Placement by graduation:	n/av
Placement within 9 months:	97% of class
Average starting salary:	$30,000 to $150,000
Areas of placement:	
Private practice 2-10 attorneys	26%
Private practice 11-25 attorneys	18%
Private practice 26-50 attorneys	10%
Private practice 51-100 attorneys	5%
Government	24%
Judicial clerkships	5%
Academic	4%
Business/industry	3%
Public interest	2%
Military	2%
unknown	1%

Students

About 54% of the student body are women; 18%, minorities; 6%, African American; 3%, Asian American; 8%, Hispanic; and 1%, Native American. The majority of students come from Florida (65%). The average age of entering students is 24; age range is 20 to 51. About 50% of students enter directly from undergraduate school and 50% have worked full-time prior to entering law school. About 4% drop out after the first year for academic or personal reasons; 96% remain to receive a law degree.

SUFFOLK UNIVERSITY

Law School

120 Tremont Street
Boston, MA 02108-4977

Application Filing		Accreditation
Fall: March 1		ABA, AALS
Spring: n/app		**Degrees Granted**
Fee: $50		J.D., LL.M.

Enrollment 2001–2002			First-Year Class	
Men:	850	50%	Applied:	2100
Women:	865	50%	Accepted:	n/av
Minorities:	172	10%	Enrolled:	525
Out-of-State:	858	50%		

2001–02 Class Profile

LSAT Percentile: 54%
LSAT Median Score: 153
Percentage passing bar on first try: 79%

Tuition and Fees:

Resident
$24,950
Average (public)
$8,556
Average (private)
$22,915
Nonresident
$24,950
Average (public)
$16,690
Average (private)
$22,915

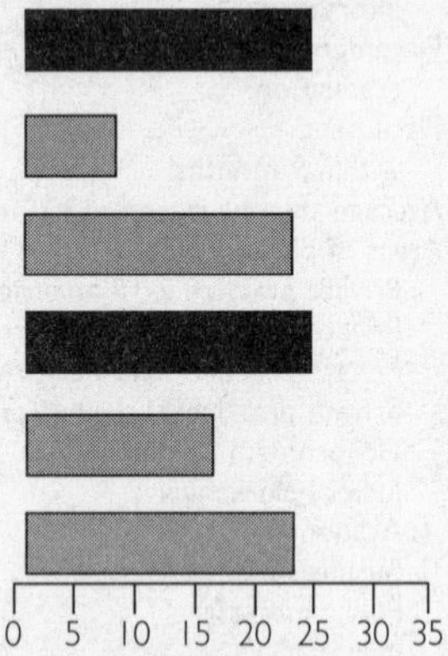

Percentage receiving financial aid: 80%

ADMISSIONS

In the fall 2001 first-year class, 2100 applied and 525 enrolled. Ten transfers enrolled. The median LSAT percentile of the most recent first-year class was 54; the median GPA was 3.2 on a scale of 4.0. The lowest LSAT percentile accepted was 32; the highest was 98. Enrollment figures in the above capsule are approximate.

Requirements

Applicants must have a bachelor's degree and take the LSAT. Minimum acceptable GPA is 3.0 on a scale of 4.0. The most important admission factors include academic achievement, GPA, and general background. No specific undergraduate courses are required. Candidates are interviewed.

Procedure

The application deadline for fall entry is March 1. Applicants should submit an application form, TOEFL, a nonrefundable application fee of $50, undergraduate letters of recommendation, and supplementary personal information for those wishing to emphasize unusual circumstances. Accepted students must pay a $200 tuition deposit by April 1; a second deposit of $300 is due June 1. Notification of the admissions decision is on a rolling basis. The latest acceptable LSAT test date for fall entry is February. The law school uses the LSDAS.

Special

The law school recruits minority and disadvantaged students by means of an admissions committee, which gives consideration to students who have overcome economic and social disadvantages. Requirements are not different for out-of-state students. Transfer students must have attended an ABA-approved law school and be in good academic standing. The application must be completed by early June. The dean of each previous law school must provide a letter of good standing and a final transcript.

Costs

Tuition and fees for the 2001-2002 academic year are $24,950 for full-time in-state students. Tuition for part-time students is $18,712 in-state. Books and supplies run about $900 annually.

Financial Aid

About 80% of current law students receive some form of aid. The average annual amount of aid from all sources combined, including scholarships, loans, and work contracts, is $22,500; maximum, $38,000. Awards are based on need and merit. Required financial statements are the CSS Profile, Suffolk University financial aid forms, and a federal income tax return. The deadline for fall entry is March 1. Special funds for minority or disadvantaged students are available through a number of financial assistance programs. First-year students are notified about their application after all documentating has been submitted.

About the Law School

Suffolk University Law School was established in 1906 and is a private institution. The campus is in an urban area in downtown Boston on the Freedom Trail. The primary mission of the law school is to produce highly skilled, ethical lawyers with a commitment to public service. In the twenty-first century, the school will connect its past strengths with its vision for the future to provide a relevant, rigorous education in contemporary legal issues combined with solid practical experience. Students have access to federal, state, county, city, and local agencies, courts, correctional facilities, law firms, and legal aid organizations in the Boston area. The Center for Continuing Professional Development serves the practicing lawyer for the purpose of continuing the legal education. There is also the Battered Women's Advocacy Project, Academic Support Program, and Strive Program. Facilities of special interest to law students include Greater Boston Legal Services, SU Clinical Legal in Chelsea Center for Juvenile Justice, and International Human Rights Project. Housing for students is not available on campus, but assistance for obtaining housing in the area is available. All law school facilities are accessible to the physically disabled.

Calendar

The law school operates on a traditional semester basis. Courses for full-time students are offered days only and must be completed within 3 years. For part-time students, courses are offered evenings only and must be completed within 4 years. New full- and part-time students are admitted in the fall. There is a 10-week summer session. Transferable summer courses are offered.

Programs

In addition to the J.D., the law school offers the LL.M. The following joint degrees may be earned: J.D./M.B.A. (Juris Doctor/Master of Business Administration), J.D./M.P.A. (Juris Doctor/Master of Public Administration), J.D./M.S.C.J. (Juris Doctor/Master of Criminal Justice), J.D./M.S.F. (Juris Doctor/Master of Science in Finance), and J.D./M.S.I.E. (Juris Doctor/Master of Science in International Economics).

Required

To earn the J.D., candidates must complete 84 total credits, of which 58 are for required courses. They must maintain a minimum GPA of 2.0 in the required courses. The following first-year courses are required of all students: Contracts, Torts, Property, Civil Procedure, Criminal Law, Legal Practice Skills, and Constitutional Law. Required upper-level courses consist of Fiduciary Relations, Evidence, and Professional Responsibility. The required orientation program for first-year students includes the Strive Program. During orientation, students are instructed in the use of the law library and legal research tools (LEXIS, NEXIS, and WESTLAW), practice in

Phone: 617-573-8144
Fax: 617-523-1367

Contact

Gail Ellis, Dean of Admissions, 617-573-8144 for general inquiries; Jocelyn Allen, Director of Financial Aid, 617-573-8147 for financial aid information.

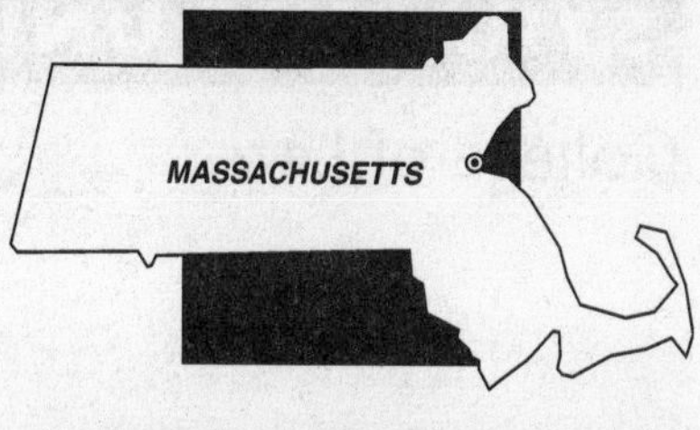

issue analysis and writing of legal memoranda, preparation of trial brief and oral arguments, an introduction to computerized legal research systems, and presentation of law school examination study and answer techniques.

Electives

The Law School offers concentrations in corporate law, criminal law, entertainment law, environmental law, family law, international law, juvenile law, labor law, litigation, media law, securities law, sports law, tax law, torts and insurance, commercial law, constitutional law, practice, property law, government regulation, trial advocacy and the legal profession, health care and biomedical law, and financial services. In addition, clinical programs, usually 3 credits, include the Suffolk Voluntary Defenders, the Prosecutor Program, and the Suffolk University Legal Assistance Bureau. Seminars are available in such areas as Advanced Contracts, Advanced Entertainment Law, and Advanced Juvenile Law. The Legal Internship Program allows students to gain 2 credits per semester for supervised legal work performed for a government or nonprofit agency (more than 500 are offered). Many students act as research assistants for individual faculty members. Work-study programs are available. Lecture series include the Donahue Lecture Series, which presents 3 to 4 different national scholars who lecture on various topics in legal education, and the Suffolk Law Forum. Study-abroad programs are offered in conjunction with law schools in Europe, Canada, South America, and Mexico. A summer study-abroad program is available at the University of Lund, Lund, Sweden. Tutorial programs are available. Minority programs include the Strive Program and the Academic Resource Center. There are multicultural groups such as the Black Law Students Association, the Asian Law Students Association, and the Hispanic Law Students Association. There are 30 special interest student groups. The most widely taken electives are Trial Advocacy, High Technology, and International Law.

Graduation Requirements

In order to graduate, candidates must have a GPA of 2.0 and have completed the upper-division writing requirement.

Organizations

The primary law review is the *Suffolk University Law Review*. Other law reviews include the *Suffolk Transnational Law Review, The Advocate*, a periodical publication, and the *High Tech Law Journal*, an on-line publication. The student newspaper is the *Dicta*. The Moot Court Board runs 5 annual intraschool programs, 7 appellate advocacy teams, and 3 trial teams. Suffolk competes in the National Trial Competition. The school is home for the National Board of Trial Advocacy, which certifies experienced trial lawyers as Civil or Criminal Trial Advocacy Specialists. The appellate advocacy teams include the Constitutional Law Team, Patent Team, International Law Team, National Team, Securities Team, and Tax Team. Student organizations include the American Trial Lawyers Association, Federalist Society, and the Student Bar Association. There are local chapters of Phi Delta Phi, National Lawyers Guild/Lawyers Guild Convocation, and the Student Bar Association.

Library

The law library contains 318,000 hard-copy volumes and 801,693 microform volume equivalents, and subscribes to 5904 serial publications. Such on-line databases and networks as DIALOG, LEXIS, NEXIS, WESTLAW, NEXIS, and membership in the New England Law Library Consortium are available to law students for research. Special library collections include a collection of biographical material on lawyers and judges, famous trials, law and literature, environmental law, criminal law, intellectual property law, biomedical law, and trial practice materials. Recently, the library moved into a building with specially designed study carrels and tables. All study seats have electrical and data hookups to the Internet. The ratio of library volumes to faculty is 5300 to 1 and to students is 185 to 1. The ratio of seats in the library to students is 1 to 1.

Faculty

The law school has 60 full-time and 114 part-time faculty members, of whom 38 are women. According to AAUP standards for Category IIA institutions, faculty salaries are well above average. About 38% of full-time faculty have a graduate law degree in addition to the J.D.; about 20% of part-time faculty have one. The ratio of full-time students to full-time faculty in an average class is 17 to 1; in a clinic, 10 to 1. The law school has a regular program of bringing visiting professors and other distinguished lecturers and visitors to campus.

Placement

J.D.s awarded:	496
Services available through: a separate law school placement center	
Services: professional directories, notices of employment, judicial clerkship information, library facilities for employment information, and panel discussions	
Special features: the fall on-campus Recruitment Program, to which the Career Services Office invites law firms, corporations, legal services offices, and state and federal agencies to interview students for employment. The school is also a member of the Massachusetts Law School Consortium, which sponsors other recruitment and career-related programs.	
Full-time job interviews:	90 employers
Summer job interviews:	65 employers
Placement by graduation:	60% of class
Placement within 9 months:	94% of class
Average starting salary:	$22,000 to $60,000
Areas of placement:	
Private practice 2-10 attorneys	12%
Private practice 11-25 attorneys	15%
Private practice 26-50 attorneys	10%
Private practice 51-100 attorneys	3%
Business/industry	28%
Government	17%
Judicial clerkships	9%
Academic	3%
Public interest	1%
Military	1%
Unknown	1%

Students

About 50% of the student body are women; 10%, minorities; 4%, African American; 4%, Asian American; and 3%, Hispanic. The majority of students come from Massachusetts (50%). The average age of entering students is 26; age range is 20 to 55. About 26% of students enter directly from undergraduate school and 13% have a graduate degree. About 8% drop out after the first year for academic or personal reasons.

SYRACUSE UNIVERSITY

College of Law

Office of Admissions and Financial Aid
Syracuse, NY 13244-1030

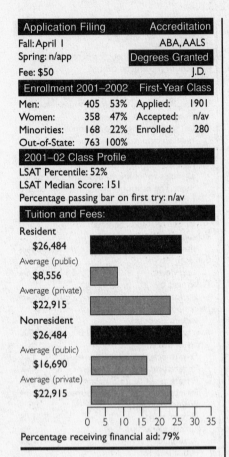

Application Filing		Accreditation
Fall: April 1		ABA, AALS
Spring: n/app		**Degrees Granted**
Fee: $50		J.D.

Enrollment 2001–2002			First-Year Class	
Men:	405	53%	Applied:	1901
Women:	358	47%	Accepted:	n/av
Minorities:	168	22%	Enrolled:	280
Out-of-State:	763	100%		

2001–02 Class Profile

LSAT Percentile: 52%
LSAT Median Score: 151
Percentage passing bar on first try: n/av

Tuition and Fees:

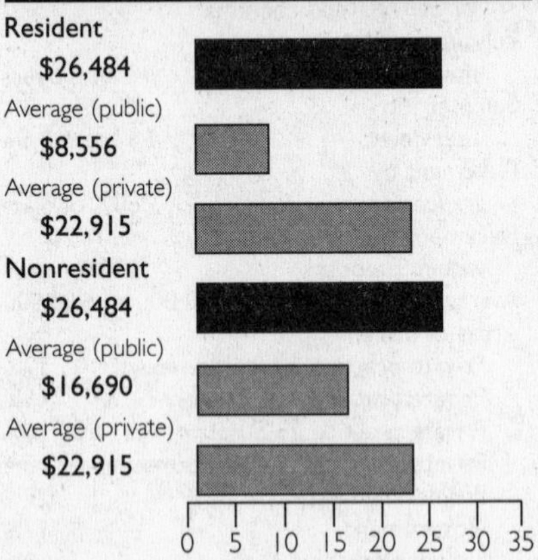

Percentage receiving financial aid: 79%

ADMISSIONS

In the fall 2001 first-year class, 1901 applied and 280 enrolled. Four transfers enrolled. The median LSAT percentile of the most recent first-year class was 52; the median GPA was 3.28 on a scale of 4.0.

Requirements

Applicants must have a bachelor's degree and take the LSAT. The most important admission factors include GPA, academic achievement, and LSAT results. No specific undergraduate courses are required. Candidates are not interviewed.

Procedure

The application deadline for fall entry is April 1. Applicants should submit an application form, LSAT results, transcripts, a nonrefundable application fee of $50, 3 letters of recommendation, and a personal statement. Notification of the admissions decision is on a rolling basis from January to May. The latest acceptable LSAT test date for fall entry is February. The law school uses the LSDAS.

Special

The law school recruits minority and disadvantaged students by means of an inhouse Legal Education Opportunity Program, students of color law forums, the CLEO program, and by application review. Requirements are not different for out-of-state students. Transfer students must have one year of credit, a minimum GPA of 2.5, and have attended an ABA-approved law school.

Costs

Tuition and fees for the 2001-2002 academic year are $26,484 for all full-time students. Tuition for all part-time students is $1135 per credit. On-campus room and board costs about $9620 annually; books and supplies run $1100.

Financial Aid

About 79% of current law students receive some form of aid. Awards are based on need and merit. Required financial statements are the FAFSA, the College of Law application form, tax returns, and W2s. The aid application deadline for fall entry is February 1. First-year students are notified about their financial aid application at time of acceptance.

About the Law School

Syracuse University College of Law was established in 1895 and is a private institution. The campus is in an urban area 3 miles east of Syracuse. The primary mission of the law school is guided by the philosophy that the best way to train lawyers is to teach them to apply what they learn in the classroom to real legal issues, problems, and clients. Syracuse Law's goal is to promote learning through teaching, research, scholarship, and service. Students have access to federal, state, county, city, and local agencies, courts, correctional facilities, law firms, and legal aid organizations in the Syracuse area. Affordable housing is available both on and off campus. On-campus housing options include apartment complexes for law and graduate students and a single-room residence hall for law and graduate students. About 90% of the law school facilities are accessible to the physically disabled.

Calendar

The law school operates on a traditional semester basis. Courses for both full-time and part-time students are offered days only and must be completed within 4½ years. New full- and part-time students are admitted in the fall. There is a 7-week summer session. Transferable summer courses are offered.

Programs

Students may take relevant courses in other programs and apply credit toward the J.D.; a maximum of 6 credits may be applied. The following joint degrees may be earned: J.D./M.B.A. (Juris Doctor/Master of Business Administration), J.D./M.P.A. (Juris Doctor/Master of Public Administration), and J.D./M.S. (Juris Doctor/Master of Science in communications, environmental law, engineering, and computer science).

Phone: 315-443-1962
Fax: 315-443-9568
Web: www.law.syr.edu

Contact

Admissions Office, 315-443-1962 for general inquiries; Director of Financial Aid, 315-443-1963 for financial aid information.

Required

To earn the J.D., candidates must complete 87 total credits, of which 40 are for required courses. They must maintain a minimum GPA of 2.0 in the required courses. The following first-year courses are required of all students: Civil Procedure, Constitutional Law I, Contracts, Law Firm, Property, Torts, Criminal Law, and Legislation and Policy. Required upper-level courses consist of Professional Responsibility, a writing requirement, and Constitutional Law II. The required orientation program for first-year students is 2 days and includes academic programs, the first Law Firm class, and social activities.

Electives

The College of Law offers concentrations in corporate law, criminal law, environmental law, family law, international law, labor law, litigation, media law, securities law, tax law, torts and insurance, law, technology, and management, and law and economics. In addition, second- and third-year students may take clinics for 6 credits in Community Development Law, Public Interest Law, Children's Rights and Family Law, and Criminal Law. Second- and third-year students may also earn 1 to 2 credits per semester for seminars. A study-abroad summer program is available in London. Tutorial programs are offered to first-year students. Minority programs include the Legal Education Opportunity Program. The most widely taken electives are international law, trial practice, and corporations.

Graduation Requirements

In order to graduate, candidates must have a GPA of 2.0 and have completed the upper-division writing requirement.

Organizations

Law students edit the *Syracuse Law Review, Journal of International Law and Commerce, The Labor Lawyer*, and *The Digest*. Annually, students compete in the Edmund H. Lewis Appellate, Lionel O. Grossman Trial, and Jessup Moot Court competitions. Law student organizations include Black Law Students Association, Civil Liberties Union, and Asian-Pacific American Law Students Association. There are local chapters of the ABA-Law Student Division, New York State Bar Association, and the Justinian Honor Law Society.

Library

The law library contains more than 400,000 hard-copy volumes, and subscribes to more than 3200 serial publications. Such on-line databases and networks as DIALOG, LEXIS, and WESTLAW are available to law students for research. Special library collections include legal history; law, management, and technology; legal practice skills; New York state law; tax law and policy; and a selected government depository. Recently, the library adopted the NOTIS integrated system which puts OPAC, circulation, and acquisitions on-line; it added 18 WESTLAW with DIALOG stations, 10 LEXIS with NEXIS stations, and integrated on-line legal databases throughout the collection. It also added a student computer cluster containing 30 PCs and an educational training laboratory containing 11 PCs. The ratio of library volumes to faculty is 8696 to 1 and to students is 524 to 1. The ratio of seats in the library to students is 1 to 1.

Faculty

The law school has 46 full-time and 50 part-time faculty members, of whom 27 are women. According to AAUP standards for Category I institutions, faculty salaries are average. About 48% of full-time faculty have a graduate law degree in addition to the J.D. The ratio of full-time students to full-time faculty in an average class is 21 to 1; in a clinic, 10 to 1. The law school has a regular program of bringing visiting professors and other distinguished lecturers and visitors to campus. There is a chapter of the Order of the Coif.

Students

About 47% of the student body are women; 22%, minorities; 7%, African American; 7%, Asian American; 4%, Hispanic; and 4%, foreign nationals. The average age of entering students is 25; age range is 21 to 80. About 10% of students have a graduate degree.

Placement	
J.D.s awarded:	257
Services available through: a separate law school placement center	
Services: workshop on networking, career speaker series, identifying clerkship opportunities.	
Special features: individual counseling for law students, dedicated counselor for first-year students.	
Full-time job interviews:	n/av
Summer job interviews:	n/av
Placement by graduation:	73% of class
Placement within 9 months:	93% of class
Average starting salary:	$28,000 to $150,000
Areas of placement:	
Private practice 2-10 attorneys	14%
Private practice 11-25 attorneys	7%
Private practice 26-50 attorneys	7%
Private practice 51-100 attorneys	22%
Private practice firm size unknown	8%
Government	16%
Business/industry	13%
Judicial clerkships	11%
Public interest	1%
Academic	1%

TEMPLE UNIVERSITY

James E. Beasley School of Law

1719 N. Broad Street
Philadelphia, PA 19122

Application Filing		Accreditation
Fall: March 1		ABA, AALS
Spring: n/app		**Degrees Granted**
Fee: $50		J.D., LL.M.

Enrollment 2001–2002			First-Year Class	
Men:	546	51%	Applied:	3225
Women:	528	49%	Accepted:	1276
Minorities:	204	19%	Enrolled:	345
Out-of-State:	301	28%		

2001–02 Class Profile

LSAT Percentile: 74%
LSAT Median Score: 157
Percentage passing bar on first try: 75%

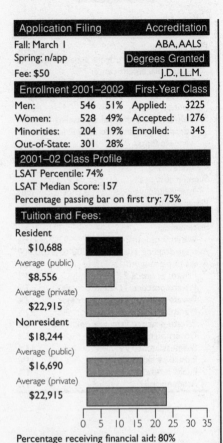

Tuition and Fees:

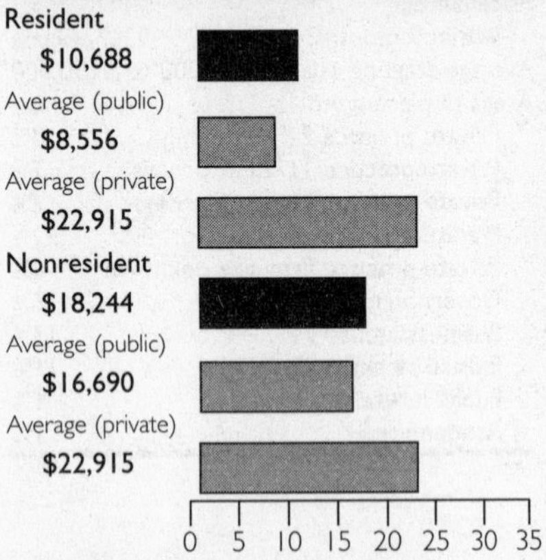

Percentage receiving financial aid: 80%

ADMISSIONS

In the fall 2001 first-year class, 3225 applied, 1276 were accepted, and 345 enrolled. Eleven transfers enrolled. The median LSAT percentile of the most recent first-year class was 74; the median GPA was 3.35 on a scale of 4.0. The lowest LSAT percentile accepted was 32; the highest was 98.

Requirements

Applicants must have a bachelor's degree and take the LSAT. Minimum acceptable LSAT percentile is 20 and minimum acceptable GPA is 2.35 on a scale of 4.0. No specific undergraduate courses are required. Candidates are interviewed.

Procedure

The application deadline for fall entry is March 1. Applicants should submit an application form, LSAT results, transcripts, TOEFL (when English is not a student's primary language), a nonrefundable application fee of $50, 3 letters of recommendation, (recommended, not required), and a personal statement. Notification of the admissions decision is 10 to 12 weeks after the file is completed. The latest acceptable LSAT test date for fall entry is February. The law school uses the LSDAS.

Special

The law school recruits minority and disadvantaged students through visits to colleges and cities with large minority populations; faculty and student contact with minority applicants; special programs at the Law School Annual Open House; LSDAS's Candidate Referral Service; and contact with college prelaw advisers. The Sp.A.C.E. program, the law school's discretionary admissions process, seeks to identify applicants whose GPA and LSAT scores may not fully represent their abilities and potential, including minority applicants and economically disadvantaged applicants. Requirements are not different for out-of-state students. Transfer students must have one year of credit, have attended an ABA-approved and an AALS member law school; and rank in the top 20% of their class after completion of 1 year. Availability of seats is also a factor in admission.

Costs

Tuition and fees for the 2001-2002 academic year are $10,688 for full-time in-state students and $18,244 for out-of-state students. Tuition for part-time students is $8626 in-state and $14,672 out-of-state. On-campus room and board costs about $6270 annually; books and supplies run $1500.

Financial Aid

About 80% of current law students receive some form of aid. The average annual amount of aid from all sources combined, including scholarships, loans, and work contracts, is $20,766; maximum, $33,644. Awards may be based on merit only, need only, or a combination of need and merit. Required financial statement is the FAFSA. The aid application deadline for fall entry is March 1. Special funds for minority or disadvantaged students consist of a limited number of partial tuition scholarships that are awarded to students admitted through the Sp.A.C.E. program (the discretionary admissions process) who have outstanding performance records and demonstrated financial need. First-year students are notified about their financial aid application after admission, and when their financial aid forms are received and processed.

About the Law School

Temple University James E. Beasley School of Law was established in 1895 and is a public institution. The 87-acre campus is in an urban area 2 miles north of downtown Philadelphia. The law school is committed to the philosophy that legal education must provide both practical and theoretical knowledge. Students have access to federal, state, county, city, and local agencies, courts, correctional facilities, law firms, and legal aid organizations in the Philadelphia area. The Temple Legal Aid Office is housed in the law school's main building. Facilities of special interest to law students include Barrack Hall, with new student services offices, classrooms, and student organization offices, a large moot court room, and 2 trial courtrooms; an 11-level open-stack law library with 2 multilevel reading rooms; 750 study carrels, and table seats, and a legal conference center. Housing for students on campus is apartment-style; many students choose off-campus housing. The Admissions Office maintains updated information on housing prospects and a list of students seeking roommates. All law school facilities are accessible to the physically disabled.

Calendar

The law school operates on a traditional semester basis. Courses for full-time students are offered days only and must be completed within 3 years. For part-time students, courses are offered both day and evening and must be completed within 4 years. New full- and part-time students are admitted in the fall. There is an 8-week summer session. Transferable summer courses are not offered.

Programs

In addition to the J.D., the law school offers the LL.M. Students may take relevant courses in other programs and apply credit toward the J.D.; a maximum of 12 credits may be applied. The following joint degrees may be earned: J.D./LL.M. (Juris Doctor/Master of Laws in taxation), J.D./LL.M. (Juris Doctor/Master of Laws in transnational law), and J.D./M.B.A. (Juris Doctor/Master of Business Administration).

Phone: 215-204-8925
800-560-1428
Fax: 215-204-1185
E-mail: *lawadmis@blue.temple.edu*
Web: *www.temple.edu/lawschool*

Contact

Admissions Staff, 215-204-8925 or 800-560-1428 for general inquiries; Financial Aid Office, 215-204-8943 for financial aid information.

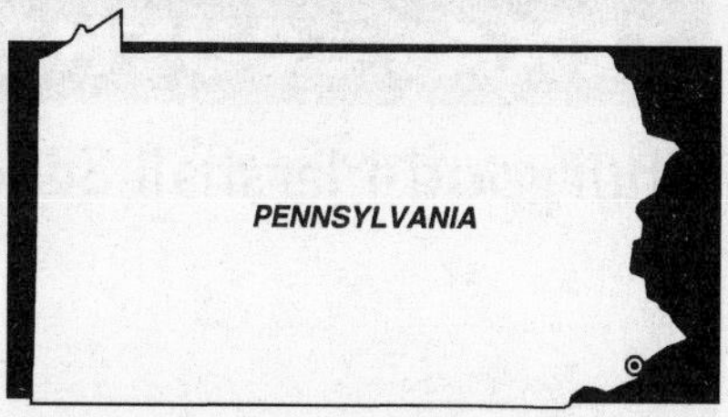

Required

To earn the J.D., candidates must complete 87 total credits, of which 39 are for required courses. They must maintain a minimum GPA of 2.0 in the required courses. The following first-year courses are required of all students: Civil Procedure I, Constitutional Law, Contracts I and II, Criminal Law I, Legal Writing and Research, Property, Torts, and Legal Decision Making. Required upper-level courses consist of Professional Responsibility and 2 writing requirements. The school offers, but does not require, participation in an extensive selection of clinical opportunities.The required orientation program for first-year students consists of a 5-day program that provides an overview of academic requirements, faculty regulations, university and law school services, financial aid, general placement information, and social activities.

Electives

The James E. Beasley School of Law offers concentrations in corporate law, criminal law, family law, international law, juvenile law, litigation, securities law, tax law, torts and insurance, public interest law, technology law, intellectual property law, constitutional and civil rights law, health care law, administrative and government law, and jurisprudence. In addition, extensive clinics worth 3 or 4 credits per semester are offered to third and fourth year students in the areas of litigation, mediation, and transactional work. There is an extensive number of writing seminar courses, each of which is worth 3 credits per semester. Special lecture series include the Fogel and Meyers lecture series, the Business Law Forum, and numerous other lectures offered by faculty members and guests of the law school. Summer sessions, worth from 2 to 6 credits, are available in Rome, Italy; Athens, Greece; and Tel Aviv, Israel. A full semester abroad is offered in Tokyo, Japan for up to 18 credits. All these sessions are open to students after their first year. Some faculty conduct guided research in a tutorial format, which is worth a maximum of 3 credits per semester. There is a faculty mentoring program for students who are having academic difficulty. Special interest group programs include Public Interest Law Programs. The most widely taken electives are Evidence, Business Associations, and Criminal Procedure.

Graduation Requirements

In order to graduate, candidates must have a GPA of 2.0, have completed the upper-division writing requirement, and Professional Responsibility.

Organizations

Students edit the *Temple Law Review, Temple International and Comparative Law Journal, Temple Environmental Law and Technology Journal, Temple Political and Civil Rights Law Review,* and the newspaper *Class Action.* Moot court competitions are the I. Herman Stern and Samuel J. Polsky Moot Court competitions held annually at the school; students also attend other competitions throughout the country. Outside competitions include the Jessup International, ABA National Negotiation, National Invitational Tournament of Champions, National Trial Competition, National Association of Criminal Defense Lawyers, and American Trial Lawyers Association competition. More than 30 different student organizations flourish at the law school. The Student Bar Association acts as the students' representative in the law school administration, and is the umbrella organization that oversees the many diverse student activities and organizations. There are local chapters of the Black Law Students Association, Moot Court, National Lawyers Guild, and Women's Law Caucus.

Library

The law library contains 529,695 hard-copy volumes and 733,797 microform volume equivalents, and subscribes to 2830 serial publications. Such on-line databases and networks as CALI, DIALOG, Dow-Jones, Infotrac, LEXIS, NEXIS, OCLC First Search, RLIN, WESTLAW, Hein Online, PA Code Online, and CCH Tax Online are available to law students for research. Special library collections include the Anglophonic collection, African collection, Rawle history collection, Ellsberg Watergate collection, and Temple Trial collection. Recently, the library installed a reference desk, innovative circulation acquisition and cataloging system, additional lighting, and renovated administrative offices. The ratio of library volumes to faculty is 8684 to 1 and to students is 493 to 1. The ratio of seats in the library to students is 1 to 2.

Placement

J.D.s awarded: 322

Services available through: a separate law school placement center

Special features: programs on federal and state judicial clerkships; specific outreach to small and medium-size firms; access to Emplawyernet and other on-line career planning resources; and co-sponsorship of regional job fairs. Temple is a founder of the Philadelphia Area Minority Job Fair. Counseling on public interest and public service careers is handed by a newly created Public Interest Law Programs Office.

Full-time job interviews:	94 employers
Summer job interviews:	94 employers
Placement by graduation:	66% of class
Placement within 9 months:	93% of class
Average starting salary:	$20,000 to $75,000

Areas of placement:

Private practice 2-10 attorneys	11%
Private practice 11-25 attorneys	3%
Private practice 26-50 attorneys	3%
Private practice 51-100 attorneys	27%
Business/industry	18%
Government	17%
Judicial clerkships	13%
Public interest	6%
Academic	2%

Faculty

The law school has 61 full-time and 155 part-time faculty members, of whom 63 are women. According to AAUP standards for Category I institutions, faculty salaries are above average. About 33% of full-time faculty have a graduate law degree in addition to the J.D. The ratio of full-time students to full-time faculty in an average class is 17 to 1. The law school has a regular program of bringing visiting professors and other distinguished lecturers and visitors to campus.

Students

About 49% of the student body are women; 19%, minorities; 9%, African American; 6%, Asian American; and 4%, Hispanic. The majority of students come from Pennsylvania (72%). The average age of entering students is 26; age range is 21 to 54. About 33% of students enter directly from undergraduate school, 14% have a graduate degree, and 65% have worked full-time prior to entering law school. About 3% drop out after the first year for academic or personal reasons; 97% remain to receive a law degree.

TEXAS SOUTHERN UNIVERSITY

Thurgood Marshall School of Law

3100 Cleburne Avenue
Houston, TX 77004

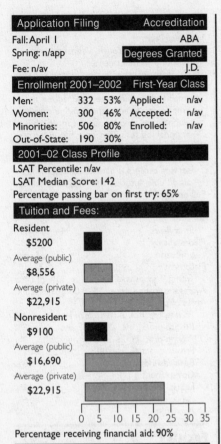

Application Filing		Accreditation
Fall: April 1		ABA
Spring: n/app		**Degrees Granted**
Fee: n/av		J.D.

Enrollment 2001–2002			First-Year Class	
Men:	332	53%	Applied:	n/av
Women:	300	46%	Accepted:	n/av
Minorities:	506	80%	Enrolled:	n/av
Out-of-State:	190	30%		

2001–02 Class Profile

LSAT Percentile: n/av
LSAT Median Score: 142
Percentage passing bar on first try: 65%

Tuition and Fees:

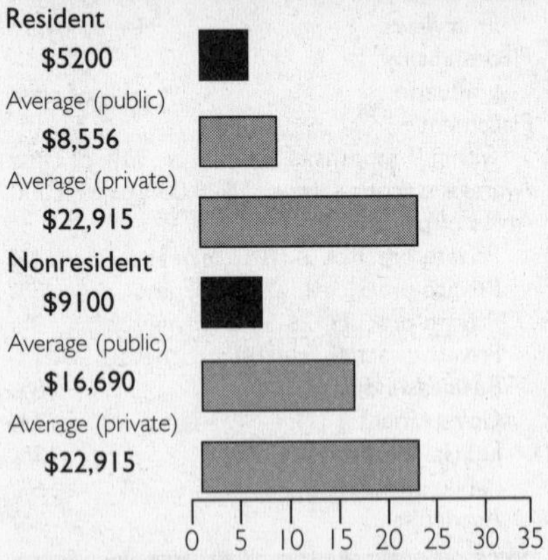

Percentage receiving financial aid: 90%

ADMISSIONS

Information in the above capsule is from an earlier year. In a recent first-year class, the median GPA was 2.7.

Requirements

Applicants must have a bachelor's degree and take the LSAT. The most important admission factors include LSAT results, GPA, and motivations. No specific undergraduate courses are required. Candidates are interviewed.

Procedure

Check with the school for current application deadlines and fee. Applicants should submit an application form, a nonrefundable fee, LSAT results, and 2 letters of recommendation. Notification of the admissions decision is between February and May (majority). The law school uses the LSDAS.

Special

The law school recruits minority and disadvantaged students through the Office of Admissions' Candidate Referral Service program and college campus visits. The majority of students are members of minority groups. Requirements are different for out-of-state students in that they must, generally, have stronger credentials. Transfer students must have attended an ABA-approved law school and have been academically successful at the first school of attendance. Preadmissions courses consist of the Legal Education Advancement Program, available during the summers by invitation.

Costs

Tuition and fees for the academic year are approximately $5200 for full-time in-state students and $9100 for out-of-state students. Books and supplies run about $1100.

Financial Aid

About 90% of current law students receive some form of aid. The average annual amount of aid from all sources combined, including scholarships, loans, and work contracts, is about $18,500 (maximum). Awards are based on need and merit. Required financial statement is the FAFSA. Check with the school for current application deadlines. Special funds for minority or disadvantaged students are available through a number of scholarships. First-year students are notified about their financial aid application at time of acceptance after the financial aid forms are processed and before enrollment if the application was submitted before the deadline.

About the Law School

Texas Southern University Thurgood Marshall School of Law was established in 1947 and is a public institution. The 6-acre campus is in an urban area 7 miles south of downtown Houston. The primary mission of the law school is in keeping with its designation by the Texas Legislature as a special purpose institution for urban programming to meet not only the needs of students in general, but of minority and disadvantaged students as well. Students have access to federal, state, county, city, and local agencies, courts, correctional facilities, law firms, and legal aid organizations in the Houston area. There are also adjunct faculty in certain areas of specialty and 2 writing-skills specialists. There is a strong clinical program and a very competitive moot court program. Facilities of special interest to law students include several computer rooms offering terminals for on-line legal research, as well as for off-line student use. Housing for students consists of a privately managed campus apartment community, for which law students receive priority consideration. All law school facilities are accessible to the physically disabled.

Calendar

The law school operates on a traditional semester basis. Courses for full-time students are offered days only and must be completed within 4 years. There is no part-time program. New students are admitted in the fall. There is a 9-week summer session. Transferable summer courses are offered.

Programs

Students may take relevant courses in other programs and apply credit toward the J.D.; a maximum of 6 credits may be applied.

Phone: 713-313-7114
Fax: 713-313-1049
E-mail: *cgardner@tsulaw.edu*
Web: *www.tsulaw.edu*

Contact

Carolyn Gardner, Admissions Officer, 713-313-7114 for general inquiries; Pamela Jones, Student Record Coordinator, 713-313-7243 for financial aid information.

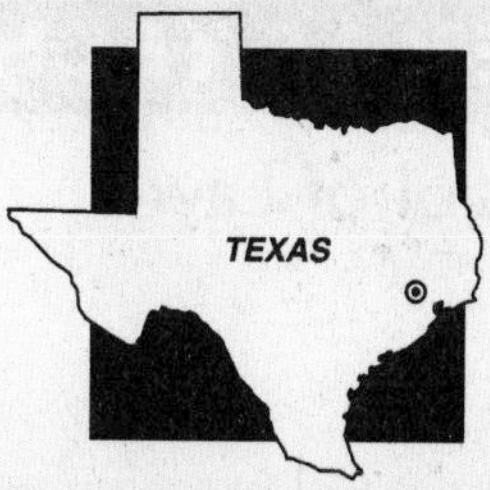

Required

To earn the J.D., candidates must complete 90 total credits, of which 70 are for required courses. They must maintain a minimum GPA of 2.0 in the required courses. The following first-year courses are required of all students: Case Analysis and Legal Writing, Civil Procedure, Property, Contracts, Torts, Constitutional Law, and Criminal Law. Required upper-level courses consist of Appellate Litigation, Evidence, Criminal Procedure, Trial Simulation, Business Associations, Commercial Law, Basic Federal Income Taxation, Professional Responsibility, Wills and Trusts, Federal Jurisdiction and Procedure, a writing seminar, Texas Practice, and Consumer Rights. The required orientation program for first-year students consists of a 1-week introduction and lectures on skills.

Electives

The Thurgood Marshall School of Law offers concentrations in litigation and tax law. In addition, clinics include criminal law, homeless advocacy law, elder law, family law, immigration law, housing law, tax law, environmental justice, AIDS law, mediation, and general civil law. Seminars include criminal trial practice; writing; First Amendment; jurisprudence; estate-planning; commercial torts; environmental law; sports law; immigration law; patent, trademarks, and copyright law; medical malpractice, and health law. Internships are available through the clinics offered, including a judicial internship with federal and state judges. Research programs allow for independent research and thesis research. A special lecture series, the Quodlibet, is a faculty- and student-sponsored program on current legal issues that are debated by faculty. Students may participate in study-abroad programs sponsored by other ABA-approved law schools. Each first-year section is assigned a student tutor who reviews substantive materials, discusses hypotheticals, and provides study help for each professor's class. The Legal Education Advancement Program (LEAP) is a 6-week summer program to develop oral and written legal analysis skills. Minority students are offered the third-year Mentor Program in which students are assigned alumni mentors in the third year through the bar examination. Academic counseling on course selection and personal goals is available. The most widely taken electives are estate planning, legal clinics, and oil and gas law.

Graduation Requirements

In order to graduate, candidates must have a GPA of 2.0 and have completed the upper-division writing requirement.

Organizations

The primary law review is the *Thurgood Marshall Law Review*. The student magazine is *The Solicitor*. The James M. Douglas Board of Advocates sponsors numerous moot court and mock trial programs. Law student organizations include the Student Bar Association, Black Law Students Association, and Chicano Law Students Association. There are local chapters of Asian Pacific American Law Students Association, Phi Alpha Delta, and Phi Delta Phi.

Library

The law library contains 229,464 hardcopy volumes and 100,536 microform volume equivalents, and subscribes to 385 serial publications. Such on-line databases and networks as DIALOG, LEXIS, WESTLAW, and Legal-Trac are available to law students for research. Special library collections include the Dominion Reports and federal government depositories. Recently, the library completed a modern, state-of-the-art research and study facility, and added an interoffice library network. The ratio of library volumes to faculty is 7402 to 1 and to students is 353 to 1. The ratio of seats in the library to students is 1 to 2.

Faculty

The law school has approximately 34 full-time and 19 part-time faculty members, of whom 14 are women. About 39% of full-time faculty have a graduate law degree in addition to the J.D. The ratio of full-time students to full-time faculty in an average class is 60 to 1; in a clinic, 10 to 1.

Placement

J.D.s awarded: 140

Services available through: a separate law school placement center

Services: participate in numerous job fairs in and out of state.

Special features: Attorneys address students about legal career opportunities and participate in interview role-playing. Resumes are also individually critiqued. In addition, mock interview seminars are conducted, as well as workshops in preparation for summer legal internships.

Full-time job interviews:	n/av
Summer job interviews:	28 employers
Placement by graduation:	72% of class
Placement within 9 months:	72% of class
Average starting salary:	$47,000
Areas of placement:	
Private practice 2-10 attorneys	88%
Government	7%
Business/industry	4%
Public interest	2%

Students

About 46% of the student body are women; 80%, minorities; 46%, African American; 3%, Asian American; 29%, Hispanic; and 2%, Native American. The majority of students come from Texas (70%). The average age of entering students is 27; age range is 25 to 35. About 60% of students enter directly from undergraduate school, 10% have a graduate degree, and 40% have worked full-time prior to entering law school. About 35% drop out after the first year for academic or personal reasons; 65% remain to receive a law degree.

TEXAS TECH UNIVERSITY

School of Law

1802 Hartford
Lubbock, TX 79409

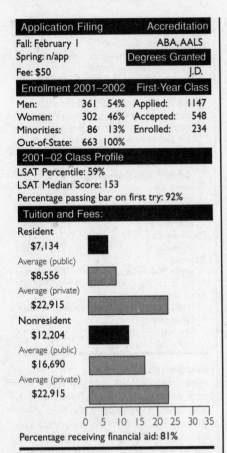

Application Filing		Accreditation
Fall: February 1		ABA, AALS
Spring: n/app		**Degrees Granted**
Fee: $50		J.D.

Enrollment 2001–2002			First-Year Class	
Men:	361	54%	Applied:	1147
Women:	302	46%	Accepted:	548
Minorities:	86	13%	Enrolled:	234
Out-of-State:	663	100%		

2001–02 Class Profile

LSAT Percentile: 59%
LSAT Median Score: 153
Percentage passing bar on first try: 92%

Tuition and Fees:

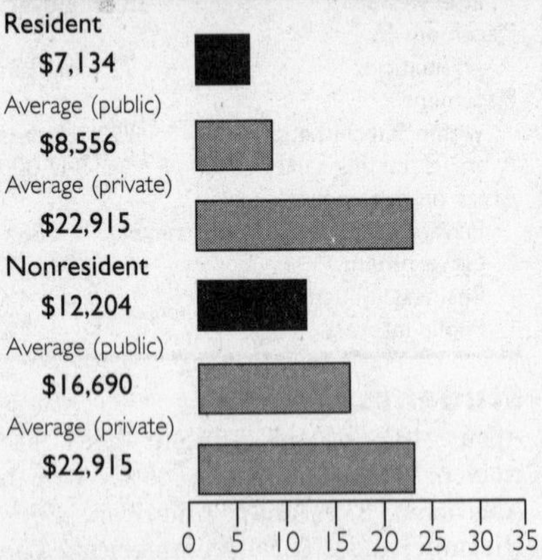

Percentage receiving financial aid: 81%

ADMISSIONS

In the fall 2001 first-year class, 1147 applied, 548 were accepted, and 234 enrolled. Nine transfers enrolled. The median LSAT percentile of the most recent first-year class was 59; the median GPA was 3.4 on a scale of 4.0. The lowest LSAT percentile accepted was 25; the highest was 96.

Requirements

Applicants must have a bachelor's degree and take the LSAT. Minimum acceptable LSAT percentile is 50 and minimum acceptable GPA is 2.5 on a scale of 4.0. The most important admission factors include LSAT results, GPA, and academic achievement. No specific undergraduate courses are required. Candidates are interviewed.

Procedure

The application deadline for fall entry is February 1. Applicants should submit an application form, LSAT results, a nonrefundable application fee of $50, and a personal statement and resume. Notification of the admissions decision begins in November. The latest acceptable LSAT test date for fall entry is February. The law school uses the LSDAS.

Special

The law school recruits minority and disadvantaged students by encouraging campus visitation by minority faculty and students and recruiting at many Texas universities. Requirements are not different for out-of-state students. Transfer students must have one year of credit, have attended an ABA-approved law school, have ranked in the upper 25% of the first-year class, and be in good standing.

Costs

Tuition and fees for the 2001-2002 academic year are $7134 for full-time in-state students and $12,204 for out-of-state students. On-campus room and board costs about $10,164 annually; books and supplies run $866.

Financial Aid

About 81% of current law students receive some form of aid. The average annual amount of aid from all sources combined, including scholarships, loans, and work contracts, is $14,642; maximum, $17,934. Awards are based on need and merit. The required financial statement is the FAFSA. The aid application deadline for fall entry is March. First-year students are notified about their financial aid application usually by late summer.

About the Law School

Texas Tech University School of Law was established in 1967 and is a public institution. The 1839-acre campus is in an urban area in Lubbock. The primary mission of the law school is to train men and women for the practice of law in the United States, whether as advocate, counselor, judge, or law teacher, in accordance with the highest traditions of professional responsibility. It is also recognized that law is used as a stepping-stone to a career in government, politics, or business. Students have access to federal, state, county, city, and local agencies, courts, correctional facilities, law firms, and legal aid organizations in the Lubbock area. Housing for students is available on-campus, as well as in plentiful rental property close to the law school and throughout the city. All law school facilities are accessible to the physically disabled.

Calendar

The law school operates on a traditional semester basis. Courses for full-time students are offered days only and must be completed within 3 years. There is no part-time program. New students are admitted in the fall. There are 2 6-week summer sessions. Transferable summer courses are offered.

Programs

Students may take relevant courses in other programs and apply credit toward the J.D.; a maximum of 12 hours credits may be applied. The following joint degrees may be earned: J.D./M.B.A. (Juris Doctor/Master of Business Administration), J.D./M.P.A. (Juris Doctor/Master of Public Administration), J.D./M.S. (Juris Doctor/Master of Science in agriculture economics), J.D./M.S.A.C. (Juris Doctor/Master of Accounting), J.D./M.S.B.T. (Juris Doctor/Master of Science in biotechnology), J.D./M.S.E.T. (Juris Doctor/Master of Science in environmental toxicology), and J.D./M.S.F.F.P. (Juris Doctor/Master of Science in family financial planning).

Phone: 806-742-3990, ext. 273
Fax: 806-742-1629
E-mail: *donna.williams@ttu.edu*
Web: *www.law.ttu.edu*

Contact

Donna Williams, Admissions Counselor, 806-742-3990, ext. 272 for general inquiries and financial aid information.

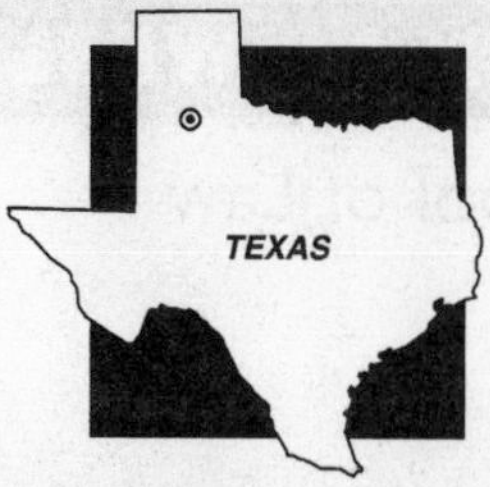

Required

To earn the J.D., candidates must complete 90 total credits, of which 55 are for required courses. They must maintain a minimum GPA of 2.0 in the required courses. The following first-year courses are required of all students: Property, Legal Practice I, Legal Practice II, Criminal Law, Constitutional Law, Civil Procedure, Torts, and Contracts. Required upper-level courses consist of Business Entities, Commercial Law, Criminal Procedure, Income Taxation, Professional Responsibility, Wills and Trusts, and Evidence. The required orientation program for first-year students is 3 days.

Electives

There are no established areas of concentration. Students select an area and take electives offered in those areas. In addition, second- and third-year students may take clinics, including low income tax clinic, worth 2 credits, and civil litigation or criminal prosecution clinics, worth 4 credits each. Second- and third-year students who have completed prerequisites may take seminar courses. A number of internships are available to second- and third-year students for credit. Independent research programs are available for advanced students for a maximum of 4 credit hours. There is a study-abroad program in Guanajuato, Mexico. A tutor is provided for each section of all first-year classes except legal practice. In addition, every first-year student will be provided with a mentor from the second- or third-year class if desired. The most widely taken electives are Family Law, Oil and Gas, and Trial Advocacy.

Graduation Requirements

In order to graduate, candidates must have a GPA of 2.0 and have completed the upper-division writing requirement.

Organizations

Students edit the *Texas Tech Law Review, the Administrative Law Journal, The Texas Bank Lawyer*, and *Texas Judges Bench Book*. Moot court competitions include the American Bar Association, Texas State Bar Association, and New York Bar Association. Other competitions include the ATLA Mock Trial, Tournament of Champions, American Bar Association Mock Trial, National Negotiations, and Client Counseling. Law student organizations include the Texas Tech Student Bar Association, Student Academic Support Services, and Criminal Trial Lawyers Association. Local chapters of national associations include Delta Theta Phi, Phi Alpha Delta, and Phi Delta Phi. Other organizations include Women In Law, Minority Law Students Association, and Board of Barristers.

Library

The law library contains 179,368 hard-copy volumes and 522,434 microform volume equivalents, and subscribes to 2341 serial publications. Such on-line databases and networks as CALI, CIS Universe, DIALOG, Dow-Jones, Infotrac, Legal-Trac, LEXIS, LOIS, Mathew Bender, NEXIS, OCLC First Search, and WESTLAW are available to law students for research. Special library collections include a federal government documents depository. Recently, the library installed multi-media technology in all classrooms in the law school, and equipped 1 classroom with distance learning capability; adopted a school-wide e-mail/calendar system, Microsoft Outlook, which is available for all students, faculty and staff; and added 14,259 linear feet of compact shelving in the library, which increased the shelving space by 55%. The ratio of library volumes to faculty is 6899 to 1 and to students, 271 to 1. The ratio of seats in the library to students is 1 to 3.

Placement

J.D.s awarded:	202
Services available through: a separate law school placement center	
Special features: participation in 4 off-campus recruitment programs in conjunction with various law schools.	
Full-time job interviews:	5 employers
Summer job interviews:	61 employers
Placement by graduation:	48% of class
Placement within 9 months:	97% of class
Average starting salary:	$40,000 to $110,000
Areas of placement:	
Private practice 2-10 attorneys	12%
Private practice 11-25 attorneys	18%
Private practice 26-50 attorneys	34%
Private practice 51-100 attorneys	17%
Government	11%
Judicial clerkships	6%
Business/industry	1%
Public interest	1%

Faculty

The law school has 26 full-time and 18 part-time faculty members, of whom 11 are women. According to AAUP standards for Category I institutions, faculty salaries are below average. About 46% of full-time faculty have a graduate law degree in addition to the J.D.; about 17% of part-time faculty have one. The ratio of full-time students to full-time faculty in an average class is 22 to 1. The law school has a regular program of bringing visiting professors and other distinguished lecturers and visitors to campus. There is a chapter of the Order of the Coif; 13 faculty and 523 graduates are members.

Students

About 46% of the student body are women; 13%, minorities; 2%, African American; 1%, Asian American; 9%, Hispanic; and 1%, Native American. The average age of entering students is 25; age range is 20 to 55. About 13% drop out after the first year for academic or personal reasons; 80% remain to receive a law degree.

TEXAS WESLEYAN UNIVERSITY

School of Law

1515 Commerce Street
Fort Worth, TX 76102

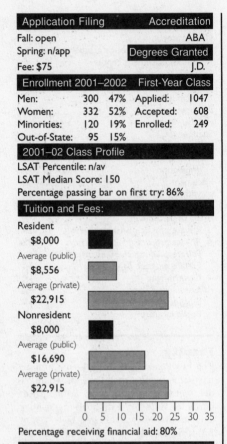

Application Filing		Accreditation
Fall: open		ABA
Spring: n/app		**Degrees Granted**
Fee: $75		J.D.

Enrollment 2001–2002			First-Year Class	
Men:	300	47%	Applied:	1047
Women:	332	52%	Accepted:	608
Minorities:	120	19%	Enrolled:	249
Out-of-State:	95	15%		

2001–02 Class Profile

LSAT Percentile: n/av
LSAT Median Score: 150
Percentage passing bar on first try: 86%

Tuition and Fees:

Resident
$8,000
Average (public)
$8,556
Average (private)
$22,915
Nonresident
$8,000
Average (public)
$16,690
Average (private)
$22,915

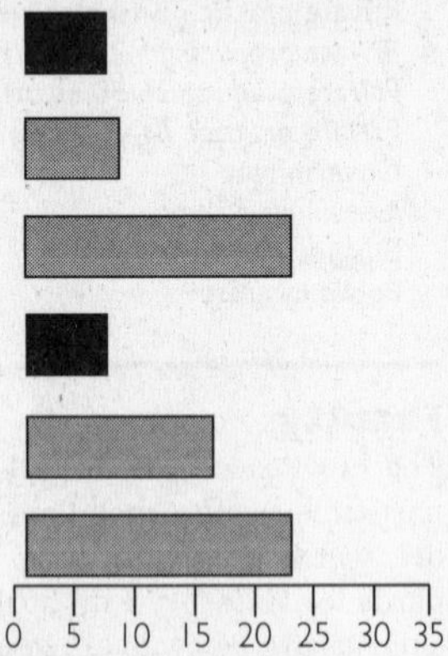

Percentage receiving financial aid: 80%

ADMISSIONS

In the fall 2001 first-year class, 1047 applied, 608 were accepted, and 249 enrolled. Eleven transfers enrolled. The median GPA of the most recent first-year class was 3.1 on a scale of 4.0.

Requirements

Applicants must have a bachelor's degree and take the LSAT. The most important admission factors include GPA, LSAT results, and academic achievement. No specific undergraduate courses are required. Candidates are not interviewed.

Procedure

The application deadline for fall entry is open. Applicants should submit an application form, LSAT results, transcripts, a nonrefundable application fee of $75, 2 letters of recommendation, a personal statement of no less than 500 words, and a letter of good standing from an undergraduate university. Notification of the admissions decision is ongoing. The latest acceptable LSAT test date for fall entry is June. The law school uses the LSDAS.

Special

The law school recruits minority and disadvantaged students through personal meetings. Requirements are not different for out-of-state students. Transfer students must have one year of credit, have a minimum GPA of 3.0, have attended an ABA-approved law school, a maximum of 30 hours transferable (no pass/fail credits transfer), a letter of good standing from the home law school, application fee, professor's recommendation, and a letter of request to transfer.

Costs

Tuition and fees for the 2001-2002 academic year are $8000 for full-time students. Tuition for part-time students is $5920 in-state. Books and supplies run about $700 annually.

Financial Aid

About 80% of current law students receive some form of aid. The average annual amount of aid from all sources combined, including scholarships, loans, and work contracts, is $20,000; maximum, $21,180. Awards are based on need and merit. The required financial statement is the FAFSA. Check with the school for current aid application deadlines. First-year students are notified about their financial aid application at the time of acceptance or time of file completion, whichever is later.

About the Law School

Texas Wesleyan University School of Law was established in 1989 and is a private institution. The campus is in an urban area in downtown Fort Worth. The primary mission of the law school is to provide legal education to a diverse student body, recognizing the need for both knowledge and skills, as well as professionalism. Students have access to federal, state, county, city, and local agencies, courts, correctional facilities, law firms, and legal aid organizations in the Fort Worth area, including the corporate headquarters of Lockheed Martin. Housing for students is at the main campus (a 10 minute drive). All law school facilities are accessible to the physically disabled.

Calendar

The law school operates on a traditional semester basis. Courses for full-time students are offered both day and evening and must be completed within 5 years. For part-time students, courses are offered both day and evening and must be completed within 6 years. New full- and part-time students are admitted in the fall. There are 2 5-week and 1 7-week summer sessions. Transferable summer courses are offered.

Programs

Required

To earn the J.D., candidates must complete 88 total credits, of which 50 are for required courses. They must maintain a minimum grade average of 70 in the required courses. The following first-year courses are required of all students: Contracts; Torts; Property; Civil Procedure; Criminal Law; Constitutional Law; Legal Analysis Research, and Writing; and Introduction to Law. Required upper-level courses consist of Professional Responsiblity, Business Associations, Criminal Procedure, Estates and Trusts, and Evidence. The required orientation program for first-year students is a 1-week orientation that includes Introduction to law class in Case Analysis, Legal History, Jurisprudence, Professionalism, Procedure, and Statutory Interpretation.

Phone: 817-212-4040
800-733-9529
Fax: 817-212-4002
E-mail: *law-admissions@law.txwes.edu*
Web: *www.law.txwes.edu*

Contact

Assistant Director of Admissions, 817-212-4040 for general inquiries; Doug Akins, Financial Aid Officer, 817-212-4090 for financial aid information.

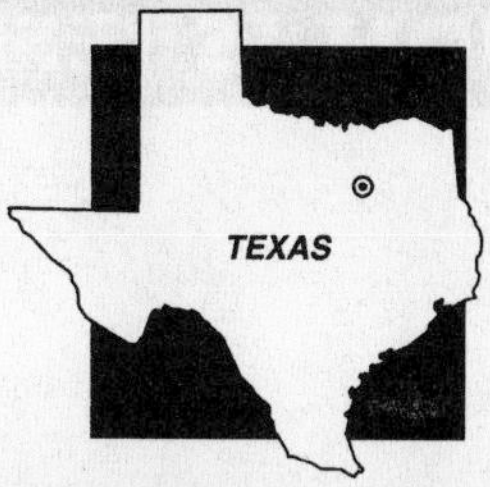

Electives

The School of Law offers concentrations in family law, tax law, and intellectual property. In addition, there is a Law Clinic, Family Mediation Clinic, and Mediation Clinic. Seminars, open to upper-level students, include Law and Elderly, Computers and Law, and Race and Racism. After completing 45 hours and maintaining a minimum grade average of 72, a student can earn up to 6 hours working with a private attorney under the supervision of a faculty member. Directed Research programs and Directed Readings are available. Special Lecture Series include the Eldon Mahon Lecture Series. An Academic Support Program provides assistance to students, including facilitated study groups and exam-taking workshops. Remedial programs include the Summer Leg-Up Program. The most widely taken electives are Tax, Family Law, and Texas Procedure.

Graduation Requirements

In order to graduate, candidates must have a minimum grade average of 70 and have completed the upper-division writing requirement.

Organizations

Students edit the *Texas Wesleyan Law Review* and *The Rambler*. There are fall and spring intraschool moot court competitions, as well as the ABA/LSD National Moot Court, Texas Young Lawyers Moot Court, and Jessup International Moot Court competitions. Other competitions include the ABA/LSD National Negotiations competition. Law student organizations include Texas Aggie Wesleyan Legal Society, Criminal Justice Society, and Intellectual Property Association. There are local chapters of Delta Theta Phi and Phi Delta Phi. Campus clubs and other organizations include HLSA, BLSA, and ABA/LSD.

Library

The law library contains 186,000 hard-copy volumes and 441,501 microform volume equivalents, and subscribes to 4168 serial publications. Such on-line databases and networks as CALI, DIALOG, Infotrac, LEXIS, NEXIS, WESTLAW, and CD-ROM towers that support '98 CD-ROM drives, which are networked to the faculty and student computer laboratories, are available to law students for research. Special library collections include Microfiche - CIS Congressional Library. Recently, the library moved to a different facility, added carrel seating, and increased its overall seating capacity. The ratio of library volumes to faculty is 7154 to 1 and to students, 294 to 1. The ratio of seats in the library to students is 1 to 2.

Faculty

The law school has 26 full-time and 28 part-time faculty members, of whom 18 are women. According to AAUP standards for Category IIA institutions, faculty salaries are above average. About 40% of full-time faculty have a graduate law degree in addition to the J.D. The ratio of full-time students to full-time faculty in an average class is 25 to 1; in a clinic, 8 to 1. The law school has a regular program of bringing visiting professors and other distinguished lecturers and visitors to campus.

Placement

J.D.s awarded:	102
Services available through: a separate law school placement center	
Special features: job fairs, career services library, job search workshop, career services handbook and packet given to students at orientation, and alumni outreach	
Full-time job interviews:	18 employers
Summer job interviews:	40 employers
Placement by graduation:	49% of class
Placement within 9 months:	83% of class
Average starting salary:	$33,000 to $80,000
Areas of placement:	
Private practice 2-10 attorneys	56%
Private practice 11-25 attorneys	9%
Private practice 26-50 attorneys	4%
Government	14%
Business/industry	12%
Judicial clerkships	3%
Public interest	1%
Academic	1%

Students

About 52% of the student body are women; 19%, minorities; 5%, African American; 2%, Asian American; 9%, Hispanic; 2%, Native American; and 6%, unknown. The majority of students come from Texas (85%). The average age of entering students is 30; age range is 21 to 68. About 10% of students have a graduate degree. About 15% drop out after the first year for academic or personal reasons; 85% remain to receive a law degree.

THOMAS JEFFERSON SCHOOL OF LAW

2121 San Diego Avenue
San Diego, CA 92110

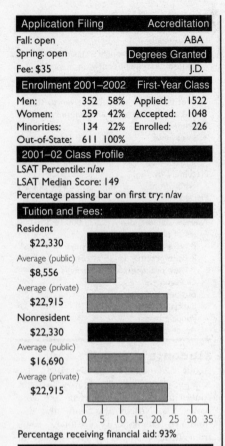

Application Filing	Accreditation
Fall: open	ABA

	Degrees Granted
Spring: open	
Fee: $35	J.D.

Enrollment 2001–2002			First-Year Class	
Men:	352	58%	Applied:	1522
Women:	259	42%	Accepted:	1048
Minorities:	134	22%	Enrolled:	226
Out-of-State:	611	100%		

2001–02 Class Profile

LSAT Percentile: n/av
LSAT Median Score: 149
Percentage passing bar on first try: n/av

Tuition and Fees:

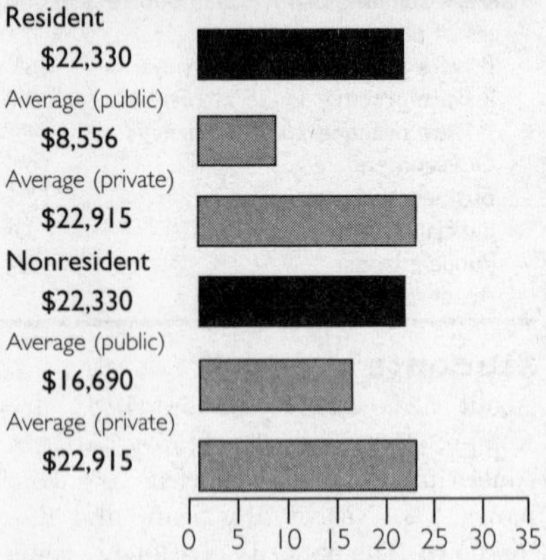

Percentage receiving financial aid: 93%

ADMISSIONS

In the fall 2001 first-year class, 1522 applied, 1048 were accepted, and 226 enrolled. The median GPA of the most recent first-year class was 2.9. The lowest LSAT percentile accepted was 9; the highest was 95.

Requirements

Generally, applicants must have a bachelor's degree from an accredited school and must take the LSAT. Minimum acceptable GPA is 2.0 on a scale of 4.0. The most important admission factors include LSAT results, academic achievement, and life experience. No specific undergraduate courses are required. Candidates are interviewed.

Procedure

The application deadline for fall entry is open. Applicants should submit an application form, LSAT results, transcripts, a nonrefundable application fee of $35, 2 letters of recommendation, and a personal statement. The latest acceptable LSAT test date for fall entry is June. The law school uses the LSDAS.

Special

Requirements are not different for out-of-state students.

Costs

Tuition and fees for the 2001-2002 academic year are $22,330 for all full-time students. Tuition for part-time students is $13,290 per year. Books and supplies run about $1074 annually.

Financial Aid

About 93% of current law students receive some form of aid. The average annual amount of aid from all sources combined, including scholarships, loans, and work contracts, is $20,703; maximum, $37,968. Awards are based on need and merit. Required financial statements are the FAFSA and institutional application. The aid application deadline for fall entry is February 15. First-year students are notified about their financial aid application at the time an application for admissions is received.

About the Law School

Thomas Jefferson School of Law was established in 1969 and is a private institution. The campus is in an urban area in the Old Town area of San Diego. The primary mission of the law school is to provide legal education for a nationally-based student body in a collegiate and supportive environment with attention to newly emerging areas of law, particularly those related to technological development, globalization, and the quest for social justice. Students have access to federal, state, county, city, and local agencies, courts, correctional facilities, law firms, and legal aid organizations in the San Diego area. There are also county law libraries available. Housing for students is not available on-site. The Student Services Department can assist with various housing alternatives. All law school facilities are accessible to the physically disabled.

Calendar

The law school operates on a traditional semester basis. Courses for full-time students are offered both day and evening and must be completed within 5 years. For part-time students, courses are offered both day and evening and must be completed within 6 years. New full- and part-time students are admitted in the fall and spring. There is an 8-week summer session. Transferable summer courses are offered.

Programs

Students may take relevant courses in other programs and apply credit toward the J.D.; a maximum of 8 credits may be applied.

Required

To earn the J.D., candidates must complete 88 total credits, of which 55 are for required courses. The following first-year courses are required of all students: Contracts I and II, Legal Writing I, Civil Procedure I and II, Torts I and II, Criminal Law, Criminal Procedure, and Property I. Required upper-level courses consist of Legal Writing II, Constitutional Law I and II, Evidence, Corporations, Property II, Remedies, and Professional Responsibility. The required orientation program for first-year students is 2 full days.

Phone: 619-297-9700
800-936-7529
Fax: 619-294-4713
E-mail: *adm@tjsl.edu*
Web: *www.tjsl.edu*

Contact

Carl Tusinski, Senior Admissions Counselor, 619-297-9700, ext. 1694 for general inquiries; Miriam Safer, Director of Financial Assistance, 619-297-9700, ext. 1353 for financial aid information.

Electives
The Thomas Jefferson School of Law offers concentrations in corporate law, criminal law, entertainment law, environmental law, family law, international law, litigation, media law, and sports law. Litigation includes dispute resolution; constitutional and civil rights; government and administrative law; intellectual property; and health law. In addition, Students can earn a maximum of 5 units by working in various government agencies, state and federal courts, or legal aid clinics. Small seminars are offered in specialty areas and are open to all students. Topics vary. A judicial internship program places qualified students in state and federal courts. Research assistantships are available through individual instructors. An Alumni Perspectives series annually features successful alumni who share their practice experience and expertise with students. Native American Law Students Association, Iranian Jurisprudence Society, Christian Legal Society, Jewish Student Union, Women's Law Association, La Raza, Pan Asian Lawyers Student Association, and Black Law Students Association offer mentoring and networking programs for minority students.

Graduation Requirements
In order to graduate, candidates must have a GPA of 2.0 and have completed the upper-division writing requirement.

Organizations

Students edit the *Thomas Jefferson Law Review*. Other publications include *The Thomas Jefferson School of Law News* and *The SBA Informer*. Moot court competitions include the National Appellate Advocacy Competition and Roger J. Traynor Moot Court Competition. Other competitions include A.T.L.A. Mock Trial, Young Texas Lawyers Association Mock Trial, San Diego Defense Lawyers, Intra-School National Mock Trial, and John Marshall Moot Court Competition. Among the student organizations are the Black Law Students Association, Pan Asian Law Students Association, and La Raza Law Students Association. Local chapters of national associations are the National Lawyers Guild, Civil Liberties Society, and ABA/Law Student Division. Campus clubs include the International Law Society, Public Interest Law Foundation, and Sports and Entertainment Law Society.

Library

The law library contains 231,301 hard-copy volumes and 124,905 microform volume equivalents, and subscribes to 2988 serial publications. Such on-line databases and networks as CALI, CIS Universe, DIALOG, Infotrac, Legal-Trac, LEXIS, LOIS, Mathew Bender, NEXIS, OCLC First Search, WESTLAW, United Nations Treaty Service, Legal Scholarship and Social Science Scholarship Network, and Hein Online are available to law students for research. Special library collections include Thomas Jefferson's writings, and books, videos, and other material about Thomas Jefferson. Recently, the library expanded its space, installed new shelving, and acquired major microform collections for Congressional documents, historical treatises, and U.S. Supreme Court documents. The ratio of library volumes to faculty is 8896 to 1 and to students is 379 to 1. The ratio of seats in the library to students is 1 to 6.

Faculty

The law school has 26 full-time and 30 part-time faculty members, of whom 22 are women. About 15% of full-time faculty have a graduate law degree in addition to the J.D. The ratio of full-time students to full-time faculty in an average class is 30 to 1. The law school has a regular program of bringing visiting professors and other distinguished lecturers and visitors to campus.

Students

About 42% of the student body are women; 22%, minorities; 4%, African American; 8%, Asian American; 11%, Hispanic; and 1%, Native American. The average age of entering students is 28.

Placement

J.D.s awarded:	128
Services available through: a separate law school placement center	
Services: several lecture series and individual lectures throughout the school year.	
Special features: n/av	
Full-time job interviews:	n/av
Summer job interviews:	n/av
Placement by graduation:	n/av
Placement within 9 months:	94% of class
Average starting salary:	$28,000 to $160,000
Areas of placement:	
Private practice 2-10 attorneys	26%
Private practice 11-25 attorneys	8%
Private practice 26-50 attorneys	5%
Private practice 100+ attorneys	11%
Business/industry	24%
Government	14%
Judicial clerkships	7%
Military	4%
Public interest	1%

THOMAS M. COOLEY LAW SCHOOL

300 South Capitol Avenue
Lansing, MI 48901

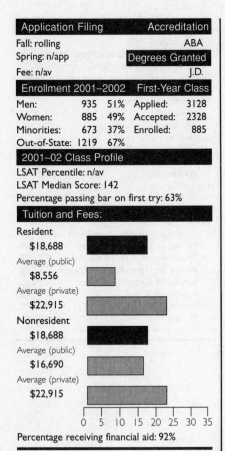

Application Filing		Accreditation
Fall: rolling		ABA
Spring: n/app		**Degrees Granted**
Fee: n/av		J.D.

Enrollment 2001–2002			First-Year Class	
Men:	935	51%	Applied:	3128
Women:	885	49%	Accepted:	2328
Minorities:	673	37%	Enrolled:	885
Out-of-State:	1219	67%		

2001–02 Class Profile

LSAT Percentile: n/av
LSAT Median Score: 142
Percentage passing bar on first try: 63%

Tuition and Fees:

Resident
$18,688
Average (public)
$8,556
Average (private)
$22,915
Nonresident
$18,688
Average (public)
$16,690
Average (private)
$22,915

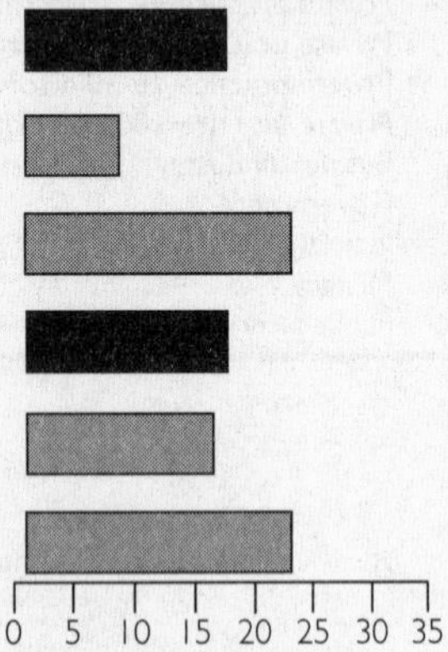

Percentage receiving financial aid: 92%

ADMISSIONS

In the fall 2001 first-year class, 3128 applied, 2328 were accepted, and 885 enrolled. Thirteen transfers enrolled. The median GPA of the most recent first-year class was 2.91.

Requirements
Applicants must take the LSAT. Minimum acceptable GPA is 2.0 on a scale of 4.0. The most important admission factors include GPA and LSAT results. No specific undergraduate courses are required. Candidates are not interviewed. A limited number of students with associate degrees are admitted, provided their qualifications are outstanding.

Procedure
The application deadline for fall entry is rolling. Applicants should submit an application form, LSAT results, and transcripts. New students pay a $25 nonrefundable enrollment fee. Notification of the admissions decision is on a rolling basis. The latest acceptable LSAT test date for fall entry is June. The law school uses the LSDAS.

Special
The Assistant to the Director of Admissions recruits minorities by attending law forums and job fairs. Requirements are not different for out-of-state students. Transfer students must have one year of credit, have a minimum GPA of 2.0, and have attended an ABA-approved law school. Students can transfer up to 30 credits for classes in which they have received a grade of C or better. They must be in good standing at their last school. An on-line prelaw course is available at *www.introlaw.cooley.edu.*

Costs

Tuition and fees for the 2001-2002 academic year are $18,688 for all full-time students. Tuition for part-time students is $13,360 per year. Books and supplies run about $800 annually.

Financial Aid

About 92% of current law students receive some form of aid. The average annual amount of aid from all sources combined, including scholarships, loans, and work contracts, is $18,500. Awards are based on need and merit. Required financial statement is the FAFSA. The aid application deadline for fall entry is rolling. Special funds for minority or disadvantaged students consist of Rosa Park and Martin Luther King, Jr. scholarships. Both are awarded based on need and merit. First-year students are notified about their financial aid application at time of acceptance.

About the Law School

Thomas M. Cooley Law School was established in 1972 and is a private institution. The campus is in an urban area in Lansing, the state capital. The primary mission of the law school is to integrate the study of law with practical experience in government, business, and the courts. Students have access to federal, state, county, city, and local agencies, courts, correctional facilities, law firms, and legal aid organizations in the Lansing area. An extensive externship program provides access to national lawyers' networks. Facilities of special interest to law students include a legal research library, opened in 1991, and an Academic Resource Center, opened in 2000. Housing for students consists of a wide variety of apartments in the Lansing area. All law school facilities are accessible to the physically disabled.

Calendar

The law school operates on a year-round basis. Courses for full-time students are offered during the day, evening, and on weekends and must be completed within 5 years. For part-time students, courses are offered days, evenings, and on weekends and must be completed within 6 years. New full- and part-time students are admitted in the fall, winter, and spring. There is a 15-week summer session. Transferable summer courses are offered.

Programs

Students may take relevant courses in other programs and apply credit toward the J.D.; a maximum of 9 (MPA) credits may be applied. The following joint degrees may be earned: J.D./M.P.A. (Juris Doctor/Master of Public Administration) through partnership with Western Michigan University.

Phone: 517-371-5140
800-874-3511
Fax: 517-334-5718
E-mail: *admissions@cooley.edu*
Web: *www.cooley.edu*

Contact

Stephanie Gregg, Assistant Dean for Admissions, 517-371-5140 ext. 2250 for general inquiries; Richard Boruszewski, Financial Aid Director, 517-371-5140 ext. 2216 for financial aid information.

Required

To earn the J.D., candidates must complete 90 total credits, of which 63 are for required courses. They must maintain a minimum GPA of 2.0 in the required courses. The following first-year courses are required of all students: Contracts I and II, Torts I and II, Criminal Law, Research and Writing, Civil Procedure I and II, Criminal Procedure, Property I and II, Professional Responsibility, and Introduction to Law I. Required upper-level courses consist of Evidence, Secured Transactions, Administrative Law or Law Practice or Sales (choose 1 of 3), Constitutional Law I and II, Business Organizations, Taxation, Wills, Estates, and Trusts, and Remedies. All students must take clinical courses. The required orientation program for first-year students is a 1-week orientation course.

Electives

The Thomas M. Cooley Law School offers concentrations in environmental law, international law, litigation, general practice, solo and small firm, administrative law, Constitutional law and civil rights, and business transactions. In addition, in-house clinics include the Sixty Plus Elder Law Clinic, Estate Planning Clinic, and Innocence Project for 3 to 6 credits. Practice seminars are conducted in civil procedure, district court practice, criminal practice, and client counseling. Traditional seminar classes include Constitutional law issues. These seminars are worth 2 to 3 credits. Students may earn up to 10 credits in externships in faculty-supervised placements around the United States. Research and Writing, Advanced Research and Writing, and Law Practice courses provide training in brief writing and oral argument conducted before sitting Circuit Court judges. Electives are available in Advanced CALR. Cooley has an extensive third-year externship program, which places senior students in work settings for 1 or 2 terms. Special lecture series include the Krinock lecture. The winter term offers study abroad in Australia and New Zealand; the summer term offers Canadian courses in Toronto. Through the Student Tutorial Services, upper-class students help new students form study groups. Faculty members may offer special seminars on study techniques. In addition, the Academic Resource Center coordinates tutorials on exam skills and study techniques and offers individual counseling. The most widely taken electives are Law Practice, Trial Workshop, and Family Law.

Graduation Requirements

In order to graduate, candidates must have a GPA of 2.0 and have completed the upper-division writing requirement.

Organizations

Students edit the *Cooley Law Review*, the *Thomas M. Cooley Journal of Practical and Clinical Law*, the *Thomas M. Cooley Green Pages*, the newspaper the *Pillar*, the *Benchmark*, a magazine published each trimester, and *Catalog*, an annual publication. The Law School competes in the Frederick Douglass Moot Court, Chicago Bar Association Moot Court, and State of Michigan Moot Court. Other competitions include Environmental Law Moot Court, Evans Competition, National Trial Competition, NACDL, and Criminal Justice Trial Advocacy Competition. The Law School has more than 30 student organizations including the Black Law Students Association, the Computer Law Society, and the Criminal Law Society. There are local chapters of the ABA-Law Student Division and Phi Delta Phi.

Library

The law library contains 429,735 hard-copy volumes and 117,732 microform volume equivalents, and subscribes to 4821 serial publications. Such on-line databases and networks as CALI, LEXIS, Mathew Bender, NEXIS, OCLC First Search, and WESTLAW are available to law students for research. Special library collections include a depository for U.S. government documents, a full set of Michigan Supreme Court records and briefs, and a Congressional Information Service Microfiche library. Recently, the library made available a large computer laboratory, 2 electronic classrooms for computer-assisted research instruction, and INNOPAC, a state-of-the-art integrated automated library system. The ratio of library volumes to faculty is 6931 to 1 and to students is 236 to 1. The ratio of seats in the library to students is 1 to 4.

Placement

J.D.s awarded:	419

Services available through: a separate law school placement center and placement office

Services: 24-hour toll-free job hotline recording; solo, small firm resource room

Special features: a complete career library including audio and visual resources, weekly workshops and programs, job bulletins from more than 123 law schools nationwide, a newsletter, mock interview program, and roommate directory.

Full-time job interviews:	19 employers
Summer job interviews:	19 employers
Placement by graduation:	23% of class
Placement within 9 months:	84% of class
Average starting salary:	$10,400 to $150,000
Areas of placement:	
Private practice 2-10 attorneys	40%
Private practice 11-25 attorneys	9%
Private practice 26-50 attorneys	3%
Private practice 51-100 attorneys	4%
Government	22%
Business/industry	11%
Judicial clerkships	6%
Public interest	3%
Academic	2%

Faculty

The law school has 62 full-time and more than 100 part-time faculty members. About 21% of full-time faculty have a graduate law degree in addition to the J.D. Most classes mix full- and part-time students. The law school has a regular program of bringing visiting professors and other distinguished lecturers and visitors to campus.

Students

About 49% of the student body are women; 37%, minorities; 22%, African American; 5%, Asian American; 6%, Hispanic; and 1%, Native American. Most students come from Michigan (33%). The average age of entering students is 29; age range is 20 to 69. About 7% of students have a graduate degree. About 30% drop out after the first year for academic or personal reasons; 70% remain to receive a law degree.

TOURO COLLEGE

Jacob D. Fuchsberg Law Center

300 Nassau Road
Huntington, NY 11743

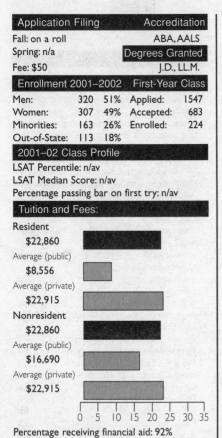

Application Filing		Accreditation
Fall: on a roll		ABA, AALS
Spring: n/a		**Degrees Granted**
Fee: $50		J.D., LL.M.

Enrollment 2001–2002			First-Year Class	
Men:	320	51%	Applied:	1547
Women:	307	49%	Accepted:	683
Minorities:	163	26%	Enrolled:	224
Out-of-State:	113	18%		

2001–02 Class Profile

LSAT Percentile: n/av
LSAT Median Score: n/av
Percentage passing bar on first try: n/av

Tuition and Fees:

Resident
$22,860
Average (public)
$8,556
Average (private)
$22,915
Nonresident
$22,860
Average (public)
$16,690
Average (private)
$22,915

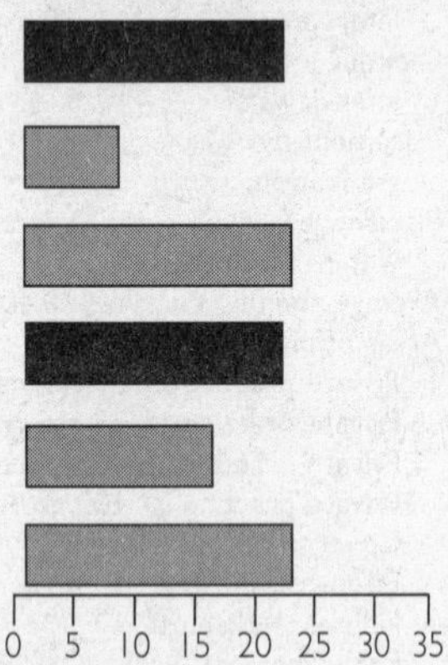

Percentage receiving financial aid: 92%

ADMISSIONS

In the fall 2001 first-year class, 1547 applied, 683 were accepted, and 224 enrolled. Twenty-two transfers enrolled. The lowest LSAT percentile accepted was 15; the highest was 86.

Requirements

Applicants must have a bachelor's degree and take the LSAT. The most important admission factors include academic achievement, LSAT results, and general background. No specific undergraduate courses are required. Candidates are interviewed.

Procedure

The application deadline for fall entry is on a rolling basis. Applicants should submit an application form, LSAT results, transcripts, a nonrefundable application fee of $50, optional letters of recommendation, and a personal statement. Notification of the admissions decision is on a rolling basis. The latest acceptable LSAT test date for fall entry is June. The law school uses the LSDAS.

Special

The law school recruits minority and disadvantaged students by means of visits to historically black colleges, as well as colleges and universities with significant minority populations; the use of Law Services' Candidate Referral Service; Council on Legal Education Opportunity (CLEO); the Legal Education Access Program; and other projects. Requirements are not different for out-of-state students. Transfer students must have one year of credit and be in good academic standing, and submit a copy of the LSDAS Report, an official transcript, and a letter of good standing from the law school currently attended.

Costs

Tuition and fees for the 2001-2002 academic year are $22,860 for all full-time students. Tuition for part-time students is $17,830 per year. Books and supplies run about $1600 annually.

Financial Aid

About 92% of current law students receive some form of aid. The average annual amount of aid from all sources combined, including scholarships, loans, and work contracts, is $18,500; maximum, $40,330. Awards are based on need and merit. The required financial statement is the FAFSA. The aid application deadline for fall entry is April 15. Special funds for minority or disadvantaged students consist of the Touro Grant, awarded based on financial need; Perkins Loan and College Work Study, awarded based on need; and incentive awards, based on need and merit. First-year students are notified about their financial aid application after acceptance, but before enrollment.

About the Law School

Touro College Jacob D. Fuchsberg Law Center was established in 1980 and is a private institution. The 11.1-acre campus is in a suburban area 25 miles east of New York City. The primary mission of the law school is to produce graduates ready for real-world practice. The student experience is characterized by extensive faculty-student interaction, innovative student support systems, and a commitment to a lawyer's moral and ethical obligations. Students have access to federal, state, county, city, and local agencies, courts, correctional facilities, law firms, and legal aid organizations in the Huntington area. The school is planning to relocate to become part of the Central Islip court complex, with a state-of-the-art interactive facility. Facilities of special interest to law students include law firms, local and New York City attorneys' offices, and public interest agencies and firms. Housing for students is available on-campus and off-campus. The school's Housing Information Network and mailings identify available accommodations and students who wish to share housing. About 98% of the law school facilities are accessible to the physically disabled.

Calendar

The law school operates on a traditional semester basis. Courses for full-time students are offered days only and must be completed within 6 years. For part-time students, courses are offered both day and evening and must be completed within 6 years. New full- and part-time students are admitted in the fall. There is a 4- and 7-week summer session. Transferable summer courses are offered.

Programs

In addition to the J.D., the law school offers the LL.M. and *LL.M. in U.S. legal studies for foreign law graduates and in general studies. The following joint degrees may be earned: J.D./M.B.A. (Juris Doctor/Master of Business Administration), J.D./M.P.A. (Juris Doctor/Master of Public Administration in health care), and J.D./M.S.W (Juris Doctor/Master of Social Work, with State University of New York at Stony Brook University, C.W. Post Campus, and Dowling College).

Required

To earn the J.D., candidates must complete 87 total credits, of which 55 to 56 are for required courses. They must maintain a minimum GPA of 2.0 in the required courses. The following first-year courses are required of all students: Torts I and II, Civil Procedure I and II, Contracts I and II, Legal Methods I and II, Criminal Law I, and Property I. Required upper-level courses consist of Property II, Constitutional Law I and II, Professional Responsibility, a perspective requirement, advanced writing requirement, public interest requirement, Business Organizations I, Evidence, Sales, Trusts and Estates, and Second-year Writing Tutorial. All students may satisfy the public interest requirement by taking a clinical course, and are strongly encouraged to do so. The required orientation program for first-year students is a 5- to 6-day orientation program that deals mostly with legal methods and provides an introduction to law; case assignments are given in advance for students to read, brief, and discuss.

Phone: 631-421-2244 ext. 312
Fax: 631-421-9708
E-mail: *admissions@tourolaw.edu*
Web: *http://www.tourolaw.edu*

Contact

Grant W. Keener, Director of Admissions, 631-421-2244, ext. 312 for general inquiries; Lydia Marcantonio, Associate Director of Financial Aid, 631-421-2244, ext. 322 for financial aid information.

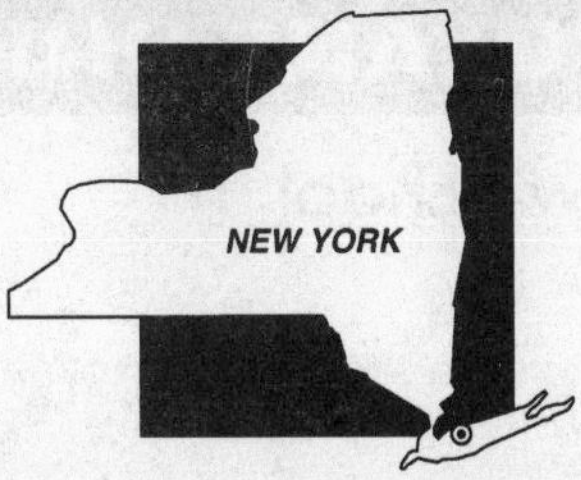

Electives

The Jacob D. Fuchsberg Law Center offers concentrations in corporate law, criminal law, family law, international law, litigation, public interest and civil rights, intellectual property, real estate, health law, and immigration law. In addition, clinical offerings include Family Law (6 credits), Elder Law, Criminal Law, Civil Practice, and Judicial Clerkship (5 credits each); Civil Rights Litigation (3 or 6 credits): International Human Rights/ Immigration Litigation (4 credits), and Not-For-Profit Corporation Law (2 credits). Seminars are open to all students who have satisfied the prerequisites: Law and Medicine: Selected Topics in Law, Medicine, and Ethics; Patent Practice Seminar; and Supreme Court. Internships are arranged through the Career Planning Office for positions during the semester and in the summer. Externships are also available in-house, at the Law Center's Domestic Violence Project and at the Housing Rights Project. Second- and third-year students may apply to be paid research assistants for a faculty member. Also, students may take Independent Research for 1 to 3 credits. Field work may be done through Career Planning externships, through the pro bono requirement, and through clinical offerings. Annually, the Law Center hosts the 3 lecture series: Distinguished Jurist in Residence; Distinguished Public Interest Lawyer in Residence; and Distinguished Israeli Jurist in Residence. Any student in good academic standing may take up to 6 credits at an ABA-approved summer program. Such programs are evaluated on a case-by-case basis. The Office of Student Affairs arranges summer placements abroad in London, Paris, Lisbon, Brussels, Cork, Tel Aviv, Jerusalem, and Moscow. The Writing Clinic provides writing specialists to assist students. The Professional Development Program, designed to help first-year students adapt to the rigors of law school, provides teaching assistants in most required courses, as well as TA mentors and TA tutors for writing skills. Minority students may take advantage of the Legal Education Access Program (LEAP), which offers an orientation program, a lecture series, discussion groups, mentor program, and individual counseling. Special interest groups include the Institute for Jewish Law and the Institute of Local and Suburban Law. The most widely taken electives are New York Practice, Family Law, and Criminal Procedure.

Graduation Requirements

In order to graduate, candidates must have a GPA of 2.0, have completed the upper-division writing requirement, and have successfully completed 87 credits, including all the required courses and additional requirements (Perspective Requirement, Public Interest Requirement, and Advanced Writing Requirement).

Organizations

Students edit the *Touro Law Review, Touro International Law Review, Journal of the Suffolk Academy of Law* (produced in conjunction with the Suffolk County Bar Association), the newspaper *The Restatement*, and the yearbook *Res Ipsa*. Students compete in the ABA-National Moot Court Competition, Benjamin N. Cardozo National Moot Court in Entertainment Law, and Brooklyn Law School's Jerome Prince Invitational Evidence Competition. Other competitions include the New York State Bar Association Legal Ethics Writing Competition, the Nathan Burkan Copyright Law, Association of Trial Lawyers of America, and ABA Negotiation and Counseling competitions. Law student organizations include the Student Bar Association, Delta Theta Phi International Law Fraternity, and Women's Bar Association. There are local chapters of ABA-Law Student Division, National Jewish Students Network, and American Civil Liberties Union. Other organizations include Minority Students Bar Association, Federalist Society, and International Law Society.

Library

The law library contains 400,000 hard-copy volumes, and subscribes to 1400 serial publications. Such on-line databases and networks as CALI, DIALOG, Legal-Trac, LEXIS, NEXIS, OCLC First Search, WESTLAW, and Full Internet access, Dow Jones News Retrieval, and Auto-Cite are available to law students for research. Special library collections include an official depository for selected U.S. government publications, a New York State depository, an extensive Judaica collection, and rare English, American, and foreign legal works. Recently, the library added titles, volumes, and physical space. The ratio of library volumes to faculty is 10,811 to 1 and to students, 638 to 1. The ratio of seats in the library to students is 1 to 2.

Placement

J.D.s awarded:	153
Services available through: a separate law school placement center	
Services: employer panels, resource library, judicial clerkship screening committee, job prospectus, and alumni newsletter on-line daily.	
Special features: Computers, laser printers, on-line services, Directories on Disk, and Pro Bono Students America.	
Full-time job interviews:	13 employers
Summer job interviews:	10 employers
Placement by graduation:	n/av
Placement within 9 months:	89% of class
Average starting salary:	$37,500 to $67,500
Areas of placement:	
Private practice 2-10 attorneys	26%
Private practice 11-25 attorneys	7%
Private practice 26-50 attorneys	3%
Private practice 51-100 attorneys	6%
Private practice 100+ attorneys	3%
Government	19%
Business/industry	18%
Unknown	9%
Public interest	4%
Judicial clerkships	3%
Military	1%
Academic	1%

Faculty

The law school has 37 full-time and 30 part-time faculty members, of whom 19 are women. About 33% of full-time faculty have a graduate law degree in addition to the J.D. The ratio of full-time students to full-time faculty in an average class is 35 to 1; in a clinic, 8 to 1. The law school has a regular program of bringing visiting professors and other distinguished lecturers and visitors to campus. There is a chapter of the Order of the Coif; 2 faculty are members.

Students

About 49% of the student body are women; 26%, minorities; 12%, African American; 5%, Asian American; and 8%, Hispanic. The majority of students come from New York (82%). The average age of entering students is 29; age range is 19 to 57. About 40% of students enter directly from undergraduate school, 16% have a graduate degree, and 64% have worked full-time prior to entering law school. About 5% drop out after the first year for academic or personal reasons; 90% remain to receive a law degree.

TULANE UNIVERSITY

Law School

Weinmann Hall, 6329 Freret Street
New Orleans, LA 70118

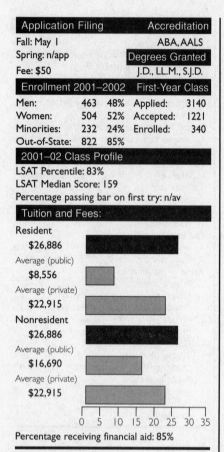

Application Filing	Accreditation
Fall: May 1	ABA, AALS
Spring: n/app	**Degrees Granted**
Fee: $50	J.D., LL.M., S.J.D.

Enrollment 2001–2002			First-Year Class	
Men:	463	48%	Applied:	3140
Women:	504	52%	Accepted:	1221
Minorities:	232	24%	Enrolled:	340
Out-of-State:	822	85%		

2001–02 Class Profile

LSAT Percentile: 83%
LSAT Median Score: 159
Percentage passing bar on first try: n/av

Tuition and Fees:

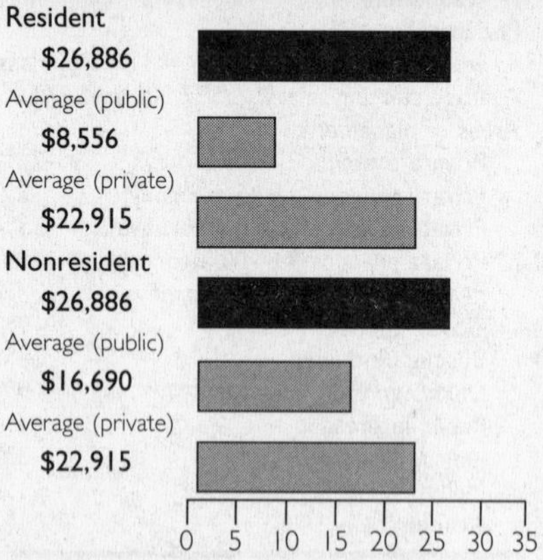

Percentage receiving financial aid: 85%

ADMISSIONS

In the fall 2001 first-year class, 3140 applied, 1221 were accepted, and 340 enrolled. The median LSAT percentile of the most recent first-year class was 83; the median GPA was 3.4 on a scale of 4.0. The lowest LSAT percentile accepted was 25; the highest was 99.

Requirements

Applicants must take the LSAT. Minimum acceptable LSAT percentile is 25 and minimum acceptable GPA is 2.0 on a scale of 4.0. The most important admission factors include academic achievement, LSAT results, and GPA. No specific undergraduate courses are required. Candidates are interviewed.

Procedure

The application deadline for fall entry is May 1. Applicants should submit an application form, LSAT results, transcripts, LSDAS report, a nonrefundable application fee of $50. Notification of the admissions decision is from January 15 through the summer. The latest acceptable LSAT test date for fall entry is February. The law school uses the LSDAS.

Special

The law school recruits minority and disadvantaged students by actively visiting undergraduate schools, using the CRS, and following up. Requirements are not different for out-of-state students. Transfer students must have one year of credit and have a good law school record.

Costs

Tuition and fees for the 2001-2002 academic year are $26,886 for all full-time students. On-campus room and board costs about $7325 annually; books and supplies run $800.

Financial Aid

About 85% of current law students receive some form of aid. Loans are based on need, while scholarships are based on merit and on need and merit combined. The required financial statement is the FAFSA. The aid application deadline for fall entry is February 15. Special funds for minority or disadvantaged students are available. First-year students are notified about their financial aid application in the spring.

About the Law School

Tulane University Law School was established in 1847 and is a private institution. The 110-acre campus is in an urban area in uptown New Orleans. The primary mission of the law school is to provide the best possible professional training so that graduates will become effective and ethical lawyers with skills that qualify them to practice law anywhere in the United States or the world. Students have access to federal, state, county, city, and local agencies, courts, correctional facilities, law firms, and legal aid organizations in the New Orleans area. There are five levels of courts in New Orleans: state trial, appellate, and supreme, and federal trial and appellate. Facilities of special interest to law students are the Reily Recreation Center, the Freeman School of Business, and numerous cultural opportunities throughout the city. Housing for students is available on and off campus. About 95% of the law school facilities are accessible to the physically disabled.

Calendar

The law school operates on a traditional semester basis. Courses for full-time students are offered days only with some elective courses offered during the evening and must be completed within 6 semesters, although limited leaves are permitted. There is no part-time program. New students are admitted in the fall. There is a 6-week summer session in New Orleans and 2- and 4-week study-abroad sessions. Transferable summer courses are offered.

Programs

In addition to the J.D., the law school offers the LL.M., S.J.D., and LL.M. in admiralty, energy and environment, and international comparative law. The following joint degrees may be earned: J.D./M.A. (Juris Doctor/Master of Arts in Latin American studies and in political science), J.D./M.Acc (Juris Doctor/Master of Accounting), J.D./M.B.A. (Juris Doctor/ Master of Business Administration), J.D./M.H.A. (Juris Doctor/ Master of Health Administration), J.D./M.P.H. (Juris Doctor/ Master of Public Health in environmental health), and J.D./M/S.W. (Juris Doctor/Master of Social Work).

Phone: 504-865-5930
Fax: 504-865-6710
E-mail: *admissions@law.tulane.edu*
Web: *www.law.tulane.edu*

Contact

Susan Krinsky, Associate Dean for Admissions, 504-865-5930 for general inquiries; Georgia Whiddon, 504-865-5931 for financial aid information.

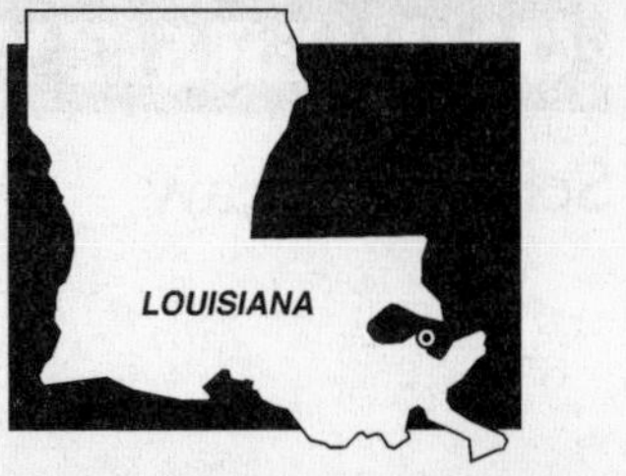

Required

To earn the J.D., candidates must complete 88 total credits, of which 31 are for required courses. They must maintain a minimum GPA of 2.0 in the required courses. The following first-year courses are required of all students: Criminal Law, Constitutional Law, Civil Procedure, Property (Civil or Common), Contracts I, Legal Profession (can be taken in the first year or later), Torts, Contracts II or Obligations I, and Legal Research and Writing. Required upper-level courses consist of 20 hours of community service. The required orientation program for first-year students is 1½ days of logistical information plus sessions on case briefing.

Electives

Students must take 15 to 16 credits in their area of concentration. The Law School offers concentrations in environmental law, maritime law, sports law, European legal studies, and civil law. In addition, 7 different clinics, including representation of actual clients, are available for third-year students for 8 credits. Second- and third-year students may earn 2 to 3 credits for seminars that are offered in various advanced legal areas and typically require an extensive research paper. Judicial and other externships, 1-year (2-semester) externship programs worth 4 credits, are offered to third-year students. Upper-level students may undertake directed research with individual faculty members for a maximum of 3 credits. Field work in some courses, particularly advanced environmental law is offered. Many special lecture series are also offered each year. Students may earn 3 to 6 credits for the summer study-abroad program, offered in 8 countries and held for 2 to 4 weeks. In addition, some semester-long exchange programs are available with universities abroad. Selected first-year students may take the tutorial course, Legal Analysis, for 1 credit. Support and placement programs for minority students are sponsored by the school, including an assistant dean. Special interest group programs are provided by 20 student organizations. The most widely taken electives are Business Enterprises, Evidence, and Trusts and Estates.

Graduation Requirements

In order to graduate, candidates must have a GPA of 2.0, have completed the upper-division writing requirement (starting with the '05 class), and have performed 20 hours of mandatory pro bono work.

Organizations

Students edit the *Tulane Law Review, Tulane Maritime Law Journal, Tulane Environmental Law Journal, Journal of Law and Sexuality, Tulane Journal of International and Comparative Law, Civil Law Forum, Sports Law Journal, Journal of American Arbitration,* and the student newspaper *Dicta*. There are separate intraschool trial and appellate competitions for second- and third-year students, plus a variety of interschool competitions, including the Jessup International, Negotiations, and Trial competitions. Law student organizations include the Environmental Law Society, Public Interest Law Foundation, and International Law Society. There is a local chapter of the American Civil Liberties Union.

Library

The law library contains 500,000 hard-copy volumes, and subscribes to 3000 serial publications. Such on-line databases and networks as DIALOG, LEXIS, and WESTLAW are available to law students for research. Special library collections include canon law, European law, civil law, and maritime law. Recently, the library opened a law school building and law library with excellent computer facilities for student use. The ratio of library volumes to faculty is 10,000 to 1 and to students, 517 to 1. The ratio of seats in the library to students is 1 to 2.

Placement

J.D.s awarded: 321

Services available through: a separate law school placement center

Services: videotaped mock interviews, law firm tours and orientations, job fairs and placement consortia, and introduction to new cities.

Special features: a minority clerkship program and individual sessions with career services staff.

Full-time job interviews:	n/av
Summer job interviews:	n/av
Placement by graduation:	60% of class
Placement within 9 months:	92% of class
Average starting salary:	$33,189 to $125,000
Areas of placement:	
Private practice 2-100 attorneys	48%
Judicial clerkships	16%
Government	12%
Business/industry	10%
Unknown	10%
Public interest	2%
Academic	2%

Faculty

The law school has 50 full-time and 49 part-time faculty members, of whom 21 are women. According to AAUP standards for Category I institutions, faculty salaries are above average. About 26% of full-time faculty have a graduate law degree in addition to the J.D.; about 18% of part-time faculty have one. The ratio of full-time students to full-time faculty in an average class is 34 to 1; in a clinic, 8 to 1. The law school has a regular program of bringing visiting professors and other distinguished lecturers and visitors to campus. There is a chapter of the Order of the Coif; 100 faculty and 30 graduates are members.

Students

About 52% of the student body are women; 24%, minorities; 11%, African American; 5%, Asian American; and 6%, Hispanic. Most students come from the South (42%). The average age of entering students is 24; age range is 21 to 55. About 33% of students enter directly from undergraduate school, 5% have a graduate degree, and 65% have worked full-time prior to entering law school. About 5% drop out after the first year for academic or personal reasons; 92% remain to receive a law degree.

UNIVERSITY OF AKRON

School of Law

Corner of Wolf Ledges and
University Avenue
Akron, OH 44325-2901

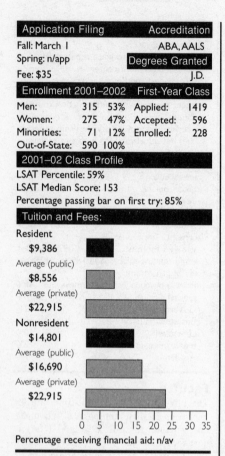

Application Filing		Accreditation
Fall: March 1		ABA, AALS
Spring: n/app		**Degrees Granted**
Fee: $35		J.D.

Enrollment 2001–2002			First-Year Class	
Men:	315	53%	Applied:	1419
Women:	275	47%	Accepted:	596
Minorities:	71	12%	Enrolled:	228
Out-of-State:	590	100%		

2001–02 Class Profile

LSAT Percentile: 59%
LSAT Median Score: 153
Percentage passing bar on first try: 85%

Tuition and Fees:

Resident
$9,386
Average (public)
$8,556
Average (private)
$22,915
Nonresident
$14,801
Average (public)
$16,690
Average (private)
$22,915

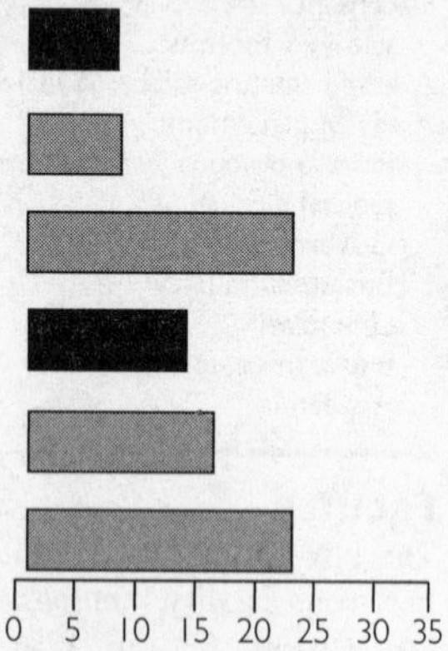

Percentage receiving financial aid: n/av

ADMISSIONS

In the fall 2001 first-year class, 1419 applied, 596 were accepted, and 228 enrolled. The median LSAT percentile of the most recent first-year class was 59; the median GPA was 3.19 on a scale of 4.0.

Requirements

Applicants must have a bachelor's degree and take the LSAT. Minimum acceptable GPA is 2.0 on a scale of 4.0. The most important admission factors include general background, GPA, and LSAT results. No specific undergraduate courses are required. Candidates are not interviewed.

Procedure

The application deadline for fall entry is March 1. Applicants should submit an application form, LSAT results, transcripts, TOEFL and TSE for applicants whose first language is not English, a nonrefundable application fee of $35. Letters of recommendation are not required but 2 to 3 are strongly recommended, and The application fee is waived for on-line applications. Notification of the admissions decision is 4 to 6 weeks after the application is complete. The latest acceptable LSAT test date for fall entry is June. The law school uses the LSDAS.

Special

The law school recruits minority and disadvantaged students by means of visiting colleges with a large percentage of minority students, sending mailings, holding recruitment days, participating in minority law fairs, publishing a minority brochure, granting scholarships, and advertising in various publications. In addition, minority law students call minority admittees to welcome them. Requirements are not different for out-of-state students. Transfer students must have one year of credit, have attended an ABA-approved law school, and show strong academic performance. Preadmissions courses consist of optional legal skills workshops, traditionally offered in the summer.

Costs

Tuition and fees for the 2001-2002 academic year are $9386 for full-time in-state students and $14,801 for out-of-state students. Tuition for part-time students is $7541 in-state and $11,873 out-of-state. Books and supplies run about $600 annually.

Financial Aid

The average annual amount of aid from all sources combined, including scholarships, loans, and work contracts, is $14,950; maximum, $27,232. Awards are based on need and merit. The required financial statements are the FAFSA and the institutional aid application. The aid application deadline for fall entry is May 1. First-year students are notified about their financial aid application some time prior to April 1 for scholarships; as early as possible for loans.

About the Law School

University of Akron School of Law was established in 1921 and is a public institution. The 170-acre campus is in an urban area 40 miles south of Cleveland. The primary mission of the law school is to prepare students to become outstanding members of the bench and bar. Students have access to federal, state, county, city, and local agencies, courts, correctional facilities, law firms, and legal aid organizations in the Akron area. There is the Akron Municipal Court, Summit County Court, Ninth District Court of Appeals, and Federal Court. Facilities of special interest to law students include the Legal Clinic law library. Housing for students is available on campus in graduate housing; many off-campus affordable housing options are available within walking distance or a short drive. All law school facilities are accessible to the physically disabled.

Calendar

The law school operates on a traditional semester basis. Courses for full-time students are offered both day and evening and must be completed within 5 years. For part-time students, courses are offered evenings only and must be completed within 6 years. New full- and part-time students are admitted in the fall. There are 5- and 10-week summer sessions. Transferable summer courses are offered.

Programs

Students may take relevant courses in other programs and apply credit toward the J.D.; a maximum of 6 graduate level credits may be applied. The following joint degrees may be earned: J.D./M.B.A. (Juris Doctor/Master of Business Administration), J.D./M.H.R. (Juris Doctor/Master of Human Resources), J.D./M.P.A. (Juris Doctor/Master of Public Administration), and J.D./M.Tax. (Juris Doctor/Master of Taxation).

Required

To earn the J.D., candidates must complete 88 total credits, of which 44 are for required courses. They must maintain a minimum GPA of 2.0 in the required courses. The following first-year courses are required of all students: Civil Procedure I and II; Contracts I and II; Criminal Law; Property I and II; Torts I and II; Legal Research; Introduction: Law and Legal Systems; and Legal Analysis, Research, and Writing I and II. Required upper-level courses consist of Constitutional Law I and II, Evidence, a general writing requirement, Legal Drafting, Advanced Legal Research, and Professional Responsibility. An elective course, which is offered for 2 or 3 credits and may be repeated up to 6 credits, includes Trial Litigation Clinic, Appellate Review, Inmate Assistance Program, and external placements in government and non-

Phone: 330-972-7331
800-4-AKRON-U
Fax: 330-258-2343
E-mail: *lawadmissions@uakron.edu*
Web: *www.uakron.edu/law*

Contact

Lauri S. File, Director of Admissions and Financial Assistance, 330-972-7331, 800-4-AKRON-U for general inquiries; University Financial Aid Office, 330-972-7032 for financial aid information.

profit organizations. The required orientation program for first-year students introduces students to professional responsibility, the U.S. Legal System, and common law systems. Introduction to Law and Legal Systems is a 1-week course held during the first week of classes. Students are provided with a framework for understanding the basic premises of our system of law, both substantive and procedural, and the ways in which law is made to assist in studying law. The course includes a mock law class, a discussion of how to brief and outline, and study tips for final exams.

Electives

The School of Law offers concentrations in corporate law, criminal law, international law, labor law, litigation, tax law, and intellectual property and technology, and public interest. In addition, the Trial Litigation Clinic allows third-year students to be certified legal interns; in the Clinical Seminar, students with strong academic records may clerk for judges. There is also a clinic in Appellate Review. Clinic students may be placed in-house or externally for credit after their first year. Students with an intern certificate may represent clients in civil and misdemeanor cases in court. Seminars include Feminist and Race Theory, International Investment, and Business Planning. Internships and research programs are offered through the School of Law Career Planning Office. Field work is offered through the School of Law Legal Clinic or the Career Planning and Placement Office. Individual studies and research may be taken under the guidance of a faculty member. Upper-division students may apply to become a research assistant for a law faculty member. Special lecture series are held during the fall and spring semesters with an emphasis on intellectual property and constitutional law. Study abroad is only available through another ABA-accredited law school's study-abroad program. With permission of the associate dean, students may assume visiting status at another ABA-accredited law school and transfer credits back to Akron. Tutoring is available through the Academic Success Program. The Black Law Student Association (BLSA) sponsors outlining and exam-taking seminars, adopt-a-school, scholarships, an annual dinner/dance, regional job fairs, Frederick Douglass Moot Court Competition, and travel to regional and national BLSA events. The most widely taken electives are Administration of Criminal Justice, Wills, Trusts and Estates, and Corporations.

Graduation Requirements

In order to graduate, candidates must have a GPA of 2.0, have completed the upper-division writing requirement, and fulfill residency weeks requirements as established by the ABA.

Organizations

Students edit the *Akron Law Review* and the *Akron Tax Journal*. The moot court team attends the ABA/LSD-National Appellate Advocacy competition, National Moot Court competition (N.Y. Bar Association), and Jessup International Law Competition. A trial team attends competitions sponsored by the American College of Trial Lawyers, the American Trial Lawyers Association, National Institute for Trial Advocacy, the Academy of Trial Lawyers of Allegheny County, PA, and other associations. There is also a negotiation team. Law student organizations include the International Law Society, Student Bar Association, and Law Association for Women's Rights. Local chapters of national organizations incude the Intellectual Property and Technology Law Association, National Association of Criminal Defense Lawyers, and Sports and Entertainment Law Society. Campus clubs include Phi Alpha Delta, Delta Theta Phi, and Phi Delta Phi.

Library

The law library contains 267,581 hardcopy volumes and 385,300 microform volume equivalents, and subscribes to 3149 serial publications. Such on-line databases and networks as CALI, CIS Universe, Infotrac, Legal-Trac, LEXIS, Mathew Bender, NEXIS, WESTLAW, 100 databases on Ohiolink, CCH web-based databases on business, finance, human resources management, and tax are available to law students for research. Special library collections include a government documents depository (intellectual property). Recently, the library installed a wireless network in the law library to allow students to use wireless laptops to access the Internet. The ratio of library volumes to faculty is 8919 to 1 and to students, 454 to 1. The ratio of seats in the library to students is 1 to 2.

Placement

J.D.s awarded: 144

Services available through: a separate law school placement center, the university placement center, and the College of Business Placement Center

Services: Alumni and Student Affairs Committee, Judicial Clerkship Programs, Reference Letter Program, Mentor Program, preparatory career planning workshops and seminars, and mock interview program.

Special features: individualized one-to-one counseling and assisting students with all phases of the job search; computerized job postings, participation in off-campus hiring programs for intellectual property and public interest law, participation in several off-campus hiring programs for minority students; and coordination with the Ohio Law Placement Consortium (OLPC).

Full-time job interviews:	11 employers
Summer job interviews:	18 employers
Placement by graduation:	47% of class
Placement within 9 months:	90% of class
Average starting salary:	$18,000 to $150,000
Areas of placement:	
Private practice 2-10 attorneys	28%
Private practice 11-25 attorneys	8%
Private practice 26-50 attorneys	2%
Private practice 51-100 attorneys	5%
Private practice, Self employed/ Solo practice	4%
Government	17%
Business/industry	17%
Judicial clerkships	9%
Academic	3%

Faculty

The law school has 30 full-time and 42 part-time faculty members, of whom 30 are women. According to AAUP standards for Category I institutions, faculty salaries are below average. The ratio of full-time students to full-time faculty in an average class is 18 to 1.

Students

About 47% of the student body are women; 12%, minorities; 7%, African American; 3%, Asian American; and 2%, Hispanic. The average age of entering students is 26; age range is 21 to 60. About 20 to 30% drop out after the first year for academic or personal reasons; 70 to 80% remain to receive a law degree.

UNIVERSITY OF ALABAMA

School of Law

Box 870382
Tuscaloosa, AL 35487-0382

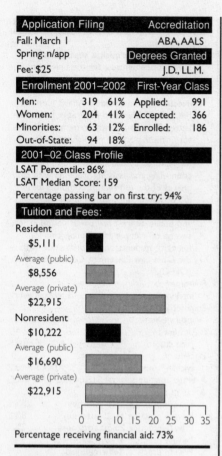

Application Filing		Accreditation
Fall: March 1		ABA, AALS
Spring: n/app		**Degrees Granted**
Fee: $25		J.D., LL.M.

Enrollment 2001–2002			First-Year Class	
Men:	319	61%	Applied:	991
Women:	204	41%	Accepted:	366
Minorities:	63	12%	Enrolled:	186
Out-of-State:	94	18%		

2001–02 Class Profile

LSAT Percentile: 86%
LSAT Median Score: 159
Percentage passing bar on first try: 94%

Tuition and Fees:

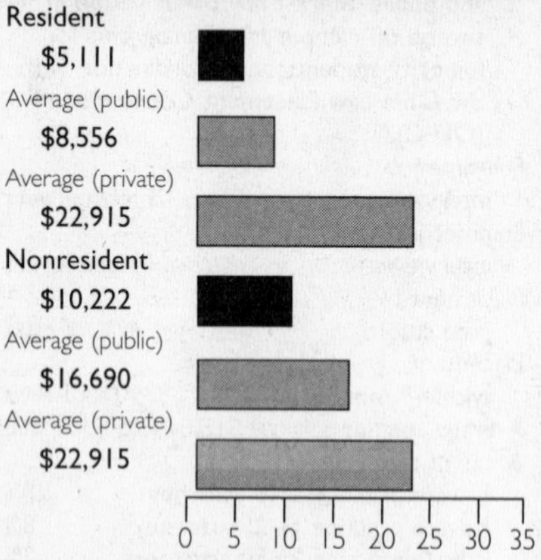

Percentage receiving financial aid: 73%

ADMISSIONS

In the fall 2001 first-year class, 991 applied, 366 were accepted, and 186 enrolled. Two transfers enrolled. The median LSAT percentile of the most recent first-year class was 86; the median GPA was 3.3 on a scale of 4.0.

Requirements

Applicants must have a bachelor's degree and take the LSAT. The most important admission factors include LSAT results, GPA, and academic achievement. No specific undergraduate courses are required. Candidates are not interviewed.

Procedure

The application deadline for fall entry is March 1. Applicants should submit an application form, LSAT results, transcripts, the TOEFL for M.C.L. candidates, a nonrefundable application fee of $25, 2 personal statements, correspondence cards, and a personal information card. Notification of the admissions decision is on a rolling basis, beginning in November. The latest acceptable LSAT test date for fall entry is February. The law school uses the LSDAS.

Special

The law school recruits minority and disadvantaged students by means of recruiters visiting undergraduate institutions and participating annually in the Law Forums. Requirements are different for out-of-state students. Because it is a state school, more residents than nonresidents are admitted to The University of Alabama School of Law. Transfer students must have one year of credit, have attended an ABA-approved law school, and have a collegiate academic record and an LSAT score that would have qualified the student for entry-level admission to the school. They must be in good standing at the current law school, as evidenced by a letter from the dean of that school, must not be on any kind of probationary status, and must rank academically high at that school.

Costs

Tuition and fees for the 2001-2002 academic year are $5111 for full-time in-state students and $10,222 for out-of-state students. On-campus room and board costs about $5275 annually; books and supplies run $930.

Financial Aid

About 73% of current law students receive some form of aid. The average annual amount of aid from all sources combined, including scholarships, loans, and work contracts, is $10,000; maximum, $18,500. Awards are based on need and merit. The School of Law provides significant scholarship support. Outstanding nonresident students may receive a nonresident fee waiver. The required financial statement is the FAFSA. The aid application deadline for fall entry is March 1. First-year students are notified about their financial aid application at the time of acceptance.

About the Law School

University of Alabama School of Law was established in 1872 and is a public institution. The campus is in a small town 60 miles south of Birmingham. The primary mission of the law school is to prepare future lawyers for their critical role in society, as well as to become a dynamic part of the community. Students have access to federal, state, county, city, and local agencies, courts, correctional facilities, law firms, and legal aid organizations in the Tuscaloosa area. Facilities of special interest to law students include the moot court and trial advocacy rooms, student lounge, and student areas. Housing for students is available in residence halls and university-owned and operated apartments and efficiency units. The majority of the law students live off campus. All law school facilities are accessible to the physically disabled.

Calendar

The law school operates on a traditional semester basis. Courses for full-time students are offered days only and must be completed within 3 years. There is no part-time program. New students are admitted in the fall. There is a 7-week summer session. Transferable summer courses are not offered.

Programs

In addition to the J.D., the law school offers the LL.M. and LL.M. in taxation. Students may take relevant courses in other programs and apply credit toward the J.D.; a maximum of 6 credits may be applied. The following joint degree may be earned: J.D./M.B.A. (Juris Doctor/ Master of Business Administration).

Required

To earn the J.D., candidates must complete 90 total credits, of which 36 are for required courses. They must maintain a minimum GPA of 2.0 in the required courses. The following first-year courses are required of all students: Contracts, Property, Torts, Criminal Law, Civil Procedure, Constitutional Law, Legal Writing, Moot Court, Legal Research, and Federal Income Tax. Required upper-level courses consist of Evidence, The Legal Profession, and seminar. The required orientation program for first-year students is a 4-day program geared toward making the transition into law school as smooth as possible.

Phone: 205-348-5440
Fax: 205-348-3917
E-mail: *admissions@law.ua.edu*
Web: *www.law.ua.edu*

Contact

Betty McGinley, Admissions Coordinator, 205-348-5440 for general inquiries; Noah Funderburg, Assistant Dean, 205-348-4508 for financial aid information.

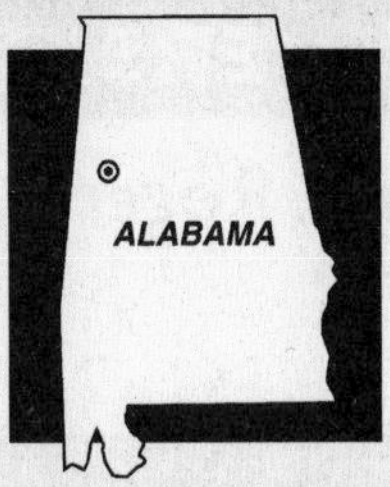

Electives

The School of Law offers concentrations in corporate law, criminal law, environmental law, international law, litigation, and tax law. In addition, clinics are offered for 3 credit hours. Students may take 2-credit hour internships under the Alabama Student Practice Rule, in which a student clerks for a judge. Seminars are usually small groups of third-year students. Instruction is on a more informal and advanced basis than in basic courses. A written paper is required. First-year students are required to carry out a closely supervised program in legal research and writing. They must also participate in a moot court program in appellate advocacy involving substantial library research. A course in advanced legal research is offered as a 2-hour elective for upper-level students. Several minority programs support a diversified student body. Special lecture series include the Hugo L. Black Lecture, established in 1996 to honor the U.S. Supreme Court Justice Hugo L. Black, who was a 1906 graduate of the law school, and the Daniel J. Meador Lecture, established in 1994 to honor Professor Meador, a 1951 graduate. Study abroad is available through a 4½-week program at the University of Friborerg. Students take 2 2-hour classes for 4 hours of credit. Externships are available in a variety of placements. Special interest group programs include the Future Trial Lawyers Association, Dorbin Association (women's support group), Black Law Students Association, and Alabama Public Interest Law Association. The most widely taken electives are Family Law, Criminal Procedure, and Trial Advocacy.

Graduation Requirements

In order to graduate, candidates must have a GPA of 2.0 and have completed the upper-division writing requirement.

Organizations

Students edit the *Alabama Law Review, Law and Psychology Review, Journal of the Legal Profession*, and *American Journal of Tax Policy*. The student newspaper is *Alabama Column*. The school participates annually in the John A. Campbell Moot Court, National Moot Court, Phillip C. Jessup International Law Moot Court, and Frederick Douglass Moot Court competitions. The law school also participates in 3 to 4 trial advocacy competitions each year and in 3 to 5 moot court competitions. Student organizations include the Bench and Bar Society, Environmental Law Society, and Law Spouses Club. There is a local chapter of the American Civil Liberties Union. Legal fraternities include Phi Alpha Delta, Phi Delta Phi, and Delta Theta Phi.

Library

The law library contains 395,318 hard-copy volumes and 122,762 microform volume equivalents, and subscribes to 3284 serial publications. Such on-line databases and networks as CALI, DIALOG, Infotrac, Legal-Trac, LEXIS, NEXIS, OCLC First Search, and WESTLAW are available to law students for research. Special library collections include all decisions of appellate-level state and federal courts, all state and federal codes, Alabama and federal rules and regulations, and the decisions of selected agencies and of principal courts of the Commonwealth nations. There are also extensive treatise holdings. Recently, the library reassigned or upgraded many library staff to enhance technical services, and added a new Special Collections area. The ratio of library volumes to faculty is 10,403 to 1 and to students, 756 to 1. The ratio of seats in the library to students is 1 to 1.

Faculty

The law school has 38 full-time and 42 part-time faculty members, of whom 11 are women. According to AAUP standards for Category I institutions, faculty salaries are below average. About 30% of full-time faculty have a graduate law degree in addition to the J.D.; about 14% of part-time faculty have one. The ratio of full-time students to full-time faculty in an average class is 18 to 1; in a clinic, 5 to 1. The law school has a regular program of bringing visiting professors and other distinguished lecturers and visitors to campus. There is a chapter of the Order of the Coif; 23 faculty are members.

Placement

Placement	
J.D.s awarded:	181
Services available through: a separate law school placement center	
Special features: fall and spring on-campus interviewing and resume forwarding programs and participation in job fairs, seminars, various publications, telephone and message/mail delivery service, LEXIS and WESTLAW computers, and programs in nontraditional law.	
Full-time job interviews:	20 employers
Summer job interviews:	61 employers
Placement by graduation:	70% of class
Placement within 9 months:	99% of class
Average starting salary:	$26,000 to $125,000
Areas of placement:	
Private practice 2-10 attorneys	25%
Private practice 11-25 attorneys	11%
Private practice 26-50 attorneys	4%
Private practice 51-100 attorneys	4%
Private practice 100+ attorneys	5%
Private practice unknown size	5%
Private practice, solo	2%
Judicial clerkships	17%
Government	10%
Business/industry	10%
Public interest	4%
Academic	3%

Students

About 41% of the student body are women; 12%, minorities; 9%, African American; 1%, Asian American; 1%, Hispanic; and 1%, Native American. The majority of students come from Alabama (82%). The average age of entering students is 25. About 49% of students enter directly from undergraduate school, 9% have a graduate degree, and 49% have worked full-time prior to entering law school. About 2% drop out after the first year for academic or personal reasons; 98% remain to receive a law degree.

UNIVERSITY OF ARIZONA

James E. Rogers College of Law

Mountain and Speedway
P.O. Box 210176
Tucson, AZ 85721-0176

Application Filing	Accreditation
Fall: March 1	ABA, AALS
Spring: n/app	**Degrees Granted**
Fee: $50	J.D., LL.M.

Enrollment 2001–2002			First-Year Class	
Men:	246	49%	Applied:	1870
Women:	257	51%	Accepted:	430
Minorities:	121	24%	Enrolled:	162
Out-of-State:	151	30%		

2001–02 Class Profile

LSAT Percentile: 87%
LSAT Median Score: 161
Percentage passing bar on first try: 94%

Tuition and Fees:

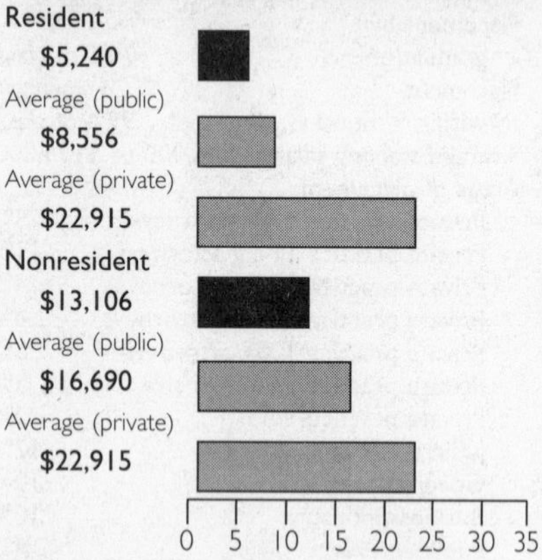

Percentage receiving financial aid: 85%

ADMISSIONS

In the fall 2001 first-year class, 1870 applied, 430 were accepted, and 162 enrolled. Eight transfers enrolled. The median LSAT percentile of the most recent first-year class was 87; the median GPA was 3.48 on a scale of 4.0. The lowest LSAT percentile accepted was 36; the highest was 99.

Requirements

Applicants must have a bachelor's degree and take the LSAT. The most important admission factors include academic achievement and LSAT results. No specific undergraduate courses are required. Candidates are not interviewed.

Procedure

The application deadline for fall entry is March 1. Applicants should submit an application form, LSAT results, transcripts, TOEFL for foreign applicants, a nonrefundable application fee of $50, 2 letters of recommendation, and use of the LSDAS, a personal statement, and a resume. Notification of the admissions decision is January through May. The latest acceptable LSAT test date for fall entry is February. The law school uses the LSDAS.

Special

The law school recruits minority and disadvantaged students through a strong recruitment and retention program. Ethnicity is one of many qualitative factors considered by the Admissions Committee. Requirements are different for out-of-state students in that there are a limited number of openings for nonresident students. Generally, 70% of enrollees are residents and 30% are nonresidents; however, approximately 50% of admission offers go to nonresidents. Transfer students must have one year of credit, have attended an ABA-approved law school, and should be ranked in the top tenth to top quarter of their class. Space in the class and nature of law school attended are always factors, as are undergraduate record, LSAT score, admissibility as a first-year applicant, personal statement, and letters of recommendation from law faculty with whom the applicant has studied.

Costs

Tuition and fees for the 2001-2002 academic year are $5240 for full-time in-state students and $13,106 for out-of-state students. On-campus room and board costs about $7554 annually; books and supplies run $720.

Financial Aid

About 85% of current law students receive some form of aid. The average annual amount of aid from all sources combined, including scholarships, loans, and work contracts, is $10,000; maximum, $18,500. Awards are based on need and merit. The required financial statement is the FAFSA. The aid application deadline for fall entry is March 1. Special funds for minority or disadvantaged students include special scholarships for Native Americans. First-year students are notified about their financial aid application between acceptance and enrollment; generally between February and June.

About the Law School

University of Arizona James E. Rogers College of Law was established in 1925 and is a public institution. The 325-acre campus is in an urban area near downtown Tucson. The primary mission of the law school is to integrate the study of modern issues with the traditional legal course of study in a small law school of approximately 480 students, with a rigorous yet collegial atmosphere. Students have access to federal, state, county, city, and local agencies, courts, correctional facilities, law firms, and legal aid organizations in the Tucson area. In addition, Arizona is home to many Native American tribes, all with their own tribal governments and tribal court systems. Facilities of special interest to law students include videotape-equipped classrooms, a moot court room, seminar rooms, a student lounge, a library, a computer laboratory for students, and a fully equipped computerized courtroom. Housing for students includes plenty of affordable off-campus rental housing. About 99% of the law school facilities are accessible to the physically disabled.

Calendar

The law school operates on a traditional semester basis. Most courses for full-time students are offered days only; there are some late afternoon and early evening elective courses. Course work must be completed within 3 years. There is no part-time program. New students are admitted in the fall. There is a 5-week summer session. Transferable summer courses are offered.

Programs

In addition to the J.D., the law school offers the LL.M., LL.M. in international trade law, and LL.M. in indigenous peoples' law and policy. Students may take relevant courses in other programs and apply credit toward the J.D.; a maximum of 6 credits may be applied. The following joint degrees may be earned: J.D./M.A. (Juris Doctor/Master of Arts in economics, American Indian studies, and Latin American studies), J.D./M.B.A. (Juris Doctor/Master of Business Administration), J.D./M.P.A. (Juris Doctor/Master of Public Administration), and J.D./Ph.D. (Juris Doctor/Doctor of Philosophy in psychology, philosophy, and economics).

Required

To earn the J.D., candidates must complete 85 total credits, of which 39 are for required courses. They must maintain a minimum GPA of 2.0 in the required courses. The following first-year courses are required of all students: Contracts; Torts; Civil Procedure; Criminal Procedure; Property; Constitutional Law; and Legal Analysis, Writing and Research.

Phone: 520-621-3477
Fax: 520-621-9140
E-mail: *admissions@law.arizona.edu*
Web: *www.law.arizona.edu*

Contact

Dan Nunez, Admissions Office, 520-621-3477 for general inquiries; Henrietta Stover, Assistant Dean, Financial Services, 520-626-8101 for financial aid information.

Required upper-level courses consist of Evidence, Professional Responsibility, and an advanced writing seminar. The required orientation program for first-year students is 2 days and encompasses academic and cultural aspects of the law school experience; 3 follow-up sessions during the first 2 weeks of school are held on ethics, stress, and various other matters.

Electives

The James E. Rogers College of Law offers concentrations in corporate law, criminal law, environmental law, family law, international law, litigation, securities law, tax law, torts and insurance, Indian law, and human rights. In addition, clinics include Domestic Violence, Child Advocacy, Indian law, Immigration Law, Prosecution, and Defense (3 to 5 units per credit). Students work for legal aid, the county and city prosecutor's office, public defender's office, and the state attorney general's office. Additionally, the College has an active legal clinic program with several Native American tribes located in Arizona. The College has a diverse set of offerings for its advanced research and writing seminars, ranging from the Warren Court to a death penalty seminar. Also offered are a rich variety of small seminars and colloquia. Internships may be taken with the state legislature and with the offices of U.S. senators, and on the Navajo, Tohono O'odham, and White Mountain Apache reservations. Students may take up to 6 units of independent study with faculty supervision. Students may hear special lectures through the Isaac Marks Memorial Lectures, Rosenstiel Scholar-in-Residence Program, McCormick Society lectures, and the Jeanne Kiewit Taylor Visiting Faculty Program. Chief Justice William Rehnquist teaches the History of the U.S. Supreme Court each January. Study abroad is possible in London and Puerto Rico at the University of Puerto Rico Law School. The college accepts credit for participation in ABA-approved international programs sponsored by other schools. All first-year students may participate in tutorial programs. Special scholarship efforts, mentoring, tutorial assistance, and a weeklong bridge program are offered to all students. The most widely taken electives are Federal Income Tax, Corporations, and Employment Law.

Graduation Requirements

In order to graduate, candidates must have a GPA of 2.0 and have completed the upper-division writing requirement. All students must write a paper of "publishable quality" to fulfill the upper-division writing requirement.

Organizations

The primary law review is the *Arizona Law Review*. Students also edit *The Arizona Journal for International Law*, and *The Journal of Psychology, Public Policy and Law. The Arizona Advocate* is the student newspaper. Other publications include *Environmental Law Newsletter* and *The Bulletin*. Students may participate in a wide range of regional, national, and international moot court competitions. Other competitions include Richard Grand Damages, Grand Writing, and Jenkes competitions. Law student organizations include the Student Bar Association, Minority Law Students Association, Law Women's Association, Phi Alpha Delta, and Phi Delta Phi. There are local chapters of the American Civil Liberties Union and ABA-Law Student Division. Other law student organizations include Black Law Students Association, LaRaza/Hispanic National Bar Association, and Native American Law Student Association.

Library

The law library contains 380,000 hard-copy volumes and 426,000 microform volume equivalents, and subscribes to 3650 serial publications. Such on-line databases and networks as CALI, DIALOG, LEXIS, NEXIS, and WESTLAW are available to law students for research. Special library collections include an extensive collection of materials on Latin American law. Recently, the library refurbished and recarpeted the computer laboratory and library. Ther are also extensive electronic databases. The ratio of library volumes to faculty is 12,667 to 1 and to students, 755 to 1. The ratio of seats in the library to students is 1 to 1.

Faculty

The law school has 30 full-time and 55 part-time faculty members, of whom 36 are women. According to AAUP standards for Category I institutions, faculty salaries are above average. About 47% of full-time faculty have a graduate law degree in addition to the J.D.; about 2% of part-time faculty have one. The ratio of full-time students to full-time faculty in an average class is 15 to 1; in a clinic, 7 to 1. The law school has a regular program of bringing visiting professors and other distinguished lecturers and visitors to campus. There is a chapter of the Order of the Coif; 15 faculty and 350 graduates are members.

Placement

J.D.s awarded: 152

Services available through: a separate law school placement center

Services: extensive career counseling and direction, creative programming, and participation of faculty and alumni

Special features: the college has a very active Career Services Office with 2 full-time attorneys on staff. The office takes a proactive approach to career services, educating, and assisting students.

Full-time job interviews:	70 employers
Summer job interviews:	110 employers
Placement by graduation:	65% of class
Placement within 9 months:	94% of class
Average starting salary:	$39,818 to $79,652

Areas of placement:

Private practice 2-10 attorneys	5%
Private practice 11-25 attorneys	8%
Private practice 26-50 attorneys	20%
Private practice 51-100 attorneys	18%
Judicial clerkships	19%
Government	15%
Business/industry	4%
Academic	4%
Unknown	3%
Public interest	2%
Military	2%

Students

About 51% of the student body are women; 24%, minorities; 3%, African American; 6%, Asian American; 11%, Hispanic; 4%, Native American; and 5%, foreign nationals (including indigenous peoples, Latin Americans and Asians). The majority of students come from Arizona (70%). The average age of entering students is 26; age range is 20 to 59. About 40% of students enter directly from undergraduate school, 22% have a graduate degree, and 60% have worked full-time prior to entering law school. About 1% drop out after the first year for academic or personal reasons; 98% remain to receive a law degree.

UNIVERSITY OF ARKANSAS

School of Law

Robert A. Leflar Law Center,
Waterman Hall
Fayetteville, AR 72701

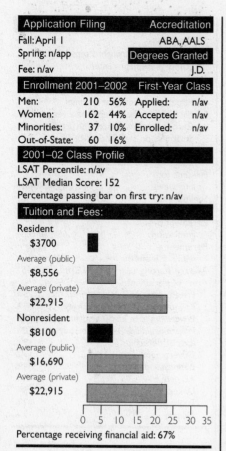

Application Filing		Accreditation
Fall: April 1		ABA, AALS
Spring: n/app		**Degrees Granted**
Fee: n/av		J.D.

Enrollment 2001–2002			First-Year Class	
Men:	210	56%	Applied:	n/av
Women:	162	44%	Accepted:	n/av
Minorities:	37	10%	Enrolled:	n/av
Out-of-State:	60	16%		

2001–02 Class Profile

LSAT Percentile: n/av
LSAT Median Score: 152
Percentage passing bar on first try: n/av

Tuition and Fees:

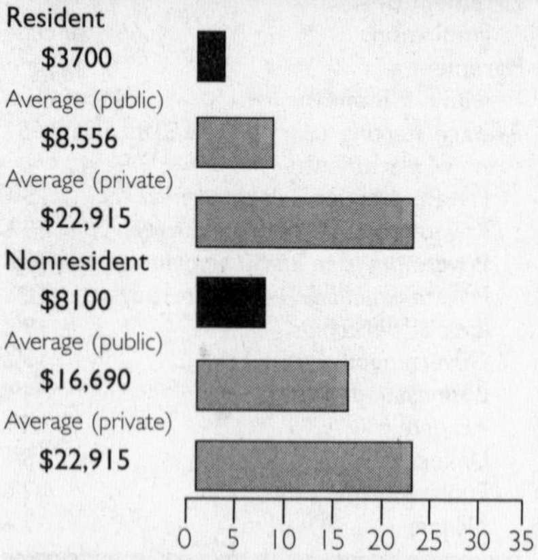

Percentage receiving financial aid: 67%

ADMISSIONS

Information in the above capsule is from an earlier year. In a recent first-year class, four transfers enrolled. The median GPA of a recent first-year class was 3.3.

Requirements

Applicants must have a bachelor's degree and take the LSAT. The most important admission factors include GPA and LSAT results. No specific undergraduate courses are required. Candidates are not interviewed.

Procedure

Check with the school for current application deadlines and fee. Applicants should submit an application form, LSAT results, and transcripts. Accepted students must submit a nonrefundable preregistration fee, which is applied to the regular registration fee for the semester. Notification of the admissions decision is on a rolling basis. The law school uses the LSDAS.

Special

Requirements are different for out-of-state students in that index admission is granted to those nonresident applicants who have prediction indexes of 200 or above on the 120-180 scale. If space permits, index admission is offered to other applicants. A small number of nonresidents who do not qualify for index admission may be admitted by the Admissions Committee. Transfer students must have one year of credit, have attended an ABA-approved law school, and apply to the Dean of the School of Law, indicating previous attendance at another school. Transfer students must complete the last 4 semesters at the University of Arkansas School of Law.

Costs

Tuition and fees for the academic year are approximately $3700 for full-time in-state students and $8100 for out-of-state students. On-campus room and board costs about $3900 annually; books and supplies run about $1000.

Financial Aid

About 67% of current law students receive some form of aid. Awards are based on need and merit, along with the probability of success in law school. Check with the school for current deadlines. Special funds for minority or disadvantaged students consist of selected scholarships.

About the Law School

University of Arkansas School of Law was established in 1924 and is a public institution. The campus is in a small town. The primary mission of the law school is to prepare students as lawyers who will provide professional service to their clients, who are interested in and capable of advancing legal process and reform, and who are prepared to fill the vital role of the lawyer as a community leader. Students have access to federal, state, county, city, and local agencies, courts, correctional facilities, law firms, and legal aid organizations in the Fayetteville area. Housing for students consists of on-campus residence halls, sorority and fraternity houses, and 2-bedroom units. Housing for married students is limited. A housing service helps students find off-campus housing.

Calendar

The law school operates on a traditional semester basis. Courses for full-time students are offered days only and must be completed within 3 years. There is no part-time program. New students are admitted in the fall. There is a summer session. Transferable summer courses are offered.

Programs

In addition to the J.D., the law school offers the LL.M. in agricultural law. The following joint degrees may be earned: J.D./M.B.A. (Juris Doctor/Master of Business Administration) and J.D./M.P.A. (Juris Doctor/Master of Public Administration).

Phone: 501-575-3102
Web: *http://law.uark.edu/*

Contact

James Miller, Associate Dean for Students, 501-575-3102 for general inquiries; Terry Finney, Director of Financial Aid, 501-575-3806 for financial aid information.

Required

To earn the J.D., candidates must complete 90 total credits, of which 43 are for required courses. They must maintain a minimum GPA of 2.0 in the required courses. The following first-year courses are required of all students: Legal Research and Writing I, Contracts A and B, Criminal Law, Torts, Property A and B, Civil Procedure A and B, and Legal Research and Writing II. Required upper-level courses consist of Constitutional Law, Legal Research and Writing III, and Professional Responsibility. The required orientation program for first-year students is a 6-day introduction to the study of law that includes an introduction to the library, law school, campus tours, university rescources, and student life planning suggestion.

Electives

The School of Law offers concentrations in agricultural law. In addition, students with 48 or more hours who have completed Civil Procedure A and B, Criminal Procedure, Basic Evidence and Professional Responsibility may take a civil or criminal clinic. Upper-level students who have Professsional Responsibility may take Fedreral Practice clinic. Seminars for 2 or 3 hours of credit are available to upper-level students. Seminars offered include Bankruptcy, Bioethics, Comparative Law, Criminal Law, Elder Law, Indian Law, Judicial Administration Jurisprudence, Juvenile Justice, Privacy Law, Supreme Court, and UCC. Faculty may hire research assistants. Several scholarships are available for minority students.

Graduation Requirements

In order to graduate, candidates must have a GPA of 2.0, have completed the upper-division writing requirement, and completed an upper-level research and writing project. Seminar papers may be used to satisfy this requirement. Grades are usually based on a single final exam.

Organizations

Students edit the *University of Arkansas Law Review*. The school participates in a variety of national and regional moot court competitions. Student organizations include the Student Bar Association, the Women's Law Student Association, Arkansas Coalition for Public Interest Law, and Christian Legal Society. Local chapters of national associations include Phi Alpha Delta, Phi Delta Phi, Black Law Students Association, Delta Theta Phi, and the Student Honor Council.

Library

The law library contains 243,962 hard-copy volumes and 43,584 microform volume equivalents, and subscribes to 2240 serial publications. Such on-line databases and networks as LEXIS and WESTLAW are available to law students for research. Special library collections include a growing collection of agricultural law materials developed through the National Center for Agricultural Law Research and Information. The Young Law Library is a depository for federal documents. Recently, the library expanded the Leflar Law Center, which created additional library space. The ratio of library volumes to faculty is 5433 to 1 and to students is 511 to 1. The ratio of seats in the library to students is 1 to 105.

Faculty

The law school has approximately 35 full-time and 5 part-time faculty members, of whom 9 are women. About 26% of full-time faculty have a graduate law degree in addition to the J.D.

Students

About 44% of the student body are women and 10% are minorities. The majority of students come from Arkansas (84%). The average age of entering students is 26.

Placement

J.D.s awarded:	136
Services available through: a separate law school placement center and the university placement center	
Special features: monthly placement newsletters, including internships and fellowships, and alumni and monthly job list postings by mail or e-mail, including those exchanged at other schools.	
Full-time job interviews:	18 employers
Summer job interviews:	37 employers
Placement by graduation:	48% of class
Placement within 9 months:	95% of class
Average starting salary:	$18,000 to $82,000
Areas of placement:	
Private practice 2-10 attorneys	32%
Private practice 11-25 attorneys	9%
Private practice 51-100 attorneys	3%
Business/industry	21%
Government	14%
Judicial clerkships	9%
Public interest	2%
Academic	2%

UNIVERSITY OF ARKANSAS AT LITTLE ROCK

UALR William H. Bowen School of Law

1201 McMath Avenue
Little Rock, AR 72202-5142

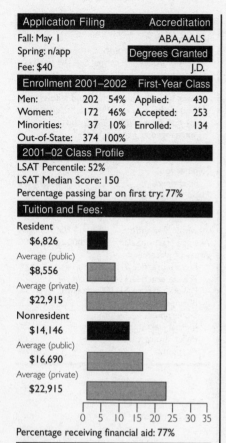

Application Filing		Accreditation
Fall: May 1		ABA, AALS
Spring: n/app		**Degrees Granted**
Fee: $40		J.D.

Enrollment 2001–2002			First-Year Class	
Men:	202	54%	Applied:	430
Women:	172	46%	Accepted:	253
Minorities:	37	10%	Enrolled:	134
Out-of-State:	374	100%		

2001–02 Class Profile

LSAT Percentile: 52%
LSAT Median Score: 150
Percentage passing bar on first try: 77%

Tuition and Fees:

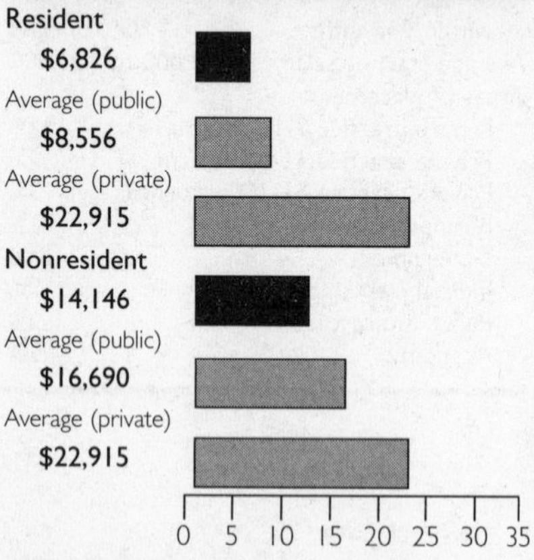

Percentage receiving financial aid: 77%

ADMISSIONS

In the fall 2001 first-year class, 430 applied, 253 were accepted, and 134 enrolled. Two transfers enrolled. The median LSAT percentile of the most recent first-year class was 52; the median GPA was 3.4 on a scale of 4.0. The lowest LSAT percentile accepted was 23; the highest was 90.

Requirements

Applicants must have a bachelor's degree and take the LSAT. The most important admission factors include LSAT results, GPA, and life experience. No specific undergraduate courses are required. Candidates are not interviewed.

Procedure

The application deadline for fall entry is May 1. Applicants should submit an application form, LSAT results, transcripts, a nonrefundable application fee of $40, 2 letters of recommendation, and a prescribed-format personal statement. Notification of the admissions decision is on a rolling basis. The latest acceptable LSAT test date for fall entry is June. The law school uses the LSDAS.

Special

The law school recruits minority and disadvantaged students by means of scholarships that take diversity of life experiences into account. Requirements are not different for out-of-state students. Transfer students must have attended an ABA-approved law school and have an official law school transcript showing completion of 20 semester hours, a letter of good standing stating class rank, LSAT score, official undergraduate transcript, a letter explaining the need to transfer, an application, and the $40 application fee.

Costs

Tuition and fees for the 2001-2002 academic year are $6826 for full-time in-state students and $14,146 for out-of-state students. Tuition for part-time students is $4426 in-state and $8818 out-of-state. Books and supplies run about $750 annually.

Financial Aid

About 77% of current law students receive some form of aid. The average annual amount of aid from all sources combined, including scholarships, loans, and work contracts, is $15,000; maximum, $16,800 for residents; $23,800 for non-residents. Awards are based on need and merit. Required financial statement is the FAFSA. The aid application deadline for fall entry is March 1. Special funds for minority or disadvantaged students include Bowen Scholarships. First-year students are notified about their financial aid application at the time of admission application request.

About the Law School

University of Arkansas at Little Rock UALR William H. Bowen School of Law was established in 1975 and is a public institution. The 5-acre campus is in an urban area downtown, 6 miles from the main campus. The primary mission of the law school is to provide a high-quality legal education that equips students with the knowledge, skills, and ethical concepts to function as competent attorneys, public officials, business persons, and other professionals, and to think critically about the efficacy of the law and legal institutions and to work for their improvement. Students have access to federal, state, county, city, and local agencies, courts, correctional facilities, law firms, and legal aid organizations in the Little Rock area. Little Rock is Arkansas's capital city; thus, students have a wide range of employment opportunities, from all branches of state government to legal services to law firms. Housing for students consists of many rental properties varying in cost. All law school facilities are accessible to the physically disabled.

Calendar

The law school operates on a traditional semester basis. Courses for full-time students are offered principally day, with some upper-level electives, and must be completed within 6 years. For part-time students, courses are offered principally evenings, with some upper-level electives and must be completed within 6 years. New full- and part-time students are admitted in the fall. There is an 8-week summer session. Transferable summer courses are offered.

Programs

Students may take relevant courses in other programs and apply credit toward the J.D.; a maximum of 6 credits may be applied for the joint degree. The following joint degrees may be earned: J.D./M.B.A. (Juris Doctor/Master of Business Administration) and J.D./M.P.A. (Juris Doctor/Master of Public Administration).

Phone: 501-324-9439
Fax: 501-324-9433
E-mail: *lawadm@ualr.edu*
Web: *ualr.edu/~lawschool*

Contact

Jean M. Probasco, Director of Admissions and Registrar, 501-324-9439 for general inquiries; John Noah, Director of Student Services, (501) 569-3130 for financial aid information.

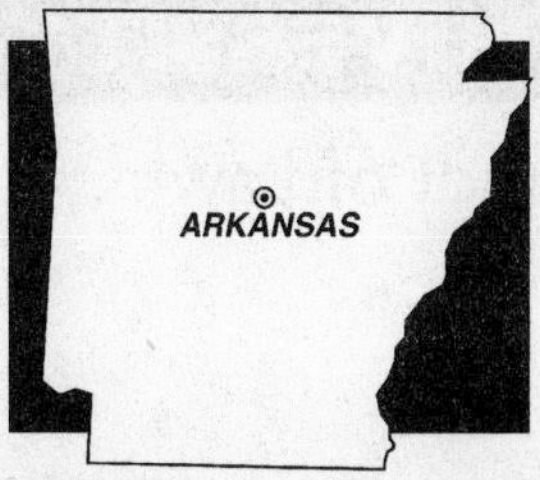

Required

To earn the J.D., candidates must complete 90 total credits, of which 48 are for required courses. They must maintain a minimum GPA of 2.0 in the required courses. The following first-year courses are required of all students: Contracts I and II; Torts I and II; Civil Procedure I and II; Property I and II; Legal Research I and II; and Reasoning, Writing, and Advocacy I and II. Required upper-level courses consist of Constitutional Law I and II, Legal Profession, Evidence, Lawyering skills, and Criminal law. The required orientation program for first-year students is 4 days long and covers the academic and personal skills needed to succeed in law school.

Electives

Of special curricular note are the 2 clinics, litigation (worth 6 hours) and mediation (worth 4 hours). The latter is offered at night as well as in the day. Upper-level students can choose from a number of highly interesting seminar topics (worth 2 credits), as well as writing their own independent paper (1 credit) under the supervision of a faculty member. Outside speakers participate in an annual symposium, and nationally notable speakers offer several lectures a year as well. An ABA-approved summer program at the University of Haifa offers courses in comparative law (6 credits). A number of scholarships are available to students. Many factors are considered in the awarding of scholarships, including race, ethnicity, and background. An ongoing tutorial program directed by the assistant dean and staffed by upper-level students who teach study skills is available to first-year students. An academic mentoring program is available to all first-year students. The most widely taken electives are Family Law, Debtor-Creditor, and Business Associations.

Graduation Requirements

In order to graduate, candidates must have a GPA of 2.0, completed the upper-division writing requirement, and upper-level jurisprudential requirement, which can be fulfilled by a number of courses, e.g., jurisprudence or legal history.

Organizations

During the current year there are 12 registered student organizations which sponsor various activities during the school year, ranging from community service to bringing in outside speakers. Organizations include the Student Bar Association, Black Law Students Association, Criminal Law Society, Environmental Law Society, Community Outreach Opportunities League, and The Federalist Society. Local chapters of national associations include Phi Alpha Delta, Phi Delta Phi, and Delta Theta Phi. In addition to the student organizations, students edit the *UALR Law Review*, a quarterly publication containing scholarly articles. The*Journal of Appellate Practice and Process*, is faculty edited; other publications include *The Student Bar Association Forum* and *Hearsay*, an alumni publication. Students staff the Moot Court Board, which sends several teams each year to participate in national competitions. Since its inception, UALR has also sent teams to the National Trial Competition. Each year UALR and UAF student trial teams compete in the Henry Woods competition. Other competitions include First Amendment, National Moot Court, Bankruptcy, an intraschool Moot Court, and an Advocacy Slam.

Library

The law library contains 168,938 hard-copy volumes and 534,284 microform volume equivalents, and subscribes to 3421 serial publications. Such on-line databases and networks as CALI, CIS Universe, DIALOG, Legal-Trac, LEXIS, LOIS, NEXIS, OCLC First Search, WESTLAW, and Wilsonline Indexes are available to law students for research. Special library collections include a federal documents depository, a state documents depository going back to 1993, and Arkansas Supreme Court records and briefs for 1836-1926. Recently, the library added a wireless network, on-line interlibrary loan, and expanded access to electronic resources. The ratio of library volumes to faculty is 6034 to 1 and to students, 452 to 1. The ratio of seats in the library to students is 1 to 1.

Placement

J.D.s awarded: 109

Services available through: a separate law school placement center

Services: computer access to WESTLAW, NALPLine, brown-bag lunches on various aspects of career planning and the job search.

Special features: an annual graduate brochure that is mailed to all judges and attorneys in Arkansas. The brochure features each student's picture along with information on GPA, honors, past work experience, type of legal practice desired, and geographic preference.

Full-time job interviews:	4 employers
Summer job interviews:	8 employers
Placement by graduation:	n/av
Placement within 9 months:	95% of class
Average starting salary:	$18,480 to $100,000
Areas of placement:	
Private practice 2-10 attorneys	31%
Private practice 11-25 attorneys	6%
Private practice 26-50 attorneys	3%
Private practice 51-100 attorneys	3%
Private practice, other	8%
Government	20%
Business/industry	13%
Judicial clerkships	11%
Public interest	3%
Military	1%
Academic	1%

Faculty

The law school has 28 full-time and 29 part-time faculty members, of whom 22 are women. About 32% of full-time faculty have a graduate law degree in addition to the J.D.; about 13% of part-time faculty have one. The ratio of full-time students to full-time faculty in an average class is 13 to 1; in a clinic, 8 to 1. The law school has a regular program of bringing visiting professors and other distinguished lecturers and visitors to campus.

Students

About 46% of the student body are women; 10%, minorities; 6%, African American; 1%, Asian American; and 2%, Hispanic. The average age of entering students is 28; age range is 21 to 69. About 1% drop out after the first year for academic or personal reasons; 99% remain to receive a law degree.

UNIVERSITY OF BALTIMORE

School of Law

1420 North Charles Street
Baltimore, MD 21201-5779

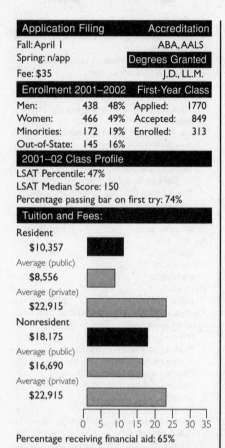

Application Filing		Accreditation
Fall: April 1		ABA, AALS
Spring: n/app		**Degrees Granted**
Fee: $35		J.D., LL.M.

Enrollment 2001–2002			First-Year Class	
Men:	438	48%	Applied:	1770
Women:	466	49%	Accepted:	849
Minorities:	172	19%	Enrolled:	313
Out-of-State:	145	16%		

2001–02 Class Profile

LSAT Percentile: 47%
LSAT Median Score: 150
Percentage passing bar on first try: 74%

Tuition and Fees:

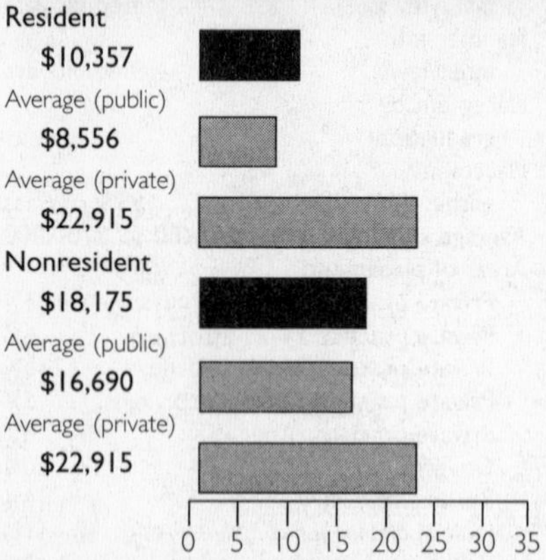

Percentage receiving financial aid: 65%

ADMISSIONS

In the fall 2001 first-year class, 1770 applied, 849 were accepted, and 313 enrolled. Sixteen transfers enrolled. The median LSAT percentile of the most recent first-year class was 47; the median GPA was 2.9 on a scale of 4.0. The lowest LSAT percentile accepted was 17; the highest was 92.

Requirements

Applicants must have a bachelor's degree and take the LSAT. The most important admission factors include work experience, LSAT results, and GPA. No specific undergraduate courses are required. Candidates are not interviewed.

Procedure

The application deadline for fall entry is April 1. Applicants should submit an application form, LSAT results, transcripts, a nonrefundable application fee of $35, 2 letters of recommendation. LSAT scores and transcripts must come through the LSDAS. Notification of the admissions decision is on a rolling basis. The latest acceptable LSAT test date for fall entry is February. The law school uses the LSDAS.

Special

The law school recruits minority and disadvantaged students by means of an on-campus minority law forum, recruiting at historically black colleges, recruiting minorities during visits to undergraduate institutions, and through the Baltimore Scholar Program. Requirements are not different for out-of-state students. Transfer students must have one year of credit, have attended an ABA-approved law school, and have files individually reviewed by committee, which does so subject to availability of space. The Summer Institute, a conditional admission program, offers the opportunity to demonstrate ability for law school through successful completion of an intensive case analysis and legal writing program to individuals whose grades or test scores may be somewhat lower than those ordinarily required for admission.

Costs

Tuition and fees for the 2001-2002 academic year are $10,357 for full-time in-state students and $18,175 for out-of-state students. Books and supplies run about $850 annually.

Financial Aid

About 65% of current law students receive some form of aid. The average annual amount of aid from all sources combined, including scholarships, loans, and work contracts, is $18,000; maximum, $30,000. Awards are based on need and merit; need only for federal programs. Scholarships are based on need and/or merit. The required financial statement is the FAFSA. The aid application deadline for fall entry is April 1. First-year students are notified about their financial aid application in mid-June.

About the Law School

University of Baltimore School of Law was established in 1925 and is a public institution. The campus is in an urban area in Baltimore. The primary mission of the law school is to draw together students and faculty from a variety of backgrounds in a common search for knowledge and understanding. Students have access to federal, state, county, city, and local agencies, courts, correctional facilities, law firms, and legal aid organizations in the Baltimore area. Area corporations and nonprofit organizations are also accessible. Facilities of special interest to law students consist of 2 small personal computer laboratories for student use and on-line databases and networks. Housing for students is available off campus; there is a roommate referral service offered. Nearby, many apartments range from inexpensive studios to luxury apartment buildings. About 95% of the law school facilities are accessible to the physically disabled.

Calendar

The law school operates on a traditional semester basis. Courses for full-time students are offered both day and evening and must be completed within 5 years. For part-time students, courses are offered both day and evening and must be completed within 6 years. New full- and part-time students are admitted in the fall. There is a 6- and 8-week summer session. Transferable summer courses are offered.

Programs

In addition to the J.D., the law school offers the LL.M. Students may take relevant courses in other programs and apply credit toward the J.D.; a maximum of 6 credits may be applied. The following joint degrees may be earned: J.D./M.B.A. (Juris Doctor/ Master of Business Administration), J.D./M.P.A. (Juris Doctor/ Master of Public Administration), J.D./M.S. (Juris Doctor/Master of Science in criminal justice and negotiations, and conflict management), and J.D./Ph.D. (Juris Doctor/ Doctor of Philosophy in policy sciences).

Required

To earn the J.D., candidates must complete 90 total credits, of which 39 are for required courses. They must maintain a minimum GPA of 2.0 in the required courses. The following first-year courses are required of all students: Civil Procedure I and II; Contracts I and II; Criminal Law; Property; Torts; Legal Analysis, Research, and Writing I and II; and Con-

Phone: 410-837-4459
Fax: 410-837-4450
E-mail: *lwadmiss@ubmail.ubalt.edu*
Web: *www.law.ubalt.edu*

Contact

Christina Cantu, Assistant Director of Admission (interim), 410-837-4459 for general inquiries; 410-837-4763, for financial aid information.

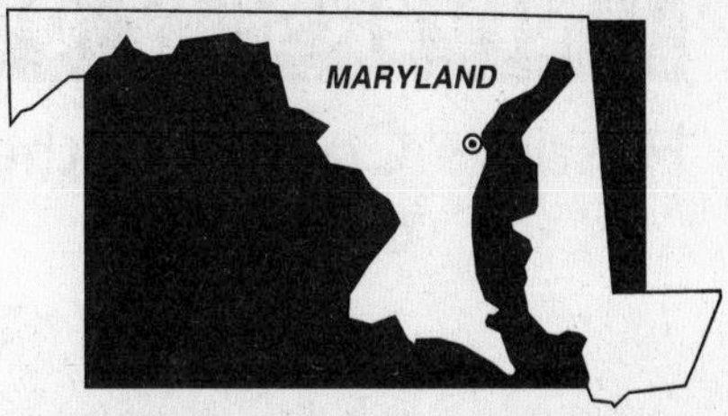

stitutional Law. Required upper-level courses consist of Evidence; Professional Responsibility; an advocacy requirement; 2 upper-level research and writing projects; and Legal Analysis, Research, and Writing III (Moot Court). All students take clinics as part of upper-level elective courses.The required orientation program for first-year students is 4 days; students meet with faculty and peer advisers, attend case analysis and other seminars, and attend an Information Fair on school services and student activities.

Electives

Students must take 36 credits in their area of concentration. The School of Law offers concentrations in corporate law, criminal law, environmental law, family law, international law, litigation, securities law, tax law, torts and insurance, civil rights, estate planning, public and government law, property, general practice, real estate practice, and theories of the law. In addition, clinics offer the opportunity to work under the direct supervision of attorneys. Upper-level students undertake the representation of real clients in actual cases and perform all tasks necessary for proper representation. Students earn 6 credits in the Criminal Practice Clinic, Family Law Clinic, Appellate Advocacy Clinic, Civil Litigation Clinic, Tax Clinic, and Community Development Clinic. Seminars are 3-credit advanced discussion classes that require independent research, writing, and discussion leadership by students. The Internship Program allows upper-level students to learn about the lawyering and judicial process by working closely with supervising attorneys and judges. Internships are open to any upper-level student in good standing and are worth 3 to 4 credits. Special lecture series include the Liss Memorial Lectures, A.M. Law Series, Hoffberger Center for Professional Ethics, and the Center for International and Comparative Law. Study abroad is open to any student after the first year of study. The school offers a program in international comparative law in conjunction with the University of Aberdeen, Scotland. First-year students may receive tutorial assistance through the Law Achievement Workshop, which consists of weekly tutorial sessions for almost every first-year class. Other tutorial programs are handled on an individual basis. Programs for minority students include the Law Achievement Workshop, Attorney Mentors, Exam Writing Workshop, Afro-American Lectures in Law, and Black Law Student Orientation. The most widely taken electives are Business Organization, Criminal Procedure I, and Family Law.

Graduation Requirements

In order to graduate, candidates must have a GPA of 2.0, have completed the upper-division writing requirement, and fulfill the upper-level advocacy requirement.

Organizations

Students edit *The University of Baltimore Law Review*, the *University of Baltimore Law Forum*, the *University of Baltimore Journal of Environmental Law*, the *University of Baltimore Intellectual Property Journal*, and the newspaper *The Advance Sheet*. Annually, teams compete at the American Trial Lawyers Association and Trial Advocacy and Client Counseling competitions, as well as the Client Negotiation Moot Court, Pace National Environmental Law Moot Court, Tax Moot Court, and Trial Advocacy competitions. Law student organizations include the Intellectual Property Legal Society, Christian Legal Society, and Criminal Law Association. There are local chapters of Phi Alpha Delta, Phi Delta Kappa, and Phi Delta Phi. Campus clubs and other organizations include BLSA, APALSA, and WBA.

Library

The law library contains 320,526 hardcopy volumes and 561,053 microform volume equivalents, and subscribes to 3250 serial publications. Such on-line databases and networks as CALI, CIS Universe, Legal-Trac, LEXIS, LOIS, NEXIS, OCLC First Search, WESTLAW, and Wilsonline Indexes are available to law students for research. Special library collections include a U.S. government selective depository. Recently, the library added a 28-seat PC laboratory with offline LEXIS and WESTLAW printers. The ratio of library volumes to faculty is 6968 to 1 and to students, 355 to 1. The ratio of seats in the library to students is 1 to 3.

Placement

J.D.s awarded:	320
Services available through: a separate law school placement center	
Services: some 20 different panels and workshops on job search techniques, specialty areas, and career opportunities	
Special features: Public Interest Career Fair and the Small Employer Career Fair, a joint program with the University of Maryland, and EXPLOR, a summer legal experience program for first year students.	
Full-time job interviews:	15 employers
Summer job interviews:	30 employers
Placement by graduation:	77% of class
Placement within 9 months:	88% of class
Average starting salary:	$44,577
Areas of placement:	
Private practice 2-10 attorneys	15%
Private practice 11-25 attorneys	6%
Private practice 26-50 attorneys	3%
Private practice 51-100 attorneys	4%
Private practice 100+ lawyers	3%
Judicial clerkships	26%
Government	22%
Business/industry	16%
Unknown	3%
Public interest	2%

Faculty

The law school has 46 full-time and 79 part-time faculty members, of whom 38 are women. About 30% of full-time faculty have a graduate law degree in addition to the J.D. The ratio of full-time students to full-time faculty in an average class is 19 to 1; in a clinic, 6 to 1. The law school has a regular program of bringing visiting professors and other distinguished lecturers and visitors to campus.

Students

About 49% of the student body are women; 19%, minorities; 13%, African American; and 4%, Asian American. The majority of students come from Maryland (84%). Some 16% are from out of state with the majority from the Northeast. The average age of entering students is 28; age range is 21 to 56. About 14% of students have a graduate degree. About 2% drop out after the first year for academic or personal reasons; 93% remain to receive a law degree.

UNIVERSITY OF CALIFORNIA

Hastings College of the Law

200 McAllister Street
San Francisco, CA 94102

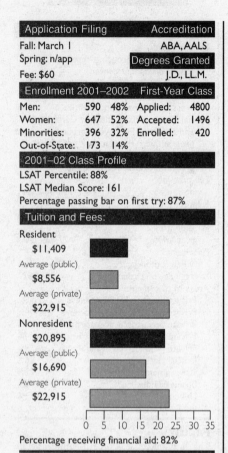

Application Filing		Accreditation
Fall: March 1		ABA, AALS
Spring: n/app		**Degrees Granted**
Fee: $60		J.D., LL.M.

Enrollment 2001–2002			First-Year Class	
Men:	590	48%	Applied:	4800
Women:	647	52%	Accepted:	1496
Minorities:	396	32%	Enrolled:	420
Out-of-State:	173	14%		

2001–02 Class Profile

LSAT Percentile: 88%
LSAT Median Score: 161
Percentage passing bar on first try: 87%

Tuition and Fees:

Resident
$11,409
Average (public)
$8,556
Average (private)
$22,915
Nonresident
$20,895
Average (public)
$16,690
Average (private)
$22,915

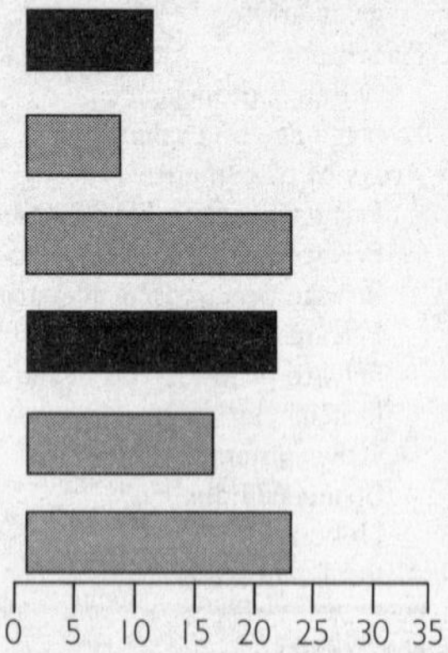

Percentage receiving financial aid: 82%

ADMISSIONS

In the fall 2001 first-year class, 4800 applied, 1496 were accepted, and 420 enrolled. The median LSAT percentile of the most recent first-year class was 88; the median GPA was 3.5 on a scale of 4.0. The lowest LSAT percentile accepted was 23; the highest was 100.

Requirements

Applicants must have a bachelor's degree and take the LSAT. The most important admission factors include academic achievement, LSAT results, and GPA. No specific undergraduate courses are required. Candidates are not interviewed.

Procedure

The application deadline for fall entry is March 1. Applicants should submit an application form, LSAT results, a nonrefundable application fee of $60, and optional letters of recommendation. Notification of the admissions decision is January through May. The latest acceptable LSAT test date for fall entry is February. The law school uses the LSDAS.

Special

The law school recruits minority and disadvantaged students by enrolling 20% of the class through the LEOP program, an alternative means of evaluating disadvantaged students. Requirements are not different for out-of-state students. Transfer students must have one year of credit, have a minimum GPA of 3, have attended an ABA-approved law school, and the school must be AALS-approved.

Costs

Tuition and fees for the 2001-2002 academic year are $11,409 for full-time in-state students and $20,895 for out-of-state students. On-campus room and board costs about $10,800 annually; books and supplies run $840.

Financial Aid

About 82% of current law students receive some form of aid. The average annual amount of aid from all sources combined, including scholarships, loans, and work contracts, is $18,500; maximum, $31,800. Awards are based on need and merit. The required financial statements are the FAFSA and the entering student financial aid supplement form. The aid application deadline for fall entry is March 1. First-year students are notified about their financial aid application as soon after acceptance as possible.

About the Law School

University of California Hastings College of the Law was established in 1878 and is a public institution. The campus is in an urban area in San Francisco. The primary mission of the law school is to prepare new members of the legal profession who are capable of and willing to serve all segments of the public as lawyers, judges, legislators, legal scholars, and in other roles in society. Students have access to federal, state, county, city, and local agencies, courts, correctional facilities, law firms, and legal aid organizations in the San Francisco area. Facilities of special interest to law students include the Public Interest Clearinghouse, the Public Law Research Institute, and the Land Conservation Institute. Housing for students is offered at McAllister Tower, which accommodates approximately 450 students. There are studios, 1-bedroom, and 2-bedroom units available. About 90% of the law school facilities are accessible to the physically disabled.

Calendar

The law school operates on a traditional semester basis. Courses for full-time students are offered days only and must be completed within 3 years. There is no part-time program. New students are admitted in the fall. There is no summer session. Transferable summer courses are not offered.

Programs

In addition to the J.D., the law school offers the LL.M. The following joint degrees may be earned: J.D./M.B.A. (Juris Doctor/Master of Business Administration).

Required

To earn the J.D., candidates must complete 86 total credits, of which 34 are for required courses. They must maintain a minimum GPA of 2.0 in the required courses. The following first-year courses are required of all students: Criminal Law, Torts, Contracts, Property, Civil Procedure, Legal Writing and Research, Moot Court, and a statutory course,

Phone: 415-565-4623
Fax: 415-565-4863
E-mail: *admiss@uchastings.edu*
Web: *u.c.hastings.edu*

Contact

Akira Shiroma, Director of Admissions, 415-565-4885 for general inquiries; Linda Bisesi, Director of Financial Aid, 415-565-4624 for financial aid information.

either Employment Discrimination, Environmental, Food and Drug, or Taxation. Required upper-level courses consist of Professional Responsibility and a seminar or independent study with a substantial writing component. The required orientation program for first-year students is a 2 ½-day program that includes mock classes taught by first-year faculty, assignments, and discussions of study habits, test-taking, and diversity issues.

Electives

The Hastings College of the Law offers concentrations in corporate law, criminal law, entertainment law, environmental law, international law, litigation, media law, securities law, tax law, and public interest law. In addition, upper-level students may act as a judicial extern for one of the state or federal courts. Students also may participate in a clinical seminar and gain practice experience under the supervision of an attorney. Clinics include Civil Justice, Civil Practice, Criminal Practice, Environmental Law, Workers' Rights, Immigration, and Local Government Law. Enrollment in seminars is limited to 24 second- and third-year students. Upper-level students whose academic work is of superior quality may conduct research under the supervision of a full-time faculty member. There are exchange programs with Leiden University in the Netherlands and the University of British Columbia. Outstanding second- or third-year students may be chosen by the dean to serve as discussion group leaders for each of the first-year classes and for certain elective courses. The Legal Education Opportunity Program (LEOP) offers academic support to selected students with backgrounds that include some serious disadvantage that has been encountered and overcome. Incoming students have a special 1-week orientation introducing them to case briefing, legal writing, and analysis. Other programming for LEOP students includes the First-Year Study Program for the California bar examination, which is taught by and for LEOP students. An exchange program in Environmental Law is offered with Vermont Law School. The most widely taken electives are Constitutional Law, Evidence, and Criminal Procedure.

Graduation Requirements

In order to graduate, candidates must have a GPA of 2.0 and have completed the upper-division writing requirement.

Organizations

Students edit the *Hastings Law Journal, The Constitutional Law Quarterly, International and Comparative Law Review, Communications and Entertainment Law Journal, Women's Law Journal*, and *North/Northwest Journal of Environmental Law and Policy*. The student newspaper is the *Hastings Law News*. Moot court competitions include the Giles Sutherland Rich Moot Court, National Appellate Advocacy, and the Frederick Douglass Moot Court. Two credit hours are awarded for participation. Among the 40 student organizations are the Associated Students of Hastings, La Raza Law Students Association, and the Black Law Students Association. There are local chapters of the National Lawyers Guild, Phi Delta Phi, and Amnesty International.

Library

The law library contains 653,988 hard-copy volumes and 1,322,970 microform volume equivalents, and subscribes to 8036 serial publications. Such on-line databases and networks as DIALOG, LEXIS, WESTLAW, and NEXIS, InfoTrac, EPIC, and First Search are available to law students for research. Special library collections include a state and federal depository, a state and federal records and briefs collection, and documents of the U.S. Supreme Court and U.S. Court of Appeals for the Ninth Circuit and California appellate courts. Recently, the library expanded student computer facilities for legal research and word processing at the Learning Resources Center. Students access to e-mail is now available in the library. The ratio of library volumes to faculty is 14,217 to 1 and to students, 529 to 1. The ratio of seats in the library to students is 1 to 1.

Placement

J.D.s awarded:	445
Services available through: a separate law school placement center	
Special features: The center is a co-sponsor of an annual public interest and public service conference; it also conducts on-campus interviewing twice a year.	
Full-time job interviews:	200 employers
Summer job interviews:	225 employers
Placement by graduation:	57% of class
Placement within 9 months:	95% of class
Average starting salary:	$26,000 to $90,000
Areas of placement:	
Private practice 2-10 attorneys	15%
Private practice 11-25 attorneys	4%
Private practice 26-50 attorneys	5%
Private practice 51-100 attorneys	8%
Private practice 101-500 attorneys	24%
Business/industry	13%
Government	10%
Unknown	10%
Judicial clerkships	7%
Public interest	3%
Academic	1%

Faculty

The law school has 46 full-time and 88 part-time faculty members, of whom 39 are women. According to AAUP standards for Category I institutions, faculty salaries are above average. About 28% of full-time faculty have a graduate law degree in addition to the J.D. The ratio of full-time students to full-time faculty in an average class is 20 to 1; in a clinic, 18 to 1. The law school has a regular program of bringing visiting professors and other distinguished lecturers and visitors to campus. There is a chapter of the Order of the Coif; 48 faculty and 1622 graduates are members.

Students

About 52% of the student body are women; 32%, minorities; 4%, African American; 19%, Asian American; 8%, Hispanic; and 1%, Native American. The majority of students come from California (86%). The average age of entering students is 24; age range is 20 to 49. About 7% of students have a graduate degree. About 5% drop out after the first year for academic or personal reasons; 93% remain to receive a law degree.

UNIVERSITY OF CALIFORNIA AT BERKELEY

Boalt Hall

5 Boalt Hall
Berkeley, CA 94720

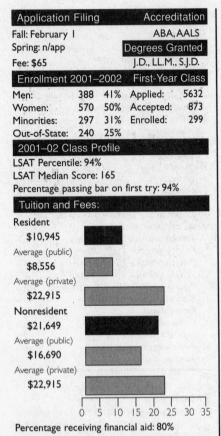

Application Filing		Accreditation
Fall: February 1		ABA, AALS
Spring: n/app		**Degrees Granted**
Fee: $65		J.D., LL.M., S.J.D.

Enrollment 2001–2002			First-Year Class	
Men:	388	41%	Applied:	5632
Women:	570	50%	Accepted:	873
Minorities:	297	31%	Enrolled:	299
Out-of-State:	240	25%		

2001–02 Class Profile

LSAT Percentile: 94%
LSAT Median Score: 165
Percentage passing bar on first try: 94%

Tuition and Fees:

Resident
$10,945
Average (public)
$8,556
Average (private)
$22,915
Nonresident
$21,649
Average (public)
$16,690
Average (private)
$22,915

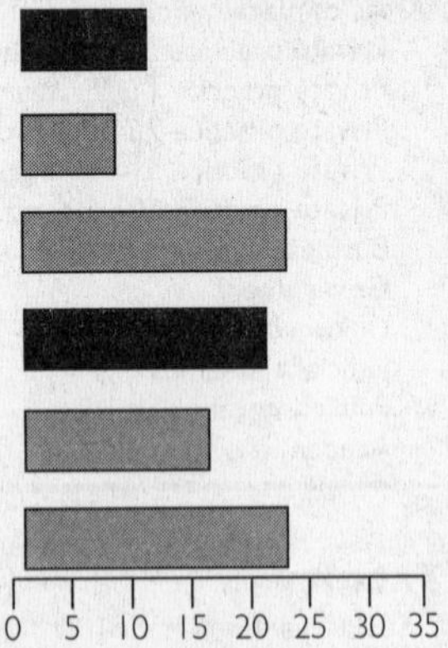

Percentage receiving financial aid: 80%

ADMISSIONS

In the fall 2001 first-year class, 5632 applied, 873 were accepted, and 299 enrolled. Sixty-four transfers enrolled. The median LSAT percentile of the most recent first-year class was 94; the median GPA was 3.73 on a scale of 4.0. The lowest LSAT percentile accepted was 22; the highest was 99.

Requirements

Applicants must have a bachelor's degree and take the LSAT. The most important admission factors include academic achievement, LSAT results, and life experience. No specific undergraduate courses are required. Candidates are not interviewed.

Procedure

The application deadline for fall entry is February 1. Applicants should submit an application form, LSAT results, transcripts, a nonrefundable application fee of $65, and a personal statement. Although letters of recommendation are not mandatory, they are highly recommended. Notification of the admissions decision is from January to May. The latest acceptable LSAT test date for fall entry is December. The law school uses the LSDAS.

Special

The law school recruits minority and disadvantaged students by means of special programs for statewide visits and outreach, and national recruitment via mail campaigns and selected visits. Requirements are not different for out-of-state students. Transfer students must have one year of credit, have attended an ABA-approved law school, and be in the top 5% at their home law school.

Costs

Tuition and fees for the 2001-2002 academic year are $10,945 for full-time instate students and $21,649 for out-of-state students. On-campus room and board costs about $11,258 annually; books and supplies run $1170.

Financial Aid

About 80% of current law students receive some form of aid. The average annual amount of aid from all sources combined, including scholarships, loans, and work contracts, is $21,995; maximum, $37,871. Awards are based on need and merit. The required financial statements are the FAFSA and supplemental aid application (if applicable). The aid application deadline for fall entry is March 2. First-year students are notified about their financial aid application in late spring.

About the Law School

University of California at Berkeley Boalt Hall was established in 1903 and is a public institution. The campus is in an urban area 12 miles east of San Francisco. The primary mission of the law school is to educate men and women not only for the practice of law, but for all the varied roles lawyers perform in a modern society. Students have access to federal, state, county, city, and local agencies, courts, correctional facilities, law firms, and legal aid organizations in the Berkeley area. All other facilities of the Berkeley campus are available to law students. Housing for students is available at the law studio apartment complex, International House, and off campus. All law school facilities are accessible to the physically disabled.

Calendar

The law school operates on a traditional semester basis. Courses for full-time students are offered days only and must be completed within 3 years. There is no part-time program. New students are admitted in the fall. There is no summer session. Transferable summer courses are not offered.

Programs

In addition to the J.D., the law school offers the LL.M. and S.J.D. Students may take relevant courses in other programs and apply credit toward the J.D.; the maximum number of credits that may be applied varies. The following joint degrees may be earned: J.D./M.A. (Juris Doctor/Master of Arts in Asian studies, jurisprudence and social policy; economics and area studies; information management and systems), J.D./M.A.L.D. (Juris Doctor/Master of Arts in law and diplomacy), J.D./M.B.A. (Juris Doctor/Master of Business Administration), J.D./M.C.P. (Juris Doctor/Master of City Planning), J.D./M.J. (Juris Doctor/Master of Journalism), J.D./M.P.P. (Juris Doctor/Master of Public Policy), and J.D./Ph.D. (Juris Doctor/Doctor of Philosophy in legal history, jurisprudence).

Phone: 510-642-2274
Fax: 510-643-6222
Web: *www.law.berkeley.edu*

Required
To earn the J.D., candidates must complete 85 total credits, of which 30 are for required courses. The following first-year courses are required of all students: Civil Procedure; Contracts; Criminal Law; Legal Writing, Research, and Advocacy; Property; and Torts. Required upper-level courses consist of Professional Responsibility. The required orientation program for first-year students consists of 2 days of basic material for new students including the curriculum and services.

Electives
The number of credits students must take in their area of concentration varies. Boalt Hall offers concentrations in environmental law, international law, law and technology, and social justice/public interest. In addition, many clinics, with varying credit, mostly open to second-and third-year students, are available. Research programs can be undertaken at the Earl Warren Legal Institute, whereas field work may be done at the Berkeley Community Law Center or Boalt Hall's International Human Rights Clinic. Special lecture series are offered through the Sho Sato Japanese Legal Studies Program and the Berkeley-Cologne Program. Additionally, tutorials are offered by the Academic Support Program.

Graduation Requirements
In order to graduate, candidates must have completed the upper-division writing requirement.

Contact

Director, 510-642-2274 for general inquiries; 510-642-1563 for financial aid information.

Organizations

Students edit *The California Law Review, Ecology Law Quarterly, Berkeley Technology Law Journal, Berkeley Journal of Employment and Labor Law, Berkeley Journal of International Law, Berkeley Women's Law Journal, African American Law and Policy Report, La Raza Law Journal*, and *Asian Law Journal*. The *Cross-Examiner* is the student newspaper. Annual moot court competitions are held at the school and include the McBaine and Jessup competitions. Among the student organizations are the Asian Pacific American Law Students, Law Students of African Descent, and La Raza. There are local chapters of the Federalist Society, Phi Alpha Delta, and the ABA/Law Student Division.

Library

The law library contains 680,000 hardcopy volumes and 660,000 microform volume equivalents, and subscribes to 7000 serial publications. Such on-line databases and networks as DIALOG, LEXIS, WESTLAW, and Legal-trac are available to law students for research. Special library collections include the Robbins Collection of ecclesiastical, foreign, comparative, and international law, and the Goodrich and Matthew collections of commercial, conservation, and ecology law. Recently, the library increased word processing facilities for students. The ratio of library volumes to faculty is 11,148 to 1 and to students, 710 to 1. The ratio of seats in the library to students is 1 to 3.

Faculty

The law school has 61 full-time and 102 part-time faculty members, of whom 51 are women. According to AAUP standards for Category I institutions, faculty salaries are well above average. About 10% of full-time faculty have a graduate law degree in addition to the J.D.; about 2% of part-time faculty have one. The ratio of full-time students to full-time faculty in an average class is 25 to 1; in a clinic, 6 to 1. The law school has a regular program of bringing visiting professors and other distinguished lecturers and visitors to campus. There is a chapter of the Order of the Coif; 22 faculty are members.

Placement

J.D.s awarded: 279

Services available through: a separate law school placement center and the university placement center

Services: A searchable job listing database is available on the school's web site.

Special features: fall and spring on-campus interview programs, a career symposium for first year students, a mentor program, mock interviews, a speaker series on law specialties, as well as individual counseling sessions with counselors who have all practiced law themselves. A full-time counselor focuses on public interest/public sector careers, fellowships, and judicial clerkship advising.

Full-time job interviews:	198 employers
Summer job interviews:	342 employers
Placement by graduation:	93% of class
Placement within 9 months:	98% of class
Average starting salary:	$25,000 to $145,000

Areas of placement:

Private practice 2-10 attorneys	1%
Private practice 11-25 attorneys	2%
Private practice 26-50 attorneys	1%
Private practice 51-100 attorneys	7%
Private practice 101+ attorneys	43%
Private practice, unknown size	18%
Judicial clerkships	14%
Government	6%
Public interest	4%
Business/industry	3%
Academic	1%

Students

About 50% of the student body are women; 31%, minorities; 5%, African American; 14%, Asian American; 11%, Hispanic; and 1%, Native American. The majority of students come from California (75%). The average age of entering students is 24; age range is 18 to 48. About 19% of students have a graduate degree.

UNIVERSITY OF CALIFORNIA AT DAVIS

School of Law

Martin Luther King, Jr. Hall - 400 Mrak Hall Drive
Davis, CA 95616-5201

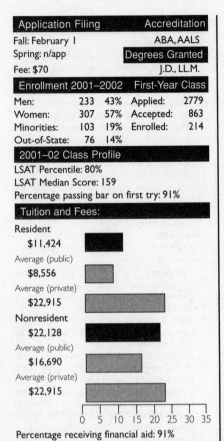

Application Filing		Accreditation
Fall: February 1		ABA, AALS
Spring: n/app		**Degrees Granted**
Fee: $70		J.D., LL.M.

Enrollment 2001–2002			First-Year Class	
Men:	233	43%	Applied:	2779
Women:	307	57%	Accepted:	863
Minorities:	103	19%	Enrolled:	214
Out-of-State:	76	14%		

2001–02 Class Profile

LSAT Percentile: 80%
LSAT Median Score: 159
Percentage passing bar on first try: 91%

Tuition and Fees:

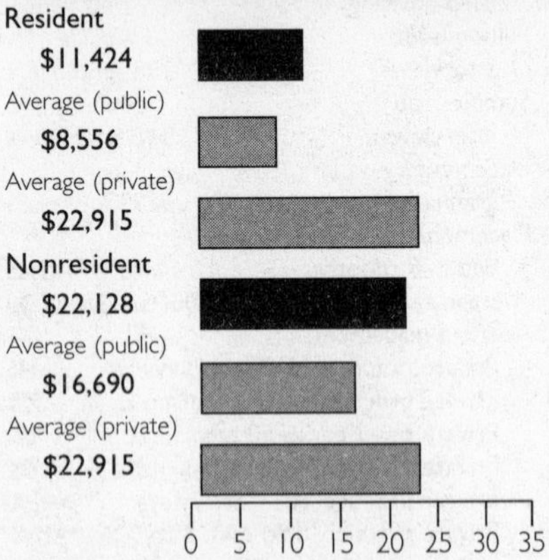

Percentage receiving financial aid: 91%

ADMISSIONS

In the fall 2001 first-year class, 2779 applied, 863 were accepted, and 214 enrolled. Seven transfers enrolled. The median LSAT percentile of the most recent first-year class was 80; the median GPA was 3.55 on a scale of 4.0. The lowest LSAT percentile accepted was 25; the highest was 99.

Requirements

Applicants must have a bachelor's degree and take the LSAT. The most important admission factors include LSAT results, GPA, and a personal statement. No specific undergraduate courses are required. Candidates are not interviewed.

Procedure

The application deadline for fall entry is February 1. Applicants should submit an application form, LSAT results, a nonrefundable application fee of $70, 2 letters of recommendation, and a personal statement; applicants should directly submit supplementary transcripts covering the fall semester, and successful applicants must submit a final transcript showing the receipt of a bachelor degree. Notification of the admissions decision is from January to May. The latest acceptable LSAT test date for fall entry is December prior to August enrollment. The law school uses the LSDAS.

Special

The law school recruits minority and disadvantaged students by means of visits to undergraduate campuses, the Candidate Referral Service, graduate/professional information days, and the LSAC forums and various outreach events. Requirements are different for out-of-state students in that they pay tuition not required of California residents. All admission requirements are the same. Transfer students must have one year of credit, have attended an ABA-approved law school, with admitted students usually in the top 5% to 10% of their first-year class.

Costs

Tuition and fees for the 2001-2002 academic year are $11,424 for full-time in-state students and $22,128 for out-of-state students. Books and supplies run about $937 annually.

Financial Aid

About 91% of current law students receive some form of aid. The average annual amount of aid from all sources combined, including scholarships, loans, and work contracts, is $18,596; maximum, $32,205. Awards are based on need. The required financial statement is the FAFSA. The aid application deadline for fall entry is March 2. First-year students are notified about their financial aid application once they have been admitted.

About the Law School

University of California at Davis School of Law was established in 1965 and is a public institution. The 5200-acre campus is in a small town 15 miles west of Sacramento. The primary mission of the law school is to combine the best of traditional legal education and modern, practical techniques with nationally and internationally recognized scholars and teachers who have meaningful practical experience. Students have access to federal, state, county, city, and local agencies, courts, correctional facilities, law firms, and legal aid organizations in the Davis area. Facilities of special interest to law students include the instructional computer laboratory; the library, which allows 24-hour access; a day care co-op where care is provided by parents for children 12 months and younger; and wireless Internet access in specific locations. Housing for students is available through university housing facilities for single graduate students and student families; off campus housing is available through the ASUCD Community Housing Listing Service and a variety of community resource listings (e.g., newspapers); rental rates are reasonable and consistently lower than those in San Francisco and Los Angeles. All law school facilities are accessible to the physically disabled.

Calendar

The law school operates on a traditional semester basis. Courses for full-time students are offered days only and must be completed within 3 years, unless there are extenuating circumstances with approval by the Dean. There is no part-time program. New students are admitted in the fall. There is no summer session. Transferable summer courses are not offered.

Programs

In addition to the J.D., the law school offers the LL.M. Students may take relevant courses in other programs and apply credit toward the J.D.; a maximum of 10 semester units may be applied. The following joint degrees may be earned: J.D./M.A. (Juris Doctor/Master of Arts in most programs offered by UC Davis Graduate Studies Division) and J.D./M.B.A. (Juris Doctor/Masters in Business Administration).

Required

To earn the J.D., candidates must complete 88 total credits, of which 33 are for required courses. They must maintain a minimum GPA of 2.0 in the required courses. The following first-year courses are required of all students: Introduction to Law, Property, Contracts, Civil Procedure, Torts, Constitutional Law, Criminal Law, and Legal Research and Legal

Phone: 530-752-6477
E-mail: *lawadmissions@ucdavis.edu*
Web: *kinghall.ucdavis.edu*

Contact

Sharon L. Pinkney, Admissions Director, 530-752-6477 for general inquiries; Lawrence Gallardo, Financial Aid Director, 530-752-6573 for financial aid information.

Writing. Required upper-level courses consist of Professional Responsibility and an advanced legal writing project. The required orientation program for first-year students is an introductory week that includes meeting the Academic Assistance Program tutors, a tour of the law library, a photo session, class registration, a financial aid information session, dean's orientation, and social activities. The primary focus is a 1-unit course, Introduction to Law.

Electives

Students must take 15 credits in their area of concentration. The School of Law offers concentrations in environmental law, international law, and a certificate program in public interest law; the law school provides for a number of specialized studies including intellectual property and business law. In addition, clinics are open to upper-level students. Placements are available with selected public agencies, judges, and some private attorneys through such formal clinical programs as Administration of Criminal Justice (2 to 6 or 12 units), Civil Rights (2 to 6 units), and Employment Relations (2 to 6 units). Seminars for 2 or 3 credits, open to upper-level students, include areas of constitutional law, criminal law, and estate planning. An extensive array of seminars for 2 to 3 credits are open to upper-level students. Internships are available through clinics; additional opportunities are available in tax and public interest. In the second or third year, all students must complete a writing project (an individually authored work of rigorous intellectual effort). Special lecture series include Bodenheimer Lecture on the Family and Barrett Lecture on Constitutional Law. Study abroad is available with the Dean's permission; credit is given for participation in programs offered at other ABA law schools. There is an Academic Assistance Program whereby a second- or third-year student is assigned to each first-year class. The tutors are available for assistance with substantive course work as well as note taking, briefing, and outlining skills. There are no minority programs, but there is an active minority student body and organizations. Special interest group programs include the King Hall Pro Bono Program and the Public Interest Law Program. The most widely taken electives are Negotiations, Trial Practice, and Evidence.

Graduation Requirements

In order to graduate, candidates must have a GPA of 2.0, have completed the upper-division writing requirement, and the required courses.

Organizations

Students edit the *UC Davis Law Review*; the newspaper, *Advocate*; the *Environs*, a publication of the Environmental Law Society; the *Journal of International Law and Policy*, a publication of the International Law Society; and the *Journal of Juvenile Law and Policy*. Moot court competitions held annually include the Moot Court Trial Competition, Client Counseling, and National Moot Court. Student organizations include the Law Student Association, ABA-Law Student Division, and American Civil Liberties Union. There are local chapters of Phi Alpha Delta, Phi Delta Phi, and Tax Law Society. Other campus organizations include the Alumni Association, Advocates for the Rights of Children, and Criminal Law Association.

Library

The law library contains 282,566 hard-copy volumes and 676,254 microform volume equivalents, and subscribes to 4814 serial publications. Such on-line databases and networks as CALI, CIS Universe, DIALOG, Legal-Trac, LEXIS, LOIS, Mathew Bender, NEXIS, OCLC First Search, RLIN, WESTLAW, MELVYL-UC system, First Search, WORLDCAT, CQ, and MEDLINE are available to law students for research. Special library collections include federal and California documents depositories. Special emphasis is in intellectual property and environmental law. Recently, the library added wireless access to the Internet and on-line resources through the library. The ratio of library volumes to faculty is 9419 to 1 and to students, 523 to 1. The ratio of seats in the library to students is 1 to .7.

Faculty

The law school has 30 full-time and 20 part-time faculty members, of whom 16 are women. According to AAUP standards for Category I institutions, faculty salaries are well above average. About 3% of full-time faculty have a graduate law degree in addition to the J.D. The ratio of full-time students to full-time faculty in an average class is 40 to 1; in a clinic, 10 to 1. The law school has a regular program of bringing visiting professors and other distinguished lecturers and visitors to campus. There is a chapter of the Order of the Coif; 26 faculty and 448 graduates are members.

Placement

J.D.s awarded:	164
Services available through: a separate law school placement center	
Special features: NEXIS and LEXIS systems are available for student use; there is a career services library as well as career-related panels and presentations. UC Davis is a member of the Public Interest Clearinghouse's Public Interest Law Certificate Program, which includes specialized job listings and career advising.	
Full-time job interviews:	n/av
Summer job interviews:	125 employers
Placement by graduation:	66% of class
Placement within 9 months:	99% of class
Average starting salary:	$30,000 to $200,000
Areas of placement:	
Private practice 2-10 attorneys	13%
Private practice 11-25 attorneys	9%
Private practice 26-50 attorneys	6%
Private practice 51-100 attorneys	4%
Private practice 101+ attorneys	25%
Government	15%
Business/industry	12%
Judicial clerkships	7%
Public interest	5%
Academic	1%

Students

About 57% of the student body are women; 19%, minorities; 2%, African American; 13%, Asian American; 4%, Hispanic; and 1%, Native American. The majority of students come from California (86%). The average age of entering students is 25; age range is 20 to 52. About 38% of students enter directly from undergraduate school and 13% have a graduate degree. About 6% drop out after the first year for academic or personal reasons; 90% remain to receive a law degree.

UNIVERSITY OF CALIFORNIA AT LOS ANGELES

School of Law

P.O. Box 951445
Los Angeles, CA 90095-1445

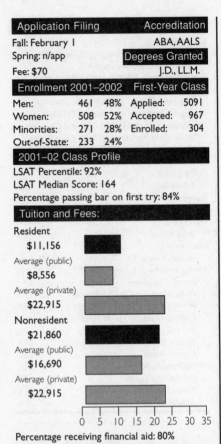

Application Filing	Accreditation
Fall: February 1	ABA, AALS
Spring: n/app	**Degrees Granted**
Fee: $70	J.D., LL.M.

Enrollment 2001–2002			First-Year Class	
Men:	461	48%	Applied:	5091
Women:	508	52%	Accepted:	967
Minorities:	271	28%	Enrolled:	304
Out-of-State:	233	24%		

2001–02 Class Profile

LSAT Percentile: 92%
LSAT Median Score: 164
Percentage passing bar on first try: 84%

Tuition and Fees:

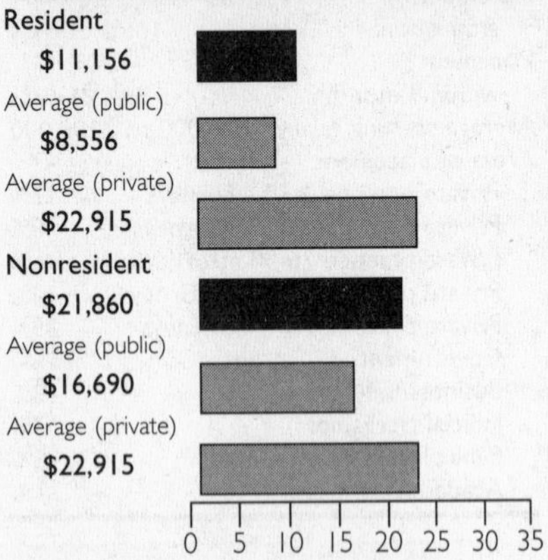

Percentage receiving financial aid: 80%

ADMISSIONS

In the fall 2001 first-year class, 5091 applied, 967 were accepted, and 304 enrolled. Thirty-three transfers enrolled. The median LSAT percentile of the most recent first-year class was 92; the median GPA was 3.63 on a scale of 4.0. The lowest LSAT percentile accepted was 47; the highest was 99.

Requirements

Applicants must have a bachelor's degree and take the LSAT. The most important admission factors include GPA, LSAT results, and academic achievement. No specific undergraduate courses are required. Candidates are not interviewed.

Procedure

The application deadline for fall entry is February 1. Applicants should submit an application form, LSAT results, transcripts, a nonrefundable application fee of $70, at least 1 but no more than 3 letters of recommendation, and a resume. Notification of the admissions decision is from January through late May. The latest acceptable LSAT test date for fall entry is December. The law school uses the LSDAS.

Special

The law school recruits minority and disadvantaged students by means of visits to undergraduate schools, participation in LSAC forums, and programs arranged by law school student organizations. Requirements are not different for out-of-state students. Transfer students must have one year of credit, have attended an ABA-approved law school, and must have an outstanding academic performance in the first year of law school. The law school offers a limited enrollment, 8-day summer program designed for students who are the first in their family to attend college or law school, those who have been out of school for a number of years, or those who are unfamiliar with the American legal system.

Costs

Tuition and fees for the 2001-2002 academic year are $11,156 for full-time in-state students and $21,860 for out-of-state students. On-campus room and board costs about $9351 annually; books and supplies run $1425.

Financial Aid

About 80% of current law students receive some form of aid. The average annual amount of aid from all sources combined, including scholarships, loans, and work contracts, is $18,500; maximum, $26,156. Awards are based on need; departmental scholarships are awarded on the basis of need and merit. The required financial statement is the FAFSA. Check with the school for current application deadlines. Graduate Opportunity Fellowship Program funds are available to disadvantaged students. First-year students are notified about their financial aid application some time prior to the beginning of the semester.

About the Law School

University of California at Los Angeles School of Law was established in 1948 and is a public institution. The 419-acre campus is in an urban area in Los Angeles. The primary mission of the law school is to admit outstanding students who will bring a wide range of backgrounds to the classroom and the legal profession. UCLA's central purpose is to train attorneys of professional excellence and integrity who will exercise civic responsibility. Students have access to federal, state, county, city, and local agencies, courts, correctional facilities, law firms, and legal aid organizations in the Los Angeles area. Housing for students is widely available. They may choose from privately owned rental housing, university-owned apartments, and graduate student apartments and dormitories. About 99% of the law school facilities are accessible to the physically disabled.

Calendar

The law school operates on a traditional semester basis. Courses for full-time students are offered days only and must be completed within 5 years. There is no part-time program. New students are admitted in the fall. There is no summer session. Transferable summer courses are not offered.

Programs

In addition to the J.D., the law school offers the LL.M. Students may take relevant courses in other programs and apply credit toward the J.D.; 6 credits may be applied, but with petition, 12. The following joint degrees may be earned: J.D./M.A. (Juris Doctor/Master of Arts in American Indian studies, urban planning, and Afro-American studies), J.D./M.B.A. (Juris Doctor/Master of Business Administration), J.D./M.P.H. (Juris Doctor/Master of Public Health (specialization in Health Services), J.D./M.P.P. (Juris Doctor/Master of Public Policy), and J.D./M.S.W. (Juris Doctor/Master of Social Welfare).

Required

To earn the J.D., candidates must complete 87 total credits, of which 35 are for required courses. They must maintain a minimum GPA of 1.7 in first year required courses, 1.9 thereafter. The following first-year courses are required of all students: Constitutional Law I, Contracts, Lawyering Skills, Torts, Criminal Law, Property, and Civil Procedure. Required upper-level courses consist of Legal Profession. All students must take clinical courses. Clinical training is part

Phone: 310-825-2080
Fax: 310-825-9450
E-mail: *admissions@law.ucla.edu*
Web: *www.law.ucla.edu*

Contact

Andrea Sossin-Bergman Assistant Dean for Admissions, 310-825-2080 for general inquiries; Veronica Wilson, 310-825-2459 for financial aid information.

of the required first-year "Lawyering Skills" course. Upper-division courses are optional. There is a required 2-day orientation program designed to acquaint first-year students with classmates, professors and deans, and with the study of law and to handle a variety of administrative tasks. It incorporates a law skills workshop, panel and group discussions, and a substantive course lecture.

Electives

The School of Law offers concentrations in corporate law, criminal law, entertainment law, environmental law, family law, international law, juvenile law, labor law, litigation, media law, securities law, sports law, tax law, torts and insurance, critical race studies, public interest law and policy, and corporate law. In addition, clinics are offered to advanced students in environmental law, trial advocacy, public policy advocacy, and corporate transactional law. Credit ranges from 4 to 13 units, depending on the course. Seminars are offered to advanced students and credit ranges from 2 to 4 units, depending on the course. Full-time externships are offered to students in their fourth and fifth semesters and are worth 13 units: 11 units for the placement and 2 units for a related seminar or tutorial taught by a faculty member. The externships range from the State Department's Office of General Counsel, the White House Counsel, government law offices, and public interest law firms, to nonprofit agencies and the chambers of many federal judges. Directed research, for which students must produce original scholarship of publishable quality, is worth 1 to 5 units. Students may obtain credit for summer study abroad at foreign programs offered by ABA-approved law schools. Academic support programs that include tutorials are available. Student organizations offer other academic enrichment programs. Summer programs for students admitted on a diversity basis are available. The most widely taken electives are those subjects tested on the California bar exam, such as Evidence, Constitutional Criminal Procedure, and Wills and Trusts.

Graduation Requirements

In order to graduate, candidates must have a GPA of 1.9, and have 6 semesters of residence credit in regular session.

Organizations

Students edit the *UCLA Law Review* and the newspaper, the *Docket*. Other student edited publications include the *Asian Pacific American Law Journal, Journal of Environmental Law and Policy, National Black Law Journal, Pacific Basin Law Journal, Women's Law Journal, Chicano/Latino Law Review, Entertainment Law Review, UCLA Journal of International Law and Foreign Affairs*, and the online *Bulletin of Law and Technology*. There is a Moot Court Honors Program, a Roscoe Pound Competition, and the National Hispanic Moot Court Competition. Law student organizations include Student Bar Association, PILF, and El Centro Legal. Other organizations include the American Indian Law Students Association, Immigration Law Society, and Health Care Law Society. Local chapters of national associations include Phi Alpha Delta and Phi Delta Phi.

Library

The law library contains 512,769 hard-copy volumes and 403,651 microform volume equivalents, and subscribes to 7013 serial publications. Such on-line databases and networks as CALI, DIALOG, Infotrac, Legal-Trac, LEXIS, Mathew Bender, NEXIS, OCLC First Search, RLIN, WESTLAW, and Wilsonline Indexes are available to law students for research. Special library collections include a U.S. government depository, a California depository, an East Asian law collection, a Latin American law collection, and treaties. The expanded and renovated Hugh and Hazel Darling Law Library creates one of the largest and most beautiful law libraries in the country. The ratio of library volumes to faculty is 6178 to 1 and to students, 529 to 1. The ratio of seats in the library to students is 1 to 1.

Faculty

The law school has 83 full-time and 26 part-time faculty members, of whom 33 are women. According to AAUP standards for Category IIA institutions, faculty salaries are well above average. About 10% of full-time faculty have a graduate law degree in addition to the J.D.; about 15% of part-time faculty have one. The ratio of full-time students to full-time faculty in an average class is 12 to 1; in a clinic, 6 to 1. The law school has a regular program of bringing visiting professors and other distinguished lecturers and visitors to campus. There is a chapter of the Order of the Coif; 32 faculty and 1050 graduates are members.

Placement

J.D.s awarded:	324
Services available through: a separate law school placement center	
Services: a twice-yearly on-campus interview program. The office hosts public interest, government, and small firm events as well.	
Special features: individual counseling and workshops on career planning and interviewing skills. Job listings can be accessed by students and alumni by the Internet.	
Full-time job interviews:	230 employers
Summer job interviews:	350 employers
Placement by graduation:	90% of class
Placement within 9 months:	98% of class
Average starting salary:	$30,000 to $180,000
Areas of placement:	
Private practice 2-10 attorneys	8%
Private practice 11-25 attorneys	6%
Private practice 26-50 attorneys	4%
Private practice 51-100 attorneys	7%
Private practice 101-500+ attorneys	49%
Private practice, size unknown	2%
Judicial clerkships	8%
Business/industry	7%
Government	4%
Public interest	3%
Academic	1%
Unknown	1%

Students

About 52% of the student body are women; 28%, minorities; 2%, African American; 18%, Asian American; 7%, Hispanic; and 1%, Native American. The majority of students come from California (76%). The average age of entering students is 25; age range is 16 to 42. About 35% of students enter directly from undergraduate school and 13% have a graduate degree. About 1% drop out after the first year for academic or personal reasons; 99% remain to receive a law degree.

UNIVERSITY OF CHICAGO

Law School

1111 East 60th Street
Chicago, IL 60637

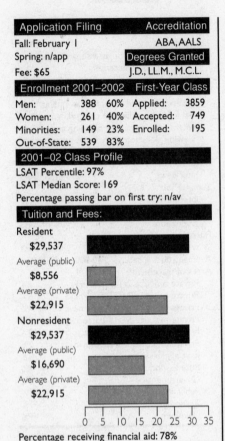

Application Filing		Accreditation
Fall: February 1		ABA, AALS
Spring: n/app		**Degrees Granted**
Fee: $65		J.D., LL.M., M.C.L.

Enrollment 2001–2002			First-Year Class	
Men:	388	60%	Applied:	3859
Women:	261	40%	Accepted:	749
Minorities:	149	23%	Enrolled:	195
Out-of-State:	539	83%		

2001–02 Class Profile

LSAT Percentile: 97%
LSAT Median Score: 169
Percentage passing bar on first try: n/av

Tuition and Fees:

Resident
$29,537
Average (public)
$8,556
Average (private)
$22,915
Nonresident
$29,537
Average (public)
$16,690
Average (private)
$22,915

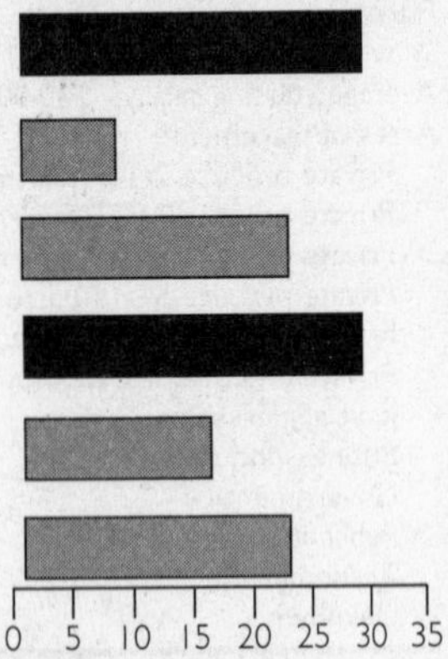

Percentage receiving financial aid: 78%

ADMISSIONS

In the fall 2001 first-year class, 3859 applied, 749 were accepted, and 195 enrolled. Fifteen transfers enrolled. The median LSAT percentile of the most recent first-year class was 97; the median GPA was 3.62 on a scale of 4.0.

Requirements

Applicants must have a bachelor's degree and take the LSAT. No specific undergraduate courses are required. Candidates are interviewed.

Procedure

The application deadline for fall entry is February 1. Applicants should submit an application form, LSAT results, transcripts, a nonrefundable application fee of $65, 2 letters of recommendation, a personal statement, and a resume. The latest acceptable LSAT test date for fall entry is December for most cases. The law school uses the LSDAS.

Special

The law school recruits minority and disadvantaged students by using the Law School Data Assembly Service's Candidate Referral Service and outreach at law school forums, colleges, and minority fairs. Requirements are not different for out-of-state students. Transfer students must have one year of credit, have attended an ABA-approved law school, and must be planning to spend at least 2 years at the school.

Costs

Tuition and fees for the 2001-2002 academic year are $29,537 for all full-time students. On-campus room and board costs about $11,105 annually; books and supplies run $1575.

Financial Aid

About 78% of current law students receive some form of aid. Awards are based on need and merit. The required financial statement is the FAFSA. The aid application deadline for fall entry is March 1.

About the Law School

University of Chicago Law School was established in 1902 and is a private institution. The 203-acre campus is in an urban area 7 miles from downtown Chicago. The primary mission of the law school is not to certify lawyers but to train well-rounded, critical, and socially conscious thinkers and doers. Three cornerstones provide the foundation for Chicago's educational mission: the life of the mind, participatory learning, and interdisciplinary inquiry. Students have access to federal, state, county, city, and local agencies, courts, correctional facilities, law firms, and legal aid organizations in the Chicago area. Housed in the Arthur Cane Center, Chicago's clinics involve more than 100 students each year and permit them to represent clients with real-world legal problems under the guidance of clinical faculty. Facilities of special interest to law students include the law quadrangle, made up of buildings surrounding a reflecting pool and housing the law library, classrooms, offices, the legal aid clinics, an auditorium, and a moot court room. Housing for students About a third of first-year students live in the school's dormitory, located 2 blocks from the school. Half of the first-year students and half of the upper-class students live in Hyde Park's 3-story walk-ups, highrises, single-family homes, and townhouses. The remainder commute from other neighborhoods in Chicago.

Calendar

The law school operates on a quarter basis. Courses for full-time students are offered days only and must be completed within a 3-year course of study. There is no part-time program. New students are admitted in the fall. There is no summer session. Transferable summer courses are not offered.

Programs

In addition to the J.D., the law school offers the LL.M., M.C.L., J.S.D., and D.C.L. Students may take relevant courses in other programs and apply credit toward the J.D.; a maximum of 12 credits may be applied.

Phone: 773-702-9484
Fax: 773-834-0942
E-mail: *admissions@law.uchicago.edu*
Web: *law.uchicago.edu*

Contact

Genita Robinson, Admissions Office, 773-702-9484 for general inquiries; Joyce Wilson, Financial Aid Administration, 773-702-9484 for financial aid information.

Required

To earn the J.D., candidates must complete 105 total credits, of which 40 are for required courses. They must maintain a minimum grade average of 68 in the required courses. The following first-year courses are required of all students: Elements of the Law, Contracts, Criminal Law, Civil Procedures, Property, Torts, Legal Research and Writing, and 1 elective. All upper-level courses are elective with the exception of a professional responsibility course. The optional orientation program for first-year students consists of 4 days of presentations, tours, and social events, including a dinner, a Lake Michigan boat cruise, a picnic, and a visit to the Second City Comedy Review.

Electives

The school's clinical program includes the Mandel Legal Aid Clinic, the Institute for Justice Clinic on Entrepreneurship, and the MacArthur Justice Center. These clinics are open to second- and third-year students. Credit is given for both the classroom and the practical component. Sixty-eight of the school's 155 courses are seminars. They are open to second- and third-year students. Examples include Cyberlaw, Race and Criminal Justice, Entrepreneurship, and Issues in International Refugee Law. The Career Services Center helps students locate summer internships. Approximately 95% of first-year students and 99% of second-year students are employed during the summer. The Chicago Law Foundation, a student-run charitable organization, awards grants to students working in public-interest jobs during the summer. The school encourages student and faculty research in the law as well as the social sciences. Faculty-supervised research may be done in the Individual Research program for credit. Lectures, open to the law school community, occur several times a year in workshops such as Constitutional Law, International Law, Law and Economics, Law and Philosophy, and regular lunch-time lectures with a variety of speakers. The Director of Academic Support works with students who need help with their academic skills. The most widely taken electives are Evidence, Constitutional Law, and Taxation of Individual Income.

Graduation Requirements

In order to graduate, candidates must have a minimum grade average of 68 (on a 100 point scale), have completed the upper-division writing requirement, and have completed a Professional Responsibility course.

Organizations

Students edit *The University of Chicago Law Review, The University of Chicago Legal Forum, The University of Chicago Roundtable*, and *The Chicago Journal of International Law*. There are 4 faculty-edited journals: the *Supreme Court Review, Journal of Law and Economics, Journal of Legal Studies*, and *Law and Economics: Working Papers*. The student newspaper is *The Phoenix*. While first-year students have moot court practice in their Legal Research and Writing class, upper-level students participate in the Hinton Moot Court Program. Other competitions include the annual trivia contest. The school has about 45 student organizations that include the Intellectual Property and Entertainment Law Society, International Law Society, and the Law and Internet Forum. Local chapters of national associations include the Black Law Students Association, the Federalist Society, and American Constitution Society. Other organizations include Habitat for Humanity, Outdoor Adventure Club, and Simply Theater.

Library

The law library contains 651,822 hard-copy volumes and 64,007 microform volume equivalents, and subscribes to 8429 serial publications. Such on-line databases and networks as CALI, CIS Universe, DIALOG, Dow-Jones, Infotrac, Legal-Trac, LEXIS, NEXIS, OCLC First Search, RLIN, and WESTLAW are available to law students for research. Special library collections include a federal document depository, Supreme Court briefs and records, and Karl Llewellyn Papers. Recently, the library updated to a new integrated on-line catalog for all campus libraries. The ratio of library volumes to faculty is 13,036 to 1 and to students, 1004 to 1. The ratio of seats in the library to students is 1 to 1.

Placement	
J.D.s awarded:	195
Services available through: a separate law school placement center	
Services: seminars and publications	
Special features: clerkship counseling	
Full-time job interviews:	185 employers
Summer job interviews:	336 employers
Placement by graduation:	99% of class
Placement within 9 months:	100% of class
Average starting salary:	$15,000 to $165,000
Areas of placement:	
Private practice	66%
Judicial clerkships	28%
Government	2%
Business/industry	2%
Public interest	1%
Academic	1%

Faculty

The law school has 50 full-time and 21 part-time faculty members. According to AAUP standards for Category I institutions, faculty salaries are well above average. The law school has a regular program of bringing visiting professors and other distinguished lecturers and visitors to campus. There is a chapter of the Order of the Coif.

Students

About 40% of the student body are women; 23%, minorities; 4%, African American; 10%, Asian American; 9%, Hispanic; and 1%, Native American. Most students come from the Midwest (29%). The average age of entering students is 24; age range is 21 to 42. About 29% of students enter directly from undergraduate school. About 1% drop out after the first year for academic or personal reasons; 99% remain to receive a law degree.

UNIVERSITY OF CINCINNATI

College of Law

P.O. Box 210040
Cincinnati, OH 45221-0040

Application Filing		Accreditation
Fall: April 1		ABA, AALS
Spring: n/app		**Degrees Granted**
Fee: $35		J.D.

Enrollment 2001–2002			First-Year Class	
Men:	165	45%	Applied:	1124
Women:	201	55%	Accepted:	404
Minorities:	66	18%	Enrolled:	97
Out-of-State:	128	35%		

2001–02 Class Profile

LSAT Percentile: n/av
LSAT Median Score: 160
Percentage passing bar on first try: 92%

Tuition and Fees:

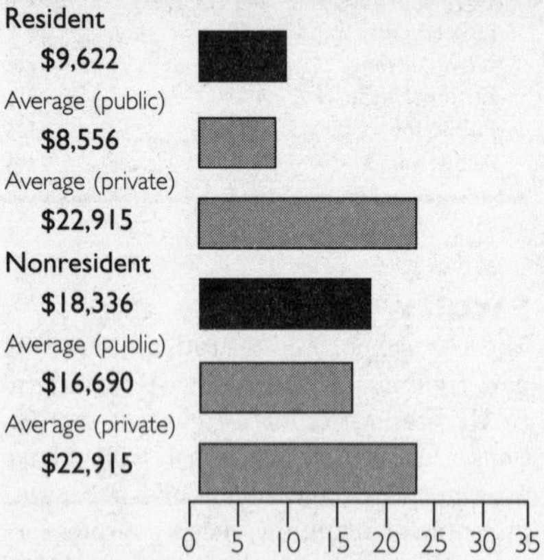

Percentage receiving financial aid: 70%

ADMISSIONS

In the fall 2001 first-year class, 1124 applied, 404 were accepted, and 97 enrolled. Fifteen transfers enrolled. The median GPA of the most recent first-year class was 3.44. The lowest LSAT percentile accepted was 147; the highest was 173.

Requirements

Applicants must have a bachelor's degree and take the LSAT. The most important admission factors include GPA, LSAT results, and academic achievement. No specific undergraduate courses are required. Candidates are not interviewed.

Procedure

The application deadline for fall entry is April 1. Applicants should submit an application form, LSAT results, transcripts, TOEFL for international applicants, and WES transcript analysis, a nonrefundable application fee of $35, and 2 letters of recommendation (through LSAC). Notification of the admissions decision is on a rolling basis. The latest acceptable LSAT test date for fall entry is February. The law school uses the LSDAS.

Special

The law school recruits minority and disadvantaged students by giving special consideration to competitive applications for admission by candidates from minority groups under-represented in the legal profession. Particular effort is made to provide adequate financial assistance to minority students. Requirements are not different for out-of-state students. Transfer students must have one year of credit, have attended an ABA-approved law school, supply their class rank, give the reason(s) for the transfer, and generally be in the top 20% of the class.

Costs

Tuition and fees for the 2001-2002 academic year are $9622 for full-time in-state students and $18,336 for out-of-state students. On-campus room and board costs about $6648 annually; books and supplies run $771.

Financial Aid

About 70% of current law students receive some form of aid. Awards are based on need and merit. The required financial statements are the FAFSA and the scholarship application. The aid application deadline for fall entry is March 1. First-year students are notified about their financial aid application within 2 weeks of acceptance.

About the Law School

University of Cincinnati College of Law was established in 1833 and is a public institution. The campus is in an urban area in the Clifton area of Cincinnati. The primary mission of the law school is to provide students with an opportunity to equip themselves for effective and creative participation in the roles lawyers play in society. Students have access to federal, state, county, city, and local agencies, courts, correctional facilities, law firms, and legal aid organizations in the Cincinnati area. Students also have access to a variety of legal externships in Cincinnati coordinated through the Office of Public Service and Professional Development. Facilities of special interest to law students are the U.S. Court of Appeals for the Sixth Circuit and the District Court for the Southern District of Ohio; the 3000-plus members of the Cincinnati Bar Association; the more than 300 law firms; and the Legal Aid Society of Cincinnati. Housing for students is plentiful, and most law students live off campus in housing within walking distance of campus. The average rent is $375 to $425 a month. All law school facilities are accessible to the physically disabled.

Calendar

The law school operates on a traditional semester basis. Courses for full-time students are offered days only. There is no part-time program. New students are admitted in the fall. There is no summer session. Transferable summer courses are offered.

Programs

Students may take relevant courses in other programs and apply credit toward the J.D.; a maximum of 8 credits may be applied. The following joint degrees may be earned: J.D./M.A. (Juris Doctor/Master of Arts in women's studies), J.D./M.B.A. (Juris Doctor/Master of Business Administration), and J.D./M.C.P. (Juris Doctor/Master of Community Planning).

Phone: 513-556-6805
E-mail: *admissions@law.uc.edu*
Web: *www.law.uc.edu*

Contact

Al Watson, Assistant Dean and Director of Admission, 513-556-6805 for general inquiries; and financial aid information.

Required

To earn the J.D., candidates must complete 90 total credits, of which 35 are for required courses. They must maintain a minimum GPA of 2.0 in the required courses. The following first-year courses are required of all students: Introduction to Law, Civil Procedure I and II, Constitutional Law I and II, Contracts, Legal Research and Writing, Torts, Advocacy, Criminal Law, and Property. Required upper-level courses consist of Professional Responsibility and 2 writing requirements. The required orientation program for first-year students lasts 1 week and includes the Introduction to Law course, registration, a photo identification session, a tour of the facilities, assignment of faculty and student advisers, a meeting with student advisers, a social event with upper-level students, information about the law library, and bar association membership opportunities.

Electives

The College of Law offers concentrations in corporate law, environmental law, international law, litigation, tax law, intellectual property, and international human rights. In addition, seminar topics can include corporate law, constitutional law, and banking. An externship program is offered to 50 or 60 students and is worth 3 credit hours. Speakers can be heard at the Human Rights Institute, which invites international human rights scholars, the Center for Corporate Law, the Center for Mental Health Law, and the Health Care Law symposium. Study abroad may be done at any ABA/AALS-approved program with special permission. A maximum of 8 credit hours from outside the law school can be applied toward the J.D. An academic support program is also available. Minority programs include the Minority Access Program and a summer clerkship program with federal judges, local corporations, and law firms. The most widely taken electives are Corporations and Evidence.

Graduation Requirements

In order to graduate, candidates must have a GPA of 2.0, have completed the upper-division writing requirement, and have completed the Professional Responsibility course.

Organizations

Students edit the *University of Cincinnati Law Review, Immigration and Nationality Law Review*, and *Human Rights Quarterly*. Students compete at the Jessup International Law Moot Court, the J. Braxton Craven, Jr. Memorial Moot Court, and the Giles Sutherland Rich Moot Court in patent law. Also, the College of Law hosts the National Product Liability Competition and participates in all other national competitions. Law student organizations include the ABA-Law Student Division, International Law Society, and Intellectual Property Society. There are local chapters of Order of the Barristers and Order of the Coif.

Library

The law library contains 394,852 hard-copy volumes and 783,306 microform volume equivalents, and subscribes to 2320 serial publications. Such on-line databases and networks as CALI, CIS Universe, LEXIS, NEXIS, OCLC First Search, and WESTLAW are available to law students for research. Special library collections include the Urban Morgan Human Rights Collection; the Segoe Collection on Land Use and Urban Planning; the Goldstein Collection on the Law of Church and State; manuscript collections: papers of William J. Butler, trustee and benefactor of the Urban Morgan Institute for Human Rights; papers of Nationiel R. James of the U.S. Court of Appeals for the Sixth Circuit; records of the 1987 Merit Plan constitutional amendment campaign regarding judicial selection in Ohio; and the U.S. federal government depository since 1978. Recently, the library participated in Ohio Link, a statewide resource-sharing network comprising more than 75 other academic libraries; created a College of Law Intranet *http://intranet.law.uc.edu*; and implemented wireless access to the law school's LAN. The ratio of library volumes to faculty is 16,452 to 1 and to students, 1079 to 1. The ratio of seats in the library to students is 1 to 1.

Placement

J.D.s awarded:	128
Services available through: a separate law school placement center	
Special features: focused career planning and career counseling sessions, an extensive library on career issues including nonlegal and specialty practice, a federal job options program, and a local government/public interest career fair.	
Full-time job interviews:	30 employers
Summer job interviews:	45 employers
Placement by graduation:	60% of class
Placement within 9 months:	94% of class
Average starting salary:	$24,500 to $140,000
Areas of placement:	
Private practice 2-10 attorneys	12%
Private practice 11-25 attorneys	9%
Private practice 26-50 attorneys	6%
Private practice 51-100 attorneys	5%
Private practice 101+ attorneys	23%
Prosecutor/Public Defender	13%
Judicial clerkships	10%
Business/industry	10%
Public interest	4%
Government	4%
Academic	4%

Faculty

The law school has 24 full-time faculty members, of whom 10 are women. According to AAUP standards for Category I institutions, faculty salaries are average. About 38% of full-time faculty have a graduate law degree in addition to the J.D. The ratio of full-time students to full-time faculty in an average class is 13 to 1. The law school has a regular program of bringing visiting professors and other distinguished lecturers and visitors to campus. There is a chapter of the Order of the Coif.

Students

About 55% of the student body are women; 18%, minorities; 9%, African American; 4%, Asian American; 4%, Hispanic; and .3%, Native American. The majority of students come from Ohio (65%). The average age of entering students is 24; age range is 20 to 50. About 45% of students enter directly from undergraduate school, 10% have a graduate degree, and 55% have worked full-time prior to entering law school. About 1% drop out after the first year for academic or personal reasons; 96% remain to receive a law degree.

UNIVERSITY OF COLORADO

School of Law

Campus Box 403
Boulder, CO 80309-0403

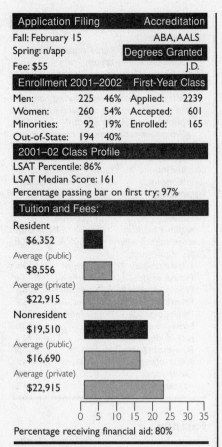

Application Filing		Accreditation
Fall: February 15		ABA, AALS
Spring: n/app		**Degrees Granted**
Fee: $55		J.D.

Enrollment 2001–2002			First-Year Class	
Men:	225	46%	Applied:	2239
Women:	260	54%	Accepted:	601
Minorities:	92	19%	Enrolled:	165
Out-of-State:	194	40%		

2001–02 Class Profile

LSAT Percentile: 86%
LSAT Median Score: 161
Percentage passing bar on first try: 97%

Tuition and Fees:

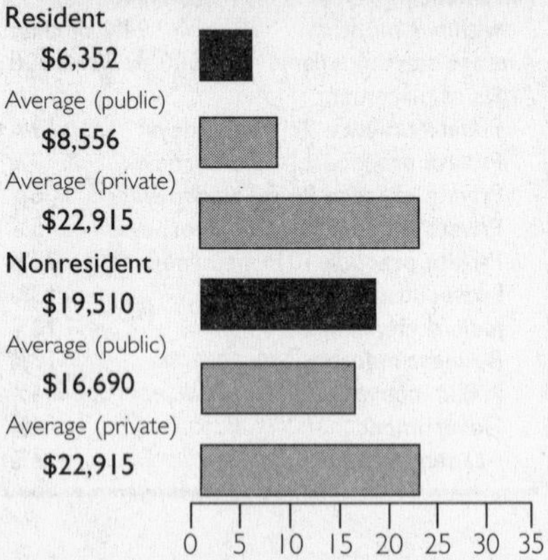

Percentage receiving financial aid: 80%

ADMISSIONS

In the fall 2001 first-year class, 2239 applied, 601 were accepted, and 165 enrolled. Four transfers enrolled. The median LSAT percentile of the most recent first-year class was 86; the median GPA was 3.55 on a scale of 4.0.

Requirements

Applicants must have a bachelor's degree and take the LSAT. No specific undergraduate courses are required. Candidates are not interviewed.

Procedure

The application deadline for fall entry is February 15. Applicants should submit an application form, LSAT results, transcripts, a nonrefundable application fee of $55, 1 letter of recommendation, and a personal statement. Notification of the admissions decision is mid-January through May. The latest acceptable LSAT test date for fall entry is December. The law school uses the LSDAS.

Special

The law school recruits minority and disadvantaged students by means of law school forums, candidate referral services through LSAS, and special outreach by the Associate Dean for Student Affairs/Professional Programs. Requirements are not different for out-of-state students. Transfer students must have one year of credit and have attended an ABA-approved law school, and it is recommended that students be in the top 10% to 20% of their current law school class.

Costs

Tuition and fees for the 2001-2002 academic year are $6352 for full-time in-state students and $19,510 for out-of-state students. On-campus room and board costs about $7776 annually; books and supplies run $1100.

Financial Aid

About 80% of current law students receive some form of aid. The average annual amount of aid from all sources combined, including scholarships, loans, and work contracts, is $18,943 (resident); maximum, $31,753 (nonresident). Awards are based on need and merit, loans are based on need. Scholarships are usually based on a combination of need and merit. Required financial statements are the FAFSA and tax returns. The aid application deadline for fall entry is March 1. First-year students are notified about their financial aid application at the time of the initial inquiry; information on financial aid is included in the catalog. Admitted students are encouraged to apply for financial aid as early as possible.

About the Law School

University of Colorado School of Law was established in 1892 and is a public institution. The 873-acre campus is in a small town 30 miles northwest of Denver. The primary mission of the law school is to develop the skills, ethics, and habits of mind to be an excellent lawyer with a strong sense of the legal profession's greatest traditions and to develop an equal dedication to public service. Students have access to federal, state, county, city, and local agencies, courts, correctional facilities, law firms, and legal aid organizations in the Boulder area. Facilities of special interest to law students include the law school facility, which contains all aspects of academic, administrative, clinical, research, career services, social, and audiovisual offerings under one roof. Housing for students is primarily in apartments within 10 minutes of the law school. Less expensive accommodations are available in nearby towns. About 95% of the law school facilities are accessible to the physically disabled.

Calendar

The law school operates on a traditional semester basis. Courses for full-time students are offered days only and must be completed within 5 years. There is no part-time program. New students are admitted in the fall. There are 3- and 5-week summer sessions. Transferable summer courses are offered.

Programs

Students may take relevant courses in other programs and apply credit toward the J.D.; the maximum number of credits that may be applied varies. The following joint degrees may be earned: J.D./M.B.A. (Juris Doctor/Master of Business Administration), J.D./M.I.A. (Juris Doctor/Master of International Affairs), and J.D./M.P.A. (Juris Doctor/Master of Public Administration).

Phone: 303-492-7203
Web: *www.colorado.edu/law*

Contact
Carol Nelson-Douglas, Assistant Dean for Admissions and Financial Aid, Admissions Office, 303-492-7203 for general inquiries and financial aid information.

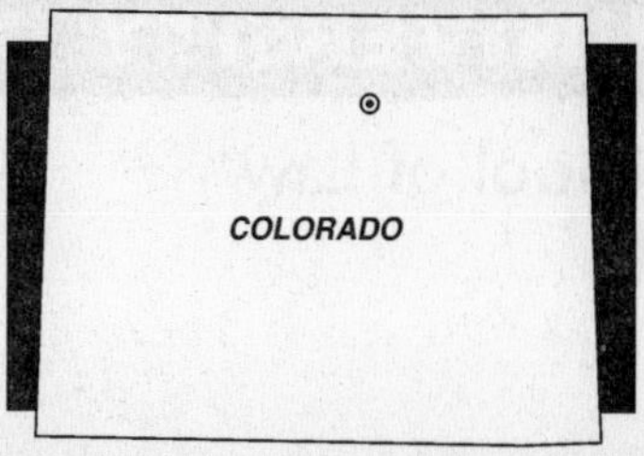

Required

To earn the J.D., candidates must complete 89 total credits, of which 43 are for required courses. They must maintain a minimum grade average of 60 in the required courses. The following first-year courses are required of all students: Contracts I and II, Torts, Civil Procedure I and II, Property I and II, Criminal Law, Legal Writing, and Appellate Court Advocacy. Required upper-level courses consist of Constitutional Law, Evidence, Professional Responsibility, and a seminar and practice requirement. All students must take clinical courses. The required orientation program for first-year students is 4 days and includes class registration, legal writing exercises, social activities, and an introduction to faculty, law school, and university facilities.

Electives

The School of Law offers concentrations in corporate law, criminal law, environmental law, family law, international law, juvenile law, labor law, litigation, media law, securities law, tax law, torts and insurance, and natural resources. In addition, clinics are available for either a year or 1 semester and a maximum of 11 credits may be awarded. Clinics include the Indian Law, Appellate Advocacy, Entrepreneurial Law, Natural Resource Litigation, and Legal Aid (civil and criminal practice). A minimum of 1 seminar must be chosen from a variety of subjects. Externships allow students to earn up to 4 hours of academic credit for work in a governmental agency, private nonprofit institution or a private law office. Independent study is permitted for 1 credit. Field work is offered through some seminars, externships, and clinics. Special no-credit lectures are offered to all students on a variety of topics. There is one tutor per each first-year class section. Students on academic probation are furnished with tutors. The most widely taken electives are Natural Resources and Environmental Law, Corporate Law, and Telecommunication/Intellectual Property.

Graduation Requirements

In order to graduate, candidates must have a minimum grade average of 72, complete the upper-division writing requirement, and submit a paper of publishable quality for the required seminar.

Organizations
Students edit the *University of Colorado Law Review, Colorado Journal of International Environmental Law and Policy*, the *Independent Legal Research: Journal on Telecommunications and High Technology Law* and the newspaper, *Class Action*. The most successful teams in the Rothgerber Moot Court Competition participate in the National Moot Court Competition. The school also competes in the Jessup Moot Court, held each year regionally, nationally, and internationally, and the Carrigan Cup Competition, an internal competition in which participants are selected for regional competitions leading to the national mock trial competition sponsored by the ABA. Other competitions deal with environmental law, Indian law, and trademark law. The Student Bar Association is an umbrella group for many student organizations. There are local chapters of Phi Alpha Delta—Julius Gunther Chapter, ABA, and ACLU.

Library
The law library contains 383,000 hard-copy volumes and 725,704 microform volume equivalents, and subscribes to 970 serial publications. Such on-line databases and networks as CALI, DIALOG, LEXIS, and WESTLAW are available to law students for research. Special library collections include a federal publications depository and strengths in environmental and Native American Law and Constitutional Law. Recently, the library installed a wireless LAN that allows students to check out laptops, or use their own, to access the Internet via a radio frequency. The ratio of library volumes to faculty is 9575 to 1 and to students, 790 to 1. The ratio of seats in the library to students is 1 to 1.

Faculty
The law school has 40 full-time and 30 part-time faculty members, of whom 23 are women. According to AAUP standards for Category I institutions, faculty salaries are average. About 2% of full-time faculty have a graduate law degree in addition to the J.D.; about 4% of part-time faculty have one. The ratio of full-time students to full-time faculty in an average class is 14 to 1; in a clinic, 12 to 1. The law school has a regular program of bringing visiting professors and other distinguished lecturers and visitors to campus. There is a chapter of the Order of the Coif; 39 faculty and 573 graduates are members.

Placement

J.D.s awarded:	156
Services available through: a separate law school placement center	
Services: group information in addition to individual advising; access to computer career search resources; written documents providing job search information	
Special features: an on-campus interview program, lunch-time informational sessions on job-seeking skills and various types of employment (traditional and nontraditional), Internet access to job postings, career workshops for law school graduates, a mock interview program, annual legal career options day program, and government/public interest career fair.	
Full-time job interviews:	30 employers
Summer job interviews:	67 employers
Placement by graduation:	60% of class
Placement within 9 months:	97% of class
Average starting salary:	$27,000 to $125,000
Areas of placement:	
Private practice 2-10 attorneys	17%
Private practice 11-25 attorneys	5%
Private practice 26-50 attorneys	4%
Private practice 51-100 attorneys	18%
Private practice 100 + attorneys	13%
Judicial clerkships	19%
Government	9%
Business/industry	9%
Public interest	5%
Military	1%
Academic	1%

Students
About 54% of the student body are women; 19%, minorities; 5%, African American; 4%, Asian American; 7%, Hispanic; and 3%, Native American. The majority of students come from Colorado (60%). The average age of entering students is 26; age range is 21 to 50. About 36% of students enter directly from undergraduate school, 12% have a graduate degree, and 58% have worked full-time prior to entering law school. About 5% drop out after the first year for academic or personal reasons; 90% remain to receive a law degree.

UNIVERSITY OF CONNECTICUT

School of Law

55 Elizabeth Street
Hartford, CT 06105

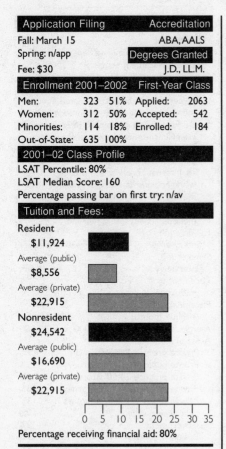

Application Filing		Accreditation
Fall: March 15		ABA, AALS
Spring: n/app		**Degrees Granted**
Fee: $30		J.D., LL.M.

Enrollment 2001–2002			First-Year Class	
Men:	323	51%	Applied:	2063
Women:	312	50%	Accepted:	542
Minorities:	114	18%	Enrolled:	184
Out-of-State:	635	100%		

2001–02 Class Profile

LSAT Percentile: 80%
LSAT Median Score: 160
Percentage passing bar on first try: n/av

Tuition and Fees:

Resident
$11,924
Average (public)
$8,556
Average (private)
$22,915
Nonresident
$24,542
Average (public)
$16,690
Average (private)
$22,915

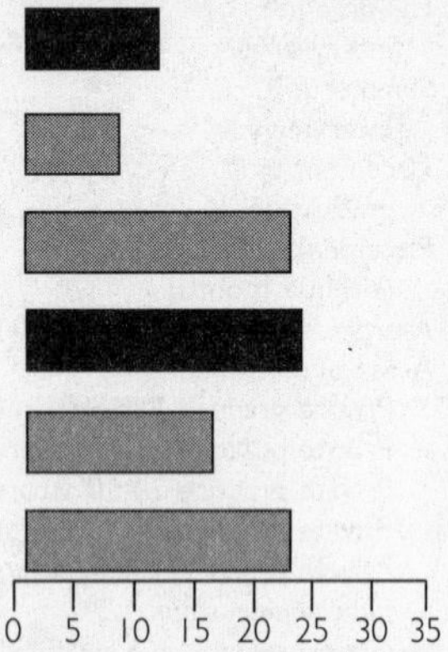

Percentage receiving financial aid: 80%

ADMISSIONS

In the fall 2001 first-year class, 2063 applied, 542 were accepted, and 184 enrolled. The median LSAT percentile of the most recent first-year class was 80; the median GPA was 3.34 on a scale of 4.0.

Requirements

Applicants must have a bachelor's degree and take the LSAT. The most important admission factors include LSAT results, GPA, and writing ability. No specific undergraduate courses are required. Candidates are not interviewed.

Procedure

The application deadline for fall entry is March 15. Applicants should submit an application form, LSAT results, transcripts, a nonrefundable application fee of $30, 2 letters of recommendation, and a personal statement. Notification of the admissions decision is January through May. The latest acceptable LSAT test date for fall entry is February. The law school uses the LSDAS.

Special

The law school recruits minority and disadvantaged students by means of an annual Minority Law Day sponsored by BLSA, ALSA, and LLSA students, and contacts with various minority undergraduate student organizations, centers, and advisers. Requirements are not different for out-of-state students. Transfer students must have one year of credit, have attended an ABA-approved law school, should be within the top 10% of their class, and must show compelling reason(s) for transfer.

Costs

Tuition and fees for the 2001-2002 academic year are $11,924 for full-time in-state students and $24,542 for out-of-state students. Books and supplies run about $1000 annually.

Financial Aid

About 80% of current law students receive some form of aid. The average annual amount of aid from all sources combined, including scholarships, loans, and work contracts, is $12,100; maximum, $36,000. Awards are based on need, but some loans are non-need-based. The required financial statements are the FAFSA and institutional financial aid application. The aid application deadline for fall entry is March 15. Special funds for minority or disadvantaged students consist of several grants that are awarded each year to entering students from economically and educationally disadvantaged backgrounds who demonstrate promise. First-year students are notified about their financial aid application at the time of acceptance.

About the Law School

University of Connecticut School of Law was established in 1921 and is a public institution. The 21-acre campus is in an urban area 100 miles southwest of Boston. The primary mission of the law school is to provide a legal education of high quality, serve the state and the bar, and prepare students to practice law in any jurisdiction. Students have access to federal, state, county, city, and local agencies, courts, correctional facilities, law firms, and legal aid organizations in the Hartford area. Housing for students is ample and affordable in the surrounding areas; there are no on-campus housing facilities.

Calendar

The law school operates on a traditional semester basis. Courses for full-time students are offered both day and evening and days and evenings after the first year and must be completed within 5 years. For part-time students, courses are offered both day and evening and must be completed within 6 years. New full- and part-time students are admitted in the fall. There is a 4½-week summer session. Transferable summer courses are offered.

Programs

In addition to the J.D., the law school offers the LL.M. Students may take relevant courses in other programs and apply credit toward the J.D.; a maximum of 6 credits may be applied. The following joint degrees may be earned: J.D./LL.M. (Juris Doctor/Master of Laws, Insurance Law), J.D./M.A. (Juris Doctor/Master of Public Policy), J.D./M.B.A. (Juris Doctor/Master of Business Administration), J.D./M.L.S. (Juris Doctor/Master of Library Science), J.D./M.P.A. (Juris Doctor/Master of Public Affairs Administration), J.D./M.P.H. (Juris Doctor/Master of Public Health), and J.D./M.S.W. (Juris Doctor/Master of Social Work).

Phone: 860-570-5159
Fax: 860-570-5153
E-mail: *admit@law.uconn.edu*
Web: *www.law.uconn.edu*

Contact

Karen DeMeola, Director of Admissions, 860-570-5159 for general inquiries; Roberta Frick, Director of Financial Aid, 860-570-5147 for financial aid information.

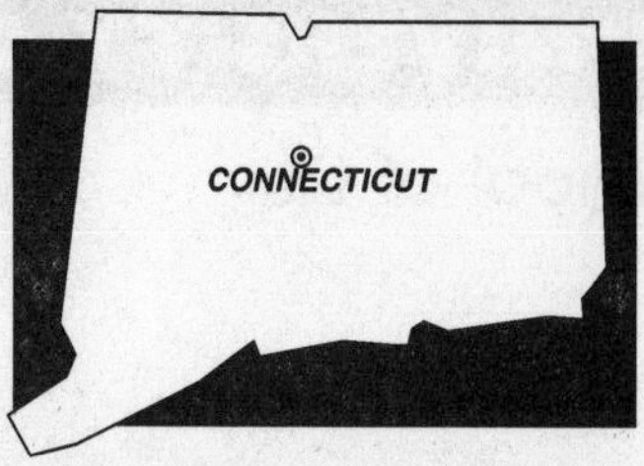

Required

To earn the J.D., candidates must complete 86 total credits, of which 36 are for required courses. They must maintain a minimum GPA of 2.3 in the required courses. The following first-year courses are required of all students: Civil Procedure, Contracts, Criminal Law, Torts, Moot Court, Property, Constitutional Law, Lawyering Process, and Statuatory/Regulatory Class. Required upper-level courses consist of Legal Profession and the upper-class writing requirement. The required orientation program for first-year students is a 1 day event including presentations by the dean, faculty members, financial aid and career services offices, as well as facility tours.

Electives

The School of Law offers concentrations in corporate law, criminal law, environmental law, family law, international law, juvenile law, labor law, litigation, tax law, torts and insurance, and legal theory, intellectual property, information technology law, and property and land use law. In addition, clinics provide hands-on, practical training to upper-level students who earn up to 10 credits for their work; strong and widely recognized Civil Rights and Criminal Law clinics are available. Seminars in a multitude of different substantive areas are available to upper-level students for about 3 credits. Internships, research programs, and field work are available to upper-level students. Research positions are open to upper-level students under the direction of a faculty adviser. Field work is available to upper-level students. Special lecture series include Intellectual Property Teas; Law Review Symposia; and various human rights, international, and insurance law series. Study abroad is open to upper-level students for 1 semester in various countries, including England; the Netherlands; Ireland; France; Germany; or Puerto Rico. Exchange programs in environmental law with the University of Vermont Law School and University of London are also available. Special admission students and students having academic difficulty meet weekly with a faculty or student tutor to review case briefing, writing, legal analysis, and exam techniques. No credit is granted. An Academic Support Program is offered for special admissions students that includes 2 mini-courses designed to introduce case briefing, writing, and legal analysis. In the fall, special admission students meet in small groups with a professor to explore criminal law materials. No credit is granted. Special interest group programs include the Tax Certificate Program and Intellectual Property Certificate Program. The most widely taken electives are Evidence, Intellectual Property, and International Law.

Graduation Requirements

In order to graduate, candidates must have a GPA of 2.3 and have completed the upper-division writing requirement.

Organizations

Students edit the *Connecticut Law Review, Connecticut Journal of International Law, Connecticut Insurance Law Journal, Public Interest Law Journal,* and the newspaper, *Public Forum*. Moot court competitions include the Alva P. Loiselle, William H. Hastie, and Willem Vis International Moot Court. Other competitions include the National Appellate Advocacy Competition, Family Law Competition, Craven Competition, and National Moot Court Competition. A wide range of intellectual, political, social, and special interest organizations and activities are available to students, including the Student Bar Association, Black Law Students Association, and National Italian American Bar Association. Other organizations include Health Law Interest Group, Public Interest Law Group, and Arts, Sports and Entertainment Law Society. Among many others, there are local chapters of the Federalist Society, National Lawyers Guild, and Lambda Law Alliance.

Library

The law library contains 471,556 hard-copy volumes and 976,556 microform volume equivalents, and subscribes to 5994 serial publications. Such on-line databases and networks as DIALOG, LEXIS, WESTLAW, NEXIS, RLN, OCLC, CIS-Masterfile, Innovative Interfaces OPAC, CTLAWNET (on-line catalog), and CD-ROM are available to law students for research. Special library collections include a federal depository, Connecticut materials, an international collection, and an insurance law collection. Recently, the library completed a $23 million law library. The ratio of library volumes to faculty is 9068 to 1 and to students, 743 to 1. The ratio of seats in the library to students is 1 to 1.

Faculty

The law school has 52 full-time and 74 part-time faculty members. According to AAUP standards for Category I institutions, faculty salaries are well above average. About 33% of full-time faculty have a graduate law degree in addition to the J.D. The ratio of full-time students to full-time faculty in an average class is 11 to 1; in a clinic, 8 to 1. The law school has a regular program of bringing visiting professors and other distinguished lecturers and visitors to campus.

Students

About 50% of the student body are women; 18%, minorities; 5%, African American; 5%, Asian American; 5%, Hispanic; and 1%, Native American. The average age of entering students is 25; age range is 21 to 63. About 17% of students have a graduate degree. About 1% drop out after the first year for academic or personal reasons; 95% remain to receive a law degree.

Placement

J.D.s awarded:	175
Services available through: a separate law school placement center	
Services: alumni mentor program, job bulletins, newsletter	
Special features: summer and permanent job resume bank; presentations, workshops, seminars on career-related and job search projects.	
Full-time job interviews:	n/av
Summer job interviews:	n/av
Placement by graduation:	n/av
Placement within 9 months:	95% of class
Average starting salary:	$28,000 to $101,000
Areas of placement:	
Private practice 2 - 100 attorneys	58%
Government	13%
Business/industry	13%
Judicial clerkships	8%
Public interest	4%
Academic	3%
Military	1%

UNIVERSITY OF DAYTON

School of Law

300 College Park
Dayton, OH 45469-2760

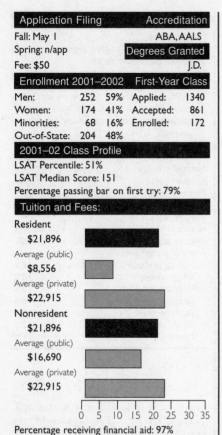

Application Filing	Accreditation
Fall: May 1	ABA, AALS
Spring: n/app	**Degrees Granted**
Fee: $50	J.D.

Enrollment 2001–2002			First-Year Class	
Men:	252	59%	Applied:	1340
Women:	174	41%	Accepted:	861
Minorities:	68	16%	Enrolled:	172
Out-of-State:	204	48%		

2001–02 Class Profile

LSAT Percentile: 51%
LSAT Median Score: 151
Percentage passing bar on first try: 79%

Tuition and Fees:

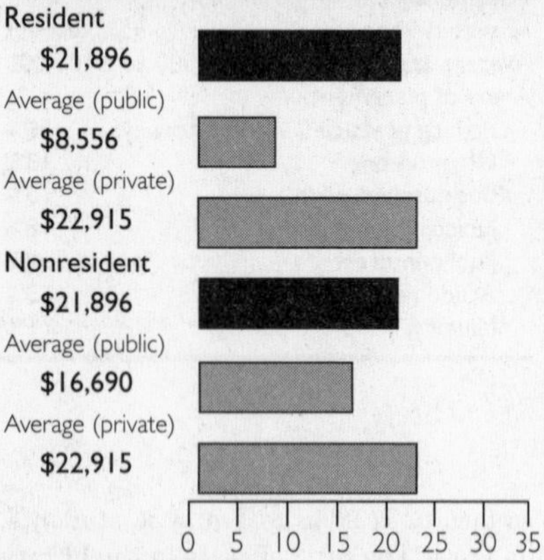

Percentage receiving financial aid: 97%

ADMISSIONS

In the fall 2001 first-year class, 1340 applied, 861 were accepted, and 172 enrolled. Two transfers enrolled. The median LSAT percentile of the most recent first-year class was 51; the median GPA was 3.01 on a scale of 4.0. The lowest LSAT percentile accepted was 7; the highest was 99.

Requirements

Applicants must have a bachelor's degree and take the LSAT. The most important admission factors include writing ability, GPA, and LSAT results. No specific undergraduate courses are required. Candidates are not interviewed.

Procedure

The application deadline for fall entry is May 1. Applicants should submit an application form, LSAT results, transcripts, a nonrefundable application fee of $50 (fee is waived if using UDSL online application), 2 letters of recommendation, and a personal statement. Notification of the admissions decision is usually within 6 to 8 weeks after application completion. The latest acceptable LSAT test date for fall entry is February. The law school uses the LSDAS.

Special

The law school recruits minority and disadvantaged students by means of targeted mailings, recruiting at undergraduate schools, and meeting with targeted student organizations. Requirements are not different for out-of-state students. Transfer students must have one year of credit and have attended an ABA-approved law school. Applications are reviewed on a case-by-case basis, with class rank and the school attended being primary considerations.

Costs

Tuition and fees for the 2001-2002 academic year are $21,896 for all full-time students. On-campus room and board costs about $7900 annually; books and supplies run $900.

Financial Aid

About 97% of current law students receive some form of aid. The average annual amount of aid from all sources combined, including scholarships, loans, and work contracts, is $25,000; maximum, $32,116. Awards are based on need and merit. The required financial statement is the FAFSA. The aid application deadline for fall entry is March 1. Special funds for minority or disadvantaged students include Legal Opportunity Scholarships, used to diversify the class. Loan packages are awarded to first-year students in the summer, scholarships at the time of acceptance.

About the Law School

University of Dayton School of Law was established in 1974 and is a private institution. The 110-acre campus is in an urban area 1 mile south of downtown Dayton. The primary mission of the law school is to enroll a diverse group of women and men who are intellectually curious, who possess self-discipline, and who are well motivated, and to rigorously educate them in the substantive and procedural principles of public and private law. Students have access to federal, state, county, city, and local agencies, courts, correctional facilities, law firms, and legal aid organizations in the Dayton area. Area corporations regularly employ students in their legal departments; some students are interns with the Ohio Supreme Court. Facilities of special interest to law students include the School of Law and University cafeterias, recreation areas, computer laboratories, child care, health services, and more than 100 university-owned apartments within 2 blocks of the School of Law. Housing for students is convenient and readily available both on campus and off campus. University and private housing is within 5 to 15 minutes from the School of Law. All law school facilities are accessible to the physically disabled.

Calendar

The law school operates on a traditional semester basis. Courses for full-time students are offered both day and evening and must be completed within 3 years. There is no part-time program. New students are admitted in the fall. There is a 6-week summer session. Transferable summer courses are offered.

Programs

Students may take relevant courses in other programs and apply credit toward the J.D.; a maximum of 6 credits may be applied. The following joint degree may be earned: J.D./M.B.A. (Juris Doctor/Master of Business Administration).

Phone: 937-229-3555
Fax: 937-229-4194
E-mail: *lawinfo@udayton.edu*
Web: *www.law.udayton.edu*

Contact

Admissions Office, 937-229-3555 for general inquiries; Janet L. Hein, Assistant Dean, Director of Admissions and Financial Aid, 937-229-3555 for financial aid information.

Required
To earn the J.D., candidates must complete 87 total credits, of which 36 are for required courses. They must maintain a minimum GPA of 2.0 in the required courses. The following first-year courses are required of all students: Constitutional Law I, Contracts I and II, Legal Profession I and II, Legislation, Property, and Torts I and II. Required upper-level courses consist of Constitutional Law II, Legal Profession III, and Professional Responsibility. The required orientation program for first-year students is a 3-day program primarily aimed at introducing students to the structure of their course of studies, to administrative matters such as registration and notebook computer set-up, and to provide them with an opportunity to gather in social settings to establish relationships with fellow students, faculty, and staff.

Electives
The School of Law offers concentrations in corporate law, criminal law, litigation, tax law, intellectual property, patent law, and computer/cyberspace law. In addition, clinics worth 5 credits are available to any third-year student who possesses an intern's license. Seminars are open to any student with upper-level standing. Topics include poverty law, product liability, health care law, complex litigation, cyberspace law, and e-commerce law. An internship in the area of patent law is open to upper-level students who have taken a patent law course. Research programs may be undertaken with individual law faculty members. Second- and third-year law students are able to act as law clerks to area judges for 3 credits. Special lecture series include the Law and Technology Symposium and the Law and Technology Scholar-in-Residence. The voluntary Academic Excellence Program is designed to assist first-year students from educationally or economically disadvantaged backgrounds and is conducted by law faculty and upper-level teaching assistants for no credit. A summer clerkship program, in conjunction with the Dayton Bar Association, is intended to provide legal employment for some minority students. The Thurgood Marshall Society provides mentors for minority students. The most widely taken electives are Evidence, Tax, Corporations, Criminal Law, and Criminal Procedure.

Graduation Requirements
In order to graduate, candidates must have a GPA of 2.0 and have completed the upper-division writing requirement.

Organizations

Students edit the *University of Dayton Law Review* and the student newspaper, *Equitable Relief*. Students typically participate in moot court competitions including tax, criminal, patent, and international law. The School of Law also hosts the Carl A. Stickel National Cybercrimes Moot Court competition. There is also a mock trial competition. Law student organizations include the Student Bar Association, Cyberspace Law Association, and the Women's Caucus. There are local chapters of Phi Alpha Delta, Delta Theta Phi, and Phi Delta Phi. Other law student organizations include Public Interest Law Organization, the Thomas More Society, and Black Law Students Association.

Library

The law library contains 283,994 hard-copy volumes and 700,794 microform volume equivalents, and subscribes to 4590 serial publications. Such on-line databases and networks as CALI, CIS Universe, DIALOG, LEXIS, LOIS, NEXIS, WESTLAW, and Ohio LINK are available to law students for research. Recently, the library opened the Zimmerman Law Library, which offers data and power outlets at each seat; students are able to access the Law School Network and online research services from 500 different locations within the library. The ratio of library volumes to faculty is 10,143 to 1 and to students, 667 to 1. The ratio of seats in the library to students is 1 to 1.

Faculty

The law school has 28 full-time and 32 part-time faculty members, of whom 17 are women. According to AAUP standards for Category IIA institutions, faculty salaries are well above average. About 43% of full-time faculty have a graduate law degree in addition to the J.D.; about 16% of part-time faculty have one. The ratio of full-time students to full-time faculty in an average class is 15 to 1; in a clinic, 8 to 1. The law school has a regular program of bringing visiting professors and other distinguished lecturers and visitors to campus.

Placement	
J.D.s awarded:	151
Services available through: a separate law school placement center	
Full-time job interviews:	25 employers
Summer job interviews:	26 employers
Placement by graduation:	n/av
Placement within 9 months:	92% of class
Average starting salary:	$23,000 to $115,000
Areas of placement:	
Private practice 2-10 attorneys	25%
Private practice 11-25 attorneys	8%
Private practice 26-50 attorneys	7%
Private practice 51-100 attorneys	4%
Private practice 101+ attorneys	7%
Private practice solo	1%
Business/industry	20%
Government	14%
Judicial clerkships	7%
Academic	4%
Military	2%
Public interest	1%

Students

About 41% of the student body are women; 16%, minorities; 7%, African American; 3%, Asian American; 5%, Hispanic; and 1%, Native American. The majority of students come from the Midwest (67%). The average age of entering students is 25; age range is 21 to 52. About 49% of students enter directly from undergraduate school, 6% have a graduate degree, and 51% have worked full-time prior to entering law school. About 6% drop out after the first year for academic or personal reasons; 94% remain to receive a law degree.

UNIVERSITY OF DENVER

College of Law

7039 E. 18th Avenue
Denver, CO 80220

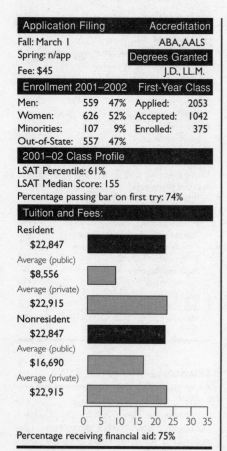

Application Filing		Accreditation
Fall: March 1		ABA, AALS
Spring: n/app		**Degrees Granted**
Fee: $45		J.D., LL.M.

Enrollment 2001–2002			First-Year Class	
Men:	559	47%	Applied:	2053
Women:	626	52%	Accepted:	1042
Minorities:	107	9%	Enrolled:	375
Out-of-State:	557	47%		

2001–02 Class Profile

LSAT Percentile: 61%
LSAT Median Score: 155
Percentage passing bar on first try: 74%

Tuition and Fees:

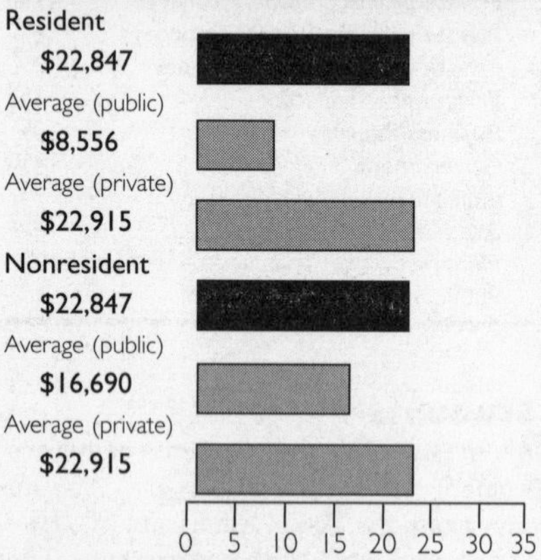

Percentage receiving financial aid: 75%

ADMISSIONS

In the fall 2001 first-year class, 2053 applied, 1042 were accepted, and 375 enrolled. Thirty transfers enrolled. The median LSAT percentile of the most recent first-year class was 61; the median GPA was 3.1 on a scale of 4.0. The lowest LSAT percentile accepted was 33; the highest was 98.

Requirements

Applicants must have a bachelor's degree and take the LSAT. The most important admission factors include LSAT results and GPA. No specific undergraduate courses are required. Candidates are not interviewed.

Procedure

There is no application deadline, but March 1 is suggested. Applicants should submit an application form, a nonrefundable application fee of $45, 2 letters of recommendation, a personal statement, and a resume. Notification of the admissions decision is on a rolling basis. The latest acceptable LSAT test date for fall entry is February. The law school uses the LSDAS.

Special

The law school recruits minority and disadvantaged students by means of special scholarships and the intervention and support of the Assistant Dean of Student Affairs' office. Requirements are not different for out-of-state students. Transfer students must have one year of credit and have attended an ABA-approved law school.

Costs

Tuition and fees (including a technology fee) for the 2001-2002 academic year are $22,847 for all full-time students. Tuition for part-time students is $14,740 per year. Books and supplies run about $900 annually.

Financial Aid

About 75% of current law students receive some form of aid. The average annual amount of aid from all sources combined, including scholarships, loans, and work contracts, is $20,000; maximum, $36,580. Awards are based on need and merit, along with Award letters offer aid (scholarships, loans, workstudy) up to cost of attendance. The required financial statement is the FAFSA. The aid application deadline for fall entry is February 15. First-year students are notified about their financial aid application shortly after receipt of the admissions application.

About the Law School

University of Denver College of Law was established in 1892 and is a private institution. The 33-acre campus is in an urban area 10 minutes from downtown Denver. The primary mission of the law school is to support and foster significant legal research while being actively involved in the profession and in the society it serves. Students have access to federal, state, county, city, and local agencies, courts, correctional facilities, law firms, and legal aid organizations in the Denver area. Facilities of special interest to law students include the Lowell Thomas Law Building, which houses the law library, classrooms and auditorium, faculty offices, and courtrooms. Adjoining buildings provide space for administration, student examination, dining facilities, student residences, and apartments. Housing for students is on campus and consists of apartments and dormitories. About 85% of the law school facilities are accessible to the physically disabled.

Calendar

The law school operates on a traditional semester basis. Courses for full-time students are offered days only and must be completed within 4 years. For part-time students, courses are offered evenings only and must be completed within 5 years. New full- and part-time students are admitted in the fall. There is an 11-week summer session. Transferable summer courses are offered.

Programs

In addition to the J.D., the law school offers the LL.M. Students may take relevant courses in other programs and apply credit toward the J.D.; a maximum of 10 credits may be applied. The following joint degrees may be earned: J.D./G.S.I.S. (Juris Doctor/Graduate School International Studies), J.D./M.A. (Juris Doctor/Master of Arts in geography and judicial administration), J.D./M.B.A. (Juris Doctor/Master of Business Administration), J.D./M.I.M. (Juris Doctor/Master of International Management), J.D./M.T. (Juris Doctor/Master in Taxation), and J.D./MSLA (Juris Doctor/ Master of Legal Administration).

Phone: 303-871-6135
Fax: 303-871-6100
E-mail: *khigganb@law.du.edu*
Web: *www.law.du.edu*

Contact

Karen Higganbotham, Associate Director of Admissions, 303-871-6135 for general inquiries; Iain Davis, 303-871-6136 for financial aid information.

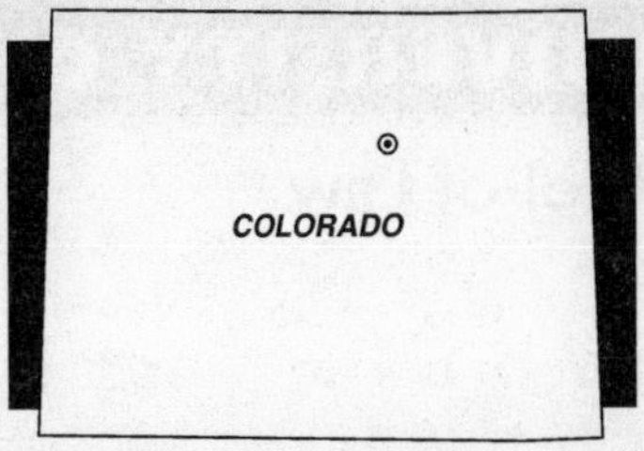

Required

To earn the J.D., candidates must complete 90 total credits, of which 44 are for required courses. They must maintain a minimum GPA of 2.0 in the required courses. The following first-year courses are required of all students: Contracts, Torts, Civil Procedure, Criminal Law, Property, Lawyering Process, and a perspective elective. Required upper-level courses consist of Constitutional Law, Evidence, Administrative Law, and Legal Profession and Legal Writing. The required orientation program for first-year students orients students to law school programs, facilities, organizations, and procedures and is 3 days long.

Electives

The College of Law offers concentrations in corporate law, criminal law, environmental law, international law, litigation, tax law, and business and commercial law, natural resources, advocacy skills, transportation law, and public interest law. In addition, upper-level students receive 5 credit hours for a clinic. Clinic topics include public interest, civil, criminal, human rights, and mediation/arbitration. Seminars, offered to upper-level students, are worth 2 to 3 credit hours. Seminar topics include Criminal Justice, Advertising Regulations, and Appellate Advocacy. Internships, open to upper-level students for 3 credits, are available in the offices of prosecutors; public defenders; the attorney general; and judicial, legislative, corporate, immigration, and natural resources agencies. Directed research may be undertaken under a professor's supervision. Research positions are open only to upper-level students for 2 to 3 credits. Externships are equal to 10 credits and are available to upper-level students. A study-abroad option is available. The no-credit Academic Achievement Program is a tutorial program offered to first-year students. The most widely taken electives are Basic Tax, Corporations, and Trusts and Estates.

Graduation Requirements

In order to graduate, candidates must have a GPA of 2.0.

Organizations

Students edit the *University of Denver Law Journal, Water Court Reporter, Transportation Law Journal, Denver Journal of International Law and Policy*, and the newspaper, *Student Writ*. Moot court competitions running through the school year include the Negotiations Competition, Jessup International Law Competition, and Hoffman Cup Trial Competition. Among the student organizations are Christian Legal Society, Colorado Council of Mediators Organization, and Entertainment Law Society. Chapters of national associations include the Delta Theta Phi, Phi Alpha Delta, and Phi Delta Phi.

Library

The law library contains 274,284 hard-copy volumes and 48,685 microform volume equivalents, and subscribes to 3100 serial publications. Such on-line databases and networks as DIALOG, LEXIS, NEXIS, and WESTLAW are available to law students for research. Special library collections include a government document selective depository and the Hughes Rare Book Room. Recently, the library upgraded computer equipment and rearranged seating to maximize outside lighting. The ratio of library volumes to faculty is 5598 to 1 and to students is 231 to 1. The ratio of seats in the library to students is 1 to 1.

Faculty

The law school has 49 full-time and 66 part-time faculty members, of whom 28 are women. According to AAUP standards for Category I institutions, faculty salaries are below average. About 25% of full-time faculty have a graduate law degree in addition to the J.D.; about 5% of part-time faculty have one. The ratio of full-time students to full-time faculty in an average class is 14 to 1; in a clinic, 8 to 1. The law school has a regular program of bringing visiting professors and other distinguished lecturers and visitors to campus.

Placement	
J.D.s awarded:	298
Services available through: a separate law school placement center	
Services: self-assessment	
Special features: out-of-town alumni networks, DU alumni links, mentors, and individualized networking strategies.	
Full-time job interviews:	43 employers
Summer job interviews:	n/av
Placement by graduation:	84% of class
Placement within 9 months:	93% of class
Average starting salary:	$20,000 to $125,000
Areas of placement:	
Private practice 2-10 attorneys	17%
Private practice 11-25 attorneys	5%
Private practice 26-50 attorneys	3%
Private practice 51-100 attorneys	2%
Private practice 101+ attorneys; 6% unknown	14%
Business/industry	30%
Government	12%
Judicial clerkships	6%
Unknown	6%
Public interest	3%
Military	2%

Students

About 52% of the student body are women; 9%, minorities; 1%, African American; 2%, Asian American; 4%, Hispanic; and 1%, Native American. Most students come from Colorado (53%). The average age of entering students is 25; age range is 18 to 58. About 25% of students enter directly from undergraduate school, 15% have a graduate degree, and 40% have worked full-time prior to entering law school. About 4% drop out after the first year for academic or personal reasons; 95% remain to receive a law degree.

School of Law

651 East Jefferson Avenue
Detroit, MI 48226

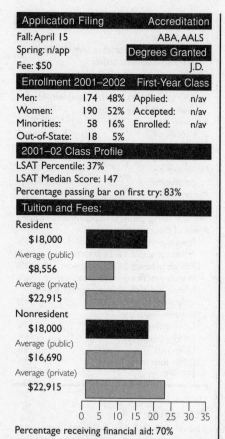

Application Filing	Accreditation
Fall: April 15	ABA, AALS
Spring: n/app	**Degrees Granted**
Fee: $50	J.D.

Enrollment 2001–2002			First-Year Class	
Men:	174	48%	Applied:	n/av
Women:	190	52%	Accepted:	n/av
Minorities:	58	16%	Enrolled:	n/av
Out-of-State:	18	5%		

2001–02 Class Profile

LSAT Percentile: 37%
LSAT Median Score: 147
Percentage passing bar on first try: 83%

Tuition and Fees:

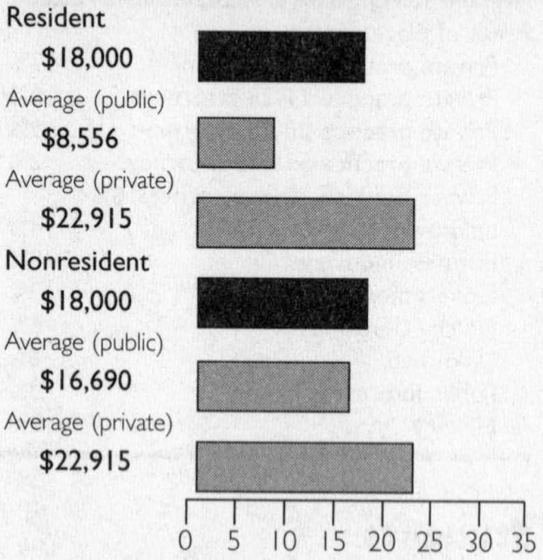

Percentage receiving financial aid: 70%

ADMISSIONS

Information in the above capsule is from an earlier year. In a recent first-year class, two transfers enrolled. The median LSAT percentile of a recent first-year class was 37; the median GPA was 3 on a scale of 4.0. The lowest LSAT percentile accepted was 15; the highest was 81.

Requirements

Applicants must have a bachelor's degree and take the LSAT. The most important admission factors include academic achievement, LSAT results, and GPA. No specific undergraduate courses are required. Candidates are not interviewed.

Procedure

Check with the school for current application deadlines and fee. Applicants should submit an application form, LSAT results, transcripts, a nonrefundable application fee, and 2 letters of recommendation. TOEFL may be required in some instances. Notification of the admissions decision is on a rolling basis. The law school uses the LSDAS.

Special

The law school recruits minority and disadvantaged students by attending law fairs at colleges and universities targeted to reach students of color by using the LSAC Candidate Referral Service. Requirements are not different for out-of-state students. Transfer students must have one year of credit, have attended an ABA-approved law school, and be in good standing at his or her current law school. Preadmissions courses consist of an 8-week conditional admission program offered during the summer for minority and disadvantaged students who do not meet current admission standards, but who demonstrate potential for success in law school. Satisfactory demonstration of ability in the program permits admission as a regular student in the fall semester.

Costs

Tuition and fees for the academic year are approximately $18,000 for all full-time students. Tuition for part-time students is $13,000 per year. Books and supplies run about $900.

Financial Aid

About 70% of law students receive some form of aid. The average annual amount of aid from all sources combined, including scholarships, loans, and work contracts, is about $18,500; maximum, $32,500. Scholarships are based on merit; all other aid, except unsubsidized loans, is based on need. Required financial statement is the FAFSA. Check with the school for current deadlines. First-year students are notified about their financial aid application at time of acceptance. Students are asked to apply for financial aid when they apply for admission. Awards are made after the student has been accepted and the file completed.

About the Law School

University of Detroit Mercy School of Law was established in 1912 and is a private institution. The 4-acre campus is in an urban area in downtown Detroit. The primary mission of the law school is to provide a rigorous, value-oriented education in the Jesuit tradition. Students have access to federal, state, county, city, and local agencies, courts, correctional facilities, law firms, and legal aid organizations in the Detroit area. The career services office provides a wide array of resources to enable students to obtain short-and long-term positions in these areas. A full range of extracurricular activities and organizations like the St. Thomas More Society, the Student Bar Association, the Black Law Student's Association, and Phi Alpha Delta offer the chance to exercise leadership skills and perform community service. There is a large quantity of apartments and housing within walking distance of the law school. For students who do not mind a short commute, there are many residential suburbs from which to choose. The School of Law assists students with housing needs. All law school facilities are accessible to the physically disabled.

Calendar

The law school operates on a traditional semester basis. Courses for full-time students are offered both day and evening and must be completed within 3 years. For part-time students, courses are offered both day and evening and must be completed within 5 years. New full- and part-time students are admitted in the fall. There is a 7-week summer session. Transferable summer courses are offered.

Programs

The following joint degrees may be earned: J.D./M.B.A. (Juris Doctor/Master of Business Administration).

Required

To earn the J.D., candidates must complete 90 total credits, of which 49 are for required courses. They must maintain a minimum GPA of 2.0 in the required courses. The following first-year courses are required of all students: Contracts, Civil Procedure, Property, Torts, and Applied Legal Theory and Analysis. Required upper-level courses consist of Tax A, Criminal Law I and II, Constitutional Law I, Evidence, Professional Responsibility, and a seminar course. The required orientation program for first-year students is a 3-day session that includes presentations by faculty and administrators, alumni panel discussions, and an overview of the first-year curriculum.

Phone: 313-596-0264
Fax: 313-596-0280
E-mail: *udmlawao@udmercy.edu*
Web: *www.law.udmercy.edu*

Contact

Kathleen H. Caprio, Assistant Dean, Admissions and Student Affairs, 313-596-0264 for general inquiries; Denise Daniel, Financial Aid Coordinator, 313-596-0214 for financial aid information.

Electives

The School of Law offers concentrations in corporate law, criminal law, entertainment law, environmental law, family law, international law, labor law, litigation, tax law, torts and insurance, health law, constitutional law, and intellectual property law. The Urban Law Clinic (clinical intern program) is available to upper-level students who have successfully completed at least 30 credits; Criminal Procedure and Evidence courses are prerequisites for eligibility for 1 of the 12 slots each semester for the 4-credit Urban Law Clinic course. Upper-level students who have successfully completed all of their first-year courses and who meet the upper-level course prerequisites for any given seminar may apply for 1 of the 16 slots in any of the 2-credit seminars offered each semester. A variety of 2-credit clinical externships is also available to upper-class students. Students with a GPA of 2.5 may work under the supervision of faculty attorneys in preparing cases for local civil and criminal courts, federal district courts, and state and federal administrative courts. The clinic places students with such agencies as the Wayne County Prosecutor's Office, the U.S. Attorney's Office, the Attorney Grievance Commission, the American Civil Liberties Union, the City of Detroit Law Department, and local health care systems. Students may undertake independent research projects through the Urban Law Clinic. A special program gives students credit for teaching law to high school students. One feature of the Applied Legal Theory and Analysis course is the Analytical Tools Section Lectures, including Structure of Legal Argument, History of Legal Education, The Common Law, Equity, and American Reception of the Common Law. The School of Law also hosts the annual McElroy Lecture on Law and Religion. The University of Detroit Mercy School of Law London Law Program offers second- and third-year students from UDM and other ABA-accredited law schools, an opportunity to study international and comparative law abroad for a fall or spring semester. The Associate Director of Recruitment and Academic Support is available to provide individual tutorial sessions to students in an effort to assist students in improving study skills. Minority and disadvantaged students who do not meet the standard of those currently being admitted, but who have strong qualifications that indicate possible success in law school, may be admitted to the Special Summer Program (SSP). Students who successfully complete the SSP may matriculate with the fall class. Through a consortium with 2 other law schools, students interested in intellectual property law may choose from a wide array of intellectual property law electives. The most widely taken electives are Trial Practice, Estates and Trusts, and Criminal Procedure.

Graduation Requirements

In order to graduate, candidates must have a GPA of 2.0 and have completed the upper-division writing requirement.

Organizations

The primary law review is *The University of Detroit Mercy Law Review*. Another law review is the *Michigan Business Law Journal*. The student newspaper is *In Brief*. Moot court competitions include the Gallagher Competition, the G. Mennen Williams Annual Moot Court Competition, and the Professional Responsibility Competition. Law student organizations include the Student Bar Association, the St. Thomas More Society, and the Black Law Students Association. Local chapters of national associations include Phi Alpha Delta and Delta Theta Phi. Other organizations include the Justice Frank Murphy Honor Society (named for a former faculty member who became a U.S. Attorney General and Associate Justice of the U.S. Supreme Court), intramural team sports, and the Film Society.

Library

The law library contains 307,767 hard-copy volumes and 94,430 microform volume equivalents, and subscribes to 3537 serial publications. Such on-line databases and networks as DIALOG, LEXIS, WESTLAW, and LANs are available to law students for research. Special library collections include English and Canadian Law, government documents, records, legal periodical indexes on CD-ROM, and several hundred databases in related fields. Recently, the library installed 38 state-of-the-art Y2K compliant computers for student use. The ratio of library volumes to faculty is 16,200 to 1 and to students is 845 to 1. The ratio of seats in the library to students is 1 to 1.

Placement	
J.D.s awarded:	127
Services available through: a separate law school placement center	
Special features: The Career Services Office operates on-campus interview programs in the fall and spring, provides seminars and individual advice on such topics as interviewing and resume preparation, and sponsors the weekly "Lunch with a Lawyer" series and the Alumni Mentor Program. The Career Services Office also provides employment letters for alumni and students and an alumni job telephone hotline.	
Full-time job interviews:	17 employers
Summer job interviews:	32 employers
Placement by graduation:	n/av
Placement within 9 months:	85% of class
Average starting salary:	$41,000
Areas of placement:	
Private practice 2-10 attorneys	18%
Private practice 11-25 attorneys	5%
Private practice 26-50 attorneys	2%
Private practice 51-100 attorneys	3%
Government	20%
Business/industry	20%
Judicial clerkships	9%
Public interest	3%
Academic	3%

Faculty

The law school has approximately 19 full-time and 20 part-time faculty members, of whom 11 are women. About 18% of full-time faculty have a graduate law degree in addition to the J.D. The ratio of full-time students to full-time faculty in an average class is 23 to 1; in a clinic, 12 to 1. The law school has a regular program of bringing visiting professors and other distinguished lecturers and visitors to campus.

Students

About 52% of the student body are women; 16%, minorities; 10%, African American; 3%, Asian American; and 2%, Hispanic. The majority of students come from Michigan (95%). The average age of entering students is 27; age range is 21 to 48. About 60% of students enter directly from undergraduate school, 10% have a graduate degree, and 30% have worked full-time prior to entering law school. About 10% drop out after the first year for academic or personal reasons; 90% remain to receive a law degree.

UNIVERSITY OF FLORIDA

College of Law

325 Holland Hall P.O. Box 117622
Gainesville, FL 32611-7622

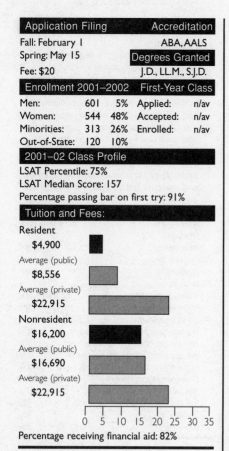

Application Filing	Accreditation
Fall: February 1	ABA, AALS
Spring: May 15	**Degrees Granted**
Fee: $20	J.D., LL.M., S.J.D.

Enrollment 2001–2002			First-Year Class	
Men:	601	5%	Applied:	n/av
Women:	544	48%	Accepted:	n/av
Minorities:	313	26%	Enrolled:	n/av
Out-of-State:	120	10%		

2001–02 Class Profile

LSAT Percentile: 75%
LSAT Median Score: 157
Percentage passing bar on first try: 91%

Tuition and Fees:

Resident
$4,900
Average (public)
$8,556
Average (private)
$22,915
Nonresident
$16,200
Average (public)
$16,690
Average (private)
$22,915

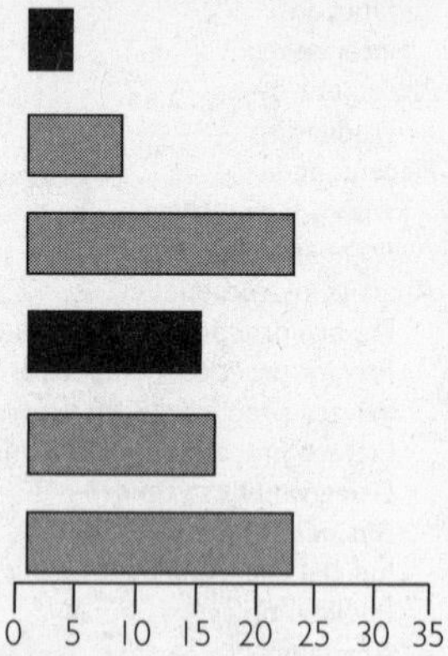

Percentage receiving financial aid: 82%

ADMISSIONS

Information in the above capsule is from an earlier year. In a recent first-year class, twenty-three transfers enrolled. The median LSAT percentile of a recent first-year class was 75; the median GPA was 3.5 on a scale of 4.0.

Requirements
Applicants must have a bachelor's degree and take the LSAT. All admission factors are considered. No specific undergraduate courses are required. Candidates are not interviewed.

Procedure
Check with the school for application deadlines and fee. Applicants should submit an application form, LSAT results, transcripts, a nonrefundable application fee, 3 letters of recommendation (recommended, but not required), and a personal statement to the Admissions Committee. Candidates are strongly encouraged to use the LSDAS letter option. Notification of the admissions decision is in April for fall; July for spring. The law school uses the LSDAS.

Special
The College of Law is represented at a large number of Law Day programs in Florida and other southern states. This activity is supplemented by individual campus visits and other visits to historically black colleges in Florida and the south. The law school actively seeks a diverse student body. Requirements are different for out-of-state students in that their credentials must be significantly better. State law limits non-Floridian enrollment to 10%. Transfer students must have one year of credit, have attended an ABA-approved law school, and must rank in at least the top ⅛ of their class to be considered.

Costs

Tuition and fees for the academic year are approximately $4900 for full-time in-state students and $16,200 for out-of-state students. On-campus room and board costs about $9200 annually; books and supplies run about $700.

Financial Aid

About 82% of law students receive some form of aid. The average annual amount of aid from all sources combined, including scholarships, loans, and work contracts, is about $13,000; maximum, $27,000. Awards are based on need and merit. Required financial statement is the FAFSA. Check with the school for current deadlines. Special funds for minority or disadvantaged students include the Minority Participation in Legal Education (MPLE) Scholarship of $15,000, the Virgil Hawkins Scholarship of $15,000, and the Florida Bar Foundation Council on Legal Education Opportunity. First-year students are notified about their financial aid application at time of acceptance or at some time after acceptance, but prior to enrollment.

About the Law School

University of Florida College of Law was established in 1909 and is a public institution. The 2000-acre ca mpus is in a small town 70 miles southwest of Jacksonville, Florida. The primary mission of the law school is to prepare students for a life of creative problem solving, dispute resolution, planning, and counseling. Students have access to federal, state, county, city, and local agencies, courts, correctional facilities, law firms, and legal aid organizations in the Gainesville area. Housing for students is available in university dormitories, family housing, and apartments. About 90% of the law school facilities are accessible to the physically disabled.

Calendar

The law school operates on a traditional semester basis. Courses for full-time students are offered days only and must be completed within 5 years. There is no part-time program. New students are admitted in the fall and spring. There is an 8-week summer session. Transferable summer courses are offered.

Programs

In addition to the J.D., the law school offers the LL.M. and S.J.D. Students may take relevant courses in other programs and apply credit toward the J.D.; a maximum of 6 credits may be applied. The following joint degrees may be earned: J.D./Ph.D. (Juris Doctor/Doctor of Philosophy in psychology and educational leadership), J.D./Certificate (Juris Doctor/Program in gender studies), J.D./M.A. (Juris Doctor/Master of Arts in accounting, mass communication), J.D./M.A. (Juris Doctor/Master of Arts, in history, Latin American Studies, and political science), J.D./M.Acc. (Juris Doctor/Master of Accounting), J.D./M.B.A. (Juris Doctor/ Master of Business Administration), J.D./M.D. (Juris Doctor/Doctor of Medicine), J.D./M.H.A. (Juris Doctor/Master of Health Administration), J.D./M.S. (Juris Doctor/Master of sciences in anthropology, environment, engineering), J.D./M.U.R.P. (Juris Doctor/Master of Urban and Regional Planning), and J.D./Ph.D (Juris Doctor/Doctor of Philosophy in history, educational leadership).

Phone: 352-392-2087
Fax: 352-392-2087
E-mail: *patrick@law.ufl.edu*
Web: *www.law.ufl.edu*

Contact

J. Michael Patrick, Assistant Dean for Admissions, 352-392-2087 for general inquiries; Trish Varnes, Director of Financial Aid, 352-392-0421 for financial aid information.

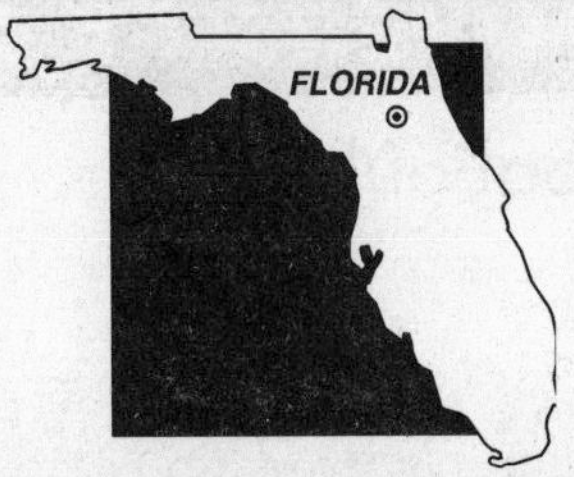

Required

To earn the J.D., candidates must complete 88 total credits, of which 34 are for required courses. They must maintain a minimum GPA of 2.0 in the required courses. The following first-year courses are required of all students: Contracts, Torts, Civil Procedure, Property, Constitutional Law, Legal Research and Writing, Appellate Advocacy, and Introduction to Law. Required upper-level courses consist of Legal Drafting and Professional Responsibility. The required orientation program for first-year students is incorporated into the 4-day (1-credit) Introduction to Law class.

Electives

The College of Law offers concentrations in corporate law, criminal law, entertainment law, environmental law, family law, international law, juvenile law, labor law, litigation, maritime law, media law, securities law, sports law, tax law, and torts and insurance. Clinics include the Virgil Hawkins Civil Clinic for 9 credits, Prosecutor-Criminal Clinic for 6 credits, and Public Defender-Criminal Clinic for 6 credits. The clinics are open to students who have completed at least 48 hours and Professional Responsibility. Criminal Clinics also require Trial Practice. Seminars are available in a variety of legal topics for 2 credits and are open to students who have completed the first-year curriculum. The Council of Ten is a non-credit tutorial program for any first year student. Academic support workshops for students at risk of being placed on academic probation are available. The program is open to any student who has completed at least 1 semester of law school; no credit. The Virgil Hawkins Summer Program is available to any African American admitted for the following fall class, with no credit. The most widely taken electives are legal skills courses.

Graduation Requirements

In order to graduate, candidates must have a GPA of 2.0, have completed the upper-division writing requirement, and a senior writing project seminar.

Organizations

Students edit the *Florida Law Review*, the *Florida International Law Journal*, *Journal of Law and Public Policy*, the *Florida Tax Review*, *FLA-LAW*, and the student newspaper, *The Docket*. Law student organizations include the Justice Campbell Thornal Moot Court Team, Trial Competition Team, and Achieving a Barrier Free Legal Education. Local chapters of national associations include The National Lawyers Guild, Phi Alpha Delta, and Phi Delta Phi.

Library

The law library contains 592,000 hard-copy volumes and 200,000 microform volume equivalents, and subscribes to 8100 serial publications. Such on-line databases and networks as DIALOG, LEXIS, WESTLAW, and Internet access are available to law students for research. Special library collections include tax, Latin American, U.S. government documents, and video and multimedia collections. Recently, the library installed an extensive computer system for on-line searching and student e-mail access throughout the law complex. The ratio of library volumes to faculty is 7283 to 1 and to students is 432 to 1. The ratio of seats in the library to students is 1 to 1.

Faculty

The law school has approximately 69 full-time and 18 part-time faculty members, of whom 28 are women. According to AAUP standards for Category I institutions, faculty salaries are above average. About 32% of full-time faculty have a graduate law degree in addition to the J.D. The ratio of full-time students to full-time faculty in an average class is 18 to 1; in a clinic, 10 to 1. There is a chapter of the Order of the Coif.

Placement

J.D.s awarded: 388

Services available through: a separate law school placement center

Services: mock interviews, off-campus job fairs; on-line interview sign-up/job listings available 24/7.

Special features: Large numbers of on campus interviewers and on-line job listings; three full-time professionals to advise students, mock interviews, and off-campus job fairs.

Full-time job interviews:	153 employers
Summer job interviews:	165 employers
Placement by graduation:	65% of class
Placement within 9 months:	85% of class
Average starting salary:	$28,000 to $75,000

Areas of placement:

Private practice 2-10 attorneys	9%
Private practice 11-25 attorneys	7%
Private practice 26-50 attorneys	5%
Private practice 51-100 attorneys	5%
Government	19%
Judicial clerkships	6%
Business/industry	6%
Public interest	1%

Students

About 48% of the student body are women; 26%, minorities; 9%, African American; 4%, Asian American; 12%, Hispanic; and 1%, Native American. The majority of students come from Florida (90%). The average age of entering students is 25. About 4% drop out after the first year for academic or personal reasons.

UNIVERSITY OF GEORGIA

School of Law

Hirsch Hall, 225 Herty Drive
Athens, GA 30602-6012

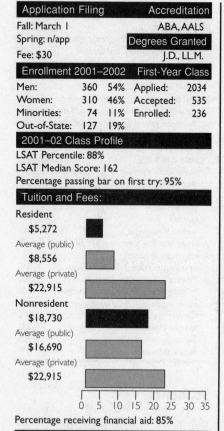

Application Filing		Accreditation
Fall: March 1		ABA, AALS
Spring: n/app		**Degrees Granted**
Fee: $30		J.D., LL.M.

Enrollment 2001–2002			First-Year Class	
Men:	360	54%	Applied:	2034
Women:	310	46%	Accepted:	535
Minorities:	74	11%	Enrolled:	236
Out-of-State:	127	19%		

2001–02 Class Profile

LSAT Percentile: 88%
LSAT Median Score: 162
Percentage passing bar on first try: 95%

Tuition and Fees:

Resident
$5,272
Average (public)
$8,556
Average (private)
$22,915
Nonresident
$18,730
Average (public)
$16,690
Average (private)
$22,915

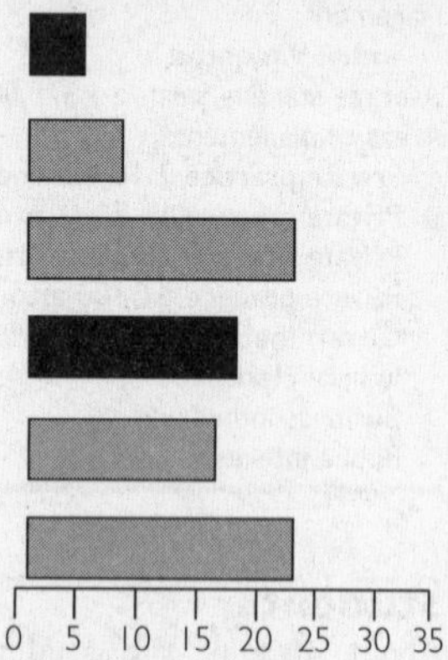

Percentage receiving financial aid: 85%

ADMISSIONS

In the fall 2001 first-year class, 2034 applied, 535 were accepted, and 236 enrolled. Twelve transfers enrolled. The median LSAT percentile of the most recent first-year class was 88; the median GPA was 3.65 on a scale of 4.3. The lowest LSAT percentile accepted was 20; the highest was 99.

Requirements

Applicants must take the LSAT. Minimum acceptable GPA is 2.0 on a scale of 4.0. No specific undergraduate courses are required. Candidates are not interviewed.

Procedure

The application deadline for fall entry is March 1. Applicants should submit an application form, LSAT results, transcripts, a nonrefundable application fee of $30, 2 letters of recommendation, and a 200-word statement indicating the applicant's reasons for obtaining a legal education. Notification of the admissions decision is from October through August. The latest acceptable LSAT test date for fall entry is February. The law school uses the LSDAS.

Special

The law school recruits minority and disadvantaged students by means of the Candidate Referral Service of Law Services, LSAC Law Forums, and campus visitations. Requirements are not different for out-of-state students. Transfer students must have one year of credit, have attended an ABA-approved law school, and transfer from an AALS member school. A copy of the LSDAS Law School Report, law school transcript, dean's certification letter, and 2 letters of recommendation must be submitted.

Costs

Tuition and fees for the 2001-2002 academic year are $5272 for full-time in-state students and $18,730 for out-of-state students. On-campus room and board costs about $7770 annually; books and supplies run $1000.

Financial Aid

About 85% of current law students receive some form of aid. Awards are based on need and merit. The required financial statement is the FAFSA. First-year students are notified about their financial aid application on or about March 1 for academic scholarships; on or about June 1 for need-based aid.

About the Law School

University of Georgia School of Law was established in 1859 and is a public institution. The 1289-acre campus is in a small town 65 miles northeast of Atlanta. Students have access to federal, state, county, city, and local agencies, courts, correctional facilities, law firms, and legal aid organizations in the Athens area. Facilities of special interest to law students are the Dean Rusk Center for International and Comparative Law, the Institute for Continuing Legal Education, and the Institution for Continuing Judicial Education. Housing for students is available on campus for single students in residence halls; students with a spouse and/or children may live in University Village, an on-campus apartment complex. About 99% of the law school facilities are accessible to the physically disabled.

Calendar

The law school operates on a traditional semester basis. Courses for full-time students are offered days only and must be completed within 5 years. There is no part-time program. New students are admitted in the fall. There is a 7-week summer session. Transferable summer courses are offered.

Programs

In addition to the J.D., the law school offers the LL.M. Students may take relevant courses in other programs and apply credit toward the J.D.; a maximum of 4 credits may be applied. The following joint degrees may be earned: J.D./M.B.A. (Juris Doctor/Master of Business Administration), J.D./M.H.P. (Juris Doctor/Master of Historic Preservation), and J.D./M.P.A. (Juris Doctor/Master of Public Administration).

Phone: 706-542-7060
E-mail: *ugajd@arches.uga.edu*
Web: *www.law.uga.edu*

Contact

Giles W. Kennedy, Director of Law Admissions, 706-542-7060 for general inquiries; Susan Little, Director, Office of Student Financial Aid, 706-542-6147 for financial aid information.

Required

To earn the J.D., candidates must complete 88 total credits, of which 33 are for required courses. They must maintain a minimum GPA of 1.7 in the required courses. The following first-year courses are required of all students: Civil Procedure, Contracts and Sales, Criminal Law, Legal Research and Writing, Property, and Torts. Required upper-level courses consist of Legal Profession. The required orientation program for first-year students is a 2-day program that provides an introduction to the school's activities, programs, and requirements, to the case method and legal study, and to new and returning students.

Electives

The School of Law offers concentrations in corporate law, criminal law, entertainment law, environmental law, family law, international law, juvenile law, labor law, litigation, sports law, tax law, torts and insurance, and intellectual property law. Upper-level students may take Legal Aid and Defender Clinic, Civil Clinic, and Prosecutorial Clinic; credit varies. Seminars, worth 2 credits, and supervised research and independent projects worth a maximum of 4 credits, are also open to upper-level students. Internships, worth variable credits, include the Civil Externship; Public Interest Practicum; and Protective Order Project. The Dean Rusk Center for International and Comparative Law provides research programs for variable credit. Field work includes a summer clerkship program for students in England. All students may attend the following special, non-credit lecture series offered on a number of topics: Horace Sibley Lecture Series and Edith House Lecture Series. Study-abroad programs may be undertaken with permission; the law school is a member of the London Law Consortium, and sponsor of Brussels Seminar on Law and Institutions of the European Union and Community. Several tutorial and mentoring programs are offered for no credit. The most widely taken electives are Constitutional Law I and II, Evidence, and Federal Income Tax.

Graduation Requirements

In order to graduate, candidates must have a GPA of 1.7 and have completed the upper-division writing requirement.

Organizations

Students edit the *Georgia Law Review, Georgia Journal of International and Comparative Law*, and *Journal of Intellectual Property Law*. Annually, moot court teams participate in 8 moot court competitions, including the National and the Phillip C. Jessup Moot Courts and the ABA National Moot Court competitions. Other competitions are the American Trial Lawyers Association and National Mock Trial competitions. Law student organizations include the Christian Legal Society, Jewish Law Students Association, and Federalist Society. There are local chapters of Black Law Students Association, Phi Alpha Delta, and ABA-Law Student Division. Campus clubs and other organizations include Equal Justice Foundation, Women Law Students Association, and Student Bar Association.

Library

The law library contains 360,950 hard-copy volumes and 504,653 microform volume equivalents, and subscribes to 7223 serial publications. Such on-line databases and networks as CALI, CIS Universe, Legal-Trac, LEXIS, LOIS, NEXIS, WESTLAW, Wilsonline Indexes, and more than 100 databases are available to law students for research. Special library collections include complete English and Canadian law collections and a European Community depository library. Recently, the library upgraded wiring for computers. The ratio of library volumes to faculty is 7520 to 1 and to students, 539 to 1. The ratio of seats in the library to students is 1 to .80.

Faculty

The law school has 48 full-time and 36 part-time faculty members, of whom 23 are women. According to AAUP standards for Category I institutions, faculty salaries are average. About 39% of full-time faculty have a graduate law degree in addition to the J.D.; about 10% of part-time faculty have one. The ratio of full-time students to full-time faculty in an average class is 18 to 1; in a clinic, 6 to 1. The law school has a regular program of bringing visiting professors and other distinguished lecturers and visitors to campus. There is a chapter of the Order of the Coif.

Placement

J.D.s awarded:	224
Services available through: a separate law school placement center	
Services: 12 off-campus job fairs, a computer and laser printer laboratory, Internet, LEXIS, WESTLAW access, e-mail, and Web distribution of job announcements	
Special features: a career lecture series and videotaping of mock interviews, shadow programs, mentor programs, and 12 or more interviewing consortiums.	
Full-time job interviews:	58 employers
Summer job interviews:	103 employers
Placement by graduation:	74% of class
Placement within 9 months:	96% of class
Average starting salary:	$20,000 to $82,000
Areas of placement:	
Private practice 2-10 attorneys	22%
Private practice 11-25 attorneys	11%
Private practice 26-50 attorneys	6%
Private practice 51-100 attorneys	4%
Private practice 100+ attorneys	13%
Judicial clerkships	16%
Business/industry	14%
Government	6%
Public interest	4%

Students

About 46% of the student body are women; 11%, minorities; 10%, African American; 3%, Asian American; 1%, Hispanic; and 8%, unknown. The majority of students come from the South (90%). The average age of entering students is 24; age range is 21 to 47. About 46% of students enter directly from undergraduate school, 6% have a graduate degree, and 54% have worked full-time prior to entering law school. About 5% drop out after the first year for academic or personal reasons; 95% remain to receive a law degree.

UNIVERSITY OF HAWAII AT MANOA

William S. Richardson School of Law

2515 Dole Street
Honolulu, HI 96822

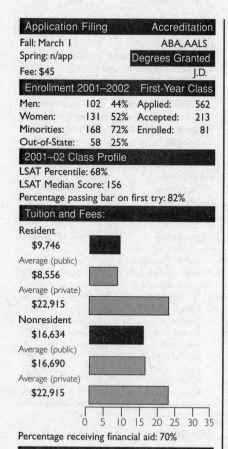

Application Filing		Accreditation
Fall: March 1		ABA, AALS
Spring: n/app		**Degrees Granted**
Fee: $45		J.D.

Enrollment 2001–2002			First-Year Class	
Men:	102	44%	Applied:	562
Women:	131	52%	Accepted:	213
Minorities:	168	72%	Enrolled:	81
Out-of-State:	58	25%		

2001–02 Class Profile

LSAT Percentile: 68%
LSAT Median Score: 156
Percentage passing bar on first try: 82%

Tuition and Fees:

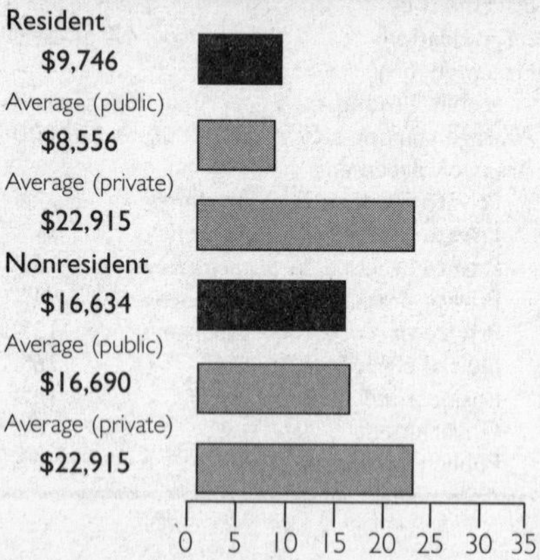

Percentage receiving financial aid: 70%

ADMISSIONS

In the fall 2001 first-year class, 562 applied, 213 were accepted, and 81 enrolled. Four transfers enrolled. The median LSAT percentile of the most recent first-year class was 68; the median GPA was 3.4 on a scale of 4.0. The lowest LSAT percentile accepted was 21; the highest was 99.

Requirements

Applicants must have a bachelor's degree and take the LSAT. The most important admission factors include academic achievement, GPA, and LSAT results. No specific undergraduate courses are required. Candidates are not interviewed.

Procedure

The application deadline for fall entry is March 1. Applicants should submit an application form, LSAT results, transcripts, TOEFL (if applicable), a nonrefundable application fee of $45, 2 letters of recommendation, and residency declaration. Notification of the admissions decision is in early April. The latest acceptable LSAT test date for fall entry is February. The law school uses the LSDAS.

Special

The law school recruits minority and disadvantaged students by means of the Pre-Admission Program and by targeting certain affinity and ethnic groups. Requirements are different for out-of-state students in that there is a higher admission threshold on LSAT scores and the GPA for nonresidents. Transfer students must have one year of credit, have attended an ABA-approved law school, and have a law school rank in at least the top half of their class, 2 letters of recommendation including one from a law professor, and a completed application. Preadmissions courses consist of a 1-year course for 12 students selected from groups underrepresented in the Hawaii Bar. Students enroll in Contracts I and II, Civil Procedure I and II, tutorials for each of those 4 courses, Legal Bibliography, and a Pre-Admission Seminar, held each semester, which is designed for the group.

Costs

Tuition and fees for the 2001-2002 academic year are $9746 for full-time in-state students and $16,634 for out-of-state students. On-campus room and board costs about $7550 annually; books and supplies run $800.

Financial Aid

About 70% of current law students receive some form of aid. The average annual amount of aid from all sources combined, including scholarships, loans, and work contracts, is $12,680; maximum, $23,614. Awards are based on need, with some merit grants available. Required financial statement is the FAFSA. Check with the school for current application deadlines. Special funds for minority or disadvantaged students consist of grants from the Bishop Estate for Native Hawaiians and, through the university, special tuition waivers for state residents; native Hawaiians qualify for resident tuition rates regardless of residency. Most first-year students are notified about their financial aid application in June.

About the Law School

The William S. Richardson School of Law was established in 1973 and is a public institution. The 300-acre campus is in a suburban area 2 miles east of downtown Honolulu. The primary mission of the law school is to provide a legal education for the state and her people, as well as those committed to the state, while developing special programs in Pacific and Asian law and ocean and environmental law. Students have access to federal, state, county, city, and local agencies, courts, correctional facilities, law firms, and legal aid organizations in the Honolulu area. Students have full access to virtually every aspect of the legal community as the law school is Hawaii's only law school; the legal community is active at the school via adjunct teaching, live client clinics, mentoring, and speaking. Facilities of special interest to law students consist of expertise, degree programs, research units in ocean studies, resource management, land use, water resources, natural energy, and marine biology. Additionally, there are Centers for Chinese, Hawaiian, Japanese, Korean, Pacific Island, Philippine, South Asian, and South East Asian Studies. Housing for students is very limited on campus; nearly all law students live off campus in nearby apartments. All law school facilities are accessible to the physically disabled.

Calendar

The law school operates on a traditional semester basis. Courses for full-time students are offered primarily during the day with a few evening courses, and must be completed within 5 years. There is no part-time program. New students are admitted in the fall. There is no summer session. Transferable summer courses are not offered.

Programs

Students may take relevant courses in other programs and apply credit toward the J.D.; various credits may be applied. The following joint degrees may be earned: J.D./M.A. (Juris Doctor/Master of Arts in Asian studies), J.D./M.B.A. (Juris Doctor/Master of Business Adminstration), J.D./M.P.H. (Juris Doctor/Master of Public Health), J.D./M.S.W. (Juris Doctor/Master of Social Work), J.D./ M.U.R.P. (Juris Doctor/Master of Urban

Phone: 808-956-7966
Fax: 808-956-3813
E-mail: *lawadm@hawaii.educ*

Contact

Assistant Dean, 808-956-7966 for general inquiries; Gail Koki, Director of Financial Aid, (808) 956-7251 for financial aid information.

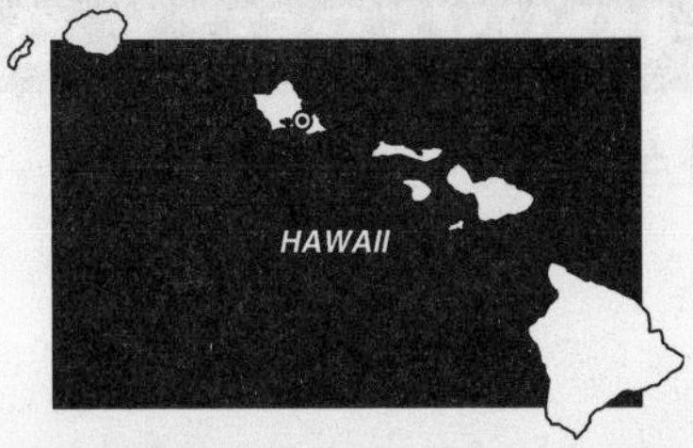

and Regional Planning), and J.D./Ph.D. (Juris Doctor/Doctor of Philosophy in psychology).

Required

To earn the J.D., candidates must complete 89 total credits, of which 42 are for required courses. They must maintain a minimum GPA of 2.0 in the required courses. The following first-year courses are required of all students: Torts Process I and II, Contracts I and II, Civil Procedure I and II, Criminal Justice, Real Property Law I, Legal Method Seminar, Appellate Advocacy, and Legal Bibliography. Required upper-level courses consist of Constitutional Law I, Second Year Seminar, Professional Responsibility, one clinical course, and Pro Bono legal service (60 hours). All students must take clinical courses. The required orientation program for first-year students is 1 week consisting of introductions to faculty, students, career issues, registration, and academic regulations; discussion of stress and personal issues; and a group introduction to the Legal Method Seminar.

Electives

The William S. Richardson School of Law offers concentrations in corporate law, criminal law, environmental law, family law, international law, labor law, litigation, maritime law, tax law, torts and insurance, and Pacific Asian legal studies. In addition, clinics for 3 or 4 credits each are assigned by lottery to upper-level students who meet the prerequisites. Clinics include Prosecution, Elder Law, Native Hawaiian Rights, and others. Upper-level students are offered a variety of seminars in advanced legal studies and Pacific-Asian Legal Studies for 1 to 3 credits per seminar. The required Second Year Seminar is offered for 4 credits. One externship per semester may be taken by upper-level students; a maximum of 2 externships may be taken for 2 credits each. Alternatively, a 14-credit externship in an approved Pacific Island jurisdiction may taken. Under the directed studies program, any upper-level student may elect to conduct special research for 1 to 3 credits. Research can be repeated. Field work is linked to those clinics that include live client representation as well as actual court appearances under a special state Supreme Court rule. Special lecture series are offered for no credit; any student may attend. Annually, there is a Distinguished Fujiyama Visiting Professor, a George Johnson visiting Scholar, and Jurist-in-Residence Program. There is also a Pacific-Asian Legal Studies lecture series for visiting Asian legal scholars. Study abroad can be accomplished by special arrangement for varying credits or by a full-semester externship in certain Pacific Island jurisdictions for 14 credits. Tutorial programs are available and administered through the Student Bar Association for no credit. The Pre-Admission is a 1-year program prior to matriculation for 12 students from among those groups underrepresented in the Hawaii Bar; Special interst group programs, offered for no credit, include the Filipino Law Students Association, 'Ahahui 'O Hawai'i (a Native Hawaiian organization), Advocates for Public Interest Law, and the Pacific-Asian Legal Studies Organization. The most widely taken electives are Evidence, Wills and Trusts, and Corporations.

Graduation Requirements

In order to graduate, candidates must have a GPA of 2.0 and have completed the upper-division writing requirement.

Organizations

Students edit the *University of Hawaii Law Review* and the *Pacific Asian Legal Journal*. Students participate in the annual Susan McKay Moot Court Competition, held internationally and in Honolulu; the Environmental Law Moot Court, held in New York; and the Jessup International Moot Court competition. Other competitions include client counseling and Mock Trial. Law student organizations include the Student Bar Association, Environmental Law Society, and Hawaii Association of Women Law Students. Local chapters of national associations include the American Inns of Court, ABA-Student Division, and Phi Delta Phi, Rutherford chapter.

Library

The law library contains 248,838 hardcopy volumes and 875,305 microform volume equivalents, and subscribes to 2736 serial publications. Such on-line databases and networks as DIALOG, LEXIS, WESTLAW, and NEXIS, LEGAL TRAC, ERIC, ABI/INFORM are available to law students for research. Special library collections include a partial federal government depository. Recently, the library upgraded its computer lab. The ratio of library volumes to faculty is 13,097 to 1 and to students is 1046 to 1. The ratio of seats in the library to students is 1 to 1.

Placement

J.D.s awarded:	80
Services available through: a separate law school placement center	
Services: career information series	
Special features: Nearly all placement activity is focused on the Hawaii market, as are on-campus interviews, because 95% of graduates remain in the state.	
Full-time job interviews:	n/av
Summer job interviews:	n/av
Placement by graduation:	n/av
Placement within 9 months:	96% of class
Average starting salary:	$24,000 to $70,000
Areas of placement:	
Private practice 2-10 attorneys	13%
Private practice 11-25 attorneys	8%
Private practice 26-50 attorneys	7%
Private practice 51-100 attorneys	8%
Judicial clerkships	36%
Government	15%
Business/industry	12%
Public interest	3%

Faculty

The law school has 19 full-time and 29 part-time faculty members, of whom 16 are women. About 37% of full-time faculty have a graduate law degree in addition to the J.D.; about 25% of part-time faculty have one. The ratio of full-time students to full-time faculty in an average class is 13 to 1; in a clinic, 12 to 1.

Students

About 52% of the student body are women; 72%, minorities; 1%, African American; 47%, Asian American; 1%, Hispanic; 1%, Native American; and 22%, Hawaiian and Pacific Islander. The majority of students come from Hawaii (75%). The average age of entering students is 27; age range is 22 to 56. About 37% of students enter directly from undergraduate school, 15% have a graduate degree, and 63% have worked full-time prior to entering law school. About 5% drop out after the first year for academic or personal reasons; 92% remain to receive a law degree.

UNIVERSITY OF HOUSTON

Law Center

100 Law Center
Houston, TX 77204-6060

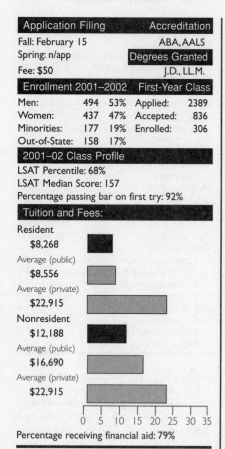

Application Filing		Accreditation
Fall: February 15		ABA, AALS
Spring: n/app		**Degrees Granted**
Fee: $50		J.D., LL.M.

Enrollment 2001–2002			First-Year Class	
Men:	494	53%	Applied:	2389
Women:	437	47%	Accepted:	836
Minorities:	177	19%	Enrolled:	306
Out-of-State:	158	17%		

2001–02 Class Profile

LSAT Percentile: 68%
LSAT Median Score: 157
Percentage passing bar on first try: 92%

Tuition and Fees:

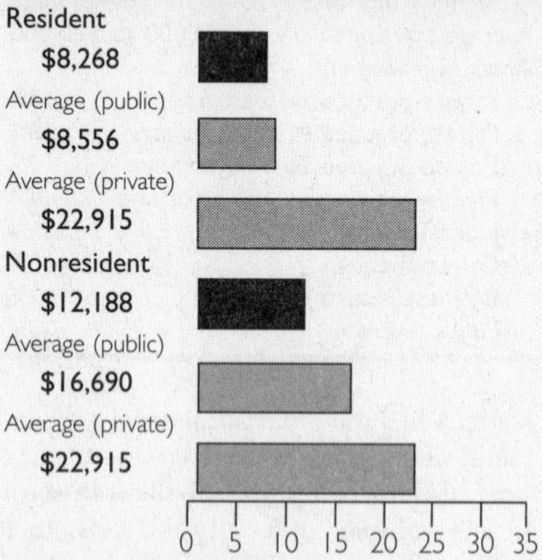

Percentage receiving financial aid: 79%

ADMISSIONS

In the fall 2001 first-year class, 2389 applied, 836 were accepted, and 306 enrolled. Forty-three transfers enrolled. The median LSAT percentile of the most recent first-year class was 68; the median GPA was 3.4 on a scale of 4.0. The lowest LSAT percentile accepted was 27; the highest was 99.

Requirements

Applicants must have a bachelor's degree and take the LSAT. The most important admission factors include LSAT results, GPA, and general background. No specific undergraduate courses are required. Candidates are not interviewed.

Procedure

The application deadline for fall entry is February 15. Applicants should submit an application form, a nonrefundable application fee of $50, a personal statement, resume, and the LSDAS report. Letters of recommendation are optional. Notification of the admissions decision is December to May. The latest acceptable LSAT test date for fall entry is February. The law school uses the LSDAS.

Special

The law school recruits minority and disadvantaged students through a strong support system on campus, well-funded BLSA, HLSA, and ALSA organizations, and by visiting various colleges and hosting programs. Requirements are different for out-of-state students in that there is a 20% cap for nonresident students. Transfer students must have one year of credit, have attended an ABA-approved law school, and rank typically within the top 10%.

Costs

Tuition and fees for the 2001-2002 academic year are $8268 for full-time in-state students and $12,188 for out-of-state students. Tuition for part-time students is $6108 in-state and $8908 out-of-state. On-campus room and board costs about $5150 annually; books and supplies run $864.

Financial Aid

About 79% of current law students receive some form of aid. The average annual amount of aid from all sources combined, including scholarships, loans, and work contracts, is $14,559; maximum, $16,948. Awards are based on need and merit; need-based financial aid is handled by the University's Director of Financial Aid. Scholarships are handled by the Assistant Dean for Student Affairs at the Law Center. The Financial Aid Counselor at the Law Center assists students with their paperwork. The required financial statement is the FAFSA. The aid application deadline for fall entry is April 1. First-year students are notified about their financial aid application on a rolling basis as their financial aid file is complete.

About the Law School

University of Houston Law Center was established in 1947 and is a public institution. The 540-acre campus is in an urban area 3 miles south of downtown Houston. The primary mission of the law school is to attract a student body characterized by social and ethnic diversity that will be exposed to a diverse educational and social experience and that will enter the legal profession in positions of responsibility. Students have access to federal, state, county, city, and local agencies, courts, correctional facilities, law firms, and legal aid organizations in the Houston area. Special attention is given to accommodating students with disabilities. Housing for students is available, including housing for married students. About 98% of students live 15 to 20 minutes from campus. About 95% of the law school facilities are accessible to the physically disabled.

Calendar

The law school operates on a traditional semester basis. Courses for full-time students are offered both day and evening and must be completed within 4 years. For first-year students, courses are offered days only. For part-time students, courses are offered both day and evening and must be completed within 6 years. For first-year students, courses are offered evenings only. New full-time students are admitted in the fall; part-time, summer. There are 2 6-week summer sessions and 1 12-week summer session. Transferable summer courses are offered.

Programs

In addition to the J.D., the law school offers the LL.M. Students may take relevant courses in other programs and apply credit toward the J.D.; a maximum of 12 hours of credits may be applied. The following joint degrees may be earned: J.D./M.A. (Juris Doctor/Master of Arts in history), J.D./M.B.A. (Juris Doctor/Master of Business Administration), J.D./M.P.H. (Juris Doctor/Master of Public Health), J.D./M.S.W. (Juris Doctor/Master of Social Work), and J.D./Ph.D. (Juris Doctor/Doctor of Philosophy in criminal justice and in medical humanities).

Phone: 713-743-2280
Fax: 713-743-2194
E-mail: *admission@www.law.uh.edu*
Web: *www.law.uh.edu*

Contact

Sondra R. Tennessee, Assistant Dean for Admissions, 713-743-2280 for general inquiries; Laura Neal, Financial Aid Counselor, 713-743-2269 for financial aid information.

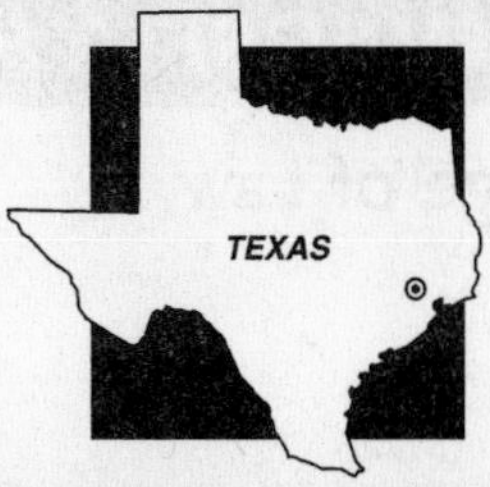

Required

To earn the J.D., candidates must complete 90 total credits, of which 35 are for required courses. They must maintain a minimum GPA of 2.0 in the required courses. The following first-year courses are required of all students: Torts I and II, Criminal Law, Contracts I and II, Legal Research, Procedure, Property I and II, Legal Writing, and Constitutional Law. Required upper-level courses consist of Professional Responsibility and the senior writing requirement. The required orientation program for first-year students is 2 days of general information and mock classroom instruction taught by faculty, plus ongoing activities throughout the semester.

Electives

The Law Center offers concentrations in corporate law, criminal law, environmental law, international law, litigation, tax law, and health law, and intellectual property. In addition, students may choose among 20 to 25 clinics, both civil and criminal, including the Health Law Clinic and Environmental Law Clinic. Seminar courses are available in all areas. There are judicial internships at federal, state, district, and county municipal levels. Research programs include the Environmental Liability Law Program, Health Law and Policy Institute, National Institute of Trial Advocacy (NITA), Institute of Higher Education Law and Governance, Intellectual Property Institute, and International Law Institute. There is a Young Scholars lecture series. Study abroad may be done through the North American Consortium of Legal Education (NACLE). The Academic Enrichment Program provides tutorial assistance. The most widely taken electives are Commercial Transactions, Business Organizations, and Evidence.

Graduation Requirements

In order to graduate, candidates must have a GPA of 2.0 and have completed the upper-division writing requirement.

Organizations

Students edit the *Houston Law Review, Houston Journal of International Law, Houston Journal of Health Law and Policy, Houston Business and Tax Law Journal, Texas Consumer Law Journal, Environmental Resource Newsletter, Environmental Law Society, Health Law News, Environmental Liability Law Report, International Law in Houston*, and the newspaper *Legalese*. Intrascholastic moot court competitions include the Blakely, Hippard, and Newhouse Mediation competitions. Law student organizations include Advocates, Corporate Law Society, and Environmental Law Society. There are local chapters of ABA-Law Student Division, Phi Alpha Phi, and Order of the Coif. Other organizations include Student Bar Association, Black Law Students Association, and Hispanic Law Students Association.

Library

The law library contains 460,569 hard-copy volumes and 911,626 microform volume equivalents, and subscribes to 2750 serial publications. Such on-line databases and networks as DIALOG, LEXIS, and WESTLAW are available to law students for research. Special library collections include a U.S. government depository, Mexican Law Collection, Admiralty and Maritime Law Collection, and John R. Brown Archives. Recently, the library added additional computer laboratories and expanded the law school network. Major renovation of the law library building was completed in 1996. The ratio of library volumes to faculty is 10,012 to 1 and to students is 495 to 1. The ratio of seats in the library to students is 1 to 1.

Faculty

The law school has 46 full-time and 67 part-time faculty members, of whom 29 are women. According to AAUP standards for Category I institutions, faculty salaries are well below average. About 28% of full-time faculty have a graduate law degree in addition to the J.D.; about 13% of part-time faculty have one. The ratio of full-time students to full-time faculty in an average class is 19 to 1; in a clinic, 5 to 1. The law school has a regular program of bringing visiting professors and other distinguished lecturers and visitors to campus. There is a chapter of the Order of the Coif; 26 faculty and 337 graduates are members.

Placement

J.D.s awarded: 336

Services available through: a separate law school placement center

Services: Public Interest/Public Sector Fellowship Program

Special features: A comprehensive career education series is held every spring, and includes networking events, speaker panels and mock interviews for first year students. UHLC participates in 6 off-campus recruitment programs during the year.

Full-time job interviews:	56 employers
Summer job interviews:	121 employers
Placement by graduation:	70% of class
Placement within 9 months:	93% of class
Average starting salary:	$45,000 to $78,000
Areas of placement:	
Private practice 2-10 attorneys	27%
Private practice 11-25 attorneys	15%
Private practice 26-50 attorneys	9%
Private practice 51-100 attorneys	3%
Other private practice	9%
Business/industry	19%
Government	13%
Judicial clerkships	4%
Public interest	1%

Students

About 47% of the student body are women; 19%, minorities; 3%, African American; 6%, Asian American; 9%, Hispanic; and 1%, Native American. The majority of students come from Texas (83%). The average age of entering students is 25; age range is 19 to 48. About 60% of students enter directly from undergraduate school and 13% have a graduate degree. About 3% drop out after the first year for academic or personal reasons; 85% remain to receive a law degree.

College of Law

P.O. Box 442321
Moscow, ID 83844-2321

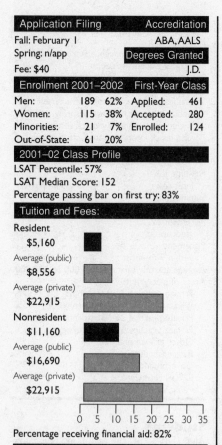

Application Filing		Accreditation
Fall: February 1		ABA, AALS
Spring: n/app		**Degrees Granted**
Fee: $40		J.D.

Enrollment 2001–2002			First-Year Class	
Men:	189	62%	Applied:	461
Women:	115	38%	Accepted:	280
Minorities:	21	7%	Enrolled:	124
Out-of-State:	61	20%		

2001–02 Class Profile

LSAT Percentile: 57%
LSAT Median Score: 152
Percentage passing bar on first try: 83%

Tuition and Fees:

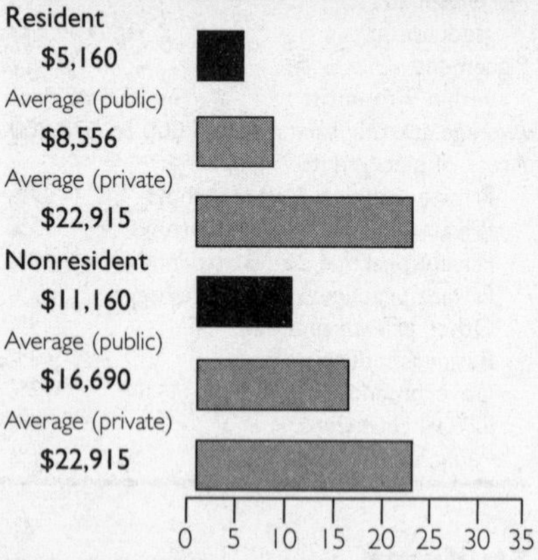

Percentage receiving financial aid: 82%

ADMISSIONS

In the fall 2001 first-year class, 461 applied, 280 were accepted, and 124 enrolled. Two transfers enrolled. The median LSAT percentile of the most recent first-year class was 57; the median GPA was 3.31 on a scale of 4.0. The lowest LSAT percentile accepted was 13; the highest was 94.

Requirements

Applicants must have a bachelor's degree and take the LSAT. Exceptional students may be admitted after completing 75% of credits necessary for a bachelor's degree, if the degree will be granted upon completion of the first year of law school. The most important admission factors include GPA, LSAT results, and state or country of residence. No specific undergraduate courses are required. Candidates are interviewed.

Procedure

The application deadline for fall entry is February 1. Applicants should submit an application form and a nonrefundable application fee of $40. LSDAS registration is required. Personal statements are encouraged, as well as current resumes and letters of recommendation. Notification of the admissions decision is by April 1. The latest acceptable LSAT test date for fall entry is December. The law school uses the LSDAS.

Special

The law school recruits minority and disadvantaged students by means of the Candidate Referral Service, law Fairs and forums, and the minority recruiting event, "Law by Day, Jazz by Night." Requirements are not different for out-of-state students. Transfer students must have one year of credit, have attended an ABA-approved law school, submit a letter of good standing, rank in the top half of class, and have competitive LSAT results and UGPA.

Costs

Tuition and fees for the 2001-2002 academic year are $5160 for full-time in-state students and $11,160 for out-of-state students. On-campus room and board costs about $4000 annually; books and supplies run $750.

Financial Aid

About 82% of current law students receive some form of aid. The average annual amount of aid from all sources combined, including scholarships, loans, and work contracts, is $13,000; maximum, $18,500. Awards are based on need and merit. The required financial statements are the FAFSA and University of Idaho special forms. The aid application deadline for fall entry is February 15. Special funds for minority or disadvantaged students consist of scholarships.

About the Law School

University of Idaho College of Law was established in 1909 and is a public institution. The 160-acre campus is in a small town 85 miles southeast of Spokane, Washington. The primary mission of the law school is to prepare students for the practice of law and leadership in the community. Students have access to federal, state, county, city, and local agencies, courts, correctional facilities, law firms, and legal aid organizations in the Moscow area. Facilities of special interest to law students include the law building, which is especially designed for the study of law. Law students also have access to the extensive university athletic facilities. Housing for students is available and includes university graduate student dorms, married student housing, and apartments in the local community. All law school facilities are accessible to the physically disabled.

Calendar

The law school operates on a traditional semester basis. Courses for full-time students are offered days only and must be completed within 6 years. There is no part-time program. New students are admitted in the fall. There is an 8-week summer session. Transferable summer courses are not offered.

Programs

Students may take relevant courses in other programs with approval of the Associate Dean and apply credit toward the J.D.; a maximum of 6 credits may be applied. The following joint degrees may be earned: J.D./M.Acc. (Juris Doctor/Master of Accounting), J.D./M.B.A. (Master of Business Administration from Washington State University College of Business and Economics (Concurrent)), and J.D./M.S. (Master of Environmental Science (Concurrent)).

Phone: 208-885-6423
Fax: 208-885-5709
E-mail: *erickl@uidaho.edu*
Web: *www.uidaho.edu*

Contact

Erick Larson, Admissions Coordinator, 208-885-6423 for general inquiries; Rodd Dunn, Associate Director, 208-885-6312 for financial aid information.

Required

To earn the J.D., candidates must complete 88 total credits, of which 37 are for required courses. They must maintain a minimum GPA of 2.0 in the required courses. The following first-year courses are required of all students: Introduction to Law, Property I and II, Torts I and II, Legal Research and Writing, Procedure, Contracts I and II, and Criminal Law. Required upper-level courses consist of Professional Responsibility, an upper-division writing requirement, and Constitutional Law I and II. The required orientation program for first-year students is a 3-day introduction to the study of law which includes professional responsibility, the court system, and trial process.

Electives

The College of Law offers concentrations in corporate law, environmental law, litigation, and lawyering skills. In addition, Third-year students may take general practice clinic, tax clinic, United States Court of Appeals for the Ninth Circuit, and Nez Perce Indian Reservation defense clinics for a maximum of 8 credits. Second- and third-year students may take seminars for 1 to 3 credits. The school offers class and non-class, and resident credit for semesters with the U.S. Attorney, the Attorney General, federal and state district and appellate courts, and other similar work environments. Second- and third-year students may participate in research programs for 1 to 2 credits. Third year students may participate in a semester in practice externship in Boise for up tp 12 classroom credits and residential credit. The Sherman Bellwood Lecture is a program to bring learned individuals to the state of Idaho and the University of Idaho campus in order to allow students the opportunity to discuss, examine, and debate subjects related to the justice system. The speakers are prominent and highly regarded local, regional, and national leaders who cover a wide range of topics. Tutorial programs are provided to first-year students as requested. Minority programs are sponsored by the Minority Law Student Association. The most widely taken electives are Natural Resources, Lawyering Skills, and bar courses.

Graduation Requirements

In order to graduate, candidates must have a GPA of 2.0 and have completed the upper-division writing requirement.

Organizations

The *Idaho Law Review* is the student-edited, student-managed law publication. Teams compete in the National Moot Court, Duberstein Bankruptcy Moot Court, and Environmental Law Moot Court competitions. Teams regularly compete in the National competition and then either the Bankruptcy or Environmental competition. Other competitions include the McNichols Moot Court, ATLA trial, and regional negotiation and mediation competitions. Law student organizations include the ABA-Law Student Division, American and Idaho Trial Lawyers Association, and Environmental Law Society. Other organizations include the Student Bar Association and the Board of Student Advocates. There are local chapters of Delta Theta Phi, Phi Delta Phi, and Phi Alpha Delta.

Library

The law library contains 180,892 hard-copy volumes, and subscribes to 2820 serial publications. Such on-line databases and networks as DIALOG, LEXIS, NEXIS, and WESTLAW are available to law students for research. Special library collections include archives of Idaho materials. Recently, the library added carrells, compact shelving, a computer laboratory, and renovated the third floor. The ratio of library volumes to faculty is 11,306 to 1 and to students, 595 to 1. The ratio of seats in the library to students is 1 to 1.

Faculty

The law school has 1 part-time and 16 full-time and 1 part-time faculty members, of whom 8 are women. According to AAUP standards for Category I institutions, faculty salaries are below average. About 1% of full-time faculty have a graduate law degree in addition to the J.D. The ratio of full-time students to full-time faculty in an average class is 40 to 1; in a clinic, 10 to 1. The law school has a regular program of bringing visiting professors and other distinguished lecturers and visitors to campus.

Placement	
J.D.s awarded:	80
Services available through: a separate law school placement center	
Full-time job interviews:	41 employers
Summer job interviews:	n/av
Placement by graduation:	69% of class
Placement within 9 months:	93% of class
Average starting salary:	$35,385 to $49,677
Areas of placement:	
Private practice 2-10 attorneys	25%
Private practice 11-25 attorneys	5%
Private practice 26-50 attorneys	1%
Private practice 51-100 attorneys	4%
Private practice (unknown size)	13%
Judicial clerkships	23%
Government	18%
Business/industry	5%
Unknown	3%
Public interest	2%
Academic	1%

Students

About 38% of the student body are women; 7%, minorities; 1%, African American; 2%, Asian American; 2%, Hispanic; and 1%, Native American. The majority of students come from Idaho (80%). The average age of entering students is 28; age range is 21 to 56. About 9% drop out after the first year for academic or personal reasons; 90% remain to receive a law degree.

UNIVERSITY OF ILLINOIS

College of Law

504 East Pennsylvania Avenue
Champaign, IL 61820

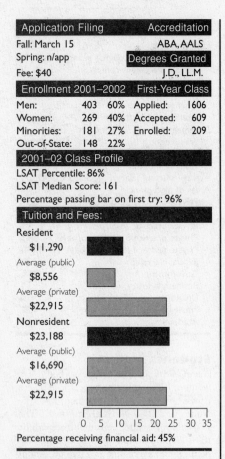

Application Filing		Accreditation
Fall: March 15		ABA, AALS
Spring: n/app		**Degrees Granted**
Fee: $40		J.D., LL.M.

Enrollment 2001–2002			First-Year Class	
Men:	403	60%	Applied:	1606
Women:	269	40%	Accepted:	609
Minorities:	181	27%	Enrolled:	209
Out-of-State:	148	22%		

2001–02 Class Profile

LSAT Percentile: 86%
LSAT Median Score: 161
Percentage passing bar on first try: 96%

Tuition and Fees:

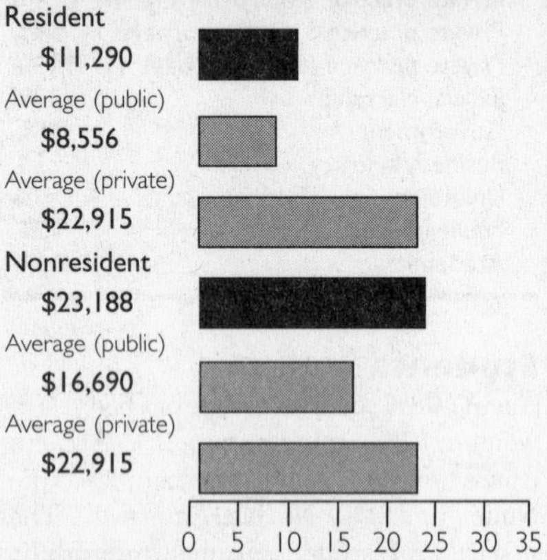

Percentage receiving financial aid: 45%

ADMISSIONS

In the fall 2001 first-year class, 1606 applied, 609 were accepted, and 209 enrolled. Eighteen transfers enrolled. The median LSAT percentile of the most recent first-year class was 86; the median GPA was 3.4 on a scale of 4.0. The lowest LSAT percentile accepted was 33; the highest was 99.

Requirements

Applicants must have a bachelor's degree and take the LSAT. The most important admission factors include LSAT results, GPA, and undergraduate curriculum. No specific undergraduate courses are required. Candidates are not interviewed.

Procedure

The application deadline for fall entry is March 15. Applicants should submit an application form, LSAT results, transcripts, a nonrefundable application fee of $40, 2 letters of recommendation, a personal statement, and a resume. Notification of the admissions decision is on a rolling basis from December to May. The latest acceptable LSAT test date for fall entry is February. The law school uses the LSDAS.

Special

The law school recruits minority and disadvantaged students by participating in recruiting fairs and visiting schools where there are a large number of minority students. Requirements are not different for out-of-state students. Transfer students must have one year of credit, have a minimum GPA of 3.0, and have attended an ABA-approved law school. Preadmissions courses consist of the Law Minority Access Program to expose college juniors to law school. Students take classes in legal analysis and legal research and writing for 4 weeks and then spend 4 weeks as interns with Chicago law firms. Another program, Minority Access to Law School, has a similar intent but is designed for college sophomores.

Costs

Tuition and fees for the 2001-2002 academic year are $11,290 for full-time in-state students and $23,188 for out-of-state students. On-campus room and board costs about $7848 annually; books and supplies run $960.

Financial Aid

About 45% of current law students receive some form of aid. The maximum annual amount of aid from all sources combined, including scholarships, loans, and work contracts, is $18,500. Loans are need based and scholarships are merit based. Required financial statement is the FAFSA. The aid application deadline for fall entry is March 15. Special funds for minority or disadvantaged students are available. First-year students are notified about their financial aid application at the time application is made, and again in a letter of acceptance.

About the Law School

University of Illinois College of Law was established in 1897 and is a public institution. The 710-acre campus is in an urban area 130 miles south of Chicago. The primary mission of the law school is to foster excellence in legal education through a close community of professors and students, where teaching goes hand in hand with scholarship and public service. Students have access to federal, state, county, city, and local agencies, courts, correctional facilities, law firms, and legal aid organizations in the Champaign area. Housing for students is available in inexpensive apartments in Champaign-Urbana. Two graduate student dormitories are available for law students. All law school facilities are accessible to the physically disabled.

Calendar

The law school operates on a traditional semester basis. Courses for full-time students are offered days only and must be completed within 3 years. There is no part-time program. New students are admitted in the fall. There is an 11-week summer session. Transferable summer courses are not offered.

Programs

In addition to the J.D., the law school offers the LL.M. Students may take relevant courses in other programs and apply credit toward the J.D.; a maximum of 12 credits may be applied. The following joint degrees may be earned: J.D./D.V.M. (Juris Doctor/ Doctor of Veterinary Medicine), J.D./M.A. (Juris Doctor/Master of Arts in education and in journalism), J.D./M.S. (Juris Doctor/. Master of Science in chemistry and in natural resources), J.D./M.A.L.I.R. (Juris Doctor/ Master of Arts in Labor and Industrial Relations), J.D./M.B.A. (Juris Doctor/ Master of Business Administration), J.D./M.D. (Juris Doctor/ Doctor of Medicine), J.D./M.Ed. (Juris Doctor/ Master of Education), J.D./M.U.P. (Juris Doctor/Master of Urban Planning), and J.D./Ph.D. (Juris Doctor/ Doctor of Philosophy in Education).

Phone: 217-244-6415
Fax: 217-244-1478
E-mail: *admissions@law.uiuc.edu*
Web: *www.law.uiuc.edu*

Contact

Maggie D. Austin, Director of Admissions, 217-244-6415 for general inquiries; Ann K. Perry, Assistant Dean for Student Affairs, 217-333-6438 for financial aid information.

Required

To earn the J.D., candidates must complete 90 total credits, of which 34 are for required courses. They must maintain a minimum GPA of 2.0 in the required courses. The following first-year courses are required of all students: Contracts, Property, Criminal Law and Procedure, Civil Procedure, Torts, Legal Research and Writing, Introduction to Advocacy, Constitutional Law I, and statutory interpretation electives. Required upper-level courses consist of Professional Responsibility and upper-level writing. The required orientation program for first-year students lasts 2 days and is designed to familiarize students with the college. Mock class and group discussions introduce students to law study.

Electives

The College of Law offers concentrations in corporate law, criminal law, environmental law, family law, international law, labor law, litigation, securities law, sports law, tax law, torts and insurance, intellectual property, and public interest law. In addition, clinics are open to second- and third-year students for 4 credit hours. Seminar enrollment is generally limited to 12 students. Numerous seminars are offered each semester and are open to second- and third-year students for 2 to 3 credit hours. Student interns may receive up to 4 credit hours for working in such agencies as a local legal services agency, the state's attorney's office, and the public defender's office. Students may also work as research assistants for faculty members and may receive up to 4 credit hours for independent research projects working with individual faculty members. Field work may be carried out through the Prisoners' Rights Research Project, where students provide legal research for federal and state inmates in Illinois institutions; no academic credit is offered. The David C. Baum Memorial Lectures are presented twice each year by distinguished scholars in the areas of civil liberties and civil rights. Paul M. Van Arsdell, Jr. presents an annual lecture on litigation and the legal profession. Students may receive credit for ABA-approved study-abroad programs. The most widely taken electives are Trial Advocacy, Business Organizations, and Evidence.

Graduation Requirements

In order to graduate, candidates must have a GPA of 3.0, have completed the upper-division writing requirement, and have 90 weeks residency, 90 semester hours of passing grades, and 56 hours earned from the University of Illinois.

Organizations

Students edit the *University of Illinois Law Review, Elder Law Journal, Journal of Law, Technology, and Policy*, and the newspaper *Pro Se*; law students write the "Recent Decisions" section of the *Illinois Bar Journal*. Teams are sent to the National Moot Court, Philip C. Jessup International Moot Court, and Environmental Moot Court competitions. Other competitions are the ABA Negotiations and ABA Client Counseling competitions. Law student organizations are the Public Interest Law Foundation, Sports Law Society, and Student Bar Association. Local chapters of national associations include Black Law Students Association, ABA-Law Student Division, and Christian Legal Society. Other campus clubs include intramural basketball and darts, Law Revue, and Volunteer Outreach Program.

Library

The law library contains 565,660 hard-copy volumes and 775,212 microform volume equivalents, and subscribes to 8190 serial publications. Such on-line databases and networks as LEXIS and WESTLAW are available to law students for research. Special library collections include a federal government depository and a European union depository. Recently, the library added 2 public terminals and a government document workstation and wired south balcony carrels for network access. The ratio of library volumes to faculty is 12,570 to 1 and to students is 842 to 1.

Placement

J.D.s awarded:	185
Services available through: a separate law school placement center, the university placement center, and other college placement offices.	
Special features: the Alumni-Student Job Search Conference, where 50 alumni provide counseling and programs for students about the job search process.	
Full-time job interviews:	62 employers
Summer job interviews:	108 employers
Placement by graduation:	70% of class
Placement within 9 months:	96% of class
Average starting salary:	$19,000 to $148,000
Areas of placement:	
Private practice 2-10 attorneys	11%
Private practice 11-25 attorneys	13%
Private practice 26-50 attorneys	6%
Private practice 51-100 attorneys	12%
Business/industry	21%
Judicial clerkships	19%
Government	16%
Public interest	2%

Faculty

The law school has 45 full-time and 33 part-time faculty members. About 10% of full-time faculty have a graduate law degree in addition to the J.D. The ratio of full-time students to full-time faculty in an average class is 17 to 1; in a clinic, 7 to 1. The law school has a regular program of bringing visiting professors and other distinguished lecturers and visitors to campus. There is a chapter of the Order of the Coif; 40 faculty and 20 graduates are members.

Students

About 40% of the student body are women; 27%, minorities; 9%, African American; 9%, Asian American; 8%, Hispanic; and 1%, Native American. The majority of students come from Illinois (78%). The average age of entering students is 24; age range is 21 to 43. About 1% drop out after the first year for academic or personal reasons; 99% remain to receive a law degree.

UNIVERSITY OF IOWA

College of Law

276 Boyd Law Building, Melrose at Byington Street
Iowa City, IA 52242

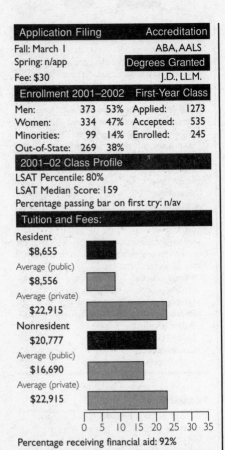

Application Filing		Accreditation
Fall: March 1		ABA, AALS
Spring: n/app		**Degrees Granted**
Fee: $30		J.D., LL.M.

Enrollment 2001–2002			First-Year Class	
Men:	373	53%	Applied:	1273
Women:	334	47%	Accepted:	535
Minorities:	99	14%	Enrolled:	245
Out-of-State:	269	38%		

2001–02 Class Profile

LSAT Percentile: 80%
LSAT Median Score: 159
Percentage passing bar on first try: n/av

Tuition and Fees:

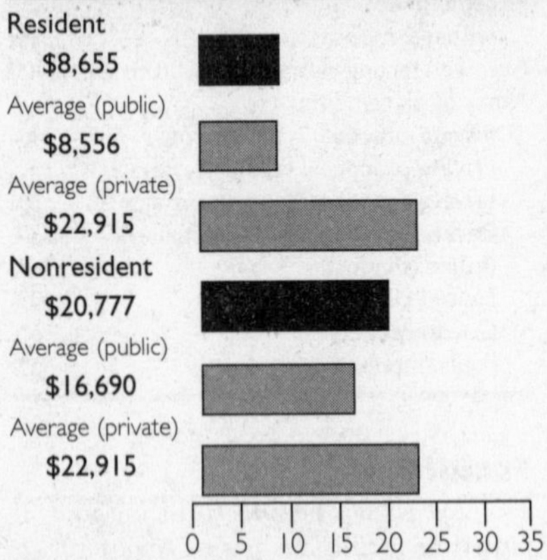

Percentage receiving financial aid: 92%

ADMISSIONS

In the fall 2001 first-year class, 1273 applied, 535 were accepted, and 245 enrolled. Three transfers enrolled. The median LSAT percentile of the most recent first-year class was 80; the median GPA was 3.57 on a scale of 4.0.

Requirements

Applicants must have a bachelor's degree and take the LSAT. The most important admission factors include academic achievement, LSAT results, and motivation. No specific undergraduate courses are required. Candidates are not interviewed.

Procedure

The application deadline for fall entry is March 1. Applicants should submit an application form, LSAT results, and transcripts. Prior standardized test scores may be submitted as well as and TOEFL, for foreign applicants who have not received a degree from a U.S. institution, and a nonrefundable application fee of $30. and 3 are recommended letters of recommendation are recommended. Notification of the admissions decision is begins in October but usually no later than April. The latest acceptable LSAT test date for fall entry is February, although a February score will put applicants at a slight disadvantage. The law school uses the LSDAS.

Special

In addition to extensive travel, the law school has sponsored, for more than 20 years, "Bridging the Gap," a minority pre-law conference held at the law school. The law school participates in, and supports, CLEO and PLSI. Requirements are different for out-of-state students in that preference is given to applicants who are residents of Iowa. Approximately 70% of the entering class is comprised of Iowa residents. Transfer students must have one year of credit, have attended an ABA-approved law school, have credentials that would have made the students admissible as first-year students, and have attended an AALS- and ABA-approved law school.

Costs

Tuition and fees for the 2001-2002 academic year are $8655 for full-time in-state students and $20,777 for out-of-state students. On-campus room and board costs about $4870 annually; books and supplies run $1440.

Financial Aid

About 92% of current law students receive some form of aid. The average annual amount of aid from all sources combined, including scholarships, loans, and work contracts, is $19,293; maximum, $31,415. Awards are based on need and merit. The required financial statements are the FAFSA, students' federal tax returns, and the institutional form. The aid application deadline for fall entry is on a rolling basis after January 1. The Law Opportunity Fellowship program funds a limited number of 3-year tuition and research assistant positions to persons from groups and backgrounds historically underrepresented in the legal profession. First-year students are notified about their financial aid application after admission, and once all required financial aid documents are submitted to the university.

About the Law School

University of Iowa College of Law was established in 1865 and is a public institution. The 1900-acre campus is in a small town 125 miles east of Des Moines. The primary mission of the law school is to challenge students to set high standards for themselves and to strive for the best professional education they can obtain from the curriculum, the faculty, and the academic environment. Students have access to federal, state, county, city, and local agencies, courts, correctional facilities, law firms, and legal aid organizations in the Iowa City area. Facilities of special interest to law students include the $25 million law building that features state-of-the-art computer equipment, audiovisual technology, and 3 full-scale courtrooms. Housing for students is available as family housing for married or single parent students, as dormitory housing offered through Residence Services, and as apartments, rooms, and duplexes off campus. All law school facilities are accessible to the physically disabled.

Calendar

The law school operates on a traditional semester basis. Courses for full-time students are offered days only and must be completed within 3 years. There is no part-time program. New students are admitted in the fall and summer. There is an 11-week summer session. Transferable summer courses are offered.

Programs

In addition to the J.D., the law school offers the LL.M. Students may take relevant courses in other programs and apply credit toward the J.D.; a maximum of 6 credits may be applied. The following joint degrees may be earned: J.D./M.A. (Juris Doctor/Master of Arts in urban and regional planning and health administration), J.D./M.B.A. (Juris Doctor/Master of Business Administration), J.D./M.H.A. (Juris Doctor/Master of Health Administration), and J.D./M.P.H. (Juris Doctor/Master of Public Health).

Required

To earn the J.D., candidates must complete 90 total credits, of which 35 are for required courses. The following first-year courses are required of all students: Contracts I and II, Property I and II, Criminal Law, Torts, Civil Procedure, Constitution-

Phone: 319-335-9095 or 319-335-9142
553-IOWA, ext. 9095
Fax: 319-335-9019
E-mail: *law-admissions@uiowa.edu*
Web: *www.law.uiowa.edu*

Contact

College of Law Admissions Staff, 319-335-9095 or 319-335-9142 for general inquiries; Susan Palmer, Director of Financial Aid and Acting Director of Admissions, 319-335-9142 for financial aid information.

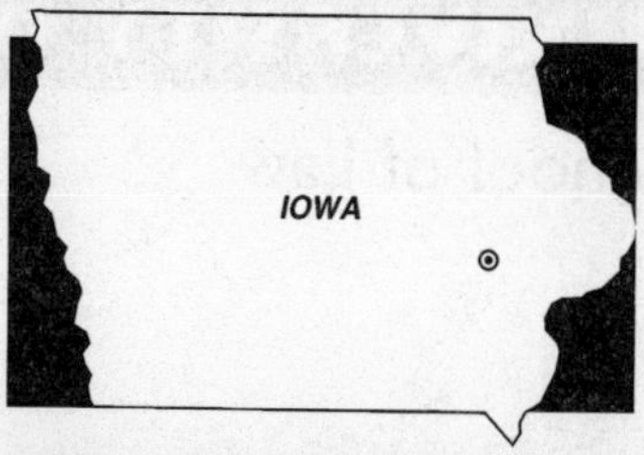

al Law I, and Introduction to Legal Reasoning. Required upper-level courses consist of Appellate Advocacy I, Professional Responsibility, and Constitutional Law II. The required orientation program for first-year students is 1 week; the course component covers an overview of the American legal system, legal education, the legal profession and perspectives on law. The program component covers academic and other support services, bar requirements, dealing with stress, professional conduct standards, and social events.

Electives

There are no formal concentrations areas. There is a variety of civil and criminal law programs, including specialized clinics representing financially distressed farmers and persons with HIV-related problems. Clinics are open to students in the second half of their law study for up to 15 credit hours. Seminars are offered in a variety of subject areas. They normally run for 2 semesters; 5-credits and an upper-level writing credit are awarded. If there is overenrollment in the seminars, priority is given to third-year students and those seeking maximum credit. Occasionally, externship placements are approved with nonprofit entities that offer a strong educational experience. They may be arranged in the summer or during the academic year. Credit is normally 6 hours, though a maximum of 15 credits may be awarded in extraordinary circumstances. Students may arrange an independent research project with faculty members in areas of mutual interest. The Academic Achievement Program sponsors an academic skills lecture series throughout the year, which is open to all students, though the emphasis is on the needs of first-year students. The college participates in the London Law Consortium and sponsors a summer semester in Archachon, France. In addition, many students transfer credits from programs sponsored by other institutions. Faculty members provide mentoring for students needing special assistance. In addition, the Writing Center works with students individually. Students of color are involved in the full array of opportunities offered by the law school, as well as in the minority student organizations. Minority and special interest programming is also sponsored by student organizations. The most widely taken electives are Clinics, Trial Advocacy, and Evidence.

Graduation Requirements

In order to graduate, candidates must have a minimum grade average of 65 and have completed the upper-division writing requirement.

Organizations

Students edit the *Iowa Law Review*, the *Journal of Corporation Law*, *Journal of Transnational Law and Contemporary Problems*, and the *Iowa Journal of Gender, Race, and Justice*. Newsletters are produced by the Student Bar Association and the Organization of Women Law Students. Moot court competitions include The Baskerville Competition, whose winners comprise the Chicago Moot Court team, The Van Oosterhout, to select the National Moot Court team, and the Jessup International Law Competition. Additionally, the Stepenson Competition is a competitive version of the full trials completing the trial advocacy course. Law student organizations include OUTLAWS, Organization of Women Law Students and Staff, and Iowa Society of International Law and Affairs. Campus clubs and other organizations include the National Lawyers Guild, Equal Justice Foundation, and the Federalist Society. There are local chapters of Phi Delta Phi and Phi Alpha Delta.

Library

The law library contains 678,130 hard-copy volumes and 317,212 microform volume equivalents, and subscribes to 8958 serial publications. Such on-line databases and networks as CIS Universe, DIALOG, Infotrac, Legal-Trac, LEXIS, LOIS, Mathew Bender, NEXIS, OCLC First Search, RLIN, WESTLAW, and Wilsonline Indexes are available to law students for research. Special library collections include a U.S. Government Printing Office and Iowa depositories as well as a United Nations collection. Recently, the library wired all 381 student carrels with access to LAN (Internet, WESTLAW, LEXIS, OPAC, and so on). The ratio of library volumes to faculty is 13,297 to 1 and to students, 959 to 1. The ratio of seats in the library to students is 1 to 1.

Placement

J.D.s awarded:	202
Services available through: a separate law school placement center	
Services: 2 full-time professionals provide individual advising and mock interview training.	
Special features: weekly programs on career areas in the law.	
Full-time job interviews:	251 employers
Summer job interviews:	n/av
Placement by graduation:	86% of class
Placement within 9 months:	100% of class
Average starting salary:	$40,213 to $170,000
Areas of placement:	
Private practice 2-10 attorneys	16%
Private practice 11-25 attorneys	6%
Private practice 26-50 attorneys	5%
Private practice 51-100 attorneys	3%
Private practice 100+ attorneys and solo practice	28%
Judicial clerkships	16%
Business/industry	13%
Government	8%
Academic	2%
Unknown	2%
Public interest	1%

Faculty

The law school has 51 full-time and 29 part-time faculty members, of whom 26 are women. According to AAUP standards for Category I institutions, faculty salaries are above average. About 20% of full-time faculty have a graduate law degree in addition to the J.D.; about 10% of part-time faculty have one. The ratio of full-time students to full-time faculty in an average class is 12 to 1; in a clinic, 7 to 1. The law school has a regular program of bringing visiting professors and other distinguished lecturers and visitors to campus. There is a chapter of the Order of the Coif; 50 faculty and 830 graduates are members.

Students

About 47% of the student body are women; 14%, minorities; 5%, African American; 5%, Asian American; 3%, Hispanic; and 1%, Native American. The majority of students come from the Midwest (87%). The average age of entering students is 25; age range is 21 to 53. About 14% of students have a graduate degree. About 3% drop out after the first year for academic or personal reasons; 94% remain to receive a law degree.

UNIVERSITY OF KANSAS

School of Law

205 Green Hall
Lawrence, KS 66045

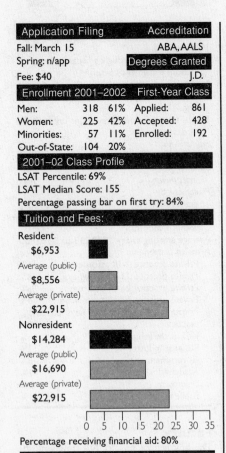

Application Filing	Accreditation
Fall: March 15	ABA, AALS
Spring: n/app	**Degrees Granted**
Fee: $40	J.D.

Enrollment 2001–2002			First-Year Class	
Men:	318	61%	Applied:	861
Women:	225	42%	Accepted:	428
Minorities:	57	11%	Enrolled:	192
Out-of-State:	104	20%		

2001–02 Class Profile

LSAT Percentile: 69%
LSAT Median Score: 155
Percentage passing bar on first try: 84%

Tuition and Fees:

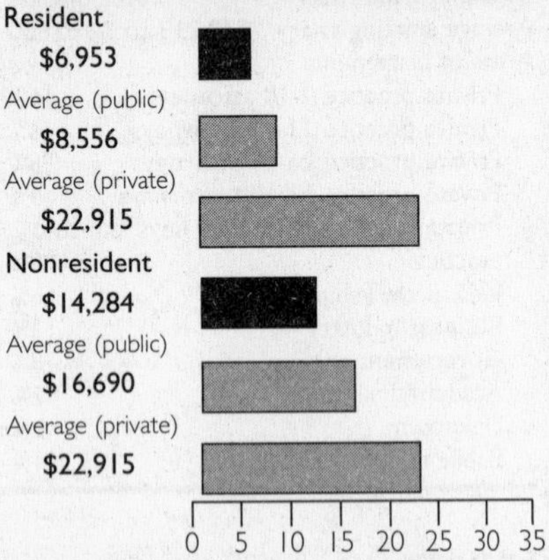

Percentage receiving financial aid: 80%

ADMISSIONS

In the fall 2001 first-year class, 861 applied, 428 were accepted, and 192 enrolled. Five transfers enrolled. The median LSAT percentile of the most recent first-year class was 69; the median GPA was 3.3 on a scale of 4.0. The lowest LSAT percentile accepted was 20; the highest was 99.

Requirements

Applicants must have a bachelor's degree and take the LSAT. The most important admission factors include GPA, LSAT results, and letter of recommendation. No specific undergraduate courses are required. Candidates are not interviewed.

Procedure

The application deadline for fall entry is March 15, but early application is encouraged. Applicants should submit an application form, LSAT results, a nonrefundable application fee of $40, 1 letter of recommendation, and a personal statement. Notification of the admissions decision is on a rolling basis. The latest acceptable LSAT test date for fall entry is February; however, December is preferred. The law school uses the LSDAS.

Special

The law school recruits minority and disadvantaged students by means of minority scholarship opportunities. The law school also sponsors a Minority-in-Law Day program. Letters are sent to students from the Western Name Exchange program. The Law Service Candidate Referral Service is also used. In addition, the law school recruits in areas with a large minority population and recruits at CLEO institutes. Requirements are different for out-of-state students in that preference is given to Kansas residents. Transfer students must have one year of credit, have a minimum GPA of 3.0, and have attended an ABA-approved law school. No more than 31 hours from the student's previous law school can be transferred.

Costs

Tuition and fees for the 2001-2002 academic year are $6953 for full-time in-state students and $14,284 for out-of-state students. On-campus room and board costs about $6546 annually; books and supplies run $800.

Financial Aid

About 80% of current law students receive some form of aid. The average annual amount of aid from all sources combined, including scholarships, loans, and work contracts, is $8500; maximum, $18,500. Awards are based on need and merit. The required financial statement is the FAFSA. The aid application deadline for fall entry is March 1. Special funds for minority or disadvantaged students consist of an amount close to tuition, which is generally available. First-year students are notified about their financial aid application at any point in time from acceptance through the time of enrollment.

About the Law School

University of Kansas School of Law was established in 1878 and is a public institution. The 1000-acre campus is in a suburban area 40 miles west of Kansas City. The primary mission of the law school is to prepare students for practice in the legal profession by focusing on a general education in the law as well as on the details of legal rules and practice. Students have access to federal, state, county, city, and local agencies, courts, correctional facilities, law firms, and legal aid organizations in the Lawrence area. Facilities of special interest to law students is the Paul E. Wilson Defender Project, which allows students to counsel and perform legal service for indigent inmates of the U.S. Penitentiary at Leavenworth, the Kansas State Penitentiary, and Kansas Correctional Institution; the project was the first of its kind in the country. Housing for students is available in a university residence hall or apartment complex and also in apartments or houses off campus. Married student housing is also available. All law school facilities are accessible to the physically disabled.

Calendar

The law school operates on a traditional semester basis. Courses for full-time students are offered days only and must be completed within 5 years. There is no part-time program. New students are admitted in the fall and summer. There are 2 5-week summer sessions. Transferable summer courses are offered.

Programs

Students may take relevant courses in other programs and apply credit toward the J.D.; a maximum of 6 hours credits may be applied. The following joint degrees may be earned: J.D./M.A. (Juris Doctor/Master of Arts in economics and in philosophy), J.D./M.B.A. (Juris Doctor/Master of Business Administration), J.D./M.P.A. (Juris Doctor/Master of Public Administration), J.D./M.S. (Juris Doctor/Master of Science in health services administration), J.D./M.S.W. (Juris Doctor/Master of Social Work), and J.D./M.U.P. (Juris Doctor/Master of Urban Planning).

Phone: 785-864-4378
Fax: 785-864-5054
E-mail: *reitz@law.wpo.ukans.edu*
Web: *www.law.ukans.edu*

Contact
Rachel Reitz, Director of Admissions, 866-864-4378 for general inquiries; Diane Del Buono, Director of Financial Aid, 866-864-4700 for financial aid information.

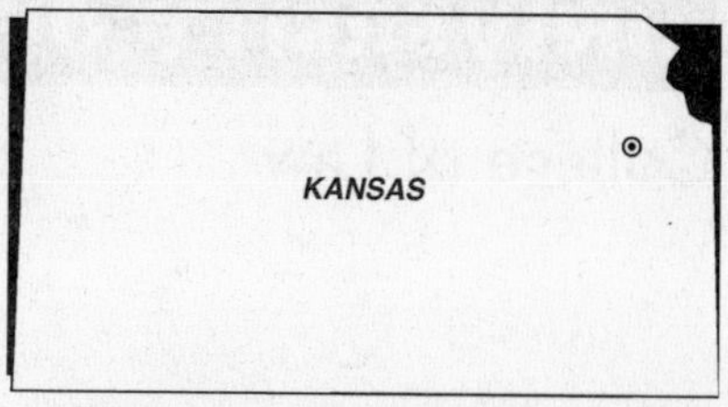

Required
To earn the J.D., candidates must complete 90 total credits, of which 43 to 45 are for required courses. They must maintain a minimum GPA of 2.0 in the required courses. The following first-year courses are required of all students: Civil Procedure I and II, Contracts I and II, Criminal Law, Criminal Procedure, Property I and II, Torts I, and Lawyering I and II. Required upper-level courses consist of Commercial Law I, Constitutional Law *or* Constitutional Law A and B, Evidence, Professional Responsibility, and a writing requirement. The required orientation program for first-year students is a 1 ½-day program that includes sessions on preparing for class, briefing and studying techniques, a mock class, small group sessions, and tours of the library and building.

Electives
The School of Law offers concentrations in corporate law, criminal law, environmental law, family law, international law, juvenile law, labor law, litigation, media law, securities law, tax law, torts and insurance, agricultural law, civil rights law, constitutional law, energy law, industrial relations law, tribal law and patent law. In addition, clinics are offered to second- and third-year students for 1 to 3 hours of credit. Clinics include Criminal Justice, the Paul E. Wilson Defender Project, and the Legal Aid Clinic. Periodically, research workshops are offered for all students. Second- and third-year students may take advantage of available internship opportunities; usually no academic credit is awarded. Independent research seminars are available. Guest lecture programs are offered for no credit. Students may study at University College in London through the London Law Consortium, of which the University of Kansas is a member. Students may also study at the Summer Institute in Cambridge, England. They may also participate in other ABA-approved study-abroad programs. Tutorial programs are voluntary. Academic support programs are available for students who may be in need of assistance. The most widely taken electives are Business Associations I and II, Income Tax, and Family Law.

Graduation Requirements
In order to graduate, candidates must have a GPA of 2.0and fulfill the upper-division writing requirement by successfully completing 2 hours of independent research, and a 2- to 3-hour seminar, workshop, clinic, or other course that a faculty member has certified involves close faculty supervision of writing, or publishing a student note or comment in the law review or journal.

Organizations
Students edit the *Kansas Law Review, Kansas Journal of Law and Public Policy*, and the newspaper, *Brief Briefs*. Other publications include *KU Laws*, the alumni newsletter. There is an in-house moot court competition for second-year students who compete for the Robert C. Foulston and George Siefkin Prizes for Excellence in Appellate Advocacy. The National Moot Court Competition is held annually in the fall, whereas the Jessup International Moot Court Competition is held annually in the spring. Other competitions include the Client Counseling Competition. Student organizations include the American Trial Lawyers Association, Black Law Students Association, and Environmental Law Society. Local chapters of national associations include Phi Alpha Delta, Phi Delta Phi, and National Lawyers Guild.

Library
The law library contains 325,000 hard-copy volumes and 333,169 microform volume equivalents, and subscribes to 4165 serial publications. Such on-line databases and networks as DIALOG, LEXIS, and WESTLAW are available to law students for research. Special library collections include selective government depositories for both state and federal documents. Recently, the library wired study carrels for Internet access. The ratio of library volumes to faculty is 9559 to 1 and to students, 623 to 1. The ratio of seats in the library to students is 1 to 1.

Placement

J.D.s awarded:	166
Services available through: a separate law school placement center	
Special features: a mentoring program that matches current law students with practicing alumni..	
Full-time job interviews:	150 employers
Summer job interviews:	n/av
Placement by graduation:	n/av
Placement within 9 months:	94% of class
Average starting salary:	$23,000 to $52,000
Areas of placement:	
Private practice 2-10 attorneys	26%
Private practice 11-25 attorneys	14%
Private practice 26-50 attorneys	6%
Private practice 51-100 attorneys	11%
Business/industry	26%
Judicial clerkships	7%
Public interest	4%
Government	2%
Military	2%
Academic	2%

Faculty
The law school has 34 full-time and 7 part-time faculty members, of whom 11 are women. According to AAUP standards for Category I institutions, faculty salaries are average. About 28% of full-time faculty have a graduate law degree in addition to the J.D.; about 50% of part-time faculty have one. The ratio of full-time students to full-time faculty in an average class is 16 to 1; in a clinic, 10 to 1. The law school has a regular program of bringing visiting professors and other distinguished lecturers and visitors to campus. There is a chapter of the Order of the Coif; 17 faculty and 450 graduates are members.

Students
About 42% of the student body are women; 11%, minorities; 3%, African American; 3%, Asian American; 3%, Hispanic; and 1%, Native American. The majority of students come from Kansas (80%). The average age of entering students is 23; age range is 20 to 52. About 51% of students enter directly from undergraduate school, 8% have a graduate degree, and 40% have worked full-time prior to entering law school. About 3% drop out after the first year for academic or personal reasons; 94% remain to receive a law degree.

UNIVERSITY OF KENTUCKY

College of Law

209 Law Building
Lexington, KY 40506-0048

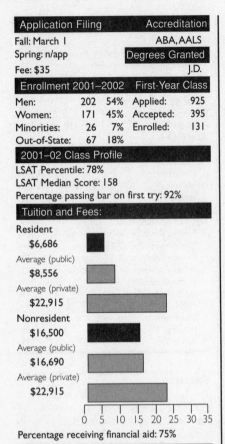

Application Filing		Accreditation
Fall: March 1		ABA, AALS
Spring: n/app		**Degrees Granted**
Fee: $35		J.D.

Enrollment 2001–2002			First-Year Class	
Men:	202	54%	Applied:	925
Women:	171	45%	Accepted:	395
Minorities:	26	7%	Enrolled:	131
Out-of-State:	67	18%		

2001–02 Class Profile

LSAT Percentile: 78%
LSAT Median Score: 158
Percentage passing bar on first try: 92%

Tuition and Fees:

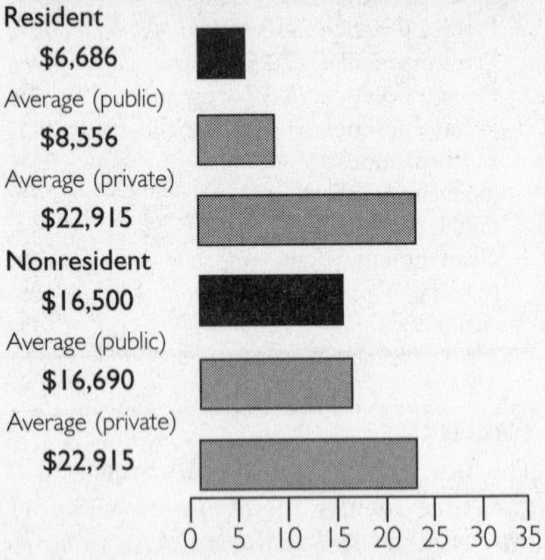

Percentage receiving financial aid: 75%

ADMISSIONS

In the fall 2001 first-year class, 925 applied, 395 were accepted, and 131 enrolled. Eight transfers enrolled. The median LSAT percentile of the most recent first-year class was 78; the median GPA was 3.5 on a scale of 4.0. The lowest LSAT percentile accepted was 30; the highest was 98.

Requirements

Applicants must have a bachelor's degree and take the LSAT. Minimum acceptable LSAT percentile is 30 and minimum acceptable GPA is 2.4 on a scale of 4.0. The most important admission factors include GPA, LSAT results, and writing ability. No specific undergraduate courses are required. Candidates are not interviewed.

Procedure

The application deadline for fall entry is March 1. Applicants should submit an application form, LSAT results, transcripts, TOEFL if a foreign student, a nonrefundable application fee of $35; 2 letters of recommendation are recommended but not required. Notification of the admissions decision is weekly on a rolling basis. The latest acceptable LSAT test date for fall entry is February. The law school uses the LSDAS.

Special

The law school recruits minority and disadvantaged students by means of the Fall Minority Visitation Conference, scholarships and stipends, visits to campuses, participation in CLEO, the provision of tutors during the first year, and general academic support offerings. Requirements are not different for out-of-state students. Transfer students must have one year of credit, have a minimum GPA of 2.7, and must provide reasons for wanting to transfer. As transfers are not encouraged, applications are reviewed on a case-by-case basis. Preadmissions courses consist of a 1-week summer workshop prior to the first day of classes.

Costs

Tuition and fees for the 2001-2002 academic year are $6686 for full-time in-state students and $16,500 for out-of-state students. On-campus room and board costs about $7400 annually; books and supplies run $650.

Financial Aid

About 75% of current law students receive some form of aid. The average annual amount of aid from all sources combined, including scholarships, loans, and work contracts, is $17,000; maximum, $30,500. Awards are based on need and merit. Special funds are available that have specific criteria that must be met by the applicants. The required financial statement is the FAFSA. The aid application deadline for fall entry is April 1. Special funds for minority or disadvantaged students consist of tuition and monthly stipends available through the combined efforts of the college's and university's administration. First-year students are notified about their financial aid application 1 month after acceptance for scholarships, and in June for loans.

About the Law School

University of Kentucky College of Law was established in 1908 and is a public institution. The 673-acre campus is in an urban area 80 miles east of Louisville and 75 miles south of Cincinnati, Ohio. The primary mission of the law school is to provide a legal education to individuals so that they might render a high quality of professional service to Kentucky and the nation. Students have access to federal, state, county, city, and local agencies, courts, correctional facilities, law firms, and legal aid organizations in the Lexington area. Additional opportunities are available in state agencies and the state judicial system. The U.S. District Courts for both the Eastern and Western districts of Kentucky, and the sixth Circuit Court of Appeals is 80 miles north. Facilities of special interest to law students include a civil law clinic; students have their own clients and caseloads under the supervision of a former trial attorney. Housing for students is plentiful both on and off campus. Most law students choose off-campus housing, some of which is located across the street from the law school. All law school facilities are accessible to the physically disabled.

Calendar

The law school operates on a traditional semester basis. Courses for full-time students are offered days only and are usually completed within 3 to 4 years. There is no part-time program. New students are admitted in the fall. There is an 8-week summer session. Transferable summer courses are offered.

Programs

Students may take relevant courses in other programs and apply credit toward the J.D.; a maximum of 6 credits may be applied. The following joint degrees may be earned: J.D./M.B.A. (Juris Doctor/Master of Business Administration) and J.D./M.P.A. (Juris Doctor/Master of Public Administration).

Required

To earn the J.D., candidates must complete 90 total credits, of which 34 are for required courses. They must maintain a

Phone: 606-257-7938
Fax: n/av
E-mail: *dbakert@uky.edu*
Web: *http://www.uky.edu/law*

Contact

Jeanie Powell, Admissions Associate, 859-257-1678 for general inquiries; University of Kentucky Student Financial Aid Office, 606-257-3172 for financial aid information.

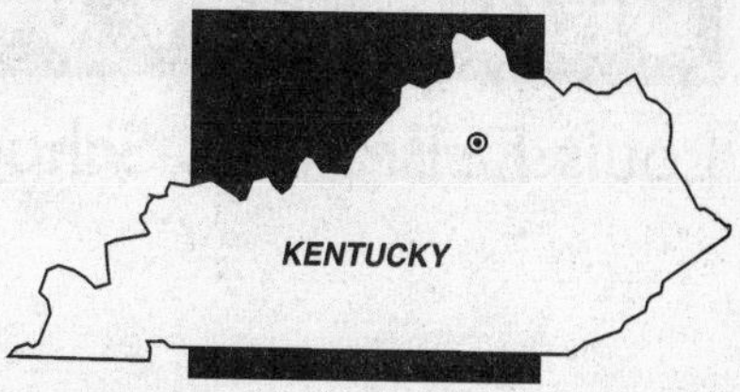

minimum GPA of 2.0 in the required courses. The following first-year courses are required of all students: Contracts and Sales I and II, Torts, Property, Criminal Law, Constitutional Law I, Civil Procedure I and II, and Legal Research and Writing. Required upper-level courses consist of Professional Responsibility and a seminar with a writing requirement. The required orientation program for first-year students is 2 days and includes an introduction to the community, to the case method, to the faculty, and to the current students.

Electives

The College of Law offers concentrations in corporate law, criminal law, environmental law, family law, international law, juvenile law, labor law, litigation, securities law, sports law, tax law, and torts and insurance. In addition, clinics include Prison Counsel for upper-level students for 3 credit hours and Civil-Law Clinic for upper-level students for 3 credit hours. Numerous seminars are offered, including Gender Discrimination, Housing Law, and Intellectual Property. Third-year students may participate in internships with prosecutors and with state and federal judges for 3 credit hours. An Innocence Project with the state public defender's office for 3 credit hours is also offered. Independent research may be done on topics of special interest for 1 to 3 credit hours. Third-year students receive 1 to 3 credit hours for clerking with judges in state district, circuit, and appellate division courts, or in either of 2 federal district courts. Third-year students also receive 1 to 3 credit hours working with local prosecutors and in the prison internship program. The Roy Ray and Virginia Ray lecture series brings national figures to speak at the college. Other lecture series are given by scholars such as Dean Guido Calabresi and the Honorable Justice William H. Rehnquist. Study abroad is available via transient work at a number of ABA-approved law schools. Academic support is offered for all first-year students in the first semester and in later semesters for those in academic difficulty. An academic success program and tutorials are offered to minority students. The most widely taken electives are Evidence, Business Associations, and Tax.

Graduation Requirements

In order to graduate, candidates must have a GPA of 2.0 and have completed the upper-division writing requirement.

Organizations

Students edit the *Kentucky Law Journal*, the *Journal of Natural Resources and Environmental Law*, and the newspaper *Week in Brief*. Students compete in the National Moot Court Competition, Jessup Competition, and Frederick Douglass Black Law Student Association Competition. Other competitions include the Trial Advocacy Competition, the Wilhelm Vis International Commercial Law Moot Court, and competitions in sports law, space law, and telecommunications law. Student organizations include the Student Bar Association, Environmental Law Society, and Womens' Law Caucus. Other organizations include Appalachian Law Students, Health Law Society, and International Law Society. Henry Clay Inns of Court and several legal fraternities have local chapters.

Library

The law library contains 437,233 hard-copy volumes and 195,875 microform volume equivalents, and subscribes to 3805 serial publications. Such on-line databases and networks as CALI, CIS Universe, DIALOG, Dow-Jones, Legal-Trac, LEXIS, LOIS, Mathew Bender, NEXIS, OCLC First Search, and WESTLAW are available to law students for research. Special library collections include human rights and mineral law and policy, as well as a selective government document depository. Recently, the library made laptops available for student check-out and added a 42-carrel study room wired for laptop use of the Internet, LEXIS, WESTLAW, and other library resources. The ratio of library volumes to faculty is 15,615 to 1 and to students, 1172 to 1. The ratio of seats in the library to students is 1 to 1.

Placement	
J.D.s awarded:	130
Services available through: a separate law school placement center	
Services: computer database on Kentucky law firms and 5 recruitment conferences	
Special features: individual attention from an associate dean with 8 years of practice experience in a law firm setting.	
Full-time job interviews:	100 employers
Summer job interviews:	175 employers
Placement by graduation:	60% of class
Placement within 9 months:	100% of class
Average starting salary:	$23,000 to $127,000
Areas of placement:	
Solo practice	1%
Private practice 2-10 attorneys	22%
Private practice 11-25 attorneys	7%
Private practice 26-50 attorneys	10%
Private practice 51-500 attorneys	20%
Judicial clerkships	17%
Government	10%
Business/industry	9%
Public interest	2%
Military	2%

Faculty

The law school has 28 full-time and 20 part-time faculty members, of whom 16 are women. According to AAUP standards for Category I institutions, faculty salaries are average. About 25% of full-time faculty have a graduate law degree in addition to the J.D.; about 10% of part-time faculty have one. The ratio of full-time students to full-time faculty in an average class is 14 to 1; in a clinic, 8 to 1. The law school has a regular program of bringing visiting professors and other distinguished lecturers and visitors to campus. There is a chapter of the Order of the Coif; 23 faculty and 443 graduates are members.

Students

About 45% of the student body are women; 7%, minorities; 5%, African American; 1%, Asian American; 1%, Hispanic; and 1%, Native American. The majority of students come from Kentucky (82%). The average age of entering students is 23; age range is 21 to 50. About 6% drop out after the first year for academic or personal reasons; 92% remain to receive a law degree.

UNIVERSITY OF LOUISVILLE

Louis D. Brandeis School of Law

University of Louisville
Belknap Campus-Wilson W. Wyatt Hall
Louisville, KY 40292

Application Filing		Accreditation
Fall: March 1		ABA, AALS
Spring: n/app		**Degrees Granted**
Fee: $40		J.D.

Enrollment 2001–2002			First-Year Class	
Men:	200	52%	Applied:	796
Women:	183	48%	Accepted:	271
Minorities:	322	84%	Enrolled:	129
Out-of-State:	69	18%		

2001–02 Class Profile

LSAT Percentile: 70%
LSAT Median Score: 156
Percentage passing bar on first try: 82%

Tuition and Fees:

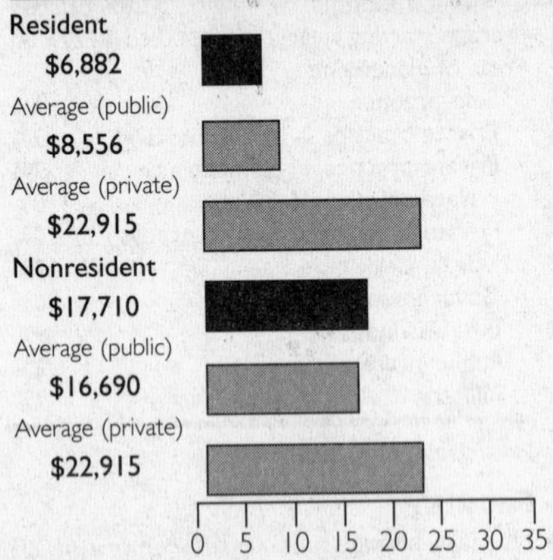

Percentage receiving financial aid: 80%

ADMISSIONS

In the fall 2001 first-year class, 796 applied, 271 were accepted, and 129 enrolled. Fourteen transfers enrolled. The median LSAT percentile of the most recent first-year class was 70; the median GPA was 3.3 on a scale of 4.0. The lowest LSAT percentile accepted was 16; the highest was 99.

Requirements

Applicants must have a bachelor's degree and take the LSAT. Minimum acceptable GPA is 2.0 on a scale of 4.0. The most important admission factors include academic achievement, LSAT results, and GPA. No specific undergraduate courses are required. Candidates are not interviewed.

Procedure

The application deadline for fall entry is March 1. Applicants should submit an application form, a nonrefundable application fee of $40, and a personal statement. Recommendations are suggested, but not required. Notification of the admissions decision is on a rolling basis. The latest acceptable LSAT test date for fall entry is February. The law school uses the LSDAS.

Special

The law school recruits minority and disadvantaged students by sponsoring a minority prelaw day and attending minority fairs and programs at other schools. Requirements are not different for out-of-state students. Transfer students must have one year of credit, have attended an ABA-approved law school, be in good standing, have met entrance requirements for the school had they applied for initial admission, and be in the upper quarter of their law school class. Preadmissions courses vary from year to year.

Costs

Tuition and fees for the 2001-2002 academic year are $6882 for full-time in-state students and $17,710 for out-of-state students. Tuition for part-time students is $5840 in-state and $14,880 out-of-state. On-campus room and board costs about $6504 annually; books and supplies run $854.

Financial Aid

About 80% of current law students receive some form of aid. Awards are based on need and merit. The required financial statement is the FAFSA. The aid application deadline for fall entry is June 1. Special funds for minority or disadvantaged students consist of a number of recruiting scholarships. First-year students are notified about their financial aid application at the time of acceptance.

About the Law School

University of Louisville Louis D. Brandeis School of Law was established in 1846 and is a public institution. The campus is in an urban area 4 miles south of downtown Louisville. The primary mission of the law school is to provide students with a quality legal education and prepare them for professional life through a curriculum that emphasizes fundamental lawyering skills and the development of professional values, while also affording students the opportunity to take advanced courses in a wide variety of specialty areas. Students have access to federal, state, county, city, and local agencies, courts, correctional facilities, law firms, and legal aid organizations in the Louisville area. Facilities of special interest to law students include the school's physical facility that provides students with a large, comfortable environment in which to attend class and study. Many student gathering places and study group rooms are available. Housing for students is available in a university dormitory and in affordable rental housing close to campus. All law school facilities are accessible to the physically disabled.

Calendar

The law school operates on a traditional semester basis. Courses for full-time students are offered days only, but full-time students may enroll in evening classes after the first year; courses and must be completed within 5 years. For part-time students, courses are offered evenings only, but part-time students may enroll in day classes and must be completed within 6 years. New full- and part-time students are admitted in the fall. There is an 8-week summer session. Transferable summer courses are offered.

Programs

The following joint degrees may be earned: J.D./M.A. (Juris Doctor/Master of Arts in humanities), J.D./M.B.A. (Juris Doctor/Master of Business Administration), J.D./M.Div. (Juris Doctor/Master of Divinity), and M.S.S.W./J.D. (Master of Science in Social Work/Juris Doctor).

Phone: 502-852-6364
334-8634
Fax: 502-852-0862
E-mail: *lawadmissions@louisville.edu*
Web: *www.louisville.edu/brandeislaw/*

Contact

Admissions Office, 502-852-6364 for general inquiries; Connie Shumake, Assistant Dean for Law Admissions, 502-852-6391 for financial aid information.

Required

To earn the J.D., candidates must complete 90 total credits, of which 44 are for required courses. They must maintain a minimum GPA of 2.0 in the required courses. The following first-year courses are required of all students: Basic Legal Skills, Civil Procedure, Contracts, Torts, Property, Legal Research, and Criminal Law. Required upper-level courses consist of Professional Responsibility, Constitutional Law I and II, a perspective course, a writing requirement, and 24 hours of core courses. The required orientation program for first-year students is 2½ days devoted to skills development and orientation to legal education and the profession. There is also time for social events.

Electives

The Louis D. Brandeis School of Law offers concentrations in corporate law, criminal law, family law, international law, labor law, securities law, and tax law. In addition, there is a required pro bono program (minimum 30 hours of work). Externships in the courts and the P.D. and D.A. offices are available to those who have completed 60 credit hours. A wide variety of seminars are offered to second-, third-, and fourth-year students in specialized fields of law; 2 to 3 credit hours are awarded. Several internships, worth 2 to 4 hours, are available, including a judicial internship and a civil and criminal internship. All students are required to complete Legal Research, a 3-hour Basic Legal Skills course, and a seminar that requires a substantial research paper. Special lecture series include the Brandeis and Harlan Lecture Series. Students may earn credit for participation in foreign study in an ABA-accredited program. Students with adequate language abilities may be foreign exchange students with several law schools throughout the world. An academic support program is offered to provide tutorial assistance to students with academic problems. Tutors run study sessions in first-year courses. The school has several minority recruiting activities each year and a number of scholarships for minority students. A diversity committee presents programs to the student body on topics such as gay/lesbian issues and women in politics. The most widely taken electives are Tax, Evidence, and Business Organizations.

Graduation Requirements

In order to graduate, candidates must have a GPA of 2.0, have completed the upper-division writing requirement, and have performed 30 hours of law-related public service at a placement approved by the school.

Organizations

Students edit the *Brandeis Law Journal*, the *Brandeis Brief Magazine*, and in conjunction with the University of South Carolina, the *Journal of Law and Education*. Annually, students participate in the National Moot Court, the Jessup International Law, and the American Association of Trial Lawyers Mock Trial. Other competitions include a Trial Advocacy Moot Court exercise in a student's first year and the Pirtle-Washer Moot Court in a student's second year. Law student organizations include the Student Bar Association, Environmental Law Society, and the International Law Society. There are local chapters of Delta Theta Phi, Phi Alpha Delta, and the Federalist Society.

Library

The law library contains 385,367 hardcopy volumes and 8461 microform volume equivalents, and subscribes to 5378 serial publications. Such on-line databases and networks as CALI, CIS Universe, DIALOG, LEXIS, NEXIS, OCLC First Search, WESTLAW, and 213 databases available through the university libraries are available to law students for research. Special library collections include the Justice Brandeis papers, Justice Harlan papers, Supreme Court briefs, and a U.S. government documents depository. The ratio of library volumes to faculty is 11,678 to 1 and to students, 1006 to 1. The ratio of seats in the library to students is 1 to 1.

Placement

J.D.s awarded:	96
Services available through: a separate law school placement center	
Special features: participation in recruiting consortia in the southeast and Kentucky.	
Full-time job interviews:	16 employers
Summer job interviews:	17 employers
Placement by graduation:	69% of class
Placement within 9 months:	96% of class
Average starting salary:	$23,500 to $85,000
Areas of placement:	
Private practice 2-10 attorneys	31%
Private practice 11-25 attorneys	10%
Private practice 26-50 attorneys	9%
Private practice 51-100 attorneys	15%
Business/industry	15%
Government	13%
Public interest	3%
Judicial clerkships	2%
Military	1%
Academic	1%

Faculty

The law school has 33 full-time and 8 part-time faculty members, of whom 14 are women. According to AAUP standards for Category I institutions, faculty salaries are below average. About 33% of full-time faculty have a graduate law degree in addition to the J.D. The ratio of full-time students to full-time faculty in an average class is 7 to 1. The law school has a regular program of bringing visiting professors and other distinguished lecturers and visitors to campus.

Students

About 48% of the student body are women; 84%, minorities; 6%, African American; 3%, Asian American; 2%, Hispanic; and 1%, Native American. The majority of students come from Kentucky (82%). The average age of entering students is 24; age range is 21 to 52. About 44% of students enter directly from undergraduate school.

UNIVERSITY OF MAINE

School of Law

246 Deering Avenue
Portland, ME 04102

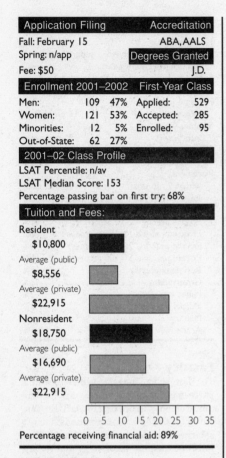

Application Filing		Accreditation
Fall: February 15		ABA, AALS
Spring: n/app		**Degrees Granted**
Fee: $50		J.D.

Enrollment 2001–2002			First-Year Class	
Men:	109	47%	Applied:	529
Women:	121	53%	Accepted:	285
Minorities:	12	5%	Enrolled:	95
Out-of-State:	62	27%		

2001–02 Class Profile

LSAT Percentile: n/av
LSAT Median Score: 153
Percentage passing bar on first try: 68%

Tuition and Fees:

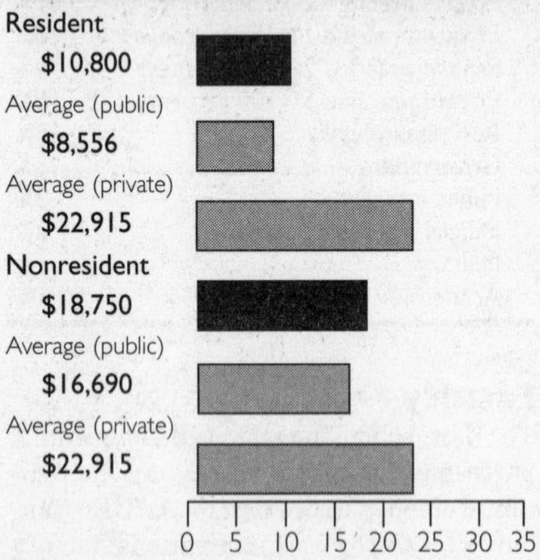

Percentage receiving financial aid: 89%

ADMISSIONS

In the fall 2001 first-year class, 529 applied, 285 were accepted, and 95 enrolled. Three transfers enrolled. The median GPA of the most recent first-year class was 3.26 on a scale of 4.0. The lowest LSAT percentile accepted was 16; the highest was 98.

Requirements

Applicants must have a bachelor's degree and take the LSAT. The most important admission factors include academic achievement. No specific undergraduate courses are required. Candidates are not interviewed.

Procedure

The application deadline for fall entry is February 15. Applicants should submit an application form, LSAT results, transcripts, a nonrefundable application fee of $50, and 1 letter of recommendation. Notification of the admissions decision is mid-April. The latest acceptable LSAT test date for fall entry is February. The law school uses the LSDAS.

Special

The law school recruits minority and disadvantaged students through law school admissions forums, scholarship assistance, and contacts with law school minority organizations, and mailings to minority candidates through Law Service's C.R.S. Requirements are not different for out-of-state students. Transfer students must have one year of credit, have attended an ABA-approved law school, and have superior academic credentials.

Costs

Tuition and fees for the 2001-2002 academic year are $10,800 for full-time in-state students and $18,750 for out-of-state students. On-campus room and board costs about $9296 annually; books and supplies run $851.

Financial Aid

About 89% of current law students receive some form of aid. The average annual amount of aid from all sources combined, including scholarships, loans, and work contracts, is $19,277; maximum, $31,980. Awards are based on need. The required financial statement is the FAFSA. The aid application deadline for fall entry is February 1. Special funds for minority or disadvantaged students consist of 3 full-tuition scholarships available for each class. First-year students are notified about their financial aid application when a nonrefundable deposit is due.

About the Law School

University of Maine School of Law was established in 1962 and is a public institution. The campus is in an urban area in Portland. The primary mission of the law school is to educate students to serve the public and private sectors with distinction; to contribute to the advancement of the law through scholarly and professional research and writing; and to engage in public services aimed at improving the legal system. Students have access to federal, state, county, city, and local agencies, courts, correctional facilities, law firms, and legal aid organizations in the Portland area. Portland is the major urban and legal center in the state. Facilities of special interest to law students are the Cumberland County Superior Court, the Maine Supreme Judicial Court, and the Federal District Court. Housing for students is available in university dorms, but most students prefer to find housing in and around Portland. All law school facilities are accessible to the physically disabled.

Calendar

The law school operates on a traditional semester basis. Courses for full-time students are offered days only and must be completed within 3 years. For part-time students, courses are offered days only and must be completed within 5 years. New full- and part-time students are admitted in the fall. There is a 7-week summer session. Transferable summer courses are offered.

Programs

Students may take relevant courses in other programs and apply credit toward the J.D.; the maximum of credits that may be applied varies, and must be approved by the curriculum committee. The following joint degree may be earned: J.D./M.A. (Juris Doctor/Master of Arts in public policy and management, health policy management, and community planning and development).

Phone: 207-780-4341
E-mail: *mainelaw@usm.maine.edu*
Web: *www.law.usm.maine.edu*

Contact

Barbara Gauditz, Assistant Dean, 207-780-4341 for general inquiries; Norma Catalano, Assistant Director, 207-780-5250 for financial aid information.

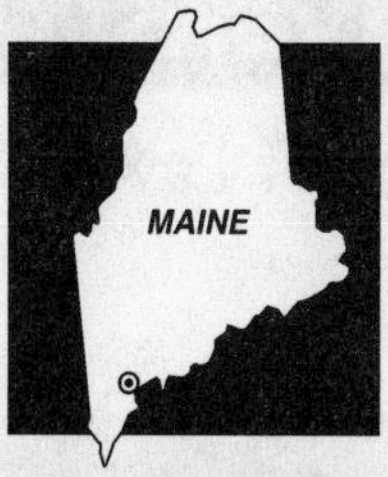

Required

To earn the J.D., candidates must complete 89 total credits, of which 40 are for required courses. They must maintain a minimum GPA of 2.0 in the required courses. The following first-year courses are required of all students: Constitutional Law I, Contracts I and II, Civil Procedure I and II, Property, Torts, Criminal Law, and Legal Research and Writing I and II. Required upper-level courses consist of Professional Responsibility, a perspectives course, an independent writing requirement, and Constitutional Law II. The required orientation program for first-year students is 2 days. The first day includes mini-classes, then discussion with alumni on the same case, and small group discussions with faculty; the second day is information on university services, student organizations, and a session on professional responsibility.

Electives

There are no formal concentration areas. A number of clinics are offered: General Practice Clinic is open to third-year students for 6 credits; Criminal Law and Family Law practicums are open to third-year students for 6 credits; and the Environmental Law Clinic is open to second- and third-year students for 3 credits. Seminars in commercial law, consumer law, constitutional law, and international law are open to second- and third-year students. The Frank M. Coffin Lecture on Law and Public Service is held annually, along with the Godfrey Distinguished Visiting Lecturer and the Deans Distinguished Lecture Series. The Student Bar Association and other student organizations also offer guest lectures. There is a 1-semester option at Dalhousie Law School in Halifax, Nova Scotia; the University of New Brunswick, Canada; University College, Galway, Ireland; University of Buckingham, England; Université du Maine, LeMans, France; or Université de Cergy in Ponceoise, Paris. Tutorial assistance is available for students identified as requiring additional work in writing skills and legal analysis. The most widely taken electives are Trial Practice, Business Associations, and Evidence.

Graduation Requirements

In order to graduate, candidates must have a GPA of 2.0, have completed the upper-division writing requirement, and which may be fulfilled with *Law Review, Ocean and Coastal Law Journal*, Moot Court, or an independent writing project; and have taken Constitutional Law II, one course that places the law in a broader philosophic, historic, or comparative context, and a course in professional responsibility.

Organizations

Students edit the *Maine Law Review, Ocean and Coastal Law Journal*, and *The Advocate*, the weekly career services newsletter. The second-year Moot Court Board is chosen by internal competition. Board members compete in a number of regional, national, and international competitions, such as the National Moot Court Competition, Jessup International, and the Trilateral Moot Court competition with Canadian law schools. Other competitions include the National Mock Trial Competition. Student organizations include the Environmental Law Society; Lesbian, Gay and Bisexual Law Caucus; and Maine Association for Public Interest Law. Local chapters of national associations include the National Lawyers Guild, International Law Society, and the Federalist Society.

Library

The law library contains 336,000 hard-copy volumes and 16,300 microform volume equivalents, and subscribes to 3700 serial publications. Such on-line databases and networks as LEXIS, RLIN, and WESTLAW are available to law students for research. Special library collections include a U.S. government publications depository and Canadian and British Commonwealth law reports and statutes. Recently, the library completed an addition that provides more shelf space and student study space. The ratio of library volumes to faculty is 21,000 to 1 and to students, 1461 to 1.

Placement

J.D.s awarded:	89
Services available through: a separate law school placement center	
Full-time job interviews:	40 employers
Summer job interviews:	53 employers
Placement by graduation:	n/av
Placement within 9 months:	80% of class
Average starting salary:	$20,000 to $50,000
Areas of placement:	
Private practice 2-100 attorneys	37%
Judicial clerkships	19%
Government	15%
Business/industry (non-legal)	15%
Business/industry (legal); 2% unknown	9%
Public interest	3%
Unknown	2%

Faculty

The law school has 16 full-time and 3 part-time faculty members, of whom 7 are women. About 30% of full-time faculty have a graduate law degree in addition to the J.D. The ratio of full-time students to full-time faculty in an average class is 40 to 1; in a clinic, 6 to 1. The law school has a regular program of bringing visiting professors and other distinguished lecturers and visitors to campus.

Students

About 53% of the student body are women; 5%, minorities; 2%, African American; 1%, Asian American; 1%, Hispanic; and 1%, Native American. The majority of students come from Maine (73%). The average age of entering students is 29; age range is 20 to 61. About 20% of students enter directly from undergraduate school, 22% have a graduate degree, and 82% have worked full-time prior to entering law school. About 3% drop out after the first year for academic or personal reasons; 97% remain to receive a law degree.

UNIVERSITY OF MARYLAND

School of Law

500 West Baltimore Street
Baltimore, MD 21201

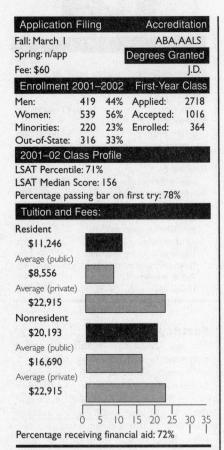

Application Filing		Accreditation
Fall: March 1		ABA, AALS
Spring: n/app		**Degrees Granted**
Fee: $60		J.D.

Enrollment 2001–2002			First-Year Class	
Men:	419	44%	Applied:	2718
Women:	539	56%	Accepted:	1016
Minorities:	220	23%	Enrolled:	364
Out-of-State:	316	33%		

2001–02 Class Profile

LSAT Percentile: 71%
LSAT Median Score: 156
Percentage passing bar on first try: 78%

Tuition and Fees:

Resident
$11,246
Average (public)
$8,556
Average (private)
$22,915
Nonresident
$20,193
Average (public)
$16,690
Average (private)
$22,915

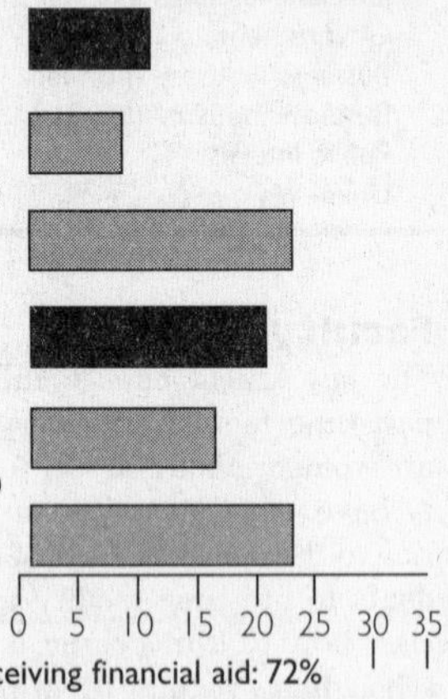

Percentage receiving financial aid: 72%

ADMISSIONS

In the fall 2001 first-year class, 2718 applied, 1016 were accepted, and 364 enrolled. The median LSAT percentile of the most recent first-year class was 71; the median GPA was 3.4 on a scale of 4.0. The lowest LSAT percentile accepted was 10; the highest was 99.

Requirements

Applicants must have a bachelor's degree and take the LSAT. Outstanding applicants, at minimum age 23 with 3 years of college, are also considered. The most important admission factors include GPA, general background, and faculty recommendation. No specific undergraduate courses are required. Candidates are not interviewed.

Procedure

The application deadline for fall entry is March 1. Applicants should submit an application form, LSAT results, transcripts, a nonrefundable application fee of $60, 2 letters of recommendation, and a personal statement. Notification of the admissions decision is January through April. The latest acceptable LSAT test date for fall entry is February. The law school uses the LSDAS.

Special

The law school recruits minority and disadvantaged students by encouraging applications from African Americans and other students of color, and from disadvantaged persons who will enrich the law school and the profession. Requirements are not different for out-of-state students. Transfer students must have one year of credit, have attended an ABA-approved law school, and have competitive academic credentials.

Costs

Tuition and fees for the 2001-2002 academic year are $11,246 for full-time in-state students and $20,193 for out-of-state students. Tuition for part-time students is $8478 in-state and $15,186 out-of-state. On-campus room and board costs about $11,291 annually; books and supplies run $1500.

Financial Aid

About 72% of current law students receive some form of aid. The average annual amount of aid from all sources combined, including scholarships, loans, and work contracts, is $21,042. Awards are based on need and merit. The average financial package is $21,042, based on need. There are a limited number of merit scholarships awarded through the admissions process. The required financial statement is the FAFSA. The aid application deadline for fall entry is March 1. Special funds for minority or disadvantaged students consist of grants that are available for students whose enrollment would add significantly to student diversity. First-year students are notified about their financial aid application at the time of acceptance.

About the Law School

University of Maryland School of Law was established in 1816 and is a public institution. The 24-acre campus is in an urban area in downtown Baltimore. The primary mission of the law school is to prepare students for professional leadership as lawyers, legislators, and other public policymakers, community advocates, and agents of social, political, and economic progress. Students have access to federal, state, county, city, and local agencies, courts, correctional facilities, law firms, and legal aid organizations in the Baltimore area. The law school is within walking distance of local and federal courthouses. It is less than an hour from Annapolis, the state capital, and Washington, D.C. Facilities of special interest to law students include clinical programs that involve student practice, under close faculty supervision, in courts and government agencies; Certificate programs in environmental law and health care law are also offered. Housing for students is available in campus apartments and at the Baltimore Student Union; board is not offered. The university's Residence Life Office assists in finding off-campus housing. All law school facilities are accessible to the physically disabled.

Calendar

The law school operates on a traditional semester basis. Courses for full-time students are offered day only for required courses; day and evening for electives. They must be completed within 3 years. For part-time students, courses are offered evening only for required courses; day and evening for electives. Courses must be completed within 4 years. New full- and part-time students are admitted in the fall. There is a 7-week summer session. Transferable summer courses are offered.

Programs

Students may take relevant courses in other programs and apply credit toward the J.D.; a maximum of 9 credits may be applied. The following joint degrees may be earned: J.D./M.A. (Juris Doctor/Master of Arts in criminal justice, liberal education, applied and professional ethics, community planning, and public management), J.D./M.B.A. (Juris Doctor/Master of Business Administration), J.D./M.S.W. (Juris Doctor/Master of Social Work), J.D./Ph.D. (Juris Doctor/Doctor of Philosophy in policy science), and J.D./Pharm. D. (Juris Doctor/Doctor of Pharmacy).

Required

To earn the J.D., candidates must complete 85 total credits, of which 36 to 38 are for required courses. They must maintain a minimum GPA of 1.67 in the required courses. Among the required first-year courses are: Contracts; Torts; Property; Legal Analysis, Writing and Research (LAWR I and II); and Civil Procedure. Required upper-level courses include Constitutional Law: Individual Rights; Legal Analysis; and Writing and Research (LAWR I and II). Required courses for first-year evening students consist of Contracts; Torts; Criminal Law; Legal Analysis, Writing and Research (LAWR I and II); Legal Profession; Advanced Legal

Phone: 410-706-3492
Fax: 410-706-4045
E-mail: *admissions@law.umaryland.edu*
Web: *http://www.law.umaryland.edu*

Contact

Patricia A. Scott, Director of Admissions, 410-706-3492 for general inquiries; Mary S. Vansickle, 410-706-7347 for financial aid information.

Research; Advanced Writing requirement; and an additional elective. All students must take clinical courses. Full-time day students are required to take the Cardin Program, which integrates traditional classroom learning with live client contact. The Clinical Law Program (live—client—student representation) is an elective. The optional orientation program for first-year students is a brief introduction to case analysis and synthesis, including a sample class, a lunch with faculty, and a small group meeting with upper-class peer advisers. The program lasts 2½ days.

Electives

Students must take 40 credits in their area of concentration. The School of Law offers concentrations in corporate law, criminal law, environmental law, family law, international law, juvenile law, labor law, litigation, securities law, tax law, torts and insurance. Clinical practice offers more than 15 specialties. Approximately 60 seminars are offered. Externships are available in public agencies and nonprofit organizations for 1 to 13 credits. Externships are coordinated with classroom discussion and a writing requirement. Research may be undertaken through 4 legal journals, through independent research/writing under faculty supervision, by acting as research assistants for faculty, and in courses and seminars. Several annual lectures are sponsored by alumni gifts, student organizations, law school faculty/administration, and campus administration. A summer abroad program is held at Aberdeen, Scotland and a semester-long program is available in South Africa. Also, credits are accepted for work done in other ABA-approved summer programs. Tutorial programs may be done as independent study on a topic of choice for 1 to 7 credits. The writing center provides support for all students on an appointment basis. Administration/faculty and student initiatives provide a supportive learning environment for the 25% of students who identify as members of minority groups. Mentoring and social support is provided through a wide variety of student groups. There is a varied and diverse group of student organizations that sponsors events such as the BLSA Banquet and the MPILP Auction. The most widely taken electives are Business, Environmental, and Health Law related courses.

Graduation Requirements

In order to graduate, candidates must have a GPA of 1.67, have completed the upper-division writing requirement, and meet the residency requirements of 6 semesters of attendance (full-time students) and 8 semesters (part-time).

Organizations

The primary law review is the *Maryland Law Review*. Other law reviews include the *Journal of Health Care Law and Policy, The Business Lawyer*, a joint publication of the law school and the ABA Section of Business Law, and *Margins*. The student newspaper is *The Raven*. Moot court competitions include the Morris B. Myerowitz Competition, the Albert R. Mogel National Tax Moot Court Competition, and the Pace University National Environmental Law Moot Court Competition. Other competitions include Health Law Moot Court, Robert R. Merhige, Jr. National Environmental Negotiations Competition, Jessup International Moot Court, American College of Trial Lawyers, and Association of Trial Lawyers of America. Law student organizations include the Student Bar Association, Women's Bar Association (Student Chapter), and Phi Alpha Delta. There are local chapters of Asian/Pacific-American Law Students Association, Black Law Students Association, and Latino Law Students Association. Campus clubs and other organizations include the University Student Government Association (USGA), International Student Organization (ISO), and A Bridge to Excellence.

Library

The law library contains 283,743 hard-copy volumes and 106,876 microform volume equivalents, and subscribes to 4037 serial publications. Such on-line databases and networks as CALI, DIALOG, Infotrac, Legal-Trac, LEXIS, LOIS, NEXIS, OCLC First Search, and WESTLAW are available to law students for research. See *www.law.umaryland.edu/marshall/marshall_index.asp* for a list of other databases and networks. Special library collections include a partial federal government depository. The ratio of library volumes to faculty is 4892 to 1 and to students, 296 to 1.

Placement

J.D.s awarded:	237
Services available through: a separate law school placement center	
Services: job fairs, on-line Jobs/Internship database	
Special features: Career Development staff assists in developing job search strategies, facilitates on-campus interviewing, and provides workshops and seminars.	
Full-time job interviews:	41 employers
Summer job interviews:	64 employers
Placement by graduation:	81% of class
Placement within 9 months:	97% of class
Average starting salary:	$45,000 to $75,000
Areas of placement:	
Private practice 2-10 attorneys	10%
Private practice 11-25 attorneys	3%
Private practice 26-50 attorneys	1%
Private practice 51-100 attorneys	3%
Private practice 101-500 attorneys	18%
Firm size unknown	4%
Judicial clerkships	24%
Government	17%
Business/industry	15%
Public interest	4%
Academic	4%

Faculty

The law school has 58 full-time and 98 part-time faculty members, of whom 57 are women. According to AAUP standards for Category I institutions, faculty salaries are below average. About 22% of full-time faculty have a graduate law degree in addition to the J.D.; about 4% of part-time faculty have one. The ratio of full-time students to full-time faculty in an average class is 14 to 1; in a clinic, 8 to 1. The law school has a regular program of bringing visiting professors and other distinguished lecturers and visitors to campus. There is a chapter of the Order of the Coif.

Students

About 56% of the student body are women; 23%, minorities; 12%, African American; 8%, Asian American; and 2%, Hispanic. The majority of students come from Maryland (67%). The average age of entering students is 26; age range is 20 to 60. About 32% of students enter directly from undergraduate school, 15% have a graduate degree, and 68% have worked full-time prior to entering law school. About 1% drop out after the first year; 94% remain to receive a law degree.

UNIVERSITY OF MEMPHIS

Cecil C. Humphreys School of Law

207 Humphreys Law School
Memphis, TN 38152-3140

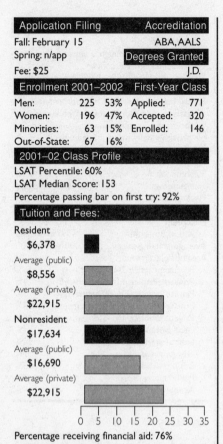

Application Filing		Accreditation
Fall: February 15		ABA, AALS
Spring: n/app		**Degrees Granted**
Fee: $25		J.D.

Enrollment 2001–2002			First-Year Class	
Men:	225	53%	Applied:	771
Women:	196	47%	Accepted:	320
Minorities:	63	15%	Enrolled:	146
Out-of-State:	67	16%		

2001–02 Class Profile

LSAT Percentile: 60%
LSAT Median Score: 153
Percentage passing bar on first try: 92%

Tuition and Fees:

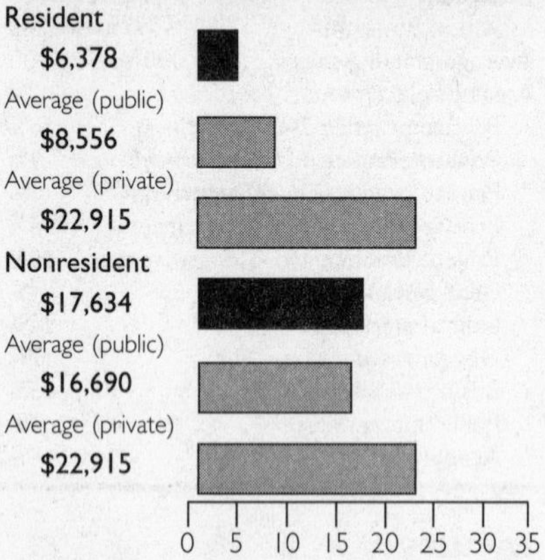

Percentage receiving financial aid: 76%

ADMISSIONS

In the fall 2001 first-year class, 771 applied, 320 were accepted, and 146 enrolled. Three transfers enrolled. The median LSAT percentile of the most recent first-year class was 60; the median GPA was 3.29 on a scale of 4.0. The lowest LSAT percentile accepted was 11; the highest was 99.

Requirements

Applicants must have a bachelor's degree and take the LSAT. Minimum acceptable GPA is 2.0 on a scale of 4.0. The most important admission factors include LSAT results, GPA, and academic achievement. No specific undergraduate courses are required. Candidates are not interviewed.

Procedure

The application deadline for fall entry is February 15. Applicants should submit an application form, LSAT results, transcripts, a nonrefundable application fee of $25, 1 letter of recommendation, a dean's certification form, a personal statement, and a domicile certificate. Notification of the admissions decision is from January to May. The latest acceptable LSAT test date for fall entry is February. The law school uses the LSDAS.

Special

The law school recruits minority and disadvantaged students by means of the Tennessee Pre-Law Fellowship Program, graduate and professional fairs, law school forums, workshops, and a candidate referral service with Law Services. Out-of-state students in that out-of-state applicants may be required to have higher GPA and LSAT results. Transfer students must have one year of credit, have attended an ABA-approved law school, and meet the admission index set by the school or be in the upper quarter of their class.

Costs

Tuition and fees for the 2001-2002 academic year are $6378 for full-time in-state students and $17,634 for out-of-state students. Tuition for part-time students is $5510 in-state and $14,726 out-of-state. On-campus room and board costs about $6570 annually; books and supplies run $1300.

Financial Aid

About 76% of current law students receive some form of aid. The average annual amount of aid from all sources combined, including scholarships, loans, and work contracts, is $17,980; maximum, $29,053. Awards are based on need and merit. The required financial statement is the FAFSA. The aid application deadline for fall entry is April 1. Special funds for minority or disadvantaged students include law stipends for African-American Tennessee residents. First-year students are notified about their financial aid application after seat deposit and orientation fees are paid, usually May 1.

About the Law School

University of Memphis Cecil C. Humphreys School of Law was established in 1962 and is a public institution. The campus is in a suburban area located within Memphis. The primary mission of the law school is to provide a sound, traditional, and quality study of law and to promote legal scholarship and research. Students have access to federal, state, county, city, and local agencies, courts, correctional facilities, law firms, and legal aid organizations in the Memphis area. Other resources include the University of Memphis library and departmental libraries. Facilities of special interest to law students are the law school and library, which are housed in a single building on the north side of campus. Housing for students consists of traditional residence halls as well as on-campus apartments and townhouses. Local privately owned apartments are available off campus. All law school facilities are accessible to the physically disabled.

Calendar

The law school operates on a traditional semester basis. Courses for full- and part-time students are offered days only, though limited elective courses are offered in the evenings, and must be completed within 6 years. New full- and part-time students are admitted in the fall. There is an 8-week summer session. Transferable summer courses are offered.

Programs

The following joint degree may be earned: J.D./M.B.A. (Juris Doctor/Master of Business Administration).

Phone: 901-678-5403
Fax: 901-678-5210
E-mail: *lawadmissions@spc75.law.memphis.edu*
Web: *http://www.law.memphis.edu*

Contact

Office of Law Admissions, 901-678-5403 for general inquiries; Karen Smith, Assistant Director, Office of Student Financial Aid, 901-678-4825, direct line 901-678-3687 for financial aid information.

Required

To earn the J.D., candidates must complete 90 total credits, of which 56 are for required courses. They must maintain a minimum GPA of 2.0 in the required courses. The following first-year courses are required of all students: Contracts I and II, Torts I and II, Property I and II, Civil Procedure I and II, Legal Method I and II, and Criminal Law. Required upper-level courses consist of Income Tax, Secured Transactions, Criminal Procedure I, Evidence, Constitutional Law, Business Organizations I, Decedents' Estates, Professional Responsibility, and Advanced Research. The required orientation program for first-year students consists of a 2-day program that takes place immediately before the beginning of fall classes.

Electives

The Cecil C. Humphreys School of Law offers concentrations in corporate law, criminal law, entertainment law, environmental law, family law, international law, juvenile law, labor law, litigation, securities law, tax law, torts and insurance, commercial law, and real estate law. In addition, clinics on subject areas that include civil litigation, elder law, juvenile law, domestic violence, and criminal law (worth 3 credit hours each) are available to upper-class students as an elective. Second- or third-year students may select from 16 seminars, worth 2 credit hours each. Seminars satisfy the upper-division research requirement. Internships, worth 2 hours each, are available with the National Labor Relations Board, U.S. Attorney, and Bankruptcy Court. Two research programs are available: Research I and Law Review. Field work consists of the Bankruptcy, National Labor Relations Board, U.S. Attorney, Death Penalty, Criminal Justice, and Judicial externships. There is an annual alumni distinguished lecture series and an academic support program offered on a voluntary basis to first-year students for required curriculum courses. The Tennessee Pre-Law Fellowship Program is available to African-Americans who are Tennessee residents, beginning in their sophomore year of undergraduate school. Study abroad is available through a summer program in Beijing. The most widely taken electives are Sales, Commercial Paper, and Trial Advocacy.

Graduation Requirements

In order to graduate, candidates must have a GPA of 2.0 and have completed the upper-division writing requirement.

Organizations

The primary law review is *The University of Memphis Law Review*. The Tennesse Journal of Practice and Procedure is also published. The *Docket* is published by the Dean's office to provide information to students. Moot court competitions include Intraschool Trial, Intraschool Advanced, and First-Year Intraschool. Other competitions include National Environmental Moot Court, Frederick Douglass Moot Court, ATLA National Mock Trial, and National Mock Trial. Law student organizations include the Student Bar Association, International Law Society, and Environmental Law Society. There are local chapters of Phi Delta Phi, Phi Alpha Delta, and Black Law Students Association. Campus clubs and other organizations include the American Trial Lawyers Association, Entertainment Law Society, and the Association of Women Attorneys.

Library

The law library contains 273,360 hardcopy volumes and 602,670 microform volume equivalents, and subscribes to 2496 serial publications. Such on-line databases and networks as CALI, CIS Universe, DIALOG, Legal-Trac, LEXIS, NEXIS, OCLC First Search, WESTLAW, current Index to Legal Periodicals, BNA (selected titles), CCH, and Environmental Law Report are available to law students for research. Special library collections include a selective federal depository. Recently, the library renovated the computer laboratory to include 22 computers and an upgraded training laboratory with 15. The ratio of library volumes to faculty is 11,885 to 1 and to students, 649 to 1. The ratio of seats in the library to students is 1 to 1.5.

Placement

J.D.s awarded:	161
Services available through: a separate law school placement center	
Services: workshops, seminars, and nontraditional legal career advice	
Special features: membership in regional, national, and minority law placement consortiums	
Full-time job interviews:	20 employers
Summer job interviews:	27 employers
Placement by graduation:	60% of class
Placement within 9 months:	96% of class
Average starting salary:	$24,000 to $140,000
Areas of placement:	
Private practice 2-10 attorneys	42%
Private practice 11-25 attorneys	7%
Private practice 26-50 attorneys	4%
Private practice 51-100 attorneys	1%
Private practice 101+ attorneys	3%
Solo practice	1%
Government	12%
Business/industry	12%
Judicial clerkships	8%
Military	5%
Public interest	1%
Academic	1%

Faculty

The law school has 23 full-time and 34 part-time faculty members, of whom 17 are women. According to AAUP standards for Category I institutions, faculty salaries are below average. About 60% of full-time faculty have a graduate law degree in addition to the J.D.; about 32% of part-time faculty have one. The ratio of full-time students to full-time faculty in an average class is 19 to 1; in a clinic, 9 to 1.

Students

About 47% of the student body are women; 15%, minorities; 13%, African American; 1%, Asian American; and 1%, Hispanic. The majority of students come from Tennessee (84%). The average age of entering students is 26; age range is 20 to 53. About 43% of students enter directly from undergraduate school, 12% have a graduate degree, and 60% have worked full-time prior to entering law school. About 8 to 10% drop out after the first year for academic or personal reasons; 90% remain to receive a law degree.

UNIVERSITY OF MIAMI

School of Law

P.O. Box 248087, 1311 Miller Drive
Coral Gables, FL 33124-8087

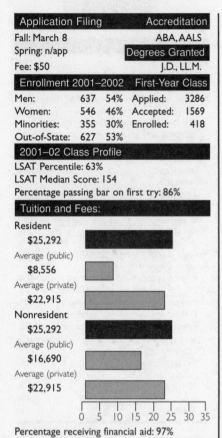

Application Filing		Accreditation
Fall: March 8		ABA, AALS
Spring: n/app		**Degrees Granted**
Fee: $50		J.D., LL.M.

Enrollment 2001–2002			First-Year Class	
Men:	637	54%	Applied:	3286
Women:	546	46%	Accepted:	1569
Minorities:	355	30%	Enrolled:	418
Out-of-State:	627	53%		

2001–02 Class Profile

LSAT Percentile: 63%
LSAT Median Score: 154
Percentage passing bar on first try: 86%

Tuition and Fees:

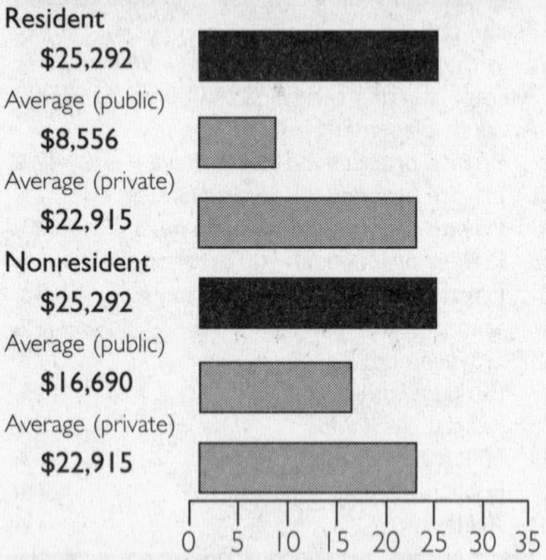

Percentage receiving financial aid: 97%

ADMISSIONS

In the fall 2001 first-year class, 3286 applied, 1569 were accepted, and 418 enrolled. Fourteen transfers enrolled. The median LSAT percentile of the most recent first-year class was 63; the median GPA was 3.3 on a scale of 4.0. The lowest LSAT percentile accepted was 7; the highest was 95.

Requirements

Applicants must have a bachelor's degree and take the LSAT. No specific undergraduate courses are required. Candidates are not interviewed.

Procedure

The application deadline for fall entry is March 8. Applicants should submit an application form, LSAT results, TOEFL for foreign students, a nonrefundable application fee of $50, and 2 letters of recommendation. Graduates from foreign institutions should submit transcript evaluations. All students must possess a bachelor's degree or its equivalent from a regionally accredited institution prior to the first day of classes. Notification of the admissions decision is on a rolling basis. The latest acceptable LSAT test date for fall entry is June. The law school uses the LSDAS.

Special

The law school recruits minority and disadvantaged students by means of a committee reviewing all files, sending information to prelaw advisers at historically minority institutions, hosting diversity admissions fairs, and participating in recruiting events at historically black schools and locations at schools where minority population is strong; also, current minority students call newly admitted minority students. Requirements are not different for out-of-state students. Transfer students must have one year of credit, have a minimum GPA of 3.0, have attended an ABA-approved law school, be in the top fifth of their forst-year class, and have their LSAT and undergraduate performance reviewed.

Costs

Tuition and fees for the 2001-2002 academic year are $25,292 for all full-time students. Tuition for part-time students is $18,708 per year. On-campus room and board costs about $9360 annually; books and supplies run $1000.

Financial Aid

About 97% of current law students receive some form of aid. The average annual amount of aid from all sources combined, including scholarships, loans, and work contracts, is $37,500; maximum, $41,622. Awards are based on need and merit, but the majority of scholarships are merit-based. The required financial statement is the FAFSA. The aid application deadline for fall entry is March 1. Special funds for minority or disadvantaged students include need-based scholarships and merit scholarships, both institutional and donor, including the Colson Scholarship Fund, Florida Bar Minority Scholarships, and the Spellman and Baker McKenzie scholarships. First-year students are notified about their financial aid application on a rolling basis as the files are complete.

About the Law School

University of Miami School of Law was established in 1926 and is a private institution. The 260-acre campus is in an urban area 7 miles south of Miami. The primary mission of the law school is to teach students the craft as well as the theory of law, develop the research and writing skills necessary to the legal profession, and expose students to other skills necessary for effective professional service, such as client counseling, fact investigation, and trial skills. Students have access to federal, state, county, city, and local agencies, courts, correctional facilities, law firms, and legal aid organizations in the Coral Gables area. The legal institutions and firms of Miami, Fort Lauderdale, and the Palm Beach areas are also available to students. Facilities of special interest to law students include the Litigation Skills and Clinical programs, the Moot Court Board, which runs one of the nation's largest mock trial competitions, 7 LL.M. programs, the London Summer Program, the Summer Program in Spain, and the Summer Public Interest Program. Housing for students is available on campus in limited quantities. Ample apartments are available in the area, and roommate referral and apartment listings are supplied to admitted students. About 98% of the law school facilities are accessible to the physically disabled.

Calendar

The law school operates on a traditional semester basis. Courses for full- and part-time students are offered both day and evening; (evening courses offered after the first year only), and must be completed within 5 years. New full- and part-time students are admitted in the fall. There is a 7-week summer session. Transferable summer courses are offered.

Programs

In addition to the J.D., the law school offers the LL.M. and LL.M. in comparative law; tax; real estate; estate planning; ocean and coastal; inter-American; and international law. Students may take relevant courses in other programs and apply credit toward the J.D.; a maximum of 6 credits may be applied. The following joint degrees may be earned: J.D./M.B.A. (Juris Doctor/Master of Business Administration), J.D./M.P.H. (Juris Doctor/Master of Public Health), and J.D/M.S. (Juris Doctor/Master of Marine Science).

Required

To earn the J.D., candidates must complete 88 total credits, of which 73 are for required courses. They must maintain a minimum GPA of 2.0 in the required courses. The following first-year courses are required of all students: Contracts, Torts, Elements, Civil Procedure I, Legal Writing and Research I and II, Property, Criminal Procedure, Constitutional Law

Phone: 305-284-2523
E-mail: *admissions@law.miami.edu*
Web: *law.miami.edu*

Contact

Therese Lambert, Director of Student Recruiting, 305-284-6746 for general inquiries; Felicita Colon, Director of Financial Aid, 305-284-3115; *finaid@law.miami.edu* for financial aid information.

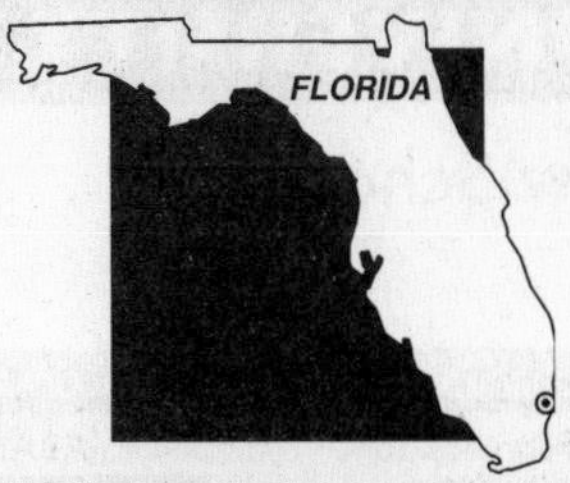

I, and a first-year elective. Required upper-level courses consist of Legal Professions, Personal and Business Transactions, public law and process courses, and perspective courses. The required orientation program for first-year students is a 2-day formal program combined with a writing seminar and various activities organized by students.

Electives

The School of Law offers concentrations in corporate law, criminal law, entertainment law, environmental law, family law, international law, labor law, litigation, maritime law, securities law, sports law, tax law, and torts and insurance. In addition, clinical placement is worth 6 credits and Litigations Skills I is a prerequisite. Students are placed in one of 45 clinical internships and handle actual cases under the supervision of agency attorneys. A Children's and Youth Law Clinic is sponsored by the School of Law. Seminars providing intensive study, research, and writing opportunities in specialized areas are worth 2 credits and are open to second- and third-year students. The summer Public Interest Seminar Program focuses on a public interest topic; students are selected through an application and interview process. Second- and third-year students are also able to take part in individual research projects, worth 1 to 3 credits. The Cole Lecture Series brings distinguished jurists such as U.S. Supreme Court Justices to campus. Other special lectures bring distinguished judges, scholars, and practicing attorneys from around the world to the campus. Study abroad is possible through the London and Tour de Espana Summer Programs, intensive 7-week, 6-credit program. The London program is offered at University College, London; the Tour de Espana in Barcelona, Fuengirola on the Costa del Sol, and Madrid. Selected minority students may be chosen to participate in the James Weldon Johnson Institute. This is a 5-week summer fellowship program designed to develop legal, analytical, and writing skills. The Institute is held prior to the beginning of fall classes and all financial aspects are covered by grants. A special orientation for first-year African-American students is conducted by the Black Law Students Association. The most widely taken electives are Litigation Skills and Clinical Program, Civil Procedure II, and Evidence.

Graduation Requirements

In order to graduate, candidates must have a GPA of 2.0, and have completed the upper-division writing requirement. Many offerings in the upper division require substantial papers.

Organizations

Student-edited publications include the *University of Miami Law Review; Inter-American Law Review; Business Law Review; International and Comparative Law Review; Psychology, Public Policy, and Law Journal; Res Ispa Loquitur* (newspaper), *Amicus Curiae* (yearbook), and *The Hearsay* (weekly newsletter). The Moot Court Board runs one of the nation's largest mock trial competitions, involving more than 200 experienced lawyers. This organization also sponsors several local, state, and regional moot court competitions, as well as negotiation and client counseling competitions. Other competitions include International Moot Court. Law student organizations include Black Law Students Association, Association of Caribbean Law Students, and Asian/Pacific Law Students Association. Local chapters of national associations include Phi Delta Phi, Phi Alpha Delta, and The Federalist Society. Other law student organizations include Hispanic Law Students, Entertainment and Sports Law Society, and Maritime Law Society.

Library

The law library contains 368,011 hard-copy volumes and 846,350 microform volume equivalents, and subscribes to 6381 serial publications. Such on-line databases and networks as CALI, CIS Universe, DIALOG, Dow-Jones, Legal-Trac, LEXIS, LOIS, Mathew Bender, NEXIS, OCLC First Search, RLIN, WESTLAW, and Wilsonline Indexes are available to law students for research. Special library collections include taxation, estate planning, labor theory, ocean law, international law, the law of Latin American and Caribbean countries, Soia Mentschikoff papers, and Everglades litigation files. Recently, the law school expanded and renovated the law library, which features a 600-node local area network for accessing on-line legal research, communications, and internal library systems. The ratio of library volumes to faculty is 6456 to 1 and to students, 311 to 1. The ratio of seats in the library to students is 1 to 1.4 (742 seats).

Placement

J.D.s awarded: 292

Services available through: a separate law school placement center, the university placement center, the graduate business school placement center, and reciprocal programs with other law schools

Services: off-campus interview programs/job fairs

Special features: a professional staff consisting of 5 attorneys and a certified career counselor; a minority mentor program; a public interest program; a judicial internship program; an on- and off-campus interview program, including lottery selections for students, and various job fairs nationwide.

Full-time job interviews:	49 employers
Summer job interviews:	61 employers
Placement by graduation:	52% of class
Placement within 9 months:	91% of class
Average starting salary:	$29,000 to $250,000
Areas of placement:	
Private practice 2-100 attorneys	62%
Government	14%
Business/industry	8%
Unknown	7%
Public interest	4%
Judicial clerkships	3%
Military	1%
Academic	1%

Faculty

The law school has 57 full-time and 103 part-time faculty members, of whom 41 are women. According to AAUP standards for Category I institutions, faculty salaries are average. About 7% of full-time faculty have a graduate law degree in addition to the J.D. The ratio of full-time students to full-time faculty in an average class is 23 to 1; in a clinic, 15 to 1. The law school has a regular program of bringing visiting professors and other distinguished lecturers and visitors to campus. There is a chapter of the Order of the Coif; 29 graduates are members.

Students

About 46% of the student body are women; 30%, minorities; 8%, African American; 4%, Asian American; 17%, Hispanic; and 1%, Native American. The majority of students come from the South (64%). The average age of entering students is 26; age range is 19 to 60. About 40% of students enter directly from undergraduate school. About 5% drop out after the first year for academic or personal reasons; 90% remain to receive a law degree.

UNIVERSITY OF MICHIGAN

Law School

625 South State Street
Ann Arbor, MI 48109-1215

Application Filing		Accreditation
Fall: February 15		ABA, AALS
Spring: n/app		**Degrees Granted**
Fee: $60		J.D., LL.M., M.C.L., S.J.D.

Enrollment 2001–2002			First-Year Class	
Men:	627	57%	Applied:	4022
Women:	471	43%	Accepted:	1169
Minorities:	253	23%	Enrolled:	361
Out-of-State:	824	75%		

2001–02 Class Profile

LSAT Percentile: 95%
LSAT Median Score: 166
Percentage passing bar on first try: n/av

Tuition and Fees:

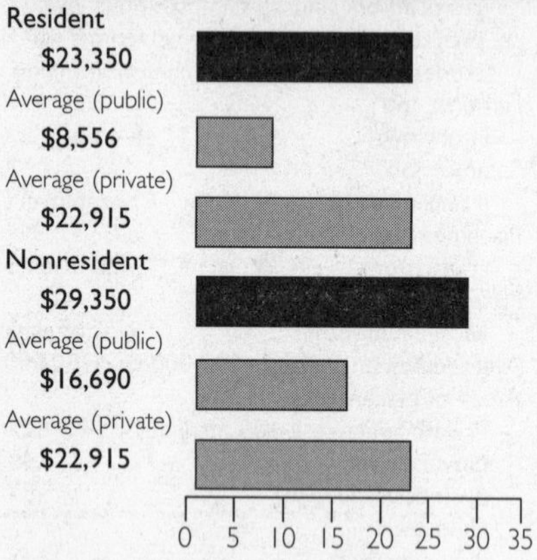

Percentage receiving financial aid: 93%

ADMISSIONS

In the fall 2001 first-year class, 4022 applied, 1169 were accepted, and 361 enrolled. Twenty-five transfers enrolled. The median LSAT percentile of the most recent first-year class was 95; the median GPA was 3.51 on a scale of 4.0.

Requirements

Applicants must have a bachelor's degree and take the LSAT. While academic acheivement and LSAT results are very important, the University of Michigan considers many factors in the admissions process. No specific undergraduate courses are required. Candidates are not interviewed.

Procedure

The application deadline for fall entry is February 15. Applicants should submit an application form, LSAT results, transcripts, a nonrefundable application fee of $60, 1 (although 3 are encouraged) letter of recommendation, and a personal statement. Transcripts and LSAT results must be sent via LSDAS. Notification of the admissions decision is on a rolling basis from December 1. The latest acceptable LSAT test date for fall entry is December at the latest; September is encouraged. The law school uses the LSDAS.

Special

The law school recruits minority and disadvantaged students by reaching out to student populations that are likely to consist of minority or economically disadvantaged students in significant concentrations. Specific means of recruiting minority students include attending minority Law Days, writing to all admissible minority students who participate in the candidate referral service, and holding alumni receptions in various nationwide settings. The Law School attempts to attract economically disadvantaged students by providing need-based financial aid packages, as well as some merit-based financial aid awards. Requirements are different for out-of-state students in that Michigan residency is a slight advantage in the admissions process. Typically one-third of the entering class will be Michigan residents. Credentials of matriculating residents and nonresidents are comparable. Transfer students must have one year of credit, have attended an ABA-approved law school, and typically must be in top 5% to 10% of their first-year class.

Costs

Tuition and fees for the 2001-2002 academic year are $23,350 for full-time in-state students and $29,350 for out-of-state students. On-campus room and board costs about $8150 annually; books and supplies run $830.

Financial Aid

About 93% of current law students receive some form of aid. The average annual amount of aid from all sources combined, including scholarships, loans, and work contracts, is $29,119; maximum, $55,937. Awards are based on need and merit. Most aid is need-based, but a small number of merit-based grants are awarded each year. Required financial statement is the FAFSA. First-year students are notified about their financial aid application 3 to 5 working days from the acceptance date or March 15, whichever is later.

About the Law School

University of Michigan Law School was established in 1859 and is a public institution. The 2665-acre campus is in a suburban area 45 miles west of Detroit. The primary mission of the law school is to bring human insight to the study of law and its institutions. It seeks to share with its students a knowledge of past and present forms and functions of law, and an engaged understanding of the law's evolution and future development. Students have access to federal, state, county, city, and local agencies, courts, correctional facilities, law firms, and legal aid organizations in the Ann Arbor area. Other resources come from the school's integration in an international university. Facilities of special interest to law students include the law libraries, containing study space for each student, and extensive mainframe and computer facilities. Housing for students is available at the Lawyers Club, in university family housing, in graduate dormitories, and in other dormitories as resident advisers. Off-campus housing is also available. All law school facilities are accessible to the physically disabled.

Calendar

The law school operates on a traditional semester basis. Courses for full-time students are offered days only and must be completed within 5 years. There is no part-time program. New students are admitted in the fall and summer. There is a 11-week summer session. Transferable summer courses are not offered.

Programs

In addition to the J.D., the law school offers the LL.M., M.C.L., and S.J.D. Students may take relevant courses in other programs and apply credit toward the J.D.; a maximum of 9 credits may be applied. The following joint degrees may be earned: J.D./A.M. (Juris Doctor/Master of Arts in world politics), J.D./M.A. (Juris Doctor/ Master of Arts in Russian and East European studies), J.D./M.B.A. (Juris Doctor/Master of Business Administration), J.D./M.H.S.A. (Juris Doctor/Master of Health Services Administration), J.D./M.P.H. (Juris Doctor/Master of Public Health), J.D./M.P.P. (Juris Doctor/Master of Public Policy Studies), J.D./M.S. (Juris Doctor/Master of Science in natural resources), J.D./M.S.I. (Juris Doctor/Master of Science in Information), J.D./M.S.W. (Juris Doctor/Masters in Social Work), J.D./M.U.P (Juris Doctor/Master of Urban Planning), and J.D./Ph.D. (Juris Doctor/Doctor of Philosophy in economics).

Required

To earn the J.D., candidates must complete 80 total credits, of which 32 are for required courses. They must maintain a minimum GPA of 2.0 in the required courses. The following first-year courses are required of all students: Civil Procedure, Criminal Law, Introduction to Constitutional Law, Legal Practice I and II,

Phone: 734-764-0537
Fax: 734-647-3218
E-mail: *law.jd.admissions@umich.edu*

Contact
Sarah C. Zearfoss, Assistant Dean, Director of Admissions, 734-764-0537 for general inquiries; Katherine Gottschalk, Assistant Dean for Financial Aid, 734-764-5289 for financial aid information.

Torts, an elective, Contracts, Property, and Transnational Law. Required upper-level courses consist of 1 seminar and a course meeting the professional responsibility requirement. The required orientation program for first-year students consists of 2 days of presentations by deans, faculty, and upper-class students; tours; information about the school and Ann Arbor; and an introduction to the study of law. The school day of orientation has traditionally become "Service Day." New students, along with participating orientation leaders, administrators and faculty, are brought to various sites in the Ann Arbor and Detroit area to engage in a community service project.

Electives

The Law School offers concentrations in corporate law, criminal law, environmental law, family law, international law, juvenile law, labor law, litigation, media law, securities law, sports law, tax law, torts and insurance, and civil rights, feminist legal theory, law and literature, psychology, sociology, economic commercial law, intellectual property, Japanese Law, asylum and refugee law. In addition, upper-class students may take clinical and externship courses for up to 12 hours of credit. These clinics include Child Advocacy Law Clinic, Criminal Appellate Clinic, Environmental Law Clinic, Legal Assistance for Urban Communities Clinic. Students must take at least one seminar in their second or third year; most recently, 71 seminars were offered. Externships may be arranged for up to 12 hours of credit, 3 of which are devoted to a significant research paper. Under the supervision of a school faculty member, students may pursue up to 6 hours of independent research. Many non-credit opportunities exist for field work, including the Family Law Project and Public Service Law Network Worldwide (PSLAWNET). Special lecture series include the William W. Cook Lecture Series, Thomas M. Cooley Lectureship, Helen L. DeRoy Fellowship, and Sunderland Faculty Fellowship. Study abroad is available at Leiden University in the Netherlands, University College in London, Bucerius Law School, Hamburg, Katholiecke University in Leuven, Belgium, and the University of Paris II in France; special fellowships support student-initiated study for third-year students and recent graduates.The Minority Affairs Program (MAP) represents a commitment by the Law School to its students of color. The voluntary program permits interested students to receive academic and social support from upper-class students who serve as MAP instructors. The most widely taken electives are Enterprise Organizations, Jurisdiction, and Choice of Law.

Graduation Requirements

In order to graduate, candidates must have a GPA of 2.0, have completed the upper-division writing requirement, and Transnational Law, a required course for graduation.

Organizations
Students edit the *Michigan Law Review, Michigan Journal of International Law, University of Michigan Journal of Law Reform, Michigan Journal of Gender and Law, Michigan Journal of Race and Law, Michigan Telecommunications and Technology Law Review*, and the newspaper *Res Gestae*. Annual moot court competitions include the Henry M. Campbell Memorial, the Philip C. Jessup International Moot Court, and the ABA Negotiation Competition. Other competitions include the Client Counseling Competition. Law student organizations include the Environmental Law Society, Law School Student Senate, and Women's Law Student Association. There are local chapters of Phi Alpha Delta, Phi Delta Phi, and the ABA-Law Student Division.

Library
The law library contains 876,822 hard-copy volumes and 1,245,320 microform volume equivalents, and subscribes to 9315 serial publications. Such on-line databases and networks as CIS Universe, DIALOG, Dow-Jones, Infotrac, Legal-Trac, LEXIS, LOIS, NEXIS, OCLC First Search, RLIN, WESTLAW, and Wilsonline Indexes are available to law students for research. Special library collections include a depository for U.S. and European Union documents, all documents from U.N. and other supranational authorities, as well as U.S. state and federal material. There are also extensive Special Collections in the fields of Roman law, canon law, comparative law, indigenous nations, trials, biography, and legal bibliography. Recently, the library added an on-line public access catalog, Lexcalibur. Also added were a separate secure area for EC documents, reserved books, a new rare book room, and study carrels. The ratio of library volumes to faculty is 12,178 to 1 and to students is 799 to 1. The ratio of seats in the library to students is 1 to 77.

Placement

J.D.s awarded: 355

Services available through: a separate law school placement center

Services: databases to assist in job searches and mailings.

Special features: a separate office dedicated to public interest placement, and access to an innovative nationwide database program that helps students obtain volunteer legal experience under the supervision of lawyers in a variety of nonprofit offices, government agencies, and law firms..

Full-time job interviews:	728 employers
Summer job interviews:	n/av
Placement by graduation:	94% of class
Placement within 9 months:	99% of class
Average starting salary:	$41,834 to $155,000
Areas of placement:	
Private practice	76%
Judicial clerkships	16%
Business/industry	4%
Government	2%
Public interest	1%
Academic	1%

Faculty
The law school has 72 full-time and 50 part-time faculty members, of whom 33 are women. According to AAUP standards for Category I institutions, faculty salaries are above average. About 43% of full-time faculty have a graduate law degree in addition to the J.D.; about 46% of part-time faculty have one. The ratio of full-time students to full-time faculty in an average class is 14 to 1; in a clinic, 8 to 1. The law school has a regular program of bringing visiting professors and other distinguished lecturers and visitors to campus. There is a chapter of the Order of the Coif.

Students
About 43% of the student body are women; 23%, minorities; 8%, African American; 10%, Asian American; 4%, Hispanic; and 2%, Native American. The majority of students come from the Midwest (50%). The average age of entering students is 24; age range is 21 to 40. About 1% drop out after the first year for academic or personal reasons; 99% remain to receive a law degree.

UNIVERSITY OF MINNESOTA

Law School

229 19th Avenue S.
Minneapolis, MN 55455

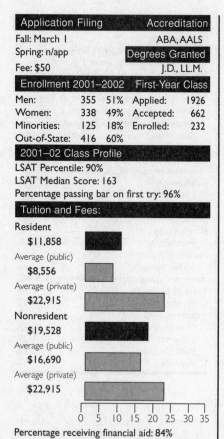

Application Filing		Accreditation
Fall: March 1		ABA, AALS
Spring: n/app		**Degrees Granted**
Fee: $50		J.D., LL.M.

Enrollment 2001–2002			First-Year Class	
Men:	355	51%	Applied:	1926
Women:	338	49%	Accepted:	662
Minorities:	125	18%	Enrolled:	232
Out-of-State:	416	60%		

2001–02 Class Profile

LSAT Percentile: 90%
LSAT Median Score: 163
Percentage passing bar on first try: 96%

Tuition and Fees:

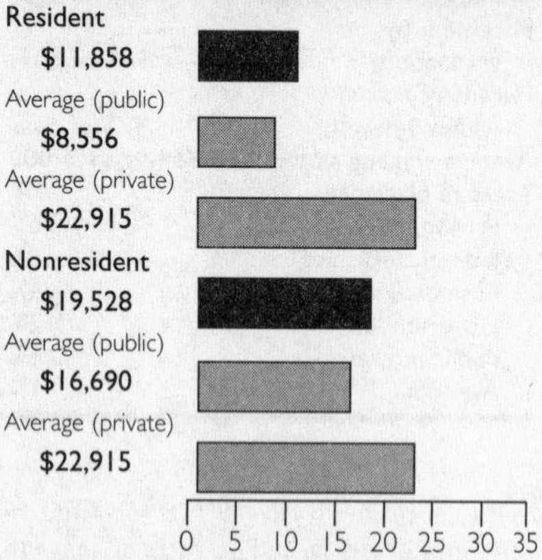

Percentage receiving financial aid: 84%

ADMISSIONS

In the fall 2001 first-year class, 1926 applied, 662 were accepted, and 232 enrolled. Twenty transfers enrolled. The median LSAT percentile of the most recent first-year class was 90; the median GPA was 3.6 on a scale of 4.0.

Requirements

Applicants must have a bachelor's degree and take the LSAT. The most important admission factors include academic achievement, letter of recommendation, and motivations. No specific undergraduate courses are required. Candidates are interviewed.

Procedure

The application deadline for fall entry is March 1. Applicants should submit an application form, LSAT results, transcripts, a nonrefundable application fee of $50, 2 letters of recommendation, and a personal statement. Notification of the admissions decision is on a rolling basis. The latest acceptable LSAT test date for fall entry is February. The law school uses the LSDAS.

Special

The law school recruits minority and disadvantaged students by means of national recruitment, CLEO, Candidate Referral Service, and the National Name Exchange. Requirements are different for out-of-state students in that admission standards are slightly higher. Transfer students must have one year of credit, have attended an ABA-approved law school, have credentials to be admitted as a first-year law student, and exhibit good standing with quality work at a comparable law school.

Costs

Tuition and fees for the 2001-2002 academic year are $11,858 for full-time in-state students and $19,528 for out-of-state students. Off-campus room, board, and personal expenses are about $8378 annually; books and supplies run $1666.

Financial Aid

About 84% of current law students receive some form of aid. The average annual amount of aid from all sources combined, including scholarships, loans, and work contracts, is $21,400; maximum, $29,572. Awards are based on need and merit. The required financial statement is the FAFSA. The aid application deadline for fall entry is March 15. Special funds for minority or disadvantaged students are available. First-year students are notified about their financial aid application some time between March and June.

About the Law School

The University of Minnesota Law School was established in 1888 and is a public institution. The campus is in an urban area in Minneapolis. The primary mission of the law school is to provide students with the theoretical, analytical, and practical skills necessary to contribute professionally and creatively to U.S. and international society. Students have access to federal, state, county, city, and local agencies, courts, correctional facilities, law firms, and legal aid organizations in the Minneapolis area. Facilities of special interest to law students consist of the clinic law office, 2 courtrooms, 24-hour library access, a computer laboratory, the placement office, a bookstore, group study rooms, student publication and organization offices, cafe, and multiple lounge areas with an adjoining outdoor plaza. Housing for students is plentiful. Apartments, efficiencies, houses near campus, and on-campus housing, are available. Most of the law school facilities are accessible to the physically disabled.

Calendar

The law school operates on a traditional semester basis. Courses for full-time students are offered days only and must be completed within 5 years. There is no part-time program. New students are admitted in the fall. There is an 8-week summer session. Transferable summer courses are offered.

Programs

In addition to the J.D., the law school offers the LL.M. and foreign law degrees and a Master of Arts in American Legal institutions. Students may take relevant courses in other programs and apply credit toward the J.D.; a maximum of 6 credits may be applied. The following joint degrees may be earned: J.D./M.A. (Juris Doctor/Master of Arts), J.D./M.B.A. (Juris Doctor/Master of Businss Administration), J.D./M.P. (Juris Doctor/Master of Planning), J.D./M.P.P. (Juris Doctor/Master of Public Policy), J.D./M.S. (Juris Doctor/Master of Science), and J.D./Ph.D. (Juris Doctor/Doctor of Philosophy).

Required

To earn the J.D., candidates must complete 88 total credits, of which 32 are for required courses. They must maintain a minimum GPA of 8.0 (on a 16-point scale) in the required courses. The following first-year courses are required of all students: Constitutional Law, Contracts, Criminal Law, Civil Procedure, Property, Torts, and Legal Research and Writing. Required upper-level courses consist of Professional Responsibility. Clincal courses are not required but they are popular, with a 65% participation rate.The required orientation program for first-year students consists of 3½ days in which the entering class is introduced to each other and the law school faculty and staff.

Phone: 612-625-3487
Fax: 612-626-1874

Contact

Collins Byrd, Admissions Director, 612-625-3487 for general inquiries; Office of Admissions, 612-625-3487 for financial aid information.

Electives

The Law School offers concentrations in corporate law, criminal law, environmental law, family law, international law, juvenile law, labor law, litigation, securities law, tax law, torts and insurance, and commercial transactions, real estate, estate planning, theories of law, and public law. In addition, second- and third-year students may enroll in 17 separate clinics in such areas as bankruptcy, child advocacy, and civil practice. Through these clinics, students receive academic credit while also providing more than 18,000 hours of pro bono legal assistance to low income individuals in the Twin Cities each year. More than 50 seminars, averaging 2 credits each, are available each year to upper-level students. The Law School houses 6 research institutes: Human Rights Center, Institute on Criminal Justice, Institute on Race and Poverty, Kommerstad Center for Business Law and Entrepreneurship, Minesota Center for Legal Studies, and Consortium on Law and Values in Health, Envirnoment, and the Life Sciences. The Judicial Externship Program places students with local federal and state court judges. There is a variety of endowed lecture programs that bring special speakers to the Law School each year. In addition, the Minnesota Supreme Court and the U.S. Court of Appeals for the Eight Circuit preside over special hearings at the Law School each year. Study abroad is available in France, Sweden, Germany, Ireland, the Netherlands, and Spain. Tutorial programs are available. A structured study group program is available to all first-year students. The most widely taken electives are Business/Corporations, Tax, and Evidence.

Graduation Requirements

In order to graduate, candidates must have a GPA of 8.0 on a 16-point scale and have completed the upper-division writing requirement.

Organizations

Students edit the *Minnesota Law Review, Law and Inequality: A Journal of Theory and Practice; Minnesota Journal of Global Trade*; and the *Minnesota Intellectual Property Review.* Moot court competitions include Jessup International Law, Giles S. Rich Intellectual Property Moot Court, and the William McGee Civil Rights Moot Court. Other competitions include National Moot Court, Wagner Labor Law Moot Court, Environmental Law Moot Court, ABA Moot Court, and Maynard Pirsig Moot Court. There are 25 law student organizations, including Law Council, Black Law Students Association, and Student Intellectual Property Law Association. The ABA, National Lawyers Guild, and Federalist Society have local chapters.

Library

The law library contains 923,000 hardcopy volumes and 304,000 microform volume equivalents, and subscribes to 9720 serial publications. Such on-line databases and networks as CALI, CIS Universe, DIALOG, Legal-Trac, LEXIS, LOIS, NEXIS, OCLC First Search, RLIN, WESTLAW, and LUMINA, an online library catalog of University of Minnesota libraries, and LEGI-SLATE are available to law students for research. Special library collections include a U.S. documents depository as well as collections on the United Nations, European Community, and human rights; American Indian Law collection; Rare Books collection (especially early English and American law), and Canon Law. Recently, the library installed a wireless network and built a rare-books facility. The ratio of library volumes to faculty is 21,465 to 1 and to students is 1332 to 1. The ratio of seats in the library to students is 1 to 1.

Placement

J.D.s awarded:	239
Services available through: a separate law school placement center	
Special features: extensive career programming, an alumni networking program for students, and listings of employers by type, size, and city.	
Full-time job interviews:	190 employers
Summer job interviews:	190 employers
Placement by graduation:	90% of class
Placement within 9 months:	99% of class
Average starting salary:	$28,100 to $150,000
Areas of placement:	
Private practice 2-10 attorneys	8%
Private practice 11-25 attorneys	7%
Private practice 26-50 attorneys	3%
Private practice 51-100 attorneys	8%
Private practice 100 + attorneys	29%
Judicial clerkships	24%
Government	9%
Business/industry	5%
Public interest	5%
Military	2%
Academic	1%

Faculty

The law school has 43 full-time and 112 part-time faculty members, of whom 54 are women. According to AAUP standards for Category I institutions, faculty salaries are above average. About 42% of full-time faculty have a graduate law degree in addition to the J.D. The ratio of full-time students to full-time faculty in an average class is 43 to 1; in a clinic, 7 to 1. The law school has a regular program of bringing visiting professors and other distinguished lecturers and visitors to campus. There is a chapter of the Order of the Coif; 13 faculty are members.

Students

About 49% of the student body are women; 18%, minorities; 3%, African American; 11%, Asian American; 3%, Hispanic; and 1%, Native American. The majority of students come from the Midwest (66%). The average age of entering students is 25; age range is 21 to 53. About 4% drop out after the first year for academic or personal reasons; 98% remain to receive a law degree.

UNIVERSITY OF MISSISSIPPI

L.Q.C. Lamar Hall

Grove Loop
University, MS 38677

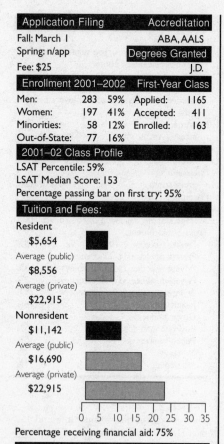

Application Filing		Accreditation
Fall: March 1		ABA, AALS
Spring: n/app		**Degrees Granted**
Fee: $25		J.D.

Enrollment 2001–2002			First-Year Class	
Men:	283	59%	Applied:	1165
Women:	197	41%	Accepted:	411
Minorities:	58	12%	Enrolled:	163
Out-of-State:	77	16%		

2001–02 Class Profile

LSAT Percentile: 59%
LSAT Median Score: 153
Percentage passing bar on first try: 95%

Tuition and Fees:

Resident
$5,654
Average (public)
$8,556
Average (private)
$22,915
Nonresident
$11,142
Average (public)
$16,690
Average (private)
$22,915

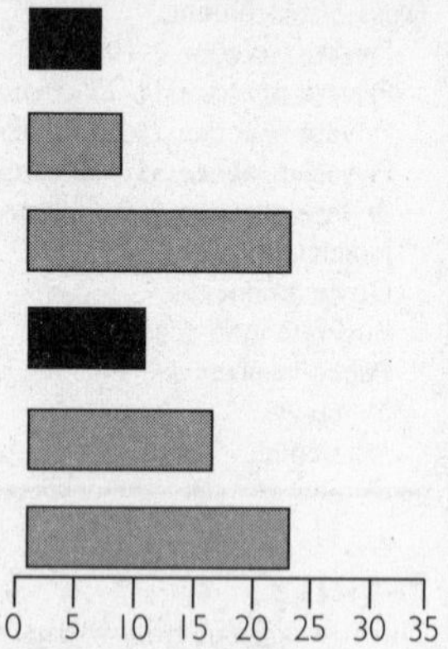

Percentage receiving financial aid: 75%

ADMISSIONS

In the fall 2001 first-year class, 1165 applied, 411 were accepted, and 163 enrolled. The median LSAT percentile of the most recent first-year class was 59; the median GPA was 3.53 on a scale of 4.0. The lowest LSAT percentile accepted was 6; the highest was 99.

Requirements
Applicants must have a bachelor's degree and take the LSAT. The most important admission factors include state or country of residence, LSAT results, and GPA. No specific undergraduate courses are required. Candidates are not interviewed.

Procedure
The application deadline for fall entry is March 1. Applicants should submit an application form, LSAT results, transcripts, TOEFL for non-U.S. citizens whose native language is not English, a nonrefundable application fee of $25, and letters of recommendation (not required, but strongly recommended). Notification of the admissions decision is no later than April 15. The latest acceptable LSAT test date for fall entry is December. (February might be considered depending on pool of applicants.) The law school uses the LSDAS.

Special
The law school recruits minority and disadvantaged students by means of an extensive recruiting program aimed at historically black colleges and universities in Mississippi and in other states, as well as participation in Law School Forums. Requirements are different for out-of-state students in that slightly higher credentials are required and the percentage of nonresidents admitted is limited. Transfer students must have one year of credit and the law school from which the transfer is made must be both ABA and AALS accredited.

Costs

Tuition and fees for the 2001-2002 academic year are $5654 for full-time in-state students and $11,142 for out-of-state students. On-campus room and board costs about $7228 annually; books and supplies run $1000.

Financial Aid

About 75% of current law students receive some form of aid. The average annual amount of aid from all sources combined, including scholarships, loans, and work contracts, is $10,000; maximum, $18,500. Awards are based on need and merit. Required financial statements are the CSS Profile and the FAFSA. The aid application deadline for fall entry is March 1. Special funds for minority or disadvantaged students are available as tuition grants; some grants, based on both merit and need, exceed tuition. First-year students are notified about their financial aid application at time of acceptance.

About the Law School

University of Mississippi L.Q.C. Lamar Hall was established in 1854 and is a public institution. The 1900-acre campus is in a small town 80 miles southeast of Memphis, Tennessee. The primary mission of the law school is to provide a quality legal education that prepares graduates for the practice of law in the United States and for entry into government and public service or any profession in which a legal education is a helpful or necessary background. Students have access to federal, state, county, city, and local agencies, courts, correctional facilities, law firms, and legal aid organizations in the University area. Housing for students is primarily off campus and is adequate and reasonably priced. All law school facilities are accessible to the physically disabled.

Calendar

The law school operates on a traditional semester basis. Courses for full-time students are offered days only. There is no part-time program. New students are admitted in the fall and summer. There is an 8-week summer session. Transferable summer courses are offered.

Programs

Students may take relevant courses in other programs and apply credit toward the J.D.; a maximum of 6 credits may be applied. The following joint degrees may be earned: J.D./M.B.A. (Juris Doctor/Master of Business Administration).

Required
To earn the J.D., candidates must complete 90 total credits, of which 54 to 57 are for required courses. They must maintain a minimum GPA of 2.0 in the required courses. The following first-year courses are required of all students: Contracts, Torts, Civil Procedure I, Property, Constitutional Law, Legal Research and Writing I and II, and Criminal Law. Required upper-level courses consist of Civil Procedure II, Evidence, Legal Profession, Moot Court, 2 business/commercial courses, 1 procedure course, 1 perspective course, and 1 senior skills/writing course. The required orientation program for first-year students is a 2-day program incorporating an introduction to the study of law, analytical and case briefing skills, and exam-taking skills.

Phone: 601-915-6910
Fax: 601-915-1289
E-mail: *bvinson@olemiss.edu*

Contact

Barbara Vinson, Director of Admissions, Office of Law Admissions, 601-915-6910 for general inquiries; Laura Diven-Brown, Director of Financial Aid, 601-915-7175 for financial aid information.

Electives

The L.Q.C. Lamar Hall offers concentrations in corporate law, criminal law, labor law, litigation, and tax law. In addition, The Poverty Law Clinic, worth 3 to 6 credit hours, provides legal referral and assistance to indigent clients. A Constitutional Law seminar is offered. Public Service Internships, awarding 6 hours of pass/fail credit, are offered to senior students with more than 60 hours, a GPA of 2.2, and the permission of the Director. Law students work with judges, prosecuting attorneys, and public defenders under the Student Limited Practice Act. The Mississippi Law Research Institute, operated as an auxiliary program, offers students the opportunity to perform legal research. Students receive wages for their work, but no law school credit. Field work opportunities are available. Special lectures include the Dunbar Lectures in Philosophy and the Law, the Currie lectures, which relate law, religion, and the behavioral sciences, and the McClure Memorial Lectures in Law. Upper-class students may take 6 hours in the study-abroad program in Cambridge, England, where various courses are offered. Students may also earn up to 6 hours in the summer study program in Hawaii. All first-year students may take advantage of a tutorial program in which upper-class students serve as teaching assistants. The program is under the direction of the Assistant to the Dean. Minority programs consist of the Minority Tuition Scholarship Program and those offered through the Black Law Students Association (BLSA). There are various active special interest organizations. The most widely taken electives are Wills and Estates; Mississippi Civil Practice; Pretrial Practice.

Graduation Requirements

In order to graduate, candidates must have a GPA of 2.0 and have completed the upper-division writing requirement.

Organizations

Student-edited publications include the *Mississippi Law Journal, National Security Law Journal*, the student newspaper *The Solicitor*, and *The Advocate*, the School of Law yearbook. Moot court competitions include the Steen-Reynolds Competition in the fall semester and trial competitions and appellate competitions each semester. Other competitions include the National Moot Court, Douglass Moot Court, Student Trial, Craven Moot Court, Heidelberg, Woodliff Oral Advocacy, and Jessup International Law. Law student organizations include the Lamar Society of International Law, Moot Court Board, and Law School Student Body Association as well as student divisions of ABA, Delta Theta Phi, and Phi Delta Phi. Other law student organizations include Christian Legal Society, Environmental Law Society, and Women in Law.

Library

The law library contains 314,929 hardcopy volumes and 155,585 microform volume equivalents, and subscribes to 2554 serial publications. Such on-line databases and networks as CALI, CIS Universe, DIALOG, Infotrac, Legal-Trac, LEXIS, Mathew Bender, NEXIS, OCLC First Search, WESTLAW, Benner Full Authority, CIS Universe, and *mslawyer.com* are available to law students for research. Special library collections include a depository of federal documents and a space law collection. Recently, the library added lab computers and upgraded network connectivity. The ratio of library volumes to faculty is 9842 to 1 and to students is 656 to 1.

Faculty

The law school has 32 full-time and 17 part-time faculty members, of whom 13 are women. According to AAUP standards for Category I institutions, faculty salaries are below average. About 35% of full-time faculty have a graduate law degree in addition to the J.D.; about 15% of part-time faculty have one. The ratio of full-time students to full-time faculty in an average class is 15 to 1; in a clinic, 8 to 1.

Placement

J.D.s awarded: 136

Services available through: a separate law school placement center

Services: a course in general practice offers insight into establishing a solo practice.

Special features: personalized service based on the small student body.

Full-time job interviews:	15 employers
Summer job interviews:	47 employers
Placement by graduation:	71% of class
Placement within 9 months:	98% of class
Average starting salary:	$30,000 to $115,000
Areas of placement:	
Private practice 2-10 attorneys	35%
Private practice 11-25 attorneys	5%
Private practice 26-50 attorneys	6%
Private practice 51-100 attorneys	7%
Private practice 101 - 250 attorneys	5%
Judicial clerkships	14%
Business/industry	9%
Government	5%
Public interest	3%
Military	3%
Academic	1%

Students

About 41% of the student body are women; 12%, minorities; 10%, African American; 1%, Asian American; 1%, Hispanic; and 1%, Native American. The majority of students come from Mississippi (84%). The average age of entering students is 24; age range is 21 to 44. About 75% of students enter directly from undergraduate school, 5% have a graduate degree, and 25% have worked full-time prior to entering law school. About 9% drop out after the first year for academic or personal reasons; 90% remain to receive a law degree.

UNIVERSITY OF MISSOURI-COLUMBIA

School of Law

103 Hulston Hall
Columbia, MO 65211

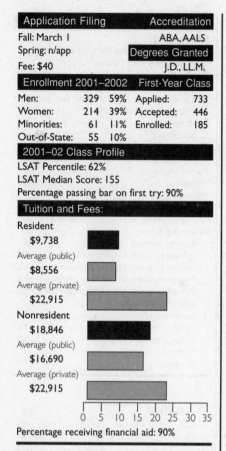

Application Filing		Accreditation
Fall: March 1		ABA, AALS
Spring: n/app		**Degrees Granted**
Fee: $40		J.D., LL.M.

Enrollment 2001–2002			First-Year Class	
Men:	329	59%	Applied:	733
Women:	214	39%	Accepted:	446
Minorities:	61	11%	Enrolled:	185
Out-of-State:	55	10%		

2001–02 Class Profile

LSAT Percentile: 62%
LSAT Median Score: 155
Percentage passing bar on first try: 90%

Tuition and Fees:

Resident
$9,738
Average (public)
$8,556
Average (private)
$22,915
Nonresident
$18,846
Average (public)
$16,690
Average (private)
$22,915

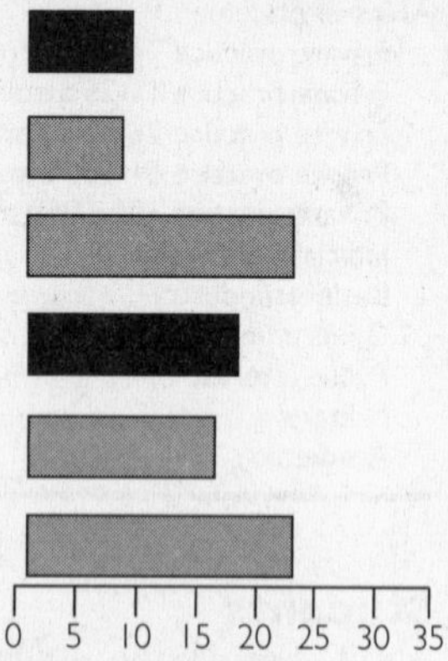

Percentage receiving financial aid: 90%

ADMISSIONS

In the fall 2001 first-year class, 733 applied, 446 were accepted, and 185 enrolled. Nine transfers enrolled. The median LSAT percentile of the most recent first-year class was 62; the median GPA was 3.36 on a scale of 4.0. The lowest LSAT percentile accepted was 28; the highest was 99.

Requirements

Applicants must have a bachelor's degree and take the LSAT. Minimum acceptable LSAT percentile is 30. The most important admission factors include LSAT results, GPA, and academic achievement. No specific undergraduate courses are required. Candidates are not interviewed.

Procedure

The application deadline for fall entry is March 1. Applicants should submit an application form, LSAT results, transcripts, a nonrefundable application fee of $40. First deposit of $200 is due on April 15; the second deposit of $200 is due on June 1; the deposits are credited toward tuition. Notification of the admissions decision is usually by April 1. The latest acceptable LSAT test date for fall entry is February. The law school uses the LSDAS.

Special

The law school recruits minority and disadvantaged students actively and has a special admissions policy. Requirements are not different for out-of-state students. Transfer students must have one year of credit, have attended an ABA-approved law school, and must be in good standing.

Costs

Tuition and fees for the 2001-2002 academic year are $9738 for full-time in-state students and $18,846 for out-of-state students. On-campus room and board costs about $6912 annually; books and supplies run $1200.

Financial Aid

About 90% of current law students receive some form of aid. The average annual amount of aid from all sources combined, including scholarships, loans, and work contracts, is $15,200; maximum, $23,182. Awards are based on need and merit. Required financial statement is the FAFSA. The aid application deadline for fall entry is March 1. Special funds for minority or disadvantaged students consist of need- and merit-based law school scholarships, ranging from $500 to full tuition. First-year students are notified about their financial aid application at time of acceptance.

About the Law School

University of Missouri-Columbia School of Law was established in 1872 and is a public institution. The 1348-acre campus is in a suburban area 125 miles west of St. Louis. The primary mission of the law school is to educate students about the fundamentals of legal thinking, including the analysis and synthesis of court opinions, preparation and argument of cases, and the resolution of client problems and ethical issues that attorneys must face. Students have access to federal, state, county, city, and local agencies, courts, correctional facilities, law firms, and legal aid organizations in the Columbia area. Housing for students is available in on- and off-campus apartments and dormitories. All law school facilities are accessible to the physically disabled.

Calendar

The law school operates on a traditional semester basis. Courses for full-time students are offered days only. There is no part-time program. New students are admitted in the fall. There is a 7-week summer session. Transferable summer courses are offered.

Programs

In addition to the J.D., the law school offers the LL.M. Students may take relevant courses in other programs and apply credit toward the J.D.; a maximum of 3 to 6 credits may be applied. The following joint degrees may be earned: J.D./M.A. (Juris Doctor/Master of Arts in economics, library and information sciences, journalism, health administration, and educational leadership and policy analysis), J.D./M.B.A. (Juris Doctor/Master of Business Administration), J.D./M.P.A. (Juris Doctor/Master of Public Administration), and J.D./Ph.D. (Juris Doctor/Doctor of Philosophy in journalism).

Required

To earn the J.D., candidates must complete 89 total credits, of which 57 are for required courses. They must maintain a minimum grade average of 70 in the required courses. The following first-year courses are required of all students: Contracts I and II, Torts I and II, Civil Procedure I and II, Criminal Law, Property I and II, Legal Research and Writing, and Advocacy and Research. Required upper-level courses consist of Evidence, Constitutional Law, Professional Responsibility, Legislation, Public Law Module (Administrative Law or Criminal Procedure), Transactions Module (Business Organizations and Real Estate Finance), Law of Personal Relationships (Estates and Trusts or Family Law), and Skills Module (Trial Practice,

Phone: 573-882-6042
888-685-2948
Fax: 573-882-9625
E-mail: *CatheyA@missouri.edu*
Web: *www.law.missouri.edu*

Contact

Andrea Cathey, Admissions Representative, 573-882-6042 or 888-MULAW4U (685-2948) for general inquiries; Financial Aid Adviser, 573-882-1383 for financial aid information.

Pretrial Litigation, Arbitration, and completion of a writing requirement). The required 3-day orientation program for first-year students consists of meeting with administration, faculty, and student organizations; learning rules and regulations; and learning to brief a case.

Electives

The School of Law offers concentrations in corporate law, criminal law, environmental law, family law, labor law, litigation, securities law, tax law, torts and insurance, and trial law. In addition, the school offers a criminal clinic, a domestic violence clinic, and a mediation clinic. Internship programs are available to upper-level students who wish to experience the practice of civil and criminal law in various state and federal agencies; 3 credit hours are offered. Seminars are open to upper-level students on Communication Law, Criminal Law, and Environmental Law. Upper-level students may perform independent research for a faculty member and earn up to 3 credit hours. The main lecture series at the Law School is the Nelson Lecture, in which noted national legal scholars deliver a major address. There are also annual lectures in dispute resolution and dispute resolution brown bag lunches. The School of Law participates in the London Law Consortium, in cooperation with the universities of Kansas, Utah, Iowa, Arizona, Indiana, IIT Chicago-Kent, and Georgia. A semester in the Bloomsbury district of London, each January through May, is available to second- and third-year law students in good standing; the courses are taught by regular faculty from the participating American universities. Students also may enroll in classes taught by British professors. The school has a full-time academic counselor available to assist students with academic concerns. Remedial programs include Legal Reasoning. Minority scholarship funds are available; the Law School is a sustaining institution in CLEO and participates in the ABA legal opportunity scholarship program. The most widely taken electives are Trial Practice, Family Law, and Secured Transactions.

Graduation Requirements

In order to graduate, candidates must have completed the upper-division writing requirement.

Organizations

Students edit the *Missouri Law Review*, the *Environmental Law and Policy Review*, and the *Journal of Dispute Resolution*. The student newspaper is the *Student Bar Association Newsletter* and *The Gavel*. Moot court competitions include the Midwest Moot Court Competition, National Moot Court, and the ABA Moot Court. Other competitions are the Negotiation, Trial, Client Counseling, and First Year Moot Court. Student organizations include the Board of Advocates, the Student Bar Association, and the Women's Law Association. Campus clubs and other organizations include the Black Law Student Association, Non-Traditional Law Student Association, and Entertainment Law. Phi Alpha Delta, the ABA-Law School Division, and the Association of Trial Lawyers of America have local chapters.

Library

The law library contains 331,663 hard-copy volumes and 444,865 microform volume equivalents, and subscribes to 3637 serial publications. Such on-line databases and networks as DIALOG, LEXIS, WESTLAW, OCLC, Merlin, Legal-Trac, LOIS, the Internet, and World Wide Web are available to law students for research. Special library collections include U.S. and Missouri state documents and a nineteenth-century criminal trial collection. Recently, the library upgraded its computer laboratory to Windows NT and Netware 5, and added carrel seating and a wireless network. The ratio of library volumes to faculty is 9213 to 1 and to students is 600 to 1.

Faculty

The law school has 36 full-time and 15 part-time faculty members, of whom 16 are women. According to AAUP standards for Category I institutions, faculty salaries are average. About 14% of full-time faculty have a graduate law degree in addition to the J.D.; about 2% of part-time faculty have one. The ratio of full-time students to full-time faculty in an average class is 16 to 1; in a clinic, 8 to 1. The law school has a regular program of bringing visiting professors and other distinguished lecturers and visitors to campus. There is a chapter of the Order of the Coif; 45 faculty and 533 graduates are members.

Placement

J.D.s awarded: 153

Services available through: a separate law school placement center, the university placement center, and Business and Public Administration Career Services

Services: access to electronic and hard copy resume databases; counseling on professional development and career growth; and programming on law and lifestyles

Special features: Individual counseling for each student, an active and successful judicial clerkship committee, and active alumni support.

Full-time job interviews:	37 employers
Summer job interviews:	56 employers
Placement by graduation:	70% of class
Placement within 9 months:	92% of class
Average starting salary:	$25,000 to $140,000

Areas of placement:

Private practice 2-10 attorneys	24%
Private practice 11-25 attorneys	8%
Private practice 26-50 attorneys	1%
Private practice 51-100 attorneys	15%
Government	22%
Judicial clerkships	14%
Business/industry	13%
Public interest	1%
Academic	1%
LL.M. program	1%

Students

About 39% of the student body are women; 11%, minorities; 6%, African American; 2%, Asian American; 1%, Hispanic; and 1%, Native American. The majority of students come from Missouri (90%). The average age of entering students is 23; age range is 20 to 50. About 80% of students enter directly from undergraduate school, 10% have a graduate degree, and 20% have worked full-time prior to entering law school. About 3% drop out after the first year for academic or personal reasons; 97% remain to receive a law degree.

UNIVERSITY OF MISSOURI-KANSAS CITY

School of Law

500 East 52nd Street
Kansas City, MO 64110-2499

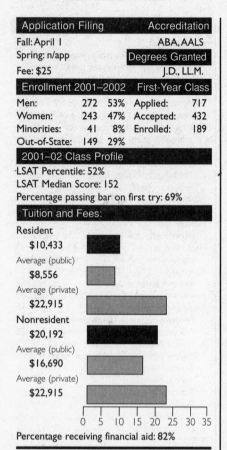

Application Filing		Accreditation
Fall: April 1		ABA, AALS
Spring: n/app		**Degrees Granted**
Fee: $25		J.D., LL.M.

Enrollment 2001–2002			First-Year Class	
Men:	272	53%	Applied:	717
Women:	243	47%	Accepted:	432
Minorities:	41	8%	Enrolled:	189
Out-of-State:	149	29%		

2001–02 Class Profile

LSAT Percentile: 52%
LSAT Median Score: 152
Percentage passing bar on first try: 69%

Tuition and Fees:

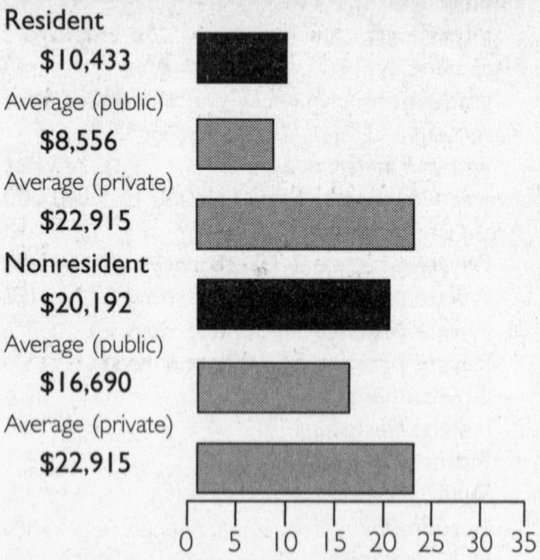

Percentage receiving financial aid: 82%

ADMISSIONS

In the fall 2001 first-year class, 717 applied, 432 were accepted, and 189 enrolled. Eight transfers enrolled. The median LSAT percentile of the most recent first-year class was 52; the median GPA was 3.2 on a scale of 4.0. The lowest LSAT percentile accepted was 20; the highest was 99.

Requirements

Applicants must take the LSAT. Minimum acceptable LSAT percentile is 45 and minimum acceptable GPA is 2.0 on a scale of 4.0. The most important admission factors include LSAT results, GPA, and academic achievement. Factors that bring diversity to a class are also considered. No specific undergraduate courses are required. Candidates are interviewed.

Procedure

The application deadline for fall entry is April 1. Applicants should submit an application form, LSAT results, transcripts, a nonrefundable application fee of $25, 2 letters of recommendation, and a personal statement. Notification of the admissions decision is on a rolling basis. The latest acceptable LSAT test date for fall entry is June. The law school uses the LSDAS.

Special

The law school recruits minority and disadvantaged students by means of minority recruitment, forums, personal letters, and telephone calls to potential applicants. Requirements are not different for out-of-state students. Transfer students must have one year of credit, have a minimum GPA of 2.7, and have attended an ABA-approved law school. Had the student not been admissible when applying for initial admission to the school, then a minimum GPA of 3.0 is required.

Costs

Tuition and fees for the 2001-2002 academic year are $10,433 for full-time in-state students and $20,192 for out-of-state students. Books and supplies run about $500 annually.

Financial Aid

About 82% of current law students receive some form of aid. The average annual amount of aid from all sources combined, including scholarships, loans, and work contracts, is $6775. Awards are based on need and merit. Required financial statement is the FAFSA. Check with the school for current application deadlines. Special funds for minority or disadvantaged students include special admissions scholarships and out-of-state tuition waivers for minority students. First-year students are notified about their financial aid application at time of acceptance.

About the Law School

University of Missouri-Kansas City School of Law was established in 1895 and is a public institution. The 93-acre campus is in an urban area in Kansas City. The primary mission of the law school is to prepare men and women for the general practice of law and for policy-forming functions in government, business, and organization community life, while providing a sound curriculum that offers a rigorous learning experience for students to obtain knowledge and skills in breadth and depth. Students have access to federal, state, county, city, and local agencies, courts, correctional facilities, law firms, and legal aid organizations in the Kansas City area. Clerkship opportunities are available in the numerous nearby law firms and government agencies. Facilities of special interest to law students include "virtual office" suites shared by faculty and students, designed to foster the exchange of ideas and promote collegiality between faculty and students. The school has more than 121,000 square feet of space, including the E.E. "Tom" Thompson Courtroom, which is equipped with audiovisual equipment, used to augment the advocacy training program of the school. Digital classrooms with wireless computer access enhance the learning experience for students. In addition, students have a spacious commons area, including an outdoor courtyard and a vending area. The Leon E. Bloch Law Library is a modern facility that combines the traditions of print with electronic media. Housing for students is limited on campus, while a large selection of housing is available off campus from private owners. About 95% of the law school facilities are accessible to the physically disabled.

Calendar

The law school operates on a traditional semester basis. Courses for full-time students are offered both day and evening, with most courses being offered during the day, and must be completed within 3 years. For part-time students, courses are offered both day and evening, with most courses being offered during the day, and must be completed within 5 years. New full- and part-time students are admitted in the fall. There is an 8-week summer session. Transferable summer courses are not offered.

Programs

In addition to the J.D., the law school offers the LL.M. in 3 emphasis areas: tax, general, and estate planning. Students may take relevant courses in other programs and apply credit toward the J.D.; a maximum of 10 credits may be applied. The following joint degrees may be earned: J.D./LL.M. (Juris Doctor/Master of Laws in estate planning), J.D./LL.M. TAX (Juris Doctor/Master of Laws in taxation), and J.D./M.B.A. (Juris Doctor/Master of Business Administration).

Phone: 816-235-1644
Fax: 816-235-5276
E-mail: *brooksdv@umkc.edu*
Web: *law.umkc.edu*

Contact

Debbie Brooks, Admissions Director, 816-235-1672 for general inquiries; Pat McTee, Director of Financial Aid, 816-235-1154 for financial aid information.

Required

To earn the J.D., candidates must complete 91 total credits, of which 52 are for required courses. They must maintain a minimum GPA of 2.0 in the required courses. The following first-year courses are required of all students: Contracts I and II, Property I and II, Introduction to Law I and II, Criminal Law, Constitutional Law, Torts, Advanced Torts, and Civil Procedure I. Required upper-level courses consist of Business Organizations, Civil Procedure II, Evidence, Criminal Procedure, Professional Responsibility, a jurisprudential requirement, Commercial Transactions or Secured Transactions, and Federal Taxation. The required orientation program for first-year students is a 2-day program that introduces students to all aspects of law school, legal study, and registration and rules, and includes discussion groups and lunch with members of the local judiciary and bar.

Electives

The School of Law offers concentrations in corporate law, criminal law, entertainment law, environmental law, family law, international law, labor law, litigation, securities law, sports law, tax law, torts and insurance, urban affairs, estates and trust/planning. In addition, clinics from 2 to 6 credit hours include legal aid, public defender trial, and death penalty. Other In-house clinics, worth 2 to 6 credit hours, include Family Violence, Wrongful Convictions, Entrepreneurial Clinic, Family and Child Services. Seminars for 2 or 3 credit hours include Civil Rights Litigation, Gender and Justice, and Famous Trials. Research is conducted as part of the research and writing requirement for all students. Introduction to Law and Legal Processes, for 5 credit hours, requires all students to engage in research case analysis and synthesis, and Advanced Legal Writing, a 3-credit-hour course for upper-level students, focuses on drafting seminars in corporate law and litigation. Structured study groups are offered in one substantive course in each first-year section. Trained upper-level study leaders model effective learning strategies and assist with writing/synthesis skills. An academic enrichment program, focusing on analytical, organization, and exam-writing skills, also is offered. Credit may be given for independent study/research projects conducted under faculty supervision, and which may include empirical studies/data gathering. The Cohen and Gage Lecture Series are given and study abroad is possible at Bejing and Oxford Universities and the University of Dublin. The most widely taken electives are Family Law, Debtor-Creditor, Trial Advocacy, Estates and Trusts, and Consitutional Law II.

Graduation Requirements

In order to graduate, candidates must have a GPA of 2.0, have completed the upper-division writing requirement, the jurisprudential requirement, and the advanced torts requirement.

Organizations

Students edit the *UMKC Law Review*, the *Urban Lawyer*, and the *Journal of the American Academy of Matrimonial Lawyers*. Annual moot court competitions include the National Moot Court, Jessup International Law, and Giles Sutherland Rich. Other competitions include the National Trial, ATLA Trial, Environmental Law, Frederick Douglass Moot Court, Client Counseling, and the yearly ABA Negotiation. Student organizations include the ABA/Law School Division, Black Law Students Association, International Law Society, Association of Women Law Students, Public Interest, Law Association, and Environmental Law Society. Local chapters of national associations include Phi Alpha Delta, Delta Theta Phi, and The Federalist Society.

Library

The law library contains 202,809 hard-copy volumes and 89,195 microform volume equivalents, and subscribes to 3802 serial publications. Such on-line databases and networks as CALI, DIALOG, Legal-Trac, LEXIS, Mathew Bender, NEXIS, and WESTLAW are available to law students for research. Special library collections include a depository for federal, Missouri, and Kansas documents, an urban law collection, and a tax law concentration. Recently, the library provided a LAN for students, access to the Internet, and a computer word-processing lab. The ratio of library volumes to faculty is 7243 to 1 and to students is 394 to 1. The ratio of seats in the library to students is 1 to 1.

Placement	
J.D.s awarded:	157
Services available through: a separate law school placement center	
Services: career services news bulletin and the career services library	
Full-time job interviews:	39 employers
Summer job interviews:	n/av
Placement by graduation:	60% of class
Placement within 9 months:	89% of class
Average starting salary:	$24,960 to $100,000
Areas of placement:	
Private practice 2-10 attorneys	18%
Private practice 11-25 attorneys	5%
Private practice 26-50 attorneys	2%
Private practice 51-100 attorneys	3%
Private practice 100+ attorneys	13%
Government	29%
Business/industry	16%
Judicial clerkships	3%
Military	3%
Academic	2%
Public interest	1%

Faculty

The law school has 28 full-time and 42 part-time faculty members, of whom 14 are women. According to AAUP standards for Category I institutions, faculty salaries are below average. About 42% of full-time faculty have a graduate law degree in addition to the J.D. The ratio of full-time students to full-time faculty in an average class is 16 to 1; in a clinic, 6 to 1. The law school has a regular program of bringing visiting professors and other distinguished lecturers and visitors to campus.

Students

About 47% of the student body are women; 8%, minorities; 3%, African American; 2%, Asian American; 1%, Hispanic; and 1%, Native American. The majority of students come from the Midwest (92%). The average age of entering students is 25; age range is 20 to 52. About 12% of students have a graduate degree. About 12% drop out after the first year for academic or personal reasons; 88% remain to receive a law degree.

UNIVERSITY OF MONTANA

School of Law

Missoula, MT 59812

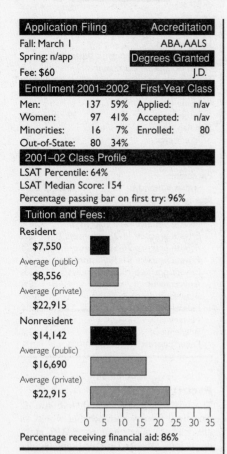

Application Filing	Accreditation
Fall: March 1	ABA, AALS
Spring: n/app	**Degrees Granted**
Fee: $60	J.D.

Enrollment 2001–2002			First-Year Class	
Men:	137	59%	Applied:	n/av
Women:	97	41%	Accepted:	n/av
Minorities:	16	7%	Enrolled:	80
Out-of-State:	80	34%		

2001–02 Class Profile

LSAT Percentile: 64%

LSAT Median Score: 154

Percentage passing bar on first try: 96%

Tuition and Fees:

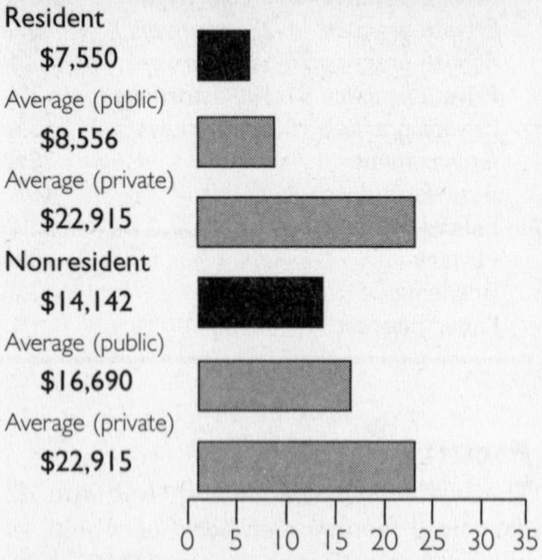

Percentage receiving financial aid: 86%

ADMISSIONS

Some information in the above capsule is from an earlier year. In the fall 2001 first-year class, 80 enrolled. Six transfers enrolled. The median LSAT percentile of the most recent first-year class was 64; the median GPA was 3.2 on a scale of 4.0. The lowest LSAT percentile accepted was 17; the highest was 97.

Requirements

Applicants must have a bachelor's degree and take the LSAT. The most important admission factors include LSAT results, academic achievement, and writing ability. No specific undergraduate courses are required. Candidates are not interviewed.

Procedure

The application deadline for fall entry is March 1. Applicants should submit an application form, LSAT results, transcripts, TOEFL for foreign applicants, a nonrefundable application fee of $60, 3 letters of recommendation, and personal statements. Notification of the admissions decision is from October to April. The latest acceptable LSAT test date for fall entry is February. The law school uses the LSDAS.

Special

The law school recruits minority and disadvantaged students by means of special recruiting efforts aimed at Native American and other minority students. Requirements are not different for out-of-state students. Transfer students must have one year of credit and a minimum GPA of 2.0.

Costs

Tuition and fees for the 2001-2002 academic year are $7550 for full-time in-state students and $14,142 for out-of-state students. On-campus room and board costs about $7450 annually; books and supplies run $950.

Financial Aid

About 86% of current law students receive some form of aid. The average annual amount of aid from all sources combined, including scholarships, loans, and work contracts, is $14,254; maximum, $18,500. Awards are based on need and merit. Required financial statement is the FAFSA. The aid application deadline for fall entry is March 1. Special funds for minority or disadvantaged students consist of Native American fee waivers and scholarships. First-year students are notified about their financial aid application at a time determined by the University Financial Aid Office.

About the Law School

University of Montana School of Law was established in 1911 and is a public institution. The campus is in a small town Missoula, Montana. The primary mission of the law school is to teach a competency-based curriculum. Legal writing, trial practice, and clinical programs require students to demonstrate their abilities to apply highly technical legal knowledge to practical situations. Students have access to federal, state, county, city, and local agencies, courts, correctional facilities, law firms, and legal aid organizations in the Missoula area. Students in clinics benefit from natural resource groups and Native American tribal courts and governments. Facilities of special interest to law students include a computerized courtroom facility and first-year moot "law firms." Housing for students is available in university housing; apartments and houses are available for rent in the community. All law school facilities are accessible to the physically disabled.

Calendar

The law school operates on a traditional semester basis. Courses for full-time students are offered days only and must be completed within 3 years. There is no part-time program. New students are admitted in the fall. There is a 6-week summer session. Transferable summer courses are not offered.

Programs

Students may take relevant courses in other programs and apply credit toward the J.D.The following joint degrees may be earned: J.D./M.B.A. (Juris Doctor/Master of Business Administration), J.D./M.P.A. (Juris Doctor/Master of Public Administration), and J.D./M.S. (Juris Doctor/Master of Science in environmental studies).

Phone: 406-243-2698
E-mail: *lawadmis@selway.umt.edu*
Web: *http://www.umt.edu/law*

Contact

Heidi Fanslow, Director of Admissions, 406-243-2698 for general inquiries; Connie Bowman, 406-243-5524 for financial aid information.

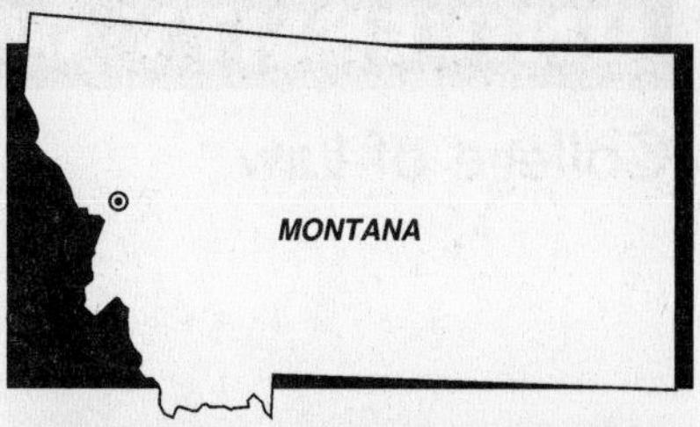

Required

To earn the J.D., candidates must complete 90 total credits, of which 56 are for required courses. They must maintain a minimum GPA of 2.0 in the required courses. The following first-year courses are required of all students: Civil Procedure I and II, Contracts I and II, Legal Writing I, Torts I and II, Legal Research and Analysis, Pre-Trial Advocacy I and II, and Criminal Law and Procedure I and II. Required upper-level courses consist of Business Organizations, Federal Tax, Constitutional Law I and II, Evidence, a Commercial requirement, Estate Planning, Professional Responsibility, Trial Practice, clinical training, Property I and II, advanced writing component, and Business Transactions. All students must take clinical courses. The required orientation program for first-year students is 7 days and includes concepts of jurisprudence, the role of lawyers in society, legal history, and other topics.

Electives

The School of Law offers concentrations in corporate law, criminal law, environmental law, family law, labor law, litigation, tax law, torts and insurance, and Indian law. In addition, clinics, field work, and internships include the Criminal Defense Clinic, Montana Legal Services, and Natural Resource Clinic for 1 to 4 credit hours for third-year students. Seminars include Contemporary Problems in Constitutional Law, Problems in Estate Planning, and Problems in Indian Law Regulation for 2 credit hours each, open to second- and third-year students. Independent study programs designed by law students and professors for 1 to 2 credit hours for third-year students and periodic law reform projects for second- and third-year students, for no credit hours, are available. Special lectures include the Blankenbaker Lecture in Ethics and the Judge William B. Jones and Judge Edward A. Tamm Judicial Lecture Series. Tutorial programs include the Academic Assistance Program. Minority programs are sponsored by the Native American Law Students Association. Periodic programs are offered by the Federalist Society, Women's Law Caucus, Phi Delta Phi, Student Bar Association, and 8 other student groups. The most widely taken electives are Family Law, Environmental Law, and Real Estate Transactions.

Graduation Requirements

In order to graduate, candidates must have a GPA of 2.0 and have completed the upper-division writing requirement.

Organizations

Students edit the *Montana Law Review* and the *Public Land and Resource Law Review*. Moot court competitions include National Moot Court Team, NALSA Moot Court Team, Pace Environmental Moot Court Team, and International Law Moot Court Team (Jessup). Other competitions include ATLA Trial Team, ABA Negotiations Team, and ABA Client Counseling Team. Student organizations include the Student Bar Association, Phi Delta Phi, and Women's Law Caucus. Local chapters of national organizations include American Trial Lawyers and ACLU.

Library

The law library contains approximately 108,599 hard-copy volumes and 57,584 microform volume equivalents, and subscribes to 1717 serial publications. Such on-line databases and networks as LEXIS, WESTLAW, and MontLaw are available to law students for research. Recently, the library increased staffing, added computers, and completed renovation of a basement that added seminar rooms and a presentation center. The ratio of library volumes to faculty is 3109 to 1 and to students is 464 to 1. The ratio of seats in the library to students is 1 to 1.

Faculty

The law school has 19 full-time and 16 part-time faculty members, of whom 10 are women. According to AAUP standards for Category I institutions, faculty salaries are well below average. About 43% of full-time faculty have a graduate law degree in addition to the J.D.; about 27% of part-time faculty have one. The ratio of full-time students to full-time faculty in an average class is 19 to 1; in a clinic, 10 to 1. The law school has a regular program of bringing visiting professors and other distinguished lecturers and visitors to campus.

Placement	
J.D.s awarded:	72
Services available through: a separate law school placement center	
Special features: semiannual on-campus recruitment conferences.	
Full-time job interviews:	40 employers
Summer job interviews:	n/av
Placement by graduation:	n/av
Placement within 9 months:	96% of class
Average starting salary:	$33,750
Areas of placement:	
Private practice 2-10 attorneys	44%
Solo practice	4%
Judicial clerkships	24%
Government	17%
Business/industry	6%
Unknown	4%
Academic	1%

Students

About 41% of the student body are women; 7%, minorities; 1%, African American; 1%, Asian American; 2%, Hispanic; and 4%, Native American. The majority of students come from Montana (66%). The average age of entering students is 28; age range is 21 to 60. About 22% of students enter directly from undergraduate school, 14% have a graduate degree, and 60% have worked full-time prior to entering law school. About 1% drop out after the first year for academic or personal reasons; 99% remain to receive a law degree.

UNIVERSITY OF NEBRASKA

College of Law

P.O. Box 830902
Lincoln, NE 68583-0902

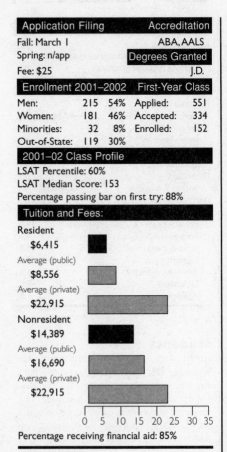

Application Filing		Accreditation
Fall: March 1		ABA, AALS
Spring: n/app		**Degrees Granted**
Fee: $25		J.D.

Enrollment 2001–2002			First-Year Class	
Men:	215	54%	Applied:	551
Women:	181	46%	Accepted:	334
Minorities:	32	8%	Enrolled:	152
Out-of-State:	119	30%		

2001–02 Class Profile

LSAT Percentile: 60%
LSAT Median Score: 153
Percentage passing bar on first try: 88%

Tuition and Fees:

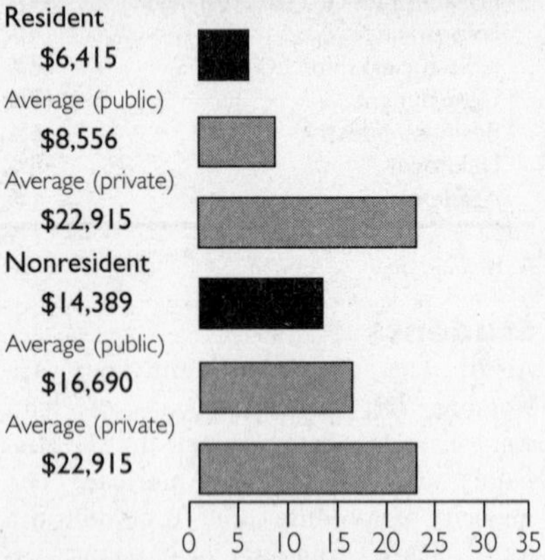

Percentage receiving financial aid: 85%

ADMISSIONS

In the fall 2001 first-year class, 551 applied, 334 were accepted, and 152 enrolled. Three transfers enrolled. The median LSAT percentile of the most recent first-year class was 60; the median GPA was 3.6 on a scale of 4.0. The lowest LSAT percentile accepted was 11; the highest was 99.

Requirements

Applicants must have a bachelor's degree unless they are applying under the 3/3 combined program, and take the LSAT. The most important admission factors include LSAT results, GPA, and academic achievement. No specific undergraduate courses are required. Candidates are not interviewed.

Procedure

The application deadline for fall entry is March 1. Applicants should submit an application form, LSAT results, transcripts, a nonrefundable application fee of $25, and 2 letters of recommendation (recommended, not required). Notification of the admissions decision is on a rolling basis. The latest acceptable LSAT test date for fall entry is February. The law school uses the LSDAS.

Special

The law school recruits minority and disadvantaged students through sponsoring an annual Diversity Law Day and participating in career fairs and the CLEO program. The college takes special care when evaluating applications from members of minority groups that historically have not been well represented in the legal profession. Requirements are not different for out-of-state students. Transfer students must have one year of credit, have attended an ABA-approved law school, and must be in good standing at the end of a full year of study and eligible to continue at their current law school. Other requirements may apply.

Costs

Tuition and fees for the 2001-2002 academic year are $6415 for full-time in-state students and $14,389 for out-of-state students. On-campus room and board costs about $5365 annually; books and supplies run $1040.

Financial Aid

About 85% of current law students receive some form of aid. The maximum annual amount of aid from all sources combined, including scholarships, loans, and work contracts, is $22,405. Awards are based on need and merit. Required financial statement is the FAFSA. The aid application deadline for fall entry is March 1. Special funds for minority or disadvantaged students consist of college funds for need-based grants and opportunity grants. First-year students are notified about their financial aid application from January to April for scholarships and grants, and May through August for loans.

About the Law School

University of Nebraska College of Law was established in 1888 and is a public institution. The campus is in a suburban area on the east campus of the University of Nebraska-Lincoln. The primary mission of the law school is to provide an excellent, affordable legal education with a balance between legal theory and professional skills in the atmosphere of a small law school. Students have access to federal, state, county, city, and local agencies, courts, correctional facilities, law firms, and legal aid organizations in the Lincoln area. As Lincoln is the state capital, the legislature, the State Supreme Court, and the Intermediate Court of Appeals are nearby. Facilities of special interest to law students include 2 clinical programs: 1 clinic is located at the college, providing civil legal services to low income clients, and the other clinic is located within the Lancaster County Attorney's Office, permitting third-year students to prosecute misdemeanor cases. The federal and state appellate courts frequently hear cases at the college. The Shermon S. Welpton, Jr. courtroom is used for actual trials as well as practical skills training. Housing for students is available both as on-campus graduate housing and off-campus apartments and homes. All law school facilities are accessible to the physically disabled.

Calendar

The law school operates on a traditional semester basis. Courses for full-time students are offered days only and must be completed within 5 years; 3 years is normal. There is no part-time program. New students are admitted in the fall. There are 2 5-week summer sessions and 1 3-week session. Transferable summer courses are offered.

Phone: 402-472-2161
Fax: 402-472-5185
E-mail: *lawadm@unl.edu*
Web: *www.unl.edu/lawcoll*

Contact

Glenda J. Pierce, Associate Dean, 402-472-2161 for general inquiries and financial aid information.

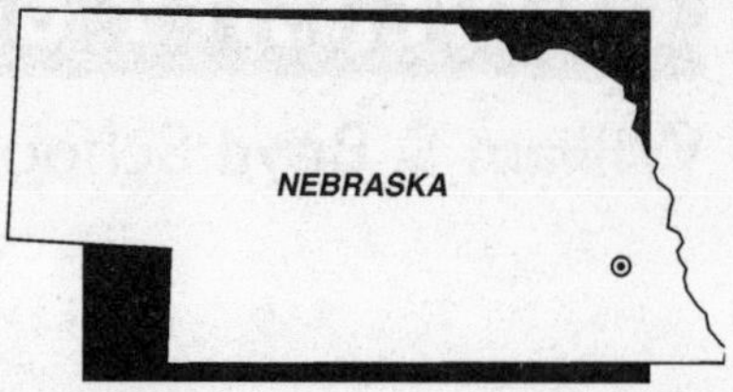

Programs

In addition to the J.D., the law school offers the M.L.S.(Master of Legal Studies). Students may take relevant courses in other programs and apply credit toward the J.D.; a maximum of 3 nonlaw graduate level credits may be applied. The following joint degrees may be earned: J.D./M.A. (Juris Doctor/Master of Arts in psychology, economics, political science, and international affairs), J.D./M.B.A. (Juris Doctor/Master of Business Administration), J.D./M.C.R.P. (Juris Doctor/Master of Community and Regional Planning), J.D./M.P.A. (Juris Doctor/Master of Professional Accountancy), and J.D./Ph.D (Juris Doctor/Doctor of Philosophy in psychology and educational administration).

Required

To earn the J.D., candidates must complete 96 total credits, of which 45 are for required courses. They must maintain a minimum GPA of 4.0 (C) in the required courses. The following first-year courses are required of all students: Torts, Civil Procedure, Contracts, Legal Process, Criminal Law, Legal Research and Writing, and Property. Required upper-level courses consist of Constitutional Law I, Legal Professional Responsibility, and a seminar with substantial writing requirements. The required orientation program for first-year students is 2 days prior to the beginning of the fall semester. Students listen to speakers, tour the college, meet faculty and upper-level students, and attend a legal writing class.

Electives

The College of Law offers concentrations in corporate law, criminal law, environmental law, international law, labor law, litigation, and tax law. In addition, students who have obtained senior standing are eligible to take either a 6-credit hour civil or criminal clinic. Second- or third-year students must take a 3-credit-hour seminar with a substantial writing requirement. A 3-credit-hour research program in a selected field under the supervision of a faculty member is available to any upper-level student. Any student may apply to have transfer credit for courses taken in a summer abroad program where the student received a grade of C or better. The Academic Resource Program offers a non-credit skills seminar for first-year students to assist in developing such skills as note taking, case briefing, and exam taking. Participation in the program is by invitation. Minority programs include a voluntary day "introduction to law school and legal methodology" for which no credit is given. The most widely taken electives are Corporations, Evidence, and Wills and Trusts.

Graduation Requirements

In order to graduate, candidates must have a GPA of 4.0 (C), have completed the upper-division writing requirement, have taken the Legal Professional Responsibility course and Constitutional Law I, and have completed 96 credit hours.

Organizations

Students edit the *Nebraska Law Review*. Moot court competitions include the Allen Moot Court Competition for first-year students, Fall Grether Moot Court Competition for second-year students, and the National Moot Court competition. Other competitions include Client Counseling and National Trial. Student organizations include the Black Law Students Association, American Civil Liberties Union Chapter of Nebraska, and Community Legal Education Project. Delta Theta Phi, ABA-Law Student Division, and Phi Alpha Delta have local chapters. Other organizations include the Multi-Cultural Legal Society, Allies and Advocates for GLBT Equality, and Equal Justice Society.

Library

The law library contains 217,729 hardcopy volumes and 158,056 microform volume equivalents, and subscribes to 2833 serial publications. Such on-line databases and networks as CALI, CIS Universe, DIALOG, Legal-Trac, LEXIS, WESTLAW, and Expanded Academic Index Full Text are available to law students for research. Special library collections include a selected federal government depository and the Great Plains Tax Library. The ratio of library volumes to faculty is 7776 to 1 and to students is 550 to 1. The ratio of seats in the library to students is 1 to 2.

Placement	
J.D.s awarded:	116
Services available through: a separate law school placement center	
Full-time job interviews:	34 employers
Summer job interviews:	43 employers
Placement by graduation:	56% of class
Placement within 9 months:	98% of class
Average starting salary:	$20,000 to $110,000
Areas of placement:	
Private practice 2-10 attorneys	26%
Private practice 11-25 attorneys	8%
Private practice 26-50 attorneys	3%
Private practice 51-100 attorneys	4%
Government	19%
Business/industry	11%
Unknown	11%
Judicial clerkships	8%
Military	3%
Academic	3%
Public interest	1%

Faculty

The law school has 28 full-time and 28 part-time faculty members, of whom 15 are women. According to AAUP standards for Category I institutions, faculty salaries are average. About 18% of full-time faculty have a graduate law degree in addition to the J.D. The ratio of full-time students to full-time faculty in an average class is 20 to 1; in a clinic, 12 to 1. The law school has a regular program of bringing visiting professors and other distinguished lecturers and visitors to campus. There is a chapter of the Order of the Coif; 11 faculty and 662 graduates are members.

Students

About 46% of the student body are women; 8%, minorities; 2%, African American; 2%, Asian American; 2%, Hispanic; and 2%, Mexican-American, 2% Foreign National. The majority of students come from the Midwest (86%). The average age of entering students is 24; age range is 20 to 47. About 41% of students enter directly from undergraduate school, 3% have a graduate degree, and 59% have worked full-time prior to entering law school. About 8% drop out after the first year for academic or personal reasons; 92% remain to receive a law degree.

UNIVERSITY OF NEVADA, LAS VEGAS

William S. Boyd School of Law

4505 Maryland Parkway, Box 451003
Las Vegas, NV 89154-1003

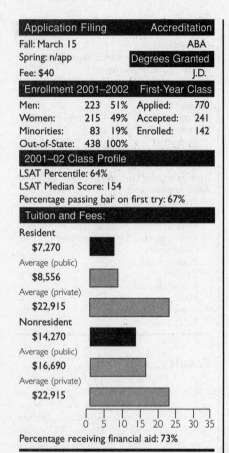

Application Filing		Accreditation
Fall: March 15		ABA
Spring: n/app		**Degrees Granted**
Fee: $40		J.D.

Enrollment 2001–2002			First-Year Class	
Men:	223	51%	Applied:	770
Women:	215	49%	Accepted:	241
Minorities:	83	19%	Enrolled:	142
Out-of-State:	438	100%		

2001–02 Class Profile

LSAT Percentile: 64%
LSAT Median Score: 154
Percentage passing bar on first try: 67%

Tuition and Fees:

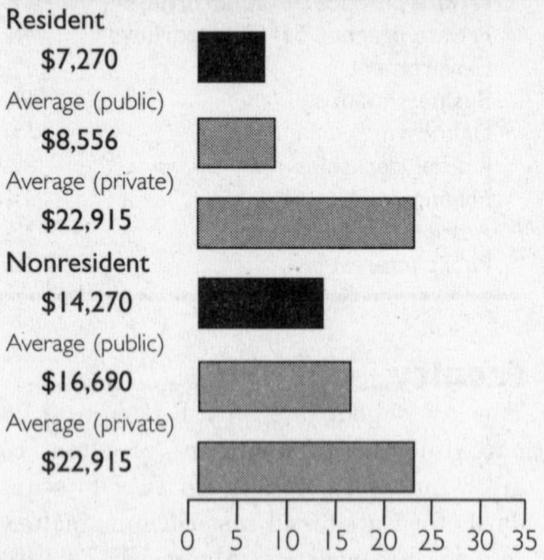

Percentage receiving financial aid: 73%

ADMISSIONS

In the fall 2001 first-year class, 770 applied, 241 were accepted, and 142 enrolled. Five transfers enrolled. The median LSAT percentile of the most recent first-year class was 64; the median GPA was 3.36 on a scale of 4.0. The lowest LSAT percentile accepted was 96; the highest was 23.

Requirements

Applicants must have a bachelor's degree and take the LSAT.

Procedure

The application deadline for fall entry is March 15. Applicants should submit an application form, LSAT results, transcripts, an application fee of $40, 1 letter of recommendation, a personal statement, and resume. Notification of the admissions decision is April. The latest acceptable LSAT test date for fall entry is generally February. The law school uses the LSDAS.

Special

The law school recruits minority and disadvantaged students through reaching out to various individuals and community organizations to generate a large and diverse applicant pool. Requirements are not different for out-of-state students. Transfer students must have one year of credit, have attended an ABA-approved law school, and have an admissions committee review.

Costs

Tuition and fees for the 2001-2002 academic year are $7270 for full-time in-state students and $14,270 for out-of-state students. Tuition for part-time students is $4720 in-state and $9220 out-of-state. On-campus room and board costs about $6640 annually; books and supplies run $850.

Financial Aid

About 73% of current law students receive some form of aid. The average annual amount of aid from all sources combined, including scholarships, loans, and work contracts, is $14,033; maximum, $25,880. Awards are based on need and merit. Required financial statement is the FAFSA. The aid application deadline for fall entry is February 1. First-year students are notified about their financial aid application on a rolling basis.

About the Law School

University of Nevada, Las Vegas William S. Boyd School of Law was established in 1998 and is a public institution. The 335-acre campus is in a fast-growing metropolitan area. The primary mission of the law school is to train ethical and effective lawyers and leaders, to stress community service, professionalism, and the roles, responsibilities, skills, and values of lawyers to produce excellent scholarship, to involve students and faculty in community service projects, and to provide leadership on important issues of public policy, dispute resolution, the law, and legal practice. Students have access to federal, state, county, city, and local agencies, courts, correctional facilities, law firms, and legal aid organizations in the Las Vegas area. Facilities of special interest to law students include a centrally located facility on the main campus that is equipped to permit students access to the law school computer network from classrooms, library study carrels, and home. Housing for students not available on-campus, but is abundantly available off-campus. All law school facilities are accessible to the physically disabled.

Calendar

The law school operates on a traditional semester basis. Courses for full-time students are offered both day and evening and must be completed within 5 years. For part-time students, courses are offered both day and evening and must be completed within 6 years. New full- and part-time students are admitted in the fall. There is a 10-week summer session. Transferable summer courses are offered.

Programs

Students may take relevant courses in other programs and apply credit toward the J.D.; a maximum of 6 credits may be applied.

Required

To earn the J.D., candidates must complete 86 total credits, of which 44 are for required courses. They must maintain a minimum GPA of 2.0 in the required courses. The following first-year courses are required of all students: Introduction to Law, Civil Procedure/Alternative Dispute Resolution I, Civil Procedure/Alternative Dispute Resolution II, Contracts I, Contracts II, Lawyering Process I, Lawyering Process II, Property I, Property II, Torts I, and Torts II. Required upper-level courses consist of Constitutional Law I, Criminal Law, Lawyering Process III, and Professional Responsibility. The required orientation program for first-year students is a 1-week course, Introduction to Law.

Phone: 702-895-3671
Fax: 702-895-1095
E-mail: request@law.unlv.edu
Web: www.law.unlv.edu

Contact

Frank Durand, Assistant Dean, Admissions and Financial Aid, 702-895-3671 for general inquiries; Christopher Kypuros, Senior Coordinator, Professional Program and Debt Counseling, 702-895-0630 for financial aid information.

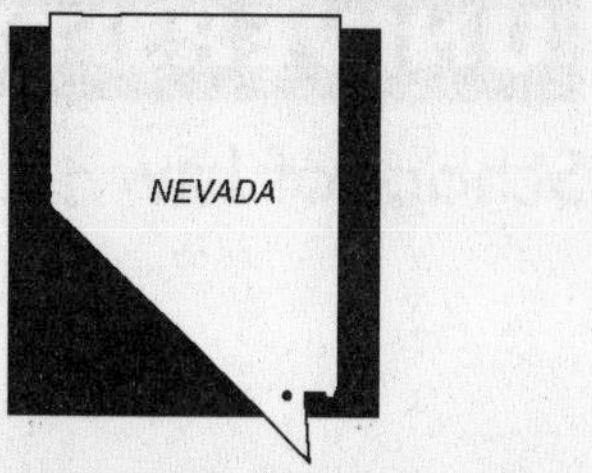

Electives

The Child Welfare Clinic and Juvenile Justice Clinics, worth 3 credits each, afford students the opportunity to represent clients in real-life settings, under faculty supervision. Each clinic also has a classroom component. In the Child Welfare Clinic, students represent clients in civil litigation regarding child protection, termination of parental rights, adoption or other related matters. In the Juvenile Justice Clinic, students represent juveniles in juvenile court and district court proceedings involving charges of criminal conduct. Students must be licensed under Nevada's student practice rule to appear in court. Seminars include First Amendment Rights and Bioethics, worth 2 to 3 credits each, and Gaming Policy, worth 1 to 3 credits. Congressional and judicial externships, worth 3 to 6 credits, legislative externships worth 1 to 12 credits, and government/public interest externships, worth 1 to 6 credits, are also offered. Research programs include Directed Readings, where students complete readings under faculty supervision for 1 credit, or Directed Research, where they research and write on a legal topic of their choice under faculty supervision, for 1 to 3 credits. The Barrick Lecture Series brings well-known persons to the university for free public lectures on a variety of topics. Lecturers have included Walter Cronkite, Louis Rukeyser, and Benazir Bhutto. The series has also featured academicians such as Stephen Jay Gould, Carl Sagan, and Richard Leakey. The law school provides an academic support program open to all students, on topics such as learning styles, class preparation, outlining, general exam-taking skills, and practice exams in specific doctrinal areas. Although the program is open to all students, those having academic difficulty may be required to take advantage of some parts of the program. The Academic Support Program supervises the Center for Academic Success and Enrichment (CASE), a student-operated and faculty-supervised program designed to facilitate learning and academic success in law school. Tutoring is available in individual subject areas. CASE is open to all students who desire mentoring, advising, or tutoring and includes a resource area with sample examinations and materials on study skills, learning theories, and learning styles. The most widely taken electives are Evidence; Criminal Procedure; Wills, Trusts, and Estates.

Graduation Requirements

In order to graduate, candidates must have a GPA of 2.0, have completed the upper-division writing requirement, and have completed community service and writing requirements.

Organizations

Students edit the *Nevada Law Journal*. Moot court competitions include ABA-LSD National Appellate Advocacy, National Criminal Procedure, and Bar Association of the City of New York National. Other competitions include the ABA-LSD Negotiation Competition. Law student organizations include the Student Bar, Minority Law Students, and Public Interest Law Associations. Local chapters of national associations include ACLU, Phi Alpha Delta, and the Federalist Society. Campus clubs include the Environmental Law Society, Sports and Entertainment Law Association, and Organization of Women Law Students.

Library

The law library contains 202,277 hard-copy volumes and 138,618 microform volume equivalents, and subscribes to 830 serial publications. Such on-line databases and networks as CALI, Legal-Trac, LEXIS, LOIS, NEXIS, OCLC First Search, and WESTLAW are available to law students for research. Recently, the library added a facility. The ratio of library volumes to faculty is 6525 to 1 and to students is 462 to 1. The ratio of seats in the library to students is 1 to 2.

Faculty

The law school has 31 full-time and 13 part-time faculty members, of whom 19 are women. According to AAUP standards for Category IIA institutions, faculty salaries are well above average. About 1% of full-time faculty have a graduate law degree in addition to the J.D. The ratio of full-time students to full-time faculty in an average class is 17 to 1; in a clinic, 8 to 1. The law school has a regular program of bringing visiting professors and other distinguished lecturers and visitors to campus. There is a chapter of the Order of the Coif; 12 faculty are members.

Placement

J.D.s awarded:	89
Services available through: a separate law school placement center	
Services: Utilizes web-based recruiting and placement software program accessible 24 hours a day to students and employers; has established mentorship program, matching more than 100 experienced attorneys with current law students; maintains Career Services Library and Resource Center (including a computer terminal allowing students to access job search options in Lexis and Westlaw); conducts legal career options day; maintains judicial clerkship notebook pertaining to hiring practices of the Nevada and federal judiciary.	
Full-time job interviews:	n/av
Summer job interviews:	n/av
Placement by graduation:	n/av
Placement within 9 months:	n/av
Average starting salary:	n/av
Areas of placement:	n/av

Students

About 49% of the student body are women; 19%, minorities; 4%, African American; 4%, Asian American; 9%, Hispanic; and 3%, Native American. The average age of entering students is 30; age range is 20 to 56. About 22% of students enter directly from undergraduate school and 20% have a graduate degree.

UNIVERSITY OF NEW MEXICO

School of Law

1117 Stanford Drive N.E.
Albuquerque, NM 87131-1431

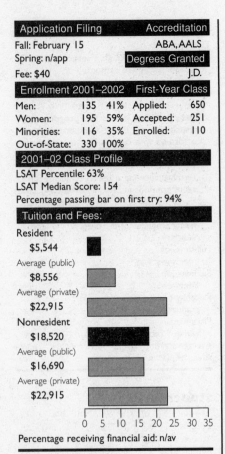

Application Filing		Accreditation
Fall: February 15		ABA, AALS
Spring: n/app		**Degrees Granted**
Fee: $40		J.D.

Enrollment 2001–2002			First-Year Class	
Men:	135	41%	Applied:	650
Women:	195	59%	Accepted:	251
Minorities:	116	35%	Enrolled:	110
Out-of-State:	330	100%		

2001–02 Class Profile

LSAT Percentile: 63%
LSAT Median Score: 154
Percentage passing bar on first try: 94%

Tuition and Fees:

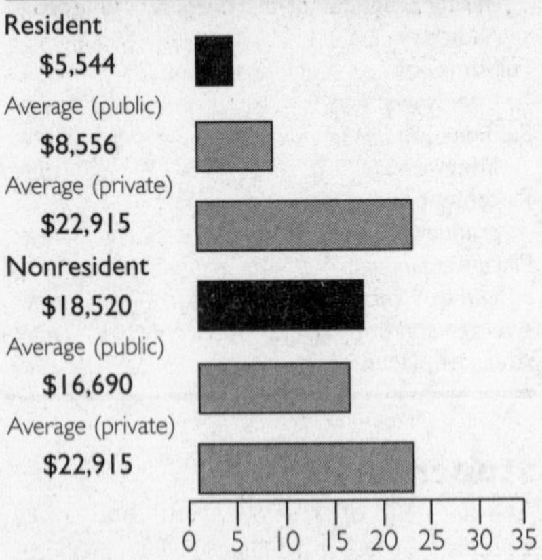

Percentage receiving financial aid: n/av

ADMISSIONS

In the fall 2001 first-year class, 650 applied, 251 were accepted, and 110 enrolled. Six transfers enrolled. The median LSAT percentile of the most recent first-year class was 63; the median GPA was 3.24 on a scale of 4.0. The lowest LSAT percentile accepted was 16; the highest was 99.

Requirements

Applicants must have a bachelor's degree and take the LSAT. No specific undergraduate courses are required. Candidates are not interviewed.

Procedure

The application deadline for fall entry is February 15. Applicants should submit an application form, a nonrefundable application fee of $40, 1 letter of recommendation, a personal statement, and the LSDAS report. Notification of the admissions decision is on a rolling basis. The latest acceptable LSAT test date for fall entry is December (preferred). The law school uses the LSDAS.

Special

Requirements are not different for out-of-state students. Transfer students must have one year of credit, have attended an ABA-approved law school, and a letter from the dean of the previously attended school. The applicant must be in good academic standing.

Costs

Tuition and fees for the 2001-2002 academic year are $5544 for full-time in-state students and $18,520 for out-of-state students. On-campus room and board costs about $6604 annually; books and supplies run $864.

Financial Aid

Awards are based on need and merit. Required financial statements are the FAFSA and Need Access. The aid application deadline for fall entry is March 1. Special funds for graduate fellowships for minority or disadvantaged students are available through the Office of Graduate Studies. First-year students are notified about their financial aid application after acceptance.

About the Law School

The University of New Mexico School of Law was established in 1947 and is a public institution. The 600-acre campus is in an urban area in the city of Albuquerque. The primary mission of the law school is to offer a legal education that combines training in legal doctrine, theory, and policy with the development of practical lawyering skills. Emphasis is placed on student-faculty interaction. Students have access to federal, state, county, city, and local agencies, courts, correctional facilities, law firms, and legal aid organizations in the Albuquerque area. A facility of special interest to law students is Bratton Hall, which, in addition to housing the classrooms, seminar rooms, and faculty, staff, and student organization offices, is home to the Natural Resources Center, the American Indian Law Center, and the Law Practice Clinic. Housing for students consists of off-campus rental homes and apartments where most students live and 200 student family apartments. The university helps with finding housing.

Calendar

The law school operates on a traditional semester basis. Courses for full-time students are offered days only and must be completed within 3 years. There is no part-time program. New students are admitted in the fall. There is a summer session.

Programs

Students may take relevant courses in other programs and apply credit toward the J.D.; a maximum of 6 to 9 credits may be applied. The following joint degrees may be earned: J.D./M.A., M.S., or Ph.D (all degrees are available in various academic fields), J.D./M.A.L.A.S. (Juris Doctor/Master of Arts in Latin American Studies), J.D./M.B.A. (Juris Doctor/Master of Business Administration), and J.D./M.P.A. (Juris Doctor/Master of Public Administration).

Phone: 505-277-0572
Fax: 505-277-9958

Contact

Susan Mitchell, Director of Admissions and Financial Aid, 505-277-0959 for general inquiries and for financial aid information.

Required

To earn the J.D., candidates must complete 86 total credits, of which 41 are for required courses. They must maintain a minimum GPA of 2.0 in the required courses. The following first-year courses are required of all students: Contracts I, Historical Introduction to Law, Property I, Legislative and Administrative Process, Criminal Law, Torts, Civil Procedure I, Advocacy, and Legal Reasoning, Research, and Writing. Required upper-level courses consist of Constitutional Law, a course in Professional Responsibility, and 6 hours of clinical courses. All students must take clinical courses. The required orientation program for first-year students lasts 3 days.

Electives

The School of Law offers concentrations in Indian law, with natural resources and environmental law certificate programs offered. In addition, UNM's Clinical Law Program is a requirement for the J.D. degree. Students, supervised by faculty members, may counsel and advise clients and appear in state, federal, and tribal courts in New Mexico. The District Attorney Clinic involves supervised prosecution of misdemeanor cases in Bernalillo County Metropolitan Court. The program is jointly sponsored by the law school and the District Attorney's Office and is trial oriented, in addition to having a classroom component. Emphasis is placed on improving students' knowledge and experience in criminal procedure, evidence, and trial practice. Judicial and law office externships are available. Individual research, worth from 1 to 3 credits, is available under faculty direction. There is also an Advanced Legal Research elective. Summer-abroad programs are available through the Guanajuato Summer Law Institute. Tutorials are available to first-year students for each substantive course.

Graduation Requirements

In order to graduate, candidates must have a GPA of 2.0, have completed the upper-division writing requirement, and have at least 3 full academic years in residence. Ethics and Constitutional Law courses must be taken.

Organizations

The primary law review is the *New Mexico Law Review*, which is published 3 times a year. Students also edit the *Natural Resources Journal, Tribal Law Journal* and *U.S.-Mexico Law Journal*. Moot court teams attend the Native American Law Student Association, Hispanic, and National Moot Court Competitions. Law student organizations include the Student Bar Association, Environmental Law Society, International Law Students Association, Mexican American Law Students Association, Black Law Students Association, and Native American Law Students Association. There are campus chapters of Phi Alpha Delta, Phi Delta Phi, and Association of Trial Lawyers of America/New Mexico.

Library

The law library contains 412,694 hard-copy volumes and 31,691 microform volume equivalents, and subscribes to 3113 serial publications. Such on-line databases and networks as CALI, CIS Universe, Legal-Trac, LEXIS, LOIS, Mathew Bender, NEXIS, OCLC First Search, and WESTLAW are available to law students for research. Special library collections include extensive collection of New Mexico appellate briefs and records, American Indian law, Mexican and Latin American law, and land-grant law. Recently, the library added a PC for researcher access to the Internet and electronic subscriptions. All carrels were wired for network access. The ratio of library volumes to faculty is 12,138 to 1 and to students is 1251 to 1. The ratio of seats in the library to students is 1 to 1.

Faculty

The law school has 34 full-time and 29 part-time faculty members, of whom 25 are women. According to AAUP standards for Category I institutions, faculty salaries are below average. About 21% of full-time faculty have a graduate law degree in addition to the J.D.; about 5% of part-time faculty have one. The ratio of full-time students to full-time faculty in an average class is 11 to 1; in a clinic, 8 to 1. The law school has a regular program of bringing visiting professors and other distinguished lecturers and visitors to campus. There is a chapter of the Order of the Coif; 33 faculty and 330 graduates are members.

Placement	
J.D.s awarded:	106
Services available through: a separate law school placement center, the university placement center, and	
Services: autumn job fair	
Full-time job interviews:	8 employers
Summer job interviews:	17 employers
Placement by graduation:	n/av
Placement within 9 months:	87% of class
Average starting salary:	$18,000 to $100,000
Areas of placement:	
Private practice 2-10 attorneys	31%
Private practice 11-25 attorneys	4%
Private practice 26-50 attorneys	4%
Private practice 51-100 attorneys	1%
Private practice solo	5%
Government	30%
Judicial clerkships	11%
Business/industry	6%
Public interest	4%
Military	1%

Students

About 59% of the student body are women; 35%, minorities; 3%, African American; 2%, Asian American; 23%, Hispanic; and 7%, Native American. The average age of entering students is 27; age range is 21 to 63. About 17% of students enter directly from undergraduate school and 20% have a graduate degree.

UNIVERSITY OF NORTH CAROLINA AT CHAPEL HILL

School of Law

Campus Box 3380, 101 Van Hecke-Wettach Hall
Chapel Hill, NC 27599-3380

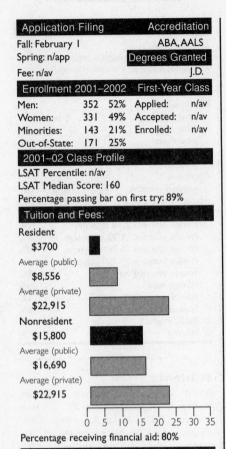

Application Filing		Accreditation
Fall: February 1		ABA, AALS
Spring: n/app		**Degrees Granted**
Fee: n/av		J.D.

Enrollment 2001–2002			First-Year Class	
Men:	352	52%	Applied:	n/av
Women:	331	49%	Accepted:	n/av
Minorities:	143	21%	Enrolled:	n/av
Out-of-State:	171	25%		

2001–02 Class Profile

LSAT Percentile: n/av
LSAT Median Score: 160
Percentage passing bar on first try: 89%

Tuition and Fees:

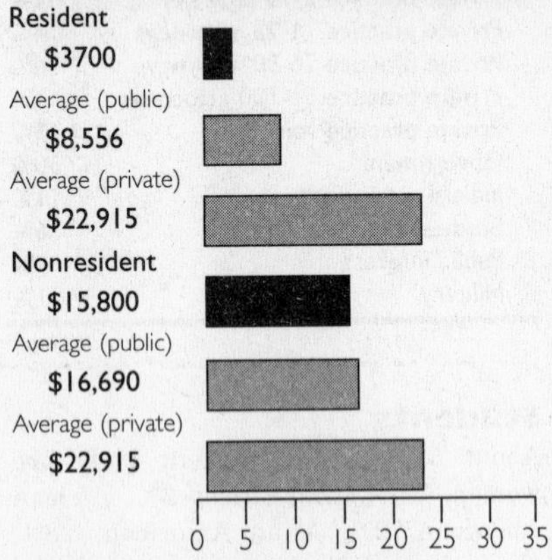

Percentage receiving financial aid: 80%

ADMISSIONS

Information in the above capsule is from an earlier year. In a recent first-year class, one transfer enrolled. The median GPA of a recent first-year class was 3.6. The lowest LSAT percentile accepted was 24; the highest was 99.

Requirements

Applicants must have a bachelor's degree and take the LSAT. The most important admission factors include LSAT results, GPA, and academic achievement. No specific undergraduate courses are required. Candidates are not interviewed.

Procedure

Check with the school for current application deadlines and fee. Applicants should submit an application form, LSAT results, transcripts, and 2 letters of recommendation. Notification of the admissions decision is on a rolling basis from January. The law school uses the LSDAS.

Special

The law school recruits minority and disadvantaged students by means of the Candidate Referral Service and a special open house for minority students. Requirements are not different for out-of-state students. Transfer students must have one year of credit, have attended an ABA-approved law school, have a superior academic performance, be in good academic standing, and have been originally admissible.

Costs

Tuition and fees for the academic year are approximately $3700 for full-time in-state students and $15,800 for out-of-state students. On-campus room and board costs about $11,300 annually.

Financial Aid

About 80% of current law students receive some form of aid. Awards are based on need. Required financial statement is the FAFSA. Check with the school for current application deadlines. Special funds for minority or disadvantaged students consist of the Minority Presence Grant Program. First-year students are notified about their financial aid application in June.

About the Law School

University of North Carolina at Chapel Hill School of Law was established in 1845 and is a public institution. The 700-acre campus is in a small town 23 miles northwest of Raleigh. The primary mission of the law school is to educate future practitioners and leaders of the bench and bar. Students have access to federal, state, county, city, and local agencies, courts, correctional facilities, law firms, and legal aid organizations in the Chapel Hill area. Housing for students is available in the residence hall for graduate and professional students located near the law school; there are also many apartments in the area.

Calendar

The law school operates on a traditional semester basis. Courses for full-time students are offered days only and must be completed within 3 years. There is no part-time program. New students are admitted in the fall. There is a 6-week summer session. Transferable summer courses are not offered.

Programs

Students may take relevant courses in other programs and apply credit toward the J.D.; a maximum of 3 credits may be applied. The following joint degrees may be earned: J.D./M.B.A. (Juris Doctor/Master of Business Administration), J.D./M.P.A. (Juris Doctor/Master of Public Administration), J.D./M.P.H. (Juris Doctor/Master of Public Health), J.D./M.P.P.S. (Juris Doctor/Master of Public Policy Sciences), J.D./M.R.P. (Juris Doctor/Master of Regional Planning), and J.D./M.S.W. (Juris Doctor/Master of Social Work).

Required

To earn the J.D., candidates must complete 86 total credits, of which 33 are for required courses. They must maintain a minimum GPA of 1.7 in the required courses. The following first-year courses are required of all students: Civil Procedure, Contracts, Property, Torts, Criminal Law, and Research and Writing. Required upper-level courses consist of Professional Responsibility. The required orientation program for first-year students is 2 ½ days and includes an introduction to case study method and briefing, and social activities.

Phone: 919-962-5109
Fax: 919-843-7939
E-mail: *law_admission@unc.edu*
Web: *www.law.unc.edu*

Contact

Winston Crisp, Associate Dean, 919-962-5109 for general inquiries; Sue Burdick, Financial Aid Officer, 919-962-8396 for financial aid information.

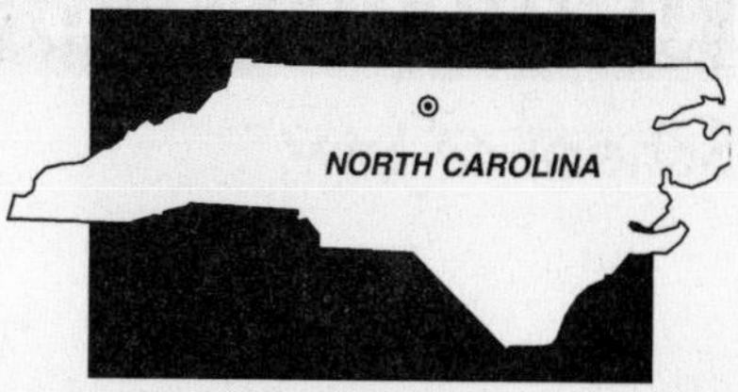

Electives

The School of Law offers concentrations in corporate law, criminal law, environmental law, family law, international law, juvenile law, labor law, litigation, securities law, and tax law. In addition, third-year students may participate in Trial Advocacy to gain experience in pretrial and trial settings. Some 24 students participate in the Criminal Law Clinic, representing defendants and convicted prisoners under faculty supervision. The Civil Law Clinic is also open to some 24 students. There are approximately 40 seminars offered to upper-level students for 3 credit hours; preference is given to third-year students, then second-year students. Research may be undertaken for no more than 3 credit hours and only with faculty permission. Students may study in Lyon, France; Nijmegen, The Netherlands; Glasgow, Scotland; Mexico City, Mexico; or Manchester, England during the spring semester of the second or third year for 12 credit hours. Courses focus on international law. The LEAP program is a first-year academic support program for a select group of entering students.

Graduation Requirements

In order to graduate, candidates must have a GPA of 1.7, have completed the upper-division writing requirement, and the seminar requirement in the third year.

Organizations

Students edit the *North Carolina Law Review, North Carolina Journal of International Law and Commercial Regulation*, the student newspaper *Mere Dictum*, and *The Banking Institute*. The Holderness Moot Court Bench consists of the negotiations team, client counseling team, invitational team, national team, constitutional team, and international team, and sponsors the annual Craven Moot Court competition. Other competitions include American Jurisprudence Award, Block Improvement, Burkan Memorial, Millard S. Breckenridge, Judge Heriot Clarkson, Chief Justice Walter Clark, Albert Coates, Investors Title Insurance, William T. Jayner, James William Morrow III, U.S. Law Week, and West Group. Law student organizations include Order of the Barristers, Environmental Law Project, and the Federalist Society.

Library

The law library contains 447,320 hard-copy volumes and 11,302 microform volume equivalents, and subscribes to 5926 serial publications. Such on-line databases and networks as LEXIS and WESTLAW are available to law students for research. Special library collections include Anglo-American legal materials.

Faculty

The law school has approximately 44 full-time and 35 part-time faculty members, of whom 29 are women. According to AAUP standards for Category I institutions, faculty salaries are well above average. The ratio of full-time students to full-time faculty in an average class is 20 to 1. There is a chapter of the Order of the Coif.

Students

About 49% of the student body are women; 21%, minorities; 13%, African American; 4%, Asian American; 2%, Hispanic; and 1%, Native American. The majority of students come from North Carolina (75%). The average age of entering students is 23; age range is 21 to 53. About 12% of students have a graduate degree. About 1% drop out after the first year for academic or personal reasons; 95% remain to receive a law degree.

Placement

J.D.s awarded:	233
Services available through: a separate law school placement center and the university placement center	
Special features: associate director for public service employment opportunities.	
Full-time job interviews:	117 employers
Summer job interviews:	n/av
Placement by graduation:	73% of class
Placement within 9 months:	98% of class
Average starting salary:	$23,000 to $100,000
Areas of placement:	
Private practice 2-10 attorneys	15%
Private practice 11-25 attorneys	4%
Private practice 26-50 attorneys	4%
Private practice 51-100 attorneys	4%
Government	11%
Judicial clerkships	10%
Business/industry	10%
Public interest	6%
Military	1%
Academic	1%

UNIVERSITY OF NORTH DAKOTA

School of Law

Box 9003
Grand Forks, ND 58202

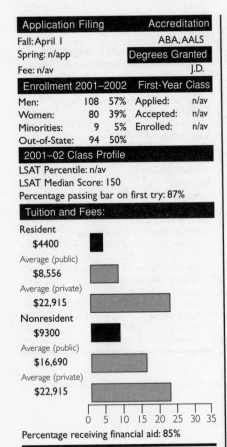

Application Filing
Fall: April 1
Spring: n/app
Fee: n/av

Accreditation
ABA, AALS

Degrees Granted
J.D.

Enrollment 2001–2002			First-Year Class	
Men:	108	57%	Applied:	n/av
Women:	80	39%	Accepted:	n/av
Minorities:	9	5%	Enrolled:	n/av
Out-of-State:	94	50%		

2001–02 Class Profile
LSAT Percentile: n/av
LSAT Median Score: 150
Percentage passing bar on first try: 87%

Tuition and Fees:

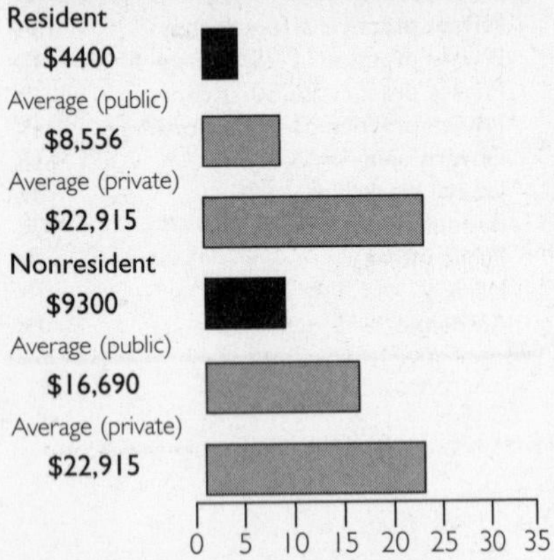

Percentage receiving financial aid: 85%

ADMISSIONS

Information in the above capsule is from an earlier year. In a recent first-year class, two transfers enrolled. The median GPA of a recent first-year class was 3.3. The lowest LSAT percentile accepted was 11; the highest was 95.

Requirements

Applicants must have a bachelor's degree and take the LSAT. The most important admission factors include academic achievement, GPA, and LSAT results. No specific undergraduate courses are required. Candidates are not interviewed.

Procedure

Check with the school for current application deadlines and fee. Applicants should submit an application form and a nonrefundable fee. Notification of the admissions decision is on a rolling basis. The latest acceptable LSAT test date for fall entry is that which ensures the score is received by the application deadline. The law school uses the LSDAS.

Special

The law school recruits minority and disadvantaged students as part of the school's philosophy of promoting diversity in the student body. Requirements are different for out-of-state students in that preference is given to qualified state residents, depending on the number of applications received. Transfer students must have a minimum GPA of 2.0 and have attended an ABA-approved law school. Generally, no more than 2 semesters of course work are eligible for transfer.

Costs

Tuition and fees for the academic year are approximately $4400 for full-time in-state students and $9300 for out-of-state students. On-campus room and board costs about $7300 annually; books and supplies run about $800.

Financial Aid

About 85% of current law students receive some form of aid. The average annual amount of aid from all sources combined, including scholarships, loans, and work contracts, is about $9300; maximum, $14,500. Awards are based on need and merit. Required financial statement is the FAFSA. Check with the school for current application deadlines. Special funds for minority or disadvantaged students include Cultural Diversity Tuition Waivers. First-year students are notified about their financial aid application at time of acceptance.

About the Law School

University of North Dakota School of Law was established in 1899 and is a public institution. The campus is in a small town 320 miles northwest of Minneapolis-St. Paul. The primary mission of the law school is to provide education and training in legal analysis and the application of legal principles leading to professional competence. Students have access to federal, state, county, city, and local agencies, courts, correctional facilities, law firms, and legal aid organizations in the Grand Forks area. Housing for students is in residence halls, single-student apartments, family housing apartments, and a trailer court, all adjacent to the campus. About 95% of the law school facilities are accessible to the physically disabled.

Calendar

The law school operates on a traditional semester basis. Courses for full-time students are offered days only and must be completed within 5 years. There is no part-time program. New students are admitted in the fall. There is a 6-week summer session. Transferable summer courses are offered.

Programs

Students may take relevant courses in other programs and apply credit toward the J.D.; a maximum of 6 credits may be applied. The following joint degrees may be earned: J.D/M.P.A. (Juris Doctor/Master of Public Administration).

Phone: 701-777-2104
Fax: 701-777-2217
E-mail: *linda.kohoutek@thor.law.und.nodak.edu*
Web: *www.law.und.nodak.edu*

Contact

Linda D. Kohoutek, Admissions and Records Associate, 701-777-2260 for general inquiries; Mark Bricksom, Student Financial Aid Officer, 701-777-2269 for financial aid information.

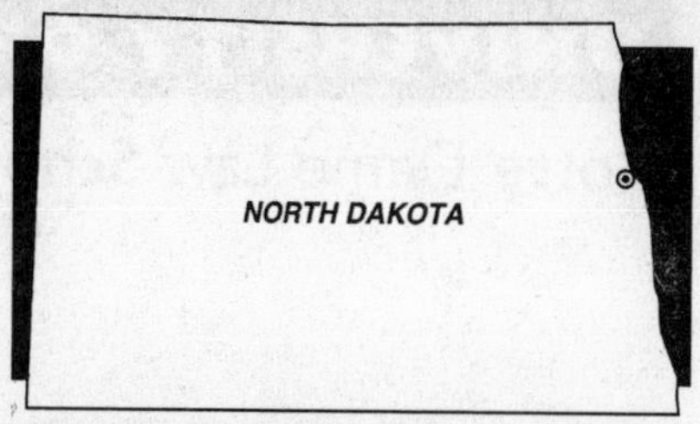

Required

To earn the J.D., candidates must complete 90 total credits, of which 34 are for required courses. They must maintain a minimum GPA of 2.0 in the required courses. The following first-year courses are required of all students: Brief Writing and Appellate Advocacy, Civil Procedure, Contracts I and II, Criminal Law, Legal Process, Property I and II, Torts I and II, and Constitutional Law I and II. Required upper-level courses consist of Professional Responsibility. The required orientation program for first-year students lasts 1 week.

Electives

Clinics are conducted under the supervision of the Director of Legal Aid, and other clinical instructors, including a family law clinic and a Native American law project. Clinical Education I, II, III, and IV are also available. Internships are available with the North Dakota District Court, North Dakota Legislative Assembly, Grand Forks County States Attorney, and the Office of the Staff Judge Advocate at the Grand Forks Air Force Base. Various supervised research projects are available through the Special Projects Committee. Also, Central Legal Research employs second- and third-year students to work on current legal research questions. The Rocky Mountain Mineral Law Foundation, through grants, scholarships, seminars, and publications, promotes research in natural resources law. The Fode Lecture is a special lecture series. Students may receive credit for summer law study at the University of Oslo, Norway. The Canadian-American Law Institute encourages interchange among law students and faculty from North Dakota and several Canadian provinces. The most widely taken electives are bar courses, skills courses, and trial advocacy.

Graduation Requirements

In order to graduate, candidates must have a GPA of 2.0, have completed the upper-division writing requirement, and have completed Legal Process, Brief Writing, and Professional Responsibility, have completed 2 significant writing projects, and have completed the residency requirements of the last 4 semesters of study at the school.

Organizations

Students edit the *North Dakota Law Review* and the student newspaper, *Rhadamanthus.* The North Dakota Agricultural Law Institute serves the state's agricultural industry by publishing bulletins related to agriculture. Members of the Moot Court Association participate in an appellate moot court intraschool competition. During the past few years, members have also participated in the National Moot Court Competition, the Tulane Sports Law Competition, and various regional competitions. Student organizations include the Student Bar Association, Native American Law Students Association, Christian Law Students Society, the Federalist Society, Student Trial Lawyers Association, and the Law Women's Caucus. There are campus chapters of Phi Alpha Delta, Phi Delta Phi, and Order of the Coif.

Library

The law library contains 251,320 hardcopy volumes and 129,554 microform volume equivalents, and subscribes to 2710 serial publications. Such on-line databases and networks as DIALOG, LEXIS, WESTLAW, OCLC, ODIN, Internet, CALI, Legal-Trac are available to law students for research. Special library collections include a good Canadian collection, partial U.S. government documents depository, and a Norwegian law collection. Recently, the library added a computer laboratory and walk-up computer information kiosks. The ratio of library volumes to faculty is 10,927 to 1 and to students is 1315 to 1. The ratio of seats in the library to students is 1 to 1.

Faculty

The law school has approximately 14 full-time and 9 part-time faculty members, of whom 8 are women. About 29% of full-time faculty have a graduate law degree in addition to the J.D. There is a chapter of the Order of the Coif.

Students

About 39% of the student body are women; 5%, minorities; 1%, African American; 1%, Asian American; 1%, Hispanic; and 3%, Native American. Most students come from North Dakota (50%). The average age of entering students is 26; age range is 21 to 48. About 6% drop out after the first year for academic or personal reasons.

Placement

J.D.s awarded: 66

Services available through: a separate law school placement center

Services: job board, on which full- and part-time positions are listed

Special features: a job-seeking resource and reference library, files on individual firms or organizations, and files on job bulletins from more than 80 other law schools around the nation. Internet, legal, and job-seeking sites are bookmarked from the school's web page.

Full-time job interviews:	6 employers
Summer job interviews:	10 employers
Placement by graduation:	60% of class
Placement within 9 months:	100% of class
Average starting salary:	$19,000 to $70,000
Areas of placement:	
Private practice 2-10 attorneys	32%
Private practice 11-25 attorneys	3%
Private practice 26-50 attorneys	2%
Judicial clerkships	35%
Business/industry	14%
Government	10%
Military	4%

Notre Dame Law School

P.O. Box R
Notre Dame, IN 46556-0780

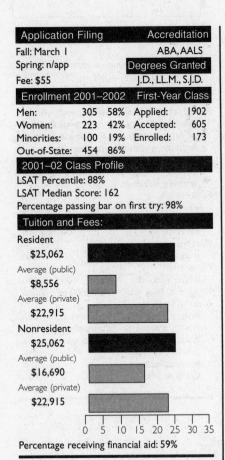

Application Filing		Accreditation
Fall: March 1		ABA, AALS
Spring: n/app		**Degrees Granted**
Fee: $55		J.D., LL.M., S.J.D.

Enrollment 2001–2002			First-Year Class	
Men:	305	58%	Applied:	1902
Women:	223	42%	Accepted:	605
Minorities:	100	19%	Enrolled:	173
Out-of-State:	454	86%		

2001–02 Class Profile

LSAT Percentile: 88%
LSAT Median Score: 162
Percentage passing bar on first try: 98%

Tuition and Fees:

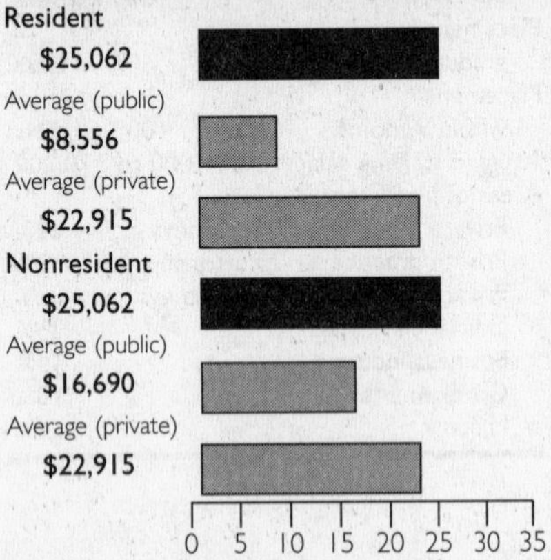

Percentage receiving financial aid: 59%

ADMISSIONS

In the fall 2001 first-year class, 1902 applied, 605 were accepted, and 173 enrolled. Seven transfers enrolled. The median LSAT percentile of the most recent first-year class was 88; the median GPA was 3.51 on a scale of 4.0. The lowest LSAT percentile accepted was 36; the highest was 100.

Requirements

Applicants must have a bachelor's degree and take the LSAT. The most important admission factors include academic achievement, college extracurricular activities, and LSAT results. No specific undergraduate courses are required. Candidates are not interviewed.

Procedure

The application deadline for fall entry is March 1. Applicants should submit an application form, LSAT results, transcripts, a nonrefundable application fee of $55, 2 letters of recommendation, and a personal statement. Notification of the admissions decision is on a rolling basis. The latest acceptable LSAT test date for fall entry is February. The law school uses the LSDAS.

Special

The law school recruits minority and disadvantaged students by considering as positive factors an applicant's ethnic or minority background and economic disadvantage. Requirements are not different for out-of-state students. Transfer students must have one year of credit and have attended an ABA-approved law school.

Costs

Tuition and fees for the 2001-2002 academic year are $25,062 for all full-time students. On-campus room and board costs about $5285 annually; books and supplies run $1050.

Financial Aid

About 59% of current law students receive some form of aid. Awards are based on need and merit. Required financial statement is the FAFSA. The aid application deadline for fall entry is March 1. Special grants are available for minority or disadvantaged students. First-year students are notified about their financial aid application as soon as possible after acceptance and after financial documents are received.

About the Law School

The University of Notre Dame Law School was established in 1869 and is a private institution. The 1250-acre campus is in a small town just north of South Bend. The primary mission of the law school is to provide capable and compassionate lawyers for practice in the profession, and to play a leadership role in legal education and in the development of the law. Students have access to South Bend offices of federal, state, county, city, and local agencies, courts, correctional facilities, law firms, and legal aid organizations, as well as the courts and legal aid clinics of Chicago and Michigan. Housing for students is available as on-campus apartments for single students. There are also apartments for married students and townhouses for graduate and law students. The university assists students in finding off-campus housing. About 90% of the law school facilities are accessible to the physically disabled.

Calendar

The law school operates on a traditional semester basis. Courses for full-time students are offered days only and must be completed within 5 years. There is no part-time program. New students are admitted in the fall. There is a 6-week summer session in London. Transferable summer courses are offered.

Programs

In addition to the J.D., the law school offers the LL.M. and S.J.D. Students may take relevant courses in other programs and apply credit toward the J.D.; a maximum of 9 credits may be applied. The following joint degrees may be earned: J.B./M.B.A. (Juris Doctor/Master of Business Administration), J.D./M.A. (Juris Doctor/Master of Arts in English and law and peace studies), and J.D./M.S. (Juris Doctor/Master of Science in Engineering).

Phone: 574-631-6626
Fax: 574-631-5474
E-mail: *lawadmit@nd.edu*
Web: *www.law.nd.edu*

Contact

Charles W. Roboski, Director, Admissions and Financial Aid, 574-631-6626 for general inquiries and for financial aid information.

Required

To earn the J.D., candidates must complete 90 total credits, of which 42 are for required courses. They must maintain a minimum GPA of 2.0 in the required courses. The following first-year courses are required of all students: Criminal Law, Torts I and II, Contracts I and II, Legal Research I and II-Moot Court, Legal Writing, Ethics I, Civil Procedure I and II, Property, and Constitutional Law. Required upper-level courses consist of Jurisprudence, Ethics II, Business Associations, and Federal Income Taxation. The required orientation program for first-year students is 2 days.

Electives

The Notre Dame Law School offers concentrations in corporate law, criminal law, international law, and litigation. In addition, clinical training is avaiable in Indiana and Michigan through Legal Aid, Apellate Advocacy, Criminal Practice, Public Interest Practice, and Trial Advocacy programs. Special seminars are offered in criminal law, trial advocacy, business law, and general law. Internships are available through the Public Defender and Prosecutor's office. A study-abroad program allows students to take their second year or a summer session at the law school's London campus. Tutorial programs are tailored to meet the needs of individual students. Diversity groups are actively involved in the law school. The most widely taken electives are Evidence, Trial Advocacy, and Trusts.

Graduation Requirements

In order to graduate, candidates must maintain a GPA of 2.0.

Organizations

Students edit the *Notre Dame Law Review*, published 5 times a year. Other publications are the *American Journal of Jurisprudence, Journal of Legislation, Journal of College and University Law,* and the *Journal of Law, Ethics, and Public Policy*. Moot court competitions include the National Moot Court and the Jessup International Moot Court competitions. Other competitions include the National Trial Competition and Client Counseling. Law student organizations include Phi Alpha Delta. There are chapters of the Black Law Students of Notre Dame, Hispanic Law Students Association, Asian Law Students Association, and the Native American Law Students Association. Other organizations include Federalist Society, Irish Law Society, and Women's Law Forum.

Library

The law library contains 563,174 hardcopy volumes and 1,548,800 microform volume equivalents, and subscribes to 5447 serial publications. Such on-line databases and networks as CALI, CIS Universe, Legal-Trac, LEXIS, LOIS, NEXIS, OCLC First Search, RLIN, and WESTLAW are available to law students for research. Special library collections include the U.S. Civil Rights Commission archived records. There is also an auxiliary library in London. Recently, the library renovated a computer laboratory and installed a wireless network. The ratio of library volumes to faculty is 16,091 to 1 and to students is 1067 to 1. The ratio of seats in the library to students is 1 to 1.

Faculty

The law school has 35 full-time and 29 part-time faculty members, of whom 14 are women. According to AAUP standards for Category I institutions, faculty salaries are well above average. About 4% of full-time faculty have a graduate law degree in addition to the J.D. The ratio of full-time students to full-time faculty in an average class is 20 to 1; in a clinic, 4 to 1. The law school has a regular program of bringing visiting professors and other distinguished lecturers and visitors to campus.

Placement	
J.D.s awarded:	186
Services available through: a separate law school placement center	
Services: conducting seminars and surveys, maintaining a library, and networking through a national alumni network	
Full-time job interviews:	216 employers
Summer job interviews:	180 employers
Placement by graduation:	75% of class
Placement within 9 months:	99% of class
Average starting salary:	$75,000 to $125,000
Areas of placement:	
Private practice 2-10 attorneys	5%
Private practice 11-25 attorneys	6%
Private practice 26-50 attorneys	3%
Private practice 51-100 attorneys	6%
Unknown	63%
Judicial clerkships	7%
Government	5%
Public interest	4%
Academic	1%

Students

About 42% of the student body are women; 19%, minorities; 3%, African American; 7%, Asian American; 7%, Hispanic; and 1%, Native American. The majority of students come from the Midwest (33%). The average age of entering students is 24; age range is 20 to 38. About 65% of students enter directly from undergraduate school, 4% have a graduate degree, and 30% have worked full time prior to entering law school. About 1% drop out after the first year for academic or personal reasons; 99% remain to receive a law degree.

UNIVERSITY OF OKLAHOMA

College of Law

300 Timberdell Road
Norman, OK 73019

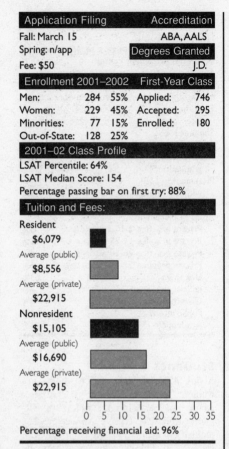

Application Filing		Accreditation
Fall: March 15		ABA, AALS
Spring: n/app		**Degrees Granted**
Fee: $50		J.D.

Enrollment 2001–2002			First-Year Class	
Men:	284	55%	Applied:	746
Women:	229	45%	Accepted:	295
Minorities:	77	15%	Enrolled:	180
Out-of-State:	128	25%		

2001–02 Class Profile

LSAT Percentile: 64%
LSAT Median Score: 154
Percentage passing bar on first try: 88%

Tuition and Fees:

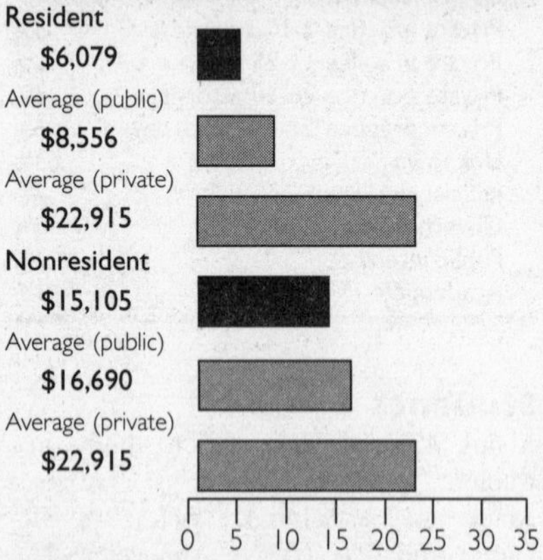

Percentage receiving financial aid: 96%

ADMISSIONS

In the fall 2001 first-year class, 746 applied, 295 were accepted, and 180 enrolled. Thirteen transfers enrolled. The median LSAT percentile of the most recent first-year class was 64; the median GPA was 3.45 on a scale of 4.0.

Requirements

Applicants must have a bachelor's degree and take the LSAT. The most important admission factors include GPA, LSAT results, and academic achievement. No specific undergraduate courses are required. Candidates are not interviewed.

Procedure

The application deadline for fall entry is March 15. Applicants should submit an application form, LSAT results, transcripts, a nonrefundable application fee of $50, and 2 letters of recommendation. Notification of the admissions decision is from late October until mid-May. The latest acceptable LSAT test date for fall entry is February. The law school uses the LSDAS.

Special

The law school recruits minority and disadvantaged students through prelaw fairs and counseling days at undergraduate institutions and through personal correspondence and contacts. Requirements are different for out-of-state students. A state Regents' mandate limits nonresident admissions to 15%. Further, the college is prohibited from admitting a nonresident whose scores are lower than those of a resident to whom admission has been denied. Transfer students must have one year of credit and have attended an ABA-approved law school.

Costs

Tuition and fees for the 2001-2002 academic year are $6079 for full-time in-state students and $15,105 for out-of-state students. On-campus room and board costs about $6600 annually; books and supplies run $899.

Financial Aid

About 96% of current law students receive some form of aid. The average annual amount of aid from all sources combined, including scholarships, loans, and work contracts, is $15,409; maximum, $18,500. Awards are based on need. Required financial statement is the FAFSA. The aid application deadline for fall entry is March 1. First-year students are notified about their financial aid application at time of acceptance.

About the Law School

University of Oklahoma College of Law was established in 1909 and is a public institution. The campus is in a small town 20 miles south of Oklahoma City. The primary mission of the law school is to prepare qualified students to practice law or to use the law in their disciplines, to enable law graduates to remain qualified; and to promote further understanding of law and legal institutions. Students have access to federal, state, county, city, and local agencies, courts, correctional facilities, law firms, and legal aid organizations in the Norman area. Housing for students is in dormitories and nearby off-campus apartments. All law school facilities are accessible to the physically disabled.

Calendar

The law school operates on a traditional semester basis. Courses for full-time students are offered days only and must be completed within 5 years. There is no part-time program. New students are admitted in the fall. There is an 8-week summer session. Transferable summer courses are offered.

Programs

The following joint degrees may be earned: J.D./M.B.A. (Juris Doctor/Master of Business Administration), J.D./M.P.H. (Juris Doctor/Master of Public Health), and J.D./M.S. (Juris Doctor/Master of Science in health administration, environmental science, and occupational health).

Required

To earn the J.D., candidates must complete 90 total credits, of which 42 are for required courses. They must maintain a minimum GPA of 4 on a scale of 12 in the required courses. The following first-year courses are required of all students: Contracts I; Contracts II, Property, Civil Procedure I; Civil Procedure II, Torts I; Torts II, Legal Research, & Writing I; Legal Research and Writing II, Constitutional Law, and Criminal Law. Required upper-level courses consist of Professional Responsibility, Evidence, a graduation writing requirement, and Criminal Procedure I. No clinical courses are required. The required orientation program for first-year students is a 1-day orientation that provides a basic introduction to legal study and the OU Law Center.

Phone: 405-325-4726
888-298-0891
Fax: 405-325-0502
E-mail: *kmadden@ou.edu*
Web: *www.law.ou.edu*

Contact

Kathie Madden, Admissions Coordinator, 405-325-4728 for general inquiries; 405-325-4521, for financial aid information.

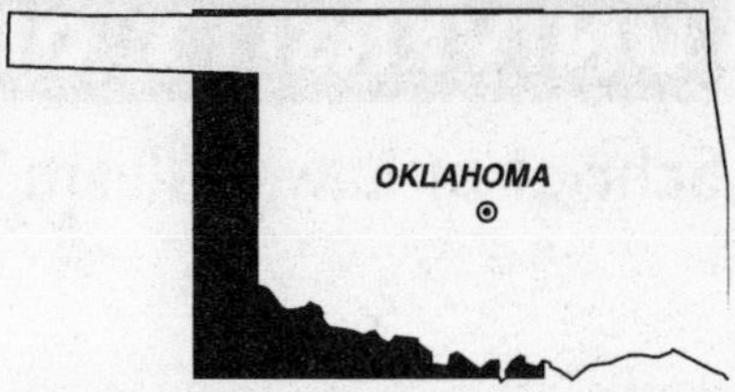

Electives

The College of Law offers concentrations in corporate law, criminal law, environmental law, family law, international law, labor law, litigation, media law, securities law, sports law, tax law, and torts and insurance. In addition, the Civil Clinic and the Criminal Defense Clinic are available for 3 hours per semester. The Judicial Clinic (employment with a judge) is limited to 3 hours. All students, who have completed their first year of law studies, may take seminars. Each semester several are offered for 2 credit hours each. There is no limit, though students generally take no more than 2 or 3. Federal Indian Law and Environmental Law internships are available for 12 credit hours. Second- and third-year students may be research assistants for law professors for no credit while receiving an hourly wage. All students may attend enrichment programs for no credit. A summer program is available at Brasenose College, Oxford University, Oxford, England. In addition, students have the opportunity to study abroad for a semester or full academic year after they have completed at least the first year of law studies and are in good academic standing. Students can create individual study programs at foreign law schools, and if approved by the College of Law and the American Bar Association, they can receive up to 30 hours of credit. Such study programs are particularly relevant to students who have an interest in international law or international business. Tutorial programs are available for all first year students and all upper-level students as needed. The Early Admission Program (EAP) of 15 to 20 students is a special admission program designed to provide a small class environment, mentoring, and head start for students prior to joining the regular fall class. Minority law student organizations host programs for undergraduates throughout the academic year. The most widely taken electives are Corporations, Commercial Law, and Remedies.

Graduation Requirements

In order to graduate, candidates must have a GPA of 4 on a scale of 12 and have completed the upper-division writing requirement.

Organizations

Students edit the *Oklahoma Law Review* and the *American Indian Law Review*. Moot court competitions include the National Moot Court, ABA NAAC, and Jessup International. Other competitions include first-year competitions within the law school. Law student organizations include the Student Bar Association, Board of Advocates, and Association of Public Interest Lawyers. Local chapters of national associations include Phi Alpha Delta, Phi Delta Phi, and ABA/Law Student Division. Campus clubs and other organizations include BALSA, OAWL, and Federalist Society.

Library

The law library contains 331,510 hard-copy volumes and 80,970 microform volume equivalents, and subscribes to 4573 serial publications. Such on-line databases and networks as CALI, CIS Universe, DIALOG, Dow-Jones, Infotrac, Legal-Trac, LEXIS, NEXIS, OCLC First Search, WESTLAW, and Wilsonline Indexes are available to law students for research. Special library collections include the Native Peoples Collection, GPO Depository, and Oil and Gas Law Collection. Recently, the library replaced all student computers, added 2 laser printers and a variety of software, and provided access to the Internet. The ratio of library volumes to faculty is 10,046 to 1 and to students is 646 to 1. The ratio of seats in the library to students is 1 to 2.

Faculty

The law school has 33 full-time and 20 part-time faculty members, of whom 13 are women. According to AAUP standards for Category I institutions, faculty salaries are below average. About 50% of full-time faculty have a graduate law degree in addition to the J.D. The ratio of full-time students to full-time faculty in an average class is 25 to 1; in a clinic, 12 to 1. The law school has a regular program of bringing visiting professors and other distinguished lecturers and visitors to campus. There is a chapter of the Order of the Coif; 33 faculty and 856 graduates are members.

Placement	
J.D.s awarded:	188
Services available through: a separate law school placement center	
Special features: personal student counseling and on-campus seminars.	
Full-time job interviews:	10 employers
Summer job interviews:	30 employers
Placement by graduation:	60% of class
Placement within 9 months:	97% of class
Average starting salary:	$20,000 to $80,000
Areas of placement:	
Private practice 2-10 attorneys	27%
Private practice 11-25 attorneys	9%
Private practice 26-50 attorneys	4%
Private practice 51-100 attorneys	5%
Government	21%
Business/industry	12%
Unknown	8%
Judicial clerkships	5%
Public interest	4%
Academic	4%
Military	1%

Students

About 45% of the student body are women; 15%, minorities; 3%, African American; 1%, Asian American; 1%, Hispanic; and 9%, Native American. The majority of students come from Oklahoma (75%). The average age of entering students is 24; age range is 20 to 54. About 80% of students enter directly from undergraduate school, 7% to 10% have a graduate degree, and 7% to 10% have worked full-time prior to entering law school. About 4% drop out after the first year for academic or personal reasons; 95% remain to receive a law degree.

UNIVERSITY OF OREGON

School of Law, William W. Knight Law Center

1515 Agate Street
Eugene, OR 97403-1221

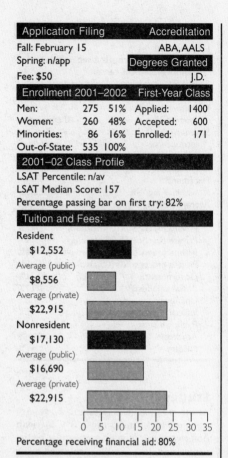

Application Filing		Accreditation
Fall: February 15		ABA, AALS
Spring: n/app		**Degrees Granted**
Fee: $50		J.D.

Enrollment 2001–2002			First-Year Class	
Men:	275	51%	Applied:	1400
Women:	260	48%	Accepted:	600
Minorities:	86	16%	Enrolled:	171
Out-of-State:	535	100%		

2001–02 Class Profile

LSAT Percentile: n/av
LSAT Median Score: 157
Percentage passing bar on first try: 82%

Tuition and Fees:

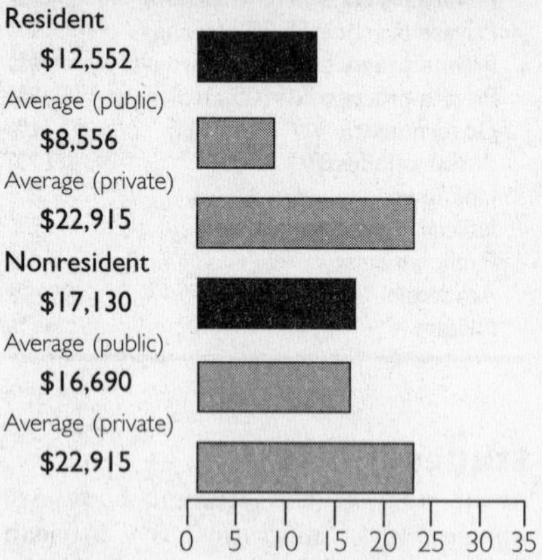

Percentage receiving financial aid: 80%

ADMISSIONS

In the fall 2001 first-year class, 1400 applied, 600 were accepted, and 171 enrolled. The median GPA of the most recent first-year class was 3.5. The lowest LSAT percentile accepted was 17; the highest was 96.

Requirements

Applicants must have a bachelor's degree and take the LSAT. The most important admission factors include GPA, LSAT results, and academic achievement. No specific undergraduate courses are required. Candidates are not interviewed.

Procedure

The application deadline for fall entry is February 15. Applicants should submit an application form, LSAT results, transcripts, a nonrefundable application fee of $50, 2 letters of recommendation, and a personal statement and resume. Notification of the admissions decision is January through May. The latest acceptable LSAT test date for fall entry is February. The law school uses the LSDAS.

Special

The law school recruits minority and disadvantaged students by attending law school fairs throughout the country and contacting minority prospective applicants who attend; having students and alumni contact admitted minorities; inviting qualified minorities and disadvantaged students to apply to the law school through the LSAS's Candidate Referral Service (CRS); and by eliciting recruitment support from current students of color. Requirements are not different for out-of-state students. Transfer students must have one year of credit, have attended an ABA-approved law school. The Admissions Committee considers each application on an individual basis.

Costs

Tuition and fees for the 2002-2003 academic year are $12,552 for full-time instate students and $17,130 for out-of-state students.

Financial Aid

About 80% of current law students receive some form of aid. Awards are based on need and merit. Required financial statement is the FAFSA. Check with the school for current application deadlines. Special funds for minority or disadvantaged students in the form of scholarships and loans, specifically, Derrick Bell, Jr. scholarships are available through the Oregon State Bar. Other general university scholarships and loans are possible. First-year students are notified about their financial aid application as early as possible after acceptance.

About the Law School

The University of Oregon School of Law, William W. Knight Law Center was established in 1884 and is a public institution. The 250-acre campus is in a small town in Eugene. The primary mission of the law school is to serve the state, the nation, and the world through a constantly renewed commitment to excellence. Students are challenged to excel in the service of both clients and community. The school is committed to providing a technological as well as a legal education. Students have access to federal, state, county, city, and local agencies, courts, correctional facilities, law firms, and legal aid organizations in the Eugene area. The law school is aggressive in its commitment to nationwide networks that provide both summer and permanent employment. Housing for students readily available. All law school facilities are accessible to the physically disabled.

Calendar

The law school operates on a traditional semester basis. Courses for full-time students are offered days only and must be completed within 3 years. There is no part-time program. New students are admitted in the fall. There is an 8-week summer session. Transferable summer courses are offered.

Programs

Students may take relevant courses in other programs and apply credit toward the J.D.; a maximum of 5 credits may be applied. The following joint degrees may be earned: J.D./M.B.A. (Juris Doctor/Master of Business Administration) and J.D./M.S. (Juris Doctor/Master of Science).

Phone: 541-346-1553
800-825-6687
Fax: 541-346-3984
E-mail: *admissions@law.uoregon.edu*
Web: *www.uoregon.edu*

Contact

Katherine A. Jernberg, Director of Admissions, 541-346-1553 for general inquiries; Katrina Schmidt, Financial Aid Counselor, 541-346-3221 or 800-760-6953 for financial aid information.

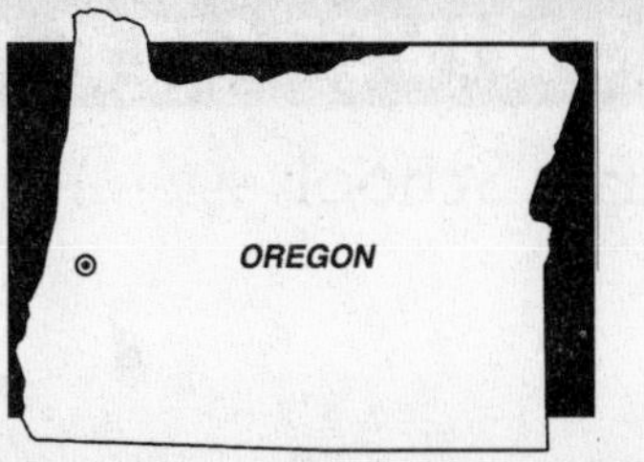

Required

To earn the J.D., candidates must complete 85 total credits, of which 37 are for required courses. They must maintain a minimum GPA of 2.0 in the required courses. The following first-year courses are required of all students: Civil Procedure, Contracts, Criminal Law, Legal Research and Writing, Legislative and Administrative Processes, Property, and Torts. Required upper-level courses consist of Legal Profession, a comprehensive writing requirement, a basic writing requirement, and Constitutional Law. The required orientation program for first-year students consists of a 2-day orientation and registration before the first day of classes. Orientation includes a convocation, small group sessions, peer advising sessions, a library tour, and an all-school picnic. Peer and faculty advising continues throughout the J.D. program.

Electives

The School of Law, William W. Knight Law Center, offers concentrations in corporate law, criminal law, environmental law, family law, international law, juvenile law, labor law, litigation, maritime law, securities law, tax law, torts and insurance, and legal theory and ethics, litigation and procedure, property and estate, public law and policy, business law, clinical programs, and transnational legal problems. In addition, a variety of clinics is offered. The Civil clinic is with the Legal Aid Office; the Prosecution clinic involves working with local prosecutors; and the Criminal Defense clinic involves working through the public defender services. More than 20 seminars are offered. Students have excellent opportunities for internships as a result of an established network and alumni relationships. Faculty-supervised research may be done for a total of 6 credits, but no more than 3 per semester. A reciprocal study-abroad exchange has been established with the University of Adelaide in Australia. The Academic Support Program, offered on a voluntary basis, addresses the needs of nontraditional law students. It involves a 2-week summer orientation prior to registration and tutorial assistance during the academic year. Minority programs include a Minority Law Students Association (MLSA) and an Oregon State Bar Affirmative Action Program, which offers financial assistance through scholarships and loans. Additionally, the law school offers placement assistance, scholarships, and partial fee waivers to minority students.

Graduation Requirements

In order to graduate, candidates must have a GPA of 2.0 and have completed the upper-division writing requirement.

Organizations

Students edit the *Oregon Law Review*, the *Journal of Environmental Law and Litigation*, and the newspaper *The Weekly Dissent*. There is an alumni magazine, the *Oregon Lawyer* and a monthly administrative publication for students, *In The Loop*. Students compete at the Client Counseling Competition, Mock Trial Competition, and Environmental Moot Court Competition. Other competitions are held for appointments to the *Oregon Law Review* and the *Journal of Environmental Law and Litigation*. Student organizations are the Black American Law Students Association, Christian Legal Society, and Federalist Society. There are local chapters of Phi Alpha Delta, Phi Delta Phi, and Partners and Spouses.

Library

The law library contains 177,409 hardcopy volumes and 169,187 microform volume equivalents, and subscribes to 3092 serial publications. Such on-line databases and networks as DIALOG, LEXIS, WESTLAW, and EPIC, OLIS, BRS, FirstSearch, Internet are available to law students for research. Special library collections include a selected U.S. government depository, an Ocean and Coastal Law Library, and a rare book collection. Recently, the library installed 78 drop sites for laptop computer access to a local area network. The ratio of library volumes to faculty is 4126 to 1 and to students is 338 to 1. The ratio of seats in the library to students is 1 to 3.

Placement

J.D.s awarded:	n/av
Services available through: a separate law school placement center	
Services: a Career Services Library with more than 500 references, and information on fellowships, graduate and summer writing programs, and writing competitions.	
Special features: weekly bulletin of job notices to students; semimonthly bulletin for interested alumni.	
Full-time job interviews:	n/av
Summer job interviews:	n/av
Placement by graduation:	n/av
Placement within 9 months:	92% of class
Average starting salary:	$40,000 to $80,000
Areas of placement:	n/av

Faculty

The law school has 32 full-time and 11 part-time faculty members, of whom 10 are women. According to AAUP standards for Category I institutions, faculty salaries are below average. About 19% of full-time faculty have a graduate law degree in addition to the J.D. The ratio of full-time students to full-time faculty in an average class is 5 to 1; in a clinic, 10 to 1. There is a chapter of the Order of the Coif.

Students

About 48% of the student body are women; 16%, minorities; 2%, African American; 14%, Asian American; 4%, Hispanic; 1%, Native American; and 2%, foreign nationals. The average age of entering students is 25; age range is 20 to 49. About 2% drop out after the first year for academic or personal reasons; 98% remain to receive a law degree.

UNIVERSITY OF PENNSYLVANIA

Law School

3400 Chestnut Street
Philadelphia, PA 19104-6204

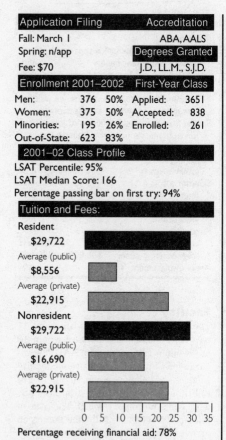

Application Filing		Accreditation
Fall: March 1		ABA, AALS
Spring: n/app		**Degrees Granted**
Fee: $70		J.D., LL.M., S.J.D.

Enrollment 2001–2002			First-Year Class	
Men:	376	50%	Applied:	3651
Women:	375	50%	Accepted:	838
Minorities:	195	26%	Enrolled:	261
Out-of-State:	623	83%		

2001–02 Class Profile

LSAT Percentile: 95%
LSAT Median Score: 166
Percentage passing bar on first try: 94%

Tuition and Fees:

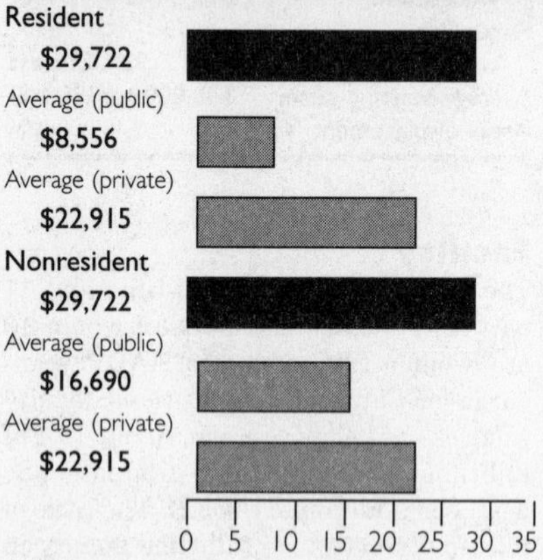

Percentage receiving financial aid: 78%

ADMISSIONS

In the fall 2001 first-year class, 3651 applied, 838 were accepted, and 261 enrolled. Fourteen transfers enrolled. The median LSAT percentile of the most recent first-year class was 95; the median GPA was 3.6 on a scale of 4.0. The lowest LSAT percentile accepted was 45; the highest was 99.

Requirements

Applicants must have a bachelor's degree and take the LSAT. The most important admission factors include academic achievement, LSAT results, and undergraduate curriculum. No specific undergraduate courses are required. Candidates are not interviewed.

Procedure

The application deadline for fall entry is March 1. Applicants should submit an application form, LSAT results, transcripts, a nonrefundable application fee of $70, 2 letters of recommendation, and a Dean's letter. Accepted students must pay two $250 deposits to hold a place in the class. Notification of the admissions decision is on a rolling basis. The latest acceptable LSAT test date for fall entry is December. The law school uses the LSDAS.

Special

The law school recruits minority and disadvantaged students as part of the school's policy to achieve diversity in the student body. Requirements are not different for out-of-state students. Transfer students must have one year of credit, have attended an ABA-approved law school, and the school must be AALS-approved.

Costs

Tuition and fees for the 2001-2002 academic year are $29,722 for all full-time students. On-campus room and board costs about $9345 annually; books and supplies run $850.

Financial Aid

About 78% of current law students receive some form of aid. The average annual amount of aid from all sources combined, including scholarships, loans, and work contracts, is $10,600. Awards are based on need and merit. Required financial statements are the FAFSA and the institution's financial aid form. The aid application deadline for fall entry is March 1. First-year students are notified about their financial aid application shortly after acceptance.

About the Law School

University of Pennsylvania Law School was established in 1852 and is a private institution. The 260-acre campus is in an urban area 2 miles from central Philadelphia. The primary mission of the law school is to prepare students for effective, enlightened, and socially responsible careers in law. The school is sensitive to the problems confronting society. Students have access to federal, state, county, city, and local agencies, courts, correctional facilities, law firms, and legal aid organizations in the Philadelphia area. The Pennsylvania Supreme Court is in Philadelphia. The federal courthouse is the headquarters for the U.S. District Court for the Eastern District of Pennsylvania and the Court of Appeals for the Third Circuit. Housing for students is available in on-campus facilities for single and married students in 2 high-rise apartment residences and an international house for international students. About 95% of the law school facilities are accessible to the physically disabled.

Calendar

The law school operates on a traditional semester basis. Courses for full-time students are offered both day and evening and must be completed within 3 years. There is no part-time program. New students are admitted in the fall. There is no summer session. Transferable summer courses are not offered.

Programs

In addition to the J.D., the law school offers the LL.M., S.J.D., and LL.C.M. Students may take relevant courses in other programs and apply credit toward the J.D.; a maximum of 12 credits may be applied. The following joint degrees may be earned: J.D./M.A. (Juris Doctor/Master of Arts in Islamic studies), J.D./M.B. (Juris Doctor/Master of Bioethics), J.D./M.B.A. (Juris Doctor/Master of Business Administration), J.D./M.C.P. (Juris Doctor/Master of City Planning), J.D./M.D. (Juris Doctor/Doctor of Medicine), J.D./M.S.W. (Juris Doctor/Master of Social Work), and J.D./Ph.D. (Juris Doctor/Doctor of Philosophy in economics, public policy, and in American legal history).

Phone: 215-898-7400
E-mail: *admissions@oyez.law.upenn.edu*
Web: *www.law.upenn.edu*

Contact

Janice Austin, Assistant Dean, Admissions and Financial Aid, 215-898-7400 for general inquiries; 215-898-7743, for financial aid information.

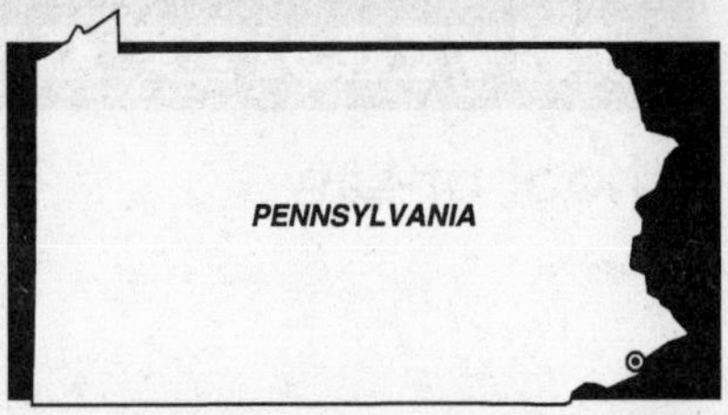

Required

To earn the J.D., candidates must complete 89 total credits, of which 28 are for required courses. The following first-year courses are required of all students: Civil Procedure, Contracts, Criminal Law, Torts, Constitutional Law, Property, and Legal Writing. Required upper-level courses consist of Professional Responsibility. The required orientation program for first-year students lasts 2 days.

Electives

The Law School offers concentrations in corporate law, criminal law, family law, international law, labor law, securities law, tax law, and regulation of business, property and land development, perspectives on the law, law and the health services, constitutional law, courts and administration of justice, commercial law, urban and public interest law, and clinical, professional responsibility, and co-curricular courses. In addition, clinics and extern programs are available for credit in law-related agencies outside of the school. The clinical program includes courses in litigation, small-business planning, legislative process, and mediation and criminal defense. Seminars are available to second- and third year students. First-year students may enroll for a perspective elective during their second semester. Each year a substantial number of students are employed as research assistants for faculty members. The Center for Advanced Studies in Legal History encourages teaching, research, and scholarship in legal history. The school requires that all students complete 70 hours of service in public interest.

Graduation Requirements

In order to graduate, candidates must have completed the upper-division writing requirement.

Organizations

Students edit the *University of Pennsylvania Law Review*, *Journal of Employment and Labor Law*, the *Journal of International Economic Law*, the *Constitutional Law Journal*, the *Hybrid: A Journal of Law and Social Change*, and the newspaper *The Forum*. The student Moot Court Board, made up of third-year students, administers the Moot Court Program, which holds a voluntary intramural competition for the Edwin R. Keedy Trophy. The school also participates in several competitions sponsored by bar associations or other law schools, including the Jessup International Moot Court Competition, the Frederick Douglass Moot Court Competition, and others. Law student organizations include Council of Student Representatives, International Law Students Association, and Light Opera Company. Local chapters of national associations include National Lawyers Guild, Association of Trial Lawyers of America, ABA/Law Student Division. Campus clubs include JD/MBA Society and Penn Advocates for the Homeless.

Library

The law library contains 742,009 hardcopy volumes and 940,251 microform volume equivalents, and subscribes to 3370 serial publications. Such on-line databases and networks as CALI, CIS Universe, DIALOG, Legal-Trac, LEXIS, LOIS, NEXIS, OCLC First Search, RLIN, WESTLAW, and Wilsonline Indexes are available to law students for research. Special library collections include foreign, international, and rare book collections, archives of the American Law Institute and the National Conference of Commissioners on Uniform State Laws, and the papers of Judge Bazelon and Bernard G. Segal. The Biddle Library incorporates a variety of study environments totaling 525 seats and more than 650 computer ports. The ratio of library volumes to faculty is 11,416 to 1 and to students is 988 to 1. The ratio of seats in the library to students is 1 to 2.

Placement	
J.D.s awarded:	269
Services available through: a separate law school placement center	
Services: Placement library contains material on a wide variety of subjects and includes all major legal press.	
Special features: Students work individually with counselors on their career searches. The office holds panel discussions and small group meetings during the year to explore the practice of law and career opportunities. Additionally, first-year students work in small groups on issues such as resume writing and career opportunities.	
Full-time job interviews:	340 employers
Summer job interviews:	340 employers
Placement by graduation:	98% of class
Placement within 9 months:	100% of class
Average starting salary:	$30,000 to $100,000
Areas of placement:	
Private practice 26-50 attorneys	1%
Private practice 51-100 attorneys	70%
Judicial clerkships	19%
Business/industry	5%
Public interest	3%
Government	1%
Unknown	1%

Faculty

The law school has 65 full-time and 52 part-time faculty members, of whom 32 are women. According to AAUP standards for Category I institutions, faculty salaries are well above average. About 3% of full-time faculty have a graduate law degree in addition to the J.D. The ratio of full-time students to full-time faculty in an average class is 12 to 1. The law school has a regular program of bringing visiting professors and other distinguished lecturers and visitors to campus. There is a chapter of the Order of the Coif; 10 graduates are members.

Students

About 50% of the student body are women; 26%, minorities; 10%, African American; 8%, Asian American; and 8%, Hispanic. Most students come from the Northeast (44%). The average age of entering students is 24. About 33% of students enter directly from undergraduate school and 12% have a graduate degree. About 1% drop out after the first year for academic or personal reasons; 99% remain to receive a law degree.

UNIVERSITY OF PITTSBURGH

School of Law

3900 Forbes Avenue
Pittsburgh, PA 15260

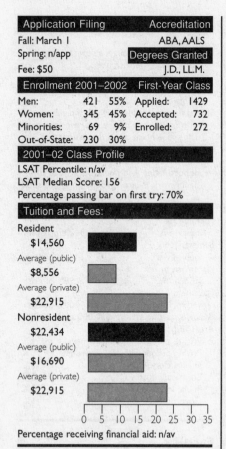

Application Filing	Accreditation
Fall: March 1	ABA, AALS
Spring: n/app	**Degrees Granted**
Fee: $50	J.D., LL.M.

Enrollment 2001–2002			First-Year Class	
Men:	421	55%	Applied:	1429
Women:	345	45%	Accepted:	732
Minorities:	69	9%	Enrolled:	272
Out-of-State:	230	30%		

2001–02 Class Profile

LSAT Percentile: n/av
LSAT Median Score: 156
Percentage passing bar on first try: 70%

Tuition and Fees:

Resident
$14,560
Average (public)
$8,556
Average (private)
$22,915
Nonresident
$22,434
Average (public)
$16,690
Average (private)
$22,915

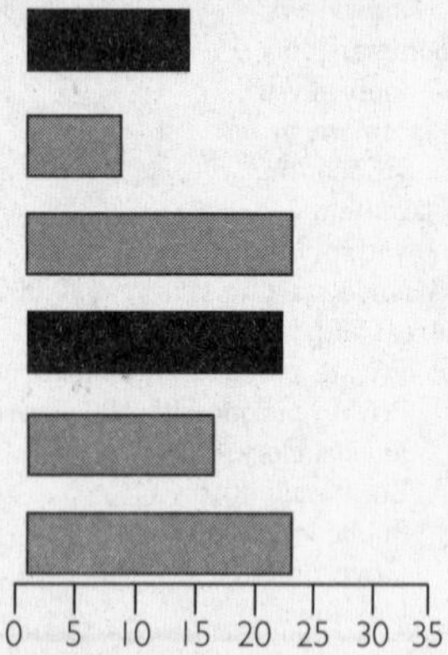

Percentage receiving financial aid: n/av

ADMISSIONS

In the fall 2001 first-year class, 1429 applied, 732 were accepted, and 272 enrolled. Fifteen transfers enrolled. The median GPA of the most recent first-year class was 3.3. The highest LSAT percentile was 99.

Requirements
Applicants must have a bachelor's degree and take the LSAT. The most important admission factors include LSAT results, GPA, and academic achievement. No specific undergraduate courses are required. Candidates are not interviewed.

Procedure
The application deadline for fall entry is March 1. Applicants should submit an application form, LSAT results, transcripts, a nonrefundable application fee of $50, and 3 suggested letters of recommendation. Notification of the admissions decision is on a rolling basis. The latest acceptable LSAT test date for fall entry is February. The law school uses the LSDAS.

Special
The law school recruits minority and disadvantaged students by means of in-house programs, visits to minority institutions, direct mail, phone solicitation, and Candidate Referral Service. Requirements are not different for out-of-state students. Transfer students must have one year of credit, have attended an ABA-approved law school, and must have maintained a B average or be in the top 25% of their class.

Costs

Tuition and fees for the 2001-2002 academic year are $14,560 for full-time in-state students and $22,434 for out-of-state students. Books and supplies run about $1150 annually.

Financial Aid

The average annual amount of aid from all sources combined, including scholarships, loans, and work contracts, is $18,500. Awards are based on need and merit. Required financial statement is the FAFSA. The aid application deadline for fall entry is March 1. Special funds for minority or disadvantaged students are available through scholarships provided by the school and the university. First-year students are notified about their financial aid application at time of acceptance.

About the Law School

University of Pittsburgh School of Law was established in 1895 and is a public institution. The campus is in an urban area 3 miles from downtown Pittsburgh. The primary mission of the law school is to provide education, research, and public service. Students have access to federal, state, county, city, and local agencies, courts, correctional facilities, law firms, and legal aid organizations in the Pittsburgh area. the county law library. Facilities of special interest to law students are the law library, classrooms, seminar rooms, courtroom complex, student lounge, student activities offices, meeting rooms, and administrative offices. Housing for students is in rental apartments that cost $400 to $500 and are available within 1 to 3 miles of the law school. On-campus housing is not available. All law school facilities are accessible to the physically disabled.

Calendar

The law school operates on a traditional semester basis. Courses for full-time students are offered days only and must be completed within 3 years. For flex-time students, courses are offered days and must be completed within 5 years. New full- and part-time students are admitted in the fall. There is no summer session. Transferable summer courses are not offered.

Programs

In addition to the J.D., the law school offers the LL.M. Students may take relevant courses in other programs and apply credit toward the J.D.; a maximum of 6 credits may be applied. The following joint degrees may be earned: J.D./M.A. (Juris Doctor/Master of Arts in bioethics), J.D./M.B.A. (Juris Doctor/ Master of Business Administration), J.D./M.P.A. (Juris Doctor/ Master of Public Administration), J.D./M.P.H. (Juris Doctor/ Master of Public Health), J.D./ M.P.I.A. (Juris Doctor/ Master of Public and International Affairs), J.D./M.S. (Juris Doctor/Master of Science in law and public management), and J.D./ M.S.I.A. (Juris Doctor/ Master of Science in industrial management).

Required
To earn the J.D., candidates must complete 88 total credits, of which 34 are for required courses. They must maintain a minimum GPA of 2.0 in the required courses. The following first-year courses are required of all students: Contracts, Torts, Property, Legal Process and Civil Procedure, Legal Analysis and Writing, Criminal Law, Criminal Procedure, and Constitutional Law. Required upper-level courses consist of Legal Profession and an upper-level writing requirement. The

Phone: 412-648-1400
Fax: 412-648-2647
E-mail: *admissions@law.pitt.edu*
Web: *www.pitt.law.edu*

Contact

Fredi G. Miller, Assistant Dean For Admissions, 412-648-1412 for general inquiries; Michelle Vettorel, Assistant Director of Financial Aid, 412-648-1415 for financial aid information.

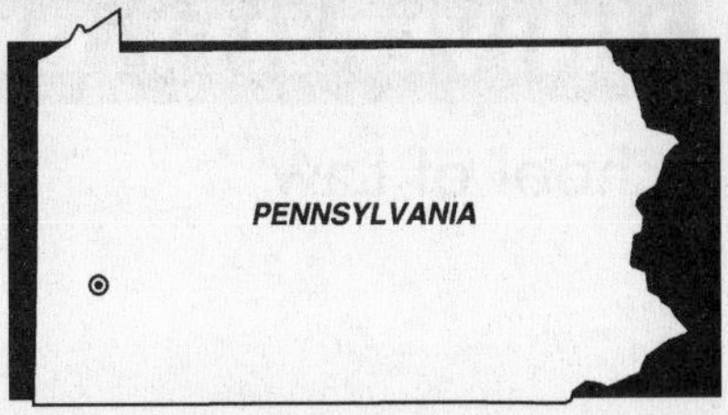

required orientation program for first-year students is conducted over a 2-day period including a formal program, diversity training, discussion groups, family and friends orientation, and a cookout.

Electives
The School of Law offers concentrations in corporate law, criminal law, environmental law, family law, international law, labor law, litigation, tax law, torts and insurance, and health law. In addition, clinical offerings consist of the Tax Clinic, Environmental Law Clinic, and Family Support Clinic. Second- and third-year students may receive 2 credits for a variety of seminars, which can satisfy the upper-level writing requirement. Externship opportunities are available with 62 federal and state judges, 34 other judges throughout Pennsylvania, and 34 judges in other states. Students are also placed in 91 Pennsylvania and federal agencies and out-of-state agencies; including Legal Aid Societies, the Urban Redevelopment Authority, U.S. Attorneys, neighborhood legal services, public defenders, the National Labor Relations Board, hospitals, and housing authorities. The Colloquium Committee sponsors the Caplan Lecture, the Mellon Lecture, a Faculty Colloquium series, and the Martin Luther King Lecture annually. The Law School sponsors a lecture in honor of Black History Month. The University of Brussels and University of Augsburg provide both faculty and student exchange. A Law at Sea program, in which each student is required to take 7 credits of law school courses, is also available. The Law School invites minority and other students to participate in the Mellon Legal Writing Program, which is designed to provide additional academic and social support for students confronting special challenges. The Law School has been cosponsor of the CLEO (The Council for Legal Educational Opportunity) Institute. The Law School hosted the Institute in 1993, 1995, 1998, and 2000. Student organizations sponsor programs reflecting the interests of the group, such as Sports and Entertainment Law, International Law, Environmental Law, Health Law, Business Law, and Family Law. The most widely taken electives are Federal Income Tax, Corporations, and Evidence.

Graduation Requirements
In order to graduate, candidates must have a GPA of 2.0, have completed the upper-division writing requirement, and Legal Profession Ethics course.

Organizations

Students edit the *University of Pittsburgh Law Review, University of Pittsburgh Journal of Law and Commerce, Pittsburgh Journal of Technology*, and *Law and Policy*. Moot court competitions include the Murray S. Love Trial Moot Court Competition, the National Health Law Moot Court Competition, and the BMI/Cardoza Entertainment Law Moot Court Competition. Law student organizations include Black Law Students Association, Environmental Law Association, and Women's Association. There are local chapters of the Student Bar Association, International Law Society, and Phi Alpha Delta.

Library

The law library contains 379,723 hard-copy volumes, and subscribes to 4674 serial publications. Such on-line databases and networks as CALI, CIS Universe, DIALOG, Dow-Jones, Infotrac, Legal-Trac, LEXIS, Mathew Bender, NEXIS, OCLC First Search, WESTLAW, Wilsonline Indexes, and more than 75 separate databases available through the University of Pittsburgh Digital Library are available to law students for research. Special library collections include international law, tax and labor law, health law, and a selective federal depository. Recently, the library installed a law school local area network with a CD-ROM server, added CIS legislative history archives collection on microfiche, and a coffee bar. The ratio of library volumes to faculty is 9041 to 1 and to students is 496 to 1. The ratio of seats in the library to students is 1 to 1.65.

Faculty

The law school has 42 full-time and 38 part-time faculty members, of whom 23 are women. According to AAUP standards for Category I institutions, faculty salaries are average. About 24% of full-time faculty have a graduate law degree in addition to the J.D.; about 14% of part-time faculty have one. The ratio of full-time students to full-time faculty in an average class is 23 to 1; in a clinic, 8 to 1. The law school has a regular program of bringing visiting professors and other distinguished lecturers and visitors to campus. There is a chapter of the Order of the Coif.

Placement

J.D.s awarded: 206

Services available through: a separate law school placement center

Services: computerized job search, weekly workshops, publication of a weekly student newletter as well as a monthly alumni bulletin, formal assessment availability, mock videotaped interviews, and participation in minority and other specialized job fairs

Special features: an emphasis on exploring career options and long-range career planning and developing and refining job procurement and retention skills. The professional staff consists of an assistant dean and the director of placement and public interest opportunities, both of whom remain active in state and local bar associations and bring an array of legal practice experience to their work.

Full-time job interviews:	25 employers
Summer job interviews:	65 employers
Placement by graduation:	60% of class
Placement within 9 months:	99% of class
Average starting salary:	$26,000 to $125,000
Areas of placement:	
Private practice 2-10 attorneys	32%
Private practice 11-25 attorneys	8%
Private practice 26-50 attorneys	2%
Private practice 51-100 attorneys	24%
Private practice 101+ attorneys	19%
Business/industry	6%
Judicial clerkships	4%
Public interest	2%
Military	2%
Government	1%

Students

About 45% of the student body are women; 9%, minorities; 5%, African American; 3%, Asian American, and 1%, Hispanic. The majority of students come from Pennsylvania (70%). The average age of entering students is 24; age range is 20 to 59. About 40% of students enter directly from undergraduate school and 10% have a graduate degree. About 3% drop out after the first year for academic or personal reasons; 95% remain to receive a law degree.

UNIVERSITY OF PUERTO RICO

School of Law

P.O. Box 23349, UPR Station
Rio Piedras, PR 00931-3349

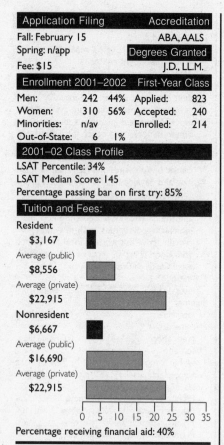

Application Filing		Accreditation
Fall: February 15		ABA, AALS
Spring: n/app		**Degrees Granted**
Fee: $15		J.D., LL.M.

Enrollment 2001–2002			First-Year Class	
Men:	242	44%	Applied:	823
Women:	310	56%	Accepted:	240
Minorities:	n/av		Enrolled:	214
Out-of-State:	6	1%		

2001–02 Class Profile

LSAT Percentile: 34%
LSAT Median Score: 145
Percentage passing bar on first try: 85%

Tuition and Fees:

Resident
$3,167
Average (public)
$8,556
Average (private)
$22,915
Nonresident
$6,667
Average (public)
$16,690
Average (private)
$22,915

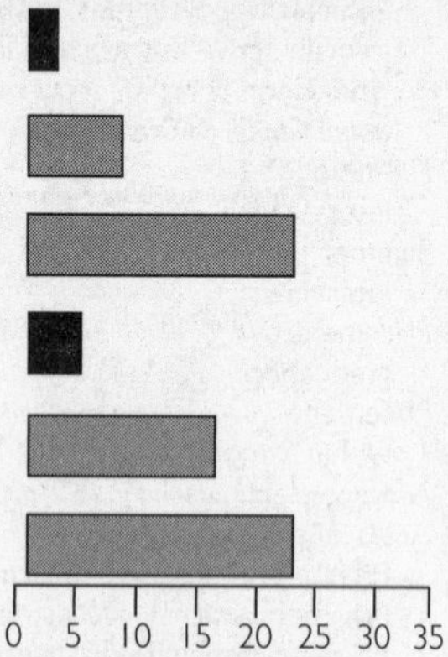

Percentage receiving financial aid: 40%

ADMISSIONS

In the fall 2001 first-year class, 823 applied, 240 were accepted, and 214 enrolled. Eleven transfers enrolled. The median LSAT percentile of the most recent first-year class was 34; the median GPA was 3.5 on a scale of 4.0. The lowest LSAT percentile accepted was 4; the highest was 99.

Requirements

Applicants must have a bachelor's degree and take the LSAT. (GPA, LSAT, and PAEG are considered.) Minimum acceptable GPA is 2.0 on a scale of 4.0. No specific undergraduate courses are required. Candidates are not interviewed.

Procedure

The application deadline for fall entry is February 15. Applicants should submit an application form, LSAT results, transcripts, PAEG, and a nonrefundable application fee of $15. Accepted students must pay a $45 seat deposit. Notification of the admissions decision is in May. The latest acceptable LSAT test date for fall entry is February. The law school uses the LSDAS.

Special

Requirements are not different for out-of-state students. Transfer students must have a minimum GPA of 3.3, have attended an ABA-approved law school, and have completed at least 60 credit hours in residence.

Costs

Tuition and fees for the 2001-2002 academic year are $3167 for full-time in-state students and $6667 for out-of-state students. Tuition for part-time students is $1967 in-state. Books and supplies run about $2000 annually.

Financial Aid

About 40% of current law students receive some form of aid. The average annual amount of aid from all sources combined, including scholarships, loans, and work contracts, is $2000; maximum, $8000. Awards are based on need and merit. Required financial statement is the CSS Profile. The aid application deadline for fall entry is May 1. First-year students are notified about their financial aid application at time of acceptance.

About the Law School

University of Puerto Rico School of Law was established in 1913 and is a public institution. The 5-acre campus is in an urban area in metropolitan San Juan. The primary mission of the law school is to train competent lawyers and jurists with a strong sense of professional, ethical, and social responsibility. Students have access to federal, state, county, city, and local agencies, courts, correctional facilities, law firms, and legal aid organizations in the Rio Piedras area. Housing for students is available in dormitories on campus. About 95% of the law school facilities are accessible to the physically disabled.

Calendar

The law school operates on a traditional semester basis. Courses for full-time students are offered both day and evening and must be completed within 6 semesters. For part-time students, courses are offered both day and evening and must be completed within 8 semesters. New full- and part-time students are admitted in the fall. There is a 6-week summer session. Transferable summer courses are not offered.

Programs

In addition to the J.D., the law school offers the LL.M. Students may take relevant courses in other programs and apply credit toward the J.D.; a maximum of 6 credits may be applied. The following joint degrees may be earned: J.D./Lic. en Derecho (dual degree program with the University of Barcelona), J.D./M.B.A. (Juris Doctor/Master of Business Administration), J.D./M.D. (Juris Doctor/Doctor of Medicine), and J.D./M.P.P. (Juris Doctor/Master of Public Policy).

Phone: 787-772-1472
Fax: 787-764-4360
E-mail: *wandi_perez@hotmail.com*

Contact

Wanda Perez Alvarez, Director of Admissions, (787)-764-0000, ext. 2413 or (787)-764-1655 for general inquiries; Michael Ayala, (787)-764-0000, ext 3148-2413; (787) 764-1655 for financial aid information.

Required

To earn the J.D., candidates must complete 92 total credits, of which 46 are for required courses. They must maintain a minimum GPA of 2.0 in the required courses. The following first-year courses are required of all students: Introduction to Law, Torts, Property, Family Law, Legal Research, Criminal Law, Obligations and Contracts Law, Civil Procedure, Constitutional Law, and Problems in International Law. Required upper-level courses consist of Evidence, Theory of Law, Business Associations and Corporations, and Legal Aid Clinic I and II. All students must take clinical courses. The required orientation program for first-year students lasts 1 week and includes information on financial aid, required courses, and exchange programs.

Electives

All students are required to take clinics on civil, criminal, or federal law, worth 6 credits, and 2 2-credit seminars. During the summer an elective legal practice workshop is offered; it is worth 2 credits. Legal research in urban planning, housing, poverty, and related subjects is encouraged in a number of courses. There is a summer course in Barcelona, worth up to 5 credits, that is open to all students in good standing. There is also a double-degree program with the University of Barcelona. The most widely taken electives are Bankruptcy, Taxation, and Criminology.

Graduation Requirements

In order to graduate, candidates must have a GPA of 2.0 and have completed the upper-division writing requirement.

Organizations

Students edit the *University of Puerto Rico Law Review* and the newspaper *El Nuevo Jurista*. Moot court competitions include the Annual Pace University School of Law National Environmental, NACDL Katty Bennet Criminal Trial, and Philip C. Jessup International. Law student organizations include the Student Council, which is an elected student government; the National Association of Law Students; and ABA-Law Student Division. Student representatives chosen by the student council serve on all law school committees, except the personnel committee.

Library

The law library contains 223,000 hard-copy volumes and 152,000 microform volume equivalents, and subscribes to 4487 serial publications. Such on-line databases and networks as DIALOG, LEXIS, and WESTLAW are available to law students for research. Special library collections include extensive collections in Latin American and comparative law, a U.S. government depository, Specialized European Communities Documentation Centre, and a depository for the Central American Parliament. Recently, the library was developing a comprehensive collection of legal materials from Mexico, Central America, Colombia, Venezuela, and the jurisdictions of the Caribbean. The ratio of library volumes to faculty is 6371 to 1 and to students is 404 to 1. The ratio of seats in the library to students is 1 to 1.

Faculty

The law school has 35 full-time and 29 part-time faculty members, of whom 15 are women. According to AAUP standards for Category IIB institutions, faculty salaries are below average. About 70% of full-time faculty have a graduate law degree in addition to the J.D.; about 50% of part-time faculty have one. The ratio of full-time students to full-time faculty in an average class is 15 to 1; in a clinic, 13 to 1. The law school has a regular program of bringing visiting professors and other distinguished lecturers and visitors to campus.

Students

About 56% of the student body are women. The majority of students come from Puerto Rico (99%). The average age of entering students is 23; age range is 20 to 60. About 91% of students enter directly from undergraduate school, 9% have a graduate degree, and 14% have worked full-time prior to entering law school. About 5% drop out after the first year for academic or personal reasons; 95% remain to receive a law degree.

Placement

J.D.s awarded:	143
Services available through: a separate law school placement center	
Full-time job interviews:	n/av
Summer job interviews:	n/av
Placement by graduation:	n/av
Placement within 9 months:	n/av
Average starting salary:	$28,000 to $35,000
Areas of placement:	
Private practice 2-10 attorneys	9%
Private practice 11-25 attorneys	13%
Private practice 26-50 attorneys	15%
Private practice 51-100 attorneys	16%
Unknown	35%
Judicial clerkships	10%
Business/industry	1%
Public interest	1%

UNIVERSITY OF RICHMOND

The T.C. Williams School of Law

University of Richmond, VA 23173

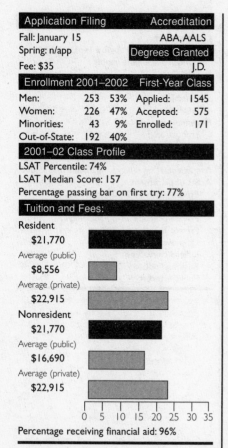

Application Filing		Accreditation
Fall: January 15		ABA, AALS
Spring: n/app		**Degrees Granted**
Fee: $35		J.D.

Enrollment 2001–2002			First-Year Class	
Men:	253	53%	Applied:	1545
Women:	226	47%	Accepted:	575
Minorities:	43	9%	Enrolled:	171
Out-of-State:	192	40%		

2001–02 Class Profile

LSAT Percentile: 74%
LSAT Median Score: 157
Percentage passing bar on first try: 77%

Tuition and Fees:

Resident
$21,770
Average (public)
$8,556
Average (private)
$22,915
Nonresident
$21,770
Average (public)
$16,690
Average (private)
$22,915

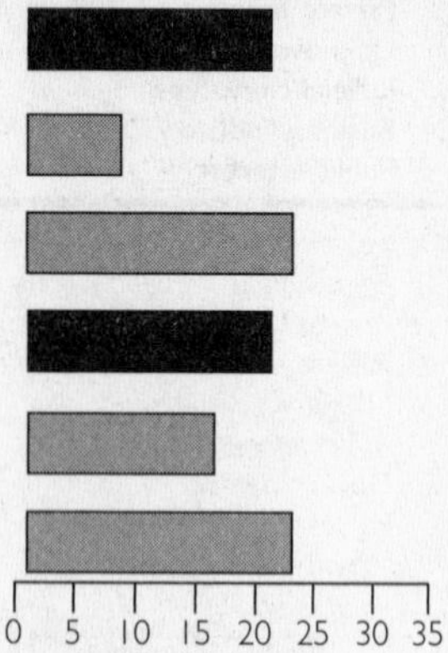

Percentage receiving financial aid: 96%

ADMISSIONS

In the fall 2001 first-year class, 1545 applied, 575 were accepted, and 171 enrolled. Eighteen transfers enrolled. The median LSAT percentile of the most recent first-year class was 74; the median GPA was 3.2 on a scale of 4.0. The highest LSAT percentile was 96.

Requirements

Applicants must have a bachelor's degree and take the LSAT. No specific undergraduate courses are required. Candidates are not interviewed.

Procedure

The application deadline for fall entry is January 15. Applicants should submit an application form, LSAT results, transcripts, a nonrefundable application fee of $35, 2 optional letters of recommendation, and a narrative statement. Notification of the admissions decision is by May 1. The latest acceptable LSAT test date for fall entry is February. The law school uses the LSDAS.

Special

The law school recruits minority and disadvantaged students by attending minority law forums, being a Council for Legal Education Opportunity (CLEO) sponsor, being a CLEO Regional Summer Institute site (3 of last 7 years), and visiting historically black colleges and universities. Requirements are not different for out-of-state students. Transfer students must have one year of credit, have attended an ABA-approved law school, and must be in good standing at an ABA-approved law school.

Costs

Tuition and fees for the 2001-2002 academic year are $21,770 for all full-time students. Part-time students pay $1050 per credit. On-campus room and board costs about $4730 annually; books and supplies run $1100.

Financial Aid

About 96% of current law students receive some form of aid. The average annual amount of aid from all sources combined, including scholarships, loans, and work contracts, is $26,530. Awards are based on need and merit. All admitted students who file the FAFSA by February 25 of each year are considered for grants based on both merit and need at the time they enter the law school. Required financial statement is the FAFSA. The aid application deadline for fall entry is February 25. Special funds for minority or disadvantaged students consist of scholarships. First-year students are notified about their financial aid application at time of acceptance.

About the Law School

University of Richmond The T.C. Williams School of Law was established in 1870 and is a private institution. The 350-acre campus is in a suburban area 2 miles west of Richmond. The primary mission of the law school is to train its graduates to practice law. Its relatively small size helps fashion a close and open relationship between students and faculty. Students have access to federal, state, county, city, and local agencies, courts, correctional facilities, law firms, and legal aid organizations in the University of Richmond area. Facilities of special interest to law students include the law library with a legal research and writing computer laboratory, and individualized study carrels that are electronically networked via students' personal computers to the Legal Information Center, a schoolwide computer system that gives instant access to the electronic age in law. Housing for students is available in 2 law dormitories with 27 single rooms. Attractively-priced apartments are available very close to the campus. All law school facilities are accessible to the physically disabled.

Calendar

The law school operates on a traditional semester basis. Courses for all full-time and part-time students are offered days only and must be completed within 5 years. New full- and part-time students are admitted in the fall and summer. There is a 3- and 8-week summer session. Transferable summer courses are offered.

Programs

Students may take relevant courses in other programs and apply credit toward the J.D.; a maximum of up to 9 credits may be applied. The following joint degrees may be earned: J.D./M.B.A. (Juris Doctor/Master of Business Administration), J.D./M.H.A. (Juris Doctor/Master of Health Administration with Medical College of Virginia), J.D./M.P.A. (Juris Doctor/Master of Public Administration with Virginia Commonwealth), J.D./M.S.W. (Juris Doctor/Master of Social Work with Virginia Commonwealth), and J.D./M.U.R.P. (Juris Doctor/Master of Urban and Regional Planning with Virginia Commonwealth).

Required

To earn the J.D., candidates must complete 86 total credits, of which 38 are for required courses. The following first-year courses are required of all students: Contracts, Constitutional Law, Property, Civil Procedure, Lawyering Skills I and II, Criminal Law, Torts, and Environmental Law. Required upper-level courses consist of Professional Responsibility, upper-level writing requirements, and upper-level Lawyering Skills III and IV. The required orientation program for first-year students lasts 3 days and includes network and computer training and an introduction to lawyering skills as well as the law school administration, faculty, staff, student organizations, and law student advisers.

Phone: 804-289-8189
E-mail: *admissions@uofrlaw.richmond.edu*
Web: *law.richmond.edu*

Contact

Michelle L. Rahman, Admissions Director, 804-289-8189 for general inquiries; C. Deffenbaugh, Director of Financial Aid, 804-289-8438 for financial aid information.

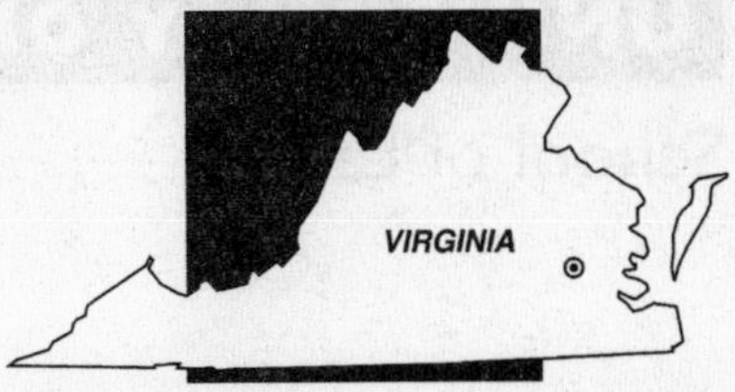

Electives

The T.C. Williams School of Law offers concentrations in corporate law, criminal law, entertainment law, environmental law, family law, international law, juvenile law, labor law, litigation, maritime law, securities law, sports law, tax law, and torts and insurance. In addition, third-year students may participate in either the outplacement clinic or the school's in-house Youth Advocacy and Mental Disabilities clinics. The outplacement clinic allows students to work in various legal offices in the community, and is complemented by a classroom component. The Youth Advocacy and Mental Disabilities clinics, supervised by a staff attorney, allow students to represent clients in business, civil, criminal, and judicial matters. Students may also participate in the D.C. Summer Environmental Internship Program in Washington, D.C. Credit varies for these programs. Special lecture series include the Allen Chair Lecture, Emroch Lecture, Austin Owen Lecture, and Legal Forum. There is a study-abroad option. Students may study international law for 5 weeks at Emmanuel College in Cambridge, England or for a semester at any one of 9 foreign universities with which the law school has an exchange program. There is an academic support program.

Graduation Requirements

In order to graduate, candidates must have a GPA of 2.0 and have completed the upper-division writing requirement.

Organizations

Students edit the *University of Richmond Law Review, Journal of Law Technology* (which is completely on-line), *Perspectives on Law and the Public Interest, Journal of International Law and Business*, and the newspaper, *Juris Publici*. Moot court teams attend the Appellate Advocacy Moot Court Competition in the fall, and the Motions and Interscholastic Motions Competition in the spring as well as the Judge John R. Brown Admiralty Moot Court Competition. There are intramural competitions in both client counseling and negotiations. The winning teams enter respective ABA competitions. Annually, the National Environmental Negotiation Competition is entered. The school has hosted the ABA regional competition. Law student organizations include the Student Bar Association, Client Counseling and Negotiation Board, American Constitution Society, and Federalist Society for Law and Public Policy Studies. There are local chapters of ABA-Student Division, the Black Law Students Association, and Phi Alpha Delta. Additionally, there are intramural sports including soccer and softball.

Library

The law library contains 311,084 hard-copy volumes and 126,941 microform volume equivalents, and subscribes to 4169 serial publications. Such on-line databases and networks as CALI, CIS Universe, DIALOG, Infotrac, Legal-Trac, LEXIS, LOIS, NEXIS, OCLC First Search, WESTLAW, Wilsonline Indexes, Hein Online, and Michie's Virginia Law on Disc are available to law students for research. Special library collections include a U.S. government documents depository, Robert R. Merhige, Jr. judicial papers, and Tokyo war crimes tribunal. Recently, the library has added completely wired study carrels for each student for the entire 3 years. A Novell computer network for e-mail, file transfers, WESTLAW and LEXIS searching, information sharing, notice boards, course discussions, and so on, has been installed, linking all computers in the law school, including student computers in the carrels. There is also a wireless network in the reading room and a special collection facility. The ratio of library volumes to faculty is 10,369 to 1 and to students is 649 to 1. The ratio of seats in the library to students is 1 to 1.

Faculty

The law school has 30 full-time and 69 part-time faculty members, of whom 30 are women. According to AAUP standards for Category IIA institutions, faculty salaries are well above average. About 47% of full-time faculty have a graduate law degree in addition to the J.D. The ratio of full-time students to full-time faculty in an average class is 15 to 1; in a clinic, 6 to 1. The law school has a regular program of bringing visiting professors and other distinguished lecturers and visitors to campus.

Placement

J.D.s awarded:	163
Services available through: a separate law school placement center and the university placement center	
Services: programs on law practice areas, minority job and career fairs, specialty fairs, and job search programs with national speakers and specialty career fairs.	
Special features: Individual attention available to all students with 3 professional staff members in career services office.	
Full-time job interviews:	52 employers
Summer job interviews:	68 employers
Placement by graduation:	62% of class
Placement within 9 months:	100% of class
Average starting salary:	$30,000 to $130,000
Areas of placement:	
Private practice 2-10 attorneys	25%
Private practice 11-25 attorneys	3%
Private practice 26-50 attorneys	5%
Private practice 51-100 attorneys	8%
Private practice 100+ attorneys	12%
Judicial clerkships	21%
Business/industry	13%
Government	10%
Public interest	1%
Military	1%
Academic	1%

Students

About 47% of the student body are women; 9%, minorities; 3%, African American; 3%, Asian American; 1%, Hispanic; and 2%, Native American. The majority of students come from Virginia (60%). The average age of entering students is 25; age range is 19 to 40. About 46% of students enter directly from undergraduate school, 10% have a graduate degree, and 54% have worked full-time prior to entering law school. About 1% drop out after the first year for academic or personal reasons; 99% remain to receive a law degree.

UNIVERSITY OF SAN DIEGO

School of Law

5998 Alcala Park
San Diego, CA 92110

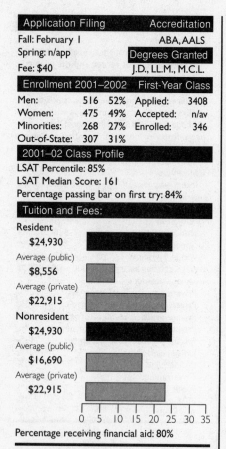

Application Filing		Accreditation
Fall: February 1		ABA, AALS
Spring: n/app		**Degrees Granted**
Fee: $40		J.D., LL.M., M.C.L.

Enrollment 2001–2002			First-Year Class	
Men:	516	52%	Applied:	3408
Women:	475	49%	Accepted:	n/av
Minorities:	268	27%	Enrolled:	346
Out-of-State:	307	31%		

2001–02 Class Profile

LSAT Percentile: 85%
LSAT Median Score: 161
Percentage passing bar on first try: 84%

Tuition and Fees:

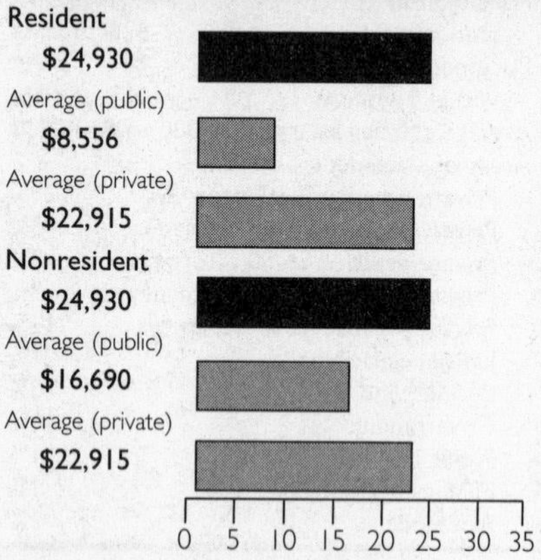

Percentage receiving financial aid: 80%

ADMISSIONS

In the fall 2001 first-year class, 3408 applied and 346 enrolled. The median LSAT percentile of the most recent first-year class was 85; the average GPA was 3.5 on a scale of 4.0.

Requirements
Applicants must have a bachelor's degree and take the LSAT. The most important admission factors include academic achievement, GPA, and LSAT results. No specific undergraduate courses are required. Candidates are not interviewed.

Procedure
The application deadline for fall entry is February 1. Applicants should submit an application form, LSAT results, a nonrefundable application fee of $40, a personal statement, and any other information that the applicant wants to provide. Notification of the admissions decision is January through mid-April. The latest acceptable LSAT test date for fall entry is February (day program) and June (evening program). The law school uses the LSDAS.

Special
The law school recruits minority and disadvantaged students by welcoming and respecting those whose lives are formed by different traditions, recognizing that diversity of viewpoint, background, and experience (including race, ethnicity, cultural diversity, gender, religion, age, socioeconomic status, and disability) among its student body is essential to the full and informed exchange of ideas and to the quality of legal education it seeks to provide. Requirements are not different for out-of-state students. Transfer students must have one year of credit, have attended an ABA-approved law school, and should have a rank in the top quintile of the first-year class.

Costs

Tuition and fees for the 2001-2002 academic year are $24,930 for all full-time students. Tuition for part-time students is $17,700 per year. On-campus room and board costs about $12812 annually; books and supplies run $750.

Financial Aid

About 80% of current law students receive some form of aid. The average annual amount of aid from all sources combined, including scholarships, loans, and work contracts, is $12,878; maximum, $38,492. Awards are based on need and merit. Required financial statement is the FAFSA. The aid application deadline for fall entry is March 2. Special funds for minority or disadvantaged students include need-based, full- and partial-tuition scholarships available to entering students. These scholarships are based on the applicant's academic promise, financial need, potential for service to the community, and contribution of diversity to the student body. First-year students are notified about their financial aid application at time of acceptance, upon completion of their financial aid file.

About the Law School

University of San Diego School of Law was established in 1954 and is a private institution. The 180-acre campus is in a suburban area 5 miles north of downtown San Diego. The primary mission of the law school is to foster an environment of stimulating and rigorous intellectual exchange between teacher and student in which teaching and learning engage the full attention of faculty and students while maintaining concern for the broader personal and moral development of the law student. Students have access to federal, state, county, city, and local agencies, courts, correctional facilities, law firms, and legal aid organizations in the San Diego area. Housing for students is available in safe and affordable accommodations near campus. The Admissions Office maintains a listing of students seeking roommates and other resources. About 90% of the law school facilities are accessible to the physically disabled.

Calendar

The law school operates on a traditional semester basis. Courses for full-time students are offered days only and must be completed within 5 years. For part-time students, courses are offered evenings only and must be completed within 5 years. New full- and part-time students are admitted in the fall. There is an 8-week summer session. Transferable summer courses are offered.

Programs

In addition to the J.D., the law school offers the LL.M., M.C.L., LL.M in Taxation; LL.M. in International Law; LL.M. in Comparative Law; and LL.M. in Business and Comparative Law. Students may take relevant courses in other programs and apply credit toward the J.D.; a maximum of 6 credits may be applied. The following joint degrees may be earned: J.D./I.M.B.A. (Juris Doctor/Int'l. Master of Business Administration), J.D./M.A (Juris Doctor/Master of Arts in international relations), and J.D./M.B.A. (Juris Doctor/Master of Business Administration).

Phone: 619-260-4528
248-4873
Fax: 619-260-2218
E-mail: *jdinfo@sandiego.edu*
Web: *sandiego.edu/usdlaw*

Contact

Carl J. Eging, Director of Admissions and Financial Aid, 619-260-4528 for general inquiries; 619-260-4570 for financial aid information.

Required

To earn the J.D., candidates must complete 85 total credits, of which 48 are for required courses. They must maintain a minimum grade average of 75 in the required courses. The following first-year courses are required of all students: Civil Procedure, Contracts, Criminal Law, Lawyering Skills I, Property, and Torts. Required upper-level courses consist of Constitutional Law, Criminal Procedure I, Evidence, Professional Responsibility, and Tax I. The optional orientation program for first-year students is offered to incoming students, who attend a 1-day orientation hosted by the Student Bar Association. Many topics are presented for discussion, including Socratic method, time management, and how to study for law school exams.

Electives

The School of Law offers concentrations in corporate law, criminal law, environmental law, family law, international law, juvenile law, labor law, litigation, tax law, torts and insurance, and public interest/children's advocacy. In addition, students may enroll for up to 10 credits of clinical field work. They represent actual clients in consumer, housing, family, administrative, mental health, environmental, immigration, criminal, juvenile, and tax law matters. Several seminar courses are offered each semester. Internships are available in-house through the Clinical Education Program, as well as with local agencies, government offices, and law firms in a variety of areas. Research programs are available at the Center for Public Interest Law, Patient Advocacy Program, and the Children's Advocacy Institute. Field work may be done for credit through the Clinical Education Program as well as the Summer Community Service grants. Students may also receive credit for judicial field placements with state and federal courts. Special lecture series include the Nathanson Series, featuring such speakers as U.S. Supreme Court Justices Sandra Day O'Connor and Antonin Scalia, and the Seigan Series, featuring such speakers as Nobel Laureate Milton Friedman and Judge Robert Bork. The Institute on International and Comparative Law sponsors the Summer Law Study Programs, held in England, France, Ireland, Italy, and Spain. Internships for credit are available in England France. The Academic Support Program makes special services available to eligible students. A faculty member provides academic counseling and sets up study groups for each class. Minority programs include a Multicultural Law Day. Pro Bono Legal Advocates promote diversity in the bar and donate students' talent and time to clients who cannot afford a lawyer. The most widely taken electives are courses relevant to international law, environmental law, and corporate law.

Graduation Requirements

In order to graduate, candidates must have a grade average of 75 and have completed the upper-division writing requirement.

Organizations

Students edit the *San Diego Law Review*, the newspaper *Motions*, the *Journal of Contemporary Legal Issues* published by the law school; and *Legal Theory*, a quarterly journal published by Cambridge University Press in conjunction with Yale, Harvard, and USD law schools. Moot court competitions include the Alumni Tort, Annual USD National Criminal Procedure Competition, and Jessup International Law. All are held annually on the university campus, except for the National, which is held at the San Diego Court House. Other competitions include Advanced Trial Advocacy, Mock Trial, Lou Kerig Criminal Law, Thomas More Constitutional Law, National Crimninal Procedure, and John Winters competitions. Student organizations include American Trial Lawyers Association, Pro Bono Legal Advocates, Women's Law Caucus, Student Bar Association, Environmental Law Society, and International Law Society. Phi Delta Phi and Phi Alpha Delta have local chapters.

Library

The law library contains 453,301 hard-copy volumes and 1,415,092 microform volume equivalents, and subscribes to 5305 serial publications. Such on-line databases and networks as CALI, DIALOG, Legal-Trac, LEXIS, NEXIS, and WESTLAW are available to law students for research. Special library collections include state and federal depositories, tax collection, and California collection.

Placement	
J.D.s awarded:	286
Services available through: a separate law school placement center	
Special features: panel discussions sponsored by the Alumni Association that focus on law practice, alternative careers, and law clerk training.	
Full-time job interviews:	n/av
Summer job interviews:	n/av
Placement by graduation:	n/av
Placement within 9 months:	89% of class
Average starting salary:	$30,000 to $85,000
Areas of placement:	
Private practice 2-10 attorneys	29%
Private practice 11-25 attorneys	14%
Private practice 26-50 attorneys	9%
Private practice 51-100 attorneys	11%
Government	17%
Business/industry	15%
Judicial clerkships	2%
Public interest	1%
Military	1%
Academic	1%

Recently, the library installed a computer instructional lab that provides state-of-the-art access to legal research tools, the Internet, and law office technology. It also participates in a consortium. The ratio of library volumes to faculty is 7431 to 1 and to students is 457 to 1.

Faculty

The law school has 61 full-time and 56 part-time faculty members, of whom 36 are women. The ratio of full-time students to full-time faculty in an average class is 20 to 1. The law school has a regular program of bringing visiting professors and other distinguished lecturers and visitors to campus. There is a chapter of the Order of the Coif; 62 faculty and 187 graduates are members.

Students

About 49% of the student body are women; 27%, minorities; 2%, African American; 13%, Asian American; 8%, Hispanic; and 2%, Native American. The majority of students come from California (69%). The average age of entering students is 24; age range is 19 to 57. About 16% drop out after the first year for academic or personal reasons; 84% remain to receive a law degree.

UNIVERSITY OF SAN FRANCISCO

School of Law

2130 Fulton Street
San Francisco, CA 94117-1080

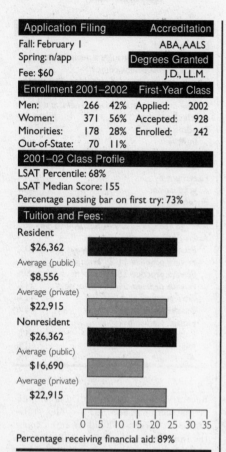

Application Filing		Accreditation
Fall: February 1		ABA, AALS
Spring: n/app		**Degrees Granted**
Fee: $60		J.D., LL.M.

Enrollment 2001–2002			First-Year Class	
Men:	266	42%	Applied:	2002
Women:	371	56%	Accepted:	928
Minorities:	178	28%	Enrolled:	242
Out-of-State:	70	11%		

2001–02 Class Profile

LSAT Percentile: 68%
LSAT Median Score: 155
Percentage passing bar on first try: 73%

Tuition and Fees:

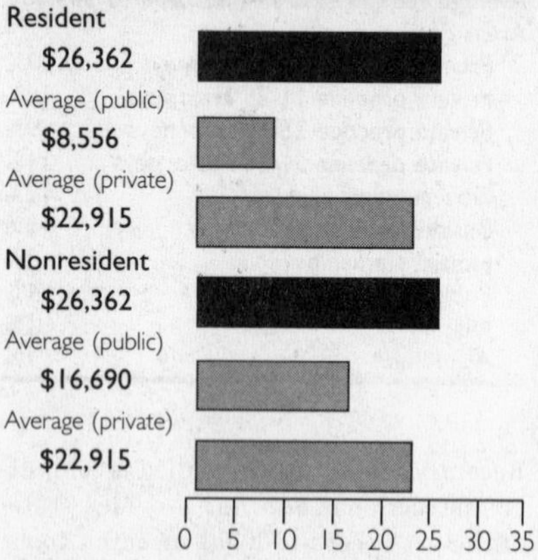

Percentage receiving financial aid: 89%

ADMISSIONS

In the fall 2001 first-year class, 2002 applied, 928 were accepted, and 242 enrolled. The median LSAT percentile of the most recent first-year class was 68; the median GPA was 3.2 on a scale of 4.0.

Requirements

Applicants must have a bachelor's degree and take the LSAT. The most important admission factors include LSAT results, GPA, and academic achievement. No specific undergraduate courses are required. Candidates are not interviewed.

Procedure

The application deadline for fall entry is February 1. Applicants should submit an application form, LSAT results, transcripts, a nonrefundable application fee of $60, 2 letters of recommendation, and personal essay. Notification of the admissions decision is on a rolling basis. The latest acceptable LSAT test date for fall entry is February. The law school uses the LSDAS.

Special

The law school recruits minority and disadvantaged students by actively recruiting under the special admissions program. Requirements are not different for out-of-state students. Transfer students must have one year of credit, have attended an ABA-approved law school; deadline for transfer is July 1.

Costs

Tuition and fees for the 2001-2002 academic year are $26,362 for full-time in-state students. Tuition for part-time students is $21,723 in-state. On-campus room and board costs about $9120 annually; books and supplies run $800.

Financial Aid

About 89% of current law students receive some form of aid. The average annual amount of aid from all sources combined, including scholarships, loans, and work contracts, is $30,000; maximum, $37,144. Awards are based on merit. Required financial statement is the FAFSA. The aid application deadline for fall entry is rolling. The Special Admissions Program provides a grant that varies in amount not to exceed $5000. First-year students are notified about their financial aid application at time of acceptance.

About the Law School

University of San Francisco School of Law was established in 1912 and is a private institution. The 55-acre campus is in an urban area in the center of San Francisco, adjacent to Golden Gate Park. The primary mission of the law school is to educate students to be skilled lawyers with a social conscience and a global perspective, emphasizing analytical ability and other fundamental skills, along with full awareness of special obligations to society. Students have access to federal, state, county, city, and local agencies, courts, correctional facilities, law firms, and legal aid organizations in the San Francisco area. The law school is minutes away from federal, state, and municipal courts as well as cultural, social, and recreational resources in San Francisco and throughout the greater Bay Area. Facilities of special interest to law students are the law building, Kendrick Hall, which contains classrooms, the library, and faculty and administrative offices. An addition houses a moot court room, seminar rooms, offices, and library space. The Koret Center, a large health and recreational center on campus, is available to all law students. Housing for students limited on campus; listings of off-campus accommodations are also available.

Calendar

The law school operates on a traditional semester basis. Courses for full-time students are offered both day and evening and must be completed within 5 years; required courses are offered during the day, and elective courses, both day and evening. For part-time students, courses are offered both day and evening (mostly evenings) and must be completed within 5 years. New full- and part-time students are admitted in the fall. There is an 8-week summer session. Transferable summer courses are offered.

Programs

In addition to the J.D., the law school offers the LL.M. The following joint degrees may be earned: J.D./M.B.A. (Juris Doctor/ Master of Business Administration).

Phone: 415-422-6586
Fax: 415-422-6433
Web: *www.law.usfca.edu*

Contact

Josie Martin, Associate Director of Admissions, 415-422-6586 for general inquiries; Office of Financial Aid, 415-422-6210 for financial aid information.

Required

To earn the J.D., candidates must complete 86 total credits, of which 48 are for required courses. They must maintain a minimum GPA of 2.0 in the required courses. The following first-year courses are required of all students: Civil Procedure I and II, Contracts I and II, Criminal Law (second-year part time), Torts I and II, Legal Research, Writing, and Analysis I and II, Criminal Procedure (second-year part time), and Moot Court (second-year part time). Required upper-level courses consist of Property I and II, Constitutional Law I and II, Evidence, Professional Responsibility, and a research and writing requirement. The required orientation program for first-year students is a 1-week program.

Electives

The School of Law offers concentrations in corporate law, criminal law, environmental law, family law, international law, juvenile law, labor law, litigation, maritime law, securities law, tax law, torts and insurance, and intellectual property (including entertainment, sports, and media law). Clinics include the USF Law Clinic, a teaching law firm staffed by faculty and students with a caseload half criminal, half civil; the narcotics prosecution clinic, with the city's District Attorney's office; the Mediation Clinic, with Family Court Services; and the Judicial Clerkship and Externship. The Cambodian Law and Democracy Project allows law students to assist efforts to reestablish legal institutions and legal education in Cambodia through research into American and foreign legal systems. Summer research and tutoring positions are available in Phnom Penh for interested USF law students. Summer study-abroad programs are offered at Trinity College, Dublin; Charles University, Prague; and Udayana University, Bali. Tutorial programs are available for special admission program's students through the Academic Support Program. There is a special Admission Program to promote enhanced opportunity for students who have been deprived of equal educational opportunity or who are members of groups underrepresented in higher education. Special interest group programs include the Street Law Project, a program to promote legal literacy among 30 Bay Area high schools, and Asian Pacific Legal Studies Program, a special international law focus on Pacific Rim nations. The most widely taken electives are Corporations, Wills and Trusts, and Remedies.

Graduation Requirements

In order to graduate, candidates must have a GPA of 2.0 and have completed the upper-division writing requirement.

Organizations

Students edit the *University of San Francisco Law Review*, and the *University of San Francisco Maritime Law Journal*, one of only 2 maritime law reviews published in the United States. The student newspaper is *The Forum*. Students participate in the National Moot Court, Jessup International Law Moot Court, and Roger Memorial Moot Court competitions. Other competitions include the Advocate of the Year and the Nathan Burkan Memorial competitions. Law student organizations include the McAuliffe Honor Society, Student Bar Association, and Admiralty and Maritime Law Society. There are local chapters of Environmental Law Society, American Trial Lawyers Association, and Intellectual Property Association. Campus clubs and other organizations include the Public Interest Law Foundation, St. Thomas More Society, and Entertainment Law Society.

Library

The law library contains 295,317 hardcopy volumes and 161,252 microform volume equivalents, and subscribes to 2693 serial publications. Such on-line databases and networks as DIALOG, LEXIS, WESTLAW, and Innovative OPAC are available to law students for research. Special library collections include California and federal government documents depository collections. Recently, the library installed a CD-ROM network, a computer lab network, and a web-based integrated automated library system (Millennium II). The ratio of library volumes to faculty is 10,938 to 1 and to students is 491 to 1. The ratio of seats in the library to students is 1 to 2.

Placement	
J.D.s awarded:	200
Services available through: a separate law school placement center	
Services: career seminars, on-campus interviewing	
Special features: Mentor Program, Public Interest Law Program.	
Full-time job interviews:	25 employers
Summer job interviews:	45 employers
Placement by graduation:	n/av
Placement within 9 months:	94% of class
Average starting salary:	$60,000 to $107,500
Areas of placement:	
Private practice 2-10 attorneys	60%
Private practice 101 to 501+ attorneys	7%
Business/industry	15%
Government	7%
Judicial clerkships	5%
Public interest	5%
Academic	1%

Faculty

The law school has 33 full-time and 63 part-time faculty members, of whom 26 are women. About 15% of full-time faculty have a graduate law degree in addition to the J.D.; about 5% of part-time faculty have one. The ratio of full-time students to full-time faculty in an average class is 20 to 1; in a clinic, 8 to 1. The law school has a regular program of bringing visiting professors and other distinguished lecturers and visitors to campus.

Students

About 56% of the student body are women; 28%, minorities; 4%, African American; 14%, Asian American; 7%, Hispanic; and 3%, multi-ethnic. The majority of students come from California (89%). The average age of entering students is 25; age range is 20 to 42. About 19% of students enter directly from undergraduate school and 5% have a graduate degree. About 9% drop out after the first year for academic or personal reasons; 90% remain to receive a law degree.

UNIVERSITY OF SOUTH CAROLINA

School of Law

Main and Greene Streets
Columbia, SC 29208

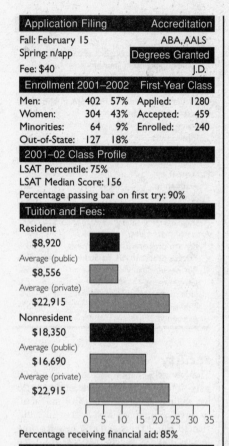

Application Filing		Accreditation
Fall: February 15		ABA, AALS
Spring: n/app		**Degrees Granted**
Fee: $40		J.D.

Enrollment 2001–2002			First-Year Class	
Men:	402	57%	Applied:	1280
Women:	304	43%	Accepted:	459
Minorities:	64	9%	Enrolled:	240
Out-of-State:	127	18%		

2001–02 Class Profile

LSAT Percentile: 75%
LSAT Median Score: 156
Percentage passing bar on first try: 90%

Tuition and Fees:

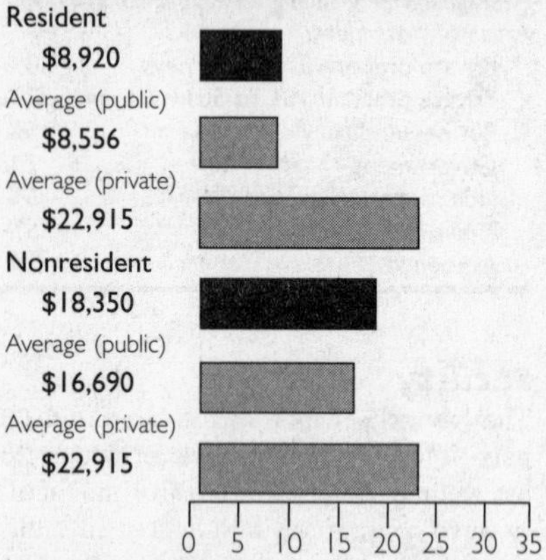

Percentage receiving financial aid: 85%

ADMISSIONS

In the fall 2001 first-year class, 1280 applied, 459 were accepted, and 240 enrolled. Fifteen transfers enrolled. The median LSAT percentile of the most recent first-year class was 75; the median GPA was 3.2 on a scale of 4.0. The highest LSAT percentile was 99.

Requirements

Applicants must have a bachelor's degree and take the LSAT. Minimum acceptable GPA is 2.0 on a scale of 4.0. The most important admission factors include life experience, GPA, and LSAT results. No specific undergraduate courses are required. Candidates are interviewed.

Procedure

The application deadline for fall entry is February 15. Applicants should submit an application form, LSAT results, transcripts, a nonrefundable application fee of $40, 2 letters of recommendation, a personal statement, and dean's certification. Notification of the admissions decision is from mid-December to May. The latest acceptable LSAT test date for fall entry is February. The law school uses the LSDAS.

Special

The law school recruits minority and disadvantaged students through campus visits and a minority recruitment day that is held on campus in the fall; students are invited to attend. Requirements are different for out-of-state students in that their LSAT and GPA scores must be better than residents' scores. Transfer students must have one year of credit, have a minimum GPA of 3, have attended an ABA-approved law school, be in good standing, and be eligible to return to their current law school.

Costs

Tuition and fees for the 2001-2002 academic year are $8920 for full-time in-state students and $18,350 for out-of-state students. Books and supplies cost about $500 annually.

Financial Aid

About 85% of current law students receive some form of aid. The average annual amount of aid from all sources combined, including scholarships, loans, and work contracts, is $12,000; maximum, $19,302. Awards are based on need and merit. Required financial statements are the FAFSA and the School of Law scholarship application. The aid application deadline for fall entry is April 15. Special funds for minority or disadvantaged students are provided through the Minority Scholarship program and other law school sources. First-year students are notified about their financial aid application at time of acceptance and other awards are made in late summer.

About the Law School

University of South Carolina School of Law was established in 1866 and is a public institution. The campus is in an urban area in downtown Columbia, South Carolina. The primary mission of the law school is to develop professional competence and responsibility. The school seeks to qualify its graduates for the highest opportunities in professional legal services and to instill a sense of perspective about what the law is capable of doing for the good of society. Students have access to federal, state, county, city, and local agencies, courts, correctional facilities, law firms, and legal aid organizations in the Columbia area. The U.S. Department of Justice's Legal Education Program has moved from Washington, D.C. to Columbia and is affiliated with the law school. Facilities of special interest to law students are the 2 courtrooms in the school. One is designed as a moot courtroom, and the other is an actual courtroom periodically used by the state court system. There is also a computer lab for student use. Housing for students is available in numerous apartments within commuting distance of the school. The university has apartments for married students near the campus. All law school facilities are accessible to the physically disabled.

Calendar

The law school operates on a traditional semester basis. Courses for full-time students are offered days only and must be completed within 3 years. There is no part-time program. New students are admitted in the fall. There is an 8-week summer session. Transferable summer courses are offered.

Programs

Students may take relevant courses in other programs and apply credit toward the J.D.; a maximum of 9 hours credits may be applied. The following joint degrees may be earned: J.D./H.R.M. (Juris Doctor/Master of Human Resource Management), J.D./I.M.B.A. (Juris Doctor/Master of International Business Administration), J.D./M.C.J. (Juris Doctor/Master of Criminal Justice), J.D./M.E.S. (Juris Doctor/Master of Environmental Science), J.D./M.P.A. (Juris Doctor/Master of Public Administration), J.D./M.S.W. (Juris Doctor/Master of Social Work), and J.D./M.T. (Juris Doctor/Master of Taxation).

Phone: 803-777-6605
Fax: 803-777-7751
E-mail: *usclaw@law.law.sc.edu*
Web: *www.law.sc.edu*

Contact

Admissions Office, School of Law, Assistant Dean for Admissions, 803-777-6605 for general inquiries; Director of Financial Aid, 803-777-6605 for financial aid information.

Required

To earn the J.D., candidates must complete 90 total credits, of which 46 are for required courses. They must maintain a minimum GPA of 2.0 in the required courses. The following first-year courses are required of all students: Civil Procedure, Constitutional Law, Contracts I and II, Property I and II, Torts I and II, Introduction to Legal System and Legal Writing, and Introduction to Legal Research and Lawyering. Required upper-level courses consist of Criminal Process, Professional Responsibility, a perspective course, and a writing requirement. The required orientation program for first-year students is 1 day before the start of classes. Accepted students are also invited to a reception in the spring prior to the start of the first fall semester.

Electives

The School of Law offers concentrations in corporate law, labor law, litigation, tax law, and business law, commercial law and bankruptcy, probate and estate planning, and real estate. In addition, there are several types of clinics, usually for 3 credits hours. Examples are Consumer Bankruptcy and Criminal Practice. Students gain closely supervised training experience in the representation of clients. A number of seminars are offered each semester, such as Death Penalty and Environmental Law. All have limited enrollment, require a paper to be written, and are for 3 credit hours. In the area of research programs, students may take the course Supervised Legal Research for 2 credit hours. It is an independent study performed under the supervision of a faculty member and requires a research paper. Many upper-level students clerk for law firms during the school year. A special lecture series is open to all students. First-year students are offered a tutorial program. A minority peer assistance tutorial program is also available. Special interest group programs include the Pro Bono Program, which provides opportunities for volunteer law students to obtain practical legal training. The most widely taken electives are litigation, business, and commercial law.

Graduation Requirements

In order to graduate, candidates must have a GPA of 2.0 and have completed the upper-division writing requirement.

Organizations

The primary law review is the *South Carolina Law Review*; the other law reviews are *ABA Real Property, Probate, and Trust Journal* and *The South Carolina Environmental Law Journal*. The student newspapers are the *Gavel Raps* and *The Forum*. The school sponsors teams in the National, International, American Bar Association, and Labor Law Moot Court competitions as well as the National Trial competitions. It also competes in the J. Woodrow Lewis Intramural Moot Court competition in appellate advocacy. The law student organizations are the Student Bar Association, Black Law Students, and Women in Law. The local chapters of national associations are Phi Alpha Delta, Christian Legal Society and Phi Delta Phi. Campus clubs and other organizations include the Society of International Law, Wig and Robe, and the Federalist Society.

Library

The law library contains 330,000 hardcopy volumes and 2718 microform volume equivalents, and subscribes to 972 serial publications. Such on-line databases and networks as DIALOG, LEXIS, NEXIS, and WESTLAW are available to law students for research. Special library collections include a South Carolina legal history collection and a selective GPO depository. Recently, the library added 2 electronic classrooms. The ratio of library volumes to faculty is 7674 to 1 and to students is 467 to 1.

Faculty

The law school has 43 full-time and 26 part-time faculty members, of whom 9 are women. According to AAUP standards for Category I institutions, faculty salaries are average. About 55% of full-time faculty have a graduate law degree in addition to the J.D. The ratio of full-time students to full-time faculty in an average class is 45 to 1; in a clinic, 12 to 1. The law school has a regular program of bringing visiting professors and other distinguished lecturers and visitors to campus. There is a chapter of the Order of the Coif; 19 faculty and 281 graduates are members.

Placement	
J.D.s awarded:	197
Services available through: a separate law school placement center	
Services: eAttorney/OCI	
Special features: free job opportunities postings on the web site, eAttorney job listings and searchable web site of legal employers; reciprocity with other law schools.	
Full-time job interviews:	31 employers
Summer job interviews:	46 employers
Placement by graduation:	60% of class
Placement within 9 months:	94% of class
Average starting salary:	$19,500 to $105,000
Areas of placement:	
Private practice 2-10 attorneys	25%
Private practice 11-25 attorneys	6%
Private practice 26-50 attorneys	4%
Private practice 51-100 attorneys	5%
Private practice 100+ attorneys	11%
Judicial clerkships	25%
Government	13%
Business/industry	8%
Public interest	1%
Military	1%
Academic	1%

Students

About 43% of the student body are women; 9%, minorities; 7%, African American; and 1%, Asian American. The majority of students come from South Carolina (82%). The average age of entering students is 23; age range is 21 to 57. About 55% of students enter directly from undergraduate school, 8% have a graduate degree, and 45% have worked full-time prior to entering law school. About 3% drop out after the first year for academic or personal reasons; 97% remain to receive a law degree.

UNIVERSITY OF SOUTH DAKOTA

School of Law

414 East Clark Street
Vermillion, SD 57069-2390

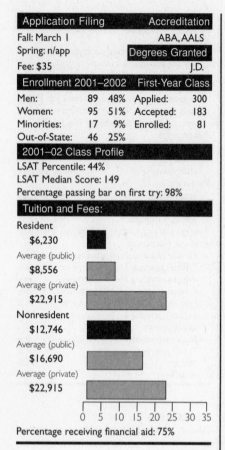

Application Filing		Accreditation
Fall: March 1		ABA, AALS
Spring: n/app		**Degrees Granted**
Fee: $35		J.D.

Enrollment 2001–2002			First-Year Class	
Men:	89	48%	Applied:	300
Women:	95	51%	Accepted:	183
Minorities:	17	9%	Enrolled:	81
Out-of-State:	46	25%		

2001–02 Class Profile

LSAT Percentile: 44%
LSAT Median Score: 149
Percentage passing bar on first try: 98%

Tuition and Fees:

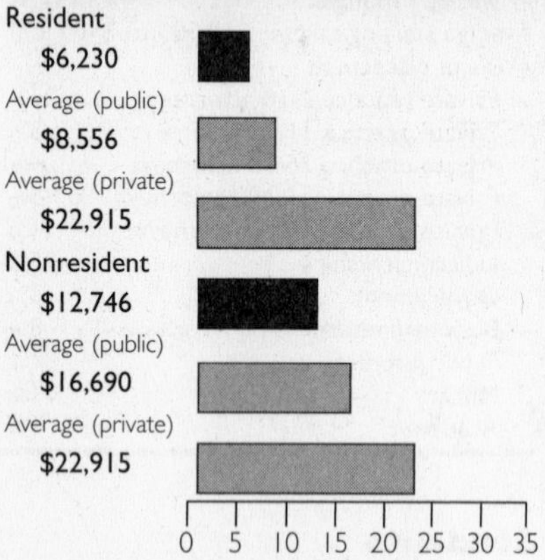

Percentage receiving financial aid: 75%

ADMISSIONS

In the fall 2001 first-year class, 300 applied, 183 were accepted, and 81 enrolled. One transfer enrolled. The median LSAT percentile of the most recent first-year class was 44; the median GPA was 3.3 on a scale of 4.0. The lowest LSAT percentile accepted was 9; the highest was 97.

Requirements

Applicants must have a bachelor's degree and take the LSAT. The most important admission factors include LSAT results, GPA, and character, personality. Undergraduate courses that require writing reports and papers, and logical, analytic reasoning are helpful. In addition, an understanding of the basic principles of accounting may be helpful for the practice of business-related law. Candidates are not interviewed.

Procedure

The application deadline for fall entry is March 1. Applicants should submit an application form, use LSDAS for LSAT and transcripts, a nonrefundable application fee of $35, 2 letters of recommendation, a personal statement, and the LSDAS report. Notification of the admissions decision is on a rolling basis. The latest acceptable LSAT test date for fall entry is February. The law school uses the LSDAS.

Special

The law school recruits minority and disadvantaged students by mail solicitation and meeting in person with prospects. Requirements are not different for out-of-state students. Transfer students must have one year of credit, have attended an ABA-approved law school, and be in good standing at their present law school.

Costs

Tuition and fees for the 2001-2002 academic year are $6230 for full-time in-state students and $12,746 for out-of-state students. On-campus room and board costs about $4000 annually; books and supplies run $1250.

Financial Aid

About 75% of current law students received some form of aid in a recent year. The maximum annual amount of aid from all sources combined, including scholarships, loans, and work contracts, is $17,284 (resident). Awards are based on need and merit. Required financial statement is the FAFSA. Check with the school for current aid application deadlines. First-year students are notified about their financial aid application at time of acceptance.

About the Law School

University of South Dakota School of Law was established in 1901 and is a public institution. The 216-acre campus is in a small town 50 miles south of Sioux Falls. The primary mission of the law school is to prepare students for the practice of law and to train professionally competent graduates capable of achieving their career goals and serving their profession. Students have access to federal, state, county, city, and local agencies, courts, correctional facilities, law firms, and legal aid organizations in the Vermillion area. Housing for students is adequate. All law school facilities are accessible to the physically disabled.

Calendar

The law school operates on a traditional semester basis. Courses for full-time students are offered days only and must be completed within 6 semesters. For part-time students, courses are offered days only and must be completed within 10 semesters. New full- and part-time students are admitted in the fall. There is a 6-week summer session. Transferable summer courses are offered.

Programs

Students may take relevant courses in other programs and apply credit toward the J.D.; a maximum of 9 credits may be applied. The following joint degrees may be earned: J.D./M.A. (Juris Doctor/Master of Arts in English, history, psychology, and political science), J.D./M.B.A. (Juris Doctor/Master of Business Administration), J.D./M.P.A. (Juris Doctor/Master of Public Administration), J.D./M.P.Acc. (Juris Doctor/Master of Professional Accountancy), and J.D./M.S.A.S. (Juris Doctor/Master of Science in Administrative Studies).

Phone: 605-677-5443
Fax: 605-677-5417
E-mail: *lawreq@usd.edu*
Web: *www.usd.edu/law*

Contact

Jean Henriques, Admission Officer/Registrar, 605-677-5443 for general inquiries; University Financial Aid Office, 605-677-5446 for financial aid information.

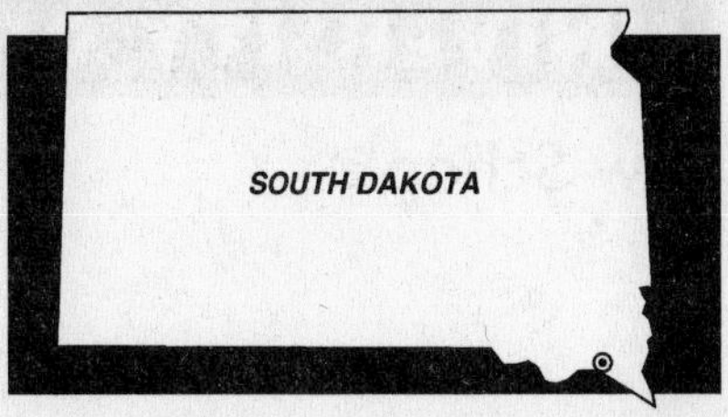

Required

To earn the J.D., candidates must complete 90 total credits, of which 43 are for required courses. They must maintain a minimum grade average of 60 in the required courses. The following first-year courses are required of all students: Torts, Contracts, Property, Criminal Law and Procedure, Civil Procedure, Legal Writing, Legal Research, Appellate Advocacy, and Introduction to the Study and Practice of Law. Required upper-level courses consist of Constitutional Law, Evidence, Legal Profession, and code course (Commercial Law, Secured Transactions, or Federal Income Tax). The required orientation program for first-year students lasts for 2½ days.

Electives

The School of Law offers concentrations in corporate law, environmental law, tax law, Indian law, and trial advocacy. Research programs, amounting to 1 or 2 hours of credit, are available for second- and third-year students. Externships are available for third-year students, and a federal judicial externship is available for first-year students. The most widely taken electives are Trusts and Wills, Advanced Torts, and Commercial Law.

Graduation Requirements

In order to graduate, candidates must have a grade average of 70 and have completed the upper-division writing requirement.

Organizations

The primary law review is the *South Dakota Law Review*. Other publications include the *Great Plains Natural Resources Journal*. Moot court competitions are the New York Bar, ABA, and Health Law competitions. Other competitions include ABA-LSD Competitions (Negotiations, Client Counseling, Mediation) and the Robert R. Merhige, Jr. National Negotiation Competition. Law student organizations include Native American Law Students Association, Black Law Students Association, and Federalist Society. Campus clubs and other organizations include Women in Law, R.D. Hurd Pro Bono Society, and Student Bar Association.

Library

The law library contains 192,397 hard-copy volumes and 12,052 microform volume equivalents, and subscribes to 755 serial publications. Such on-line databases and networks as CALI, DIALOG, LEXIS, and WESTLAW are available to law students for research. Special library collections include a government documents depository collection, which is an extension of the main university library's collection. Other collections include reference, reserve, and Indian law. Recently, the library provided students and faculty with 24/7 access to the library. The ratio of library volumes to faculty is 12,826 to 1 and to students is 1045 to 1. The ratio of seats in the library to students is 1 to 1.

Faculty

The law school has 15 full-time and 2 part-time faculty members, of whom 3 are women. According to AAUP standards for Category 1 institutions, faculty salaries are well below average. About 27% of full-time faculty have a graduate law degree in addition to the J.D. The ratio of full-time students to full-time faculty in an average class is 13 to 1. The law school has a regular program of bringing visiting professors and other distinguished lecturers and visitors to campus.

Students

About 51% of the student body are women; 9%, minorities; 1%, African American; 1%, Asian American; 1%, Hispanic; 10%, Native American; and 1%, African. The majority of students come from South Dakota (75%). The average age of entering students is 27; age range is 22 to 52. About 48% of students enter directly from undergraduate school and 5% have a graduate degree. About 8% drop out after the first year for academic or personal reasons; 92% remain to receive a law degree.

Placement	
J.D.s awarded:	59
Services available through: a separate law school placement center and the university placement center	
Special features: alumni network, weekly career services, and alumni newsletter.	
Full-time job interviews:	5 employers
Summer job interviews:	22 employers
Placement by graduation:	56% of class
Placement within 9 months:	90% of class
Average starting salary:	$33,600 to $39,500
Areas of placement:	
Private practice 2-10 attorneys	23%
Private practice 11-25 attorneys	3%
Private practice 51-100 attorneys	1%
Judicial clerkships	35%
Government	18%
Business/industry	8%
Unknown	7%
Public interest	4%
Military	1%

UNIVERSITY OF SOUTHERN CALIFORNIA

Law School

Los Angeles, CA 90089-0074

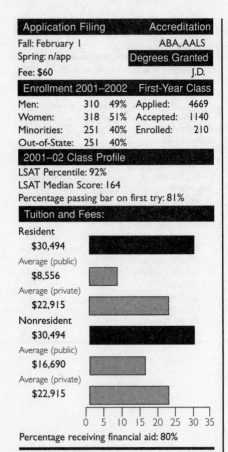

Application Filing		Accreditation
Fall: February 1		ABA, AALS
Spring: n/app		**Degrees Granted**
Fee: $60		J.D.

Enrollment 2001–2002			First-Year Class	
Men:	310	49%	Applied:	4669
Women:	318	51%	Accepted:	1140
Minorities:	251	40%	Enrolled:	210
Out-of-State:	251	40%		

2001–02 Class Profile

LSAT Percentile: 92%

LSAT Median Score: 164

Percentage passing bar on first try: 81%

Tuition and Fees:

Resident

$30,494

Average (public)

$8,556

Average (private)

$22,915

Nonresident

$30,494

Average (public)

$16,690

Average (private)

$22,915

Percentage receiving financial aid: 80%

ADMISSIONS

In the fall 2001 first-year class, 4669 applied, 1140 were accepted, and 210 enrolled. The median LSAT percentile of the most recent first-year class was 92; the median GPA was 3.55 on a scale of 4.0.

Requirements

Applicants must have a bachelor's degree and take the LSAT. No specific undergraduate courses are required. Candidates are not interviewed.

Procedure

The application deadline for fall entry is February 1. Applicants should submit an application form, LSAT results, transcripts, a nonrefundable application fee of $60, 2 letters of recommendation, and a personal statement. Notification of the admissions decision is in the spring. The latest acceptable LSAT test date for fall entry is December. The law school uses the LSDAS.

Special

The law school recruits minority and disadvantaged students by means of mail outreach campaigns, school visits, and minority receptions; the minority student organizations also help recruit and retain qualified candidates. Requirements are not different for out-of-state students. Transfer students must have one year of credit, have attended an ABA-approved law school, and be in the top 20% of their first-year class.

Costs

Tuition and fees for the 2001-2002 academic year are $30,494 for all full-time students. Room and board costs about $12988.

Financial Aid

About 80% of current law students receive some form of aid. The average annual amount of aid from all sources combined, including scholarships, loans, and work contracts, is $27,124; maximum, $47,466. Awards are based on need and merit. Required financial statements are the FAFSA and the Law School financial aid application. The aid application deadline for fall entry is February 15. Special funds for minority or disadvantaged students consist of scholarships that are used in part to assist disadvantaged and minority students. First-year students are notified about their financial aid application at time of acceptance.

About the Law School

University of Southern California Law School was established in 1900 and is a private institution. The 150-acre campus is in an urban area 3½ miles south of downtown Los Angeles. The primary mission of the law school is to offer an innovative program focusing on the law as an expression of social values and as an instrument for implementing social goals. Students have access to federal, state, county, city, and local agencies, courts, correctional facilities, law firms, and legal aid organizations in the Los Angeles area. Facilities of special interest to law students include a computer laboratory, multimedia classrooms, large and high-tech library facilities, a spacious student lounge, and clinical law offices. The USC campus features a 24-hour library, fitness center, specialty libraries, theaters, and restaurants. Housing for students consists of an on-campus apartment house designated for law students.

Calendar

The law school operates on a traditional semester basis. Courses for full-time students are offered days only and must be completed within 4 years. There are no part-time programs. New students are admitted in the fall. There is no summer session. Transferable summer courses are not offered.

Programs

Students may take relevant courses in other programs and apply credit toward the J.D.; a maximum of 12 credits may be applied. The following joint degrees may be earned: J.D./M.A. (Juris Doctor/Master of Arts in economics, international relations, communications, management, religion, political science), J.D./M.A.P. (Juris Doctor/Master of Philosophy), J.D./M.B.A. (Juris Doctor/Master of Business Administration), J.D./M.B.T. (Juris Doctor/Master of Business Taxation), J.D./M.P.A. (Juris Doctor/Master of Public Administration), J.D./M.P.P. (Juris Doctor/Master of Public Policy), J.D./M.R.E.D. (Juris Doctor/Master of Real Estate Development), J.D./M.S. (Juris Doctor/Master of Science in gerontology), J.D./M.S.W. (Juris Doctor/Master of Social Work), J.D./Ph.D. (Juris Doctor/Doctor of Philosophy in Economics), J.D./Ph.D. (Juris Doctor/Doctor of Philosophy in political science), and J.D./Ph.D. (Juris Doctor/Doctor of Pharmacy).

Required

To earn the J.D., candidates must complete 88 total credits, of which 33 are for required courses. They must maintain a minimum grade average of 70 in the required courses. The following first-year courses are required of all students: Law Language and Ethics, Torts I, Civil Procedure, Contracts, Criminal Law, Constitutional Law, Property, Legal Research and Introduction to Lawyering Skills, and Legal Profession. Required upper-level courses consist of a writing requirement. The required orientation program for first-year students is a 1-day program that includes a welcoming address, luncheon, financial aid counseling, meetings with second-year advisers assigned to incoming students, and a barbecue. A student-run mentor program for first-year students has year-round activities.

Phone: 213-740-2523
Web: *www.usc.edu/law*

Contact

William J. Hoye, Associate Dean, 213-740-2523 for general inquiries; Mary Bingham, Director of Financial Aid, 213-740-7331 for financial aid information.

Electives

The Law School offers concentrations in corporate law, criminal law, entertainment law, environmental law, family law, international law, juvenile law, labor law, litigation, media law, securities law, tax law, torts and insurance, public interest, constitutional law, and civil rights. In addition, in-house and simulated clinics are available for upper-level students. In-house clinics include the Post-Conviction Justice project, the Children's Legal Issues Clinic, and the Employer Legal Advice Clinic. Seminars, available to upper-level students, are offered on many topics and facilitate intensive discussions in small groups. Internships, worth up to 4 credits, are available for upper-level students with government or public interest nonprofit organizations. Judicial externships allow students to clerk for a state or federal judge. The Law School cosponsors the Pacific Center for Health Policy and Ethics research program; Center for Communications Law and Policy; Center for the Study of Law and Politics; Center for Law, History and Culture, and Center for Law, Economics and Organization. Special lecture series include the annual Roth lecture, Olin faculty workshops, and Centers. There is no study-abroad program, but credit may be given for work done in other accredited law schools' study-abroad programs. Tutorials are arranged on a case-by-case basis. The school also offers a 5-part workshop on studying. An exam-taking skills course is offered to first-year students in the spring and upper-division students in the fall. Minority student organizations and minority alumni associations collaborate on a range of social and educational programs as well as networking opportunities. Student-run organizations geared at specific areas of the legal profession include the Entertainment Law Society, International Law Society, Corporate Law Society, and Public Interest Law Foundation. The most widely taken electives are Entertainment Law, What Lawyers Should Know About Business, and Gender Discrimination.

Graduation Requirements

In order to graduate, candidates must have completed the upper-division writing requirement.

Organizations

Students edit the *Southern California Law Review, Southern California Interdisciplinary Law Journal, Southern California Review of Law and Womens Studies*, and the newspaper, *The Law Street Journal. Advance Sheet*, a weekly newsletter, and *USC Law*, a semiannual alumni magazine. All first-year students participate in moot court competitions; the 40 best advocates are selected to compete, in their second year, in the Hale Moot Court Honors Program. In addition, the best advocates from the Hale Moot Court Competition participate in numerous national competitions. Student organizations include the Public Interest Law Foundation; Sports, Music and Entertainment Law Society; and Street Law. Local chapters of national associations are Phi Alpha Delta, Phi Delta Phi, and Order of the Coif.

Library

The law library contains 381,032 hardcopy volumes and 89,917 microform volume equivalents, and subscribes to 4319 serial publications. Such on-line databases and networks as DIALOG, LEXIS, NEXIS, RLIN, and WESTLAW are available to law students for research. Special library collections include a selected depository. Among the important holdings are health law/bioethics, law and economics, law and philosophy, law and social sciences, taxation, preventive law and historic documents concerning President Lincoln. Recently, the library expanded and renovated facilities including additional computer laboratories and classrooms, and increased seating and study areas; library carrels are wired for laptop Internet access. The ratio of library volumes to faculty is 7938 to 1 and to students is 607 to 1.

Faculty

The law school has 48 full-time and 54 part-time faculty members, of whom 24 are women. According to AAUP standards for Category I institutions, faculty salaries are well above average. The ratio of full-time students to full-time faculty in an average class is 15 to 1; in a clinic, 5 to 1. The law school has a regular program of bringing visiting professors and other distinguished lecturers and visitors to campus. There is a chapter of the Order of the Coif; 15 faculty and 10% of all graduates are members.

Placement

J.D.s awarded: 193

Services available through: a separate law school placement center

Services: lists of public interest contacts, counseling regarding a wide array of alternatives, a major on-campus placement program, videotaped practice interviews, 1-to-1 mentor program with graduates for first-year students in the second semester

Special features: 1-on-1 counseling session for each first-year student; the Career Services Office's *Guide to Public Interest Law* for its students/graduates; Alumni-Student Mock Interview Program.

Full-time job interviews:	110 employers
Summer job interviews:	188 employers
Placement by graduation:	90% of class
Placement within 9 months:	96% of class
Average starting salary:	$75,000 to $125,000
Areas of placement:	
Private practice 2-10 attorneys	5%
Private practice 11-25 attorneys	5%
Private practice 26-50 attorneys	1%
Private practice 51-100 attorneys	2%
Private practice 100+ attorneys	61%
Business/industry	12%
Judicial clerkships	8%
Government	3%
Public interest	2%
Academic	1%

Students

About 51% of the student body are women; 40%, minorities; 11%, African American; 17%, Asian American; 11%, Hispanic; and 1%, Native American. The majority of students come from California (60%). The average age of entering students is 24; age range is 20 to 50. About 40% of students enter directly from undergraduate school, 25% have a graduate degree, and 35% have worked full-time prior to entering law school. About 1% drop out after the first year for academic or personal reasons; 99% remain to receive a law degree.

UNIVERSITY OF TENNESSEE

College of Law

1505 W. Cumblerland Avenue
Knoxville, TN 37996-1810

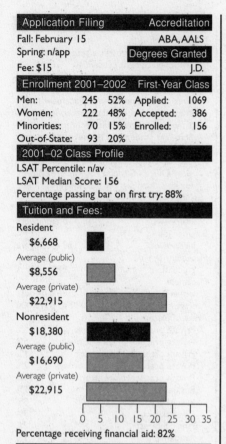

Application Filing		Accreditation
Fall: February 15		ABA, AALS
Spring: n/app		**Degrees Granted**
Fee: $15		J.D.

Enrollment 2001–2002			First-Year Class	
Men:	245	52%	Applied:	1069
Women:	222	48%	Accepted:	386
Minorities:	70	15%	Enrolled:	156
Out-of-State:	93	20%		

2001–02 Class Profile

LSAT Percentile: n/av
LSAT Median Score: 156
Percentage passing bar on first try: 88%

Tuition and Fees:

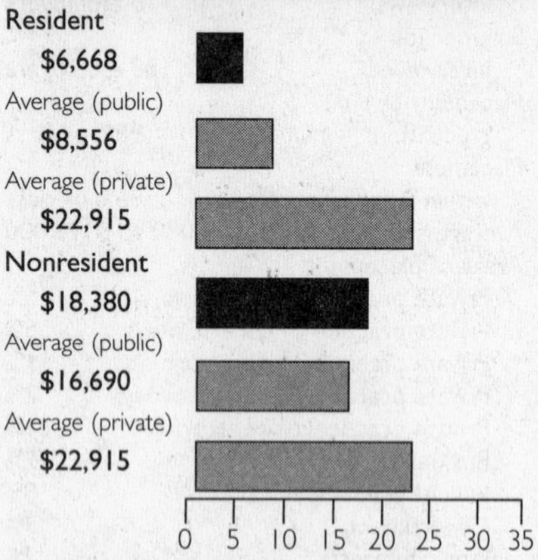

Percentage receiving financial aid: 82%

ADMISSIONS

In the fall 2001 first-year class, 1069 applied, 386 were accepted, and 156 enrolled. One transfer enrolled. The median GPA of the most recent first-year class was 3.46. The lowest LSAT score accepted was 139; the highest was 174.

Requirements

Applicants must have a bachelor's degree and take the LSAT. Admission factors are not ranked; all are considered during a review of each application. No specific undergraduate courses are required. Candidates are not interviewed.

Procedure

The application deadline for fall entry is February 15. Applicants should submit an application form, LSAT results, transcripts, a nonrefundable application fee of $15, 2 letters of recommendation, personal statement, an essay, and a dean's certification form. Notification of the admissions decision varies. The latest acceptable LSAT test date for fall entry is December. The law school uses the LSDAS.

Special

The law school recruits minority and disadvantaged students through a number of initiatives, including on-campus visits, LSAC forums, on-campus workshops, Tennessee Pre-Law Day (each spring), and LSAC CRS Service. Requirements are not different for out-of-state students. Transfer students must have one year of credit, have a minimum GPA of 2, and have attended an ABA-approved law school. Transfer admission is limited and very competitive.

Costs

Tuition and fees for the 2001-2002 academic year are $6668 for full-time in-state students and $18,380 for out-of-state students. On-campus room and board costs about $6216 annually; books and supplies run $1244.

Financial Aid

About 82% of current law students receive some form of aid. The average annual amount of aid from all sources combined, including scholarships, loans, and work contracts, is $15,636; maximum, $27,188. Awards are based on need and merit. Required financial statement is the FAFSA. The aid application deadline for fall entry is March 1. Special funds for minority or disadvantaged students consist of scholarships that are awarded on the basis of demonstrated financial need and merit. First-year students are notified about their financial aid application before acceptance, usually in January.

About the Law School

University of Tennessee College of Law was established in 1890 and is a public institution. The 417-acre campus is in an urban area in Knoxville, Tennessee, in the heart of the university. The primary mission of the law school is to provide a first-rate legal education to a diverse group of students. Students have access to federal, state, county, city, and local agencies, courts, correctional facilities, law firms, and legal aid organizations in the Knoxville area. The College of Law is located approximately 1 mile from the courts and legal employers in downtown Knoxville. Facilities of special interest to law students include a law center, which houses civil and criminal clinics, a mediation program, the center for entrepreneurial law, classrooms, law library, and faculty offices. Several off-campus university apartment complexes are available to single and married students. Seven apartment complexes are located within a 5-mile radius of the campus. All law school facilities are accessible to the physically disabled.

Calendar

The law school operates on a traditional semester basis. Courses for full-time students are offered days only and must be completed within 5 years. There is no part-time program. New students are admitted in the fall. There is an 8-week summer session. Transferable summer courses are offered.

Programs

Students may take relevant courses in other programs and apply credit toward the J.D.; a maximum of 6 credits may be applied. The following joint degrees may be earned: J.D./M.B.A. (Juris Doctor/Master of Business Administration).

Phone: 865-974-4131
Fax: 865-974-1572
E-mail: *lawadmit@libra.law.utk.edu*
Web: *www.law.utk.edu*

Contact

Carolyn Dossett, Admissions Assistant, 865-974-4131 for general inquiries; Janet Hatcher, Admissions and Financial Aid Adviser, 865-974-4131 for financial aid information.

Required

To earn the J.D., candidates must complete 89 total credits, of which 46 are for required courses. They must maintain a minimum GPA of 2.0 in the required courses. The following first-year courses are required of all students: Introduction to the Study of Law, Civil Procedure I and II, Contracts I and II, Criminal Law, Legal Process I and II, Torts I and II, and Property. Required upper-level courses consist of Constitutional Law, Legal Profession, a perspective course, an expository writing course, and a planning and drafting course. The Introductory Period begins with orientation, offers 3½ days of mini courses in Civil Litigation Process and Case Analysis and Briefing, and concludes with one regular class meeting in Criminal Law, Contracts, and Torts.

Electives

The College of Law offers concentrations in business transactions, advocacy and dispute resolution. In addition, an advocacy clinic is open to third-year students who have completed trial practice. Students receive 6 hours of credit. A mediation clinic is open to all upper-division students for 3 hours of credit. A variety of seminars is available for 2 hours credit. An experimental prosecutorial internship is open to third-year students, who preferably have completed both Criminal Procedure I and II. Students receive 4 credit hours. An advanced legal research course is offered. Special lecture series include the Alumni Distinguished Lecture in Jurisprudence, the Charles Henderson Miller Lecture in Professional Responsibility, and the Speaker Series, which hosts nationally known speakers to address issues of importance to a wide spectrum of Tennesseans. Any student may study abroad through ABA-approved summer abroad programs. A maximum of 8 credit hours may be transferred. Students with a first-semester average below 2.0 are invited to participate, in the second semester, in tutorials in Contracts, Civil Procedure, and Torts. First-year students may attend a series of Law School Success Skills seminars on topics such as Managing Time and Energy in Law School; Outlining; sample exams in Civil Procedure, Torts, and Contracts; and Final Exams. The most widely taken electives are Commercial Law, Trial Practice, and Criminal Procedure.

Graduation Requirements

In order to graduate, candidates must have a GPA of 2.0, have completed the upper-division writing requirement, and the perspective requirement, and the planning and drafting requirement.

Organizations

Students edit the *Tennessee Law Review* and the student newspapers *The Informant* and *UTK Daily Beacon*. Moot court competitions include the National Moot Court, National Trial, and Jerome Prince Evidence. Other competitions include the Jenkins Trial and Advocates Prize Moot Court. Law student organizations include the American Bar Association—Law Student Division, Association of Trial Lawyers of America—Student Chapter, and Hamilton Barrett Chapter of the American Inns of Court. There are local chapters of the Black Law Students Association, Phi Delta Phi, and Tennessee Association for Public Interest Law.

Library

The law library contains 498,656 hard-copy volumes and 1,216,308 microform volume equivalents, and subscribes to 6636 serial publications. Such on-line databases and networks as CALI, CIS Universe, Infotrac, Legal-Trac, LEXIS, Mathew Bender, NEXIS, OCLC First Search, WESTLAW, and Wilsonline Indexes are available to law students for research. Special library collections include a selective federal document depository and a Tennessee depository. Recently, the library upgraded to the millennium library system. The ratio of library volumes to faculty is 16,622 to 1 and to students is 1068 to 1. The ratio of seats in the library to students is 1 to 1.

Faculty

The law school has 30 full-time and 26 part-time faculty members, of whom 19 are women. According to AAUP standards for Category I institutions, faculty salaries are average. About 37% of full-time faculty have a graduate law degree in addition to the J.D.; about 5% of part-time faculty have one. The ratio of full-time students to full-time faculty in an average class is 13 to 1; in a clinic, 8 to 1. The law school has a regular program of bringing visiting professors and other distinguished lecturers and visitors to campus. There is a chapter of the Order of the Coif.

Placement

J.D.s awarded:	163

Services available through: a separate law school placement center and law students also may use the UTK placement center.

Services: off-campus recruiting events, the Southeastern Minority Job Fair, the Southeastern Law Placement Consortium, National Association for Public Interest Law Career Information Fair, Mid-South Law Placement Consortium, Patent Law Interview Program, and the Nashville Bar Association Minority Clerkship Program

Special features: small-group orientations; the Career Services Handbook; a resource library with more than 1000 employer files, books, and videotapes; an annual picturebook of students; a booklet series of alumni career narratives; and a web-based information system.

Full-time job interviews:	26 employers
Summer job interviews:	64 employers
Placement by graduation:	61% of class
Placement within 9 months:	89% of class
Average starting salary:	$29,400 to $125,000

Areas of placement:

Private practice 2-10 attorneys	28%
Private practice 11-25 attorneys	11%
Private practice 26-50 attorneys	5%
Private practice 51-100 attorneys	4%
Private practice 100+ attorneys and solo practice	13%
Judicial clerkships	15%
Government	12%
Business/industry	8%
Public interest	2%
Military	1%
Academic	1%

Students

About 48% of the student body are women; 15%, minorities; 11%, African American; 2%, Asian American; 2%, Hispanic; and 1%, ethnicity unknown/unreported. The majority of students come from Tennessee (80%). The average age of entering students is 25; age range is 20 to 51. About 71% of students enter directly from undergraduate school, 6% have a graduate degree, and 29% have worked full-time prior to entering law school. About 3% drop out after the first year for academic or personal reasons; 97% remain to receive a law degree.

UNIVERSITY OF TEXAS AT AUSTIN

School of Law

727 East Dean Keeton Street
Austin, TX 78705

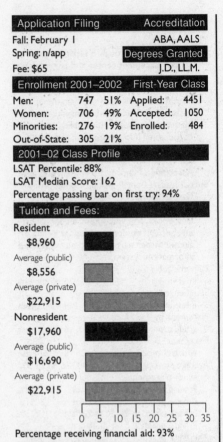

Application Filing	Accreditation
Fall: February 1	ABA, AALS
Spring: n/app	**Degrees Granted**
Fee: $65	J.D., LL.M.

Enrollment 2001–2002			First-Year Class	
Men:	747	51%	Applied:	4451
Women:	706	49%	Accepted:	1050
Minorities:	276	19%	Enrolled:	484
Out-of-State:	305	21%		

2001–02 Class Profile

LSAT Percentile: 88%
LSAT Median Score: 162
Percentage passing bar on first try: 94%

Tuition and Fees:

Resident
$8,960
Average (public)
$8,556
Average (private)
$22,915
Nonresident
$17,960
Average (public)
$16,690
Average (private)
$22,915

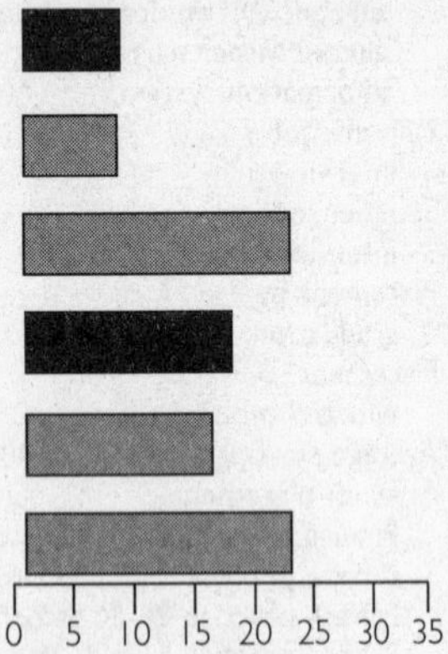

Percentage receiving financial aid: 93%

ADMISSIONS

In the fall 2001 first-year class, 4451 applied, 1050 were accepted, and 484 enrolled. Twenty-three transfers enrolled. The median LSAT percentile of the most recent first-year class was 88; the median undergraduate GPA was 3.68 on a scale of 4.0. The lowest LSAT percentile accepted was 16; the highest was 100.

Requirements

Applicants must have a bachelor's degree and take the LSAT. Minimum acceptable GPA is 2.2 on a scale of 4.0. No specific undergraduate courses are required. Candidates are interviewed.

Procedure

The application deadline for fall entry is February 1. Applicants should submit an application form, a nonrefundable application fee of $65, and registration with LSDAS by January 10 or by October 10 for early decision. Payment of $200 as an enrollment fee for admitted students, a personal statement, and a resume are required. Notification of the admissions decision is December to May. The latest acceptable LSAT test date for fall entry is December. The law school uses the LSDAS.

Special

The law school recruits minority and disadvantaged students through campus visits and law forums, and special mailings and phone calls. Requirements are different for out-of-state students in that Texas' state legislature limits nonresident enrollment to 20% of the entering class. Therefore, nonresidents face tougher competition. Transfer students must have one year of credit, have a minimum GPA of 2.2, have attended an ABA-approved law school, demonstrate good cause for the transfer, and have a strong academic record prior to and during law school.

Costs

Tuition and fees for the 2001-2002 academic year are $8960 for full-time in-state students and $17,960 for out-of-state students. On-campus room and board costs about $7332 annually; books and supplies run $898.

Financial Aid

About 93% of current law students receive some form of aid. The average annual amount of aid from all sources combined, including scholarships, loans, and work contracts, is $20,258; maximum, $26,578. Awards are based on need and merit. Required financial statement is the FAFSA. The aid application deadline for fall entry is March 31. First-year students are notified about their financial aid application at time of acceptance. The application and guide are mailed at the time of acceptance; they can be mailed earlier if requested by a student.

About the Law School

University of Texas at Austin School of Law was established in 1883 and is a public institution. The 40-acre campus is in an urban area within Austin. The primary mission of the law school is to educate students for the practice of law by advancing knowledge of the law as an institution to effect social change. Students have access to federal, state, county, city, and local agencies, courts, correctional facilities, law firms, and legal aid organizations in the Austin area. Facilities of special interest to law students include Townes Hall, and Tarlton Law Library, which is housed in the Joseph D. Jamail Center for Legal Research, 2 connected buildings that house the law library, classrooms, seminar rooms, student organization areas, and other support facilities. Off-campus housing is available. Few students select on-campus housing. All law school facilities are accessible to the physically disabled.

Calendar

The law school operates on a traditional semester basis. Courses for full-time students are offered days only and must be completed within within five years. There is no part-time program. New students are admitted in the fall. There is a 6-week summer session. Transferable summer courses are offered.

Programs

In addition to the J.D., the law school offers the LL.M. Students may take relevant courses in other programs and apply credit toward the J.D.; a maximum of 6 credits may be applied. The following joint degrees may be earned: J.D./M.A. (Juris Doctor/Master of Arts in Latin American, Middle Eastern, Russian, East European, and Eurasian studies), J.D./M.B.A. (Juris Doctor/Master of Business Administration), J.D./M.P.A. (Juris Doctor/Master of Public Affairs), and J.D./M.S. (Juris Doctor/Master of Science in community and regional planning).

Required

To earn the J.D., candidates must complete 86 total credits, of which 38 are for required courses. They must maintain a minimum GPA of 1.9 in the required courses. The following first-year courses are required of all students: Contracts, Criminal Law, Torts, Property, Legal Research and Legal Writing, Civil Procedure, and Constitutional Law I. Re-quired upper-level courses consist of Professional Responsibility, a writing seminar, and Constitutional Law II. The required orientation program for first-year students is a 3-day program that familiarizes them with the physical facilities, rules, and procedures of the law school and the university. Students attend a general welcome and social event.

Phone: 512-232-1200
Fax: 512-471-6988
E-mail: *admissions@mail.law.utexas.edu*
Web: *www.utexas.edu/law*

Contact

Terrie Pinkerton, Admissions Office Manager, 512-232-1200 for general inquiries; Linda Alba, Financial Aid Counselor, 512-232-1130 for financial aid information.

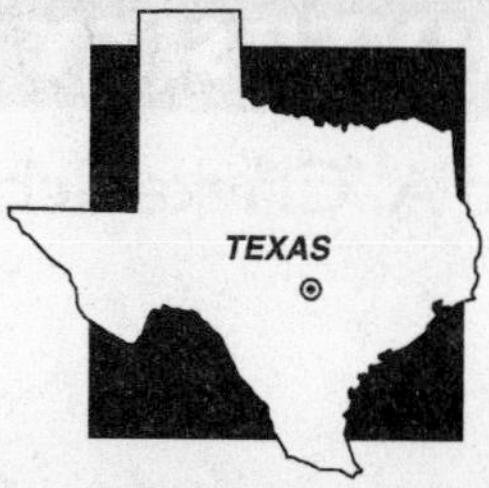

Electives

The School of Law offers concentrations in corporate law, criminal law, entertainment law, family law, international law, juvenile law, labor law, litigation, maritime law, media law, securities law, tax law, torts and insurance, natural resources law, civil liberties, commercial law, and intellectual property law. In addition, clinics are offered in Capital Punishment, Children's Rights, Criminal Defense, Elder Law, Fair Housing, Juvenile Justice, and Mental Health. A writing seminar is a requirement for graduation. Judicial internships are available with the Texas Supreme Court, the Texas Court of Criminal Appeals, and the Texas Court of Appeals through which a small number of students earn law school credit for work done under the supervision of an individual justice. Empirical legal research projects sponsored and directly supervised by a faculty member are available. An advanced student may also conduct individual research projects. The school has a semester-long exchange program with Queen Mary College and Westfield College, which are both colleges of the University of London. Up to 30 upper-class students enroll for 4 approved courses in international or comparative law. Students can create their own study abroad program as well. Students on scholastic probation and second-semester first-year students in danger of being placed on scholastic probation, are assigned tutors. There are student organizations focusing on almost any area of the law. The most widely taken electives are Wills and Estates, Business Associations, and Federal Income Tax.

Graduation Requirements

In order to graduate, candidates must have a GPA of 1.9, have completed the upper-division writing requirement, and 86 credit hours, of which 38 are required courses.

Organizations

Students edit the *Texas Law Review*, *Texas International Law Journal*, *American Journal of Criminal Law*, *The Review of Litigation*, the *Texas Forum on Civil Liberties and Civil Rights*, *Texas Environmental Law Journal*, *Texas Intellectual Property Law Journal*, *Texas Journal of Women and the Law*, *Texas Journal of Hispanic Law and Policy*, *Texas Review of Law and Politics*, *Texas Review of Entertainment and Sports Law*, and the SBA newsletter, *The Writ*. The Board of Advocates directs a range of moot court, mock trial, and client counseling contests both in the school and with other law schools. Law student organizations include the Student Bar Association, Thurgood Marshall Legal Society, and Chicano/Hispanic Law Students Association. Campus clubs and other organizations include Public Interest Law Association, Board of Advocates, and Assault and Flattery.

Library

The law library contains 992,745 hard-copy volumes and 766,572 microform volume equivalents, and subscribes to 9045 serial publications. Such on-line databases and networks as CALI, CIS Universe, DIALOG, Dow-Jones, Infotrac, Legal-Trac, LEXIS, LOIS, Mathew Bender, NEXIS, OCLC First Search, RLIN, WESTLAW, and Wilsonline Indexes are available to law students for research. Special library collections include an extensive collection of foreign law (Western Europe, Latin America), papers of Tom C. Clark, Associate Justice of the U.S. Supreme Court; ABA Gavel Committee Award Entries; EU depository; law in popular culture; U.S. Supreme Court briefs; Canadian Government Document Depository. Recently, the library added web access to its collection through TALLONS (Tartlton Law Library Online System), and to the resources of the other UT libraries and the Harry Ransom Humanities Research Center through UTCAT. The Law Library's Computer Learning Center (CLC) provides a networked environment for research, e-mail, and word processing applications with laser-printed output. The CLC has doubled in size, with more than 100 networked PCs now available for student use. The ratio of library volumes to faculty is 13,599 to 1 and to students is 683 to 1. The ratio of seats in the library to students is 1 to 1.

Faculty

The law school has 73 full-time and 102 part-time faculty members, of whom 51 are women. According to AAUP standards for Category I institutions, faculty salaries are above average. About 19% of full-time faculty have a graduate law degree in addition to the J.D.; about 5% of part-time faculty have one. The ratio of full-time students to full-time faculty in an average class is 17 to 1; in a clinic, 9 to 1. The law school has a regular program of bringing visiting professors and other distinguished lecturers and visitors to campus. There is a chapter of the Order of the Coif; 57 graduates are members.

Placement

J.D.s awarded: 450

Services available through: a separate law school placement center

Services: Mentor Program/Directory, Judicial Clerkship Program, approximately 60 student programs/workshops per year.

Special features: Founding member of *www.PSLaw.net*, use of *www.eAttorney.com*, 1 of 9 original law schools participating in Treeba Virtual Interview Portal.

Full-time job interviews:	265 employers
Summer job interviews:	450 employers
Placement by graduation:	93% of class
Placement within 9 months:	100% of class
Average starting salary:	$33,000 to $100,946

Areas of placement:

Private practice 2-10 attorneys	5%
Private practice 11-25 attorneys	4%
Private practice 26-50 attorneys	3%
Private practice 51-100 attorneys	6%
Private practice 100+ attorneys	35%
Judicial clerkships	13%
Business/industry	10%
Government	7%
Public interest	2%
Military	2%
Academic	2%

Students

About 49% of the student body are women; 19%, minorities; 3%, African American; 6%, Asian American; and 10%, Hispanic. The majority of students come from Texas (79%). The average age of entering students is 23; age range is 19 to 46. About 54% of students enter directly from undergraduate school and 12% have a graduate degree. About 1% drop out after the first year for academic or personal reasons; 98% remain to receive a law degree.

UNIVERSITY OF THE DISTRICT OF COLUMBIA

David A. Clarke School of Law

4200 Connecticut Avenue, N.W.
Washington, DC 20008

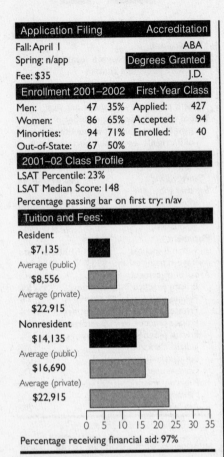

Application Filing		Accreditation
Fall: April 1		ABA
Spring: n/app		**Degrees Granted**
Fee: $35		J.D.

Enrollment 2001–2002			First-Year Class	
Men:	47	35%	Applied:	427
Women:	86	65%	Accepted:	94
Minorities:	94	71%	Enrolled:	40
Out-of-State:	67	50%		

2001–02 Class Profile

LSAT Percentile: 23%
LSAT Median Score: 148
Percentage passing bar on first try: n/av

Tuition and Fees:

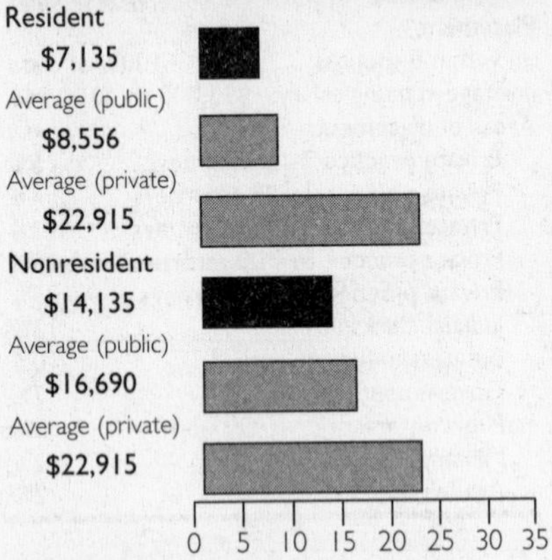

Percentage receiving financial aid: 97%

ADMISSIONS

In the fall 2001 first-year class, 427 applied, 94 were accepted, and 40 enrolled. One transfer enrolled. The median LSAT percentile of the most recent first-year class was 23; the median GPA was 2.78 on a scale of 4.0. The lowest LSAT percentile accepted was 13; the highest was 98.

Requirements

Applicants must have a bachelor's degree and take the LSAT. Minimum acceptable GPA is 2.5 on a scale of 4.0. The most important admission factors include general background, GPA, and LSAT results. No specific undergraduate courses are required. Candidates are interviewed.

Procedure

The application deadline for fall entry is April 1. Applicants should submit an application form, LSAT results, transcripts, a nonrefundable application fee of $35, 2 letters of recommendation, and 3 essays. Notification of the admissions decision is on a rolling basis. The latest acceptable LSAT test date for fall entry is February. The law school uses the LSDAS.

Special

The law school recruits minority and disadvantaged students by direct mail recruitment campaigns, such as LSAC Candidate Referral Service and GRE Minority Locator Service; through visits to historically black and minority institutions; by maintaining contact with local community groups and organizations; holding Law Day and Open House programs; and through ads in school papers and local government periodicals. Requirements are not different for out-of-state students. Transfer students must have one year of credit, have a minimum GPA of 2.0, and have attended an ABA-approved law school. The school offers a pre-admission summer program, including courses in Legal Writing and Analysis, Torts, and tutorials.

Costs

Tuition and fees for the 2001-2002 academic year are $7135 for full-time in-state students and $14,135 for out-of-state students. Books and supplies run about $4500 annually.

Financial Aid

About 97% of current law students receive some form of aid. The average annual amount of aid from all sources combined, including scholarships, loans, and work contracts, is $23,000; maximum, $35,010. Awards are based on need and merit. Students may apply for non-need-based alternative loans with eligibility based on credit worthiness. Required financial statements are the FAFSA and NEED ACCESS required for institutional scholarships. The aid application deadline for fall entry is May 1. Special funds for minority or disadvantaged students are available through need-based named scholarships donated to the law school's scholarship fund for minority student awards. First-year students are notified about their financial aid application at time of acceptance.

About the Law School

University of the District of Columbia David A. Clarke School of Law was established in 1987 and is a public institution. The campus is in an urban area in upper northwest Washington D.C. The primary mission of the law school is to represent the legal needs of low-income persons, particularly those who reside in the District of Columbia, while recruiting, enrolling, and training persons from racial, ethnic, or other population groups that have been traditionally underrepresented at the Bar to become public interest, public policy, and public service lawyers. Students have access to federal, state, county, city, and local agencies, courts, correctional facilities, law firms, and legal aid organizations in the Washington area. Other resources include the Supreme Court, Capitol Hill, Library of Congress, and public interest groups and organizations. Facilities of special interest to law students include local and federal government offices, courts and administrative agencies, public interest organizations, and Capitol Hill. There is no on-campus housing. The School of Law assists incoming students with locating housing in the Washington D.C. metropolitan area. All law school facilities are accessible to the physically disabled.

Calendar

The law school operates on a traditional semester basis. Courses for full-time students are offered both day and evening and must be completed within 5 years. There is no part-time program. New students are admitted in the fall. There is an 8- to 10-week summer session. Transferable summer courses are offered.

Programs

Students may take relevant courses in other programs and apply credit toward the J.D.; a maximum of 30 credits may be applied.

Phone: 202-274-7341
Fax: 202-274-5583
E-mail: *vcanty@law.udc.edu*
Web: *www.law.udc.edu*

Contact

Vivian W. Canty, 202-274-7341 for general inquiries; Anne El-Shazli, Financial Aid Officer, 202-274-7337 for financial aid information.

Required

To earn the J.D., candidates must complete 90 total credits, of which 66 are for required courses. They must maintain a minimum GPA of 2.0 in the required courses. The following first-year courses are required of all students: Civil Procedure I and II, Contracts I and II, Criminal Law, Lawyering Process I and II, Torts, Criminal Procedure, and Law and Justice. Required upper-level courses consist of Evidence, Clinic I and II, Property, Constitutional Law I and II, Professional Responsibility, and Moot Court. Students must complete 2 semesters of clinic totaling 700 hours and 14 credits. The required orientation program for first-year students is approximately 2 weeks in length, in early to mid-August. It includes the courses Lawyering Process I and Law and Justice, as well as activities such as tours of the Supreme Court and D.C. Superior Court, student and faculty presentations, and a dean's reception.

Electives

The David A. Clarke School of Law offers concentrations in criminal law, juvenile law, litigation, and public interest law. In addition, clinics are offered for 7 credits each in topics including Juvenile and Special Education, Small Business, and AIDS/HIV Law. Seminars are offered each semester. A 2-credit internship seminar is required of all students who do an internship. Internships with public or nonprofit private agencies, for 4 to 8 credits, are offered for advanced students who have completed 14 credits of clinic and are in good standing. Students may be selected to be research assistants on faculty research projects. The clinics involve students in various forms of field work. In addition, the internship program provides full-time field work, such as in the School's Immigration Law Project. Special lecture series include the Dean's Lecture Series. The Career Services Office and student organizations also organize guest speakers' visits and programs. The Academic Support Program provides small group and individual tutorials for first-year students. The Program requires students to examine the analytic processes needed to solve legal problems. It also provides diagnostic testing, counseling, and tutoring for students whose GPA falls below 2.0. The Academic Support Program (Mason Enhancement Program) also makes use of CALI exercises and diagnostic exercises on the computer, which were designed at the school. The most widely taken electives are Race and The Law, Business Organizations I, and Uniform Commercial Code.

Graduation Requirements

In order to graduate, candidates must have a GPA of 2.0 and have completed the upper-division writing requirement.

Organizations

Students edit *The District of Columbia Law Review, The Advocate*, and the newspaper, *The Sidebar*. Law student organizations include the UDC-DCSL Student Bar Association, Women's Society, and Joseph Raub Equal Justice Fund. There are local chapters of the American Trial Lawyers Association, Delta Theta Phi, and Federalist Society.

Library

The law library contains 205,000 hard-copy volumes and 90 microform volume equivalents, and subscribes to 550 serial publications. Such on-line databases and networks as BNA, CALI, CIS Universe, Infotrac, Legal-Trac, LEXIS, LOIS, Mathew Bender, NEXIS, WESTLAW, and the Internet are available to law students for research. Special library collections include District of Columbia law. Recently, the library has expanded its computer laboratory and audiovisual department, and has automated its public catalog and other library operations. In addition, the library has undergone renovation. The ratio of library volumes to faculty is 11,389 to 1 and to students is 1541 to 1. The ratio of seats in the library to students is 1 to 1.

Faculty

The law school has 18 full-time and 18 part-time faculty members, of whom 15 are women. About 10% of full-time faculty have a graduate law degree in addition to the J.D.; about 22% of part-time faculty have one. The ratio of full-time students to full-time faculty in an average class is 10 to 1; in a clinic, 8 to 1. The law school has a regular program of bringing visiting professors and other distinguished lecturers and visitors to campus.

Placement	
J.D.s awarded:	48
Services available through: a separate law school placement center	
Services: lists of judicial clerkships, fellowships, and writing competitions. Bar exam applications and information are also available.	
Special features: personalized career counseling.	
Full-time job interviews:	20 employers
Summer job interviews:	6 employers
Placement by graduation:	60% of class
Placement within 9 months:	85% of class
Average starting salary:	$27,000 to $102,000
Areas of placement:	
Solo practice	5%
Private practice 2-10 attorneys	30%
Private practice 11-25 attorneys	5%
Government	30%
Business/industry	10%
Public interest	10%
Judicial clerkships	5%
Military	2%
Academic	2%
Unknown	1%

Students

About 65% of the student body are women; 71%, minorities; 57%, African American; 3%, Asian American; and 11%, Hispanic. Most students come from the District of Columbia (50%). The average age of entering students is 30; age range is 21 to 65. About 38% of students enter directly from undergraduate school, 15% have a graduate degree, and 50% have worked full-time prior to entering law school. About 15% drop out after the first year for academic or personal reasons; 85% remain to receive a law degree.

UNIVERSITY OF THE PACIFIC

McGeorge School of Law

3200 Fifth Avenue
Sacramento, CA 95817

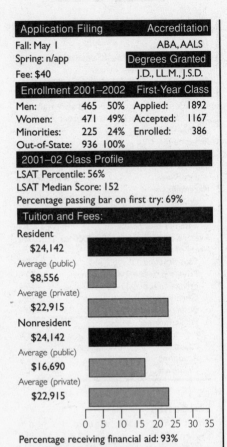

Application Filing		Accreditation
Fall: May 1		ABA, AALS
Spring: n/app		**Degrees Granted**
Fee: $40		J.D., LL.M., J.S.D.

Enrollment 2001–2002			First-Year Class	
Men:	465	50%	Applied:	1892
Women:	471	49%	Accepted:	1167
Minorities:	225	24%	Enrolled:	386
Out-of-State:	936	100%		

2001–02 Class Profile

LSAT Percentile: 56%
LSAT Median Score: 152
Percentage passing bar on first try: 69%

Tuition and Fees:

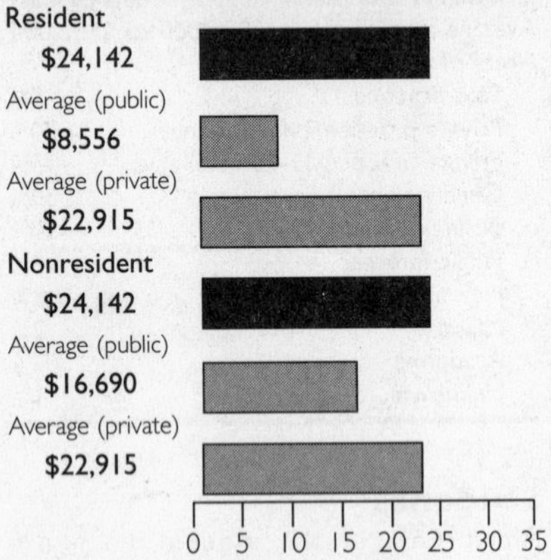

Percentage receiving financial aid: 93%

ADMISSIONS

In the fall 2001 first-year class, 1892 applied, 1167 were accepted, and 386 enrolled. Eight transfers enrolled. The median LSAT percentile of the most recent first-year class was 56; the median GPA was 3.12 on a scale of 4.3. The lowest LSAT percentile accepted was 22; the highest was 99.

Requirements

Senior undergraduates, who have not yet earned a bachelor's degree, with compelling reasons for admission, may be considered. Applicants must take the LSAT. The most important admission factors include academic achievement, LSAT results, and general background. No specific undergraduate courses are required. Candidates are not interviewed.

Procedure

The application deadline for fall entry is May 1. Applicants should submit an application form, LSAT results, transcripts, a nonrefundable application fee of $40, optional (2 are suggested) letters of recommendation, and personal statement. Notification of the admissions decision begins in January. The latest acceptable LSAT test date for fall entry is February; June if space is available. The law school uses the LSDAS.

Special

The law school recruits minority and disadvantaged students through recruiting events, publications, letters, contacts with McGeorge students, and scholarship and grant programs. Requirements are not different for out-of-state students. Transfer students must have one year of credit. Acceptance of transfer students is dependent upon space availability; preference is given to students with compelling reasons to request transfer.

Costs

Tuition and fees for the 2001-2002 academic year are $24,142 for all full-time students. Tuition for part-time students is $16,062 per year. Books and supplies run about $610 annually.

Financial Aid

About 93% of current law students receive some form of aid. The average annual amount of aid from all sources combined, including scholarships, loans, and work contracts, is $24,737; maximum, $38,204. Awards are based on need and merit. Required financial statement is the FAFSA. The aid application deadline for fall entry is open. Diversity factors are considered in the award of scholarships and grants. First-year students are notified about their financial aid application at time of acceptance, assuming a completed application is on file.

About the Law School

University of the Pacific McGeorge School of Law was established in 1924 and is a private institution. The 22-acre campus is in a suburban area in Sacramento, California. The primary mission of the law school is to educate practice-ready graduates, able to represent clients skillfully and ethically, through a rigorous curriculum that unifies classroom study with development of professional skills. Students have access to federal, state, county, city, and local agencies, courts, correctional facilities, law firms, legal aid organizations in the Sacramento area, state capital internships and on-campus administrative justice offices. Special facilities include the trial courtroom, the LawLab equipped with computer technology, the "live-client" clinical facilities, student center with food service, library with ample study and computer areas, and recreational facilities. Housing for students consists of 158 on-campus apartments; housing off campus is readily available in the Sacramento area at a reasonable cost. About 95% of the law school facilities are accessible to the physically disabled.

Calendar

The law school operates on a traditional semester basis. Courses for full-time students are offered both day and evening and must be completed within 4 years. For part-time students, courses are offered both day and evening and must be completed within 5 years. New full- and part-time students are admitted in the fall. There is a 7 1/2-week summer session. Transferable summer courses are offered.

Programs

In addition to the J.D., the law school offers the LL.M. and J.S.D. Students may take relevant courses in other programs and apply credit toward the J.D.; a maximum of 30 from an ABA law school credits may be applied. The following joint degrees may be earned: J.D./M.A. or M.S. (Juris Doctor/Master of Arts or Master of Science), J.D./M.B.A. (Juris Doctor/Master of Business Administration), and J.D./M.P.P.A. (Juris Doctor/Master of Public Policy and Administration).

Required

To earn the J.D., candidates must complete 88 total credits, of which 58 are for required courses. They must maintain a minimum GPA of 2.3 in the required courses. The following first-year courses are required of all students: Civil Procedure, Contracts, Criminal Law, Legal Process, Property, and Torts. Required upper-level courses consist of Business Associations, Constitutional Law, Criminal Procedure, Evidence, Professional Responsibility, Remedies, Community Property, Appellate or International Advocacy, and Decedents' Estates and Trusts. The required orientation program for first-year students is a 3-day program at the beginning of the year

Phone: 916-739-7105
Fax: 916-739-7134
E-mail: *admissionsmcgeorge@uop.edu*
Web: *www.mcgeorge.edu*

Contact

Elizabeth J. Travis, Assistant Director of Admissions, 916-739-7105 for general inquiries; Financial Aid Office, 916-739-7158 for financial aid information.

that includes orientation classes, small group sessions, and social activities. First-year faculty provide special feedback programs, including practice examinations, throughout the first year.

Electives

The McGeorge School of Law offers concentrations in corporate law, criminal law, environmental law, family law, international law, juvenile law, litigation, tax law, torts and insurance, intellectual property, and governmental affairs. On-campus clinics include Community Legal Services, which provides legal services for those not otherwise able to afford them; it is available to advanced students, carries a 2-semester commitment and is worth 6 credits. Other campus-based clinics available to advanced students for 2 or 3 credits each semester are Administrative Adjudication Clinic; Parole Representation Clinic; and Legislative Process. A number of elective courses are in a seminar format with limited enrollment. Of particular interest are Advanced Intellectual Property; Negotiations and Settlement; California Law Revision; Reorganization, Recapitalization and Insolvency; and International Water Resources Law. More than 75 off-campus internships are available in non-profit and local, state, and federal governmental offices and agencies. Internships are available to advanced students and are worth 2 or 3 credits per semester. Directed research, available as an elective for advanced students, is offered for 1 or 2 credits. Individual professors also have student research assistants. Additionally, the Research Pool undertakes research projects for practitioners. Lecture series such as the Distinguished Speaker's Series, Hefner Memorial Lecture Series, and Lou Ashe Symposium bring outstanding guest speakers to campus. The Institute on International Legal Studies is a 3-week program in Salzburg, Austria, in cooperation with the University of Salzburg. International and comparative law courses are offered in public and commercial law fields. For more than a decade, Anthony M. Kennedy, Associate Justice of the U.S. Supreme Court has co-taught "Fundamental Rights in Europe and the U.S." Tutorial programs include the Skills Hour Program and the Practice Examination Program offered in the fall of the student's first year. A voluntary Minority Support Program provides a peer support and networking system as well as special orientation sessions, student-led discussion groups, and course review sessions. The most widely taken electives are Trial Advocacy, clinical offerings, and business courses.

Graduation Requirements

In order to graduate, candidates must have a GPA of 2.3 and have completed the upper-division writing requirement.

Organizations

Students edit the *McGeorge Law Review* and the *Transnational Lawyer*. McGeorge teams compete in the National and ABA Moot Court competitions, and the Philip Jessup International Moot Court Competition. Other competitions include Willem C. Viz International Commercial Arbitration in Vienna; San Diego Defense Lawyers; William Daniel Mock Trial; San Diego Consumer Attorneys Mock Trial; Michigan State Competition; ABA Texas Young Lawyers National Trial Competition Nationals; ATLA National Student Advocacy Competition Nationals; ABA Client Counseling, and ABA Negotiation. Law student organizations include the Student Bar Association, Public Legal Services Society, and Government Affairs Student Association. There are local chapters of ABA-Law Student Division, Federalist Society, and Phi Alpha Delta fraternity. Campus clubs and other organizations include Entertainment Law Society, Women's Caucus, and International Law Society.

Library

The law library contains 454,775 hard-copy volumes and 1,189,824 microform volume equivalents, and subscribes to 4509 serial publications. Such on-line databases and networks as CALI, CIS Universe, DIALOG, Legal-Trac, LEXIS, Mathew Bender, NEXIS, OCLC First Search, RLIN, WESTLAW, CCH, and BNA are available to law students for research. Special library collections include California legal materials, California and U.S. documents depository, and tax and international law special collections. Recently, the library expanded and remodeled 6000 square feet that provided room for automated systems, LEXIS/WESTLAW Permanent Learning Centers, additional study rooms, microform/media/CD-ROM Center, expanded circulation, and upgraded photocopy facilities. The ratio of library volumes to faculty is 10,336 to 1 and to students is 486 to 1. The ratio of seats in the library to students is 1 to 1.

Placement

J.D.s awarded:	308
Services available through: a separate law school placement center	
Special features: Practice interview program; alumni network program; first-year Career Development orientation program.	
Full-time job interviews:	70 employers
Summer job interviews:	n/av
Placement by graduation:	58% of class
Placement within 9 months:	87% of class
Average starting salary:	$25,000 to $135,000
Areas of placement:	
Private practice 2-10 attorneys	56%
Government	20%
Business/industry	13%
Judicial clerkships	4%
Public interest	2%
Military	2%
Academic	1%

Faculty

The law school has 44 full-time and 64 part-time faculty members, of whom 29 are women. According to AAUP standards for Category IIA institutions, faculty salaries are well above average. About 30% of full-time faculty have a graduate law degree in addition to the J.D.; about 11% of part-time faculty have one. The ratio of full-time students to full-time faculty in an average class is 24 to 1; in a clinic, 10 to 1. The law school has a regular program of bringing visiting professors and other distinguished lecturers and visitors to campus. There is a chapter of the Order of the Coif; 31 faculty and 686 graduates are members.

Students

About 49% of the student body are women; 24%, minorities; 4%, African American; 10%, Asian American; 8%, Hispanic; and 2%, Native American. The average age of entering students is 24; age range is 20 to 52. About 76% of students enter directly from undergraduate school and 1% have a graduate degree. About 26% drop out after the first year for academic or personal reasons.

UNIVERSITY OF TOLEDO

College of Law

2801 West Bancroft Street
Toledo, OH 43606-3390

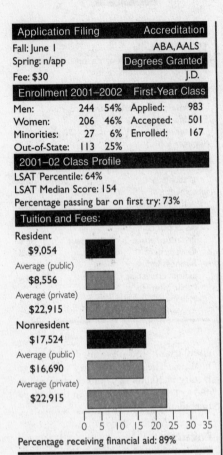

Application Filing		Accreditation
Fall: June 1		ABA, AALS
Spring: n/app		**Degrees Granted**
Fee: $30		J.D.

Enrollment 2001–2002			First-Year Class	
Men:	244	54%	Applied:	983
Women:	206	46%	Accepted:	501
Minorities:	27	6%	Enrolled:	167
Out-of-State:	113	25%		

2001–02 Class Profile

LSAT Percentile: 64%
LSAT Median Score: 154
Percentage passing bar on first try: 73%

Tuition and Fees:

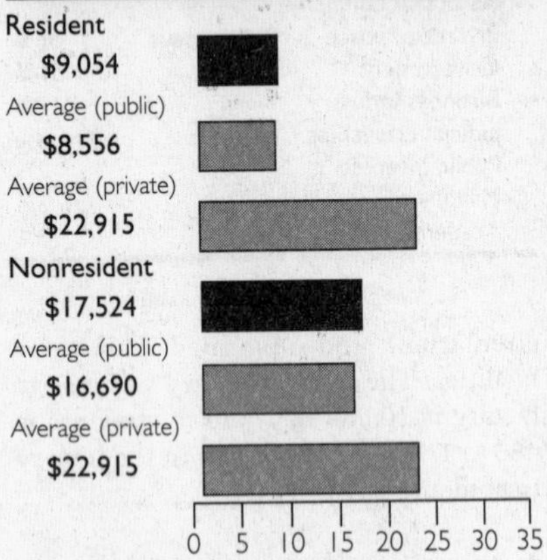

Percentage receiving financial aid: 89%

ADMISSIONS

In the fall 2001 first-year class, 983 applied, 501 were accepted, and 167 enrolled. Five transfers enrolled. The median LSAT percentile of the most recent first-year class was 64; the median GPA was 3.31 on a scale of 4.0. The lowest LSAT percentile accepted was 26; the highest was 99.

Requirements

Applicants must have a bachelor's degree and take the LSAT. Graduate study is considered. Minimum acceptable GPA is 2.0 on a scale of 4.0. No specific undergraduate courses are required. Candidates are not interviewed.

Procedure

The application deadline for fall entry is June 1. Applicants should submit an application form, LSAT results, transcripts, a nonrefundable application fee of $30 (free on-line), 2 letters of recommendation, and should indicate preference for full- or part-time study. Accepted applicants must submit a $75 nonrefundable deposit, which is credited toward tuition. Notification of the admissions decision is on a rolling basis. The latest acceptable LSAT test date for fall entry is February. The law school uses the LSDAS.

Special

Requirements are not different for out-of-state students. Transfer students must have attended an ABA-approved law school and be in good standing at the previous school.

Costs

Tuition and fees for the 2001-2002 academic year are $9054 for full-time in-state students and $17,524 for out-of-state students. Tuition for part-time students is $7545 in-state and $14,603 out-of-state. Books and supplies run about $1025 annually.

Financial Aid

About 89% of current law students receive some form of aid. The average annual amount of aid from all sources combined, including scholarships, loans, and work contracts, is $15,770; maximum, $36,694. Awards are based on need and merit. Required financial statement is the FAFSA. The aid application deadline for fall entry is July 1. First-year students are notified about their financial aid application at time of acceptance.

About the Law School

University of Toledo College of Law was established in 1906 and is a public institution. The 210-acre campus is in a suburban area west of downtown Toledo, adjacent to Ottawa Hills. The primary mission of the law school is to familiarize prospective lawyers with the major areas of the law while at the same time introducing them to the basic skills for competent lawyering. The college integrates theory and practice. Students have access to federal, state, county, city, and local agencies, courts, correctional facilities, law firms, and legal aid organizations in the Toledo area. Facilities of special interest to law students include a state-of-the-art mock courtroom, which is available for trial practice and appellate advocacy programs, renovated classrooms, and the wireless Web. Housing for students consists of living accommodations located near the campus. The university assists students in finding housing. All law school facilities are accessible to the physically disabled.

Calendar

The law school operates on a traditional semester basis. Courses for full-time students are offered both day and evening and are usually completed within 5 years. For part-time students, courses are offered both day and evening and must be completed within a maximum of 6 years. New full- and part-time students are admitted in the fall. There is a 10-week summer session. Transferable summer courses are offered.

Programs

Students may take relevant courses in other programs and apply credit toward the J.D.; a maximum of 7 credits may be applied. The following joint degrees may be earned: J.D./M.B.A. (Juris Doctor/Master of Business Administration), J.D./M.E. (Juris Doctor/Master of Engineering), and J.D./M.P.A. (Juris Doctor/Master of Public Administration).

Required

To earn the J.D., candidates must complete 89 total credits, of which 42 are for required courses. They must maintain a minimum GPA of 2.0 in the required courses. The following first-year courses are required of all students: Civil Procedure I and II, Contracts I and II, Torts, Legal Research, Writing, and Appellate Advocacy I and II, Criminal Law, Constitutional Law, and Property. Required upper-level courses consist of Constitutional Law II, Evidence, and Legal Ethics and Professional Responsibility. The required orientation program for first-year students lasts 2 days.

Phone: 419-530-4131
Fax: 419-530-4345
E-mail: *law.utoledo.edu*
Web: *www.utlaw.edu*

Contact

Carol E. Frendt, Assistant Dean of Law Admission, 419-530-4131 for general inquiries; Beth Solo, Assistant Director, Law Financial Aid, 419-530-7929 for financial aid information.

Electives

The College of Law offers concentrations in corporate law, criminal law, environmental law, family law, international law, juvenile law, labor law, sports law, tax law, torts and insurance, business and commercial law, civil practice and procedure, estate and trust law, governmental regulation, health care law, intellectual property, jurisprudence, legal history and philosophy, personal and family law, property/real estate law, public interest law, public law, skills and values. In addition, clinical programs include the College of Law Legal Clinic, the Criminal Law Practice Program, and the Dispute Resolution Clinic. These are offered to all upper-level students for 4 to 6 hours of credit. An upper-level writing requirement provides maximum flexibility in meeting the needs and interests of students. Internships are available through the Criminal Law Practice Program. A Public Service Externship Program offers field experience in the chambers of a federal judge or magistrate or state appellate judge. The college offers a number of research assistantships to students who have completed 1 academic year. Individual research programs allow students to develop their own research projects, which are pursued in consultation with a faculty committee. The Cannon Lecture Series and the Stranghan National Issues Forum have hosted individuals of national prominence who provide the college and general public with timely discussions of legal and policy issues. The College of Law, in cooperation with the Inns of Court Law School in London, arranges summer internships with British barristers and solicitors. A special first-year course for academically disadvantaged students is available. The most widely taken electives are Administrative Law, Corporations, and Evidence.

Graduation Requirements

In order to graduate, candidates must have a GPA of 2.0 and have completed the upper-division writing requirement.

Organizations

Students edit the *University of Toledo Law Review, Toledo Transcript, The Toledo Journal of Great Lakes' Law, Sciences and Policy*, and the student/newspaper *No Holds Bar Review*. The Moot Court program helps build skills in the arts of brief writing and oral advocacy through participation in national and intraschool competitions, such as the Charles W. Fornoff Intra-School Competition. Competitions are managed by a student Moot Court Board. Law student organizations include the Student Bar Association, Business Law Society, and Federalist Society. There are local chapters of The Order of the Coif, Delta Theta Phi, and Phi Alpha Delta. The Law Alumni Association has more than 5000 members across the country.

Library

The law library contains 327,663 hardcopy volumes and 128,622 microform volume equivalents, and subscribes to 3290 serial publications. Such on-line databases and networks as CALI, CIS Universe, Legal-Trac, LEXIS, NEXIS, WESTLAW, and Index Master are available to law students for research. Special library collections include significant holdings of primary materials for the United Kingdom, Canada, Australia, and New Zealand, and primary and secondary materials for studying international law; the library is a federal depository. Recently, the library upgraded 30 of 45 networked computers to support various kinds of on-line legal research and installed compact shelving for historical library materials. The ratio of library volumes to faculty is 9929 to 1 and to students is 728 to 1. The ratio of seats in the library to students is 1 to 1.

Faculty

The law school has 33 full-time and 29 part-time faculty members, of whom 19 are women. According to AAUP standards for Category I institutions, faculty salaries are below average. About 20% of full-time faculty have a graduate law degree in addition to the J.D.; about 1% of part-time faculty have one. The ratio of full-time students to full-time faculty in an average class is 14 to 1; in a clinic, 5 to 1. The law school has a regular program of bringing visiting professors and other distinguished lecturers and visitors to campus. There is a chapter of the Order of the Coif; 37 faculty and 321 graduates are members.

Placement	
J.D.s awarded:	166
Services available through: a separate law school placement center	
Services: arrange interviews using video conferencing equipment, organize mentor program, and arrange for reciprocity with other law schools	
Special features: the Law Career Services Employment Resource Library and the Law Career Services Student Handbook.	
Full-time job interviews:	10 employers
Summer job interviews:	25 employers
Placement by graduation:	80% of class
Placement within 9 months:	95% of class
Average starting salary:	$18,000 to $125,000
Areas of placement:	
Private practice 2-10 attorneys	25%
Private practice 11-25 attorneys	4%
Private practice 26-50 attorneys	4%
Private practice 51-100 attorneys	1%
Business/industry	22%
Government	18%
Unknown	11%
Public interest	6%
Academic	5%
Judicial clerkships	3%
Military	1%

Students

About 46% of the student body are women; 6%, minorities; 4%, African American; 1%, Asian American; and 1%, Hispanic. The majority of students come from Ohio (75%). The average age of entering students is 26; age range is 22 to 65. About 85% of students enter directly from undergraduate school and 15% have a graduate degree. About 5% drop out after the first year for academic or personal reasons; 97% remain to receive a law degree.

UNIVERSITY OF TULSA

College of Law

3120 East Fourth Place
Tulsa, OK 74104-2499

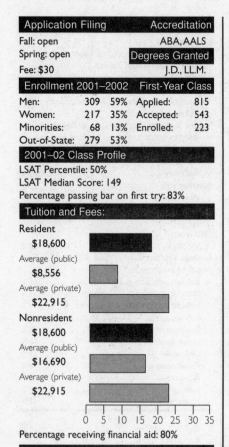

Application Filing		Accreditation
Fall: open		ABA, AALS
Spring: open		**Degrees Granted**
Fee: $30		J.D., LL.M.

Enrollment 2001–2002			First-Year Class	
Men:	309	59%	Applied:	815
Women:	217	35%	Accepted:	543
Minorities:	68	13%	Enrolled:	223
Out-of-State:	279	53%		

2001–02 Class Profile

LSAT Percentile: 50%
LSAT Median Score: 149
Percentage passing bar on first try: 83%

Tuition and Fees:

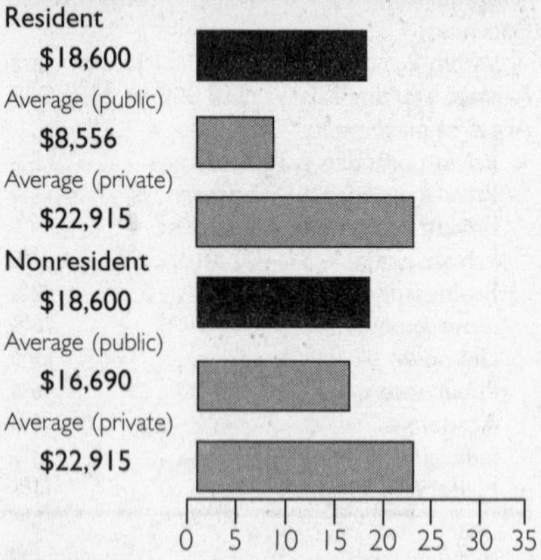

Percentage receiving financial aid: 80%

ADMISSIONS

In the fall 2001 first-year class, 815 applied, 543 were accepted, and 223 enrolled. Twenty transfers enrolled. The median LSAT percentile of the most recent first-year class was 50; the median GPA was 3.1 on a scale of 4.0. The lowest LSAT percentile accepted was 25; the highest was 94.

Requirements

Applicants must have a bachelor's degree and take the LSAT. Minimum acceptable GPA is 2.0 on a scale of 4.0. The most important admission factors include GPA, LSAT results, and general background. No specific undergraduate courses are required. Candidates are not interviewed.

Procedure

The application deadline for fall entry is open. Applicants should submit an application form, LSAT results, transcripts, a nonrefundable application fee of $30 (free on-line), 2 letters of recommendation, and a personal statement. Notification of the admissions decision is on an ongoing basis. The latest acceptable LSAT test date for fall entry is June. The law school uses the LSDAS.

Special

The law school recruits minority and disadvantaged students through CLEO and an academic success program in summer and recruitment at minority schools. Requirements are not different for out-of-state students. Transfer students must have one year of credit and have attended an ABA-approved law school.

Costs

Tuition and fees for the 2001-2002 academic year are $18,600 for all full-time students. Tuition for part-time students is $12,167 per year. On-campus room and board costs about $9580 annually; books and supplies run $1500.

Financial Aid

About 80% of current law students receive some form of aid. The average annual amount of aid from all sources combined, including scholarships, loans, and work contracts, is $24,000; maximum, $30,000. Awards are based on need and merit. Required financial statement is the FAFSA. The aid application deadline for fall entry is open. Special funds for minority or disadvantaged students consist of need-based scholarship awards. First-year students are notified about their financial aid application at time of acceptance.

About the Law School

University of Tulsa College of Law was established in 1923 and is a private institution. The 160-acre campus is in a suburban area 3 miles east of Tulsa. The primary mission of the law school is to provide an education responsive to the legal affairs of the country, particularly in the areas of energy development, natural resources, environmental ethics, international and comparative law, dispute resolution, American Indian law and history, health law, and public policy and regulation. Students have access to federal, state, county, city, and local agencies, courts, correctional facilities, law firms, and legal aid organizations in the Tulsa area. Housing for students is available in dormitories and university apartments. Accommodations are available in non-university facilities at reasonable cost. All law school facilities are accessible to the physically disabled.

Calendar

The law school operates on a traditional semester basis. Courses for full-time students are offered both day and evening and must be completed within 3 years. For part-time students, courses are offered both day and evening and must be completed within 5 years. New full- and part-time students are admitted in the fall and spring. There is an 8-week summer session. Transferable summer courses are offered.

Programs

In addition to the J.D., the law school offers the LL.M. Students may take relevant courses in other programs and apply credit toward the J.D.; a maximum of 6 credits may be applied. The following joint degrees may be earned: J.D./M.A. (Juris Doctor/Master of Arts in anthropology, history, psychology, and English), J.D./M.B.A. (Juris Doctor/Master of Business Administration), and J.D./M.S. (Juris Doctor/Master of Science in biological sciences, geosciences, taxation, and accountancy).

Required

To earn the J.D., candidates must complete 88 total credits, of which 42 are for required courses. They must maintain a minimum GPA of 2.0 in the required courses. The following first-year courses are required of all students: Civil Procedure I and II, Contracts I and II, Criminal Law and Administration, Legal Authorities, Introduction to Legal Reasoning and Writing, Torts, Property I and II, and Legal Reasoning and Writing. Required upper-level courses consist of Constitutional Law I and II, Introduction to Appellate Advocacy, and electives. The required orientation program for first-year students is the week-long Legal Authorities course. It starts 1 week before the beginning of other courses.

Phone: 918-631-2709
Fax: 918-631-3630
E-mail: *george-justice@utulsa.edu*
Web: *www.utulsa.edu/law*

Contact

George Justice, Assistant Dean, 918-631-2709 for general inquiries; Kristi Emerson, Assistant Director of Financial Aid, 918-631-3325 for financial aid information.

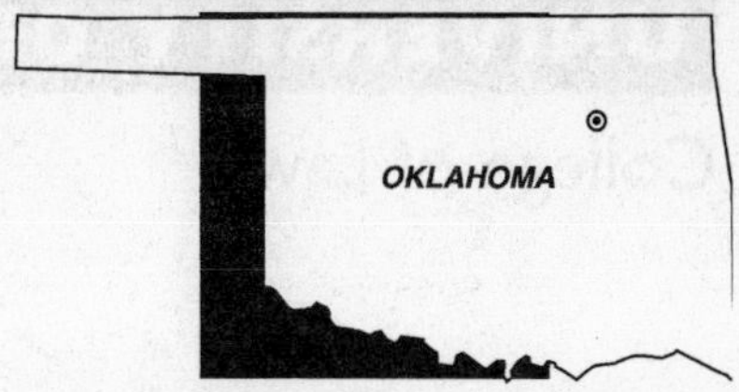

Electives

The College of Law offers concentrations in corporate law, criminal law, environmental law, family law, international law, juvenile law, labor law, litigation, securities law, sports law, tax law, torts and insurance, Indian law, health law, and lawyering skills. At the University of Tulsa Legal Clinic, students represent needy clients in a variety of civil cases. All students are supervised by a faculty member, and credit is offered. The Neighbor-to-Neighbor clinic offers the opportunity to provide volunteer assistance to low-income clients on issues such as landlord-tenant, consumer fraud, benefit problems, and domestic disputes. Seminars offered have a limited enrollment. Topics include banking, corrections, and criminal justice. Through the college's Legal Internship Program, students may obtain academic credit for practical experience gained under the supervision of practicing attorneys and the college. The Judicial Internships program offers students supervised educational experience in the Oklahoma District Court, Oklahoma Court of Appeals, U.S. District Court, U.S. Magistrate's Office, and U.S. Bankruptcy Court. There are also advanced appellate advocacy, law journal, and legal internships. Qualified students may pursue independent study in specific areas of the law under the supervision of 2 law professors. In addition, all entering students are invited to participate in the Enrichment Program, an orientation program developed by the college and the BLSA. Minority programs include the Indian Law Certificate, in which students learn to do legal work on issues of importance to Native Americans. The Comparative and International Law Center coordinates and develops activities related to study and research in international law and teaching and research. The Center on Dispute Resolution offers a resource for students, attorneys, judges, and the general public in the field of dispute resolution.

Graduation Requirements

In order to graduate, candidates must have a GPA of 2.0 and have completed the upper-division writing requirement.

Organizations

Students edit the *Tulsa Law Journal*, *Energy Law Journal*, *International Law Journal*, and the newspaper *Baculus*. The First Board of Advocates sponsors 7 moot court competitions, including the first-year Client Counseling, Client Counseling (regional and national), and ABA Negotiation (regional and national). Student organizations include ABA-Law Student Division, Federalist Society, and Student Bar Association. Campus clubs and other organizations include Native American Law Student Association, Black Law Student Association, and Hispanic Law Student Association. There are local chapters of Delta Theta Phi, Phi Alpha Delta, and Phi Delta Phi.

Library

The law library contains 290,669 hardcopy volumes and 688,772 microform volume equivalents, and subscribes to 4059 serial publications. Such on-line databases and networks as DIALOG, LEXIS, NEXIS, and WESTLAW are available to law students for research. Special library collections include literature and information on environmental law and Indian law. Recently, the College of Law completed construction of a major addition to the law library, the Mabee Legal Information Center. Existing library space was completely renovated, and two additional floors were constructed. The addition permits the College of Law to nearly double its library collection space, increase seating capacity to accommodate the entire student body, introduce expanded technologies, provide additional facilities for law school programs, and offer more services to members of Tulsa's professional legal community who use the library extensively. The ratio of library volumes to faculty is 10,765 to 1 and to students is 553 to 1. The ratio of seats in the library to students is 1 to 1.

Faculty

The law school has 27 full-time and 28 part-time faculty members, of whom 19 are women. According to AAUP standards for Category IIA institutions, faculty salaries are above average. About 50% of full-time faculty have a graduate law degree in addition to the J.D.; about 13% of part-time faculty have one. The ratio of full-time students to full-time faculty in an average class is 20 to 1; in a clinic, 6 to 1. The law school has a regular program of bringing visiting professors and other distinguished lecturers and visitors to campus.

Placement

Placement	
J.D.s awarded:	180
Services available through: a separate law school placement center and the university placement center	
Services: seminars and panel presentations on various aspects of law practice and career options.	
Special features: video library and taping equipment; the *Career Counseling Handbook*; and career services library resources, including directories, reference books, computer terminals, equipped with WESTLAW, LEXIS, the Internet, and word-processing software, job advertisements, periodicals, and job sharing with 99 other law schools.	
Full-time job interviews:	10 employers
Summer job interviews:	20 employers
Placement by graduation:	49% of class
Placement within 9 months:	81% of class
Average starting salary:	$42,000
Areas of placement:	
Private practice 2-10 attorneys	40%
Private practice 11-25 attorneys	4%
Private practice 26-50 attorneys	2%
Private practice 51-100 attorneys	1%
Business/industry	25%
Government	11%
Unknown	9%
Public interest	4%
Judicial clerkships	2%
Military	2%

Students

About 35% of the student body are women; 13%, minorities; 6%, African American; 3%, Asian American; 4%, Hispanic; and 9%, Native American. Most students come from Oklahoma (47%). The average age of entering students is 27; age range is 20 to 58. About 40% of students enter directly from undergraduate school, 11% have a graduate degree, and 50% have worked full-time prior to entering law school. About 2% drop out after the first year for academic or personal reasons; 98% remain to receive a law degree.

UNIVERSITY OF UTAH

College of Law

332 South 1400 East Front Room 101
Salt Lake City, UT 84112

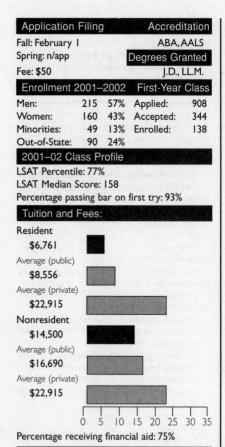

Application Filing		Accreditation
Fall: February 1		ABA, AALS
Spring: n/app		**Degrees Granted**
Fee: $50		J.D., LL.M.

Enrollment 2001–2002			First-Year Class	
Men:	215	57%	Applied:	908
Women:	160	43%	Accepted:	344
Minorities:	49	13%	Enrolled:	138
Out-of-State:	90	24%		

2001–02 Class Profile

LSAT Percentile: 77%
LSAT Median Score: 158
Percentage passing bar on first try: 93%

Tuition and Fees:

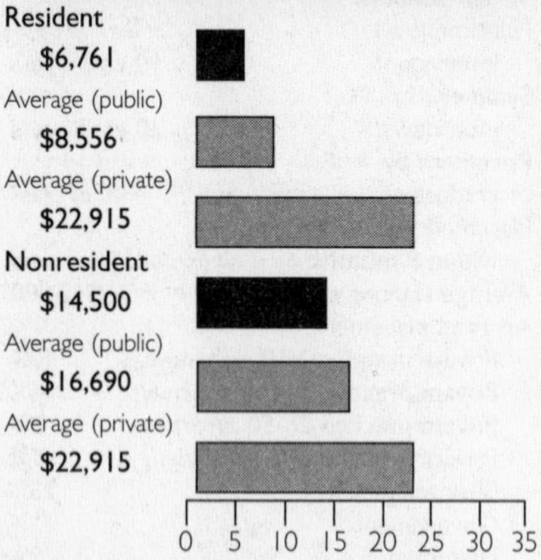

Percentage receiving financial aid: 75%

ADMISSIONS

Enrollment figures in the above capsule ae approximate. In the fall 2001 first-year class, 908 applied, 344 were accepted, and 138 enrolled. Fourteen transfers enrolled. The median LSAT percentile of the most recent first-year class was 77; the median GPA was 3.53 on a scale of 4.0. The lowest LSAT percentile accepted was 21; the highest was 99.

Requirements

Applicants must have a bachelor's degree and take the LSAT. The most important admission factors include academic achievement, writing ability, and GPA. No specific undergraduate courses are required. Candidates are not interviewed.

Procedure

The application deadline for fall entry is February 1. Applicants should submit an application form, LSAT results, transcripts, a nonrefundable application fee of $50, 1 letter of recommendation, a personal statement, and a resume. Notification of the admissions decision is from January on. The latest acceptable LSAT test date for fall entry is December. The law school uses the LSDAS.

Special

The law school recruits minority and disadvantaged students through extensive mailing to prospective applicants located through the Candidate Referral Service of LSAC and through special targeted recruitment programs. Council on Legal Opportunity fellows are recruited. Requirements are not different for out-of-state students. Transfer students must have one year of credit, have attended an ABA-approved law school, and be in the top 30% of the first-year class.

Costs

Tuition and fees for the 2001-2002 academic year are $6761 for full-time in-state students and $14,500 for out-of-state students. On-campus room and board costs about $6264 annually; books and supplies run $1200.

Financial Aid

About 75% of current law students receive some form of aid. The average annual amount of aid from all sources combined, including scholarships, loans, and work contracts, is $18,300; maximum, $25,500. Awards are based on need and merit. Required financial statements are the FAFSA and College of Law need-based scholarship application. The aid application deadline for fall entry is March 15. Special funds for minority or disadvantaged students include need and merit scholarships, stipend for a summer intern program, and tuition waivers that accompany CLEO fellowships. First-year students are notified about their financial aid application between April and June.

About the Law School

University of Utah College of Law was established in 1913 and is a public institution. The 1535-acre campus is in an urban area 1½ miles east of downtown Salt Lake City. The primary mission of the law school is to educate students to deal effectively with the complex legal, social, and ethical problems of modern society. Students have access to federal, state, county, city, and local agencies, courts, correctional facilities, law firms, and legal aid organizations in the Salt Lake City area. Facilities of special interest to law students include the library, which features individual study carrels with connections to laptop computers and extensive computing and online facilities. Housing for students is abundant and affordable on and off campus in safe neighborhoods within walking distance of campus. All law school facilities are accessible to the physically disabled.

Calendar

The law school operates on a traditional semester basis. Courses for full-time students are offered days only and must be completed within 6 semesters. There is no part-time program. New students are admitted in the fall. There are 2 6-week summer sessions. Transferable summer courses are offered.

Programs

In addition to the J.D., the law school offers the LL.M. Students may take relevant courses in other programs and apply credit toward the J.D.; a maximum of 15 credits may be applied. The following joint degrees may be earned: J.D./M.B.A. (Juris Doctor/Master of Business Administration), J.D./M.P.A. (Juris Doctor/Master of Public Administration), and others (by special arrangement).

Required

To earn the J.D., candidates must complete 88 total credits, of which 40 are for required courses. They must maintain a minimum GPA of 2.0 in the required courses. The following first-year courses are required of all students: Contracts, Torts, Property, Criminal Law, Constitutional Law, Civil Procedure, and Legal Writing and Research. Required upper-level courses consist of Advanced Constitutional Law, seminar, perspective course, and Professional Ethics. They are, however, strongly encouraged to participate.The required orientation program for first-year students is a 4-day course before classes begin to help students understand the role of law, the tasks of a lawyer, and the method of legal education and study.

Phone: 801-581-7479
800-444-8638 ext. 1-7479
Fax: 801-581-6897
E-mail: *aguilarr@law.utah.edu*
Web: *www.law.utah.edu*

Contact

Reyes Aguilar, Associate Dean, 801-581-7479 for general inquiries; Marie Eastman, Law School Financial Aid Counselor, 801-585-5828 for financial aid information.

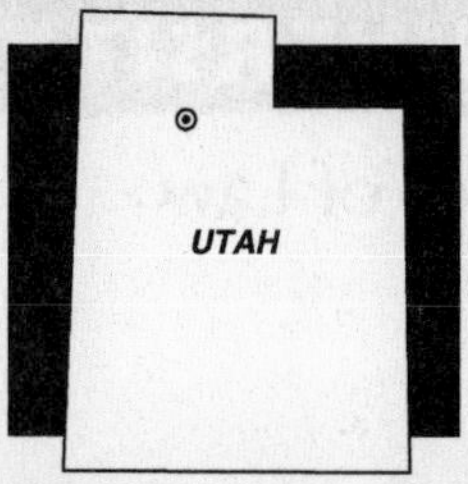

Electives

The College of Law offers concentrations in corporate law, criminal law, environmental law, family law, labor law, litigation, natural resources, public lands and energy, and constitutional law. In addition, live and simulation component clinics are offered for 2 to 4 credit hours. Clinics may be criminal, in which students work at the offices of the county attorney or Salt Lake Legal Defenders; civil, in which students represent actual clients from a public-interest law firm; or judicial, in which students act as law clerks to state and federal judges. In seminars, students perform closely supervised research, analysis, and writing. Topics have included American Legal History, Appellate Advocacy, Civil Rights, and Law and Economics. Students may spend a semester as full-time law clerks in the Judical Extern Program as part of the Judicial Clinic. Numerous opportunites exist for students to be paid as research assistants for faculty, or to undertake directed research for credit or advanced legal research courses. Field placements with a public interest law office, Utah Legal Services, Legal Aid Society of Salt Lake, Legal Center for People with Disabilities, Catholic Community Services, and the ACLU are part of the clinical program. Special lecture series include the Leary Lecture, Fordham Debate, Distinguished Jurist in Residence, Law Review Symposium, and the Natural Resources Law Forum. Study abroad is possible for upper-level students in the London Law Consortium, a 1-semester, ABA-approved program. The Academic Support Program is available for eligible students and includes a legal process tutorial course, organized study groups, and academic counseling. The college sponsors a summer intern program, funded with private donations, for minority students. Selected students intern with major Salt Lake City law firms for 10 weeks following the completion of their first year and receive a $3000 stipend. The college has hosted and regularly recruits participants from the Council on Legal Education Opportunity summer institute. Special interest groups include the Natural Resources Law Forum and the Family Law Symposium. The most widely taken electives are Evidence, Criminal Procedure, and Business Organization.

Graduation Requirements

In order to graduate, candidates must have a GPA of 2.0 and have completed the upper-division writing requirement.

Organizations

Students edit the *Utah Law Review, Journal of Law and Family Studies, Journal of Land Resources and Environmental Law*, and the newspaper *Utah Law Forum*. Moot court competitions include the annual Traynor Moot Court and National Moot Court. In addition, several writing and research competitions are offered in connection with scholarships and awards. Law student organizations include the Natural Resources Law Forum, Women's Law Caucus, and Minority Law Caucus. Campus clubs and other organizations include Native American Law Student Association, Federalist Society, and American Inns of Court. There are local chapters of Phi Alpha Delta, Phi Delta Phi, and the Federalist Society.

Library

The law library contains 300,000 hard-copy volumes and 98,000 microform volume equivalents, and subscribes to 1280 serial publications. Such on-line databases and networks as DIALOG, LEXIS, NEXIS, and WESTLAW are available to law students for research. Special library collections include environmental and natural resources law, Utah/Western United States law, tax and commercial law, U.S. government document depository, energy and public utilities regulation, and labor and employment law. Recently, the library expanded the reference room to provide additional workstations for access to legal research databases, added shelving, and attached network nodes to study carrels. The ratio of library volumes to faculty is 10,714 to 1 and to students is 813 to 1. The ratio of seats in the library to students is 1 to 1.

Faculty

The law school has 28 full-time and 32 part-time faculty members, of whom 16 are women. According to AAUP standards for Category I institutions, faculty salaries are average. About 35% of full-time faculty have a graduate law degree in addition to the J.D. The ratio of full-time students to full-time faculty in an average class is 30 to 1; in a clinic, 12 to 1. The law school has a regular program of bringing visiting professors and other distinguished lecturers and visitors to campus. There is a chapter of the Order of the Coif; 15 faculty and 10 graduates are members.

Placement

J.D.s awarded:	125
Services available through: a separate law school placement center	
Services: pro bono initiative	
Special features: Computer-maintained records of current and former students may be transmitted to prospective employers to facilitate both on- and off-campus recruiting. The Legal Career Services Office offers personal counseling, maintains a resource library, and sponsors seminars to aid students in their self-directed job search.	
Full-time job interviews:	n/av
Summer job interviews:	70 employers
Placement by graduation:	71% of class
Placement within 9 months:	96% of class
Average starting salary:	$19,000 to $150,000
Areas of placement:	
Private practice 2-10 attorneys	9%
Private practice 11-25 attorneys	22%
Private practice 26-50 attorneys	16%
Private practice 51-100 attorneys	6%
Government	17%
Judicial clerkships	16%
Business/industry	10%
Public interest	2%
Military	1%
Academic	1%

Students

About 43% of the student body are women; 13%, minorities; 2%, African American; 4%, Asian American; 7%, Hispanic; and 1%, Native American. The majority of students come from the West (79%). The average age of entering students is 28; age range is 20 to 54. About 60% of students enter directly from undergraduate school, 12% have a graduate degree, and 36% have worked full-time prior to entering law school. About 3% drop out after the first year for academic or personal reasons; 97% remain to receive a law degree.

UNIVERSITY OF VIRGINIA

School of Law

580 Massie Road
Charlottesville, VA 22903-1789

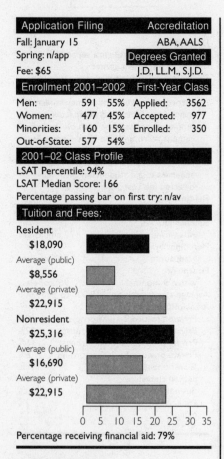

Application Filing		Accreditation
Fall: January 15		ABA, AALS
Spring: n/app		**Degrees Granted**
Fee: $65		J.D., LL.M., S.J.D.

Enrollment 2001–2002			First-Year Class	
Men:	591	55%	Applied:	3562
Women:	477	45%	Accepted:	977
Minorities:	160	15%	Enrolled:	350
Out-of-State:	577	54%		

2001–02 Class Profile

LSAT Percentile: 94%
LSAT Median Score: 166
Percentage passing bar on first try: n/av

Tuition and Fees:

Resident
$18,090
Average (public)
$8,556
Average (private)
$22,915
Nonresident
$25,316
Average (public)
$16,690
Average (private)
$22,915

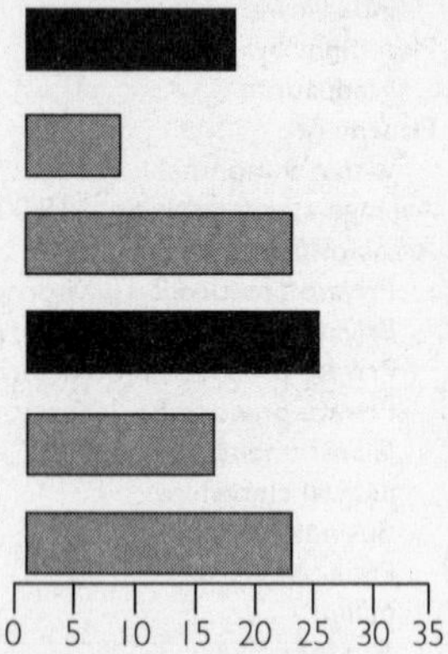

Percentage receiving financial aid: 79%

ADMISSIONS

In the fall 2001 first-year class, 3562 applied, 977 were accepted, and 350 enrolled. Twenty-one transfers enrolled. The median LSAT percentile of the most recent first-year class was 94; the median GPA was 3.64 on a scale of 4.0.

Requirements

Applicants must have a bachelor's degree and take the LSAT. Unusual training or backround is considered. No specific undergraduate courses are required. Candidates are interviewed.

Procedure

The application deadline for fall entry is January 15. Applicants should submit an application form, LSAT results, transcripts, a nonrefundable application fee of $65, 2 letters of recommendation, a personal statement, and a dean's certification form. Notification of the admissions decision is by April 15. The latest acceptable LSAT test date for fall entry is December. The law school uses the LSDAS.

Special

The law school recruits minority and disadvantaged students through the Candidate Referral Service and by providing scholarship aid. Requirements are not different for out-of-state students, but in-state and out-of-state applicant pools are looked at separately. Transfer students must have one year of credit and be in the top 5% of their class.

Costs

Tuition and fees for the 2001-2002 academic year are $18,090 for full-time in-state students and $25,316 for out-of-state students. On-campus room and board costs about $11,280 annually; books and supplies run $800.

Financial Aid

About 79% of current law students receive some form of aid. The average annual amount of aid from all sources combined, including scholarships, loans, and work contracts, is $24,260. Awards are based on need and merit. Required financial statements are the FAFSA and institutional forms. The aid application deadline for fall entry is February 15. Need is an important factor in scholarship allocations. First-year students are notified about their financial aid application beginning in March.

About the Law School

University of Virginia School of Law was established in 1826 and is a public institution. The 1050-acre campus is in a suburban area 120 miles southwest of Washington D.C. and 70 miles west of Richmond. The primary mission of the law school is to help build a new dedication in society to the classic roles and skills of lawyering, and to foster an intellectual environment rich in the transmission of traditional values and character as well as immersed in new and creative legal thinking, analysis, and research. Students have access to federal, state, county, city, and local agencies, courts, correctional facilities, law firms, and legal aid organizations in the Charlottesville area. The Public Service Center and numerous student organizations offer pro bono opportunities and other practice situations. Facilities of special interest to law students include an extensive library, modern classrooms, moot courtrooms, student organization offices, lounges, computer laboratories, and outdoor gardens and recreational areas. Housing for students is available in university housing for both single and married students; the Off-Grounds Housing Office also helps students find off-campus accommodations. All law school facilities are accessible to the physically disabled.

Calendar

The law school operates on a traditional semester basis. Courses for full-time students are offered days only and must be completed within a time set on a case-by-case basis. There is no part-time program. New students are admitted in the fall. There is no summer session. Transferable summer courses are not offered.

Programs

In addition to the J.D., the law school offers the LL.M., S.J.D., and LL.M. in the Judicial Process. Students may take relevant courses in other programs and apply credit toward the J.D.; a maximum of 12 credits may be applied. The following joint degrees may be earned: J.D./M.A. (Juris Doctor/Master of Arts in several areas), J.D./M.B.A. (Juris Doctor/Master of Business Administration), J.D./M.P. (Juris Doctor/Master of Planning with the Architecture School), and J.D./M.S. (Juris Doctor/Master of Science in accounting).

Phone: 804-924-7351
Fax: 804-982-2128
E-mail: *lawadmit@virginia.edu*
Web: *http://www.law.virginia.edu*

Contact

Elaine M. Hadden, Associate Dean, 434-924-7343 for general inquiries; Jerome Stokes, Assistant Dean, 434-924-7805 for financial aid information.

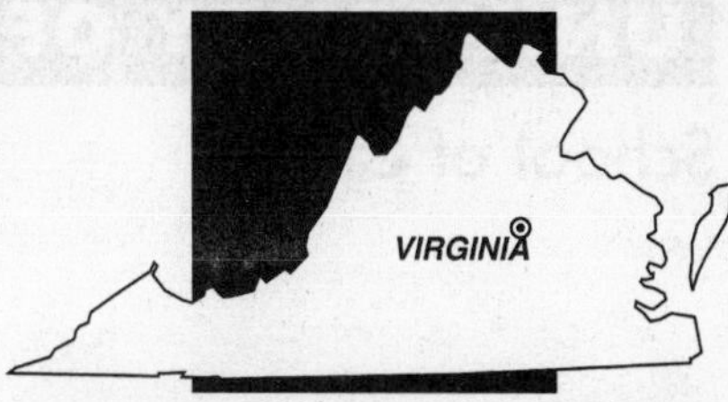

Required

To earn the J.D., candidates must complete 86 total credits, of which 27 are for required courses. They must maintain a minimum GPA of 2.3 in the required courses. The following first-year courses are required of all students: Criminal Law, Civil Procedure, Constitutional Law, Contracts, Property, Torts, and Legal Writing. Required upper-level courses consist of Professional Responsibility and a writing requirement. The required orientation program for first-year students is one day, scheduled the week classes begin.

Electives

The School of Law offers concentrations in corporate law, criminal law, family law, international law, labor law, litigation, media law, tax law, administrative law and regulations, business organizations and finance, commercial, constitutional, health, human rights and civil liberties, intellectual property, legal history, jurisprudence and comparative law. In addition, clinical offerings include the family law clinic, criminal practice clinic, and housing law. More than 80 seminar offerings are available each year, two-thirds taught by full-time faculty. A special program of seminars in ethical values is also offered. Students may work with local judges in the surrounding jurisdictions, in commonwealth attorneys' offices, and with public defenders. Students may also work with individual faculty on independent research projects and may also assist faculty in research and publication projects. There are numerous special lecture series held throughout the year, including the Contemporary Legal Thought series. Students may also gain experience through the University of Virginia's Legal Assistance Society, the Post-Conviction Assistance Project, the John M. Olin Program in Law and Economics, the Center for Oceans Law and Policy, the Institute of Law, Psychiatry, and Public Policy, the Center for Environmental Studies, and the Center for National Security Law. The most widely taken electives are Corporations, Evidence, and Federal Income Tax I.

Graduation Requirements

In order to graduate, candidates must have a GPA of 2.3 and have completed the upper-division writing requirement.

Organizations

Students edit the *Virginia Law Review; Virginia Tax Review; Virginia Environmental Law Journal; Virginia Journal of International Law*, the oldest continuously published student-edited international law review in the country; *Journal of Law and Politics; Virginia Journal of Social Policy and the Law; Journal of Law and Technology; Virginia Sports and Entertainment Law Journal*; and the newspaper *Virginia Law Weekly*. Students participate in in-house, intramural, and national competitions with more than 100 teams entered in the William Minor Lile moot court competition. Law student organizations include the John B. Moore Society of International Law, Environmental Law Forum, and Student Bar Association. National societies with chapters on campus are Delta Theta Phi, Phi Alpha Delta, and Phi Delta Phi.

Library

The law library contains 827,768 hard-copy volumes and 1,174,043 microform volume equivalents, and subscribes to 12,192 serial publications. Such on-line databases and networks as DIALOG, Infotrac, Legal-Trac, LEXIS, WESTLAW are available to law students for research. Special library collections include oceans law and historic preservation law materials as well as U.S. government documents. Recently, the library added a 3-story main reading room, expanded space with updated furnishings and more seating, and installed additional computer terminals. The ratio of library volumes to faculty is 11,825 to 1 and to students is 775 to 1. The ratio of seats in the library to students is 1 to 1.

Faculty

The law school has 70 full-time and 59 part-time faculty members, of whom 22 are women. According to AAUP standards for Category I institutions, faculty salaries are well above average. The law school has a regular program of bringing visiting professors and other distinguished lecturers and visitors to campus. There is a chapter of the Order of the Coif; 1250 graduates are members.

Placement

J.D.s awarded:	359
Services available through: a separate law school placement center	
Special features: Computer network-based information on law firms and other employment opportunities, on-line interview sign-ups, and an extensive public service opportunities database. There is also an active and extensive national alumni network.	
Full-time job interviews:	500 employers
Summer job interviews:	850 employers
Placement by graduation:	97% of class
Placement within 9 months:	100% of class
Average starting salary:	$32,000 to $145,000
Areas of placement:	
Unknown	76%
Judicial clerkships	17%
Government	2%
Business/industry	2%
Military	2%
Public interest	1%

Students

About 45% of the student body are women; 15%, minorities; 7%, African American; 6%, Asian American; 2%, Hispanic; and 1%, Native American. Most students come from Virginia (46%). The average age of entering students is 24; age range is 21 to 44. About 9% of students have a graduate degree.

UNIVERSITY OF WASHINGTON

School of Law

1100 Northeast Campus Parkway
Seattle, WA 98105-6617

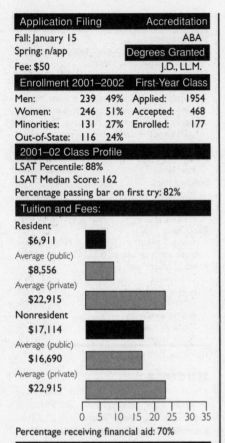

Application Filing		Accreditation
Fall: January 15		ABA
Spring: n/app		**Degrees Granted**
Fee: $50		J.D., LL.M.

Enrollment 2001–2002			First-Year Class	
Men:	239	49%	Applied:	1954
Women:	246	51%	Accepted:	468
Minorities:	131	27%	Enrolled:	177
Out-of-State:	116	24%		

2001–02 Class Profile

LSAT Percentile: 88%
LSAT Median Score: 162
Percentage passing bar on first try: 82%

Tuition and Fees:

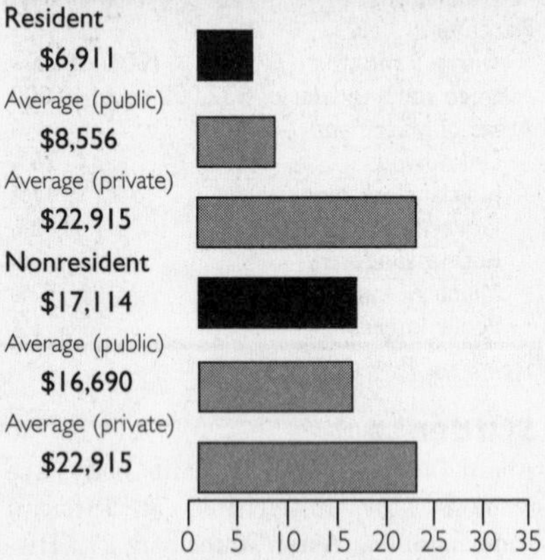

Percentage receiving financial aid: 70%

ADMISSIONS

In the fall 2001 first-year class, 1954 applied, 468 were accepted, and 177 enrolled. Two transfers enrolled. The median LSAT percentile of the most recent first-year class was 88; the median GPA was 3.62 on a scale of 4.0. The lowest LSAT percentile accepted was 138; the highest was 175.

Requirements

Applicants must have a bachelor's degree and take the LSAT. The most important admission factors include LSAT results, GPA, and academic achievement. No specific undergraduate courses are required. Candidates are not interviewed.

Procedure

The application deadline for fall entry is January 15. Applicants should submit an application form, LSAT results, transcripts, a nonrefundable application fee of $50, 2 optional letters of recommendation, a dean's certificate, and a personal statement. Notification of the admissions decision is April 1. The latest acceptable LSAT test date for fall entry is December. The law school uses the LSDAS.

Special

The law school recruits minority and disadvantaged students through West Coast law fairs, Washington undergraduate schools, law forums, and personal referrals. Requirements are not different for out-of-state students. Transfer students must have one year of credit and have attended an ABA-approved law school.

Costs

Tuition and fees for the 2001-2002 academic year are $6911 for full-time in-state students and $17,114 for out-of-state students. On-campus room and board costs about $9111 annually; books and supplies run $924.

Financial Aid

About 70% of current law students receive some form of aid. The average annual amount of aid from all sources combined, including scholarships, loans, and work contracts, is $18,500; maximum, $30,134 (for nonresidents). Awards are based on need. Required financial statement is the FAFSA. The aid application deadline for fall entry is February 28. Special funds for minority or disadvantaged students include scholarships that are available from the school's privately donated scholarship funds. Scholarships are awarded based on demonstrated financial need. First-year students are notified about their financial aid application in late spring for on-time applicants who have been admitted.

About the Law School

University of Washington School of Law was established in 1899 and is a public institution. The 20-acre campus is in an urban area 3 miles from downtown Seattle. The primary mission of the law school is a commitment to excellence in teaching, scholarship, and public service. Students have access to federal, state, county, city, and local agencies, courts, correctional facilities, law firms, and legal aid organizations in the Seattle area. Facilities of special interest to law students include a well-stocked law library. Housing for students is available for single and married students to a limited degree in university housing; the Student Housing Affairs Office maintains listings of off-campus accommodations. All law school facilities are accessible to the physically disabled.

Calendar

The law school operates on a quarter basis. Courses for full-time students are offered days only and must be completed within 3 years. There is no part-time program. New students are admitted in the fall. There are 2 4-week summer sessions. Transferable summer courses are offered.

Phone: 206-543-4078
E-mail: *admissions@law.washington.edu*
Web: *www.law.washington.edu*

Contact

Kathy Swinehart, Admissions Supervisor, 206-543-4078 for general inquiries; Financial Aid Coordinator, 206-543-4552 for financial aid information.

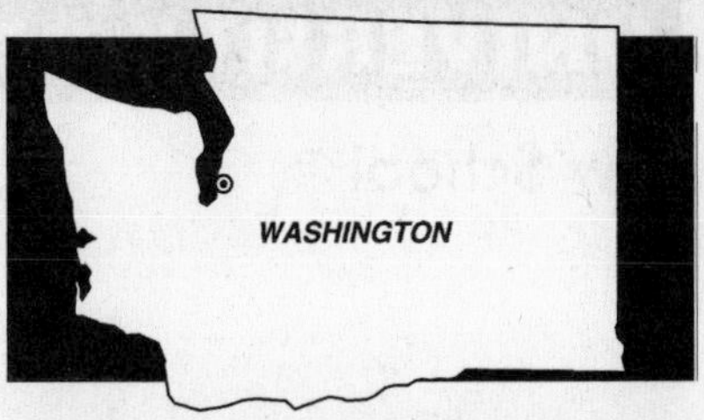

Programs

In addition to the J.D., the law school offers the LL.M. and Ph.D in Asian law. Students may take relevant courses in other programs and apply credit toward the J.D.; a maximum of 15 quarter credits credits may be applied. Joint degree programs can be set up with 90 other graduate programs at the school.

Required

To earn the J.D., candidates must complete 135 quarter total credits. The following first-year courses are required of all students: Contracts, Civil Procedure, Property, Torts, Criminal Law, Basic Legal Skills, and Constitutional Law. Required upper-level courses consist of Advanced Writing, Professional Responsibility, and 60 hours of pro bono legal work. The required orientation program for first-year students is 2 days.

Electives

The School of Law offers concentrations in corporate law, criminal law, environmental law, family law, international law, labor law, litigation, securities law, tax law, and torts and insurance. In addition, clinics open to second- and third-year students for 7 or 8 credits are available in mediation, child advocacy, unemployment, criminal law, low-income taxpayer, immigration, refugee and immigrant advocacy law, and Indian law. Seminars earning 3 to 6 credits and internships worth 1 to 15 credits are also open to second- and third-year students. Also available are independent research programs earning 1 to 6 credits. The most widely taken electives are Trial Advocacy, Payment Systems, and Evidence.

Graduation Requirements

In order to graduate, candidates must have completed the upper-division writing requirement and 9 quarters in residence.

Organizations

Students edit the *Washington Law Review*, and the *Pacific Rim and Policy Journal*. Moot court competitions include the Jessup and International Jessup. Law student organizations include the Student Bar Association, Women's Law Caucus, and Minority Law Students Association. Other organizations include International Law Society, Innocence Project Northwest, and Public Interest Law Association.

Library

The law library contains 539,771 hard-copy volumes and 163,030 microform volume equivalents, and subscribes to 1559 serial publications. Such on-line databases and networks as LEXIS, WESTLAW, and full Internet access are available to law students for research. Special library collections include Japanese and other East Asian law materials. The library has been designated as a depository for U.S. government documents. The ratio of library volumes to faculty is 12,533 to 1 and to students is 1113 to 1. The ratio of seats in the library to students is 1 to 2.

Faculty

The law school has 43 full-time faculty members, of whom 14 are women. According to AAUP standards for Category I institutions, faculty salaries are above average. About 25% of full-time faculty have a graduate law degree in addition to the J.D. The ratio of full-time students to full-time faculty in an average class is 18 to 1. The law school has a regular program of bringing visiting professors and other distinguished lecturers and visitors to campus. There is a chapter of the Order of the Coif.

Students

About 51% of the student body are women; 27%, minorities; 3%, African American; 15%, Asian American; 8%, Hispanic; and 3%, Native American. The majority of students come from Washington (76%). The average age of entering students is 25; age range is 17 to 50. About 20% of students enter directly from undergraduate school, 20% have a graduate degree, and 70% have worked full-time prior to entering law school. About 2% drop out after the first year for academic or personal reasons; 98% remain to receive a law degree.

Placement

J.D.s awarded:	151
Services available through: a separate law school placement center	
Special features: first-year student job workshops, first-year student mock interview program, and other career programs throughout the school year.	
Full-time job interviews:	32 employers
Summer job interviews:	79 employers
Placement by graduation:	82% of class
Placement within 9 months:	96% of class
Average starting salary:	$35,000 to $80,000
Areas of placement:	
Private practice 2-10 attorneys	6%
Private practice 11-25 attorneys	6%
Private practice 26-50 attorneys	7%
Private practice 51-100 attorneys	7%
Unknown	20%
Government	19%
Judicial clerkships	16%
Business/industry	7%
Public interest	6%
Military	1%
Academic	1%

UNIVERSITY OF WISCONSIN

Law School

975 Bascom Mall
Madison, WI 53706

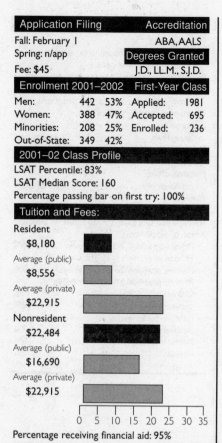

Application Filing		Accreditation
Fall: February 1		ABA, AALS
Spring: n/app		**Degrees Granted**
Fee: $45		J.D., LL.M., S.J.D.

Enrollment 2001–2002			First-Year Class	
Men:	442	53%	Applied:	1981
Women:	388	47%	Accepted:	695
Minorities:	208	25%	Enrolled:	236
Out-of-State:	349	42%		

2001–02 Class Profile

LSAT Percentile: 83%
LSAT Median Score: 160
Percentage passing bar on first try: 100%

Tuition and Fees:

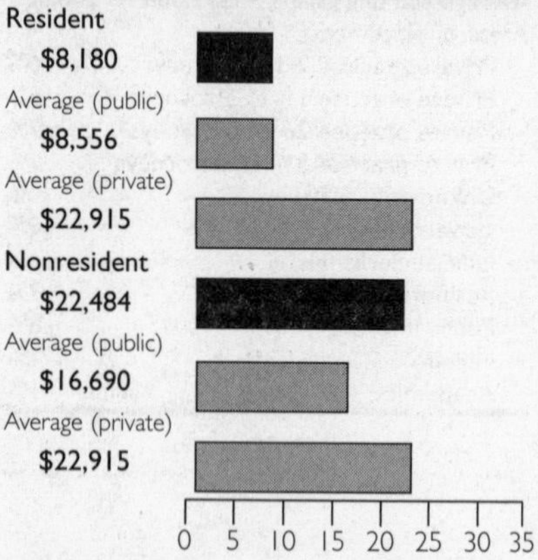

Percentage receiving financial aid: 95%

ADMISSIONS

In the fall 2001 first-year class, 1981 applied, 695 were accepted, and 236 enrolled. Nine transfers enrolled. The median LSAT percentile of the most recent first-year class was 83; the median GPA was 3.38 on a scale of 4.0. The lowest LSAT percentile accepted was 23; the highest was 88.

Requirements

Applicants must have a bachelor's degree and take the LSAT. The most important admission factors include academic achievement, general background, and LSAT results. No specific undergraduate courses are required. Candidates are not interviewed.

Procedure

The application deadline for fall entry is February 1. Applicants should submit an application form, LSAT results, transcripts, a nonrefundable application fee of $45, 2 to 3 letters of recommendation, resume, and personal statement. Notification of the admissions decision is rolling admissions policy. The latest acceptable LSAT test date for fall entry is February. The law school uses the LSDAS.

Special

The law school recruits minority and disadvantaged students through mailings, law school and graduate school days, minority career fairs, and a network of alumni and current students. Requirements are not different for out-of-state students. Transfer students must have one year of credit and have attended an ABA-approved law school. Due to enrollment pressures, transfer applications are accepted primarily on the basis of class rank in the transferring law school, or, if class rank is unavailable, on the basis of other evidence of academic performance.

Costs

Tuition and fees for the 2001-2002 academic year are $8180 for full-time in-state students and $22,484 for out-of-state students. On-campus room and board costs about $1820 annually; books and supplies run $6290.

Financial Aid

About 95% of current law students receive some form of aid. The average annual amount of aid from all sources combined, including scholarships, loans, and work contracts, is $18,500; maximum, $31,000. Awards are based on need and merit. Required financial statement is the FAFSA. The aid application deadline for fall entry is February 1. Special funds for minority or disadvantaged students are available. First-year students are notified about their financial aid application at the time they apply to law school.

About the Law School

University of Wisconsin Law School was established in 1868 and is a public institution. The 933-acre campus is in an urban area 120 miles northwest of Chicago. The primary mission of the law school is its *law-in-action* tradition. The law school pioneered the belief that law must be studied in action as it relates to society, and not in isolation. The law school focuses on helping its students understand how law both affects and is affected by every other institutional force in society. Students have access to federal, state, county, city, and local agencies, courts, correctional facilities, law firms, and legal aid organizations in the Madison area. All of the resources of the University of Wisconsin, including educational, cultural, and social opportunities, are available to law students. Facilities of special interest to law students include the state capitol, state supreme court, federal district court, and county court located in Madison, less than 1 mile from the law school. Housing for students is available at the university, but most students live in private rental property close to campus. All law school facilities are accessible to the physically disabled.

Calendar

The law school operates on a traditional semester basis. Courses for both full-time and part-time students are offered both day and evening and must be completed within 6 years. New full- and part-time students are admitted in the fall. There is a 13-week summer session. Transferable summer courses are offered.

Programs

In addition to the J.D., the law school offers the LL.M., S.J.D., and M.L.I. (Master of Arts or Master of Science in Legal Institutions). Students may take relevant courses in other programs and apply credit toward the J.D.; a maximum of 6 credits, unless student credits are in a joint degree program, may be applied. The following joint degrees may be earned: (Law and Business), (Law and Environmental Studies), (Law and Industrial Relations), (Law and Latin American and Iberian Studies), (Law and Library and Information Services), (Law and Philosophy (Ph.D. level only)), (Law and Public Af-fairs), (Law and Sociology (Ph.D.) and Rural Sociology), J.D./M.B.A. (Juris Doctor/Law and Business), and others at the student's request.

Phone: 608-262-5914
Fax: 608-262-5485
E-mail: *admissions@law.wisc.educ*
Web: *www.law.wisc.educ*

Contact

Heather Check, Admissions Coordinator, 608-262-5914 for general inquiries; Dorothy Davis, 608-262-1815 for financial aid information.

Required

To earn the J.D., candidates must complete 90 total credits, of which 30 to 31 are for required courses. They must maintain a minimum grade average of 77 in the required courses. The following first-year courses are required of all students: Contracts, Introduction to Substantive Criminal Law, Civil Procedure, Criminal Procedure, Torts, Legal Research and Writing, and Property. Other required courses consist of Legal Process and Professional Responsibilities. An extensive selection of clinical courses is available for students who wish to participate.The required orientation program for first-year students is a 3-day program that includes a check-in with the Admissions Office staff, community service day, case briefing workshop, first-year convocation, informal gatherings, and student photos.

Electives

The Law School offers concentrations in corporate law, criminal law, environmental law, family law, international law, juvenile law, labor law, litigation, securities law, torts and insurance, public interest law; intellectual property; and estate planning. In addition, clinics include Legal Assistance to Institutionalized Persons, Legal Defense Project, and Labor Law. Numerous seminars are available, as well as internships, research programs, field work, tutorial programs, and special interest group programs. Study abroad is possible through the Germany, Holland, Italy, Chile, South Africa, and Asia programs. An individualized instruction service, offering writing assistance, workshops on study skills, test taking, time management, research papers, and other topics, is available to all students. The Legal Education Opportunities Program is available for students of color. Many special interest programs are available. The most widely taken electives are Evidence, Business Organizations, and Trusts and Estates.

Graduation Requirements

In order to graduate, candidates must have a grade average of 77 and graduates who meet certain course requirements are admitted to the bar without taking a bar examination. An upper-division writing requirement is recommended.

Organizations

Students edit the *Wisconsin Law Review, Environmental Law Journal, Wisconsin International Law Journal, Women's Law Journal*, and the creative writing journal *Praxis*. Moot court competitions include the Philip C. Jessup International Law, Evan A. Evans Constitutional Law, and Thomas Tang. There are numerous writing competitions. Law student organizations include the ABA-Law School Division, Association of Trial Lawyers of America-Student Division, and National Lawyers Guild. Other law student organizations include Intellectual Property Students Association, Wisconsin Public Interest Law Foundation, and Business and Tax Law Association. Campus clubs include Black Law Students, Indian Law Students, and Latino Law Students Associations.

Library

The law library contains 513,573 hard-copy volumes and 812,276 microform volume equivalents, and subscribes to 4694 serial publications. Such on-line databases and networks as CALI, CIS Universe, DIALOG, Legal-Trac, LEXIS, LOIS, NEXIS, OCLC First Search, WESTLAW, Wilsonline Indexes, and local and Internet access to a wide range of resources are available to law students for research. Special library collections include criminal justice, foreign and international law materials, and a federal depository. Recently, the library was expanded and redesigned, and added staff and additional resources to the student computer lab. The ratio of library volumes to faculty is 10,699 to 1 and to students is 619 to 1. The ratio of seats in the library to students is 1 to 1.

Faculty

The law school has 48 full-time faculty members, of whom 13 are women. According to AAUP standards for Category I institutions, faculty salaries are well above average. About 4% of full-time faculty have a graduate law degree in addition to the J.D. The ratio of full-time students to full-time faculty in an average class is 16 to 1; in a clinic, 5 to 1. The law school has a regular program of bringing visiting professors and other distinguished lecturers and visitors to campus. There is a chapter of the Order of the Coif; 44 faculty and 10% graduates are members.

Placement

J.D.s awarded:	228
Services available through: a separate law school placement center and workshops on careers in various areas of the law, including nontraditional careers; mock interviews	
Special features: The school operates a mentoring and tag-along program in cooperation with the State Bar of Wisconsin.	
Full-time job interviews:	75 employers
Summer job interviews:	100 employers
Placement by graduation:	84% of class
Placement within 9 months:	100% of class
Average starting salary:	$24,000 to $130,000
Areas of placement:	
Private practice 2-10 attorneys	21%
Private practice 11-25 attorneys	6%
Private practice 26-50 attorneys	8%
Private practice 51-100 attorneys	4%
Private practice 100+ attorneys	27%
Judicial clerkships	8%
Government	8%
Business/industry	7%
Public interest	5%
Military	2%
Academic	2%

Students

About 47% of the student body are women; 25%, minorities; 8%, African American; 10%, Asian American; 6%, Hispanic; and 4%, Native American. Most students come from Wisconsin (58%). The average age of entering students is 26; age range is 21 to 63. About 32% of students enter directly from undergraduate school, 13% have a graduate degree, and 68% have worked full-time prior to entering law school. About 1% drop out after the first year for academic or personal reasons; 99% remain to receive a law degree.

UNIVERSITY OF WYOMING

College of Law

P.O. Box 3035
Laramie, WY 82071

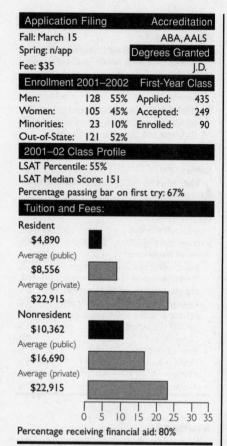

Application Filing		Accreditation
Fall: March 15		ABA, AALS
Spring: n/app		**Degrees Granted**
Fee: $35		J.D.

Enrollment 2001–2002			First-Year Class	
Men:	128	55%	Applied:	435
Women:	105	45%	Accepted:	249
Minorities:	23	10%	Enrolled:	90
Out-of-State:	121	52%		

2001–02 Class Profile

LSAT Percentile: 55%
LSAT Median Score: 151
Percentage passing bar on first try: 67%

Tuition and Fees:

Resident
$4,890
Average (public)
$8,556
Average (private)
$22,915
Nonresident
$10,362
Average (public)
$16,690
Average (private)
$22,915

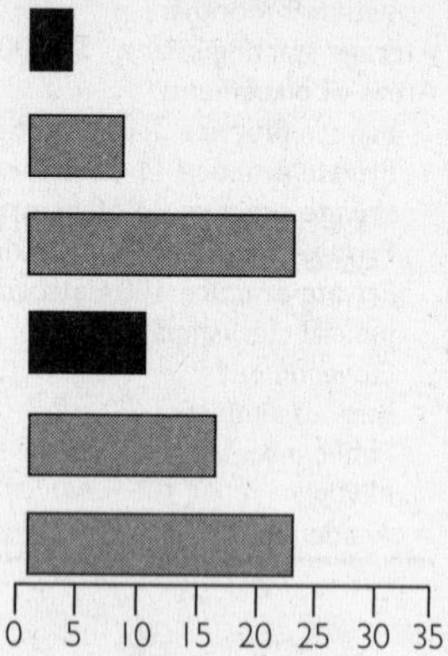

Percentage receiving financial aid: 80%

ADMISSIONS

In the fall 2001 first-year class, 435 applied, 249 were accepted, and 90 enrolled. Six transfers enrolled. The median LSAT percentile of the most recent first-year class was 55; the median GPA was 3.28 on a scale of 4.0. The lowest LSAT percentile accepted was 9; the highest was 97.

Requirements

Applicants must have a bachelor's degree and take the LSAT. The most important admission factors include academic achievement, GPA, and LSAT results. No specific undergraduate courses are required. Candidates are not interviewed.

Procedure

The application deadline for fall entry is March 15. Applicants should submit an application form, LSAT results, transcripts, a nonrefundable application fee of $35, and up to 2 letters of recommendation. Notification of the admissions decision is on a rolling basis, beginning in February. The latest acceptable LSAT test date for fall entry is February. The law school uses the LSDAS.

Special

The law school recruits minority and disadvantaged students by soliciting applications and hosting a law day session for minority undergraduate students at the university. Requirements are not different for out-of-state students. Transfer students must have one year of credit, have a minimum GPA of 2, have attended an ABA-approved law school, and have evidence of academic distinction.

Costs

Tuition and fees for the 2001-2002 academic year are $4890 for full-time in-state students and $10,362 for out-of-state students. On-campus room and board costs about $4744 annually; books and supplies run $700.

Financial Aid

About 80% of current law students receive some form of aid. The average annual amount of aid from all sources combined, including scholarships, loans, and work contracts, is $10,200. Awards are based on need and merit. Required financial statement is the FAFSA. The aid application deadline for fall entry is February 1. Special funds for minority or disadvantaged students consist of minority graduate assistantships offered on a competitive basis. First-year students are notified about their financial aid application at time of acceptance.

About the Law School

University of Wyoming College of Law was established in 1920 and is a public institution. The 735-acre campus is in a small town 125 miles north of Denver, Colorado. The primary mission of the law school is to provide students with the knowledge and training necessary to meet the responsibilities of the profession; students must secure a broad and basic knowlege of legal principles, understand the social and economic factors underlying these principles, and learn to judge the effectiveness of these principles in solving client and societal problems. Students have access to federal, state, county, city, and local agencies, courts, correctional facilities, law firms, and legal aid organizations in the Laramie area. Housing for students is available in a university residence hall for single students. The university also maintains 2-bedroom furnished apartments for married students. About 95% of the law school facilities are accessible to the physically disabled.

Calendar

The law school operates on a traditional semester basis. Courses for full-time students are offered days only and must be completed within 3 years. There is no part-time program. New students are admitted in the fall. There is no summer session. Transferable summer courses are not offered.

Phone: 307-766-6416
E-mail: *lawadmis@uwyo.edu*
Web: *uwyo.edu/law*

Contact

Robyn Kniffen, Coordinator of Admissions, 307-766-6416 for general inquiries; Office of Student Financial Aid, 307-766-2116 for financial aid information.

Programs

Students may take relevant courses in other programs and apply credit toward the J.D.; a maximum of 6 credits may be applied. The following joint degrees may be earned: J.D./M.P.A. (Juris Doctor/Master of Public Administration).

Required

To earn the J.D., candidates must complete 88 total credits, of which 51 are for required courses. They must maintain a minimum GPA of 2.0 in the required courses. The following first-year courses are required of all students: Contracts I and II, Property I and II, Torts I and II, Criminal Law, Legal Writing and Research, Appellate Advocacy, Civil Procedure I, and Constitutional Law I. Required upper-level courses consist of Civil Procedure II, Constitutional Law II, Evidence, Professional Responsibility, and an advanced writing requirement. Students must complete 2 of the following 3 courses: Administrative Law, Business Organizations, Trusts and Estates. Students must complete 1 of the following 3 courses: Creditors' Rights, Income Taxation, and Secured Transactions. The first-year orientation program is a 1-day program including lectures on legal analysis, legal reasoning, the study of law, and case briefing sessions.

Electives

The College of Law offers concentrations in corporate law, environmental law, and litigation. In addition, Defender Aid, Legal Services, and Prosecution Assistance programs are available to third-year students; 1 clinic per semester may be taken for 3 credit hours. In order to graduate, the advanced writing requirement must be fulfilled; a variety of seminars that meet this requirement is offered for 1 to 2 credits. Second- and third-year students may participate in the externship program for 1 or 2 credit hours per semester. Externs are placed with the Wyoming Attorney General's Office, Wyoming Supreme Court, State Department of Revenue and Taxation, the U.S. District Court and Wyoming state courts. A retention program is offered each spring to first-year students who have GPAs near or below 2.0 after the first semester. The most widely taken electives are Trial Practice, Family Law, and Trusts and Estates.

Graduation Requirements

In order to graduate, candidates must have a GPA of 2.0 and have completed the upper-division writing requirement.

Organizations

Students edit the *Wyoming Law Review*. Moot court competitions include the National Moot Court, National Environmental Law Moot Court at Pace University, and Natural Resources Law Moot Court at the University of Denver. Other competitions include the National Client Counseling and the ATLA Student Trial Advocacy. Law student oraganizations include the Potter Law Club, Natural Resources Law Forum, and Women's Law Forum. There are local chapters of Phi Alpha Delta, Phi Delta Phi, and Delta Theta Phi.

Library

The law library contains 274,178 hard-copy volumes and 137,574 microform volume equivalents, and subscribes to 3031 serial publications. Such on-line databases and networks as DIALOG, LEXIS, and WESTLAW are available to law students for research. Special library collections include a selective government depository and a Roman law collection. Recently, the library increased the number of WESTLAW and LEXIS terminals. The ratio of library volumes to faculty is 19,584 to 1 and to students is 1177 to 1. The ratio of seats in the library to students is 1 to 1.

Faculty

The law school has 14 full-time faculty members, of whom 7 are women. According to AAUP standards for Category I institutions, faculty salaries are below average. About 6% of full-time faculty have a graduate law degree in addition to the J.D. The ratio of full-time students to full-time faculty in an average class is 25 to 1; in a clinic, 8 to 1. The law school has a regular program of bringing visiting professors and other distinguished lecturers and visitors to campus. There is a chapter of the Order of the Coif; 14 faculty are members.

Placement	
J.D.s awarded:	76
Services available through: a separate law school placement center and the university placement center	
Full-time job interviews:	10 employers
Summer job interviews:	11 employers
Placement by graduation:	n/av
Placement within 9 months:	93% of class
Average starting salary:	$18,000 to $110,000
Areas of placement:	
Private practice 2 - 100 attorneys	50%
Government	22%
Judicial clerkships	14%
Business/industry	12%
Public interest	2%

Students

About 45% of the student body are women; 10%, minorities; 1%, African American; 2%, Asian American; 4%, Hispanic; 2%, Native American; and 2%, Self-identified with LSDAS or on application as Other. The majority of students come from the West (75%). The average age of entering students is 27; age range is 20 to 51. About 35% of students enter directly from undergraduate school and 6% have a graduate degree. About 9% drop out after the first year for academic or personal reasons; 87% remain to receive a law degree (average of the last 3 years).

VALPARAISO UNIVERSITY

School of Law

Wesemann Hall
Valparaiso, IN 46383-6493

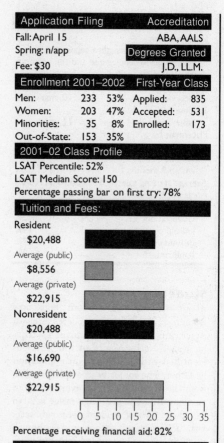

Application Filing	Accreditation
Fall: April 15	ABA, AALS
Spring: n/app	**Degrees Granted**
Fee: $30	J.D., LL.M.

Enrollment 2001–2002			First-Year Class	
Men:	233	53%	Applied:	835
Women:	203	47%	Accepted:	531
Minorities:	35	8%	Enrolled:	173
Out-of-State:	153	35%		

2001–02 Class Profile

LSAT Percentile: 52%
LSAT Median Score: 150
Percentage passing bar on first try: 78%

Tuition and Fees:

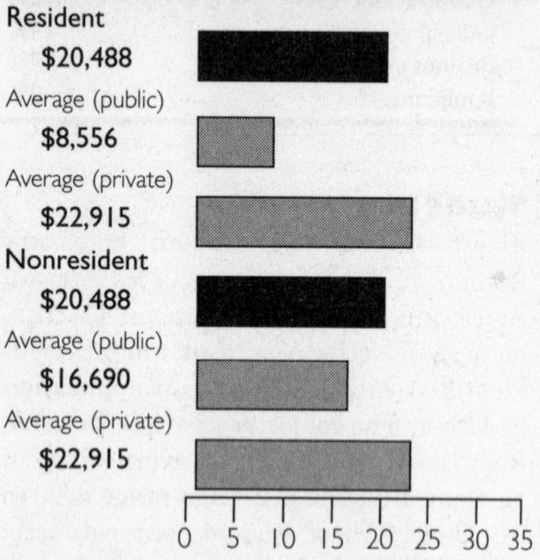

Percentage receiving financial aid: 82%

ADMISSIONS

In the fall 2001 first-year class, 835 applied, 531 were accepted, and 173 enrolled. Four transfers enrolled. The median LSAT percentile of the most recent first-year class was 52; the median GPA was 3.21 on a scale of 4.0. The lowest LSAT percentile accepted was 17; the highest was 95.

Requirements

Applicants must have a bachelor's degree and take the LSAT. The most important admission factors include academic achievement, general background, and LSAT results. No specific undergraduate courses are required. Candidates are not interviewed.

Procedure

The application deadline for fall entry is April 15. Applicants should submit an application form, LSAT results, transcripts, a nonrefundable application fee of $30, and 2 letters of recommendation. TOEFL is required of international applicants. Notification of the admissions decision is on a rolling basis. The latest acceptable LSAT test date for fall entry is February. The law school uses the LSDAS.

Special

The law school recruits minority and disadvantaged students with the assistance of the minority alumni and members of the black and Hispanic student groups, who assist the admissions office by making recruitment trips, writing letters, and making phone calls. Also, scholarships are available for qualified minority students. Requirements are not different for out-of-state students. Transfer students must have one year of credit, have a minimum GPA of 2.0, have attended an ABA-approved law school, and have their application reviewed by the admissions committee.

Costs

Tuition and fees for the 2001-2002 academic year are $20,488 for all full-time students. On-campus room and board costs about $6600 annually; books and supplies run $750.

Financial Aid

About 82% of current law students receive some form of aid. The average annual amount of aid from all sources combined, including scholarships, loans, and work contracts, is $15,000; maximum, $30,438. Awards are based on need and merit. Required financial statement is the FAFSA. The aid application deadline for fall entry is March 15. Special funds for minority or disadvantaged students are available based on academic merit and need. First-year students are notified about their financial aid application at time of acceptance and once their SAR is received.

About the Law School

Valparaiso University School of Law was established in 1879 and is a private institution. The 310-acre campus is in a suburban area 55 miles southeast of Chicago in Northwest Indiana. The primary mission of the law school is to foster a learning environment; to maintain a community of teacher-scholars committed to excellence in legal research and publication that will shape the development of the law; and to embody an interaction between demands of the law and the Lutheran heritage of Valparaiso University. Students have access to federal, state, county, city, and local agencies, courts, correctional facilities, law firms, and legal aid organizations in the Valparaiso area. Valparaiso is the county seat of Porter County. Students also have access to charitable and community organizations for volunteer/pro bono work in Porter and Lake counties, Indiana, and Cook County, Illinois (Chicago). Facilities of special interest to law students are the Wesemann Hall, which houses classrooms, a courtroom and an administrative complex; and Heritage Hall, which is listed on the National Register of historic places, housing the law clinic. Housing for students includes limited on-campus apartments; local apartments and large apartment complexes; and modest lakeside summer homes and cottages available for rent. The Admissions Office provides assistance in locating housing. About 75% of the law school facilities are accessible to the physically disabled.

Calendar

The law school operates on a traditional semester basis. Courses for both full-time and part-time students are offered both day and evening and must be completed within 5 years. New full- and part-time students are admitted in the fall. There is an 8-week summer session. Transferable summer courses are offered.

Programs

In addition to the J.D., the law school offers the LL.M. The following joint degrees may be earned: J.D./M.A. (Juris Doctor/Master of Arts in psychology and clinical mental health counseling) and J.D./M.B.A. (Juris Doctor/Master of Business Administration).

Required

To earn the J.D., candidates must complete 90 total credits, of which 46 are for required courses. They must maintain a minimum GPA of 2.0 in the required courses. The following first-year courses are required of all students: Contracts, Criminal Law, Property, Civil Procedure, Torts, Constitutional Law I, and Legal Writing, Reasoning, and Research. Required upper-level courses consist of Constitutional Law II, Jurisprudence, Legal Profession, Evidence, 1 of 7 perspective courses, 1 of 5 advanced writing courses, and a seminar. Third-year (and some second-year) law students in Indi-

Phone: 219-465-7829
888-VALPOLAW (825-7652)
Fax: 219-465-7808
E-mail: *marilyn.olson@valpo.edu*
Web: *www.valpo.edu/law/*

Contact

Marilyn R. Olson, Assistant Dean, 219-465-7829 for general inquiries; Ann Weitgenant, Financial Aid Counselor, 219-465-7818 for financial aid information.

ana are permitted to represent clients in court, under supervision. The required orientation program for first-year students is 2 days, usually the Monday and Tuesday preceeding the start of the fall semester. Formal registration and meetings with current students, deans, and faculty advisers are included.

Electives

Students must take 19 credits in their area of concentration. The School of Law offers concentrations in criminal law, entertainment law, environmental law, international law, employment/labor law, litigation, alternative dispute resolution, state and local government/civil rights, business law, elder health care, and intellectual property. In addition, clinics are available to second- and third-year students for 2 or 3 credits a semester for a maximum of 12 credit hours. A seminar is required of all third-year students not on the *Law Review*, and a substantial paper is required. Second- and third-year students may also participate in up to 15 credit hours of an extern program. The law school supports 58 externship programs. Students may assist faculty with current representation or in research assistantships in which they work one-on-one with a professor in his or her area of current interest and research. No credit is given for the 20 hours of pro bono public service. Special lecture series include the Monsanto Annual Lecture on Tort Law Reform, the annual Seegers Lecture Series, the Distinguished Visitors Program, and the annual Tabor Institute on Legal Ethics. There is a summer study-abroad program in Cambridge, England. There is also a voluntary Academic Support Program; no credit is given and participation is by invitation only. Other tutorials are led by first-year faculty with student tutors available for individual consultation. The Hispanic Law Students Association and Black Law Students Association sponsor minority programming. Special-interest group programs include the Intellectual Property Association, Health Law Association, Sports and Entertainment Law Association, Coalition for Choice, Jus Vitae, Equal Justice Alliance, Third World Legal Studies, International Law, Pastoral Ministry, ATLA, and ABA. The most widely taken electives are Trusts and Estates, Trial Advocacy, and business and commercial law courses.

Graduation Requirements

In order to graduate, candidates must have a GPA of 2.0, have completed the upper-division writing requirement, and have completed the pro bono service requirement of 20 hours, for which there is no grade or credit.

Organizations

Students edit the *Valparaiso University Law Review*. The *Third World Legal Studies* is published by the International Third World Legal Studies Association and the School of Law. The student newspaper is *The Forum*. Annually, moot court teams are sent to the Environmental Moot Court held at Pace University, the Giles Sutherland Rich Moot Court (1995 National Champions), and the Jessup International Moot Court. Other annual competitions are the Negotiations, the National Mock Trial, Association of Trial Lawyers of America, and Client Counseling. Law student organizations include the Sports and Entertainment Law Association, Midwest Environmental Law Caucus, and Christian Legal Society. Local chapters of national associations include Delta Theta Phi, Phi Alpha Delta, and Phi Delta Phi. Other groups include the Fine Arts Committee, Law Spouses Association, and Multicultural Law Students Association.

Library

The law library contains 283,803 hardcopy volumes and 774,186 microform volume equivalents, and subscribes to 2806 serial publications. Such on-line databases and networks as DIALOG, LEXIS, and WESTLAW are available to law students for research. All students are offered e-mail/Internet accounts and have access to the World Wide Web and CALI materials. Special library collections include a selected United States Government Printing Office Depository, a Readex United Nations basic law library collection, and briefs from the Indiana Supreme Court and Indiana Court of Appeals. Recently, the library expanded computer facilities; installed an integrated, automated library system; added shelving; and a staff position. The ratio of library volumes to faculty is 10,511 to 1 and to students is 651 to 1. The ratio of seats in the library to students is 1 to 8.

Placement

J.D.s awarded: 113

Services available through: a separate law school placement center

Services: annually participate in 12 job fairs, produce newsletters for students, and hold numerous seminars and workshops. Focus on personalized counseling through the "Find Your Dream Job" program. Host professional Career Day where practitioners in more than 70 legal fields come to the school to provide 1-on-1 counseling to students.

Special features: participates in NAPIL, Pro Bono Students of America, and Alliance for Justice and assists in locating intern/externships and pro bono opportunities.

Full-time job interviews:	31 employers
Summer job interviews:	40 employers
Placement by graduation:	72% of class
Placement within 9 months:	95% of class
Average starting salary:	$34,000 to $105,000

Areas of placement:

Private practice 2-10 attorneys	38%
Private practice 11-25 attorneys	11%
Private practice 26-50 attorneys	7%
Private practice 51-100 attorneys	2%
Government	12%
Unknown	11%
Judicial clerkships	7%
Business/industry	5%
Academic	3%
Public interest	2%
Military	2%

Faculty

The law school has 27 full-time and 37 part-time faculty members, of whom 24 are women. About 22% of full-time faculty have a graduate law degree in addition to the J.D. The ratio of full-time students to full-time faculty in an average class is 18 to 1; in a clinic, 8 to 1.

Students

About 47% of the student body are women; 8%, minorities; 4%, African American; 2%, Asian American; 2%, Hispanic; and 3%, International. The majority of students come from the Midwest (90%). The average age of entering students is 25; age range is 20 to 49. About 60% of students enter directly from undergraduate school and 7% have a graduate degree. About 10% drop out after the first year for academic or personal reasons; 86% remain to receive a law degree.

VANDERBILT UNIVERSITY

Law School

131 21st Avenue South
Nashville, TN 37203

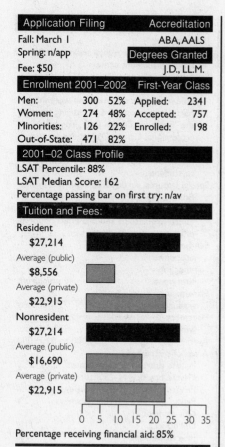

Application Filing	Accreditation
Fall: March 1	ABA, AALS
Spring: n/app	**Degrees Granted**
Fee: $50	J.D., LL.M.

Enrollment 2001–2002			First-Year Class	
Men:	300	52%	Applied:	2341
Women:	274	48%	Accepted:	757
Minorities:	126	22%	Enrolled:	198
Out-of-State:	471	82%		

2001–02 Class Profile

LSAT Percentile: 88%
LSAT Median Score: 162
Percentage passing bar on first try: n/av

Tuition and Fees:

Resident
$27,214
Average (public)
$8,556
Average (private)
$22,915
Nonresident
$27,214
Average (public)
$16,690
Average (private)
$22,915

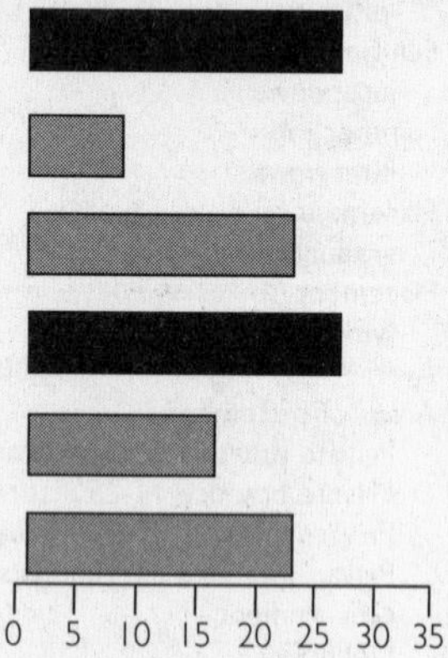

Percentage receiving financial aid: 85%

ADMISSIONS

In the fall 2001 first-year class, 2341 applied, 757 were accepted, and 198 enrolled. Twenty-two transfers enrolled. The median LSAT percentile of the most recent first-year class was 88; the median GPA was 3.68 on a scale of 4.0. The lowest LSAT percentile accepted was 22; the highest was 99.

Requirements

Applicants must have a bachelor's degree and take the LSAT. The most important admission factors include academic achievement, GPA, and LSAT results. No specific undergraduate courses are required. Candidates are not interviewed.

Procedure

The application deadline for fall entry is March 1. Applicants should submit an application form, LSAT results, transcripts, a nonrefundable application fee of $50, 2 letters of recommendation, and a personal statement. Notification of the admissions decision is by April 1. The latest acceptable LSAT test date for fall entry is February. The law school uses the LSDAS.

Special

The law school recruits minority and disadvantaged students by means of on-campus recruiting, general mailings, and LSAC Forums. Requirements are not different for out-of-state students. Transfer students must have one year of credit and have attended an ABA-approved law school. Preadmissions courses consist of none.

Costs

Tuition and fees for the 2001-2002 academic year are $27,214 for all full-time students. On-campus room and board costs about $8780 annually; books and supplies run $1256.

Financial Aid

About 85% of current law students receive some form of aid. The maximum annual amount of aid from all sources combined, including scholarships, loans, and work contracts, is $42,588. Awards are based on need and merit. Required financial statements are the CSS Profile and the FAFSA. The aid application deadline for fall entry is February 15. First-year students are notified about their financial aid application at time of acceptance.

About the Law School

Vanderbilt University Law School was established in 1874 and is a private institution. The 330-acre campus is in an urban area 1½ miles west of downtown Nashville, Tennessee. The primary mission of the law school is to educate students to become effective lawyers in a wide range of professional areas. Students have access to federal, state, county, city, and local agencies, courts, correctional facilities, law firms, and legal aid organizations in the Nashville area. Facilities of special interest to law students are local, state, and federal courts in Nashville, the state capital. Housing for students is available in off-campus and on-campus graduate facilities. All law school facilities are accessible to the physically disabled.

Calendar

The law school operates on a traditional semester basis. Courses for full-time students are offered days only and must be completed within 3 years. There is no part-time program. New students are admitted in the fall. There is no summer session. Transferable summer courses are not offered.

Programs

In addition to the J.D., the law school offers the LL.M. Students may take relevant courses in other programs and apply credit toward the J.D.; a maximum of 6 credits may be applied. The following joint degrees may be earned: J.D./M.I.V. (Juris Doctor/Master of Divinity), J.D./M.A. (Juris Doctor/Master of Arts), J.D./M.B.A. (Juris Doctor/Master of Business Administration), J.D./M.D. (Juris Doctor/Doctor of Medicine), J.D./M.T.S. (Juris Doctor/Master of Theological Studies), and J.D./Ph.D. (Juris Doctor/Doctor of Philosophy).

Phone: 615-322-6452
Fax: 615-322-1531

Contact

Sonya Smith, Assistant Dean, 615-322-6452 for general inquiries; Richelle Acker, Assistant Director of Admissions, 615-322-6452 for financial aid information.

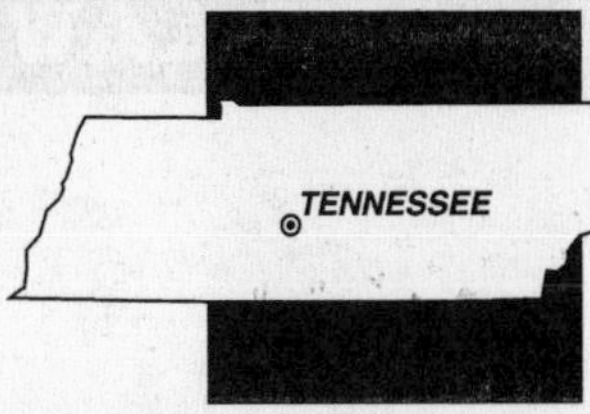

Required

To earn the J.D., candidates must complete 88 total credits, of which 37 are for required courses. They must maintain a minimum GPA of 2.0 in the required courses. The following first-year courses are required of all students: Civil Procedure, Constitutional Law, Contracts, Criminal Law, Legal Writing and Introduction to Lawyering, Property, Torts, and Legal Process and Institutions of Lawmaking. Required upper-level courses consist of Professional Responsibility. The required orientation program for first-year students consists of an informal 2-day orientation to law school; there is no academic component.

Electives

The Law School offers concentrations in law and business certificate. In addition, clinics in the areas of juvenile, family, criminal, and civil law, are elective 2- or 3-hour courses open to second- and third-year students. Many limited-enrollment courses and seminars, worth 2 or 3 credit hours, are available to second- and third-year students. Externships are available with judges and legal organizations. Research programs consist of faculty research assistantships. Several lecture series are held each year. Students may participate in summer study-abroad programs sponsored by ABA-accredited law schools. Special writing assistance is available for first-year students who need tutoring. Special interest groups include Black, Asian, Spanish-American, and Latin Law Students Associations.

Graduation Requirements

In order to graduate, candidates must have a GPA of 2.0 and have completed the upper-division writing requirement and Professional Responsibility.

Organizations

Students edit the *Vanderbilt Law Review, Journal of Transnational Law, Vanderbilt Journal of Entertainment Law and Practice*, and *VLSVENT*. Organizations that participate in moot court competitions are the National Moot Court Team, the Jessup International Moot Court Team, and the Traveling Moot Court Team. Law student organizations include the Vanderbilt Bar Association, Environmental Law Society, and the Federalist Society. There are local chapters of ABA-Law Student Division and Phi Alpha Delta.

Library

The law library contains 541,321 hard-copy volumes and 403,590 microform volume equivalents, and subscribes to 6846 serial publications. Such on-line databases and networks as DIALOG, LEXIS, NEXIS, and WESTLAW are available to law students for research. Special library collections include a federal depository and the James Cullen Looney Medico-Legal Collection. Recently, the library expanded the building, became automated, and added computers. The ratio of library volumes to faculty is 12,889 to 1 and to students is 943 to 1. The ratio of seats in the library to students is 1 to 1.

Faculty

The law school has 42 full-time and 39 part-time faculty members, of whom 23 are women. According to AAUP standards for Category I institutions, faculty salaries are above average. About 5% of full-time faculty have a graduate law degree in addition to the J.D.; about 1% of part-time faculty have one. The ratio of full-time students to full-time faculty in an average class is 15 to 1; in a clinic, 7 to 1. The law school has a regular program of bringing visiting professors and other distinguished lecturers and visitors to campus. There is a chapter of the Order of the Coif; 10 graduates are members.

Students

About 48% of the student body are women; 22%, minorities; 10%, African American; 6%, Asian American; 2%, Hispanic; and 4%, foreign nationals. The majority of students come from the South (42%). The average age of entering students is 24; age range is 21 to 53. About 60% of students enter directly from undergraduate school and 40% have worked full time prior to entering law school. About 2% drop out after the first year for academic or personal reasons; 98% remain to receive a law degree.

Placement

J.D.s awarded:	188
Services available through: a separate law school placement center	
Special features: n/av.	
Full-time job interviews:	400 employers
Summer job interviews:	400 employers
Placement by graduation:	87% of class
Placement within 9 months:	98% of class
Average starting salary:	$62,000
Areas of placement:	
Private practice 2-10 attorneys	3%
Private practice 11-25 attorneys	8%
Private practice 26-50 attorneys	15%
Private practice 51-100 attorneys	45%
Judicial clerkships	20%
Government	4%
Business/industry	2%
Academic	2%
Public interest	1%

P.O. Box 96, Chelsea Street
South Royalton, VT 05068-0096

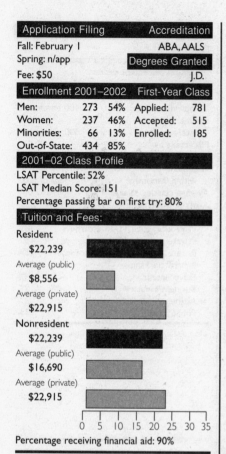

Application Filing		Accreditation
Fall: February 1		ABA, AALS
Spring: n/app		**Degrees Granted**
Fee: $50		J.D.

Enrollment 2001–2002			First-Year Class	
Men:	273	54%	Applied:	781
Women:	237	46%	Accepted:	515
Minorities:	66	13%	Enrolled:	185
Out-of-State:	434	85%		

2001–02 Class Profile

LSAT Percentile: 52%
LSAT Median Score: 151
Percentage passing bar on first try: 80%

Tuition and Fees:

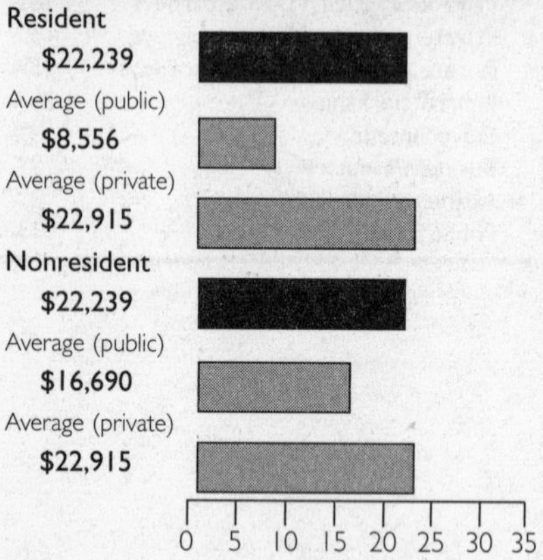

Percentage receiving financial aid: 90%

ADMISSIONS

In the fall 2001 first-year class, 781 applied, 515 were accepted, and 185 enrolled. The median LSAT percentile of the most recent first-year class was 52; the median GPA was 3 on a scale of 4.0. The lowest LSAT percentile accepted was 7; the highest was 96.

Requirements

Applicants must have a bachelor's degree and take the LSAT. The most important admission factors include academic achievement and LSAT results. No specific undergraduate courses are required. Candidates are interviewed.

Procedure

The application deadline for fall entry is February 1. Applicants should submit an application form, LSAT results, a nonrefundable application fee of $50, 2 letters of recommendation, and 3 personal statements. Notification of the admissions decision is rolling. The latest acceptable LSAT test date for fall entry is February. The law school uses the LSDAS.

Special

The law school recruits minority and disadvantaged students through the Council on Legal Education Opportunity (CLEO) program, direct mail through the Candidate Referral Service (CRS), and through participation in college minority student events and a diversity scholarship program. Requirements are not different for out-of-state students. Transfer students must be in good academic standing and eligible to return to the school from which they are transferring.

Costs

Tuition and fees for the 2001-2002 academic year are $22,239 for full-time in-state students. Books and supplies cost about $900 annually.

Financial Aid

About 90% of current law students receive some form of aid. The average annual amount of aid from all sources combined, including scholarships, loans, and work contracts, is $27,432; maximum, $37,339. All institutional aid is need-based, though some awards have a merit component. Required financial statement is the FAFSA. The aid application deadline for fall entry is February 15. Special funds for minority or disadvantaged students include the Debevoise Family Scholarship Fund, which provides grants to qualified diverse applicants from traditionally underrepresented groups with demonstrated financial need. First-year students are notified about their financial aid application as early as possible after acceptance, usually late March.

About the Law School

Vermont Law School, established in 1972, is independent. The 13-acre campus is in a small town 70 miles southeast of Burlington. The primary mission of the law school is to provide a thorough understanding of the nature and function of law in society and to equip graduates to serve their communities in positions of leadership and responsibility. The school believes lawyers should be liberally educated, ethical, competent, and committed to improving the law and its administration. Students have access to federal, state, county, city, and local agencies, courts, correctional facilities, law firms, and legal aid organizations in the South Royalton area. The South Royalton Legal Clinic is located on campus. Facilities of special interest to law students include a modern library constructed in 1992 and a new classroom building constructed in 1998. Nearby Hanover, New Hampshire, home of Dartmouth College, is a source of student cultural and social life. Child care is available on campus. Housing for students is available in private houses, apartments, or rooms in the community or nearby towns. Rental units are plentiful; the law school provides students a listing. About 75% of the law school facilities are accessible to the physically disabled.

Calendar

The law school operates on a traditional semester basis. Courses for full-time students are offered days only and must be completed within 4 years. For part-time students, courses are offered There is no part-time program. New students are admitted in the fall. There is an 8-week summer session. Transferable summer courses are offered.

Programs

In addition to the J.D., the law school offers the M.S.E.L. (Master of Studies in Environmental Law). Students may take relevant courses in other programs and apply credit toward the J.D.; a maximum of 9 credits may be applied. The following joint degrees may be earned: J.D./M.S.E.L. (Juris Doctor/Master of Studies in Environmental Law).

Required

To earn the J.D., candidates must complete 84 total credits, of which 44 are for required courses. They must maintain a minimum GPA of 2.0 in the required courses. The following first-year courses are required of all students: Civil Procedure I and II, Contracts, Introduction to the Lawyering Process, Torts, Legal Reasoning, Writing, and Research, Constitutional Law I, Criminal Law, Property, and Dispute Resolution. Required upper-level courses consist of Legal Profession, Constitutional Law II, Appellate Advocacy, 1 perspective elective, 1 skills or clinical elective, and advanced writing project. The required orientation program for first-year students is 1 week of lectures and workshops on the legal process, court systems, and sources of law, and the

Phone: 802-763-8303
888-277-5985
Fax: 802-763-7071
E-mail: *admiss@vermontlaw.edu*
Web: *www.vermontlaw.edu*

Contact

Kathy Hartman, Assiatant Dean for Admissions and Financial Aid, 802-763-8303, ext. 2239 or 888-277-5985 for general inquiries; Dino Koff, Director of Financial Aid, 802-763-8303, ext. 2235 or 888-277-5985 for financial aid information.

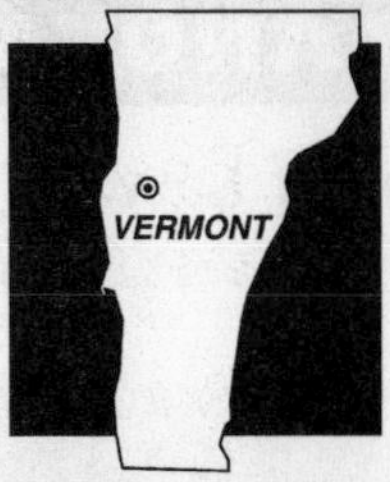

analysis and briefing of cases. It also includes an orientation to the law library, its resources and support systems, and meetings with faculty advisers.

Electives

The Vermont Law School offers concentrations in corporate law, criminal law, environmental law, family law, international law, labor law, litigation, tax law, and general practice; alternative dispute resolution; land use and real estate; and traditionally disadvantaged groups. In addition, clinics are open to second- and third-year students, but enrollment is limited. Clinics are Semester in Practice for 13 credits, Legislation Clinic for 6 credits, Environmental Semester in Washington, D.C. for 13 credits, and South Royalton Legal Clinic for 6 or 13 credits. About 20 seminars are offered annually on various topics to second- and third-year students for 2 or 3 credits each. Faculty-supervised internships are open to second- and third-year students. Credit varies and placement can be in a variety of legal settings, including private practice, government, nonprofit agencies, the judiciary, and businesses. Faculty-supervised research programs are open to second- and third-year students and culminate in a major piece of legal writing. Special lecture series include the Waterman Lectures and other lectures arranged by faculty and student organizations. There is an exchange program with McGill University, Faculty of Law in Montreal. Tutorial programs and the Program for Academic Success are offered. Workshops on topics such as time and stress management, case briefing, and exam taking are offered. Minority programs are through the Coalition for Diversity, BALSA, APALSA, NLALSA, Native American Law Society, and the Office of the Dean of Student Services and Diversity. Special interest group programs are offered through the Alliance, Animal Law League, Environmental Law Society, and other groups. The most widely taken electives are environmental law, corporations, and estates.

Graduation Requirements

In order to graduate, candidates must have a GPA of 2.0, have completed the upper-division writing requirement, the Legal Profession course, 1 perspective elective, and 1 skills or clinical elective.

Organizations

Students edit the *Vermont Law Review*, the *Environmental Law Journal*, a literary journal *Hearsay*, and the newspaper, *The Forum*. Moot court competitions include the annual Thomas M. Debevoise Moot Court, with finals argued before the Vermont Supreme Court, the annual Douglas M. Costle Environmental Moot Court, and various regional and national moot court competitions. Student organizations include the Jewish Students Group, Guardians ad Litem, and Coalition for Diversity. There are local chapters of Amnesty International, Association of Trial Lawyers of America, and Equal Justice Foundation. Campus clubs include the Barrister Bookshop, Law Partners, Chamber Music Group, Community Jazz Ensemble, Community Council, karate club, rugby club, soccer team, Ultimate Frisbee team, ice hockey team, basketball team, and softball team.

Library

The law library contains 215,000 hard-copy volumes and 95,000 microform volume equivalents, and subscribes to 1500 serial publications. Such on-line databases and networks as DIALOG, LEXIS, WESTLAW, NEXIS, ECONET, and EPIC are available to law students for research. Special library collections include environmental law, historic preservation, and alternative dispute resolution. The library added the 34,000 square-foot Cornell Library in 1992, which includes a computer room, seminar rooms, and faculty study room. The ratio of library volumes to faculty is 5972 to 1 and to students is 422 to 1. The ratio of seats in the library to students is 1 to 5.

Faculty

The law school has 36 full-time and 36 part-time faculty members, of whom 22 are women. About 20% of full-time faculty have a graduate law degree in addition to the J.D.; about 15% of part-time faculty have one. The ratio of full-time students to full-time faculty in an average class is 45 to 1; in a clinic, 6 to 1.

Placement

J.D.s awarded:	139
Services available through: a separate law school placement center	
Services: information regarding career alternatives	
Special features: Letters of application are prepared for students from an employer database, leading to computerized matching of student interests and employers. Services are characterized by individual attention, with particulary strong public interest and environmental employer listings..	
Full-time job interviews:	n/av
Summer job interviews:	n/av
Placement by graduation:	n/av
Placement within 9 months:	83% of class
Average starting salary:	$33,088 to $46,369
Areas of placement:	
Private practice 2-10 attorneys	20%
Private practice 11-25 attorneys	7%
Private practice 26-50 attorneys	9%
Private practice 51-100 attorneys	6%
Private practice 100+ attorneys	3%
Government	20%
Judicial clerkships	15%
Public interest	9%
Business/industry	7%
Military	2%
Academic	2%

Students

About 46% of the student body are women; 13%, minorities; 5%, African American; 3%, Asian American; 4%, Hispanic; 1%, Native American; and 2%, international. The majority of students come from the Northeast (50%). The average age of entering students is 26; age range is 20 to 60. About 25% of students enter directly from undergraduate school, 15% have a graduate degree and 75% have worked full-time prior to entering law school. About 8% drop out after the first year for academic or personal reasons; 92% remain to receive a law degree.

VILLANOVA UNIVERSITY

School of Law

Garey Hall
Villanova, PA 19085

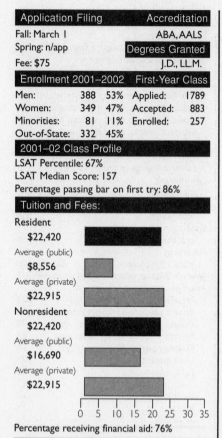

Application Filing	Accreditation
Fall: March 1	ABA, AALS
Spring: n/app	**Degrees Granted**
Fee: $75	J.D., LL.M.

Enrollment 2001–2002			First-Year Class	
Men:	388	53%	Applied:	1789
Women:	349	47%	Accepted:	883
Minorities:	81	11%	Enrolled:	257
Out-of-State:	332	45%		

2001–02 Class Profile

LSAT Percentile: 67%
LSAT Median Score: 157
Percentage passing bar on first try: 86%

Tuition and Fees:

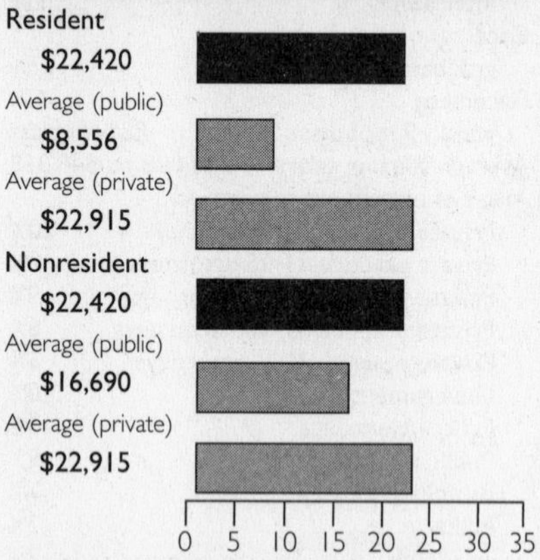

Percentage receiving financial aid: 76%

ADMISSIONS

In the fall 2001 first-year class, 1789 applied, 883 were accepted, and 257 enrolled. Twelve transfers enrolled. The median LSAT percentile of the most recent first-year class was 67; the median GPA was 3.4 on a scale of 4.0. The lowest LSAT percentile accepted was 50; the highest was 99.

Requirements

Applicants must have a bachelor's degree and take the LSAT. The most important admission factors include GPA, LSAT results, and letter of recommendation. No specific undergraduate courses are required. Candidates are not interviewed.

Procedure

The application deadline for fall entry is March 1. Applicants should submit an application form, LSAT results, transcripts, a nonrefundable application fee of $75, and A deposit is required of students after acceptance. Notification of the admissions decision is on a rolling basis beginning towards the end of December. The latest acceptable LSAT test date for fall entry is February. The law school uses the LSDAS.

Special

The law school recruits minority and disadvantaged students at LSAC forums and through the various minority student groups on campus. Requirements are not different for out-of-state students. Transfer students must have one year of credit and have attended an ABA-approved law school.

Costs

Tuition and fees for the 2001-2002 academic year are $22,420 for full-time students. Books and supplies cost about $1000 annually.

Financial Aid

About 76% of current law students receive some form of aid. The average annual amount of aid from all sources combined, including scholarships, loans, and work contracts, is $29,641; maximum, $49,767. Awards are based on need and merit. Required financial statement is the FAFSA. Special funds for minority or disadvantaged students through scholarships. First-year students are notified about their financial aid application soon after being admitted.

About the Law School

Villanova University School of Law was established in 1953 and is a private institution. The 250-acre campus is in a suburban area 15 miles west of Philadelphia. The primary mission of the law school is to provide the opportunity for students to develop an understanding of Anglo-American law in the common-law tradition as well as a knowledge of federal and state statutory and administrative developments required by the modern lawyer. The curriculum is broadly based and responsive to the needs of modern law practice. Students have access to federal, state, county, city, and local agencies, courts, correctional facilities, law firms, and legal aid organizations in the Villanova area. Facilities of special interest to law students is the library, which includes 88 Pentium computers and 21 486 computers connected to the law school network and the Internet, a microform center, and a separate facility containing the library's periodical collections. Housing for students is in off-campus apartments and other facilities. Housing is not available through the school. The university's Director of Residence Life offers to assist students in finding housing. About 90% of the law school facilities are accessible to the physically disabled.

Calendar

The law school operates on a traditional semester basis. Courses for full-time students are offered days only and must be completed within 3 years. There is no part-time program. New students are admitted in the fall. There is no summer session. Transferable summer courses are not offered.

Programs

In addition to the J.D., the law school offers the LL.M. The following joint degrees may be earned: J.D./M.B.A. (Juris Doctor/Master of Business Administration) and J.D./Ph.D. (Juris Doctor/Doctor of Philosophy in psychology).

Phone: 610-519-7010
Fax: 610-519-6291
E-mail: *admissions@law.vill.edu*
Web: *http://vls.law.vill.edu*

Contact

Assistant Dean for Admissions, 610-519-7010 for general inquiries; Wendy C. Barron,Assistant Dean for Financial Aid, 610-519-7015 for financial aid information.

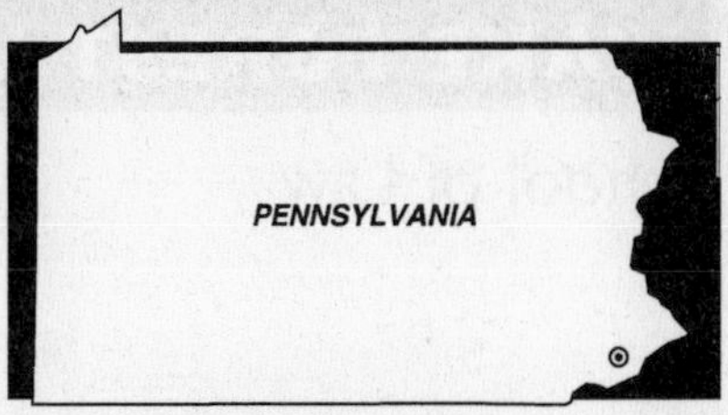

Required

To earn the J.D., candidates must complete 87 total credits, of which 44 are for required courses. The following first-year courses are required of all students: Civil Procedure, Contracts, Criminal Law, Introduction to Legal Research, Legal Writing, Property, and Torts. Required upper-level courses consist of Constitutional Law I and II, Legal Profession, a research paper course, and a practical skills/writing course, plus selection from 3 category menus. The required orientation program for first-year students is a 2-day course, Introduction to Legal Analysis and Legal Studies.

Electives

In addition, clinical offerings include Juvenile Justice, Tax, and Civil Justice Clinic. Internships/externships include U.S. Attorney (Philadelphia, Delaware); EPA, IRS, Women Against Abuse, Police Barrio Project; NJ Guardian; Philadelphia District Attorney; Judicare; and University Counsel's Office. Research assistantships are available, including special research assistants to the Reuchlein Chair. Special lecture series include the Donald A. Giannella Memorial Lecture, Law Review Symposium, Environmental Law Symposium, and Sports and Entertainment Law Symposium. The school will accept up to 6 credits from an accredited American law school summer program abroad, provided it meets the standards of the school. Academic support is provided after the first semester to students at risk. Minority programs consist of summer orientation and support throughout the student's first year. The most widely taken electives are Decedents, Corporations, and Evidence.

Graduation Requirements

In order to graduate, candidates must have a GPA of 1.7 and have completed the upper-division writing requirement.

Organizations

Law students edit the *Villanova Law Review, Villanova Environmental Law Journal, Villanova Sports and Entertainment Law Journal*, and the student newspaper *The Docket*. Annually, the school sponsors the Reimel Moot Court Competition. Other competitions include the ABA Client Interviewing and Counseling Competition, Trial Practice, and numerous moot court and trial competitions. Law student organizations include the Moot Court Board, Honor Board, and Student Bar Association. There are local chapters of Phi Delta Phi, the Black Law Student Association, and the Federalist Society. Campus clubs and other organizations include Women's Law Caucus, Public Interest Fellowship Program, and Gay-Straight Alliance.

Library

The law library contains 315,575 hard-copy volumes and 902,755 microform volume equivalents, and subscribes to 3404 serial publications. Such on-line databases and networks as CIS Universe, DIALOG, Infotrac, Legal-Trac, LEXIS, NEXIS, WESTLAW, and CCH Tax Library, RIA Checkpoint, and Social Science Research network are available to law students for research. Special library collections include a government documents depository. The ratio of library volumes to faculty is 7172 to 1 and to students is 428 to 1. The ratio of seats in the library to students is 1 to 2.

Faculty

The law school has 44 full-time and 46 part-time faculty members, of whom 30 are women. According to AAUP standards for Category IIA institutions, faculty salaries are well above average. About 29% of the full-time faculty have a graduate law degree in addition to the J.D. The ratio of full-time students to full-time faculty in an average class is 22 to 1; in a clinic, 6 to 1. The law school has a regular program of bringing visiting professors and other distinguished lecturers and visitors to campus. There is a chapter of the Order of the Coif; 35 faculty are members.

Placement

J.D.s awarded:	234
Services available through: a separate law school placement center and	
Services: sponsors career seminars and job fairs and maintains a career development and research library as well as alumni networking opportunities.	
Special features: 3 attorney-advisers on staff, 4-in-1 Interview Program, Public Interest Job Fairs, the Graduate Job Bulletin, various minority job fairs, and geographic location job fairs..	
Full-time job interviews:	100+ employers
Summer job interviews:	100+ employers
Placement by graduation:	70% of class
Placement within 9 months:	94% of class
Average starting salary:	$23,000 to $140,000
Areas of placement:	
Private practice 2-10 attorneys	12%
Private practice 11-25 attorneys	10%
Private practice 26-50 attorneys	10%
Private practice 51-100 attorneys	6%
Private practice 101+ attorneys	23%
Judicial clerkships	17%
Government	10%
Academic	6%
Business/industry	5%
Public interest	1%

Students

About 47% of the student body are women; 11%, minorities; 3%, African American; 5%, Asian American; 3%, Hispanic; and 1%, Native American. The majority of students come from Pennsylvania (55%). The average age of entering students is 23; age range is 20 to 54. About 73% of students enter directly from undergraduate school, 7% have a graduate degree, and 27% have worked full-time prior to entering law school. About 1% drop out after the first year for academic or personal reasons; 99% remain to receive a law degree.

WAKE FOREST UNIVERSITY

School of Law

P.O. Box 7206, Reynolda Station
Winston-Salem, NC 27109

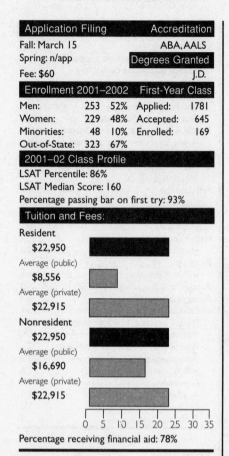

Application Filing		Accreditation
Fall: March 15		ABA, AALS
Spring: n/app		**Degrees Granted**
Fee: $60		J.D.

Enrollment 2001–2002			First-Year Class	
Men:	253	52%	Applied:	1781
Women:	229	48%	Accepted:	645
Minorities:	48	10%	Enrolled:	169
Out-of-State:	323	67%		

2001–02 Class Profile

LSAT Percentile: 86%

LSAT Median Score: 160

Percentage passing bar on first try: 93%

Tuition and Fees:

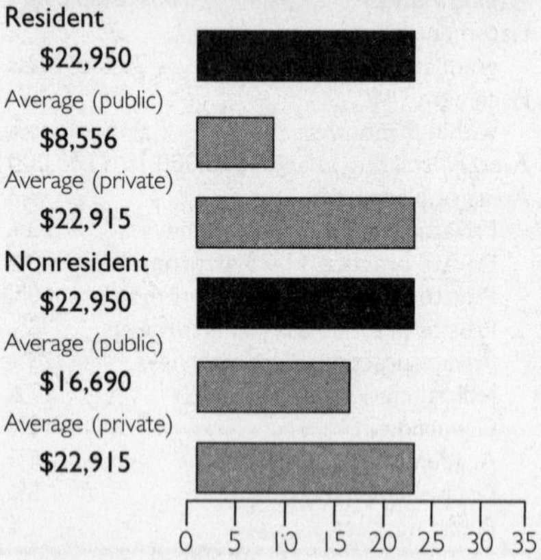

Percentage receiving financial aid: 78%

ADMISSIONS

In the fall 2001 first-year class, 1781 applied, 645 were accepted, and 169 enrolled. Eleven transfers enrolled. The median LSAT percentile of the most recent first-year class was 86; the median GPA was 3.4 on a scale of 4.0. The lowest LSAT percentile accepted was 26; the highest was 99.

Requirements

Applicants must have a bachelor's degree and take the LSAT. Important admission factors include LSAT results, GPA, and academic achievement. No specific undergraduate courses are required, but history, economics, English literature, logic, accounting, and philosophy are strongly recommended. Candidates are interviewed.

Procedure

The application deadline for fall entry is March 15. Applicants should submit an application form, LSAT results, transcripts, a nonrefundable application fee of $60, 2 letters of recommendation, and a dean's certification. Notification of the admissions decision is on a rolling basis. The latest acceptable LSAT test date for fall entry is December. The law school uses the LSDAS.

Special

The law school recruits minority and disadvantaged students through collaboration with the Black Law Students Association (BLSA), which meets with admissions on a biweekly basis and calls accepted minority candidates to discuss the school and answer questions. BLSA and the school sponsor a minority recruitment day where students visit the campus, meet with enrolled students, and attend a mock class and a moot court presentation. Also, the Placement Office works with major law firms in the state to place minority candidates for summer employment and to expedite consideration of minority applicants. Requirements are not different for out-of-state students. Transfer students must have one year of credit, have attended an ABA-approved law school and have a letter of good standing from the dean of that law school and an official transcript of first-year grades.

Costs

Tuition and fees for the 2001-2002 academic year are $22,950 for all students. Books and supplies cost about $800 annually.

Financial Aid

About 78% of current law students receive some form of aid. The average annual amount of aid from all sources combined, including scholarships, loans, and work contracts, is $25,000; maximum, $32,240. Awards are based on need and merit. Required financial statement is the FAFSA. The aid application deadline for fall entry is May 1. Special funds for minority or disadvantaged students consist of 2 full-tuition scholarships that are awarded in each entering class; candidates are eligible for all scholarships. First-year students are notified about their financial aid application at time of acceptance.

About the Law School

Wake Forest University School of Law was established in 1894 and is a private institution. The 340-acre campus is in an urban area 3 miles north of Winston-Salem. The primary mission of the law school is to graduate students eligible and qualified to practice law. Students have access to federal, state, county, city, and local agencies, courts, correctional facilities, law firms, and legal aid organizations in the Winston-Salem area. Clinical placements are with the district attorney, U.S. Attorney, Legal Aid, private practitioners, U.S. bankruptcy judge, and public defender. Housing for students is available in approximately 6000 apartment units that are within a 2 1/2 mile radius of the campus. All law school facilities are accessible to the physically disabled.

Calendar

The law school operates on a traditional semester basis. Courses for full-time students are offered days only and must be completed within 3 years. There is no part-time program. New students are admitted in the fall. There are 2 5-week summer sessions. Transferable summer courses are offered.

Phone: 336-758-5437

Contact

Melanie E. Nutt, Admissions and Financial Aid Director, 336-758-5437 for general inquiries and for financial aid information.

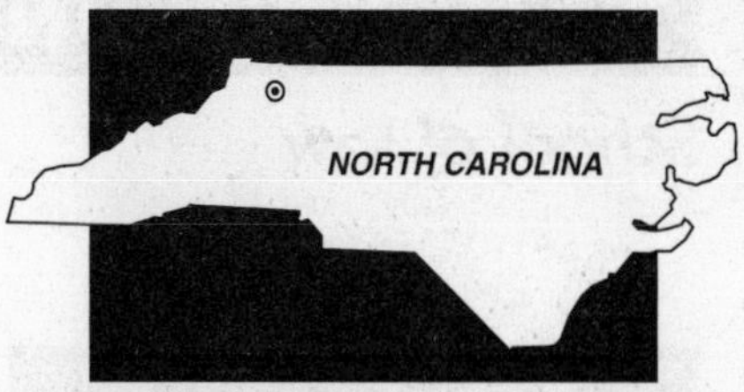

Programs

In addition to the J.D., the law school offers the LL.M. in American Law (for foreign law school graduates). Students may take relevant courses in other programs and apply credit toward the J.D.; a maximum of 6 credits may be applied. The J.D./M.B.A. (Juris Doctor/Master of Business Administration) joint degree may be earned.

Required

To earn the J.D., candidates must complete 89 total credits, of which 41 are for required courses. They must maintain a minimum GPA of 73 on a scale of 100 in the required courses. The following first-year courses are required of all students: Torts I and II, Contracts I and II, Property I and II, Civil Procedure I and II, Criminal Law I, Constitutional Law I, and Legal Research and Writing I and II. Required upper-level courses consist of Constitutional Law II, Evidence, Professional Responsibility, and Legal Writing III, plus 1 substantial writing project. The required orientation program for first-year students is a 1-week program before the beginning of classes devoted to the basics of legal research and writing.

Electives

The School of Law offers concentrations in corporate law, family law, international law, labor law, litigation, securities law, tax law, torts and insurance, and clinical law. In addition to Trial and Appellate Advocacy, the school has 2 clinics. Both are upper-level client clinics and include classroom elements. One covers the civil-criminal law spectrum for 4 credit hours; the other is an in-house clinic with the medical school serving the indigent elderly for 3 credit hours. The Constitutional Lecture Series is an annual program featuring an address by a nationally prominent figure in the field of constitutional law. Two 5-week summer programs are offered, one in London, England, and the other in Venice, Italy. Enrollment is open to all students depending on availability. A tutorial program is offered to first-year students through the Dean's Office. The most widely taken electives are Trial Practice, Decedents' Estates, and Business Organizations.

Graduation Requirements

In order to graduate, candidates must have completed the upper-division writing requirement and have written a paper or a brief to the satisfaction of the instructor in a course approved by the faculty.

Organizations

Students edit the *Wake Forest Law Review*, the student newspaper *The Hearsay*, and *The Jurist*, an alumni magazine published in the spring and fall of each year. Moot court competitions include the Marshall competition in Chicago, National Moot Court competition, and Jessup International Moot Court competition. Student organizations include ABA-Law Student Division, Environmental Law Society, and the Federalist Society. There is a local chapter of the Inns of Court.

Library

The law library contains 355,000 hard-copy volumes and 800,000 microform volume equivalents, and subscribes to 5800 serial publications. Such on-line databases and networks as DIALOG, LEXIS, WESTLAW, and NEXIS, and CCALI are available to law students for research. Special library collections include a U.S. government documents depository. The library is located in a 43,000-square-foot facility, the Worrell Professional Center. It contains 438 carrels, all of which are networked. The ratio of library volumes to faculty is 9103 to 1 and to students is 737 to 1. The ratio of seats in the library to students is 1 to 1.

Faculty

The law school has 39 full-time and 38 part-time faculty members, of whom 20 are women. According to AAUP standards for Category IIA institutions, faculty salaries are well above average. About 22% of full-time faculty have a graduate law degree in addition to the J.D.; about 10% of part-time faculty have one. The ratio of full-time students to full-time faculty in an average class is 14 to 1; in a clinic, 12 to 1. The law school has a regular program of bringing visiting professors and other distinguished lecturers and visitors to campus. There is a chapter of the Order of the Coif.

Placement	
J.D.s awarded:	153
Services available through: a separate law school placement center	
Special features: The Career Services Office sponsors an Employment Fair that targets small North Carolina legal employers and the Southeastern Minority Job Fair..	
Full-time job interviews:	122 employers
Summer job interviews:	122 employers
Placement by graduation:	n/av
Placement within 9 months:	99% of class
Average starting salary:	n/av
Areas of placement:	
Private practice 2-10 attorneys	17%
Private practice 11-25 attorneys	9%
Private practice 26-50 attorneys	6%
Private practice 51-100 attorneys	5%
Judicial clerkships	20%
Unknown	18%
Business/industry	11%
Government	9%
Military	3%
Public interest	1%
Academic	1%

Students

About 48% of the student body are women; 10%, minorities; 9%, African American; 2%, Asian American; and 2%, Hispanic. The majority of students come from North Carolina (33%). The average age of entering students is 25; age range is 20 to 45. About 50% of students enter directly from undergraduate school, 50% have a graduate degree, and 50% have worked full-time prior to entering law school. About 2% drop out after the first year for academic or personal reasons; 95% remain to receive a law degree.

WASHBURN UNIVERSITY

School of Law

1700 College
Topeka, KS 66621

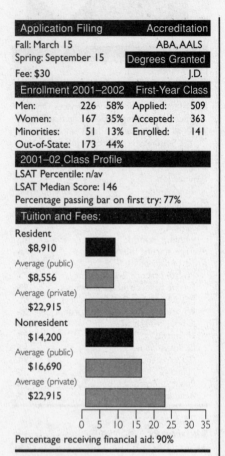

Application Filing		Accreditation
Fall: March 15		ABA, AALS
Spring: September 15		**Degrees Granted**
Fee: $30		J.D.

Enrollment 2001–2002			First-Year Class	
Men:	226	58%	Applied:	509
Women:	167	35%	Accepted:	363
Minorities:	51	13%	Enrolled:	141
Out-of-State:	173	44%		

2001–02 Class Profile

LSAT Percentile: n/av
LSAT Median Score: 146
Percentage passing bar on first try: 77%

Tuition and Fees:

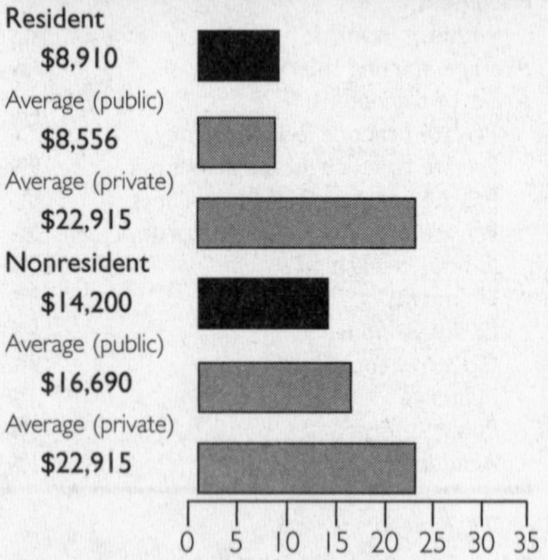

Percentage receiving financial aid: 90%

ADMISSIONS

In the fall 2001 first-year class, 509 applied, 363 were accepted, and 141 enrolled. Eight transfer students were admitted. The median GPA of the most recent first-year class was 3.51.

Requirements

Applicants must have a bachelor's degree and take the LSAT. The most important admission factors include LSAT results, GPA, and academic achievement. No specific undergraduate courses are required. Candidates are not interviewed.

Procedure

The application deadline for fall entry is March 15. Applicants should submit an application form, LSAT results, transcripts, a nonrefundable application fee of $30, 1 required (2 or 3 are recommended) letter of recommendation, and a personal statement, plus a credential evaluation for a non-U.S. bachelor's degree. Notification of the admissions decision may be sent any time from October to May for fall semester. The latest acceptable LSAT test date for fall entry is February. The law school uses the LSDAS.

Special

The law school recruits minority and disadvantaged students through CRS mailings; CLEO; law school forums in Chicago, Atlanta, New York, Dallas, Houston and accompanying workshops; law fairs at many colleges and universities; events in conjunction with BLSA, HALSA, AALSA, and NALSA; scholarships (merit and need); and through efforts with HBCU and Hispanic colleges and universities. Requirements are not different for out-of-state students. Transfer students must have one year of credit, have a minimum GPA of 2.5, have attended an ABA-approved law school, and present a copy of the LSDAS report, official undergraduate degree transcript, a letter of good standing from the dean of the law school, an official transcript of law school grades, law school class rank, and 1 letter of recommendation from a law school professor. Preadmissions courses consist of the Prelegal Education Workshop for high school sophomores and juniors, a 3-day program each June. There is an academic support program orientation held immediately prior to enrollment for admitted students. There are no provisional-admit summer courses.

Costs

Tuition and fees for the 2001-2002 academic year are $8910 for full-time in-state students and $14,200 for out-of-state students. On-campus room and board costs about $6525 annually; books and supplies run $1325.

Financial Aid

About 90% of current law students receive some form of aid. The maximum annual amount of aid from all sources combined, including scholarships, loans, and work contracts, is $25,865. Awards are based on need and merit, although federal loans up to $18,500 have no need or merit base. Factors that could increase the total award amount include number of dependents and other unusual expenses. All admitted applicants are automatically considered for academic scholarships. Required financial statements are the CSS Profile and the FAFSA. The aid application deadline for fall entry is April 1. Special funds for minority or disadvantaged students consist of need and academic scholarships. First-year students are encouraged to apply for loans and need-based scholarships at the time of application. Academic and need scholarships are usually awarded at the time of admission.

About the Law School

Washburn University School of Law was established in 1903 and is a public institution. The 160-acre campus is in an urban area 60 miles west of Kansas City, in the northeast corner of Kansas. The primary mission of the law school is to provide a foundation in the theory, doctrine, and practice of law with a strong emphasis on professionalism in an atmosphere of cooperation and congeniality. Students have access to federal, state, county, city, and local agencies, courts, correctional facilities, law firms, and legal aid organizations in the Topeka area. Facilities of special interest to law students include a 4-story library, 3 computer laboratories with 73 work stations for students, group study rooms, individual study carrels, and a special collections room. The state-of-the-art courtroom is regularly used for state administrative law hearings and occasional sittings by the Kansas Court of Appeals and the U.S. Tenth Circuit Court of Appeals. Housing for students is available in dormitories, but most students live in the many reasonably priced houses and apartments near the campus. All law school facilities are accessible to the physically disabled.

Calendar

The law school operates on a traditional semester basis. Courses for full-time students are offered days only and must be completed within 5 years. There is no part-time program. New students are admitted in the fall and spring. There is a 1 12-week summer session. Transferable summer courses are offered.

Programs

Required

To earn the J.D., candidates must complete 90 total credits, of which 37 are for required courses. They must maintain a minimum GPA of 2.0 in the required courses. The following first-year courses are required of all students: Contracts I and II, Torts, Criminal Law, Property, Civil Procedure, Constitutional Law I, Legal Analysis, Research and Writing Seminar I and II, and Criminal Procedure. Required upper-level courses consist of Evidence, Professional Responsibility, Perspectives on Law (students

Phone: 785-231-1185
800-WASHLAW
Fax: 785-232-8087
E-mail: *admissions@washburnlaw.edu*
Web: *http://washburnlaw.edu*

Contact

Director of Admissions, 785-231-1010 or 800-WASHLAW (800-927-4529) for general inquiries; Donna Winslow (scholarships) or Jannell Harris, 785-231-1185, 785-231-1151, or 800-WASHLAW for financial aid information.

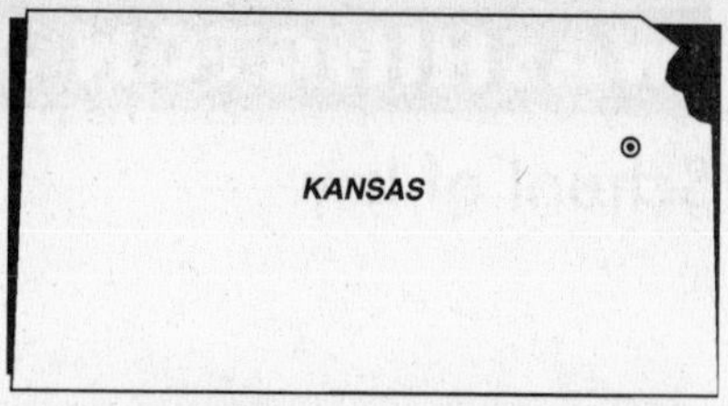

choose from 12 listed courses), a writing requirement, and an oral presentation requirement. The orientation program for first-year students is mandatory.

Electives

Students must take 15 elective credits in their area of concentration for certification. The School of Law offers concentrations in corporate law, criminal law, environmental law, family law, international law, litigation, tax law, torts and insurance, and certificates in tax law, family law, and natural resources law. In addition, clinics may be taken as an elective by third-year students for 4 to 8 credit hours. Directed clinic, available by permission for 1 to 3 credit hours after taking a clinic, concentrates on one area of practice. Second- or third-year students may take seminars for 2 to 3 credit hours in areas such as civil liberties, civil rights, constitutional litigation, family law, negotiation and settlement, and natural resources. An internship in the law library requires students to have a M.L.S. degree. There is also a U.S. Bankruptcy Court internship and a Legislative Workshop internship for 1 to 2 credit hours. There is a Kansas District Court externship for 2 credit hours, Tax Administrative Law Judge externship for 1 to 2 credit hours, and a government or private attorney externship for 1 to 2 credit hours. Research may be done through the Advanced Legal Research course for 2 credit hours or Directed Research for 1 to 3 credit hours. Clerking opportunities are available in all levels of the court system and many local firms. There is a Foulston and Siefkin Law Journal Lecture Series and special tort lectures available through the Gerald Michaud tort-chair endowment. A 6-credit-hour summer program, with various courses in comparative law, is held at the Hampstead campus of King's College, London each year. Students benefit from the academic success program that provides both individual and group tutorial and remedial assistance. All first-year students are included in the academic success program of 9 credit hours in the first year. Minority programs include the Frederick Douglass Moot Court Competition, president's scholarships, and active chapters of Black (BLSA), Asian (AALSA), Hispanic (HALSA), and Native American (NALSA) law student organizations. Special interest group programs are offered at the Rural Law Center. The most widely taken electives are Business Associations, Secured Transactions, and Decedents' Estates.

Graduation Requirements

In order to graduate, candidates must have a GPA of 2.0, have completed the upper-division writing requirement, an upper-level oral presentation, and at least 1 class from the list of 12 Perspectives on Law courses.

Organizations

The primary law review is the *Washburn Law Journal*. Students also solicit articles for and edit *The ABA Family Law Quarterly*. Students participate in 10 to 12 moot court competitions each year, including the John Marshall Privacy Law Competition, Jerome Prince Evidence Competition, New York Bar's National Moot Court Competition, Kansas Trial Lawyers, ABA Client Counseling, ABA Negotiations, Trial Advocacy, the BLSA Frederick Douglass Moot Court, and the NALSA Moot Court. Student organizations include the Washburn Environmental Law Society, Washburn Society of International Law, and Washburn Sports and Entertainment Law Society. There are local chapters of the Black Law Students Association (BLSA), Hispanic Law Students Association (HALSA), Asian-American Law Students Association (AALSA), and Native American Law Students Association (NALSA). Law students may participate in campus intramural sports.

Library

The law library contains 321,470 hardcopy volumes and 141,744 microform volume equivalents, and subscribes to 3861 serial publications. Such on-line databases and networks as DIALOG, LEXIS, WESTLAW, and the Internet, Epic, OCLC, Compuserve, and FirstSearch are available to law students for research. Special library collections include U.S. documents, Kansas documents, the Wolf Creek Collection, which is the Nuclear Regulatory Commission Depository, and 48 CD-ROM titles (70 disks). Recently, the library completed an addition that doubled its size. Three computer laboratories include 73 work stations for students. The ratio of library volumes to faculty is 11,085 to 1 and to students is 818 to 1. The ratio of seats in the library to students is 1 to 1.

Placement

J.D.s awarded:	155
Services available through: a separate law school placement center	
Services: presentations by employers and panels (for example, U.S. Attorney's Office, Judicial Clerkships, alternative careers)	
Special features: the Young Attorney's Association of Topeka conducts and critiques mock job interviews with students.	
Full-time job interviews:	60 employers
Summer job interviews:	30 employers
Placement by graduation:	n/av
Placement within 9 months:	96% of class
Average starting salary:	$22,000 to $74,000
Areas of placement:	
Private practice 2-10 attorneys	35%
Private practice 11-25 attorneys	4%
Private practice 26-50 attorneys	1%
Private practice 51-100 attorneys	6%
Government	34%
Business/industry	14%
Public interest	4%
Academic	2%

Faculty

The law school has 29 full-time and 36 part-time faculty members, of whom 16 are women. According to AAUP standards for Category IIA institutions, faculty salaries are average. About 38% of full-time faculty have a graduate law degree in addition to the J.D. The ratio of full-time students to full-time faculty in an average class is 15 to 1; in a clinic, 5 to 1. The law school has a regular program of bringing visiting professors and other distinguished lecturers and visitors to campus.

Students

About 35% of the student body are women; 13%, minorities; 5%, African American; 3%, Asian American; 4%, Hispanic; and 2%, Native American. The majority of students come from Kansas (56%). The average age of entering students is 27; age range is 20 to 55. About 37% of students enter directly from undergraduate school, 11% have a graduate degree, and 48% have worked full-time prior to entering law school. About 7% drop out after the first year for academic or personal reasons; 86% remain to receive a law degree.

WASHINGTON AND LEE UNIVERSITY

School of Law

Lewis Hall
Lexington, VA 24450

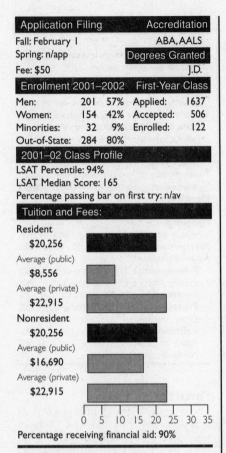

Application Filing		Accreditation
Fall: February 1		ABA, AALS
Spring: n/app		**Degrees Granted**
Fee: $50		J.D.

Enrollment 2001–2002			First-Year Class	
Men:	201	57%	Applied:	1637
Women:	154	42%	Accepted:	506
Minorities:	32	9%	Enrolled:	122
Out-of-State:	284	80%		

2001–02 Class Profile

LSAT Percentile: 94%
LSAT Median Score: 165
Percentage passing bar on first try: n/av

Tuition and Fees:

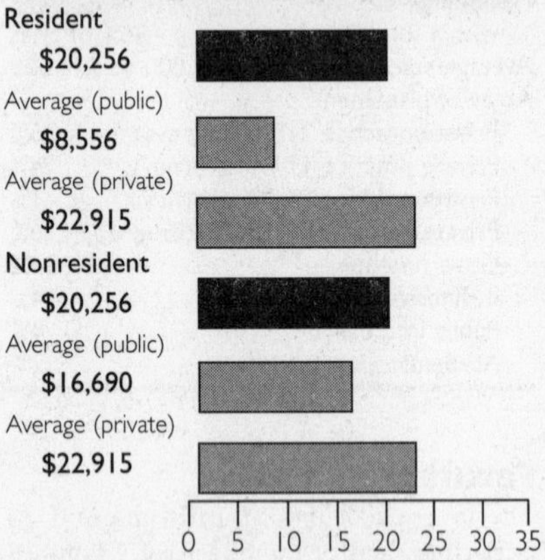

Percentage receiving financial aid: 90%

ADMISSIONS

In the fall 2001 first-year class, 1637 applied, 506 were accepted, and 122 enrolled. Five transfers enrolled. The median LSAT percentile of the most recent first-year class was 94; the median GPA was 3.42 on a scale of 4.0. The lowest LSAT percentile accepted was 35; the highest was 99.

Requirements

Applicants must have a bachelor's degree and take the LSAT. No specific undergraduate courses are required. All factors of a candidates's background are considered. Candidates are interviewed.

Procedure

The application deadline for fall entry is February 1. Applicants should submit an application form, LSAT results, transcripts, a nonrefundable application fee of $50, and 2 letters of recommendation. Notification of the admissions decision is by April 1. The latest acceptable LSAT test date for fall entry is February. The law school uses the LSDAS.

Special

The law school recruits minority and disadvantaged students through regional law forums sponsored by LSDAS and college-sponsored forums, with interviews at institutions with a substantial proportion of minority students, with direct mail, and with an open house for applicants sponsored by the law school and the Black Law Students Association. Requirements are not different for out-of-state students. Transfer students must have attended an ABA-approved law school.

Costs

Tuition and fees for the 2001-2002 academic year are $20,256 for all full-time students. On-campus room and board costs about $5700 annually; books and supplies run $850.

Financial Aid

About 90% of current law students receive some form of aid. The average annual amount of aid from all sources combined, including scholarships, loans, and work contracts, is $9311; maximum, $29,250. Awards are based on need and merit. Required financial statement is the FAFSA. The aid application deadline for fall entry is February 15. First-year students are notified about their financial aid application at time of acceptance.

About the Law School

Washington and Lee University School of Law was established in 1849 and is a private institution. The 322-acre campus is in a small town 3 hours southwest of Washington, D.C. The primary mission of the law school is to provide a rigorous, writing-intensive, and personalized legal education to each student as preparation for the legal profession in an atmosphere of mutual respect, collegiality, and appreciation for each person's dignity; and to inculcate a sense of the responsibility placed on lawyers and the ethical obligations of law practice. Students have access to federal, state, county, city, and local agencies, courts, correctional facilities, law firms, and legal aid organizations in the Lexington area. Housing for students includes on-campus apartments adjacent to the law school building for single students, and private apartments, rooms, and houses in Lexington and the surrounding area. All law school facilities are accessible to the physically disabled.

Calendar

The law school operates on a traditional semester basis. Courses for full-time students are offered days only and must be completed within 6 semesters. There is no part-time program. New students are admitted in the fall. There is no summer session. Transferable summer courses are not offered.

Programs

Required

To earn the J.D., candidates must complete 85 total credits, of which 37 are for required courses. They must maintain a minimum GPA of 1.00 in the required courses. The following first-year courses are required of all students: Criminal Law, Property, Contracts, Torts, Criminal Procedure, Civil Procedure I and II, and American Public Law Process. Required upper-level courses consist of Constitutional Law and Professional Responsibility. The required orientation program for first-year students is 3 days and includes social activities for the entire student body, introduction to the case-method and case-briefing techniques, introducton to legal research, honor system orientation, and a university orientation.

Phone: 540-463-8504
Fax: 540-463-8586
E-mail: *lawadm@wlu.edu*
Web: *www.wlu.edu*

Contact

Sidney Evans, Director of Admissions, 540-463-8504 for general inquiries; Cynthia Hintze, Assistant Director of Financial Aid, 540-463-8032 for financial aid information.

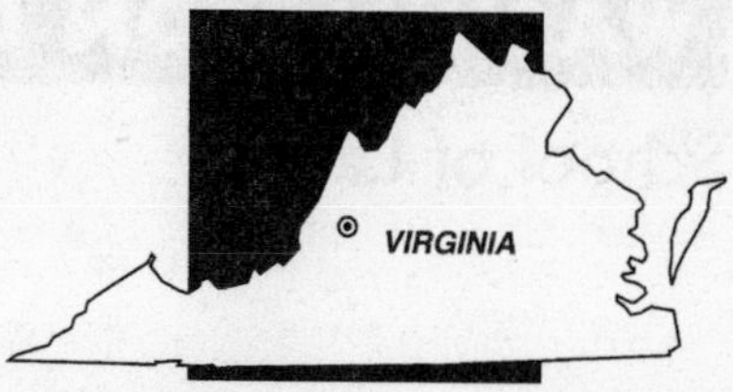

Electives

Various clinics, open to second- and third-year students, provide direct service to miners seeking black lung benefits, to patients at Western State Hospital, and to inmates of the Federal Correction Institution in Alderson, West Virginia. Credit ranges from 3 to 10 hours. Seminars, available to upper-level students, are worth 2 or 3 credits and are offered in a variety of areas. Upper-level students may perform internships with state trial court judges during the academic year for 4 graded credits or with government or nonprofit employers in the summer for 2 ungraded credits. Independent research projects may be undertaken by second- or third-year students; credit varies. The Frances Lewis Law Center sponsors research fellowships for third-year students. Bain and Shepherd Fellowships provide stipends to support collaborative research projects between students and faculty. Special lecture series include the annual John Randolph Tucker Lecture and visiting lectures sponsored by the Frances Lewis Law Center and other law student organizations in areas of special interest to their members. The school offers no study-abroad program, but may accept credit for courses taken in programs offered by other ABA-approved law schools. Tutorials are offered to upper-class students in a variety of fields. The Academic Support Program offers a series of programs introducing the case method and legal analysis, and provides continuing academic support throughout the year. Special interest group programs include Women Law Students Organization, Black Law Students Association, Christian Legal Society, and Committee on Gay and Lesbian Legal Issues. The most widely taken electives are Federal Income Tax, Family Law, and Commercial Transactions.

Graduation Requirements

In order to graduate, candidates must have a GPA of 2.0 and have completed the upper-division writing requirement.

Organizations

Students edit the *Washington and Lee Law Review, Capital Defense Digest, Virginia Environmental Law Digest* sponsored by the Virginia State Bar, *Race and Ethnic Ancestry Law Journal*, and the newspaper *Law News*. Moot court competitions include Holderness Moot Court, John W. Davis Moot Court, and Jessup International Law Moot Court. Other competitions include National Mock Trial, Client Counseling, and Negotiation competitions. Law student organizations include the Student Bar Association, International Law Society, and Environmental Law Forum. There are local chapters of Phi Alpha Delta, Phi Delta Phi, and Omicron Delta Kappa. Campus clubs and other organizations include Amnesty International, Habitat for Humanity, and Mock Convention.

Library

The law library contains 372,675 hard-copy volumes and 808,493 microform volume equivalents, and subscribes to 4638 serial publications. Such on-line databases and networks as DIALOG, LEXIS, WESTLAW, and InfoTrac, OCLC, and First Search are available to law students for research. Special library collections include the Bankruptcy Revision Act 1978 (committee papers), the John W. Davis Collection of Records and Briefs, the Impeachment of President Nixon (committee papers), and the Lewis F. Powell, Jr. Archives. Recently, the library added graphic searching of the Web and upgraded the student computer laboratory to Pentiums. The ratio of library volumes to faculty is 11,293 to 1 and to students is 1050 to 1. The ratio of seats in the library to students is 1 to 1.

Faculty

The law school has 33 full-time and 19 part-time faculty members, of whom 12 are women. According to AAUP standards for Category IIB institutions, faculty salaries are well above average. About 21% of full-time faculty have a graduate law degree in addition to the J.D.; about 5% of part-time faculty have one. The ratio of full-time students to full-time faculty in an average class is 10 to 1; in a clinic, 10 to 1. The law school has a regular program of bringing visiting professors and other distinguished lecturers and visitors to campus. There is a chapter of the Order of the Coif; 32 faculty and 310 graduates are members.

Placement

J.D.s awarded:	120
Services available through: a separate law school placement center	
Services: advice on networking, and programs on specific practice areas, (for example, corporate law, small firms, prosecution)	
Special features: one-on-one work with students on resumes, cover letters, job search advice; a brochure for student use when applying to areas where school is less well-known; mock interviews with alumni and faculty; interviews via video-conferencing; job fairs in New York, Chicago, Atlanta, and Dallas.	
Full-time job interviews:	116 employers
Summer job interviews:	n/av
Placement by graduation:	88% of class
Placement within 9 months:	98% of class
Average starting salary:	$25,000 to $125,000
Areas of placement:	
Private practice 2-10 attorneys	10%
Private practice 11-25 attorneys	7%
Private practice 26-50 attorneys	10%
Private practice 51-100 attorneys	5%
Private practice 101+ attorneys; 5%	
Unknown	24%
Judicial clerkships	27%
Government	4%
Business/industry	4%
Public interest	3%
Military	1%

Students

About 42% of the student body are women; 9%, minorities; 8%, African American; 4%, Asian American; 1%, Hispanic; 1%, Native American; and 2%, multiracial. The majority of students come from the South (35%). The average age of entering students is 24; age range is 21 to 50. About 41% of students enter directly from undergraduate school, 12% have a graduate degree, and 59% have worked full-time prior to entering law school. About 1% drop out after the first year for academic or personal reasons; 99% remain to receive a law degree.

School of Law

Box 1120, One Brookings Drive
St. Louis, MO 63130

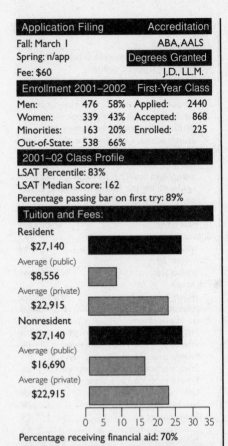

Application Filing		Accreditation
Fall: March 1		ABA, AALS
Spring: n/app		**Degrees Granted**
Fee: $60		J.D., LL.M.

Enrollment 2001–2002			First-Year Class	
Men:	476	58%	Applied:	2440
Women:	339	43%	Accepted:	868
Minorities:	163	20%	Enrolled:	225
Out-of-State:	538	66%		

2001–02 Class Profile

LSAT Percentile: 83%
LSAT Median Score: 162
Percentage passing bar on first try: 89%

Tuition and Fees:

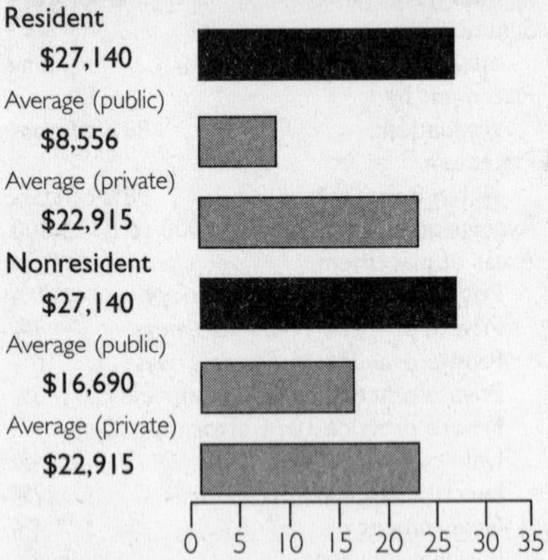

Percentage receiving financial aid: 70%

ADMISSIONS

In the fall 2001 first-year class, 2440 applied, 868 were accepted, and 225 enrolled. Eighteen transfers enrolled. The median LSAT percentile of the most recent first-year class was 83; the median GPA was 3.5 on a scale of 4.0. The lowest LSAT percentile accepted was 31; the highest was 99.

Requirements

Applicants must have a bachelor's degree and take the LSAT. Minimum acceptable GPA is 2.0 on a scale of 4.0. The most important admission factors include LSAT results, GPA, and academic achievement. No specific undergraduate courses are required. Candidates are not interviewed.

Procedure

The application deadline for fall entry is March 1. Applicants should submit an application form, a nonrefundable application fee of $60, 2 letters of recommendation, and a personal statement. Notification of the admissions decision is by April. The latest acceptable LSAT test date for fall entry is February. The law school uses the LSDAS.

Special

The law school recruits minority and disadvantaged students by means of a minority admissions counselor, specific mailings, scholarship programs, and visitation programs. Requirements are not different for out-of-state students. Transfer students must have one year of credit and have attended an ABA-approved law school.

Costs

Tuition and fees for the 2001-2002 academic year are $27,140 for all full-time students. Books and supplies cost about $1500 annually.

Financial Aid

About 70% of current law students receive some form of aid. The average annual amount of aid from all sources combined, including scholarships, loans, and work contracts, is $17,000; maximum, $32,000. Awards are based on need and merit. Required financial statement is the FAFSA. The aid application deadline for fall entry is March 1. Special funds for minority or disadvantaged students are the Minority Scholars-in-Law program, Farmer Scholarship, and the Chancellor's Fellowship. First-year students are notified about their financial aid application between the time of acceptance and enrollment.

About the Law School

Washington University in St. Louis School of Law was established in 1867 and is a private institution. The 160-acre campus is in a suburban area in St. Louis. The primary mission of the law school is to provide an enduring foundation of legal education that is useful for whatever field of law is chosen. Students have access to federal, state, county, city, and local agencies, courts, correctional facilities, law firms, and legal aid organizations in the St. Louis area. Students have access to a congressional clinic and a federal administrative agency clinic in Washington, D.C. Facilities of special interest to law students include St. Louis-based national and international corporations. Housing for students is available in surrounding neighborhoods; listings are available through an off-campus referral service. About 90% of the law school facilities are accessible to the physically disabled.

Calendar

The law school operates on a traditional semester basis. Courses for full-time students are offered days only. There is no part-time program. New students are admitted in the fall. There is a 5-week summer session. Transferable summer courses are offered.

Programs

In addition to the J.D., the law school offers the LL.M. and J.S.D. Students may take relevant courses in other programs and apply credit toward the J.D.; a maximum of 9 credits may be applied. The following joint degrees may be earned: J.D./M.A. (Juris Doctor/Master of Arts in East Asian studies, political science), J.D./M.B.A. (Juris Doctor/Master of Business Administration), J.D./M.H.A. (Juris Doctor/Master of Health Administration), J.D./M.S. (Juris Doctor/Master of Science in economics and environmental policy), and J.D./M.S.W. (Juris Doctor/Master of Social Work).

Phone: 314-935-4525
Fax: 314-935-6959
E-mail: *admiss@walaw.wash.edu*
Web: *ls.wash.edu*

Contact

Admissions Office, 314-935-4525 for general inquiries; JoAnn Eckrich, Associate Director, 314-935-4605 for financial aid information.

Required

To earn the J.D., candidates must complete 85 total credits, of which 7 are for required courses. They must maintain a minimum GPA of 75.0 in the required courses. The following first-year courses are required of all students: Contracts, Criminal Law, Legal Research and Writing, Property, Torts, Civil Procedure, and Constitutional Law I. Required upper-level courses consist of Professional Responsibility-Legal Profession and 1 additional writing seminar. The required orientation program for first-year students runs for 3 days and focuses on academic, social, and administrative components of the school.

Electives

The School of Law offers concentrations in corporate law, criminal law, environmental law, family law, international law, labor law, litigation, securities law, tax law, torts and insurance, and transactional (planning and drafting) courses. In addition, clinics are offered for 3 to 10 credit hours, including Congressional Clinic in Washington, D.C., Federal Administrative Agency in Washington, D.C., and Employment Law and Public Policy Clinic. Students may participate in research programs after the first year. Field work is performed as part of the clinics; recently, 8 clinics were offered. Special lectures include the Tyrrell Williams Memorial Lectures and the Public Interest Speakers Series. Tutorial programs are available on an individual basis. The Black Law Students Association organizes student study groups and visiting minority speakers. The most widely taken electives are Pre-trial, Trial, and Evidence.

Graduation Requirements

In order to graduate, candidates must have completed the upper-division writing requirement.

Organizations

Students edit *The Washington University Law Quarterly* and the *Journal of Law and Policy*. The student newspaper is *The Devil's Advocate*. Moot court competitions include the Wiley Rutledge Moot Court program held in the fall and spring, Environmental Moot Court, and the Jessup International Law Moot Court. Other competitions include the National Mock Trial, National Client Counseling, the Negotiation, and the Intramural Client Counseling. Student organizations include the Student Bar Association, Environmental Law Society, and International Law Society. The Federalist Society, Phi Alpha Delta, and Phi Delta Phi have local chapters. There are numerous other campus organizations.

Library

The law library contains 563,292 hardcopy volumes and 847,000 microform volume equivalents, and subscribes to 5079 serial publications. Such on-line databases and networks as DIALOG, LEXIS, and WESTLAW are available to law students for research. Special library collections include those addressing congressional, British, and state administrative regulations. Recently, the library gained access to the INNOVALQ system. The ratio of library volumes to faculty is 11,985 to 1 and to students is 691 to 1. The ratio of seats in the library to students is 1 to 1.

Faculty

The law school has 47 full-time and 50 part-time faculty members, of whom 16 are women. According to AAUP standards for Category I institutions, faculty salaries are well above average. About 32% of full-time faculty have a graduate law degree in addition to the J.D.; about 27% of part-time faculty have one. The ratio of full-time students to full-time faculty in an average class is 14 to 1. The law school has a regular program of bringing visiting professors and other distinguished lecturers and visitors to campus. There is a chapter of the Order of the Coif; 17 faculty are members.

Placement	
J.D.s awarded:	209
Services available through: a separate law school placement center	
Special features: personalized services of 4 professionals who are attorneys and have practiced law.	
Full-time job interviews:	118 employers
Summer job interviews:	n/av
Placement by graduation:	n/av
Placement within 9 months:	98% of class
Average starting salary:	$23,000 to $100,000
Areas of placement:	
Private practice 2-10 attorneys	17%
Private practice 26-50 attorneys	25%
unknown	19%
Business/industry	12%
Government	11%
Judicial clerkships	8%
Public interest	4%
Academic	3%
Military	1%

Students

About 43% of the student body are women; 20%, minorities; 10%, African American; 7%, Asian American; 2%, Hispanic; and 1%, Native American. The majority of students come from the Midwest (58%). The average age of entering students is 24; age range is 20 to 46. About 55% of students enter directly from undergraduate school and 45% have worked full-time prior to entering law school. About 7% drop out after the first year for academic or personal reasons; 92% remain to receive a law degree.

WAYNE STATE UNIVERSITY

Law School

471 W. Palmer
Detroit, MI 48202

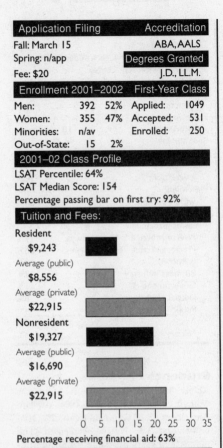

Application Filing		Accreditation
Fall: March 15		ABA, AALS
Spring: n/app		**Degrees Granted**
Fee: $20		J.D., LL.M.

Enrollment 2001–2002			First-Year Class	
Men:	392	52%	Applied:	1049
Women:	355	47%	Accepted:	531
Minorities:	n/av		Enrolled:	250
Out-of-State:	15	2%		

2001–02 Class Profile

LSAT Percentile: 64%
LSAT Median Score: 154
Percentage passing bar on first try: 92%

Tuition and Fees:

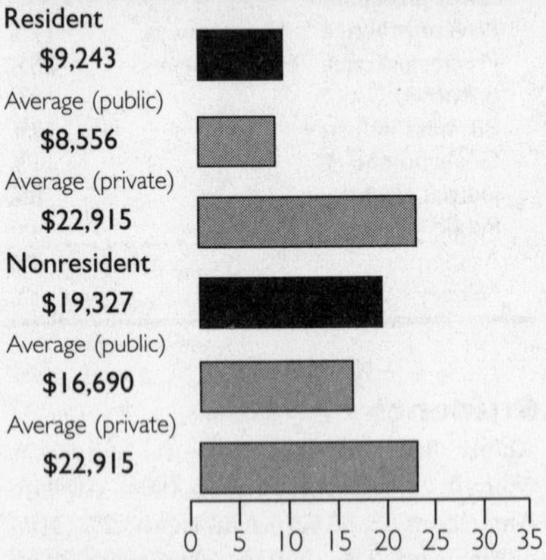

Percentage receiving financial aid: 63%

ADMISSIONS

In the fall 2001 first-year class, 1049 applied, 531 were accepted, and 250 enrolled. Two transfers enrolled. The median LSAT percentile of the most recent first-year class was 64; the median GPA was 3.33 on a scale of 4.0. The lowest LSAT percentile accepted was 20; the highest was 99.

Requirements

Applicants must have a bachelor's degree and take the LSAT. The most important admission factors include a letter of recommendation and GPA and LSAT results. No specific undergraduate courses are required. Candidates are not interviewed.

Procedure

The application deadline for fall entry is March 15. Applicants should submit an application form, LSAT results, transcripts, a nonrefundable application fee of $20, 1 letter of recommendation, and a personal statement. Notification of the admissions decision is on a rolling basis. The latest acceptable LSAT test date for fall entry is February. The law school uses the LSDAS.

Special

The law school recruits minority and disadvantaged students by means of an affirmative admission policy and by encouraging application, hosting a Minority Law Day, participating in Law Services' Atlanta Forum, and recruiting at historically black colleges and universities. Requirements are not different for out-of-state students. Transfer students must have one year of credit, have a minimum GPA of 3.4, have attended an ABA-approved law school, and have an official transcript sent from their current law school and their previous undergraduate institution, submit a letter of good standing from the dean, and submit a copy of the LSDAS report.

Costs

Tuition and fees for the 2001-2002 academic year are $9243 for full-time in-state students and $19,327 for out-of-state students. Tuition for part-time students is $6648 in-state and $14,360 out-of-state. Books and supplies cost about $900 annually.

Financial Aid

About 63% of current law students receive some form of aid. The average annual amount of aid from all sources combined, including scholarships, loans, and work contracts, is $10,000; maximum, $21,416. Awards are based on need and merit, along with outside scholarship awards. Required financial statement is the FAFSA. The aid application deadline for fall entry is April 30. Special funds for minority or disadvantaged students consist of Kenneth Cockerel, Wade McCree, and Law Alumni scholarships and fellowships. First-year students are notified about their financial aid application from mid-April through the summer, prior to fall enrollment.

About the Law School

Wayne State University Law School was established in 1927 and is a public institution. The campus is in an urban area in Detroit. The primary mission of the law school is to train lawyers for a wide variety of careers. Students have access to federal, state, county, city, and local agencies, courts, correctional facilities, law firms, and legal aid organizations in the Detroit area. Facilities of special interest to law students include the 4 buildings of the school, which house classrooms, seminar rooms, the law library, faculty and student offices, and a 250-seat auditorium (the Spencer M. Partrich Auditorium), which can be used as either a trial or appellate courtroom. Housing for students is available on campus, in the school vicinity, and throughout the metropolitan area. All law school facilities are accessible to the physically disabled.

Calendar

The law school operates on a traditional semester basis. Courses for full-time students are offered both day and evening and must be completed within 5 years. For part-time students, courses are offered both day and evening and must be completed within 6 years. New full- and part-time students are admitted in the fall. There is a 7-week summer session. Transferable summer courses are offered.

Programs

In addition to the J.D., the law school offers the LL.M. and LL.M. in taxation, labor law, and corporate. Students may take relevant courses in other programs and apply credit toward the J.D.; a maximum of 8 credits may be applied. The following joint degrees may be earned: J.D./M.A. (Juris Doctor/Master of Arts in history, public policy and dispute resolution) and J.D./M.B.A. (Juris Doctor/Master of Business Administration).

Phone: 313-577-3937
Fax: 313-577-6000
E-mail: *linda.sims@wayne.edu*

Contact

Assistant Dean for Recruitment and Admissions, 313-577-3937 for general inquiries; Financial Aid Office, 313-577-5142 for financial aid information.

Required

To earn the J.D., candidates must complete 86 total credits, of which 36 are for required courses. They must maintain a minimum GPA of 2.0 in the required courses. The following first-year courses are required of all students: Civil Procedure, Contracts, Criminal Law, Legal Writing and Research, Property, and Torts. Required upper-level courses consist of Constitutional Law I and Professional Responsibility and the Legal Profession. The required orientation program for first-year students is 3 days for students in the day program and 5 days for students in the evening program, during which students begin their legal writing classes.

Electives

The Law School offers concentrations in criminal law, international law, labor law, tax law, commercial law, and intellectual property. In addition, clinical experience is offered through the Student Trial Advocacy Program, Free Legal Aid Clinic, and the Criminal Appellate Practice Program in cooperation with the Michigan State Appellate Defender Office. There are some 28 seminars. Second- and third-year students have a choice of interning on a part-time basis with distinguished local judges and in a variety of governmental and nonprofit agencies. Students earn 2 credits per semester in these internships. Special lecture series include I. Goodman Cohen Lecture in Trial Advocacy, Driker Forum for Excellence in the Law, and Bernard Gottfried Memorial Labor Law Symposium. There is a 6-week summer exchange program with the University of Warwick, England; students may also study for 1 semester in the London Law Programme of the University of Detroit-Mercy School of Law and at The Hague, Netherlands. The Supportive Services Program offers academic and related support to students. The Intellectual Property Law Institute, a consortium with 2 other universities, offers additional intellectural property courses to law students. The most widely taken electives are Commercial Transactions, Taxation, and Evidence.

Graduation Requirements

In order to graduate, candidates must have a GPA of 2.0 and have completed the upper-division writing requirement.

Organizations

Students edit the *Wayne State Law Review, The Journal of Law and Society*, and the newspaper *The Advocate*. Moot court competitions include Jerome Prince Evidence, Craven Constitutional, and National Product Liability competitions. Law student organizations include Student Board of Governors, Black Law Students Association, and Sports and Entertainment Law Society. Other organizations include the Federalist Society, Environmental Law Society, and International Law Society. There are local chapters of National Lawyers Guild and ABA-Law Student Division.

Library

The law library contains 388,390 hard-copy volumes and 199,607 microform volume equivalents, and subscribes to 5036 serial publications. Such on-line databases and networks as CALI, CIS Universe, DIALOG, Dow-Jones, Infotrac, Legal-Trac, LEXIS, LOIS, Mathew Bender, NEXIS, OCLC First Search, WESTLAW, and Wilsonline Indexes are available to law students for research. Special library collections include a U.S. government document depository, Michigan Supreme Court records and briefs, Michigan Probate Court opinions, and Michigan Superfund Sites Collection. Recently, the library was completely renovated. There are now 14 group study rooms and increased private study space. The computer laboratory contains 22 Dell Pentium III machines and network printers. The law library home page can be accessed at *www.lib.wayne.edu/lawlibrary*. The ratio of library volumes to faculty is 11,769 to 1 and to students is 520 to 1. The ratio of seats in the library to students is 1 to 2.

Placement	
J.D.s awarded:	226
Services available through: a separate law school placement center	
Services: offers a full placement service that provides career counseling	
Special features: Students are offered free use of fax, photocopier, and telephone.	
Full-time job interviews:	72 employers
Summer job interviews:	24 employers
Placement by graduation:	63% of class
Placement within 9 months:	94% of class
Average starting salary:	$15,000 to $130,000
Areas of placement:	
Private practice 2 - 100 attorneys	56%
Business/industry	18%
Government	12%
Judicial clerkships	5%
Public interest	3%
Academic	1%

Faculty

The law school has 33 full-time and 48 part-time faculty members, of whom 20 are women. According to AAUP standards for Category I institutions, faculty salaries are average. About 25% of full-time faculty have a graduate law degree in addition to the J.D.; about 31% of part-time faculty have one. The ratio of full-time students to full-time faculty in an average class is 26 to 1; in a clinic, 12 to 1. There is a chapter of the Order of the Coif; 33 faculty and 360 graduates are members.

Students

About 47% of the student body are women; 16%, African American; 5%, Asian American; and 1%, Native American. The majority of students come from Michigan (98%). The average age of entering students is 26; age range is 20 to 56. About 15% of students have a graduate degree. About 11% drop out after the first year for academic or personal reasons; 87% remain to receive a law degree.

WEST VIRGINIA UNIVERSITY

College of Law

P.O. Box 6130
Morgantown, WV 26506

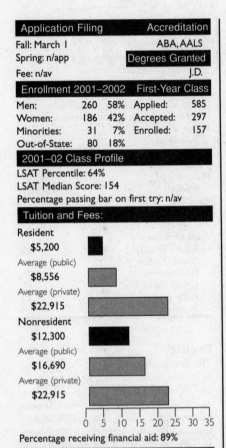

Application Filing		Accreditation
Fall: March 1		ABA, AALS
Spring: n/app		**Degrees Granted**
Fee: n/av		J.D.

Enrollment 2001–2002			First-Year Class	
Men:	260	58%	Applied:	585
Women:	186	42%	Accepted:	297
Minorities:	31	7%	Enrolled:	157
Out-of-State:	80	18%		

2001–02 Class Profile

LSAT Percentile: 64%
LSAT Median Score: 154
Percentage passing bar on first try: n/av

Tuition and Fees:

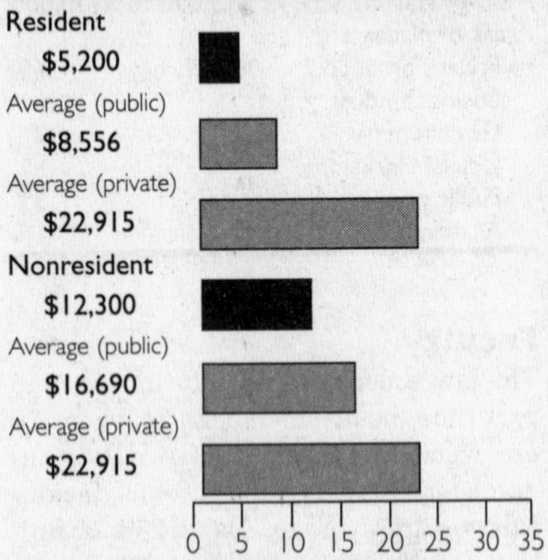

Percentage receiving financial aid: 89%

ADMISSIONS

In the fall 2001 first-year class, 585 applied, 297 were accepted, and 157 enrolled. Three transfers enrolled. The median LSAT percentile of the most recent first-year class was 64; the median GPA was 3.3 on a scale of 4.0. The lowest LSAT percentile accepted was 13; the highest was 98.

Requirements

Applicants must have a bachelor's degree and take the LSAT. The most important admission factors include LSAT results, academic achievement, and GPA. No specific undergraduate courses are required. Candidates are not interviewed.

Procedure

The application deadline for fall entry is March 1. Applicants should submit an application form, LSAT results, transcripts (submitted by LSDAS), 3 letters of recommendation, and a personal statement. Notification of the admissions decision is on a rolling basis. The latest acceptable LSAT test date for fall entry is February. The law school uses the LSDAS.

Special

The law school recruits minority and disadvantaged students through mailings, Minority Law Day, forums, and personal contacts from the school's Graduate Assistant for Minority Recruitment. Requirements are different for out-of-state students in that preference is given to West Virginia residents. Transfer students must have one year of credit and have attended an ABA-approved law school.

Costs

Tuition and fees are approximately $5200 for full-time in-state students and $12,300 for out-of-state students. Books and supplies cost about $1000 annually.

Financial Aid

About 89% of current law students receive some form of aid. The average annual amount of aid from all sources combined, including scholarships, loans, and work contracts, is $13,674; maximum, $16,859. Awards are based on need and merit. Required financial statement is the FAFSA. Special funds for minority or disadvantaged students include scholarships; additionally, vocational rehabilitation is offered to disabled and disadvantaged students. First-year students are notified about their financial aid application at time of acceptance.

About the Law School

West Virginia University College of Law was established in 1878 and is a public institution. The 1000-acre campus is in a small town 77 miles south of Pittsburgh. The primary mission of the law school is to prepare students for the practice of law and for public leadership through a curriculum that stresses basic legal principles, lawyering skills, and the responsibilities of the legal profession. Students have access to federal, state, county, city, and local agencies, courts, correctional facilities, law firms, and legal aid organizations in the Morgantown area. Facilities of special interest to law students are the Leo Carlin Computer Laboratory; the Marlyn E. Lugar Courtroom, a combination courtroom-auditorium; a mini-courtroom; 3 conference-seminar rooms; 1 large courtroom; the law library; the Meredith Career Services Center with placement interview rooms; a student lounge; and a child-care cooperative. Housing for students is available for both single and married students. The university housing office helps students find off-campus housing. All law school facilities are accessible to the physically disabled.

Calendar

The law school operates on a traditional semester basis. Courses for full-time students are offered days only and must be completed within 6 years. For part-time students, courses are offered days only and must be completed within 6 years. New full- and part-time students are admitted in the fall. There is no summer session. Transferable summer courses are not offered.

Programs

The following joint degrees may be earned: J.D./M.B.A. (Juris Doctor/Master of Business Administration, through the Department of Business and Economics) and J.D./M.P.A. (Juris Doctor/Master of Public Administration, through the Department of Public Administration).

Phone: 304-293-5304
Fax: 304-293-6891
E-mail: *lawaply@wvu.edu*
Web: *wvu.edu/~law/*

Contact

Admissions Office, 304-293-5304 for general inquiries; Joanna Hastings, Financial Counselor, 304-293-5302 for financial aid information.

Required

To earn the J.D., candidates must complete 93 total credits, of which 52 are for required courses. They must maintain a minimum GPA of 2.0 in the required courses. The following first-year courses are required of all students: Contracts I and II, Criminal Law, Property I and II, Torts, Legal Research and Writing I and II, Professional Responsibility, Civil Procedure I, and Constitutional Law. Required upper-level courses consist of Civil Procedure II, Appellate Advocacy, Evidence, Income Tax I, 2 perspective courses, a seminar, and trial advocacy or clinic. The required orientation program for first-year students is a 2 1/2-day program featuring mini-classes covering legal writing, note taking, and exams; student panels discussing first-year life and financial aid information; a picnic with upper-class students and faculty at which families are welcome; and a computer workshop for interested students.

Electives

Approved upper-class students may earn 14 credit hours in a civil legal clinic. Students may also pursue independent study under faculty supervision. The most widely taken electives are Business Organizations, Property III, and Torts.

Graduation Requirements

In order to graduate, candidates must have a GPA of 2.0 and have completed the upper-division writing requirement.

Organizations

Students edit the *West Virginia Law Review* (the fourth oldest legal journal in the United States), the *Journal of College and University Law* in conjunction with the National Association of College and University Attorneys, and the newspaper *On-Point*. Moot court competitions include the Moot Court Board, Baker Cup Competition (held annually), Marlyn E. Lugar Trial Association Mock Trial Competition (held 4 times per year), and Gourley Cup Competition. Law student organizations include the Moot Court Board, Environmental Law Society, and Labor and Employment Law Association. There are local chapters of National Lawyers Guild, Student Bar Association, and Phi Delta Phi.

Library

The law library contains 246,532 hard-copy volumes and 355,617 microform volume equivalents, and subscribes to 2791 serial publications. Such on-line databases and networks as LEXIS, WESTLAW, and CALI are available to law students for research. Special library collections include a rare book room. Recently, the library purchased 8 486DX computers and a laser printer that will support computer-assisted legal instruction and temporary training centers in the Carlin laboratory, and installed a custom-built counter that accommodates 8 computers and 2 laser printers for student word processing. The ratio of library volumes to faculty is 9482 to 1 and to students is 553 to 1. The ratio of seats in the library to students is 1 to 2.

Faculty

The law school has 26 full-time and 11 part-time faculty members, of whom 11 are women. According to AAUP standards for Category I institutions, faculty salaries are below average. About 38% of full-time faculty have a graduate law degree in addition to the J.D.; about 10% of part-time faculty have one. The ratio of full-time students to full-time faculty in an average class is 18 to 1; in a clinic, 20 to 1. There is a chapter of the Order of the Coif; 4 faculty are members.

Placement

J.D.s awarded: 139

Services available through: a separate law school placement center and the university placement center

Services: stress-management seminars, Myers-Briggs Type Indicator Administration and Interpretation, and individual counseling.

Special features: The college has a close working relationship with the West Virginia State Bar.

Full-time job interviews:	24 employers
Summer job interviews:	29 employers
Placement by graduation:	80% of class
Placement within 9 months:	90% of class
Average starting salary:	$36,610 to $72,000
Areas of placement:	
Private practice 2-10 attorneys	39%
Private practice 11-25 attorneys	10%
Private practice 26-50 attorneys	7%
Private practice 51-100 attorneys	6%
Government	18%
Business/industry	11%
Judicial clerkships	4%
Public interest	4%
Academic	1%

Students

About 42% of the student body are women; 7%, minorities; 5%, African American; and 2%, Hispanic. The majority of students come from West Virginia (82%). The average age of entering students is 26; age range is 22 to 50. About 39% of students enter directly from undergraduate school and 13% have a graduate degree.

WESTERN NEW ENGLAND COLLEGE

School of Law

1215 Wilbraham Road
Springfield, MA 01119

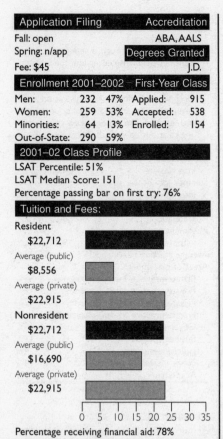

Application Filing	Accreditation
Fall: open	ABA, AALS
Spring: n/app	**Degrees Granted**
Fee: $45	J.D.

Enrollment 2001–2002			First-Year Class	
Men:	232	47%	Applied:	915
Women:	259	53%	Accepted:	538
Minorities:	64	13%	Enrolled:	154
Out-of-State:	290	59%		

2001–02 Class Profile

LSAT Percentile: 51%
LSAT Median Score: 151
Percentage passing bar on first try: 76%

Tuition and Fees:

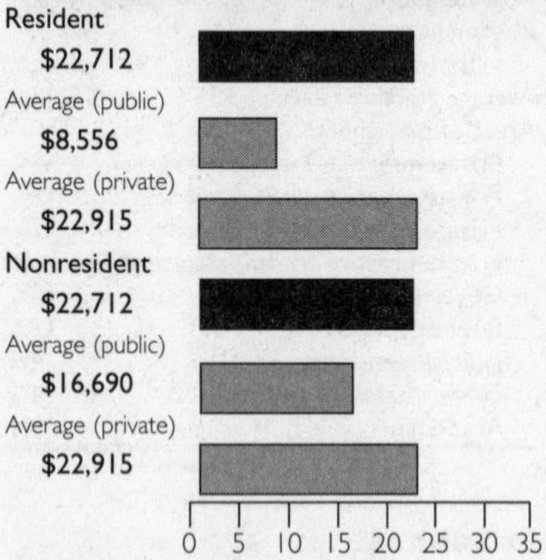

Percentage receiving financial aid: 78%

ADMISSIONS

In the fall 2001 first-year class, 915 applied, 538 were accepted, and 154 enrolled. Three transfers enrolled. The median LSAT percentile of the most recent first-year class was 51; the median GPA was 3 on a scale of 4.0. The lowest LSAT percentile accepted was 15; the highest was 94.

Requirements

Applicants must have a bachelor's degree and take the LSAT. No specific undergraduate courses are required. Candidates are not interviewed.

Procedure

The application deadline for fall entry is open. Applicants should submit an application form, LSAT results, transcripts, a nonrefundable application fee of $45, 2 letters of recommendation, and a personal statement. Notification of the admissions decision is as early as possible, usually 2 to 4 weeks after completion of the file. The latest acceptable LSAT test date for fall entry is June. The law school uses the LSDAS.

Special

The law school recruits minority and disadvantaged students by means of Law Services forums, attendance at historically black college recruiting events, mailings through the Candidate Referral Service, and limited scholarships. Requirements are not different for out-of-state students. Transfer students must have one year of credit. The school receives approximately 10 to 15 transfer applications each year, of which less than half are generally accepted. There is no minimum law school GPA used as a cutoff.

Costs

Tuition and fees for the 2001-2002 academic year are $22,712 for all full-time students. Tuition for part-time students is $16,761 per year. Books and supplies cost about $1155 annually.

Financial Aid

Some 78% of current law students receive some form of aid. The average annual amount of aid from all sources combined, including scholarships, loans, and work contracts, is $24,330; maximum, $37,282. Awards are based on need and merit. Limited merit and need-based scholarships are awarded by the law school admissions committee. Required financial statements are the FAFSA and the college financial aid application, and tax returns with W2 statements for returning law students. The aid application deadline for fall entry is rolling. Special funds for minority or disadvantaged students are awarded to students who have overcome educational, cultural, economic, or physical barriers to achieve success at the undergraduate level. First-year students are notified about their financial aid application on a rolling basis.

About the Law School

Western New England College School of Law was established in 1919 and is a private institution. The 185-acre campus is in a suburban area 25 miles north of Hartford and 90 miles west of Boston. The primary mission of the law school is to provide a practical and effective legal education in a humane and supportive environment, in which faculty and students work together in a rigorous yet rewarding educational process. Students have access to federal, state, county, city, and local agencies, courts, correctional facilities, law firms, and legal aid organizations in the Springfield area. Students have opportunities to work for federal and state judges and with government agencies and public interest organizations through the law school internship program, or to individually arrange internships. The law school also offers a legal services clinic, discrimination law clinic, criminal law clinic, and disability law clinic. Facilities of special interest to law students include a 360,000 volume law library that contains computer laboratories exclusively for student use; a moot court room used for law trial simulation classes, moot court competitions, and semiannual visits by the Massachusetts appeals court; and the Healthful Living Center, a state-of-the-art athletic and recreation facility. Housing for students is available in Springfield, which offers a variety of housing such as apartments in multifamily homes and in downtown apartment complexes. Limited on-campus housing is also available. All law school facilities are accessible to the physically disabled.

Calendar

The law school operates on a traditional semester basis. Courses for full-time students are offered both day and evening and must be completed within 4 years. For part-time students, courses are offered both day and evening and must be completed within 5 years. New full- and part-time students are admitted in the fall. There is an 8-week summer session. Transferable summer courses are not offered.

Programs

The following joint degrees may be earned: J.D./M.B.A. (Juris Doctor/Master of Business Administration in conjunction with Western New England College), J.D./M.R.P. (Juris Doctor/Master of Regional Planning in conjunction with the University of Massachusetts at Amherst), and J.D./M.S.W. (Juris Doctor/Master of Social work in conjunction with Springfield College).

Phone: 413-782-1406
800-782-6665
Fax: 413-796-2067
E-mail: *lawadmis@wnec.edu*
Web: *www.law.wnec.edu*

Contact

Associate Dean and Director of Admissions, 413-782-1406 or 800-782-6665 for general inquiries; Sandra Belanger, Financial Aid Specialist, 413-796-2080 for financial aid information.

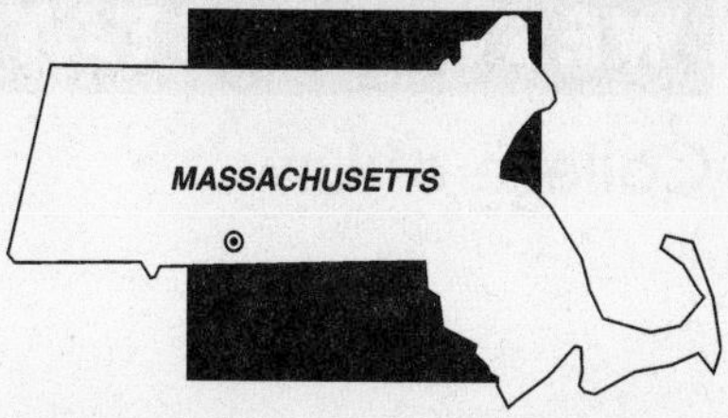

Required

To earn the J.D., candidates must complete 88 total credits, of which 46 are for required courses. They must maintain a minimum GPA of 2.0 in the required courses. The following first-year courses are required of all students: Criminal Law, Constitutional Law, Contracts, Lawyering Process, Civil Procedure, Property, and Torts. Required upper-level courses consist of Business Organizations, Income Tax, Evidence, Qualified Writing, and Legal Profession. The required orientation program for first-year students is a 3-day program at which students meet faculty members, administrators, and representatives of various student organizations and attend Lawyering Process Orientation sessions.

Electives

Upper-level students may enroll in the Legal Services Clinic for 12 credits, Criminal Law Clinic for 6 credits, Disabilities Law Clinic for 6 credits, and Discrimination Law clinic for 6 credits. There are a number of limited enrollment upper-level seminars and simulation courses offered in a broad range of subject-matter areas. Each is a 3-credit course designed to satisfy the upper-class writing requirement. Internships are available with the Massachusetts State Attorney, Connecticut State Attorney, Western Massachusetts Legal Services, Federal Judicial, U.S. Attorney, and the Internal Revenue Service's Regional Counsel Office. In independent study programs, a student may engage in advanced legal research for 2 to 3 credits under the supervision of 2 faculty members. Students may take summer programs offered by other ABA-accredited law schools. Special lecture series include the Clason Lecture Series. Students may study in tutorials with a faculty member on a mutually agreed upon subject and earn 1 to 3 credits. Remedial programs consist of a Legal Education Assistance Program, which is voluntary and available to first-year and upper-class students. The goal of the program is to provide additional assistance in legal research, writing, reasoning, and examination-taking skills. The most popular electives are Criminal Procedure, Trusts and Estates, and Trial Methods.

Graduation Requirements

In order to graduate, candidates must have a GPA of 2.0 and have completed the upper-division writing requirement.

Organizations

Students edit the *Western New England Law Review, Lex Brevis*, the student newspaper, and *Lytae*, the student-published yearbook. Annually, teams are sent to the National Moot Court, Jessup Moot Court International Law competitions, and Vale Corporate Moot Court. Other competitions include the ABA National Trial Competition and the ABA National Negotiation Competition. Organizations for law students include the Multi-Cultural Law Students Association, Women's Law Association, and Gay/Lesbian/Bisexual/Straight Alliance. Local chapters of national associations include Phi Alpha Delta, ABA-Law Student Division, and the Black Law Students Association. Other organizations include International Law Society, Environmental Law Coalition, and Criminal Law Society.

Library

The law library contains 360,000 hard-copy volumes and 169,000 microform volume equivalents, and subscribes to 4513 serial publications. Such on-line databases and networks as CALI, Dow-Jones, LEXIS, LOIS, NEXIS, OCLC First Search, WESTLAW, and Wilsonline Indexes are available to law students for research. Special library collections include a selective federal government document depository, publications of Massachusetts Continuing Legal Education, Inc., and a law and popular culture print/video/audio collection. Recently, the library added a second computer laboratory and installed a wireless network. The ratio of library volumes to faculty is 10,909 to 1 and to students is 733 to 1. The ratio of seats in the library to students is 1 to 1.

Faculty

The law school has 33 full-time and 34 part-time faculty members, of whom 26 are women. According to AAUP standards for Category IIA institutions, faculty salaries are well above average. About 15% of full-time faculty have a graduate law degree in addition to the J.D.; about 3% of part-time faculty have one. The ratio of full-time students to full-time faculty in an average class is 15 to 1; in a clinic, 10 to 1. The law school has a regular program of bringing visiting professors and other distinguished lecturers and visitors to campus.

Placement

J.D.s awarded: 153

Services available through: a separate law school placement center and

Services: advice on alternative careers and practice in various areas of the law.

Special features: networking functions, video-taped individual mock interviews, various panels and workshops presented on conducting the job search and on career options, a weekly Career Services newsletter containing part- and full-time job openings for students and alumni, articles of interest, and notices of writing competitions, summer study, study abroad, fellowships, clerkships, and internships. The school is an active member of 2 law school placement consortia, 1 state and 1 regional.

Full-time job interviews:	10 employers
Summer job interviews:	11 employers
Placement by graduation:	59% of class
Placement within 9 months:	89% of class
Average starting salary:	$18,000 to $106,000
Areas of placement:	
Private practice 2-10 attorneys	21%
Private practice 11-25 attorneys	2%
Private practice 26-50 attorneys	2%
Private practice 51-100 attorneys	2%
Private Practice 101 - 500 attorneys	4%
Business/industry	25%
Government	21%
Judicial clerkships	12%
Public interest	4%
Military	3%
Academic	3%

Students

About 53% of the student body are women; 13%, minorities; 6%, African American; 2%, Asian American; 4%, Hispanic; 1%, Native American; and 2%, Middle Eastern. The majority of students come from the Northeast (46%). The average age of entering students is 27; age range is 20 to 58. About 26% of students enter directly from undergraduate school. About 9% drop out after the first year for academic or personal reasons; 91% remain to receive a law degree.

WESTERN STATE UNIVERSITY

College of Law

1111 North State College Blvd
Fullerton, CA 92831

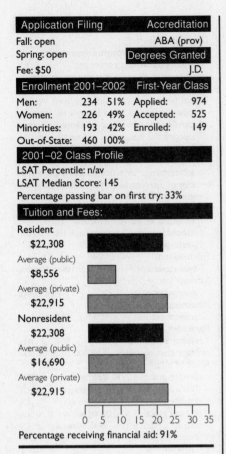

Application Filing		Accreditation
Fall: open		ABA (prov)
Spring: open		**Degrees Granted**
Fee: $50		J.D.

Enrollment 2001–2002			First-Year Class	
Men:	234	51%	Applied:	974
Women:	226	49%	Accepted:	525
Minorities:	193	42%	Enrolled:	149
Out-of-State:	460	100%		

2001–02 Class Profile

LSAT Percentile: n/av
LSAT Median Score: 145
Percentage passing bar on first try: 33%

Tuition and Fees:

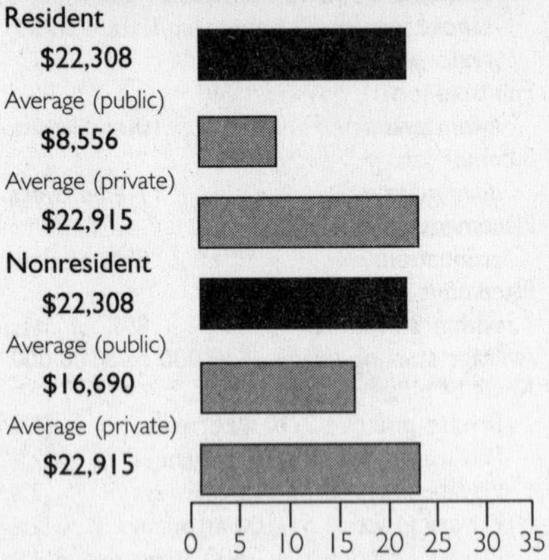

Percentage receiving financial aid: 91%

ADMISSIONS

In the fall 2001 first-year class, 974 applied, 525 were accepted, and 149 enrolled. Eighteen transfers enrolled. The median GPA of the most recent first-year class was 2.9.

Requirements

Applicants must have a bachelor's degree and take the LSAT. The most important admission factors include writing ability, GPA, and LSAT results. No specific undergraduate courses are required. Candidates are interviewed.

Procedure

The application deadline for fall entry is open. Applicants should submit an application form, LSAT results, transcripts, a nonrefundable application fee of $50, and 2 letters of recommendation. Notification of the admissions decision is 2 weeks after file is completed. The latest acceptable LSAT test date for fall entry is June. The law school uses the LSDAS.

Special

The law school recruits minority and disadvantaged students through a minority recruitment program and forums. Requirements are not different for out-of-state students. Transfer students must have a minimum GPA of 2 and good standing at an accredited law school.

Costs

Tuition and fees for the 2001-2002 academic year are $22,308 for all full-time students. Tuition for part-time students is $15,060 per year. Books and supplies cost about $1620 annually.

Financial Aid

About 91% of current law students receive some form of aid. The average annual amount of aid from all sources combined, including scholarships, loans, and work contracts, is $24,298; maximum, $38,432. Awards are based on need and merit. Required financial statements are the FAFSA and an institutional application. The priority aid application deadline for fall entry is March 1. First-year students are notified about their financial aid application at the time of acceptance.

About the Law School

Western State University College of Law was established in 1966 and is a private institution. The 4-acre campus is in a suburban area midway between Los Angeles and San Diego. The primary mission of the law school is to provide the highest quality legal education, based on an innovative program of studies designed to develop the tools of careful legal analysis and to foster a broad understanding of law, law practice, and legal theory. Students have access to federal, state, county, city, and local agencies, courts, correctional facilities, law firms, and legal aid organizations in the Fullerton area. Facilities of special interest to law students include county, state, city, and federal agencies, courts, correctional facilities, law firms, and legal aid organizations. Housing for students is widely available in a university environment adjacent to Western State and California State University of Fullerton. About 98% of the law school facilities are accessible to the physically disabled.

Calendar

The law school operates on a traditional semester basis. Courses for full-time students are offered days only and must be completed within 5 years. For part-time students, courses are offered both day and evening and must be completed within 6 years. New full- and part-time students are admitted in the fall and spring. There is an 8- plus 2-week summer session. Transferable summer courses are offered.

Programs

Required

To earn the J.D., candidates must complete 88 units, of which 58 are for required courses. They must maintain a minimum GPA of 2.0 in the required courses. The following first-year courses are required of all students: Criminal Law, Torts I and II, Civil Procedure I and II, Property I and II, Contracts, and Professional Skills I and II. Required upper-level courses consist of Criminal Procedure, Sales, Professional Responsibility, Advocacy, Constitutional Law, Evidence, Remedies, and Advanced Professional Skills. The orientation program for first-year students is mandatory.

Phone: 714-738-1000, ext. 2600
800-978-4529
Fax: 714-441-1748
E-mail: *paulb@wsulaw.edu*
Web: *wsulaw.edu*

Contact

Paul D. Bauer, Assistant Dean of Admission, (714) 738-1000, ext. 2600 for general inquiries; Donna Espinoza, Director of Student Finance, 714-738-1000, ext. 2356 for financial aid information.

Electives

The College of Law offers concentrations in criminal law. In addition, Research programs are available to all students for up to 2 credits. All students are eligible for externships (worth 5 to 8 credits) once prerequisites have been met. Study abroad is available to all students for a maximum of 6 credits. Noncredit tutorial and remedial programs are available to all students. There is an academic support program for minority students. The most widely taken electives are First Amendment courses in the Entrepreneurial Law Center and the Criminal Law Practice Center.

Graduation Requirements

In order to graduate, candidates must have a GPA of 2.0 and have completed the upper-division writing requirement and Advocacy course.

Organizations

Students edit the *Western State University Law Review*, *The Dictum*, and the newspaper, *SBA Connections*. Moot court competitions include Ferguson Moot Court, Jessup Moot Court, and California Moot Court. Other competitions include Traynor Moot Court and ABA Tax Section Young Lawyer's Forum. Student organizations include Women's Law Association, Black Law Student Association, and Student Bar Association. Local chapters of national organizations include ABA Law Student Division, Delta Theta Phi, and Phi Alpha Delta. Campus clubs include Criminal Law Association, Christian Legal Society, and Tax Law Society.

Library

The law library contains 174,569 hardcopy volumes and 44,237 microform volume equivalents, and subscribes to 846 serial publications. Such on-line databases and networks as CALI, DIALOG, Legal-Trac, LEXIS, LOIS, Mathew Bender, NEXIS, and WESTLAW are available to law students for research. Recently, the library was expanded to include 27,176 square feet and 312 networked connections. The ratio of library volumes to faculty is 8313 to 1 and to students is 380 to 1. The ratio of seats in the library to students is 1 to 1.

Faculty

The law school has 21 full-time and 50 part-time faculty members, of whom 30 are women. About 32% of full-time faculty have a graduate law degree in addition to the J.D. The ratio of full-time students to full-time faculty in an average class is 18 to 1. The law school has a regular program of bringing visiting professors and other distinguished lecturers and visitors to campus.

Students

About 49% of the student body are women; 42%, minorities; 6%, African American; 18%, Asian American; 17%, Hispanic; 1%, Native American; and 12%, Mexican-American. The average age of entering students is 28; age range is 21 to 62. About 24% of students enter directly from undergraduate school and 6% have a graduate degree. About 35% drop out after the first year for academic or personal reasons; 55% remain to receive a law degree.

Placement	
J.D.s awarded:	103
Services available through: a separate law school placement center	
Special features: public service program, externship program, data terminals, alumni mentors.	
Full-time job interviews:	15 employers
Summer job interviews:	15 employers
Placement by graduation:	n/av
Placement within 9 months:	88% of class
Average starting salary:	$41,000 to $175,000
Areas of placement:	
Private practice 2-10 attorneys	17%
Private practice 11-25 attorneys	12%
Private practice 26-50 attorneys	5%
Private practice 51-100 attorneys	5%
Private practice (solo)	6%
Business/industry	28%
Government	18%
Academic	5%
Judicial clerkships	1%
Public interest	1%
Military	1%

WHITTIER COLLEGE

School of Law

3333 Harbor Blvd.
Costa Mesa, CA 92626

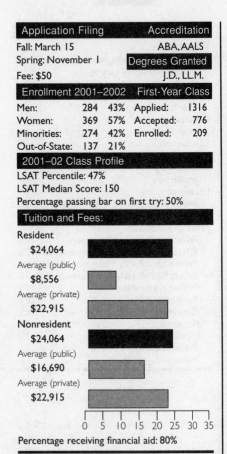

Application Filing	Accreditation
Fall: March 15	ABA, AALS
Spring: November 1	**Degrees Granted**
Fee: $50	J.D., LL.M.

Enrollment 2001–2002			First-Year Class	
Men:	284	43%	Applied:	1316
Women:	369	57%	Accepted:	776
Minorities:	274	42%	Enrolled:	209
Out-of-State:	137	21%		

2001–02 Class Profile

LSAT Percentile: 47%
LSAT Median Score: 150
Percentage passing bar on first try: 50%

Tuition and Fees:

Resident
$24,064
Average (public)
$8,556
Average (private)
$22,915
Nonresident
$24,064
Average (public)
$16,690
Average (private)
$22,915

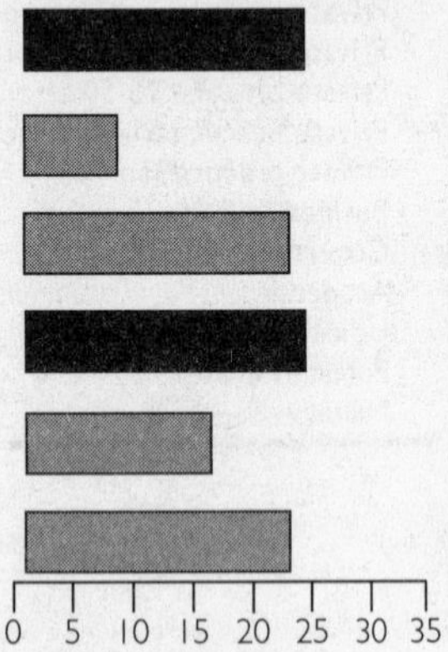

Percentage receiving financial aid: 80%

ADMISSIONS

In the fall 2001 first-year class, 1316 applied, 776 were accepted, and 209 enrolled. Ten transfers enrolled. The median LSAT percentile of the most recent first-year class was 47; the median GPA was 3 on a scale of 4.0. The lowest LSAT percentile accepted was 11; the highest was 95.

Requirements

Applicants must have a bachelor's degree, except in rare instances, and take the LSAT. Minimum acceptable GPA is 2.0 on a scale of 4.0. The most important admission factors include academic achievement, GPA, and LSAT results. No specific undergraduate courses are required. Candidates are not interviewed.

Procedure

The application deadline for fall entry is March 15. Applicants should submit an application form, LSAT results, transcripts, TOEFL, if English is not the primary language, a nonrefundable application fee of $50, 2 letters of recommendation, and a personal statement; if foreign, the applicant must have his/her foreign degree reviewed by an evaluation service approved by the school. Moreover, transcripts must be presented at matriculation. Notification of the admissions decision is as decisions are made. The latest acceptable LSAT test date for fall entry is June. The law school uses the LSDAS.

Special

The law school recruits minority and disadvantaged students by means of extensive fall recruiting, mass mailings targeted at minority groups, and diversity scholarships. Requirements are not different for out-of-state students. Transfer students must have one year of credit and have attended an ABA-approved law school.

Costs

Tuition and fees for the 2001-2002 academic year are $24,064 for all full-time students. Tuition for part-time students is $14,452 per year. Books and supplies run about $675 annually.

Financial Aid

About 80% of current law students receive some form of aid. The average annual amount of aid from all sources combined, including scholarships, loans, and work contracts, is $32,321; maximum, $53,234. Awards are based on need and merit. Required financial statement is the FAFSA. The aid application deadline for fall entry is June 1. Special funds for minority or disadvantaged students include a limited number of diversity scholarships that are available. First-year students are notified about their financial aid application at time of acceptance.

About the Law School

Whittier College School of Law was established in 1975 and is a private institution. The 15-acre campus is in a suburban area in Costa Mesa, California. The primary mission of the law school is in the Quaker tradition of Whittier College, stressing concern for the individual student's intellectual and ethnic development. The Law School expresses this concern through a low student-to-faculty ratio, which allows for considerable interaction with students, and by training socially and professionally responsible lawyers. Students have access to federal, state, county, city, and local agencies, courts, correctional facilities, law firms, and legal aid organizations in the Costa Mesa area. Facilities of special interest to law students include approximately 150 law firms that exist within a 5-mile radius of campus. Orange County courts provide abundant opportunities for externships, clerkships, and other associations for students. Substantial resources are also available in nearby Los Angeles. Housing for students is not available on campus but is available and affordable in surrounding areas. The Office of Student Affairs assists students seeking housing accommodations. All law school facilities are accessible to the physically disabled.

Calendar

The law school operates on a traditional semester basis. Courses for full-time students are offered both day and evening and must be completed within 5 years. For part-time students, courses are offered both day and evening and must be completed within 6 years. New full-time students are admitted in the fall and spring; part-time, fall. There is an 8-week summer session. Transferable summer courses are offered.

Programs

In addition to the J.D., the law school offers the LL.M. Students may take relevant courses in other programs and apply credit toward the J.D.; a maximum of 6 credits may be applied.

Required

To earn the J.D., candidates must complete 87 total credits, of which 40 are for required courses. They must maintain a minimum grade average of 77 in the required courses. The following first-year courses are required of all students: Contracts, Torts, Criminal Law, Real Property, Civil Procedure, Legal Process, and Legal Skills/Legal Bibliography. Required upper-level courses consist of Constitutional Law and Professional Responsibility Practicum. The required orientation program for first-year students a week-long program that includes

Phone: 714-444-4141, ext. 121
808-8188
Fax: 714-444-0250
E-mail: *info@law.whittier.edu*
Web: *law.whittier.edu*

Contact

Patricia Abracia, Director of Admissions, 714-444-4141, ext. 123 for general inquiries; Jennifer Pham, Director of Financial Aid, 714-444-4141, ext. 203, 205 for financial aid information.

introductions to and presentations by faculty, the administration, the library, financial aid office, and student organizations, plus a lecture entitled, "How to Survive in Law School."

Electives

Students must take 10 to 15 units in their area of concentration. The School of Law offers concentrations in environmental law, health law, Center for Children's Rights, and intellectual property. In addition, 3 clinics are offered. The Children's Rights Clinic offers 10 law students the opportunity to provide pro bono legal assistance to children in selected cases on such matters as guardianship, custody, and adoption, under faculty supervision. The Special Education Clinic affords students the opportunity to assist special-needs children with formal mediation with local school districts, in mediation sessions, and administrative hearings. The Legal Policy Clinic is a "clientless" clinic permitting students to advocate legal positions in the student's area of interest. Seminars are available including First Amendment, Health Law, and Adoption. Internships are permitted after the completion of 30 units. Students can earn up to 6 units working in the offices of county, state, city, and federal agencies and courts, such as the City Attorney's office, District Attorney's office, Department of Corporations, and the public defender's office. Students may take up to 3 units of independent study with a full-time professor. Field placements with various public and private nonprofit legal entities are available. Special lecture series include International Law, Health Law, and Center for Children's Rights Fellow Program. Summer-abroad programs are offered in Israel and Spain. Exchange programs are available at University of Paris, and University of Cantabria and University of Seville in Spain. Students are also permitted to enroll in ABA-approved study-abroad programs sponsored by other law schools for a maximum credit of 6 units. Each semester during the first year of law school, students are invited to attend extensive exam writing workshops. In addition, teaching assistants are available in most first-year classes for one-on-one and group tutorials. The Academic Success Program is designed to meet students needs in mastering writing and other skills. Special interest group programs include International Law, Environmental Law, Center for Children's Rights, and Intellectual Property. The most widely taken electives are Criminal Procedure, Evidence, Wills and trusts.

Graduation Requirements

In order to graduate, candidates must have a grade average of 77, and have completed the upper-division writing requirement. Students are required to take a 4-unit Professional Responsibility Course, which includes a 1-unit writing skills component.

Organizations

Students edit the *Whittier Law Review*, the *Whittier Journal of Child and Family Advocacy*, and the student newspaper, *The Barrister*. Moot court teams are sent to the National Moot Court, National Criminal Procedure, and Jessup International Moot Court competitions, among others. Whittier also hosts the National Juvenile Law and Sonnenberg First Year Moot Court competitions. Law student organizations include the Alternative Dispute Resolution Group, Asian and Pacific Islander Law Students Association, and Trial Advocacy Honors Board, and local chapters of Delta Theta Phi, Phi Alpha Delta, and Phi Delta Phi. Other law student organizations include Middle Eastern Law Students Organization, and Black Law Students and Women's Law Associations.

Library

The law library contains 356,086 hardcopy volumes and 168,765 microform volume equivalents, and subscribes to 4864 serial publications. Such on-line databases and networks as CALI, DIALOG, Infotrac, Legal-Trac, LEXIS, LOIS, Mathew Bender, NEXIS, RLIN, WESTLAW, and Wilsonline Indexes are available to law students for research. Special library collections include a federal and a California state depository. Recently, the library installed Innovative Interfaces library automation system. The ratio of library volumes to faculty is 12,717 to 1 and to students is 545 to 1. The ratio of seats in the library to students is 1 to 59.

Faculty

The law school has 28 full-time and 43 part-time faculty members, of whom 31 are women. According to AAUP standards for Category IIB institutions, faculty salaries are well above average. About 18% of full-time faculty have a graduate law degree in addition to the J.D.; about 5% of part-time faculty have one. The ratio of full-time students to full-time faculty in an average class is 19 to 1; in a clinic, 10 to 1. The law school has a regular program of bringing visiting professors and other distinguished lecturers and visitors to campus.

Placement

J.D.s awarded:	167
Services available through: a separate law school placement center	
Services: a mentor program, mock interviews, informational programs, a comprehensive library of directories and other materials; host Intellectual Property Job Fair	
Special features: member of Law School Career Advisors of Southern California (LSCA), a group of 11 law schools that sponsors career programs.	
Full-time job interviews:	n/av
Summer job interviews:	n/av
Placement by graduation:	67% of class
Placement within 9 months:	79% of class
Average starting salary:	$35,000 to $250,000
Areas of placement:	
Private practice 2-10 attorneys	41%
Private practice 11-25 attorneys	3%
Private practice 26-50 attorneys	4%
Private practice 51-100 attorneys	4%
Solo practice and private practice 100+ attorneys	8%
Business/industry	25%
Government	6%
Judicial clerkships	4%
Academic	4%
Public interest	1%

Students

About 57% of the student body are women; 42%, minorities; 1%, African American; 19%, Asian American; 15%, Hispanic; 1%, Native American; and 1%, foreign nationals. The majority of students come from California (79%). The average age of entering students is 25; age range is 19 to 23. About 30% of students enter directly from undergraduate school. About 30% drop out after the first year for academic or personal reasons; 70% remain to receive a law degree.

WIDENER UNIVERSITY

School of Law

4601 Concord Pike, P.O. Box 7474
Wilmington, DE 19803

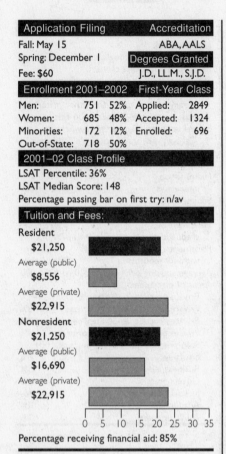

Application Filing		Accreditation
Fall: May 15		ABA, AALS
Spring: December 1		**Degrees Granted**
Fee: $60		J.D., LL.M., S.J.D.

Enrollment 2001–2002			First-Year Class	
Men:	751	52%	Applied:	2849
Women:	685	48%	Accepted:	1324
Minorities:	172	12%	Enrolled:	696
Out-of-State:	718	50%		

2001–02 Class Profile

LSAT Percentile: 36%
LSAT Median Score: 148
Percentage passing bar on first try: n/av

Tuition and Fees:

Resident
$21,250
Average (public)
$8,556
Average (private)
$22,915
Nonresident
$21,250
Average (public)
$16,690
Average (private)
$22,915

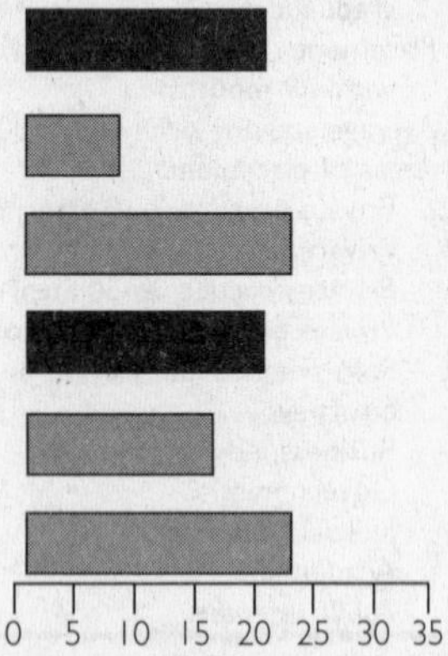

Percentage receiving financial aid: 85%

ADMISSIONS

Information in the above capsule and the following profile applies to both campuses unless otherwise stated. In the fall 2001 first-year class, 2849 applied, 1324 were accepted, and 696 enrolled. Twelve transfers enrolled. The median LSAT percentile of the most recent first-year class was 36; the median GPA was 3.03 on a scale of 4.0. The lowest LSAT percentile accepted was 7; the highest was 95.

Requirements

Applicants must have a bachelor's degree and take the LSAT. There are special admission opportunities for graduates of the 14 universities in the Pennsylvania State System. The most important admission factors include LSAT results, GPA, and academic achievement. A personal statement is highly recommended. No specific undergraduate courses are required. Candidates are not interviewed.

Procedure

The application deadline for fall entry is May 15. Applicants should submit an application form, LSAT results, transcripts, a nonrefundable application fee of $60, letters of recommendation, and a personal statement (both strongly suggested). Notification of the admissions decision is on a rolling basis. The latest acceptable LSAT test date for fall entry is June. The law school uses the LSDAS.

Special

The law school recruits minority and disadvantaged students through the availability of scholarships to members of minority groups underrepresented in the bar. The Trial Admissions Program is designed to identify and assist qualified minority students, and the school recruits students at programs sponsored by colleges and universities across the country. Requirements are not different for out-of-state students. Transfer students must have attended an ABA-approved law school and a certified transcript and letter of good standing must be submitted. A maximum of 35 qualified credits will be accepted in transfer. Transfer candidates must be in the top-third of their law school class.

Costs

Tuition and fees for the 2001-2002 academic year are $21,250 for all full-time students. Tuition for part-time students is $15,900 per year. On-campus room and board costs about $3900 annually; books and supplies run $1000.

Financial Aid

About 85% of current law students receive some form of aid. The average annual amount of aid from all sources combined, including scholarships, loans, and work contracts, is $19,676; maximum, $32,220. Awards are based on need and merit. A number of substantial scholarships are awarded to outstanding applicants and continuing students. Required financial statement is the FAFSA. The aid application deadline for fall entry is open for first-year students. Merit scholarships are available to minority and disadvantaged students. Deferred tuition loans are offered to students maintaining a satisfactory GPA. First-year students are notified about their financial aid application at time of acceptance.

About the Law School

Widener University School of Law is a private institution. There are 2 campuses. The 40-acre campus in suburban Delaware is 3 miles from downtown Wilmington; the 25-acre Harrisburg, Pennsylvania campus is 7 miles from the capital at 3800 Vartan Way, Harrisburg, PA 17110, phone 717-541-3999. The primary mission of the law school is to emphasize the development of legal writing and practice skills through an extensive curriculum of traditional courses, skills training, clinics and externships, and specialized advanced seminars, with teaching as the highest priority. Students have access to federal, state, county, city, and local agencies, courts, correctional facilities, law firms, and legal aid organizations in the Wilmington area. In addition, students have access to the numerous resources available at the university's main campus. Both campuses provide extensive clinical and skills programs, moot court rooms, law libraries, audiovisual centers, recreational facilities, and student dining centers. The Wilmington campus has on-campus residence halls and townhouse apartments. Area apartments are widely available. Student housing in Harrisburg consists of several apartment complexes within walking distance. About 90% of the law school facilities are accessible to the physically disabled.

Calendar

The law school operates on a traditional semester basis. Courses for full-time students are offered days only and must be completed within 5 years. Evening classes are offered on a space-available basis. For part-time students, courses are offered both day and evening; some classes are offered on Saturdays, and must be completed within 6 years. New full-time students are admitted in the fall and spring (DE campus); part-time, fall. There is a 7-week summer session. Transferable summer courses are offered.

Programs

In addition to the J.D., the law school offers the LL.M., S.J.D., and M.J. (Master of Jurisprudence), D.L. (Doctor of Laws). Students may take relevant courses in other programs and apply credit toward the J.D.; a maximum of 9 credits may be applied. The following

Phone: 302-477-2162 (DE); 717-541-3903 (PA)
1-888-WIDENER
Fax: 302-477-2224 (DE); 717-541-3999 (PA)
E-mail: *law.admissions@law.widener.edu*
Web: *http://www.widener.edu/law/law.html*

Contact

Barbara Ayars, Assistant Dean for Admissions, 302-477-2162 for general inquiries; Anthony Doyle, Assistant Dean for Financial Aid, 302-477-2272 for financial aid information.

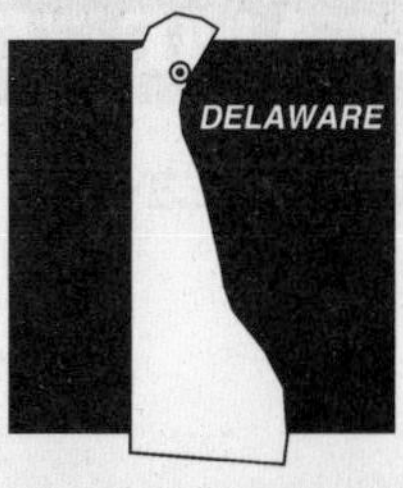

joint degrees may be earned: J.D./M.B.A. (Juris Doctor/Master of Business Administration), J.D./M.M.P. (Juris Doctor/Master of Marine Policy), J.D./M.L.S. (Juris Doctor/Master of Library Science), and J.D./Psy.D. (Juris Doctor/Doctor of Psychology in Law).

Required

To earn the J.D., candidates must complete 87 total credits, of which 64 (55, DE campus) are for required courses. They must maintain a minimum GPA of 2.0 in the required courses. Check with the individual campus for the most current list of required courses. The required orientation program for first-year students 1-week that includes an introduction to law course and informational sessions on information technology, the legal information center, and other topics.

Electives

Students must take 12 to 18 credits in their area of concentration. The School of Law offers concentrations in corporate law, criminal law, environmental law, family law, international law, juvenile law, labor law, litigation, securities law, tax law, torts and insurance, and law and government, commercial, property and probate, health law. Clinics for up to 8 credits are offered and clinical education also includes a comprehensive trial advocacy training program. Seminars are offered in most areas of concentration. Students may take part in externships with legislative and state agencies, district attorneys, public defenders, legal aid societies, and state and local courts. All students must complete a major research paper or directed research project. The school's legal journals, moot court, and trial advocacy program, and the many institutes and organizations provide additional opportunities for scholarly research. Check with the school for study abroad and field work opportunities. The most widely taken electives are Wills and Trusts, Family Law and Secured Transactions.

Graduation Requirements

In order to graduate, candidates must have a GPA of 2.0 and have completed the upper-division writing requirement.

Organizations

The primary law reviews are *Delaware Journal of Corporate Law* (Wilmington); *Widener Journal of Public Law* (Harrisburg); also publishes the *Annual Survey of Pennsylvania Administrative Law* and the *Widener Law Symposium Journal (Wilmington)*. The student newspaper is *The Law Forum*. The Health Law Institute publishes the *Newsletter of the Society of Health Care Attorneys*. The Law and Government Institute publishes the *Administrative Law Bulletin* of the Pennsylvania Bar Association. The Moot Court Honor Society sponsors the G. Fred DiBona Competition, the Delaware-Harrisburg Moot Court Competition, and Ruby R. Vale Interschool Corporate Moot Court Competition. The Moe Levine Trial Advocacy Honor Society sponsors the Hugh B. Pearce Memorial Trial Advocacy Competition and qualifying competitions for the Gorby Moot Court and National Association of Criminal Defense Counsel. Student organizations include the Student Bar Association, Juvenile Justice Society, and Business Law Society. There are local chapters of ATLA, Phi Alpha Delta, and Public Interest Law Alliance.

Library

The law library contains 322,141 hard-copy volumes and 293,021 microform volume equivalents, and subscribes to 8434 serial publications. Such on-line databases and networks as CALI, CIS Universe, DIALOG, Infotrac, Legal-Trac, LEXIS, LOIS, Mathew Bender, NEXIS, WESTLAW, and FIS On-line, among others, are available to law students for research. Special library collections include state and federal depository materials, U.S. Supreme Court records and briefs, CIS congressional library, corporate law, law and government, and health law collections. The Wilmington campus library was completely renovated during 1998-2000 to accommodate present and future technology needs of students. In Harrisburg, a renovation project was completed in 2000 to accommodate the growth of the collection. The library has developed and maintains the Delaware Corporate Law Clearinghouse web site. The ratio of library volumes to faculty is 7690 to 1 and to students, 488 to 1. The ratio of seats in the library to students is 1 to 2.

Faculty

The law school has 80 full-time and 110 part-time faculty members, of whom 68 are women. According to AAUP standards for Category IIA institutions, faculty salaries are above average. About 24% of full-time faculty have a graduate law degree in addition to the J.D.; about 18% of part-time faculty have one. The ratio of full-time students to full-time faculty in an average class is 12 to 1; in a clinic, 10 to 1. The law school has a regular program of bringing visiting professors and other distinguished lecturers and visitors to campus.

Placement	
J.D.s awarded:	355
Services available through: a separate law school placement center	
Services: career resource library that includes books, directories, periodicals, and videotapes; lists of all area judges.	
Special features: Alumni-student mentor program; free faxing, photocopying and telephone usage; videotaped mock interviews; career panels on various career options; specialized programs for minority students; and a weekly e-mail alumni employment newsletter. All professional staff possess J.D. degrees..	
Full-time job interviews:	19 employers
Summer job interviews:	30 employers
Placement by graduation:	62% of class
Placement within 9 months:	89% of class
Average starting salary:	$20,000 to $350,000
Areas of placement:	
Private practice 2-10 attorneys	14%
Private practice 11-25 attorneys	5%
Private practice 26-50 attorneys	2%
Private practice 51-100 attorneys	2%
Business/industry	22%
Other	22%
Judicial clerkships	16%
Government	14%
Public interest	1%
Academic	1%

Students

About 48% of the student body are women; 12%, minorities; 6%, African American; 1%, Asian American; and 1%, Hispanic. The majority of students come from the Northeast (91%). The average age of entering students is 25; age range is 21 to 66. About 35% of students enter directly from undergraduate school. About 8% drop out after the first year for academic or personal reasons; 92% remain to receive a law degree.

WILLAMETTE UNIVERSITY

College of Law

245 Winter Street S.E.
Salem, OR 97301

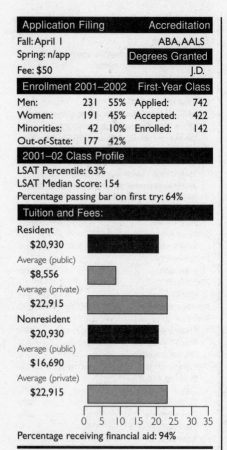

Application Filing		Accreditation
Fall: April 1		ABA, AALS
Spring: n/app		**Degrees Granted**
Fee: $50		J.D.

Enrollment 2001–2002			First-Year Class	
Men:	231	55%	Applied:	742
Women:	191	45%	Accepted:	422
Minorities:	42	10%	Enrolled:	142
Out-of-State:	177	42%		

2001–02 Class Profile

LSAT Percentile: 63%
LSAT Median Score: 154
Percentage passing bar on first try: 64%

Tuition and Fees:

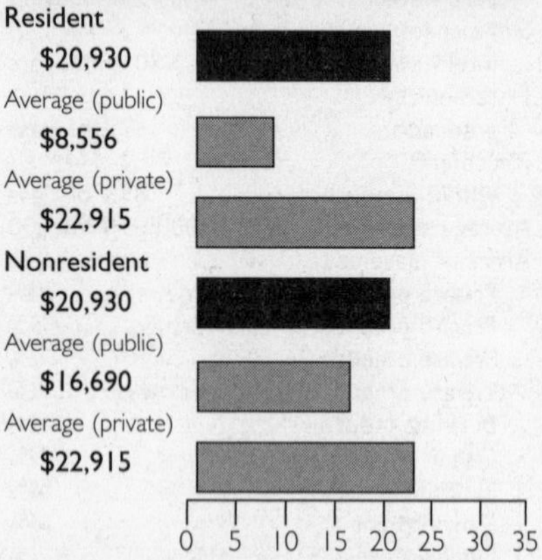

Percentage receiving financial aid: 94%

ADMISSIONS

In the fall 2001 first-year class, 742 applied, 422 were accepted, and 142 enrolled. Seven transfers enrolled. The median LSAT percentile of the most recent first-year class was 63; the median GPA was 3.24 on a scale of 4.0. The highest LSAT percentile was 97.

Requirements

Applicants must have a bachelor's degree and take the LSAT. The most important admission factors include LSAT results, GPA, and academic achievement. No specific undergraduate courses are required. Candidates are not interviewed.

Procedure

The application deadline for fall entry is April 1. Applicants should submit an application form, LSAT results, transcripts, a nonrefundable application fee of $50, 2 letters of recommendation, and a personal statement. Notification of the admissions decision is begun by March 15. The latest acceptable LSAT test date for fall entry is February. The law school uses the LSDAS.

Special

The law school recruits minority and disadvantaged students through programs, scholarships, and alumni contacts. Requirements are not different for out-of-state students. Transfer students must have attended an ABA-approved law school, be in good standing academically, and be eligible to return to their current law school.

Costs

Tuition and fees for the 2001-2002 academic year are $20,930 for all full-time students. On-campus room and board costs about $6030 annually; books and supplies run $1250.

Financial Aid

About 94% of current law students receive some form of aid. The average annual amount of aid from all sources combined, including scholarships, loans, and work contracts, is $28,253; maximum, $43,387. Awards are based on need and merit. Required financial statement is the FAFSA. The aid application deadline for fall entry is February 1. Special funds for minority or disadvantaged students include 2 full-tuition renewable waivers for qualified minority students in the entering class. First-year students are notified about their financial aid application approximately 2 weeks after acceptance.

About the Law School

Willamette University College of Law was established in 1883 and is a private institution. The 57-acre campus is in an urban area 45 miles south of Portland in Salem, the state capital. The primary mission of the law school is to provide legal training that is broad-based in content in an environment that promotes competition and encourages collaboration. Students have access to federal, state, county, city, and local agencies, courts, correctional facilities, law firms, and legal aid organizations in the Salem area. The college is located across the street from the state capitol and is within walking distance of the tax court, Oregon Supreme Court, the Supreme Court Library, the Oregon Court of Appeals, and virtually all state agencies and departments. Facilities of special interest to law students include several county and 2 federal courts located within approximately 1 hour of Williamette University. Housing for students includes a limited number of on-campus single rooms, an apartment building on campus offering 1-bedroom apartments, and reasonably priced off-campus housing. All law school facilities are accessible to the physically disabled.

Calendar

The law school operates on a traditional semester basis. Courses for full-time students are offered days only and must be completed within 3 years. There is no part-time program. New full- and part-time students are admitted in the fall. There is a 7-week summer session. Transferable summer courses are offered.

Programs

In addition to the J.D., the law school offers the International and Comparative Legal Studies Certificate; Law and Business Certificate, Law and Government Certificate, and Dispute Resolution Certificate. Students may take relevant courses in other programs and apply credit toward the J.D.; a maximum of 6 credits may be applied. The following joint degrees may be earned: J.D./M.M. (Juris Doctor/Master of Management).

Phone: 503-370-6282
Fax: 503-370-6375
E-mail: *law-admission@willamette.edu*

Contact

Lawrence Seno, Jr., Director of Admission, 503-370-6282 for general inquiries; Jim Eddy, Financial Aid Director, 503-370-6273 for financial aid information.

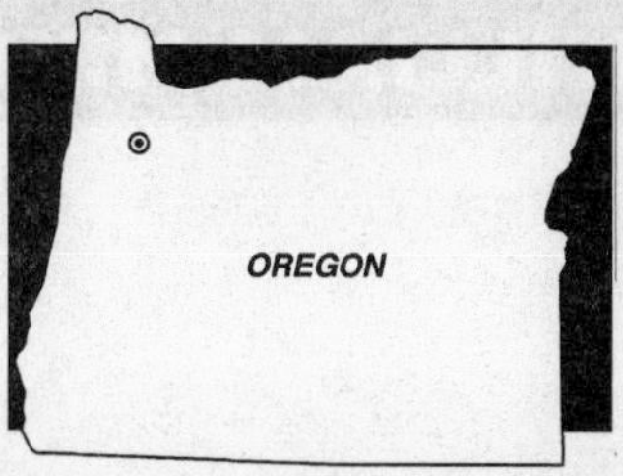

Required

To earn the J.D., candidates must complete 92 total credits, of which 39 are for required courses. They must maintain a minimum GPA of 2.0 in the required courses. The following first-year courses are required of all students: Civil Procedure, Property, Criminal Law, Contracts, Torts, Constitutional Law I and II, Dispute Resolution, and Legal Research and Writing. Required upper-level courses consist of Evidence, Professional Responsibility, and Constitutional Law II. The required orientation program for first-year students lasts 2 days and consists of an introduction to the law program and to legal research and writing.

Electives

The College of Law offers concentrations in corporate law, criminal law, environmental law, family law, international law, labor law, litigation, tax law, torts and insurance, alternative dispute resolution, real estate finance and development, law and government, commercial law, and estate planning and elder law. In addition, there are live client clinics worth 3 hours of credit each. Seminars, worth 2 hours of credit, are offered to second- and third-year students on such topics as law and education, American Indian law, and state constitutional law. An externship program places students in civil or criminal practice environments under the supervision of the school's field instructors. There is an Annual Lecture Series, Dispute Resolution Series, and Paulus Lecture Series. A Summer in China study program, worth 5 hours of credit, is offered to second- and third-year students. In addition, individual students, with ABA approval, may spend a semester at a leading law school in Quito, Ecuador, or in Hamburg, Germany. Special student assistants are available for students in legal research and writing. Along with a prelaw school study program, the college of law has an active minority student organization that sponsors a Martin Luther King dinner involving the community at large. The college offers simulation courses on negotiations, mediation, arbitration, interviewing and counseling, and trial practice. The most widely taken electives are Negotiation, Mediation, and Arbitration.

Graduation Requirements

In order to graduate, candidates must have a GPA of 2.0 and have completed the upper-division writing requirement.

Organizations

Students edit the *Willamette Law Review* and the *Williamette Bulletin of International Law and Dispute Resolution.* Students participate in a number of moot court competitions, including the National Appellate Competition, the Jessup International, and the Labor Law Appellate Competition. The student-run Moot Court Board provides or assists with other competitions in trial and appellate practice, including the National Trial Competition, Criminal Law, ATLA Trial, Business Trial, First Year Appellate, and Envrionmental Appellate competitions. Law student organizations include Willamette Women's Law Caucus, National Lawyers Guild, and Oregon Trial Lawyers Association. There are local chapters of Phi Delta Phi, Phi Alpha Delta, and Inns of Court. Other campus clubs include the Student Bar Association, law class organizations, and the Joint Degree Students Organization.

Library

The law library contains 272,000 hard-copy volumes and 866,000 microform volume equivalents, and subscribes to 1340 serial publications. Such on-line databases and networks as LEXIS, WESTLAW, and ORBIS are available to law students for research. Special library collections include a federal depository, Public International Law, and labor collections. Recently, the library added a wireless network. The ratio of library volumes to faculty is 11,333 to 1 and to students is 645 to 1. The ratio of seats in the library to students is 1 to 1.

Faculty

The law school has 24 full-time and 5 part-time faculty members, of whom 8 are women. About 10% of full-time faculty have a graduate law degree in addition to the J.D. The ratio of full-time students to full-time faculty in an average class is 24 to 1; in a clinic, 12 to 1.

Placement

J.D.s awarded: 131

Services available through: a separate law school placement center

Services: extensive mentor program with practicing attorneys; a first- year honors program; clerkship stipends; a fellowship program for minority students through the Oregon State Bar; and a separate Matching Funds program for public interest employment.

Special features: a director of career services, with special knowledge of the disabled. Services are coordinated for Joint Degree Students with Atkinson Graduate School of Management. There are career services newsletters with job hunting tips, workshop information, and job postings published every 2 weeks for students and monthly for alumni.

Full-time job interviews:	19 employers
Summer job interviews:	24 employers
Placement by graduation:	44% of class
Placement within 9 months:	84% of class
Average starting salary:	$22,880 to $112,500
Areas of placement:	
Private practice 2-10 attorneys	24%
Private practice 11-25 attorneys	8%
Private practice 26-50 attorneys	5%
Private practice 51-100 attorneys	2%
Private practice size unknown	3%
Government	30%
Business/industry	12%
Judicial clerkships	10%
Public interest	3%
Military	3%

Students

About 45% of the student body are women; 10%, minorities; 2%, African American; 5%, Asian American; 1%, Hispanic; and 1%, Native American. Most students come from Oregon (58%). The average age of entering students is 26; age range is 21 to 57. About 9% drop out after the first year for academic or personal reasons; 92% remain to receive a law degree.

WILLIAM MITCHELL COLLEGE OF LAW

875 Summit Avenue
St. Paul, MN 55105-3076

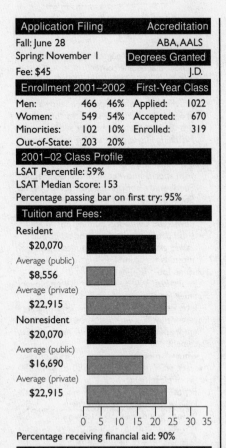

Application Filing		Accreditation
Fall: June 28		ABA, AALS
Spring: November 1		**Degrees Granted**
Fee: $45		J.D.

Enrollment 2001–2002			First-Year Class	
Men:	466	46%	Applied:	1022
Women:	549	54%	Accepted:	670
Minorities:	102	10%	Enrolled:	319
Out-of-State:	203	20%		

2001–02 Class Profile

LSAT Percentile: 59%
LSAT Median Score: 153
Percentage passing bar on first try: 95%

Tuition and Fees:

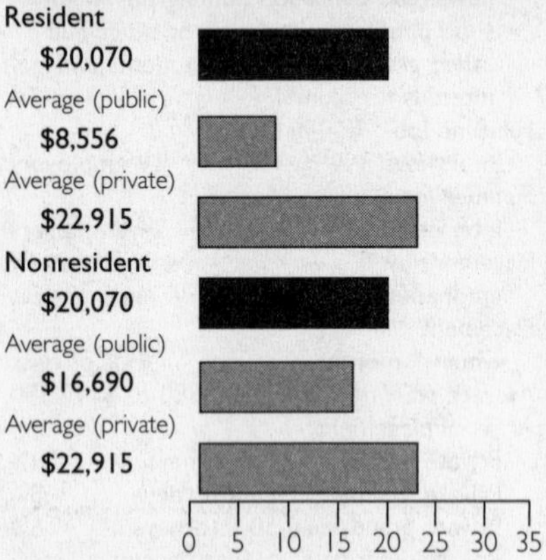

Percentage receiving financial aid: 90%

ADMISSIONS

In the fall 2001 first-year class, 1022 applied, 670 were accepted, and 319 enrolled. Twenty-eight transfers enrolled. The median LSAT percentile of the most recent first-year class was 59; the median GPA was 3.2 on a scale of 4.0. The lowest LSAT percentile accepted was 8; the highest was 99.

Requirements

Applicants must have a bachelor's degree and take the LSAT. The most important admission factors include academic achievement, LSAT results, and life experience. No specific undergraduate courses are required. Candidates are not interviewed.

Procedure

The application deadline for fall entry is June 28. Applicants should submit an application form, LSAT results, transcripts, TOEFL if English is a second language, a nonrefundable application fee of $45, 2 (3 preferred) letters of recommendation, and a personal essay, a resume, and a $150 nonrefundable deposit if accepted and planning to attend. Notification of the admissions decision is on a rolling basis. The latest acceptable LSAT test date for fall entry is June. The law school uses the LSDAS.

Special

The law school recruits minority and disadvantaged students through a general policy of admissions that encourages diversity in the student body and on-campus visits. Requirements are not different for out-of-state students. Transfer students must have one year of credit, have a minimum GPA of 2, have attended an ABA-approved law school, and submit a letter of good standing from the dean of the previously attended school. 24 credits must by completed at William Mitchell. Preadmissions courses consist of the Summer Partnership in Law (SPIL) for college sophomores and juniors. Introduction to Legal Theory is also taught.

Costs

Tuition and fees for the 2001-2002 academic year are $20,070 for all full-time students. Tuition for part-time students is $14,660 per year. Books and supplies run about $694 annually.

Financial Aid

About 90% of current law students receive some form of aid. The average annual amount of aid from all sources combined, including scholarships, loans, and work contracts, is $19,129. Awards are based on need and merit. Required financial statements are the FAFSA and the institutional application. The aid application deadline for fall entry is March 15. Special funds for minority or disadvantaged students are available through the William Mitchell Access Scholarships and many named scholarships. First-year students are notified about merit and access awards at time of acceptance; need-based after financial aid applications are processed.

About the Law School

William Mitchell College of Law was established in 1900 and is a private institution. The 7-acre campus is in an urban residential area of St. Paul. The primary mission of the law school is to provide a rigorous legal education that fully integrates practical skills, theory, and ethics; prepares students to serve clients and community and to promote justice and the public good; and accommodates the career, family, and other needs of students. Students have access to federal, state, county, city, and local agencies, courts, correctional facilities, law firms, and legal aid organizations in the St. Paul area. Facilities of special interest to law students are the Warren E. Burger Library, completed in 1990; high-tech classrooms; and Legal Practicum with model law firm offices. Housing for students is available in the neighborhood and elsewhere in Minneapolis-St. Paul. About 98% of the law school facilities are accessible to the physically disabled.

Calendar

The law school operates on a traditional semester basis. Courses for all full-time and part-time students are offered both day and evening and must be completed within 6 years. New full- and part-time students are admitted in the fall. There is a 7-week summer session. Transferable summer courses are offered.

Programs

Students may take relevant courses in other programs and apply credit toward the J.D.; a maximum of 62 credits may be applied. The following joint degrees may be earned: J.D./M.P.A. (Juris Doctor/Master of Arts in Public Administration).

Required

To earn the J.D., candidates must complete 86 total credits, of which 46 are for required courses. They must maintain a minimum GPA of 2.0 in the required courses. The following first-year courses are required of all students: Civil Procedure, Property I and II, Torts I and II, Contracts, Writing and Representation: Advice, and Writing and Representation: Persuasion. Required upper-level courses consist of Constitutional Law-Powers, Constitutional Law-Liberties, Professional Responsibility, Lawyering, a skills

Phone: 651-290-6476
888-WMCL-LAW
Fax: 651-290-6414
E-mail: *admissions@wmitchell.edu*
Web: *www.wmitchell.edu*

Contact

Dr. James H. Brooks, Dean of Students, 651-290-6362 for general inquiries; Jeanette Maynard Nelson, Director of Financial Aid, 612-290-6358 for financial aid information.

course, 2 statutory courses, Advanced Research and Writing, and Writing and Representation: Advocacy. The required orientation program for first-year students lasts 2 days and covers an introduction to law school, tours, the first class, and writing and representation.

Electives

The William Mitchell College of Law offers concentrations in corporate law, criminal law, environmental law, family law, international law, labor law, litigation, securities law, tax law, torts and insurance, and constitutional law, property, intellectual property, estates, jurisprudence, civil procedure, administrative and legislative process, and poverty law. In addition, there are clinics in Administrative Law, Business Law, and Immigration Law. Other opportunities are available for students as appellate and judicial interns working for the Attorney General and by participating in an independent clinic, among others. Seminars are available in law and sexuality, biomedical ethics, and the First Amendment. Independent research projects are available for 1 to 4 credits; students may do a maximum of 2 projects. Study abroad consists of a summer program in London. A summer tutorial program allows students to benefit from introductory courses emphasizing the legal process. First-year-subject tutors are also available. First-year students at academic risk can participate in Compass I, a noncredit course providing students with study and exam taking skills. The curriculum involves learning legal analysis using tort doctrine, does not require students to prepare additional legal materials, requires frequent written assignments, and gives students individualized feedback. Minority programs are provided by the Black Law Students Association, Hispanic Law Students Association, Gay-Lesbian Student Association, and the American Indian Law Student Association. Special interest group programs are provided by the Student Intellectual Property Association, Christian Law Fellowship, Jewish Law Society, Minnesota Public Interest Research Group, National Lawyers Guild, Minnesota Justice Foundation, and Women Law Students Association. The most widely taken electives are criminal law and procedure, evidence, and intellectual property survey.

Graduation Requirements

In order to graduate, candidates must have a GPA of 2.0 and have completed the upper-division writing requirement.

Organizations

The primary law review is the *William Mitchell Law Review* and the student newspaper is the *Opinion*. Teams participate in the National Civil Rights Moot Court, Tax Moot Court, and Philip C. Jessup International Moot Court. Other competitions include Rosalie Wahl Moot Court, ABA Client Counseling, ABA Negotiations, and ATLA Trial Advocacy. Law student organizations include the Student Bar Association, WMCL Democrats, and the Federalist Society. There are local chapters of Delta Theta Phi, Phi Alpha Delta, and Phi Delta Phi. Other law student organizations include Association for International Law, Health Law Society, and Women's Law Student Association.

Library

The law library contains 313,093 hardcopy volumes and 139,351 microform volume equivalents, and subscribes to 2085 serial publications. Such on-line databases and networks as DIALOG, LEXIS, WESTLAW, NEXIS, OCLC, the Internet, and Congressional Universe are available to law students for research. Special library collections include a federal depository library and a comprehensive collection of federal government documents covering legal materials from the federal courts, U.S. government agencies, Congress, and the executive branch. There is also an extensive tax collection. Recently, the library added approximately 75 network access points at study tables and carrels. The ratio of library volumes to faculty is 8697 to 1 and to students is 308 to 1. The ratio of seats in the library to students is 1 to 66.

Faculty

The law school has 36 full-time and 160 part-time faculty members, of whom 78 are women. About 17% of full-time faculty have a graduate law degree in addition to the J.D. The ratio of full-time students to full-time faculty in an average class is 51 to 1; in a clinic, 5 to 1. The law school has a regular program of bringing visiting professors and other distinguished lecturers and visitors to campus.

Placement

J.D.s awarded:	289
Services available through: a separate law school placement center	
Services: career panels, resource library, out-of-state job-search resources, on-line resources on the web site.	
Special features: comprehensive career-planning program; "Graduate Bulletin" (newsletter) courtesy subscription to all recent graduates.	
Full-time job interviews:	23 employers
Summer job interviews:	60 employers
Placement by graduation:	90% of class
Placement within 9 months:	94% of class
Average starting salary:	$20,800 to $260,000
Areas of placement:	
Private practice 2-10 attorneys	20%
Private practice 11-25 attorneys	4%
Private practice 26-50 attorneys	4%
Private practice 51-100 attorneys	3%
Private practice 100+ attorneys	12%
Business/industry	24%
Judicial clerkships	17%
Government	10%
Public interest	2%
Academic	2%
Military	1%

Students

About 54% of the student body are women; 10%, minorities; 4%, African American; 4%, Asian American; 2%, Hispanic; and 1%, Native American. The majority of students come from Minnesota (80%). The average age of entering students is 29; age range is 20 to 54. About 2% drop out after the first year for academic or personal reasons; 90% remain to receive a law degree.

Yale Law School

P.O. Box 208329
New Haven, CT 06520-8329

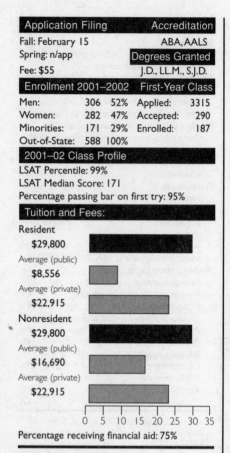

Application Filing		Accreditation
Fall: February 15		ABA, AALS
Spring: n/app		**Degrees Granted**
Fee: $55		J.D., LL.M., S.J.D.

Enrollment 2001–2002			First-Year Class	
Men:	306	52%	Applied:	3315
Women:	282	47%	Accepted:	290
Minorities:	171	29%	Enrolled:	187
Out-of-State:	588	100%		

2001–02 Class Profile

LSAT Percentile: 99%
LSAT Median Score: 171
Percentage passing bar on first try: 95%

Tuition and Fees:

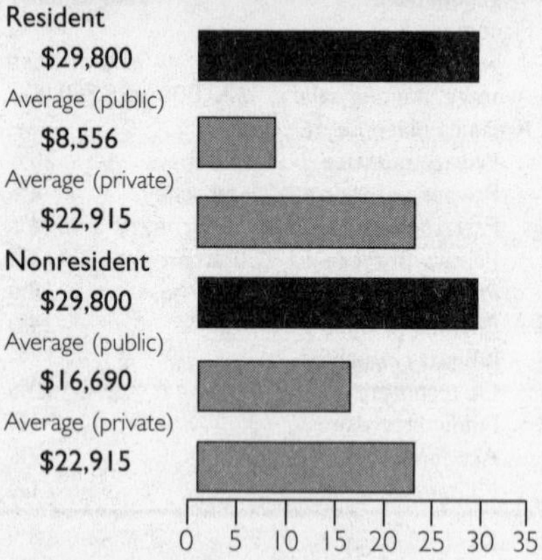

Percentage receiving financial aid: 75%

ADMISSIONS

In the fall 2001 first-year class, 3315 applied, 290 were accepted, and 187 enrolled. Eight transfers enrolled. The median LSAT percentile of the most recent first-year class was 99; the median GPA was 3.84 on a scale of 4.0. The highest LSAT percentile was 99.

Requirements

Applicants must have a bachelor's degree and take the LSAT. No specific undergraduate courses are required. Candidates are not interviewed.

Procedure

The application deadline for fall entry is February 15. Applicants should submit an application form, LSAT results, transcripts, a nonrefundable application fee of $55 to $70, 2 letters of recommendation, and an essay. Notification of the admissions decision is on a rolling basis. The latest acceptable LSAT test date for fall entry is December. The law school uses the LSDAS.

Special

The law school recruits minority and disadvantaged students by means of Candidate Referral Services through Law Services. Requirements are not different for out-of-state students. Transfer students must have one year of credit, have attended an ABA-approved law school, and have a weighted average of not less than B.

Costs

Tuition and fees for the 2001-2002 academic year are $29,800 for all full-time students. On-campus room and board costs about $9680 annually; books and supplies run $820.

Financial Aid

About 75% of current law students receive some form of aid. The average annual amount of aid from all sources combined, including scholarships, loans, and work contracts, is $27,000; maximum, $45,000. Awards are based on need. Required financial statement is the FAFSA. The aid application deadline for fall entry is March 15. First-year students are notified about their financial aid application at time of acceptance.

About the Law School

Yale University Yale Law School was established in 1801 and is a private institution. The campus is in an urban area in New Haven on the block bounded by Grove, High, Wall, and York streets. The primary mission of the law school is to train lawyers and leaders in the public and private sectors, and to encourage research in the law. The law school seeks to train lawyers for public service and teaching as well as for private practice, and to advance inquiry at the boundaries of the law as to inculcate knowledge at the core in a setting hospitable to a wide variety of intellectual currents. Students have access to federal, state, county, city, and local agencies, courts, correctional facilities, law firms, and legal aid organizations in the New Haven area. Facilities of special interest to law students include a renovated law library and computer facility; the Jerome W. Frank Legal Services Organization; the Orville H. Shell, Jr. Center for International Human Rights; the Center for Studies in Law, Economics, and Public Policy; numerous endowed lecture programs that bring distinguished speakers from around the world to Yale; and access to the university's 10.8 million-volume library system, and to its cultural, social, intellectual, and athletic facilities and activities. Limited housing space is available in the law school dormitories. The majority of students live in off-campus housing. Additionally, some family housing is available from the university. The university also has a housing office that assists students in locating housing. About 85% of the law school facilities are accessible to the physically disabled.

Calendar

The law school operates on a traditional semester basis. Courses for full-time students are offered days only and must be completed within 6 terms. There is no part-time program. New students are admitted in the fall. There is no summer session. Transferable summer courses are not offered.

Programs

In addition to the J.D., the law school offers the LL.M., J.S.D., and M.S.L., Master of Studies in Law, including fellowships in law for journalists and other scholars. Students may take relevant courses in other programs and apply credit toward the J.D.; a maximum of 15 credits may be applied. The following joint degrees may be earned: J.D./M.A. (Juris Doctor/Master of Arts), J.D./M.A.R. (Juris Doctor/Master of Arts in religion), J.D./M.B.A. (Juris Doctor/Master of Business Administration), J.D./M.D. (Juris Doctor/Doctor of Medicine), J.D./M.Div. (Juris Doctor/Master of Divinity), J.D./M.E.S. (Juris Doctor/Master of Environmental Studies), and J.D./Ph.D. (Juris Doctor/Doctor of Philosophy).

Required

To earn the J.D., candidates must complete 82 total credits, of which 19 are for required courses. The following first-year courses are required of all students: Constitutional Law, Contracts, Procedure, and Torts. Required upper-level courses consist of Criminal Law and Administration, Professional Responsibility and Legal Ethics Reading Group, and supervised analytic writing paper.

Phone: 203-432-4995
E-mail: *admissions.law@yale.edu*
Web: *www.law.yale.edu*

Contact
Jean K. Webb, Director of Admissions, 203-432-4995 for general inquiries; Patricia Barnes, Director of Financial Aid, 203-432-1688 for financial aid information.

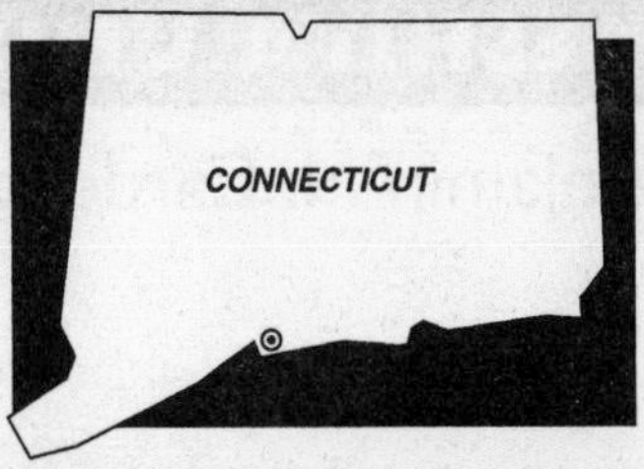

The optional orientation program for first-year students consists of a weekend prior to registration at which life at the law school and in New Haven is discussed.

Electives
The Yale Law School offers concentrations in corporate law, criminal law, entertainment law, environmental law, family law, international law, juvenile law, labor law, litigation, media law, securities law, sports law, tax law, torts and insurance, administrative law, constitutional law, comparative law, legal history, torts, criminal procedure, bankruptcy, law and economics, employment discrimination, property, health, antitrust, evidence, and international business. In addition, clinical opportunities are offered through the Jerome N. Frank Legal Services Orgainzation, which links law students with individuals in need of legal help who cannot afford private attorneys. Faculty-supervised students interview clients, write briefs, prepare witnesses, try cases, negotiate settlements, and argue appeals in state and federal courts, including the U.S. Court of Appeals for the Second circuit and the Connecticut Supreme Court. There are eight main projects: Advocacy for Parents and Children, Advocacy for People with Disabilities, Community Legal Services, Housing and Community Development, Immigration, Landlord/Tenant, Legal Assistance, and Prisons. Students also participate in independent projects at 2 local prosecutors' offices (the New Haven State Attorney and the U.S. Attorney) and at other public service law offices. Other clinics include the Environmental Protection Clinic and the Allard K. Lowenstein International Human Rights Law Clinic. In addition to the many seminars offered during the fall and spring terms, groups of six or more students may submit proposals for research and legislative drafting seminars. Also, fourth-and fifth-term students may elect to take the Intensive Semester Program. Research programs and independent reading may be undertaken after the first term with faculty permission. Numerous special lecture series are held annually, including the Timothy B. Atkerson Environmental Practitioner in Residence: the Cover Lecture in Law and Religion; the Ralph Gregory Elliot First Amendment Lecture; the Preiskel/Silverman Program on the Practicing Lawyer and the Public Interest; and the Robert L. Bernstein Lecture in International Human Rights. In the second term students may begin participation in programs managed primarily by students under the supervision of a faculty adviser. These include the Capital Defense Project, the Domestic Violence Temporary Restraining Order Project, the Greenhaven Prison Project, Street Law, Thomas Swan Barristers' Union Morris Tyler Moot Court of Appeals, and numerous reviews and journals.

Graduation Requirements
In order to graduate, candidates must have completed the upper-division writing requirement.

Organizations
Student-edited publications include the *Yale Law Journal, Yale Journal of International Law, Yale Journal of Law and Feminism, Yale Journal of Law and Humanities, Yale Journal on Regulation, Yale Human Rights and Development Law Journal,* and *Yale Law and Policy Review*. Moot court competitions include the Thurman Arnold Appellate Compettiton Prize, the Benjamin N. Cardozo Prize, and the John Fletcher Caskey, John Currier Gallagher, Potter Stewart, and Harlan Fiske Stone prizes. Other competitions or prizes include the Albom, Brody, Burkan Memorial, Cohen, Connecticut Attorneys' Title Insurance Company, Cullen, Egger, Emerson, Gherini, Gruter, Jewell, Khosla, Lemkin, Massey, Miller, Munson, Olin, Parker, Peres, Porter, Robbins Memorial, Scharps, Townsend, Wang, and Wayland. Law student organizations include the Asia Law Forum, the Initiative for Public Interest Law at Yale, and the Yale Law and Technology Society. There are local chapters of the Black Law Students Association, the Federalist Society, and the Native American Law Students Association.

Library
The law library contains 798,200 hardcopy volumes and 2583 microform volume equivalents, and subscribes to 9598 serial publications. Such on-line databases and networks as LEXIS, WESTLAW, ORBIS (Yale University catalog), MORRIS (Yale Law School catalog) are available to law students for research. Special library collections include a 200,000-volume foreign and international law collection. Recently, the library underwent a major renovation as part of a comprehensive, $90 million renovation of the Sterling Law Building. The ratio of library volumes to faculty is 11,913 to 1 and to students is 1357 to 1. The ratio of seats in the library to students is 2 to 3.

Faculty
The law school has 67 full-time and 39 part-time faculty members, of whom 28 are women. According to AAUP standards for Category I institutions, faculty salaries are well above average. The ratio of full-time students to full-time faculty in an average class is 12 to 1. The law school has a regular program of bringing visiting professors and other distinguished lecturers and visitors to campus.

Students
About 47% of the student body are women; 29%, minorities; 9%, African American; 11%, Asian American; 8%, Hispanic; and 1%, Native American. The average age of entering students is 25.

Placement

J.D.s awarded:	198
Services available through: a separate law school placement center	
Services: judicial clerkship counseling and programs, public interest counseling and programs, career counseling, publications, recruiting events, resource library	
Special features: a professional counseling staff, comprehensive individual career counseling, a program resource library, publications, and recruiting events.	
Full-time job interviews:	185 employers
Summer job interviews:	n/av
Placement by graduation:	n/av
Placement within 9 months:	96% of class
Average starting salary:	n/av
Areas of placement:	
Private practice 2-100 attorneys	36%
Judicial clerkships	45%
Business/industry	7%
Public interest	7%
Academic	3%
Government	2%

YESHIVA UNIVERSITY

Benjamin N. Cardozo School of Law

55 Fifth Avenue
New York, NY 10003

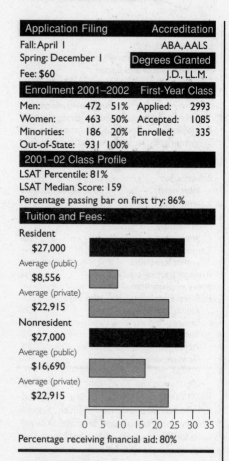

Application Filing		Accreditation
Fall: April 1		ABA, AALS
Spring: December 1		**Degrees Granted**
Fee: $60		J.D., LL.M.

Enrollment 2001–2002			First-Year Class	
Men:	472	51%	Applied:	2993
Women:	463	50%	Accepted:	1085
Minorities:	186	20%	Enrolled:	335
Out-of-State:	931	100%		

2001–02 Class Profile

LSAT Percentile: 81%
LSAT Median Score: 159
Percentage passing bar on first try: 86%

Tuition and Fees:

Resident
$27,000
Average (public)
$8,556
Average (private)
$22,915
Nonresident
$27,000
Average (public)
$16,690
Average (private)
$22,915

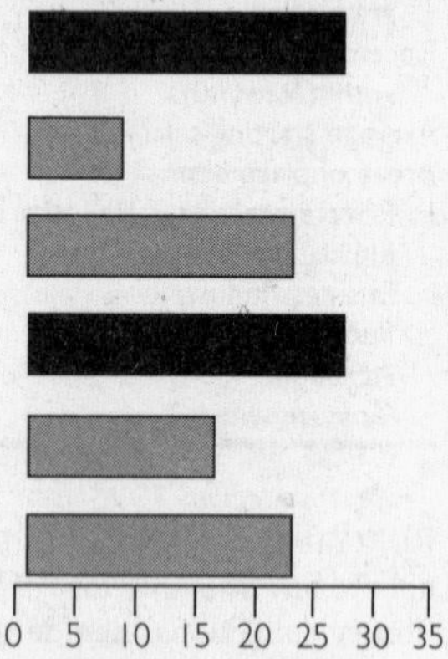

Percentage receiving financial aid: 80%

ADMISSIONS

In the fall 2001 first-year class, 2993 applied, 1085 were accepted, and 335 enrolled. Twelve transfers enrolled. The median LSAT percentile of the most recent first-year class was 81; the median GPA was 3.4 on a scale of 4.0.

Requirements

Applicants must have a bachelor's degree and take the LSAT. No specific undergraduate courses are required. Candidates are not interviewed.

Procedure

The application deadline for fall entry is April 1. Applicants should submit an application form, LSAT results, transcripts, a nonrefundable application fee of $60, 2 letters of recommendation, a dean's certification form, and a personal statement. Notification of the admissions decision is on a rolling basis. The latest acceptable LSAT test date for fall entry is February. The law school uses the LSDAS.

Special

The law school recruits minority and disadvantaged students by means of Candidate Referral Service searches, special mailings, attendance at law fairs and receptions, and an Opportunities for Minority Students brochure. Requirements are not different for out-of-state students. Transfer students must have one year of credit and have attended an ABA-approved law school. Most of the emphasis in the admissions decision is placed on first-year performance.

Costs

Tuition and fees for the 2001-2002 academic year are $27,000 for all full-time students. Books and supplies cost about $989 annually.

Financial Aid

About 80% of current law students receive some form of aid. The average annual amount of aid from all sources combined, including scholarships, loans, and work contracts, is $25,340; maximum, $48,716. Awards are based on need and merit. Required financial statements are the FAFSA and Need Access. The aid application deadline for fall entry is April 15. Special funds for minority or disadvantaged students are available. First-year students are notified about their financial aid application at time of acceptance, as long as the FAFSA and Need Access have been received.

About the Law School

Yeshiva University's Benjamin N. Cardozo School of Law was established in 1976 and is a private institution. The campus is in an urban area in the heart of Greenwich Village in lower Manhattan. The primary mission of the law school is to enhance the student's understanding of the legal profession and of the ethical dilemmas and professional responsibilities for a lawyer in today's society. Students have access to federal, state, county, city, and local agencies, as well as courts, correctional facilities, law firms, and legal aid organizations in the New York area. Students benefit from the school's proximity to city, state, and federal bar associations and from reciprocal library privileges with numerous area law schools. Facilities of special interest to law students include the New York Stock Exchange, American Stock Exchange, the United Nations, and New York's many cultural institutions. Housing for students is available through assistance from the Admissions office, a housing booklet, and a newsletter. A residence hall is located 1 block from the law school. All law school facilities are accessible to the physically disabled.

Calendar

The law school operates on a traditional semester basis. Courses for full-time students are offered days only and must be completed within 7 semesters or 5 years. For part-time students, courses are also offered days only. New students are admitted in the summer. There is a 13-week summer session. Transferable summer courses are not offered.

Programs

In addition to the J.D., the law school confers the LL.M. Students may take relevant courses in other programs and apply credit toward the J.D.; a maximum of 12 credits may be applied. The following joint degrees may be earned: J.D./M.A. (Juris Doctor/Master of Arts in political science, sociology, economics, or philosophy), J.D./M.S. (Juris Doctor/Master of Science in management), and J.D./M.S.W (Juris Doctor/Master of Social Work).

Required

To earn the J.D., candidates must complete 84 total credits, of which 38 are for required courses. They must maintain a minimum GPA of 2.2 in the required courses. The following first-year courses are required of all students: Torts, Contracts, Property, Civil Procedure, Elements of the Law, Legal Writing and Moot Court, Criminal Law, and Constitutional Law. Required upper-level courses consist of Professional Responsibility, upper-level legal research, upper-level writing requirement, and distribution requirements. Clinics are offered but are not required. The required orientation program for first-year students consists of 3 days of orientation activities.

Phone: 212-790-0274
Fax: 212-790-0482
E-mail: *lawinfo@ymail.yu.edu*
Web: *www.cardozo.yu.edu*

Contact

Office of Admissions, 212-790-0274 for general inquiries; Thomas Curtin, Financial Aid Director, 212-790-0392 for financial aid information.

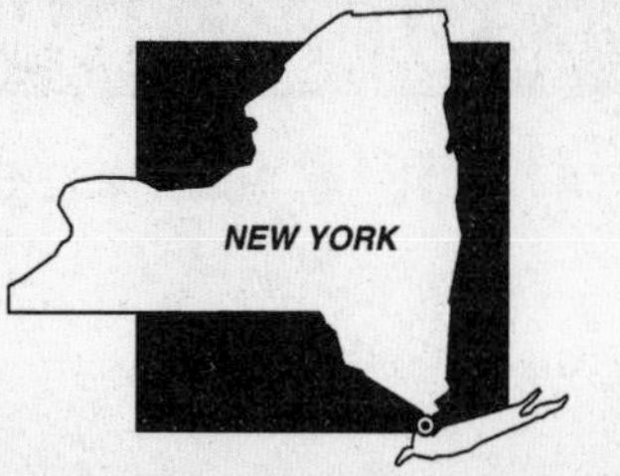

Electives

Students must take 10 to 15 credits in their area of concentration. The Benjamin N. Cardozo School of Law offers concentrations in corporate law, criminal law, entertainment law, family law, international law, litigation, media law, tax law, intellectual property law, commercial law, constitutional law, jurisprudence, legal history, property and real estate law, and public law. In addition, clinics include the Criminal Law Clinic at the Manhattan Criminal Court, the Criminal Appeals Clinic in which students represent indigent appellants, and the Prosecutor Practicum in which students assist the Manhattan district attorney. Special courses and seminars are offered in human rights, federal regulation of the media, and bioethics and the law. A wide variety of internships is offered during the academic year as well as through the Summer Institute. Research assistants are hired by professors. Field work is offered through the Criminal Law Clinics at the Manhattan Criminal Court, the Brooklyn Mediation Center through the Mediation Clinic, and the U.S. Tax Court through the Tax Clinic. Many seminars and conferences are held each year. Study abroad is provided through the Uri and Caroline Bauer Israel Program at Hebrew University and programs in Budapest, Hungary, Paris, France, and at Oxford University, England. For students at risk, the law school offers academic support, counseling, and workshops in legal methods, and requires a directed studies academic program. Minority programs include activities of the Black, Asian, and Latino Law Student Association (BALLSA). There is an Intellectual Property Law Program, which encompasses traditional courses, unusual externships, and ground-breaking symposia and lectures, and the Samuel and Ronnie Heyman Center on Corporate Governance. The most widely taken electives are entertainment, communications, and corporate and tax law.

Graduation Requirements

In order to graduate, candidates must have a GPA of 2.2 and have completed the upper-division writing requirement, the upper-division legal research, Professional Responsibility, and distribution requirements.

Organizations

Students edit the *Cardozo Law Review, Arts and Entertainment Law Journal, Cardozo Women's Law Journal, Cardozo Journal of International and Comparative Law, On-line Journal of Conflict Resolution, Cardozo Studies in Law and Literature, New York Real Estate Reporter*, and the newspaper *The Insider*. Moot court competitions include the ABA-sponsored National, Jessup International, and Labor Law. Other competitions include the Advocacy and Monrad Paulsen competitions and the Cardozo/BMI Moot Court Competition in communications and entertainment law. Law student organizations include Sports and Entertainment Law Students Association, Public Interest Law Students Association, and Cardozo Advocates for Battered Women. Campus clubs and other organizations include the Bwketsell Club, Environmental Law Society, and International Law Students Society. There are local chapters of the American Constitutional Law Society; Black, Asian, and Latino law student associations; and Cardozo Dispute Resolution Society.

Library

The law library contains 465,353 hard-copy volumes and 1,178,352 microform volume equivalents, and subscribes to 8054 serial publications (1702 periodicals, 6352 serial subscriptions). Such online databases and networks as CALI, DIALOG, LEXIS, LOIS, NEXIS, WESTLAW, CCH Tax, Hein-on-Line, and U.N. are available to law students for research. Special library collections include the Louis and Ida Shlansky Family Foundation Library of Jewish and Israeli Law and U.S. government depository. Recently, the library added 1 floor and renovated another floor. The ratio of library volumes to faculty is 10,576 to 1 and to students is 500 to 1. The ratio of seats in the library to students is 1 to 2.

Faculty

The law school has 44 full-time and 52 part-time faculty members, of whom 25 are women. About 16% of full-time faculty have a graduate law degree in addition to the J.D. The ratio of full-time students to full-time faculty in an average class is 18 to 1; in a clinic, 8 to 1. The law school has a regular program of bringing visiting professors and other distinguished lecturers and visitors to campus. There is a chapter of the Order of the Coif; 12 faculty and 170 graduates are members.

Placement

Placement	
J.D.s awarded:	296
Services available through: a separate law school placement center	
Services: nationally renowned on-line job placement system and computerized databases for student and alumni use, and on-line registration system for on-campus recruitment.	
Special features: large number of counselors with J.D.'s and practice experience offer a wide array of services including but not limited to mock video interviews, a summer institute combining an internship and seminar, extensive assistance with summer and postgraduate federal and state judicial clerkships, a public interest resource center, and a separate career resource library.	
Full-time job interviews:	140 employers
Summer job interviews:	1 employer
Placement by graduation:	n/av
Placement within 9 months:	99% of class
Average starting salary:	$37,500 to $150,000
Areas of placement:	
Private practice 2-10 attorneys	5%
Private practice 11-25 attorneys	9%
Private practice 26-50 attorneys	7%
Private practice 51-100 attorneys	9%
Private practice 101 - 500+ attorneys	27%
Government	15%
Business/industry	13%
Public interest	7%
Judicial clerkships	5%
Academic	0.4%

Students

About 50% of the student body are women; 20%, minorities; 4%, African American; 10%, Asian American; and 6%, Hispanic. The average age of entering students is 24; age range is 20 to 50. About 50% of students enter directly from undergraduate school. About 4% drop out after the first year for academic or personal reasons; 96% remain to receive a law degree.

CHAPTER 14

Law Schools Not Approved by the ABA

AN OVERVIEW

Although the vast majority of law school students attend institutions approved by the American Bar Association, a distinct minority attend schools that have not received ABA accreditation. Applicants frequently wonder whether it will make a difference if they attend a nonapproved school. The answer to this question requires an understanding of what it means for a law school to be accredited.

For nearly a century, the American Bar Association has developed educational standards for law schools, reviewed institutional adherence to those standards, and approved law schools that complied with the standards. The standards themselves have evolved out of the crucible of experience with input from legal educators, practitioners, and judges. The standards, while sometimes mystifying to those who do not understand legal education, represent well-reasoned statements of policy aimed at assuring that individuals who enter the practice of law undertake a rigorous curriculum in an intellectually demanding setting. Over the years the ABA approval process has established and maintained a basic set of standards for entry into the practice of law that is accepted by bar licensing authorities, practitioners, and the courts.

Recognizing the value of the accreditation process in upholding the quality of legal education and ultimately the legal profession, most states require candidates for the bar examination to have graduated from an ABA-approved law school. Some other states certify graduates of law schools located in the state but not approved by the ABA to sit for the bar exam in that state. It is virtually impossible for graduates of a nonapproved law school to take the bar outside the state where they attended law school.

The non-ABA schools generally fall into three groups: new schools seeking ABA approval, state-approved schools, and unapproved schools. New law schools seeking ABA accreditation must go through an initial review and provisional accreditation before becoming fully approved. During this period of several years the school undergoes strict scrutiny, and students who enroll run the risk that the institution may never meet ABA standards. In recent years, more than a few such schools have dissolved when they could not secure ABA approval. If this happens, students may lose all their law school credits, and, worse, find that they cannot take a bar examination anywhere. On the other hand, if the school gains ABA approval, the risk will turn out to have been worthwhile.

The differences between state-approved and unapproved schools may seem murky. In most states where graduates of non-ABA schools can take the bar, there are only one or two non-ABA schools. Whether these schools are accredited by a state accrediting agency or whether the graduates simply are certified by the bar examiners is probably immaterial to most students. In California, however, the distinction does have ramifications. Significantly, that state has the largest number of lawyers as well as the largest number of non-ABA schools. In California, the state approves law schools using a procedure similar to but different from the ABA. State-approved law schools are treated within the state much like ABA schools; outside California the graduates of these schools usually will be considered like graduates of any other non-ABA approved school. Schools in California that have not been approved by either the state or the ABA represent a separate group within that state, and graduates face additional restrictions on (but not prohibition from) bar admission.

Why would you choose to attend a non-ABA law school? The most common reason might be that you do not gain admission to an ABA school. There is definitely a pecking order among law schools from elite schools like Harvard or Yale down to the unapproved schools. Generally, the more prestigious the law school, the more competitive it will be, and, conversely, the lower the school's perceived ranking, the less stringent will be the admission standards. Legal educators frequently warn prelaw students to beware of law school rankings because they often are based on reputations decades old rather than the current state of legal education at the schools. Rankings also overlook distinctions among schools that make different schools the best choice for different students. In this sense you should evaluate the quality of education at an unapproved school the same way you would evaluate an approved school. The point here is that some students whose traditional qualifications (such as undergraduate GPA and LSAT percentile) will not get them into an approved school may be able to secure a seat at an unapproved one. Some candidates may decide not to attend law school at all if they are not accepted at an ABA school; others may want a law degree so much that they select one of the non-ABA institutions.

A second reason that some students give for attending an unapproved school is cost. Because they are not bound by ABA requirements, non-ABA schools frequently rely heavily on part-time instructors, who cost less than full-time professors. In addition, non-ABA schools may provide more spartan facilities (the library, for example). This bargain basement approach to education can mean tuition savings for students.

Because classes are taught by practitioners, non-ABA schools may offer a more practice-oriented education. There are tradeoffs learning from part-time instructors who have full-time jobs in law firms, government, or corporations. You may gain from the practical experiences of these teachers but miss the indepth attention that full-time teachers can provide.

On the negative side, attendance at a non-ABA law school will inevitably restrict the jurisdictions in which graduates may be licensed. Therefore, it is unwise to enroll in a non-ABA law school in a state where you are unwilling to live and practice. You should carefully check the bar admission requirements for all the jurisdictions you consider prior to entering any law school that is not fully approved by the ABA.

Those considering attending an unapproved law school should consider also the educational experience they will receive. Since many such schools provide a bare bones education, applicants should scrutinize the academic program of the school at least as carefully as they would that of an ABA-approved school. While many non-ABA schools have existed for many years and maintain sound local reputations, other schools have less than solid foundations.

A final consideration that anyone contemplating attending a non-ABA-approved law school should address involves the career opportunities available to graduates. Not only is the bar passage rate lower at some non-ABA schools, thereby limiting career opportunities, but also the placement patterns of the graduates may be significantly different. The bottom line is that anyone considering law school should carefully investigate and research all aspects of each potential school before applying.

PROFILES OF SELECTED LAW SCHOOLS

Brief profiles of selected law schools not approved by the ABA appear on the following pages. The pros and cons of such law schools are discussed above. Only schools responding to our request for current information are included here.

Each profile begins with the name of the law school, its address and phone and fax numbers, and e-mail and Web addresses if provided. The capsule of basic information about the law school presents the following information.

Application Filing Fall and spring application deadlines and the application fee are given.

Accreditation Any professional accreditation is noted. (See **Abbreviations and Degrees** on page vii).

Degrees Granted Degrees are nearly always limited to the J.D.

Enrollment Enrollment breakdowns for 2001–2002 include men, women, minorities, and out-of-state students.

First-Year Class The applied, accepted, and enrolled figures refer to the number of students applying for the 2001–2002 entering class.

Class Profile This section includes the median LSAT percentile and the median LSAT score of freshmen in the 2001–2002 entering class, as well as the percentage of a recent graduating class that passed the bar on the first attempt.

Tuition and Fees Tuition and Fees figures given here are annual amounts, unless otherwise indicated. (NOTE: None of the schools featured in this edition are public institutions.) Because tuition charges change periodically, it is important to check with the school for current figures. This section also features the percentage of current students receiving financial aid.

Contact The person or position to whom inquiries should be directed is given, along with appropriate phone numbers.

AMERICAN COLLEGE OF LAW

1717 South State College
Boulevard #100
Anaheim, CA 92672

Phone: 714-634-3699
Fax: 714-634-3894
E-mail: *ccuffy@aol.com*
Web: *www.aclaw.com*

Application Filing	Accreditation
Fall: August 15	no
Spring: January 7	**Degrees Granted**
Fee: $25	J.D.

Enrollment 2001–2002			First-Year Class	
Men:	51	58%	Applied:	21
Women:	37	42%	Accepted:	19
Minorities:	15	17%	Enrolled:	19
Out-of-State:	0	0%		

2001–02 Class Profile

LSAT Percentile: 67%
LSAT Median Score: n/av
Percentage passing bar on first try: 27%

Tuition and Fees:

Resident
$325 (per credit)

Average (public)
$8,556

Average (private)
$22,915

Nonresident
$325 (per credit)

Average (public)
$16,690

Average (private)
$22,915

0 5 10 15 20 25 30 35

Percentage receiving financial aid: n/av

Contact

Janice Cowan, Academics Department, 714-634-3699 for general inquiries and financial aid information.

BARRY UNIVERSITY SCHOOL OF LAW

(Accredited by the ABA in February 2002)

6441 East Colonial Drive
Orlando, FL 32807

Phone: (407) 275-2000, ext. 237
Fax: (407) 275-2010
E-mail: *lawinfo@mail.barry.edu*
Web: *http://barry.edu/law*

Application Filing	Accreditation
Fall: March 30	ABA
Spring: n/app	**Degrees Granted**
Fee: $50	J.D.

Enrollment 2001–2002			First-Year Class	
Men:	117	57%	Applied:	158
Women:	90	44%	Accepted:	68
Minorities:	81	39%	Enrolled:	24
Out-of-State:	27	13%		

2001–02 Class Profile

LSAT Percentile: 29%
LSAT Median Score: 147
Percentage passing bar on first try: n/av

Tuition and Fees:

Resident
$21,380

Average (public)
$8,556

Average (private)
$22,915

Nonresident
$21,380

Average (public)
$16,690

Average (private)
$22,915

0 5 10 15 20 25 30 35

Percentage receiving financial aid: 83%

Contact

John Agett, Director of Admissions and Financial Aid, 407-275-2000, ext. 237 for general inquiries; John Agett or Maureen McFarlane, Financial Aid Counselor, 407-275-2000, ext. 264 for financial aid information.

CALIFORNIA NORTHERN

School of Law

1395 Ridgewood Drive, Suite 100
Chico, CA 95973

Phone: 530-891-6900
Fax: 530-891-3429
E-mail: *info@calnorthern.edu*
Web: *www.calnorthern.edu*

Application Filing	Accreditation
Fall: June 1	no
Spring: n/app	**Degrees Granted**
Fee: $50	J.D.

Enrollment 2001–2002			First-Year Class	
Men:	26	37%	Applied:	45
Women:	44	62%	Accepted:	32
Minorities:	1	1%	Enrolled:	29
Out-of-State:	0	0%		

2001–02 Class Profile

LSAT Percentile: 40%
LSAT Median Score: 148
Percentage passing bar on first try: 29%

Tuition and Fees:

Resident
$5,200 (P/T)

Average (public)
$8,556

Average (private)
$22,915

Nonresident
$5,200 (P/T)

Average (public)
$16,690

Average (private)
$22,915

0 5 10 15 20 25 30 35

Percentage receiving financial aid: 5%

Contact

Marty Gosling, Administrative Assistant, 530-891-6900 for general inquiries.

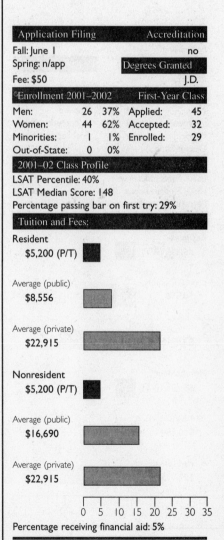

EMPIRE COLLEGE

School of Law

3035 Cleveland Avenue
Santa Rosa, CA 95403

Phone: 707-546-4000
Fax: 707-546-4058
E-mail: *alute@empirecollege.com*
Web: *www.empirecollege.com*

Application Filing / **Accreditation**
Fall: rolling — no
Spring: n/app
Degrees Granted
Fee: $95 — J.D.

Enrollment 2001–2002			First-Year Class	
Men:	64	48%	Applied:	n/av
Women:	70	52%	Accepted:	n/av
Minorities:	n/av		Enrolled:	n/av
Out-of-State:	n/av			

2001–02 Class Profile
LSAT Percentile: n/av
LSAT Median Score: n/av
Percentage passing bar on first try: 71%

Tuition and Fees:

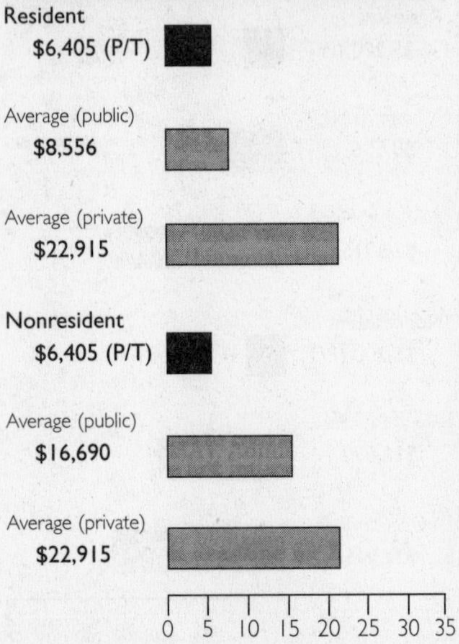

Percentage receiving financial aid: n/av

Contact

Aimee M. Lute, Admissions Officer, 707-546-4000 for general inquiries; Patricia Spaeth, Student Accounts, 707-546-4000 for financial aid information.

FAULKNER UNIVERSITY

Thomas Goode Jones School of Law

5345 Atlanta Highway
Montgomery, AL 36109

Phone: 334-386-7210
800-879-9816
Fax: 334-386-7223
E-mail: *psmith@faulkner.edu*

Application Filing / **Accreditation**
Fall: May 1 — no
Spring: n/app
Degrees Granted
Fee: $25 — J.D.

Enrollment 2001–2002			First-Year Class	
Men:	126	57%	Applied:	128
Women:	96	43%	Accepted:	94
Minorities:	29	13%	Enrolled:	73
Out-of-State:	4	2%		

2001–02 Class Profile
LSAT Percentile: 36%
LSAT Median Score: 147
Percentage passing bar on first try: n/av

Tuition and Fees:

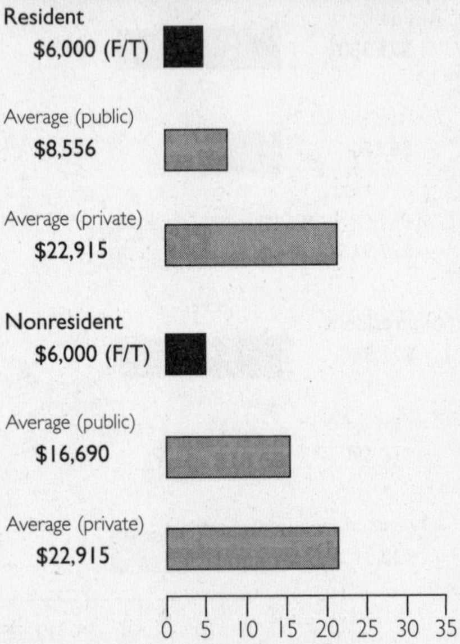

Percentage receiving financial aid: 73%

Contact

Paul M. Smith, Assistant Dean, 334-386-7210 for general inquiries; William G. Jackson, Director of Financial Aid, 334-386-7195 for financial aid information.

HUMPHREYS COLLEGE

School of Law

6650 Inglewood
Stockton, CA 95207

Phone: 209-478-0800
Fax: 209-478-8721

Application Filing / **Accreditation**
Fall: July 1 — no
Spring: n/app
Degrees Granted
Fee: $35 — J.D.

Enrollment 2001–2002			First-Year Class	
Men:	34	57%	Applied:	59
Women:	26	43%	Accepted:	33
Minorities:	34	57%	Enrolled:	20
Out-of-State:	n/av			

2001–02 Class Profile
LSAT Percentile: n/av
LSAT Median Score: n/av
Percentage passing bar on first try: 55%

Tuition and Fees:

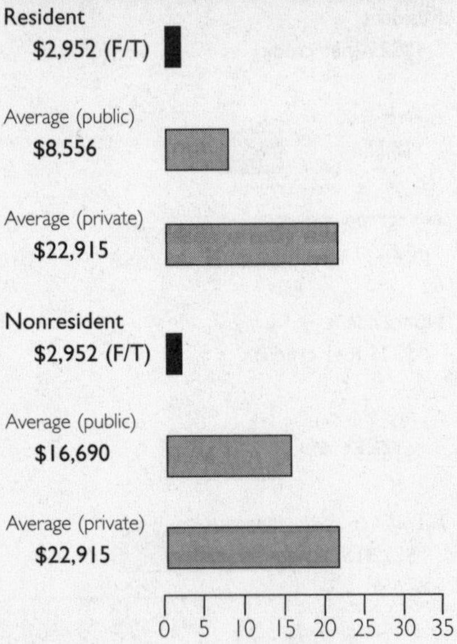

Percentage receiving financial aid: n/av

Contact

JOHN F. KENNEDY UNIVERSITY

School of Law

547 Ygnacio Valley Road
Walnut Creek, CA 94596

Phone: 925-258-2213
Fax: 925-254-6964
E-mail: *proginfo@jfku.edu*
Web: *www.jfku.edu*

Application Filing		Accreditation
Fall: May 30		no
Spring: November 30		**Degrees Granted**
Fee: $50		J.D.

Enrollment 2001–2002			First-Year Class	
Men:	131	45%	Applied:	102
Women:	158	55%	Accepted:	80
Minorities:	113	39%	Enrolled:	69
Out-of-State:	3	1%		

2001–02 Class Profile

LSAT Percentile: n/av
LSAT Median Score: n/av
Percentage passing bar on first try: 18%

Tuition and Fees:

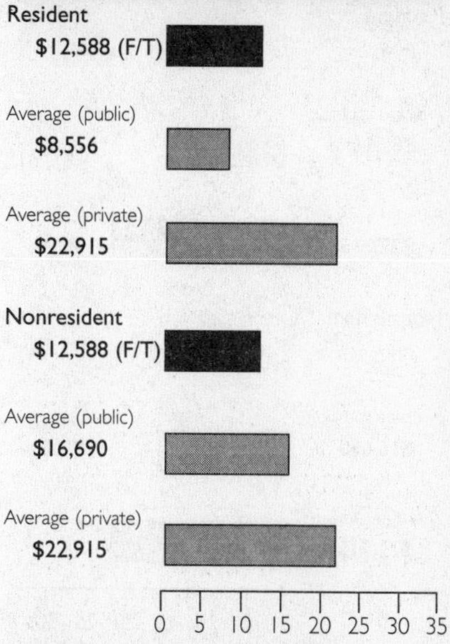

Percentage receiving financial aid: 62%

Contact

Director of Admissions, 925-258-2213 for general inquiries; Mindy Bergeron, 925-258-2385 for financial aid information.

JOHN MARSHALL LAW SCHOOL - ATLANTA

John Marshall Law School

1422 W. Peachtree St., NW
Atlanta, GA 30309

Phone: 404-872-3593
866-872-5657
Fax: 404-872-1555
E-mail: *skeef@johnmarshall.edu*
Web: *www.johnmarshall.edu*

Application Filing		Accreditation
Fall: n/av		no
Spring: n/app		**Degrees Granted**
Fee: $50		J.D.

Enrollment 2001–2002			First-Year Class	
Men:	80	61%	Applied:	189
Women:	51	39%	Accepted:	104
Minorities:	43	33%	Enrolled:	71
Out-of-State:	7	5%		

2001–02 Class Profile

LSAT Percentile: n/av
LSAT Median Score: 144
Percentage passing bar on first try: n/av

Tuition and Fees:

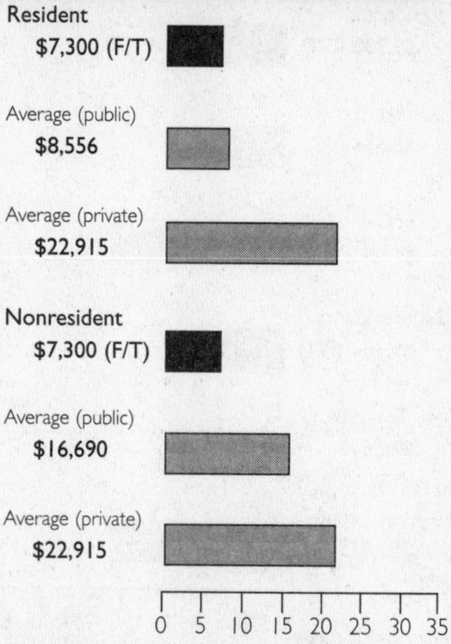

Percentage receiving financial aid: 82%

Contact

Sharon M. Keef, Interim Director of Admissions, 404-872-3593 for general inquiries; Janine Robinson, Director of Student Services/Registrar, 404-872-3593 for financial aid information.

LINCOLN LAW SCHOOL OF SACRAMENTO

3140 J Street
Sacramento, CA 95816

Phone: 916-446-1275
Fax: 916-446-5641
E-mail: *lincolnlaw@lincolnlaw.edu*
Web: *www.lincolnlaw.edu*

Application Filing		Accreditation
Fall: June 15		no
Spring: November 15		**Degrees Granted**
Fee: $30		J.D.

Enrollment 2001–2002			First-Year Class	
Men:	117	53%	Applied:	150
Women:	104	47%	Accepted:	122
Minorities:	152	69%	Enrolled:	102
Out-of-State:	n/av			

2001–02 Class Profile

LSAT Percentile: 30%
LSAT Median Score: 145
Percentage passing bar on first try: 35%

Tuition and Fees:

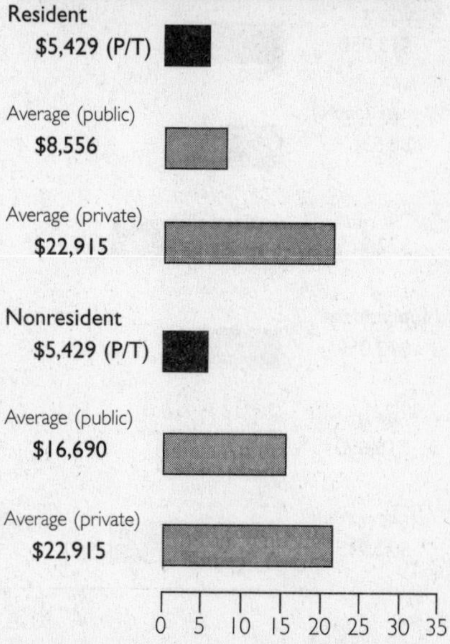

Percentage receiving financial aid: 20%

Contact

Erin O'Brien, Secretary, 916-446-1275 for general inquiries; Melissa Fuller, Assistant Registrar, 916-446-1275 for financial aid information.

MASSACHUESTTS SCHOOL OF LAW

500 Federal Street
Andover, MA 01810

Phone: (978) 681-0800
Fax: (978) 681-6330
E-mail: *pcolby@mslaw.edu*
Web: *www.mslaw.edu*

Application Filing	Accreditation
Fall: July 30	AALS
Spring: January 1	**Degrees Granted**
Fee: $40	J.D.

Enrollment 2001–2002			First-Year Class	
Men:	350	5%	Applied:	200
Women:	350	50%	Accepted:	170
Minorities:	175	25%	Enrolled:	150
Out-of-State:	140	20%		

2001–02 Class Profile

LSAT Percentile: n/av
LSAT Median Score: n/av
Percentage passing bar on first try: 60%

Tuition and Fees:

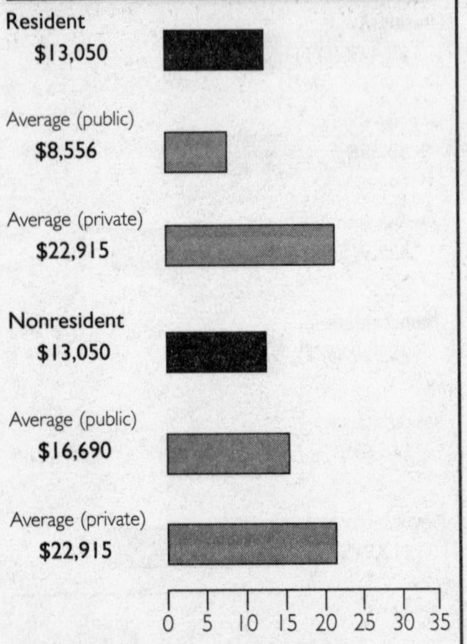

Percentage receiving financial aid: 70%

Contact

Paula Colby-Clements, Director of Admissions, 978-681-0800 for general inquiries; Lynn Bowab, Director of Financial Aid, 978-681-0800 for financial aid information.

MONTEREY COLLEGE OF LAW

404 West Franklin Street
Monterey, CA 93940

Phone: (831) 373-3301
Fax: (831) 373-0143
E-mail: *wfl@montereylaw.edu*
Web: *www.montereylaw.edu*

Application Filing	Accreditation
Fall: June 1	no
Spring: n/app	**Degrees Granted**
Fee: $75	J.D.

Enrollment 2001–2002			First-Year Class	
Men:	40	55%	Applied:	65
Women:	33	45%	Accepted:	40
Minorities:	18	25%	Enrolled:	28
Out-of-State:	4	5%		

2001–02 Class Profile

LSAT Percentile: 45%
LSAT Median Score: n/av
Percentage passing bar on first try: 33%

Tuition and Fees:

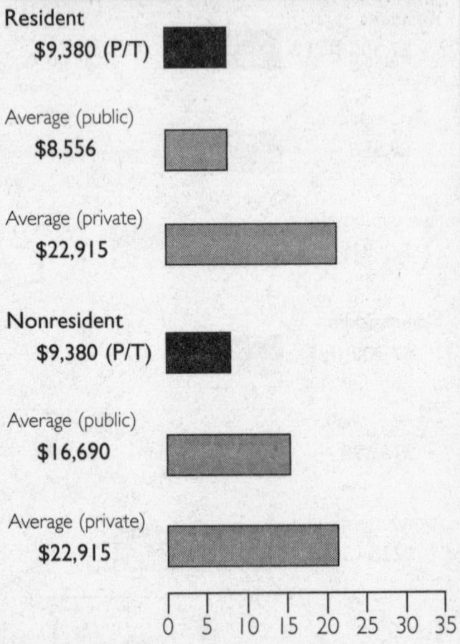

Percentage receiving financial aid: n/av

Contact

Director of Admissions and Student Services, 831-373-3301 for general inquiries.

NEW COLLEGE OF CALIFORNIA

School of Law

50 Fell Street
San Francisco, CA 94102

Phone: (415) 241-1314
Fax: (415) 241-1353
E-mail: *lawinfo@newcollege.edu*
Web: *www.newcollege.edu*

Application Filing	Accreditation
Fall: May 1	no
Spring: n/app	**Degrees Granted**
Fee: $45	J.D.

Enrollment 2001–2002			First-Year Class	
Men:	n/av		Applied:	n/av
Women:	n/av		Accepted:	60
Minorities:	84	70%	Enrolled:	40
Out-of-State:	120	100%		

2001–02 Class Profile

LSAT Percentile: 35%
LSAT Median Score: 148
Percentage passing bar on first try: 33%

Tuition and Fees:

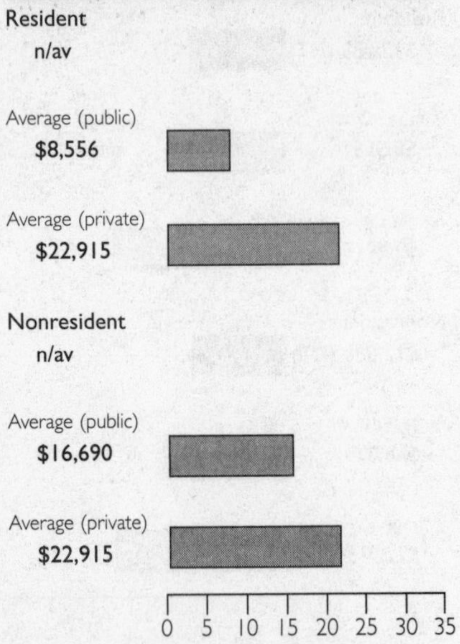

Percentage receiving financial aid: n/av

Contact

Assistant Dean, 415-241-1314 for general inquiries; Juanita Marshall-Bell, Director, 415-437-3442 for financial aid information.

PRESIDENT'S COLLEGE

School of Law

123 S. Market Street
Wichita, KS 67202

Phone: (316) 267-9000 ext. 213
Fax: (316) 267-8825
E-mail: *shenderson@presidentscollege.edu*
Web: *www.presidentscollege.edu*

Application Filing | **Accreditation**

Fall: August 23 — no
Spring: n/app
Fee: $35

Degrees Granted: J.D.

Enrollment 2001–2002			First-Year Class	
Men:	53	65%	Applied:	63
Women:	28	35%	Accepted:	58
Minorities:	17	21%	Enrolled:	53
Out-of-State:	n/av			

2001–02 Class Profile

LSAT Percentile: 32%
LSAT Median Score: 145
Percentage passing bar on first try: n/av

Tuition and Fees:

Resident
$7,000 (P/T)
Average (public) $8,556
Average (private) $22,915

Nonresident
$7,000 (P/T)
Average (public) $16,690
Average (private) $22,915

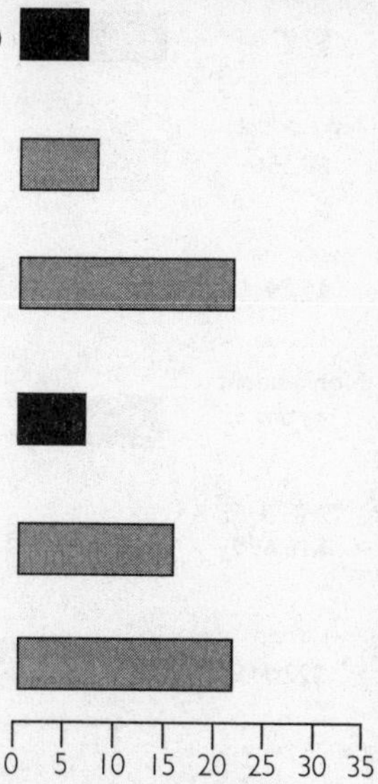

Percentage receiving financial aid: 90%

Contact

Director of Admissions, 316-267-9000, ext. 213 for general inquiries; Michael Foster, Director of Student Services, 316-267-9000, ext. 215 for financial aid information.

SAN FRANCISCO LAW SCHOOL

20 Haight Street
San Francisco, CA 94102

Phone: 415-626-5550 ext. 123
Fax: 415-626-5584
E-mail: *admin@sfls.edu*
Web: *www.sfls.edu*

Application Filing | **Accreditation**

Fall: November 15 — no
Spring: June 15
Fee: $50

Degrees Granted: J.D.

Enrollment 2001–2002			First-Year Class	
Men:	54	56%	Applied:	51
Women:	42	44%	Accepted:	31
Minorities:	39	41%	Enrolled:	17
Out-of-State:	1	1%		

2001–02 Class Profile

LSAT Percentile: 26%
LSAT Median Score: n/av
Percentage passing bar on first try: 40%

Tuition and Fees:

Resident
$3,280 (P/T)
Average (public) $8,556
Average (private) $22,915

Nonresident
$3,280 (P/T)
Average (public) $16,690
Average (private) $22,915

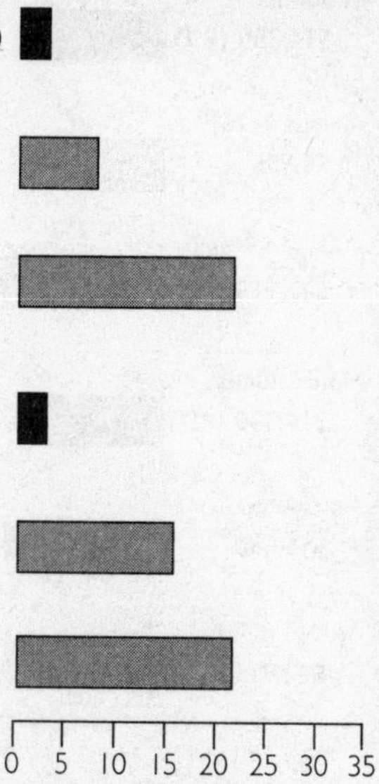

Percentage receiving financial aid: 40%

Contact

Registrar, 415-626-5550, ext. 122 for general inquiries; Deborah McIntyre, 415-626-5550, ext. 121 for financial aid information.

SANTA BARBARA AND VENTURA COLLEGES OF LAW

Ventura College of Law

4475 Market Street
Ventura, CA 93003

Phone: 805-658-0511
Fax: 805-658-0529
E-mail: *bdoyle@venturalaw.edu*
Web: *www.venturalaw.edu*

Application Filing | **Accreditation**

Fall: June 1 — no
Spring: December 1
Fee: $45

Degrees Granted: J.D.

Enrollment 2001–2002			First-Year Class	
Men:	34	38%	Applied:	33
Women:	55	62%	Accepted:	24
Minorities:	24	27%	Enrolled:	19
Out-of-State:	n/av			

2001–02 Class Profile

LSAT Percentile: n/av
LSAT Median Score: n/av
Percentage passing bar on first try: 25%

Tuition and Fees:

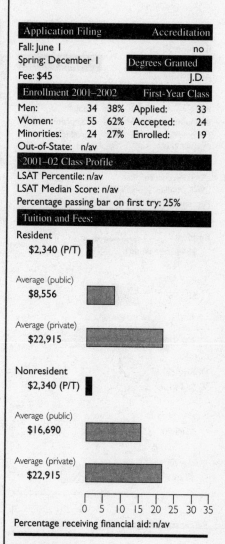

Resident
$2,340 (P/T)
Average (public) $8,556
Average (private) $22,915

Nonresident
$2,340 (P/T)
Average (public) $16,690
Average (private) $22,915

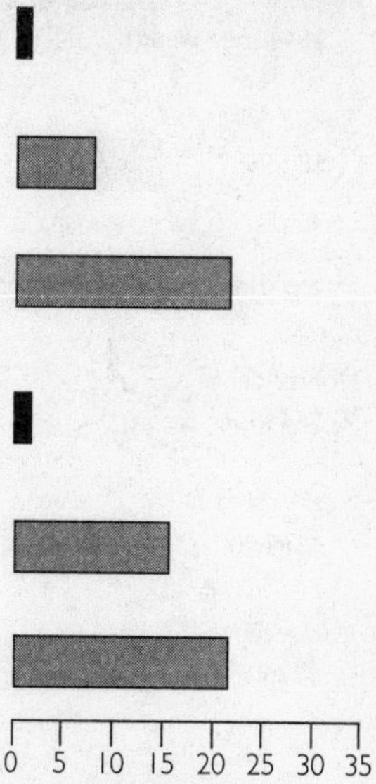

Percentage receiving financial aid: n/av

Contact

Assistant Dean, 805-658-0511 for general inquiries.

SOUTHERN NEW ENGLAND SCHOOL OF LAW

333 Faunce Corner Road
North Dartmouth, MA 02747

Phone: 508-998-9400
800-213-0060
Fax: 508-998-9561
E-mail: *cvidal@snesl.edu*
Web: *www.snesl.edu*

Application Filing	Accreditation
Fall: June 30	no
Spring: n/app	**Degrees Granted**
Fee: $50	J.D.

Enrollment 2001–2002			First-Year Class	
Men:	70	45%	Applied:	174
Women:	86	50%	Accepted:	152
Minorities:	16	10%	Enrolled:	63
Out-of-State:	55	35%		

2001–02 Class Profile

LSAT Percentile: n/av
LSAT Median Score: 140
Percentage passing bar on first try: 60%

Tuition and Fees:

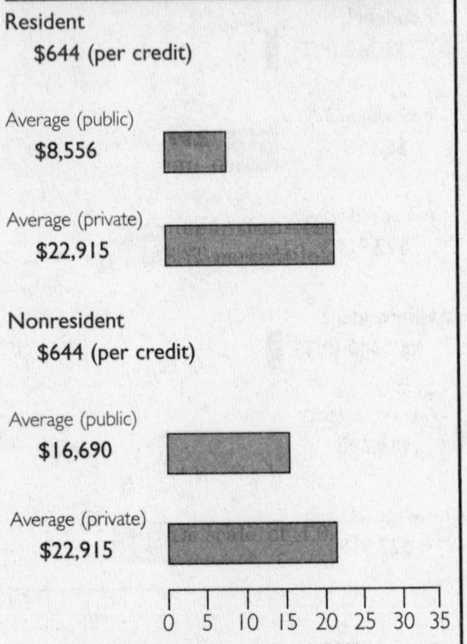

Percentage receiving financial aid: 50%

Contact

Carol A. Vidal, Registrar, 508-998-9600 for general inquiries; Sandra Leger Silva, Director of Financial Aid, 508-998-9600, ext. 112 for financial aid information.

TRINITY INTERNATIONAL UNIVERSITY

Trinity Law School

2200 North Grand Avenue
Santa Ana, CA 92705

Phone: (714) 796-7100
Fax: (714) 796-7190
E-mail: *tls@tiu.edu*
Web: *tiu.edu/law*

Application Filing	Accreditation
Fall: July 1	no
Spring: December 1	**Degrees Granted**
Fee: $30	J.D.

Enrollment 2001–2002			First-Year Class	
Men:	94	61%	Applied:	107
Women:	59	39%	Accepted:	62
Minorities:	70	46%	Enrolled:	36
Out-of-State:	2	1%		

2001–02 Class Profile

LSAT Percentile: 18%
LSAT Median Score: 142
Percentage passing bar on first try: 13%

Tuition and Fees:

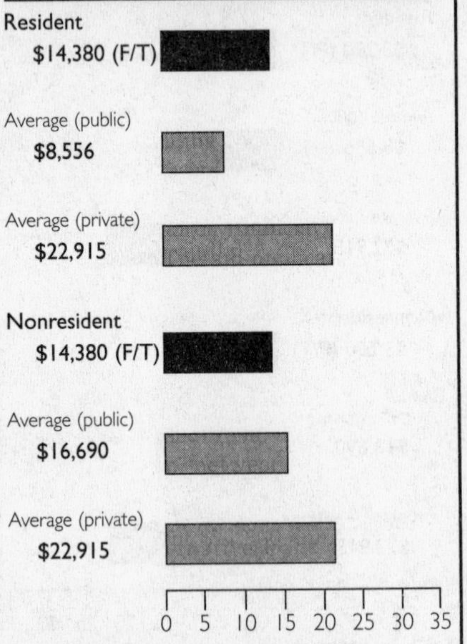

Percentage receiving financial aid: 78%

Contact

Admissions Office, 714-796-7100 for general inquiries; Maria Mancillas, 714-796-7120 for financial aid information.

UNIVERSITY OF LA VERNE

San Fernando Valley College of Law

21300 Oxnard Street
Woodland Hills, CA 91367

Phone: 818-830-0529
800-830-0529
Fax: 818-883-8142
E-mail: *murphy@sfvlaw.edu*
Web: *www.sfvlaw.edu*

Application Filing	Accreditation
Fall: January 1	AALS
Spring: October 1	**Degrees Granted**
Fee: $45	J.D.

Enrollment 2001–2002			First-Year Class	
Men:	101	56%	Applied:	124
Women:	80	43%	Accepted:	106
Minorities:	43	24%	Enrolled:	77
Out-of-State:	0	0%		

2001–02 Class Profile

LSAT Percentile: 24%
LSAT Median Score: 142
Percentage passing bar on first try: 23%

Tuition and Fees:

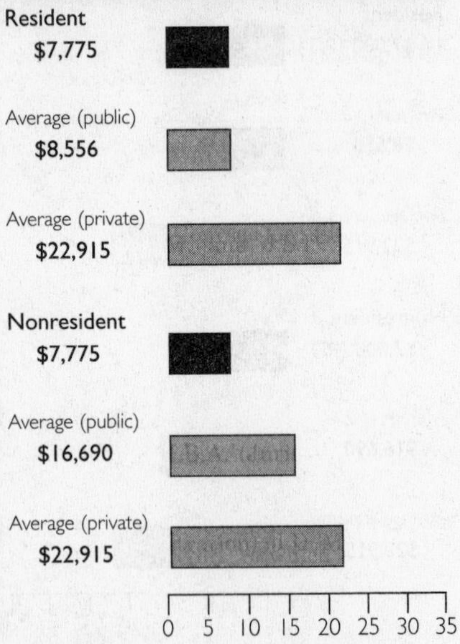

Percentage receiving financial aid: 90%

Contact

Director of Admissions, 800-830-0529 for general inquiries; Financial Aid Counselor, 909-593-3511 for financial aid information.

UNIVERSITY OF NORTHERN CALIFORNIA

Lorenzo Patino School of Law

1012 J Street
Sacramento, CA 95814

Phone: (916) 441-4485
Fax: (916) 441-0175

Application Filing		Accreditation
Fall: August 15		no
Spring: January 7		**Degrees Granted**
Fee: $25		J.D.

Enrollment 2001–2002			First-Year Class	
Men:	n/av		Applied:	28
Women:	n/av		Accepted:	28
Minorities:	n/av		Enrolled:	24
Out-of-State:	75	100%		

2001–02 Class Profile

LSAT Percentile: n/av
LSAT Median Score: n/av
Percentage passing bar on first try: n/av

Tuition and Fees:

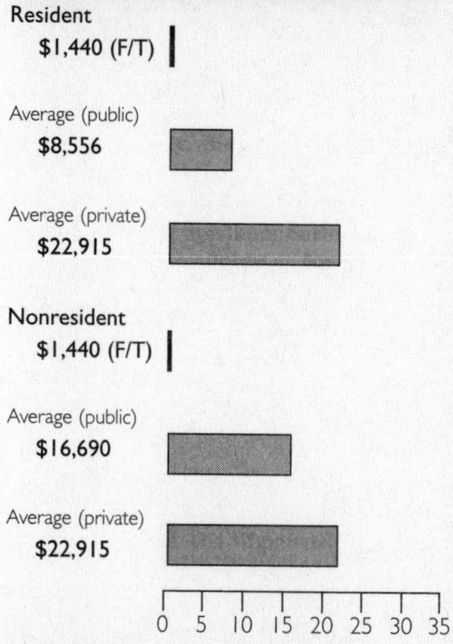

Percentage receiving financial aid: n/av

Contact

Crescenzo Vellucci, Registrar's Office, (916) 441-4485 for general inquiries.

UNIVERSITY OF WEST LOS ANGELES

School of Law

1155 W. Arbor Vitae Street
Inglewood, CA 90301-2902

Phone: 310-342-5254
Fax: 310-342-5295
E-mail: *kcerv@uwla.edu*
Web: *www.uwla.edu*

Application Filing		Accreditation
Fall: rolling		no
Spring: n/app		**Degrees Granted**
Fee: $55		J.D.

Enrollment 2001–2002			First-Year Class	
Men:	83	53%	Applied:	161
Women:	75	47%	Accepted:	86
Minorities:	66	42%	Enrolled:	65
Out-of-State:	0	0%		

2001–02 Class Profile

LSAT Percentile: 31%
LSAT Median Score: n/av
Percentage passing bar on first try: 25%

Tuition and Fees:

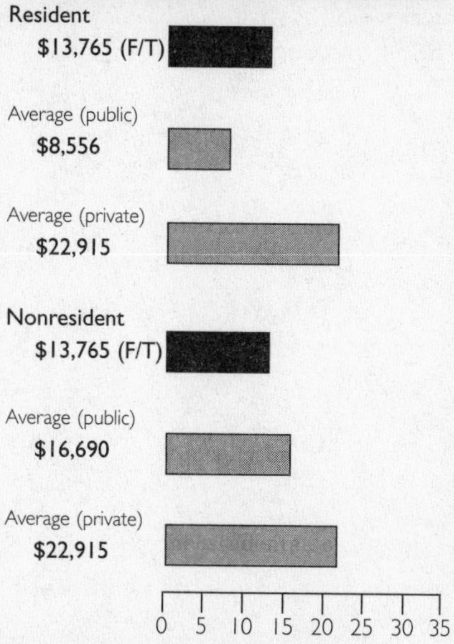

Percentage receiving financial aid: 90%

Contact

Kathi Cervi, 310-342-5210 for general inquiries; Ed Reed, Director, 310-342-5257 for financial aid information.

WILLIAM HOWARD TAFT UNIVERSITY

201 E. Sandpointe Avenue
Santa Ana, CA 92707

Phone: (714) 850-4800
800-882-4555
Fax: (714) 708-2082
E-mail: *admissions@taftu.edu*
Web: *taftu.edu*

Application Filing		Accreditation
Fall: rolling		no
Spring: rolling		**Degrees Granted**
Fee: $35		J.D., LL.M.

Enrollment 2001–2002			First-Year Class	
Men:	188	79%	Applied:	360
Women:	50	27%	Accepted:	324
Minorities:	64	27%	Enrolled:	159
Out-of-State:	102	43%		

2001–02 Class Profile

LSAT Percentile: n/av
LSAT Median Score: n/av
Percentage passing bar on first try: 22%

Tuition and Fees:

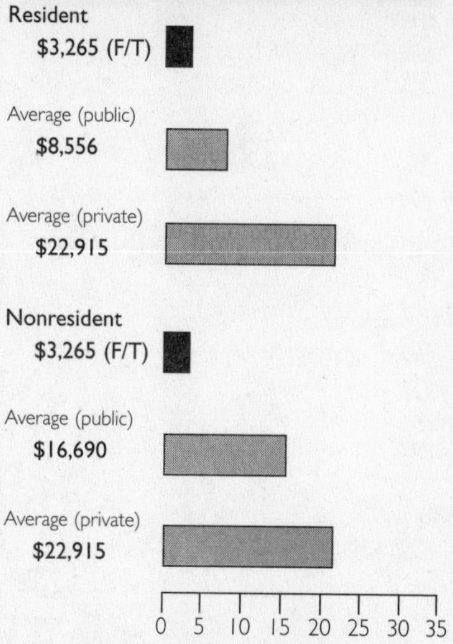

Percentage receiving financial aid: n/av

Contact

Director of Student Services, 714-850-4800 or 800-882-4555 for general inquiries; Joy Stark, Accounting, 800-882-4555 for financial aid information.

INDEX

Entries set in roman type are law schools approved by the American Bar Association.
Entries set in italic type are law schools not approved by the American Bar Association.